# THE ROUTLEDGE COMPANION TO MEDIA AND GENDER

*The Routledge Companion to Media and Gender* offers a comprehensive examination of media and gender studies, charting its histories, investigating ongoing controversies, and assessing future trends.

The 59 chapters in this volume, written by leading researchers from around the world, provide scholars and students with an engaging and authoritative survey of current thinking in media and gender research.

The *Companion* includes the following features:

- With each chapter addressing a distinct, concrete set of issues, the volume includes research from around the world to engage readers in a broad array of global and transnational issues and intersectional perspectives.
- Authors address a series of important questions that have consequences for current and future thinking in the field, including postfeminism, sexual violence, masculinity, media industries, queer identities, video games, digital policy, media activism, sexualization, docusoaps, teen drama, cosmetic surgery, media Islamophobia, sport, telenovelas, news audiences, pornography, and social and mobile media.
- A range of academic disciplines inform exploration of key issues around production and policymaking, representation, audience engagement, and the place of gender in media studies.

*The Routledge Companion to Media and Gender* is an essential guide to the central ideas, concepts, and debates currently shaping media and gender research.

**Contributors:** Ben Aslinger, Shakuntala Banaji, Susan Berridge, Gargi Bhattacharyya, Denise D. Bielby, Anita Biressi, Tanja Bosch, Karen Boyle, Shelley-Jean Bradfield, Sara Bragg, Carolyn M. Byerly, Lisa Marie Cacho, Tanja Carstensen, Cynthia Carter, Shira Chess, Lisa M. Cuklanz, Dawn H. Currie, Christine Daviault, Josephine Dolan, Tim Edwards, Nahed Eltantawy, Matthew B. Ezzell, Margaret Gallagher, Rosalind Gill, J. Robyn Goodman, Esther Hamburger, Dustin Harp, Radha S. Hegde, Joke Hermes, Larissa Hjorth, Ursula Huws, Iam-Chong Ip, Veronika Kalmus, Sahar Khamis, Youna Kim, Oi-Wan Lam, Dafna Lemish, Marion Leonard, Koen Leurs, Sonia Livingstone, Catharine Lumby, Lisa McLaughlin, Brenton J. Malin, Vicki Mayer, Toby Miller, Isabel Molina-Guzmán, Annabelle Mooney, Dara Persis Murray, Heather Nunn, Laurie Ouellette, Radhika Parameswaran, Sandra Ponzanesi, Andrea L. Press, Rosa Reitsamer, Karen Ross, David Rowe, Julie Levin Russo, Katharine Sarikakis, Gareth Schott, Katherine Sender, Leslie Regan Shade, Tamara Shepherd, Linda Steiner, Kairi Talves, Francesca Tripodi, Angharad N. Valdivia, Milly Williamson, Audrey Yue, Elke Zobl

**Cynthia Carter** is Senior Lecturer in the Cardiff School of Journalism, Media and Cultural Studies, Cardiff University, UK. She has published widely on feminist news studies, children and news, and media violence. She is founding co-editor, with Lisa McLaughlin, of the journal *Feminist Media Studies*.

**Linda Steiner** is Professor of Journalism at the University of Maryland, USA. Her primary research areas are alternative media, gendered media employment, women and technology, citizen journalism, and ethics. She has written/co-authored three books, and over 85 book chapters and journal articles.

**Lisa McLaughlin** is Associate Professor in the Department of Media, Journalism, and Film and the Women's, Gender, and Sexuality Studies program at Miami University-Ohio, USA. Her research focuses on transnational feminism, the public sphere, political economy, and women, work, and information technologies.

# THE ROUTLEDGE COMPANION TO MEDIA AND GENDER

*Edited by*
*Cynthia Carter, Linda Steiner and*
*Lisa McLaughlin*

Routledge
Taylor & Francis Group

LONDON AND NEW YORK

First published in paperback 2015
First published 2014
by Routledge
2 Park Square, Milton Park, Abingdon, Oxon, OX14 4RN

and by Routledge
711 Third Avenue, New York, NY 10017

*Routledge is an imprint of the Taylor & Francis Group, an informa business*

*British Library Cataloguing in Publication Data*
A catalogue record for this book is available from the British Library

*Library of Congress Cataloging in Publication Data*
The Routledge companion to media and gender / edited by Cynthia Carter,
Linda Steiner and Lisa McLaughlin
pages cm
Includes bibliographical references and index.
1. Sex role in mass media 2. Mass media and culture. I. Carter, Cynthia, 1959- editor
of compilation. II. Steiner, Linda, editor of compilation. III. McLaughlin, Lisa, editor
of compilation.
P96.S5R68 2014
305.3–dc23
2013023812

ISBN: 978-0-415-52769-9 (hbk)
ISBN: 978-1-138-84912-9 (pbk)
ISBN: 978-0-203-06691-1 (ebk)

Typeset in Goudy
by Taylor & Francis Books

Printed and bound in Great Britain by
TJ International Ltd, Padstow, Cornwall

# CONTENTS

*List of illustrations*                                                  xi
*List of contributors*                                                   xii

**Introduction: re-imagining media and gender**                          1
CYNTHIA CARTER, LINDA STEINER,
AND LISA MCLAUGHLIN

PART I
Her/histories                                                            21

1  **Media and the representation of gender**                            23
   MARGARET GALLAGHER

2  **Mass media representation of gendered violence**                    32
   LISA M. CUKLANZ

3  **Lone wolves: masculinity, cinema, and the man alone**              42
   TIM EDWARDS

4  **To communicate is human; to chat is female: the feminization
   of US media work**                                                    51
   VICKI MAYER

5  **Rediscovering twentieth-century feminist audience research**        61
   JOKE HERMES

6  **Historically mapping contemporary intersectional feminist
   media studies**                                                       71
   ISABEL MOLINA-GUZMÁN AND LISA MARIE CACHO

7  **Sexualities/queer identities**                                      81
   AUDREY YUE

8  **Gender, media, and trans/national spaces**                          92
   RADHA S. HEGDE

PART II
Media industries, labor, and policy                                          103

 9 Women and media control: feminist interrogations at the macro-level      105
   CAROLYN M. BYERLY

10 Risk, innovation, and gender in media conglomerates                      116
   BEN ASLINGER

11 Putting gender in the mix: employment, participation, and role
   expectations in the music industries                                     127
   MARION LEONARD

12 Gender inequality in culture industries                                  137
   DENISE D. BIELBY

13 Shifting boundaries: gender, labor, and new information and
   communication technology                                                147
   URSULA HUWS

14 Gendering the commodity audience in social media                        157
   TAMARA SHEPHERD

15 Youthful white male industry seeks "fun"-loving middle-aged women
   for video games—no strings attached                                     168
   SHIRA CHESS

16 Boys are ... girls are ... : how children's media and merchandizing
   construct gender                                                        179
   DAFNA LEMISH

17 Girls' and boys' experiences of online risk and safety                  190
   SONIA LIVINGSTONE, VERONIKA KALMUS,
   AND KAIRI TALVES

18 Holy grail or poisoned chalice? Three generations of
   men's magazines                                                         201
   ANNABELLE MOONEY

19 Making public policy in the digital age: the sex industry as a
   political actor                                                         211
   KATHARINE SARIKAKIS

20 Gender and digital policy: from global information infrastructure
   to internet governance                                                  222
   LESLIE REGAN SHADE

CONTENTS

21  Gender and media activism: alternative feminist media in Europe      233
    ELKE ZOBL AND ROSA REITSAMER

22  Between legitimacy and political efficacy: feminist counter-publics
    and the internet in China                                            245
    IAM-CHONG IP AND OI-WAN LAM

PART III
Images and representations across texts and genres                       257

23  Buying and selling sex: sexualization, commerce, and gender          259
    KAREN BOYLE

24  Class, gender, and the docusoap: *The Only Way Is Essex*             269
    HEATHER NUNN AND ANITA BIRESSI

25  *Society*'s emerging femininities: neoliberal, postfeminist, and
    hybrid identities on television in South Africa                      280
    SHELLEY-JEAN BRADFIELD

26  A nice bit of skirt and the talking head: sex, politics,
    and news                                                             290
    KAREN ROSS

27  Transgender, transmedia, transnationality: Chaz Bono in
    documentary and *Dancing with the Stars*                             300
    KATHERINE SENDER

28  Celebrity, gossip, privacy, and scandal                              311
    MILLY WILLIAMSON

29  "Shameless mums" and universal pedophiles: sexualization and
    commodification of children                                          321
    SARA BRAGG

30  Glances, dances, romances: an overview of gendered sexual
    narratives in teen drama series                                      332
    SUSAN BERRIDGE

31  Smoothing the wrinkles: Hollywood, "successful aging," and the
    new visibility of older female stars                                 342
    JOSEPHINE DOLAN

32  Perfect bodies, imperfect messages: media coverage of cosmetic
    surgery and ideal beauty                                             352
    J. ROBYN GOODMAN

CONTENTS

33 Globalization, beauty regimes, and mediascapes in the
   New India                                                        363
   RADHIKA PARAMESWARAN

34 Narrative pleasure in *Homeland*: the competing femininities of
   "rogue agents" and "terror wives"                                374
   GARGI BHATTACHARYYA

35 Above the fold and beyond the veil: Islamophobia in
   Western media                                                    384
   NAHED ELTANTAWY

36 Sport, media, and the gender-based insult                        395
   DAVID ROWE

PART IV
Media audiences, users, and prosumers                              407

37 Subjects of capacity? Reality TV and young women                 409
   LAURIE OUELLETTE

38 Telenovelas, gender, and genre                                   419
   ESTHER HAMBURGER

39 Gendering and selling the female news audience in a digital age  430
   DUSTIN HARP

40 Looking beyond representation: situating the significance of gender
   portrayal within game play                                       440
   CHRISTINE DAVIAULT AND GARETH SCHOTT

41 Textual orientation: queer female fandom online                  450
   JULIE LEVIN RUSSO

42 Delivering the male—and more: fandom and media sport             461
   TOBY MILLER

43 Men's use of pornography                                         473
   MATTHEW B. EZZELL

44 Gender and social media: sexism, empowerment, or the irrelevance
   of gender?                                                       483
   TANJA CARSTENSEN

45 Slippery subjects: gender, meaning, and the Bollywood audience   493
   SHAKUNTALA BANAJI

# CONTENTS

46 Asian women audiences, Asian popular culture, and media
    globalization                                                503
    YOUNA KIM

47 Women as radio audiences in Africa                            514
    TANJA BOSCH

48 Reading girlhood: opportunities for social literacy          523
    DAWN H. CURRIE

49 Investigating users' responses to Dove's "real beauty" strategy:
    feminism, freedom, and Facebook                              533
    DARA PERSIS MURRAY

50 Feminism in a postfeminist world: women discuss who's
    "hot"—and why we care—on the collegiate "Anonymous
    Confession Board"                                            543
    ANDREA L. PRESS AND FRANCESCA TRIPODI

51 Gendered networked visualities: locative camera phone cultures in
    Seoul, South Korea                                           554
    LARISSA HJORTH

52 Gendering the Arab Spring: Arab women journalists/activists,
    "cyberfeminism," and the sociopolitical revolution           565
    SAHAR KHAMIS

PART V
Gendered media futures and the future of gender                  577

53 Latinas on television and film: exploring the limits and possibilities
    of inclusion                                                 579
    ANGHARAD N. VALDIVIA

54 Postfeminist sexual culture                                   589
    ROSALIND GILL

55 Post-postfeminism                                             600
    CATHARINE LUMBY

56 Policing the crisis of masculinity: media and masculinity at the
    dawn of the new century                                      610
    BRENTON J. MALIN

57 Glassy architectures in journalism                            620
    LINDA STEINER

# CONTENTS

58  Intersectionality, digital identities, and migrant youths: Moroccan
    Dutch youths as digital space invaders                          632
    KOEN LEURS AND SANDRA PONZANESI

59  Online popular anti-sexism political action in the UK and USA:
    the importance of collaborative anger for social change         643
    CYNTHIA CARTER

    *Index*                                                          654

# LIST OF ILLUSTRATIONS

## Figures

21.1   *Riot Grrrl London* zine (Issue 3, 2003)                                    237
58.1   Hyves groups that Midia links to on her Hyves profile page
       (April 15, 2009)                                                            639

## Tables

9.1    Women's representation at policy level in large global media
       conglomerates (data assembled from company websites and
       other industry data, 2012)                                                  108
17.1   Children's internet access, use, and skills, by gender                      191
17.2   Children's experience of online risk and harm, by gender                    192
17.3   Children's risky online activities, by gender                               194
17.4   Coping strategies among those bothered by online risks, by gender           195
17.5   Strategies of parental mediation for sons and daughters, according
       to child and parent (means)                                                 196
17.6   Boys' and girls' experiences of online risks and harm (according
       to child) correlated with strategies of parental mediation (according
       to parent)                                                                  197
21.1   Features of feminist media: Lievrouw's (2011) genre framework for
       alternative and activist new media extended to feminist media
       production on- and off-line                                                 242

# LIST OF CONTRIBUTORS

**Ben Aslinger** is an Associate Professor in the Department of English and Media Studies at Bentley University, USA. He is co-editor of the collections *Gaming Globally: Production, Play, and Place* (2013) and *Locating Emerging Media* (forthcoming, Routledge).

**Shakuntala Banaji** is Lecturer in the Department of Media and Communications at the London School of Economics and Political Science, UK. She lectures in Development and Communication, International Media and Film. She publishes widely on Hindi cinema, audiences, creativity, youth and online civic participation. She is co-author of *Media Cultures* (2012) and *The Civic Web* (2013), and editor of *South Asian*.

**Susan Berridge** is Lecturer in Film and Media at the University of Leeds, UK. She completed her Ph.D. at Glasgow University in 2010. She previously taught in the Media Arts department at Royal Holloway, UK, the University of London, UK, and at the University of Stirling, UK.

**Gargi Bhattacharyya** is Professor of Sociology at the University of East London, UK. She has published on race and racism, sexuality, globalization, and the war on terror. Her books include *Sexuality and Society* (2002), *Traffick, the Illicit Movement of People and Things* (2005), and *Dangerous Brown Men: Exploiting Sex, Violence and Feminism in the War on Terror* (2008).

**Denise D. Bielby** is Professor of Sociology and Affiliated Faculty in Film & Media Studies at the University of California, Santa Barbara, USA. Her research focuses on the culture industries of television and film, audiences and popular criticism, and media, aging, and the life course.

**Anita Biressi** is Reader in Media Cultures at the University of Roehampton, UK. Her research interests include popular factual television, tabloid culture, and class and culture. She is the co-author with Heather Nunn of *Class and Contemporary British Culture* (2013).

**Tanja Bosch** is Lecturer in the Centre for Film and Media Studies at the University of Cape Town, South Africa. She completed her MA in International Affairs while a Fulbright Scholar at Ohio University, where she also graduated with a Ph.D. in Mass

Communication. She teaches journalism, research methods, and researches radio, youth, gender, and mobile and online media.

**Karen Boyle** is Professor of Feminist Media Studies at the University of Stirling, UK. She is author of *Media & Violence: Gendering the Debates* (2005) and the editor of *Everyday Pornography* (2010).

**Shelley-Jean Bradfield** is Assistant Professor of Media Studies at Central College, Iowa, USA. Her research and teaching employ feminist critical and cultural studies to analyze media representations of identities and globalized media institutions, texts, and audiences.

**Sara Bragg** is a Senior Research Fellow in the Education Research Centre at the University of Brighton, UK. Her research has focused on media education, youth voice and participation, school ethos, and "creative" research methods, as well as debates about the "sexualization" of childhood.

**Carolyn M. Byerly** is Professor in the School of Communications, Howard University, USA. She teaches graduate seminars in media theory, research methods, and political communication, and studies the relationship between social movements and media, and race and gender issues in media policy.

**Lisa Marie Cacho** is Associate Professor of Asian American Studies and Latina/Latino Studies at the University of Illinois, USA, and author of *Social Death: Racialized Rightlessness and the Criminalization of the Unprotected* (2012).

**Tanja Carstensen** is a sociologist and post-doc researcher at the research group Work–Gender–Technology, Hamburg University of Technology, Germany. Research interests include gender relations, intersectionality and internet, digitalization of work, social media at workplaces, subject constructions and digital culture, and human–technology interactions.

**Cynthia Carter** is Senior Lecturer in the Cardiff School of Journalism, Media and Cultural Studies, Cardiff University, UK. She has widely published on feminist news studies, children and news, and media violence. She is co-author of *Violence and the Media* (2003) and recently co-edited *Current Perspectives in Feminist Media Studies* (2013). She is founding co-editor, with Lisa McLaughlin, of the journal *Feminist Media Studies*.

**Shira Chess** is Assistant Professor of Mass Media Arts at the University of Georgia, USA. She received her Ph.D. in Communication and Rhetoric from Rensselaer Polytechnic Institute, USA. Her research has been published in *Critical Studies in Media Communication*, *Feminist Media Studies*, and *Information, Communication & Society*, as well as several essay collections.

**Lisa M. Cuklanz** is Professor and Chair of the Communication Department at Boston College, USA. She is former Director of the Women's Studies Program at Boston College, and is author or editor of three books and numerous articles on gendered violence in media.

**Dawn H. Currie** is Professor of Sociology at the University of British Columbia, Canada. Her research interests include girl cultures and feminist media education. She is author of *Girl Talk: Adolescent Magazines and Their Readers* (1999) and co-author of *"Girl Power": Girls Reinventing Girlhood* (2009), as well as a number of journal articles and book chapters on girl cultures, feminist theory, and feminist methodology.

**Christine Daviault** is in the last stages of her Ph.D. in Communication at the University of Otago, New Zealand. Her research examines the relationship between video game players and the avatars they control/embody, and the persistent non-player characters they encounter and use to progress in the game.

**Josephine Dolan** is Senior Lecturer in Film Studies at the University of the West of England, Bristol, UK. She specializes in British Cinema. A founding member of the Women, Ageing, Media research network, her recent publications on gender and old age include *Aging Femininities: Troubling Representations* (2012).

**Tim Edwards** is Senior Lecturer in Sociology in the Department of Sociology at the University of Leicester, UK. He has lectured and published widely on topics including gender and masculinities, fashion, and consumer culture. He is author of *Cultures of Masculinity* (2006) and *Fashion in Focus* (2011), and editor of *Cultural Theory* (2007).

**Nahed Eltantawy** is an Egyptian American who is on the journalism faculty at High Point University, USA. She earned a Ph.D. at Georgia State University, USA. Her research covers media portrayals of Arabs and Muslims, the Arab Spring, and social media.

**Matthew B. Ezzell** is Assistant Professor of Sociology at James Madison University, USA. His research and teaching focus on the study of race, class, and gender inequality, with specific attention on media, identity, and men's violence against women.

**Margaret Gallagher** is a freelance researcher and writer in the UK specializing in gender and media. She has worked as a consultant for the United Nations and its agencies, the European Commission, the Council of Europe, development agencies and media organizations.

**Rosalind Gill** is Professor at City University, London, UK. She is known for research in gender and media, the body, sexuality, cultural labor, new technologies, and mediated intimacy. She leads an ESRC research seminar about the "sexualization" of culture and is working with others to explore how girls negotiate a "sexualized" culture.

**J. Robyn Goodman** is Associate Professor of Advertising at the University of Florida, USA. Having earned her Ph.D. at the University of Texas, USA, she has authored numerous journal articles and book chapters on cosmetic surgery, eating disorders, ideal beauty, and the media.

**Esther Hamburger** is Professor of History and Theory of Cinema and Television in the School of Communication Arts at the University of São Paulo, Brazil. She is author of *O Brasil Antenado* (2005) and articles in the journals *Framework* and *Television and New Media*.

**Dustin Harp** is Assistant Professor in the Department of Communication, the University of Texas, Arlington, USA. She conducts research related to issues of power and voice in the public sphere. Her research focuses on women and marginalized groups, journalism, and digital/social media.

**Radha S. Hegde** is Associate Professor, Department of Media, Culture and Communication, New York University, USA. Her research and teaching center on gender, globalization, migration, and global media flows. She is co-editor of *Circuits of*

*Visibility: Gender and Transnational Media Cultures* (2011). Her work has appeared in various journals and in book chapters.

**Joke Hermes** is Professor of practice-based research in media, culture, and citizenship at Inholland University, Netherlands, and she teaches media and popular culture at the University of Amsterdam. She is founding co-editor of the *European Journal of Cultural Studies*.

**Larissa Hjorth** is an artist, digital ethnographer, and Associate Professor in the School of Media & Communication, RMIT University, Australia. Her research centers on gendered mobile, social, and gaming practices in the Asia-Pacific. She is author of *Mobile Media in the Asia-Pacific* (2009) and *Games & Gaming* (2010).

**Ursula Huws** is Professor of Labour and Globalisation at the University of Hertfordshire Business School, UK, and editor of the journal *Work Organisation, Labour and Globalisation*.

**Iam-Chong Ip** is Senior Teaching Fellow of Cultural Studies at Lingnan University, Hong Kong. He is the editor of *Social Media Uprising in the Chinese-Speaking World* (2011). His research interests include NGOs, statism, and neoliberalism in China.

**Veronika Kalmus** is Professor of Media Studies at the Institute of Social Studies, University of Tartu, Estonia. Her research interests are socialization and intergenerational relationships in the information society. She participates in several national and international projects, including EU Kids Online.

**Sahar Khamis** is Associate Professor in the Department of Communication at the University of Maryland, College Park, USA. An expert on Arab and Muslim media and the former department head at Qatar University, she recently was a visiting professor at the University of Chicago.

**Youna Kim** is Professor of Global Communications at the American University of Paris, France. She is author of *Women, Television and Everyday Life in Korea: Journeys of Hope* (2005); *Media Consumption and Everyday Life in Asia* (2008); *Transnational Migration, Media and Identity of Asian Women: Diasporic Daughters* (2011); *The Korean Wave: Korean Media Go Global* (2013); and edited *Women and the Media in Asia: The Precarious Self* (2012).

**Oi-Wan Lam** is Northeast Asia editor at globalvoicesonline.org and a part-time instructor for the Master Program of Global Communication at the School of Journalism and Communication in the Chinese University of Hong Kong. She has carried out action researches on independent media and citizen online participation regarding the development of civil society in Chinese-speaking communities.

**Dafna Lemish** is Professor and Dean of the College of Mass Communication and Media Arts at Southern Illinois University, USA, and founding editor of the *Journal of Children and Media*. She has published extensively on children and media and gender representations.

**Marion Leonard** is Senior Lecturer in the School of Music at the University of Liverpool, UK. She is author of *Gender in the Music Industry* (2007). Her popular music research engages with gender, the music industries, heritage, and museum practice.

**Koen Leurs** is a Marie Curie Postdoctoral Fellow at the London School of Economics, UK. He is the author of *Digital Passages: How Diaspora, Gender and Youth Culture Intersect*

*Online* (2015) co-editor of *Everyday Feminist Research Praxis* (2014) and guest co-editor of the special issue *Digital Crossings in Europe* published in *Crossings: Journal of Migration and Culture* (2014). He publishes on digital networks, youth culture, multiculturalism, migration and gender. See www.koenleurs.net.

**Sonia Livingstone** is Professor in the Department of Media and Communications, London School of Economics, UK. She leads the EU Kids Online network for the European Commission, and is co-author of *Children and the Internet* (2009) and *Media Regulation* (2012), and co-editor of *International Handbook of Children's Media Culture* (2008).

**Catharine Lumby** is Professor of Media at Macquarie University, Sydney, Australia. She is the author and co-author of six books and one edited collection. A former journalist, her research interests include gender and ethics, online and social media, and young people and media consumption.

**Lisa McLaughlin** is Associate Professor with appointments in the Department of Media, Journalism, and Film and the Women's, Gender, and Sexuality Studies program at Miami University-Ohio, USA. She has published on transnational feminism, the public sphere, political economy, and women, work, and information technologies. She is founding co-editor, with Cynthia Carter, of the journal *Feminist Media Studies*.

**Brenton J. Malin** is Associate Professor of Communication at the University of Pittsburgh, USA, with a focus on media theory, history, and criticism. He is the author of *American Masculinity under Clinton: Popular Media and the Nineties "Crisis of Masculinity"* (2005).

**Vicki Mayer** is Professor of Communication at Tulane University, USA. Her publications, including authored and co-edited books and articles, examine how media production and consumption reflect political economic transformations of media industries. She is editor of the journal *Television & New Media*.

**Toby Miller** is Distinguished Professor of Media and Cultural Studies at the University of Southern California, Riverside, USA. He is author of over 30 books and numerous articles and chapters. His latest authored book is *Blow Up the Humanities* (2012) and he co-authored, with Richard Maxwell, *Greening the Media* (2012). See www.toby miller.org.

**Isabel Molina-Guzmán** is Associate Professor of Latina/Latino Studies and Media & Cinema Studies at the University of Illinois, USA, and author of *Dangerous Curves: Latina Bodies in the Media* (2010).

**Annabelle Mooney** is Reader in Sociolinguistics at the University of Roehampton, UK. Her current work focuses on law and human rights.

**Dara Persis Murray** is a doctoral candidate specializing in Media Studies at Rutgers University, USA, where she also completed a Certificate in Women's and Gender Studies. Her work has appeared in *Feminist Media Studies*, *Celebrity Studies*, and several edited collections.

**Heather Nunn** is Professor of Culture and Politics at the University of Roehampton, UK. Her research interests include gender and politics, documentary and reality TV, cultural studies and social class. She is the co-author with Anita Biressi of *Class and Contemporary British Culture* (2013).

**Laurie Ouellette** is Associate Professor in the Department of Communication Studies at the University of Minnesota, USA. She is co-author of *Better Living through Reality TV: Television and Post-Welfare Citizenship* (2008) and editor of the forthcoming *A Companion to Reality Television*.

**Radhika Parameswaran** is Professor in the School of Journalism at Indiana University, Bloomington, USA. She has authored two monographs and eight book chapters and published articles in leading journals in media studies and communication. She is editor of the forthcoming encyclopedia *Audience and Interpretation in Media Studies*.

**Sandra Ponzanesi** is Associate Professor at the Department of Media and Culture Studies, Utrecht University, Netherlands. She is author of *Paradoxes of Postcolonial Culture* (2004) and *The Postcolonial Cultural Industry* (2014), and co-editor of *Migrant Cartographies* (2005), *Postcolonial Cinema Studies* (2012), *Deconstructing Europe* (2012), and *Gender, Globalization and Violence: Postcolonial Conflict Zones* (2014). See www. ponzanesi.com.

**Andrea L. Press** is Professor of Media Studies and Sociology at the University of Virginia, USA. She is the author or co-author of several books, including *The New Media Environment* (2010). She is co-editor of the academic journal *The Communication Review*. She is working on a book about representations of feminism/postfeminism in popular media, and their reception.

**Rosa Reitsamer** is Assistant Professor at the Institute for Music Sociology at the University of Music and Performing Arts, Vienna, Austria. Her most recent authored book is *Die Do-it-yourself-Karrieren der DJs: Über die Arbeit in elektronischen Musikszenen* (2013).

**Karen Ross** is Professor of Media at the University of Northumbria at Newcastle, UK. She teaches, researches, and has written extensively about gender, media, and politics. Her latest book is the co-edited volume *A Handbook of Gender, Sex and Media* (2011).

**David Rowe** is Professor of Cultural Research, Institute for Culture and Society, University of Western Sydney, Australia. He is author of *Sport, Culture and the Media* (2nd edition, 2004) and *Global Media Sport* (2011), co-author of *Sport Beyond Television* (2012), and co-editor of *Digital Media Sport* (2013) and *Sport, Public Broadcasting, and Cultural Citizenship* (2014).

**Julie Levin Russo** is a Member of the Faculty at the Evergreen State College. She received her Ph.D. at Brown University, USA, and served as Acting Assistant Professor of Film & Media Studies at Stanford University, USA, and as an Associate of the Five College Women's Studies Research Center at Mount Holyoke College, USA.

**Katharine Sarikakis** is Professor of Media Governance, Department of Communication, University of Vienna, Austria, and formerly Senior Lecturer in Media Policy at the University of Leeds, UK, where she led the Centre for International Communication Research. She is co-editor of the *Journal of Media and Cultural Politics* and publishes on media governance and the political economy of the media industry.

**Gareth Schott** is Senior Lecturer in the School of Arts at the University of Waikato, New Zealand. He has published widely in the field of game studies since its inception in 2001. He is co-author of *Computer Games: Text, Narrative and Play* (2006).

**Katherine Sender** is a Professor in the Department of Film, Television and Media Studies at the University of Auckland, New Zealand. She has written extensively on reality television and GLBT media and marketing, including *Business Not Politics: The Making of the Gay Market* (2004).

**Leslie Regan Shade** is Associate Professor in the Faculty of Information at the University of Toronto, Canada. Her research and teaching are concerned with the social and policy aspects of information and communication technologies, with a particular focus on gender, youth, and political economy.

**Tamara Shepherd** is a Postdoctoral Fellow at the Rogers School of Information Technology Management, Ryerson University, Canada. She has published on aspects of labor and literacy in social media from a feminist political economy perspective.

**Linda Steiner** is Professor of Journalism at the University of Maryland, USA. Her primary research areas are alternative media, gendered media employment, women and technology, citizen journalism, and ethics. She has written or co-authored three books, and over 85 book chapters and journal articles. Her most recent co-edited book is *Key Concepts in Critical-Cultural Studies* (2010).

**Kairi Talves** is a Researcher at the Institute of Social Studies, University of Tartu, Estonia. Currently she is working on her Ph.D. in Sociology and her research is focused on gendered patterns of socialization and intergenerational relationships in the information society.

**Francesca Tripodi** is a Ph.D. student in sociology with a focus in media studies at the University of Virginia, USA. Her dissertation examines "integrated audiences"—the responses of groups directly represented in popular media. She studies how gender, class, and sexuality come into play in the integrated audience phenomenon.

**Angharad N. Valdivia** is Research Professor, Head of Media and Cinema Studies, and Interim Director of the Institute of Communications Research at the University of Illinois, USA. She is author of *A Latina in the Land of Hollywood* (2000) and *Latina/os and the Media* (2010), and editor of *Feminism, Multiculturalism and the Media* (1995), *A Companion to Media Studies* (2005), and *Latina/o Communication Studies Today* (2008).

**Milly Williamson** is Senior Lecturer in Film and TV Studies at Brunel University, UK. She teaches and researches in the areas of horror, celebrity culture, gender, racism and the media, television studies and fan culture. She is the author of *The Lure of the Vampire* (2005) and *Celebrity: The Politics of the Popular* (forthcoming).

**Audrey Yue** is Associate Professor in Screen and Cultural Studies at the University of Melbourne, Australia. She is author of *Ann Hui's Song of the Exile* (2010), and co-author of *Queer Singapore: Illiberal Citizenship and Mediated Cultures* (2012) and *Transnational Australian Cinema: Ethics in the Asian Diasporas* (2013). She is Chief Investigator in two current Australian Research Council funded projects.

**Elke Zobl** is Assistant Professor at the Department of Communication and head of the program area "Contemporary Arts & Cultural Production" at the University of Salzburg (in cooperation with Mozarteum University), Austria. She recently co-edited the anthology *Feminist Media: Participatory Spaces, Networks and Cultural Citizenship* (2012).

# Introduction

## Re-imagining media and gender

# Cynthia Carter, Linda Steiner, and Lisa McLaughlin

Media commentators often claim that feminism largely has achieved its initial aims of equality between men and women. This assertion sometimes tends to support the view that in Westernized, "postfeminist" societies media and communication scholars no longer need to interrogate gendered media forms, practices, and consumption processes. It is true that, in many parts of the world over the past few decades, public perceptions of gender roles, opportunities, and life expectations have substantially changed. Nevertheless, many important problems remain unresolved. Meanwhile, of course, new concerns, debates, and tensions cry out for scholarly investigation. The opening premise of *The Routledge Companion to Media and Gender* is that gender continues to matter and that issues related to the gender–media nexus are more complicated than ever, necessitating more nuanced and multifaceted understandings.

A rapidly growing body of evidence undermines the claim that equality between men and women has been achieved. For instance, in most countries a pay gap between men and women persists (ITUC 2008; AAUW 2013; European Commission 2013). Despite women's economic gains in particular fields in certain countries, the feminization of poverty worldwide is increasing (Moghadam 2005). More to the point, women, especially women of color and poor women, tend to remain especially disadvantaged in new global communication economies. Media production and distribution systems remain primarily in the hands of white, elite men; and global information and capital flows still largely privilege their views, preoccupations, and economic goals. Not enough women are in charge of major corporations, including in the media, for researchers to be able to say whether women act in significantly different (and better) ways as leaders and managers than men. The research on this question is mixed. But, in the meantime, the numbers of women who have broken through what is widely referred to as the "glass ceiling," especially at the very top levels, is miniscule compared to the number of men who have been able to advance into positions of power and decision-making.

What we can say is that media constructions of masculine identities are still widely articulated with violence, power, and control, as witnessed in the broad-ranging discussions in North America, for instance around "rape culture" and feminist responses to the problem, such as a Slut Walk initiative launched in Toronto in 2011. Critics, journalists, and popular commentators are exploring claims that masculinity is currently—that is, once again—in a state of "crisis" and needs to be reinvented, although various versions of so-called hegemonic masculinity do not greatly differ. Meanwhile, feminists have successfully dislodged a single hegemonic femininity, if not a single beauty ideal. Several chapters in this volume note the increasing global circulation of narrow ideas of beauty.

Nonetheless, concern is growing around the sexualization of girls and women and, to a lesser extent, of boys and men. Commentators often blame this problem on the media. Additionally, the normalization of pornographic representations in "everyday" mainstream culture is getting increasing attention. Even a cursory look at the mainstream media reveals that the ubiquitous, repetitive sexualization of women reinforces the common perception that they are sexual objects always "up for it," while at the same time positioning women who are sexually assaulted as somehow being out of line or to blame for such violence precisely because they have asserted their sexual agency. Further, there is now an enormous body of evidence that journalists tend to portray men and women running for political office differently: Men tend to be judged on the basis of issues and political records and women on appearance and marital status, thus undermining women's participation in democratic public spheres. Gender difference has in some ways become much more fixed and rigid, as media clearly demarcate between the feminine and masculine.

Nowhere is this more apparent than in the ways in which children are encouraged to adopt very narrow forms of gender identity in terms of media, toys, games, and so forth. Video gaming is deeply gendered in relation to the development of gendered genres—largely divided between violent video games for boys and relationship-oriented games for girls. Despite the claim—indeed the promise—that the internet, blogging, and social and mobile media would finally open up more discursive space for fluid identifications and expressions of gender identity, such technophilic, technologically deterministic prophecies fail to take into account the impact of offline social worlds on online interactions and vice versa. Even an open "information" space as heralded as Wikipedia, with its Wild West culture, seems to have isolated, and even alienated, women. Some 78 percent of Wikipedia contributors are men, largely accounting for the fact that over 80 percent of the individual biographies on Wikipedia are about men (Glott et al. 2010). Women are using the internet and social media for entrepreneurial, activist, journalistic, and intellectual pursuits, especially as new technologies become cheaper, more portable, and easier to learn. Nonetheless, the democratizing and feminist potential of new media may be exaggerated, while the promise of a non-gendered cyberspace so embraced by technophiles in the 1990s remains largely unrealized.

Journalists also report on gender problems in the wider society, sometimes galvanizing solutions. This occurs even in sports, a domain generally assumed to be invulnerable to criticism. Relevant to discussions of gender-based insults in sport, recently the men's basketball coach at Rutgers, the State University of New Jersey, was fired after journalists exposed how he insulted the masculinity of his players (as well as hitting them). On the other hand, at least as of this writing, journalists' persistent attention to abuse of women athletes by the new Athletic Director (as a coach she called them "whores") brought in to clean up Rutgers's problem has not yet resulted in an abrogation of her high-paying contract, despite seemingly massive expression of outrage.

Despite growing interest in interrogating the intersections of gender, race, ethnicity, sexual orientation, and transnational feminism, much more work is needed to address the issues identified by this research, including in digital spaces, and the varying forms of activism associated with intersectional approaches. Representations of gender and sexuality in entertainment forms still tend to reinforce sexual difference and imbalances of power in ways that disadvantage gay, lesbian, bisexual, and transgendered people. Media policy and political economy remain areas which are under-researched in gendered terms, and this research deficit is both more pronounced when considered in relation to other dimensions of difference and "othering," particularly around questions of race and ethnicity.

In addressing questions around media and gender equality, this volume features contributions asking a seemingly endless series of questions that persist in discussions of gender and media: Why and under what circumstances do ideas and ideologies offered up in media content about gender, gender differences, gender roles, and gender identity persist, or change? Where and for whom are these changing? How do different groups of people construct gender identities and how, when, and to what extent do media representations offer either useful resources or unattainable standards? How do professionals working within the media push back against stultifying notions of gender, as well as under what conditions might such challenges be possible? Additionally, how do audiences variously respond, resist, use, discard, transform, or poach media messages about gender? Indeed, several of the authors in this volume ask, both more and less explicitly, what do we want? Feminist and gender scholars have long argued that women and men are constricted by gender identities, both "traditional" and not so traditional. What happened to the feminist idea—the hope—that gender would become a meaningless concept? How do progressive or liberating ideas about sex, sexuality, and sexual relationships coexist and confront dominant ideologies in a social environment of gendered contradictions?

*The Routledge Companion to Media and Gender* explores the role of a broad range of media forms, practices, and consumption processes that reproduce as well as resist conventional notions of gender, and reinforce or challenge gendered inequalities. Since the emergence of what is often referred to as "second-wave feminism," particularly in industrialized economies, women around the world have made important social, economic, and political gains. Men have changed, too. Nevertheless, much more needs to be done to enhance the lives of women and men, and to make the world more just and fair for everyone.

Researchers contributing to this volume offer innovative, engaging insights into old questions around media and gender, exploring some of the key factors that have shaped the current state of gender, gender identity, and gender relations worldwide. The volume engages with a broad span of issues, conceptual frameworks, and methodological approaches to studying a diverse range of media audiences; media forms, including television, newspapers, radio, magazines, video games, mobile media, and the internet; and media institutions and professional practices, as well as questions of media ownership, control, and regulation. These issues concern—or certainly should concern—scholars, activist groups, media producers, pressure groups, government, and policymakers.

## This volume

Much of the research in this field has been conducted in North America and Western Europe, as well as in Australia and New Zealand. *The Routledge Companion to Media and Gender* addresses this constraint by bringing together in the volume a series of issues, ideas, and themes currently shaping the field of media and gender studies from a broad range of conceptual and methodological approaches drawn from research around the world. Fostering an international dialogue among media and gender researchers and activists will broaden and deepen our understandings in international, global, and transnational terms. Encouraging more transnational forms of feminist media research is central to challenging rosy views of an ideal postfeminist state of being and to critiquing mediated prescriptions for ideal or normative masculine and feminine bodies.

Part I, "Her/histories," provides an historical overview of media and gender research across conceptual and methodological frameworks. This section critiques the scholarly work that informs contemporary studies in the field and pays homage to the pioneering groundwork foundational to the field of feminist media studies. Part II turns to a consideration of "Media industries, labor, and policy" and explores the social, economic, and political contexts in which the gendered division of labor and sex segregation have implications for the deep gender inequalities that characterize patterns of media ownership, employment opportunities and disparities, the construction of the audience commodity, and policy decision-making, as well as ignite forms of activism against media concentration, violations of privacy, and censorship. Chapters in Part III, "Images and representations across texts and genres," examine media texts from a range of conceptual approaches and media forms. Textual analysis is probably the most theoretically elaborated, so the chapters here hint at some of the diversity in media and gender research. Part IV, "Media audiences, users, and prosumers," investigates media audiences, including the so-called "prosumers" who self-consciously and explicitly bridge and blur the lines between media consumption and production in their engagement with media. Finally, Part V, "Gendered media futures and the future of gender," looks ahead to trends and themes in media and gender research, some already emerging and others of crucial consequence for future engagement.

## Structure and contents

### Part I: Her/histories

This opening part of the *Companion* focuses on the histories of key topics in media and gender research. Margaret Gallagher (Chapter 1) observes that since the 1970s feminists have critiqued how media discourses help to silence women in a process that both reflects and shapes gender power relations in society. Media representations have diversified over the years, Gallagher explains, from the early template of "hearth and home" as women's natural sphere to those which show women in more varied roles in both the private and public spheres. Additionally, feminist ideas have been absorbed into media practice, reproducing them within an ideology of individual choice, women's empowerment, and sexual freedom.

Gallagher herself has been active in organizing systematic, international media monitoring through the Global Media Monitoring Project (GMMP), which has since 1995 provided empirical data demonstrating various patterns of gender representation in the news. One such pattern, Gallagher notes, is that of women as victims of violence. Lisa M. Cuklanz (Chapter 2) investigates this topic with regard to the historical pervasiveness of representations of gendered violence, particularly rape, in the US mass media. Specifically, she argues that the mainstreaming of pornography and pornography-style representations, the increasingly problematic relationships between media representations of sexuality and sexual violence, the gap between legal changes in the national and international sphere and media representations, and the enormous range and reach of US media products featuring gender-based violence all play a role in normalizing sexual violence. The focus on the gendered nature of violent media representations also forms a central theme in Tim Edwards' exploration of representations of masculinity, especially in film (Chapter 3). Edwards complicates the frequently heard claim that representations of masculinity reinforce traditional notions of patriarchy, men's power over women, or simply set up ideal types of masculinity. He notes a growing number of films that feature men in crisis or distressed men. Such portrayals of emotionally incapacitated loners appear to be linked to wider public discourses around the "crisis of masculinity." Men no longer know what it is to be a man, some suggest, leading to increasing public and personal reflections on the social construction of masculinity. Edwards's analysis of three films which feature the lone male as the central protagonist concludes that such texts offer emotionally powerful portraits of men that complicate the view that representations of masculinity in cinema are overwhelmingly about men's violence and power over others.

Vicki Mayer (Chapter 4) considers research on the feminization of labor, focusing on the invisibility and dismissal of forms of work that are not considered "labor," from cooking and cleaning to comfort and caretaking. She contends that the feminization of work has been part of an ongoing trajectory in US media and communication industries that correlates visibility with work performance. Beginning with the lessons learned from early telecommunications industries and the role of the telephone operator, communication work has become feminized. Even as these positions have become more competitive, outsourced, and less gender segregated, the roles themselves continue to be feminized. Joke Hermes (Chapter 5) similarly argues for the importance of understanding the gendered history of media audiences' labor. Contributing to what became referred to as the "ethnographic turn" in media and cultural studies in the 1980s, she suggests, feminist audience research started from recognition of the complexity of everyday life worlds and the need to theorize the descriptions and interpretations of real-life media users. Contemporary feminist audience studies, she claims, call for greater sensitivity not only around gender, but also with regard to the ways in which gender intersects with ethnicity, class, sexuality or any other means of differentiating individuals by their perceived worth and level of equality.

Isabel Molina-Guzmán and Lisa Marie Cacho (Chapter 6) maintain that since the 1980s feminist media scholarship has increasingly embraced the concept of "intersectionality" to discuss how race, class, gender, and sexuality need to be analyzed in relationship to one another rather than as individual or additive identities. They argue for the significance of intersectional feminist media scholarship in an increasingly diverse, global, and digitally networked world. Molina-Guzmán and Cacho highlight three dimensions in research: foregrounding media interpretations by women of color; focusing on the multiple interactions of vectors of inequality; and exploring the relationship between media as an institution and the production of inequalities. Audrey Yue (Chapter 7) also focuses on the global in highlighting the ways that sexualities and queer identities are forged in the relation between media texts and audiences, as seen in the representations of Asian refugees, gay Asian porn, and equal love campaigns from Asian Diasporas. Specifically, Yue considers the mutually constitutive categories of sexuality and race as a set of practices, as desire, and as identity and post-identity politics. She critiques contemporary articulations on biopolitics and homonationalism, and questions the politics of sexualized racialism and radicalized sexuality that govern current practices of queer neoliberalism. On a related note, Radha S. Hegde (Chapter 8) argues that neoliberal globalization and new communication technologies are foregrounding gender and sexuality issues in new ways. To illustrate how the globalized, gendered subject surfaces through particular mobilizations of nation, mobility, and modernity, she investigates the sensational news media coverage of the 2011 scandal that unfolded after Dominique Strauss-Kahn, then head of the International Monetary Fund, was charged with raping a hotel maid in New York City. The story circulated around the world. More political and transnational readings of the politics of gender and mediated environments are necessary, Hegde concludes.

## Part II: Media industries, labor, and policy

In their well-known edited book on feminist political economy of media, Meehan and Riordan (2002) wrote that feminist communications scholars largely had abandoned political-economic issues, perhaps because, as women, they were unwelcome in overtly political and economic domains. Indeed, at that time and in the present, feminist media scholars have been reluctant to explore media economics, industries, and policy, along with issues including capitalism, labor, and class (McLaughlin 1999). Areas such as media industries, labor, finance, market creation, and policy traditionally have been the realm of men—or perhaps masculinism. Part II reveals that we have made significant strides since 2002; yet, as the authors point out, women continue to be marginalized within both media industries and the fields of political economy and policy. For feminists, understanding how global capitalism and its local manifestations affect women's lives as citizens, producers, and consumers is crucial. Feminist political economy reveals how material and ideological factors are the basis for social inequalities and progressive social change (Steeves and Wasko 2002). Although Part II is roughly divided into intersections of gender with media industries, media labor, audience commodification, and policy, within the field of feminist political economy of communication, each clearly informs the other.

Carolyn M. Byerly (Chapter 9) provides a compelling argument for conducting more research on women's entry into and influence on the macro level of media. Policymaking, finance, and ownership are the media and communications arenas where decision-making power is most efficacious. Given the growth in holdings of a small number of huge media conglomerates, the marginalization of women continues in the form of unequal pay and underrepresentation across occupational ranks, especially those associated with decision-making. However, putting women into more media decision-making positions does not necessarily prompt progressive changes in media content or employment related to gender. Ben Aslinger (Chapter 10) maintains that, although media conglomerates are risk averse, conglomerates can override local homophobia or sexism in ways and at a scale often unavailable to local minority producers. Yet their search for niche markets of significant size results in the production of texts that often elide differences and diversity within minority target markets, privileging the representations of gender, sexuality, race, and ethnicity that most closely resemble ideal consumer subjects, while potentially distorting these same representations. Analyzing riot grrrl, queercore, and Latino/a music, Aslinger concludes that the risk and innovation dialectic affects which cultural producers have access to capital and which narratives are told.

Focusing on the association of rock music with notions of masculinity, Marion Leonard (Chapter 11) explores how gendered expectations influence rock musicians and contemporary music practice. Leonard interviewed eight women in particularly sex-segregated areas of music employment—artist management, artist and repertoire (A&R), tour management, and promotion—about how they navigated the continuing male dominance in these spheres. Although the achievements of women in the music industries should be appreciated, Leonard shows how persistent gender inequalities have real effects on the experiences and earning potential of women working in the music industry.

Denise D. Bielby (Chapter 12) describes how representations and relations of gender and sexuality are critical to the definition and workings of media conglomerates. She uses analyses of film and television writers' employment and ethnographic accounts of their production culture in order to explain how gender inequalities in culture industries are created and sustained. She focuses on distinctive gatekeeping organizational mechanisms that make invisible the organizational structures and policies that block career advancement based on distorted notions of gender, age, and other demographic characteristics.

Ursula Huws (Chapter 13) shifts the focus to the "information society," addressing the complex and shifting interrelationship between, on the one hand, the gender division of labor in unpaid work and paid work and, on the other hand, transformations in the technical and spatial division of labor that have accompanied the spread of information and communications technologies (ICTs), the liberalization of world trade, and globalization. She concludes that changes in the boundaries of paid and unpaid work, as well as in the location of work in the new media industries, have not resulted in gender equality; nor have they eased time pressures for women.

Huws urges more attention to gendered divisions of labor in the new ICTs, but also to the interactions among class, nationality, and ethnicity.

The next three chapters turn to the media industry's vision and construction of the audience as consumers and commodities. Tamara Shepherd (Chapter 14) describes how the users of social media are constructed as gendered commodities. Social media technologies, she writes, can be viewed as platforms for creativity and communication (e.g. Facebook, YouTube, Twitter, Pinterest, and Instagram). As profit-seeking corporations, however, these sites use sophisticated data-mining practices that harness significant stores of user information for targeted marketing campaigns. The user becomes both a laborer, by constituting part of their immense web traffic and populating them with content, and a product or commodity. Social media users are commodified according to gender and other intersecting axes of identity, she suggests, in ways that appropriate their labor and participation within institutionalized systems of inequality.

While Shepherd offers an important conceptual framework for understanding digital media's acumen for constructing users as gendered commodities, Shira Chess (Chapter 15) illustrates this phenomenon through an account of a Martha Stewart avatar introduced into the role-playing video game *Castleville* in order to target women interested in Martha Stewart products. Chess describes video game industries' propensity for misunderstanding and alienating women as video game consumers by assuming that women share similar tastes and desires. As Chess explains, with women representing only 11 percent of the video game workforce, it is no wonder that most games are geared to men. The industry is now trying to include more women as developers and as game characters; however, the primary result has been to reify traditional stereotypes of femininity and narrow definitions of womanhood. Chess urges the gaming industry to engender more diversity and abandon the ill-conceived dichotomy between "casual" women players and "hardcore" men players.

Adding to the strong case that sex/gender segregation exists in, and is sustained by, media industries, Dafna Lemish (Chapter 16) maintains that a large portion of children's media and related merchandizing produced, distributed, and consumed around the world promotes traditional and stereotypical constructs of marginalized femininity and masculinity. Her analysis of gender representations in children's culture demonstrates that the same issues dominating critiques of adult media are relevant to those targeting children. The political economy of media explains key factors driving this segregation, and the restrictive narratives offered by the media industry to boys and girls for their own construction of gender identity influence socialization processes.

Given that gender equality in a networked world requires considerations of online risk and safety, Sonia Livingstone, Veronika Kalmus, and Kairi Talves (Chapter 17) address gender differences in girls' and boys' experiences of online risk (including exposure to pornography, bullying, sexual messaging, potentially harmful user-generated content, and meeting online contacts offline). Drawing on the EU Kids Online project, which surveyed 1,000 children aged 9–16 years old in 25 European countries, the authors studied girls' and boys' behaviors online and specifically how children cope when bothered by online risks. The authors found some important differences, including that while girls were slightly more likely to be bullied online, boys received slightly more sexual messages. Girls were more upset by sexting than were boys. Boys also were more sensation-seeking online, for example seeking online contacts beyond their familiar social circle and sharing more personal information online than did girls. The latter invested more in protecting their sexual reputation online. They also found that parents "mediated" or regulated the internet use of sons and daughters differently: Girls got more of all types of parental mediation (with the exception of technical mediation) than did boys. The authors urge policymakers to avoid gender-stereotyped views of children's experiences of the internet and advocate policy initiatives which recognize heterogeneity among children, schooling that teaches about online and offline social relations, and government and industry efforts to develop online safety tools.

Annabelle Mooney (Chapter 18) focuses on men's magazines. The "old man" phase of men's magazines in the 1940s and 1950s turned men into consumers, even though consumption was considered a feminine domain. Those magazines, as did the later "new man" and "new lad" magazines, objectified and sexualized women. While the "new man" magazines had a relatively limited advertising base, the construction of the "new lad" reader of the 1990s expanded the market for male consumers by linking discourses of masculinity to the crisis of masculinity as part of the backlash against feminism. Despite some grassroots campaigns, Mooney finds little interest in regulation, because the magazines are packaged as "authentic" and "manly." This allows them to use "irony" and commercial arguments for promotional purposes.

Katharine Sarikakis (Chapter 19) sees an urgent need for rethinking the technological, sociocultural and political economic conditions and frameworks within which modern-day pornography operates. Although pornography has been at the center of polarization and intense politicization for over three decades, she defines the pornography industry as a political actor; as such, it can protect and promote its economic interests. The pornography industry can govern the conditions of its own regulation because of both regulatory vacuums and conflicts, and its intervention in politics, through lobbying and creating informal alliances with civil society groups.

Traditionally, policy and regulation nearly are oxymoronic to activism. However, as Leslie Regan Shade (Chapter 20) writes, digital policy issues related to internet rights and freedoms are increasingly on the agenda of many global activists. Taking feminist political economy as the lens to examine systemic and structural power dynamics related to digital policy, which emanate from industry, international policy regimes, and civil society, Shade explores the development of policies and programs in both transnational and national contexts. Following the 2012 United Nations Human Rights Council resolution, Shade advocates the importance of viewing internet access as a human right. Such a right embraces access to ICTs, privacy rights, communication security, and freedom from surveillance.

Elke Zobl and Rosa Reitsamer (Chapter 21) show how alternative and activist women-led and feminist media offer participatory forums and political, social, and cultural exchange between those who otherwise would be marginalized within mainstream debates. They explore how the young generation of feminist media producers in Europe use media such as blogs and e-zines to challenge the status quo and create social change. As with second-wave efforts, these new ones aim to challenge power structures, transform social roles, and encourage small-scale, collaborative, DIY economies based in subcultural literacy. Although these new feminist media producers position themselves in relation to second-wave feminism, with little reference to the "third wave," their networking is virtual, transnational, and dependent upon new social media.

Iam-chong Ip and Oi-wan Lam (Chapter 22) question the relationship between activism and official policy and politics in the Chinese context. Taking an approach that diverges from the largely Western project of focusing on cosmopolitan democracy as a sign of *transnational* democracy, they argue that Chinese feminists' new cosmopolitanism features their creative appropriation of global feminist ideas for *local and national uses*. Their analysis, based in an examination of archive documentation and unstructured interviews, reveals that counter-publics not only contribute to the civil rights movement but also engage in more subtle struggles against state feminism *and* for trans-institutional spaces within the state. Exploring this largely neglected dimension in the literature on Chinese politics is crucial for understanding the tension between legitimacy and efficacy facilitated by the new political-economic realities of authoritarian countries.

## Part III: Images and representations across texts and genres

Many of the arguments connected to gender and media turn on issues about the representations of women and men, and of masculinity and femininity. Indeed, although the evidence for assuming "effects" is uneven at best (and considered passé by most critical scholars), many of the arguments about the gender (or intersections of gender with race, ethnicity, national origin, or sexual orientation) of the producers of media content assume that this matters in some way to the content they produce and also that representations of gender have some impact on their audiences. Certainly, women and men are not always represented dichotomously, and should not be represented as such. Nor are representations static over time or stable across space, platform, or audience. Content does not have a predictable, much less direct, impact on audiences. The premise of Part III, however, is that representations of women and men, of masculinity and femininity, become the basis for the stories told about what it means to be a woman or man in a specific time and place. Sophisticated and nuanced analyses illustrate a broad set of issues regarding how gender is represented differently in cultural formations across the globe.

One of the major themes is sex and sexualization, although this issue is complicated and our authors often turn arguments on their head. Leading off, Karen Boyle (Chapter 23) challenges the usual arguments about "sex for its own sake" and the "sexualization of culture" in order to highlight the significant differences between the place (and power) of heterosexual women and men in the sexual marketplace. Boyle offers several examples of products sold to heterosexuals that claim to enhance sexual pleasure either directly (sex toys, such as the "Rabbit" vibrator, whose sales rocketed after it was featured on *Sex and the City*) or indirectly (e.g. pole dancing exercise classes that promise to remodel women's bodies). Unsettling casual equivalences sometimes are made between commercial sex, pornography, and "sex shows," while contemporary women, allegedly "empowered" by their sexualized consumption (or even by high-pay sex work), still face power inequalities.

Heather Nunn and Anita Biressi (Chapter 24) examine the popular British docu-soap series *The Only Way Is Essex (TOWIE)*, i.e. a semi-scripted highly structured hybrid combining highly realistic observation with a continuing narrative about its working class characters. Early working class docusoap characters often worked in unglamorous, low-reward jobs and were judged on the basis of their authenticity. No longer needing to be genuine, the new reality docusoaps such as *TOWIE* are set in glamorous media, consumer, and service industries. More to the point, their performers are judged for their elaborate and costly grooming and participation in consumer culture, thus encouraging individuals—including men—to regard makeover practices as the route to social success and recognition. Similarly, Shelley-Jean Bradfield (Chapter 25) looks at distinctly post-apartheid South African femininities in the miniseries *Society*. Bradfield critiques *Society*'s complicated postfeminist sensibility of sexual choice and empower-ment, for example with a television "weather girl" character who must rely on a pos-sessive boyfriend to pay her rent. In particular, Bradfield notes how a neoliberal focus on the individual (but also a preference for "traditional" community and family values) ignores systemic constraints, making women responsible for their failures.

Karen Ross (Chapter 26), who herself ran for political office, examines news cov-erage of political candidates. Journalists increasingly adopt the salacious tone of tabloids regarding *all* politicians, and some women politicians receive gender-neutral or even "positive" coverage. Nonetheless, Ross generally finds journalists obsessed with women's coiffure, couture, and conjugal relations, thereby still ignoring their policy positions. Thus, women achieve their political ambitions *despite* news media, not *because* of them. Ross suspects a variety of factors are in play, including gender-based stereotypes, the male-ordered nature of many newsrooms, and the reliance on the "usual suspects" as sources and subjects for news discourse. In examining tele-vised representations of Chaz Bono's transition to a transgendered self, however, Katherine Sender (Chapter 27) finds Bono having skillfully put his "brand" into cir-culation on a transnational basis. Sender predicts that gay, lesbian, bisexual, and transgender (GLBT) media representations produced at the media "center" will be most normative: gender conforming, family oriented, non-sexual, and apolitical. At the margins of this center, low-budget reality television both allows and demands riskier GLBT images. Self-funded media at the periphery, for microniche audiences, can circulate the widest range of GLBT images. Accordingly, Bono's transgender narrative emerged differently in two documentaries (marginal media), as contestant on *Dancing with the Stars* (media center), a memoir, as well as print, television, and online news media.

Milly Williamson's (Chapter 28) history of female celebrity and scandal—since sexualized scandal and concentration on the personality are not new—emphasizes the paradox and contradictions at the heart of the bourgeois society from which modern fame emerged: it expresses growing freedom and democracy but also shows the limits of freedom and democracy, including that of women. Media treatment of women celebrities continues a social hierarchy based on class, race, and gender, and significantly expresses the economic needs of commercial entertainment and media. So while celebrity culture seemingly provides women with social mobility and increasing opportunity to participate in the public sphere, Williamson underscores the limits to social mobility.

Sara Bragg (Chapter 29) challenges the terms of public debates about the "sexualization" and "commercialization" of childhood, exposing how some standard views of contemporary consumer culture are often simplistic, unreflexive, and (wrongly) reiterating the same old story about how "sex sells." To Bragg, the view that children are inherently more vulnerable to media influence than adults is patronizing, ignores children's own views, and proposes problematic pedagogy. The media cannot directly cause social ills, so literacy will not ameliorate them. Being critical will not "cure" children of their attachments to disapproved cultural texts. Analyzing constructions of female and male sexuality in teenage-oriented television dramas, Susan Berridge (Chapter 30) implicitly agrees with Bragg. Berridge also rejects a patronizing, simplistic notion of a cause-and-effect relationship between what viewers watch and their behavior. That said, she finds that dramas for teens "naturalize" distinctions between male and female teenage sexuality. Male sexuality is presented as unstoppable, something boys cannot control, thus removing culpability for their actions. In contrast, female sexuality is portrayed as devoid of desire; girls are responsible for their sexual actions—and less entitled to sexual pleasure—thus rendering sexual violence a girl's personal problem.

Moving to representations of older women, Josephine Dolan (Chapter 31) notes that as early as 1973 Molly Haskell observed that, given the conflation by Hollywood and other national film industries of beauty and youth, women stars were, at the first visible signs of aging, deemed too old to be cast except as a marginalized mother or older sister. The same was not true for similarly aged men, who continue to be cast and often romantically coupled with much younger women. Dolan points out that old(er) women stars currently enjoy visibility—but only in the context of discourses about "successful aging," which requires and naturalizes "cosmeceutical enhancement" and age-appropriate decorum. Women are protected from pathologized abjection, but only if they conform to a "beauty myth" now extended into old age. Meanwhile, J. Robyn Goodman (Chapter 32) highlights the practices that ideologically promote these perfect bodies. Over the past 20 years, cosmetic surgery has grown dramatically worldwide, despite safety concerns and risks. In 2010, more than six million people worldwide had liposuction, breast augmentation, and surgery on their eyelids, nose, or abdomen; millions more had minimally invasive skin procedures. Goodman emphasizes the media's role as an information source for, and influence on, cosmetic surgery and ideal beauty; indeed, a single global beauty ideal for women. Since sociocultural pressures are behind cosmetic surgery's growth, and media are behind these pressures, Goodman blames media for not discussing risks and complications while overemphasizing social and psychological benefits, and finds that media emphasizing how easily, painlessly, and magically we can be transformed into the ideal.

Radhika Parameswaran (Chapter 33) turns to beauty regimes in India—not the "old" India, with its condemnation of conspicuous consumption as sinful and its suspicions of the West, but a "new" India, which embraces affluent Western lifestyles (and beauty products) and a capitalist climate favoring the middle classes. Returning to the sleepy hometown in Hyderabad she left 20 years ago to illustrate the contradictory ways beauty culture intersects with cultural imperialism, nationalism, and glocalization, Parameswaran offers a personal account of the beauty choices of her upwardly mobile niece, who disdained shabby Indian-style beauty parlors, with their "third-rate Indian products," in favor of high-end salons where Western-attired English-speaking professionals offered products imported from Europe and America.

Gargi Bhattacharyya (Chapter 34) argues that the "war on terror" has shaped popular culture representations of sexualized racism. To show the links between discourses around personal and national security with those of feminism, race, and sexuality, she contrasts the narratives of the first series of the immensely popular and influential US television program *Homeland* with news media representations of women who have been associated with UK terrorist suspects. Bhattacharyya concludes that, in the name of the security state, we are witnessing a replaying of older mythologies of good and bad girls and of domesticated and disorderly femininity across the media, drawing on certain features from popular feminism in the name of securitization. Examining the potential effects of media images on audiences, Nahed Eltantawy (Chapter 35) criticizes Western media's dominant portrayal of Muslim women, covered in the traditional black abaya, eyes peering out from black veils. She blames such one-dimensional images, especially after 9/11, for encouraging dread, dislike, and mystification of Muslim women. She concludes that Western cartoons, news, and editorial columns portray the Muslim woman as an enigma, an oppressed victim, or a faceless clone. Moreover, she says, even Western feminists wrongly view the veil as signaling Muslim women's oppression.

Finally, David Rowe (Chapter 36) analyzes the gender-based insult in sport, where slurs denigrating (male) athletes' masculinity are so common that their use neither shocks nor incurs widespread condemnation. Journalists and media commentators usually focus on more "spectacular" narratives in sport of racial abuse, yet gender-based insults are typically treated as deplorable but almost banal. Organized, institutionalized sport has always been a major domain of sex/gender hierarchy; men put themselves at the center, sexualize women, and position femininity as inferior and contemptible. Rowe finds increasing evidence that gender-based insults are routine even within men's team sports that are subjected to intense scrutiny, whose official associations are mandated to foster respect, and despite policies dedicated to eradicating sexual and gender inequality.

## Part IV: Media audiences, users, and prosumers

Audience studies have long been a central feature of media and gender research, with enquiries ranging from quantitative surveys of gendered media consumption habits to qualitative analyses of the ways in which men and women make sense of media messages. While in the past the demarcation between media producers and consumers was regarded as clear, today the line between them is increasingly blurred. Media and gender research on "prosumers," or those who use and create media content, often in online environments, extends audience research beyond the traditional production/consumption binary. This part of the *Companion* addresses such issues, beginning with chapters that focus on the ways in which the imagined and often commodified audience shapes decisions about media production in gendered ways. Later chapters report on empirical audience studies interrogating how certain users and prosumers make sense of and reconfigure media output through their active and often creative use of new media.

Laurie Ouellette (Chapter 37) looks at the imagined, commodified audience for reality television, which she analyzes as a "cultural technology." Focusing on the contradictory ways in which young women are addressed and regulated as "subjects of capacity," she investigates MTV's network programs *Jersey Shore*, *16 and Pregnant*, and *Teen Mom* to reveal tensions between the display of young women's sexual freedom and empowerment and the proliferation of programs claiming to help prevent teenage pregnancy by instilling in girls the right choices, behaviors, and technologies of self-regulation. Ouellette situates reality television within neoliberalist and postfeminist frames, showing how institutional constructions of the "audience" reflect (sometimes conflicting) consumer agendas and governmental goals.

Taking up similar points, Esther Hamburger (Chapter 38) notes that since the mid-1970s Brazilian television companies have exported telenovelas; the genre has since become one of the most popular and economically successful in the world. Although telenovelas attract both male and female audiences in Brazil, they remain defined in gendered terms as "feminine" by producers, market researchers, and audiences. Hamburger's analysis suggests that telenovelas often provide audiences with progressive narratives that question the binaries of feminine and masculine, melodrama and newscast, private and public, mass culture and modernism.

The need to sell audiences to advertisers has long driven journalistic choices in the packaging of news, argues Dustin Harp (Chapter 39). In the 1890s, US newspaper publishers started segregating content related to women by creating special pages for them, although many newspapers dropped women's sections or renamed them in the face of arguments against segregating gendered content. She finds that "women's content" remains marginalized and isolated, thereby reinforcing gender divisions and inequalities. So, little has changed from previous generations in arguments both for and against separating "women's content" from the rest of the news. Therefore, what started as a way to attract women readers to sell to advertisers remains a standard means for attracting women readers to newspapers in a way, for the sake of advertising revenue.

The significance of gender portrayal as part of the wider experience of game play is explored by Christine Daviault and Gareth Schott (Chapter 40). Despite the perceived gender imbalance in terms of the greater numbers of male players, most critical research has focused on girls and women, with very little attention paid to male characters and their impact on male players. The authors conclude that the experience of play does not necessarily permit the player to engage in extensive interpretive work.

Discussing queer female fandom, Julie Levin Russo (Chapter 41) focuses on the development from its pre-digital roots to its present-day internet bounty, emphasizing both internal diversity and external dynamics. The phenomenon of fandom asks us to consider the value of subtext, she argues. In mainstream media, boosting the visibility of marginalized groups goes hand in hand with boosting their commercial profile. Russo's historical survey of fan communities, and analysis of their current exploits and conflicts, points to some of the vitality and multiplicity of queer female fandom.

Toby Miller (Chapter 42) interrogates the question of who is the implied spectator for the *bourgeois* media's coverage of sport. Sport and masculinity, he suggests, jumble together in a complex and protean weave of contradictory commodification. As part of the desire to address media spectators and capture their attention for adver-tisers, the masculine body has become an object of lyrical rhapsody. Sculpted mas-culine features, chiseled waistlines, dreamy eyes, administered hair, and an air of casual threat are the currency of the day. Like beauty and fitness of all kinds, Miller predicts that the media will identify new names, new bodies, new Eros, new Euros.

Matthew B. Ezzell (Chapter 43) examines men's use of pornography. Pornographic images, he explains, are produced primarily for heterosexual men by and through a global, multibillion dollar industry. Men's choices to consume pornography, he adds, express a patriarchal masculinity that reinforces sex inequality. So, while men who consume pornography are caught up in an equation that provides a collective economic gain for men as a class, this exacts an individual cost. Ezzell calls for more research on the male pornography "refuser."

Gender researchers have long questioned whether the internet would become a male domain and reinforce gender inequality or, conversely, strengthen feminist politics. Tanja Carstensen (Chapter 44) shows how both older and newer technolo-gies have shaped the gendered access, use, design, identities, and politics of the web. She argues that gender no longer seems to play a significant role regarding access to and usage of social media. And while social media have become male domains rein-forcing gender inequalities, social media also provide opportunities for feminist politics and political activism.

Shakuntala Banaji (Chapter 45) reports on her research with young viewers of Hindi films. Critical studies of gender representation in Hindi films often assume that male viewers all identify with a limited number of sexist—and heterosexist—discursive positions mapped out in these films. Banaji argues that, although some-times equally worrying or retrograde, other contextual and sociocultural identities and experiences—from race and ethnicity through geography and surroundings to sexuality and class—complicate young audiences' responses to and uses of gender representation in Bollywood films.

What grasp do we have of the relationship between the consumption of media and the shaping of individual lives and identities, asks Youna Kim (Chapter 46)? What do we know about the experience of non-Western women? Based on her ethnographic studies, Kim analyzes the consequences of women's media consumption at a time when the political, economic, and technological contexts in which the media operate are becoming increasingly global. She argues that media globalization in Asia needs to be recognized as a proliferating, indispensable, yet highly complex and contra-dictory resource for the construction of gender identity within the lived experience of women's everyday lives.

While gendered audiences for film and television are the subject of considerable research, few scholars work with radio audiences. Tanja Bosch (Chapter 47) notes that in Africa talk radio has contributed to the development of a range of public spheres (based on gender, ethnicity, sexuality, social background, and region); diverse and sometimes geographically disparate audiences use radio as a platform for deliberation. Bosch shows how radio listening is integrated into women's daily routines, contributing in many positive ways to their gendered sense of self-worth.

Dawn H. Currie (Chapter 48) explores the ways that girls read adolescent fashion and beauty magazines. Adults' plausible and legitimate concerns with how these magazines address girl readers as "young women" have resulted in calls for "media education" to "inoculate" girls against the harms of popular culture. However, Currie rejects the "protectionist" approach. Instead she argues for acknowledging and mobilizing the agency of girls as readers. Having shown how commercial media work through girls' reading pleasure, she proposes harnessing this pleasure to promote critical media literacy. The shaping of self-perceptions in commerce is also a concern for Dara Persis Murray (Chapter 49). Her focus is the Dove Campaign for Real Beauty (CFRB), which she says communicates problematic messages of beauty and feminism to audiences. Though people who posted on the campaign's Facebook page may consider CFRB a liberating philosophy of resistance to dominant ideologies of beauty, because it showcases "real" women with diverse sizes, colors, and ages, Murray concludes that such "liberation" encourages an individualized pursuit which necessitates work on the self, a focus that detracts from the feminist argument for collective thinking and structural change.

Andrea L. Press and Francesca Tripodi (Chapter 50) analyze posts related to women's sexual attractiveness on a US-based university online message board, Collegiate ABC. While women's bodies and sexual behaviors are targeted for praise and critique, few women have raised objections to these discourses. Most think they know sexism when they see it, the authors' research found. Meanwhile, their focus group interviews suggested that young women want to claim the freedom to be "hot," to enjoy when friends are so labeled, and to enjoy the status of associating with such women. The entrenched nature of sexism in media culture demands continuing attention, Press and Tripodi conclude.

As camera phones become more commonplace—as well as social media like microblogging and location-based services (LBS)—new types of visuality are overlaid onto place as part of users' personal journeys and forms of self-expression, maintains Larissa Hjorth (Chapter 51). LBS camera phone practices take on new gendered visual cartographies that rehearse and revise traditional Korean notions of place (*bang*) and intimacy (*ilchon*). Hjorth considers how Korean women use LBS games and camera phone images, which are generating new cartographies of place-making overlaid with playful socialities.

Sahar Khamis (Chapter 52), drawing on in-depth interviews, examines how young Arab women journalists/activists from Egypt, Syria, Libya, Yemen, and Bahrain are engaging with social media to redefine their activism, empowerment, and resistance. These women have used "cyberfeminism" to launch a parallel *sociopolitical* revolution which challenges discrimination, harassment, and gendered abuse. While new media are relevant to processes of sociopolitical change, she argues that they are *catalysts*, not *magical tools*. Arab women's activism will bring about social change, she concludes, through their challenging gender discrimination and facing real risks in the struggle for women's rights.

### Part V: Gendered media futures and the future of gender

So, where do we go from here? What should be done? Indeed, what do we want? Chapters in this final part of the collection disrupt and complicate the oversimplified, polarized debates over key issues and concepts. The authors urge us to move beyond outmoded concepts, assumptions, and paradigms and to reject exaggerated either/or dichotomies that forbid researchers or activists from embracing ambivalence. People make choices and are constrained by economic, social, and political circumstances.

Angharad N. Valdivia (Chapter 53) explores the implicit utopia guiding much of the activism as well as research about production, representations, and audience interpretation. Her points about Latina/o studies apply equally well to debates in ethnic studies and gender studies: The narrow line separating demeaning stereotype from merely easily recognizable discourse generates seemingly insolvable tensions. We prefer complex characters that suggest diversity and heterogeneity. Yet, again referring to Latinas, although we disdain stereotypes, we want a recognizable Latina presence. Moreover, if that presence is too subtle, we complain that she has been whitened or assimilated. Valdivia's television and film examples illustrate the ruptures and continuities in the limits and possibilities of inclusion of Latinas. She shows that we can say what we dislike—stereotypes of Latinas as aberrant or abnormal. But what *specific* type of presence we want has not been clearly articulated beyond a vague and unsustainable cry for authenticity.

Anxieties about the "sexualization of culture" have been addressed by journalists, policymakers, and academics, including feminists. Others, too, worry that societies—and not merely in the West—are becoming saturated by sexual representations, with practices like lap dancing and pole dancing now becoming respectable and regular features of corporate entertainment or recreational activity. Describing herself as neither anti-sex nor anti-porn, but rather "anti-sexist," Rosalind Gill (Chapter 54) criticizes the concept of "sexualization." Rhetoric about sexualization pushes moralistic rather than political solutions and homogenizes significant differences in the way bodies are figured in the media. Gill suggests that we are neither helpless cultural dopes nor autonomous agents who are made immune to sexual content through media literacy.

Catharine Lumby (Chapter 55) analogously challenges the polarized and polarizing debates within feminism over the term "postfeminism." Some celebrate how postfeminism marks liberation from feminism's outdated ideological shackles; others say it represents a panicked backlash against feminism. Her position is that, at least in the West, feminism made fundamental inroads in law, public policy, and education. Rejecting the feminist/postfeminist debate in media studies that unproductively opposes woman as sexual object and as sexual subject, Lumby emphasizes that popular media representations of women and the pleasures women may (or may not) take in them cannot be neatly categorized as either authentically "feminist" or flippantly "postfeminist." Instead, as in everyday life, popular culture is often a site of ambivalent pleasure for women. Urging feminist researchers to move beyond the putative feminist/postfeminist binary into a new "post-postfeminist" phase, Lumby urges careful attention to the speaking positions we adopt, being aware of the forms of power we enjoy, with their specific claims to authority, and how others are disempowered. Indeed, when we listen actively to others, we learn to hear more clearly how we sound when we speak.

Brenton J. Malin (Chapter 56) focuses on changes in media representations of manhood, suggesting the elasticity of dominant conceptions of masculinity in the

West, where after the late 1980s there was much discussion of a "crisis of masculinity," indicating dissatisfaction with the so-called traditional manhood, whose hypermasculine toughness and emotional control were increasingly seen as problematic. Therefore, a sensitive, "metrosexual" masculinity was constructed. But the new ideal man, except for his alleged emotional expressiveness, reiterated most of the dominant categories of traditional, hegemonic masculinity: He was white, heterosexual and enjoyed middle-class cultural capital. Malin notes that the media's inability to think beyond narrow dichotomous stereotypes highlights a lack of creativity and betrays the media's interest in economically and politically safe images, i.e. that do not upset advertisers.

Linda Steiner (Chapter 57) critiques several theories that use problematic and universalizing gender binaries to explain why more women are not executives in US news media and why women journalists or women leaders have not had more impact on journalism. These theories assume not only that representations reflect their makers, but also that women always want to produce content that is different from men's content. The leading theory was that until women comprise at least one-third of staffs they cannot challenge prevailing practices, so cannot achieve significant organizational change. Now that women are at least one-third of newsroom staffs, the paucity of women in the upper echelons of news organizations is referenced to explain why women and men do not produce significantly different news. Steiner objects to what she regards as claims about women's superiority, arguing that fairness should be sufficient. She criticizes binary understandings of gender for obscuring how sexism and discrimination prevent women from being hired and promoted, and for enforcing implausible distinctions between men's and women's topics.

Koen Leurs and Sandra Ponzanesi (Chapter 58) apply intersectional analysis and postcolonial theorizing to Moroccan Dutch youths who use online social networking sites to articulate their online identities. They first look at a short video that presented an exaggerated inventory of the consequences—according to prevailing Islamophobic stereotypes cultivated by sensationalist news media—of what the Netherlands would look like if all Moroccans left the country. Media discourse constructs "Moroccan youth" as a danger, problem, financial burden, or nuisance. Rejecting mainstream understandings of digital culture as either liberating or disenfranchising, their multi-method research shows how these youths both understood and subverted intersecting digital spatial hierarchies. Such intersectional approaches are well suited to showing how power relationships get organized, reorganized, and reformed online.

Online power relations are also a central feature of Cynthia Carter's (Chapter 59) examination of online anti-sexism political action initiatives in the UK and USA. She highlights how feminist anger around media sexism is helping to fuel the establishment of a growing number of online gender education initiatives, databases about women experts, and targeted anti-sexism campaigns. While much of it is constructive and progressive, in some instances anger over media sexism effectively closes down discussion. Future advances toward fairer gender relations are partly contingent, Carter concludes, on turning personal and collective anger into positive, constructive political achievements, with women and men working both separately and collaboratively toward this goal.

Each chapter of *The Routledge Companion to Media and Gender* addresses concrete issues in ways that illuminate important aspects of our current understanding of the relationships between media and gender. The time is long overdue for revisiting and re-imagining many of the issues and concerns first noted by researchers several decades ago and which continue to be significant in considerations of media and gender. The *Companion* offers an extensive examination of a wide array of contemporary critical perspectives and diverse contexts in the field of media and gender studies. Given the stated aim of reinvigorating current debates related to the place and importance of media and gender research, innovative thinking that reflects cutting-edge developments is of the utmost value for students, scholars, and practitioners.

## References

AAUW (2013) "The Simple Truth about the Gender Pay Gap." http://www.aauw.org/files/2013/02/The-Simple-Truth-2013.pdf.

European Commission (2013) "Gender Pay Gap Statistics." http://epp.eurostat.ec.europa.eu/statistics_explained/index.php/Gender_pay_gap_statistics.

Glott, R., P. Schmidt, and R. Ghosh (2010) *Wikipedia Survey – Overview of Results*, United Nations University-Merit. http://www.wikipediasurvey.org/docs/Wikipedia_Overview_15March2010-FINAL.pdf.

Haskell, M. (1973) *From Reverence to Rape: The Treatment of Women in the Movies*, Chicago: University of Chicago Press.

ITUC (2008) "The Global Gender Pay Gap." http://www.tuc.org.uk/equality/tuc-14409-f0.cfm.

McLaughlin, L. (1999) "Beyond 'Separate Spheres': Feminism and the Cultural Studies/Political Economy Debate," *Journal of Communication Inquiry* 23(4): 327–54.

Meehan, E. R. and E. Riordan (2002) *Sex and Money: Feminism and Political Economy in the Media*, Minneapolis: University of Minnesota Press.

Moghadam, V. M. (2005) "The Feminization of Poverty and Women's Human Rights," Paris: UNESCO. http://www.unesco.org/new/fileadmin/MULTIMEDIA/HQ/SHS/pdf/Feminization_of_Poverty.pdf.

Steeves, H. L. and J. Wasko (2002) "Feminist Theory and Political Economy: Toward a Friendly Alliance," in E. R. Meehan and E. Riordan (eds.) *Sex and Money: Feminism and Political Economy in the Media*, Minneapolis: University of Minnesota Press, pp. 16–29.

# Part I
# HER/HISTORIES

# 1

# Media and the representation of gender

## Margaret Gallagher

### Image and reality

"How can the media be changed? How can we free women from the tyranny of media messages limiting their lives to hearth and home?" Media sociologist Gaye Tuchman ends her celebrated essay "The Symbolic Annihilation of Women by the Mass Media" with these two questions (Tuchman 1978: 38). Straightforward, confident, and unambiguous, from today's vantage point the questions may seem naïve in their formulation. Yet in essence they encapsulate the concerns that continue to drive much feminist media analysis around the world almost four decades later. Despite enormous transformations in national and global media landscapes, and the development of infinitely more sophisticated approaches to media analysis and theorizing, the fundamental issues remain those that preoccupied Tuchman and her colleagues: power, values, representation, and identity.

Feminist cultural politics is a common thread running through much work on image and representation, from its origins to the present. The edited collection *Hearth and Home: Images of Women in the Mass Media*, in which Tuchman's "symbolic annihilation" essay appears, was motivated by "an interest in the progress we are making toward the full social equality of women" and by "the rise of the women's movement" (Kaplan Daniels 1978: v). These early analyses argued that the US media are deeply implicated in the patterns of discrimination operating against women in society—patterns which, through the absence, trivialization or condemnation of women in media content, amounted to their "symbolic annihilation." The term, originally coined by George Gerbner in 1972, became a powerful and widely used metaphor to describe the ways in which media images make women invisible. This mediated invisibility, it was argued, is achieved not simply through the non-representation of women's points of view or perspectives on the world. When women are "visible" in media content, the manner of their representation reflects the biases and assumptions of those who define the public—and therefore the media—agenda.

Much of this early work attempted to establish the extent to which media content departed from "reality." Some of the earliest analysis was driven by personal experience. In the early 1960s, former magazine journalist Betty Friedan, introducing her study of how the cultural definition of femininity in the USA shifted between the 1940s and 1950s, explained: "There was a strange discrepancy between the reality of our lives as women and the image to which we were trying to conform, the image that I came to call the feminine mystique" (Friedan 1963: 9). A decade later, more systematic studies of basic stereotypes were providing a basis from which to argue that the media provided idealized versions of femininity that were "false." For instance, the editors of *Hearth and Home* concluded: "Televised images of women are in large measure false, portraying them less as they really are, more as some might want them to be" (Franzwa 1978: 273).

Despite the use of terms that today we might find lack nuance, these early studies were not necessarily as unsophisticated as they are sometimes characterized. The notion that women were being portrayed "as some might want them to be" theorizes the media as part of a system "that cultivates the images fitting the established structure of social relations," a system whose function is to create cultural resistance to change—in this case, change in the status of women (Gerbner 1978: 46–8). Gerbner identifies three main tactics of resistance to change used in media imagery of women—discrediting, isolating, and undercutting. He says that the result is a "counterattack on the women's movement as a social force for structural change" (1978: 50). Betty Friedan, too, was concerned with the interplay between media images, social change, and gender identity. Asking why the "spirited New Woman" who dominated women's magazines of the 1940s had, by the 1950s, given way to the "happy Housewife Heroine," while, over the same period, educational and employment opportunities for middle-class white American women had greatly expanded, she concluded: "When a mystique is strong, it makes its own fiction of fact. It feeds on the very facts which might contradict it, and seeps into every corner of culture" (Friedan 1963: 53). What many of these early studies were grappling with, without naming it as such, was the ideological role of the media.

## Ideology and representation

In many respects the contemporary field of feminist media scholarship looks vastly different from the relatively straightforward terrain occupied by the "women and media" studies of the 1970s and 1980s. The inadequacies of studies that conflate the condition of white, heterosexual, middle-class women with the condition of all women are now acknowledged, and contemporary media research has tried to grapple with more complex understandings of gender identity and experience. As Marsha Houston has put it:

> Women of color do not experience sexism *in addition* to racism, but sexism *in the context of* racism; thus they cannot be said to bear an *additional* burden that white women do not bear, but to bear an altogether *different* burden from that borne by white women.
>
> (Houston 1992: 49)

Most early studies of "women and media" had analyzed *only* women's representation, thereby appearing to assume that the representation of men's experience was unproblematic. As feminist media critique developed and deepened, it became clear that masculinity was also represented in quite specific ways in media content. Rosalind Gill contends that studies of masculinities developed as a direct result of feminism's critique, literally "transforming research on women and media into something that is properly about gender and media" (2007: 32; see also Carter 2012).

The crossing of intellectual and disciplinary boundaries that characterizes much of today's work can actually be traced back to some of most creative points of departure in feminist media studies. As far back as 1977 Noreen Janus critiqued the theoretical shortcomings of white, middle-class, liberal research into "sex-role stereotypes." Janus advocated more holistic studies of media content, allied with analyses of the economic imperatives of the media industries and with studies of the perceptions of different audience groups, and the linking of media-related questions to other kinds of social analysis. This type of integrated interdisciplinary research agenda will seem familiar to many feminist media scholars today. Yet its implementation has demanded the location and articulation of a distinct feminist voice. This has involved a difficult and protracted struggle to achieve intellectual legitimacy within the general field of media and communication studies (see Gallagher 2003).

A move towards analyses of the socioeconomic contexts of media structures and processes during the 1990s signaled feminism's recognition that media representations and gender discourses take shape within particular, and changing, socioeconomic formations which must themselves be analyzed and understood. Indeed, one of feminism's significant contributions to the overall field has been its emphasis on the relationship between gender and class. The interplay between gender and class in the creation of contemporary consumerist identities was central to much feminist scholarship of the 1990s (for example Basu 2001; Nag 1991). By demonstrating how, in an era of globalizing capitalism, "middle-class women in particular are at the epicentre of the unfolding struggle over the terms of (the) transition" towards consumer modernity, feminist research provided an important entry point for a revitalized and urgently needed class analysis of contemporary change in the organization of communications and culture (Murdock 2000: 24). For instance, studies of the effects of the German unification process on media structures and content noted a new emphasis on women as mothers and housewives, although in the former German Democratic Republic media portrayals generally depicted women as capable of combining paid employment and family life (Rinke 1994). Data from Central and Eastern Europe suggested that the transformations of 1989 and the adaptation of the media to market-oriented demands resulted in previously absent representations of women that emphasized sexuality, mixing entrenched patriarchal conventions with new sexist language and images (Ibroscheva and Stover 2012; Zabelina 1996; Zarkov 1997).

Going beyond the issue of socioeconomic formations, feminists also grappled with the wider concept of political ideology, focusing on how women's representation is frequently a site on which wider, public meanings are inscribed. At the simplest level, it is clear that in all parts of the world, at different times in history, representations and images of women have been used as symbols of political aspirations and social change. An obvious example was the widespread use of particular asexual, "emancipated" female images in Soviet culture: the confident, sturdy woman on her tractor, on the farm, or in the factory. Images of this kind reflected an idealized political vision: "the social realist tradition was intended to create an ideal reality and utilized this model to portray the exemplary woman of the radiant Communist future" (Lipovskaya 1994: 124; see also Ibroscheva and Stover 2012). In such a situation female imagery becomes a metaphor for a particular political ideology, rather than a representation of women's lives.

A clear contemporary example of these political and ideological tensions is to be found in media representations of veiled Muslim women (see Jiwani 2005; Macdonald 2006). In the wake of 9/11, images of women in chadors, burqas, and hijabs proliferated in the Western media. Feminist analysis has focused on how these images have been used to justify wars of "liberation" in Afghanistan and Iraq (Stabile and Kumar 2005; Winegar 2005). Evelyn Alsultany has analyzed these images in terms of its "ideological work" in justifying political agendas and the so-called war on terror (2012). She argues that apparently sympathetic representations of oppressed Muslim women feed a public sense of outrage:

> If we are outraged at the treatment of the oppressed Muslim woman, we are far more likely to support U.S. interventions in Muslim countries in the name of saving the women. ... This highly mediated evocation of outrage for the plight of the oppressed Muslim woman inspires support of U.S. interventions against Muslim men and barbaric Islam.
>
> (Alsultany 2012: 99)

Alsultany concludes that media representations of Muslim women and Muslim men are "mirror images" of one another, encouraging public sympathy for the former and moral disengagement from the latter. Crucial to the impact of these "simplified complex representations," she argues, is the way in which discourses of multiculturalism and feminism have been co-opted by the media and by political institutions. This co-optation, she contends, has "helped to form a new kind of racism, one that projects antiracism and multiculturalism on the surface but simultaneously produces the logics and affects necessary to legitimize racist policies and practices" (Alsultany 2012: 16).

## Feminist discourse and media empowerment

The "tyranny of media messages" against which pioneers of feminist criticism railed has, over the past half-century, given way to something infinitely more complex and sophisticated. Contemporary media content frequently draws on and invokes feminism itself, and feminist vocabulary, in a "post-feminist" discourse implying that feminism has been "taken into account" (McRobbie 2009: 12). The result is a paradox. On the one hand, ostensibly feminism has become part of the cultural field. On the other, modern media narratives frequently present feminism as irrelevant to today's social struggles, and indeed as something to be repudiated—albeit often in a humorous or ironic tone, which of course makes feminist counter-critique particularly difficult (Gill 2007: 268).

With few exceptions, however, feminist discourse in the media remains conservative. Relying heavily on notions of women's individual choice, empowerment and personal freedom, it fits perfectly within a vocabulary of neoliberalism. Cultural theorist Angela McRobbie describes this as "disarticulation"—a process which, through its insistent focus on female individualism and consumerism, unpicks the seams of connection between groups of women who might find common cause, and "makes unlikely the forging of alliances, affiliations or connections," whether locally, nationally, or internationally (2009: 26). This analysis is shared by feminist theorist Nancy Fraser, who distinguishes between feminism as a social movement and feminism as discourse (2009). In the context of neoliberal capitalism, Fraser argues, feminism in the discursive sense has "gone rogue." As a result, today's feminist movement is "increasingly confronted with a strange shadowy version of itself, an uncanny double that it can neither simply embrace nor wholly disavow" (Fraser 2009: 114).

These twenty-first-century paradoxes and contradictions—in particular the incorporation of feminist ideas into media discourse—oblige feminists to confront the question of how, despite apparent changes, media images and representations intertwine with political and social ideologies to reaffirm relatively stable gender positions in society. For although media narratives regularly suggest that the struggles launched by the women's movement of the 1970s are no longer relevant, no country in the world has achieved gender equality. The 2012 Global Gender Gap Report, which since 2006 has measured progress on tackling gender gaps in health, education, economic and political participation, found that in 13 of the 111 countries for which it had data (12 percent), the overall gender gap has actually widened since 2006 (Hausmann *et al.* 2012: 17).

This tension between the lived experience of inequality and its representation in the media is as obvious today as it was 50 years ago. For example, the 1995 Beijing Platform for Action (BPfA), which acknowledged the media as one of 12 "critical areas of concern" that stand in the way of gender equality, was a breakthrough. It moved beyond the concept of women's "advancement" (within taken-for-granted, existing structures) as expressed in earlier international documents, to that of women's "empowerment" (implying the potential to transform those structures). The empowerment of women, as advocated in the BPfA, is a radical demand. It depends on "the full realization of all human rights and fundamental freedoms of all women" (United Nations 1995: para. 9). Yet in the years after Beijing the concept was soon emptied of its radical essence. Empowerment became "the word of the moment" across a range of social and political institutions, including the media.

It is a stripped-out, neutered version of "women's empowerment" that we find in a great deal of contemporary media discourse, which explicitly equates empowerment with sexual assertiveness, buying power, and individual control. For instance, the Dove "Campaign for Real Beauty," devised by advertising agency Ogilvie & Mather, in its later stages involved online contests that promised women "empowerment" and "creative control" by contributing their own advertisements to promote the Dove Supreme Cream Oil Body Wash (Duffy 2010). In this highly conservative version of empowerment, which chimes fully with the neoliberal economic model, gender equality becomes confused with individual "lifestyle" choices. Told that "you have the power to be what you want to be," the modern media woman responds logically: "Today. I decided to stop being fat. My decision. My weight loss" (Lazar 2006: 510). The false-feminist rhetoric in these exhortations to exercise "choice" gives the illusion of progress, while reaffirming the age-old centrality of the female body in media discourse.[11]

As for feminist discourse, this has been incorporated in various ways across all media genres—from advertising to newspapers to television. Analyzing those global patterns of incorporation is central to a large body of contemporary feminist scholarship (for example Ball 2012; Mendes 2012; Bucciferro 2012). These developments have resulted in a vast diversity of media content which, in terms of the challenge it presents for critical practice, is immeasurably more complicated than that which confronted the first feminist media scholars.

## Activism, scholarship, and change

In the final part of her groundbreaking study of gender and media, Rosalind Gill turns to the issue of feminist cultural politics. Recalling the strategies of activism used in the 1970s and 1980s, she asks what kind of strategies would be appropriate for critiquing contemporary media representations. It is a difficult question to answer, and Gill concludes that "only by understanding the dynamics of contemporary sexism will we know which political tools might be useful" (Gill 2007: 270). Yet neither the sophistication of today's media scholarship, nor the complexity of representations in today's media, need produce a sense of futility in the search for change.

Feminism is a "double-edged" social movement—both an interest group that struggles for change and an intellectual force that challenges cultural definitions (van Zoonen 1994: 152). This means that feminists may engage with the media in ways that appear to be completely unconnected but that can inform each other within a shared political framework. The connections are important, but as yet have been insufficiently explored. Carolyn Byerly notes that feminist media scholarship has tended to ignore "the process of struggle represented by women's media activism," arguing that this must be examined if the "dialectical nature of gender relations with respect to the media" is to be fully understood (2012: 15).

In their study of women's media activism in 20 countries, Carolyn Byerly and Karen Ross (2006) identify a number of "pathways" through which women's agency has opened up spaces for change in the media. This, they argue, is part of a broader political process in which women media activists envisage a world in which "women's influence shapes everything from culture to social policy, advancing women in the process" (2006: 232). For instance, "women's movement media" have certainly played a crucial role in women's struggle around the world. Part of a global networking, consciousness-raising, and knowledge-creation project, they have allowed women to communicate through their own words and images. Women's radio has been immensely important in this project and, with the possibilities opened up by internet radio, can make new connections between local and global feminist struggles (Mitchell 2004). Women's news services on the web—Women's eNews, World Pulse, Women's News Network, Women's Views on News, to name but a few— have introduced content and opinions different from those found in "mainstream" media. There are also signs that policymaking, one of the most intractable areas for feminists, can respond to sustained activist effort. A number of recent pieces of legislation—for example in Spain and Latin America—include provisions to restrain media content that encourages violence against women and, in an innovative departure for legislators, the concept of "symbolic violence" has been included in Argentina's 2009 Law on Violence Against Women (see Gallagher 2011).

Another important development has been the use of media monitoring as a tool in the pursuit of accountability. There is nothing new about media monitoring. It was one of the earliest strategies used by the National Organization for Women (NOW) as part of its 1970s campaign to file "petitions-to-deny" the license renewals of local television stations across the USA on grounds of discrimination against women (Perlman 2007). In the 1980s and 1990s activists in many countries began to monitor gender representation in their media, at both national and local levels (Gallagher 2001). Mobilization around these issues grew in the early 1990s, coalescing in what was to become one of the most far-reaching collective enterprises of the global women's movement—the Global Media Monitoring Project (GMMP). Conceived in 1994, the plan was to monitor the representation of women and men in the news on television, radio, and the press on one "ordinary" day, in the widest possible range of countries. The results of the first study were released at the 1995 Beijing Conference.

The significance of the GMMP has been enormous. The monitoring has been repeated every five years, with the number of participant countries increasing from 71 in 1995 to 108 in 2010. Over that period the percentage of women in the news was found to increase from 17 percent to just 24 percent, with very little variation across different regions. Global, longitudinal studies like the GMMP are rare. They are important because they can show how patterns of inequality change over time and across continents (Ross and Carter 2011: 1161). However, the GMMP is unprecedented in terms of not simply its geographical scope, but also its execution. From scholars and researchers, to activists and lobbyists, to journalists and other media professionals—some with considerable research experience, others with none—groups and individuals from a wide spectrum of backgrounds have taken part. The GMMP is thus much more than a data-collection exercise. By putting simple but reliable monitoring tools in the hands of activists, and developing media literacy and advocacy skills through the monitoring process, it aims to be genuinely transformational.

In their analysis of the ways in which transnational networks try to bring about change, Keck and Sikkink (1998) identify four commonly used strategies: information politics, symbolic politics, leverage politics, and accountability politics. The GMMP combines all four (see Gallagher 2014). Accountability politics is at the heart of the GMMP. The consistency of its findings over time, along with the regularity of the monitoring exercise, gives activists a powerful rationale for periodically reminding media professionals and decision-makers of policy commitments, obligations to their audiences, or statements of support for gender equality—and for pressuring them to review their practices.

While the media activist approach may seem to sit uneasily with that of methodologically sophisticated feminist scholarship, each must be considered in terms of the different interpretations and understandings of media content that it aims to produce. Since the earliest days there has been a continuous process of push and pull between theorizing, research, and activism in feminist media criticism. This is one of the field's great strengths, sustaining a political dimension whose commitment to change—whether explicit or implicit—is integral to its identity.

# References

Alsultany, E. (2012) *Arabs and Muslims in the Media: Race and Representation after 9/11*, New York: New York University Press.

Ball, V. (2012) "The 'Feminization' of British Television and the Re-Traditionalization of Gender," *Feminist Media Studies* 12(2): 248–64.

Basu, S. (2001) "The Blunt Cutting-edge: The Construction of Sexuality in the Bengali 'Feminist' Magazine *Sananda*," *Feminist Media Studies* 1(2): 179–96.

Bucciferro, C. (2012) "Chilean Women in Changing Times: Media Images and Social Understandings," in K. Ross (ed.) *The Handbook of Gender, Sex and Media*, Malden, MA: Wiley-Blackwell, pp. 20–34.

Byerly, C. M. (2012) "The Geography of Women and Media Scholarship," in K. Ross (ed.) *The Handbook of Gender, Sex and Media*, Malden, MA: Wiley-Blackwell, pp. 3–19.

Byerly, C. M. and K. Ross (2006) *Women & Media: A Critical Introduction*, Malden, MA: Blackwell Publishing.

Carter, C. (2012) "Sex/Gender and the Media: From Sex Roles to Social Construction and Beyond," in K. Ross (ed.) *The Handbook of Gender, Sex and Media*, Malden, MA: Wiley-Blackwell, pp. 365–82.

Duffy, B. E. (2010) "Empowerment through Endorsement? Polysemic Meaning in Dove's User-Generated Advertising," *Communication, Culture & Critique* 3(1): 26–43.

Franzwa, H. (1978) "Image of Women in Television: An Annotated Bibliography," in G. Tuchman, A. Kaplan Daniels, and J. Benét (eds.) *Hearth and Home: Images of Women in the Mass Media*, New York: Oxford University Press, pp. 272–300.

Fraser, N. (2009) "Feminism, Capitalism and the Cunning of History," *New Left Review* 56: 97–117.

Friedan, B. (1963) *The Feminine Mystique*, London: Victor Gollancz.

Gallagher, M. (2001) *Gender Setting: New Agendas for Media Monitoring and Advocacy*, London: Zed Books.

——(2003) "Feminist Media Perspectives," in A. N. Valdivia (ed.) *A Companion to Media Studies*, Malden, MA: Blackwell Publishing, pp. 19–39.

——(2011) "Gender and Communication Policy: Struggling for Space," in R. Mansell and M. Raboy (eds.) *The Handbook of Global Media and Communication Policy*, Malden, MA: Wiley-Blackwell, pp. 451–66.

——(2014) "Reframing Communication Rights: Why Gender Matters," in C. Padovani and A. Calabrese (eds.) *Communication Rights and Social Justice: Historical Reflections on Transnational Mobilizations*, Basingstoke: Palgrave Macmillan, pp. 234–48.

Gerbner, G. (1978) "The Dynamics of Cultural Resistance," in G. Tuchman, A. Kaplan Daniels, and J. Benét (eds.) *Hearth and Home: Images of Women in the Mass Media*, New York: Oxford University Press, pp. 46–50.

Gill, R. (2007) *Gender and the Media*, Cambridge: Polity Press.

Hausmann, R., L. D. Tyson, and S. Zahidi (2012) *The Global Gender Gap Report 2012*, Geneva: World Economic Forum.

Houston, M. (1992) "The Politics of Difference: Race, Class, and Women's Communication," in L. F. Rakow (ed.) *Women Making Meaning: New Feminist Directions in Communication*, New York: Routledge, pp. 45–59.

Ibroscheva, E. and M. Stover (2012) "The Girls of Parliament: A Historical Analysis of the Press Coverage of Female Politicians in Bulgaria," in K. Ross (ed.) *The Handbook of Gender, Sex and Media*, Malden, MA: Wiley-Blackwell, pp. 35–52.

Janus, N. Z. (1977) "Research on Sex-roles in the Mass Media: Toward a Critical Approach," *Insurgent Sociologist* 7(3): 19–30.

Jiwani, Y. (2005) "'War Talk' Engendering Terror: Race, Gender and Representation in Canadian Print Media," *International Journal of Media and Cultural Politics* 1(1): 15–21.

Kaplan Daniels, A. (1978) "Preface," in G. Tuchman, A. Kaplan Daniels, and J. Benét (eds.) *Hearth and Home: Images of Women in the Mass Media*, New York: Oxford University Press, pp. v–viii.

Keck, M. E. and K. Sikkink (1998) *Activists Beyond Borders: Advocacy Networks in International Politics*, Ithaca, NY: Cornell University Press.

Lazar, M. M. (2006) "'Discover the Power of Femininity': Analyzing Global 'Power Femininity' in Local Advertising," *Feminist Media Studies* 6(4): 505–17.

Lipovskaya, O. (1994) "The Mythology of Womanhood in Contemporary 'Soviet' Culture," in A. Posadskaya (ed.) *Women in Russia: A New Era in Russian Feminism*, London: Verso, pp. 123–34.

Macdonald, M. (2006) "Muslim Women and the Veil: Problems of Image and Voice in Media Representations," *Feminist Media Studies* 6(1): 7–23.

McRobbie, A. (2009) *The Aftermath of Feminism: Gender, Culture and Social Change*, London: Sage Publications.

Mendes, K. (2012) "'Feminism Rules! Now, Where's My Swimsuit?' Re-evaluating Feminist Discourse in Print Media 1968–2008," *Media, Culture & Society* 34(5): 554–70.

Mitchell, C. (2004) "'Dangerously Feminine?' Theory and Praxis of Women's Alternative Radio," in K. Ross and C. M. Byerly (eds.) *Women and Media: International Perspectives*, Malden, MA: Blackwell Publishing, pp. 157–84.

Murdock, G. (2000) "Reconstructing the Ruined Tower: Contemporary Communications and Questions of Class," in J. Curran and M. Gurevitch (eds.) *Mass Media and Society*, London: Arnold, pp. 7–26.

Nag, D. (1991) "Fashion, Gender and the Bengali Middle Class," *Public Culture* 3(2): 93–112.

Perlman, A. (2007) "Feminists in the Wasteland: The National Organization for Women and Television Reform," *Feminist Media Studies* 7(4): 413–31.

Rinke, A. (1994) "Wende-Bilder: Television Images of Women in Germany in Transition," in E. Boa and J. Wharton (eds.) *Women and the WENDE: Social Effects and Cultural Reflections on the German Reunification Process*, Amsterdam: Rodopi, BV, pp. 124–38.

Ross, K. and C. Carter (2011) "Women and News: A Long and Winding Road," *Media, Culture & Society* 33(8): 1148–65.

Stabile, C. A. and D. Kumar (2005) "Unveiling Imperialism: Media, Gender and the War on Afghanistan," *Media, Culture & Society* 27(5): 765–82.

Tuchman, G. (1978) "Introduction: The Symbolic Annihilation of Women by the Mass Media," in G. Tuchman, A. Kaplan Daniels, and J. Benét (eds.) *Hearth and Home: Images of Women in the Mass Media*, New York: Oxford University Press, pp. 3–38.

United Nations (1995) *Beijing Declaration and Platform for Action*, New York: United Nations.

van Zoonen, L. (1994) *Feminist Media Studies*, London: Sage Publications.

Winegar, J. (2005) "Of Chadors and Purple Fingers: US Visual Media Coverage of the 2005 Iraqi Elections," *Feminist Media Studies* 5(3): 391–5.

Zabelina, T. (1996) "Sexual Violence towards Women," in H. Pilkington (ed.) *Gender, Generation and Identity in Contemporary Russia*, London: Routledge, pp. 169–86.

Zarkov, D. (1997) "Pictures on the Wall of Love: Motherhood, Womanhood and Nationhood in Croatian Media," *European Journal of Women's Studies* 4(3): 305–39.

# 2
# Mass media representation of gendered violence

## Lisa M. Cuklanz

Unfortunately, one of the most obvious and historically consistent elements of gender in media is the notable pervasiveness of representations of gender-based violence (GBV). The linkages in US media representation between masculinity and violence, and between femininity and victimization, are frequently discussed and much studied. Feminist scholars have been examining such representations for several decades, since the 1970s, when groundbreaking analyses, including Laura Mulvey's essay "Visual Pleasure and Narrative Cinema" (1975), Molly Haskell's book *From Reverence to Rape* (1974), and Gaye Tuchman's essay on "The Symbolic Annihilation of Women in the Mass Media" (1978), highlighted the hostile and violent treatment of women across many media forms, including US prime-time television and Hollywood film. Since that time, scholarship on GBV in pornography, Hollywood film, music videos, computer and video games, news coverage of sexual assault and domestic violence, and certain television genres, including soap operas, forensic and police dramas, made-for-TV movies, and reality policing programs, has become well established. Feminist scholars assert that the objectification of women in mass media not only is a pervasive problem, but also in many instances can be considered a form of violence against women. By treating female characters as objects to be observed, handled, used, abused, and even discarded, mass media encourage us to think of women and girls as less than human. Mainstream media tend to reinforce blaming of individual perpetrators and victims and to lack structural analysis and social explanations for gender-based violence, to circulate stereotypes of helpless victims, and to project cultural superiority when different nations or ethnic groups are involved.

This chapter surveys our basic understanding of GBV in genres and forms that have been carefully researched, and outlines some areas in which further investigation is needed. Particular focus is placed on newly emerging areas of emphasis, including the mainstreaming of pornography and pornography-style representation, increasingly problematic relationships between sexuality and sexual violence, and representations of global and international forms of GBV, including rape as a crime of war and human trafficking of sex workers. These emerging areas of investigation constitute the most significant recent developments in our understanding of media representations of gender-based violence.

While each of these three approaches has some advantages and information to contribute to our general understanding of GBV representation, analytical approaches to the meanings generated through these various discourses on GBV have proven to be more substantive than empirical approaches that focus on cause–effect relationships between violent media images and real-world effects, or empirical approaches that focus on numerical understanding of these representations. This is because the establishment of cause–effect relationships between media imagery and real-world effects, such as changes in cognition and behavior, are difficult to establish and/or prove; findings from such experiments have limited generalizability. The second type of research on GBV in mass media, empirical content-analyses of media imagery that are broad based (for instance studying every episode of every crime drama during a particular year and counting how many acts of violence of different types occurred in them) can be helpful in establishing a framework of understanding of the scope of the issues related to media representation of GBV, but this approach tells us little about why imagery is important and how the details of representation differ from one text, genre, or medium to another. The most well-developed and more currently active areas of study are focused on analyzing images and their meanings within texts rather than in interaction with the world outside of those texts. I focus on knowledge about representations of GBV that has been generated through such textual analysis. I outline basic findings in a broad range of texts and genres, drawing on the most recent examples of scholarship in key areas in which scholarship on mass media representation of GBV is currently developing.

## Scholarship on the representation of women as victims

Targeted examinations of the representation of gender in mass media began in the USA, UK, and elsewhere in the 1970s pursuant to the insights and criticisms of the second wave of the Western women's movement in relation to gender biases in mainstream culture. Many works have shown how such representations share several common elements: female characters who are victims have usually been depicted as having little agency to help themselves, have few support networks or female friends and family, are often assisted by stronger and more competent males, and are frequently blamed, at least in part, for their own victimization. Historically, mainstream media discourses, including news, have maintained elements of racial bias in pointing to men of color as perpetrators and white women as victims, both in the choice of cases for public attention and in the terms in which coverage is written. Sujata Moorti's *Color of Rape* (2002) documents these biases across media prior to 2000, while Carole Stabile (2006) provides a deep historical account of racial bias in news coverage from the 1830s to the present. Numerous studies of news and fictional television discourses surrounding sexual assault and domestic violence (see Benedict 1992; Carter 1998; Cuklanz 1996, 2000; Moorti 2002; Projansky 2001) have exposed how news and television discourses historically have marginalized victim voices, blamed victims, depicted and normalized extreme cases, and only slowly

accepted the insights embedded in rape law reforms. Meyers (2004) reveals limitations in coverage of intersections of race, class, and gender in news coverage of
sexual assault. More recently, Jane Monckton-Smith (2010) shows how the British
press placed sex at the center of coverage on a range of themes.

Media representations of domestic violence have been found to blame victims and
treat perpetrators with sympathy, although more recent narratives have done a
better job of recognizing and understanding patterns of behavior based on power
dynamics in abusive relationships. Marian Meyers (1994) illustrates the ways in
which mainstream news discourses blamed domestic violence victims for their pre-
dicaments and failed to understand the power dynamics of abusive relationships.
Analysis of domestic violence in reality TV programs (Carmody 1998; Rapping
2003) shows that these programs favor individualized explanations for crime while
omitting references to larger social issues and problems, and also tend to provide
images that fit easily into preconceived audience stereotypes of racial, ethnic, and
immigrant minority populations. More recent work on the representation of
domestic violence in US reality crime programs such as *Cops*, daytime talk shows
such as *Sally Jessie Raphael*, and women's magazines also documents the representation of domestic violence as a private matter rather than a social issue. As such, they
state or imply that the victim is to blame. The focus on individual rather than
structural causes (such as unequal distribution of resources, power imbalances in
interpersonal relationships, and lack of support structures for victims and survivors)
for gender-based violence, including battering, has made it more difficult for victims
to get the help they need. In recent years, attention has increased in many parts of
the world to the problem of media and domestic violence (Berns 2004; Heeren and
Messing 2009). Additionally, Josephine Hendin (2004) examines mainstream narratives featuring women perpetrators of intimate violence, while M. Cristina Alcalde
(2009) examines news coverage of battered women in Peru.

A subcategory of scholarship on domestic/family violence focuses on public
representations of incest, much of which has centered on issues related to memory,
recovered memory, and the controversial construction "false memory syndrome"
(see Kitzinger 1998). Looking at texts dealing with incest, Janet Walker notes that
"prior to the age of the personal home page and Internet link, television was the
premier medium for widely shared discourse on incestuous assault and recovery"
(2005: 54). Jane Kilby notes that these television treatments were able to "turn classical
tropes toward feminist ends" by showing "female therapists and social workers
advocating their client's autonomy from family" (2007: 54). During this period, Kilby
asserts, television films did not focus on, or sometimes even mention, "false
memory syndrome," and in fact even presented real but repressed memories as keys
to legal success and recovery for survivors. Mediated discourses have generally been
unable to convey the complexity of repressed and recovered memories, which may
suppress or bring to light some aspects of a traumatic experience while remaining
unable to encompass everything one might like to know about a trauma from the
past. McKinney (2006) and Kilby (2007) provide more recent analyses in the spheres
of law and policy. Henry (2011) offers a thorough discussion of the complexity of
public understanding of some of the same issues of traumatic memory in relation to
traumas created in situations of war and genocide.

A growing number of studies examine mass mediated representations of sex trafficking and/or human trafficking more broadly, uncovering several notable patterns of imagery and meaning across a wide range of depictions. While sympathy for victims is emphasized, this is often exaggerated through the use of extreme cases and excessive examples of violence. These selected examples, in turn, establish the helplessness of victims and their need for external rescue, often from "ethical johns" or from journalists themselves. Finally, the blame for trafficking is placed not on the commodification and exploitation of women and their bodies in developed Western nations such as the USA, but rather on unethical traffickers, backward nations and cultural norms, and desperate uneducated women who make unwise choices. As Jo Doezema notes, "narratives of trafficking in women, like those of white slavery, appear to be descriptions of reality, but are actually mythical narratives closely bound up with ideologies concerning sexuality, race, and the state" (2010: 46). Jane Arthurs (2010) examines the use of irony in sex-trafficking campaign films, while Wendy Hesford (2011) emphasizes limitations typical of media coverage of gender-based violence, and examines the ways in which US media tend to focus on individuals rather than structural elements:

> Stereotypes of prostitutes as social deviants or as helpless victims maintain their rhetorical appeal because they keep the audience's focus on the other and thereby deflect attention from the national and international policies, economic and sociopolitical forces, and cultural traditions that contribute to the material conditions that drive many women to work in the sex industry.
>
> (Hesford 2011: 32)

Julietta Hua (2011) shows how news coverage, while expressing sympathy for victims and outrage at their treatment, also subtly suggests that trafficking is in part caused by backward cultures in which female children are not valued, and even by the somewhat deluded notions of trafficked women, whose hopes for a better future are desperately distorted. "Even when the framing of sex trafficking is attentive to the combination of globalization, militarism, and colonialism all as reasons for trafficking, the suggestion is that these political formations simply exacerbate already present cultural conditions that enable trafficking" (Hua 2011: 61). Furthermore, the cultures of origin for trafficked women described in news stories appear to take more blame for trafficking than the "culture of complicity" from which traffickers originate and in which they operate. Although patriarchy is defined as an important part of the problem, it is situated in these stories only within cultures of origin.

Felicity Schaeffer-Grabiel (2011) similarly shows how these products, and particularly anti-trafficking media campaigns, have worked to depict the West as the endpoint and potential "savior" of trafficked women, how "foreign" trafficked persons are identified as "incompatible" and therefore in need of relocation, and the bolstering of the "moral authority" of the nation-state. In particular, several media forms, including films, documentaries, and reality-based television re-enactments, attempt to recruit viewer assistance in the project of eliminating prostitution by trafficked women within US borders. "The desire to rid exploitation is entangled in the longing to purge the scene (and, by extension, the nation) of suffering and, therefore, of the racialized subjects attached to the pain" (2011: 108). Most significantly, she observes that "[t]rafficking campaigns inadvertently shift the focus from the masses of migrants who are exploited every day as cheap laborers to saving 'duped' female migrants shuttled into the commerce of underground prostitution" (2011: 104). Hua and Schaeffer-Grabiel examine Western news coverage of GBV in a global context, confirming Western media biases that tend to blame victims and treat immigrants as unwanted newcomers into developed nations.

Scholarship on media representations of rape as a war crime are also emerging, although this subject warrants further attention as the range and magnitude of war crimes involving rape is not reflected in the scholarship on media representations, and there is still very little scholarship on news coverage of these issues. As with news coverage of domestic violence, particularly incest, coverage of rape as a crime of war has often focused on issues related to traumatic memory and the recovery of lost memories (see Stables 2003). Régine Michelle Jean-Charles (2009) examines narratives of rape in feature films dealing with the Rwandan genocide. More recently, although she does not address media coverage specifically, Nicola Henry (2011) provides an excellent discussion of issues related to public understanding of memory and rape as a war crime. Yaschica Williams and Janine Bower (2009) note that in US newspapers the conflict in Yugoslavia received much more coverage, and much more intense coverage, than did the conflict in Rwanda. Furthermore, "the articles surveyed contained no references to individualized motives, such as sexual urges or genetic predisposition," but rather they "treated the problem in relation to larger political events" (2009: 172). The themes of rape and ethnic cleansing seemed to be chosen because they "evoke public reaction," whereas other forms of violence, such as torture, were not covered or received much less attention within these stories.

## Scholarship on the objectification of women in mass media

In film studies, cinematic linkages between the male gaze, male desire, and female victimization have been explored extensively. Particularly problematic have been the ways in which mainstream mass media conflate male power and masculinity with violence, in a range of interpersonal relations, including sexual interactions. When mass media images depict violence as a part of consensual sex, or blur the lines between rape and consent, or depict an intimate interaction as beginning with force and ending with mutual desire, they encourage viewers to think of violence as a natural part of sex, to think of men as incapable of non-violent intimacy, and to think of women as desirous of sexual violation. These sorts of depictions are common and occur across many media and genres.

While Molly Haskell's book *From Reverence to Rape* (1974) examines victimization and several tropes of filmic depiction of women in Hollywood prior to the 1970s, Laura Mulvey's 1975 article "Visual Pleasure and Narrative Cinema," originally published in the film journal *Screen*, is usually considered the start of a coherent feminist theory of gender and representation in Hollywood film. Mulvey showed how female characters were habitually presented as displays for male visual enjoyment. Further, she explored the associations between such representations and identification with male audience members, who, she argued, were invited to identify with the male characters on screen and join them in their visual enjoyment of female characters. Mulvey's work has been taken up by a legion of scholars interested in exploring the extent and limits of her insights about the gendered nature of the act of looking (as masculine), now commonly referred to as the "male gaze," and being looked at (as feminine). Jane Gaines (1988) investigated the relationships between racial identity and the male gaze, while Carol Clover (1992) considered the relationships between the young male audience and the female victims. Clover's work shows how the male gaze in horror films is operationalized as violence that stands in for sex, but she also theorized that these films depicting violent and prolonged attacks on women allowed young male audience members to explore feelings of identification with the young terrified women on screen. She noted that the established grammar of Hollywood films already made "abject terror" something feminine, such that horror films would be more frightening with female victims rather than male. Clover explained how the acts of objectifying, fantasizing, sexualizing, dehumanizing, and sexually violating women are clearly interconnected in the fictional world of mainstream film.

Sarah Projansky's book *Watching Rape* (2001) importantly establishes the centrality of rape narratives to a wide range of Hollywood genres prior to 1980. Although scholarship on rape and its representation as a seemingly natural byproduct of normal sexual desires of objectified women and violent men has mostly centered on Hollywood feature films, these linkages are made even more explicit in pornography, where women appear not only to wish for, but also to enjoy, violent assault and extreme degradation. In his analysis of the mainstreaming of recent pornography, including extreme "gonzo" porn texts, Stephen Maddison argues that the central narrative of the film *Forced Entry*, typical of most porn films, "doesn't have sufficient meaning to dislodge the identification with the violence and sexual sadism of the [central] character" (2009: 49). These films, furthermore, do not include any visible "kind of genital act that would signify female sexual pleasure that isn't a function of phallic performativity," and this is usually accompanied by acts of extreme degradation of the woman as well as explicit acts of violence such as strangling, kicking, spitting, and verbal vilification (2009: 49). Contemporary scholarship on pornography has focused on the mainstreaming of porn-style representations of sex. Maddison points not only to the increased degradation of women and increasing intensity of the relationship between sex and violence in hardcore representations, but also to the increasingly harmful effects on the women who perform in hardcore porn, such as the transmission of HIV. Simon Hardy observes further that while "one of the defining power structures of pornography has been the relation of male-as-subject to women-as-object," some contemporary examples demonstrate how this "relation is fractured but not broken" due to the "increasingly active internalization by women of their status within this dynamic" (2009: 15–16).

The increasing prevalence and intensity of violence in relation to sex in recent pornography is also examined by Gail Dines in her book *Pornland: How Pornography has Hijacked our Sexuality* (2010). Dines explores the mainstreaming and intensification of pornography due largely to the influence of the internet. She offers several notable examples of how mainstream media, particularly Hollywood film, and pornography, have begun to overlap and how mainstream media products increasingly employ both stars and norms of representation formerly relegated to porn. Strategies for implementing this goal of mainstreaming include efforts "to garner publicity in mainstream media by placing stories, people, and products that advertise the porn industry" (2010: 54). Examples include instances in which characters in mainstream films read or consume pornography; mainstream news media offer interviews with former porn actors who find roles in mainstream films. Porn stars, most notably Jenna Jameson, have been featured in mainstream magazines such as *People* and *US*, and have appeared in advertisements for companies such as Abercrombie and Fitch (2010: 34–5). In addition, "many have noted hip hop culture's crossover into the $11 billion pornographic film industry" (Sharpley-Whiting 2007: 61).

Objectification to the point of victimization and degradation of women has been a central issue in the analysis of music videos and hip hop culture. Kimberle Crenshaw's (1997) analysis of media discussion of 2 Live Crew emphasized the ways in which two important elements of hip hop misogyny are usually not fully understood. Crenshaw notes that it is important to critique hip hop products for their misogyny and also to understand that treating these products as "worse than" or more to blame for other forms of abuse of women in mainstream culture is a form of racist logic. In *Pimps Up, Ho's Down*, T. Denean Sharpley-Whiting concurs with Crenshaw's findings and observes what many have noted about the disproportionate attention given to the abusive treatment of women in hop hop culture:

> [H]ip hop culture is no more or less violent and sexist than other American cultural products (think Playboy, prime-time news and television, the flourishing Hooters restaurant chain and now-bankrupt airline, The O'Reilly Factor, hard rock, country music, the blues, Abercrombie and Fitch catalogues). However, it is more dubiously highlighted by the media as the source of violent misogyny in American youth culture.
>
> (Sharpley-Whiting 2007: 58)

Sharpley-Whiting documents the links between the hip hop and porn industries and catalogues violent and misogynist lyrics and actions by recent rappers.

## Representations of gendered violence

Scholarship on the gendered nature of violence in mass media representations has frequently taken up the analysis and critique of associations between masculinity and violence. Research on masculinity in US mainstream media products, for instance, has focused on the extreme nature of depictions of masculinity as violent, emotionless, machine-like, and result oriented, although evolving over time. My own work, for example, shows how prime-time detective dramas in the 1970s and 1980s presented their protagonist male detectives as shifting over time into more well-rounded characters who could work with female colleagues and express emotions (Cuklanz 2000). Rape narratives in these programs, however, were centered more on delineating forms of masculinity than on examining victims of sexual assault and their post-traumatic experiences of distress and recovery. Erica Scharrer (2001) also examines tough masculinity in detective programs. Masculinity in these media products is understood to shift in relation to social and political changes in the mainstream culture, but always retains the elements of competitiveness, effectivity, action orientation, and use of violence to solve certain problems. Barna William Donovan (2010) further explores these themes in relation to Hollywood action films.

Scholars have also examined depictions in which typical gender roles with respect to violent action are reversed or exchanged, such that female characters take on the role usually reserved for violent masculinity. Many have taken up this topic, with Yvonne Tasker (1993) and Sherrie Inness (1999) as early examples. Hilary Neroni (2005) examines violent women in Hollywood cinema in relation to romance narratives, showing how these characters disrupt the usual relation of complementarity between violent masculinity and passive/rescued femininity, such that violent female characters must be either eliminated or redirected back into patriarchal family structures and renounce their violent ways. Sara Crosby (2004) similarly shows how female heroines in gothic television dramas such as *Buffy the Vampire Slayer* can take on roles of violent heroism once reserved for male characters, but within certain proscribed limits: the heroines do not enjoy these roles and perform them out of a sense of altruism and care for others. Linda Mizejewski (2004) also observes how the "female dick" disrupts the usual order of detective fiction and is thus seldom the protagonist in this television genre. Josephine Hendin goes further, asserting that "[t]he emergence of remorseless, violent women in pop culture serves to deny the actual vulnerability of women, justify male violence, and project a world without sensibility that sanctions aggression" (2004: 291). Although few studies of female criminals have been undertaken, Lisa Cuklanz and Sujata Moorti (2006) explore the meanings generated through women criminals on prime-time detective fiction, noting that these characters serve to express the underlying misogyny of programs that are in other ways pro-feminist.

## Conclusion

Beginning with the insights of Western second-wave feminism in the 1970s, explorations of gender-based violence in the mainstream mass media have explored many genres, themes, and issues from the role of violence in basic cultural understandings of gender, to representations of real-world instances of violence, to gendered viewing of mediated sexuality. Because GBV continues to pervade mass media as well as to feature prominently in significant world events, we can expect this area of scholarship to continue its rapid expansion into realms increasingly focused on issues of globalization and new media forms and genres.

## References

Alcalde, M. C. (2009) "Ripped from the Headlines: Newspaper Depictions of Battered Women in Peru," in L. Cuklanz and S. Moorti (eds.) *Local Violence, Global Media: Feminist Analyses of Gendered Representations*, New York: Peter Lang, pp. 46–64.

Arthurs, J. (2010) "Deliciously Consumable: The Uses and Abuses of Irony in 'Sex-Trafficking' Campaign Films," in K. Ross (ed.) *The Handbook of Gender, Sex, and the Media*, Oxford: Wiley-Blackwell, pp. 470–86.

Benedict, H. (1992) *Virgin or Vamp: How the Press Covers Sex Crimes*, New York: Oxford University Press.

Berns, N. (2004) *Domestic Violence Media and Social Problems*, New York: Aldine de Gruyter.

Carmody, D. C. (1998) "Mixed Messages: Images of Domestic Violence on 'Reality' Television," in M. Fishman and G. Cavender (eds.) *Entertaining Crime: Television Reality Programs*, New York: Aldine de Gruyter, pp. 159–74.

Carter, C. (1998) "When the 'Extraordinary' Becomes the 'Ordinary': Everyday News of Sexual Violence," in C. Carter, G. Branston, and S. Allan (eds.) *News, Gender and Power*, New York: Routledge, pp. 219–32.

Clover, C. (1992) *Men, Women, and Chain Saws: Gender in the Modern Horror Film*, Princeton, NJ: Princeton University Press.

Crenshaw, K. W. (1997) "Beyond Racism and Misogyny: Black Feminism and 2 Live Crew," in D. Meyers (ed.) *Feminist Social Thought*, New York: Routledge, pp. 245–63.

Crosby, S. (2004) "The Cruelest Season: Female Heroes Snapped into Sacrificial Heroines," in S. Inness (ed.) *Action Chicks: New Images of Tough Women in Popular Culture*, New York: Palgrave Macmillan, pp. 153–80.

Cuklanz, L. (1996) *Rape on Trial: How the Mass Media Construct Legal Reform and Social Change*, Philadelphia: University of Pennsylvania Press.

——(2000) *Rape on Prime Time: Television, Masculinity, and Sexual Violence*, Philadelphia: University of Pennsylvania Press.

Cuklanz, L. and S. Moorti (2006) "Television's New Feminism: Prime Time Representations of Women and Victimization," *Critical Studies in Media Communication* 23(4) (October): 302–21.

Dines, G. (2010) *Pornland: How Pornography has Hijacked our Sexuality*, Boston: Beacon Press.

Doezema, J. (2010) *Sex Slaves and Discourse Masters: The Construction of Trafficking*, London: Zed Books.

Donovan, B. W. (2010) *Blood, Guns, and Testosterone: Action Films, Audiences, and a Thirst for Violence*, Toronto: Scarecrow Press.

Gaines, J. (1988) "White Privilege and Looking Relations: Race and Gender in Feminist Film Theory," *Screen* 29(4): 12–27.

Hardy, S. (2009) "The New Pornographies: Representation or Reality," in F. Attwood (ed.) *Mainstreaming Sex: The Sexualization of Western Culture*, London: I. B. Tauris, pp. 3–18.

Haskell, M. (1974) *From Reverence to Rape: The Treatment of Women in the Movies*, London: Routledge.

Heeren, J. W. and J. T. Messing (2009) "Victims and Sources: Newspaper Reports of Mass Murder in Domestic Contexts," in D. Humphries (ed.) *Women, Violence, and the Media: Readings in Feminist Criminology*, Boston: Northeastern University Press, pp. 206–23.

Hendin, J. G. (2004) *Heartbreakers: Women and Violence in Contemporary Culture and Literature*, New York: Palgrave Macmillan.

Henry, N. (2011) *War and Rape: Law, Memory, and Justice*, New York: Routledge.

Hesford, W. (2011) *Spectacular Rhetorics: Human Rights Visions, Recognitions, Feminisms*, Durham, NC: Duke University Press.

Horek, T. (2004) *Public Rape: Representing Violation in Fiction and Film*, New York: Routledge.

Hua, J. (2011) *Trafficking and Women's Human Rights*, Minneapolis: University of Minnesota Press.

Inness, S. A. (1999) *Tough Girls: Women Warriors and Wonder Women in Popular Culture*, Philadelphia: University of Pennsylvania Press.

Jean-Charles, R. M. (2009) "Beneath the Layers of Violence: Representations of Rape and Rwandan Genocide," in L. Cuklanz and S. Moorti (eds.) *Local Violence, Global Media: Feminist Analyses of Gendered Representations*, New York: Peter Lang, pp. 246–66.

Kilby, J. (2007) *Violence and the Cultural Politics of Trauma*, Edinburgh: Edinburgh University Press.

Kitzinger, J. (1998) "The Gender-Politics of News Production: Silenced Voices and False Memories," in C. Carter, G. Branston, and S. Allan (eds.) *News, Gender and Power*, New York: Routledge, pp. 186–203.

McKinney, D. (2006) "Malignant Memories: It's a Long Road Back to Recovery from Incest," in R. Simpson and W. Cote (eds.) *Covering Violence: A Guide to Ethical Reporting about Victims and Trauma*, 2nd edition, New York: Columbia University Press.

Maddison, S. (2009) "Choke on It, Bitch! Porn Studies, Extreme Gonzo, and the Main-streaming of Hardcore," in F. Attwood (ed.) *Mainstreaming Sex: The Sexualization of Western Culture*, London: I. B. Tauris, pp. 37–54.

Meyers, M. (1994) "News of Battering," *Journal of Communication* 44(2): 47–63.

——(2004) "African American Women and Violence: Gender, Race, and Class in the News," *Critical Studies in Media Communication* 21(2): 95–118.

Mizejewski, L. (2004) *Hard-boiled and High-heeled: The Woman Detective in Popular Culture*, New York: Routledge.

Monckton-Smith, J. (2010) *Relating Rape and Murder: Narratives of Sex, Death, and Gender*, London: Palgrave Macmillan.

Moorti, S. (2002) *Color of Rape: Gender and Race in Television's Public Spheres*, Albany: State University of New York Press.

Mulvey, L. (1975) "Visual Pleasure and Narrative Cinema," *Screen* 16(3): 6–18.

Neroni, H. (2005) *The Violent Woman: Femininity, Narrative, and Violence in Contemporary American Cinema*, Albany: State University of New York Press.

Projansky, S. (2001) *Watching Rape: Film and Television in Postfeminist Culture*, New York: New York University Press.

Rapping, E. (2003) *Law and Justice as Seen on TV*, New York: New York University Press.

Schaeffer-Grabiel, F. (2011) "Transnational Media Wars over Sex Trafficking: Abolishing the 'New Slave Trade' or the New Nativism," in R. Hegde (ed.) *Circuits of Visibility: Gender and Transnational Media Cultures*, New York: New York University Press, pp. 103–23.

Scharrer, E. (2001) "Tough Guys: The Portrayal of Hypermasculinity and Aggression in Televised Police Dramas," *Journal of Broadcasting and Electronic Media* 45: 615–34.

Sharpley-Whiting, T. D. (2007) *Pimps Up, Ho's Down: Hip Hop's Hold on Young Black Women*, New York: New York University Press.

Stabile, C. A. (2006) *White Victims, Black Villains: Gender, Race, and Crime News in US Culture*, New York: Routledge.

Stables, G. (2003) "Justifying Kosovo: Representations of Gendered Violence and U.S. Military Intervention," *Critical Studies in Media Communication* 20(1): 92–115.

Tasker, Y. (1993) *Spectacular Bodies: Gender, Genre, and Action Cinema*, New York: Routledge.

Tuchman, G. (1978) "The Symbolic Annihilation of Women in the Mass Media," in G. Tuchman, A. K. Daniels, and J. Benet (eds.) *Hearth and Home: Images of Women in the Mass Media*, New York: Oxford University Press, pp. 3–38.

Walker, J. (2005) *Trauma Cinema: Documenting Incest and the Holocaust*, Berkeley: University of California Press.

Williams, Y. and Bower, J. (2009) "Media Images of Wartime Sexual Violence: Ethnic Cleansing in Rwanda and the Former Yugoslavia," in D. Humphries (ed.) *Women, Violence, and the Media: Readings in Feminist Criminology*, Boston: Northeastern University Press, pp. 156–74.

# 3
# Lone wolves
## Masculinity, cinema, and the man alone

## Tim Edwards

Studies of representations of masculinity, particularly in film, exploded in the 1980s and onwards. There were perhaps two dimensions to this: first, a continued theoretical engagement with the ideas of feminist film scholar Laura Mulvey and the applications of psychoanalytic theory to cinema more widely; and, second, a more empirical concern with the rise of the action hero and the spectacle of the male body—and more particularly its muscles—that dominated many of the box office hits of the time, from *Rambo* and the *Terminator* series to the career of Tom Cruise and, later, Brad Pitt (Cohan and Hark 1993; Jeffords 1994; Mulvey 1975). In relation to the first dimension, the work of Kaja Silverman in exploring the psychoanalytic aspects of cinema, this time in relation to masculinity and not femininity as in the case of Mulvey, and Richard Dyer's influential studies of the instabilities of representations of masculinity across a variety of media forms, were critical (Dyer 1989; Silverman 1992). The overall thrust of this work was to question the extent to which traditional notions of masculinity were reinforced in cinema, tending to assert that many filmic representations at once set up patriarchal notions of male power yet also disrupted them and pointed to their internal contradictions.

Masculinity and the media is thus a relatively recent yet expanding area of study mostly, though certainly not exclusively, focused on the ways in which various media forms may (re)present masculinity in relation to sexual politics and second-wave feminism (Craig 1992). Thus a range of cultural texts from adverts to movies and from television to pop music are considered for the ways in which they do, or do not, reinforce traditional notions of patriarchy and men's power over women, or simply set up ideal types of masculinity. Consequently, this area of study is for the most part focused on the consumption rather than production of media. Prior to developing this further it is worth outlining the ways in which masculinity and the media may connect more widely. This chapter will primarily focus on cinema, yet the mapping of issues here may equally pertain to many other media forms.

First and foremost, masculinity may pertain to the production of media given the underrepresentation of women as film directors and producers, and their relative preponderance in roles such as costume designers and make-up artists, such that this work is stereotyped as women's. Kathryn Bigelow's winning of an Oscar for her direction of *The Hurt Locker* was the exception rather than the rule in gender terms and often played out by journalists as a personal competition with her ex-husband James Cameron. Second, as is commonly known, roles for women actors are more limited and less well paid. The woman actor is often valued more for her youthful looks, so roles disappear particularly in middle age, until old age, when her looks are of less concern. Few women manage to survive this intact—even Meryl Streep's career dipped. Dame Judi Dench and Dame Maggie Smith, and a few others, find renaissance in film only when much older. Similarly, this maps onto the roles offered to female actors, which may play on wider stereotypes of femininity—as a love interest to the male hero, as leads in romantic comedies aimed at a female audience, or, conversely, as some kind of monstrous man-hating femme fatale. The legacy here of bitchiness associated with the likes of Bette Davis through to the bunny boiling stereotyping of Glenn Close in *Fatal Attraction* and horrors of female power played out through Sigourney Weaver in the science fiction *Alien* movies is only rarely counteracted by all-female lead movies such as *Thelma and Louise* or TV series *Sex and the City*, the latter raising a disproportionate media furor. These more production-driven elements clearly impact upon the consumption of gender through media as they limit the scope and remit of the representations offered. Furthermore, this *positioning* of men and women differently within many media formats and most clearly in film may play out into the wider sense in which masculinity and femininity are consumed differently in a structured and patterned way.

I will develop these matters shortly. How these factors connect to questions of masculinity is of concern here, however; for this we need to briefly survey the work on masculinity before applying this to one, more contemporary, concern in some recent films—the lone male as a figure of crisis or distress. The lone male—or wolf, given his often prowling sense of sexual allure—is not necessarily new. Hollywood cinema is littered with "wild" male figures whom women wish to "tame," from the mythology of the cowboy through to the brooding heroes of film noir and James Bond, who may get shaken but never stirs. What often characterizes these figures is their silence, rarely speaking of some unknown trauma they have suffered. Their emotional reticence somehow makes them all the more alluring. The grist to my mill here is that this is now shifting in a more nuanced, narcissistic, and complex direction.

## Masculinity and film

The study of masculinities is now vast, yet what most share is an emphasis on masculinity as a social construct or as a set of associations and characteristics that shift over time and pertain to social and cultural phenomena, even women, and not merely male bodies (see Edwards 2006). The problematic raised by film studies underpins this sense in which the spectacle of the male—and his body—is used to somehow symbolize, signify, or (re)construct masculinity. Underpinning this, in turn, is second-wave feminism's critique of the problem of sexual objectification, i.e. the idea that film creates, perpetuates, or reinforces the positioning of women as (sexual) objects. Sexual objectification in turn depends upon the positioning of women more widely, not only as objects but also as objects *to be looked at* by men. The problem of objectification is effectively a double one: first, in constructing the person as an object lacking in subjectivity and devoid of emotion; and, second, in setting up that person as passive and helpless, or at least disempowered, to resist that construction. One of the most influential analyses of this process has come from film studies, and the analysis of femininity and female subjectivity as being the object of the (male) gaze is premised almost entirely upon Mulvey's famous essay "Visual Pleasure and Narrative Cinema" (1975).

The visual pleasure offered through cinema for Mulvey is essentially twofold: first, scopophilia or the voyeuristic pleasure derived through looking; and, second, narcissism, or the pleasure developed from recognition and identification. Yet the true cut of her thrust appears when these concepts are overlaid in gendered terms. Put more simply, men, the male subject, and masculinity *look*, whilst women, the female object, and femininity are *looked at*. The more particular problematic that then ensues is the idea that the male and the masculine "cannot bear the burden of sexual objectification" (Mulvey 1975: 12). Similarly, narrative plotlines are also seen to reinforce the activity of the male subject, often conceived as heroic or powerful, and the passivity of the female object, who mostly serves the purpose of providing erotic interest.

Perhaps not surprisingly, Mulvey's work has since received a barrage of criticism. First and foremost, her approach is seen to underplay the importance of female pleasure in looking and indeed the significance of women's spectatorship more widely; so her analysis of looking relations is regarded as overly simplistic in its emphasis upon a strictly polarized gender divide in viewing relations (MacKinnon 1997; Silverman 1992). Second, the perspective she develops deflects attention away from more complex forms of identification that may exist (Neale 1982). Following from this, men as well as women may engage in various viewing positions that exist *across* any strict gender divide (Neale 1983). More significantly, the tendency to deflect the visual and sexual objection of men within cinema may be motivated as much, if not more, by the disavowal of male homoeroticism as by the heterosexual imperative to objectify femininity and women (Green 1984). Third, her use of psychoanalytic theory, particularly Freud's work around ambivalent identifications and polymorphous sexuality, is criticized (Rodowick 1982). Most severely, her analysis is seen by some as overly Westernized, middle class, and ⬚⬚⬚alized in its emphasis and examples (Gai⬚⬚ ⬚⬚⬚⬚⬚ the *way* men and women look and ⬚⬚⬚⬚⬚nd. In sum, *how* we look is often ⬚⬚⬚⬚⬚ t and vice versa.

Two important collections, as well as the work of Jeffords in particular, challenged these ideas more in relation to masculinity: figures as diverse as Tarzan and Rambo were seen to exhibit contradictory qualities, macho yet wimpy, as their outward aggression and swagger became seen primarily as a defensive response to more internal masculine insecurities (Cohan and Hark 1993; Jeffords 1994; Kirkham and Thumin 1993). One factor rather skimmed over in such analyses, however, is what I would like to call the cinematic *trope*—or symbol through use of a recurring character or ideal type. Of course many tropes exist. Yet one key figure here is that of the lone male, historically located within the Western genre in the figure of the cowboy, and now played out in other genres with similar, and also differing, consequences.

## Man alone: *Drive* (dir. Winding Refn, 2011), *Shame* (dir. McQueen, 2011), and *A Single Man* (dir. Ford, 2010)

At first glance these three films have little in common: Winding Refn's *Drive* is a tale of a Hollywood stunt driver and part-time criminal taxi service, punctuated by scenes of extreme violence; Steve McQueen's second major directorial offering, *Shame*, tells the provocative story of a "sex addict" in contemporary New York; whilst Tom Ford's *A Single Man* is a highly stylized remaking of Christopher Isherwood's novel into a near-existential contemplation on the grief of a gay academic in California. However, the films all focus centrally and pivotally on the figure of a man alone, struggling to relate to his fellow human beings and enduring severe psychological crisis. The result is near-death in two out of three cases and near-death by association in the other.

Nicolas Winding Refn's film *Drive* is based on the novel of the same name by James Sallis. The film, about a Hollywood stunt driver who at night becomes a getaway driver, was released in 2011 to rave reviews, particularly at the Cannes Film Festival, and further catapulted Ryan Gosling into the spotlight. Specific content aside, it furthers the career of Winding Refn as a director specializing in existential character portraits of men, previously seen in *Valhalla Rising*, and adds to his knack of spotting and developing new talent, previously seen with Tom Hardy in *Bronson*. The film's plotline is fairly simple and arguably unremarkable. The driver falls in love with his neighbor, Irene, played by Carey Mulligan, who is helping her ex-con partner and father to her child escape his past and pay off his debts in one last heist. Suffice to say, the pawn shop heist goes wrong and the driver is then engaged in trying to protect the girl and her child from the violent criminal world of which he has otherwise been a part.

What characterizes the film and makes the unremarkable extraordinary are three things: (1) Refn's direction and Hossein Amini's screen writing; (2) the casting and indeed dressing of Ryan Gosling; and (3) the electro synth pop soundtrack co-developed with Cliff Martinez of the Red Hot Chili Peppers. Refn's direction is characterized by a near-constant juxtaposing of wide angle and close-up shots, with characters often positioned off centre. Of particular significance here is the filming of the driver himself, frequently framed within mirrors and other prop devices or literally within the car rather than outside of it. For example, early on in the film the conversation between the driver and Irene is conducted through a mirror in her apartment, the driver's face is often seen through the car's rear-view mirror, and it is later seen at the film's denouement framed within the door to the criminal gang's pizzeria.

The overall effect of such devices is to make the film feel at once intimate and yet simultaneously surreal and mysterious. The direction is also, above all else, intensely self-conscious, from the toothpick-chewing cowboy mythmaking of Sergio Leone films starring Clint Eastwood and the violence characterizing Tarantino's work, to the interior scenes devoid of dialogue derived from David Lynch and the fetishism of cars and clothing used in Anger's *Scorpio Rising*. Complementing all of this is Amini's relentlessly stripped-back dialogue—the driver barely speaks and, when he does, does so with huge delays and pauses. Complementing this imagery is the similarly inflected use of electro synth pop that dominates the score. This music is well known for its associations with the 1980s and its later development into gay-oriented euro disco. More significantly, it plays upon the human/electronic, expressive/repressive and feminine/masculine ambiguities that dominate the character of the driver—he is never entirely coherent but lurches violently from one extreme to the other.

What drives the film, to pardon the pun, is not the plot or the cars but the mystery that surrounds the driver himself—a nameless, past-less, future-less character often hidden behind masks, shades, the theatrical costumery for the film parts he plays, or—if nothing else—Gosling's impassive gaze. The casting of Gosling is critical here. Gosling exudes a blue-eyed innocence that is juxtaposed with his slightly feminized yet physically toned sexuality. It appeals to gay men and women in a way not dissimilar to David Beckham. This juxtaposing of innocence with sexually and or violently inflected knowingness is what characterizes much of Gosling's on-screen presence. The dressing of Gosling is critical here and acknowledged by Refn to be overtly fetishized. He dons a silver satin jacket with a gold scorpion imprinted on the back whenever he is engaged in his more criminally related activities, clearly nodding towards Anger's use of the same symbolism in *Scorpio Rising*, as well as the wider myth of the scorpion and the frog crossing the river (which is cited at one point). He wears perfectly fitted jeans, sometimes with a matching denim jacket, and leather gloves that literally stretch and creak at various otherwise-silent points in the film. The sexuality here is both blatantly erotic and ambiguous. If it were not for his near-chaste relationship with Irene one could equally code the driver's sexuality as gay. Refn's lingering direction would seem to give Gosling the same double b(l)uff appeal of a young James Dean. Of significance, then, is the sense in which the presentation of Gosling as the driver is far more nuanced, feminized, and sexually ambiguous than that of many of his predecessors.

What does any of this tell us concerning masculinity? In the first instance, the film plays on a traditional tale of a bad guy tamed by the love of a woman who tries to go good but doesn't quite manage it. At the same time it clearly invokes the archetype of the cowboy loner, down to the toothpicks he chews, who drives rather than rides into town and then out again. What gives all this a far newer twist, however, are the three elements above that scratch at the surface of the character of the unnamed driver and render him both far more mysterious and yet infinitely more emotionally vulnerable than any latter-day cowboy. Key within this are the overtly feminizing influences of the music, the casting and dressing of Gosling, and the knowing yet sparse direction and writing of Refn and Amini that—combined—speak volumes about the ambiguities of a young man alone.

*Shame* is the second major film directed by Steve McQueen, whose earlier work, *Hunger*, was highly acclaimed. Unlike the other two films under consideration here, it is an original piece co-written by Abi Morgan and concerns the supposed "sex addiction" of Brandon, a successful advertising executive, played by Michael Fassbender. His highly controlled life of porn, sex, and work comes under fire when his sister Sissy, interestingly also played by Carey Mulligan, comes to stay; meanwhile his computer at work comes under investigation due to a virus, revealing excessive use of pornography. Again, the plotline is fairly simple as Brandon becomes overly stressed. He cracks under the pressure of exposure. His sister is also clearly mentally unwell and later attempts suicide. Whilst the film was mostly positively reviewed, some criticized the lack of back story explaining the unstable behavior of the brother and sister, although there are a few vague allusions to earlier abuse. A subplot concerns Brandon's relationship with Marianne, a co-worker, who is attracted to him, and they go on an awkward dinner date. Brandon is, however, impotent afterwards and returns to his use of casual encounters and prostitutes for sex. The overriding theme of the film is that Brandon cannot connect and, whilst surrounded by multiple sex partners, is effectively emotionally isolated.

The film is not perhaps as remarkable in its direction or writing as it is controversial; yet it contains some defining, and very moving, scenes. The most notable of these are set on the subway, where Brandon encounters a woman, played by Lucy Walters, with whom he exchanges glances and who he then pursues at the station. She returns, wearing red lipstick, in the final scene in the film, where she is far more assertive, in a repetition of the earlier scene, their hands (again showing her engagement ring) meet on the train's grip pole. What dominates these scenes are the long shot-reverse-shots of the two characters and the overlay of Escott's score—a repetitive string-based refrain set against the ticking of a clock. These elements are also echoed in the film's denouement, which starts around 75 minutes into the running time. McQueen intercuts footage of Brandon deliberately provoking an attack from a girl's boyfriend whom he meets in a bar, his visitation of a gay sex club where he gets a young man he sees on the street to go down on him, his receipt of phone messages from his sister crying for help, and his visit with a group of prostitutes. The scene with the prostitutes is particularly extended, ending with a close-up of Brandon's increasingly desperate expression. Again Escott's score is used to full effect. The opening of the film deploys the same temporal intercutting technique, showing Brandon on the subway, having sex with a prostitute, using the bathroom, and ignoring phone messages from his sister. The impression gained from this is that Brandon himself is equally fragmented, whilst the more constant element throughout is the music.

This temporal intercutting, use of sound effects and/or music, and near-total absence of dialogue is what gives the film its curiously intense yet distant feeling, heightening Brandon's all too evident isolation. The only dialogue that invades such scenes is pertinent to the film's main themes: "You're disgusting" at the end of the film's opening; and the oft-quoted line from his sister, "We're not bad people; we just come from a bad place." Given McQueen's avoidance of explanations and back story, the film inculcates a debate concerning sex addiction and problems of intimacy in the age of the internet or, perhaps more widely, a crisis of white Western middle-class masculinity as previously explored in films such as *Fight Club* and *American Psycho*. There is a clear nod to the latter in McQueen's portrayal of Brandon wandering naked in a minimalist New York apartment and using the bathroom, a scene identical to the set-up used in Hannon's earlier film. Given the traditional portrayal of male promiscuity as merely playboy hedonism, the film radically overturns this into a depiction of such practices as nervy and compulsive, thereby shifting the terrain of masculinity quite significantly.

*A Single Man*, a slightly older film, indeed takes aging as one of its key themes. Based on Isherwood's book of the same name, it tells the story of one day in the life of George Falconer, an English university lecturer in Los Angeles. George, played by BAFTA award winning and Academy nominated Colin Firth, is aging and—more to the point—grieving for the loss of his relationship with Jim, who died in a car crash around eight months earlier. The story is told in part linear and part flashback fashion, sticking in large part like glue to the original novel, except for the potential suicide plotline that director Tom Ford added. Like *Shame* and indeed *American Psycho* it opens with the protagonist waking in bed, using the bathroom, showering, and performing mundane morning routines. Yet, unlike those films, *A Single Man* for the most part stays on precisely this terrain. What also makes George's grief all the more excruciating is Isherwood's and indeed Ford's excoriating drilling into the loneliness that goes with it. The film's first full—and perhaps most powerful—scene shows George receiving the news by phone that his lover has been killed. He is also told that the funeral is for family members only and that one of their dogs is dead and the other is missing. Given this is the early 1960s, gay sexuality is neither legal nor liberated and George is forced to endure his grief in silence, other than for the support of his equally lonely but alcoholically enlivened friend Charley, played by a typically on-form Julianne Moore. Ford does not shy away from portraying this. The extended and uncut scene of Firth's face as the sad news is painfully and silently realized is one of the film's highlights. Thus the film is more forward than many of its predecessors in portraying explicitly male emotion and vulnerability.

Various conversations throughout the film refer to his and other minorities' "invisibility," set against a backdrop of paranoia and fear around the Cuban missile crisis and the legacy of McCarthyism. This more political point is juxtaposed with the film's existentialism. The paradox of the film, and what gives it its existential edge, is that George's day actually goes rather well, full of new and potentially exciting encounters—particularly with one of his students, the very beautiful and clearly rather flirty student Kenny, dinner with a friend, and even skinny dipping on a warm summer's night—and yet the punch line is that he never gets to choose suicide or even life as his body decides it for him. This theme is echoed throughout in Ford's use of the sound of a heartbeat, recurrent shooting of scenes of bodies under water, and—again as in *Shame*—the use of a ticking clock.

The film marks the debut of Tom Ford, otherwise known for his work as a globally renowned fashion designer. It was a critical and commercial success, yet some critics likened it to an advert, given Ford's meticulous attention to every conceivable aspect of *mise-en-scène* from clothing and make-up to lighting and interior decoration in a way often likened to the hit television series *Mad Men*. In addition, Ford's most original and distinctive trick is to change the hue according to mood. When George is about his mundane or grieving activities he and his surroundings are immersed in dull sepia. All springs into Technicolor whenever he is happier, enlivened, or diverted from his grief. This is particularly striking in the scene where he visits a local liquor store, meets a woman with the same breed of dog that he had with his partner, and then a handsome wannabe actor-cum-rent boy named Carlos. His kissing of the dog and admiration of the boy's body see the entire screen flood with color. This fades to grey as he returns to his suicidal preparations. Similarly, the film's denouement, where he encounters Kenny in the same bar where he met Jim and goes skinny dipping, is shot with a constant near-orange glow that literally drains from the screen at the end. Like the other films mentioned, the languid and lyrical score—this time by Academy Award nominee Able Korzeniowski—also plays a part.

## Conclusions: lone wolves

What do these films tell us concerning contemporary masculinities or, perhaps more accurately, their representation? My earlier work on film highlighted the sense in which many particularly American films were beginning to focus on the so-called crisis of masculinity thesis, where men are seen to be "in trouble" due to the rise of feminism and the decline of the traditional male role (Edwards 2006). Examples of this included *American Beauty*, where the Kevin Spacey character regresses into a kind of hippie, *Fight Club*, where men attempt to reclaim a more physical masculinity in a world of consumerist narcissism, and *American Psycho*, where Patrick Bateman is at once a groomed Wall Street city boy and a serial killer. The films considered here would seem to play on similar themes as their lead characters crack and dissolve, yet also harken back to an older trope of the man alone most strongly played out in the cowboy myth and the film career of Clint Eastwood, for example. Their crises are related to typically masculine emotional reticence yet are perhaps less crises of masculinity *per se*.

The films also continue to raise questions concerning Mulvey's thesis regarding the male gaze. All three protagonists are the object as well as the active subject here in the driver's fetishized dress, Brandon's nakedness, and George's immaculate suits. What also emerges is an inflection of Willemen's (1994) frictions or the fracturing of the gaze into parts, from camera to actor, actor to actor, viewer to actor, and ultimately actor to viewer. The facial close-ups in all three films are key here as the actors are not looking at anyone else but rather at us. Thus, part of the paradox of Mulvey's thesis is that if men are active their passive subjective worlds become all the more mysterious—rather like hollow men they have all the hard exterior of acting out yet almost nothing at their center. The three films I have examined in this chapter start to scratch at this predicament as, most fundamentally, character portraits of flawed men who are alone and struggling with how they feel. Their emotions are not told so much as shown through the way in which they are filmed—impassive, often silent, and put in situations that should provoke enormous reaction yet frequently do not—whilst shot-making, music, and silence somehow tell us what they are feeling. We are and are not on new territory here—men as emotionally incapacitated loners that directors portray tumbling into crisis. A more complete gender revolution would involve men discussing their feelings in some sort of *Sex and the City* for men where all the women do is yap on about such things non-stop—admittedly George does some of this, but primarily to himself—and falling apart rather than heroically holding it together.

What limits this discussion and much of what has preceded it is that we are still dealing with a specifically white, Western and often North American form of masculinity and indeed its Hollywood representation. Thus, in many ways these studies of masculinity in film echo wider populist concerns about "men in crisis" that in sum focus on a rather particular complaint. What these characters may suffer as a crisis of identity may for others be nothing more than routine experience. However, these lyrical—and often emotionally powerful—portraits still inflect their male protagonists with a few more levels of complication than before.

# References

Cohan, S. and I. A. Hark (eds.) (1993) *Screening the Male: Exploring Masculinities In Hollywood Cinema*, London: Routledge.

Craig, S. (ed.) (1992) *Men, Masculinity and the Media*, London: Sage.

Dyer, R. (1989) "Don't Look Now: The Instabilities of the Male Pin-Up," in A. McRobbie (ed.) *Zoot Suits and Second-Hand Dresses: An Anthology of Fashion and Music*, London: Macmillan, pp. 198–208.

Edwards, T. (2006) *Cultures of Masculinity*, London: Routledge.

Gaines, J. (1986) "White Privilege and Looking Relations: Race and Gender," *Cultural Critique* (Fall): 59–79.

Green, I. (1984) "Male Function: A Contribution to the Debate On Masculinity," *Screen* 25(4–5): 36–48.

Jeffords, S. (1994) *Hard Bodies: Hollywood Masculinity in the Reagan Era*, New Brunswick, NJ: Rutgers University Press.

Kirkham, P. and J. Thumin (eds.) (1993) *You Tarzan: Masculinity, Movies and Men*, London: Lawrence & Wishart.

MacKinnon, K. (1997) *Uneasy Pleasures: The Male as Erotic Object*, London: Cynus Arts.

Mulvey, L. (1975) "Visual Pleasure and Narrative Cinema," *Screen* 16(3): 6–18.

Neale, S. (1982) "Images of Men," *Screen* 23(3–4): 47–53.

——(1983) "Masculinity as Spectacle: Reflections on Men and Mainstream Cinema," *Screen* 24(6): 2–16.

Rodowick, D. (1982) "The Difficulty of Difference," *Wide Angle* 5(1): 4–15.

Silverman, K. (1992) *Male Subjectivity at the Margins*, London: Routledge.

Willemen, P. (1994) *Looks and Frictions: Essays in Cultural Studies and Film Theory*, London: BFI Publishing; Bloomington: Indiana University Press.

# 4

# To communicate is human; to chat is female

## The feminization of US media work

## *Vicki Mayer*

[T]he telephone girl solved the vexing problem of making the wonderful invention practical and successful. It was she who was cleverly represented as bringing order out of chaos; her deft fingers, her sweet voice and courteous tones transforming the pandemonium of the early operating to the orderly quiet of the modern Exchange.

(Dewhurst 1913: 9)

A 1913 article in the *Bell Telephone News* titled "The Unseen Force: Our Operators" directly addressed the "girls of the switchboard" about a play then being performed in Chicago celebrating their achievement in making "the telephone service the greatest convenience of the age." Written by the regular correspondent, a woman by the name Mrs. F. E. Dewhurst, the company trade magazine felt the performance recognized telephone operators' labor as women, although it's unlikely many nationally would have seen the local production. Herein lies the rub of feminized media labor: its invisibility, even to those who do it.

Today, as in the above quotation, much of feminized labor is characterized as a service, a dedication, and a natural extension of one's body and emotional capacities. In other words, what feminizes labor is the adaptation of unwaged forms of work associated with female sex and gender characteristics into a labor market, where these forms are less valued and subordinate to other kinds of work. The feminization of labor legitimates material inequalities that are related to sexism in the labor force. Yet for newcomers to a formal wage economy, it also can be a source of recognition, even status, at least for a time.

I will first focus on this ontological question as to what constitutes feminized labor in the next section of this chapter. I then examine what makes feminized labor attractive to employers and employees alike in media and communication industries: namely the mutual benefits that both thought they were getting from having women dominate a particular job role. I begin with an extended case study of telephone girls; the early experience of telephone operators demonstrates that for employers and employees, the key aspect of a feminized workforce was its ability to take qualities associated with domestic duties and apply them in serving others. My perspective on feminized labor as a negotiation between employers and employees differs from some accounts that stress only exploitation of women's work. It thus provides insight into why women would seek, even defend, these particular jobs in media industries. Last, I examine the overall feminization of media industry work. Throughout media industries, many occupations remain sex segregated, with women concentrated in occupations least likely to be seen by others as work based on individual merit or job performance. At the same time, far more media work has become feminized, which has involved increasing numbers of men in the negotiations over the gendering of service-based work.

## Feminized work

Scholarly assertions of feminization in labor markets do not reflect necessarily what the term "feminization" means or how it may be usefully applied across cultures, historical eras, or types of waged work roles. While longstanding disparities exist between men and women in earnings and status, definitions of feminized work vary based on location and time as well as the intersections between sex and gender, age, marital status, education and class, religion, and so on (Mills 2003). Given these differences, three criteria have typically been used to define feminized work:

1 Feminized work is that which is associated with domestic duties of housework and childcare. In the US, these duties were disseminated and standardized through highly prescriptive forms of popular culture during the nineteenth century (McHugh 1999). Although the taylorization or uniform mechanization and routinization of daily tasks put "women's work" in a market-oriented framework, its unpaid nature made it a "labor of love," subject to sentimentalization. As wages for housework advocates would later argue (Edmond and Fleming 1975), without wages societies would fail to recognize mothering as arguably the most important job of all: that of societal reproduction. Jobs that focus on organizational duties, interpersonal and time management skills, and the ability to do multiple tasks at once (multi-tasking) tend to be framed as feminized work.
2 Feminized work tends to emphasize affective performances associated with serving, assisting, or caring for others. Hochschild (1983) developed the phrase "emotional labor" to signal the ways many jobs in which women dominated—secretaries and flight attendants, for example—required a particular kind of female performance, or deep acting, in which people sublimated their own emotions to make others feel more comfortable and pleased. These affects seem not only to lack value in terms of the marketplace, but they are so ephemeral they seem invisible to a labor economy, if not a distraction: "Embodied affective labor is simultaneously constructed in the workplace and made invisible *as work that adds value*, to the extent that affective labor is construed as part of women's biology" (Otis 2012: 17). These performances today are largely associated with the service economy, where women predominate in positions of direct contact with customers, though others have extended emotional labor to a wide range of professionals (Gregg 2011).

3 Because feminized work defined in points 1 and 2 tends to be assigned to women by virtue of gender, and thus overlooked as trained skills or performances, feminized work tends to be devalued and degraded relative to non-feminized work (Kemp 1994). So while all work to some extent involves communication and social interactions, feminized work tends to frame these universals as "gossip," "chatting," or "banter," degrading their worth as part of a work role. This is true despite the importance of social networking and social media in many work roles that arguably stress the importance of feminized forms of conversation.

The definition of feminized work thus extends past the strict division between what women actually do in the marketplace to encompass a host of job duties that people of all genders do. The equal numbers of men and women in the workforce, combined with the dissolution of strict separate spheres between home and work, means that feminized work combines residual notions of femininity and domesticity with work roles that may be performed by men or women. The boundaries of feminized work are indeed arbitrary. Architects, chefs, and psychoanalysts all have roles that could easily be associated with the home, the domestic, or the private sphere, respectively. But that has not made those occupations more open to women or female claims of superiority in those roles. Furthermore, due to the fact that the feminization of some job roles seems an outgrowth of women's roles in the home, for example those stressing service, these connections have to be actively forged and enforced by both employers and employees alike.

Feminized workers can particularly emphasize the practices within job roles as having gendered or sexual connotations. Hence, the worker who stresses her ability to satisfy a customer, to be polite and well groomed, over her ability to make deals, negotiate, and drive a hard bargain may be stressing the feminized aspects of her work role: those associated with femininity over masculinity. This is not a stable binary categorization either. After all, virtually all work that involves some sort of social interaction, whether as an angel of the household or as an advertising executive, involves knowing when to serve others and when to stand your ground. If we look at the emphasis throughout the economy on sociality, good service, appearance, nearly any job could be said to be feminizing. What seems crucial in defining feminized work, whether as a telephone operator or as film casting agent, is the way that employers and employees concur in gendering the work, thereby stressing characteristics of the job that may help certain workers' entry into the workforce, while restricting their mobility later.

## The telephone girl

About a century ago, the telephone girl exemplified aspects of feminization that precede the ways in which communication and media industries feminize job roles today. The telephone girl was not a real woman, but a socially constructed ideal of a worker in an advanced capitalist society. This ideal reflected cultural assumptions about gender and work, taking aspects of communication associated with home and family, and applying those to a segment of the labor force. Employers reproduced those assumptions through workforce selection and management techniques. Female workers also reinforced the ideal in their own work performances and in disciplining other workers to follow suit. The telephone girl exists residually today in the ways that job requirements become gendered, creating an ideal of which gender is perceived as excelling in different roles in media industries.

In the late nineteenth century, a certain segment of young women came to dominate the labor market for telephone operation: "By 1900, over 80 percent of operators were single, white, native-born females" (Lipartito 1994: 1085). These women were high-school educated, taking advantage of the boom in universal secondary education. For the female graduates, work options were limited. Domestic work and factory jobs were abundant, but their educational training socialized them to aspire to something more than what they could get without an education. Their families had aspirations for them too. High school had sheltered girls from the dangers they would find in public. Social concerns fit the Victorian ideology of separate spheres for men and women, with the latter group assigned to the domestic sphere of hearth and home. A "respectable" woman needed to take care to be faithful to her domestic role later in life. The best remaining options at the time were teaching, clerical work, or being a telephone operator (Martin 1988: 154). Of these, the latter paid the best wages and thus most assured a path to the middle class, and later back to domestic motherhood.

This last point, that telephone operators balanced their positions between the home and the workplace, was most salient in determining that the job was most appropriate for women. Although some young women had worked in telegraph operation, the feminization of the work roles associated with telephone operators came in a relatively short time-span and transformed the ways that work done outside of a formal labor market came to be economically valuable and socially respectable in a formal labor market. As Marvin (1990: 61) writes, the introduction of the telephone into American society was fraught with the moral panic over the dissolution of the proper boundaries between public and private spheres. Tales of romantic courtship over the telegraph and telephone accompanied fears of class (and racial) transgressions in social interactions (1990: 62). The unsightly wiring of public space, combined with the fear that users would lose their intimate interactions, privacy, and community, made all telecommunications companies suspect.

To "domesticate" the new technology, women seemed to offer telephone companies the crucial characteristics needed in bridging the gap between being an efficient facilitator of the technology and being an assuring and trustworthy member of the community. The skill set associated with "the cult of domesticity" (McHugh 1999)— the nurturing care of familial others combined with the efficient conduct of routine tasks in the home—made the "angel of the household" an ideal worker in the communications industry. As Martin (1988: 145) notes, the operator had to play an awkward mediating role in connecting two people in a private conversation. On one hand, they had to act neutrally as an efficient part of the switching technology. On the other hand, this human intervention required some degree of tact and assurances of trustworthiness, given their intimate knowledge of people's telephone use. Comparing young female operators with young male operators, employers decided early on that the women would be more willing to submit themselves to both a routinized efficiency and politeness in doing the job. The social construction of the "telephone girl" was born.

The Bell Company, later AT&T, reinforced this construction with its selection, training, and disciplining of new workers. Telephone girls were to be white and native born. The company required applicants' education and physical records. They had to be unmarried; at times supervisors checked the marital status of employees to ensure they did not combine their work and domestic roles (Vallas 1993). This requirement for telephone girls benefited the company in two ways. First, single women could be more easily integrated into the company as their new "family" without the distractions of childcare. Second, the image of the single telephone operator no doubt held some marketing appeal to customers, who in the early 1900s were largely middle-class men. Training taught the workers to further accentuate these characteristics that would help callers identify them as "feminine," including patience, genteel manners, and a sweet voice. Emphasizing that "your voice is your smile" (Martel 2004), corporate training films instructed women to focus primarily on their speech (tonality, volume, and pitch) to communicate a pleasing attitude. Conversely, all other physical motions were to be unnoticeable, made fast and efficient to facilitate these men's communication. "When a girl passes her plug to the girl next to her to complete a connection, her eyes must not follow in that direction. She must never turn her head … . The service must be kept up at any costs," wrote one corporate inspector in 1915 (Vallas 1993: 48). This micro training of the body took months to perfect and was under constant monitoring for improvements on the job (Lipartito 1994). The telephone girl's agency would thus be sublimated to serving others in a seemingly natural and effortless way.

At the same time, the feminization of the operator role de-emphasized the operator's ability with regard to tasks associated with masculinity, namely: control the technology and manage the clients. Many early operators assumed the duties of repairing their precarious systems, from untangling the lines in high winds to fixing the switchboard, thus taking over male-dominated tasks in the organization (Vallas 1993: 44). Even as the technology improved, the telephone company provided operators with their own how-to manuals for repairing the system (Martin 1988: 155). Similarly, operators did many other tasks beyond simply chatting and connecting callers. Many acted as news reporters, knowledge brokers, even giving wake-up calls to the telephone subscribers (Marvin 1990: 75). One operator described her role as "a personal service bureau and general guide to the city of New York" (Schmidt quoted in Vallas 1993: 44). Still, these skills as job requirements were subordinate to those associated with feminine charm, courtesy, and submission "to make clear … that she was only a servant, not truly a member of the class to whose secrets she had access" (Marvin 1990: 76).

The idealization of the feminine worker and the feminization of the workforce was under constant negotiation in real work settings. In fact both men and women on the job were routinely disciplined for striking the wrong balance between streamlined and excessive communication. In an 1885 letter to future AT&T president Theodore Vail, the soon-to-be US chief patent attorney Thomas Lockwood admitted the advantages of female operators, who "exceed the males in civility," while noting their failure to always act as efficient switching technologies: "The young ladies also appear fond of airing their voices, and sometimes prolong conversations, to talk with subscribers, again losing time" (quoted in Vallas 1993: 39). Similarly, employers' assumptions that women would be more passive or docile than men were frequently confounded. Scholars have recorded numerous strikes between 1890 and 1929, all mobilized by what other craft workers derisively called the "petticoat unions" (Vallas 1993: 50). In all of these cases, the figure of idealized telephone girl meant that the company would strictly and stubbornly seek to recruit, train, and reform the women workers to fit the ideal.

Many women defended, even touted, the feminization of their work. The moral regulation of women in the public workplace was frequently framed by men and women alike as a "labour of love" (Martin 1988: 143). Dismissing the capacities of men to be patient operators, one female operator defined the labor force as "women who have put their femininity to the service of the community" (quoted in Martin 1988: 156). In other words, the very same rationales used in excluding women from work roles based on sex-assigned characteristics became the same bases for claiming a sector of the communications industry as a female-privileged turf. Women who met the basic qualifications of race, education, native status, and so on could collude with the idealized expectations for the feminized worker to limit the labor pool and gain power in negotiating better terms for employment. They were so successful, Lipartito (1994) claims, that the Bell Company and later AT&T were loath to automate the switching equipment for some 40 years, even to save costs. Operators had helped create their own golden handcuffs, because employers and customers alike expected a female operator.

For many women of this generation, the company's discrimination in choosing them as employees verified their suitability for the job and its associated class expectations. Many women migrated to cities for these desirable jobs. During their time as operators, they had some autonomy from their families and from the restrictions faced in their home communities. Being a "telephone girl" carried as much an air of fantasy as respect; they could look forward to the courtships and adventures that independence afforded in this new semi-public/semi-private sphere (Marvin 1990). At the same time, telephone operators could harbor their fantasies in a relatively safe and sheltered environment. In response to middle-class reformers and to protect their well-cultivated workforce, the company provided free meals, boarding, and healthcare as standard benefits. Libraries, reading circles, athletic clubs, and vegetable gardens were further amenities in some locations. For employers and employees, operators' education, good health, and moral well-being could be seen as meritorious in the workplace, providing opportunities for promotion. Within this paternalist framework, the growing monopoly power of the company led to expanded opportunities for female operators as supervisors. These women, frequently personified as "Ma Bell" (Vallas 1993: 60), were complicit in the moral regulation of gender distinction as a kind of mothering over the telephone girls while uplifting them into the middle class. Although the kind of work varied regionally and by company, the telephone operator was an occupation in which educated women could expect upward class mobility, at least before leaving the labor market to return to a life in the domestic sphere. Herein lay the rub of becoming an operator: the assumption that this was a temporary stage on the way to women's real roles as mothers and housewives. Telephone operators' relatively high status was always circumscribed by this notion of its temporariness.

The feminization of work requires an ample supply of employers and employees willing to defend its gendered assumptions. The definition of the feminized worker, exemplified in the negotiated ideal of the telephone girl, was unique in that for a segment of women entering the labor force it held the promise of class mobility while preserving sex-defined characteristics that would otherwise be invisible and unwaged. It also naturalized these characteristics, rendering them as part of "human nature" as opposed to a merit-based skill. That is, the feminization of telephone operation, or of comparable communication jobs at the time, can be identified in the multiple ways that aspects of the job were promoted as organic, unskilled, or effortless, and thus subordinate to jobs that stress learned application, skills, and personal merit. Despite the benefits of being able to claim a sector of the labor market as one's own, the feminization of work ultimately results in pigeonholing and a glass ceiling for women who want to advance beyond it. These have left their mark on media and communications industries as a residual culture (Williams 1980) that correlates the value of the worker with the visibility of the work performed on the job.

## Media workers today

The composition of the labor market for media jobs today roughly mirrors that of the late nineteenth century: a large number of educated young people are seeking employment for the first time. In my university communication classes over the past decade, women have always outnumbered men by a ratio of roughly three to one, including courses on the political economy of media industries, creative industry policy, and law. So it is not surprising that women make up nearly half of all US employees in communications and media industries. Women in communications and media industries also tend to earn more than the average US working woman in non-executive roles (Lovell et al. 2006: 2–3). Clearly a massive labor pool has been largely absorbed into jobs that earn more, and likely carry more status, than the vast majority of other jobs where women work.

At the same time, few people, including myself, can name many, if any, female film directors or producers, news editors, publishers, or other types of media executives. At the top of each media industry's occupational hierarchy, few women preside as managers or professional executives. In radio, television, and cable, approximately one-third of professional management staffers are women; 35 percent in motion pictures and video industries (Lovell et al. 2006: 23). Women fare better in newspaper industries, where they are nearly half of journalists and publishing managers, but make on average far less than similarly skilled jobs in film, radio, or television (Lovell et al. 2006: 24). As we move up these hierarchies, the numbers of women at the apex of their chosen industries dwindle. In US network television, for example, fewer than one-fifth of prime-time creators or directors are women; fewer than one-quarter of executive producers (Lauzen 2011). These statistics suggest an abundance of women in media industries, but they are concentrated in positions of lower status (and pay grade) than men in these same industries. Sex segregation of media jobs and the feminization of media work conspire to render women in media industries less visible relative to a handful of men whose names we are more likely to know as the movers, shakers, and newsmakers.

One example of how the continuing sex segregation in media industry occupations renders women less visible is casting, which plays a crucial role in finding talent for film and television productions. Approximately 80 percent of the Casting Society of America (CSA) are women. The organization, which represents casting directors and associates in film, television, and theater, has status on par with a creative guild in these industries. Casting stands above many of the non-professionalized occupations in visual media production. However, casting stands apart from other creative professionals, such as directors, screenwriters, producers, and acting talent, in that they are not recognized by any major awards organization for film and television production, including the Academy Awards, the Golden Globes, and the Emmys (Jaher 2012). The invisibility of casters is reinforced by the social construction of the work, which stresses the organizational and emotional skills of casters as feminine. In my own research (Mayer 2011), casters were extremely proud of their success in their field and touted their abilities as natural to their identities: largely as women as well as gay men. In this case, the feminization of the work promoted women into better compensated occupations in film and television production, while keeping them in an occupational ghetto with little opportunity for movement into creative fields that garnered more public recognition.

While sex segregation continues in particular occupations, such as casting, wardrobe, and make-up, the feminization of work can be witnessed in media industries overall in which employees and employers tout feminized skills either to fend off competition or to justify temporary employment. From the rise of new media applications to the intense marketing efforts used to bring consumers from one media platform to another, media industries demand workers with the skills once associated with telephone operation. "Gossip," in terms of both its production and its distribution, is now central to media industries' strategies for the management of information (Harrington and Bielby 1995). Workers need to become skilled at decoding the truthfulness of gossip and maintaining the social connections with sources, while preserving the reputation of the outlet. Similarly, media workers need to preserve their reputations as particular types of eager, sociable, and responsive servants to their employers and clients (McRobbie 2004). Over the past two decades, full-time and unionized employee positions across print, music, and all other media industries have been replaced by part-time contractors, freelancers, and interns, through a process called casualization. Despite the stress and insecurity of the employment, media workers can justify their investment as a labor of love for the entertainment industries they themselves enjoy, admire, or even revere (McRobbie 2002). Much like the telephone operators of the past, they know their jobs are presumed to be temporary, but this pool of young and eager workers may not know that their employers expect them to move on, not up.

Of these casualized workers, the number of interns has grown exponentially to capture the large numbers of communication and media graduates looking for work. Historically these jobs stem from the role of the "assistant," who was a woman. Female assistants of film studios, for example, "were called upon to use wifely, motherly or daughterly skills to nurture co-workers, to mitigate the emotional content of messages, to communicate pleasantly, and to exercise an influence under the guise of feminine passivity, all the while rendering their efforts virtually invisible through other aspects of gendered performance—such as chatter, flirtation, and gossip associated with girlish pleasure and leisure" (Hill 2013: 407). Today the spread of assistantships in the guise of internships and apprenticeships has meant the spread of feminized work for men and women alike, putting both in competition for supposedly lowly jobs. Hill employs the term "creative support" to identify the job requirements associated with the feminine cult of domesticity in the service of other workers' production capacities and vision. Despite the roughly equitable proportions of men and women in PA positions across the industry, creative support, also called apprenticeships or internships, remains a feminized labor market in the sense that the work is both invisible and devalued relative to others in those same industries.

To suggest that telephone operators of yesterday have much in common with media industry workers today might seem ludicrous. The low associations that middle-class Americans have of call center work, with its high levels of surveillance and minimum wages, would seem the diametric opposite of the optimistic, if not glamorous, associations these same people make with working in television, film, music, and new media industries. Yet set in the appropriate historical context, the differences seem less startling. Media industries seek a continuous stable of young, educated people for work that is not presumed to be a lifetime career. In return for loyalty and self-sacrifice, many media industry workers get certain perks, a per diem if on the road or a company playroom if tied to an office. Yet the biggest perk of all is precisely the fact that media work is respectable. At a time when more college-educated youth in the US seek jobs than ever before, the appeal of working as a free intern in a media corporation supersedes that of waiting tables for minimum wage, even if the latter job is actually sustaining the former.

What is clear is that feminized labor is a relational concept that does not stand in easy opposition to some stable conception of the masculine. Rather, feminization is contingent on a host of class and other social dynamics. That means that while a feminized role in media production may be lower in status to the highest parts of the industry, it is also better than being on the bottom, or not having a job at all. Within a labor hierarchy, feminized roles may seem to put women in a double bind. On the one hand, women who enter these jobs may see themselves as uniquely qualified by virtue of their gender. On the other, these same women may have difficulty advancing from the role or negotiating from a position of their "natural" qualifications. After all, it is very difficult to demand payment for something that comes naturally.

At the same time, the interesting paradox about gendered labor is that by limiting the entire workforce to only one particular segment of the market able to play gendered roles, media industries potentially give the in-group more power to demand higher wages and better working conditions. Histories of the telephone girls reveal that, far from submissive servants, they resisted their exploitation, went on strike, and continuously negotiated the terms by which they would labor. In this respect, the telephone girls of yesterday might have some tips about labor resistance to pass on to today's struggling media workers, if only as a secret between friends.

# References

Dewhurst, F. E. (1913) "The Unseen Force: Our Operators," *Bell Telephone News* 3(4): 9.

Edmond, W. and S. Fleming (1975) *All Work and No Pay: Wages, Housework and the Wages Due*, London: Power of Women Collective and the Falling Wall Press.

Gregg, M. (2011) *Work's Intimacy*, London: Polity.

Harrington, L. and D. Bielby (1995) "Where Did You Hear That? Technology and the Social Organization of Gossip," *Sociological Quarterly* 36: 607–28.

Hesmondhalgh, D. (2010) "User-generated Content, Free Labor and the Cultural Industries," *Ephemera* 10: 267–84.

Hill, E. (2013) "Distributed Assistanthood: Dues-paying Apprentices and 'Desk Slaves'," in V. Mayer (ed.) *The International Handbook on Media Studies: Production*, London: Blackwell, pp. 404–10.

Hochschild, A. (1983) *The Managed Heart: The Commercialization of Human Feeling*, Berkeley: University of California Press.

Jaher, D. (2012) "The Casting Director as Decision-maker," paper presented at Console-ing Passions: International Conference for Television and Media, Boston, MA, July 19.

Kemp, A. (1994) *Women's Work: Degraded and Devalued*, Englewood Cliffs, NJ: Prentice Hall.

Lauzen, M. (2011) "Boxed In: Employment of Behind-the-Scenes and On-Screen Women in the 2010–11 Prime-time Television Season," Report for the Center for the Study of Women in Film and Television, San Diego State University.

Lipartito, K. (1994) "When Women Were Witches: Technology, Work, and Gender in the Telephone Industry," *American Historical Review* 99: 1075–111.

Lovell, V., H. Hartmann, and J. Koski (2006) "Making the Right Call: Jobs and Diversity in the Communications and Media Sector," Report, Institute for Women Policy Research, Washington, DC: IWPR.

McHugh, K. A. (1999) *American Domesticity: From How-to Manual to Hollywood Melodrama*, New York: Oxford University Press.

McRobbie, A. (2002) "From Holloway to Hollywood: Happiness at Work in the New Cultural Economy," in P. DuGay and M. Pryke (eds.) *Cultural Economy*, London: Sage, pp. 97–114.

——(2004) "Making a Living in London's Small-scale Creative Economy," in D. Power and A. Scott (eds.) *Cultural Industries and the Production of Culture*, London: Routledge, pp. 130–44.

Martel, C. (dir.) (2004) *Phantom of the Operator*, New York: Women Make Movies.

Martin, M. (1988) "Feminisation of the Labour Process in the Communication Industry: The Case of the Telephone Operators, 1876–1904," *Labour/Le Travail* 22: 139–62.

Marvin, C. (1990) *When Old Technologies Were New*, Chicago: University of Chicago Press.

Mayer, V. (2011) *Below the Line: Producers and Production Studies in the New Television Economy*, Durham, NC: Duke University Press.

Mills, M. B. (2003) "Gender and Inequality in the Global Labor Force," *Annual Review of Anthropology* 32: 41–62.

Otis, E. (2012) *Markets and Bodies: Women, Service Work, and the Making of Inequality in China*, Palo Alto, CA: Stanford.

Vallas, S. P. (1993) *Power in the Workplace: The Politics of Production at AT&T*, Albany: State University of New York Press.

Williams, R. (1980) *Problems in Materialism and Culture: Selected Essays*, London: Verso.

# 5

# Rediscovering twentieth-century feminist audience research

## *Joke Hermes*

Qualitative audience studies have arguably been the best possible expression of feminist engagement in media studies. Seminal studies such as Janice Radway's *Reading the Romance* (1984), Ien Ang's *Watching Dallas* (1985), and David Morley's *Family Television* (1986) can all be categorized as audience research that allowed for the voice of "ordinary women" (and sometimes "ordinary men") to be heard. This research bears witness to a spirit of solidarity and recognition of unequal gender relations without imposing ideological dogma or political correctness.

The qualitative audience researchers of the 1980s took on more than the heritage of the new social movements of the 1960s and 1970s that queried unequal relations having to do with class, race, and gender. They were also pathfinder studies for the exploration of new (qualitative) methods in media research and prompted a shift in academic thinking about how media texts have meaning. In the 1970s, there was little reason to suppose that the stark division between media producers and consumers was to come to an end. Although "alternative" and "minority media" (underground and subcultural broadsheets, magazines, community radio and television stations; see Downing 1984 or Jankowski 2006) existed, they mostly shifted the boundary between media makers and users. But they did not dispute the boundary itself and did not initially foresee what mediated communication was to become. Their investment was in participatory democracy, not in the unpredictability of practices of meaning making by audience members or producers. The convergence of these concerns marks out a highly relevant research area that now tends to be colonized by business-driven research. Exceptions to this are, for instance, Christine Hine's *Virtual Ethnography* (2000), which questions "net life," its meanings and participatory possibilities. The court case against Louise Woodward, a British *au pair* who was charged with shaking a baby to death, and the debate this spurred on newsgroups and early "homemade" websites form the central focus of the book.

In today's mixed field, in which broadcast and platform or network media exist side by side, different versions of reality clearly can exist side by side as well. Audience research pointed to sometimes entirely different sets of meaning that audiences constructed around texts (Hall 1980 [1973]; Morley 1980); neither authorities nor media have full control over meaning making. It made clear that audiences were bound in doing so by the means at their disposal (given their education, class background, and so on). They will, from time to time, use the space to read "against the grain." Making room for new insights and method, qualitative audience research also started engaging viewers in, for example, video production, to reconstruct how particular genres were meaningful to them (Drotner 1989). Beyond a voice, viewers have been given *credit* for their interpretations and criticisms of media texts. Qualitative audience research in the 1980s is a veritable treasure trove for academic investigation in today's media landscape, offering instruction in how to wield theoretical tools delicately, to respect how others experience everyday reality, and to understand how we are bound by rules not of our own making even as today's neoliberalism tries to convince us that we are in charge of our own fate.

Another reason to revisit what was briefly called "the new audience research" (Corner 1991) of the 1980s is its fiercely anti-essentialist notion of gender. Rather than taking it as a given, these studies took gender as a product of power relations, bound up with ethnicity and class. The women's movement has a less powerful presence today than in the 1970s and 1980s but this is not to say that gender has ceased to be one of the primary disciplining tools for individuals or that the position of specific groups of women and men has ameliorated to the point that feminism has become superfluous.

After briefly introducing early feminist audience research, this chapter will offer an example of a research area that can benefit greatly from this previous research. I do not propose to undertake a direct inquiry into women or men and the media, but instead to offer an example of an area in which considering gender and gendered practices of representation and media use may yield more theoretically interesting results. What from the early 1990s onwards is often referred to as "feminist audience research" is not preoccupied with gender *per se* but instead with when and how gender is used as a disciplining mechanism. Contemporary studies call for great sensitivity concerning gender, ethnicity, class, sexuality, or any other means of differentiating individuals and the ways in which that shapes their positions unequally. This can entail understanding social phenomena and texts as gendered where this is not obviously the case, but it is also to see how practices that at face value appear to be "neutral" may be built on gendered logics that ultimately will result in women and men being ruled by their gender, or, perhaps more precisely, by the consequences of being gendered.

## A poststructuralist political project

When done well, qualitative audience studies teach us if, when, and how gender matters. An example is Ann Gray's (1992) research on the introduction of the VCR in households. While some of her informants claimed that the new machine was male terrain because its timer function was too difficult to operate, those same informants could prepare meals on complicated cookers involving as much technical dexterity. Early qualitative audience research makes clear that we need to always be willing to consider the role and importance of gender, and the ways in which gender "works" by providing us with suitable identities and activities to take up, and is dictated by contexts of time and place. In Gray's study, as in Morley's *Family Television*, class position and working outside the home are also important in whether and how "gender" has meaning in relation to the use of household media technology. In these and other feminist audience studies gendered *practices* matter rather than gender as such as a significant attribute of individuals. Looking at the body of "feminist audience research" this may not be immediately clear. Quite a sizable part of this body of work specifically engages with women's media or approaches primarily women as its informants. For instance, Ang (1985) advertised in a young women's magazine for viewer comments on the television series *Dallas*. Radway (1984) focused on Harlequin romances, which may be the most gender-divided medium in its practice of use. Why did they focus on women and women's genres?

Feminist audience research was inspired by feminist criticism of male-dominated science (hence the choice of women's genres and women as the main group of informants) and a material force in emancipating popular culture more generally. Popular culture, particularly those forms which were made to appeal to female audiences, was largely regarded as unworthy of academic consideration. General conclusions pertaining to entire populations had primarily been based on research that included only men. Standards for behavior and for achievements tended to be based on what was expected of white, middle-class males (Archer and Lloyd 1982). Feminist audience research aimed to remedy these wrongs.

Despite great advances, three decades later women still tend to earn far less than men for the same jobs for which they hold the same qualifications across the globe (World Economic Forum 2012). Although women's lives have changed since the onset of second-wave feminism in the late twentieth century, sexism remains a thorny issue. What we see today are gender regimes that target both women and men, and that require men to meet levels of discipline and achievement across social, emotional, and professional performance that are far more demanding than they used to be. Personal hygiene and the standards of the well-toned male body are good examples: while soap, aftershave, and Brylcream were used by my father's generation, men of my generation were socialized into using deodorants, colognes, facial creams, specialized shampoos, and other hair products of which Brylcream was a lonesome early predecessor. A Global Insight report in 2007 speaks approvingly of a "burgeoning male consumer marketplace" (2007: 14).

Social, political, and academic contexts matter to how a body of research comes into being. Of particular relevance here is how feminist *media* (not audience) studies became a label for a particular type of research in the late 1980s and early 1990s, and how "feminist audience research" solidified as a separate but related field of academic inquiry (Steeves 1987; van Zoonen 1994, 1991; Walters 1995). Central to feminist media studies were debates over how to understand gender: as a (natural) given or as a social construction. The women's movement developed highly distinct streams in which radical feminism, liberal feminism, and socialist feminism were the main approaches. They differed in their views on gender, taking various positions on whether gender is innate and biologically defined or a social construction. If gender is a social construction and the product of socialization and stereotyping in the media, and merely *one* of the differences (alongside class and race) through which power in patriarchal-capitalist societies is enacted, differences amongst women matter as much as those between men and women. Such a constructivist (rather than essentialist) approach underscores that gender is not destiny. As the French feminist Simone de Beauvoir said in 1949 in her famous book *La Deuxième Sexe*: "On ne naît pas femme, on le devient" (one is not born but rather becomes a woman).

Liesbet van Zoonen remarked that feminist media studies is divided, with post-structuralism (bearer of the constructivist approach) marking a more or less clear fault line (1994: 4). On one side of the divide, gender is regarded as the product of power and therefore not in itself relevant; on the other, gender is the very reason for power differences between women and men. In such an essentialist view men are jealous of women and wish to control their progeny and child-bearing more generally. A second fault line coheres around popular culture, with some suggesting that it must be taken seriously and studied academically. Others view popular culture and mainstream media as principal causes of women's oppression. The media are claimed to oppress women by celebrating and objectifying a particular type of women's body, while reserving serious programming, such as news and public affairs, almost exclusively for men (Davies *et al.* 1987).

The qualitative audience research on women and particular media and media genres discussed here is unified by its "constructivist" perspective regarding gender and popular culture. It is unified in its assumption that dominant gender definitions in the media can be and are challenged by audience members even if they cannot change media regimes altogether. Crucially, this point of view allows both for recognizing agency on the part of individuals and for understanding individuals as always subjected to regimes of power that are more encompassing than they seem to be. Looking at societies in this manner, it makes sense to do audience research that centers on how particular (groups of) individuals give meaning to media and media texts, and to understand how these practices of meaning making are grounded in shared cultural knowledge and bound by social structures. For instance, Camille Bacon-Smith (1992) and Marie Gillespie (1995) produced important ethnographies that do so. Bacon-Smith examined the culture produced by female fans of popular culture in fanzines. Gillespie investigated migrant and diasporic cultures through long interviews, focusing on a West London Punjabi community and its use of television.

Other studies focused on readers of women's and men's magazines; readers were asked about what made these texts meaningful (Hermes 1995; Jackson *et al.* 1999). Helen Taylor undertook research with fans of *Gone with the Wind*, placing ads in journals and newspapers to reach these fans. She asked her participants to write to her about their memories, experiences, and views of book and film and to reconstruct "how *GWTW* lives in the imagination, memories and experiences of individuals and groups" (1989: 17). Jacqueline Bobo (1992) interviewed black women viewers of the much contested Spielberg movie based on Alice Walker's novel *The Color Purple*. The film and novel were widely regarded as including unacceptable, racist depictions of black men. Bobo's audience research, however, highlighted how her participants made sense of "the savage and brutal depiction of black men in the film" and "black family instability." She found that they largely embraced the film and used their own reconstructed meaning as a way to "empower themselves and their social group" (1992: 90–2).

## Gender as a theory building tool

After the exciting work of the 1980s and 1990s, new audience studies since the millennium appear to have become less innovative and critical. With a small number of exceptions (such as Duits's 2007 *Multi-Girl-Culture* and Herbert and Gillespie's 2011 themed journal issue on religion, media, and social change), few book-length feminist audience studies have been recently published. In part, this may have had to do with changing circumstances in academic publishing. Single peer-reviewed journal articles are rapidly coming to be regarded by many academic institutions as more important than books. Feminist audience studies, however, fit more comfortably in a full-length monograph, given that the validity and the quality of theorization can more easily be borne out by supplying the reader with enough direct quotations from informants and detailed warrants for methodological choices. Given my focus here on the early feminist audience research, the important question is what exactly was achieved by the earlier work? Generally speaking, these studies all considered media through the eyes and perceptions of viewers and readers. It meant an end to the dominance of textual criticism where the media text was concerned; the suggestion is also clearly that practices of media use are always also social practices and of interest in that sense.

Charlotte Brunsdon has argued that David Morley's findings in *Family Television* "conform so tightly to what might be guessed to be stereotypical masculine and feminine behavior as to be almost unbelievable" (Brunsdon 1986, cited in van Zoonen 1994: 123). Morley convinces, however, because a small number of exceptions emerged to the pattern of male domination in households that he finds. In the few cases where women hold more cultural capital than men, the pattern does not hold (van Zoonen 1994: 114), a case of exceptions proving a rule. That rule, however, had little to do with either television or innate gender qualities but instead with the ritual renewal of social expectations and what Bourdieu (1984) called "distinction." Bourdieu uses the concept to theorize how class differences are maintained by claiming specific tastes and ways of being for a particular group or class. Gender difference can be argued to be perpetuated in much the same way. The mechanism of "distinction" ensures that individuals will live up to what they feel is expected of them given their professional or social position. As social beings we have learned that we need to distinguish ourselves: from other genders, from other social classes, from other professions. Even in such mundane activities as watching television we continue to do so.

Likewise Ang's study of the nighttime soap opera *Dallas* (1985) showed how the tragic structure of feeling in the soap text is connected yet highly different from the melodramatic imagination viewers bring to bear on the series. By understanding the depiction of characters and relationships in the series as realism in disguise, viewers connect what they see on the screen to everyday experience. Ang calls this "emotional realism." Making matters even more complex is the ideological inscription of the melodramatic imagination: disavowed by some using ironic distancing mechanisms, espoused by others using a populist ideology. Radway's (1984) romance readers were also more discerning consumers of culture than those who do not read romance novels would expect. By reconstructing top tens of the best and worst romances readers recollected reading, Radway can show how romance reading is a means of rewriting patriarchal masculinity by imagining the romantic hero as both very masculine and strong and highly caring. Paying close attention to gender in audience research allowed for theorization of power, genre, and affect with a far wider reach than the media text or mediated communication.

There was no secret ingredient to these studies, no shared methodology or theoretical apparatus used by all. *Reading the Romance* (1984) was written before Radway became acquainted with British cultural studies, which did provide for much of the framework that was used in later audience research. While Morley employed qualitative media sociological approaches in his research, Ang was schooled in social psychology. Radway is an American studies scholar who used both quantitative and qualitative methods in her work. What connects them is something that might be called "ethnographic spirit": a willingness to engage with other worlds, to not be bothered by others' preconceptions and prejudices, and to take the time to understand what those engaging with it find meaningful and pleasurable about popular media culture. In that sense this work is the opposite of textual analysis, which often *assumes* how a text will be understood without actually asking its readers or viewers whether that is indeed the case. As a reward for their ethnographic spirit, Radway, Ang, and Morley found much more than accounts of media use. They introduced us to audience members we might not ordinarily come across. They use the insights gained, including surprise and dismay, not only in strong understanding of media and media making, but also in theorization of identity formation and subjectivity.

To keep coming up with exceptional insights in the way these 1980s feminist audience studies did, as well as those that followed, would be difficult. Treating gender with a light hand and making clear that gender (like ethnicity or age) does not *always* matter, or matter in the exact same way, is also difficult (see Ang and Hermes 1991; van Zoonen 1994). A light hand and paying careful attention to gender were not always achieved in the 1980s and 1990s. Some of the work important to the development of feminist media studies was criticized for not doing so, such as John Fiske's (1987) work on television and popular culture. Initially Fiske became known for two books on television and its role in (post)modern culture, *Reading Television* (1978), co-authored with John Hartley, and *Television Culture* (1987). Neither contains audience research but *Television Culture* does offer extensive theorization of the "resistant" reader and of feminine and masculine genres, suggesting its relevance to feminist audience studies.

Fiske claims that the soap operas show how "power may be achieved by feminine values" (1987: 188). Unfortunately he also suggests such a strong link between the soap opera as text and its viewers that Elspeth Probyn finds the liberating power of this claim a mockery. Fiske may well suggest that readers resist dominant meanings and thus hegemonic power relations (Probyn 1993) but apparently the text continues to have the power to construct its female viewers as feminine subjects: "For all of Fiske's vaunting of the resisting and negotiating reader, there is little room for any semiotic manipulation, let alone warfare, in his model. These texts construct their feminine readers, rather than the other way around" (Probyn 1993: 53). Fiske thus undermines feminist audience studies' double claim that making contact with audiences matters and that gender may be constructed differently in different viewing practices, despite the seeming uniformity of mass media texts. Both claims have remained important and need paying careful attention to, up until today.

## Uses of feminist audience research today

The ethnographic spirit in 1980s and 1990s audience research shows itself in its recognition of the complexity of everyday life worlds, and the need to theorize the experience and interpretations of media users (Clifford and Marcus 1986; Hammersley and Atkinson 1995 [1983]). In the second decade of the twenty-first century, new questions around gender and audiences are coming to the fore. The broadcast logic of mass media production and consumption that defined the audience as the end station of communication processes is no longer seen to be all powerful, as it was widely regarded in media research several decades ago. The widespread availability of multi-platform, increasingly interactive media undermine transmission models of communication, which view communication in terms of a chain of cause and effect, from powerful producers to passive consumers. Today, media production tends to blur with media consumption (which some refer to as "prosumption") as networked friends pass content on to one another (Green and Jenkins 2011). Can the "ethnographic perspective" of yesteryear still help us to understand gender and gendered identities in relation to the logics of both broadcast and multi-platform media?

The ethnographic approach needs to be rethought, I suggest, to engage with this new media landscape. Audience researchers may usefully borrow from governmentality studies to understand power and power relations, or affect theory to make sense of what binds us to specific identities and subjectivities that we share in and through the media. A newly energized perspective would combine authenticity, a separate but strong voice for academic interpretation, and an invitation to critical dialogue and public discussion. It would include an acceptance that while gendered identities in media content and in everyday life have changed, gender equality has by no means been achieved, whilst the disciplining of individuals by means of gender coding and public sexualities has become intense. It would for that reason challenge older perceptions of gender difference and the power imbalance between men and women in everyday life.

It is not up to audience researchers to set social or moral norms for individuals. Whilst they may be highly critical of social inequality, of particular media practices and texts, basic respect for media users must be the bottom line. The project of media and gender research from an audience research perspective has to do with understanding, not with prescription or finding fault. The changing media environment allows media users to also be producers and co-designing participants—all the more reason not just to take audiences seriously but to be aware of what can be gained by paying close attention to "bad taste," sexism, and the meanings and pleasures of media texts and practices that celebrate gender inequality. John Fiske, criticized for the way in which he defended soap opera, does point the way to the continuing need to pay close theoretical attention to what may seem to be counterproductive and sexist content from a feminist perspective. The changing media landscape offers new possibilities to do so. Media users who are also media producers might also be considered co-producers in research. Broadening the scope of research methodology to participant design tools could help in getting a deeper understanding of how, where, and why audience members cling to traditional gender roles and appear to welcome their reinvention across conventional storytelling in television and new media practices on, e.g., social networks.

Through the use of contemporary participant design tools feminist audience research has potential to be highly useful outside of what conventionally has been its domain. For instance, participant design feminist audience research would be able to understand more thoroughly how media literacy is not merely a question of knowledge and competences but also a domain of power inequality. Power often uses gendered connotations to distinguish strong from weak, and good from bad. Reasoned (masculine) is opposed to emotional and sensationalist (feminine). Gender does not come into being in a contained, fenced-off arena. On the contrary, gender ideology permeates most other social domains. David Buckingham's and Sara Bragg's respective studies with and on young people are of particular significance here (Bragg *et al.* 2011; Buckingham *et al.* 2010). Not only is their use of mixed methods and sensitivity to the kind of knowledge that different research methods produce a strong example of work that has continued the tradition of late twentieth-century feminist audience research, it also points our attention to an area that as a whole could benefit from being defined as research on gender and media.

In two small studies, Annika van den Berg, Marloes Mol, and I found media literacy to be a reference to highly conservative practices: parents from almost all (class) backgrounds amongst our informants rejected television viewing for young children in favor of reading books to them. Twelve-year-olds had learned to carefully replicate this type of talk about television (television is bad for children, it offers bad examples) but insisted there was also much to learn from television especially if a program was also funny (Hermes *et al.* 2013). The parents and the 12-year-olds shared a strong investment in the need for distinction: whether between age groups, social classes, or indeed the genders. By making television disputable terrain, the children had learned to carefully distinguish between good and bad television but also how "bad" television is handled well (by using reason, of course). Tilting this research material a quarter circle allows for better understanding of how we continue gender coding in our own lives and practices as media users, as children, and as their parents even when we are not aware we are doing so. Quite possibly, too, the issue of media literacy becomes more exciting when approached not from a perspective of concern but from a perspective of everyday creativity and waywardness, because and in spite of all the conventions surrounding it. The tradition of feminist audience research offers most promising ways and means to do so. While the current dominance of neoliberalism would at face value appear to discourage any attention to social inequality, it would support the uncovering of hidden mechanisms that hinder individuals in reaching their full potential. What better way to do so than the open, respectful, and theoretically engaging method of qualitative audience research developed in feminist media studies?

# References

Ang, I. (1985) *Watching Dallas: Soap Opera and the Melodramatic Imagination*, London: Methuen.

Ang, I. and J. Hermes (1991) "Gender and/in Media Consumption," in J. Curran and M. Gurevitch (eds.) *Mass Media and Society*, London: Arnold, pp. 307–29.

Archer, J. and B. Lloyd (1982) *Sex and Gender*, Harmondsworth: Penguin.

Bacon-Smith, C. (1992) *Enterprising Women: Television Fandom and the Creation of Popular Myth*, Philadelphia: University of Pennsylvania Press.

Bobo, J. (1992) "*The* Color Purple: Black Women as Cultural Readers," in E. Deirdre Pribham (ed.) *Female Spectators*, London: Verso.

Bourdieu, P. (1984) *Distinction: A Social Critique of the Judgement of Taste*, Cambridge, MA: Harvard University Press.

Bragg, S., D. Buckingham, R. Russell, and R. Willett (2011) "Too Much, Too Soon? Children, 'Sexualization' and Consumer Culture," *Sex Education: Sexuality, Society and Learning* 11(3): 279–92.

Buckingham, D. and S. Bragg (2004) *Young People, Sex and the Media: The Facts of Life?*, Basingstoke: Palgrave Macmillan.

Buckingham, D., R. Willett, S. Bragg, and R. Russell (2010) "Sexualised Goods Aimed at Children: A Report to the Scottish Parliament Equal Opportunities Committee," Scottish Parliament Equal Opportunities Committee, Edinburgh.

Clifford, J. and G. E. Marcus (1986) *Writing Culture: The Poetics and Politics of Ethnography*, Berkeley: University of California Press.

Corner, J. (1991) "Meaning, Genre and Context: The Problematic of 'Public Knowledge' in the New Audience Research," in J. Curran and M. Gurevitch (eds.) *Mass Media and Society*, London: Arnold, pp. 267–306.

Davies, K., J. Dickey, and T. Stratford (eds.) (1987) *Out of Focus: Writing on Women and the Media*, London: The Women's Press.

Downing, J. (1984) *Radical Media: The Political Experience of Alternative Communication*, Cambridge, MA: South End Press.

Drotner, K. (1989) "Girl Meets Boy: Aesthetic Production, Reception and Gender Identity," *Cultural Studies* 1(2): 208–25.

Duits, L. (2007) *Multi-Girl-Culture: An Ethnography of Doing Identity*, Amsterdam: Amsterdam University Press.

Fiske, J. (1987) *Television Culture: Popular Pleasures and Politics*, New York: Routledge.

Fiske, J. and J. Hartley (1978) *Reading Television*, London: Methuen.

Gillespie, M. (1995) *Television, Ethnicity and Cultural Change*, London: Routledge.

Global Insight (2007) "A Study of the European Cosmetics Industry, Final Report." http://ec.europa.eu/enterprise/newsroom/cf/_getdocument.cfm?doc_id=4976.

Gray, A. (1992) *Video Playtime: The Gendering of a Leisure Technology*, London: Routledge.

Green, J. and H. Jenkins (2011) "Spreadable Media: How Audiences Create Value and Meaning in a Networked Economy," in V. Nightingale (ed.) *The Handbook of Media Audiences*, Malden, MA: Wiley-Blackwell, pp. 109–26.

Hall, S. (1980) "Encoding/Decoding," in S. Hall, D. Hobson, A. Lowe, and P. Willis (eds.) *Culture, Media, Language*, London: Hutchinson, pp. 128–38.

Hammersley, M. and P. Atkinson (1995 [1983]) *Ethnography: Principles in Practice*, 2nd edition, London: Routledge.

Herbert, D. and M. Gillespie (2011) "Editorial. Special Issue on Religion, Media and Social Change," *European Journal of Cultural Studies* 14(6): 601–9.

Hermes, J. (1995) *Reading Women's Magazines: An Analysis of Everyday Media Use*, Cambridge: Polity Press.

Hermes, J., A. van den Berg, and M. Mol (2013) "Sleeping with the Enemy: Audience Studies and Critical Literacies," *International Journal of Cultural Studies* 16: 457–73.

Hine, C. (2000) *Virtual Ethnography*, London: Sage.

Jackson, P., K. Brooks, and N. Stevenson (1999) "Making Sense of Men's Lifestyle Magazines," *Society and Space* 17(3): 353–68.

Jankowski, N. (2006) "Creating Community with Media: Histories, Theories and Scientific Investigations," in L. Lievrouw and S. Livingstone (eds.) *The Handbook of New Media*, London: Sage, pp. 55–74.

Katz, E. and T. Liebes (1990) *The Export of Meaning: Cross-Cultural Readings of Dallas*, New York and Oxford: Oxford University Press.

Morley, D. (1980) *The Nationwide Audience*, London: The British Film Institute.

——(1986) *Family Television: Domestic Leisure and Cultural Power*, London: Comedia.

Probyn, E. (1993) *Sexing the Self: Gendered Positions in Cultural Studies*, London and New York: Routledge.

Radway, J. (1984) *Reading the Romance: Women, Patriarchy and Popular Culture*, Chapel Hill: University of North Carolina Press.

Steeves, L. (1987) "Feminist Theories and Media Studies," *Critical Studies in Mass Communication* 42(2): 95–135.

Taylor, H. (1989) *Scarlett's Women: Gone with the Wind and Its Female Fans*, New Brunswick, NJ: Rutgers University Press.

van Zoonen, L. (1991) "Feminist Perspectives on the Media," in J. Curran and M. Gurevitch (eds.) *Mass Media and Society*, London: Arnold, pp. 33–54.

——(1994) *Feminist Media Studies*, London: Sage.

Walters, S. D. (1995) *Material Girls: Making Sense of Feminist Cultural Theory*, Berkeley: University of Los Angeles Press.

World Economic Forum (2012) "The Global Gender Gap Report 2012" (R. Hausmann, Harvard University, L. D. Tyson, University of California, Berkeley, S. Zahidi, World Economic Forum). http://www.weforum.org/issues/global-gender-gap. Accessed Spring 2013.

# 6

# Historically mapping contemporary intersectional feminist media studies

## Isabel Molina-Guzmán and Lisa Marie Cacho

On March 6, 2012 the *Guardian* reported on the withdrawal of "Growing Together," a viral high-budget online video promoting EU unity by targeting young adults (Watt 2012). The video featured a white woman of indeterminate ethnicity wearing a tight-fitting suit reminiscent of the one Uma Thurman wore in *Kill Bill: Volume 1* (2003). She stares in fright as a Chinese-looking man, an Indian-looking man, and a black man wearing dreadlocks—all of them practicing a martial art—surround her. In response to the threat, the woman multiplies herself, transforming into the stars in the EU flag, surrounding the men, who then give up their pursuit and are erased by the EU emblem and the slogan "the more we are, the stronger we are." Responding to the ensuing controversy, the European Commission issued an apology stating the video was innocently meant to appeal to younger voters.

The video might appear to be simply about youth or female empowerment. But an intersectional media analysis discredits this facile explanation of the Commission's "innocent" intentions. The ad represents the "threats" to European unity as aggressive, racialized, hyper-masculine figures in culturally conspicuous non-European costumes. Since the EU is represented through the body of a young white woman, the "threat" is not only that of physical violence but also that of sexual violence. Drawing on historical narratives that construct white women's desirable bodies as perpetually in need of protection from the colonized other, this particular juxtaposition of race, gender, and nation also brings to mind other phobias. If the EU were represented by a woman of color or a white man, this advertisement would not evoke the same degree of racialized peril and backlash.

Against the global backdrop of increases in anti-immigration laws, hate crimes against Muslim citizens, and state violence against women and undocumented im/migrants, the racialized and gendered threat of sexual and cultural miscegenation to racial and Euro-homogeneity, intersectionality continues to be a significant theoretical tool for analyzing the media. This chapter reviews literature on women of color feminism and queer of color critique to develop a usable and working definition of intersectionality. Next, we showcase some contemporary interdisciplinary scholarship by queer and feminist scholars in media studies and related fields that utilizes intersectionality effectively. We conclude with a discussion of the continued importance of intersectional feminist media scholarship to social justice in an increasingly diverse, global, and digitally networked environment.

## Defining intersectionality

The concept "intersectionality" challenges predominant understandings of race and gender as discrete social identities shaped by and formative of distinct social experiences. When race and gender are viewed as parallel, rather than as intersecting, institutional discrimination can only be recognized when it occurs along one axis, as due to either race or gender, but never both. Critical legal scholar Kimberlé Crenshaw, who coined the term "intersectionality," refers to this as a "'but for' analysis"—I would have received that job "but for" my race; I would have gotten that promotion "but for" my gender (1989: 151). This single-axis framework is problematic because such discrimination can only be read for persons privileged in all aspects except their racial or gender difference. This cannot address how women of color can and do face multiple forms of discrimination, making impossible to understand, let alone remedy, discrimination against women of color (Crenshaw 1989: 149).

As Crenshaw details in three separate US court cases, black women's experiences exceed the logic of legal redress. In one case, *DeGraffenreid v. General Motors*, the court refused to acknowledge that black women could face discrimination as black women, as a combination of race and sex discrimination. In *Moore v. Hughes Helicopter, Inc.*, the courts claimed that black women could not represent "women" as a class in sex discrimination cases, while *Payne v. Travenol* determined that black women could not be representatives for race discrimination because they may have faced the combination of race and sex discrimination. When read relationally, the three court cases clearly contradicted one another, revealing that black women are not just unprotected as a class but actually illegible in US anti-discrimination law.

Intersectionality speaks to the unique position of women of color, who, as multiply marginalized, cannot always pinpoint how, why, and from where discrimination occurs. Sometimes discriminatory policies target women of color as women of color while having little to no impact on white women or men of color. But the concept of intersectionality reminds us that this is only *one* of the ways in which women of color experience discrimination. They can also experience race and gender discrimination as compounded if, for instance, a company has policies that affect people of color and different policies that affect women in different ways. Additionally, women of color can also face discrimination as women or as people of color.

Intersectionality, thus, is not about women of color *per se*, but about the kind of intersecting oppressions that defies the *logic of redress* not only in anti-discrimination law but also in progressive politics both in and outside the United States. For example, building on the work of Crenshaw, Fernández de Vega, Emanuela Lombardo, and Rolandsen Agustín (2008) critique the European Union's contemporary "equality policies":

> The EU has adopted mainly a separate and unitary approach to inequalities and is developing a multiple and additive approach (see Hancock 2007). The concept of "multiple discrimination" is increasingly used to refer to additional social inequalities faced by people. But intersecting social inequalities are most of the time treated from separate different political approaches, far from addressing the multiple factors causing female social disadvantages together.
>
> (Fernández de Vega *et al.* 2008: 3)

As an analytic, intersectionality can also be used to examine how structures of domination intersect, such as racism and heteropatriarchy. In other words, the concept of intersectionality is not limited to evidence that can showcase an embodied positionality. As scholars, we are not dependent on the bodies of women of color to analyze media from an intersectional standpoint. Patricia Hill Collins has explained that we need to see how systems of oppression interlock in order to avoid the additive paradigm for analyzing race and gender (1990: 225). Like the single-axis framework, the additive paradigm not only simplifies the oppressions facing women of color (i.e. as white women's experiences "added to" men of color's experiences), but it also cannot address how oppression and privilege are relational, such as how the privileges of white womanhood are contingent on and defined in relation to the multiple oppressions faced by women of color (Carby 1987).

To show how oppressions interlock to both undermine and reinforce one another—in which case they are neither additive nor equivalent—we turn to contemporary work that deploys a "queer of color critique" (Ferguson 2004; Reddy 2011). Using an intersectional analysis, Siobhan Somerville (2005) illustrates why we cannot read today's US anti-gay marriage laws as "just like" the anti-miscegenation laws of the past. When we view oppressions premised on identities as parallel rather than interlocking, we assume the court case, *Loving v. Virginia* (1967), that legalized interracial marriage in the United States can be used as an obvious and logical precedent for today's fights against anti-gay marriage laws. But, as Somerville explains, reading *Loving* as only about race fails to see that *Loving* is *also* about naturalizing and universalizing heterosexuality. Lifting the racial restriction on marriage helped to re-establish the primacy of heterosexual, monogamous, and state-sanctioned intimate relationships during an era when the institution of marriage was losing its currency (Somerville 2005: 357–8). Somerville notes the irony that *Loving* is utilized in the contemporary era as a symbol and precedent for gay marriage activism, given that normalizing race through formalizing interracial marriage simultaneously reinforced and naturalized heteropatriarchy during a historical moment when homosexuals were being actively excluded and deported under US immigration and naturalization law.

Below, we explain the concept of intersectionality as deployed by scholars of media and culture, first by reviewing key foundational texts, which not only shifted how women of color in the media could be analyzed, but also utilized the concept of intersectionality to analyze relational oppressions beyond race and gender. Subsequent sections take up those questions of relationality. Because it is not necessarily tied to embodied identities, intersectionality is also an approach to thinking about the ways in which power works relationally and how responses to marginalization must negotiate how oppression and privilege are interdependent. Power works through securing privileges and promising rights as much as it does through denial, dehumanization, and disenfranchisement. In other words, sometimes racism and sexism work through or in concert with other forms of oppression, such as colonialism or nativism. At other times, race and gender are products or remnants of state violence, capital exploitation, or haunting historical hurts. Last, sometimes intersectionality really is about embodiment—about negotiating a sense of self through pre-scripted social identities disseminated by media and popular culture, or about claiming power for oneself that legible social identities, whether empowering or problematic, make possible. The texts we cite are models of either how the concept of intersectionality operates in media scholarship and/or how an intersectional approach to media and culture provides us with nuanced insights of and new interpretive frames for understanding the workings of power in the media and society at large.

## Foundations of intersectional media studies scholarship

Taking on the work of feminist media scholars and British critical cultural studies for their single-axis analyses of race or gender during the 1970s and 1980s, women of color scholars in the US and European feminist scholars began the paradigmatic shift towards intersectionality (Yuval-Davis 2006). While US media scholars engaged in research and theory-making that moved away from analyses of media production and reception that looked only at race or at gender and rarely dealt with the ways in which gender is racialized and race is gendered, European feminist scholars privileged how the relational experiences of race, gender, class, and sexuality together shape agency and power and connect to broader issues of social justice.

In her groundbreaking book *Black Women as Cultural Readers*, Jacqueline Bobo (1995) parted with feminist media studies that engage gender but either lack analysis of race or focus exclusively on white women, or British cultural studies that examine race or class but ignore gender. Indeed, she radically introduces an intersectional analytic to media studies by complicating dominant media theories of text and audience reception, such as Stuart Hall's (1973) encoding–decoding model. Bobo calls for re-theorizing media scholarship by situating black women as having diverse reading strategies and differential experiences of race and gender often complicated by class. Particularly instructive is Bobo's reception analysis of the films *The Color Purple* and *Daughters of the Dust*. With regards to the *The Color Purple*, for instance, Bobo illustrates how some black men were more categorically negative of the film's portrayal of black masculinity and black family life; while black women had negotiated responses to the film based on sexual identity, education, and socioeconomic class that resulted in criticism of some elements of the film while celebrating the broader cinematic visibility of black women (1995: 4). In doing so, Bobo complicates critical and feminist approaches by calling for a relational analysis of race, gender, and class in studying how texts are read and interpreted by audiences.

Another canonical work in intersectional media studies, bell hooks's *Reel to Real: Race, Sex, and Class at the Movies* (1996), explores racial and gender discrimination by foregrounding the multiple oppressions reinforced through mainstream media discourses of white femininity and black masculinity. For example, hooks proposes that one cannot make sense of Madonna without recognizing how she benefits from the commodification of queer youth of color; likewise, one cannot read Spike Lee without acknowledging how his cinematic production of black masculinity reinforces the ways gender and racial hegemonies work together to marginalize the social and political experiences of black women and black gay men (1996: 34, 214). Thus, she suggests, both Madonna and Spike Lee are complicit in maintaining the ideological power structures of the media by marginalizing black women and queers.

Finally, in *Unthinking Eurocentrism: Multiculturalism and the Media* (1994), Ella Shohat and Robert Stam further complicate intersectional media studies through a postcolonial "ethnicities in relation" approach that foregrounds non-European cultures and anti-colonialist scholarship. As Shohat and Stam define it, such an approach moves away from thinking about one racial or cultural group in isolation from others and instead seeks to break from racial, gender, and cultural binaries by looking for key linkages, differences, and "overlapping multiplicities" outside of a conflictual frame (1994: 6). Shohat and Stam's "ethnicities in relation" approach opened the door for feminist media scholars working within and outside the United States, such as Radha Hegde (2005) and Radhika Parameswaran (2001). Through ethnographic work in India, for example, Parameswaran documents how gender as a category is informed by local and global culture and in the Indian context must be further problematized through the intersection of class/caste, religious, and political identities. Parameswaran and other postcolonial feminist media scholars look at the global flows of gender through an intersectional lens to illustrate how analyses of gender must take into account gendered and racialized discourses and the geopolitical spaces in which cultural texts are produced and interpreted. Other scholars engage an ethnicities-in-relation intersectional analytics to complicate media representations of gender and ethnicity. For instance, Valdivia's tranformative *A Latina in the Land of Hollywood and Other Essays on Media Culture* (2000) maps out how gender, age, and nationality intersect to differentially position Latinidad. By examining the media discourses about Guatemalan Rigoberta Menchu in relation to representations of Puerto Rican actress Rosie Perez, Valdivia takes an "ethnicities in relation" approach to analyze oppression and, more significantly, pleasure across Latina identities as they are shaped by nationality, citizenship, ethnicity, and race.

Together these scholars illustrate the problematics of studying gender or race alone by avoiding single-axis, additive, or multiple analyses of gender and race to study the production of alternative interpretative frameworks in textual interpretation and audience reception as well as the role of media and culture in producing oppression and marginalization. We suggest that intersectional media studies scholarship exhibits one or more of the following characteristics: it foregrounds women of color as interpreters and audiences; emphasizes how gender(s) intersect sexuality, class, race, nationality, or citizenship; and/or illustrates how gendered representations in the media are significant in the production of social, political, or cultural inequalities.

## Intersectionality, interdisciplinarity, and culture

We begin our mapping of contemporary intersectional media scholarship with scholars working outside the discipline of media studies who situate the media more broadly as a cultural text rather than as a medium of mass communication. Lisa Marie Cacho, Celine Parreñas Shimizu, Ruby Tapia, and other scholars bring interdisciplinary training to study media performances and narratives of gender as an identity that must always take into account its relationship to sex, sexuality, ethnicity, race, class, and, increasingly, citizenship.

Exploring cultural performances of gender from a sexualized and racialized perspective, Shimizu examines how Asian and Asian American femininity is represented and performed in pornography. She complicates notions of agency and subjectivity by looking at how Asian and Asian American women in the pornography industry engage racial stereotypes to augment their economic prospects even as they recognize their exclusion from the white male-centered power structure of the industry and its primary consumers. Thus, gender gains its meaning or value not solely through the category of woman but in its intersection with heterosexuality and Asian-ness.

From a comparative ethnic studies angle, Cacho's work exemplifies an intersectional analysis of gender as it is connected to racialized masculinity, ethnicity, criminalization, and citizenship. For example, discussing Southeast Asian refugee gangs in her book *Social Death: Racialized Rightlessness and the Criminalization of the Unprotected* (2012), Cacho reveals how sympathetic journalists downplay young gang members' acts of sexual violence because mainstream media rationalized that Southeast Asian gang violence could be traced to an abusive and hyper-patriarchal Southeast Asian culture. To challenge representations of Southeast Asian culture as intrinsically violent and hyper-patriarchal, Cacho explains, reporters discredited women's allegations of rape by demonizing female gang members, rendering their bodies as somehow unable to be sexually violated. Her scholarship reveals that our notions of citizenship and social justice cannot be disentangled from how gender, race, nationality, and legal status work together and differentially to produce social value and evoke public sympathy.

Finally, entering intersectionality from a women's studies perspective informed by ethnic studies, Tapia analyzes how figures of motherhood inform audiences' understanding of death through racial frameworks. In *American Piètas: Visions of Race, Death, and the Maternal*, Tapia examines how figurations of motherhood work ideologically in ways that enable audiences to apprehend "the imaged chaos of death" through racial ways of knowing (2011: 14). For instance, Tapia's chapter "*Beloved* Therapies" analyzes how Oprah Winfrey's film adaption (1998) of Toni Morrison's Pulitzer Prize winning novel *Beloved* (1987) conceals and heals the sexualized and gendered violence inherent in mothering children born into slavery. Unlike the novel, which demands we never forget, the film transforms an historically horrific era of US racial violence into "universal" messages of love and transcendence. Tapia argues that this transformation and erasure are possible in part because of the public persona of Winfrey as America's psychiatrist. Because Winfrey plays the film's main character Sethe, audiences cannot *not* visualize Sethe as Winfrey. They cannot visually disentangle a distraught slave mother who commits infanticide from America's therapist who forgives us all.

## Intersectionality, inequality, and media studies

Using more traditional feminist media and communication studies frameworks and methodologies, contemporary communication scholars are increasingly engaging inter-sectionality to theorize gendered texts and performances in the media as significant elements in the production of social, political, or cultural inequalities. For example, in *Dangerous Curves: Latina Bodies in the Media*, Molina-Guzmán (2010) conducts a cross-media textual and audience analysis of popular Latinas in news, television, and film to illustrate the various and dynamic conflicts between media producers and media consumers over how racial and gendered meanings are not only fabricated and assimilated but also reified and instrumentalized. Racialized and gendered meanings of Latina femininity and Latinidad are co-produced in media, Molina-Guzmán argues, through the dynamic interplay of "symbolic colonization" and "symbolic rupture." "Symbolic colonization" refers to the ideological processes that flatten representations of gendered ethnicity into one-dimensional tropes through racialization. Recognizing that symbolic colonization can never be absolute, she also examines the ways in which online and journalistic audiences from different gender, race, ethnicity, and national subject-positions read symbolically colonized media texts. People sometimes disrupt the intended meanings of media producers, thus engaging in the process of "symbolic rupture." While media producers "symbolically colonize" images of Latini-dad, media consumers will actively interrogate and negotiate those same images, which can "symbolically rupture" the ideological processes at work. Molina-Guzmán moves beyond analysis of gender to analyze how gender, race, and ethnicity function together to co-produce meaning as well as spaces that challenge the processes involved in making and stabilizing the meanings of race, gender, ethnicity, nation, and sexuality.

Ralina Joseph (2012) disarticulates performances of blackness through an intersec-tional frame applied to television, film, and literature. Joseph extends critical mixed-race studies to cultural meaning making around blackness. Her readings of *The L Word* and *America's Next Top Model*, for example, problematize the ways the gendering and racializing surrounding mixed-race women who are read as black produce troubling discourses of either exceptional deviance or exceptional citizenship. In doing so, she critiques dominant biological constructions of race, in particular blackness and black femininity. Joseph's work suggests that scholars must understand how the mutually dependent relationship of race and gender produces cultural meaning and ideological value that in turn destabilize popular definitions of gender and race.

Finally, US scholars such as Jillian Báez, Bernadette Calafell, Aisha Durham, and Lucilla Vargas foreground the significance of intersectionality to the role of women of color as cultural interpreters and media audiences. Vargas's *Latina Teens, Migration, and Popular Culture* (2009) is a groundbreaking critical ethnography documenting how readings of gender and ethnicity for young Latina media consumers are com-plicated by class, language, nationality, migration, and citizenship, what she refers to as "multi-layered" identity (2009: 68). For example, she documents how the musical consumption of recent Latina immigrants from poor to working-class backgrounds is influenced by their relationship to US national identity (immigrants identifying with Latin America listen to Shakira and immigrants identifying with the US listen to Britney Spears) and constrained by their economic access to technology (sharing a radio with the family vs. owning an individual MP3 player). These young women privileged music and celebrities that reaffirmed their subjectivities, for instance by listening to a mainstream English artist to affirm an "American" identity, such as Eminem, or Selena as a symbol of Mexican respectability or Ja Rule as a sign of a non-white "Americanness" (2009: 70–6). Thus, Vargas proposes that gender subjectivity for these Latina teenagers is intimately interconnected to migration and class.

Among some of the most innovative contemporary work informed by inter-sectionality is the scholarship of women of color working within the auto-ethnographic and performative tradition, such as Bernadette Calafell (2012) and Aisha Durham (2012). Durham's work on "hip-hop feminism" and comparative work with Jillian Báez (2007) (on the sexualization of racialized women) compel us to account for the ways the lived experiences of women of color are always informed by nation, gender, race, and class. That is, Báez and Durham's qualitative research on how women of color interpret some of the most globally visible celebrity representations of their communities (Beyoncé and Jennifer Lopez) illustrates how women of color do not have the interpretative privilege of reading race and gender as mutually exclusive.

Through her auto-ethnographic work on the "monstrous Other," Calafell continues the intersectional intervention. Calafell interprets her own experiences as a queer Chicana whose scholarship and body are othered and marginalized in the academy against depictions of female monsters, specifically the woman werewolf. For Calafell the desire of fellow academics to code her identity and her performative research as sexually and racially aberrant and therefore less intellectually valuable positions her and women of color as monsters and monstrous. Yet Calafell's analysis suggests that the refusal to be silenced, the involuntary insistence to speak up in departmental meetings and conferences, and the desire to write/publish research validating the experiences of women of color provide us with an agency that is equally monstrous in that it cannot be easily contained or controlled. Through the embodied scholarship of Báez, Calafell, and Durham among others, we see intersectionality as both a lived experience and a significant theory and method of analysis.

Similarly, European feminist communication scholars are engaging in intersectional and performative approaches. Marjo Buitelaar (2006) provides a compelling example of the ways in which this US-origin paradigm is being applied in the European context, for example. Using a narrative analysis, Buitelaar examines intersectional identity discourses by exploring the "life-story" of a popular Moroccan Dutch political figure who uses a headscarf. Buitelaar avoids additive narratives of identity through the complex debates that surround Moroccan, Turkish, and Muslim women in the Netherlands who choose to perform their identity in part through wearing the headscarf. Contextualizing her study within the increase of North African immigration and the rise of anti-Islamic sentiments in the Netherlands, her analysis troubles notions of gender and citizenship through understanding their intimate intersectional linkages to ethnicity, race, religion, and nationhood.

## Conclusion

Too often media studies scholarship on gender continues to position hegemonic whiteness and white women as the default category even though demographics in

Europe and the United States point to the growing complexities surrounding ethnic and diasporic women, who are many times racialized and sexualized as culturally, socially, and politically undesirable, irrelevant, and undeserving of equality. Intersectionality as theoretical concept and framework for analysis calls into focus those very experiences and centers the interpretative practices of quickly growing communities, such as Latinas and Asians in the United States, and African and Muslim women in Europe, among others. Furthermore, contemporary interdisciplinary scholarship that engages with intersectionality sometimes foregrounds the importance of decentering the category of gender itself through queering whiteness or racializing masculinity to illustrate how systems of gender and racial oppression interlock. Finally, intersectionality calls for problematizing research on ethnicity and race by asking that gender be taken into account not as a variable to be added but as a complex interdependent identity central to making sense of gender, race, citizenship, and nationality.

Thus, the works presented in this chapter are only a few among the growing body of scholarship in which "intersectionality" figures centrally to both theory and method, though not uniformly. Indeed, the concept necessarily destabilizes the very categories upon which its intelligibility depends, making it an unproductive exercise to delimit how it can be used. For instance, in this chapter, intersectionality provides us the language we need to talk about women of color as producers and consumers of media, but it has also functioned as a reading practice to make sense of media's relationship to social, cultural, and political inequalities. At times, intersectionality also works as an analytic to uncover what we know is there but cannot see. The examples we chose highlight the ways in which intersectionality (whether invoked or not) has been used in a variety of contexts and has been adapted to complement various methods of gathering and analyzing evidence. Therefore, *how* intersectionality is used is not what these texts have in common. Rather, what they have in common is *why* intersectionality is an important interpretive frame to examine media, its effects, and its audiences. It is important because an intersectional approach requires us to ask the difficult, sometimes unpopular, questions, to write the insightful but sometimes shaming answers, to research responsibly as well as thoroughly, and to hold ourselves accountable to those who make our work possible.

# References

Báez, J. and A. Durham (2007) "A Tail of Two Women: Exploring the Contours of Difference in Popular Culture," in S. Springgay and D. Freedman (eds.) *Curriculum and the Cultural Body*, New York: Peter Lang, pp. 131–45.

Bobo, J. (1995) *Black Women as Cultural Readers*, New York: Columbia University Press.

Buitelaar, M. (2006) "'I Am the Ultimate Challenge': Accounts of Intersectionality in the Lifestory of a Well-known Daughter of Moroccan Migrant Workers in the Netherlands," *European Journal of Women's Studies* 13: 259–76.

Cacho, L. (2012) *Social Death: Racialized Rightlessness and the Criminalization of the Unprotected*, New York: New York University Press.

Calafell, B. (2012) "Monstrous Femininity: Women of Color in the Academy," *Journal of Communication Inquiry* 36(2): 111–30.

Carby, H. (1987) *Reconstructing Womanhood: The Emergence of the Afro-American Woman Novelist*, New York: Oxford University Press.

Collins, P. H. (1990) *Black Feminist Thought: Knowledge, Consciousness, and the Politics of Empowerment*, Boston: UnwinHyman.

Crenshaw, K. (1989) "Demarginalizing the Intersection of Race and Sex: A Black Feminist Critique of Antidiscrimination Doctrine, Feminist Theory and Antiracist Politics," *University of Chicago Legal Forum*: 139–67.

Durham, A. (2012) "Check On It," *Feminist Media Studies* 12(1): 35–49.

Ferguson, R. (2004) *Aberrations in Black: Toward a Queer of Color Critique*, Minneapolis: University of Minnesota Press.

Fernández de Vega, A., E. Lombardo, and L. Ronaldsen Agustín (2008) "Report Analysing Intersectionality in Gender Equality Policies for the EU," QUING Project, Vienna: Institute for Human Sciences (IWM). http://www.quing.eu/files/results/ir_eu.pdf.

Hall, S. (1973) *Encoding and Decoding in the Television Discourse*, Birmingham: Centre for Contemporary Cultural Studies.

Hegde, R. (2005) "Disciplinary Spaces and Globalization: A Postcolonial Unsettling," *Global Media and Communication* 1(1): 59–62.

hooks, b. (1996) *Reel to Real: Race, Sex, and Class at the Movies*, New York: Psychology Press.

——(1999) *Black Looks and Representation*, Cambridge: South End Press.

Joseph, R. (2012) *Transcending Blackness: From the New Millennium Mulatta to the Exceptional Multiracial*, Durham, NC: Duke University Press.

Molina-Guzmán, I. (2010) *Dangerous Curves: Latina Bodies in the Media*, New York: New York University Press.

Parameswaran, R. (2001) "Feminist Media Ethnography in India: Exploring Power, Gender, and Culture in the Field," *Qualitative Inquiry* 7(1): 69–103.

Prins, B. (2006) "Narrative Accounts of Origins: A Blind Spot in the Intersectional Approach?," *European Journal of Women's Studies* 13: 277–90.

Reddy, C. (2011) *Freedom with Violence: Race, Sexuality, and the U.S. State*, Durham, NC: Duke University Press.

Shimizu, C. P. (2001) *The Hypersexuality of Race: Performing Asian/Asian American Women on Screen and Scene*, Durham, NC: Duke University Press.

Shohat, E. and R. Stam (1994) *Unthinking Eurocentrism: Multiculturalism and the Media*, New York: Routledge.

Somerville, S. (2005) "Queer Loving," *GLQ: A Journal of Gay and Lesbian Studies* 11: 335–70.

Tapia, R. (2011) *American Piètas: Visions of Race, Death, and the Maternal*, Minneapolis: University of Minnesota Press.

Valdivia, A. (2000) *A Latina in the Land of Hollywood and Other Essays on Media Culture*, Tucson: University of Arizona Press.

Vargas, L. (2009) *Latina Teens, Migration, and Popular Culture*, New York: Peter Lang.

Watt, N. (2012) "European Commission Criticized for 'Racist' Ad," *Guardian*, March 12. http://www.guardian.co.uk/world/2012/mar/06/european-commission-criticised-racist-ad.

Yuval-Davis, N. (2006) "Intersectionality and Feminist Politics," *European Journal of Women's Studies* 13: 193–206.

# 7

# Sexualities/queer identities

## *Audrey Yue*

From the mainstream success of the US cable network Showtime's lesbian television series *The L Word*, to the global embrace of the *It Gets Better* project aimed at lesbian, gay, bisexual, and transgender youth, the media are central to the mainstreaming and re-visioning of sexual identity. Niche television programming and interactive social media have also opened up new arenas to showcase heterogeneous sexual practices. Of particular significance in this chapter is the representation of racialized queer identities. In the two decades since the emergence of queer race studies, scholarship on queer identities has developed in tandem with sexuality, postcolonial, and diasporic studies. I will explore the limitations, exclusions, and possibilities of queer identities through the connections between these theoretical fields, considering the mutually constitutive categories of sexuality and race as a set of practices; as desire; and as identity and post-identity politics.

This chapter revisits the history of queer race studies in the light of today's "post-gay" and "post-racial" environment with two focal points. The first attends to the specific methods and sites in which queer race interventions have emerged, in particular media analyses on interracial sexual encounters, such as independent art house and experimental cinema, and gay Asian porn. The second explores media in terms of queer race identities in relation to neoliberalism and postmodern racism; specifically, practices of queer mobility illustrated by marriage equality and sexual migration. These aims highlight changes in the way racialized sexualities have been constituted, from the early margins of subcultural media, to the center of mainstream forces that mediate new power hierarchies of inclusion and exclusion.

I begin with independent film, online porn, magazines, and situated media, looking back to radicalized sexuality as a set of practices tied to the emergence of modern sex and racism, and examining "Oriental sex" as a form of Western desire. Second, I examine black gay cinema and photography. I problematize identity politics by locating the critical combinations of voice, enunciation, and intersectionality as central to early scholarship on queer race studies. Third, I evaluate media texts of queer mobility as represented in gay travel guidebooks, queer asylum reports, and newspapers. I situate historical developments of racialized sexuality and identity politics against contemporary articulations on homonationalism, and question the politics of sexualized racism that govern practices of queer neoliberalism. I argue that the challenge for a post-identity queer race studies is to attend to the politics of a queer mobility that resists assimilation to a "post-gay" and "post-racial" settlement.

## As desire: from modern sex and race to racialized sexuality and Oriental sex

The historical construction of sexuality as a discourse bringing together the biological, cultural, and corporeal provides an important conceptual framework for discussions on the overlapping identities of race and sexuality (Weeks 2003: 7). For Foucault, the schema that regulated life—bio-power—was the same process that regulated race (1978: 140). Technologies of sex that supported the bio-power of life were the same technologies that justified racism: "Through surveillance of sex, racial supremacy was also maintained: sex as an instrumental target, racism an effect" (Stoler 1995: 35). Underpinning this biopolitics of race is the historical invention of race as a signifier or marker of difference. It constructed a language that manipulated arbitrary classifications and exacerbated the complex relationships in cultural differences: "Race has become a trope of ultimate, irreducible difference between cultures, linguistic groups, or groups with specific belief systems" (Gates 1985: 5). Overlapping sexual and racial identities have resulted in new practices of racialized sexuality, in particular the colonial desire for Oriental sex.

Observing European writers who traveled to the Orient, postcolonial scholar Said writes:

> What they looked for often, correctly I think—was a different type of sexuality, perhaps more libertine and less guilt-ridden, but even that quest, if repeated by enough people, could (and did) become as regulated and uniform as learning itself. In time "Oriental sex" was as standard a commodity as any other available in the mass culture.
>
> (Said 1985: 190)

"Oriental sex" was the product of the European invention of Orientalism—the idea that Middle Eastern, Asian, and North African countries are traditional, undeveloped, uncivilized, and irrational in contradistinction to the West, which is regarded as modern, developed, civilized, and rational. Through the frame of Orientalism, the West assumed a superior position as the Sovereign Self inside the Occident–Orient relation.

David Cronenberg's critically acclaimed film M. Butterfly (1993) offers a clear example of Orientalism. It was adapted from the 1988 play by David Henry Hwang, about a real-life scandal between a junior French diplomat and a Chinese transvestite whom the former never realized was a man. The narrative suggests the political and economic dominance of Western imperialism and its ideology of racial supremacy, a trope established in the opening credits and from the first conversation between Song (the Chinese opera singer/transvestite) and Gallimard (the French diplomat). With the camera facing Song from Gallimard's point of view, Song tells Gallimard, "It's your fantasy, isn't it? The submissive Oriental woman and the cruel white man … I am your slave, you are my master."

Researchers tend to use two main approaches when seeking to demonstrate how sexuality is constituted through racial difference: the construction of Oriental fantasy (exoticism of the Other) and the panic of homosexuality (psychotic anxiety said to be experienced by those who are the object of unwanted homosexual advances). In the first, Suner demonstrates the "colonization of the feminine and feminization of the colonized" by looking at how Hwang's story replicates the colonial patterns of romance based on the Western hierarchies of gender, race, and sexuality, and spatially feminizes China as exotic and mysterious (1999: 51). De Lauretis suggests the postmodern film opens up "cultural issues of gender, race, and sexuality in a postcolonial West" by using the cross-cultural and cross-dressing motifs of gender performativity to reveal the white man's construction of the East (1999: 311). Similarly, Chow elaborates on the undoing of the white man's fantasy by deconstructing its performance of Enlightenment (1998: 95). San Juan (2002) offers insights drawn from political economy to discuss Orientalism as a part of the global system of exchange value and commodity fetishism that has its roots in imperial conquest and racialized violence.

In discussions around homosexual panic, scholars read the film through homosexual disavowal and the reification of heterosexuality. Grist (2003) focuses on the film's gender ambiguity and sexual transgression to highlight how heterosexuality is supported through emphasizing the crisis of masculinity and sidelining homosexuality. Drawing on the racial castration of the Chinese man to show how white heterosexuality is maintained, Eng suggests the white man is made more masculine through the disavowal of the Asian penis: "this curious crossing of castration with race," he concludes, makes possible a heterosexual relationship between a white man and woman (2001: 150). M. *Butterfly* questions the desire for the cultural and racial other, as well as "differences" between the sexes. For Gallimard, the fantasy of Oriental sex makes possible a relationship with an idealized, non-white woman. For Song, it enables a homosexual relationship with a straight man in a time and context when such a relationship would have been considered unacceptable. Performed through his role as an opera singer, transvestitism is assumed as a masquerade for spying, for crossing the borders between male/female, West/East, and homosexuality/heterosexuality (Garber 1992). The Oriental Other and colonial master are both agents and effects of dominant cultural fantasies.

Contemporary gay Asian porn repeats the performativity and complicity of Oriental sex. Performativity is a process that exposes how identities are socially constructed and naturalized through everyday practices of repetition. To be complicit in the performance of Oriental sex is to self-consciously participate in the ideologies that have constructed the stereotype of Asian passivity. Notwithstanding the 15 years that have passed since queer theorist Richard Fung's seminal treatise on the de-sexualization of Asian men, "Asians ... are [still] undersexed [and] defined by a striking absence down there" (1996: 184–5). On popular interracial online porn sites such as Asian Twinks and AsianBoyNation, labels like "teen," "cute," and "smooth" are commonly used to trade on the prepubescent youthfulness of Asian men. Notably, these sites are marketed to the West—for example, Asian Twinks is owned by London-based Pacific Panorama, which advertises itself as the exclusive producer and distributor of gay Asian porn; and AsianBoyNation is owned by San

Francisco-based company Imagi-Nation, which has made about 75 films featuring interracial gay porn. Images on these sites recall Fung's (1996) discussion of Asian American porn star Sum Yung Mahn, popular in the 1980s in the gay porn industry, who was always positioned as the "bottom" in sexual acts.

This stereotype persists despite the trend towards gay cult masculinity. Although contemporary porn stars such as Brandon Lee, Andy Honda, and Archer Quan showcase a more muscular body than Sum, they are still featured as the "bottom" in interracial sexual encounters. Quan, for example, despite sporting a soldier crew cut and a six pack abdomen, is featured in two Titan videos—*Fixation* (dir. Brian Mills, 2011) and *Punch and Pounded* (dir. Paul Wilde, 2011)—as the submissive receiver. In *Punch and Pounded*, even his tough-looking SM leather straps are no match for Dirk Caber, the white protagonist (presumably playing the role of a white colonel), in military camouflage pants.

Not only do these videos repeat the sediments of Oriental sex that suspend the gay Asian man in symbolic emasculation, even "progressive" magazines such as the now defunct *OG* (*Oriental Guys*) are also complicit in rehearsing this discourse. In circulation between 1989 and 2004, the Australia-based magazine enjoyed popular readership in cities such as Taipei, Singapore, and Bangkok. Promoted as a gay Asian lifestyle magazine, it featured stories and biographies about gay Asian men. Some magazine covers show young muscle men as clones of the Western twink (young gay male with a slim and hairless body), while others feature slender effete men under the aesthetic guise of "beauty." Whether Oriental passivity or globally queer, this diversity discourse reveals the two forces of colonial Orientalism and postcolonial complicity: the first performs the stereotype while the second participates in collusion. Both equally maintain the power structures of inequality that condition the modernity of Western sex and race. More recently, these stereotypes are made explicit by the online sexual racism of social networking applications such as Grindr or chat rooms such as gay.com, where sexual preferences such as "no GAMS" (Gay Asian Males), "seeking other similar good looking masculine guys, no fems, no Asians please," and "not interested in arrogant, effeminate guys, Asians or guys with attitude" proliferate and thrive (Paul *et al.* 2010).

## Identity politics and the politics of identity: from voice to enunciation and intersection

Against this backdrop, queer race studies has emerged as a form of identity politics. Identity politics is a political process of self- and collective expression centered on the shared experiences and social concerns that arise from a person's or a group's identity determinants, such as race, gender, and sexuality. Coming out of Western social movements in the 1960s that promoted a mode of organizing based on the oppression of social groups, identity politics was mobilized around the politics of recognition (Taylor 1992) and difference (Young 1990). The identity politics of racialized sexuality built on the civil rights, gay liberation, and model minority multicultural movements, and came to the fore in the wake of the AIDS crisis in the late 1980s. Western-based filmmakers, writers, and scholars of color such as Marlon

Riggs, Isaac Julien, Kobena Mercer, and Gloria Anzaldúa have carved out critical tools that question the politics of identity and set the theoretical beginnings for queer race studies.

Riggs was a black gay video filmmaker who "[produced] some of the most innovative and challenging work on the subject of identity" (Mercer 1994: 221). Making eight videos between 1987 and 1994, such as *Ethnic Notions* (1987), *Tongues Untied* (1989), *Anthem* (1990), *Affirmations* (1991), *Non, Je Ne Regrette Rien* (1992), *Color Adjustment* (1993), and *Black Is ... Black Ain't* (1994), his work "interrupts commonsense essentialism in favor of a relational and dialogic view of the constructed character of any social identity" (Mercer 1994: 222). In particular, *Tongues Untied* is acclaimed as "the most powerful examination of Black sexual identity ever produced" (Jones 1993: 256). The film, in mixing the genres of documentary, autobiography, and fiction, uses the strategy of "unsilencing" to voice the black sexuality of gay men unable to express themselves because of the prejudices in mainstream heterosexual and white homosexual society. Juxtaposing images of gay pride with the poetry of Essex Hemphill, his own account of his gay sexuality and his sadness over the deaths of his friends from AIDS, the film highlights the link between AIDS and whiteness at the site of the black gay body as a repository for homophobia, sexism, and racism, as well as white gay seduction (Gerstner 2011: 190).

Cultural theorist Mercer's work intervenes in the politics of looking and speaking. He twice responded to Robert Mapplethorpe's 1980 controversial "Man in a Polyester Suit" photograph. In "Just Looking for Trouble: Robert Mapplethorpe and Fantasies of Race," Mercer describes his shock at the sight of the black penis (1992: 96). This response exposes the hypersexualization of the black man who is always already "fixed in terms of the genital" (Fanon 1991: 165). In "Skin Head Sex Thing: Racial Difference and the Homoerotic Imaginary," Mercer offers a different viewpoint, suggesting that the image evokes "the experience of aesthetic ambivalence" (1991: 169). The image can confirm a racist reading as easily as an anti-racist one. That is, it can be homophobic or homoerotic because the penis, as both aesthetic and erotic, keeps the viewer suspended between danger and beauty. He calls for "a politics of enunciation" to locate the specificity of the photographer/audience (1991: 195).

The politics of enunciation refers to the strategy of being attentive to the power structures of cultural locations that inform a subject's speaking-position. This strategy is important to understanding sexuality and queer identities because the media represent an important arena for the production of and challenge to hegemonic images and desires that have shaped the experiences of sexual minorities. For marginal subjects, media may be used to reveal dominant regimes of representation. Similarly, mainstream media may provide opportunities to cultivate a self-reflexivity necessary to the ethics of looking and speaking. As part of the broader critical framework on the politics of location (Frankenberg and Mani 1993; Rich 1985), the politics of enunciation has been one of the influential theoretical foundations not only for identity politics studies, but also for feminist film spectatorship and cross-cultural media reception.

Alongside strategies of voice and enunciation is intersectionality, which examines how various social and culturally constructed categories such as gender, race, class, sexuality, and other axes of identity combine and interact on multiple levels and contribute to systemic inequality (Crenshaw 1991). "[A]s a nexus of social location, linked to structural phenomenon, it suggests identity determinants exist not as sealed entities but parts of an interwoven intersection" (Taylor *et al.* 2010: 4). Central to critical race theory, and feminist, legal, and health studies, it has underpinned the first generation of queer race scholarship. In 1998, North America-based queer scholars revised this framework as "the intersection of racial and (homo)sexual difference" to express queer and Asian American identities (Eng and Hom 1998: 1, parenthesis in original). The following year, Australia-based gay scholars Jackson and Sullivan examined the country's multicultural policy in relation to a collective queer identity to explore how people from minority racial backgrounds view their sexual identities (1999: 1). Anzaldúa's (2007) concept of mestiza consciousness, as a critical third border-space for race, gender, and sexuality, has also gained critical traction as a tool of intersection. These interventions are succinctly summarized in *Queer Race*: "Sexuality is always racially marked, as every racial marking is always imbued with a specific sexuality. ... [R]ace is always already sexualized and sexuality is always already raced" (Barnard 2004: 2).

In the last two decades, identity politics has enabled the development and legitimation of practices associated with minority racialized queer constituencies. Not without its critics, identity politics has come under fire by the Right and Left in the West. The former accuses it of being a politically correct essentialist fad; the latter deplores its preoccupation with moral suffering and inability to address capitalist structures of class (Brown 1995). It is against this backlash that post-identity politics has emerged.

## As post-identity: queer mobility

Post-identity politics departs from subject-centered identities. Rather than self and group identities based on the fixed determinants of race, gender, and sexuality, post-identity politics focuses on the contextual and symbolic specificity of identity. The editors of *Post Identity* refer to "the disappearance of distinction" that frames "cohesive" essentialist paradigms (Rombes *et al.* 1997, n.p.). It seeks to substitute the fixity of identity "for the fluidity and flexibility of 'affiliations'" (Bramen 2002: 6), in favor of universalism (Lott 2000) and cosmopolitanism (Hollinger 2006). Queer theorist Puar's maneuver from intersectionality to assemblage is incisive of this shift. She defines assemblage as "a series of dispersed but mutually implicated and messy networks [that draw] together enunciation and dissolution, causality and effect, organic and non-organic forces" (Puar 2007: 211). Sex and race are viewed not as intersections but as "outside the parameters of identity ... as assemblages, as *events*" (2007: 211, emphasis in original).

Two media events on queer mobility in Australia—the sexual migration of queer asylum and the marriage equality campaign—illustrate post-identity struggles on the question of subject embodiment and its implications for racialized and sexualized minorities. I have chosen to examine queer mobility here because it is an important arena for considering contemporary media and racialized sexuality. From the uses of mobile technologies by gay and lesbian communities, the rise of pink tourism to the material forces that condition queer social visibility and subjectivity, the media are central to queer mobility, helping to unravel how race has been incorporated and fetishized in progressive articulations of sexual identity. I consider how discourses and practices of equal love and sexual migration are represented in gay travel guidebooks, queer asylum reports, and newspapers. These media demonstrate queer mobility in two ways: as practices of non-heteronormative (and irregular) sexual migration and as a rights-based process of how gays and lesbians have potentially overcome homophobia and gained recognition as equal citizens.

Diverse media texts are used for official verification in sexual identity-based asylum applications. Following the development of the humanitarian migration category of asylum, gays, lesbians, and transsexuals can seek refugee protection on the basis of their membership of "a particular social group" if they can demonstrate a fear of persecution based on that membership. Key to the application is the construction of a personal narrative that documents an individual's sexual identity, membership of the social group, and history of public persecution. An applicant is more likely to be believed if the personal narrative can fit with the narratives in other sources. Newspapers in West and East, and global gay lifestyle magazines that report on the tightening or loosening of homosexual laws in source countries, are regularly used by officials for corroboration. Between 1994 and 2000, the Australian authorities referred to the *Spartacus International Gay Travel Guide* as a source of independent evidence of homosexual tolerance in 24 percent of the cases, and 90 percent of these were unsuccessful (Dauvergne and Millbank 2003: 309, 318). Ten cases of the 26 cases involved lesbians, and each of these was unsuccessful. In the three cases involving Chinese lesbians, the authorities quoted the guide by noting a gradual liberalization of attitudes towards homosexuals in Shanghai, and listing an emerging gay scene as evidence of increasing tolerance (see Refugee Review Tribunal 1998a, 1998b, 1999).

Queer travel guidebooks have become a popular resource with the rise of queer tourism as a niche industry marketed to increasingly international and upwardly mobile gays and lesbians, an industry estimated to be worth about US$55 billion a year (Madan 2007). The guidebook lists destinations popular with queer travelers; some are global cities, while others are more exclusive gay neighborhoods, or special events such as the Gay Games or gay cruises. In publication since 1970, the Germany-based annual *Spartacus* is one of the most established. The 2009 edition is a 1,200-page guide containing listings for at least 160 countries with information about homosexual laws, hotels, saunas, beats, beaches, bars, and support hotlines, and covers about 22,000 businesses.

When travel guidebooks are used in asylum cases to verify the context of homosexual persecution, tribunal decisions follow the globally queer narrative of sexual liberation, and ignore the racial and sexual contexts of source countries that create the conditions of persecution. The post-identity logic signaled follows the universalizing tendency of Western globalization: race and sex emerge as sites that make present queer mobility as a contradictory force of liberation and containment, simultaneously legitimating the sexual uplifting of queer tourism and the progressive spread of the post-Stonewall paradigm of rights and emancipation while also containing in its sexual and racial hierarchy those who do not fit its logic. A few claims have been successful, such as that of a Cambodian-Vietnamese lesbian who was granted a protection visa. However, more than 30 different corroborating sources—including academic journals, US-based Vietnamese queer activists, gay websites, newspapers and sex encyclopedias—stated that Vietnam has no laws against homosexuality (Refugee Review Tribunal 2008). Thus, homonationalism—as a process that removes homophobia by championing the sexual openness of a nation-state—legitimates the hierarchical sexualization and racialization of the refugee other. The logic of queer mobility that underpins sexual identity-based asylum exposes the complicity of homonormativity (Luibhéid 2008: 180).

Homonormativity describes how gay and lesbian politics have moved closer to the standards of normative heterosexuality by using a human rights discourse to mask the economic inequalities of neoliberal capitalism (Duggan 2003). This ideology provides the ballast for current equal love campaigns that have seen Australia, which had already passed its laws recognizing same-sex partnerships, join in the global fight to achieve marriage equality. Key to this campaign, and central to sexual law reform, is the equal rights claims of queer mobility. On December 14, 2011 a Chinese lesbian, hailed as a rights advocate, appeared on the front page of the Australian newspaper *The Age* (Murphy 2011). Current Senator and ex-Minister for Finance, Penny Wong, a Malaysian Chinese Australian, and her Australian partner, Sophie Allouache, had just become parents to their first child, a daughter conceived through IVF. The photo that accompanies the article has Wong sitting next to birth mother Allouache; both beam as they cradle their baby. It should be noted that while Wong is the first Asian and openly gay member of the Australian parliament, she herself never used her sexuality or race as diversity tools. The innocuous celebrity pose for the newspaper, with no linguistic sign alluding to the obvious sexual and racial otherness, reflects the universality of homonormativity. With both women wearing similar shades of gray, it connotes a sameness synonymous with the homonormalizing claims of same-sex marriage family rights. Herein manifests the "post-racial" and "post-gay" milieu of contemporary queer neoliberalism and homonationalism.

For some, the notion "post-racial" is used to problematize issues of race and racism which are deemed no longer relevant for discussions (Kaplan 2011); for others, it suggests a more insidious form of postmodern racism where racial difference is no longer biologically attributed but culturally assigned (Back and Solomos 2000). The "post-gay" is also understood in similar terms. In the West, it refers to the linear trajectory where the stage of liberatory gay identities has passed and identification is claimed through similarities with heterosexuals (Ghaziani 2011). These post-identity claims resonate with the practices of queer neoliberalism and homonationalism that seek to erase the specificity of and remove the homophobic stigma associated with minority sexualized (and racialized) identities, by drawing on its successful assimilation into the heteronormative mainstream. It refers to a new sexual politics that has moved away from rights-based political activism towards a new normalization emphasizing individual rights; it is motivated by desire to reach "equality with," rather than "tolerance from," the mainstream (Richardson 2005: 516). As queer theorist Duggan suggests, it "does not contest dominant heteronormative assumptions and institutions but upholds and sustains them while promising the possibility of a demobilized gay constituency and a privatized, depoliticized gay culture anchored in domesticity and consumption" (2002: 179).

## Conclusion

I have revisited the foundations of queer race studies to consider the media futures confronting our current "post-gay" and "post-racial" milieu, with a focus on how race and sexuality have shaped queer identities as desire, as identity, and as post-identity. At the heart of the interdisciplinary queer race project, from unraveling the practices of biopolitics and Oriental sex to critical tools of voice, enunciation, and intersectionality, is the politics of racialized sexuality. Situating these legacies against the backdrop of contemporary queer neoliberalism, and explicating how race and sex have emerged as post-identitarian sites for the conditioning of homonationalism, I present new approaches in media and cultural studies that are equally exigent and proposed interventions in the practices of queer mobility. The challenge for queer race studies is to continue to attend to these media vectors that not only cut across and materialize the re-embodiments of race and sex, but also resist the assimilation to a "post-gay" and "post-racial" future.

## References

Anzaldúa, G. (2007) *Borderlands/La Frontera: The New Mestiza*, San Francisco: Aunt Lute Books.

Back, L. and J. Solomos (eds.) (2000) *Theories of Race and Racism: A Reader*, New York: Routledge.

Barnard, I. (2004) *Queer Race: Cultural Interventions in the Racial Politics of Queer Theory*, New York: Peter Lang.

Bramen, C. T. (2002) "Turning Point: Why the Academic Left Hates Identity Politics," *Textual Practice* 16(1): 1–11.

Brown, W. (1995) *States of Injury: Power and Freedom in Late Modernity*, Princeton, NJ: Princeton University Press.

Chow, R. (1998) *Ethics after Idealism*, Bloomington: Indiana University Press.

Crenshaw, K. (1991) "Mapping the Margins: Intersectionality, Identity Politics, and Violence against Women of Color," *Stanford Law Review* 43(6): 1241–99.

Dauvergne, C. and J. Millbank (2003) "Burdened by Proof: How the Australian Refugee Review Tribunal Has Failed Lesbian and Gay Asylum Seekers," *Federal Law Review* 31(2): 299–342.

De Lauretis, T. (1999) "Popular Culture, Public and Private Fantasies: Femininity and Fetishism in David Cronenberg's M. *Butterfly*," *Signs* 24(2): 303–34.

Duggan, L. (2002) "The New Homonormativity: The Sexual Politics of Neoliberalism," in R. Castronovo and D. Nelson (eds.) *Materializing Democracy: Towards a Revitalized Cultural Politics*, Durham, NC: Duke University Press, pp. 175–94.

——(2003) *Neoliberalism, Cultural Politics, and the Attack on Democracy*, Boston: Beacon Press.

Eng, D. (2001) *Racial Castration: Managing Masculinity in Asian America*, Durham, NC: Duke University Press.

Eng, D. and A. Hom (eds.) (1998) *Q&A: Queer in Asian America*, Philadelphia: Temple University Press.

Fanon, F. (1991) *Black Skin, White Masks*, New York: Grove Weidenfeld.

Foucault, M. (1978) *The History of Sexuality: An Introduction*, Harmondsworth: Penguin.

Frankenberg, R. and L. Mani (1993) "Crosscurrents, Crosstalk: Race, 'Postcoloniality' and the Politics of Location," *Cultural Studies* 7(2): 291–308.

Fung, R. (1996) "Looking for My Penis: The Eroticized Asian in Gay Video Porn," in R. Leong (ed.) *Asian American Sexualities: Dimensions of Gay and Lesbian Experience*, New York: Routledge, pp. 180–91.

Garber, M. (1992) *Vested Interests: Cross-Dressing and Cultural Anxiety*, New York: Penguin.

Gates, H. L. (1985) "Editor's Introduction: Writing 'Race' and the Difference It Makes," *Critical Inquiry* 12(1): 1–20.

Gerstner, D. A. (2011) *Queer Pollen: White Seduction, Black Male Homosexuality, and the Cinematic*, Urbana: University of Illinois Press.

Ghaziani, A. (2011) "Post-Gay Collective Identity Construction," *Social Problems* 58(1): 99–125.

Grist, L. (2003) "'It's Only a Piece of Meat': Gender Ambiguity, Sexuality, and Politics in *The Crying Game* and *M. Butterfly*," *Cinema Journal* 42(4): 3–28.

Hollinger, D. (2006) *Cosmopolitanism and Solidarity: Studies in Ethnoracial, Religious, and Professional Affiliation in the United States*, Madison: University of Wisconsin Press.

Jackson, P. and G. Sullivan (eds.) (1999) *Multicultural Queer: Australian Narratives*, New York: Haworth Press.

Jones, J. (1993) "The Construction of Black Sexuality: Towards Normalizing the Black Cinematic Experience," in M. Diawara (ed.), *Black America Cinema*, New York: Routledge, pp. 247–56.

Kaplan, R. (2011) *The Myth of Post-Racial America: Searching for Equality in the Age of Materialism*, Lanham, MD: Rowman & Littlefield.

Lott, E. (2000) "After Identity, Politics: The Return of Universalism," *New Literary History* 31(4): 665–7.

Luibhéid, E. (2008) "Queer/Migration: An Unruly Body of Scholarship," *GLQ: A Journal of Lesbian & Gay Studies* 14(2/3): 169–90.

Madan, R. (2007) "Philadelphia Refines Its Pitch to Gay Tourists," *USA Today*. http://www.usatoday.com/travel/destinations/2007-08-01-gay-tourism_N.htm.

Mercer, K. (1991) "Skin Head Sex Thing: Racial Difference and the Homoerotic Imaginary," in Bad Object-Choices (ed.), *How Do I Look: Queer Film and Video*, Seattle: Bay Press, pp. 169–222.

——(1992) "Just Looking for Trouble: Robert Mapplethorpe and Fantasies of Race," in L. Segal and M. McIntosh (eds.) *Sex Exposed: Sexuality and the Pornography Debate*, London: Virago, pp. 92–110.

——(1994) *Welcome to the Jungle: New Positions in Black Cultural Studies*, New York: Routledge.

Murphy, K. (2011) "Wong's Joyous Vote for New Parenthood," *The Age*, December 14. http://www.theage.com.au/action/printArticle?id=2837254.

Paul, J. P., G. Ayala, and K. H. Choi (2010) "Internet Sex Ads for MSM and Partner Selection Criteria: The Potency of Race/Ethnicity Online," *Journal of Sex Research* 47(6): 528–38.

Puar, J. (2007) *Terrorist Assemblages: Homonationalism in Queer Times*, Durham, NC: Duke University Press.

Refugee Review Tribunal (1998a) N97/16390 RRTA [1998] 4379 (September 23), Refugee Review Tribunal of Australia Decisions. http://www.austlii.edu.au/cgi-bin/sinodisp/au/cases/cth/RRTA/1998/4379.html?stem=0&synonyms=0&query=Chinese%20lesbian.

——(1998b) N97/17155 [1998] RRTA 4386 (September 23), Refugee Review Tribunal of Australia Decisions. http://www.austlii.edu.au/cgi-bin/sinodisp/au/cases/cth/RRTA/1998/4386.html?stem=0&synonyms=0&query=Chinese%20lesbian.

——(1999) N99/27818 [1999] RRTA 1607 (June 29), Refugee Review Tribunal of Australia Decisions. http://www.austlii.edu.au/cgi-bin/sinodisp/au/cases/cth/RRTA/1999/1607.html?stem=0&synonyms=0&query=Chinese%20lesbian.

——(2008) 071862642 [2008] RRTA 40 (February 19), Refugee Review Tribunal of Australia Decisions. http://www.austlii.edu.au/cgi-bin/sinodisp/au/cases/cth/RRTA/2008/40.html?stem= 0&synonyms=0&query=Chinese%20lesbian.

Rich, A. (1985) "Notes Towards a Politics of Location," in M. Diaz-Diocaretz and O. Zavala (eds.) *Women's Feminist Identity and Society in the 1980s*, Amsterdam: John Benjamins, pp. 7–22.

Richardson, D. (2005) "Desiring Sameness? The Rise of a Neoliberal Politics of Normalisation," *Antipode* 37(3): 515–35.

Rombes, N., H. C. Nicholas, and J. A. Howard (1997) "Otherwise: An Editorial Welcome," *Post Identity* 1(1): n.p. http://hdl.handle.net/2027/spo.pid9999.0001.101.

Said, E. (1985) *Orientalism*, Harmondsworth: Penguin.

San Juan, E., Jr. (2002) "Symbolic Violence and the Fetishism of the Sublime: A Metacommentary on David Hwang's M. *Butterfly*," *Journal of Intercultural Studies* 23(1): 33–46.

Stoler, A. (1995) *Race and the Education of Desire*, Durham, NC: Duke University Press.

Suner, A. (1999) "Postmodern Double Cross: Reading David Cronenberg's M. *Butterfly* as a Horror Story," *Cinema Journal* 37(2): 49–64.

Taylor, C. (1992) *Multiculturalism and "The Politics of Recognition,"* Princeton, NJ: Princeton University Press.

Taylor, Y., S. Hines, and M. Casey (2010) "Introduction," in Y. Taylor, S. Hines, and M. E. Casey (eds.) *Theorizing Intersectionality and Sexuality*, New York: Palgrave Macmillan, pp. 1–14.

Weeks, J. (2003) *Sexuality*, 2nd edition, London: Routledge.

Young, I. M. (1990) *Justice and the Politics of Difference*, Princeton, NJ: Princeton University Press.

# 8

# Gender, media, and trans/national spaces

## Radha S. Hegde

As local worlds are inserted into larger social and economic configurations, gender issues gain new forms of visibility and invisibility. Feminist interventions into these conditions entail the navigation of multiple publics, media imaginaries, and geographies, all of which are embedded within dispersed and shifting relations of power. However, these critical mappings of the gender politics are fraught with challenges. First of all, for the most part, discussions of globalization simply bypass the subject of gender (Basu *et al.* 2001). Instead of developing inclusive perspectives, the tendency is to either normalize the status quo or perpetuate binary logics of differentiation. This simplification, as Scott notes, gives "schematic coherence to the messy entanglements of local, national, regional and international politics" (2002: 5). Yet these developments and perspectives are the very reason to rethink the ways in which questions of gender and sexuality are currently contested within global assemblages and their histories. The convergence of the neoliberal economy, commodity flows, and the global media apparatus poses specific types of asymmetries that warrant the attention of scholars of media and gender. In this chapter, I elaborate on some key issues that need to be considered for a nuanced transnational mapping of the politics of gender and mediated environments.

## Global ecology

Over the last decade, most accounts of globalization from different intellectual traditions have emphasized, among other things, the importance of acknowledging the elements of space, time, structure, scale, and global networks (see Castells 2000; Giddens 1999; Wallerstein 2004). Held writes that economic globalization is about the "widening, intensifying, speeding up and growing impact of worldwide interconnectedness" (2002: 306). In the process, other linked formations of power, which are often both racialized and gendered, are naturalized in order to support the rapid flow of capital. Feminist scholars, therefore, have argued for the need to expose the asymmetries that globalization has either created or exacerbated (Alexander and

Mohanty 1997) and the importance of grappling with "scattered hegemonies" of power (Grewal and Kaplan 1994). According to Katz, globalization reworks existing social relations and material practices and produces a precarious political ecology (2001: 1228). The global reach of media plays a crucial role in the circulation of these connected systems of power, as seen in a sensational case that unfolded in New York City and on screens around the world. The highly publicized incident that the media dubbed the "DSK affair" illustrates how complex intersections of power and gendered precarity are constituted in highly mediated contexts of the global economy.

In May 2011, images of a hand-cuffed Dominique Strauss-Kahn, then chief of the International Monetary Fund (IMF), arrested in a dramatic turn of events by the New York Police Department, began to circulate in the global media. A hotel housekeeper, Nafissatou Diallo, a 32-year-old Muslim immigrant woman from Guinea, West Africa, had accused Strauss-Kahn of rape and sexual assault. As news about the alleged assault made headlines around the world, speculations soared about what exactly had transpired in a hotel room in the ritzy Sofitel hotel in New York City. The media were abuzz with conjectures whether the encounter between the housekeeper and the IMF chief was forced or consensual. Some people wondered if an opportunistic immigrant had schemed the fall of a highly visible and powerful man. A steady stream of discourse emerged connecting issues of race, class, nation, and gender. Eventually, Ms. Diallo's excessive media appearances and inconsistencies in her account cast her as an unworthy victim in public perception. Her credibility was even further compromised when media revelations emerged that she had fabricated or embellished the violence she had experienced in Guinea in order to gain asylum in the United States. While this led to a dismissal of the charges against Strauss-Kahn, the so-called "DSK affair" brought into view a number of issues that are endemic to neoliberal globalization.

First of all, the story highlighted the presence and vulnerability of social actors who fall below the radar screen of dominant accounts of globalization. More specifically, it revealed the lives of immigrants in the global city whose bodies and labor increasingly constitute the hidden infrastructure of global cities (Sassen 1991). Their disempowered lives and situations stand as proof of the economic inequalities that have resulted from the conditions both defined and exacerbated by capitalist structures of colonialism and, more recently, neoliberal globalization. Next, the unfolding saga of violence, sex, and power exemplified the deep entanglements of geography and history that frame the economic divide between the Global North and South—a renewed reminder about how economic and sexual power are intertwined. Finally, the mediatized spectacle reinforces the need to parse how the intersecting logics of race, class, gender, and nation are reproduced on the global stage. Sassen (2008) calls for more inclusive accounting of actors and processes that are coded outside the scale of the global, but are, in fact, constitutive of it. Therefore, she notes, we need "conceptual architectures that allow us to detect what we might think of as countergeographies of globalization" (2008: 82). As this example revealed, gender issues are a case in point, where local articulations almost always have to be situated within larger cross-border dynamics (see also Hegde 2012).

The materiality of gendered lives has to be contextualized within the crossfire of transnational forces and the mediated circulation of gendered discourses. To do this, the transparency of categories cannot be assumed. Certain normative stances that surface repeatedly, in both scholarly and popular sources, need to be problematized. For instance, the global is conflated with the modern, which, in turn, is identified as a narrative emanating from the West. Considered to stand at the frontier of enlightened rationality, the West becomes, by extension, the site of progressive sexual politics. In addition, the discourse on globalization tends to privilege the new as modern and this leads to the overall discounting of history. As Hall puts it dramatically, "we suffer increasingly from a process of historical amnesia in which we think that just because we are thinking about an idea it has only just started" (1997: 19–20). The repercussions to these assumptions are both gendered and transnational.

A set of global thematics need to be addressed by feminist scholars of globalization and media. This includes the deterritorialization of cultures, privatization of services, deregulation, flexibilization of labor, and the emergence of the consumer-citizen. In addition, informal social and economic processes are set into motion by the dispersed formations of transnational capital, which intensify the nature of gendered exclusions on a global scale. Lowe and Lloyd state that while global capitalism might seem to have penetrated all social terrains, exhausting the possibilities for resistance, transnational capitalism, "like colonial capitalism before it, continues to produce sites of contradiction and the dynamics of its own negation and critique" (1997: 21). Feminist and queer scholarship have begun to respond with a critique of the issues posed by the new global conjunctures. The moment has inspired a diverse body of work within media and cultural studies, which maps the ways in which the global media cultures and technology participate in the reproduction of the private and public dimensions of gendered life and identity.

This emerging knowledge base on globalization, gender, and sexuality builds on previous scholarship that spoke to the absences and silences about gender in dominant knowledge structures. For example, ideas of intersectionality (Crenshaw 1991) and the border (Anzaldúa 1990) suggested how racial and sexual identities together impact the materialities of everyday life. Postcolonial and subaltern scholarship has been very influential in historicizing representations of the non-Western gendered body and challenging the normativity of Euro modernity (Chow 1993; Spivak 1990; Sunder Rajan 1993). Others have extensively analyzed the civilizational matrix that frames the global divide between the West and the Rest (Mohanty 1991; Narayan 1997). However, the theoretical task of producing more nuanced representations of cross-border dynamics is also complicated by the lingering influence of the area studies model in the social sciences, where the domestic and the global are demarcated as separate and distinct (Grewal et al. 1999). The logic of area studies, a legacy from the knowledge production of the Cold War, has had significant consequences for the type of knowledge produced about genders and sexualities located in the non-West. As Mohanty (2003) and others have argued, the power of Western modernity is premised on the systematic containment of the Other. The dynamics and density of the interconnections between cultures today exceed these dichotomous descriptions.

Cross-border issues require an optics that goes beyond the familiar polarities of the West/non-West or local/global. Research on global issues now has to transnationally track the ways in which issues of gender and sexuality are drafted through the various political configurations, geographical and virtual spaces. Unlike a comparative approach, the focus on linkages across cultural contexts, according to Kim-Puri (2005), does not presuppose equivalence. The notion of the transnational focuses attention on the contested connections and lines of power that cut across contexts. Categories such as gender, nation, modernity, tradition, and culture are being rethought in more pliable ways that decenter naturalized definitions and take into account the ideological work that is reproduced through the normalization of categories (see Briggs *et al.* 2008). The challenge is to find ways to highlight how the politics of gender and sexuality are situated at the interstices of complex social histories and within the cross-cutting public formations of modernity, neoliberal cultures, and mediated worlds (Hegde 2011). I next turn to describe each of these conjunctures and the particular transnational locations that both receive and demand attention.

## Modernity and its formulaic other

Geopolitical events of the last decade have renewed attention on issues of gender. Whether it is about justification for war, integration of immigrants or gauging civilizational progress, the mediated gaze circles back to gender and sexuality. Issues get conflated when geographical areas are explained away in essentialist terms as unchanging and fixed. This pits cultures in opposition, designating some as forward-looking and others as lacking the ability to participate in a modern present. Modernity is asserted in opposition to that which is outside, apart, and in need of being rescued through a civilizing process. As Mitchell writes, "the modern occurs only by performing the distinction between the modern and the non-modern, the West and the non-West, each performance opening the possibility of what is figured as non-modern contaminating the modern, displacing it, or disrupting its authority" (2000: 26). This logic of Euro-modernity, now strengthened by the circulatory power of media technologies, reproduces the West as the site of progressive gender politics. In the context of war and the articulation of American exceptionalism, there has also been a linking of nationalism, race, and heteronormativity to define the acceptable citizen.

Describing the complex trajectory of the production of sexuality in the "war on terror," Puar writes that "the terrorist figure is not merely racialized and sexualized; the body must appear improperly racialized (outside the norms of multiculturalism) and perversely sexualized in order to materialize as the terrorist in the first place" (2007: 38). The logic of regulation and benevolence work together within an Orientalist, neocolonial paradigm, both defining and disciplining non-Western intimacies and sexualities in relation to Western scripts (Massad 2002). As Wilson (2006) notes, due to being intertwined with political, economic, and cultural power, Western sexual discourse, both normative and radical, is able to exert a strong global influence.

The transnational travels of Western sexual modernity are best seen in recent discourses around gendered Muslim bodies. The visual trope of the veiled Muslim woman, out of pace with the modern, has become a staple topic of public discourse.

A position on the veil has turned into what Scott terms "an ideological litmus test" and "having an opinion about it serves to establish one's credentials on the heady topics of individualism, secularism and the emancipation of women" (2007: 17). The media coverage of the veiled Muslim women waiting to be saved reached a feverish pitch after the US attacks on Afghanistan in 2001. In her radio address, Laura Bush (2001) talked of the war against terror as being fought for the rights of women. Due to the military intervention by the United States, Mrs. Bush stated, Afghan women can listen to music and teach their daughters without fear of punishment.

Feminist scholars have since critiqued these claims and benevolent postures. Analyzing the media frameworks used to represent Afghan women, Stabile and Kumar show how the convergence of discourses around protectionism and Orientalism erase the political struggles of Afghan women and replace them with those of women in the West, whose struggles center on the rights and "the eternal virtues of Western civilization" (2005: 766). Others argue that by homogenizing the experiences of diverse populations of Muslim women, the reductive discourses about the veil in the United States reproduce a paternalistic imperialist logic (Ayotte and Husain 2005). In addition to the victim narrative, the veiled Muslim female body is sometimes read from a postfeminist stance that equates bodily display with sexual liberation. This explains the reductive consumerist summaries, such as that Afghan women cannot paint their nails or wear lipstick, that are highlighted over the structural oppression in their lives (Macdonald 2006).

The mediated flow of these visual spectacles continues to tether the gendered non-Western subject within a narrative of transition and waiting. Recently, these themes had another airing with the global circulation of horror and support for the teenaged Pakistani activist and student, Malala Yousafzai, who was shot by the Taliban as she was coming home from school. In a world of converging media, the story went viral. Celebrities including Barack Obama, Asif Ali Zardari, Hamid Karzai, and Hillary Clinton have made public statements about Malala and her courage. Former British prime minister Gordon Brown, as the current UN Special Envoy on Global Education, presented the Pakistani government with one million signatures attached to a petition, "I am Malala," urging Islamabad to provide education for all children (Sayah 2012). The speed and extent to which this story circulated exemplify the media circuits that frame the arrival of the gendered non-Western subject on the global radar screen. While the rallying cry of "I am Malala" drummed up some immediate support, the viral circulation also diminishes the structural and geopolitical issues at play, and contributes to an overall flattening of the politics and its particularities. Adding to the publicity, the movie star Angelina Jolie wrote a piece titled "We Are All Malala" (2012), where she draws attention to Malala's plight and documents her own children's responses. As Malala lay in a coma, Madonna added her support as well by way of a striptease and flashed the words MALALA emblazoned on her back (Yousafzai 2012). Media and markets set the conditions under which gendered causes come into visibility. The "I am Malala" campaign is emblematic of the way in which a superficial sense of transnational community is created and circulated without anchors to history and the politics of material specificities. Media coverage of undifferentiated landscapes of backwardness in contrast to images of Western benevolence in fact reinforce a racialized civilizational discourse that reproduces old colonial logics of difference combined with postfeminist celebrity spectacle (see Duvall 2011).

## Transnational layering of consumption

Cosmopolitan forms of desire shaped by the global flow and reach of commodity capitalism have added more transnational layers to the politics of gender and its intersection with modernity. As Sunder Rajan argues, modernity is never simply the time of the present; rather, it is "a complex historical and cultural situation defined against the past, the traditional, and the 'West' with different kinds of value attached to what it represents" (1999: 7). This reworking of the relationship between tradition and modernity is best seen in the context of gendered consumer cultures which are being shaped worldwide according to the dictates of market logics. With the increasing importance of privatization in the neoliberal economy and the eroding of the sense of the collective, the shaping of the citizen as consumer is a global project. Commodity culture is the site where new sensibilities and gendered modes of participation in a global modernity are crafted. Media and new technologies become the instruments that transport neoliberal ideologies of narcissism and self-regulation. Desires and newly imagined subjectivities are being forged transnationally through the circulation of images, ideologies, and commodities flowing via multiple global media platforms.

With the expansion of neoliberal capitalism in emerging economies like China and India, and in former socialist countries, there is an active circulation and reproduction of values and lifestyle associated with a form of consumption identified with the West. The West itself is reproduced as an imagined space of freedom and being on the cutting-edge of progress (see Grewal 2005). With the market offering possibilities for the re-imagination of the self, consumption becomes the site of magical transformation and choice in the media-saturated global environment. Structural constraints are rendered superfluous and material realities such as racism and homophobia are rendered in exclusively personal terms (Gill 2007). Promoting the cult of the individual and the persuasive message that consumption signifies liberation, neoliberalism has also introduced a postracial and postfeminist worldview. The rationality of neoliberalism, writes Wendy Brown, is "a mode of governance encompassing but not limited to the state, and one which produces subjects, forms of citizenship and behavior, and a new organization of the social" (2003: 3).

The cultural consequences of this new social organization and its transnational entanglements have been significant. Gender and sexuality once again are positioned at the center of these discourses of transformation when local cultures both collide and redefine global modernity. For example, since the early 1920s, the image of the "modern girl"—provocative, recognizable, and fashionable—has been a subject of visual representations, in cities including Tokyo, Bombay, Shanghai, and Berlin (Weinbaum et al. 2008). In a global context, the paradigm of the modern girl continues to travel, transported by the power of digital technology, media, and markets. As the market recruits more women and minorities as workers and consumers, the experience of the modern is promoted through material objects and media cultures. With the flexibilization of work and digital technologies enabling new forms of offshore work, young men and women in call centers in India and the Philippines, for example, are now fully entrenched in the transnational equation. With disposable income, they are regarded as the new class of consumer citizens, a readymade market for the global economy and media circuits. They service customers in the West and partake of the world through consumption; as such they are deeply implicated within the economic and social structures of the West. Luxury malls springing up in places like Shanghai, Bangalore, Rio de Janeiro, and Manila reach out to this growing consuming demographic with appeals to the alluring construct of a universally connected, sexually liberated, cosmopolitan lifestyle that comes alive with the possession of mobile phones, branded clothes, and digital accessories. Gendered norms and sexuality are now to be negotiated within local contexts against the presence of this global force.

Sexual politics today is played out in a space where cultures, economies, and histories are deeply intertwined and traverse borders. Illustrative of this development is the growing global appeal of whiteness as evidenced through the marketing of skin lightening creams. A visual economy of images shapes the aspirations and longings of consumers in emerging economies such as India (see Mazzarella 2003). Commodities become the route to magical transformation and alignment with a transnational modernity. For instance, the juxtaposition of tradition and modernity takes interesting transnational detours in the case of the growing media genre of "chick lit" catering to the global postfeminist reader. Global "chick lit" is springing up in Latin America, China, India, and Eastern Europe, with similar themes that unite young urban women in a global community of consumers who, as Chen argues, are eager to imbibe a "Western-style cosmopolitan lifestyle, coded as progress, empowerment and freedom" (2012: 217). Religion is another interesting site where tradition is being repackaged with adaptations for cosmopolitan living and consuming (Echchaibi 2011). The fashion merchandising and the interest of fashion houses worldwide in catering to Islamic women's fashion and religious sensibility (Tarlo 2010) is a case in point where tradition gets recoded as transnational modern. The modern emerges as a style statement and lifestyle forged through transnational linkages and mediated negotiations.

While universalist narratives of Western modernity are being actively worked into aspirational narratives of consumers, there is also considerable local contestation with such transformations as they meet with local ideologies. The sexualized body becomes the site on which other anxieties about globalization are played out. For example, gay and lesbian identities as they are formed outside of the West are highly contested and articulate a different politics of inhabiting sexual identities. Queer theorists have made compelling arguments for understanding the flow and politics of desire in a transnational frame (Gopinath 2005; Manalansan 2003). Or, for instance, the heightened sexual visibility of the young workforce of global corporations is confronted by violence, such as in the tragedy of femicide in the maquiladoras of Ciudad Juárez (Wright 1999) and the aggressive, negative public responses in India about the Westernization of young women (Hegde 2011). The public visibility of women and the place of tradition in the context of a rapidly changing society were again debated and contested after the rape of a young woman in Delhi, which set off a national movement around gendered violence in India. The subject of gender, tradition, and modernity is resurrected repeatedly in various ways in the global arena. These examples once again show that the local and the global are by no means transparent or self-evident categories; rather, they should be viewed as processes animated by multiple vectors of power, contestation, and ideological conflict.

## Conclusion

The forces of transnational capital, migration, and urbanization have radically altered the conditions of everyday life and how the terms under the subject of gender and sexuality are defined and mobilized. Globalization is already a gendered process which has thrown territorial views of culture, communication, identity, and community into crisis. Media are pivotal to the understanding of the gendered politics of globalization as they both frame and provoke contestations between local and transnational processes. Media and technology are never mere conduits for information but are instead part of the larger social discourse, where media forms, gendered cultures, and material experiences of everyday life are intricately and globally connected. Hence, the manner in which gendered bodies and meaning are being defined or deployed within shifting fields of power merits nuanced attention from scholars of gender and media.

Mapping the global, especially with a view to producing gendered knowledge that resists normative explanations and universalist frameworks, is intellectually challenging. I have tried to advance a case for a more expansive theorizing of gender politics in the context of highly mediated global environments. Although the term transnational is defined variously, it serves as a powerful heuristic to think critically about and beyond established categories, and to contextualize overlapping and interconnected fields and flows of power. It is through following linkages, tracking circuits, and historicizing conjunctures that we can understand the dialectics of gender in the contemporary global context.

## References

Alexander, M. J. and C. T. Mohanty (1997) "Genealogies, Legacies, Movements," in M. J. Alexander and C. T. Mohanty (eds.) *Feminist Genealogies, Colonial Legacies, Democratic Futures*, New York: Routledge, pp. xiii–xlii.

Anzaldúa, G. (ed.) (1990) *Making Face, Making Soul/Haciendo Caras: Creative and Critical Perspectives by Feminists of Color*, San Francisco: Aunt Lute Books.

Ayotte, K. and M. E. Husain (2005) "Securing Afghan Women: Neocolonialism, Epistemic Violence and the Rhetoric of the Veil," *NWSA* 17(3): 112–33.

Basu, A., I. Grewal, and L. Malki (eds.) (2001) "Editorial," *Signs* special issue 26(4): 943–8.

Briggs, L., G. McCormick, and J. T. Way (2008) "Transnationalism: A Category of Analysis," *American Quarterly* 60(3): 625–48.

Brown, W. (2003) "Neo-liberalism and the End of Liberal Democracy," *Theory and Event* 7(1): 1–19.

Bush, L. (2001) Radio Address Online. http://georgewbush-whitehouse.archives.gov/news/releases/2001/11/20011117.html.

Castells, M. (2000) *The Rise of The Network Society: The Information Age: Economy, Society and Culture*, vol. 1, 2nd edition, Hoboken, NJ: Wiley-Blackwell.

Chen, E. (2012) "Shanghai(ed) Babies: Geopolitics, Biopolitics and the Global Chick Lit," *Feminist Media Studies* 12(2): 214–28.

Chow, R. (1993) *Writing Diaspora: Tactics of Intervention in Contemporary Cultural Studies*, Bloomington: Indiana University Press.

Crenshaw, K. (1991) "Mapping the Margins: Intersectionality, Identity Politics, and Violence against Women of Color," *Stanford Law Review* 43(6): 1241–99.

Duvall, S.-S. (2011) "Celebrity Travels: Media Spectacles and Construction of a Transnational Politics of Care," in R. S. Hegde (ed.) *Circuits of Visibility: Gender and Transnational Media Cultures*, New York: New York University Press, pp. 103–23.

Echchaibi, N. (2011) "Gendered Blueprints: Muslim Masculinities in Televangelist Cultures," in R. S. Hegde (ed.) *Circuits of Visibility: Gender and Transnational Media Cultures*, New York: New York University Press, pp. 89–102.

Giddens, A. (1999) *The Runaway World: How Globalization is Reshaping Our Lives*, London: Profile Books.

Gill, R. (2007) "Postfeminist Media Culture: Elements of a Sensibility," *European Journal of Cultural Studies* 10(2): 147–66.

Gopinath, G. (2005) *Impossible Desires: Queer Diasporas and South Asian Public Cultures*, Durham, NC: Duke University Press.

Grewal, I. (2005) *Transnational America: Feminisms, Diasporas, Neoliberalisms*, Durham, NC: Duke University Press.

Grewal, I. and C. Kaplan (1994) *Scattered Hegemonies: Postmodernity and Transnational Feminist Practice*, Minneapolis: University of Minnesota Press.

——(2001) "Global Identities: Theorizing Transnational Studies of Sexuality," *GLQ: A Journal of Lesbian and Gay Studies* 7(4): 663–79.

Grewal, I., A. Gupta and A. Ong (1999) "Introduction: Asian Transnationationalities," *Positions* 7(3): 799–826.

Hall, S. (1997) "The Local and the Global: Globalization and Ethnicity," in A. D. King (ed.) *Culture, Globalization and the World-system*, Minneapolis: University of Minnesota Press.

Hegde, R. S. (2011) "Spaces of Exception: Violence, Technology and the Transgressive Gendered Body in India's Global Call Centers," in R. S. Hegde (ed.) *Circuits of Visibility: Gender and Transnational Media Cultures*, New York: New York University Press, pp. 178–95.

——(2012) "Gender, Globalization and the Politics of Visibility," in T. Maier, M. Thiele, and C. Linke (eds.) *Medien, Öffentlichkeit und Geschlecht in Bewegung: Forschungsperspektiven der kommunikations- und medienwissenschaftlichen Geschlechterforschung (Media, the Public Sphere and Gender in Motion. Research Perspectives in Gender and Media Studies)*, Belefeld, Germany: Transcript, pp. 17–24.

Held, D. (2002) "Cosmopolitanism: Ideas, Realities and Deficits," in D. Held and A. McGrew *Governing Globalization: Power, Authority and Global Governance*, Cambridge: Polity, pp. 305–23.

Jolie, A. (2012) "We Are All Malala." http://www.thedailybeast.com/articles/2012/10/16/angelina-jolie-we-all-are-malala.html.

Katz, C. (2001) "On the Grounds of Globalization: A Topography for Feminist Political Engagement," *Signs: Journal of Women in Culture and Society* 26: 1213–34.

Kim-Puri, H. J. (2005) "Conceptualizing Gender-Sexuality-State-Nation: An Introduction," *Gender & Society* 19(2): 137–59.

Lowe, L. and D. Lloyd (eds.) (1997) *The Politics of Culture in the Shadow of Capital*, Durham, NC: Duke University Press.

Macdonald, M. (2006) "Muslim Women and the Veil: Problems of Image and Voice in Media Representations," *Feminist Media Studies* 6(1): 7–23

Manalansan, M. (2003) *Global Divas: Filipino Gay Men in the Diaspora*, Durham, NC: Duke University Press.

Massad, J. (2002) "Re-orienting Desire: The Gay International and the Arab World," *Public Culture* 14(2): 361–85.

Mazzarella, W. (2003) *Shovelling Smoke: Advertising and Globalization in Contemporary India*, Durham, NC: Duke University Press.

Mitchell, T. (2000) "The Stage of Modernity," in T. Mitchell (ed.) *Questions of Modernity*, Minneapolis: University of Minnesota Press, pp. 1–34.

Mohanty, C. T. (1991) "Under Western Eyes: Feminist Scholarship and Colonial Discourse," in C. T. Mohanty, A. Russo, and L. Torres (eds.) *Third World Women and the Politics of Feminism*, Bloomington: Indiana University Press, pp. 51–80.

——(2003) *Feminism without Borders: Decolonizing Theory, Practicing Solidarity*, Bloomington: Indiana University Press.

Narayan, U. (1997) *Dislocating Cultures: Identities, Traditions and Third World Feminism*, New York: Routledge.

Parameswaran, R. (2011) "E-Racing Color: Gender, Transnational Visual Economies of Beauty in India," in R. S. Hegde (ed.) *Circuits of Visibility: Gender and Transnational Media Cultures*, New York: New York University Press, pp. 68–86.

Povinelli, E. and George Chauncey (1999) "Thinking Sexuality Transnationally," *GLQ: A Journal of Lesbian and Gay Studies* 5(4): 439–50.

Puar, J. (2007) *Terrorist Assemblages: Homonationalism in Queer Times*, Durham, NC: Duke University Press.

Sassen, S. (1991) *The Global City: New York, London, Tokyo*, Princeton, NJ: Princeton University Press.

——(2008) "The Many Scales of the Global: Implications for Theory and for Politics," in R. Krishnaswamy and J. C. Hawley (eds.) *The Post-colonial and the Global*, Minneapolis: University of Minnesota Press, pp. 82–93.

Sayah, R. (2012) "Ex-UK PM Brown Supports Malala's Call for Girls' Education in Pakistan," November 10. http://www.cnn.com/2012/11/10/world/asia/pakistan-malala-gordon-brown/index.html?iid=article_sidebar.

Scott, J. W. (2002) "Feminist Reverberations," *Differences* 13(3): 1–23.

Scott, K. (2007) *Politics of the Veil*, Princeton, NJ: Princeton University Press.

Shohat, E. (2001) "Area Studies, Transnationalism and the Feminist Production of Knowledge," *Signs* 26: 1269–72.

Spivak, C. (1990) *Postcolonial Critic: Interviews, Strategies, Dialogues*, New York: Routledge.

Stabile, C. and D. Kumar (2005) "Unveiling Imperialism: Media, Gender and the War on Afghanistan," *Media, Culture & Society* 27(5): 765–82.

Sunder, R. (1993) *Real and Imagined Women: Gender, Culture, Postcolonialism*, New York: Routledge.

——(ed.) (1999) *Signposts: Gender Issues in Post-independence India*, New Delhi: Kali for Women Press.

Tarlo, E. (2010) *Visibly Muslim: Fashion, Politics, Faith*, London: Berg.

Wallerstein, I. (2004) *World Systems Analysis: An Introduction*, Durham, NC: Duke University Press.

Weinbaum, A. E., L. M. Thomas, P. Ramamurthy, L. M. Poiger, M. Y. Dong, and T. Barlow (2008) *The Modern Girl around the World: Consumption, Modernity and Globalization*, Durham, NC: Duke University Press.

Wilson, A. (2006) "Queering Asia," *Intersections: Gender, History and Culture in the Asian Context* (November) 14. http://intersections.anu.edu.au/issue14/wilson.html.

Wright, M. W. (1999) "The Dialectics of Still Life: Murder, Women and Maquiladoras," *Public Culture* 11(3): 453–73.

Yousafzai, S. (2012) "Malal: With Friends Like Madonna." http://www.thedailybeast.com/articles/2012/10/22/malala-with-friends-like-madonna.html.

# Part II

# MEDIA INDUSTRIES, LABOR, AND POLICY

# 9

# Women and media control
## Feminist interrogations at the macro-level

## Carolyn M. Byerly

> The shrinking ownership of media outlets worldwide into the hands of even fewer (white, western) men ... not only puts issues about news content into a new context, but impacts on the career prospects of its workers, reducing the variety of job opportunities.
>
> (North 2009)

Louise North's (2009) study of the effects of neoliberalism in the news industry in Australia has sweeping implications for women's relationship to the media in other nations as well. In this chapter I explore neoliberalism's broader reach, building on the work that North and other critical media scholars (both women and men) have laid out for feminist media scholarship in the macro-level. That level includes the policy, financial, and ownership structures that together create the environment within which the major media companies operate and produce their products for public consumption.

I explore the three aspects of the macro-level—policy, finance, ownership—and situate women and women's interest within them. Because the macro-level today exists in a climate of neoliberalism, I briefly explain neoliberal philosophy and its impact on women in the media macro-level. This is an ideal time to take stock of the women-and-media relationship at the macro-level. The times demand it. Striving for a global perspective, I review some of the current dynamics, including what is happening within the industries with respect to conglomeration, and explore how these impact women in different parts of the world. Last, a chapter on this subject would be remiss without acknowledging the dialectical nature of women's relationship to media and mentioning some of the ways that women have advanced their agendas for change at the media macro-level. Thus, my overarching mission is to demystify the macro-level for feminist scholars and to encourage further examinations of the many unexplored problems and issues that are so much a part of women's right to communicate in the world.

### Shifting course

Some readers might ask what is the fuss about macro-level media concerns? Indeed, the relative inattention to the macro-level by feminist media researchers since the

1970s has created a kind of invisibility for the broader concerns; this might lead us to think they are less important than the messages and images that have dominated feminist media scholarship. Messages and images (and other properties associated with content) comprise the *micro-level* and should be understood as existing only as the product of human activities and forces. I have already problematized this dominance of content-driven research, suggesting the need for greater feminist analysis of the meso- and macro-levels of mass communication (Byerly 2006, 2012a, 2012b; Byerly and Ross 2006), where the activities and forces responsible for production exist. This is not to say that the micro-level is unimportant. Audiences connect with and react to ideas and meanings purveyed by the media through the content. No wonder that media content, with all of its multiple problematic representations of women, has so often been the subject of both popular and academic feminist criticism. The problematic representations include the enduring issues of distortion, stereotyping, and omission of women's lives in news and other media content. All of these content-oriented issues have required documentation and analysis by feminist media scholars, whose work over some four decades has formed a rich, eclectic international literature.

Some lesser amount of feminist media research has focused on the *meso-level of media*, which is found at the organizational level and comprises the relations of production within the media companies, including professional routines, standards of quality, and a range of technical and creative processes associated with creating content. The meso-level also takes in employee–employer relations, the way that work is organized, and the organizational culture. It is in this realm of the meso-level where content is imagined, made, and imbued with meaning by those carrying out distinct practices in the creative processes, and where that content is disseminated to audiences (Hall 1980; Jeurissen 1997).

Numerous scholars have researched women's employment in media industries. In the United States, this has included Lafky (1993), Johnson (1993), Nicholson (2007) and Cramer (2007), among others. In Canada, women's employment in media has been investigated by Robinson (2005) and McKercher and Mosco (2007), among others. Joseph's (2000) research on women in Indian journalism assesses women's employment on the subcontinent. Gallagher's (1995) 43-nation study, Gender Links' (2010) 15-nation study, and Byerly's (2011) 59-nation study are examples of global-level comparative research on women's employment in media.

## Macro-level and women

The micro- and meso-levels are not necessarily where feminist researchers should choose to look for a deeper analysis of gender in the forces and processes that shape the contemporary commercial media organizations, their employment practices, or their production of content. Gender relations have long been a neglected aspect of media research in the macro-level. Why this is so remains open to speculation. Riordan (2002: 3) posits the possibility that feminist communication scholars have done so little to shine a light on the political, economic, and other structural issues (in the macro-level) because they have historically been unwelcome in overtly economic and political domains reserved for men. She argues for a feminist political economy of media that is ultimately concerned with praxis, i.e. changing what does not serve women's interests (Riordan 2002: 11). Mosco (1996) and McKercher and Mosco (2007) write that feminist analysis at the macro-level should consider women's access to the production of media content (e.g. through decision-making in the industries) as well as to the consumption of that content. Recognizing women media professionals as knowledge workers, Mosco (1996) and McKercher and Mosco (2007) argue for the greater valuing of women's labor in industries where they have been historically marginalized and underpaid. The struggle of women employed in communication industries to gain access, promotion, advancement into decision-making roles, and pay commensurate with that of men is clearly in need of more attention by critical and feminist scholars across the globe. It is within these relations of production at the meso-level that female knowledge workers can also both contest and shape meanings in news and other content in their own interest, as research indicates they have tried to do for many decades (see, for example, Byerly and Ross 2006; Byerly 2012b). However, women cannot exert even limited influence on company policies at the meso-level without strong union backing, and in most nations this has not been forthcoming (particularly under anti-union neoliberalism, as shall be shown).

The macro-level landscape of mass communications is formed by activities and structures associated with finance, investment, ownership and related activities, as well as the varied activities constituting policymaking and governance. This second group of activities determines how media may be owned and operated and whose interests the media industries shall serve. Critical scholars sometimes collapse all of these features into the expression "political economy of the media." For the most part, this realm will be examined in its constituent parts, with specific respect to women's involvement (or not) and interests.

Women's relationship to the macro-level of media matters. Both enormous wealth and enormous power are to be found there. What part of the wealth and power belong to women? Marx's and Engels' (1947: 64) observation that "the class which has the means of material production at its disposal, has control at the same time of the mental production" (i.e. the ideas arising from that production) has always had particular relevance for women, whose realities have been shaped by the ideas of the men who owned the presses and, more recently, the communication industries, and who thereby had the power to determine which messages and images circulated to broader publics. The telecommunications industries today are second only to pharmaceuticals in producing the highest annual revenues in the world (Byerly 2006). Their vast holdings in cable, cellular, broadcast, print news, book publishing, broadband, magazines, film, and other communication formats were expected to reach $2.1 trillion in 2012, growing at a rate of 5.3 percent annually, in spite of global economic uncertainty (Epstein 2012; RCR Wireless 2012). Because all societies, developing and developed alike, are so reliant on telecommunications in its many forms, telecommunications companies are a facilitating factor in socioeconomic development and political process. However, the few data that do exist suggest that women have only the merest presence in the ownership and decision-making levels of these corporations the world over.

CAROLYN M. BYERLY

*Table 9.1* Women's representation at policy level in large global media conglomerates (data assembled from company websites and other industry data, 2012)

| Media conglomerate | Headquarters | Ownership | Estimated assets (US$) | Total on board of directors | Number of women | Percentage women |
|---|---|---|---|---|---|---|
| Disney | USA | Investors | $72.1 billion (2011) | 10 | 4 | 40% |
| News Corp | USA | Investors | $61.9 billion (2011) | 17 | 1 | 6% |
| Vivendi | France | Investors | $55.7 billion (2011) | 12 | 4 | 33% |
| Time Warner | USA | Investors | $48.3 billion (2011) | 11 | 2 | 18% |
| Bertelsmann AG | Germany | Family | $27.0 billion (2012) | 21 | 5 | 24% |
| Viacom | USA | Investors | $14.9 billion (2011) | 11 | 2 | 18% |
| Grupo Televisa | Mexico | Investors | $14.7 billion (2011) | 20 | 2 | 10% |
| Times of India Group | India | Family | $1 billion (2009) | 9 | 3 | 33% |
| Lagardère | France | Investors | $10.9 billion (2011) | 6 | 1 | 17% |
| Naspers | South Africa | Investors | $8.5 million (2010) | 14 | 3 | 21% |

In fact, women are grossly underrepresented in the policymaking positions of the world's largest media conglomerates, as shown in Table 9.1. The table, composed of data from company websites, contains the very largest players on the global stage (Disney, News Corp, Vivendi, and Time Warner), together with the largest players in several specific nations. Table 9.1 illustrates several points relevant to this chapter's concerns. The first is that media conglomeration is dominated by huge American and European companies. This phenomenon was much a part of critical scholarship on cultural imperialism in the 1970s and 1980s (e.g. Schiller 1989), as well as a major part of the call by leaders in non-aligned (developing) nations for a New World Information and Communications Order that could begin to shift greater power and information resources from the Global North to the Global South (Gallagher 2011).

The second point illustrated by Table 9.1 is the extent to which women are marginalized in media governance around the world. This is not to say that such is true in all companies, or in all nations. As recent research (Byerly 2011) revealed, the representation of women at the top (ownership, policy, and management) of a few of the 522 news companies surveyed by researchers in 59 nations showed considerable progress, or even relative parity for men and women in governance and top management. Such was true in Russia, for example, where women hold 42 percent of the positions in governance and 59 percent of the positions in top management among the 14 Russian news companies surveyed (Byerly 2011: 297–8). But the overwhelming finding in Byerly's study for International Women's Media Foundation was that men held three-fourths of the seats on governing boards and in executive

108

ranks at the vast majority of the companies surveyed. This finding echoed and reaffirmed Gallagher's (1995) earlier research on 239 media companies in 43 nations.

Among the largest conglomerates, as shown in Table 9.1, the trend is marginalization of women at the occupational levels associated with policy setting and other decision-making. Only the Disney company shows progress toward gender parity in its board of directors, with 4 of 10 directors female (40 percent)—a stark comparison with giant News Corporation's one female on its 17-member board (6 percent). Whether or not women in governance at Disney possess a feminist conscience and/or are able to exert a pro-female perspective on the creative aspects of the company is open to question. Miami University's Department of Psychology, which hosts the Psybersite website, raises cogent feminist issues about how Disney films portray women as subservient and submissive. It says:

> Typically women are shown in a position of princess, queen, or homemaker ...
> [and] subservient to the male characters who typically display forceful
> behaviors to get what they want ... [Women always become] the possession
> of their husband or another male. For instance, Ariel is handed over from
> her father to Prince Eric [in *The Little Mermaid*], Jasmine to Aladdin, and
> Belle to the Beast [in *Beauty and the Beast*].
>
> (Psybersite 1999)

In fact, Meehan's (2002) feminist political economy research on Disney has led her to conclude that the corporation's primary concern about women is their role as consumers, i.e. as the audience for women-oriented programming on Disney's Lifetime cable channel or in theatrical films, or as the buyer of Disney's extensive line of products for children and adults. In Meehan's analysis, women's ability to increase Disney profits is foremost among the company's gender concerns. The largest media conglomerate in the world, Disney Corporation's tentacles reach into all corners of the globe. In 2011, Disney owned 12 film and theater studios, 2 music companies, 37 television networks or stations (one-third of them ESPN-related sports networks), 27 radio stations, 10 book publishing houses, 10 theme parks and resorts, and 19 other entities, including apparel, toys, food, stationery, and other lines ("Who Owns What" 2011).

Steeves (2007: 197) reminds us of research showing that simply putting more women in decision-making levels of the media is a panacea for women's marginalization neither in employment (meso-level) nor in media content (micro-level). As she writes, "Patriarchal political-economic power structures are so entrenched in all aspects of society that other kinds of change are also needed." Among the strategies for resistance and change she mentions are political activism, alternative media, and policy changes.

## Economics and policy

Economist Hazel Henderson (1995) is among the feminist scholars who look around the world and proclaim that the vast global financial system is a woman's issue. In considering the location of the media in that global system, media scholar Robin

Mansell (2009: 35) further observes that economic and political forces "give rise to the social dynamics of exclusion." These observations, taken together, help us to problematize women's marginal financial relationship to media systems today.

Not only do women in major media companies around the world hold few policy-related positions, but women at the top as well as in other ranks are underpaid. While information and communication technologies continue to be a driving force for development and change in societies today, women have little to do with financial or policy decisions. In one recent study of women's status in these highly significant digital (i.e. cable and other informational) industries, the European Commission (2009) concluded that not only were women underrepresented in top jobs (e.g. those on boards) of the largest information and communications technology (ICT) companies, but the gender pay gap was greatest for women in managerial positions. Women's greatest relationship to the new digital world, the report said, was as users of the internet and other services—not as owners, managers, or even researchers or developers of the technologies.

One irony in this is that new research by Credit Suisse AG Research Institute (2012) indicates that companies benefit financially from having more women in top roles. After studying 2,400 companies around the world, the Swiss-based Institute found that companies with at least one woman on their boards delivered higher average returns on equity and better average growth in the six years examined. More relevant here is that the fewest women on boards were found in the information technology sector (out of ten sectors examined), where 52.5 percent of companies studied had no women on their boards and another 47.5 percent had between one and three women (Credit Suisse 2012: 9). The greatest exclusion of women from corporate boards was in Emerging Asia, Developed Asia, and Latin America. The Swiss study recognized that progress has been made in many companies since 2005 (the beginning point for analysis); national policies requiring gender equity and women's advancement to the top of the corporate ladder seem to be correlated (Credit Suisse 2012: 25).

In fact, women's lack of access to the organizational and economic realms of most media companies signifies the broader problem of their marginalization within these realms societally. In other words, even when women do corner an amount of capital for a media project, it is typically smaller in scale and less secure in its future than those of men. The Swiss study cited barriers to women's financial equality responsible for institutionalizing gender disparity as being social typecasting (i.e. stereotypes of women's inferiority), the double burden (i.e. dual responsibilities of workplace and home), and lack of social structures to support working women (e.g. tax breaks, on-site nurseries, job sharing options, etc.). Steeves (2007) is among those who point out that under capitalism (i.e. the "free market," which institutionalizes patriarchy organizationally and economically) women's labor has always been exploited and women have had lower status in their societies. This situation has deepened under neoliberal reforms since the 1970s.

## Neoliberalism

British communication scholar Nick Couldry (2010) defines neoliberalism as public policy strongly dedicated to the free market, including "strong fiscal discipline, reductions in public expenditures, tax reform to encourage market investors, interest rates determined by markets and not the state, competitive exchange rates, trade liberalization, the encouragement of foreign direct investment, privatization of public services and assets, deregulation of financial and other markets, and the securing of private property rights" (Couldry 2010: 5). Neoliberalism has roots going back to the 1940s, but its principles found traction in a number of nations in the 1960s and 1970s, when conservative business leaders were trying to reverse successful gains being made by trade unions, women, and minority rights groups. Harvey (2005) puts neoliberalism's defining moment in 1973 with General Pinochet's successful coup against Chile's democratically elected socialist President Salvador Allende. The coup was preceded by several years of systematic consolidation of Latin American business associations in Peru and Chile by business elites who were able to institutionalize pro-corporate laws and regulatory reforms in government (Silva and Durand 1998). Neoliberal measures came into practice globally through the administrations of President Ronald Reagan in the United States and Prime Minister Margaret Thatcher in Great Britain during the 1980s. Reagan and Thatcher instituted privatization and pro-corporate policies that laid the groundwork for deregulation of media and other industries, leading to widespread mergers and acquisitions that would continue through to the present time.

Today's mega-media corporations are one result: only a handful of giant conglomerates own the majority of newspapers, magazines, broadcast, cable, book publishing, film, computer software, and other media. Most of these media companies are global enterprises with extensive reach into other nations. In the case of US-based conglomerates, which are the largest and most powerful, their products become the vehicles for global distribution of American culture and values in films, television programs, magazines, etc. Table 9.1 illustrates this in better detail, showing the extent of US and other Western corporate dominance in mass communication. German-based Bertelsmann AG, for example, owns book publishing companies, television and radio stations, and other media in 63 nations. The problem of media conglomeration also manifests itself regionally, as with Mexico-based Grupo Televisa, which has a dominant presence throughout Latin America (Free Press 2012). Media conglomeration under neoliberalism has eliminated untold numbers of jobs in news and other media industries, and limited the number of voices and political perspectives. Couldry (2010) and McChesney (2004) are among those who point out the anti-democratic threats bound up in these dynamics. After all, where is dissent to be voiced on any scale under corporate media hegemony? While alternative media (including women's media) have historically served this purpose, their reach has always been limited.

## Charting harm, struggle, and change

Neoliberalism is a deeply gendered phenomenon, and women have suffered the most, the world over. Caribbean feminist economist Peggy Antrobus (2004) emphasizes that the neoliberal agenda put a choke hold on broad-based socioeconomic development, particularly in the Third World, depriving women of advancement.

The United States, Great Britain, and those who marched with them used the mechanisms of the International Monetary Fund (IMF) and World Bank to impose pro-market structural reforms on indebted nations. Antrobus said that this "policy framework demonstrated as nothing had done before, the gender and class biases inherent in an economic model that focused on economic growth while apparently ignoring social, cultural, and political factors" (Antrobus 2004: 68). Nations receiving loans were required to eliminate social spending, for example, which was used to fund health and other family services, nutritional programs for children, and expansion of education (including to females), among other things. Africa, the Caribbean, and Latin America were particularly hard hit. Labor unions, which had championed expanded employment and better wages (including for women) were targeted and substantially weakened under neoliberalism. The assertion of macro-economic policies on weaker nations by the powerful ones also ushered in what Antrobus calls a "pattern of neo-colonial relations that were to be more insidious than those of colonialism" (2004: 74).

Neoliberal policies in all sectors, including media, have been carried out, for the most part, without women's broader understanding or involvement, at either the national or international levels. In the US, which prides itself on freedom of press and speech, the problem is no less serious than elsewhere as regards women's exclusion from the policy arena. Female representation in the Congress, the national bi-cameral legislative body, is still only 17 percent. At any given time only one or two women are likely to sit on the five-member Federal Communications Commission which regulates media ownership (among other things). There is no evidence these women have been able to influence media policy on women's behalf. Even a vibrant, well-orchestrated citizens' media justice and reform movement, which formed in 2003 specifically to protest media conglomeration and its effects, has not been able to move the broader public's, including women's, media ownership agendas forward. Today, 95 percent of the broadcast (radio, television) companies in the United States licensed to serve the public interest are owned and operated by very wealthy men and their mega-corporations (US GAO 2008), as are nearly all major daily newspapers and other media firms. While this is an established fact, neither Congress (through new laws) nor the Federal Communication Commission (through incentives or other regulatory measures) has taken steps to change the situation.

Gallagher's (2011) useful historical analysis of women's inability to enter into and exert influence at some of the major international media policy forums notes that even politically engaged women have lacked experience to help them grasp the complexity of the policy process or familiarity with the laws or other measures in the policy domain. Instead, she notes, many women have opted for smaller-scale policies within their nations, such as workplace equality or portrayal of violence against women by media companies. The strategy undertaken in Southern African nations by the Gender Links organization, which takes a multinational approach to advance greater gender equality in media companies, offers one model for an alternate way of tackling the problem. Gender Links' strategy includes training and consultation for media managers, provision of model companies, as well as research that monitors progress on a periodic basis, and an annual awards ceremony that recognizes companies that have demonstrated greater gender equality (Gender Links 2012).

As I have shown, indicators are available that women have not been able to enter fully into the media macro-level in finance, policymaking or ownership. And yet the research that bears these indicators is still greatly incomplete. Feminist media scholars are challenged to research the subject using diverse methodologies. We still lack baseline studies on where women are located in financial, policymaking and governance roles associated with media, as well as whether women in such roles are able to effect changes that benefit women in some way. Some recent research along this line has been cited throughout this chapter, but the area remains ripe for further examination. We also lack case study research on where and when women's organized effort to institute gender equality in national media or company-level media policies has been successful or failed. These efforts need careful documentation and analysis from a feminist perspective. Geertsema's (2010) examination of Gender Links' campaigns in Southern Africa offers a model for similar studies. We also lack comparative analysis of national-level policies to determine how workplace laws affect women in media companies, as well as to identify media-related laws and regulations that enable women to more fully participate in media operations. Research by Sarikakis and Nguyen (2009) on European Union media policy is a beacon for what might be done on other nations and regions. It is in the interest of feminist scholarship that this important body of work be undertaken soon.

# References

Antrobus, P. (2004) *The Global Women's Movement*, London and New York: Zed Books.

Byerly, C. M. (2006) "Feminist Research in an Era of Globalization," *Revista de Estudios para el Desarrollo Social de la Comunicación* 3: 39–52.

——(2011) *Global Report on the Status of Women in News Media*, Washington, DC: International Women's Media Foundation.

——(2012a) "Gender, Justice and the Media: Shifting Our Agendas to Media Ownership," *Derecho a Comunicar* (special issue on women and communication studies) 4: 21–32.

——(2012b) "Women and the Geography of Media Scholarship," in K. Ross (ed.) *The Handbook of Gender, Sex and the Media*, Chichester: Wiley-Blackwell, pp. 3–19.

Byerly, C. M. and K. Ross (2006) *Women and Media: A Critical Introduction*, Malden, MA: Blackwell.

Cotter, C. (2011) "Women's Place at the Fourth Estate: Constraints on Voice, Text, and Topic," *Journal of Pragmatics* 43: 2519–33.

Couldry, N. (2010) *Why Voice Matters: Culture and Politics after Neoliberalism*, Los Angeles, CA: Sage Publications.

Council of Europe (2009) "Not Enough News Coverage of Women, Says PACE," Parliamentary Assembly, Council of Europe, March 24. http://www.assembly.coe.int/ASP/NewsManager.

Cramer, J. (2007) "Radio: The More Things Change ... The More They Stay the Same," in P. J. Creedon and J. Cramer (eds.) *Women in Mass Communication*, 3rd edition, Thousand Oaks, CA: Sage Publications, pp. 59–72.

Credit Suisse (2012) *Gender Diversity and Corporate Performance*, Zurich, Switzerland: Credit Suisse Research Institute, July 13. https://www.credit-suisse.com/newsletter/doc/gender_diversity.pdf.

Epstein, Z. (2012) "Global Telecommunications Industry Revenue to Reach $2.1 trillion in 2012." http://www.bgr.com/2012/01/05/global-telecommunications-industry-revenue-to-reach-2-1-trillion-in-2012/.

European Commission (2009) "Women and ICT Status Report." http://ec.europa.eu/information_ society/activities/itgirls/doc/women_ict_report.pdf.

Fourth Bi-Annual European PWN Boardwomen Monitoring (2011) Women on Boards, February 25. http://www.europeanpwn.net/index.php?article.id=8.

Free Press (2012) "Ownership Chart." http://www.freepress.net/ownership/chart/.

Freedman, D. (2008) The Politics of Media Policy, Cambridge: Polity.

Gallagher, M. (1995) An Unfinished Story: Gender Patterns in Media Employment, Paris: UNESCO.

——(2001) Gender-Setting: New Agendas for Media Monitoring and Advocacy, London: Zed Books.

——(2011) "Gender and Communication Policy: Struggling for Space," in R. Mansell and M. Raboy (eds.) The Handbook of Global Communication Policy, Malden, MA: Wiley-Blackwell, pp. 451–66.

Geertsema, M. (2010) "Challenging the Lion in Its Den: Dilemmas of Gender and Media Activism in South Africa," Ecquid Novi: African Journalism Studies 31(1): 68–88.

Gender Links (2010) "Glass Ceiling Research." http://www.genderlinks.org.za/page/media-glass-ceiling-research.

——(2012) Gender Links website. http:// genderlinks.org.za/.

Hall, S. (1980) "Encoding/Decoding," in S. Hall, D. Hobson, A. Love, and P. Willis (eds.) Culture, Media, Language, London: Hutchinson.

Harvey, D. (2005) A Brief History of Neoliberalism, Oxford: Oxford University Press.

Henderson, H. (1995) "Opportunities in the Global Casino," in N. Heyzer (ed.) A Commitment to the World's Women: Perspectives on Development for Beijing and Beyond, New York: UN Development Fund for Women (Unifem), pp. 185–90.

Jeurissen, R. (1997) "Integrating Micro, Meso and Macro Levels in Business Ethics," Ethical Perspectives 4(2): 246–54.

Johnson, S. (1993) "Magazines: Women's Employment and Status in the Magazine Industry," in P. Creedon (ed.) Women in Mass Communication, 2nd edition, Newbury Park, CA: Sage Publications, pp. 134–53.

Joseph, A. (2000) Making News: Women in Journalism, New Delhi: Penguin Books.

Lafky, S. A. (1993) "The Progress of Women and People of Color in the U.S. Journalistic Workforce," in P. Creedon (ed.) Women in Mass Communication, 2nd edition, Newbury Park, CA: Sage Publications, pp. 87–103.

Lopez, V. (2001) "Women Bring a Certain Look and Feeling to News," Nieman Reports (Winter): 100–2.

Mansell, R. (2009) "Media and Global Divides: An Introduction," Nordicom Review 30: 35–7.

Marx, K. and F. Engels (1947) The German Ideology: Part One, New York: International Publishers.

McChesney, R. W. (2004) The Problem of the Media, New York: Monthly Review Books.

McKercher, C. and V. Mosco (2007) Knowledge Workers in the Information Society, Lanham, MD: Lexington Books.

Meehan, E. R. (2002) "Gendering the Commodity Audience: Critical Media Research, Feminism, and Political Economy," in E. R. Meehan and E. Riordan (eds.), Sex & Money: Feminist Political Economy in the Media, Minneapolis: University of Minnesota Press, pp. 209–22.

Mosco, V. (1996) The Political Economy of Communication, Thousand Oaks, CA: Sage Publications.

Nicholson, J. O. (2007) "Women in Newspaper Journalism (Since the 1990s)," in P. J. Creedon and J. Cramer (eds.) Women in Mass Communication, 3rd edition, Thousand Oaks, CA: Sage Publications, pp. 35–46.

North, L. (2009) "Gendered Experiences of Industry Change and the Effects of Neoliberalism," Journalism Studies 10(4): 506–21.

Psybersite (1999) Department of Psychology, Miami University. http://www.units.muohio.edu/psybersite/disney/disneygender.shtml.

RCR Wireless (n.d.) "Global Telecom Industry Revenue to Grow at 5.3% Annually." http://www.rcrwireless.com.

Riordan, E. (2002) "Intersections and New Directions: On Feminism and Political Economy," in E. R. Meehan and E. Riordan (eds.) *Sex & Money: Feminism and Political Economy in the Media*, Minneapolis: University of Minnesota Press, pp. 3–15.

Robinson, G. J. (2005) *Gender, Journalism and Equity: Canadian, U.S. and European Perspectives*, Cresskill, NJ: Hampton Press.

Sarikakis, K. and E. T. Nguyen (2009) "The Trouble with Gender: Media Policy and Gender Mainstreaming in the European Union," *European Integration* 31(2): 201–16.

Schiller, H. I. (1989) *Culture, Inc.: The Corporate Takeover of Public Expression*, Oxford: Oxford University Press.

Silva, E. and F. Durand (1998) "Organized Business and Politics in Latin America," in F. Durand and E. Silva (eds.) *Organized Business, Economic Change, Democracy in Latin America*, Miami, FL: North-South Center Press, University of Miami, pp. 1–50.

Steeves, L. (2007) "Global Context of Women in Communication," in P. J. Creedon and J. Cramer (eds.) *Women in Mass Communication*, 3rd edition, Thousand Oaks, CA: Sage Publications, pp. 191–206.

Sturm, L. (n.d.) *The Interaction between Micro-, Meso- and Macro-levels*. http://www.tiss.zdv.uni-tue bingen.de/webroot/sp/barrios/themeB1b.html.

US GAO (2008) *Media Ownership*, Washington, DC: United States Government Accounting Office, March.

"Who Owns What" (2011) *Columbia Journalism Review* website. http://www.cjr.org/resources/?c=disney.

"Woman on Board" (2012) Women Elect website. http://womenelect.org/2012/06/27/woman-on-board/.

# 10

# Risk, innovation, and gender in media conglomerates

## Ben Aslinger

This chapter examines how the dialectic of risk and innovation in media conglomerates and large media firms affects the representation and construction of gender and sexuality in media texts. A key dimension of this analysis is an exploration of how feminist and queer cultural labor are enabled and channeled through operational norms governing production and distribution in media firms. Media conglomerates are poised to subsidize and fund representations of gender and sexuality that are, or will, become mass mediated, but they also are risk averse. Conglomerates can override local homophobia or sexism in ways often unavailable to local minority producers, but in their search for niche markets of significant size, texts produced within conglomerates often elide differences (and diversity) within minority target markets even as they privilege particular types of male, female, and queer subjects that most closely resemble ideal consumers. These erasures affect which types of cultural producers have access to capital, which styles and modes of audiovisual production are most common, and which narratives are told. In this chapter, I examine the ways in which many feminist and queer perspectives on media conglomeration occupy a middle ground between the binary of neoliberal capital and anti-monopoly dreams of hyperlocal media. I then illustrate how norms and practices in the music industry render music scenes and forms comprehensible to a larger public while potentially distorting the ties of these forms and scenes to gender, sexuality, race, and ethnicity.

## Conglomeration in media studies

Beginning with the pioneering work of Herbert Schiller (1989, 1992), media scholars and political economists have worked to assess the state of diversity in media ownership as well as the level of competition in local, national, and global media markets. Scholars such as Ben Bagdikian (1997) and Robert McChesney (1999, 2004) joined Schiller in the critique of the decreasing diversity of major media owners and raised concerns about what an oligopoly of media firms does (or can do) to local, national, and transnational media cultures. Popular-music scholar and historian

David Sanjek argues that "efforts at monopolization of all media by transglobal enterprises transform individuals from citizens into consumers and consumers alone" (1998: 176). McChesney's (2004) focus on news and public affairs programming and his focus on resuscitating forms of media localism have gained significant traction in the media reform movement.

In the USA, practices of media deregulation accelerated through the decisions of the 1980s Federal Communication Commission (FCC), whose chairman, Mark Fowler, infamously called television "a toaster with pictures." Such policies were advanced even further during Michael Powell's tenure at the FCC, when ownership caps and other regulations were lifted. The passage of the Telecommunications Act of 1996 kicked off a mergers and acquisitions frenzy that further reduced the number of major media owners and resulted in an even smaller oligarchy of mainstream media owners in the United States. The passage of the Digital Millennium Copyright Act (DMCA) in 1998 worked to protect major media industries' intellectual property holdings while effectively trapping the development of new media enterprises in a convoluted legal web.

To many scholars of political economy as well as global and transnational media studies the increase in conglomeration and an oligopoly of media owners raises fears of cultural imperialism—fears that local media diversity will be trampled and that global media cultures might become homogenized. Fears of cultural imperialism often are based in ideas of Americanization, given the historical power of Hollywood studios, broadcast networks, and US-based major recording labels. However, Americanization visited upon other countries by the US is not the only potential form of cultural imperialism. While I focus primarily on Anglophone media in North American contexts, Koichi Iwabuchi (2002), who focuses on Japanization as a cultural and sociotechnical force, encourages us to think about the possibility of other "-izations" besides Americanization. While I barely scratch the surface of the impact of media conglomeration on locally inflected understandings of gender and sexuality in this essay, Mizuko Ito's work on the "media mix" in Japan (2006) and the emerging work on the Korean wave (also known as Hallyu) point to the ways in which corporate control and economic flows motivating other "-izations" may impact the production and expression of gender, youth culture, and transnational media exchange.

Conglomeration has been praised by industrial forces who seek to maximize efficiencies and maximize profits. Robert Burnett writes:

> Upstream vertical integration implies broadcasters moving into production, developing their own skills and buying library programmes; hardware manufacturers moving into production, mainly through acquisitions; and distributors buying into production. Downstream vertical integration refers to producers moving into broadcasting through mergers and acquisitions; and broadcasters moving into distribution.
>
> (Burnett 1996: 14)

Perfect synergy is seen as the ideal marriage of vertical integration and horizontal integration. If synergy promised pie-in-the-sky economic returns and reduced risk, it failed to live up to its proponents' utopian hopes. Sanjek argues, "The commercial prospects of many media conglomerates have proven to pale in light of the excessive debt connected to mergers, the inability to cut overhead or put efficiency plans in action, and the failure of much of the product placed before an oversaturated public" (1998: 177). Sanjek points to the 1990s struggles and upheavals in the Warner Music Group to illustrate that "self-destructive practices can lie behind the corporate façade" (1998: 177).

Techno-utopian pundits and Silicon Valley evangelists often take issue with claims of media conglomeration's effects, but discussions of contemporary media must take seriously the political economies of emerging media. Graeme Turner writes of the academic popularization of digital media studies: "Convergence culture and new media studies are both based on a conviction that the new media operate in ways that are more participatory, more community-oriented, and less commercially venal than the 'Big Media' conglomerates that prevailed during the pre-Internet, broadcasting era" (2012: 94). I take issue with Turner's claim that digital media scholars, analysts, and participants are not interested in power; digital media studies acknowledges the ways that "Big Media" have resisted disintermediation by investing in, acquiring, or becoming stakeholders in disruptive "new" and "social" media firms. Turner does not acknowledge how scholars raise concerns about the corporate takeover and control of web-based communication and the shift of the internet from a grassroots, peer-to-peer (P2P) gift economy. As Nancy Baym (2011) argues, user-generated content only makes sense as an expression because so much content is professionally created and geared towards greasing the wheels of commerce. As Aida Hozic (1999) notes, in our contemporary world it may make sense to think about the economic and cultural clout, not of Hollywood, but of Siliwood—a marriage of firms belonging to the imaginary of Silicon Valley and firms belonging to the imaginary of Hollywood. Regardless of whether one attributes cultural hegemony or homogenizing force to neoliberal media capital, more and more mainstream media firms are owned by fewer and fewer companies. The ownership, control, and design of digital media platforms and experiences create affordances while constraining communication.

I close this section by profiling a middle-of-the-road position between those who argue that media conglomeration and ownership are no longer as important as they used to be and those who posit that corporate ownership directly leads to negative media effects. Scholars such as John Caldwell (2008) and David Hesmondhalgh (2007) think through the connections between ownership, the generation and evolution of corporate cultures, and media production and distribution. Writing about music industry strategies in the 1990s, Keith Negus profiles Time Warner's late 1990s strategy of "divesting themselves of repertoire catalogues (dumping artists and songs) and using the money to buy into new distribution networks (the routes along which the artists and songs will travel)" (1999: 33). He also examines Bertelsmann Music Group's (BMG's) conservatism, where funds were not made available for expansion and speculative investment in the acquisition of labels, but executives were "encouraged to operate with a small artist roster, maximizing the potential of performers such as Annie Lennox rather than signing new artists" (1999: 39). Of these and other recording industry strategies, Negus argues, "It is necessary to think away from organizational culture in a narrow sense and towards the broader cultural patterns that intersect with an organization, to think away from *culture within an industry* and towards an *industry within culture*" (1999: 82; italics in original). In Negus's examples, it is not that conglomeration necessarily and/or inherently leads to particular strategies of risk aversion or of channeled visibility for particular groups of creative laborers (even though conglomeration does seem to lead firms down the path towards these outcomes). Rather, particular cultures of management and investment in media conglomerates (relationships between corporate divisions and headquarters, sector autonomy, and division capitalization) result in outcomes with important implications for creative labor and for the representation of gendered, racial, and sexual identities in mass media.

## Feminist and queer perspectives on media conglomeration and consumption

Perhaps striking is the concurrent evolution of feminist and queer perspectives on the constitutive role of consumption, especially media consumption, with concerns about how media capital and ownership limit what can be produced and said about gender and sexuality. Carolyn Byerly (2004) notes the long trajectory of feminist scholarship in "gendering neoliberalism." Michael Curtin notes the complicated connections and disjunctures between the structure of media markets and gender when he writes: "Media firms actually benefit from the transnational circulation of multiple and alternative representations of feminine desire. Although this does not necessarily democratize media, in most societies it significantly expands the range of feminine imagery available in popular culture" (1999: 55). He chronicles a move from the organization of media industries "under the rubric of Fordism" to the current period of transition, "paradoxically characterized by both transnationalization and fragmentation" (1999: 60). Media scholars and critics interested in the limitations and constraints on media capital must contend with the enabling centrifugal forces of capital that have helped give rise to and/or popularized alternative constructions of gender and embodiment and gendered and sexual identifications while at the same time recognizing that representations of gender and sexuality are embedded within power relations.

Consumption (even of mainstream texts and consumer experiences) is seen as something that helps subjects identify and construct their gendered and sexual identities. Scholarship points to the foundational role of capital, specifically media capital, in the project of self-making. For example, John D'Emilio (1993) observed that changes within American capitalism enabled new forms of queer subjectivity and queer world-making. Nan Enstad (1999) examined how working-class women used the tools of consumer culture. Kelly Schrum (2004) examined the ways that mainstream industries helped create the idea of the teenager and enabled the formation of teen girl culture in the 1920–45 period. On the other hand, Amy Villarejo argues that we cannot lose sight of the fact that media scholars analyze "*industrially produced* sexual rhetoric, queerness literally brought to you by Sony or GE (General Electric)" (2009: 51–2). Rosemary Hennessy argues that "not only is much recent gay visibility aimed at producing new and potentially lucrative markets, but, as in most marketing strategies, money, not liberation, is the bottom line" (2000: 112). Danae Clark expressed this sentiment in arguing that advertisements invite in gay viewers only as consumers, thus negating any gay politics. Gay advertisements champion "a liberal discourse of choice that separates sexuality from politics and connects them both with consumerism" (1995: 147–8). However, Villarejo also argues that the antithesis of media conglomeration, a hyperlocal citizen-driven form of media regulation and organization, will leave little space for gender and sexual alterity:

> But "the people" have never been very pro-queer, especially those in "the labour movement" (what labour movement, by the way?) McChesney hopes will lead the digital revolution. Neither do many media activists want to remake educational television into sexual education, or into a haven for gender nonconformity: PBS consistently withdraws support for queer programming.
>
> (Villarejo 2009: 59)

Independently produced work is great, but, as Hesmondhalgh argues, many "indie" firms go under; those who work in them burn out, leaving established firms as the major long-term players in defining production and distribution norms and in representing possible identities and identifications. Thus, indie firms deal with issues such as professionalization and whether to partner or collaborate with larger firms if they wish to grow or stay afloat (1999: 36). Megan Mullen (2003) and others have argued that local media are most diverse in localities that are the most diverse, meaning that local media are at their best in communities like San Francisco and New York, where local media can reach a diverse audience. Conglomerates have the ability to program, produce, and distribute materials that might never see the light of day in local communities (e.g. substantive African American media content in northern rural Maine) but that can reach audiences on a national or transnational level. While texts such as *Will and Grace* or *Glee* have problems and elisions, the fact that these series introduced many viewers (including me) to discussions about the nature of gender and sexuality cannot be ignored. As Villarejo notes, texts like these are unlikely to emerge out of a media system grounded in and based on localism.

Villarejo's ambivalence is endemic in feminist and queer media scholarship as scholars seek to criticize and understand both systems of representations and systems of production. Our ambivalence about conglomeration may have something to do with the fact that when we talk about conglomeration, we may be talking about conglomeration in the "mainstream" national and transnational media industries, conglomeration in minority/niche media ownership and distribution, or a hybrid of the two. All forms of conglomeration raise concerns about risk versus innovation, but the second form more acutely raises concerns regarding how identity politics, profit-making imperatives, and firm survival mix.

Drawing on Bagdikian's work to address mainstream media monopolization, Joshua Gamson (2003) urges more research on ownership patterns in minority media. He writes, "The dynamics and impact of media ownership in the media systems of marginalized or minority groups are not well understood" (2003: 257). More importantly, Gamson asserts that "the gay and lesbian 'monopoly' controversy points out how much remains to be understood about the dynamics and impact of ownership concentration in the media of marginalized groups" (2003: 257). Increasing conglomeration in publishing, audiovisual production, and web-based products and services made LGBT media more visible and arguably more widely available, but observers worried that conglomeration resulted in a chilling effect on news and political debate and that conglomeration would further reify dominant constructions of LGBT markets, demographics, and taste cultures (Aslinger 2010; Sender 2004).

Fred Fejes and Kevin Petrich encourage scholars concerned with LGBT representations to analyze gay media with the goal of assessing how elements of "heterosexually-defined homosexuality" work to make the creation of "affirmative gay and lesbian identities" more difficult (1993: 412). Gay media must be analyzed in order to show that when "political pressure to conform to heterosexist assumptions about sexuality and the media increases," "the creative vitality and diversity of the community decreases" (1993: 412). It may seem obvious that representations of LGBT identity emerging from publicly traded media conglomerates and their respective divisions have been authored, financed, and/or regulated by "straights." This concern becomes even more pointed if and when firms, publications, or platforms previously controlled by members of the queer community suddenly become parts of a bigger machine that may or may not privilege the same social, political, and cultural values of queer authorship and community as the original owners. In the case of ventures such as Logo, which was constructed within the Viacom empire as a network for queer audiences and attracted cultural producers such as Patrik-Ian Polk (Aslinger 2009), a conglomerate's attention to gender and/or sexual minorities may wane if the return on investment is insufficient; at the time of this writing, rumors abound that Logo's programming is intended to focus more on the tastes of straight women than those of LGBT demographics.

Queer media also pose problems both to the privileging of the local in media reform movements and to any easy celebration of consumer culture. Local indie media texts in feminist and queer media may take a hegemonic position within the local community (especially in the queer metropoles of New York, San Francisco, and Los Angeles), while texts with wider national or international audiences can move beyond the tastes of the local majority to address a wider swath of gay viewers. However, many texts that reach more readers/viewers still suffer from a focus on specific forms of LGBT urbanity. Mary Gray writes, "Mass media consistently narrate rural LGBT identities as out of place, necessarily estranged from authentic (urban) queerness. These images teach rural youth to look anywhere but homeward for LGBT identities" (2009: 12). Katherine Sender notes:

> Marketers frequently made urban-coastal, rural-heartland comparisons, and displayed what seemed to me a false modesty along the lines of "this is what we do (think, feel, wear) in the city, but we don't really know what goes on there," but have few intentions of going "there" to find out. Claiming a lack of knowledge about the heartland may actually elevate gay marketers' subcultural capital, because it suggests their immersion in a particularly hip urban subculture.
>
> (Sender 2004: 80)

For Sender, such assumptions, knowledges, and biases generate notions of the LGBT audience and the kinds of texts, platforms, and experiences that both big gay media and big media offer up for public consumption and consideration.

## The limits of riot grrrl, queercore, and Latin music

Mainstream music firms often provide opportunities for previously marginalized cultural producers to break the national sound barrier. Nevertheless, the ways that firms manage tensions between risk and innovation provide interesting illustrations of the complicated politics of feminist and queer perspectives on media capital. For example, the emergence of M.I.A. as a hip hop artist and the creation of her star text is both symptomatic of transnational flows in the age of conglomerate capital and critical of the very systems that enable and fuel her claim to celebrity. Conglomerate culture makes it difficult to make sense of artists such as M.I.A. who embody transgressive politics and positionalities but help line major label coffers.

An interesting illustration of the tensions surrounding gender and sexuality in the recording industry is the 1990s emergence of riot grrrl. Emerging as a movement inspired by punk and fueled by a do-it-yourself (DIY) ethos, riot grrrl sought to give girls and women increased access to music making and safer access to concert going. Bands such as Bikini Kill, Sleater-Kinney, and Le Tigre melded music with feminist politics and reclaimed hard rock instrumentation and generic styles most often associated with an aggressive, masochistic masculinity. Riot grrrl musicians and artists were worried about the refraction and/or potential reduction of gender, genre, performance style, content, musical meaning, and modes of cultural production if their music moved from the margins closer to the center and came under the control of mainstream musical capital and the power of executives at the major record labels. Joanne Gottlieb and Gayle Wald write, "Such major-label recognition can be construed as particularly threatening to the musical, stylistic and political integrity of women performers, who are simultaneously pressured to tone down their music (through 'softer sounds,' less guitar feedback, and more elaborate, even cosmetic production) and to dress up their image (through new hairstyles, makeup, and clothing)" (1994: 251). While the major labels had the most power to get music in front of millions of the very young women riot grrrl musicians sought to inspire, many riot grrrl bands valued independence over reach. The nationalization of riot grrrl and its mainstreaming risked diminishing the control over the movement by women (Kearney 1997). In a radio landscape increasingly defined by data-driven (and often reductive) constructions of format, artists risked being asked to tone down the rough edges of their sound or alter their music to make it more commercially palatable to mass audiences. Given constructions of artist and repertoire personnel as "A&R men" in corporate lore and industrial jargon, riot grrrl performers, promoters, and organizers risked exchanging their feminist-inspired local, DIY, and networked scenes for a masculinized corporate reach enabled by the gendering of the professionalization of artist discovery and talent grooming.

While riot grrrl musicians were sometimes approached by the major labels, the rise of homocore or queercore (queer hard rock and alternative music production) posed a different challenge (Ciminelli and Knox 2005). Commodity capital wants to capitalize on risk and edge but does not always know how to integrate risk and edge into established hegemonic constructions of the audience. Queercore artists had difficulty interacting with labels because many label executives thought straight punk and hard rock fans would never listen to queer artists and that queer audiences either would not (or did not) listen to these musical genres. Alternative queer/gendered perspectives and modes of production such as queercore fall outside the norms of queer taste as researched and articulated by public relations and marketing firms and divisions, and challenge the kinds of industrially-produced rhetoric that have historically emerged from mainstream media companies.

Feminist and queer perspectives on conglomeration take on another layer when we consider intersections between gender/sexuality and race/ethnicity in media production and promotion. Latina feminist media studies has interrogated the visibility and representation of popular music and the representation of masculine and feminine Latino/a musical personalities such as Marc Anthony, Jennifer Lopez, Shakira, and Ricky Martin. Enabled by particular understandings of Latin music and Latino/a audiences and by a decentering of media capital that has propelled the emergence of media capitals such as Miami, Latin music's demographics have expanded, Latin music has become more visible as a pop cultural form, and Latino/a/ness has been constrained by the corporate culture of conglomerates and their desire to be as risk averse as possible. Scholars such as Mary Beltrán (2009), Arlene Davila (2001), and Angharad Valdivia (2000) have interrogated the cultural politics of Latino/a visibility and market constructions of Latino/a publics. Writing about Selena, Ramona Liera-Schwichtenberg states that "only in death did she achieve crossover success. As a result, *tejano* music, which is the variously accented expression of a borderland culture, moves from a community-based 'in-between-ness' to the media-hyped, capitalist center stage as a marketable commodity" (1998: 206). Concern over which genres and modes of musical production are rendered visible (Hanke 1998), what genres and modes are articulated with specific formations of gender, race, ethnicity, language, and nation, and how artists are represented in music video and the visual cultures of digital media have led scholars such as María Elena Cepeda (2010) to examine the complex (and sometimes challenging) ways that Latino/a masculinity and femininity are represented in the transnational aural and visual cultures of popular music.

## Conclusion

The turn to increased studies of media industries, media economics, and creative labor and production cultures opens new terrain for analyzing the interconnections between gender, sexuality, and mediated communication. Philip Napoli writes:

> Looking beyond politics to the cultural dimensions of media industries, recent research has shown how the availability of specialized content serving the interests of minority communities appears tightly tied to the demographic composition of the media markets in which the minority communities are located. Thus if minority audiences represent a relatively small proportion of the community, they are often very poorly served by their local media.
>
> (Napoli 2009: 162)

Discussions of media conglomeration in the media reform movement have been dominated by an attention to journalism and political communication. McChesney's focus on news and journalism and the privileging of the local work to erase popular culture, entertainment programming, and consumption. At the same time, the local bias of the media reform movement makes it difficult to think through the complicated ways that commodity capitalism enables and limits gendered and sexual identifications; feminist and queer media users are not necessarily happy with the state of hyper-conglomerated mainstream media culture but may receive more visibility from these sources than from local ideologues. Feminist and queer media scholars may move between the Scylla and Charybdis of strict political economic critiques and a naïve celebration of media consumption and celebratory representations (both of which are nearly nonexistent in current scholarship and now have been rendered as straw men positions), but it is only by navigating these tensions between ownership, representation, and reception that we can learn more about how the production, distribution, and exhibition of texts, platforms, and experiences dealing with gender and sexuality generate or inspire particular performances and identifications and how such texts connect with and perpetuate the industrial formations from which they spring.

## References

Aslinger, B. (2009) "Creating a Network for Queer Audiences at Logo TV," *Popular Communication* 7(2): 107–21.

——(2010) "PlanetOut and the Dichotomies of Queer Media Conglomeration," in C. Pullen and M. Cooper (eds.) *LGBT Identity and Online New Media*, New York: Routledge, pp. 113–24.

Bagdikian, B. H. (1997) *The Media Monopoly*, 5th edition, Boston: Beacon Press.

Baym, N. K. (2011) "Social Networks 2.0," in M. Consalvo and C. Ess (eds.) *The Blackwell Companion to Internet Studies*, Malden, MA: Wiley-Blackwell, pp. 384–405.

Beltrán, M. (2009) *Latina/o Stars in U.S. Eyes: The Making and Meanings of Film and TV Stardom*, Champaign: University of Illinois Press.

Burnett, R. (1996) *The Global Jukebox: The International Music Industry*, New York: Routledge.

Byerly, C. M. (2004) "Women and the Concentration of Media Ownership," in R. R. Rush, C. E. Oukrop, and P. J. Creedon (eds.) *Seeking Equity for Women in Journalism and Mass Communication Education: A 30-Year Update*, Mahwah, NJ: Lawrence Erlbaum Associates, pp. 245–62.

Caldwell, J. T. (2008) *Production Culture: Industrial Reflexivity and Critical Practice in Film and Television*, Durham, NC: Duke University Press.

Cepeda, M. E. (2010) *Musical ImagiNation: U.S.-Colombian Identity and the Latin Music Boom*, New York: New York University Press.

Ciminelli, D. and K. Knox (2005) *Homocore: The Loud and Raucous Rise of Queer Rock*, Los Angeles: Alyson Books.

Clark, D. (1995) "Commodity Lesbianism," in G. Dines and J. M. Humez (eds.) *Gender, Race, and Class in Media: A Text-Reader*, Thousand Oaks, CA: Sage Publications, pp. 142–51.

Curtin, M. (1999) "Feminine Desire in the Age of Satellite Television," *Journal of Communication* 49: 55–70.

Davila, A. (2001) *Latinos Inc.: Marketing and the Making of a People*, Berkeley: University of California Press.

D'Emilio, J. (1993) "Capitalism and Gay Identity," in H. Abelove, M. A. Barale, and D. M. Halperin (eds.) *The Lesbian and Gay Studies Reader*, New York: Routledge, pp. 467–76.

Enstad, N. (1999) *Ladies of Labor, Girls of Adventure: Working Women, Popular Culture, and Labor Politics at the Turn of the Twentieth Century*, New York: Columbia University Press.

Fejes, F. and K. Petrich (1993) "Invisibility, Homophobia, and Heterosexism: Lesbians, Gays and the Media," *Critical Studies in Mass Communication* 10: 396–422.

Gamson, J. (2003) "Gay Media, Inc.: Media Structures, the New Gay Conglomerates, and Collective Social Identities," in M. McCaughey and M. D. Ayers (eds.) *Cyberactivism: Online Activism in Theory and Practice*, New York: Routledge, pp. 255–78.

Gottlieb, J. and G. Wald (1994) "Smells Like Teen Spirit: Riot Grrrls, Revolution, and Women in Independent Rock," in A. Ross and T. Rose (eds.) *Microphone Fiends: Youth Music and Youth Culture*, New York: Routledge, pp. 250–74.

Gray, Mary L. (2009) *Out in the Country: Youth, Media, and Queer Visibility in Rural America*, New York: New York University Press.

Hanke, R. (1998) "'Yo Quiero Mi MTV!' Making Music Television for Latin America," in T. Swiss, J. Sloop, and A. Herman (eds.) *Mapping the Beat: Popular Music and Contemporary Theory*, Malden, MA: Blackwell, pp. 219–45.

Hennessy, R. (2000) *Profit and Pleasure: Sexual Identities in Late Capitalism*, New York: Routledge.

Hesmondhalgh, D. (1999) "Indie: The Institutional Politics and Aesthetics of a Popular Music Genre," *Cultural Studies* 13(1): 34–61.

——(2007) *The Cultural Industries*, Thousand Oaks, CA: Sage.

Hozic, A. A. (1999) "Uncle Sam Goes to Siliwood: Of Landscapes, Spielberg, and Hegemony," *Review of International Political Economy* 6(3): 289–312.

Ito, M. (2006) "Japanese Media Mixes and Amateur Cultural Exchange," in D. Buckingham and R. Willet (eds.) *Digital Generations*, Mahwah, NJ: Lawrence Erlbaum, pp. 49–66.

Iwabuchi, K. (2002) *Recentering Globalization: Popular Culture and Japanese Transnationalism*, Durham, NC: Duke University Press.

Kearney, M. C. (1997) "The Missing Links: Riot Grrrl-Feminism-Lesbian Culture," in S. Whiteley (ed.) *Sexing the Groove: Popular Music and Gender*, London: Routledge, pp. 207–29.

Liera-Schwichtenberg, R. (1998) "Crossing Over: Selena's Tejano Music and the Discourse of Borderlands," in T. Swiss, J. Sloop, and A. Herman (eds.) *Mapping the Beat: Popular Music and Contemporary Theory*, Malden, MA: Blackwell, pp. 205–18

McChesney, R. W. (1999) *Rich Media, Poor Democracy: Communication Politics in Dubious Times*, Urbana: University of Illinois Press.

——(2004) *The Problem of the Media: U.S. Communication Politics in the Twenty-First Century*, New York: Monthly Review Press.

Mullen, M. (2003) *The Rise of Cable Programming in the United States: Revolution or Evolution?*, Austin: University of Texas Press.

Napoli, P. M. (2009) "Media Economics and the Study of Media Industries," in J. Holt and A. Perren (eds.) *Media Industries: History, Theory, and Method*, Malden, MA: Wiley-Blackwell, pp. 161–70.

Negus, K. (1999) *Music Genres and Corporate Cultures*, New York: Routledge.

Sanjek, D. (1998) "Popular Music and Synergy of Corporate Culture," in T. Swiss, J. Sloop, and A. Herman (eds.) *Mapping the Beat: Popular Music and Contemporary Theory*, Malden, MA: Blackwell, pp. 171–86.

Schiller, H. I. (1989) *Culture, Inc.: The Corporate Takeover of Public Expression*, New York: Oxford University Press.

——(1992) *Mass Communications and American Empire*, Boulder, CO: Westview Press.

Schrum, K. (2004) *Some Wore Bobby Sox: The Emergence of Teenage Girls' Culture, 1920–1945*, New York: Palgrave Macmillan.

Sender, K. (2004) *Business, Not Politics: The Making of the Gay Market*, New York: Columbia University Press.

Turner, G. (2012) *What's Become of Cultural Studies?*, Thousand Oaks, CA: Sage.

Valdivia, A. N. (2000) *A Latina in the Land of Hollywood*, Tucson: University of Arizona Press.

Villarejo, A. (2009) "Ethereal Queer: Notes on Method," in G. Davis and G. Needham (eds.) *Queer TV: Theories, Histories, Politics*, New York: Routledge, pp. 48–62.

# 11

# Putting gender in the mix

## Employment, participation, and role expectations in the music industries

## *Marion Leonard*

Efforts to map women's participation in the music industries have been hampered by a lack of data. However, available statistics point to a continuing under-representation of women in the music industries; and the disparity is particularly acute within certain areas of practice. In 2010 the Performing Rights Society for Music (PRS), the UK's leading collection society, revealed that women accounted for only 14 percent of their registered music creators and writers. This statistic prompted the PRS Foundation to fund the "Women Make Music" initiative as a way to raise awareness of the gender gap, correct stereotypes, encourage participation, and increase the profile of women creating new music.

Research commissioned in 2008 by the Cultural Leadership Programme and published as a substantial report, found that in the UK music sector "only 20% of businesses have any form of female representation on the management team and only 10% have an all female team" (Cultural Leadership Programme 2008: 29). According to the report, women in the music sector were generally very underrepresented within positions of responsibility: the average number of female executives per firm was as low as 0.2. Such evidence of gender inequality in leadership positions within the music industries is by no means unique to the UK. In 2012 the editorial team of the Australasian Music Industry Directory (AMID), in consultation with other industry professionals, ranked for the first time the most powerful people in the Australian music industry. The criteria included who has the greatest "ability to 'shape' the scene," along with "their involvement in industry initiatives, overall career accomplishment, economic impact and public profile" (Fitzsimons 2012). The "power list" included 50 places and 56 people (some business partners held joint positions). Only six women appeared on the list, two of whom shared their place with a male colleague; overall, then, women were just under 11 percent. While the list can be critiqued for its partiality, it indicates the music industries' gender gap.

Books on women working in the music industries usually focus on women musicians and performers, often with the aim of celebrating women's contribution to the history of popular music (see, for example, Dahl 1984; Gaar 1993; Hirshey 2001; Downes 2012). In documenting women's experience, field research with musicians has shown how women have established their music careers, from acquiring instruments and learning to play, to performing and navigating the music business (see, e.g., Bayton 1998; Tucker 2000; Reddington 2007; Leonard 2007). A few specifically highlight women involved in music production and sound engineering (Sandstrom 2000; Smith 2009). Some recent work on women's changing relationship with music technologies examines how artist-producers (Wolfe 2012) and women involved in the electronic dance music scene (Farrugia 2012) have navigated a gendered sphere of practice which has historically and discursively been associated with masculinity. Music journalism has also been a focus, with critical accounts addressing the work of women music journalists and the gendered discourse of music journalism (McDonnell 1995; Davies 2001; McLeod 2001). While the literature on women musicians, journalists, DJs, and music engineers is growing, the experience of women working in other roles within the music sector is much less well documented. Indeed, Smith (2009: 308) remarks that, except for musicianship, "scholarship on gender segregation in other music industry roles has been meagre. Because of this, the gendered division of labour in the music industry is not yet adequately understood."

This chapter explores how gendered attitudes circulate within the workplace and in what ways they frame work in different sectors of the music industries. The plural term "music industries" suggests the chapter is not engaging with a unified field of practice, nor is it concerned only with the recording industry (Williamson and Cloonan 2007). I will draw on interviews with eight women who have worked in artist management, tour management, A&R (artist and repertoire), and concert promotion, although first I discuss the contexts in which these women work as a way to establish the extent to which their occupations can be broadly characterized as sex segregated.

These women work in largely under-studied but particularly sex-segregated areas of music employment. All eight were based in London, England and ranged in levels of seniority from a booking agent's assistant to a general manager of a record company. Many of the women had established portfolio careers, having worked in different roles, including radio promotion, international relations, music publishing, and marketing, so had different levels of experience in management, A&R, and concert promotion. For example, one participant worked for two years at a junior level in A&R before moving on to develop expertise in other areas, eventually becoming a general manager of a record company. Another participant began as a regional A&R scout and was promoted to A&R manager, where she stayed ten years. Therefore, they could offer a broad perspective: collectively they were engaged with international professional networks, international tour management, and the management and career development of artists building international profiles. The majority of them worked with rock bands and artists but some had worked with artists in other genres. The participants could also reflect on their experience of working with artists at different stages of career development, from new and developing bands through to major international recording stars. Seven of the approximately hour-long interviews were conducted by telephone; their responses to the open-ended questions were recorded and transcribed. One respondent offered a written response to the research questions via email. The women all seemed candid in their responses. Their comments have been anonymized; references to particular record labels, bands, or named individuals have been omitted.

## Gender and music occupations

Studies of the music industries in different countries offer an insight into gendered patterns of employment. For example, in the Nordic music industries, women's participation tends to be low in areas such as A&R and top executive positions (Power 2003: 14). In Sweden, "men tend to work as executives and with A&R activities whereas women to a larger extent tend to work as administrators and with promotion" (Power 2003: 76). Similarly, in countries in the Southern African Development Community (SADC), the music industries have clear gender divisions. Ambert found that men in the region undertook most of the production, circulation, and delivery functions; in several countries men owned "the means of production (studios, cassette and CD manufacturing, retail outlets and independent radio and TV stations)" (2003: 31). Women were generally "limited to composing and performing. Even within the ambit of these roles, women seldom play an instrument, and are clustered in backing vocals or as vocalists" (Ambert 2003: 31). Recent research in the UK (Creative & Cultural Skills 2009) has also found a considerable gender disparity: men are 66 percent of workers in the music industry. Moreover, certain roles were even more highly sex segregated. So, while retail and distribution of recordings were undertaken by a workforce that was 44 percent female, the proportion of women working in promotion, management, and agency-related activities was as low as 23 percent. While some doubt has been raised about the complete accuracy of these figures (UK Music 2012), the research nonetheless helps to highlight inequality.

Another way to gauge women's presence within different music industries is to consider membership in professional music organizations, although participation in such organizations does not necessarily reflect employment ratios. For example, the extent to which music engineering and production is male dominated is suggested by the fact that women are 4 percent of the members of the UK-based Music Producers' Guild (Savage 2012). The International Music Managers Forum (IMMF), which represents the interests of the music management profession, has five chapters in the US and 15 other national chapters worldwide. Women's membership varies in each chapter but the available information points to a generally low level of involvement. For example, 30 percent of the members of the MMF South Africa are women (Music Managers Forum South Africa 2012), while women account for just 16 percent of the membership of the UK branch (personal communication, August 28, 2012). Barry Bergman, the president of the national headquarters of the US chapters, describes women's membership in the US organization as "minimal" (personal communication, August 15, 2012). This low level of involvement is mirrored in the representation of women on the organization's board. Of the 11 members of the MMF US's executive board only one is a woman; no women serve on the advisory board.

## Experiencing the gendered workplace

While such data help identify the gender biases within music occupations, these figures cannot give insight into the specifics of how gender informs decisions about employment or how particular roles become gender typed. Statistics cannot capture the decision-making processes through which people select occupational roles, employers identify employees, and people navigate their careers by moving in or out of different jobs. For a greater understanding of how women have negotiated careers within very male-dominated areas of work, I turn now to the interviews. The research participants, while a relatively small sample group, described how their work experience, behavior, and opportunities had been shaped by gender attitudes. In considering this material I follow Ridgeway's (2011: 4) lead by "not asking the ultimate, sweeping question of *why* gender inequality has persisted, but rather the more proximate, means-focused question of *how* it has persisted." The interviewees described how gendered role expectations were common, working to shape the experience of people who were trying to break into the sector or were already in post. They discussed instances: particular situations, contexts, or work cultures in which they felt they were treated differently because they were female. As most of them had worked for a number of different employers and with a wide range of personnel, however, they did not necessarily encounter such difficulties regularly.

Their experiences also differed. For instance, a record company general manager stated that she did not feel her career had been blighted by sexism. By contrast, a tour manager described regularly encountering difficulties with men promoters and security staff when on the road. One respondent tied the issue to "age and stage" (personal communication, October 18, 2012); she had initially encountered difficulties but, as she grew more experienced and was promoted to more senior positions, she encountered these attitudes less and also felt better equipped to deal with them.

One point where sex segregation of jobs occurs is at the recruitment stage because, as Ridgeway (2011: 99) notes, "the sex segregation of jobs is an emergent structure that comes about through the job-matching processes by which applicants seek and employers place men and women into different positions in an employment organization." At this stage barriers to entry can be established which discourage women from applying for a position or prevent employers from thinking about women as ideal candidates for a job. To take these in turn, first consider how gendered role expectations about specific jobs can act as a barrier to women wishing to enter that field. For example, a recent newspaper article noted "a complete dearth of women" (Lindvall 2009) working for record companies in A&R. Women have been so absent from this field that people in this post have historically been referred to as "A&R men." The description continues to be regularly used rather than the more neutral reference to "A&R personnel." One woman with ten years of A&R experience described her frustration when newspaper reporters write A&R "men": "What I think that does, is to stop women from thinking that they could go and do that job" (personal communication, October 15, 2012). This label reinscribes the role as one naturally undertaken by men and moreover as a job *suitable* for men. To unpack this one needs to attend to assumptions about gender. Women need to negotiate a male-dominated field of practice and to face jobs carrying particular gender connotations.

The perception of certain roles as more suitable for men or women can lead people involved in the selection process to make quick decisions about the suitability of particular candidates. One research participant, reflecting on her experience of specialist music recruitment agencies, said: "They are always trying to put you into PA [personal assistant] roles or secretary roles. They are just trained to think of you as a young woman in fixed terms" (personal communication, October 18, 2012). She first entered the workplace by applying to a training program for university graduates run by a major record company. The program took several months and formed part of a very competitive recruitment process. At the end of the scheme she was offered a number of jobs, including a personal assistant role, but she declined these as she wished to work specifically in A&R. When one of the male candidates enquired if he might instead be put forward for the personal assistant job he was told: "Oh no. We would never put a guy forward for that" (personal communication, October 18, 2012). In this instance the employer had a mental picture of the ideal employee for the supportive role of a personal assistant based on previous employment patterns and gendered expectations about the qualities a woman would bring to the post. While one cannot gauge from this one account how common such instances are, it nevertheless illustrates how ideas about gender can become so ingrained within a workplace that opportunities for change are impeded.

## Gendered cultures

Once they had secured work in the sector, several women explained that, at various points in their career, they found the workplace to be not only male dominated but also one in which employees were encouraged or even expected to adopt particular patterns of gendered behavior. This resonates with Negus' 1992 description of the A&R department of a transnational record company where men executives worked in offices that opened out onto an open-plan area occupied by women secretaries and personal assistants. He observed the "casually dressed A&R men frequently strolled from their offices into this space exhibiting an informal style of working with relationships based around a bantering male camaraderie, while they were waited on by their handmaidens" (Negus 1992: 58). The number of women working in A&R roles within record and publishing companies has increased in the intervening years, including senior appointments; for example, Caroline Elleray became Head of A&R at Universal Music Publishing UK in 2007. Nevertheless, the descriptions of A&R departments in record companies given to me by women working in the music industries today were dishearteningly similar to Negus' account. One respondent, now a manager of a very successful and critically acclaimed rock band, said when she worked in A&R "it was the pretty girls out on the floor and the men in the office" (personal communication, September 4, 2012). Another woman reflected on the time she had spent in the A&R departments of different London-based record companies. She described how colleagues engaged in male social bonding rituals and how the A&R workplace culture favored stereotypically masculine behaviors of robust competitiveness and self-promotion:

> You just have to behave in a way like everyone around you is behaving or they see it as a sign of weakness, I think. So there is a lot of bragging and a lot of arrogance; and all that side of things does not come naturally to me. I'm not that kind of game player. ... In one particular record company, it was all guys in their mid-30s and then me much younger and most of the

time they seemed to spend bigging each other up, stabbing each other in the back, going to strip clubs, all these things and I had to try and keep up one way or another.

(personal communication, October 18, 2012)

As a woman in this environment she felt that she was continually marked out as different because she could not, and did not want to, engage with the performative culture of homosociality. Admittedly both of these women now work in other roles. So they were reflecting on past experience. Nonetheless, they offer an insight into a work culture in which they felt stymied on account of assumptions about gender.

Some interviewees perceived a double standard in operation, whereby certain modes of behavior might be permitted for men but were judged unacceptable when adopted by women working in the same role. For example, a tour manager, who has worked on US and European tours with numerous internationally acclaimed artists in the fields of rock and pop, remarked: "If I have a go at somebody or I lose my temper, it is seen to be 'Oh, that crazy woman. She must be PMS.' Whereas if a male reacts just the same way as I do to a situation [the response is] 'Yeah, you give 'em one!'" (personal communication, August 22, 2012). Her comments have parallels with the experiences of women rock musicians (Leonard 2007: 58–9), who describe how the history and culture of rock music supports and sustains stereotypical gendered behaviors. While instances such as the one described by the tour manager may occur only infrequently, they suggest a culture of masculinity within some music environments where gendered identities are expected and endorsed. Similarly a booking agent's assistant explained that she felt compelled to adapt her behavior in order to preserve her professional reputation. She said male colleagues judged her actions differently on account of her sex: "You need to be careful not to give the wrong impression just because we are girls. We have assistants that are boys and they can go out and get absolutely smashed with the bands. But that is fine because they are boys. We can do the same but, you know, you're definitely seen in a different way. You have to handle yourself a bit differently" (personal communication, September 4, 2012). She conceded that her understanding of the workplace as a gendered arena meant that she modified her behavior to fit in: "I think we compensate by being boyish. I don't know many women working in this industry that are super-girlie. ... Let's say we can handle a male conversation quite well. It is definitely an issue" (personal communication, September 4, 2012).

## Motherhood and work

Interviewees' comments in relation to children highlighted further inequalities in the workplace. Some discussed the negative impact of motherhood on career progression, the pressure not to take extended maternity leave because of the demands of the job, and the difficult logistics of organizing childcare and balancing work schedules. The participants discussed these parenting issues as ones that particularly affected them as women, reflecting the fact that parenthood usually has a greater impact on the careers of women than of men (Brown 2010; Ridgeway 2011). The challenges discussed here are also faced by many women in the wider workplace, but certain dimensions seemed particularly pronounced for women working in certain music sector roles. Almost all the women described the demands of their jobs as being very difficult to balance with the responsibilities of motherhood. Some even described these twin demands as completely incompatible. For example, a tour manager who did not have children said that planning long-term commitments was very difficult, "because you are on the road for a year or longer, you think in legs [of a tour]. ... So before you know it, a year and a half has gone by and then another year and a half and then another year and a half. So, for me, ten years went by and I basically didn't even notice" (personal communication, August 22, 2012). She reflected that while men tour managers and artists were able to balance parenthood and tour schedules, this was more difficult for women. Partly this was because motherhood would require periods of absence from a field of practice where job opportunities come through active participation in professional networks. Moreover, she added, the job did not allow much flexibility for people with primary responsibility for childcare and, as this is a role traditionally taken by women, it might lead some women to make decisions to move into different spheres of work. She said:

> As a tour manager you are on the road so much you know it is really, really difficult. ... And I know women who have come off the road and had babies who have said. "That's it. I can't do this." Or other people who have come off the road and said, "It's time. I need to have a relationship. I'm never going to have one if I am on the road."
>
> (personal communication, August 22, 2012)

Women working in other roles made similar points in reflecting on the future possibility of motherhood. For example, a concert promoter working mainly with rock and metal bands stated, "I am lucky enough to say I do love my job and, for the time being, going out to shows isn't a burden or a problem but, if I had my own family, it would certainly be tricky to juggle everything" (personal communication, October 25, 2012). Similarly, a booking agent's assistant commented, "My boss will do Norway, Reading festival and Manchester in three days. ... I just got married and if I am going to have a family I'm going to have to rethink ... my role. I won't be able to do everything that I do now for sure" (personal communication, September 4, 2012). These remarks parallel Gill's (2007: 7) research with new media workers, many of whom insisted that combining parenting with new media work would be "difficult, if not impossible."

Actual responsibilities for childcare or anxieties about balancing work commitments with future parenting can account for why some women may select not to work in the areas of promotion and tour management or may not feel able to continue in posts which demand long hours, travel, and regular evening work. While balancing such work commitments with childcare responsibilities is not impossible, the effort that this requires in terms of logistical planning is important to recognize. A woman who is an artist manager and has sole parenting responsibility for two children commented:

You work a lot of hours or odd hours. You'll do evenings, you'll do weekends. For example, you have got three bands on at Glastonbury [festival] and they are on the Friday lunchtime and the last one's on the Sunday evening. So you have got to … come back in the early hours of Monday morning and then get up with the kids on Monday morning because you haven't seen them since Wednesday and you have to pay for childcare.

(personal communication, September 4, 2012)

Another woman, who was a record company general manager when she had her first child, acknowledged that she could only balance her work commitments with her parenting responsibility because she could afford to pay for a nanny who could work flexible hours at very short notice:

I don't know how people do it if they can't afford to have a nanny. It is nigh on impossible, I think, to be honest. You have got to have that flexibility to be able to say, "I am running an hour late. I am really sorry. I will pay you an hour extra." You can't do that with nurseries; they expect you there at six o'clock on the dot.

(personal communication, August 28, 2012)

The cost of childcare is a salient point. A UK research report found that 78 percent of women working in music earn less than £20,000 per year, compared to 51 percent of men. Moreover, this report found, 47 percent of women working in music earn less than £10,000 a year, while only 35 percent of men in the sector are in this wage bracket (Creative & Cultural Skills 2009: 19). For some women, then, continuing to work in a low paying job is not financially worthwhile, when the costs of paying for childcare are calculated. As the same artist manager pointed out, "I have friends in major record labels who have had their first child and because childcare is so expensive and they don't get big wages in the music industry they can't afford to work and they stay at home because, as is the case in most of the world, their husbands earn more" (personal communication, September 4, 2012).

## Conclusion

Available statistics and reports from around the world highlight how women continue to be underrepresented in many key areas of the music industries. This chapter draws on interviews with women working in the areas of music management, promotion, and A&R to explore their accounts of working in highly sex-segregated roles and to consider to what extent they experienced the workplace as a gendered environment. Given the relatively small number of interviews, caution must be taken not to generalize too much from these perspectives but instead to recognize the need for further qualitative research to develop a broader understanding of the gendering of music occupations. Nevertheless the interview material offers insights into the ways in which gender has a perceptible influence on how roles, responsibilities, and expectations within the music industries are experienced and navigated. It reveals how gender stereotyping can limit access to job opportunities and how gendered behavior can be enacted within the workplace to exclude or regulate women's participation. It also supports other studies of women in the cultural industries (Gill 2007; Banks and Milestone 2011) which point to the anxieties and difficulties of many women in attempting to achieve a good balance between work commitments and the demands of parenthood. These ongoing issues confirm the need for initiatives such as the Equality and Diversity charter launched by UK Music in 2012, and the mentoring work and networking events organized by the Women in Music organization in New York. This is not to overlook or downplay the very real achievements of women in the music industries but rather to recognize that issues of gender inequality persist and have real effects on the experiences and earning potential of many women working in this sector. Identifying how gender operates within the business of music may go some ways toward dismantling the structures that support inequality.

## Acknowledgments

I would like to thank the research participants for taking the time to help with this research and for their valuable insights.

## References

Ambert, C. (2003) *Promoting the Culture Sector through Job Creation and Small Enterprise Development in SADC Countries: The Music Industry*, SEED working paper No. 49, Geneva: International Labour Office.

Banks, M. and K. Milestone (2011) "Individualization, Gender and Cultural Work," *Gender, Work and Organization* 18(1): 73–89.

Bayton, M. (1998) *Frock Rock: Women Performing Popular Music*, Oxford: Oxford University Press.

Brown, L. M. (2010) "The Relationship between Motherhood and Professional Advancement: Perceptions versus Reality," *Employee Relations* 32(5): 470–94.

Creative & Cultural Skills (2009) "Music Impact and Footprint 08–09." http://www.data-generator.co.uk.

Cultural Leadership Programme (2008) *Women in Leadership in the Creative and Cultural Sector.* http://www.culturalleadership.org.uk/uploads/tx_rtgfiles/Women_in_Leadership.pdf.

Dahl, L. (1984) *Stormy Weather: The Music and Lives of a Century of Jazzwomen*, London: Quartet Books.

Davies, H. (2001) "All Rock and Roll Is Homosocial: The Representation of Women in the British Rock Music Press," *Popular Music* 20(3): 301–19.

Downes, J. (ed.) (2012) *Women Make Noise: Girl Bands from Motown to the Modern*, Twickenham: Supernova.

Farrugia, R. (2012) *Beyond the Dance Floor: Female DJs, Technology and Electronic Dance Music Culture*, Chicago, IL: Intellect.

Fitzsimons, S. (2012) "Who Are the 50 Most Powerful People in the Music Industry?," June 26, themusic.com.au. http://themusic.com.au/news/all/2012/06/26/who-are-the-50-most-powerful-people-in-the-music-industry/.

Gaar, G. G. (1993) *She's a Rebel: The History of Women in Rock & Roll*, London: Blandford.

Gill, R. (2007) *Technobohemians or the New Cybertariat? New Media Work in Amsterdam a Decade after the Web*, Amsterdam: Institute of Network Cultures.

Hirshey, G. (2001) *We Gotta Get Out of This Place: The True, Tough Story of Women in Rock*, New York: Grove Press.

Leonard, M. (2007) *Gender in the Music Industry: Rock, Discourse and Girl Power*, Aldershot: Ashgate.

Lindvall, H. (2009) "Behind the Music: Where Are the Female A&Rs?," July 23. http://www.guardian.co.uk/music/musicblog/2009/jul/23/behind-music-female-a-rs/print.

McDonnell, E. (1995) "The Feminine Critique: The Secret History of Women and Rock Journalism," in E. McDonnell and A. Powers (eds.) *Rock She Wrote: Women Write About Rock, Pop, and Rap*, London: Plexus, pp. 15–23.

McLeod, K. (2001) "*½': A Critique of Rock Journalism in North America," *Popular Music* 20(1): 47–60.

Music Managers Forum South Africa (2012) "Our Members." http://www.mmfsa.co.za/?page_id=5.

Negus, K. (1992) *Producing Pop: Culture and Conflict in the Popular Music Industry*, London: Edward Arnold.

Power, D. (2003) *Behind the Music—Profiting from Sound: A Systems Approach to the Dynamics of Nordic Music Industry*, research report funded by the Nordic Industrial Fund. http://survey.nifu.no/step/music/DOCS/Final_Report.pdf.

PRS for Music Foundation (2012) "Background to Women Make Music." http://www.prsformusicfoundation.com/Partnerships/Flagship-Programmes/Women-Make-Music/Background-to-Women-Make-Music.

Reddington, H. (2007) *The Lost Women of Rock Music: Female Musicians of the Punk Era*, Aldershot: Ashgate.

Ridgeway, C. L. (2011) *Framed by Gender: How Gender Inequality Persists in the Modern World*, New York: Oxford University Press.

Sandstrom, B. (2000) "Women Mix Engineers and the Power of Sound," in P. Moisala and B. Diamond (eds.) *Music and Gender*, Urbana and Chicago: University of Illinois Press, pp. 289–305.

Savage, M. (2012) "Why Are Female Record Producers So Rare?," BBC News, Entertainment and Arts, August 29. http://www.bbc.co.uk/news/entertainment-arts-19284058.

Smith, D. (2009) "Deci-belles: Gender and Power in Sound Engineering for Popular Music in New Zealand," unpublished Ph.D. thesis, University of Otago, Dunedin, New Zealand.

Tucker, S. (2000) *Swing Shift: "All-Girl" Bands of the 1940s*, Chapel Hill, NC: Duke University Press.

UK Music (2012) "Equality & Diversity Charter for Music: Research." http://www.ukmusic.org/edc/ideas-and-inspiration/research12.

Williamson, J. and M. Cloonan (2007) "Rethinking the Music Industry," *Popular Music* 26(2): 305–22.

Wolfe, P. (2012) "A Studio of One's Own: Music Production, Technology and Gender," *Journal on the Art of Record Production* 7. http://arpjournal.com/2156/a-studio-of-one%e2%80%99s-own-music-production-technology-and-gender/.

# 12

# Gender inequality in culture industries

## Denise D. Bielby

Gender inequality—the unequal distribution of pay between men and women or level of women's labor force participation relative to men's—can be found across occupations and professions in industrialized countries around the globe (Charles and Grusky 2004). Although the gender gap in pay and employment and in other job-related opportunities, resources, and rewards has lessened somewhat over time for the labor force as a whole, considerable gender inequality remains at the highest levels of management in paid labor (Blau *et al.* 2006).[1] Sex segregation, which is the concentration of men and women in different kinds of work because of the division of labor in which the delegation of tasks is determined by workers' sex, is the causal mechanism that underlies differences in women's and men's employment and pay. Sex segregation occurs because of societal beliefs about the appropriateness of activities for one sex or the other.[2] Jobs become gendered—perceived as more suitable for one sex than another—through employers' conscious and unconscious beliefs (i.e. sex stereotypes) about the characteristics that various jobs require and about what tasks women and men are capable of doing. These beliefs, in turn, affect how work is organized and workers produce (Padavic and Reskin 2002). Although the gender ideology that underlies occupational sex segregation is deeply entrenched within societies, the sex segregation it creates can change over time within occupations and industries and vary cross-nationally (Blau *et al.* 2006). Reskin and Roos' (1990) seminal research on the link between sex segregation and gender inequality was based upon the study of work throughout the American occupational structure as a whole, but less is known about the distinctive mechanisms at play within culture industries.

### The distinctiveness of creative industries

While gender inequality appears throughout the paid labor force, the cause of the unequal distribution of employment and earnings between men and women in the culture industries of film, television, and music, among others such as video games, is particularly complex because of the way in which creative industries and their markets are organized. Creative industries supply goods and services that we associate with cultural, artistic, or entertainment value; their products consist of symbolic forms that connote, suggest, or imply expressive elements that may be appropriated for creation of social meanings. Cultural economist Richard Caves (2000) defines creative industries (which also include book and magazine publishing, the visual arts, the performing arts, fashion, and toys) as possessing these economic properties: (1) demand for their products is very uncertain because it is driven by fads and fashions in popular taste; (2) their creative workers invest deeply in product originality but are unable to explain their aesthetic choices a priori, which problematizes workers' appropriate level of compensation; (3) production usually requires collaborative teams of creative workers that possess diverse and specialized skills and personal tastes, which makes organization of their labor through formal contracts infeasible; (4) no two creative products are identical, which results in an infinite variety of products from which consumers may choose; (5) cultural products vary in quality, which further increases uncertainty about product choice and the valuation of creative workers' contributions; (6) because of uncertainty about consumer tastes, the economic profitability of a cultural product depends on its timely completion; and (7) the ephemerality/durability of a cultural product affects what consumers will pay for it. How do these properties of creative industries translate into institutional dynamics that create gender inequality?

First, culture industries exist in environments with career systems and networks of worker relationships that form "cultures of production" (DuGay 1997) that include gender. Coordination of the different skill sets of industry workers—creative personnel as varied as actors, musicians, and directors, craft and technical workers such as sound engineers, camera operators, and film editors, creative managers such as television producers, and administrators, executives, and unskilled labor—necessitates shared understandings of artistic conventions (Becker 1982) that are informed by how the finished product ought to comport with culturally normative expectations, including gender. Second, the oversight of artistic origination, creation, and production is difficult to regulate bureaucratically because it relies upon intangible expertise, where the quality of the work cannot be unambiguously evaluated based on technical and measurable features of the finished product (see Stinchcombe 1959, on craft administration). Instead, the quality of the work and the competence of its creator, including the gendered competence of its creator, are evaluated post hoc based on the acceptance and success of the work within the marketplace. This arrangement significantly complicates the implementation of the rational bureaucratic organizational form and its control over the creative process and labor of its employees. Third, in the competitive environment of culture industries, "careers tend to be chaotic and foster cultural innovation, and career-building and market-sensing entrepreneurs enact careers from the bottom up by starting from the margins of existing professions and conventions" (Peterson and Anand 2004: 317). Thus, career paths are highly variable and can be influenced by normative expectations about gender. Fourth, the properties of a field's cultural product determine how that field's labor is organized; as Peterson and Anand (2004: 317) explain, "such structuring produces the need for specialized gatekeepers (Hirsch 1991 [1972]) such as talent agents (Bielby and Bielby 1999), who selectively favor a subset of producers over others, thereby magnifying distortions in age, gender, and other demographic characteristics (Tuchman 1989; Bielby and Bielby 1996)." Fifth, and finally, while most creative workers are legally employees of large organizations, their employment is similar to that of outside contractors hired for short-term projects (Christopherson 1996). As a result, the organizational structures and policies that create barriers to career advancement tend to remain invisible to the employees themselves, and the lines of authority for hiring and pay decisions are often blurred. For example, the producer who approves a project is likely to be reporting directly or indirectly to executives within his or her organization who are likely to demand input into the employee's hiring and compensation. Given these multiple authorities, it is not clear who would be responsible for monitoring gender inequality or implementing a policy to minimize it.[3]

## Creative industries and gender inequality: film and television

Although Hollywood has dominated domestic and global production of media images for a century, its success as an industry could hardly have been predicted from its disorganized beginnings. In the early decades of filmmaking, the industry lacked prestige, the lines dividing production roles were fluid, and the field was "empty." As a result, women who found work within it were able to move across its tasks of scenarist, editor, director, and producer with relative ease. Even though the industry began as a loose and rather chaotic collection of motion picture shooting activities, it quickly evolved between 1915 and 1930 into Hollywood's classic organizational form of the vertically integrated studio system—"a dense interlocking system of production companies, anchored in geographic space by its own virtuous circle of endogenous growth" (Scott 2005: 11). In the late 1940s, when the studios were dismantled as a result of the Supreme Court ruling against the studios' anti-competitive practices (Stanley 1978), the industry transformed once again and organized into production companies that oversaw short-term projects staffed by vast interconnecting networks of specialized personnel. By the 1980s, talent agencies emerged as powerful deal-makers, production companies came under corporate ownership and control, and distribution became crucial to profitability.

Despite women's visible presence in the early years of the industry, they were all but pushed out by the late 1920s when the studio system emerged and film production became bureaucratized. Women's representation behind the camera has been more or less flat ever since. Statistics from 2010 reveal women accounted for just 7 percent of directors, 10 percent of writers, 15 percent of executive producers, 24 percent of producers, 18 percent of editors, and 2 percent of cinematographers, or just 16 percent of important behind-the-scenes workers in film (Lauzen 2011). Their presence as creators, executive producers, producers, writers, directors, editors, and directors of photography in the television sector, which emerged in the 1950s, is not much better at 25 percent. Among directors of episodic television women are a mere 12 percent (Yi and Dearfield 2012).

Efforts to monitor gender representation in film and television can be viewed as the legacy of Gaye Tuchman's (1978) foundational essay on the symbolic annihilation of women by the mass media. Although Tuchman's analysis focused on the *visual images* used by mass media to depict women, it was highly influential in triggering scholarly interest in the *production* of images, especially for identifying *who* determines the images that appear onscreen and *how* decisions are made about what to depict. Of considerable interest in early research on gender inequality in onscreen representation was how the gender identity of lead characters was constructed narratively. Of primary concern was the extent to which characters were conventional representations and to what extent they transcended gender roles (Signorielli 1989; Fejes and Petrich 1993). Classic writings such as Mulvey's (1975) analysis of the relevance of the male gaze, developed in her essay "Visual Pleasure and Narrative Cinema," were instrumental to explaining how the dominant male gaze constructed gender onscreen; eventually this work shaped important analyses of television characterizations more broadly (Modleski 1982; D'Acci 1987). A subsequent focus by feminist media scholars on emotional authenticity in women's narratives and its relevance to women's lived experience led to important work on audience reception and fan practices (Ang 1985; Brown 1990; Harrington and Bielby 1995; Kuhn 1984; Stacey 1994). Ultimately, though, the importance of the focus on the *who* and the *how* behind the scenes launched scholarly interest in the cultural assumptions of industry decision-makers at work. Ethnographic studies that demonstrate how representativeness is constructed through the interpretative frames of reference deployed by producers and other key behind-the-scene decision-makers have been especially valuable (see, for example, Grindstaff 2002), although access to production sites can be difficult to achieve (Levine 2001).

### Writers

Writers are crucial to film and television because without a script there is no product. Many of the most successful screenwriters of the silent film era were women—estimated at between 50 and 90 percent (Francke 1994; Martin and Clark 1987; McCreadie 1994; Mahar 2006). It is generally agreed that women screenwriters played a major role in establishing the narrative conventions of the film script. The process whereby screenwriting was transformed from a profession with substantial opportunities for women to one that became male dominated appears similar to that described by Tuchman in her account of the masculinization of authorship of the Victorian novel (Tuchman 1989). Like the occupation of novelist, screenwriting began as an "empty field" of low prestige. However, once film became more lucrative and men invaded the field, US filmmaking became industrialized, production became centralized and bureaucratized, and the skill requirements changed, pushing women out. By the late 1930s, membership statistics from the Writers Guild of America, West (Bielby and Bielby 1996) show that women accounted for less than 15 percent of those working as screenwriters. Of those employed, women were likely to be assigned to administrative or support roles such as reader or script supervisor (Francke 1994). In short, in a relatively brief period of time, women writers had become typecast by studio heads who applied sex role stereotypes about what jobs women writers were suited for and assigned them to scripting "women's films," writing dialog for female stars, and infusing the "woman's angle" into films (Francke 1994).

The decline of the studio system and the shift toward independent production in the 1950s, which theoretically should have created new opportunities for marginalized groups, had little positive impact on womens representation among screenwriters. Statistics from the Writers Guild of America, West (WGAW) reveal that in the 1950s and 1960s, which corresponds to the period when the studios were being dismantled and shifting to independent production, women constituted only about 12–13 percent of screenwriters; this persisted through the 1970s, the era of the women's movement (Bielby and Bielby 1996). When public calls for more enlightened images of women were raised during this period, women's groups within the WGA organized to advance their interests. Although these developments encouraged talented women writers to pursue careers in the industry, the early 1970s also marked the beginning of the blockbuster era, which greatly increased the financial risk involved in pursing projects with huge box office sales and ushered in a decline in the willingness of production heads to take chances. Over time, the blockbuster mentality of film production encouraged producers to seek out already established (i.e. men) directors, writers, and actors with track records of consistent success and to forgo serious consideration of unproven (i.e. women) writers.

Statistics computed from employment and earnings records of screenwriters show that these industry dynamics were highly consequential to cementing gender inequality for women writers in film. By the mid-1990s, the salaries of a small group of elite screenwriters were bid up to levels far in excess of the median earnings of women and men (Bielby and Bielby 1996: Figure 4), a pattern that persists to this day and contributes to the intractability of gender inequality in the industry. Statistical analyses over the past two decades of the earnings and employment of the vast majority of women screenwriters reveal that access to opportunity early in the career pays off more for men, causing women to experience *cumulative disadvantage* over time (Bielby and Bielby 1996).

Television was launched in the United States in the late 1940s, and by the mid-1950s the three major networks were established, dominated access to television production, and monopolized broadcast distribution. Early television programming consisted of live productions that were owned by commercial sponsors and produced at independent studios, but by a decade later ownership and control over production shifted to the networks and programming consolidated into genres (and scheduling) targeted to audience demographics (Meehan 2002). The television industry has always been dominated by men in key decision-making roles such as program procurement and financing, which is a pivotal factor in the persistence of gender inequality in this sector of the entertainment industry. The percentage of women in influential decision-making roles in the 2010–11 television season stood at 25 percent (Yi and Dearfield 2012). A report from 2007 indicates they filled less than 15 percent of the industry's high status executive producer positions (Writers Guild of America, West 2007: Figure 1). A second aspect of the television industry that places women at a disadvantage relative to men is the typecasting of writers by genre. Employment of women who defy convention by seeking to write "against type" is viewed as financially unsound by risk-averse industry executives. Executives' reliance on gender stereotypes to assess the creative capabilities of writers encapsulates writers, tying them to styles of writing that are susceptible to the cycles of popular taste that drive this industry. The combination of relative devaluation at career entry and typecasting makes women writers susceptible to *continuous disadvantage* (Bielby and Bielby 1992).

## Actors

Scholars voiced concern early on about the unrealistic standards of beauty of the actresses who portray lead characters and whether the industry undermines potentially transcendent narratives about gender through the stereotypes created by its limited casting choices (see Dyer's 1979 classic essay on the role of stereotypes). The industry's overemphasis on conventional beauty (Levy 1990) came to be regarded as even more troubling when chronological age was shown to interact definitively with gender to yield vastly different career outcomes for actresses and actors (Bazzini et al. 1997). According to a Screen Actors Guild report, in 1999 men over 40 years of age received 37 percent of all male roles in film and television, while women over 40 received only 24 percent of all female roles in the two mediums combined. A statistical analysis (Lincoln and Allen 2004) of the career trajectory of leading film actors and actresses in Hollywood over a 70-year period found that while roles drop for both men and women over the course of their careers, the decline is much more precipitous for female stars than it is for male stars. Lincoln and Allen also analyzed gender differences in *star presence*, a statistical measure they created to assess the cumulative importance of an actor through the rank of an actor's billings in the credits over several films (the larger the presence, the bigger the star). Like the decline in the number of roles for women, Lincoln and Allen found that as actresses grew older their star presence declined precipitously; in short, although growing older negatively affects the careers of both men and women, age affects the careers of actresses far more greatly. Given aging's clearly gendered impact on women's careers, Allen and Lincoln concluded that women face a double jeopardy in sustaining acting careers relative to men.

Writers and actors are just two of many occupations within creative industries that experience entrenched gender inequality. The music industry is well known for its gendered specialties; see, for example, Clawson's (1999) study of the overrepresentation of female electric bassists in alternative rock music. Other research (Schmutz and Faupel 2010) reveals that cultural assumptions about the "natural" intersection of gender and art shape the likelihood of a musician ever being recognized as an "all-time great," leaving female artists at a relative disadvantage in attaining such standing. The production of video games is another industry in which gender affects access to employment (Pham 2008; McKay and McKay 2010). Here, the not surprising nexus of men and technology has emerged much as it did in the computer industry, defining the work culture of video game production as male dominated for those considering entering the field (Stross 2008).

## Conclusion

Given reliable evidence, observing gender inequality in culture industries can be relatively straightforward, but understanding the structural factors that account for inequality or the reasons why it is so entrenched and remains so persistent is more complicated. This is so for a couple of reasons. First, as sites that produce representations of gender, creative industries rely upon cultural idioms that embody cultural assumptions about gender. Not only do these givens shape the look of a finished product (see Mears' 2011 research on modeling and the fashion industry, for example), they are embedded in the labor of cultural production itself that creates the industry's culture(s) of production (DuGay 1997; see also Caldwell 2008; Peterson and Anand 2004). Cultures of production include shared beliefs among workers about gender enactment on the job (Ridgeway and Correll 2004), which, in turn, affects access to employment, earnings, and opportunities for advancement. Once in place, these systems are powerfully self-perpetuating. Second, the distinctive features of organizational practices in cultural industries sustain gender inequality. Sociologists have observed that making work assignments in an arbitrary and subjective manner, especially where accountability for equal employment opportunity is absent, allows stereotypes to influence personnel decisions. In the corporate world this happens when managers have unfettered discretion concerning whom to hire or promote, permitting them to make personal judgments about who best fits the job. More often than not, the "best" hire matches the gender, race, and age of those already doing the job. In such circumstances interpersonal ties can determine access to advancement.

Other research provides additional insight into how structural factors account for gender inequality in culture industries. Temporary organizations such as film projects, television series, concert tours, and the like are assumed to be ephemeral and unstable. However, organization scholars show that they are sustained in part by the informal social practices workers carry from one short-term project to the next, practices that contribute to organizational stability (Bechky 2006). This research suggests the importance of understanding how a contingent labor force informally manages the "revolving door" of temporary employment through reputation, and the role of gender in this process. Other research that analyzes actors' careers as social networks of professional experiences identifies the payoff that comes from the reputational accomplishments stemming from these opportunities and how those, in turn, contribute to cumulative advantage in project-based labor markets (Rossman et al. 2010). A network analysis that specifically took gender into account (Lincoln and Allen 2011) not only confirms the importance of studying network patterns of professional experience, it also reveals how career accomplishments can be differentially shaped by national context. This research points to the importance of cross-national comparisons in order to achieve a fuller understanding of the factors that account for gender inequality within culture industries in an increasingly globalized economy.

## Notes

1 Gender inequality also persists in the division of unpaid labor.
2 More specifically, sex stereotypes (the socially shared beliefs that link various traits, attributes, and skills of one sex or the other), along with sex labeling of jobs (stereotypes about the characteristics that various jobs require) lead jobs to be labeled as either men's or women's work (Padavic and Reskin 2002: 42–4).

3 Hesmondhalgh (2007) takes some of these considerations a step further, arguing that culture industries have distinctive problems of production that include a high degree of risk and uncertainty in product success, an emphasis on creativity over commerce, high production costs and low reproduction costs, products that are semi-public goods, and the need to create scarcity. Typical organizational solutions include an overabundance of production to offset misses against hits, a reliance on publicity, the creation of artificial scarcity, formatting production through stars, genres, and serials, loose control of symbol creators, and tight control of distribution and marketing.

# References

Ang, I. (1985) *Watching Dallas: Soap Opera and the Melodramatic Imagination*, London: Methuen.

Bazzini, D. G., W. D. McIntosh, S. M. Smith, S. Cook, and C. Harris (1997) "The Aging Woman in Popular Film: Underrepresented, Unattractive, Unfriendly, and Unintelligent," *Sex Roles* 36: 531–43.

Bechky, B. (2006) "Gaffers, Gofers, and Grips: Role-Based Coordination in Temporary Organizations," *Organization Science* 17(3): 3–21.

Becker, H. (1982) *Art Worlds*, Berkeley, CA: University of California Press.

Bielby, D. and W. Bielby (1996) "Women and Men in Film: Gender Inequality among Writers in a Culture Industry," *Gender & Society* 10: 248–70.

Bielby, W. and D. Bielby (1992) "Cumulative versus Continuous Disadvantage in an Unstructured Labor Market," *Work and Occupations* 19: 366–489.

——(1999) "Organizational Mediation of Project-based Labor Markets: Talent Agencies and the Careers of Screenwriters," *American Sociological Review* 64(1): 64–85.

Blau, F., M. Brinton, and D. Grusky (2006) *The Declining Significance of Gender?*, New York: Russell Sage Foundation.

Brown, M. E. (1990) *Television and Women's Culture: The Politics of the Popular*, London: Sage.

Caldwell, J. (2008) *Production Culture: Industrial Reflexivity and Critical Practice in Film and Television*, Durham, NC: Duke University Press.

Caves, R. (2000) *Creative Industries: Contracts Between Art and Commerce*, Cambridge, MA: Harvard University Press.

Charles, M. and D. Grusky (2004) *Occupational Ghettos*, Stanford, CA: Stanford University Press.

Christopherson, S. (1996) "Flexibility and Adaptation in Industrial Relations: The Exceptional Case of the U.S. Media Entertainment Industries," in L. S. Gray and R. L. Seeber (eds.) *Under the Stars: Essays on Labor Relations in Arts and Entertainment*, New York: ILR Press, pp. 86–112.

Clawson, M. A. (1999) "When Women Play the Bass," *Gender & Society* 13(2): 193–210.

D'Acci, J. (1987) "The Case of Cagney and Lacey," in H. Baehr and G. Dyer (eds.) *Boxed In: Women and Television*, London: Pandora, pp. 203–26.

DuGay, P. (1997) *Production of Culture: Cultures of Production*, London: Sage.

Dyer, R. (1979) "The Role of Stereotypes," in Jim Cook and Mike Lewington (eds.) *Images of Alcoholism*, London: British Film Institute, pp. 15–21.

Fejes, F. and K. Petrich (1993) "Invisibility, Homophobia and Heterosexism: Lesbians, Gays, and the Media," *Critical Studies in Mass Communication* 20: 396–422.

Francke, L. (1994) *Script Girls: Women Screenwriters in Hollywood*, Bloomington: Indiana University Press.

Grindstaff, L. (2002) *The Money Shot: Trash, Class, and the Making of TV Talk Shows*, Chicago: University of Chicago Press.

Harrington, C. L. and D. D. Bielby (1995) *Soap Fans: Pursuing Pleasure and Making Meaning in Everyday Life*, Philadelphia, PA: Temple University Press.

Hesmondhalgh, D. (2007) *The Cultural Industries*, 2nd edition, London: Sage Publications.

Hirsch, P. (1991 [1972]) "Processing Fads and Fashions: An Organization-Set Analysis of Cultural Industry Systems," in C. Mukerji and M. Schudson (eds.) *Rethinking Popular Culture*, Berkeley: University of California Press, pp. 313–34.

Kuhn, A. (1984) "Women's Genres: Melodrama, Soap Opera, and Theory," *Screen* 25(1): 18–28.

Lauzen, M. (2011) "Getting Real About Reel Employment. Women's Media Center Report." http://www.womensmediacenter.com/feature/entry/getting-real-about-reel-employment.

Levine, E. (2001) "Toward a Paradigm for Media Production Research: Behind the Scenes at *General Hospital*," *Critical Studies in Media Communication* 18: 66–82.

Levy, E. (1990) "Social Attributes of American Movie Stars," *Media, Culture & Society* 12: 247–67.

Lincoln, A. and M. Allen (2004) "Double Jeopardy in Hollywood: Gender and Age Effects on the Careers of Film Actors, 1926–99," *Sociological Forum* 19: 611–31.

——(2011) "Oscar et César: Deep Consecration in French and American Film Acting Careers," in C. Mathieu (ed.) *Careers in Creative Industries*, New York: Routledge, pp. 107–37.

McCreadie, M. (1994) *Women Who Write the Movies*, New York: Birch Lane Press.

McKay, B. and K. McKay (2010) "So You Want My Job: Video Game Producer." http://artofmanliness.com/2010/09/29/so-you-want-my-job-video-game-producer/.

Mahar, K. (2006) *Regendering the Movies*, Baltimore, MD: Johns Hopkins University Press.

Martin, A. and V. Clark (1987) "What Women Wrote: Scenarios, 1912–1929," *Cinema History Microfilm Series*, Frederick, MD: University Publications of America.

Mears, A. (2011) *Pricing Beauty: The Making of a Fashion Model*, Berkeley: University of California Press.

Meehan, E. R. (2002) "Gendering the Commodity Audience: Critical Media Research, Feminism, and Political Economy," in E. R. Meehan and E. Riordan (eds.), *Sex and Money: Feminism and Political Economy in the Media*, Minneapolis: University of Minnesota Press, pp. 209–22.

Modleski, T. (1982) *Loving with a Vengeance: Mass Produced Fantasies for Women*, London: Methuen.

Mulvey, L. (1975) "Visual Pleasure and Narrative Cinema," *Screen* 16(3): 6–18.

Padavic, I. and B. Reskin (2002) *Women and Men at Work*, 2nd edition, Thousand Oaks, CA: Pine Forge Press.

Peterson, R. and N. Anand (2004) "The Production of Culture Perspective," *Annual Review of Sociology* 30: 311–34.

Pham, A. (2008) "Women Left on Sidelines of Video Game Revolution," *Los Angeles Times*, October 21: C1–C9.

Reskin, B. and P. Roos (1990) *Job Queues, Gender Queues*, Philadelphia, PA: Temple University Press.

Ridgeway, C. and S. Correll (2004) "Unpacking the Gender System: A Theoretical Perspective on Gender Beliefs and Social Relations," *Gender & Society* 18(4): 510–31.

Rossman, G., N. Esparza, and P. Bonacich (2010) "I'd Like to Thank the Academy, Team Spillovers, and Network Centrality," *American Sociological Review* 75(1): 31–51.

Schmutz, V. and A. Faupel (2010) "Gender and Cultural Consecration in Popular Music," *Social Forces* 89(2): 685–707.

Scott, A. J. (2005) *On Hollywood*, Princeton, NJ: Princeton University Press.

Screen Actors Guild (1999) "Screen Actors Guild Casting Data Find Ageism Still a Critical Issue for American Performers," Press Release, April 21, 1999. http://www.asc.upenn.edu/gerbner/Asset.aspx?assetID=464.

Signorielli, N. (1989) "Television and Conceptions about Sex Roles: Maintaining Conventionality and the Status Quo," *Sex Roles* 21: 337–56.

Stacey, J. (1994) *Star Gazing: Hollywood Cinema and Female Spectatorship*, London: Routledge.

Stanley, R. (1978) *The Celluloid Empire*, New York: Hastings House.

Stinchcombe, A. (1959) "Bureaucratic and Craft Administration of Production," *Administrative Science Quarterly* 4: 168–87.

Stross, R. (2008) "What Has Driven Women Out of Computer Science?," *New York Times*, November 15. http://www.nytimes.com/2008/11/16/business/16digi.html.

Tuchman, G. (1978) "Introduction: The Symbolic Annihilation of Women," in G. Tuchman, A. Kaplan Daniels, and J. Benet (eds.) *Hearth and Home: Images of Women in the Mass Media*, New York: Oxford University Press, pp. 3–38.

——(1989) *Edging Women Out: Victorian Novelists, Publishers, and Social Change*, New Haven, CT: Yale University Press.

Writers Guild of America, West (2007) *The 2007 Hollywood Writers Report: Whose Stories Are We Telling?*, Los Angeles, CA: Writers Guild of America West.

——(2011) "Recession and Regression: The 2011 Hollywood Writers Report." http://www.wga.org/uploadedFiles/who_we_are/hwr11execsum.pdf.

Yi, R. and C. Dearfield (2012) "The Status of Women in the U.S. Media, 2012," Women's Media Center. www.womensmediacenter.com.

# 13

# Shifting boundaries

## Gender, labor, and new information and communication technology

## *Ursula Huws*

To speak of labor is to tap into a convoluted root system of entangled meanings. The word "labor" is associated both with the affirmative exertion of giving birth and with the expenditure of physical effort on other activities, including the punishment of "hard labor." It also has more abstract collective connotations (as in "division of labor," "organized labor," or "labor movement"). Linking the concept to that of creativity adds new dimensions of complexity. A "work" can be a triumphant artistic achievement (a painting, a symphony, or a Victorian lady's needlecraft), but "working" can also refer to daily drudgery.

The tension between work as autonomous self-expression, work as necessary maintenance of the self (and others), and work as the requirement to perform externally imposed tasks is one which is played out in the context of (sometimes contested) social relationships. The more coercive these relationships, and the less power the worker has to resist this coercion, the less opportunity there is likely to be for autonomy and self-expression. Conversely, the more powerful the social position of the worker, the more likely it is that she or he can bargain for conditions that allow for some self-fulfillment through work, or pass the more mundane tasks down the line to other more vulnerable workers. These relationships may, or may not, be relationships of employment, in which work time is traded for money. However, whether this is acknowledged or not, and whether the work is paid or unpaid, these social relations shaping the character of work are likely to be strongly gendered.

The specific forms that work takes are thus shaped in a dynamic interplay between multiple forces: social relations within the household; broader social relations within which these are embedded (including those of class and ethnicity); forms of control that are exercised in the immediate employment relationship (which may be exercised hierarchically, through peer pressure, or through the design of the job itself); and, increasingly, the broader sociopolitical and economic landscape in which this employment relationship is located. This is in turn influenced by additional factors, including national legislation, cultural traditions, global market forces, and the position occupied by the employer in global value chains. The instability created by these complex interactions is further impacted by technological change, which introduces a new dimension of volatility, by changing the boundaries between paid and unpaid work, by changing the skills involved in performing it, and by introducing new options for the spatial organization of labor.

This chapter teases out some of the interactions of these multiple conflicting forces, identifies their gendered character, and outlines how they shape media work in the twenty-first century. It does this by looking at the shifting of boundaries: between paid and unpaid work; between the home and the external workplace; between production and consumption; between workers in different occupational groups; and between regions, countries, and continents.

## Shifting boundaries between paid and unpaid work

The history of the media industries can be seen as the history of a transformation of unpaid activities carried out in the home and the community, first into service industries and then into manufacturing ones (Huws 2003). For instance, domestic music-making was supplemented by the employment of professional musicians in bands and orchestras, which in turn gave way to the recorded music industry; community-based amateur performances led to professional theater, which was followed by drama delivered to its audiences via cinema and television; and word-of-mouth gossip and storytelling were supplanted by professional news and fiction-publishing industries, first in print and then on radio, television, and online. In all these transitions the general tendency was the transformation of unpaid work into paid work.

But the introduction of information and communication technologies (ICTs) has also enabled transitions in the opposite direction: the internet makes it possible for amateurs to self-publish their own writings, broadcast their own films, distribute their own recorded music, and actively contribute to the generation of content. Indeed, user-generated content is crucial to the success of some of the largest and most visible online organizations, including Wikipedia and YouTube, as well as blogging or photo-sharing sites like Wordpress, Flickr, Tumblr, and Blogger. Here, unpaid work displaces or supplements paid work.

As the same activity morphs unobtrusively between paid and unpaid status, the worker who carries it out slips in and out of "employment." The boundaries between paid and unpaid work become permeable. That permeability is blurred further in many media workplaces by the growing practice of using unpaid intern labor alongside paid employees. The fact that much of this work is carried out willingly and for pleasure, as well as for self-promotion, makes its character as labor opaque.

This ambiguous character of online unpaid labor has attracted considerable theoretical attention. In the Italian autonomist tradition (Hardt and Negri 2000, 2004) online labor is collapsed into a broader category of "immaterial labor," along with a confusingly broad range of other types of "affective labor," dissolving most workers, paid or unpaid, or involved in virtual or non-virtual work, into an amorphous "multitude." Terranova (2000) followed this approach in developing her concept of "free labor" on the internet. While acknowledging that the visibility of such unpaid work as the development of open-source software, mediating chat-room discussions, or designing websites reflects a masculine conception of work, she nevertheless fails to relate this type of unpaid labor to other forms of unpaid labor, generally carried out by women, which I have described as "reproduction work" and "consumption work" (Huws 2003), both of which have, to some extent, migrated online. Reproduction work involves the upkeep of the self and family, and can be extended to include such things as maintaining social relationships (keeping in touch with relatives, sending birthday greetings, comforting the bereaved) and education (motivating children to learn, helping them with their homework), as well as cleaning, laundry, preparing food, etc. Consumption work is an extension of reproduction work, a type of work that has grown: first, because more and more reproduction tasks have been taken over by the market and involve purchasing goods and services, rather than producing them "from scratch" in the home outside the money economy; and, second, because consumption tasks increasingly involve a substitution of self-service or self-assembly by consumers for having goods and services finished and delivered by paid service workers.

Further developing Terranova's ideas, Fuchs (2010, 2012) argues that users of social media directly produce value for companies such as Facebook by contributing to the development of the "audience commodity" (Smythe 2001) from which they make their profit. He implies that all social media users are exploited workers whose labor is expropriated, and therefore members of the "multitude." Arvidsson and Colleoni (2012) disagree, arguing that, in social media, value is created by attracting affective investments accruing to particular brands which then enhance their value on financial markets. The near-exclusive focus on social media in these debates sidelines the many other ways in which the internet has become a site for labor, whether this is freely chosen creative work (which might or might not generate an income); coercive paid work (such as online information technology or editorial work carried out on platforms such as eLance or oDesk or more low-skilled pay-per-click type work carried out through Amazon's Mechanical Turk); or unpaid reproduction or consumption work. The invisibility in these debates of the latter categories, much more likely to be done by women, reflects the more general invisibility of unpaid domestic or consumption work in society.

## Shifting boundaries between production and consumption

The shifting interface between paid and unpaid work and the changing relationship between production and consumption enabled by ICTs have implications for the labor processes and scope for creativity of both paid workers and unpaid consumers. Take, for example, one of the many websites that allows you to "design" your own garments (such as weddingdresscreator.com). Here, the customer can spend hours trying out different permutations and combinations from a range of standard ingredients (in this case, 23 neckline types, 11 midriff types, and 16 types of silhouette). As well as saving the time that would otherwise be spent trudging through shopping malls or leafing through catalogues, this can induce a sense of creativity and ownership of the final design in the consumer. But the work of the designer has been reduced to the development of standard interchangeable components, reflecting more general tendencies of standardization, intensification, and requirements to respond to customer demand found across a range of occupations in the creative industries. The same trend can be seen in the design of standard templates to be applied by bloggers using Wordpress or Blogger: an increased ability for users to achieve professional-looking results accompanying increased pressure for standardization and reduction in scope for creativity for the paid designer.

Academic debates about the blurring of the boundaries between work, consumption, and leisure, encompassed in terms such as "playbour" (Kücklich 2005), "prosumption" (Toffler 1980; Ritzer and Jurgenson 2010; Comor 2010), and "co-creation" (Prahalad and Ramaswamy 2000; Banks and Humphreys 2008), have also generally been conducted without reference to feminist debates about reproductive and consumption work (for which, see Weinbaum and Bridges 1976; Huws 2003; Oliver *et al.* 2009). Further gender-sensitive research on these interactions is clearly needed, reflecting the reality that patterns of who does what on the internet intimately reflect patterns of who does what in the real world, including the gender division of labor in housework, shopping, childcare, sustaining family networks and emotional work, as well as participation in the labor market.

## Shifting location of work: from office to home

When ICTs began to be introduced in the 1970s, one of the most widely anticipated impacts was their potential to enable work to be carried out remotely. Initially this was overwhelmingly seen as a shift of work from the office to the home, in the form of "telecommuting" (Nilles *et al.* 1976) or "teleworking" (Huws 1984). Although opinion was sharply divided on whether this would be good or bad for women (see Huws 1991 for a summary of these debates), the first wave of research on this topic, largely carried out by women with a gender-sensitive perspective (Olson 1983; Vedel 1984; Monod 1983; Zimmerman and Horwitz 1983; Huws 1985), demonstrated that this approach was over-simplistic: whether it was "good" or "bad" or both depended on the circumstances. Because of the pre-existing gender division of labor in the home, as well as in the external labor market, homeworking was for many women a way of resolving the almost irreconcilable conflicts between different demands on their time. This was illustrated in an early study of telemediated homeworking carried out in the UK, where one woman gave the same reply—"Being with the children all day"—to both the question "What is the greatest advantage of working from home?" and the question "What is the greatest disadvantage of working from home?" (Huws 1985: 50). Subsequent feminist studies of home-based teleworking (Phizacklea and Wolkowitz 1995; Gurstein 2001) confirmed the profoundly ambiguous character of the experience of working from home.

In the creative and media industries, nothing is new about working at or from one's home. For writers, and for many types of visual artists and designers, it has been unusual historically to work from anywhere else. As argued so convincingly by Virginia Woolf in *A Room of One's Own*, the availability of a suitable space in the home, combined with the time to use it autonomously, has been decisive in determining who can enter such professions. The combination of this factor with the difficulty of spending time away from home for people with parental responsibility has played a strong part in shaping the gendered patterns that, for instance, make women more likely to take up novel-writing or book illustration and men more likely to become film directors or orchestra conductors.

The ability to deliver a photoshopped image or a manuscript by email, rather than send it through the post, has, arguably, made rather little fundamental difference to the creative processes of many workers in such traditional artistic fields. The digitization of words and images, however, and the ability to transmit them electronically have, in combination with other factors, brought about fundamental changes to the character of media work, especially visible in those aspects that involve a number of different people working in a team.

## Fluidity of employment relations and occupational boundaries

Since the 1970s, media workers working at home in traditionally solitary roles have been joined by others in more collegial occupations that might in the past have been based in offices, working from their homes not so much because this is ideal for concentrated creative work (although that may still be a factor) but because they have no other affordable base. These are the growing numbers of freelance or temporary media workers flitting precariously from commission to commission, contract to contract, and job to job, for example as journalists, photographers, editors, film technicians, or web designers. Although the work itself may involve being on location with others, a temporary stint in a client's office, or nomadic roaming, these workers lack the sort of stable office base in which, in the past, their predecessors might have been able to learn new skills systematically from a mentor, form long-lasting teams, or join trade unions and negotiate secure working conditions for themselves. Technological advances have made the technology cheap enough and light enough to carry about and easy enough to learn that they can own it for themselves and transport it with them unaided. They have also eroded the clear boundaries between crafts. For instance, television presenters may now also be required to operate cameras and sound equipment and post on blogs, while editors may also design layouts and prepare files for printing or posting online.

But these same advances have also created the preconditions for atomizing and dispersing the creative workforce, making it more difficult for them to see the big picture, to organize to establish stable, collective professional identities, and to find ways to promote their joint interests. Thus the very development that opens up the possibility of being a media worker to a much wider range of people than ever before also multiplies the choices available to employers and clients. In yet another paradox, media workers thereby have been placed more sharply in competition with each other, and become more dependent on personal networks to promote themselves and obtain work, heightening the tension between the need to collaborate, on the one hand, and the urge to compete, on the other. Both the scope for networking and the self-assurance necessary for self-promotion and competition are likely to be strongly shaped by gender, class, and ethnicity.

Europe-wide research comparing the gender division of labor across different industries and occupational groups (Dahlmann *et al.* 2009) found that women in creative occupations were likely to make very different career choices from women in clerical or manual occupations. The former typically chose to sacrifice family and relationship commitments in return for a high degree of precariousness and long and unpredictable working hours. Qualitative studies bear out this picture. Clare's (2008) study of the advertising industry found that, despite the rhetoric of flexibility, egalitarianism, and non-hierarchical structures, gender was still the most important factor in facilitating career trajectories. Studying women in creative occupations, Krings (2007) found that their most common survival strategy was to adopt a "male life-style, including long hours and competitiveness, which often included giving up any thought of having children." Similar conclusions were reached in research on new media workers (Gill 2002), museum workers (Adams 2010), and fashion designers (McRobbie 1998). Studies of freelance media workers (e.g. Gill 2005; Huws *et al.* 1996; Reidl *et al.* 2007) have found that even when women can work from home and manage their own time flexibly, they are still disadvantaged in several respects, compared with men in the same occupations.

The erosion of traditional occupational demarcations in the media industries and the emergence of new occupations, based on the use of new technologies and platforms, have undoubtedly broken down many of the barriers that traditionally excluded women from a range of technical, professional, and managerial roles. However, these same changes have also eroded the bargaining power of the trade unions, resulting in a general loss of employment security and diminished earnings for all but a minority of "stars." Despite these changes, women in the "creative class" (Florida 2002) still earn considerably less than their male counterparts. Based on US data and a rather broad definition of the "creative class," Florida found that

> Women hold slightly more than half (52.3 percent) of creative class jobs and their average level of education is almost the same as men. But the pay they receive is anything but equal. Creative class men earn an average of $82,009 versus $48,077 for creative class women. This $33,932 gap is a staggering 70 percent of the average female creative class salary. Even when we control for hours worked and education in a regression analysis, creative class men out-earn creative class women by a sizable $23,700, or 49.2 percent.
>
> (Florida 2011: n.p.)

Using a narrower definition limited to "arts, design, media, entertainment and sports," the pay gap was still $9,400 (Florida 2011). This pay gap is partly related to a gender division of labor within the media but also due to the dominance of individual negotiation of fees and salaries in the media industries. Women are less able to take advantage of the terms of collective agreements and have a hard time being assertive in male-dominated environments.

## Shifting location of work: from office to home

The digitization of information and the ability to transmit it electronically that underpinned the shift of work from office to home also enabled work to be delocalized more generally. Work can now be transmitted seamlessly across regional and national borders to any location with the right infrastructure and willing workers with the right skills, speaking the right languages.

The types of telemediated offshore outsourcing that have tended to hit the headlines have been in activities such as software development, data entry, or call center work (see, for instance, UNCTAD 2002; Bardhan and Kroll 2003; Huws et al. 2005). These have attracted the attention of many researchers (e.g. Bain and Taylor 2002; Callaghan and Thompson 2002; Rainnie and Drummond 2006; Pupo and Noack 2009; Holtgrewe et al. 2009; D'Cruz and Noronha 2009; Wolff 2009), including several who bring a gender perspective to their analysis (Soares 1991; Mitter and Pearson 1992; Mazzei Nogueira 2009; Belt et al. 2000; Mirchandani 2004; Glucksman 2004). Attracting much less attention from scholars, however, has been the emergence of a highly developed international division of labor in media work. Yet, for instance, publishers based in the UK or North America often send text-editing work to India and the processing of graphs and diagrams to China. Hollywood-based film companies may (depending in part on fluctuations in the exchange rate) source their post-production visual effects from Canada and their sound post-production from the UK; and several Asian destinations are also emerging as important sources for these activities (Gurstein 2007; author's interviews with industry sources 2012).

In the Spanish-speaking world, Argentina is a center for visual special effects. Mexico acts as a Latin American production hub and is also a center for sound, because it is where dubbing and production of subtitles tend to be carried out (author's interviews with industry sources 2012). Vietnam supplies illustration and animation for Japanese manga comics and Anime films, as well as supplying graphic and website design to European companies (Huws and Flecker 2004).[1] The increasing use of platforms such as eLance and oDesk (Caraway 2010) to recruit creative media workers from a worldwide pool, regardless of location, adds another dimension of geographical complexity to the picture.

This spatial division of labor interacts with traditional gender-based patterns of job segregation in each location in complex ways. On the one hand, new opportunities may be opened up for women to enter employment in creative industries in locations where these opportunities did not exist before. On the other, the existence of a global reserve army of skilled workers may undermine the bargaining position of women workers with their employers, making it harder for them to escape from inferior positions in their local creative industries labor market. A study of the offshoring of editorial work from the UK to India found that the predominantly female workforce suffered in both locations. In the UK, the work of the majority of the workforce was deskilled and casualized, with a small minority moving into quality-control jobs. In India, although entry-level jobs were created for female graduates, the work that was created was highly stressful, with a requirement to meet tight deadlines and work antisocial hours, with the result that staff turnover was exceptionally high, job satisfaction was low, and there was a general loss in quality (Dahlmann and Huws 2007). Unfortunately, very few studies have been carried out regarding global media work from a gender perspective.

## Conclusion

We must conclude that while women are required to carry out unpaid reproductive and consumption labor, whether for pleasure or from necessity, their ambiguous relationship to paid creative work will remain constrained by time pressures and their position vis-a-vis employers will generally be weaker than that of their male counterparts. Changes in the boundaries between paid and unpaid work, as well as in the location of work in the media industries, oblige media workers to negotiate a path through a rapidly shifting and unfamiliar landscape. Further research is urgently needed to map the interplay between new developments in the gender division of labor and their interaction with class, nationality, and ethnicity.

## Note

1 Manga refers to Japanese comic art in the form of caricature, cartoon, and animation.

## References

Adams, R. (2010) "The New Girl in the Old Boy Network," in A. Levin (ed.) *Gender, Sexuality and Museums: A Routledge Reader*, London: Routledge.

Arvidsson, A. and E. Colleoni (2012) "Value in Informational Capitalism and on the Internet," *The Information Society* 28(3): 135–50.

Bain, P. and P. Taylor (2002) "Ringing the Changes? Union Recognition and Organisation in Call Centres in the UK Finance Sector," *Industrial Relations Journal* 33(3): 246–61.

Banks, J. and S. Humphreys (2008) "The Labor of User Co-creators," *Convergence* 14(4): 401–18.

Bardhan, A. and C. Kroll (2003) *The New Wave of Outsourcing*, Berkeley: Fisher Center for Real Estate & Urban Economics, University of California.

Belt, V., R. Richardson, and J. Webster (2000) "Women's Work in the Information Economy: The Case of Telephone Call Centres," *Information, Communication & Society* 3(3): 366–85.

Callaghan, G. and P. Thompson (2002) "We Recruit Attitude: The Selection and Shaping of Call Centre Labor," *Journal of Management Studies* 39(2): 233–54.

Caraway (2010) "Online Labor Markets: An Inquiry into oDesk," *Work Organisation, Labour and Globalisation* 4(2): 111–25.

Clare, K. (2008) "Management and Creativity, Chris Bilton," *Creative Industries Journal* 1(1): 81–3.

Comor, E. (2010) "Digital Prosumption and Alienation," *Ephemera* 10(3/4): 439–54.

D'Cruz, P. and E. Noronha (2009) "Experiencing Depersonalized Bullying: A Study of Indian Call-Centre Agents," *Work Organisation, Labour and Globalisation* 3: 26–46.

Dahlmann, S. and U. Huws (2007) "Sunset in the West: Outsourcing Editorial Work from the UK to India," *Work Organisation, Labour and Globalisation* 1(1): 59–75.

Dahlmann, S., U. Huws, and M. Stratigaki (2009) *Changing Patterns of Segregation and Power Relations in the Workplace*, report from the WORKS project, Leuven: Higher Institute of Labor Studies.

Florida, R. (2002) *The Rise of the Creative Class: And How It's Transforming Work, Leisure, Community and Everyday Life*, New York: Basic Books.

——(2011) "The Income Disparity of Women in the Creative Class," *Atlantic Cities*, November 2. http://www.theatlanticcities.com/jobs-and-economy/2011/11/income-disparity-women-creative-class/359/.

Fuchs, C. (2010) "Labor in Informational Capitalism and on the Internet," *The Information Society* 26: 179–96.

——(2012) "With or Without Marx? With or Without Capitalism? A Rejoinder to Adam Arvidsson and Eleanor Colleoni," *TripleC* 10(2): 633–45.

Gill, R. (2002) "Cool, Creative and Egalitarian? Exploring Gender in Project-based New Media Work in Europe," *Information, Communication & Society* 5(1): 70–89.

——(2005) "Work in the e-Society: Freelancing in New Media," *Journal für Psychologie* 13(1).

Glucksman, M. (2004) "Call Configurations: Varieties of Call Centre and Divisions of Labor," *Work, Employment and Society* 18(4): 795–811.

Gurstein, P. (2001) *Wired to the World, Chained to the Home: Telework in Daily Life*, Vancouver: UBC Press.

——(2007) "Navigating the Seamless Environment in the Global Supply Chain: Implications for Canadian Regions and Workers," *Work Organisation, Labour and Globalisation* 2(1): 76–97.

Hardt, M. and A. Negri (2000) *Empire*, Cambridge, MA: Harvard University Press.

——(2004) *Multitude: War and Democracy in the Age of Empire*, New York: Penguin.

Holtgrewe, U., J. Longen, H. Mottweiler, and A. Schönauer (2009) "Global or Embedded Service Work? The (Limited) Transnationalisation of the Call-Centre Industry," *Work Organisation, Labour and Globalisation* 3: 9–25.

Huws, U. (1984) "New Technology Homeworkers," *Employment Gazette*, January.

——(1985) *The New Homeworkers: New Technology and the Changing Location of White-Collar Work*, London: Low Pay Unit.

——(1991) "Telework: Projections," *Futures* 23 (January): 19–31.

——(2003) *The Making of a Cybertariat: Virtual Work in a Real World*, New York: Monthly Review Press.

——(2010) "Expression and Expropriation: The Dialectics of Autonomy and Control in Creative Labor," *Ephemera* 10(3/4): 504–21.

Huws, U. and J. Flecker (2004) *Asian Emergence: The World's Back Office?*, Brighton: Institute for Employment Studies.

Huws, U., S. Dahlmann, and J. Flecker (2005) *Outsourcing of ICT and Related Services in the EU*, Dublin: European Foundation for the Improvement of Living and Working Conditions.

Huws, U., S. Dahlmann, J. Flecker, U. Holtgrewe, A. Schönauer, M. Ramioul, and K. Geurts (2009) *Value Chain Restructuring in Europe in a Global Economy*, Leuven: Higher Institute of Labor Studies.

Huws, U., S. Podro, E. Gunnarsson, T. Weijers, K. Arvanitaki, and V. Trova (1996) *Teleworking and Gender*, Brighton: Institute for Employment Studies.

Krings, B.-J. (2007) "Make Like a Man: The Demands of Creative Work, Gender and the Management of Everyday Life," *Work Organisation, Labour and Globalisation* 1(1): 90–108.

Kücklich, J. (2005) "Precarious Playbour: Modders and the Digital Games Industry," *The Fibreculture Journal* 5: n.p. http://five.fibreculturejournal.org/fcj-025-precarious-playbour-modders-and-the-digital-games-industry/.

McRobbie, Angela (1998) *British Fashion Design: Rag Trade or Image Industry*, London: Routledge.

Mazzei Nogueira, C. (2009) "Double Workload: A Study of the Sexual Division of Labor among Women Telemarketing Operators in Brazil," *Work Organisation, Labour and Globalisation* 3: 66–79.

Mirchandani, K. (2004) "Practices of Global Capital: Gaps, Cracks and Ironies in Transnational Call Centres in India," *Global Networks* 4(4): 355–73.

Mitter, S. and R. Pearson (1992) *Global Information Processing: The Emergence of Software Services and Data Entry Jobs in Selected Developing Countries*, Sectoral Activities Programme Working Papers, Geneva: ILO.

Monod, E. (1983) "Le Télétravail: Une nouvelle maniere de travailler," *Datafrance*, September 15.

Nilles, J. M., F. R. Carlson, P. Gray, and G. J. Hanneman (1976) *The Telecommunications–Transportation Tradeoff*, Chichester and New York: John Wiley.

Oliver, D., C. Romm-Livermore, and F. Sudweeks (2009) *Self-Service in the Internet Age*, Heidelberg: Springer.

Olson, M. (1983) "Remote Office Work: Changing Patterns in Space and Time," *Office Workstations in the Home*, Washington, DC: National Academy of Sciences.

Phizacklea, A. and C. Wolkowitz (1995) *Homeworking Women: Gender, Racism and Class at Work*, London: Sage.

Prahalad, C. K. and V. Ramaswamy (2000) "Co-Opting Customer Competence," *Harvard Business Review*, January/February.

Pupo, N. and A. Noack (2009) "Standardising Public Service: The Experiences of Call-Centre Workers in the Canadian Federal Government," *Work Organisation, Labour and Globalisation* 3: 100–13.

Rainnie, A. and G. Drummond (2006) "Community Unionism in a Regional Call Centre: The Organizer's Perspective," in J. Burgess and J. Connell (eds.) *Developments in the Call Centre Industry: Analysis, Changes and Challenges*, New York: Routledge, pp. 136–51.

Reidl, S., H. Schiffbänker, and H. Eichmann (2007) "Creating a Sustainable Future? The Working Life of Creative Workers in Vienna," *Work Organisation, Labour and Globalisation* 1(1): 49–59.

Ritzer, G. and N. Jurgenson (2010) "Production, Consumption, Prosumption," *Journal of Consumer Culture* 10(1): 13–36.

Smythe, D. (2001 [1978]) "On the Audience Commodity and Its Work," in M. G. Durham and D. M. Kellner (eds.) *Media and Cultural Studies: Key Works*, Malden, MA and Oxford: Blackwell Publishing, pp. 253–79.

Soares, A. (1991) "The Hard Life of the Unskilled Workers in New Technologies: Data-entry Clerks in Brazil—A Case Sudy," in H.-J. Bullinger (ed.) *Human Aspects in Computing: Design and Use of Interactive Systems and Information Management*, New York: Elsevier, pp. 1219–23.

Terranova, T. (2000) "Free Labor: Producing Culture for the Digital Economy," *Social Text* 18: 33.

Toffler, A. (1980) *The Third Wave*, New York: Bantam Books.

UNCTAD (2002) *Changing Dynamics of Global Computer Software and Services Industry: Implications for Developing Countries*, New York and Geneva: UNCTAD.

Valenduc, G., P. Vendramin, B.-J. Krings, and L. Nierling (2007) *Occupational Case Studies: Synthesis Report and Comparative Analysis*, Works Project, Leuven: Higher Institute of Labor Studies.

Vedel, G. (1984) *Just Pick up a Telephone: Remote Office Work in Sweden*, Copenhagen: Copenhagen School of Economics and Business Administration.

Weinbaum, B. and A. Bridges (1976) "The Other Side of the Paycheck," *Monthly Review* 28(3): 88–103.

Wolff, S. (2009) "Looking behind the Line: Privatisation and the Reification of Work in a Brazilian Telecommunications Company," *Work Organisation, Labour and Globalisation* 3: 47–65.

Zimmerman, J. and J. Horwitz (1983) "Living Better Vicariously?," in J. Zimmerman (ed.) *The Technological Woman*, Santa Barbara, CA: Praeger.

# 14

# Gendering the commodity audience in social media

## Tamara Shepherd

### Commodification and gender in social media

Social media is a term typically used to describe a host of web-based technologies that support communication and interaction between people, or users, who both communicate using these technologies and contribute to the creation of online content. Media scholars examining social media platforms from the perspective of gender might well study the ways in which gender and sexuality influence communication behaviors, identity play, and self-promotion and branding (Consalvo and Paasonen 2002). In these respects, social media technologies can be seen as platforms for creativity and communication, as exemplified in websites such as Facebook, YouTube, Twitter, Pinterest, and Instagram. But these sites also are corporations seeking to turn a profit. The way that social media sites function as corporations is the starting point for a gendered analysis of social media's political economy.

This chapter employs a feminist political economy approach to examine how the business practices of social media, especially advertising, work to construct users as gendered commodities. Generally speaking, the political economy tradition of studying communications and the media attends to the impact of economic structures such as media ownership, government policy, and advertising models on communication as a political and social instrument of power (McChesney 2000). A feminist political economy adds to this broad perspective an understanding of economic structures as fundamentally gendered. In seeing the politics of media ownership, government policymaking, and advertising practices as following not only class divisions but also the deep-seated gender divisions that organize social relations, feminist political economy highlights the central role that gender plays in arrangements of labor (Mosco *et al.* 2008). Accordingly, the economic structures that underlie social media platforms show how these platforms are not just spaces in which gendered identities might be explored, but business models that create particular gendered identities in the interest of capital.

Typically, the business models of most major social media platforms involve advertising, where services are provided without cost so long as users look at advertisements and agree to a set of terms and conditions that allow for the collection of their information. In this context, advertising takes on new dimensions in addition to the familiar model from earlier print media or television—advertisers can know significantly more about the people using social media websites, since users share their personal and behavioral information as a condition of signing up for and using the service.

The practice whereby advertisers gain access to user data on social media websites is known as data-mining. As a market research strategy, data-mining involves the large-scale collection of the personal information that users disclose as part of participating in social media. This personal information is then aggregated so that no one is personally identifiable (i.e. it cannot be used to single out individual users), but it can show overall trends among user demographics, interests, and preferences (Chung and Grimes 2005). Broader trends within the aggregated data are used in turn to construct profiles of particular user groups, including gendered user groups, so that they may be targeted more precisely by advertisers. As advertiser-supported platforms, commercial social media websites are fundamentally built on sophisticated data-mining as their central business model (boyd and Ellison 2008; Cohen 2008). More recently, the construction of user profiles based on aggregate data has gone a step further by attempting to predict users' future consumer behavior through collecting not only personal information, but behavioral information. In this version of data-mining, known as behavioral advertising (Stallworth 2010), tracking technologies pick up how many times a user visits a particular site, or uses a particular search term, or clicks on a particular hyperlink, as part of making predictions about what kinds of consumption patterns a group of users is likely to engage in over time.

In this context, the person using social media websites becomes part of the system of exchange that supports these apparently "free" online services. The user's role in this system can be understood through Vincent Mosco's (2009) theory of "immanent commodification." Commodification is the process whereby something—an object, a piece of information, an idea, a creative work, a service, and so on—gets transformed into a good or service with a certain exchange value, as determined by market economics. Mosco looks at how social media platforms covertly deploy "new measurement and surveillance technologies to expand the production of media commodities," so that users' content, communications, personal information, and online behavior all become commodified automatically (2009: 143). For instance, mechanisms for collecting information about users, such as cookies, flash cookies, beacons, log files, and deep packet inspection, to name a few, inherently involve packaging the data collected so that it can be exchanged at market value (Shade and Shepherd forthcoming). Advertisers are keenly interested in measuring this social media user data, because it allows them to target specific groups of users with relevant ads in the most efficient, and profitable, manner.

At the same time that immanent commodification works to turn users into commodities or products for exchange, mechanisms like target marketing and behavioral advertising classify these user-commodities differentially. For example, as mentioned above, target marketing involves organizing aggregate data into discrete profiles based on demographics, interests, and preferences. Joseph Turow, citing the profiles constructed by marketing company Axciom, notes how the company's collection of segmented consumer groups like "Corporate Clout," "Soccer and SUVs," "First

Digs," and "Single City Strugglers" creates added value for its clients by arranging customers along a spectrum of income levels and lifestyles (2011: 97).

Taking target marketing a step further, behavioral advertising constructs such user groups based on predictive measures of how they might behave as consumers. So extensive are these constructed user groups that they enable advertisers to anticipate and thus shape users' needs, tastes, and purchasing habits differentially. Because of this, behavioral advertising is also referred to as "online profiling" (Stallworth 2010: 478). The differential treatment of users in social media advertising practices is not just reflective of what users are doing, but it seeks to construct their ideal consumption behaviors from the advertisers' point of view. Such constructions of ideal user profiles tend to follow certain prevailing stereotypes; this chapter focuses on gender stereotypes in particular to examine how users are constituted as gendered commodities through social media.

## The (gendered) commodity audience

> Audience power is produced, sold, purchased and consumed, it commands a price and is a commodity.
>
> (Smythe 1981: 256)

While social media platforms fundamentally constitute users as commodities in sophisticated and detailed ways, the mechanism of user or audience commodification is not entirely new. In all advertiser-supported commercial media, advertisers seek access to audiences, which they effectively rent from publishers, broadcasters, or platforms (Jhally and Livant 1986: 125). These audiences become more valuable to advertisers the more specific they are, and so media industry players have increasingly sought to gain more precise information on the make-up and behavior of audiences in order to deliver particular target markets to advertisers.

Describing the advertiser-supported media platform of television in the 1970s and early 1980s, political economist Dallas Smythe formulated the "audience commodity" as the chief product of culture industries (1977, 1981). His theory addressed what he noted was a "blindspot" in the study of communications that focused on how the culture industries produced texts, as opposed to looking at the production of audiences. Smythe instead argued that a media text, for example a television program, is only the "free lunch" that entices viewers to watch (1981: 242–3). The viewers themselves are the product being bought and sold within the commodity exchange system. Advertisers spend their money to access audiences and thus harness audience power as a kind of labor—a notion that Sut Jhally and Bill Livant (1986) further expanded upon in their account of how exactly watching television advertisements constitutes a kind of work.

Smythe's theory captures how viewers are engaged in a labor of watching advertisements, where their viewing power is produced and circulated through the economies of ratings systems. Television ratings perform the function of segmenting audiences through demographic information as well as behavioral information. For instance, in the 1980s, the television ratings firm Nielsen introduced "people meters," a device attached to a household television set that encouraged individual family members to punch in and out as a measure of how much they were watching (Jhally and Livant 1986: 139). Nielsen and other ratings firms then used this data on audience demographics and viewing habits to describe and in fact create segmented niche markets for advertisers to target by situating their ads in the most effective timeslots and programming environments.

Crucially, as Eileen Meehan (1986) underscores in her revision of Smythe's theory in what she calls the "commodity audience," ratings systems also serve to classify and categorize viewers according to gendered lines. The gathering and combination of demographic and behavioral data by firms like Nielsen, she argues, is far from a neutral practice (Meehan 1984). In the first place, ratings firms seek to measure consumers with disposable income to spend on advertised products, and so only higher-income households are measured. Second, the measurement and creation of desired audience groups do not necessarily follow actual viewing, but instead arise from power dynamics between television networks, ratings firms, and advertisers. In this way, as ratings firms negotiate market dynamics in their active construction of the most desirable audience, they transform groups of viewers into differential commodities, where "noneconomic assumptions undergird beliefs about what sorts of people *ought* to be *the* audience" (Meehan 2002: 217, emphasis in original). Moreover, the clerical work of measuring audiences was typically performed by low-status, female employees, who comprised the backstage of ratings that valued certain audience groups following "familiar patterns of discrimination on the grounds of gender, race, social status, sexual orientation, and age" (Meehan 2002: 215–17).

The process of transforming audiences into gendered commodities relies on asymmetrical market relations, and especially on the imbalance of power in the culture industries between ratings firms and viewers. In the case of television, ratings firms enjoy a relative monopoly over the practice of collecting and packaging audience data (Smythe 1977: 4–5). Meehan affirms that ratings monopolies construct audiences and their labor as "truly *manufactured* commodities whose content depend[s] on changing power relations within that market" (2002: 215, emphasis in original). These power relationships are reflected in the differential demand for certain ratings results, where a need for a common system of measurement—one that hierarchically organizes different audiences according to market value—produces monopolistic tendencies (Meehan 1993: 387–9). For example, Nielsen enjoys a relative monopoly over television ratings because the firm has succeeded in producing the ratings that advertisers want, ratings that are mostly artificially manufactured based on noneconomic assumptions about audience value. As such, ratings do not simply measure audiences but create them as commodities, reflecting gendered assumptions in demography that work to segment audiences according to institutionalized sexism (Meehan 2002: 217). In this way, the audience as commodity is always already gendered as a condition of the existing gendered constructions of meaning that take place within structures of capital accumulation.

## Social media users as gendered commodities

The concept of the gendered commodity audience, developed in relation to television viewing, can be mapped productively onto the context of social media. Here, audience members become users—an important terminological shift that signals some of the key differences between television viewing and participation in social media platforms that are important to account for in adapting the commodity audience to this new context. Examining the qualitative changes in the commodity audience from television to social media—where audience members have become users, programming has become site content, ratings systems have become data-mining, and narrowcasting has become target marketing—sheds light on how gendered assumptions work in the system of immanent commodification that characterizes commercial social media.

### Audience as users

When cast as users of networked technologies, the people that once comprised audience members are imbued with an implicit sense of agency, as "active internet contributors" (van Dijck 2009: 41; Livingstone 2004). But at the same time that the term "user" implies an active use of online media platforms, it still, like "audience," avoids any connotation of the gendered labor involved in social media participation. Jhally and Livant contend that "when the audience watches commercial television it is working for the media" (1986: 135), and the work that audiences do often follows gendered patterns. Even more so than television audience members, social media users function as workers who look at (and click on) advertisements that are targeted to specific gendered audiences, but they are also, crucially, suppliers of personal information and producers of content—particularly on a platform like Facebook, where members must disclose personal information at the outset in order to use the site, and then provide an overwhelming amount of site content as a function of their participation.

The additional layer of user labor required to populate Facebook with content adds to the complexity of the gendered commodity audience in social media, where user viewing or clicking power is bought and sold in the exchanges between the site and its advertising partners. At the same time that viewing power becomes commodified, much as it did in the context of television, the productive or creative power of Facebook users also is ripe for commercial appropriation. Consider, for example, the clauses in Facebook's Terms of Service—recently renamed its "Statement of Rights and Responsibilities"—that allow the company to retain a "non-exclusive, transferable, sub-licensable, royalty-free, worldwide license" over all content posted to the site (Facebook 2012). Facebook can appropriate users' images and text legally as part of its profit motive, and so user creativity and intellectual property become commodified along with viewing power. As Fernando Bermejo puts it with regard to online search engines, the market for viewing power has been transformed into a wider market for words in a "global language auction" (2009: 150). On Facebook, global language and image transactions contribute to the site's profit margins, while the labor of producing that content gets downplayed as everyday communication behavior among users. At the same time, the real access and privilege in digital labor remain with the mainly young, white, male "innovators" of social media platforms, like Facebook's Mark Zuckerberg or Google's Larry Page and Sergey Brin.

Moreover, the licensing agreement enshrined in Facebook's Terms further amplifies the division between user labor and the platform "owners" by invoking the legal language of End User License Agreements—the standard legal contracts that delimit the rights of users once they have agreed to use a particular software. By framing Facebook users as "end users" who contractually agree to use the service as-is, without being able to modify it, the term "user" invites a legal way of limiting people's agency and obscuring their labor. This practice of obscuring the labor involved in creating content for Facebook recalls the way that women's labor, typically performed in domestic settings, has long been obscured by cultural, ideological, and legal means (Fortunati 2007). Housework, cooking, and providing care are feminized and thus devalued as "shadow labour," despite their integral function in capitalist accumulation (Weeks 2007: 237). Yet, like women who work often invisibly to maintain the cycle of reproduction and production, user labor on Facebook is elided in order to keep the site viable as a communication network predicated upon the site content that users contribute.

### Programming as site content

Smythe famously characterized television programming as the "free lunch" that would draw audiences to watch advertisements. As Jhally and Livant further elaborate, it is not enough for the programming to be generally appealing to audiences. It must also provide the right environment for advertisements: "Advertisers seek compatible programming vehicles that stress the life-styles of consumption" (1986: 140). These lifestyles of consumption are gendered through the ways that programming targets certain audiences, where soap operas offer the quintessential example of programming that was developed as a vehicle for soap ads targeted toward "housewives" (Brown and Barwick 1988: 76). On a site like Facebook, the programming or content would seem to be less deliberate than television programming, given that, in theory, users can add whatever they wish to their profiles that constitute the network. In fact, there are a number of restrictions on the content added to Facebook, as outlined in the site's Community Guidelines and policed both by users who flag certain items as well as employees who proactively seek out and remove any content deemed "unacceptable"—with detailed guidelines around nudity, violence, hate speech, self-harm, and harassment, for example (Gillespie 2012).

Excepting these instances of unacceptable content, users enjoy relative freedom to add whatever they wish to their Facebook profiles and communicative exchanges. Yet the site does employ certain design elements that encourage an environment conducive to advertising. For instance, one of the site's trademarks is the "like" button, which allows users to "like" any content posted to site. The "like" button appears underneath wall posts, photos, and videos, and also underneath sponsored posts and sidebar advertisements. Moreover, the "like" button extends beyond Facebook itself to be integrated across many different websites for news content, e-commerce, and multimedia. The prevalence of the "like" button, along with its ease of use—just pressing "like" as opposed to formulating and writing a response in the comment box—fosters an environment of positive endorsement. There is no option to "dislike" or even to "not care"; liking something effectively feeds into the commodification structure of the site as part of users' labor of endorsement that takes place in a positive atmosphere.

Endorsement on Facebook is further supported by the individual user's personal profile as the unit of reputation that lends weight to the "like" button, by attaching a "like" to someone's identity (McGeveran 2009). Users' identities get associated with certain products, for example through clicking "like" on an e-commerce site outside of Facebook, or even certain life stages, through liking the activities of friends getting married or having children. That endorsement data is in turn connected to the vast stores of information that is networked through the site. So, for example, liking a Facebook friend's baby photos can lead to targeted ads for baby-related products, especially for women Facebook users who are listed as "married" (Delo 2012). The construction of Facebook users as commodities thus follows the patterns established more broadly in consumer targeting that naturalizes heteronormative gender roles, with the addition of much finer-grained personal and behavioral information.

### Ratings systems as data-mining

Given that users actively construct the content of a site like Facebook within the site's structure, which not only encourages a positive atmosphere of endorsement through the like button but also solicits explicitly gendered autobiographical narratives through the unit of the profile, the data to be gleaned from users represents both a quantitative and qualitative change from the data gathered through television ratings systems. Nielsen's "people meter" accounted for what programs each family member was watching and for how long; Facebook compiles personal information about a user's identity, location, work, and education, along with preferences in books, music, film, and activities, as articulated among an entire network of "friends," situated within the user's photographs, wall posts, messages, and event pages, and complemented with behavioral data on her or his "likes," clicks on hyperlinks or advertisements, and search terms. And because all of these pieces of information are transmitted digitally, they leave traces that are generated automatically and persist potentially indefinitely (Bermejo 2009: 143). Such an exponential expansion in the quantity, quality, and durability of user data means that commodification on social media sites takes place at an accelerated rate and happens immanently to participation in these sites.

When compared to this context of "big data" and increasingly sophisticated technologies for harnessing that data through the valorization of online surveillance (Cohen 2008), the television ratings systems of the past appear clumsy and quaint. But at the same time, the ways in which television audiences were segmented along gendered lines was not strictly empirical, as Meehan points out, but was a function of ratings companies' creation of particular audience groups (Meehan 2002: 215). While data-mining techniques may involve greater precision, the "exact and dispassionate measurement of audiences" remains somewhat fictional (Caraway 2011: 699). In this context, it is perhaps not surprising that the gendered segmentation of television audiences continues to influence marketers in social media. Much like the Axciom consumer profiles described by Turow, obvious gender stereotypes guide the naming of specific gendered groups for Facebook's data management partner

Datalogix, especially in groups like "Soccer Moms," "Green Consumers," and "Sports Fans" (Datalogix 2012). In turn, the categorizations of such groups based on gender (and also other stereotypical features of class, race, ethnicity, and age) function as a kind of discrimination by assigning differential value to these different target markets.

### Narrowcasting as target marketing

Organizing user groups into target markets finds its precedent in the narrowcasting strategies of cable television in the 1980s, where the gap between programming and advertising content was increasingly blurred by the targeting of both toward specific audience groups, often marked by gender (Jhally and Livant 1986: 140). Yet different audience groups were not created equally in this new television landscape, where the more valuable audiences—usually comprised of white, higher-income, male viewers—were the ones who were measured by ratings meters and thus the ones who set the benchmark market value for audience power (Meehan 1990: 132). "Narrowcasting's very foundation rests on hegemonic structuring" (Smith-Shomade 2004: 74).

In the age of online social media, this hegemonic structuring of targeted markets takes on much more detailed and sophisticated contours, where individual users may themselves be split into several niche interest groups. This micro-segmentation of the online commodity audience reflects what Tiziana Terranova traces as the way that, as broadcasting gave way to narrowcasting, narrowcasting has now given way to pointcasting—online advertisers target sub-individual units (2004: 34). But in the same manner as narrowcasting, the segmentation of user groups in pointcasting is both productive and discriminatory; pointcasting does not just reflect user desires, it produces them in ways that are differential according to already existing structures of privilege. For example, the user profiles that underlie the targeting of specific content to specific user groups also result in price and marketing discrimination (Danna and Gandy 2002). In a process known as "weblining," data-mining firms like Datalogix organize the information collected through Facebook into profile groups based on income, such as "Homeowner Status," "Presence of Children," and "Credit Card Buyers" (Datalogix 2012). In turn, these groups are presented with differential pricing or different products, based on their perceived spending power. As Anthony Danna and Oscar Gandy point out, this unfair treatment tends to involve discrimination against lower-income groups, non-whites, and women; this discrimination is particularly troubling when it extends beyond the ability to make consumer choices into the ability to access information in the public sphere (2002: 383).

## Conclusion: the social impact of gendered commodification

Returning to the concept of the gendered commodity audience is crucial in the context of social media, when not only consumer behavior but public and political behavior is increasingly shaped by social media as a key information infrastructure. When people get their information through sites like Facebook or Twitter, the way that they encounter and negotiate commodification can have far-reaching consequences. As Meehan once said of Smythe, "By looking first at Smythe's formulations in light of political economic research on the ratings industry, one finds that Smythe's basic claims have survived the tests of time and research" (1993: 379). The same might be said of Meehan today, when it is increasingly important to examine audience or user commodification from the point of view of social media labor and data collection processes that are fundamentally gendered.

While certain qualifications must be made around the gendered commodity audience when transposed from the context of television to that of social media—where audience members have become users, programming has become site content, ratings systems have become data-mining, and narrowcasting has become target marketing— the continuities between these media environments are significant. The widespread popularity of television forms a necessary precondition for the advertising environment of the web, where looking at advertisements is a long-quotidian practice and advertising is naturalized as the most efficient profit model for delivering "free" programming. This continuity between television and social media highlights how, while social media platforms often present themselves as general "means of survival," their use is designed to serve their own profit interests (Fuchs 2012: 703).

Like Smythe's initial contention about the audience commodity addressing a "blindspot" in the study of political economy, the gendered commodity audience contributes a consideration of commodification as the underlying structure of social media. Forging links between users' everyday online behaviors and the larger sub-strates that shape those behaviors and profit from them, the gendered commodity audience concept brings to light commodification processes that tend to be invisible in practice (Manzerolle and Smeltzer 2011: 334). Users function as commodities in social media sites, but are also laborers, performing the free labor necessary to uphold the advertising system as well as the content of the sites themselves (Terranova 2004; Cohen 2008; Fuchs 2012). In thinking about users as workers, and particularly as gendered workers within a system of differential commodification, the gendered commodity audience continues to be a productive framework for attending to ideological dimensions of the political economy of communication.

## References

Bermejo, F. (2009) "Audience Manufacture in Historical Perspective: From Broadcasting to Google," *New Media & Society* 11(1–2): 133–54.

boyd, d. m. and N. Ellison (2008) "Social Network Sites: Definition, History, and Scholarship," *Journal of Computer-Mediated Communication* 13(1): 210–30.

Brown, M. E. and L. Barwick (1988) "Fables and Endless Genealogies: Soap Opera and Women's Culture," *Continuum: Journal of Media & Cultural Studies* 1(2): 71–82.

Caraway, B. (2011) "Audience Labor in the New Media Environment: A Marxian Revisiting of the Audience Commodity," *Media, Culture & Society* 33(5): 693–708.

Chung, G. and S. Grimes (2005) "Data Mining the Kids: Surveillance and Market Research Strategies in Children's Online Games," *Canadian Journal of Communication* 30(4): 527–48.

Cohen, N. S. (2008) "The Valorization of Surveillance: Towards a Political Economy of Facebook," *Democratic Communiqué* 22(1): 5–22.

Consalvo, M. and S. Paasonen (eds.) (2002) *Women & Everyday Uses of the Internet: Agency and Identity*, New York: Peter Lang.

Danna, A. and O. H. Gandy (2002) "All That Glitters Is Not Gold: Digging beneath the Surface of Data Mining," *Journal of Business Ethics* 40: 373–88.

Datalogix (2012) *Audiences: Syndicated Segments for Online Consumer Targeting.* http://www.datalogix.com/audiences/online/syndicated-segments/.

Delo, C. (2012) "Does Facebook Know You're Pregnant?," *Advertising Age.* http://adage.com/article/digital/facebook-pregnant/237073/.

Facebook (2012) "Statement of Rights and Responsibilities." http://www.facebook.com/legal/terms.

Fortunati, L. (2007) "Immaterial Labour and Its Machinization," *Ephemera* 7(1): 139–57.

Fuchs, C. (2012) "Dallas Smythe Today—The Audience Commodity, the Digital Labour Debate, Marxist Political Economy and Critical Theory. Prolegomena to a Digital Labour Theory of Value," *TripleC—Cognition, Communication, Cooperation* 10(2): 692–740.

Gillespie, T. (2012) "Don't Ignore Facebook's Silly-sounding Policies," *Salon.com.* http://www.salon.com/2012/02/22/dont_ignore_facebooks_silly_sounding_policies/.

Jhally, S. and B. Livant (1986) "Watching as Working: The Valorization of Audience Consciousness," *Journal of Communication* 36(3): 124–43.

Livingstone, S. (2004) "The Challenge of Changing Audiences," *European Journal of Communication* 19(1): 75–86.

McChesney, R. (2000) "The Political Economy of Communication and the Future of the Field," *Media, Culture & Society* 22: 109–16.

McGeveran, W. (2009) "Disclosure, Endorsement, and Identity in Social Marketing," *University of Illinois Law Review* 4: 1105–66.

Manzerolle, V. and S. Smeltzer (2011) "Consumer Databases and the Mediation of Identity: A Medium Theory Analysis," *Surveillance & Society* 8(3): 323–37.

Meehan, E. (1984) "Ratings and the Institutional Approach: A Third Answer to the Commodity Question," *Critical Studies in Mass Communication* 1(2): 216–25.

——(1986) "Conceptualizing Culture as Commodity: The Problem of Television," *Critical Studies in Mass Communication* 3: 448–57.

——(1990) "Why We Don't Count: The Commodity Audience," in P. Mellencamp (ed.) *Logics of Television: Essays in Cultural Criticism,* Bloomington: Indiana University Press.

——(1993) "Commodity Audience, Actual Audience: The Blindspot Debate," in J. Wasko, V. Mosco, and M. Pendakur (eds.) *Illuminating the Blindspots: Essays Honoring Dallas W. Smythe,* Norwood, NJ: Ablex.

——(2002) "Gendering the Commodity Audience: Critical Media Research, Feminism, and Political Economy," in E. Meehan and E. Riordan (eds.) *Sex and Money: Feminism and Political Economy in the Media,* Minneapolis: University of Minnesota Press.

Mosco, V. (2009) *The Political Economy of Communication,* 2nd edition, Thousand Oaks, CA: Sage.

Mosco, V., C. McKercher, and A. Stevens (2008) "Convergences: Elements of a Feminist Political Economy of Labor and Communication," in K. Sarikakis and L. R. Shade (eds.) *Feminist Interventions in International Communication: Minding the Gap,* Lanham, MD: Rowman and Littlefield.

Shade, L. R. and T. Shepherd (forthcoming) "Tracing and Tracking Canadian Privacy Discourses: The Audience as Commodity," in K. Kozolanka (ed.) *Publicity and the State: Critical Communications Approaches,* Toronto: University of Toronto Press.

Smith-Shomade, B. E. (2004) "Narrowcasting in the New World Information Order," *Television & New Media* 5(1): 69–81.

Smythe, D. W. (1977) "Communications: Blindspot of Western Marxism," *Canadian Journal of Political and Social Theory* 1: 1–27.

——(1981) *Dependency Road: Communications, Capitalism, Consciousness and Canada,* Norwood, NJ: Ablex.

Stallworth, B. (2010) "Googling for Principles in Online Behavioral Advertising," *Federal Communications Law Journal* 62(2): 465–91.

Terranova, T. (2004) *Network Culture: Politics for the Information Age*, London: Pluto Press.

Turow, J. (2011) *The Daily You: How the New Advertising Industry Is Defining Your Identity and Your Worth*, New Haven, CT: Yale University Press.

van Dijck, J. (2009) "Users Like You? Theorizing Agency in User-generated Content," *Media, Culture & Society* 31: 41–58.

Weeks, K. (2007) "Life Within and Against Work: Affective Labor, Feminist Critique, and Post-Fordist Politics," *Ephemera* 7(1): 233–49.

# 15

# Youthful white male industry seeks "fun"-loving middle-aged women for video games—no strings attached

*Shira Chess*

## Introduction: who put Martha Stewart in my video game?

Corporate synergies can make strange bedfellows. No one would have ever expected Martha Stewart, the queen of feminine crafts and entertaining, to find a home in a video game. But in March 2012, Zynga, the most prolific of the Facebook game companies, began an unexpected synergistic collaboration: Martha Stewart became a featured character and launched a series of quests in Zynga's role-playing game *Castleville* (2011). Previous to Martha Stewart's entry, *Castleville* was a typical Zynga Facebook game: it involved using friends and acquaintances to do small quests of farming, trading and purchasing virtual goods, and crafting small items. In recent years, it has been noted, this gaming style has primarily been used to attract more women audiences to video games. In 2011, Zynga even declared that the 40-year-old woman is the "new hardcore gamer" (Crossley 2011). After Stewart joined *Castleville*, her "kingdom" was filled with rows and rows of perfectly manicured crops and artfully placed buildings. But, while Stewart's quests were not necessarily different from other quests in *Castleville*, many members of the game audience quickly grew angry over her addition to the game. They posted remarks on Facebook such as: "Castleville just crossed the line with this Martha Stewart crap. Created a snack in the gazebo for the spring points and it redirected the browser to a freakin' Martha Stewart website!" (Walkenford 2012). Another said: "Whoever told Zynga it would be a good idea to team up with Martha Stewart for the newest *Castleville* quests should be summarily beaten" (SteelCladDragon 2012). Her quests are stereotypically feminine: decorating eggs and similar crafts for an immaculately manicured "kingdom" reflecting both her ethos and her public sense of style. And, of course, products in the game link back to real Martha Stewart products. Even more amusingly, Stewart is depicted in the game in a cartoonish way, and looking 40 years younger than she does in reality.

The use (or misuse) of Martha Stewart lets us see the complete misunderstanding of women as video game consumers. In this case, Zynga did not recognize a possibility that a popular woman celebrity outside the game world might not be popular inside the game world. Women are not the only people who play casual Facebook games, and seeing Martha Stewart's (inaccurate) depiction whenever one opens up the game is an eerie reminder that Zynga games are primarily built for women audiences. While women might be the majority of players (55 percent), they are certainly not the only people playing Zynga games (Crossley 2011). Furthermore, Zynga's arrangement seems to assume that all women players have similar tastes and desires. Thus, for players who did not fall into the category of someone who enjoys Martha Stewart, the game became alienating. In short, the use of the Martha Stewart brand alienated players in a way that made many wholly reconsider if they were the proper demographic for the game in the first place.

Part of the problem with the assumptions of the creators of *Castleville* (as well as many other games aimed at women audiences) is a conflation between the sex and gender of their players. Many feminist scholars have discussed the distinction between biological (sex) difference and cultural (gendered) difference. In other words, the label "women" does not automatically map on to feminine tastes and style; these desires are culturally learned rather than biological (Beauvoir 1989 [1953]; Butler 1999 [1989]). But product development and marketing strategies often conflate biology and culture, creating products for women that stereotype the cultural expectations of femininity. Sandra Lee Bartky explains: "Women have little control over the cultural apparatus itself and are often entirely absent from its products; to the extent that we are not excluded from it entirely the images of ourselves we see reflected in the dominant culture are often truncated or demeaning" (1990: 35). As such, the use of Martha Stewart as both a character and a marketing tool in *Castleville* helped to declare that the primary target was a woman who was specifically interested in the kinds of products sold by Martha Stewart.

Despite its absurdity, the unlikely union between Martha Stewart Living Omnimedia, Inc. and Zynga, Inc. is only one recent attempt by the gaming industry to create games for women audiences given how men dominate the industry. In recent years several gaming companies have worked to attract more women gamers, with varying levels of success. The efforts of this have shifted the industry to some extent, creating and highlighting several new gaming genres that are thought to be more women friendly. While the video game industry has attempted to expand its player demographics in recent years to include women, its notions of what women want tend to be limited. The task of this chapter is to show how women are welcomed while at the same time they are simultaneously marginalized and their tastes essentialized, and how games created for them reify traditional stereotypes of femininity and narrow definitions of womanhood.

## Femininity, masculinity, and the video game industry

Many suggest that the core of the problem—the lack of understanding of women gamers—comes from male domination within the video game industry. Fron *et al.* (2007) explain the lack of diversity in video games:

The power elite of the game industry is a predominately white, and secondarily Asian, male-dominated corporate and creative elite that represents a select group of large, global publishing companies in conjunction with a handful of massive chain retail distributors. This hegemonic elite determines which technologies will be deployed and which will not; which games will be made and by which designers; which players are important to design for, and which play styles will be supported. The hegemony operates on both monetary and cultural levels.

(Fron *et al.* 2007: 309)

This hegemony and lack of diversity ultimately characterize many of the problems within the gaming industry. Because the gaming industry often involves long hours and constrained working conditions (Consalvo 2008), love of the game is what persuades people to become game designers. The most recent data suggest that only 11 percent of game industry employees are women (Consalvo 2008; Fron *et al.* 2007). The gaming industry has been so consistently male-dominated that only a handful of women are interested in being game designers, thereby limiting women's influence and maintaining the hegemony and dominant ideologies of the gaming industry's status quo.

The industry status quo, of course, need not remain as it is. According to Consalvo, finding ways to get more women developers in the industry would benefit all: "Creating and maintaining a more diverse workforce, it seems, could result in games that are more gender inclusive, and that better reflect game play styles and content that would interest a broader population of gamers" (2008: 177). At the same time, Consalvo continues, "Yet, maintaining women's active participation in the game industry on a consistent basis has met with many challenges. Beyond design elements, factors involving marketing disconnects, structural sexism, and resistance to change continue to drive many women away" (2008: 177).

Similarly, ethnographic research on women game developers suggests that industry constraints limit women's desire to be game designers (O'Donnell 2012). O'Donnell's discussions with women game developers found: "Predominantly ... it was the issue of work–life balance that discouraged their interest in the field. Nearly every woman I interviewed mentioned specifically that they selected the studio they were working at because of a positive reputation for avoiding crunch and encouraging employees to 'not live at work'" (2012: 120). This space between need for diversity and industry realities is what maintains the current hegemony of the gaming industry.

## Are you hardcore enough?

Notably, while women only make up 11 percent of video game industry employees, significantly more women are now playing games than ever. Recent statistics put the number of women gamers at 42 percent (Cross 2011)—an astonishing percentage compared to the small number of women working in the gaming industry. As previously noted, an interest in gaming often turns players into game developers. So the 42 percent predicts that the video game industry itself will eventually shift. But shifting audience expectations has created new complications and debates over different *kinds* of gaming, since most people assume that women players fall into a category known as "casual gaming" as opposed to hardcore.

In short, much of the gaming industry divides gaming into two distinct categories, although these labels actually often blur into one another. The so-called "hardcore" gamer is most commonly depicted as someone who plays video games for long periods of time, specifically playing games with greater degrees of difficulty. The stereotype of the "hardcore gamer" is someone who prefers "emotionally negative fictions like science fiction, vampires, fantasy and war, has played a large number of video games, will invest large amounts of time and resources toward playing video games, and enjoys difficult games" (Juul 2010: 29). In short, the hardcore gamer is the most favored target audience of the gaming industry, given the assumption that hardcore players will spend large amounts of money on gaming and significantly more money on game products. Conversely, casual gamers play games that are interruptible, easy to learn, replayable, forgiving of mistakes, and are inexpensive or free (Casual Connect 2007). The casual player is thought to prefer "positive and pleasant fictions, has played few video games, is willing to commit small amounts of time and resources toward playing video games" (Juul 2010: 29). There is certainly a parallel here to romance novels, which are marketed to women audiences in similar ways; Modleski's (1982) point about romance novels will be addressed in more detail on p. 174.

Games commonly categorized as "casual" include time management games (such as *Diner Dash*), free games (such as *Bejeweled* and *Tetris*), Facebook games (such as *Farmville* and the aforementioned *Castleville*), hidden object games (such as *Ravenhearst*), and many games played on the Nintendo Wii (such as *Wii Fit* and *Wii Sports*). In contrast, games that might be considered "hardcore" include games in the *Grand Theft Auto* series, *Halo*, war-themed games (such as *Call of Duty*), and sports games (such as the *Madden* series). While these examples seem to indicate precise differences in game styles, many games, such as *World of Warcraft* and *Puzzlequest*, sit at the margins.

While these stereotypes are often fluid and do not play out precisely in reality, the gaming industry often uses rhetoric suggesting that the hardcore gamer is the more valuable audience. "The terms casual and hardcore are, evidently, often used for positioning two categories of games against each other" (Juul 2010: 26). At the same time, just because players play a game considered "casual," that does not automatically define the way that they specifically play the game. Mia Consalvo's research on *Return to Ravenhearst* players notes that "many players of casual games are not at all casual in how they play or think about such games" (2009: 4), with their "thought" specifically referring to how fandom is constructed within the casual gaming community for specific game titles and brands. Consalvo recognizes, "The industry and popular press have focused on the business of casual games, touting their impressive sales figures as well as ability to reach new player demographics" (2009: 1). Nonetheless, the gaming industry unquestionably has politics in how these terms are mobilized: this process helps to gender players.

The gendering of these gaming genres is where things become complicated. No straight or rigid line can be drawn between casual games and women versus hardcore games and men. Many women play so-called "hardcore" games; some men play "casual" games. At the same time, the gaming industry tends to make cultural assumptions of this nature. For example, one editor of *Game Informer* magazine claimed in a 2007 editorial:

> You've probably been hearing about the casual gaming revolution for a while now. You've read about how much money cell phone gaming rakes in, and how middle-aged women in the suburbs love playing games on their PCs when they aren't watching *Oprah*. We've even seen companies flat-out declare that it's a priority to capture as many of these non-traditional gamers as possible. But is this really what the industry needs?
>
> (Kato 2007: 40)

In his editorial, Kato responds to his own rhetorical question, suggesting that the gaming community should remain hardcore. In referencing "middle-aged women," "the suburbs," and "*Oprah*," Kato is drawing a very specific image of the kind of "casual" player that the industry is pandering to.

So while a direct association cannot necessarily be drawn between casual gaming and women audiences, one can certainly use industry rhetoric to draw a slightly more *squiggly* line connecting them. Furthermore, industry and critical disdain for casual games as "easy" and for a relatively feminine style of play has parallels to what Modleski (1982) describes in criticisms of other media genres popular with women, such as romance novels and soap operas. She explains that criticism of "popular feminine narratives has generally adopted one of three attitudes: dismissiveness; hostility—tending unfortunately to be aimed at the consumers of the narratives; or, most frequently, a flippant kind of mockery" (1982: 14). The gaming industry's negative response to video games aimed at women audiences is similar.

That said, casual games also often repurpose common popular themes of women's popular cultural forms. For example, hidden object games (such as *Ravenhearst* and *Bitten*) use romance and Gothic genres to build their narrative structure; in fact, romance novel powerhouse Harlequin even made a hidden object game. Similarly, many time management games (such as *Diner Dash* and *Cake Mania*) feature strong female protagonists who own their own businesses. Games such as *Diaper Dash* (2009) involve childcare and babysitting. Games such as *Shopmania* and *Mall Stars* centralize their game play around stereotypes of women's desire to shop (and the "gamification" of that stereotype). And Facebook games utilize real-world friendships and relationships to push the narratives and game play forward. Thus, the game industry currently relies a great deal on genres that have appealed to women in the past to lure new audiences into gaming spaces. At the same time, many members of the video game industry are routinely dismissive of these gaming styles.

Additionally, as many researchers have discussed in detail, the depiction of female characters in video games might dissuade many (both men and women) from playing "hardcore" games. Sexualization of many women video game characters (Lara Croft, for example) might alienate women who otherwise are potentially interested in playing more hardcore games (Ray 2004; Behm-Morawitz and Mastro 2009; Dickerman *et al.* 2008). Some women still do play these games, and presumably are not conflicted by the images promoted in them. Yet, these games and depictions help to establish a pattern wherein hardcore gaming is designed for, presumably, men, and perceived as such, while casual game genres are designed with women in mind, and, again, perceived by players as such.

## Race, class, and sexuality in gendered gaming

The phrase "women's gaming" is itself misleading and presumptive. While many of the aforementioned games are generically meant to appeal to women, the games tend to essentialize race, class, and sexuality, so that "women's gaming" is almost always translated as white, middle-class, and heterosexual versions of womanhood. Games such as *Diner Dash, Wedding Dash, Love and Death: Bitten, Ravenhearst,* and similar casual games not only have female protagonists, but they tend to have white, heterosexual, middle-class female protagonists. At the same time, other races, cultures, sexualities, and lifestyles are either marginalized or avoided altogether.

The confluence of gendered gaming as white, heterosexual, and middle class is clearly seen in the Dash series of games—particularly in *Diner Dash* and *Wedding Dash.* The Dash series all take place in the fictional "Dinertown"; restaurateur Flo is the protagonist for many of the games and the mascot for others. Flo is white and financially stable enough to own her own businesses, although the primary work that she accomplishes in her restaurants—and that players do through Flo—involves menial waitressing tasks (Chess 2012).

Flo's whiteness is often in play, particularly when she is running restaurants with international cuisines. Most notably, in the first *Diner Dash* game, at level 40 a Hindu goddess approaches Flo, and asks Flo to run her Indian restaurant. The goddess—with darker skin, six arms, and a caricature of Hindu dress and style—suggests that Flo might become a goddess if she properly runs the restaurant. In turn, the game character offers Flo two more arms in order to properly run the restaurant. Flo's clothing changes in this set of levels, and she, too, becomes a caricature of Hindu culture. This essentialization and "othering" of cultural difference help to highlight Flo's whiteness. Flo, as a stand-in for players (the player plays as Flo), is a constant reminder that the game is meant not only for women players, but for *white* women players. While the many of the Dash games have characters of color, most play the role of "customer" and are rarely the player's avatar.

While Flo's sexual preference is never overtly stated in the game, sexual orientation is a primary plot-point for her roommate, Quinn, the protagonist of the game *Wedding Dash.* During the first *Wedding Dash* game, Quinn asks Flo point blank why she doesn't date more. Flo responds that she is too focused on her career. So while Flo is not necessarily heterosexual, her sexuality is eclipsed in order to discuss the dating exploits of Quinn, who is decidedly heterosexual and often pursuing men. With other games in the series, such as *Avenue Flo*, other characters' heterosexual romances are likewise spotlighted.

Similarly, nearly all of the game characters in this series are middle class. The main character of each game in Dinertown is a small business owner—a status not available to those who cannot afford this kind of investment. While "lower-class" people are never seen in the game (no homeless people live in Dinertown), upper-class customers become a point of comedy—particularly in *Diner Dash 2* and *Avenue Flo*; both games feature a businessman named "Mr. Big." Mr. Big is portrayed as greedy and uncaring. It is often Flo's job (through the player) to teach him the errors of his ways. For instance, while he is attempting a hostile takeover of all of the restaurants in Dinertown at the beginning of *Diner Dash 2*, Flo convinces him to be her assistant (and waiter) by the end of the game. Thus, the games constantly reinforce a middle-class ethos.

Other casual games, such as hidden object games (like *Ravenhearst* or *Love and Death: Bitten*), similarly reinforce themes of white, heterosexual, and middle-class values in terms of definitions of womanhood. These cues (some subtle and some not so subtle) help to define white, heterosexual, middle-class women as the most desirable audience of women gamers. Hidden object games often use Gothic and romance themes to pull the player through a loose narrative. *Ravenhearst* (2006) and *Return to Ravenhearst* (2008) are particularly well known for their use of Gothic romance: the player is hunting down clues of a 100-year-old mystery, involving a marriage gone awry. Tania Modleski says Gothic romances force the heroine to transition "from love to fear" (1982: 60). She explains the distinction between the plots of Gothic romances and the Harlequin style of romance:

> In Harlequins, the transformation is aided by the reader's own participation in the story: she knows that the heroine has nothing to fear but love and thus has a certain measure of power over the heroine and a feeling of being somewhat in control of the situation. In Gothics, on the other hand, the reader shares some of the heroine's uncertainty about what is going on and what the lover/husband is up to. The reader is nearly as powerless in her understanding as the heroine.
>
> (Modleski 1982: 60)

The common use of the Gothic romance/mystery within the hidden object game genre, then, allows game designers to tap into specific stereotypes of women's desires (and fears) regarding marriage and domestic life. At the same time, these stories normalize the heterosexuality of their protagonists.

Other romance themes creep in with games such as *Love and Death: Bitten*, where players ricochet between playing as the man and woman character after each level of the game. While this playfulness with subjectivity might seem slightly subversive, it also reinforces the heterosexuality in the romance between the main characters, whose (hetero)sexual orientation is never questioned. The hidden object game's dependence on the romance theme is necessarily heterosexual. Similar to the Dash games, nearly all characters are white and middle class. While side characters in hidden object games are occasionally people of color, for the most part these games define their style around very limited constructions of women.

Returning to *Castleville*, Martha Stewart nicely reinforced these constructions of womanhood as the desired woman gamer. The image of Martha Stewart and her products, in general, reinforce these things automatically, particularly ethnicity. In "Martha's Food: Whiteness of a Certain Kind," Ann Bentley (2001) explains that Stewart's persona and recipes constantly play at the margins of whiteness and ethnicity, while always reaffirming white privilege. She explains: "While MS [Martha Stewart] food is 'white,' it is a class-specific whiteness that transcends ethnicity and becomes accessible by cultivation rather than heritage. As such, MS food is based upon an invented artisan ethos only fully realized by those who have the luxury to perform the work, lending itself to elaborate conspicuous consumption" (Bentley 2001: 89). In other words, Stewart's brand automatically implies a certain degree of white privilege. By tapping into her brand, Zynga (via *Castleville*) constructs a specific kind of audience persona. No wonder that many felt disenfranchised upon learning that their game was being invaded by Martha Stewart.

## Stereotypes of femininity in games and marketing

White, heterosexual, middle-class versions of womanhood are not only present in the games created for women audiences. Marketing also creates stereotypes and caricatures not only of what women play, but also of *how* they play. This can be seen in not only advertisements aimed at women audiences, but also advertisements aimed at men. Similar to the game design, game advertisements help to marginalize and essentialize women audiences.

In particular, the release of the Nintendo Wii and Nintendo DS in 2008 was accompanied by a large number of magazine advertisements meant to lure more women into gaming. Elsewhere, I have argued that these advertisements aimed at women avoided pitching games and gaming systems; instead these made gaming sound "productive" by suggesting women play games to keep themselves busy in small snippets of time or use gaming products to better connect with their families (Chess 2011). For example, one campaign for the Nintendo Wii system called "My Wii Story," via the website mywiistory.com, requested that the audience submit narratives explaining how the system improved their family time.[1] Many of the responses were displayed on the mywiistory.com website; only a few were finally turned into magazine advertisements. The resulting advertisements primarily showcased whiteness, middle-class homes, and involved only heterosexual families.

A similar essentialization of gendered gaming styles emerged in a 2009 advertising campaign for the PlayStation 3 ("Dear PlayStation"). In this campaign, rather than suggesting that women should play with their families, the advertisements primarily highlighted women as non-players. In these commercials, players read letters aloud to a fictional "Kevin Butler" about their concerns regarding the PlayStation 3 gaming system. The punch line of these commercials often involved women not fully understanding the gaming systems, feeling ignored, or wanting the system for its other functionalities (such as its use as a Blu-ray system). For example, in one commercial a young Caucasian woman (labeled in the commercial "Sadie O'Dowd: Insignificant other") pleads to the camera, "Dear PlayStation, I know in *God of War 3* you're this Kratos guy seeking vengeance against the gods, but since my boyfriend got it he's been totally ignoring me" ("Lonely Girlfriend" 2010). In another, a Caucasian adolescent boy complains that his grandmother won't stop watching movies on his PS3 ("Grandma" 2010). And one advertisement for the PlayStation 3 game *Uncharted 2* shows a Caucasian man lamenting, "Dear PlayStation, I've been playing *Uncharted 2: Among Thieves*, but my girlfriend won't stop watching it because she [whispers] thinks it's a movie." Kevin Butler advises the man to give her an hour or two and she'll figure out it is a video game. The player responds, "It's been two days," as his girlfriend enters the room with popcorn.

These television advertisements exemplify how women are simultaneously courted and marginalized by the gaming industry. While these depictions acknowledge that women might be interested in the PS3, women's curiosity revolves around wanting to watch movies or misunderstanding gaming technologies. Once again, these advertisements also maintain the image of even potential players as white and middle class (all of them seem to be living in comfortable homes). And while the commercials do not use the heterosexual domestic space as a reason to get women to game (such as the My Wii Story campaign), they still primarily involve heterosexual households, where it is the girlfriend or wife who is dramatically befuddled by the gaming systems. While the gaming industry might court women, it continues to seek a specific kind of woman and image.

## Conclusion: what do women want, anyway?

Given this history and culture of tension between women and the video game industry, a decision to make Martha Stewart the temporary mascot for *Castleville* should be unsurprising. After all, Martha Stewart epitomizes the white, middle-class, heterosexual women audience that the gaming industry both yearns for and simultaneously ridicules. By placing her avatar in the game, the designers appear to be giving women what they "want." But as the Facebook comments demonstrate, the reality of what designers think women want and the reality of what players (both men and women) want are far more discursive and complex.

In order for the gaming industry to engender more diversity, several important things need to happen. First, the inclusion of women into gaming should not limit womanhood to white, heterosexual, middle-class women. Instead, games should be made for women of different ages, sexualities, ethnicities, and social classes. Second, industry divisions between "hardcore" and "casual" gamers need to be questioned. The games created out of these categories essentialize play styles and tend to map "casual" play to women and "hardcore" play to male audiences. Finally, designers should avoid repurposing tired stereotypes repeatedly used in media aimed at women audiences. Pushing at these edges might begin to create more equity of play, and more interesting games for all.

The gaming industry has spent time, money, and other resources repeatedly asking, "What do women want anyway?" Ultimately, they have missed the point entirely. Some women (and some men) might want to see Martha Stewart in their *Castleville*. Yet the category of "women players" is neither consistent nor predictable. Designers, executives, and marketers should ask better questions, reaching out to a multitude of players.

## Note

1 Mywiistory.com is no longer an active website and is currently listed as "under construction."

# References

*Avenue Flo* (video game) (2009) Encore (developer), Playfirst (publisher), Los Angeles, CA.

Bartky, S. L. (1990) *Femininity and Domination: Studies in the Phenomenology of Oppression*, New York: Routledge.

Beauvoir, S. de (1989 [1953]) *The Second Sex*, New York: Vintage Books.

Behm-Morawitz, E. and D. Mastro (2009) "The Effects of the Sexualization of Female Video Game Characters on Gender Stereotyping and Female Self-Concept," *Sex Roles* 61(11/12): 808–23.

Bentley, A. (2001) "Martha's Food: Whiteness of a Certain Kind," *American Studies* 42(2): 89–100.

Butler, J. (1999) *Gender Trouble: Feminism and the Subversion of Identity*, 10th anniversary edition, London: Routledge. Original work published 1989.

*Castleville* (video game) (2011) Zynga (developer/publisher), San Francisco, CA.

Casual Connect (2007) "Casual Games Market Report." http://www.casualconnect.org/news-content/11–2007/CasualGamesMarketReport2007_Summary.pdf.

Chess, S. (2011) "A 36-24-36 Cerebrum: Productivity, Gender, and Video Game Advertising," *Critical Studies in Media Communication* 28(3): 230–52.

——(2012) "Going with the Flo: *Diner Dash* and Feminism," *Feminist Media Studies* 12(1): 83–99.

Consalvo, M. (2008) "Crunched by Passion: Women Game Developers and Workplace Challenges," in Y. B. Kafai, C. Heeter, J. Denner, and J. Y. Sun (eds.) *Beyond Barbie and Mortal Kombat*, Cambridge, MA: MIT Press.

——(2009) "Hardcore to Casual: Game Culture Return(s) to Ravenhearst," *Proceedings from ICFDG 2009*.

Cross, T. (2011) "All the World's a Game," *Economist*. http://www.economist.com/node/21541164.

Crossley, R. (2011) "Zynga: The 40-year-old Woman Is the New Hardcore Gamer," Develop. http://www.develop-online.net/news/37278/Zynga-The-40-year-old-women-is-the-new-hardcore-gamer.

*Diaper Dash* (video game) (2009) Encore (developer), Playfirst (publisher), Los Angeles, CA.

Dickerman, C., J. Christensen, and S. Kerl-McClain (2008) "Big Breasts and Bad Guys: Depictions of Gender and Race in Video Games," *Journal of Creativity in Mental Health* 3(1): 20–9.

*Diner Dash* (video game) (2004) Encore (developer), Playfirst (publisher), Los Angeles, CA.

*Diner Dash 2: Restaurant Rescue* (video game) (2006) Encore (developer), Playfirst (publisher), Los Angeles, CA.

Fron, J., T. Fullerton, J. Morie, and C. Pearce (2007) "The Hegemony of Play," in A. Baba (ed.) *Situated Play: Proceedings from Digital Games Research Association 2007 Conference*, Tokyo: University of Tokyo, pp. 309–18.

"Grandma" (2010) Commercial for PlayStation 3, posted on November 14, 2010. http://www.youtube.com/watch?v=1tuwHi22Mz0.

Juul, J. (2010) *A Casual Revolution: Reinventing Video Games and Their Players*, Cambridge, MA: MIT Press.

Kato, M. (2007) "Space Invaders," *Game Informer Magazine* (April): 40.

"Lonely Girlfriend" (2010) Commercial for PlayStation 3, posted on March 11, 2010. http://www.youtube.com/watch?v=e9X5fX_PeXg.

Modleski, T. (1982) *Loving with a Vengeance: Mass-produced Fantasies for Women*, Hamden, CT: Archon.

*Mystery Case Files: Ravenhearst* (video game) (2006) Big Fish Games (developer/publisher), Seattle, WA.

*Mystery Case Files: Return to Ravenhearst* (video game) (2008) Big Fish Games (developer/publisher), Seattle, WA.

O'Donnell, C. (2012) "The North American Game Industry," in P. Zackariasson and T. Wilson (eds.) *The Video Game Industry: Formation, Present State, and Future*, New York: Routledge.

Ray, S. G. (2004) *Gender Inclusive Game Design: Expanding the Market*, Hingham, MA: Charles River Media.

SteelCladDragon (2012) Facebook post, posted on March 31, 2012. https://www.facebook.com/SteelCladDragon/posts/3356631831304 [note: post no longer available].

"*Uncharted 2: Among Thieves*" (2009) Commercial for PlayStation 3, posted on October 5, 2009. http://www.youtube.com/watch?v=H0q3qcLkw1A.

Walkenford, J. (2012) Facebook post, posted on March 31, 2012. https://www.facebook.com/john.walkenford/posts/1015064550737739.

# 16

# Boys are … girls are …

## How children's media and merchandizing construct gender

## *Dafna Lemish*

A large portion of children's media and related merchandizing traveling around the world is promoting a highly gender-segregated world, along traditional and stereotypical constructs of femininity and masculinity and the continuing marginalization of girlhood. This chapter explores the representations of gender in children's culture, demonstrating how the same issues that dominate critiques of adult media are equally relevant to those targeting children. I explain the political economy that is largely driving this segregation and the restrictive narratives it offers boys and girls for their own construction of gender identity. I conclude by exploring possible directions for changing this reality based on an international study of professionals of children's media.[1]

### Representations

Despite growing awareness and advocacy around the issue of gender representations in media aimed at children and consumed by them, research on the portrayals of girls and boys on television, in movies, computer and video games, advertisements, websites, toys, and media-related merchandizing points to a social world available to children that differentiates between the two genders quite systematically. Such dominant media messages in texts designed for children continue to promote the same restrictive ideologies of femininity and masculinity that characterize media in general, and say little about the multifaceted aspects of girls' and boys' lives, capabilities, and potential contributions to society.

On the whole, like adult men, boys are identified with "doing" in the public sphere, with associated characteristics such as action, rationality, forcefulness, aggressiveness, independence, ambitiousness, competitiveness, achievement, higher social status, and humorousness. Girls, like adult women, are associated with "being" in the private sphere and are characterized, generally, as passive, emotional, care-giving, childish, sexy, subordinate to males, and of lower social status. Their "girly" personality traits are depicted as being fundamentally different in nature from those of boys. Girls are portrayed as being more romantic, sensitive, dependent, vulnerable, and continue to be defined more by their appearance than by their actions (Lemish 2010).

Males—of all ages—are the main heroes of most children's programs. They succeed in overcoming everyday problems, deal successfully with all sorts of dangers, and have many adventures. Even non-gendered imaginary characters—such as creatures and animals—are considered "naturally" to be male, unless they are specifically marked as female through processes of sexualizing their appearance (e.g. hair ribbons, long eyelashes, colored lips, wasp-waists, long legs, short skirts, and high heels). Female characters in most media texts for children provide the background narrative for the adventure and are there to be saved and protected by the males. Above all, their position is defined by their meaning for the male heroes. Certain symbols, such as flowers, ponies, bunnies, and dolphins jumping in front of a sunset, are gendered in our societies and reinforced by market forces as "girlish." Other areas, such as technological prowess, action, or fighting, are almost always framed as male themes, hence reinforcing viewer expectations of masculine dominance in these domains (Lemish 2010). Acts of physical aggression are more associated with male characters, and those of social aggression more with female characters (Luther and Legg 2010).

Marketing, and, more specifically, television advertising and merchandise packaging for children, apply gendered clichés excessively in presenting goods for consumption by signaling gender intention via means such as more fades, dissolves, and glittery or pastel colors for girls, and fast cuts and action-packed dark hues for boys (Brown et al. 2009; Lamb and Brown 2007; Lewin-Jones and Mitra 2009; Seiter 1995).

The bulk of content presented to children continues to systematically promote quantified underrepresentation of females as well. For example, a study of gender prevalence and portrayal of G-rated (general viewing) films in the US found that only 28 percent of the speaking characters (both real and animated) were female; and only 17 percent of the films' narrators were female; male characters similarly outnumbered female characters by two to one in US television created for children (Smith and Cook 2008). These findings are hardly unique to the US. A comparison involving 24 countries (it analyzed over 26,000 characters in over 6,000 children's fictional programs broadcast during 2007 for children 12 years old and under) reinforced these conclusions. First, and most striking, is the fact that the sample included twice as many males as females (68 percent and 32 percent, respectively), reiterating the marginality of girls in all realms of life. This gender imbalance was evident all over the world—in public and private television, in international and domestic programming, in animated and real-life formats. Female characters were even more noticeably underrepresented as non-human characters (animals, monsters, and robots), where the biological sex of a character is clearly an arbitrary choice; whether an animal, monster, or robot is a boy or a girl is a choice producers make. Apparently, the greater the degree of creative freedom, the more the gender ratio is biased towards male characters. The study also documented the fact that girls appear much more often in groups, while males are independent loners and antagonists (Götz and Lemish 2012).

## Body and sexualization

That race and gender are heavily conflated in these images is strongly evident in the dominance of Caucasian characters around the world (72 percent) as well as the exaggerated Western body-types presented on children's television. Major gender differences related to body size were also found: girls tended to be very thin, twice as thin as boys, who were twice as frequently overweight compared to girls (Götz and Lemish 2012). This is particularly true of globally marketed animated programs. Globally, close to two out of three young female characters have extremely unrealistic figures with entirely unnatural small, wasp-like waists and long legs. What is more striking in these fabricated, unattainable figures is that they are so much alike, creating a unified model that even situates the heavily criticized Barbie figure as too curvy and full (Götz and Herche 2012).

These bodily characteristics are strongly related to an additional central feature of visual images of characters, which is the tendency to hypersexualize the appearance of young females. Females who are 11 years and under seen on TV for children have been found to be almost four times as likely as males to be shown in sexy attire. Here, too, animated stories tended to exaggerate even more the unrealistic small waist and sexy appearance of girls; at the same time animated action males were more likely to have a large chest and unrealistically masculinized physique than live action counterparts (Smith and Cook 2008). However, boy characters, as a whole, are offered a much more diversified range of personalities and appearances (Götz et al. 2012).

Over-sexualized portrayals of girls in popular culture have continued to attract public and scholarly attention (APA on the Sexualization of Girls 2007). The frequent presentation of sexy little girls or fun-seeking, fearless-sexual teenagers is entangled with myths of sexuality that link these portrayals to particular ideal body-types and youth (i.e. only girls who look a particular way are "cool" and "sexy"), as well as to beliefs about girls' exhibitionism and manipulation that attract the male gaze and potential sexual violence toward them. What Gigi Durham (2008) termed "the Lolita Effect" suggests that the media circulate and contribute to cultivation of distorted sets of myths about girls' sexuality that work to both undermine girls' healthy sexual development and at the same time keep girls in their subordinated place in society.

## Trends of change

### *"Girl power"*

Naturally, we also find changes over time (e.g. Thompson and Zerbinos 1995), as well as exceptions, in the domain of children's programming, as in adult media. The exceptions include, for example, some features of Disney's female lead characters in more recent films such as Pocahontas, Mulan, and Rapunzel, as well as the global success of *Dora Explorer*, the Latina girl in the Nickelodeon hit pre-school program. Indeed, Nickelodeon, the commercial cable network for children, has been cited for the creation and inclusion of many new, multi-dimensional girl characters (e.g.

*Clarissa, As Told By Ginger*). These exceptions, too, have been the subjects of criticism as their body images remain unchallenged. Disney's Pocahontas, for example, has been criticized for romanticizing Native American women, particularly in relation to her love for a white man (Portman and Herring 2001). Disney's "Princess Culture" in general has been heavily criticized for its gendered stereotypes and related commercialization (England *et al.* 2011; Orenstein 2011). Regardless, even these exceptions serve to highlight, by way of contrast, the routine gender bias of everyday commercial popular media around the world.

One trend in the new images is the shift of perspective from girls as victims to girls as active subjects and creative media producers (e.g. of blogs, digital images, etc.); interest in girls' "bedroom cultures" and girl studies is flourishing (Kearney 2006; Kearney 2011; Mazzarella 2005, 2010; Mazzarella and Pecora 2007; Sweeney 2003). Of particular interest are depictions of strong but feminine girl heroes in children's television and video games, such as the animated series *The Powerpuff Girls, Kim Possible, Atomic Betty*; these may have been inspired by the concept of "girl power." While Super-girls may be brave, smart, and independent, most of them also embrace the centrality of physical attractiveness (supposedly for their own pleasure) as liberated and empowered strong characters, and not as passive objects that are posing in order to please a male gaze (Lemish 1998, 2003). The highly successful *Powerpuff Girls* animation series exemplifies this evolving strategy, as it contains many contradictory messages about the coexistence of strength ("power") and femininity ("puff") while nourishing the themes of "girl power" and power feminism associated with third-wave feminism. Accordingly, being strong, brave, successful, and independent, while fighting evil forces, does not necessarily negate the pleasure of embracing "girlishness" (Hains 2008).

While the *Powerpuff Girls* are supposedly only five years old, analyses of other programs featuring "tough girls"—as warriors and super-heroines—suggest that the range of socially accepted physical appearances offered by these Super-girls is restricted, hypersexualized, and Westernized. Girls who do not conform to these expectations are often socially sanctioned in the narratives, even ostracized as outcasts. Thus, popular culture seems to be involved in an ambivalent process, wanting to depict strong girls in such a manner that they do not pose too dramatic a challenge to the traditional association between men and toughness (Inness 1999, 2004). While successful young women characters like Buffy in *Buffy the Vampire Slayer* have attracted extensive scholarly and public attention (Early 2001; Owen 1999; Ross 2004), the textual narrative and other visual markers relay the message that even strong empowered young females continue to offer girls lessons about normative feminine beauty as a key to success, popularity, and an exciting life.

### *"Brainy" girls*

Another emerging image of girls and women discussed in the recent literature is evidenced in "brainy" characters who manage to break away from their negative depiction as unattractive and unpopular. Recent children's characters in cartoons (e.g. the *Powerpuff Girls*, Lisa in *The Simpsons, Daria, Dora*) as well as in family dramas heavily consumed by children (e.g. *Gilmore Girls, Buffy the Vampire Slayer*) challenge this criticism. Defenders note being smart and "cool" are not mutually exclusive, nor do they cancel out one another (Inness 2007). This argument is also aligned with a third-wave feminism notion that the feminist and the feminine are not necessarily binary positions: one can be an independent and smart girl and still enjoy displaying girlish sensibilities and feminine performances.

Irrespective of these changes, we find ambivalence in most of the television fare viewed by children around the world about girls' intelligence and the threat it might pose to the normalized gender order, as expressed among others by the resilience of the "dumb (or bitchy) blonde" stereotype and the presentation of girls who are not as clever as their male friends. Being clever often is signified by unfashionable clothing, wearing glasses, lack of self-confidence, and the like, and is juxtaposed with romance and female nurturance. Alternatively, smart girls often use "subversive niceness" to make their intelligence less noticeable and more palatable (Hains 2007). The problem with such strategies is that they match the preconceived notions that women are "manipulative" and "conniving," using their feminine traits to get what they want.

### "Losers" and "beefy" boys

Male images in children's television have been showing some signs of change as well (Götz et al. 2012). One trend is the growing numbers of buffoons, losers, and not particularly handsome "geeks" portrayed as techno-oriented wizards who are going to rule the world through their brains and mastery of technology. Yet, scholars have noted a stronger trend towards the hyper-masculinity of animated male characters portrayed through the growing size of their bodies, for example by huge biceps and shoulders. One consequence is that such "beefy men" assume more space (both physically and symbolically) on the screen (Götz and Herche 2012).

So, while some types of traditional gender stereotypes have decreased in media for children, other stereotypes are emerging and becoming more prominent. The study of 24 countries cited above found that the vast majority of programs viewed by children around the world are imported from the US (48.5 percent), Canada (12.2 percent), and the UK (11.4 percent) (Götz and Lemish 2012). This television fare, overall, continues to offer restrictive images of young people, female and male.

## Segregated childhoods

The prevalence of gender stereotypes in children's media is particularly surprising, given the fact that professionals involved in the production of children's television in leading organizations report increasing awareness and concern for the social world they are portraying (Bryant 2007). Lemish's (2010) study of 135 producers of children's television from 65 countries includes testimonies to the intensifying complexity involved in understanding the continued prevalence of gender stereotypes in children's media; media professionals around the world believe that boys want male lead figures.

## The implied audience

One interpretation may be found in the assumption of the "implied audience" shared by the children's media community and treated as a non-debatable truism: although girls will watch boys' shows and play with boys' games and toys, boys will not watch girls' shows or play with girls' "stuff." The implications of this truism are profound as it provides a rationale—both economic as well as "moral"—for the production of more programming and computer games aimed at boys' interests and needs, under the umbrella argument of serving children's tastes and pleasures.

Children are aware of gendered play expectations from a young age and there are stronger pressures for boys to conform to gender-appropriate behaviors than for girls, for whom more flexibility is usually tolerated (Cherney and London 2006; Kahlenberg and Hein 2010; Karniol 2011). Boys like cartoons and watch them over time a lot longer than do girls. They are attracted to action/adventure content, sports, and competitions. They shy away from educational/cultural programs that are slow paced and particularly from anything with a girly touch to it in style and color (e.g. anything pink and glittery), which serve as clear demarcations of gendered content (Karniol 2011; Hull et al. 2011).

Girls, on the other hand, media professionals argue, prefer girl leads, and are attracted to displays of emotions, relationships and romance, and to narratives that are confined to the domestic world. They like princesses and fairies, dancing and music, and are drawn to pink, pastel colors, and all that is "girlish." They outgrow animation at a younger age than boys, and stay longer with educational and public television. Girls also "watch up," that is, they are willing to join an adult audience at a much earlier age than are boys. Indeed, overall, girls and boys tend to demonstrate a greater preference for contents, toys, and activities that are perceived as appropriate to their own gender: On the whole, boys prefer action/adventure and sports genres located largely in the public sphere, while girls prefer human relationships and romance and more domesticated activities (Cherney and London 2006). In general, then, boys' culture is game dominated, while girls' culture is composed of relationships and communication (e.g. Lemish et al. 2001).

## The toy and merchandizing industries

The toy and merchandizing industries play a significant role in perpetuating the gendered segregation of childhood through their co-dependency on media offerings for children (Mjos 2010). Few doubt that, in keeping with the capitalist project, children have been targeted for consumption directly and aggressively (Kapur 2004; Linn 2004; McAllister 2007; Seiter 1995; Wasko 2008); and in this process they have been constructed as knowing consumers with clearly differentiated, gender-appropriate tastes. The degree to which much of television programming is made compatible with commercial considerations that are linked to licensed merchandizing for children has been studied and documented. Research shows, for example, the industry prefers programs with "toyetic" qualities such as culturally neutral, animated characters that can be sold around the world, teams of characters that generate "collectability," backgrounds and props that can be marketed as play sets and toys, online applications that will increase brand loyalty, and educational value that will appeal to parents, etc. (Steemers 2009).

These industries continue to dwell on gender differences, play them up, exploit children's quest for gender identities, and push them to the extreme as they carve out unparalleled audience-segments for profit (Bakir *et al.* 2008; Cross 1997; Kahlenberg and Hein 2010; Sandler 2004). Girls in particular are targeted as consumers of beautification and fashion products they "must" have and use as they develop their female identity in a media culture that is so appearance and commodity centric (Hill 2011; Russell and Tyler 2005).

Thus, it is not surprising to find that advertisements, toys, and merchandizing that target children often are promoting significantly more traditional gender ideologies than the programs themselves (Kahlenberg and Hein 2010; Lemish 2010). Different packaging and different store aisles cultivate the impression that certain toys are only appropriate for boys and others only for girls, just like television programs. Boys are steered towards toys involving traditional masculine traits—action, machinery, weapons, construction—so that their play is designed to be exciting and adventurous, and to engage more in activities of the public sphere. Girls, on the other hand, are directed towards traditional feminine interests in the private sphere such as caregiving and beautification activities with dolls, household toys, and fashion and decoration products (Francis 2008; Blakemore and Centers 2005). The market pressure to conform to traditional gender roles is so strong that it is just as evident in a more egalitarian country such as Sweden (Nelson 2005). Toys and merchandizing thus provide a gendered learning environment and many gendered experiences for children.

Pressure on children to conform to normative gender stereotypes may be driven by the transnational toy industry that itself is tilted in favor of boys. This well-calculated stance is due to market findings that boys play with toys longer than girls; the more expensive toys, such as electronic ones, are purchased for them; and few toys for boys are not media driven. In interviews, media professionals suggest that boys buy more toys and their play follows television narratives more closely due to the fact that boys' programs are action packed and thus lend themselves to imitation of action (Lemish 2010). Girls' programs, on the other hand, are more about inner psychological states and relationships, thus inspiring more creative play that is not bound by the specificities of imitating an action plot. These observations were also reinforced by a study of gendered differences in the media traces found in boys' and girls' make-believe worlds (Götz et al. 2005).

## Proactive change

The dynamics of children's commercial television and related industries and the economic constraints within which they operate continue to promote a worldview where boys and girls are encouraged to inhabit different cultural spaces. They do so through the contents offered, as well as by serving as a model for younger, resource-poor television industries. Furthermore, even the exceptional transgressive border crossings, particularly by boys into girlish territories (e.g. a boy walking in the "pink aisles" in a toy store or enjoying a "chick flick"), may be heavily stigmatized and sanctioned. The accumulated research demonstrates that, indeed, children learn from the media and related industries, as well as actively negotiate what "boys are" and what "girls are" and how they are expected to perform their genders (Mazzarella 2013). The complexity involved in views of children as social actors and in situating child consumption outside of "moral panics" discourses have also raised questions about gender-related values and notions of childhood (Sparrman et al. 2012).

At the same time, however, media and popular culture can serve important roles in socializing children to gender equity as well as serving as potential social change mechanisms. Initiatives to present a more egalitarian social world that opens up possibilities for both boys and girls are available worldwide, mostly in high-quality, educational, and public broadcasting organizations and companies. Advocacy groups such as The Geena Davis Institute on Gender in Media support research and educational interventions in the media industry. As these lines are being written, *Top Toy* (which holds the franchise for *Toys "R" Us* in Sweden) has released its Christmas 2012 catalogue, which flips gender scripts: boys are playing with dolls and girls are playing with guns (Kessler 2012). The fact that even this simple, and not at all progressive, "role reversal" attracted heavy media coverage is, in and of itself, an indication of how surprisingly rare it must be, even in the more egalitarian societies such as the Nordic ones.

In the international study cited above (Lemish 2010), I offered a model of eight working principles for change, based on the accumulated wisdom of professionals of children's quality media from around the world. These include the principles of (1) *equality* of roles and opportunities while respecting differences; (2) *diversity* of characters both within and across all social categories; (3) *complexity* of characters that seeks to broaden the possibilities and traits for both boys and girls; (4) *similarities* of human traits rather than emphasizing conflict and animosity; (5) *unity* of goals and collaboration that goes well beyond romantic and sexual pursuits; (6) centrality of *family* and community as cultural contexts of connectivity and values; (7) *authenticity* of characters, narratives, and social contexts; and, finally, (8) *voicing* of children's own perspectives and inner worlds. Many successful attempts to break traditional gender constructions along these lines are already in practice. However, most of the media content traveling the world is still quite gender blind and/or struggling with heavy conservative market pressures. Deep change in the offerings of children's leisure culture remains heavily dependent on society at large, its pursuit of equality for all, and its imagination of a better future for its young.

## Note

1 This chapter is based, with permission, on earlier work, especially on Lemish (2010), with excerpts from chapters 1 and 5.

## References

APA on the Sexualization of Girls (2007) *American Psychological Association*. www.apa.org/pi/wpo/sexualization.html.

Bakir, A., J. G. Blodgett, and G. N. Rose (2008) "Children's Response to Gender-role Stereotyped Advertisements," *Journal of Advertising Research* 48: 255–66.

Blakemore, J. E. O. and R. E. Centers (2005) "Characteristics of Boys' and Girls' Toys," *Sex Roles* 53(9–10): 619–33.

Brown, L. M., S. Lamb, and M. Tappen (2009) *Packaging Boyhood: Saving Our Sons from Superheroes, Slackers, and Other Media Stereotypes*, New York: St. Martin's Press.

Bryant, J. A. (ed.) (2007) *The Children's Television Community*, Mahwah, NJ: Lawrence Erlbaum Associates.

Cherney, I. D. and K. London (2006) "Gender-linked Differences in the Toys, Television Shows, Computer Games, and Outdoor Activities of 5-to-13-year-old Children," *Sex Roles* 54: 717–26.

Cross, G. (1997) *Kids' Stuff: Toys and the Changing World of American Childhood*, Cambridge, MA: Harvard University Press.

Durham, G. (2008) *The Lolita Effect: The Media Sexualization of Young Girls and What We Can Do about It*, New York: The Overlook Press.

Early, F. H. (2001) "Staking Her Claim: *Buffy the Vampire Slayer* as Transgressive Woman Warrior," *Journal of Popular Culture* 35(3): 11–27.

England, D. E., L. Descartes, and M. A. Collier-Meek (2011) "Gender Role Portrayal at the Disney Princess," *Sex Roles* 64(7–8): 555–67.

Francis, B. (2008) "Toys, Gender and Learning," unpublished report to the Froebel Educational Institute, Roehampton University.

Götz, M. and M. Herche (2012) "'Wasp Waists and V-shape Torso': Measuring the Body of the 'Global' Girl and Boy in Animated Children's Programs," in M. Götz and D. Lemish (eds.) *Sexy Girls, Heroes and Funny Losers: Gender Representations in Children's TV around the World*, New York: Peter Lang, pp. 49–68.

Götz, M. and D. Lemish (eds.) (2012) *Sexy Girls, Heroes and Funny Losers: Gender Representations in Children's TV around the World*, New York: Peter Lang.

Götz, M., D. Lemish, A. Aidman, and H. Moon (2005) *Media and the Make-believe Worlds of Children: When Harry Potter meets Pokémon in Disneyland*, Englewood Cliffs, NJ: Lawrence Erlbaum Associates.

Götz, M., G. Neubauer, and R. Winter (2012) "Heroes, Planners and Funny Losers: Masculinities Represented in Male Characters in Children's TV," in M. Götz and D. Lemish (eds.) *Sexy Girls, Heroes and Funny Losers: Gender Representations in Children's TV around the World*, New York: Peter Lang, pp. 107–30.

Hains, R. C. (2007) "'Pretty Smart': Subversive Intelligence in Girl Power Cartoons," in S. A. Inness (ed.) *Geek Chic: Smart Women in Popular Culture*, New York: Palgrave Macmillan, pp. 65–84.

——(2008) "Power(Puff) Feminism: The Powerpuff Girls as a Site of Strength and Collective Action in the Third Wave," in M. Meyers (ed.) *Women in Popular Culture: Representation and Meaning*, Cresskill, NJ: Hampton Press, pp. 211–35.

Hill, J. A. (2011) "Endangered Childhoods: How Consumerism Is Impacting Child and Youth Identity," *Media, Culture & Society* 33: 347–62.

Hull, J. H., D. B. Hull, and C. Knopp (2011) "The Impact of Color on Ratings of 'Girl' and 'Boy' Toys," *North American Journal of Psychology* 11(3): 549–62.

Inness, S. A. (1999) *Tough Girls: Women Warriors and Wonder Women in Popular Culture*, Philadelphia: University of Pennsylvania Press.

——(ed.) (2004) *Action Chicks: New Images of Tough Women in Popular Culture*, New York: Palgrave Macmillan.

——(ed.) (2007) *Geek Chic: Smart Women in Popular Culture*, New York: Palgrave Macmillan.

Kahlenberg, S. G. and M. M. Hein (2010) "Progression on Nickelodeon? Gender-role Stereotypes in Toy Commercials," *Sex Roles* 62: 830–47.

Kapur, J. (2004) *Coining for Capital: Movies, Marketing, and the Transformation of Childhood*, New Brunswick, NJ: Rutgers University Press.

Karniol, R. (2011) "The Color of Children's Gender Stereotypes," *Sex Roles* 65: 119–32.

Kearney, M. C. (2006) *Girls Make Media*, London: Routledge.

——(ed.) (2011) *Mediated Girlhoods*, New York: Peter Lang.

Kessler, R. (2012) *Up Is Down and Girls Are Boys: Swedish Toy Ad Flips the Script on Christmas*. http://gawker.com/5963362/.

Lamb, S. and L. M. Brown (2007) *Rescuing Our Daughters from Marketers' Schemes*, New York: Macmillan.

Lemish, D. (1998) "Spice Girls' Talk: A Case Study in the Development of Gendered Identity," in S. A. Inness (ed.) *Millennium Girls: Today's Girls around the World*, New York: Rowman and Littlefield, pp. 145–67.

——(2003) "Spice World: Constructing Femininity the Popular Way," *Popular Music and Society* 26(1): 17–29.

——(2010) *Screening Gender in Children's TV: The Views of Producers around the World*, New York: Routledge.

Lemish, D., T. Liebes, and V. Seidmann (2001) "Gendered Media Meaning and Use," in S. Livingstone and M. Bovill (eds.) *Children and Their Changing Media Environment*, Hillsdale, NJ: Lawrence Erlbaum, pp. 263–82.

Lewin-Jones, J. and B. Mitra (2009) "Gender Roles in Television Commercials and Primary School Children in the UK," *Journal of Children and Media* 3(1): 35–50.

Linn, S. (2004) *Consuming Kids: The Hostile Takeover of Childhood*, New York: The New Press.

Luther, C. A. and J. R. Legg Jr. (2010) "Gender Differences in Depictions of Social and Physical Aggression in Children's Television Cartoons in the US," *Journal of Children and Media* 4(2): 191–205.

McAllister, M. P. (2007) "'Girls with a Passion for Fashion': The Bratz Brand as Integrated Spectacular Consumption," *Journal of Children and Media* 1(3): 244–58.

Mazzarella, S. (ed.) (2005) *Girls Wide Web: Girls, the Internet, and the Negotiation of Identity*, New York: Peter Lang.

——(ed.) (2010) *Girls Wide Web 2.0: Revisiting Girls, the Internet, and the Negotiation of Identity*, New York: Peter Lang.

——(2013) "Media and Gender Identities: Learning and Performing Femininity and Masculinity," in D. Lemish (ed.) *The Routledge International Handbook of Children, Adolescents and Media*, New York: Routledge, pp. 279–86.

Mazzarella, S. R. and N. Pecora (2007) "Revisiting Girls' Studies: Girls Creating Sites for Connection and Action," *Journal of Children and Media* 1(2): 105–25.

Media Education Foundation (MEF) (2002) *Tough Guise: Violence, Media and the Crisis in Masculinity with Jackson Katz* (DVD). www.mediaed.org.

Mjos, O. J. (2010) "The Symbiosis of Children's Television and Merchandising: Comparative Perspectives on the Norwegian Children's Television Channel NRK Super and the Global Disney Channel," *Media, Culture & Society* 32: 1031–42.

Nelson, A. (2005) "Children's Toy Collections in Sweden—A Less Gender Typed Country?," *Sex Roles* 52(1–2): 93–102.

Orenstein, P. (2011) *Cinderella Ate My Daughter*, New York: HarperCollins.

Owen, A. (1999) "Vampires, Postmodernity, and Postfeminism: Buffy the Vampire Slayer," *Journal of Popular Film and Television* 27(2): 24–31.

Portman, T. A. and R. Herring (2001) "Debunking the Pocahontas Paradox: The Need for a Humanistic Perspective," *Journal of Humanistic Counseling, Education and Development* 40(2): 185–200.

Ross, S. (2004) "'Tough Enough': Female Friendship and Heroism in *Xena* and *Buffy*," in S. A. Inness (ed.) *Action Chicks: New Images of Tough Women in Popular Culture*, New York: Palgrave Macmillan, pp. 237–55.

Russell, R. and M. Tyler (2005) "Branding and Bricolage: Gender, Consumption and Transition," *Childhood* 12: 221–37.

Sandler, K. S. (2004) "'A Kid's Gotta Do What a Kid's Gotta Do': Branding the Nickelodeon Experience," in H. Hendershot (ed.) *Nickelodeon Nation*, New York: New York University Press, pp. 12–133.

Seiter, E. (1995) *Sold Separately: Parents & Children in Consumer Culture*, New Brunswick, NJ: Rutgers University Press.

Smith, S. L. and C. A. Cook (2008) "Children and Gender in Film and Television," paper presented at the conference of the Geena Davis Institute on Gender in Media, Los Angeles, CA.

Sparrman, A., B. Sandin, and J. Sjöberg (eds.) (2012) *Situating Child Consumption: Rethinking Values and Notions of Children, Childhood and Consumption*, Lund, Sweden: Nordic Academic Press.

Steemers, J. (2009) "The Thin Line between Market and Quality," *TelevlZlon* 2: 53–6.

Sweeney, K. (2003) *Maiden USA: Girl Icons Come of Age*, New York: Peter Lang.

Thompson, T. L. and E. Zerbinos (1995) "Gender Roles in Animated Cartoons: Has the Picture Changed in 20 Years?," *Sex Roles* 32: 651–73.

Wasko, J. (2008) "The Commodification of Youth Culture," in K. Drotner and S. Livingstone (eds.) *The International Handbook of Children, Media and Culture*, Los Angeles: Sage, pp. 460–74.

White, C. L. and E. Hall Preston (2005) "The Spaces of Children's Programming," *Critical Studies in Media Communication* 22(3): 239–55.

# 17

# Girls' and boys' experiences of online risk and safety

## Sonia Livingstone, Veronika Kalmus, and Kairi Talves

As digital and online technologies are variously acquired and appropriated by families the world over, questions are being asked about the social shaping and social consequences of these rapid changes in everyday life. Considerable attention has centered on young people, who, while regarded as the pioneers of the new digital age, the creative and adaptable "digital natives" who leave older generations ("digital immigrants") behind, are also seen as particularly vulnerable in the face of techno-social change, supposedly assaulted by the onslaught of commercialized, sexualized, and manipulative images and invitations for which they are unprepared. And it is in this context that gender represents an important dimension of young people's experiences of the internet.

Dominant cultural representations have long positioned men and women differently in relation to technology and computer skills, influencing the construction of gender identities and privileging men's (and boys') approach to information and commu-nication technologies of all kinds (Henwood *et al.* 2000). Uotinen's (2002) study of the biographies of information technology students found that gender differences in childhood computer use, including in computer game playing, shape future career choices, resulting in gender segregation in the information and communications technologies (ICT) sector. Although theories of diffusion and development hold that economic growth and technological progress, by "lifting all boats," could alleviate social inequalities, these processes are also shaped by cultural norms, values, and beliefs (Inglehart and Norris 2003). Thus gender differences may persist even when today's younger generation of "digital natives" grows up (Helsper 2010).

Although already heavily researched, no clear picture has yet emerged of the ways in which gender might matter in relation to children's use of the internet. One challenge is that young people in heavily mediated societies do so much on the internet that the role of gender—as for age, ethnicity, culture, and class—is inevi-tably complex and multifaceted. And the place of the internet in society continues to change. Early accounts focused on the digital divide in access, finding that boys

*Table 17.1* Children's internet access, use, and skills, by gender

|  | Girls | Boys | All |
|---|---|---|---|
| Has internet access at home (%) | 86 | 87 | 87 |
| Has internet access in own bedroom (%) | 47 | 50 | 49 |
| Has internet access via mobile or handheld device (%) | 33 | 35 | 34 |
| Uses the internet every day or almost every day (%) | 58 | 61 | 60 |
| Internet use on an average day (minutes) | 85 | 91 | 88 |
| Online activities in the last month (average, out of 17) | 6.9 | 7.4 | 7.2 |
| Digital literacy and safety skills (average, out of 8)[a] | 4.0 | 4.3 | 4.2 |
| "I know more about the internet than my parents" (% very true) | 34 | 38 | 36 |

*Base*: 25,142 children aged 9–16 in Europe who use the internet.
[a] 11–16 years only.

typically gained earlier and better access to the internet at home than girls; and in schools, teachers supported boys' use of educational technologies more than they did girls' use. Although some inequalities persist (Livingstone and Helsper 2007), especially in countries where the gender gap is relatively large (Helsper 2012), researchers have moved away from static, binary approaches that contrast "haves" and "have-nots" (van Dijk 2006) to recognize more subtle ways in which gender inflects the contexts, practices, and meanings of internet use, including the development of digital literacies (Hargittai 2010), thereby possibly reproducing existing inequalities.

Here we draw on the findings of the EU Kids Online project, which surveyed 1,000 children aged 9–16 in 25 European countries about many aspects of their internet use (Livingstone *et al.* 2011; see www.eukidsonline.net). Table 17.1 reveals modest yet consistent gender differences that favor boys over girls. These measures are self-reinforcing—correlational and path analysis shows that better access supports longer use, which, in turn, is linked to broader online activities and greater digital skills (Livingstone and Helsper 2010). However, not all gender differences necessarily reveal inequalities—immersion in today's highly social media culture sustains a more shared experience for children than they have ever enjoyed before. It is also open for debate whether differences in use (girls chat online more, boys play more games) represent an inequality, or a gender preference, or opportunities for gendered identities and forms of participation. Nonetheless, the findings in Table 17.1 suggest that the combination of parental provision and children's preferences, embedded as they are in a gender-unequal society, serves to reproduce differences and also inequalities.

## Gendered dimensions of online risk encounters

In this chapter we focus on the relation between gender and online risk, contextualizing these within the literature on gender, media, and family socialization, while not forgetting that online risks and opportunities are often intertwined in the realities of daily life. What risks do girls and boys experience online? Do these mirror the agenda of public and policy concerns? Do boys' better access, greater skills, and broader use of the internet lead them to encounter a greater degree of risk? Or is society right to worry more about boys and pornography, but girls and "stranger danger"? We asked about exposure to pornography, cyberbullying, sexual messaging ("sexting"), potentially harmful user-generated content, and meeting online contacts offline ("stranger danger"). We also examined how parents respond to risks faced by their children, and how children cope with online risk, shedding light on questions of vulnerability and resilience, now part of the "digital citizenship" policy agenda.

The question of coping is important as part of a wider shift from technologically determinist discourses (of what the internet "does" to children) in favor of also recognizing children's agency. The internet is not merely an environment that affords (unequal) opportunities and risks; it is also one in which people initiate, learn, adapt, and gain resilience. Encountering risk could in itself also represent an opportunity— to become more resilient, more digitally literate, and less vulnerable to online risks (Schoon 2006). Such twists and turns in the debate are familiar to researchers who, in the debate about the "digital generation" (Buckingham and Willett 2006), have long recognized the dynamic interplay between the agency of children and young people and the forces of socialization.

Overall, four in ten children (40 percent of girls and 41 percent of boys) reported one or more of the risks we asked about. However, risk is not harm, and the conditions that explain encounters with risk could differ from those that account for experiences of harm. As Table 17.2 shows, only one in eight children had been

*Table 17.2* Children's experience of online risk and harm, by gender

| | Girls | Boys | All |
|---|---|---|---|
| "I have been bothered by something online" in the past year (%) | 13 | 11 | 12 |
| Has seen sexual images in the past year—% at all | 21 | 25 | 23 |
| (% online) | (12) | (16) | (14) |
| Has seen sexual images online and been upset by this—% all children (% upset of those who saw sexual images) | 5 (39) | 4 (26) | 4 (32) |
| Has received nasty or hurtful comments in the past year—% at all | 20 | 17 | 19 |
| (% online) | (7) | (5) | (6) |
| Has received nasty or hurtful comments online and been upset—% all children (% upset of those who received bullying comments) | 6 (87) | 4 (82) | 5 (85) |
| Has received sexual messages online—% all children | 13 | 15 | 14 |
| (% upset by this of all children, % upset of those who received messages)[a] | (4, 33) | (3, 17) | (4, 25) |
| Has gone to meet an online contact face to face—% all children | 8 | 9 | 9 |
| (% upset by this of all children, % upset of those who met someone) | (1, 9) | (1, 13) | (1, 11) |
| Has seen pro-anorexia websites[a] | 14 | 6 | 10 |
| Has seen self-harm website[a] | 7 | 8 | 7 |
| Has seen hate sites[a] | 12 | 12 | 12 |
| Someone used their password/got their personal information | 8 | 6 | 7 |

*Base*: 25,142 children aged 9–16 in Europe who use the internet.
*Note*: The wording used in this table was judged easier for children to understand, and easier to translate into 25 languages than the words "pornography," "cyberbullying," "sexting," or meeting "strangers."
[a]11–16 years only.

bothered or upset by something online in the past year (the self-report measure we used for harm)—slightly more girls than boys. As expected from other research on risks (Peter and Valkenburg 2009), the EU Kids Online survey found that boys were somewhat more likely to have seen sexual images online than girls (16 percent vs. 12 percent) while girls were a little more likely to receive bullying messages (20 percent vs. 17 percent). Further, boys received slightly more sexual messages (15 percent vs. 13 percent) and girls were considerably more likely to see pro-anorexia sites (14 percent vs. 6 percent). There were no gender differences for meeting online contacts offline, contrary to popular anxieties about girls.

The picture is rather different for self-reported harm. While online bullying—the most upsetting risk of all—was described as harmful by boys and girls equally, among those who saw sexual images, girls were more likely to be bothered or upset by this (39 percent vs. 26 percent of boys). Similarly, "sexting" upset 33 percent of girls who received sexual messages, twice as many as boys (only 17 percent were upset by such messages). Which girls report such risks? Brown *et al.* (2005) suggest that those who reach puberty earlier than their peers use media sources to explore their developing sexuality, but then find themselves unsupported by their (more slowly developing) peers and are exposed to typically sexist content alone.

Insofar as the internet provides a space for exploration of and experimentation with identities and social relations, children and young people engage in a range of online activities that are not easily classified as either opportunities or risks. The EU Kids Online project has termed these "risky online activities," recognizing the ambiguous nature of much youthful activity as well as that of the online environment (Kirwil and Laouris 2012). It is not merely difficult to determine whether, say, exposure to pornography is a risk to or an opportunity for sexual development. There are also many things young people do online which could lead to benefits or harms, depending on both the individual and context (e.g. the design or affordances of the online environment). It is precisely in this in-between space that so many online activities are positioned, permitting young people the opportunity to explore the risks surrounding them (Willett and Burn 2005); for Marwick and boyd (2011), this is essential to the "drama" of girls' peer culture. Some opportunities can still lead to risks—for example, the communicative nature of girls' internet use may increase the chance of unwanted sexual solicitation (Baumgartner *et al.* 2010; Mitchell *et al.* 2008).

In relation to a range of risky online activities, the survey revealed that boys had the edge (Table 17.3). Possibly they were generally more sensation-seeking; possibly they found face-to-face social relations more embarrassing, hence finding it a little easier to be themselves online, and so they sought online contacts beyond their familiar social circle. This might explain why they were more likely to keep their social networking profile public and to share online what they didn't share offline (Livingstone and Ólafsson 2011). While this may be framed as an opportunity, those who kept their profiles public were also more likely to reveal personal information. Indeed, risky social networking practices are associated with an increase in exposure to sexual images, receipt of sexual messages, and contact with those known online only (Staksrud *et al.* 2013).

Despite the sometimes celebratory talk that surrounds sexual expression on the internet, girls found this more problematic than boys. Wolak and Finkelhor (2011)

Table 17.3 Children's risky online activities, by gender

|  | Girls | Boys | All |
| --- | --- | --- | --- |
| Uses the internet excessively (% yes to at least 1/5 indicators)[a] | 28 | 31 | 30 |
| Has a social networking profile set to "public" (% of social networking site users only) | 23 | 30 | 26 |
| Shares private things online which doesn't share face to face[a] | 31 | 34 | 32 |
| Has made contacts online with people without connection to their lives[a] | 20 | 31 | 25 |
| Says it is "easier to be myself on the internet" than face to face[a] | 48 | 51 | 50 |

Base: 25,142 children aged 9–16 in Europe who use the internet.
[a]11–16 years only.

argue that sending sexual images is simultaneously normalized and disapproved of for girls, but not boys. In a qualitative exploration of mobile phone-related "sexting" practices among UK teenagers, Ringrose et al. (2012) argue that this is not a matter of girls' comparative prudishness (or innocence) but because the exchange of sexual content and messages is used within the peer culture as part of the sexual pressure, sexual stereotyping, and even sexual harassment exerted by boys on girls in their school or locale. Protecting their sexual reputation while avoiding being seen as rigid and unattractive is a "project" in which girls must invest energy and effort to construct just the right kind of "sexy, but not too sexy," image (Gill 2008). Such double standards can also disadvantage boys—while they are rewarded for displays of masculinity, they are also attacked (e.g. as "gay") for not joining in. Hearn (1999) argues that the construction of men's sexuality through power, aggression, objectification, and supposed "uncontrollability" creates problems of "normal boyhood." What needs further investigation is less the question of where online sexual content is located (or whether it can or should be filtered), but, rather, the social context within which girls are exposed to such content or messages and the (unwelcome) expectations that this may reinforce in the peer group.

## Gender similarities and differences in safety

Children and parents play a vital role in managing the risk of harm associated with internet use. While researchers first focused on the parental role—taking a lead from the longer tradition of research on parental mediation of children's exposure to television— recent research includes examination of children's agency, capabilities, and potential for resilience. As shown in Table 17.4, most commonly, children upset by something online talk to someone about this, as recommended by awareness-raising initiatives (Vandoninck et al. 2012). Girls were much more likely to talk to someone about being upset than boys, most often turning to their friends if they received unwanted sexual or bullying messages online. Gender differences are less within the family, with boys and girls similarly likely to tell a parent or, less commonly, a sibling about an online problem. Although other adults were rarely confided in, boys said they told a teacher more often than girls when bothered by sexual messages or offline meetings with online contacts.

*Table 17.4* Coping strategies among those bothered by online risks, by gender

| Coping strategies | | Risks | Girls | Boys | All |
|---|---|---|---|---|---|
| Fatalistic/passive coping strategies | Hope the problem would go away (%) | Sexual images | 22 | 30 | 26 |
| | | Sexual messages | 14 | 36 | 22 |
| | | Cyberbullying | 28 | 18 | 24 |
| | Stop using the internet for a while (%) | Sexual images | 29 | 22 | 25 |
| | | Sexual messages | 21 | 13 | 18 |
| | | Cyberbullying | 20 | 19 | 20 |
| Communicative strategy | Talk to somebody (%) | Sexual images | 56 | 50 | 53 |
| | | Sexual messages | 66 | 48 | 60 |
| | | Cyberbullying | 85 | 67 | 77 |
| Proactive strategies | Try to fix the problem (%) | Sexual images | 19 | 25 | 22 |
| | | Sexual messages | 29 | 23 | 27 |
| | | Cyberbullying | 41 | 30 | 36 |
| | Delete the message (%) | Sexual images | 26 | 25 | 26 |
| | | Sexual messages | 41 | 33 | 38 |
| | | Cyberbullying | 43 | 39 | 41 |
| | Block the person who sent the message (%) | Sexual images | 22 | 24 | 23 |
| | | Sexual messages | 45 | 33 | 40 |
| | | Cyberbullying | 48 | 43 | 46 |

*Source*: Adapted from Vandoninck *et al.* (2012).

Both boys and girls used "fatalistic" coping strategies. When upset by sexual content online, boys tended to do nothing, hoping that the problem would go away, while girls more often went offline altogether—a strategy unlikely to help build resilience (Vandoninck *et al.* 2012). Few gender differences exist in children's use of proactive strategies: both boys and girls deleted unwelcome messages, although girls more often blocked those who sent them. Girls also more often tried to fix a problem with cyberbullying, while boys did this more to avoid unwelcome sexual images.

Parental mediation of children's internet use may enhance the benefits and reduce the risks that children experience online. Broadly, parental mediation strategies can be divided into *social support* (help, guidance, co-use, and co-interpreting) and *rules and restrictions* (social as well as technical; Kalmus 2012). The Flash Eurobarometer 2008 survey showed that mothers more frequently than fathers talked to their children or stayed nearby when the child used the internet (Flash EB Series #248 2008). As Valcke *et al.* (2010) observed, it seems that mothers manage their children's internet usage more and give more guidance and support.

In the EU Kids Online survey, matched comparison questions about parental mediation were asked of the parent most involved in the child's internet use. This turned out to be mothers or female carers in four out of five families, reflecting European norms according to which women tend to bear most of the domestic caregiving responsibilities (Kalmus and Roosalu 2012). However, there is some evidence that parents treat sons and daughters differently in mediating their internet use. Although the analysis of single indicators of parental mediation did not reveal many differences between boys and girls (Livingstone *et al.* 2011), composite measures (the indexes of parental mediation) reveal stronger differences. Table 17.5 shows that,

Table 17.5 Strategies of parental mediation for sons and daughters, according to child and parent (means)

| Index of mediation | According to | Girls | Boys | p |
|---|---|---|---|---|
| Active mediation of internet use (5) | Child | 2.61 | 2.51 | 0.000 |
| | Parent | 2.89 | 2.84 | 0.005 |
| Active mediation of internet safety (6) | Child | 3.34 | 3.21 | 0.000 |
| | Parent | 3.66 | 3.53 | 0.000 |
| Restrictive mediation (6) | Child | 3.13 | 3.01 | 0.000 |
| | Parent | 3.5 | 3.41 | 0.001 |
| Monitoring (4) | Child | 1.02 | 0.95 | 0.000 |
| | Parent | 1.55 | 1.47 | 0.000 |
| Technical mediation (4) | Child[a] | 1.25 | 1.30 | 0.003 |
| | Parent | 1.43 | 1.45 | NS |

Base: 25,142 children aged 9–16 in Europe who use the internet.
[a] 11–16 years only.

according to both children and parents, girls received more of all types of parental mediation except technical mediation.

Neither boys nor girls felt deprived of parental interest in their online activities—just 15 percent would have liked their parent(s) to take more interest in what they did online, although nearly half of boys and girls also thought that their parents' management limited their activities (Livingstone et al. 2011). However, girls attributed slightly greater authority to their parents in internet-related matters (although social desirability may play a part in this): 46 percent of girls (41 percent of boys) said their parents knew a lot about their internet use, 63 percent of girls (61 percent of boys) thought their parents' management made their internet experience better, and only 33 percent of girls (39 percent of boys) ignored what their parents said when using the internet.

Does parental mediation reduce children's experiences of online risks and harm? Dürager and Livingstone (2012) found that children's exposure to online risks is reduced the more parents apply restrictions, although these also reduce children's online opportunities. Active mediation of the child's internet use also reduces risks, as does the use of technical restrictions, although to a lesser extent. Parental restrictions work better in reducing the likelihood of risk than they do in preventing harm from such risks. Interestingly, parental monitoring is associated with a higher incidence of online harm experienced by children of both sexes, suggesting that this type of mediation may occur retroactively, after children have had a negative online experience. As shown in Table 17.6, these findings differ little by gender. The exceptions are that, particularly among girls, the chance of encountering risks online is higher the more parents actively mediate their internet safety and the more they monitor their online activities. Also, girls' experiences of online harm are associated with higher levels of parental active mediation of internet safety and use of technical restrictions. It seems either that girls react against parental management by seeking out risks, or that parents are more inclined to intervene after their daughter encounters online risks by introducing safety strategies to prevent further negative experiences.

*Table 17.6* Boys' and girls' experiences of online risks and harm (according to child) correlated with strategies of parental mediation (according to parent)

| Index of mediation | Risks[a] | | Harm[b] | |
|---|---|---|---|---|
| | Girls | Boys | Girls | Boys |
| Active mediation of internet use (5) | −0.08*** | −0.11*** | −0.01 | −0.01 |
| Active mediation of internet safety (6) | 0.04*** | −0.02* | 0.06*** | 0.01 |
| Restrictive mediation (6) | −0.32*** | −0.33*** | −0.10*** | −0.09*** |
| Monitoring (4) | 0.03** | −0.00 | 0.04*** | 0.06*** |
| Technical mediation (4)[c] | −0.03** | −0.06*** | 0.03** | 0.00 |

[a] Child has experienced any of seven risks asked about in the EU Kids Online survey.
[b] "In the past 12 months, have you seen or experienced something on the internet that has bothered you in some way?"
Point biserial correlations: * = $p<0.05$; ** = $p<0.01$; *** = $p<0.001$.
*Base:* 25,142 children aged 9–16 in Europe who use the internet.
[c] 11–16 years only.

## Conclusions: developing policy recommendations

Children's experiences of the internet are not simply or stereotypically gendered. To those who suppose that girls and boys live very different lives online, our findings are more striking for revealing gender similarities than differences. This conclusion extends to children's experiences of online risk of harm. However, there are some subtle gender differences. In the policy debates that surround children's internet use, the intensity of public anxiety, moral panics, and media hyperbole is such that contextualized, contingent, or counter-intuitive arguments are easily lost. Thus we end with some evidence-based policy recommendations (see O'Neill *et al.* 2011) to counter the too-common policy discourses that reproduce moral panics (e.g. online pornography is inevitably harmful; lots of children are meeting strangers online) and popular myths (e.g. porn is more common online than offline; media-savvy kids know how to cope with online risks). Too often also, "children" are addressed in policy initiatives as a homogeneous rather than heterogeneous category in which gender, along with age, class, ethnicity, and other factors, all make a difference.

Schools are the main means by which a society can address digital safety and citizenship issues for all children within a structured learning environment. This requires teacher training and curriculum materials that are age appropriate, non-patronizing, technologically up-to-date, and gender and culture sensitive. In recent years, considerable efforts have been made to address cyberbullying, but schools still struggle to address sexual issues with students, including those that arise online. There is no easy line to draw between online and offline social relations, nor between cyberbullying and sexual harassment, nor indeed between empowering or entertaining content and that which is experienced as threatening or upsetting. All this makes the task of teachers especially difficult, and yet simply banning social networking or mobile phones from school or leaving safety management to parents is inadequate.

Awareness-raising—funded by governments, children's charities, or industry—has worked to provide materials, guidance, and advice to parents and children. Young people reject material that includes stereotypes, moralizing, and victim-blaming, preferring witty, topical, realistic, and thought-provoking scenarios presented through video or interactive media. Also, safety tips and advice should be gender sensitive, for example encouraging boys to talk more openly about online problems and girls to be more self-confident and independent in their relationships, both offline and online.

These materials may best be used in discussions, possibly in groups separated by gender, to permit exploration of the different pressures and concerns that girls and boys experience. Online risks do not exist in a vacuum, and adults advising young people must be confident in addressing wider issues as they arise—including sexism and sexual violence in society, and in popular culture. Both teachers and parents, we suggest, must stop regarding online risk as only originating from strangers, because risks that arise within the peer group (and the family) are more common and also upsetting.

Last, it would be naïve of policymakers to rely on either teachers or parents to ensure children's well-being in relation to so complex and fast-changing a technology as the internet. The role to be played by both government and industry remains highly contested, with cultural and political factors shaping public support for regulatory responses by both public and private sector bodies. Instances of good practice are growing—for example the provision of helplines across Europe, or the development of online safety tools on social networking sites; but instances of poor practice are also widespread, and few checks exist to evaluate what works or how well for girls and boys, or whether vulnerable children may slip through the safety net provided. Moreover, the efforts put in to safety provision by the industry are dwarfed by its efforts to develop new products and services that, it seems, are always several steps ahead of even today's fairly digitally literate children and young people. Becoming confident and competent digital citizens in a thoroughly mediated network society will remain, therefore, a significant challenge—in some ways different for girls and boys, but in other ways similar for both. It is not a challenge that they should be left to meet unsupported.

## Acknowledgments

This chapter draws on the work of the EU Kids Online network, funded by the European Commission (Directorate-General Information Society) Safer Internet plus Program (SIP-KEP-321803) (see www.eukidsonline.net), and was supported by grants from the Estonian Research Council (ESF8527 and SF0180017s07).

## References

Baumgartner, S. E., P. M. Valkenburg, and J. Peter (2010) "Unwanted Online Sexual Solicitation and Risky Sexual Online Behavior across the Lifespan," *Journal of Applied Developmental Psychology* 31: 439–47.

Brown, J. D., C. T. Halpern, and K. L. L'Engle (2005) "Mass Media as a Sexual Super Peer for Early Maturing Girls," *Journal of Adolescent Health* 36(5): 420–7.

Buckingham, D. and R. Willett (eds.) (2006) *Digital Generations*, Mahwah, NJ: Lawrence Erlbaum Associates.

Dürager, A. and S. Livingstone (2012) *How Can Parents Support Children's Internet Safety?*, London: EU Kids Online, London School of Economics and Political Science. http://eprints.lse.ac.uk/42872/.

Flash EB Series #248 (2008) *Towards a Safer Use of the Internet for Children in the EU—A Parents' Perspective. Analytical Report*, Directorate-General Communication: European Commission. http://ec.europa.eu/public_opinion/flash/fl_248_en.pdf.

Gill, R. (2008) "Empowerment/Sexism: Figuring Female Sexual Agency in Contemporary Advertising," *Feminism and Psychology* 18(1): 35–60.

Hargittai, E. (2010) "Digital Na(t)ives? Variation in Internet Skills and Uses among Members of the 'Net Generation'," *Sociological Inquiry* 80(1): 92–113.

Hearn, J. (1999) "A Crisis in Masculinity or New Agendas for Men?," in S. Walby (ed.) *New Agendas for Women*, London: Macmillan.

Helsper, E. J. (2010) "Gendered Internet Use across Generations and Life Stages," *Communication Research* 37(3): 352–74.

——(2012) "Which Children Are Fully Online?," in S. Livingstone, L. Haddon, and A. Görzig (eds.) *Children, Risk and Safety on the Internet: Research and Policy Challenges in Comparative Perspective*, Bristol: The Policy Press, pp. 45–57.

Henwood, F., S. Plumeridge, and L. Stepulevage (2000) "A Tale of Two Cultures? Gender and Inequality in Computer Education," in S. Wyatt, F. Henwood, N. Miller, and P. Senker (eds.) *Technology and In/equality: Questioning the Information Society*, London and New York: Routledge, pp. 111–28.

Inglehart, R. and P. Norris (2003) *Rising Tide: Gender Equality and Cultural Change around the World*, Cambridge: Cambridge University Press.

Kalmus, V. (2012) "Making Sense of the Social Mediation of Children's Internet Use: Perspectives for Interdisciplinary and Cross-cultural Research," in C. W. Wijnen, S. Trültzsch, and C. Ortner (eds.) *Medienwelten im Wandel: Kommunikationswissenschaftliche Positionen, Perspektiven und Konsequenzen: Festschrift für Ingrid Paus-Hasebrink (Changing Media Worlds: Positions, Perspectives and Consequences for Communication Research: Festschrift for Ingrid Paus-Hasebrink)*, Vienna: Springer VS, pp. 137–50.

Kalmus, V. and T. Roosalu (2012) "Institutional Filters on Children's Internet Use: An Additional Explanation of Cross-national Differences in Parental Mediation," in M. Walrave, W. Heirman, S. Mels, C. Timmerman, and H. Vandebosch (eds.) *e-Youth: Balancing between Opportunities and Risks*, Brussels: Peter Lang, pp. 235–50.

Kirwil, L. and Y. Laouris (2012) "Experimenting with the Self Online: A Risky Opportunity," in S. Livingstone, L. Haddon, and A. Görzig (eds.) *Children, Risk and Safety on the Internet: Research and Policy Challenges in Comparative Perspective*, Bristol: The Policy Press, pp. 113–26.

Livingstone, S. and E. J. Helsper (2007) "Gradations in Digital Inclusion: Children, Young People and the Digital Divide," *New Media & Society* 9(4): 671–96.

——(2010) "Balancing Opportunities and Risks in Teenagers' Use of the Internet: The Role of Online Skills and Internet Self-efficacy," *New Media & Society* 12(2): 309–29.

Livingstone, S. and K. Ólafsson (2011) *Risky Communication Online*, London: EU Kids Online, London School of Economics and Political Science. http://eprints.lse.ac.uk/33732/.

Livingstone, S., L. Haddon, A. Görzig, and K. Ólafsson (2011) *Risks and Safety on the Internet: The Perspective of European Children. Full Findings*, London: EU Kids Online, London School of Economics and Political Science. http://eprints.lse.ac.uk/33731/.

Marwick, A. E. and d. boyd (2011) "The Drama! Teen Conflict, Gossip, and Bullying in Networked Publics," paper presented at "A Decade in Internet Time: Symposium on the Dynamics of the Internet and Society," University of Oxford, September 21–24.

Mitchell, K. J., J. Wolak, and D. Finkelhor (2008) "Are Blogs Putting Youth at Risk for Online Sexual Solicitation or Harassment?," *Child Abuse & Neglect* 32: 277–94.

O'Neill, B., S. Livingstone, and S. McLaughlin (2011) *Final Recommendations for Policy, Methodology and Research*, London: EU Kids Online, London School of Economics and Political Science. http://eprints.lse.ac.uk/39410/.

Peter, J. and P. M. Valkenburg (2009) "Adolescents' Exposure to Sexually Explicit Internet Material and Sexual Satisfaction: A Longitudinal Study," *Human Communication Research* 35: 171–94.

Ringrose, J., R. Gill, S. Livingstone, and L. Harvey (2012) *A Qualitative Study of Children, Young People and "Sexting": A Report Prepared for the NSPCC.* http://eprints.lse.ac.uk/44216/.

Schoon, I. (2006) *Risk and Resilience: Adaptations in Changing Times*, New York: Cambridge University Press.

Staksrud, E., K. Ólafsson, and S. Livingstone (2013) "Does the Use of Social Networking Sites Increase Children's Risk of Harm?," *Computers in Human Behavior* 29(1): 40–50.

Uotinen, J. (2002) "Where Have All the Women Gone? Gender in the Biographies of IT Students," *NIKKmagasin* 3: 16–20. www.nikk.no/filestore/Publikasjoner/NIKK_magasin/mag 20023.pdf.

Valcke, M., S. Bonte, B. de Wever, and I. Rots (2010) "Internet Parenting Styles and the Impact on Internet Use of Primary School Children," *Computers & Education* 55: 454–64.

van Dijk, J. (2006) "Digital Divide Research, Achievements and Shortcomings," *Poetics* 34: 221–35.

Vandoninck, S., L. d'Haenens, and K. Segers (2012) "Coping and Resilience: Children's Responses to Online Risks," in S. Livingstone, L. Haddon, and A. Görzig (eds.) *Children, Risk and Safety Online: Research and Policy Challenges in Comparative Perspective*, Bristol: The Policy Press, pp. 203–16.

Willett, R. and A. Burn (2005) "What Exactly Is a Paedophile? Children Talking about Internet Risk," *Jahrbuch Medienpädagogik* 5: 237–54.

Wolak, J. and D. Finkelhor (2011) "Sexting: A Typology," *Research Bulletin* (March), Durham, NH: University of New Hampshire: Crimes Against Children Research Center.

# 18

# Holy grail or poisoned chalice?

## Three generations of men's magazines

## *Annabelle Mooney*

In the 1980s particularly, a general-interest men's magazine was seen as the "holy grail" for publishers (Nixon 1993). The explosion of interest in men's magazines and masculinities from the mid-1990s onwards makes it easy to forget that magazines for men have long existed although these were not targeted at "men" (Edwards 1997) and lacked large readerships (Crewe 2003b). Rather, they served readerships defined by a particular interest or hobby, such as those dealing with cars, fishing, or sporting pursuits. However, the launch of "style magazines" in the 1980s (*Arena*, *GQ*) was met with great enthusiasm. This further intensified with the launch of so-called "lads' magazines" in the UK in the 1990s. Despite several announcements that this market was disappearing or "growing up" (Carter 2000; Hodgson 2002; Marsden 2010), general-interest men's magazines appear to be surviving, if not thriving, around the world. The launch of weekly lads' magazines in the early 2000s underscores this longevity, while also providing some innovations on the older models.

That is not to deny that some have failed. A number of magazines have had very short lifespans, whether because their formula didn't quite work (e.g. *Mix*, *Jack*, *Details*, *The Hit*) or because of general competition in the market (e.g. the "new lad" monthly *Ralph* in Australia). British circulation figures for 2011 show a sharp drop for all purchased men's magazines, with the weeklies suffering most of all (Ponsford 2011). Nevertheless, the increasing availability of web-based versions of the magazines (because of changes in consumer technology) and the growing circulation of free magazines for men suggest that the market is again readjusting rather than disappearing.

Understanding contemporary publications requires charting the development of the three phases of men's magazines. While this history can be understood in terms of the innovation–imitation–saturation model (Curtin 1995), innovation needs to be understood in relation to models of masculinity circulating in the broader cultural landscape and its interaction with the broader production process. In particular, turning men into consumers and delivering them to advertisers is central to understanding the changes in this market. This relies on constructing an appropriately masculine reader, so that the risks associated with consumption can be managed. This generally relies on a binary and more or less essentialist understanding of gender: the authentic masculine male and the attractive, partially clothed woman. Perhaps because of the lack of regulation of this market and its reliance on the presence of near-naked women, a number of campaigns to lobby for changes to these magazines have been launched by feminist organizations. I focus largely on the United Kingdom, as the later magazines originate here and most research appears to have been undertaken in this context.

## Three generations of magazines

The different kinds of men's magazines suggest three phases: those targeting the old man, new man, and new lad. This ordering is roughly chronological, with the period of the "old man" (starting 1940s–1950s) establishing the techniques and frames used in the development of later kinds of magazines (Edwards 2003). This genealogy from old man to new lad can be understood as a progressive evolution in masculine subject positions, or simply as the result of producing consumers and the magazines which would sell to them (Gill 2003; Edwards 2003). Indeed, these two perspectives are linked. As Jackson, Stevenson, and Brooks note, "the images, discourses and frameworks of understanding that we borrow from the media in order to make sense of our everyday lives are embedded in wider cultures of production and media circulation" (2001: 50). In short, the quotidian nature of magazines means it is difficult to tease apart what they produce and what they reflect.

### Old man

*Esquire* is considered to have been the first magazine for men as such (Osgerby 2003). Launched in the US in 1937, it continues to be published today, not only in the US but also in the UK (since 1991). It developed and refined existing representations and discourses of the male as consumer, which can be traced back to the 1920s or even the late nineteenth century (Breazeale 1994; Osgerby 2003). As consumption is generally a feminine domain, turning men into consumers is a risky business; but it is necessary for the survival of any publication targeting men. The danger is most clearly seen in the marketing of clothing and grooming products, as this will generally involve a male model for the reader to consider. The risk, then, is the inherent femininity of consumption as well as the threat to (heterosexual) masculinity that gazing at attractive men marketing desirable products may bring. With backgrounds in marketing men's clothing, the original editors of *Esquire* were in the perfect position to manage the risks of consumption (Breazeale 1994).

*Esquire* managed these risks in at least three ways. First, the topics covered by the magazine were quintessentially masculine, including sport and traditionally male pursuits like hunting. Second, they included written contributions from "manly men" such as Ernest Hemingway. Finally, they portrayed women in a particularly objectified and sexualized manner, fusing the generally opposed genres of pornography and fine art (Breazeale 1994). In short, the editors sought to cultivate a "natural masculine character" (*Esquire*, Autumn 1933: 4, cited in Osgerby 2003: 69). These strategies, and the model of masculinity portrayed, bear a striking similarity to the much later "new lad" model, and they were picked up by many other publications, including *Playboy* (Breazeale 1994). Indeed, this strategy is more imitated than modified.

## New man

The second wave of men's magazines is connected with the figure of "new man" and often collectively called "style magazines" or "general interest men's magazines" (Nixon 1993). The two most representative titles are *Arena* and *GQ*. *Arena* was launched in 1986 by the small publisher Wagadon and can be credited with changing the attitudes of the larger publishers about what was possible for the general male market. These magazines reinvigorated the consuming male and ultimately paved the way for the third wave of magazines. In order to do this, they looked to successful women's magazines for inspiration (Nixon 1993). While never quite mainstream, these magazines are important as they coincide with changes in the consumption behavior of men. They are also linked to shifts in politics, the labor market, and demographics (Edwards 1997, 2003).

Charting the genesis of, or even describing, the new man is difficult. He is said to be a male feminist, a man in touch with his feelings, a man who wants to wear nice clothes and own nifty gadgets. But the new man has had a difficult history, in that he has been derided as a marketing construct, accused of betraying authentic masculinity, and criticized for being an identity deployed only as a way to seduce women. Nevertheless, the new man was welcomed as a model of masculinity that accepted and accommodated more equal gender relations. The term still has some currency, and may even be experiencing a comeback (Leith 2011). It seems also to be linked with class insofar as the new man is educated, articulate, and ambitious. He was created and embraced not only by men's magazines, but by popular culture more generally.

By the time the new lad came along, the new man's magazines, if not the new man himself, had already changed. Given the non-mainstream nature of new man magazines, it is unlikely that the new lad innovation was brought about by market saturation. The more likely explanation relates to expanding markets. Simply, the new man had a limited reach and a relatively niche advertising base. A new market needs a new audience. The construction of this new reader drew on discourses around masculinity which were already in circulation, including the "crisis of masculinity" (Kimmel 2006) and the related "backlash" against feminism (Faludi 1992). Gill (2009) argues, "the sudden visibility of the 'new lad' both as an emblem of a new type of masculinity and as the focus of journalistic quasi-sociological discussions, is an outcome of a number of shifts which meant that producing knowledge about gender had become 'big business'." The change was evident not only in expanding markets and new titles, but also in changes to existing titles. Specifically, in the early 1990s, both *GQ* and *Arena* began to represent women in a more sexualized way, especially on covers.

## New lad

When lads' magazines appeared, especially in the weekly formats, their popularity was seen as surprising (O'Hagan 2004). And yet all the ingredients for the form were in place, whether in the style magazines, in tabloid newspapers, or in the "shock jock" genre in American radio (Breazeale 1994). Indeed, the Australian magazine *People* (which is not the same as the US brand) encompassed a great many features of the lads' magazines long before recognition of the specific genre. Nevertheless, the formula was new, the editorial philosophy explicit, and the readership brought together in a masculine community of irony, sport, women, violence, and trust (Holmes and Nice 2012: 7).

The arrival of the new lad is commonly linked to the launch of *Loaded* magazine in the UK (1994), which was quickly followed by the rebranding of *For Him Magazine* as *FHM* (1994). *Loaded* is seen as a watershed moment in magazines for men, with founding editors James Brown and Tim Southwell generally credited with creating the new lad figure. The magazine's strapline is "for men who should know better." But it was an article in *GQ*, by Sean O'Hagan, that proclaimed the arrival of the new lad and described his mind-set. "They could defend their ideological shortcomings in socio-political terms" and were able "to switch from old lad to new man as appropriate, albeit never quite descending to the sexist depths of the 'utterly unreconstitutable' male" (cited in Crewe 2003b: 93). The early new lad had direct experience of the new man model and could apparently move between the two identities, despite their differences.

The language of the new lad, however, was not that of the new man. *Loaded*'s first editorial captured the new lad discourse in its commitment to "life, liberty, the pursuit of sex, drink, football and less serious matters" (cited in Gill 2003: 49). Another early editorial (July 1995) clearly set out the magazine's ideal content:

> *Loaded* should be rammed full of the things that people go on about in the pub and that stuff like health and perfume should be left to the adult mags. Remember, grooming is for horses.
>
> (cited in Stevenson *et al.* 2003: 121)

The link to pub culture and the rejection of grooming may suggest that the new lad is typically working class. But this ignores the problematic definition of class (Edwards 2003) and glosses over the central themes of authenticity and male community. Even so, it seems that the discourses of "honesty" and "authenticity" that underpinned the new lad led naturally to the celebration of a particular, and singular, kind of masculinity. Two aspects are worth noting in relation to the early *Loaded*. First, it explicitly rejected certain patterns of consumption, whether connected with the "new man" or with an increasingly commodified media landscape. Second, the original mock-ups for the magazine had no naked women (Crewe 2003a). This was soon to change. A magazine cannot survive without some kind of consumption, and for male markets this generally requires the presence of female flesh.

The take-up of new lad magazines was impressive, with the best-selling *FHM* having a circulation of over 700,000 copies in the first six months of 1998 (Stevenson *et al.* 2003). The magazines also traveled. For example, *Maxim* (Dennis, UK; Alpha Media Group, USA) has editions in over 20 countries. Having started in the UK (1995), it was launched in the US (1997/8) and is now the most popular men's magazine there and, as such, it is often imitated (Lambiase 2007).

### New new lad

The final evolutionary phase in men's magazines occurs with the launch of weekly men's magazines. The British launch of *Nuts* (2004, IPC Media), shortly followed by

*Zoo* (2004, Bauer Media), once again expanded the market into the "new new lad" (Crewe 2003a). For *Nuts*, this new demographic was identified through listening to British men, the so-called "Project Tribal" (Adams 2005); though this may have been as much about PR as sociological research. The weekly magazines have a lower cover price, lower production values and print quality, and a distinctive editorial approach. The latter is best exemplified in its choice of women. While the glossies tend to publish images of A-list celebrities, the weeklies use photographs of more local (national) celebrities as well as real women. This rehearses the "hierarchy" of women (Attwood 2005) while at the same time flattening this grading out, with real women taking the place of celebrities. Indeed, *Nuts* and *Zoo* both make celebrities out of real women, as they have their own "girls." There are other differences, with *Nuts* and *Zoo* being described as far "ruder and cruder" than other men's magazines or the tabloid press (Turner 2005). Even before the launch of the weeklies, a general "downward" shift in quality had been identified (Whelehan 2000). In 2005, at a journalism awards evening, founding editor of *Loaded*, James Brown, said:

> If I'd known when I started *Loaded* that the men's sector would descend into a conveyor belt of old soap stars in bikinis, I assure you I wouldn't have done it. Content wise, I think the men's sector is stale, predictable and uninspiring. It is an embarrassment.
>
> (*Press Gazette* 2005)

Nevertheless, like the monthlies, the weekly format has been adopted around the world. This is hardly surprising given the mass global markets of their advertisers. In short, if the style magazines have a scent it is Chanel or Ralph Lauren; *Zoo* and *Nuts*, in contrast, have the whiff of Lynx (the UK version of Unilever's Axe) about them.

## Creating a market, creating a man

The new lad is often understood as a reaction against the "new man" (Hodgson 2002; Benwell 2007) and symptomatic of a generalized male identity crisis. However, the evolution of men's magazines must be understood as an "attempt to find an appropriate voice in which to address their readers without antagonizing advertisers, searching for a distinctive position within the marketplace while simultaneously trying to maximise sales" (Jackson *et al.* 2001: 53–4). This results in a "series of unstable shifts back and forth" (Jackson *et al.* 2001: 53). Nevertheless, these shifts tend to have two focal points: construction of readers' masculinity and, related to this, attitudes towards women.

While the style magazines portrayed, celebrated, and encouraged a heroic masculinity, with success in all aspects of life, the lads' magazines provide a space and a subject position for the anti-hero. Ed Needham, once editor of *FHM*, puts it as follows: "The idea that it was all right to be funny and self-deprecating about, say, failure in the pursuit of women came as an enormous relief to our readers" (Needham 2007: 12). But the presentation and promotion of the anti-hero subject position requires work, especially in editorial terms. Specifically, as the anti-hero position is not one that is traditionally esteemed, it needs to be presented in a way that is both celebratory and ironic (Benwell 2004), even if readers do not identify the irony as such (Benwell 2007: 544). The subject is thus able to make a claim to authenticity which is closely connected to discourses of "cool" masculinity in the context of a very heterosexual space (Tincknell *et al.* 2003).

The theme of and claim to authenticity also fit very well with another (re)emerging discourse in popular culture: the innate qualities of men and women. Authenticity, of course, suggests an honest, natural and, most importantly, singular view of gender. (Indeed, the very concept of magazines for men or women also depends on this bifurcation.) The idea that men and women have natural ways of behaving was only consolidated by the popularity of John Gray's *Men Are from Mars, Women Are from Venus* in the 1990s, and more recently the rise of evolutionary psychology and popular-science texts which "confirm" that men and women are fundamentally different (Cameron 2010). This discourse of difference is foregrounded in editorial and commercial content as it allows "boys to be boys," to enjoy pictures of naked women, and to engage in laddish pursuits. It is a position consonant with readers' assessments of the magazines as "honest," "natural," and "unhypocritical" (Jackson *et al.* 2001: 116–17), as well as meaning that no explanation or excuse need be provided for any "natural" behavior.

Both the monthly and weekly lads' magazines include pictures of semi-clad women as part of encouraging the "natural" heterosexual male to consume the publication and the goods it advertises. Although research on the relationship between the images and purchasing behavior is not definitive (Reichert 2005), semi-clothed women remain prominent. Perspectives on the representation of women in these magazines are diverse, ranging from claims that the women are empowered, that they are making rational decisions when posing with little clothing (Whelehan 2000: 63, following Katherine Viner), to those arguing that it is exploitative (Mooney 2008). Phil Hilton (2006), then editor of *Nuts* magazine, articulates the empowerment position, arguing that the women who pose for their magazine "hope to turn modelling into a source of income. ... [Some] simply want to supplement their earnings, and some just want to get rich by being sexy. They should be free to make these choices." Other magazine editors are rather pragmatic in their arguments, while drawing on essentialist accounts of male behavior. Their explanations recite the mantra that sex sells, that men's magazines will as a matter of course include women in states of undress because it is simply part of normal male behavior to want to look at naked women. Ross Brown, then editor, admits to "a huge sliver of sexism in *FHM*," but explains, "We do it because our readers laugh at it" (quoted in Turner 2005). Certainly, some readers view the objectification of women as "complimentary" or simply as a marketing strategy (Benwell 2007: 545). This understanding is also shared by editors. According to *Zoo* editor Paul Merrill, naked women are "simply a means of attracting men to the magazine's broader content—football, facts and statistics, gadgets, and the gags" (quoted in Turner 2005), and, of course, advertisements (Crewe 2003a: 105). Thus, the use of women can be seen as a consequence of turning men into consumers – of the magazines and of their content.

## Regulation

The diversity of views about the treatment of women and the appeal to natural masculine qualities perhaps explains why there is little appetite for regulation of these publications. The partial similarity of women's magazines may also be a factor (Machin and Thornborrow 2006; Tincknell *et al.* 2003). However, while magazines for young women are highly regulated (Teenage Magazine Arbitration Panel, UK), especially in terms of any content connected with sex, the same is not true of magazines that young men read. Teenage boys read first- and (perhaps especially) second-wave lads' magazines, with the age of reader as low as 12 (Hatoum and Belle 2004: 406). While young women's magazines encourage sexual responsibility and promote respect for young men, the lads' magazines suggest sexual irresponsibility is part of "normal" masculinity and that women are sexual objects (OBJECT 2005); "Sex is guiltless fun, with little tenderness and no consequences" (Turner 2005; see also Tincknell *et al.* 2003).

This has consequences, at least in terms of readers' opinions about the publications. Specifically, recent research suggests that attitudes to sexual conduct may be closely connected to the relationship readers have with lads' magazines. In a questionnaire administered to British men, subjects were unable to discern the difference between views of women articulated by convicted rapists and those contained in lads' magazines (Horvath *et al.* 2012). The only difference is that people are less likely to label magazine content as "sexist" when they know its source, in part because they see lads' magazines as a source of advice. Thus, lads' magazines have been successful in avoiding regulation, arguably through the successful promotion of their product as "just a bit of fun." Nevertheless, because of their privileged position, lads' magazines may exert an influence on discourses of masculinity, especially in relation to women.

While there has been no regulation as such, campaigns have succeeded to greater and lesser extents. Changes to the sale or display of lads' magazines have been voluntary and only have a significant effect when such an action is taken by a large supermarket or paper shop chain, as in 2003 when Walmart in the United States withdrew *Maxim*, *Stuff*, and *FHM* from its shelves because of complaints about the nearly naked women on the covers (Younge 2003). Campaigns to obscure the nakedness of the cover woman from view with "modesty covers" have had some success, as have those which seek to move the magazines out of the eyeline of children. A UK Labour Member of Parliament did introduce a Bill in 2006 to move lads' magazines to the top shelf. While it received a deal of press coverage, the Bill was not enacted.

In the UK, the feminist group OBJECT has a long-running campaign related to lads' magazines. One particularly visible intervention was in response to Tesco supermarkets asking customers not to shop in their pajamas and nightwear as this may cause offence to other patrons. As the Tesco chain sells lads' magazines, feminist protest groups donned nightwear and danced the conga around stores chanting, "Let's get rid of lads' mags," attaching homemade modesty covers to the magazines reading, for example, "Sexism isn't Sexy," "Lads Mags? Loser Mags," and "Our Bodies Not Your Business" (Gonzales 2010). OBJECT has also developed a voluntary code for lads' magazines and tabloid newspapers that carry similar content. In early 2011, companies adopting the guidelines included the petrol station BP and major supermarket chains Tesco, Sainsbury's, Asda, Morrisons, and the Co-operative. The guidelines, however, frame the issue in terms of avoiding customer complaints, looking after the concerns of children, and being "family friendly." While the choice of such arguments may well be strategic, that this strategy is necessary underscores the lack of concern for women in this context.

Some complaints have been lodged with the UK Press Complaints Commission (PCC), but these have been rare and concern issues either of truth or of consent/privacy. Thus, a photograph of a woman's breasts was published in *Loaded* magazine without her consent. She was 15 years old when the photograph was taken. However, her complaint was not upheld as the image was already circulating on the internet (Press Complaints Commission 2010; however, see Press Complaints Commission 2007). The decision also points out that the PCC does not deal with "issues of taste or offence," as this may lead to censorship. Moreover, the PCC states that while advertisements need to be controlled as they are unavoidable, "newspapers [and presumably magazines] are actively purchased and therefore need not be subject to the same restrictions" (PCC FAQs). Other countries will no doubt vary in their views about what is culturally acceptable and this will be taken into account during the design and launch of local issues.

## Conclusion

The global reach of men's magazines, in conjunction with the fact that these texts draw on existing discourses of masculinity and femininity, means that while men's magazines may well change in future, they will probably continue to exist. While it is tempting to see the various developments in men's magazines as related to innovation born of saturation, they are more likely to be connected to expanding markets in search of a consuming audience. As was clear in the early era of men's magazines, turning males into consumers requires careful management. Editorial policy is thus just as much influenced by what can be drawn from the discourses already circulating around masculinity as it is to do with advertiser demands. The lack of regulation, despite some grassroots campaigns and superficial success, may well be to do with the particular way in which readers have been constructed. Drawing on existing resources in the publishing world and repackaging them as "authentic" and "manly" allows these magazines to use "irony" and commercial arguments as both a promotion device and an all-purpose defense against criticism.

## References

Adams, T. (2005) "New Kid on the Newsstand," *Observer*, January 23. http://observer.guardian.co.uk/.

Attwood, F. (2005) "Tits and Ass and Porn and Fighting: Male Heterosexuality in Magazines for Men," *International Journal of Cultural Studies* 8: 83–100.

Benwell, B. (ed.) (2003) *Masculinity and Men's Lifestyle Magazines*, Oxford: Blackwell.

——(2004) "Ironic Discourse: Evasive Masculinity in Men's Lifestyle Magazines," *Men and Masculinities* 7(1): 3–21.

——(2007) "New Sexism?," *Journalism Studies* 8(4): 539–49.

Breazeale, K. (1994) "In Spite of Women: 'Esquire' Magazine and the Construction of the Male Consumer," *Signs* 20(1): 1–22.

Cameron, D. (2010) "Gender, Language, and the New Biologism," *Constellations* 17(4): 526–39.

Carter, M. (2000) "Lads Magazines are Growing up," *Independent*, January 18, p. 8.

Crewe, B. (2003a) *Representing Men: Cultural Production and Producers in the Men's Magazine Market*, Oxford: Berg.

——(2003b) "Class, Masculinity and Editorial Identity in the Reformation of the UK Men's Press," in B. Benwell (ed.) *Masculinity and Men's Lifestyle Magazines*, Oxford: Blackwell.

Curtin, M. (1995) *Redeeming the Wasteland: Television Documentary and Cold War Politics*, London: Routledge.

Edwards, T. (1997) *Men in the Mirror: Men's Fashion, Masculinity and Consumer Society*, London: Cassell.

——(2003) "Sex, Booze and Fags: Masculinity, Style and Men's Magazines," in B. Benwell (ed.) *Masculinity and Men's Lifestyle Magazines*, Oxford: Blackwell.

Faludi, S. (1992) *Backlash: The Undeclared War against American Women*, London: Vintage.

Gill, R. (2003) "Power and the Production of Subjects: A Genealogy of the New Man and the New Lad," in B. Benwell (ed.) *Masculinity and Men's Lifestyle Magazines*, Oxford: Blackwell.

——(2009) "Lad Lit as Mediated Intimacy: A Postfeminist Tale of Female Power, Male Vulnerability and Toast," *Working Papers on the Web*. http://extra.shu.ac.uk/wpw/chicklit/gill.html.

Gonzales, F. (2010) "Tesco – Porn's More Harmful than Pyjamas," March 28. http://www.indy-media.co.uk.

Hatoum, I. J. and D. Belle (2004) "Mags and Abs: Media Consumption and Bodily Concerns in Men," *Sex Roles* 51(7–8): 397–407.

Hilton, P. (2006) "Lads' Mags: Porn or Good Fun?," *Telegraph*. http://www.telegraph.co.uk/culture/3653431/Lads-mags-porn-or-good-fun.html.

Hodgson, J. (2002) "The Lads Go Limp," *Guardian*, Media Pages, February 18, p. 4.

Holmes, T. and L. Nice (2012) *Magazine Journalism*, London: Sage.

Horvath, M. A. H., P. Hegarty, S. Tyler, and S. Mansfield (2012) "'Lights on at the End of the Party': Are Lads' Mags Mainstreaming Dangerous Sexism?," *British Journal of Psychology* 103(4): 454–71.

Jackson, P., N. Stevenson, and K. Brooks (2001) *Making Sense of Men's Magazines*, Cambridge: Polity.

Kimmel, M. S. (2006) *Manhood in America: A Cultural History*, 2nd edition, New York: Oxford University Press.

Lambiase, J. (2007) "Promoting Sexy Images," *Journal of Promotion Management* 13(1/2): 111–25.

Leith, W. (2011) "Has the 'New Man' Triumphed at Last?," *Guardian*, October 28. http://www.guardian.co.uk.

Machin, D. and J. Thornborrow (2006) "Lifestyle and the Depoliticisation of Agency: Sex as Power in Women's Magazines," *Social Semiotics* 16(1): 173–88.

Marsden, R. (2010) "Last of the Lads Mags," *Independent* Magazine, November 27, p. 15.

Mooney, A. (2008) "Boys Will Be Boys: Men's Magazines and the Normalisation of Pornography," *Feminist Media Studies* 8(3): 247–65.

Needham, E. (2007) "I've Had It with Men," *Guardian*, G2, June 4, p. 12.

Nixon, S. (1993) "Looking for the Holy Grail: Publishing and Advertising Strategies and Contemporary Men's Magazines," *Cultural Studies* 7(3): 466–92.

OBJECT (2005) "Teens Mags to Lads Mags." http://www.object.org.uk/files/Teen%20Mags%20to%20Lads%20Mags.pdf.

O'Hagan, A. (2004) "Disgrace Under Pressure," *London Review of Books* 26(11), June 3: 36–8.

Osgerby, B. (2003) "A Pedigree of the Consuming Male: Masculinity, Consumption and the American 'Leisure Class'," in B. Benwell (ed.) *Masculinity and Men's Lifestyle Magazines*, Oxford: Blackwell.

Ponsford, D. (2011) "Mag ABCS, Men's Titles: Big Falls for Nuts, Zoo and FHM," August 18. http://www.pressgazette.co.uk.

Press Complaints Commission (2007) Cases: A Married Couple, August 15, 2007. http://www.pcc.org.uk/.

——(2010) Cases: A Woman, May 11, 2005. http://www.pcc.org.uk/.

*Press Gazette* (2005) "Stale and Pathetic Lads' Mags Make Me Cringe," November 4. http://www.pressgazette.co.uk/node/32433.

Reichert, T. (2005) "Do Sexy Cover Models Increase Magazine Sales? Investigating the Effects of Sexual Response on Magazine Interest and Purchase Intention," *Journal of Promotion Management* 11(2/3): 113–30

Stevenson, N., P. Jackson, and K. Brooks (2003) "Reading Men's Lifestyle Magazines: Cultural Power and the Information Society," in B. Benwell (ed.) *Masculinity and Men's Lifestyle Magazines*, Oxford: Blackwell.

Tincknell, E., D. Chambers, J. V. Loon, and N. Hudson (2003) "Begging for It: 'New Femininities,' Social Agency, and Moral Discourse in Contemporary Teenage and Men's Magazines," *Feminist Media Studies* 3(1): 47–63.

Turner, J. (2005) "Dirty Young Men," *Guardian*, October 22. http://www.guardian.co.uk.

Whelehan, I. (2000) *Overloaded: Popular Culture and the Future of Feminism*, London: The Women's Press.

You and I Films (2010) "Tesco—Porn's More Harmful than Pyjamas." http://vimeo.com/10510834.

Younge, G. (2003) "When Wal-Mart Comes to Town," *Guardian*, August 18. http://www.guardian.co.uk.

# 19

# Making public policy in the digital age

## The sex industry as a political actor

## *Katharine Sarikakis*

Significant shifts in the media over the past two decades have had a global impact on the industrial and cultural context within which pornography operates. The shifts involve the privatization of communication infrastructures, followed by re-regulation, aggressive market mergers, and domination leading to ownership concentration, inter-industrial alliances, and technological convergence (Chakravartty and Sarikakis 2006; McChesney 2004; Kamalipour and Rampal 2003). Media and culture industries have developed into political actors, organized across two core political economic activities: market management and policy management. A political actor is understood to demonstrate an "observable *action* that is *purposive* ... and sufficiently *unified* so that it makes sense to speak of a single actor" (Page 1996: 20). Two parallel phenomena in the governance of pornography emerge: the sociocultural integration of pornographic imagery in everyday life, work, and "leisure" through new production, distribution processes, and consumption cultures; and the integration of pornography's economic interests into public life and policy. Across these two axes the sex industry seeks to manage the market and the regulations that affect its long-term profit potential.

Pornography has long been at the center of extensive politicization and polarization of views with respect to agency, choice and freedom, silencing, degradation, and harm, inter alia. Among the varied groups participating in pornography debates, feminists have played a key role. Yet, my premise is that contemporary pornography[1] is significantly distinct from the object of both the anti-pornography and self-censorship strands of feminist scholarship and activism in the 1970s and 1980s. In this era, pornography was critiqued strongly by anti-porn feminists for its degrading treatment of women workers, the representation of the female body and its objectification, and for causing harm through the sexualization of violence. Anti-censorship feminism feared an attack on all material around sexuality would derive from banning pornography, leading to the restriction of women's free speech. Moreover, it held that some pornography can have a subversive function and that women-made pornography can be liberating. Today's pornography also eludes the turn to "porn studies" that has been in vogue since the 1990s and which focused on the pleasures women derive from its consumption, as well as feminist uses of pornography (Kipnis 1998; Williams 2004). It is distinct in terms of the scale of its technological advancement, degree of availability, normalization and social acceptability, as well as in the broader political economic and legislative context within which it operates. Directly deriving from the pursuit of greater profit, its end-product is also more diversified, specialized, exaggerated in the "genres" it produces, and the contexts within which these are consumed.

This chapter argues that pornography's presence today cannot be viewed as a simple outcome of changes in culture, economics, and politics but rather as a major cultural product and an organized political actor. It analyzes the ways in which the regularization and normalization of pornography and the sex industry are facilitated through developments which embed sex, culture, and media industries in the new global political economy. Ultimately, within the current context, sex and pornography industries have become quite adept at influencing public policy to serve their particular interests.

## Power synergies: market, technology, and culture

The pornography industry today operates panoramically, through a highly sophisticated technological and financial infrastructure; it is seamlessly integrated into the macro-level global system of production, distribution, marketing, and consumption of media and culture products even while it operates at the micro-level of the consumer (Sarikakis and Shaukat 2008). As far as the availability of the pornographic product is concerned, the transcendence of space and time is similar to, and dependent on, the same functions of financial capital and commerce as other "products." The match between availability, "immediate" gratification, and the (false) sense of privacy and anonymity are powerful factors in this. The financial gains of the industry worldwide, from which mainstream industries benefit as well, are enormous, although difficult to pinpoint. Still, an informed estimate of the consumption trade brings pornographic content to 14 percent of all video purchases and rentals in the US, accounting for US$3.35 billion in 2006 (Covenant Eyes 2013). Moreover, US$1.55 million is spent annually for on-demand services through cable or satellite broadcasting. Hotels are among the major beneficiaries of this consumption: pornography accounts for 70 percent of their in-rooms profits (Covenant Eyes 2013). Digital delivery is the main source of increased revenue, as consumption rates increased by 25 percent from 2005 to 2006, to US$1.25 billion. Delivery via mobile phones is estimated at US$40 million in the United States (Covenant Eyes 2013).[2] As a global and powerful industry integrated into the wider world industrial complex, pornography has been widely heralded as a bullet-proof industry.

The advent of the internet has transformed the capacity of the industry for expansion—both in production and in consumption. At first glance, free online pornography would seem to challenge the profitability of the industry in hard copy or commercial online content. In fact, the opposite is true: overall, it is the business model of pornography that is changing, effectively pushing older business forms to adapt to new methods. Modern business strategies for online enterprises exploit the culture of the internet, as a space for free content, to their own benefit, while utilizing modern-day technology to gain control over consumers. The internet operates as a gigantic, ever-expanding archive of material, some of which is "free" at the point of delivery. At this point, however, where material has been accessed, the consumer is faced with various—predetermined—options demanding use of a credit card number, such as: watch the full-length product; watch it in advanced quality (high definition); gain access to other similar products (gain a "pass") on the same site; gain access to products in "affiliated" sites; "upgrade" membership through affiliate "services" that include other aspects of the sex industry; and so forth.

Still, the industry's commercial strategy does not end here. If such techniques target the intentional viewer, others target the casual surfer. Johnson (2010) candidly discusses how the sophisticated network of sex industry companies collaborates in various ways to transform a "curious clicker" into a paying customer. "The online commercial pornography industry has a very active core which functions to diversify product development, production and distribution processes. The core is surrounded by marketing tentacles designed to infiltrate and cultivate niche areas of the market" (Johnson 2010: 153). In her study of the US-based pornography industry, Johnson found that the core of the industry can be located in two mainstream corporations that coordinate most of its content: *Playboy* and *Hustler*. Joining them in a coordinating role are distribution and marketing conglomerates which provide support to the network. The network is developed further by a dense population of tentacles (smaller companies) that extend their reach through content distribution through affiliate websites, affiliate programs, and end-user sites. These specialize in niche content. With the elaborate use of push technologies, mousetrapping,[3] and affiliated programs, the industry configures users and directs them toward niche content. As Johnson (2010) argues, niche content is where the most violent pornography is found; indeed, it is where violence and degradation are used as "a bait," the means to profit-making. Pornography producers are very well aware and talk openly about the profitability of niche markets and, in particular, violent and degrading material (Sarikakis and Shaukat 2008; Sun 2008). Within this process, some amateur (non-professional) production participates in the construction of niche pornography, mimicking the industry. The latter further pushes the boundaries by accommodating and incorporating amateur production in professional production and distribution. The vicious circle of niche content generation, non-professional production, free content, and popular culture exacerbates longstanding inequalities and stereotypified masculinities (Johnson 2010; Boyle 2010).

Meanwhile, at least in the mainstream popular imaginary of the West, the sex industry has elevated its image of "dirt" or "filth" to a "respectable" and "normal" form of business and cultural product, which one may—or may not—"choose" to consume and which is regarded as part of forming one's sexual identity—indeed a personal right to pleasure and choice (Brents and Hausbeck 2007). This process is achieved through the saturation of media and cultural imageries by pornographic cues and the lowering of barriers to sexually explicit and sexualized images in everyday culture, in news, advertising, broadcasting, and fashion. The emergence of "sexualization" or "pornification" of culture (Gill 2009; APA 2007; McNair 1996,

2002; Dines *et al.* 1998) has been accompanied by the lifting of restrictions on media ownership in the US and Eastern Europe and the development of digital platforms for porn content. The outcome has been a gradual hypersexualization of female public figures in popular culture and politics, which has set new marketing and press coverage "standards" through global media and digital pornography (Levande 2007; Kronja 2006). Moreover, these "standards" are located firmly in the political economic context within which they are brought to life. The drivers for this transformation rely on broader systems of cultural values shaping understandings of femininity and masculinity, practices of self-objectification, non-professional pornographic production forms, and (self- or other-) surveillance and policing of sexual behavior in everyday culture (Peter and Valkenburg 2006). A 2009 report on corporate sexism in the United Kingdom documents the links between workplace discrimination and the sex industry. The report shows how the proliferation of cultural practices of companies revolving around the sex industry as well as the use of pornography serve to "put women in their place," survey their behaviors, and silence potential protest (Fawcett Society 2009). A study conducted in Serbia extends the links between pornography and pornified images of women in the press to the role they play in national politics characterized by extreme nationalism and sexism (Kronja 2006).

As Jacobson argues in her study of gender bias in the media and effects on young people, "there is a strong commercial interest in maintaining a conservative gender ideology. Commercialization and femininity are closely tied together" (2005: 39). This sexual economy has at its heart the sexualized female body, which serves a legitimating function. In mainstream pornography and everyday pornified imagery the body becomes the site for compartmentalization and objectification, even a site for the experimentation of physical boundaries. This experimentation occurs without involving the actual subject, except to testify to willingness or enjoyment for the benefit of the viewer.[4] In the public discourse it is "dressed up" with a feminist vocabulary of "pleasure," "empowerment," and "choice" (Walters 2009). While the very same vocabulary functions to normalize the sexual economy at large and pornography in particular, it claims a postfeminist status for self-commodification and self-sexualization as exclusively individual acts (McRobbie 2009; Paul 2005). Moreover, "the use of pornography for sex is better understood as a reiterative, irreducibly bodily practice than ... the contemplation of ideas expressed in words and images or ... an illocutionary speech act" (Mason-Grant 2004: 114).

Pornography constitutes a body of specific knowledge about human sexuality and social relations. As such, questioning the conditions under which dominant representations (and documentations) of sexuality and sexual social relations are produced, legitimized, and ultimately governed is important. The conflict of interests and negotiating power between the industry and its workforce is glaring: the industry has the capability to use all available technological, economic, and political means to extend itself, diversify, and profit. Its workers have not been the drivers of change but the objects upon which changes have been imposed: not only their financial situation but also their conditions of work have worsened in comparison to previous decades, precisely due to the industry's focus on niche market coverage and consumer demand (Sarikakis and Shaukat 2008; Grudzen and Kerndt 2007).

Adult film workers, especially women, are exposed to many risks to their physical, mental, and social health. Not only are they vulnerable to physical health injuries while at work, but they also reported serious mental health problems and high rates of physical and sexual violence; although a legal industry, the various health risks performers face are similar to sex workers in illegal industries, for example street prostitutes (Grudzen *et al.* 2008; Grudzen *et al.* 2011). Grudzen *et al.* (2008) found that certain health risks are so common that they called for immediate access to substance abuse and mental health services, as well as financial and legal assistance.

While the conditions of labor exacerbate ongoing exploitative social and economic relations, workers' unionization efforts have been hindered. Many reasons explain why this is largely still the case, including cultural factors, expressed in the lack of solidarity or motivation for association by mainstream unions; legal factors, as in the question of the legal definition of the nature of sex work as performed by self-contractors, as well as the paucity of sex worker union activists and the difficulty in maintaining unions due to workers' short career spans (Wilmet 1998; Gall 2006; Schaffauser 2010). In the UK, as recently as in 2003 the Trades Union Congress (TUC) extended its membership to sex workers; in the US, three different attempts for unionization failed in 1993, 1998, and 2003. The consequence of this is that those directly (bodily and mentally) involved in and affected by the production of pornography have very little control over its content, conditions, economic benefits, or health protection. Under such conditions the kinds of worker agency involved in the production of pornography are severely limited.

## The politics of porn: governed or governing?

The pornography industry couples its production activities with a systematic approach to public policy and debate that aims to legitimize its claims in the policy domain and normalize its practices in the public sphere. In the past decade, the industry has adopted the strategies of other businesses that aim to influence policymakers: cultivating relationships with politicians, making donations to political parties or social causes, making alliances with other groups over policy issues, and presenting a unified and respectable front to the public. It has organized itself in official representative bodies and lobbies such as the Adult Industry Trade Association in the UK, the Free Speech Coalition (FSC) in the USA, or Eros Association in Australia. In previous decades, this side of the industry was less sophisticated, with the exception perhaps of the Adult Film Association of America (AFAA), the forerunner of FSC. Legal and public representations were mostly left in the hands of a few powerful international porn media corporations, which include in their corporate portfolios publications such as *Penthouse* or *Playboy*. Over the past decade, however, the industry lobby developed to emulate other actors and enlisted prominent figures in politics and law. For example, the Executive Director of FSC, Bill Lyon, is a former defense lobbyist, while one of the organization's officers is First Amendment attorney Jon Katz. While the industry now does its own lobbying, it formerly hired the services of the Raben Group, a professional lobbying firm in Washington, DC (Goldstein 2009).

Governments have not been idle observers of the industry's pursuit of political influence. The relationship between political elites and the pornography industry takes on a more complex form than simply one actor pressuring another or a power struggle between two or more actors. In an interview on CBS's *60 Minutes*, Bill Lyon said, "[Politicians] realise that it's votes and money that we're talking about" (Kroft 2006). This is certainly the case when donations are involved. The UK's Labour Party is known to have accepted donations from Richard Desmond, the UK "Porn Baron," in 2002. More recent news stories describe government laxity[5] in monitoring these kinds of donations. In 2006, on the other side of the Atlantic, it transpired that the Republican National Committee is "a regular recipient" of donations by the pornography industry—including regular contributions from Nicholas T Boyias, the owner and CEO of the largest gay porn distributor in the US, and Marina Pacific Distributions (Marshall 2006). In January 2009, Larry Flynt, the owner of *Hustler*, and Joe Francis, the owner of Wicked Pictures, two of the most powerful porn barons in the US, if not in the world, lobbied the government for a US$5 billion bailout to counteract profit losses due to the financial crisis. This effort failed. Nonetheless, the industry managed to occupy mainstream financial press coverage and reemphasized the message that this is "business as usual." Such transactional relations allow the pornography industry to present itself in public in the professional attire of a "respectable" conglomerate.

The "habitats" within which the pornography sex industries operate certainly have national differences, and the level of political organization varies. In some cases, pornography workers have run for office, albeit almost invariably without success.[6] In Australia in 2008, the sex industry successfully formed a political party titled the Australian Sex Party (ASP). The ASP, launched at the annual sex exhibition Sexpo in Melbourne, describes itself as the "political response to the sexual needs of Australia in the 21st century" (Australian Sex Party 2010). The party has the specific agenda to intervene in public policy, especially that related to the Australian government's proposals for internet filtering. The party head, Fiona Patten, is also the CEO of the Australian sex industry lobby Eros Association, as well as its founder and its president since the early 2000s. The ASP's agenda to promote the interests of the sex industry is clearly framed within a rhetoric of positive attitudes about sex, the interests of the individual, personal choice, and liberty. The ASP policies are, unsurprisingly, focus on sexual policies, rights, and politics. The issue here is that the close relation between politics and the sex industry raises many questions with regards to the representation of *private* interests, especially in such a highly politicized area as pornography, as well as in *public* policy and the extent to which issues of societal importance are reduced to privatized behavior. It is also of particular importance when *organized* private interests in the form of lobbies (or even political parties in this case) find their way into the design of policy.

As such, the industry has been successful in shifting, blocking, and opposing regulatory proposals that affect its interests and has not been shy about allying with actors traditionally opposed to porn, such as the Church, conservative parties, and "family values" organizations, as in the case of the introduction of the ".xxx" domain (Associated Press 2013). Not only systematic interaction with politicians, but also "unholy" alliances with opposing groups have been used as tools to affect the policy game. In the US, the pornography lobby has managed to oppose "sin" taxes on pornographic materials (taxes similar to tobacco, for example) or intervention in its distribution systems, such as through cable or subscription in hotels. It has successfully pressured Congress to allow the sale of pornography on military bases and has not only fended off attempts to regulate content on the basis of obscenity law, but also effectively made pornographic content ungovernable (Kroft 2006).

Indeed, when it comes to policy initiatives to regulate content, it is noteworthy that the sex industry regularly sides with mainstream powerful industries, such as internet service providers (ISPs), the media, or communications industries. Its position is invariably negative, irrespective of motivation, intent, or rationale, whether in the US or the UK. The industry has maintained a constant anti-censorship position on the grounds of freedom of speech. This is also the meeting point for various other industries and organizations, even for "anti-anti-porn" feminists. The industry has thereby succeeded in avoiding any significant control and remained unaffected by any demands for regulation over most of its production. The pornography industry benefits from the policy vacuum and the difficulties that technology and conflicting ideas about what constitutes freedom of speech impose on legislators.

One important case of the industry's impact on public policy is the following. The US lobby has been successful in influencing the course of the 1998 Child Online Protection Act. COPA was an internet filtering law that derived from the Communications Decency Act (CDA 1996) that was found unconstitutional by the US Supreme Court irrevocably in 2009. COPA targeted US-based commercial sites by requiring them to restrict access by minors to content "harmful to minors." The requirement involved material that by "contemporary community standards" was judged to appeal to the "prurient interest," and contained sexual acts and nudity. COPA was immediately appealed and therefore not enforced; successive courts rendered it unconstitutional as violating the First Amendment. COPA was finally invalidated in 2009 (Electronic Privacy Information Center 2009). Early on, a commission consisting of a majority of communications industry representatives was formed to look at various possibilities for protecting children on the internet. This commission stated its opposition to legal provisions because "laws restricting distribution of or access to harmful to minors materials are Constitutionally suspect" (Commission on COPA 2000: 64). The Commission urged governments and industries to fund the enforcement of existing laws of obscenity. The FSC, a fierce opponent to COPA, stood safely on the same side with organizations such as Electronic Privacy Information Center (EPIC) and the American Civil Liberties Union (ACLU). Most notably, FSC was previously involved in a case of virtual child pornography: the Children Prevention Pornography Act (CPPA) (1996)[7,] which made it illegal to produce, distribute, or consume actual *and* virtual child pornography, that is, pornography where actual children were not involved. The Act was attacked as unconstitutional and challenged in the courts over a period of time. The FSC claimed that this law infringes upon free speech, since it does not concern real children. In both cases, the efforts of government to focus on crime prevention and protection of children were defeated on the grounds of free speech (Mota 2002). The Supreme Court decided against the constitutionality of the law in 2002. In contrast, both Canada and the UK have adopted regulation to criminalize child pornography (Mota 2002).

## Concluding remarks

The governance of pornography is complex and ridden with philosophical dilemmas. The industry itself, whether in systematic and sustained ways or on an ad hoc basis, utilizes a policy vacuum, technologies, and markets to extend its profitability. It is actively involved in the political and cultural domains, adopting a variety of strategies, such as political alliances, lobbying, informal transactions. These characteristics demonstrate that the industry is neither an "underground" nor a "neutral" economic actor; nor does it leave distribution and consumption as merely a matter of private, personal choices. Rather it is a *political actor* that benefits from conditions of regulatory vacuums, regulatory and constitutional conflicts, as well as mistrust between the state and citizens. In that respect, it is not simply a matter of society and laws governing the pornography industry, but rather the pornography industry governing the conditions of its own regulation and overall operation. Not coincidentally, the argument around civil liberties and freedom of speech continues to be the core issue in the debate on pornography regulation. Although obscenity does not enjoy the protection of free speech law (whether in the US or UK), it effectively is the case that almost nothing in fact is considered "obscene" currently. This should be legally problematic. The reasons for this lie in the very complexity of the process of cultural legitimation of pornography. As Mason-Grant eloquently explains:

> The cultural legitimacy of the use of pornography is not so easily localizable, not so easily tracked to a singular source. Rather the force of pornography, culturally and individually, is produced and sustained through a multiplicity of repetitive practices that extend over time and are constitutively interrelated—not only practices of using pornography but other forms of sexual or sex-defined practice. This means that the cultural extent of the practice—how common, pervasive, or routine it is—makes a difference in its productive, normalizing effects.
>
> (Mason-Grant 2004: 114)

At the heart of the regulation of pornography lies the underlying assumption that the legal subject is the individual. At the heart of digital capitalism is the individual purchaser, the sovereign consumer; at the heart of the culture industry stands the individual laborer (performer, artist, creator). In the case of pornography, its consumption is considered a private and therefore personal (individual) matter. This also is one of the reasons that not even the "community standards-oriented" obscenity law has been effective in dealing with problematic pornographic genres. Moreover, its production process is unfriendly to acknowledging communal experiences, as labor is considered an individual matter or choice and negotiation. The choice, and right, of the pornographer to express ideas is based on the individualistic conceptual premises of expression and comes at the cost of the rights of the industry laborers. Automatically equating pornography with sex, expression, or choice masks the power dynamics embedded in the production, distribution, and consumption mechanisms of the industry. Claims of "choice" and "expression" silence the critique of the conditions of production or the effects of consumption by focusing on the "individual"—instead of "the individual in society." Late capitalism operates on the basis of the individual and her/his position in the production–consumption continuum. However, the fantasy and deception of individual freedom actualized through purchasing and pleasure-seeking in digital capitalism is a powerful affective and political tool.

The pornography industry as a labor space is in many ways transformed through its intensification by communication technologies and the technologies of the body. The embodied "know-how" in the practice of pornography and its labor constitute real, immediate, and direct sites of action. But they interact with the social world outside them through a culturally tacit transformation: they become words, speech, or expression, stripped from their practice of embodiment, not only among those making the pornographic content but also among those "consuming" it. This "connection gap" leaves open significant political and cultural spaces—that lead to vacuous policies—for an organized industry to fill.

Unless we fully appreciate the power dynamics involved in pornography as a global media and culture industry, in material and symbolic terms, and its spillover into other cultural domains, the debates surrounding pornography and sexualization will remain abstract, ridden with undertones of moral panic or absolute relativism. As we have seen, the industry is an active, articulate, flexible, and networked actor that pursues its own interests in a disciplined way. These interests are not identical to those of women in either the production or the consumption sectors, or indeed of men and the construction of masculinities. In other words, very much like other media and cultural industries, the profit-making machinery of pornography does not serve those members of society on whose affect, response, and correspondence it depends.

## Notes

1 For the purposes of this discussion I do not adopt the analytical distinction between soft and hardcore pornography or pornography and erotica.
2 No similar reports for the European market are available. See Sarikakis and Shaukat (2008) for a discussion of the political economic ties of various companies in the porn trade and the sex industry, and trends in the production and consumption of porn. Also Jeffreys's 2009 *The Industrial Vagina* constitutes one of the most comprehensive sex industry analysis texts today.
3 Mousetrapping is a technical method that keeps website visitors from leaving the site.
4 See studies on male physical arousal associated with violent pornography, whereby depictions of rape and force have a physiological effect on viewers if the victim is presented as consenting or having an involuntary orgasm. For a meta-analysis of such studies, see the Rapid Evidence Assessment by Itzin *et al.* (2007).
5 See press reports, http://www.dailymail.co.uk/news/article-464679/Porn-star-quizzed-cash-honours-police-probe.html.
6 See Huffington post for a list, which includes the only successfully elected porn "star," Ilona Staller, in Italy in the 1980s. http://www.huffingtonpost.com/2010/03/02/stormy-daniels-louisiana_n_482109.html and http://www.huffingtonpost.com/2009/02/10/porn-stars-in-politics-wo_n_165730.html.
7 COPA remains active given a revision whereby minors under 12 are protected from viewing unsuitable material without parents' consent, among others (US Government 2009).

# References

American Psychological Association (APA) (2007) *Report of the APA Task Force on the Sexualisation of Girls.* http://www.apa.org/pi/wpo/sexualization.html.

Associated Press (2013) "Porn Sites and Religious Groups Unite over Internet Domain." http://www.cbc.ca/news/technology/story/2007/03/26/tech-porn.html.

Australia, The Senate, Standing Committee on Environment, Communications and the Arts (2008) *Sexualisation of Children in the Contemporary Media.* http://www.aph.gov.au/senate/committee/eca_ctte/sexualisation_of_children/report/report.pdf.

Australian Sex Party (ASP) (2010) http://www.sexparty.org.au.

Boyle, K. (ed.) (2010) *Everyday Pornography*, New York: Routledge.

Brents, B. G. and K. Hausbeck (2007) "Marketing Sex: US Legal Brothels and Late Capitalist Consumption," *Sexualities* 10(4): 425.

Chakravartty, P. and K. Sarikakis (2006) *Media Policy and Globalisation*, Edinburgh: Edinburgh University Press.

Commission on COPA (2000) "Report to Congress." http://www.copacommission.org/report/COPAreport.pdf.

Covenant Eyes (2013) "Pornography Statistics," Covenant Eyes, Owosso, MI. http://www.covenanteyes.com/pornography-facts-and-statistics/.

Dines, G., R. Jensen, and A. Russo (1998) *Pornography: The Production and Consumption of Inequality*, London: Routledge.

Electronic Privacy Information Center (EPIC) (2009) "The Legal Challenge to the Child Online Protection Act." http://epic.org/free_speech/copa/.

Fawcett Society (2009) *Corporate Sexism: The Sex Industry's Infiltration of the Modern Workplace.* http://www.fawcettsociety.org.uk/documents/Corporate%20Sexism.pdf.pdf.

Gall, G. (2006) *Sex Worker Union Organising: An International Study*, Basingstoke: Palgrave Macmillan.

Gill, R. (2009) "Supersexualize Me: Advertising and the 'Midriffs'," in F. Attwood (ed.) *Mainstreaming Sex: The Sexualization of Western Culture*, London: I. B. Tauris.

Goldstein, D. (2009) "The XXX-Files Porn Industry Lobbyists Feel out Capitol Hill in a Time of Economic Crisis," *American Prospect*, May 12. http://www.prospect.org/cs/articles?article=the_xxx_files.

Grudzen, C. R. and P. R. Kerndt (2007) "The Adult Film Industry: Time to Regulate?," *PLoS Medicine* 4(6): 0993–6.

Grudzen, C. R., G. Ryan, W. Margold, J. Torres, and L. Gelberg (2008) "Pathways to Health Risk Exposure in Adult Film Performers," *Journal of Urban Health Bulletin of the New York Academy of Medicine* 86(1): 67–78.

Grudzen, C. R., D. Meeker, J. M. Torres, Q. Du, S. Morrison, R. M. Andresen, and L. Gelberg (2011) "Comparison of the Mental Health of Female Adult Film Performers and Other Young Women In California," *Psychiatric Services* 62: 639–45.

Hunt, L. (ed.) (1996) "Introduction," in *The Invention of Pornography: Obscenity and the Origins of Modernity, 1500–1800*, New York: Zone Books.

Itzin, C., A. Taket, and L. Kelly (2007) *Evidence of Harm to Adults Relating to Exposure to Extreme Pornographic Material: A Rapid Evidence Assessment*, Ministry of Justice Research Series 11/07 UK Crown.

Jacobson, M. (2005) *Young People and Gendered Media Messages*, NORDICOM, The International Clearinghouse on Children, Youth and Media, Göteborg University.

Jeffreys, S. (2009) *The Industrial Vagina: The Political Economy of the Global Sex Trade*, Abingdon: Routledge.

Johnson, J. (2010) "To Catch a Curious Clicker: A Social Network Analysis of the Online Pornography Industry," in K. Boyle (ed.) *Everyday Pornographies*, London: Routledge.

Kamalipour, Y. R. and K. R. Rampal (eds.) (2003) *The Globalization of Corporate Media Hegemony*, New York: State University of New York Press.

Kipnis, Laura (1998) *Bound and Gagged: Pornography and the Politics of Fantasy in America*, Durham, NC: Duke University Press.

Kroft, S. (2006) "Porn in the USA," *60 Minutes*, CBS.

Kronja, I. (2006) "Politics as Porn: The Pornographic Representation of Women in Serbian Tabloids and Its Role in Politics," in N. Moranjak-Bamburać, T. Jusić, and A. Isanović (eds.) *Stereotyping: Representation of Women in Print Media in South-East Europe*, Sarajevo: MediaCentar.

Levande, M. (2007) "Women, Pop Music, and Pornography," *Meridians: Feminism, Race, Transnationalism* 8(1): 293–321.

McChesney, Robert W. (2004) *The Problem of the Media: U.S. Communication Politics in the Twenty-First Century*, New York: Monthly Review Press.

McNair, B. (1996) *Mediated Sex: Pornography and Postmodern Culture*, New York: St. Martin's Press.

——(2002) *Striptease Culture: Sex, Media and the Democratization of Desire*, New York: Routledge.

McRobbie, A. (2009) *The Aftermath of Feminism: Gender, Culture and Social Change*, London: Sage.

Marshall, J. (2006) "RNC Accepted Political Contributions from Gay Porn King?" http://www.infowars.com/articles/us/rnc_accepted_contributions_from_gay_porn_king.htm.

Mason-Grant, J. (2004) *Pornography Embodied: From Speech to Sexual Practice*, New York: Rowman and Littlefield.

Mota, A. S. (2002) "The U.S. Supreme Court Addresses the Child Pornography Prevention Act and Child Online Protection Act in Ashcroft v. Free Speech," *Federal Communications Law Journal* 55: 85–98.

Page, Benjamin I. (1996) "The Mass Media as Political Actors," *Political Science & Politics* 29(1): 20–4.

Paul, P. (2005) *Pornified: How Pornography Is Damaging Our Lives, Our Relationships, and Our Families*, New York: Owl Books.

Peter, J. and P. M. Valkenburg (2006) *Adolescents' Exposure to Sexually Explicit Material on the Internet*, Communication Research 33(2): 178–204.

Sarikakis, K. and Z. Shaukat (2008) "The Global Structures and Cultures of Pornography: The Global Brothel," in K. Sarikakis and L. Shade (ed.) *Feminist Interventions in International Communication: Minding the Gap*, New York: Rowman and Littlefield.

Schaffauser, T. (2010) "Time for Porn Stars to Self-organise," *Guardian*, March 3. http://www.guardian.co.uk/commentisfree/2010/mar/03/gay-porn-self-organise.

Smaill, B. (2009) "Documentary Investigations and the Female Porn Star," *Jump Cut: A Review of Contemporary Media* 51. http://www.ejumpcut.org/currentissue/femalePornstars/text.html.

Sun, C. F. (2008) "Fantasies Matter," in *Pornography: Driving the Demand for International Sex Trafficking*, Chicago: International Human Rights Law Institute of DePaul University College of Law.

US Government (2009) US Code Title 15 Chapter 91—Childrens Online Privacy Protection §6501–6.

Walters, N. (2009) *Living Dolls: The Return of Sexism*, London: Virago Press.

Waltman, M. (2010) "Rethinking Democracy: Legal Challenges to Pornography and Sex Inequality in Canada and the United States," *Political Research Quarterly* 63(1): 218–37.

Williams, L. (2004) *Porn Studies*, Durham, NC: Duke University Press.

Wilmet, H. J. (1998) "Naked Feminism: The Unionization of the Adult Entertainment Industry," *American University Journal of Gender, Social Policy & the Law* 7: 465.

# 20

# Gender and digital policy

## From global information infrastructure to internet governance

## *Leslie Regan Shade*

Global activism culminating in a one-day protest in January 2012 dubbed "The Great Internet Blackout" was hailed as a victory for the open internet. Major internet companies and supporters displayed black web pages and notices against proposed US legislation, the Stop Online Piracy Act (SOPA) and the PROTECT IP Act (PIPA), which critics alleged would undermine the infrastructure of the internet by allowing corporations and governments to have unprecedented control over content and services.

Pitting large media and entertainment companies against social media companies and consumers, the bills imposed stiff penalties on site owners and users accused of pirating or counterfeiting content. Media and entertainment companies argued the bills were necessary to protect their copyright and to control offshore piracy. Social media companies asserted the bills would lead to censorship and stifle freedom of expression and innovation by inhibiting online expression and user-generated content, in the process making them unreasonably responsible for their users' content and practices.

From its earnest origins as a grassroots campaign consisting of small social media companies and internet citizens, through the involvement of internet luminaries Google, Facebook, Twitter, Tumblr, and Wikipedia, to the legislation's defeat in Congress, SOPA and PIPA activism clearly demonstrated the passion of global citizens for internet rights (Electronic Frontier Foundation 2011; Goodman 2012; Weismann 2012).

Women bloggers spoke out about the impact of SOPA on their livelihoods. One remarked that women are heavier users of social media than men, reliant on blogging for household income; she mentioned 3.9 million "mommy bloggers" who monetize their content from advertisers and sponsors (Rotondi 2012). Informational control and freedom of expression were central, another said: "Regardless of gender ... if we cannot control where our voices are heard and what information we share, what does that mean for generations after us?" (Rotondi 2012). The Center for Media Justice (2012) further argued that the right to an open internet is a major human rights issue, and SOPA/PIPA would exacerbate the digital divide and threaten economic justice for communities of color and poor people.

Digital rights and freedoms are flashpoints of activism for global citizens reliant on social media for communication and social change. Digital rights are clearly entwined with women's rights, as digital media are increasingly the conduits for education, edification, and on-the-ground mobilization. Undeniably, social media intensified recent civic action—the "Arab Spring" and regime changes in the Middle East and North Africa (MENA) region, the Occupy movement, and structural changes in civil society because of global "austerity" measures (Harcourt 2012).

The fourth World Conference on Women in Beijing in 1995 recognized the importance of the nascent internet for women's equality. This coincided with discourse about a "Global Information Infrastructure," touted by the G7 nations (with head cheerleader US Vice President Al Gore). They foresaw a liberalized telecommunications sector, global free trade, and technological convergence as key for global economic prosperity. The subsequent decade, which culminated in the two-phase World Summit on the Information Society (WSIS) in 2003 and 2005, concentrated on ICT4D (information and communication technologies for development), with some attention to gender issues. Internet governance is now the arena for debating technical and socioeconomic policy issues in both scholarly and activist domains (DeNardis 2012, 2013; Mueller 2010). Feminists are now working to shape debates about gender equity in this policy space.

This chapter will sketch these early activities to the present and consider the gendered implications of digital policy, reflecting work in the scholarly and policy sectors. I briefly contextualize the digital mediascape and a brief review of feminist scholarship that takes up political economy and communications policy will follow. Feminist political economy is the lens to examine systemic and structural power dynamics in digital policy that emanate from industry, international policy regimes, and civil society. I then map out key digital policy moments where gender issues have been on the agenda, from the aforementioned early activities in the 1990s to today's contemporary climate, where access and privacy issues, in particular, manifest gendered dimensions.

## From information infrastructure to mobile media infrastructure

In the 1990s, the Global Information Infrastructure (GII) became the promotional umbrella for G7 nations touting the internet: neoliberal ideals of private investment, competition, flexible regulation, open trade, and universal service were adopted by the International Telecommunication Union (ITU) and national governments. The contemporary digital landscape is characterized by tensions inherent in the development of the internet, with commercial firms fixated on the accrual of profits, bolstered by a neoliberal policy regime favoring marketization and commercialization, while digital reform activists seek a broadened democratic space for communicative action, often at the behest of libertarian philosophies (Chakravartty and Sarikakis 2006; Mansell 2011).

Larissa Hjorth (2011) highlights how the integration of the mobile phone and social media stimulate a plethora of user-created and generated content that impacts communication, politics, and culture. The mobile media infrastructure is character-ized by personalization and an affective form of communication connecting what she describes as a *political vernacular* to a sense of place. Personalization practices are thus both political and gendered.

The panoply of popular social media tools—"Web 2.0" technologies that encourage participative communicative practices wherein users develop, collaborate, customize, rate, and distribute internet content—poses policy challenges. Social media platforms are redolent with politics. Their architecture and terms of service have significant control over the security and privacy of personal information related to data collection, retention, and distribution.

## Add feminism and shake!

A significant body of scholarship on gender and the internet has been produced in the last 20 years. Niels Van Doorn and Liesbet van Zoonen (2009), for example, categorize feminist theory as "gender as identity" and "gender as social structure." Reflecting on earlier cyberfeminist practices and their applicability to contemporary theory, Susanna Paasonen argues for "more productive engagements with contemporary technocultures in order to map out possible solutions for current social and economic inequalities" (2011: 349). Here is where feminist political economy is relevant.

Internet studies have incorporated feminist political economy (see Lee 2006, 2011; Shade 2001, among others), buoyed by the seminal collection from Eileen Meehan and Ellen Riordan (2001) and thus rectifying the feminist blind spot of mainstream political economy of communication studies. Political economy interrogates, critiques, and provides alternatives to how power and ownership of information and commu-nication resources are allocated, encouraging dynamic social change for democratic citizenship (Mosco 2009). Applying a feminist lens to crucial issues surrounding media institutions and policies deepens analyses, writes Micky Lee. To allow us "to understand how the global economy is gendered, feminists need to pay attention to production as much as, if not more than, consumption" (2011: 86). Methodologically, Lee reminds us that while this research can be confusing or boring, reading through a thicket of "documents such as congressional hearings [and] 10K reports and user terms of services" can reveal their "significant impact on our public and private lives ... [and they] are blatant in suggesting how corporations maximise their own interests whilst diminishing the public ones" (2011: 85–6). Recent feminist political economy perspectives on the labor dimensions of media (McLaughlin 2009) and social media (contingent, precarious, and affective work) are an exciting direction (Fortunati 2011).

## Getting gender into policy discourse

ICT these days isn't about teenage boys programming along in their bedrooms, it's not about how big your RAM is or how powerful your ROM. ... It's about creativity, net-works, human rights. ... It's about finding new applications, making new connections,

and having the freedom to express yourself. So, women across the world remember—
here is a sector that can help you, a sector that needs your ideas, your talent, your
enthusiasm. Remember, there are opportunities out there if you're not afraid to grab
them. And remember, there are no limits to what you can achieve.

(Neelie Kroes, in a video message for International Women's Day, 2012)

Recent digital economy agendas from national governments are redolent of earlier
discourses on global information infrastructures. Visibly absent from the debates are
gender issues. Neelie Kroes, the European Commission's Vice President for the Digital
Agenda, is an exception; but, as the quotation above reveals, when she refers to the
"sector" she is not referring to the "policy sector."

Policy has tended to be "gender blind," contends Margaret Gallagher (2011). She
advocates for feminist policy interventions to identify gaps, expand frameworks, and
create, in essence, "gender sensitive" policy to acknowledge and distinguish between
the various socioeconomic positions of men and women, recognizing gendered relations
that arise from these positions. This is policy from a feminist standpoint theory.
Despite earlier advocacy from Beijing and WSIS, Gallagher notes that current policy
rarely incorporates feminist concerns. In many instances "gender mainstreaming" is
conjured as the default solution, but seldom is the mainstreaming specified: What
are the specific gender issues: access, content, freedom?

The *Beijing Declaration and Platform for Action* (1995) recommended programs and
policies to increase digital literacy for women, especially in developing countries.
Strategic objective J.1 of the *Declaration* identified the need to "increase the participation and access of women to expression and decision-making in and through the
media and new technologies of communication" by multi-stakeholder engagement.
But at the 10th and 15th anniversaries of the Beijing Platform in 2005 and 2010
organized by the UN's Commission on the Status of Women, searching for the
elusive "J Spot" (Suárez Toro 2005) was a challenge. Heike Jensen (2010) noted a
palpable need to go beyond celebrations of social media empowerment and instead
engage in political economic analyses to critique and intervene in economic and
governance structures.

In the WSIS *Declaration* and *Plan of Action*, gender advocates were instrumental in
inserting paragraph 12 related to women's empowerment and participation in the
2003 *Plan of Action*. For the second phase, however, the Tunis Commitment document
only acknowledged a gendered digital divide. Given that WSIS, despite its claims for
multi-stakeholderism (the involvement of governments, industry, and civil society
groups), was largely led by government delegations, gender equality perspectives
were "contentious" (Gallagher 2011: 456).

Where are women in structures of policymaking? Katharine Sarikakis (2012: 364)
declares: "Gender is conspicuously absent in public policy—or at least it is absent in the
debates among powerful actors." She argues for "human centred policy scholarship" to
locate and interrogate gendered social relations promulgated by policy processes,
regulatory systems, and cultures (2012: 371). Likewise, Anita Gurumurthy, of the
Indian-based nongovernmental organization IT for Change, suggests that feminist
interventions must engage the many powerful actors "shaping the discourse" (2012: 4)
of the network society. These actors include governments, multinational organizations

(for instance the International Telecommunications Union), newer internet governance actors like ICANN (the Internet Corporation for Assigned Names and Numbers, whose core task is the management of the Internet Assigned Names Authority that allocates IP addresses), and the involvement of corporations such as Google in the global policy space.

Internet governance infrastructures are highly politicized and occur at technical and administrative levels (DeNardis 2012). The increasing interrelationship between technological design, standards and protocols, private industry, national governments, and new global institutions has stimulated debates about whether the internet should be considered a public good. While mostly invisible to the average user, these "governance infrastructures inherently embed public interest concerns such as privacy, access to knowledge, and freedom of expression" (DeNardis 2012: 726). Structures of participation in digital policymaking, even in these new spaces that integrate civil society stakeholders like the Internet Governance Forum (IGF), also raise questions about whether civil society, non-Western nations, and the concerns of marginalized groups and women can tangibly shape crucial governance debates (IT for Change 2012, Association for Progressive Communications 2012).

The IGF was established after WSIS to support the recommendation for a multi-stakeholder policy dialogue to aid the United Nations Secretary-General. Because the IGF is an unfunded mandate of the UN, voluntary contributions allow pre-paratory meetings and an annual meeting to be held. While no binding decisions are issued by the IGF, its informal recommendations and reports have impacted policy discourse. A variety of Dynamic Coalitions serve as informal issue-specific groups, including the IGF Dynamic Coalition on Gender Equality. This Coalition's goals are to ensure that gender perspectives are integrated into various governance issues, including access, privacy, content regulation, and freedom of expression. The Coalition also seeks to expand women's presence at the IGF, conduct research on IGF issues and their gendered impact, and build capacity among local, regional, and global gender advocates.

One of the main organizers of the Coalition is the Association for Progressive Communications (APC) Women's Networking Support Programme (WNSP). Since Beijing WNSP has played a key role in ICT gender advocacy (Kannengiesser 2011). In its 2012 report *Critically Absent* it documents internet governance issues related to women. Access and inclusion to diverse information, ensuring safe and secure online spaces, especially for lesbian, gay, bisexual, transgender, questioning, intersex, and asexual (LGBTQIA) groups, preventing violence against women, and mainstreaming gender in national policies are key issues essential for internet governance. As well, WNSP encourages women to become more involved in digital policy formation.

## Access

Access to digital technologies is multifaceted. A socio-technical model highlights the interrelated technical, socioeconomic, and governance infrastructures necessary for effective access; social facilitation and community intermediaries as service providers mingle with the technical layers of content, carriage, hardware, and software. Access to knowledge and involvement in processes of governance at local, regional, national, and global levels are also key (Clement and Shade 2000).

Gender divides in internet access and use are a recurring scholarly and policy concern, with early studies concerned with social inclusion in networked technologies and services (Shade 2001; Liff *et al.* 2005). Some national governments recognized that gender disparities (along with race and class) existed and digital divide programs were created to increase social inclusion in the internet (see Eubanks 2011 for a US discussion). WSIS was concerned with ICTs for development and thus the discourse of empowerment was central. Replicating earlier modernization discourses, access to ICTs was thus seen as mere technological access—connectivity—versus the provision of services, content, and policy interventions (Asiedu 2012).

But how can gender issues get on the agenda for policymakers and program analysts tasked with increasing access to digital technologies and services? Because evidence-based policymaking is the normative framework it is important to collect quantitative measures of women's access to technologies and services, especially those in developing countries. Sex-disaggregated statistics are "a necessary prerequisite to achieving a globally equitable information society. Without this information, more than 50% of the world's population may be overlooked" (Hafkin and Huyer 2007: 25). Alongside statistics enumerating access to connectivity and content (the technical infrastructure) and skills development (the social infrastructure), access to governance processes is key.

Régentic, a West African gender and ICT network, developed indicators for the gender digital divide (including connectivity, content, and skills) and for decision-making and policy. Components included gender disparities in participation at the higher echelons of ICT policymaking bodies, ICT economic bodies, and civil society organizations; whether civil society organizations were active on ICT and gender issues; and whether ICT policy and regulation explicitly referenced gender considerations. After WSIS, the terminology of digital divides shifted to digital inclusion, evoking a more holistic perception of technologies to enhance socioeconomic and cultural livelihoods. This capabilities approach fosters technological literacy to achieve equity. However, a challenge for digital inclusion policies is not "assuming sameness … supporting gender diversity without reproducing unwanted inequalities" (Sørensen and Lagesen 2011: 6).

## Privacy and surveillance

Valerie Steeves (2010a, 2014) has delineated four privacy frameworks: (1) as essential to the democratic process, necessary for individual freedom, autonomy, and citizenship; (2) as a social value allowing one to define and control personal relationships; (3) as data protection giving citizens access and control to their personal data; (4) and as a human right, an intrinsic element of civil liberties. The rights that privacy safeguards—autonomy, dignity, security, and safety—comprise citizenship. For women, this "status hinges on strong initiatives to further both their communication rights and their privacy rights in all public spheres, be they digitally mediated or not, and to protect these rights against all agents that potentially infringe on them, be it private individuals, companies or governments" (Jensen 2012: 32).

Our digital dossier is comprised of discrete bits of data compiled from administrative record-keeping, bureaucracies, consumer profiles, and voluntary disclosure from participating in social media. These technological systems control people through social sorting and discriminatory profiling—processes of surveillance that include identifying, capturing, monitoring, tracking, and informational analysis of data subjects. These surveillance practices, whether overt or covert, can be gendered. In looking at how surveillance and control are built into welfare, healthcare, and transportation infrastructures and administrative bodies, Torin Monahan observed gendered patterns insofar as they "operate on ideals of masculine control at a distance and as a result enforce a masculinization of space and practice" (2009: 299). The untrammeled increase in biometric technologies and national attempts to impose legislation that would result in the intensified cybersurveillance of citizens (see http://unlawfulaccess.net/ for a Canadian example) are just a few developments which illustrate why "the reduction of people and social practices to data that can be easily manipulated is an exercise of power that demands feminist critique and intervention" (Monahan 2009: 300).

Within social media, privacy rights and control over personal information are fraught. Surveillance by commercial entities is the norm; these ostensibly free sites surreptitiously monetize personal content to reap profits. Personal information is sold to third-party marketers, governments, law officials, and potential employees. Digital records reveal composite portraits of identities (or partial and false identities) without one's knowledge or consent. Management and control of personal privacy and information is compromised by terms of service, privacy policies, and the architectural design of social media platforms. In turn these policies impact the security and privacy of personal data related to informed consent about their collection, retention, and distribution.

Research exploring how young women negotiate and manage privacy on Facebook reveals their nuanced understandings. In one early study, young women expressed contradictory views about privacy issues; while implicitly trusting Facebook's privacy settings, for instance, they were also concerned with parental and school administrator stalking of their profiles and the tracking of their personal information by marketers. In an online space predicated on a culture of personal disclosure, these young women were enthusiastic about Facebook for sociability but did not see it as a useful space for alternative messaging (Cohen and Shade 2008). Another study of how young people manage Facebook's privacy settings concluded that "women are uncharacteristically confident in their ability to address privacy settings and somewhat more engaged in doing so than men" (boyd and Hargittai 2010: n.p.). Aside from experiences and skill, they imply that heightened sensitivity to privacy management can be causally linked to online safety campaigns primarily directed towards girls and young women.

Studying Facebook privacy negotiations by young people in their twenties, Kate Raynes-Goldie (2010) made the important distinction between social and institutional privacy. Young people, she argued, value their social privacy (control of their personal information and identity through self-management and control of context within the online space) rather than institutional privacy (such as data protection and privacy legislation). The social and economic imperative to curate a "branded" social media presence, coupled with the convenience factor, outweighs, for many, politicized scrutiny of how communicative capitalism is operational in these platforms.

Cybersurveillance infrastructures in the commercial, personal, and government realm can impact women at different levels. Domestic surveillance is prevalent with the development of technologies and software that utilize GPS or biometric technologies to monitor, control, track, and otherwise contain young people's communicative practices in social networking sites and mobile phones. They have been facilitated by promotional and media discourse that posits the young girl in need of safe techno-logical spaces (Shade 2011). Gendered commodification processes are also literally at play within digital playgrounds for young people, as these commercial sites privilege and encourage a particular type of heteronormative and hypersexualized identity. Steeves recommends that privacy literacy "illustrate the ways in which surveillance and consumerism come together to constrain girls' potential for equality and manipulate their private relationships for commercial purposes" (2010b: 18).

Privacy invasions can act as forms of violence against women (VAW) through sexual harassment, stalking, sexting, and sexual trafficking. The mobile phone has exa-cerbated these practices through new interactive technologies such as location-based tracking. The APC's WNSP Take Back the Tech! campaign is an online platform mapping digital acts of violence against women (https://www.apc.org/ushahidi/). And, in the wake of September 11, transportation security measures utilizing biometric tech-nologies pose raced and gendered implications for freedom of movement, especially through bodily and sexual discrimination (Magnet 2011; Magnet and Rodgers 2012).

## Internet rights are women's rights

In 2012 the United Nations Human Rights Council (UNHCR, a monitoring body for human rights progress and violations across all member countries) approved a resolution that internet access is a human right. Forwarded by Sweden and adopted by consensus, the resolution "affirms that the same rights that people have offline must also be protected online, in particular freedom of expression, which is applicable regardless of frontiers and through any media of one's choice," and "recognizes the global and open nature of the Internet as a driving force in accelerating progress towards development in its various forms" (United Nations General Assembly 2012).

This is an important step in recognizing the fundamental role of the internet for the lives and livelihoods, political and cultural needs of global citizens. It is a response, in part, to the widespread use of social media for global justice, poignantly and persuasively illuminated by activism in the Middle East. Online civic activism threatened repressive governments, who spitefully deployed physical (violence) and technical (internet kill-switch) tactics against their citizens. Women in MENA regions played vital roles on the streets and online. As Courtney Radsch chronicles, "Esraa Abdel Fattah was known as 'Facebook girl' for her role in launching one of the most important opposition youth groups in Egypt, the April 6 Movement. Egypt's Mona Eltahawy, Libya's Danya Bashir, Bahrain's Zeinab al-Khawaja and Maryam al-Khawaja, and many others became known as the 'Twitterrati,' as influential media and pundits dubbed their Twitter accounts as 'must-follows'" (2012: 5).

Internet rights include not just access, but privacy rights. Security of communication and freedom from surveillance, along with the ability to nourish freedom of expression, enhance democratic rights and freedoms. To achieve these goals, feminists must realize that digital policy activism is key. The issues are many: copyright, as SOPA/PIPA proved; access, as Beijing and WSIS reiterated; and privacy rights and preventing online violence against women, as the Take Back the Tech! campaign illustrates. Also critical is creating equal opportunities for women in digital policy, and making this issue central for digital activists (Löblich and Wendelin 2012). Statistics can highlight how women are intrepid internet denizens, but there is an increasing need for their voices to be heard (in scholarship, activism, and policy) on digital policy issues with material and political ramifications for their lives and within their communities.

# References

Asiedu, C. (2012) "Information Communication Technologies for Gender and Development: A Review of the Literature," *Information, Communication & Society* 15: 1186–216.

Association for Progressive Communications, Women's Networking Support Programme (APC, WNSP) (2012) *Critically Absent: Women's Rights in Internet Governance*, South Africa: APC. http://www.genderit.org/sites/default/upload/critically_absent.pdf.

*Beijing Declaration and Platform for Action* (1995) New York: United Nations. http://www.un.org/womenwatch/daw/beijing/platform/.

boyd, d. and E. Hargittai (2010) "Facebook Privacy Settings: Who Cares?," *First Monday* 15(8) (August). http://firstmonday.org/htbin/cgiwrap/bin/ojs/index.php/fm/article/viewArticle/3086/2589.

Center for Media Justice (2012) "We're Fading to Black." http://centerformediajustice.org/2012/01/17/were-fading-to-black/.

Chakravartty, P. and K. Sarikakis (2006) *Media Policy and Globalization*, Edinburgh: Edinburgh University Press.

Clement, A. and L. R. Shade (2000) "The Access Rainbow: A Social/Technical Architecture for Community Networking," in M. Gurstein (ed.) *Community Informatics: Enabling Communities with Information and Communications Technologies*, Hershey, PA: Idea Group, pp. 32–51.

Cohen, N. S. and L. R. Shade (2008) "Gendering Facebook: Privacy and Commodification," *Feminist Media Studies* 8 (June): 210–14.

DeNardis, L. (2012) "Hidden Levers of Internet Control," *Information, Communication & Society* 15: 720–38.

——(2013) "The Emerging Field of Internet Governance," in W. Dutton (ed.) *Oxford Handbook of Internet Studies*, Oxford: Oxford University Press. http://papers.ssrn.com/sol3/papers.cfm?abstract_id=1678343.

Electronic Frontier Foundation (2011) "Strike against Censorship: Stop the Internet Blacklist Bills." https://action.eff.org/o/9042/p/dia/action/public/?action_KEY=8173.

Eubanks, V. (2011) *Digital Dead End: Fighting for Social Justice in the Information Age*, Cambridge, MA: MIT Press.

Fortunati, L. (2011) "ICTs and Immaterial Labor from a Feminist Perspective," *Journal of Communication Inquiry* 35(4): 26–432.

Gallagher, M. (2011) "Gender and Communication Policy: Struggling for Space," in R. Mansell and M. Raboy (eds.) *The Handbook on Global Media and Communication Policy*, Malden, MA: Blackwell Publishing, pp. 451–66.

Goodman, A. (2012) "The SOPA Blackout Protest Makes History," *Guardian*, January 18. http://www.guardian.co.uk/commentisfree/cifamerica/2012/jan/18/sopa-blackout-protest-makes-history.

Gurumurthy, A. (2012) "The Big Deal about the Network Age: Political Economy Conversations from the CITIGEN Network," IT for Change Think Piece, April. http://www.itforchange.net/sites/default/files/ITfC/Anita_thinkpiece_polecoCITIGEN_2012.pdf.

Hafkin, N. J. and S. Huyer (2007) "Women and Gender in ICT: Statistics and Indicators for Development," *Information Technologies and International Development* 4 (Winter): 25–41.

Harcourt, W. (2012) "Editorial: The Challenge of Civic Action for Development," *Development* 55: 151–3.

Hjorth, L. (2011) "It's Complicated: Mobile Intimacy and Creativity in an Age of Social Media and Affective Technology," *Communication, Politics and Culture* 44: 45–56.

Internet Governance Forum (IGF) (n.d.) on Gender Equality. http://www.intgovforum.org/cms/dynamic-coalitions/77-gender-and-ig.

IT for Change (2012) "Gender and Citizenship in the Information Society," CITIGEN Research Programme, executive summary, IT for Change and International Development Research Centre (IDRC). http://www.gender-is-citizenship.net/sites/default/files/citigen/uploads/CITIGEN_RVM_ExecutiveSummary.pdf.

Jensen, H. (2010) "The 'J Spot' at the 54th CSW: Celebrating Women's Social Networking Is Not Enough," March 12. http://www.genderit.org/content/%E2%80%9Cj-spot%E2%80%9D-54th-csw-celebrating-womens-social-networking-not-enough#sdfootnote1sym.

——(2012) "Women and Virtual Citizenship? Gendered Experiences of Censorship and Surveillance," Bengaluru, India: IT for Change and CITIGEN Asia Research Programme. http://www.gender-is-citizenship.net/sites/.../citigen/.../Heike_TP_final.pdf.

Kannengiesser, S. (2011) "Networking for Social Change: The Association for Progressive Communications Women's Networking Support Program," *Feminist Media Studies* 11: 506–9.

Kroes, N. (2012) "Digital Agenda for Europe—International Women's Day," March 7. http://www.youtube.com/watch?v=MOwIPG4W1sA.

Lee, M. (2006) "What's Missing in Feminist Research in New Information and Communication Technologies?," *Feminist Media Studies* 6: 191–210.

——(2011) "A Feminist Political Economy of Communication," *Feminist Media Studies* 11: 83–7.

Liff, S., C. Marsden, J. Wajcman, R. E. Rice, and E. Hargittai (2005) "An Evolving Gender Digital Divide?," Oxford Internet Institute Internet Issue Brief No. 2, University of Oxford. http://www.oii.ox.ac.uk/people/?id=46.

Löblich, M. and M. Wendelin (2012) "ICT Policy Activism on a National Level: Ideas, Resources and Strategies of German Civil Society in Governance Processes," *New Media and Society* 14: 899–915.

McLaughlin, L. (2009) "Looking for Labor in Feminist Media Studies," *Television & New Media* 10: 110–13.

Magnet, S. (2011) *When Biometrics Fail: Gender, Race, and the Technology of Identity*, Durham, NC: Duke University Press.

Magnet, S. and T. Rodgers (2012) "Stripping for the State," *Feminist Media Studies* 12: 101–18.

Mansell, R. (2011) "New Visions, Old Practices: Policy and Regulation in the Internet Era," *Continuum: Journal of Media & Cultural Studies* 25: 19–32.

Meehan, E. R. and E. Riordan (2001) *Sex & Money: Feminism and Political Economy in the Media*, Minneapolis: University of Minnesota Press.

Monahan, T. (2009) "Dreams of Control at a Distance: Gender, Surveillance, and Social Control," *Cultural Studies → Critical Methodologies* 9 (April): 286–305.

Mosco, V. (2009) *Political Economy of Communications*, second edition, Thousand Oaks, CA: Sage Publications.

Mueller, M. (2010) *Networks and States: The Global Politics of Internet Governance*, Cambridge, MA: MIT Press.

Paasonen, S. (2011) "Revisiting Cyberfeminism," *Communications* 36: 335–52.

Radsch, C. C. (2012) "Unveiling the Revolutionaries: Cyberactivism and the Role of Women in the Arab Uprisings," James A. Baker III Institute for Public Policy, Rice University, May 18. http://www.bakerinstitute.org/publications/ITP-pub-CyberactivismAndWomen-051712. pdf/view.

Raynes-Goldie, K. (2010) "Aliases, Creeping, and Wall Cleaning: Understanding Privacy in the Age of Facebook," *First Monday* 15 (January). http://firstmonday.org/htbin/cgiwrap/bin/ojs/ index.php/fm/article/viewArticle/2775/2432.

Rotondi, J. P. (2012) "What SOPA and PIPA Mean for Women," *Huffington Post*, January 17. http://www.huffingtonpost.com/jessica-pearce-rotondi/sopa_b_1210581.html.

Sarikakis, K. (2012) "Stepping Out of the Comfort Zone: Unfolding Gender Conscious Research for Communication and Cultural Policy Theory," in N. Just and M. Puppis (eds.) *Trends in Communication Policy Research: New Theories, Methods & Subjects*, London: Intellect Publishing, pp. 361–75.

Shade, L. R. (2001) *Gender and Community in the Social Construction of the Internet*, New York: Peter Lang.

——(2011) "Surveilling the Girl via the Third and Networked Screen," in M. C. Kearney (ed.) *Mediated Girlhoods: New Explorations of Girls' Media Cultures*, New York: Peter Lang Publishing, pp. 261–75.

Sørensen, K. H. and V. A. Lagesen (2011) "The Digital Gender Divide and Inclusion Strategies," in W. Faulkner, E. Rommes, and K. H. Sørensen (eds.) *Technologies of Inclusion: Gender in the Information Society*, Trondheim, Norway: Tapir Academic Press. http://www. oecd.org/dataoecd/43/51/40832468.pdf.

Steeves, V. (2010a) "Privacy in a Networked Environment," in L. R. Shade (ed.) *Mediascapes: New Patterns in Canadian Communication*, third edition, Toronto: Nelson Canada, pp. 341–55.

——(2010b) "Summary of Research on Youth Online Privacy," report prepared for the Office of the Privacy Commissioner of Canada, March 28. http://www.priv.gc.ca/information/pub/ yp_201003_e.pdf.

——(2014) "Privacy in a Networked Environment," in L. R. Shade (ed.) *Mediascapes: New Patterns in Canadian Communication*, 4th edition, Toronto: Nelson Canada, pp. 304–20.

Stierch, S. (2012) "SOPA Blackout: Why Wikipedia Needs Women," *Huffington Post*, January 18. http://www.huffingtonpost.com/sarah-stierch/sopa-blackout_b_1213149.html.

Suárez Toro, M. (2005) "Looking for the 'J' Spot," *GEM News @Beijing Plus 10*, March 9. http://oldsite.genderlinks.org.za.dedi1086.nur4.host-h.net/docs/bejing/9-march-p4-5.pdf.

United Nations General Assembly (2012) "Promotion and Protection of All Human Rights, Civil, Political, Economic, Social and Cultural Rights, Including the Right to Development," Human Rights Council, Twentieth Session, agenda item 3, June 29. http://www.regeringen. se/content/1/c6/19/64/51/6999c512.pdf.

Van Doorn, N. and L. van Zoonen (2009) "Theorizing Gender and the Internet: Past, Present and Future," in A. Chadwick and P. N. Howard (eds.) *Routledge Handbook of Internet Politics*, New York: Routledge, pp. 261–74.

Weismann, J. (2012) "After an Online Firestorm, Congress Shelves Antipiracy Bills," *New York Times*, January 20. http://www.nytimes.com/2012/01/21/technology/senate-postpones-piracy-vote.html?scp=5&sq=sopa%20defeat&st=cse.

# 21

# Gender and media activism
## Alternative feminist media in Europe[1]

## *Elke Zobl and Rosa Reitsamer*

Alternative and activist women-led and feminist media offer participatory forums for debate and the exchange of politically, socially, and culturally engaged ideas by those who otherwise are marginalized within mainstream political debates. Sreberny-Mohammadi has found that "autonomous media controlled by women with women-defined output offer a challenge to existing hierarchies of power; when these media take up specific issues and campaigns, and align themselves with larger social movements, their political potential is significant" (1996: 234). Herein lies the biggest potential but also the biggest challenge for the larger feminist movement. In her book *Changing the Wor(l)d* (1997), Stacey Young conceptualizes feminist publishing as discursive politics and activism. She argues that "progressive changes in consciousness come about through discourses that challenge oppressive constructions of social phenomena" and that language acts such as publishing "can play a crucial part in bringing about individual and collective social change" (1997: 25). But how does a younger generation of feminist media producers in Europe challenge the status quo and effect social change? Can they participate in society by producing print magazines, weblogs ("blogs"), and electronic magazines ("e-zines") in grassroots, alternative, and activist contexts relating to new social movements (NSMs)? To answer these questions, we will refer to data collected through research on "Feminist Media Production in Europe," a project affiliated with the Department of Communication at the University of Salzburg from 2008 to 2012. This project included documentation at the digital archive *Grassroots Feminism*, a quantitative online survey of consumer habits with 230 persons, and 47 in-depth interviews with feminist media producers from 19 European countries. Taken together, these data enable us to contextualize and analyze feminist alternative media production in Europe.

## Feminist media projects

In *Alternative and Activist New Media* (2011), Leah Lievrouw identified several characteristics that distinguish NSMs in the postmodern era from previous social movements of the industrial age such as the labor and the anti-war/peace movements:

NSMs are of smaller scale and either tackle a wide range of issues or are focused on group identities, often supporting cultural or symbolic values and causes. Feminism—both as a movement and as a plurality of discourses in general—and feminist media in particular are profoundly cultural and represent these characteristics of NSMs.

Lievrouw regards the artistic and political practices of Dada, the Situationist International, and NSMs as the three central influences for contemporary alternative and activist uses of new media. As such, activist art movements, NSMs, and online activism are all linked by three major themes: (1) the scope or size of alternative and activist new media projects; (2) the stance of movements and projects relative to the mainstream society and culture; and (3) the nature of projects as action, and activists as agents of social change (Lievrouw 2011: 59). Lievrouw explores these themes—scope, stance, and action and agency—as a "genre framework for alternative and activist new media."

We took this distinction in scope, stance, and action and agency as a flexible toolbox and applied it to our project, thus extending Lievrouw's focus on new media to include print media, radio shows, community TV shows, and visual interventions. We identified 425 women-led and feminist grassroots media projects produced in grassroots and alternative on- and offline contexts in Europe, encompassing 150 print media, including zines, magazines, and journals; plus 140 blogs, 70 e-zines, 35 radio shows, 5 community television shows, and 17 archives, networks, and databases. We also included eight artistic or visual interventions, such as posters, stickers, adbusting (a portmanteau of *advertisement* and the verb *to bust*), and subvertising (a portmanteau of *subvert* and *advertising* referring to spoofs or parodies of corporate and political advertisements). Here we apply this framework to feminist media projects in Europe—with a main focus on the aspects of action and agency—beginning with their scope.

## The scope of feminist media projects in Europe

Lievrouw's framework suggests that feminist alternative media will be small scale along several dimensions. New media projects tend to be relatively small, low-cost projects with a do-it-yourself (DIY) aesthetic, in part because access to resources (e.g. funding and staff) is limited, but also because participants adopt a critical attitude towards dominant mass and consumer culture. Moreover, compared to "mainstream" media, the outreach of alternative and activist media projects is relatively small, enabling them to provide their audiences with a sense of familiarity and intimacy, as they address their readers as insiders (Lievrouw 2011: 62). Feminist media are overwhelmingly produced on a low-cost basis and distributed in limited size to a small group.

The second aspect of scope that Lievrouw identifies is their specific form of organization. The majority of alternative and activist new media projects are produced collaboratively by individuals and groups, and as such they are group efforts. This "new collectivism" (Lievrouw 2011: 62) is based on community building, interactivity, and participation in the design of the media, as well as on collective organization of the working processes. Such "new collectivism" is associated with postmodern artistic practices and activism. The "new collectivism" of feminist media producers becomes clear with reference to print media publishers. The majority of feminist media we studied are produced by independent collectives and groups, followed by independent women's organizations and nongovernmental organizations (NGOs), individuals, independent editors in the academic context, and small independent, self-founded corporate-structured publishers. The collaborative, shared, and volunteer nature of feminist media producers' efforts are illustrated by the co-editor of the queer print magazine *Hugs and Kisses: Tender All Your Gender*, published in German twice a year since 2007:

> *Hugs and Kisses* has many supporters. There are people for the distribution; we have several proofreaders and graphic designers. That's a good thing, as not everyone can allow themselves at any time to be part of a non-profit project, even if they want to. We have a webmaster who only attends to the homepage.

The co-editor points to the decisive group effort of feminist media projects as well as to the constraints these projects face due to limited access to resources in terms of time, funding, and staff.

Another example of a collaborative effort is *Plotki Femzine*, a post-Soviet feminist print and online zine project that is part of a larger youth-oriented media network in Central and Eastern Europe (CEE) called "Plotki." *Plotki Femzine* was launched by young women as a response to what the group saw as increasingly hierarchical and patriarchal attitudes emerging within the Plotki network. In experimental art, autobiographical essays, and critical fiction, *Plotki Femzine* brings together contributions from women in CEE countries to create an emerging, collaborative space for feminist discussions and to articulate feminist identities and connections (Chidgey *et al.* 2009).

However, the scope of feminist media projects, as well as their small-scale and collaborative nature, says little about their relationship to the "mainstream" media and hegemonic culture. Below, therefore, we describe the stance of feminist media projects in more detail, namely their heterotopic nature, their interest in subcultures, and their use of irony and humor.

## The stance of feminist media projects in Europe

Feminist media producers describe their projects often as countersites to "mainstream" media because they offer a space where people can experiment with ideas, express themselves, and describe their experiences. Michel Foucault has stated that heterotopia is "a kind of effectively enacted utopia in which ... all the other real sites that can be found with the culture are simultaneously represented, contested, and inverted. Places of this kind are outside of all places, even though it may be possible to indicate their location in reality" (Foucault 1986: 24, quoted in Lievrouw 2011: 63–4). The Belgian editor of such zines as *Flapper Gathering* and *(Different Worlds) Same Heartbeats* and organizer of "The Feminist Poster Project" articulated such an approach during her interview with us: "Zines can function as a participatory alternative medium to give alternative views on the society that can't be found in the mainstream media."

In this respect feminist media projects reflect what Lievrouw identifies as the characteristic stance of alternative and activist new media projects. First, these projects are heterotopic because they "act as 'other spaces' or 'countersites' for expression, affiliation, and creativity apart from the dominant culture" (Lievrouw 2011: 63). We see this heterotopic stance especially in feminist zines, which often function as "culturally productive, politicized counterpublic space" (Nguyen 2000) for feminist networking and reflection by a younger generation of women in different parts of the world (Zobl 2009). Zine producers discuss topics—often taboo issues—that are left out, marginalized, or underrepresented in dominant media, culture, and politics, such as abuse, incest, and complex interactions of sexism, racism, homophobia, and hatred of transgendered people. In critically discussing such issues, zine producers not only point to the challenges and conflicts of their societies but also bring to the table "new, alternative, 'other' values and practices for the rest of society" (Lievrouw 2011: 64).

Second, the heterotopic nature of feminist media projects is associated with their "subcultural quality" (Lievrouw 2011: 65), which is rooted in shared insider knowledge but also reflects pop culture. Accordingly, feminist media producers require a certain access to and knowledge of (sub)cultural codes, language, and symbols. The Love Kills Collective from Romania, which publishes the *Love Kills* zine and translates anarchist literature into Romanian, emphasizes the strong connections to queer-feminist scenes and their shared "subcultural capital" (Thornton 1995):

> The aim ... is to establish and strengthen the bounds between activists involved and interested in anarcha-feminism and to develop a network. ... Our work is visible mostly in our own small "scene"/movement and not on a large social scale. But as we are aiming towards anarchism, and as we see anarchism like an on-going emerging occurrence, we strongly believe that even the slightest effort has its own meaningful importance and contribution.

The collective understand the specific local embeddedness of their activities in the feminist-queer scenes in Romania, but they assume that their work feeds into broader, translocal cultures of social change.

A common feature of the media projects we analyzed is their reference to networking discourses through which the collectivity and affiliation of feminist groups and positions are established. Networking occurs on local, transnational, and virtual levels. In fact, this aspect of networking across national borders using the internet proves to be a major difference compared to the more restricted (in terms of geography, time, etc.) communication exchanges that took place during the era of second-wave feminism. Networking among contemporary feminist media occurs over a wide range: from linking to other media projects (where further interactions between media producers do not occur), through editorial references to other feminist media projects with similar orientations in content and perspectives, to a pooling of online and offline activities of feminist media projects which often share the same spoken language.

However, the subcultural quality of various feminist media projects also has its drawbacks and has been criticized by media producers for its structural and individual mechanisms of exclusion. The zine producer of *Masculine Femininities* (UK) points to the underrepresentation of people of color and of certain topics, as well as to the limitations of access and demographics:

> I enjoy the variety and creativity of what there is out there but ... I would like to see more people of colour, more about issues of race and sexuality, more about gender and surviving violence and things that don't get discussed much in our communities or from certain perspectives. The limiting thing about zines is getting access to them. Often they are distributed at events that are mainly white and middle class dominated ... which is problematic.

As such, by employing certain subcultural codes, language, and aesthetics, an orientation and affiliation toward a specific community occurs that involves overwhelmingly a white, middle-class and well-educated demographic. While constant failure is inscribed in processes of media production and in building networks and coalitions, the distribution of subcultural capital is essential. Feminist media producers point to the fact that these challenges need to be further negotiated and interrogated within feminist media networks.

The third characteristic Lievrouw (2011: 66) describes in relation to the stance of alternative and activist media projects is the use of irony and humor. In feminist media projects, especially zines, humor and irony manifest themselves in cut-and-paste collages that subvert and deconstruct the hegemonic representations of femininity, and

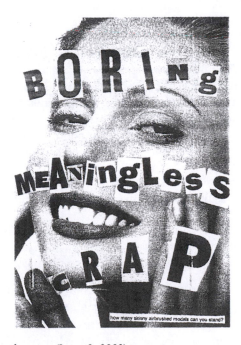

*Figure 21.1 Riot Grrrl London zine (Issue 3, 2003)*

challenge the commodification and sexualization of women's bodies as a dominant advertising and marketing strategy. The zine *Riot Grrrl London*, for example, took a black-and-white collage with an image of the face of a young, beautiful woman. Superimposed was a cut-and-paste typeface declaring, "boring meaningless crap"; juxtaposed below in small letters was the question: "How many skinny airbrushed models can you stand?" (Figure 21.1).

## Action and agency of feminist media projects

The third overarching theme of Lievrouw's framework, one connecting activist art movements, NSMs, and online activism, is *action and agency*, i.e. "the extent to which projects are conceived and executed as *action*, by participants who see themselves and their projects as *agents* of social change" (Lievrouw 2011: 68). Activist art, social movement, and alternative/activist media projects are characterized as interventionist: Their producers aim to interrupt or alter existing conditions, often by direct action and by being perishable—that is, short-lived, nomadic, ephemeral, temporary, with rapid response.

In the materials we studied, the interventionist and perishable features of action and agency are clearly exemplified by media producers who situate themselves in a DIY context of queer-feminist scenes. In the context of feminism, the 1990s riot grrrl scenes and the subsequent feminist-queer music and arts festivals such as Ladyfests developed a cultural activism based on doing-it-yourself. Here, music and skill-sharing are fused with political resistance and celebration, and the boundaries between organizer, participant, and audience are blurred (Kearney 1998; Schilt and Zobl 2008; Zobl 2010). In the UK, in activist contexts and among feminist zine producers the use of the term "DIY feminism" increased as "an umbrella term fusing together different types of feminism" which draws "on genealogies of punk cultures, grassroots movements, and the technologies of late capitalism" (Chidgey 2009). Most often, DIY feminist actions in their many forms take an anti-capitalist stance: "self/collective produced culture, politics, entertainment, and work are held as ideals, and not-for-profit voluntary/activist labour is the movement's lifeblood" (Chidgey 2009: n.p.). Emancypunx is an anarchist feminist group that runs a record label, and works as festival organizer, tour manager, and host of a zine library; it was founded in the mid-1990s in Warsaw to promote feminism and women's issues within an underground DIY distribution network. It highlights its strong anti-corporate and alternative DIY stance:

> One of the main goals is to foster the DIY hc [hardcore] punk network and to keep our ... products far from corporate business. ... Emancypunx is a non-profit, non-commercial initiative run on a voluntary and DIY basis.
>
> (Emancypunx n.d.)

Media producers who sympathize with a DIY ethos and understand their media projects as "independent" and "autonomous" often revert to discourses that are critical of society and its continuously reinforced gender relations. They build "alternative economies" (Atton 2002; Chidgey 2009), which are based on small collectives, fans-turned-entrepreneurs and volunteer labor for the non-commercial exchange of their media and as alternatives to commercial media corporations. Feminist media are circulated in a "DIY economy" in the context of feminist and anti-commercial agency, as well as in the wider alternative (sub)cultural feminist scenes and networks (Reitsamer 2012). This process of media production and networking aims to establish horizontal, non-hierarchical structures. As a result, for the overwhelming majority of feminist media producers who describe themselves as "DIY feminists," social change can only take place through a radical critique of a neoliberal system and through alternative economies outside of neoliberal exploitation logic.

Lievrouw states that alternative and activist new media projects "can either constitute intervention and action in themselves ... or invite and encourage intervention by others" (2011: 69). Because feminism(s) in itself is an intervention into hegemonic discourses, we argue that specifically *feminist* interventions do both: They aim for intervention and action within the projects themselves *and* invite and encourage interventions by others. However, they do so to various degrees.

An example that both constitutes and encourages intervention is the Italian activist collective Fikasicula, which runs the blog *Femminismo a Sud*. The blog aims to create a virtual space for sharing experiences and opinions and writing openly about the Italian conservative government. In its self-description, *Femminismo a Sud* espouses a postcolonial and intersectional perspective towards society, culture, and politics: "We think that sexism, racism and fascism are different aspects of the same hegemonic situation. And therefore we can't fight against sexism if we don't understand how sexism is interwoven with racism and fascism." The collective sees a necessity in engaging with and intervening in the many different forms of oppression that people experience in their daily lives, including violence against women and children. Therefore, the blog offers many personal stories, complemented by a variety of advice and strategies for self-empowerment. After the blog was set up in 2008, one of the group's very first steps was to provide an "ABC of technological feminism," which is a manual on how to use the internet in general and weblogs in particular for feminist, anti-racist, and anti-fascist action.

To a lesser degree, the British zine *Race Revolt* aims also for an intervention in itself, as it encourages interventions of others by calling for and accepting submissions—however, mostly from within its community. One of the zine's producers describes the media project as "an intervention into the silences around race in the queer, feminist and activist communities" and notes in the first issue (2007): "This is a beginning. A beginning of a much needed conversation that considers and addresses race within feminist, queer and DIY communities and beyond. That considers the whiteness of these communities, that finds ways for us to move forward." The editor points to the fact that in feminist media projects whiteness often appears to be an unmarked, invisible, and dominant construction of identity.

A similar focus is taken by the multilingual Austrian e-zine *Migrazine*, which has been published by MAIZ, an autonomous migrant organization in Linz, since 2006. The initial idea of *Migrazine* was to produce a feminist alternative online medium in which women with migrant backgrounds are responsible for the whole process of production. According to their website, *Migrazine* is "self-organised participation in the media landscape, intervening into the dominant discourse, (and the) democratization of information." In the center of their feminist and anti-racist self-conception stands the category "female migrant," which is understood as a political identity taking an oppositional position in society and pointing to feminist and anti-racist partiality. This self-conception, however, does not necessarily mean that all of the website's articles discuss migrant-specific issues; nor does it suggest that *Migrazine* aims to speak for women with migrant backgrounds. Rather, the editors position the experiences and knowledge production of women with migrant backgrounds at the center. As such this can in itself be seen as an intervention in the hegemonic discourse on migration (especially on female migrants).

Furthermore, a number of examples focus more on the interventionist aim within the project itself. A strategy for activist media producers seeking to underline the necessity of feminist politics and to express their own standpoint—and as such to make an intervention—is the publication of manifestos and declarations. The French activist group La Barbe note in their manifesto *Le Manifeste de la Barbe* that "it's time to revive feminism and to set out to conquer all fields of power, in all its different forms." Similarly, the French activist network Osez le féminisme speaks about the aims achieved by the women's movements and argues for the need for feminist activism, especially in times of economic crisis and instability. In their declaration "Why Pro Feminism," members of the Russian activist group ЗА ФЕМИНИЗМ—Za Feminizm (Pro Feminism) situate themselves in the tradition of feminist struggles for equal rights and the advancement of women's living conditions worldwide. The author of the Russian blog *Feminisn'ts* takes up the common phrase "I'm not a feminist, but ... " to reflect upon feminist writing, including a variety of texts dealing with feminist history and theories in Russia. Other feminist media examples focus more on the encouragement of interventions by others, especially the networking sites where users can contribute and upload their work, such as *Le Degenerate Magazine* (Italy), *Female Pressure* (Austria), or *Lo Personal es Político* (Spain), and databases such as *female:pressure*, an international electronic music resource for women djs, producers, and visual artists.

In addition, other feminist media producers see their media work as an activist practice and as an intervention into social power relations, sometimes coupled with making interventions on the content and visual level and in relation to non-commercial DIY culture; these focus on bottom-up processes through "learning by doing" and "skill-sharing."

## Feminist media as activist and interventionist practices

The social practices of the two German comic zines and comic strip producers, the artist of *Trouble X Comics* (represented at her/his insistence anonymously and with ambiguous gender) and Ka Schmitz, offer a more precise picture of feminists' self-organized participation in the media landscape and their activist and interventionist practices (see also Reitsamer and Zobl 2011; forthcoming), as well as of their self-understanding as DIY feminists.

The artist of *Trouble X Comics* and Ka Schmitz consider their drawings an activist practice. Their art is intended to break heteronormative notions of gender and sexuality in their interplay with other categories of social differentiation, so they situate their comic zines and comic strips outside the mainstream in a queer-feminist DIY culture. The two illustrators use varying publishing formats (e.g. comic zines, zines, blogs, games), address heterogeneous topics, and distribute their comic zines and comic strips through decentralized networks of queer-feminist scenes. Within the "network turn" in NSM theory such a dissemination of information and the building of temporary communities has been termed "networked activism" (Atkinson 2010: 10). As part of this "networked activism," both of the illustrators contribute to "new social movement networks" by circulating their comic zines and comic strips at cost or completely free. The two artists describe the free distribution of their comic zines and comic strips as "a kind of queer action" aimed at minimizing social inequalities. Consequently, they attempt to break through the boundaries between consumers and producers by actively involving comic zine and comic strip readers, supporting individual initiatives with "how-to" instructions, and passing along knowledge away from traditional educational institutions in self-organized workshops.

In the context of DIY culture, drawing queer-feminist comic strips becomes, through the interconnection of feminist self-empowerment strategies with a leftist critique of capitalism, an interventionist practice in social power relations. The focus is on emancipatory bottom-up processes through "learning by doing" and "skill-sharing"; the established standards for "perfect" drawings are nullified, deconstructed, and/or ignored. For example, Ka Schmitz holds comic strip workshops for girls, women, and transgendered youth. In these workshops, a low-threshold opportunity to enter into comic strip drawing and a platform for informal learning are accelerated by Ka Schmitz into a collective self-empowerment process. Drawing comic strips is dialogically and collectively conceived; it serves as a tool for individual and collective agency and action. Therefore, comic zines and workshops can be understood as an interventionist medium—although short-lived and ephemeral—for local and translocal dialogue, community and network building, and the exchange of experience and knowledge. The focus of the social practices of the DIY culture is not success in terms of the number of zine readers. The heterogeneity of voices, which is expressed in a variety of media, is crucial, as is becoming an agent of social change by producing interventionist media.

## Conclusion: feminist media agents thriving towards social change

Taking Lievrouw's framework for alternative and activist new media as a guideline, we have analyzed feminist media projects produced in on- and offline, grassroots, and alternative contexts in relation to scope, stance, agency, and action (see Table 21.1). In general, our study confirms previous research on alternative media and feminist media as they aim to challenge power structures, to transform social roles by producing "alternative" content and by reverting to a DIY-organized, alternative economy.

We were able to confirm the features of alternative and activist new media in Lievrouw's model in relation to print and online feminist media, in that they are mostly small scale, collaboratively produced, heterotopic, based on subcultural literacy, ironic, interventionist, and perishable. Yet, we have added a particular *feminist*

*Table 21.1* Features of feminist media: Lievrouw's (2011) genre framework for alternative and activist new media extended to feminist media production on- and off-line

| Scope | *small scale* | *collaborative* | |
|---|---|---|---|
| Stance | *heterotopic:* feminist media as countersites to the mainstream based on solidarity, exchange of ideas and experiences otherwise ignored by mainstream media | *subcultural literacy:* feminist media producers require access to and knowledge of (sub)cultural codes, language, and symbols certain awareness and self-critical reflection of limitations in terms of access, distribution, and audience | *ironic:* use of humour and irony in visuals (bricolages, collages) transportation of political messages and subversion of original meaning (often in zines and culture jamming) |
| Action & agency | *interventionist:* interventionist aim within the project itself and by encouraging interventions by others media production as activist practice and interventions into social power relations interventions on content and visual level and in relation to DIY culture; focus on "learning by doing" and "skill-sharing" | *perishable:* short-lived, temporary, ephemeral | |

perspective. Most feminist media producers in our study position themselves in relation to second-wave feminism; however, their strategies and discourses have changed. First, networking occurs also now on a virtual—and therefore transnational—level with the use of new and social media, which marks a major difference to the more local networks during second-wave feminism. Second, we have found that in the European context feminist media producers rarely refer to the term third-wave feminism, as it is widely discussed in the US. Rather, they are engaged in discourses on DIY feminism, intersectional perspectives of feminism, and pop feminism, the latter especially in the context of the German-speaking "new feminisms" debate (for a detailed analysis on this, see Zobl *et al.* 2012). In negotiating (interrelated) feminisms, feminist media production becomes a discursive, interventionist space that is constantly renegotiated, reinvented, and re-appropriated under neoliberal social, cultural, and economic circumstances. Thus, this comprehensive overview of the diversity of feminist media production in Europe gives insights into how a younger generation of feminist media producers negotiate neoliberal changes in society, and how they take up existing feminist discourses and practices and connect them with their own experiences in different geographic contexts.

Overall, feminist media production in online and offline contexts is characterized by a critical reflection of "mainstream" culture as much as an intervention into them. Feminist media are strongly embedded in the feminist movement as part of new social movements through their actors—the well-educated and creative participants, as well as a collective, shared identity and meaning and symbolic production—and through its action—informal, anti-hierarchical, social networks, the integration into everyday life, the widespread use of media and ICTs and "unconventional," creative, small-scale, decentralized action repertoires, and permanent, transnational campaigns (see also Lievrouw 2011: 49). The key problem of translating feminist concerns from the micro level to the meso and macro levels of wider society—and specifically the enabling of broader social participation—remains. Yet truly, as Chandra Talpade Mohanty has said, "everyday feminist, antiracist, anticapitalist practices are as important as larger, organized political movements" (2003: 4).

## Acknowledgments

Work on this report was funded as part of the stand-alone-project of the Austrian Science Fund (P 21187). This chapter has benefited from comments by Stefanie Grünangerl, Red Chidgey, and Jenny Gunnarsson Payne, for which we kindly thank them.

## Note

1 The chapter is based on a previously published report entitled "Feminist Media Production in Europe: A Research Report" in: *Feminist Media: Participatory Spaces, Networks and Cultural Citizenship* (ed. Elke Zobl and Ricarda Drüeke, 2012, Transcript). For documentation of the project, see www.grassrootsfeminism.net. All quotations in this chapter (unless otherwise indicated) stem from face-to-face or online interviews with feminist media producers. Quotes in other languages have been translated by the authors.

## References

Atkinson, J. D. (2010) *Alternative Media and Politics of Resistance: A Communication Perspective*, New York: Peter Lang.

Atton, C. (2002) *Alternative Media*, London: Sage.

Chidgey, R. (2009) "DIY Feminist Networks in Europe: Personal and Collective Acts of Resistance," *Transform! European Journal of Alternative Thinking and Political Dialogue* 5: 159–65.

Chidgey, R., J. Gunnarsson Payne, and E. Zobl (2009) "Rumours from around the Bloc: Gossip, Rhizomatic Media, and the Plotki Femzine," *Feminist Media Studies* 9(4): 477–91.

Foucault, M. (1986) "Of Other Spaces," *Diacritics* 16(1): 22–7.

Kearney, M. C. (1998) "Producing Girls: Rethinking the Study of Female Youth Culture," in S. Inness (ed.) *Delinquents and Debutantes: Twentieth-Century Girls' Cultures*, New York: New York University Press, pp. 285–310.

Lievrouw, L. (2011) *Alternative and Activist New Media*, Cambridge: Polity.

Mohanty, C. T. (2003) *Feminism without Borders: Decolonizing Theory, Practicing Solidarity*, Durham, NC: Duke University Press.

Nguyen, M. (2000) "No Title," *Punk Planet* 40. www.worsethanqueer.com/slander/pp40.html.

Reitsamer, R. (2012) "Female Pressure: A Translocal Feminist Youth-oriented Cultural Network," *Continuum: Journal of Media & Cultural Studies* 26(3): 399–408.

Reitsamer, R. and E. Zobl (2011) "Queer-feministische Comics. Produktive Interventionen im Kontext der Do-It-Yourself Kultur," in B. Eder, E. Klar, and R. Reichert (eds.) *Theorien des Comics*, Bielefeld: Transcript, pp. 365–82.

——(forthcoming) "Alternative Media Production, Feminism, and Citizenship Practices," in M. Boler and M. Ratto (eds.) *DIY Citizenship: Critical Making and Social Media*, Cambridge, MA: MIT Press.

Schilt, K. and E. Zobl (2008) "Connecting the Dots: Riot Grrrls, Ladyfests, and the International Grrrl Zine Network," in A. Harris (ed.) *Next Wave Cultures: Feminism, Subcultures, Activism*, New York: Routledge, pp. 171–92.

Sreberny-Mohammadi, A. (1996) "Women Communicating Globally: Mediating International Feminism," in D. Allen, R. R. Rush, and S. J. Kaufman (eds.) *Women Transforming Communications: Global Intersections*, Thousand Oaks, CA: Sage.

Thornton, S. (1995) *Club Cultures: Music, Media, and Subcultural Capital*, Cambridge: Polity.

Young, S. (1997) *Changing the Wor(l)d: Discourse, Politics, and the Feminist Movement*, New York: Routledge.

Zobl, E. (2009) "Cultural Production, Transnational Networking, and Critical Reflection in Feminist Zines," *Signs* 35(1) (Autumn): 1–12.

——(2010) "Zehn Jahre Ladyfest: Rhizomatische Netzwerke einer lokalen, translokale und virtuellen queer-feministischen Szene," in R. Reitsamer and W. Fichna (eds.) *"They Say I'm Different ... " Popularmusik, Szenen und ihre AkteurInnen*, Vienna: Löcker, pp. 208–27.

Zobl, E., R. Reitsamer, and S. Grünangerl (2012) "Feminist Media Production in Europe: A Research Report," in E. Zobl and R. Drüeke (eds.) *Feminist Media: Participatory Spaces, Networks and Cultural Citizenship*, Bielefeld: Transcript, pp. 21–54.

## Referenced media

Different Worlds Same Heartbeats (Belgium, since 2007) http://echoproject.110mb.com/catalog.html

Emancypunx (Poland, since 1996) http://www.emancypunx.scenaonline.org

female:pressure (Austria, since 1998) http://www.femalepressure.net

Feminisnt's—Я не феминистка, но ... (Russia, since 2008) http://feminisnts.ru

Feminist Poster Project (Belgium, since 2010) http://feministposterproject.wordpress.com

Femminismo a Sud (Italy, since 2006) http://femminismo-a-sud.noblogs.org

Flapper Gathering (Belgium, since 2002) http://echoproject.110mb.com/catalog.html

Hugs and Kisses (Germany, since 2007) http://www.hugsandkissesonline.de

La Barbe (France, since 2008) http://www.labarbelabarbe.org; Le Manifeste de la Barbe, http://labarbelabarbe.org/La_Barbe/Manifeste.html

Le Degenerate Magazine (Italy, since 2010) http://degeneremagazine.blogspot.com

Lo Personal es Político (Spain, since 2007) http://lopersonalespolitico.com

LoveKills/Dragostia Ucide (Romania, since 2003) http://aro.ecobytes.net/lovekills

Masculine Femininities (UK, since 2008) http://masculinefemininities.wordpress.com

Migrazine (Austria, since 2006) http://www.migrazine.at

Osez le féminisme! (France, since 2009) http://osezlefeminisme.fr

Plotki femzine (Germany/international, since 2006) http://plotkifemzine.wordpress.com

Race Revolt (United Kingdom, since 2007) http://www.racerevolt.org.uk.

Riot Grrrl London zine (UK, 2001–3) http://riotgrrrlonline.wordpress.com/2008/04/01/riot-girl-londons-manifesto

Za Feminizm (Russia, since 2010) http://www.zafeminizm.ru/index.php; old blog: http://www.zafeminizm.ucoz.ru.

# 22
# Between legitimacy and political efficacy
## Feminist counter-publics and the internet in China

## *Iam-Chong Ip and Oi-Wan Lam*

This chapter analyzes the dynamics of state feminist counter-publics and independent feminist groups in China, based on a conception of a public sphere as a space for political debate that is both nation based and postnational. Examining the concept and empirical reality of a counter-public sphere in the context of an authoritarian state may seem peculiar to those who are familiar with the centrality of democracy to Habermas's concept of the public sphere. Although the Western model of modernization combines a market economy with constitutional democracy, China contradicted this established paradigm throughout the 1980s, under the leadership of Deng Xiaoping, in that a fast-growing, successful market economy developed without a transition to democracy. Since then, changes such as the disintegration of the highly centralized social system and the diversification and class stratification of Chinese society have become more apparent (Hu 2007). These characteristics are indicative of a unique Chinese model that cannot be explained by established political paradigms based on Western concepts of liberalism, conservatism, political right, middle and left, public interest, democracy, rights, freedom, and individualism (Hu 2007).

Because of this unparalleled dimension of the Chinese social context, our approach diverges from the largely Western project of focusing on the struggles for transnational public spheres to emerge and thrive in a context of cosmopolitan democracy (Fraser 2007; Kidd 2003; Habermas 2001). Instead, we argue that Chinese feminists' new cosmopolitanism features their creative appropriation of global feminist ideas for local and national uses. Our work also diverges from scholarship on the impact of the internet in China and elsewhere in the world, which tends to frame discussion in terms of a civil society simply defined by its opposition to a repressive state regime (Yang 2003; Xiao 2004). Feminist counter-publics not only contribute to the civil rights movement but also engage in more subtle struggles against state feminism *and* for trans-institutional spaces within the state. Exploring this largely neglected dimension in the literature on Chinese politics is crucial for understanding the tension between legitimacy and efficacy facilitated by the new political-economic realities of authoritarian countries. We avoid adopting a technophilic understanding of new ICTs as necessarily being the conduit for oppositional politics in the interest of social change. On the one hand, ICTs enable the proliferation of counterpublics battling for political legitimacy (Dean 2003; Dahlgren 2005). On the other, as many critics point out, digitally mediated collective opinion, despite its intensified passion, neither guarantees that those in authority will be held accountable for their actions nor ensures policy change (Dean 2003; Gladwell 2010; Morozov 2010).

The arena of gender equity and women's rights in China illustrates this argument. The regime's championing of women's liberation largely endorses this field as an acceptable area for social engagement. However, women's rights are not outside the scope of state or intergovernmental intervention. Instead, state organizations, civic groups, and supranational interests collide, compete, and cooperate with one another. The issues of political legitimacy and effectiveness, rather than confined to the scope of state governance and civic domain, must be addressed and evaluated in the transnational context (Fraser 2007). This chapter focuses on the Guangdong provincial branch of the All-China Women's Federation (ACWF) and the Gender Media Action activist group, both based in the city of Guangzhou. These groups' members regularly engage in online political discussion. We consider the history and development of both groups by examining archive documentation and unstructured interviews with core organizers, whose names have been anonymized. The groups' organizational structures and political positions help assess the extent of their political legitimacy and effectiveness in fostering political change.

## The feminist public sphere in China: importing a Western concept?

The concept of the public sphere described by Jürgen Habermas in *The Structural Transformation of the Public Sphere* (1989 [1962]) is one of the most enduring concepts in critical theory and has had a longstanding impact on media studies and, more broadly, on the concept of democracy. Habermas developed the concept of public sphere around an ideal type of the Western model of a nation-state in which citizens could address issues of common concern and criticize the state through rational debate in an environment that, in principle, was free of power relations. *The Structural Transformation of the Public Sphere* begins with the eighteenth-century emergence of an independent, market-based press that published news and opinion articles that engaged public interest and prompted discussion in coffee houses and salons. Eventually, a mass society emerged that was manipulated by media that define politics as spectacle and citizens as consumers.

Particularly since the book was translated into English in 1989, Habermas's conception of the public sphere has met with numerous criticisms. We extend the discussion of two of these. First, in consideration of "the public sphere" both as a normative ideal and an empirical description of a specific historical transformation, feminist and other critical scholars argue that the eighteenth-century bourgeois public sphere described by Habermas represented an idealization of Western European society that was exclusionary. Its debaters were limited to white, propertied, and educated men. Public spheres associated with women and other marginalized groups were ignored. Feminists have responded by attempting to make visible counter-publics, or oppositional arenas recognizing and appreciating differences based on gender, race, and class, and circulating counter-discourses and counter-interpretations (Fraser 1989). Although, in the late twentieth century feminists pointed to women's groups, feminist publications, and films and videos as institutional locations and cultural practices constituting counter-publics (Fraser 1989), the rise of information and communication technologies (ICTs), along with other forces of globalization, has helped to multiply further voices that complicate and compromise established norms of political processes.

Second, largely due to the increasing prevalence of boundary-crossing new ICTs, scholars now recognize that the public sphere must be understood, not only as a nation-centered arena, but also as a potentially postnational or transnational social space. To paraphrase both Habermas and Nancy Fraser, contemporary critical theory of the public sphere must consider the normative legitimacy and political efficacy of public opinion in the postnational constellation (Fraser 2007; Habermas 2001). Our consideration of the relevance of nation-based counter-publics in a postnational context reaffirms the importance of multiple and contested sources of political legitimacy, not necessarily bounded by national territory.

National boundary-crossing is key to the introduction of concepts associated with Western thought into China in the midst of national crisis and revolutions and in the context of colonialism (Sudo 2006). Following the crumbling late-Qing dynastic power, the successor state of the Republic of China (1912–49) continued to suffer from colonial encroachment and was further plunged into internal military conflicts, notably the anti-Japanese War. Living in a crisis-ridden country, Chinese intellectuals reacted by enthusiastically adopting Western thinking as indispensable for enlightenment and national revival (Hu 2007).

One important result of the importation of Western concepts into the Chinese context was that late twentieth-century Chinese feminism was caught between women's liberation and nationalism. The urgency of rescuing the nation from colonialism helped promote the ideas of women's rights and their access to public debate. For example, the Chinese government granted women property and marriage rights, and a variety of women's organizations launched campaigns for equal opportunities, and for abolition of concubinage (the officially recognized status of mistress) (Meng 2010). Diverse voices eventually were incorporated into the revolutionary agenda put forward by the centralized state powers of Kuomintang (KMT, the nationalist revolutionary party), as they had been with the Chinese Communist Party (CCP) since the 1930s (Sudo 2006; Judge 2001), and further integrated into the latter's state bureaucracy after 1949.

In contrast with the deterioration of the rational-critical debate to the pseudo-publicity of the capitalist cultural industry, as Habermas argues, modern Chinese feminists followed a different path in transformation. The feminist debates, practices, and collectivities were largely absorbed into CCP's revolutionary theory and its leadership, which allowed no room for civic engagement and dissident views. The establishment of the ACWF is exemplary. Since the ACWF was established on March 24, 1949 at the first national People's Representative Congress of the People's Republic of China (PRC) in Beijing, all women's organizations have been placed under ACWF and its local branches, a *de facto* CCP organization for building a united front. After the Cultural Revolution, when it had ceased to function, the ACWF re-established itself as an active mass organization and contributed to building a new social order in the economic reform era, specifically by providing services for women and children in need.

The ACWF and the new communist leadership failed to mitigate the tension between political legitimacy and efficacy, which is particularly intense in postsocialist China. While the official socialist ideology has waned since economic reform started in 1978, the state increasingly relies on maintaining its political legitimacy through economic achievement within global capitalism rather than through adherence to the principles of an association of free and equal citizens. Yet, as the Enlightenment's master terms—such as freedom, rights, and democracy—have spread across the world, political cultures in China have organized and reorganized around such keywords. The shift of the party-state towards an authoritarian-capitalist system, despite its refusal to endorse Western political ideas, unintentionally has allowed more opportunities for nongovernmental processes and social engagement over the last few decades, while continuing to restrain civil liberties and formal channels of political participation. As such, newly emerging spaces for public communication often result in contested claims for moral and political legitimacy and escalating distrust in political authorities. In this chapter, apart from the Guangdong ACWF's new project of state feminism, we discuss the development and practices of Gender Media Action (GMA), a new civic group testifying to the influences of Western ideas in China.

## Guangdong ACWF: GONGO with Chinese characteristics

In the 1980s, in response to the failure of Maoist state feminism and women's deteriorating conditions during the reform era, various autonomous women's organizations emerged prior to the violent crackdown on the student movement in 1989 (Bauer et al. 1992; Bian 1987; Wang and Li 1982; Wolf 1985). After Communist Party leader Deng Xiaoping's 1992 insistence on economic reform, China hosted the United Nation's Fourth World Conference on Women and its nongovernmental organization (NGO) forum, both in 1995; this encouraged feminists to address issues related to women's NGOs (Wang 2008). Since then, the ACWF, playing the role of government-organized nongovernmental organization (GONGO), has attempted to channel women's concerns into the policymaking process. Scholars have been divided over the political nature and potential of these women organizations. Some highlight women's organizations' dependence on the party-state as hegemonic, said to compromise their advocacy work; while others say the strategies of "embeddedness" help NGOs gain support and exert influence on state policies (Cooper 2006; Lu 2007; Zhang 2009).

State-based women's organizations have had limited power in addressing the needs and concerns of marginalized women suffering from class division, exploitation, and suppression. The central and local authorities desperately have been attempting to contain social resistance and controversies, particularly those emerging on the internet. Dissident voices are not merely confined to liberal intellectual entities, but also from the grassroots. Since 2003, the civil rights movement (*weiquan yundong*) has come along with the rise of individual-centered online media such as blogging platforms and social networking sites. In some incidents, especially those related to abuse of power and corruption, the public debates have cultivated a strong awareness of "citizen's rights" and "social justice," posing challenges to the status quo featuring regularity and predictability (Beissinger 2002). The challenges, failing to bring out policy or structural changes, sometimes successfully interrupt the normalized routines of public opinion and even policymaking. As in most countries, this results in public distrust of authorities, especially local governments (Zheng 2008: 88–98, 104). As most media and means of public participation are highly restricted by the multi-level system of the party-state in China, the internet is the most accessible arena for public engagement. The party-state, despite its extensive and meticulous control over the internet, still finds it difficult to contain the online public sphere, where individual activists practice alternative citizenship in a highly unorganized and individualized manner (Yang 2009, 2003; Yu 2006).

The Guangdong ACWF, founded in February 1954, attempts to take up these new challenges by reinvigorating state feminism in this new era. It is a large organization with a staff size of 375, various specialized departments, and an extensive network with grassroots organizations in the province. Located in China's highly developed region, the Guangdong ACWF should be the site for numerous social activism opportunities. For instance, Guangdong is the world's largest export processing zone (EPZ) and hires a huge number of women from rural villages. Yet, under the leadership of the CCP, the Federation, refraining from public confrontation with the government, has to follow the policy agenda and guiding principles set by the Party. In post-Mao China, the ACWF defines its major areas as "development" and "women's *quanyi*" (rights and benefits) according to the regime's new ideology. The ACWF drafts its work plan according to the CCP's direction presented in the annual People's Congress. For example, in 2010, Wang Yang, the Party Secretary of Guangdong, following the Party slogan of "Harmonious Society," promoted the concept of "Happiness" (*xingfu*). Following this, the Guangdong ACWF conducted a public opinion survey on building harmonious families and happiness. It also receives complaints, proposes policy suggestions, and requests government departments to change their practices concerning women and children. Rather than adopting an advocacy approach, it mainly tries to solve women's problems case by case by providing advice and sometimes using its institutional networks to pressure government bodies and market enterprises.

The ACWF's activities should be characterized as "gender mainstreaming" (Wang 2008: 4). Within the context of the daily routines mentioned above, the Federation is extremely reluctant to respond to controversies. It carefully toes the Party line in making public statements and offering commentary in the media. When, in 2011, a department team leader in Guangdong ACWF mentioned in the media a sexual harassment case, his remarks were widely discussed online following approval from his supervisor. He stressed that it already was a bold move: "One has to be careful about the nature of the case and avoid crossing the line" (anonymous informant interviewed by authors on January 21, 2011 at the Guangdong ACWF office in Guangzhou).

Although the Guangdong ACWF is a registered NGO, its staff consists of civil servants recruited through an annual civil servant examination. None of our interviewees had a background in feminist politics, and they showed little interest in social and political issues. One worker in the Rights Department admitted that her background had very little to do with her current job. "I joined the ACWF by accident. I came here through public recruitment and examination. I was not clear about the Guangdong ACWF's daily work and mission. After working here for ten years, I begin to find my job meaningful and helpful. Now, I realize its mission and major functions," she said. Their knowledge about women's issues is exceptionally limited. For example, few were aware of the 1995 Beijing UN Fourth World Conference on Women and its significance to China. Not surprisingly, most have no motivation to engage in advocacy or activism.

The ACWF's value in facilitating policy changes, such as in the amendment of marriage law and the recent discussion on legislation against domestic violence, should not be completely denied. Chinese state feminism is a kind of gender negotiation involving careful plotting undertaken with a quality of secrecy within the Party power structure (Wang 2005). Due to its institutional inertia and political nature, its working style is so low profile that the work of Chinese state feminism is often seen by the public as mere propaganda.

The rise of internet politics further reveals the ACWF's predicament. Most of the Guangdong ACWF staff members whom we interviewed primarily understand ICTs as either components of a "modernized office" or tools for personal networking. Online projects facilitate the extension of official propaganda. Since 2009, the organization has started a number of online projects after Wang Yang proposed "online policy deliberation." This idea came after Wang followed President Hu Jintao's example of online dialogue with netizens. The Guangdong ACWF launched the first so-called policy deliberation website, "New Era, New Women and New Life: Guangdong ACWF Online Policy Deliberation" (gdwomen.oeeee.com/), in which the President of the Federation followed the government leaders' approach to meeting netizens online. The interaction section of its website, designed for online policy deliberation, is not genuinely "interactive" because all posts are carefully selected and largely staged. The staff told us that all posts are submitted to supervisors for revision and approval before publication. Even worse, the Guangdong ACWF's campaigns tend to be socially conservative, stressing the importance of traditional family values. For example, in 2010 it launched an online essay competition under the theme "Good Father and Good Mother." That is one reason why young feminists do not tend to regard the ACWF as "feminist."

The 2009 incident involving Deng Yujiao, a 21-year-old pedicure worker, is the most illustrative of the attitude of many young Chinese feminists. The young woman stabbed a local official to death in a hotel room in trying to rebuff several officials' sexual advances and physical assaults. The local police immediately arrested her on charges of homicide, although she claimed she acted in self-defense after three men attempted to rape her. This case aroused nationwide sympathy and public outrage over the immorality of officials across the country. Several citizens and opinion leaders, complaining about the ACWF's failure to protect women's rights, demanded the Federation make a statement and take action on the young woman's behalf

(Liu 2009; Lü Ping 2009). More than ten days after the incident happened, the Federation made a brief and moderate statement claiming that it "monitors the case closely" and expressing its "faith in the impartiality of the authority" (ACWF 2009). Probably due to social pressures, Deng was found guilty only of assault and was released.

While the ACWF's contribution to her release remains unclear, most concerned citizens, including the staff of Guangdong ACWF, were unhappy about the Federation's slow and weak response. For instance, a department team leader of Guangdong ACWF believed that more works of advocacy, notably online activism, are needed. He set up a new blog and micro-blog for public engagement in March 2011. So far, the blog, hosted under Sina (blog.sina.com.cn/u/1999442777), has not been very successful; the posts are either state-run newspaper article clippings or official announcements. Although the micro-blog (weibo.com/gdflqyb) is more popular, with 15,218 followers in seven months, it functions mainly as a form of news distribution rather than as a site for criticism of official policies or advocacy.

## Gender Media Action: a feminist network

Gender Media Action was established on November 25, 2004, the day of the Global Action against Sexual Violence. Its members first came together in a workshop titled "New Media and Gender Awareness," organized by the British Council with the support of Oxfam (Hong Kong). The network, initially founded by professional women media workers and academics, was extended to include lawyers, NGO organizers, and intellectuals from other gender studies networks. Currently, the group has more than 70 members.

GMA's limited resources and China's political environment make it impossible for the organization to be involved in grassroots organization and service provision. Its capacity for intervention into the process of policymaking is also very limited. Its strongest advantage is its ideas, knowledge, and speaking positions in news media, online forums, and state-run universities. As the group cannot be registered as an independent NGO, it operates in the form of social networking. Its main activities are seminars, talks, and training programs on topics related to women's rights and gender awareness.

When we carried out our interviews and observations, GMA was organizing an exhibition for Women's Day 2011, in which women artists, activists, and groups presented their ideas about gender violence. Despite its members' repeated emphasis on the difference between their gender awareness and the ACWF's discourse of "equality between man and woman," GMA approached the Guangdong ACWF to co-host the exhibition. Its proposal was rejected because the ACWF preferred a "celebratory mood" for its official activities, including banquets and Party leaders' speeches. Another reason is its reservation about the issues of LGBT in GMA's arts work. Indeed, the ACWF is usually reluctant to cooperate with groups outside its usual network of partners. Without the ACWF's and government's support, GMA members pulled together resources from their personal networks for their activities. They invited a number of co-organizers, including university gender studies groups, artists, LGBT, and women workers' groups for the exhibition. Although the exhibition had to be held in a private gallery on the outskirts of the city rather than in any publicly run art space, it was well covered by media and its opening was live-casted online by a commercial web portal in which some GMA members have acquaintances.

GMA's feminism has to be understood not simply in terms of its institutional position but also through its discourses and practices. It differentiates itself from the ACWF by using the term "*nüxing*" (woman), with the connotations of a gender binary and sexualities, rather than "*funü*," a Maoist category of "woman" subordinated to class and nation (Barlow 1994; Yang 1999: 39). Most members of the network have a strong background in feminism and social activism. The story of GMA founder Ai Xiaoming is most notable. Ai's intellectual path diverges from the orthodoxies of state feminism since the 1980s. She was not an active feminist until 1999, when she joined a one-year visiting program in Women Studies at a university in Tennessee. She then began to develop courses on Women's Studies and Feminism at the Sun Yat-sen University in Guangzhou. However, compared to her predecessors Li Xiaojiang and Dai Jinghua, Ai does not confine her feminism to intellectual practices but has embodied it with social activism and online politics since the early 2000s. In February 2003, the death of Huang Jing, a 21-year-old primary school teacher killed by her boyfriend, not only provided a living example of sexual violence for her but also revealed the gender bias and corruption in China's judicial system. In retrospect, the year during which she and her friends founded GMA proved to be a dramatic turn for Ai's career and life. She and her students advocated a thorough investigation of Huang's death and launched a campus-based web project, "Gender Education Forum" (http://genders.zsu.edu.cn), inspired by Huang's supporters' campaign website, Paradise Garden. In the same year, her Chinese adaptation of Eve Ensler's *Vagina Monologues* was staged in Guangzhou but was banned in Shanghai and Beijing. Initially, she picked up the video camera for recording the stage performance for teaching purposes, but she gradually developed a strong interest in documentary, eventually becoming a nationally known film-maker. Since then, she has continued to make documentaries about various topics, such as an AIDS patient village, the Sichuan Earthquake, and human rights. Ai subsequently was suspended from teaching at the university because her activism and films upset the authorities.

Despite Ai's dissidence and her influence on GMA, most members continue their institutional and professional lives and manage to sustain their personal networks through various online platforms for supporting one another and occasionally launching less politically sensitive projects together. For example, Ai's students, colleagues, and the research center she founded, although not directly involved in confrontational controversies, function as the intellectual ring of GMA. They eventually became the core of the organization after members such as Ai and others got involved in political controversies. The weak ties facilitated by the internet further help members scattered around in diverse institutional sites to maintain solidarity without any formal organization. Most campaigns are ad hoc and sometimes are built only around individuals. Hence, the political troubles encountered by individual members rarely spill over to the other members of the organization.

Without an office, GMA's members are more active than ACWF's staff in the use of ICTs; the former depends on the internet for internal discussion, planning, activity promotion, and advocacy campaigns. Few members of GMA used computers for communication until 1995. But when they feel the need, they learn to use the available media and technologies very quickly. Interestingly enough, they do not have any official website, probably because of political considerations. In China, even individual web domains require proper registration and are subject to daily censorship by the authorities. The group blog is Sina.com, a commercial portal website and an internal forum since 2009. As their personal network covers media workers, NGO workers, university teachers, lawyers, individual activists, etc., they spread information very quickly through email and social networking.

GMA members are aware of the problems of both state-run media outlets and the commercial online portals, such as political censorship from above and the gender bias of "journalistic professionalism." Despite this, they do not hesitate to make use of online resources for practical and strategic purposes. Li Jun, one of the founding members of GMA, was the first journalist who took notice of the case of Deng Yujiao. In the first few days after the incident, she became frustrated by the lukewarm responses from her colleagues and editors. This did not deter her from distributing the news on social media, which drew the media's attention to it nationwide. GMA members' critique of gender stereotypes does not prevent them from cooperating with mainstream media. Due to their personal networks, a special feature on "New Feminism" (news.163. com/special/00013R06/nvquanzhuyi.html) in the biggest Guangzhou-based online portal, Netease, was launched in 2009, and six Guangdong-based feminists, mostly GMA members, were invited to talk about gender and sexual politics in China. They successfully enabled a communication circuit of in-group deliberation, online discussion, news circulation, opinion formation, media follow-ups, and sometimes action.

The ad hoc actions launched by women activists in various institutions, particularly universities, are noteworthy. In February 2012, some college women loosely affiliated with GMA occupied a men's room at Yuexiu Park in Guangzhou to demand more toilet facilities for women. In the summer of 2012, Lü Ping, a member of GMA in Beijing, and lawyer Huang Yizhi petitioned the Ministry of Education on revealing information about adjusting the sex ratio for university entrance. They charged some universities and departments with discriminating against women in their admission exercises. After the Ministry refused to disclose further information about this, some college graduates in Beijing and Guangzhou shaved their hair in protest (*Women of China*, December 1, 2012). Although no formal press notices were issued, these campaigns were widely covered and followed up by reporters who had become well informed of the issues through GMA's online and personal networks. These advocacy and media campaigns, spontaneous and ad hoc rather than highly organized, successfully escaped governmental control and aroused public concern. In most cases, it is difficult to see any immediate effect of the individual-centered cyber-network on policy changes. It could be argued that networks engaged in informal and spontaneous venting, anger, and protests make possible challenges to the legitimacy of government authority.

## Concluding remarks

The ACWF attempts to incorporate the newly emerging groups and voices into its hierarchy and networks for channeling women's concerns into the new state project. Its political function is to negotiate with the party-state and, therefore, the organization is limited in its political scope. Its primary role is to help the government shore up legitimacy by providing services and benefits for its constituency and affiliated groups. However, with its "back-door" approach, the Federation, like the Party, faces a series of legitimacy crises at a time when there are a growing number of counter-public spheres emerging on the internet. While the crackdown on dissidents and online censorship cannot erase all dissident voices on the internet, feminist counter-publics have sown the seeds of distrust toward government authorities and even the ACWF, exacerbating the Federation's legitimacy crisis and exposing the limited political efficacy of working with and within the state.

The case of GMA demonstrates the strengths and weakness of Chinese feminist counter-publics in the information age. Working with active netizens, women activists encourage a broad vision of political consciousness by relating global feminist ideas to various notions of civil rights. However, feminist critical public opinion remains politically ineffective in terms of social change because of its individualistic tendencies, reactionary approaches to political communication and action, and feminist refusal to comply with state co-optation.

Chinese netizens prefigure citizenship by creating tension-charged events through individual-centered media. Yet, like research on the Arab Spring and the Occupy Wall Street movement (Fuchs 2012: 790; Wilson and Dunn 2011), our findings offer a more complicated and contextualized picture than that suggested by techno-optimism. For networked feminists, information becomes a resource for producing activist rallying points rather than simply a commodity for consumption as they weave their own fabric of personal and political ties in and across state-run institutions such as universities and traditional media. Chinese independent feminists' creative appropriation and uses of global feminist concepts, ICTs, ad hoc organizations, and spontaneous actions contribute to an array of emergent public spheres with the potential to operate legitimately and effectively in the social and political domains.

# References

All-China Women's Federation (ACWF) (2009) "ACWF to Monitor Government Official Stabbing Case," All-China Women's Federation Website, May 25. http://www.womenof china.cn/html/node/99134-1.htm.

Barlow, T. (1994) "Theorizing Woman: *Funü, Guojia, Jiating*," in A. Zito and T. E. Barlow (eds.) *Body, Subject and Power in China*, Chicago: University of Chicago Press, pp. 253–89.

Bauer, J., W. Feng, N. E. Riley, and X. Zhao (1992) "Gender Inequality in Urban China: Education and Employment," *Modern China* 18(3): 333–70.

Beissinger, M. (2002) *Nationalist Mobilization and the Collapse of the Soviet State*, Cambridge: Cambridge University Press.

Bian, Y. (1987) "A Preliminary Analysis of the Basic Features of the Life Style of China's Single-Child Families," *Social Sciences in China* 8: 189–209.

Cooper, C. M. (2006) "This Is Our Way In: The Civil Society of Environmental NGOs in South-west China," *Government and Opposition* 41(1): 109–36.

Dahlgren, P. (2005) "The Internet, Public Spheres, and Political Communication: Dispersion and Deliberation," *Political Communication* 22: 147–62.

Dean, J. (2003) "Why the Net Is Not a Public Sphere," *Constellations* 10(1): 95–112.

Fraser, N. (1989) "What's Critical about Critical Theory? The Case of Habermas and Gender," in *Unruly Practices: Power, Discourse, and Gender in Contemporary Social Theory*, Minneapolis: University of Minnesota Press.

——(2007) *Transnationalizing the Public Sphere: On the Legitimacy and Efficacy of Public Opinion in a Post-Westphalian World*, European Institute of Progressive Cultural Institute. http://eipcp.net/transversal/0605/fraser/en.

Fuchs, C. (2012) "Some Reflections on Manuel Castells' Book Networks of Outrage and Hope: Social Movements in the Internet Age," *Triple C: Cognition, Communication, Co-operation* 10(2): 775–97.

Gladwell, M. (2010) "Small Change: Why the Revolution Will Not Be Tweeted," *New Yorker* (October): 42–9.

Habermas, J. (1987) *The Theory of Communicative Action, Volume Two: Lifeworld and System: A Critique of Functionalist Reason*, Boston: Beacon Press.

——(1989 [1962]) *The Structural Transformation of the Public Sphere: An Inquiry of the Category of Bourgeois Society*, Cambridge, MA: MIT Press.

——(2001) *The Postnational Constellation: Political Essays*, Cambridge, MA: MIT Press.

Howell, J. (2003) "Women's Organizations and Civil Society in China," *International Feminist Journal of Politics* 5(2): 191–215.

Hu Z. (2007) "The Chinese Model and Paradigm of Media Studies," *Global Media and Communication* 3: 335–9.

Judge, J. (2001) "Talent, Virtue, and the Nation: Chinese Nationalisms and Female Subjectivities in the Early Twentieth Century," *American Historical Review* 106(3): 765–803.

Kidd, D. (2003) "Indymedia.org: A New Communications Commons," in *Cyberactivism: Online Activism in Theory and Practice*, New York: Routledge, pp. 41–69.

Liu, X. (2009) "A Public Letter to ACWF Regarding the Incident of Deng Yujiao," My1510.cn. http://www.my1510.cn/article.php?id=16844.

Lü P. (2009) "Why the Public Expects ACWF to Help Out in the Incident of Deng Yujiao," Epoch Times, May 22. http://www.epochtimes.com/b5/9/5/25/n2537839.htm.

Lu, Y. (2007) "The Autonomy of Chinese NGOs: A News Perspective," *China: An International Journal* 5(2): 173–203.

Meng, F. (2010) "A Hundred Years of Women's Liberation Movement," (Chinese). http://www.wyzxsx.com/Article/Class17/201003/135885.html.

Morozov, E. (2010) *The Net Delusion: How Not to Liberate the World*, London: Allen Lane.

Negt, O. and A. Kluge (1993) *Public Sphere and Experience: Toward an Analysis of the Bourgeois and Proletarian Public Sphere*, Minneapolis: University of Minnesota Press.

Pun, N. (2005) *Made in China: Women Factory Workers in a Global Workplace*, Durham, NC: Duke University Press.

Sudo, M. (2006) "Concepts of Women's Rights in Modern China," *Gender and History* 18(3): 472–89.

Wang, Y. and L. Jinrong (1982) "Urban Workers' Housework," *Social Sciences in China* 3: 147–65.

Wang, Z. (2005) "'State Feminism?' Gender and Socialist State Formation in Maoist China," *Feminist Studies* 31(3): 519–51.

——(2008) "Global Concepts, Local Practices: Chinese Feminism Since the Fourth UN Conference on Women," talk at the 40-Year of Women's Movement Conference at Bochum University, June 13. http://www.gwi-boell.de/downloads/Konferenzbeitrag_Bochum_Wang_Zheng_Juni_2008.pdf.

Wang, Z. and Y. Zhang (2010) "Global Concepts, Local Practices: Chinese Feminism since the Fourth UN Conference on Women," *Feminist Studies* 36(1): 499–519.

Wilson, C. and A. Dunn (2011) "Digital Media in the Egyptian Revolution: Descriptive Analysis from the Tahir Data Sets," *International Journal of Communication* 5: 1248–72.

Wolf, M. (1985) *Revolution Postponed*, Palo Alto, CA: Stanford University Press.

Xiao, Q. (2004) "The 'Blog' Revolution Sweeps across China," *New Scientist* Print Edition, November 24. http://www.newscientist.com/article/dn6707-the-blog-revolution-sweeps-across-china.html.

Yang, G. (2003) "The Internet and Civil Society in China: A Preliminary Assessment," *Journal of Contemporary China* 12(36): 453–75.

——(2009) *The Power of the Internet in China: Citizen Activism Online*, New York: Columbia University Press.

Yang, M. M. (1999) "From Gender Erasure to Gender Difference: State Feminism, Consumer Sexuality, and Women's Public Sphere in China," in M. Mei-hui Yang (ed.) *Spaces of Their Own: Women's Public Sphere in Transitional China*, Minneapolis: University of Minnesota Press, pp. 35–67.

Yu H. (2006) "From Active Audience to Media Citizenship: The Case of Post-Mao China," *Social Semiotics* 16(2): 303–26.

Zhang, L. (2009) "Chinese Women Protesting Domestic Violence: The Beijing Conference, International Donor Agencies and the Making of a Chinese Women's NGO," *Meridians* 9(2): 66–99.

Zheng, Y. (2008) *Technological Empowerment: The Internet, State and Society in China*, Palo Alto, CA: Stanford University Press.

# Part III

# IMAGES AND REPRESENTATIONS ACROSS TEXTS AND GENRES

# 23

# Buying and selling sex

## Sexualization, commerce, and gender

## *Karen Boyle*

In a 1998 episode of *Sex and the City* ("The Turtle and the Hare," 1.09), Charlotte—usually the most sexually conservative of the friends—becomes hooked on a "Rabbit" vibrator. After the episode aired, Rabbit sales rocketed. Fourteen years later, the *Sex and the City* (SATC) New York tour (http://www.screentours.com/tour.php/satc/, July 25, 2012) still includes a stop at the shop where Charlotte purchased her vibrator. This is the only "sex" on the tour, which focuses on locations associated with consumption, friendship, and romantic moments in the series and its related films.

The *Hangover* (Phillips, 2009) has been described by some as a "male *Sex and the City*."[1] Like *SATC*, it privileges conspicuous consumption. But whilst *SATC* fetishizes designer labels and luxury brands, *The Hangover* and its 2011 sequel delight in the men's casual destruction of cars, hotels, and bars, their patronage of strip clubs, and use of women and transsexuals in prostitution. Like *SATC*, the *Hangover* films have also spawned city tours, of Las Vegas and Bangkok respectively. Both tours center around strip clubs, but fans on the Vegas tour (http://vegaspartystars.com/vegaspartystars/the-hangover-tour-las-vegas/, July 25, 2012) are additionally accompanied by "hostesses" and offered the option to book a "variety of entertainers" for a private after-party. The Bangkok tour's apparent highlight is a live show in which a woman shoots ping-pong balls from her vagina (http://www.bangkokhangovertours.com/, July 25, 2012).

These examples suggest changing cultural norms around sexuality and its representations, inextricably linked to commerce. Indeed, for some commentators, the products and practices referred to in *SATC* and *The Hangover* can be understood as broadly equivalent. For example, Feona Attwood (2009a: xiv–xv) lists both strip clubs and the Rabbit as examples of "places, products and performances associated with sex for its own sake," and Clarissa Smith (2007: 167) sees the growth in the sex toy market as evidence of "the development of a sex industry for women." This chapter reconsiders these connections, distinguishing between the ways in which "sex" (or the promise of sex) is sold, and used to sell products, to women and men. This highlights the way in which ideas about "sex for its own sake" and the diversification of the "sex industry" obscure fundamental inequalities at the heart of commercial sex. Commercial sex entails the buying and selling of (sexual access to) real bodies. In its dominant forms this is profoundly gendered.

I begin not with commercial sex but, rather, with what I refer to as the "commercialization of sex:" the buying and selling of products designed to enhance the consumer's sexual pleasure either directly (e.g. sex toys) or more indirectly by remaking the body as sexually ready (e.g. pole dancing exercise classes). This allows me to examine the commercial exchange in which Charlotte and the tourists following in her well-heeled footsteps are involved. Although I begin by discussing the *things* being sold to women—particularly to heterosexual women—this leads to a broader examination of the *ideas* about sex that are at stake, drawing on a range of examples frequently mentioned in debates about the "sexualization of culture" such as pole dancing classes, erotic fiction, and intimate memoirs. My concern is not how individuals experience these (a theme dominating much feminist debate), but rather what they tell us about gender, sexuality, and power more broadly. A central question is whether it is useful to insist upon a distinction between the commercialization of sex and commercial sex. Whose interests are served by muddying these boundaries? Comparing heterosexual women's place within this marketplace to the positions offered their male contemporaries—something academic literature rarely does—sheds further light on this.

## Selling "sex" to women

When Charlotte bought her Rabbit, she bought an inanimate object, a thing. In 2012, the website of the store where Charlotte made her purchase described a new version of this object:

> The elastomer version of the original Rabbit Pearl of "Sex and the City" fame features a rotating shaft that strokes your g-spot, sensuous shuffling "pearls" to arouse your opening, and a playful wiggling rabbit to caress your clit. This fine piece of Japanese craftsmanship is adorable, of course, but also a pleasure powerhouse for those who love simultaneous internal and external stimulation. Fun Fact: Part of the episode of "Sex and the City" where Charlotte becomes addicted to her Rabbit Pearl was filmed on-location at The Pleasure Chest New York! All that, and it's made of superior-quality hypo-allergenic and phthalate-free elastomer.
> (http://www.thepleasurechest.com/vibratex-rabbit-pearl-e-7904-prd1.htm, July 25, 2012)

This marketing blurb clearly addresses female consumers. The *SATC* references sit alongside descriptions of the toy's functionality and high-end specifications. This is a piece of affordable luxury, designed for self-pleasure, consistent with discourses around female sexuality which *SATC* was widely argued to promote. While the *SATC* references have particular resonance for this store—given the store's appearance in the show—analyses of the sex toy and lingerie market for women in the UK have also indicated the ways in which women are not simply sold "sex" (or even the promise of orgasm) but, through their purchase of these goods, are invited to (re)make themselves as classed, raced, feminine subjects (Storr 2003; Attwood 2005).

A discourse of women's *right* to sexual self-pleasure is more or less explicit in different retail contexts but broadly underpins what Smith (2007: 17) calls "sex retailing" for women. Certainly, part of what is being sold to women is the promise of sexual pleasure. As such, this is retailing that is clearly *about* sex. But sex is not, *literally*, what is bought and sold: What you get for $79.95 is, at base, designed elastomer with a battery pack.

The only human presence in this blurb is the fictional Charlotte, offered as a figure of sexual identification. In much the same way, in July 2012 it is the fictional Anastasia Steele—protagonist of E. L. James's (2012) bestselling "erotic romance" *50 Shades of Grey*—whom UK-based sex retailers for women are championing. For example, high-street retailer Ann Summers (www.annsummers.com, July 25, 2012) offers a *50 Shades* button on its homepage: potential consumers who click on it are directed to a page where they can purchase both the book and a bondage kit to take their identification with the novel's protagonist one step further. Although many of the kit's pieces—adjustable rope restraints, handcuffs, solid red ball gag, and so on—could be used on men as well as women, the packaging shows women modeling the kit's uses. In the context of a company targeting heterosexual women, the invitation here is one of identification, of becoming "one of the girls" (Storr 2003). As in the SATC/Rabbit example, women are invited to buy products primarily for use on or in their own bodies. Moreover, it is women—role models, models, saleswomen—who are selling to women. These women are not simply sexual(ized) objects, nor is this discourse devoid of objectification. As we will see, whether they are being sold to women or to men, sex toys are typically marketed in relation to *women's* bodies. The equation of women with sex—but not, necessarily, with an embodied desire—remains strong.

SATC and Ann Summers's promotion of *50 Shades* suggest a female sexual culture that—while fiercely heterosexual—is also homosocial: women define for themselves and other women the possibilities of sexual pleasure and purchase. *50 Shades* may be about a heterosexual relationship but its extraordinary popularity, and its salience for Ann Summers, hinges on the way it is *shared* among women. This suggests the shared investment of (some) women in commercialized sex of this kind (Storr 2003). Indeed, questions around the nature and meaning of these investments have dominated much recent feminist scholarship on the sexualization of culture. Take, for example, research on women's experiences of pole dancing. While pole dancing originated within the sex industry, recent research has focused on its reincarnation as a sex-segregated form of exercise (Holland 2010; Whitehead and Kurz 2009). A key word in research exploring the meaning of pole dancing for women who do it for exercise—and, indeed, in debates about women and girls' engagements with sexualized cultural forms and practices more generally—is "empowerment," with participants often claiming to feel empowered in and through their participation in classes. Indeed, "empowerment" has become part of the lexicon of contemporary female sexuality and advertising (Gavey 2012; Gill 2008, 2012): something which can apparently be bought along with a vibrator or membership of a pole dancing class, and yet another sexual expectation on (young) women. As Ros Gill puts it:

> Sexual confidence and a sense of sexual power is part of the very "sexiness" ... that is normatively required of young women today. In this

sense, empowerment itself (or certainly its proxies: confidence and adventurousness) has been "sexualised" and cannot be said to operate entirely independently of "sexualisation."

(Gill 2012: 738)

The sexual confidence and adventurousness which (young) women are expected to profess are acquired and accessorized. This requires money, time, and constant upkeep. What women are being asked to buy (into) is a means of working on their/ our *own* bodies. This is perhaps not as other oriented as it once was: they/we are being asked to invest in our own pleasure and not, primarily, in men's. But within a discourse which is fundamentally *commercial*, the possibility of seeing sexual experiences and cultures in relation to broader issues of power, inequality, or oppression is side-lined in favor of individualism. As Merl Storr (2003: 31) points out: "*feeling* empowered is not the same as *being* powerful." Yet, questions about women's agency, participation, and pleasures in the sexualization of culture have become dominant in academic debates (Coy and Garner 2012). As such, it is *women's* experiences which have been fought over, whilst questions around who profits (materially and socially) from women's sexualized consumption practices are less well explored.

The above examples suggest a fairly easy distinction between "the commercialization of sex" and "commercial sex": buying a vibrator or participating in pole dancing exercise does not depend upon the bodies of *other* people. However, other examples suggest that these boundaries are less clear. What should we make of "realistic" penis-styled vibrators and dildos, for example? Analyzing women's participation in Ann Summers parties, Storr describes how these toys are discursively positioned among women. She notes that women's discussions are characterized by ambivalence: on one hand, the penis is a comic object, women's laughter undercutting the naturalization of men's power as phallic; on the other, the desirability of "realistic" vibrators depends upon that naturalization of power, strength, and authority as masculine attributes (Storr 2003: 121).

Whilst the growth in popularity of Rabbits and other non-realistic sex toys qualifies Storr's argument, the ambivalence she observes can still be found in descriptions of "realistic" sex toys for women. If product descriptions aimed at women tend to emphasize functionality, design, and materials (Attwood 2005),[2] then it is perhaps unsurprising that "realistic" toys are compared—often favorably—to the "real thing" in terms of appearance, feel, size, and ability to satisfy. The "real thing" does not always emerge well from comparisons figured in terms of materiality (length, girth) and technique (in women's hands rather than attached to men's bodies). Yet, Storr's analysis points to the ways in which these comparisons become part of women's negotiations with (rather than rejection of) patriarchy: first, they valorize vaginal orgasm during heterosex, emphasizing male technique and rendering women largely passive in the heterosexual encounter; and, second, female sexual disappointment becomes part of what she describes as an "'affectionate' post-feminist joke that 'men are useless but we love them anyway'" (2003: 175).

Importantly, nothing here suggests that women have—or should have—sexual entitlement over a man's body. "Realistic" sex toys for heterosexual women depend upon a *notional* male body. For instance, no explicit link is made to commercial sex activities or possibilities. Major "sex retailers" targeting women have not historically or primarily been known for selling pornography (Storr 2003; Attwood 2005). Although Ann Summers does now carry a range of pornography, this is euphemistically labeled ("adult" or "erotic" DVDs), the range is limited (36 titles available online in October 2012) and porn is not typically part of the offering at direct-sale parties. Within the stores porn has a very marginal presence, usually located at the rear of the store, thus remaining invisible from the street. The films sold do not—at a glance—appear to offer anything distinctive for a heterosexual female consumer. Instead, it is *women's* bodies which are on display in titles which seem to target a heterosexual male audience with the promise of female sexual availability (e.g. *Jane Bond: DD7, Dick Sucking Divas, Pump It up Me Harder, Mums and Daughters: Secrets in the Suburbs*). This is not to deny that straight women may also take pleasure in these titles, but rather to point to the fact that even within the context of sex retailing to women the gendered power dynamic at play is such that women remain the product.

An arguably more complex example of the blurring of boundaries between the "commercialization of sex" and "commercial sex" can be found in female-anchored accounts of the sex industry: sex workers' autobiographies and blogs, or television series such as *The Girls Next Door* (E!, 2005–10) and *Secret Diary of a Call Girl* (ITV2, 2007–11). Feminist media studies literature about these media emphasizes how they shift the discourse around sex work from one in which women are seen as victims to an emphasis on their choice, agency, and pleasure (e.g. Dunn 2010; Attwood 2009b, 2010). This emphasis on the experiences of individual women, their choice, agency, and pleasure, resonates with policy debates about the sexualization of culture more broadly. In this context, too, it is the choices of girls and young women which have been subjected to the most intense scrutiny, whether these choices are celebrated or censored. This emphasis on individual choice has come at the cost of a properly gendered analysis and has obscured the intersection between gender and other structural features of identity such as class, race, sexuality, and age (Gill 2012). Moreover, this has left *men's* investments in commercial sex—and in the sexualization of culture—untroubled (Boyle 2008, 2010, 2011a, 2011b).

Of particular relevance here are the ways in which the female-anchored accounts of the sex industry address women, representing commercial sex as an aspirational career choice largely made on the basis of the (non-sexual) consumption practices it allows. This was particularly explicit in ITV2's screening of the final season of *Secret Diary of a Call Girl* (February–March 2011), itself tied to a competition that played on the show's debt to *SATC* by offering a luxury shopping trip to New York as the prize. While ostensibly allowing viewers to "follow in Belle's footsteps," the prize very clearly sought to position *Secret Diary* in relation to the sexual and commercial mores of *SATC* and its female fanbase—notably, the prize was for four, although in *Secret Diary* Belle traveled to New York alone. This worked to negate the specificities of *Secret Diary*'s sexual culture. Belle sells sex; Carrie and friends do not. Admittedly, Belle says early on that her love of sex drove her choice to become a call girl. The framing questions posed in early episodes—although mainly explored through her experiences in prostitution—are, like Carrie's, general ones to which women viewers are expected to relate (e.g. "when did sex become so complicated?"). This is in line with a broader trend whereby women working in the sex industry are positioned as exemplars of modern female sexuality, experts in contemporary sexual mores.[3] Yet, female sex workers in the media frequently, and sometimes simultaneously, acknowledge that their own sexual pleasure is both immaterial to the transaction and often faked. This tension between the celebration of women's involvement in commercial sex as an expression of their sexuality and the realities of the work is also manifest in the advice sex worker narrators (real and fictional) offer to women starting out in the industry. In numerous contexts, female sex workers offer career advice alongside evidence of the multiple ways in which women are damaged by their involvement in the sex industry. As such, they imply that it is women's responsibility to avoid harm by ensuring that they enter the industry knowingly and manage their career to achieve maximum financial reward (Boyle 2011b). To the extent that these texts invite women viewers'/readers' participation in the sex industry, they invite women to make themselves products in order to become better consumers. Women are not typically figured as consumers of people, but are invited to—as porn star Jenna Jameson puts it—see themselves as the product (Jameson and Strauss 2004: 333).

## Selling "sex" to men

The previous section began with Charlotte's purchase of a *thing* and worked out from this to consider the ideas about sex being sold to women along with such purchases, before moving to consider links with commercial sex. Tellingly, here I take this journey in reverse, beginning with the purchase of *people*, arguing that the normalization of commercial sex—with the *Hangover* films and their associated tours as my examples—is then fed into the marketing of "things" (specifically, sex toys) to men.

The consumption practices privileged in *The Hangover* tours are firmly located within the sex industries of their respective cities. Underpinning both films is a tacit acceptance that stag parties in Vegas and Bangkok are necessarily defined by alcohol, drugs, gambling, and the sex industry. Moreover, girlfriends and wives (who have very marginal roles in any case) are shown to be accommodating and indulgent of men's temporary purchase of other women, who are rendered disposable on account of their class, ethnicity, or trans-status. Only Stu's girlfriend in *The Hangover* offers any critique of this dynamic and she is portrayed as controlling, shrill, and entirely unsympathetic. By the second film, Stu's new wife-to-be is appropriately accommodating. So Stu's purchase of commercial sex poses no threat to their nuptials: boys will be boys.

If the men are not entirely sympathetic characters, nonetheless their hedonistic adventures are celebrated (which is what the city tours play on) and their sense of entitlement over women is uncontested, underlined by the celebrated presence of convicted rapist Mike Tyson in both films. The purchases made by *The Hangover* tourists involve—indeed, require—the sexualized performance of real women. They (like the men on screen) are buying access to women's bodies: as patrons of strip clubs and live sex shows; as clients of "escorts." Only for the buyer can this be plausibly understood as "sex for its own sake:" for those working in the sex industry, this is—at best—consensually enacted *as labor*. For the person bought, the sex is neither for its own sake nor (again, as biographies of porn performers and escorts suggest) necessarily pleasurable.

That said, we might additionally challenge the assumption that men's purchase of sex is always pleasurable for them. Stu's sexual consumerism is accompanied by momentary regret in both cases. It is also performed without his having made a conscious choice, the central premise of both films being that the men have unknowingly taken Rohypnol (the "date rape drug"). Rohypnol functions as an alibi for behavior which the films celebrate yet recognize is excessive. But its comic function also highlights how participation in the sex industry has become such an orthodoxy for heterosexual men and boys in particular homosocial contexts (such as the stag party) that resistance is impossible, futile.

The ideas about sex being sold to men here hinge on men's sexual entitlement over women as a (if not the) marker of masculinity, particularly in homosocial contexts. These are not isolated examples. A recent study of young people's experiences of "sexting," for instance, notes that peer-produced sexualized images of girls' bodies operate as a commodity or currency in boys' relationships with each other. The authors conclude that these practices need to be linked to an analysis of wider sexist gender relations and commercial culture (Ringrose et al. 2012)—precisely my territory here.

The "sexting" example is useful because it suggests that the norms of commercial sex (here pornography) have filtered through the culture. The marketing of sex toys to men offers another set of interesting examples of the ways that commercial sex is being sold to men as an ideal.[4] As we will see, men are invited to identify with the *consumer* of commercial sex: The dominant discourse is one in which men are invited to objectify women.

On the online Hustler store, for example, clicking on the "sex toys for men" button takes you to a page of products resembling various disembodied female body parts. The first product—a torso with no head, arms, or legs—is the Pdx Mega Fuck slut, described thus:

You've always dreamt of fucking a voluptuous hottie with 36DD's, nice round hips and a super-tight waist, so what are you waiting for? Take this busty babe out of the box, push play on the hardcore DVD, get out the free lube, and pound this Mega Fuck Slut 'til you Fuck Her Silly! ... From her sexy shoulders to her wide round hips, flat stomach, and perfectly puffy pussy, *she's the perfect woman ... without the attitude and headaches! ... She's warm, she's tight, and she NEVER says no!* Real women aren't flat on the bottom side, and neither is this fuck slut! Both sides of this buxom beauty are ready for your dick! Sit her up, lay her on her side, put her on the counter top or table ... *she's ready to please you in any position you can think of.* She's *all yours* to enjoy, every inch of her! ... Face down, ass up, *that's the way she likes to fuck! She loves missionary, doggie, spooning from the side, whatever position you can come up with, she's game! ...* When you're done, blow a load deep inside her or cum all over her stomach and big tits ... *No commitments, no bullshit, and no worries about knocking her up. It's an all access, any time-any place piece of pussy and ass made for your cock!*
(http://www.hustlerstore.com/pdx-mega-fuck-slut.html,
August 2, 2012, emphasis added)

Real men do not always come off well in the comparison with realistic vibrators and dildos. But the comparisons made in this product description function rather differently. Here, the product is anthropomorphized. The potential buyer is invited to construct a fantasy around "her" perpetual sexual readiness that naturalizes his desires as "hers" and emphasizes his lack of responsibility and commitment. That this script is essentially pornographic—and, indeed, assumes that sex toys are used in conjunction with porn—should not be surprising from Hustler brand promotions. Product descriptions on Hustler's site vary in the level of pornographic detail and fantasy, but the most prominently displayed products are of women's body parts. These include Cyberskin Virtual Sweetheart in Medium (the medium referring to skin tone), which offers two "tunnels"—vaginal and anal—for disembodied penetration; the Pdx Titty Fuck Her, a pair of breasts placed directly above a vaginal-like opening; the Pdx Fuck my Face, offered in both blonde and brunette; and the Pdx Fuck Me Silly! 3, a "lifelike lower half of a woman" with pussy, ass, and long legs. Women's bodies are literally atomized here; they are holes to be penetrated, surfaces to be ejaculated on.

The relationship between product and person is further complicated by dolls featuring a screen print of a porn star's face and toys molded on the bodies of porn performers. In this latter category are "fleshlights"—so called because the product resembles a flashlight, only you remove the lid to find a masturbator, molded to resemble a vagina, mouth, or anus. Fleshlight or doll, what is being sold is not simply the promise of "sex" but an opportunity to extend the pornographic script by simulating the experience of sex with a *particular* woman who—through her existence in porn—is already understood to exist primarily as a receptacle of male fantasies (and fluids):

> The Sasha Grey blow up sex doll immortalises one of the hottest porn stars on the planet and brings her to you to enjoy at home whenever you like. A 3 hole inflatable doll featuring a screen print of Sasha's gorgeous face for maximum pleasure and play ... enjoy Sasha's pert and curvy body from the moment you pump her full of air. Made from seamed PVC with a beautiful screen printed face and hair to capture Sasha Grey's gorgeous looks, this realistic inflatable doll features moulded breasts with perky nipples to fondle during play. Standing at 5'2" feet, Sasha is beautifully petite and very flexible. Once she has been filled with air, she can be easily posed and held in place for maximum enjoyment. Sasha has 3 holes to enjoy, allowing you to emulate oral sex, anal sex and vaginal sex. Her mouth is 4.5 inches deep and fully primed to give you a slippery blow job and her tight ass and vagina both measure 5.5 inches deep and have separate entrances and inner canals for the most realistic of sensations.
>
> (www.lovehoney.com, August 2, 2012)

Doll and performer are collapsed into one. While I do not suggest that consumers would confuse one with another, the commodification of bodies here is qualitatively different than the realistic toys for women discussed above. What is being sold is an explicit extension of the pornographic fantasy in which *specific* women are not only ever-ready and ever-willing, but are also desiring of, or sated by, whatever the male consumer wants. The customer is always right.

Finally, realistic dildos and vibrators have also been molded from male porn performers. However, the overwhelming majority of "molded" toys of this kind focus on performers known primarily for gay porn. Although this article focuses on heterosexually oriented products and industries, this perhaps suggests how commodification and objectification of the bodies of others is an unexceptional aspect of the industrial construction of contemporary Western male sexuality *per se*.

## Conclusion

These examples suggest that commercial sex and the commercialization of sex are—in many ways—interlinked phenomena. However, comparing these phenomena across texts targeting male and female consumers is revealing of continuing inequalities that cannot be understood independently of a broader analysis of gender, sex, and power. Comparing women's purchase of a vibrator to men's purchase of a woman makes sense only if we are only concerned with sexual pleasure as it is experienced by those who consume. Whatever it is or is not, the sex of prostitution, pornography, and "sex shows" is not "for its own sake" for those who perform it. It is for money, status perhaps. The performer's pleasure is immaterial to the transaction.[5] To suggest simple equivalences disguises this fundamental inequality and lets men avoid answering what might be difficult questions about what they are buying (into). If we are being asked to participate in a culture—and in a culture of exchange—in which the demands made on/by men have not fundamentally changed, and, indeed, in which commercial sex is being normalized in other contexts, then no matter how "empowered" an individual woman may be by her sexualized consumption practices or her embrace of sex work it does nothing to change or challenge fundamental inequalities.

## Notes

1 See user reviews on IMDb. The link between the two franchises was commented on more fully following the close theatrical release dates of *Sex and the City 2* (Patrick King 2011) and *The Hangover Part 2* (Phillips 2011).

2 In re-viewing the female-oriented online sex businesses discussed by Attwood, as well as examining newer UK sites (lovehoney.com) and large US retailers (hustler.com and thebigsextoystore.com) for this chapter, I found that Attwood's 2005 arguments still largely pertain.

3 Whilst Dunn (2010) presents this as cause for uncritical celebration, Tyler (2011) offers a more critical and extensive feminist analysis of the connections between the pornographic and sexological construction of Western women's sexuality.

4 The positioning of male viewers as potential "johns" in television documentaries focused on the sex industry is similar (Boyle 2008).

5 This does not mean that performers never experience sexual pleasure, but this is not the premise of the transaction.

# References

Attwood, F. (2005) "Fashion and Passion: Marketing Sex to Women," *Sexualities* 8(4): 392–406.

——(ed.) (2009a) *Mainstreaming Sex: The Sexualisation of Western Culture*, London: I. B. Tauris.

——(2009b) "Intimate Adventures: Sex Blogs, Sex 'Blooks' and Women's Sexual Narration," *European Journal of Cultural Studies* 12(1): 5–20.

——(2010) "Call-girl Diaries: New Representations of Cosmopolitan Sex Work," *Feminist Media Studies* 10(1): 109–12.

Boyle, K. (2008) "Courting Consumers and Legitimating Exploitation: The Representation of Commercial Sex in Television Documentaries," *Feminist Media Studies* 8(1): 35–50.

——(2010) "Selling the Selling of Sex: *The Secret Diary of a Call Girl* on Screen," *Feminist Media Studies* 10(1): 113–16.

——(2011a) "'That's So Fun!': Selling Pornography for Men to Women in *The Girls Next Door*," in G. Dines and J. Humez (eds.) *Gender, Race, and Class in Media: A Text-Reader*, 3rd edition, Thousand Oaks, CA: Sage.

——(2011b) "Producing Abuse: Selling the Harms of Pornography," *Women's Studies International Forum* 34(6): 593–602.

Coy, M. and M. Garner (2012) "Definitions, Discourses, and Dilemmas: Policy and Academic Engagement with the Sexualisation of Popular Culture," *Gender and Education* 24(3): 285–301.

Dunn, J. (2010) "HBO's *Cathouse*: Problematising Representations of Sex Workers and Sexual Women," *Feminist Media Studies* 10(1): 105–8.

Gavey, N. (2012) "Beyond 'Empowerment'? Sexuality in a Sexist World," *Sex Roles* 66: 718–24.

Gill, R. (2008) "Empowerment/Sexism: Figuring Female Sexual Agency in Contemporary Advertising," *Feminism & Psychology* 18(1): 35–60.

——(2012) "Media, Empowerment and the 'Sexualisation of Culture' Debates," *Sex Roles* 66: 736–45.

Holland, S. (2010) *Pole Dancing, Empowerment and Embodiment*, London: Palgrave Macmillan.

Jameson, J. and N. Strauss (2004) *How to Make Love Like a Porn Star: A Cautionary Tale*, New York: HarperCollins.

Ringrose, J., R. Gill, S. Livingstone, and L. Harvey (2012) *A Qualitative Study of Children, Young People, and "Sexting,"* London: NSPCC.

Smith, C. (2007) "Designed for Pleasure: Style, Indulgence and Accessorised Sex," *European Journal of Cultural Studies* 10(2): 167–84.

Storr, M. (2003) *Latex & Lingerie: Shopping for Pleasure at Ann Summers Parties*, Oxford: Berg.

Tyler, M. (2011) *Selling Sex Short: The Pornographic and Sexological Construction of Women's Sexuality in the West*, Newcastle-upon-Tyne: Cambridge Scholars Publishing.

Whitehead, K. and T. Kurz (2009) "Empowerment and the Pole: A Discursive Investigation of the Reinvention of Pole Dancing as a Recreational Activity," *Feminism & Psychology* 19(2): 224–44.

# 24
# Class, gender, and the docusoap
## The Only Way Is Essex

## Heather Nunn and Anita Biressi

The contemporary docusoap articulates a postfeminist, neoliberal social field in which relations of class and gender are renegotiated and refashioned. Docusoaps encourage individuals to participate in consumer culture and to regard makeover practices as the route to social success. This chapter explores how this is conveyed in the successful British series *The Only Way Is Essex* (*TOWIE*, ITV2). *TOWIE*, which began in 2010, is a semi-scripted, highly structured series which, in docusoap fashion, combines "the observation and interpretation of reality found in documentary with the continuing narrative centring on a group of characters in soap opera" (Bignell and Orlebar 2005: 112). Broadcast twice weekly and focusing on a small network of friends in neighboring towns in Essex in the south of England, it quickly became a commercial success, winning an Audience British Academy Television Award (BAFTA) in 2011 and propelling its protagonists into the media spotlight. It has been referred to as both "constructed reality" and "dramality;" both terms signal its hybrid blending of dramaturgy and non-professional performers to produce multiple ongoing "real" storylines and manufactured melodramatic situations. In terms of both content and structure, *TOWIE*'s deployment of regular performers and contrived narratives have helped fuel a reinvigoration of the docusoap genre, which originally dominated British TV screens in the mid- to late 1990s.

The 1990s docusoap was a new kind of observational documentary distinguished by an emphasis on entertainment, strong personalities, soap opera style, fast editing, and a prominent voiceover (Bruzzi 2000: 76). The focus was on characters "grouped together by work, pleasure or place/institution" (Bruzzi 2000: 78). The docusoap was also notable for its focus on the ordinary and the everyday, as conveyed through close attention to participants' minor challenges, relationships, and views. While some of these deployed family settings, many more were devoted to workplace locations, as indicated by titles such as *Airport*, *Driving School*, *Hotel*, *The Cruise*, *Children's Hospital*, and *Holiday Reps*. These were series in which service, leisure, or caring duties guaranteed lively interactions between workers and the general public. While the boundaries between fact and fiction formerly established by the classic observational documentary format were somewhat relaxed, contemporaneous audiences still expected that the docusoap should not be fake; that its characters should be authentic and relatively unschooled in appearing before the camera. There was also far less expectation then than now that participants' involvement would be motivated by a desire for fame or that featuring in an observational documentary would be a route to celebrity "well-knowness" (Boorstin 1992: 57). However, the selection of characters by producers and their evident performance for the camera revealed the complex negotiation and recognition by all concerned of the creative enhancement of actuality (Kilborn 2003: 107–8). Filmmakers and audiences of the 1990s privileged the seemingly spontaneous, natural, and relatively uncontrived performances of docusoap characters, their engaging anecdotes and occasional eccentricity, and the day-to-day routine of their lives. As one media professional observed of such series, these were "structured round characters who didn't have big stories to tell, but rather round big characters with small stories to tell" (quoted in Kilborn 2003: 96).

The docusoap's depiction of the ordinary and the everyday also arguably produced narratives and scenarios of social class and class difference (albeit sometimes in displaced form). For example, early docusoaps often focused on social situations such as weddings, neighborhood disputes, and family conflicts; these knowingly exposed behaviors and attitudes rooted in snobbery, social competitiveness, over-investment in material goods, and so on (Biressi and Nunn 2005: 36–59). Docusoap characters were thereby figures of fascination because of their conduct and lifestyles, which were set out in detail across episodes and multiple storylines. Many critical responses to the early docusoaps and to reality TV (of which docusoap is a fore-runner) were "couched within discourses of (class) taste" (Holmes 2010: 251). Nearly two decades after the emergence of docusoaps, constructed reality shows such as TOWIE continue to prompt new scholarly debates about popular factual television's articulation of lifestyle and class codes. But the focus has necessarily shifted from the depiction of unremarkable subjects and their routine life (the nurse, the police officer, the hotel worker, the ordinary family) to extraordinary subjects and to the more spectacular coding of their taste and lifestyle practices, of shopping and leisure (e.g. Leppert and Wilson 2008; Grindstaff 2011; Klein 2011; Allen and Mendick 2012).

As with Jersey Shore (MTV, 2009–) and The Hills (MTV, 2006–10), to which TOWIE has been likened, TOWIE has attracted a mixed critical reception for its depiction of a particular social set by showcasing its members' lifestyles, tastes, values, ambitions, and mores. Naysayers tend to latch on to the protagonists' shallow narcissism and flashy characteristics; they explicitly link these with supposedly com-promised gender roles (feminized image-obsessed men and over-assertive women) and lower-class personal traits (tastelessness, brashness, etc.) (see Tyler 2007). So, for example, "quality TV drama" fans, who were clearly dismayed at the news that TOWIE had won the BAFTA award, made the following not untypical observations on YouTube:

> Genuinely? They? won? Over-tanned lads who pluck their own eyebrows and screaming girls who are thick as shit won … ?
>
> Thick, fake, cheap, and common as dirt. They are an absolute joke to the industry, and horrible examples for young people to follow. The fact they won an award is an indictment on a vast, shallow underclass in our

society. ... We can only watch as the next generation takes a massive cultural backward step, and men lose more respect for women.
(http://www.youtube.com/watch?v=L45o7Mzjq4k)

So while *TOWIE*'s British viewers regard the setting and activities as aspirational and even glamorous (clubs and gyms, beauty salons, high-end shopping, etc.), its characters are nonetheless coded as symbolically and culturally working or lower class (Allen and Mendick 2012: 8). As Laura Grindstaff (2011: 199) observed in relation to *Jersey Shore*, the display of cultural characteristics enables these shows to produce a kind of "social script" in which the performance of "class-as-culture" is as significant as, or even more significant than, the economic and material conditions from which class difference is said to emanate.

After describing the development of the docusoap and summarizing recent scholarship on social class, this chapter outlines recent theories of classed identities and their relationship to consumption practices. It indicates how these intersect with formations of gender and gender roles in the context of postfeminism. We then outline the establishment of Essex as a region of conspicuous consumption and celebrity ambition; media pundits read its inhabitants as emblematic class figures. We end by addressing what *TOWIE*'s representations of gender and class tell us about the manufacture of structured reality docusoap and contemporary articulations of social class.

## Class, work, consumerism, and gender

Many argue that the rise of consumerist practices, the political promotion of individual aspiration, and the expansion of employment based in the cultural, information, retail, and service industries helped produce post-class Western societies (see Joyce 1995: 3–6; Biressi and Nunn 2013). New avenues into consumption, such as easy credit, together with growing affluence, have helped to produce not so much a new way of life but new "lifestyles" in which the presentation of the self through the adoption of selected goods and services becomes fundamentally important. In 1987 Mike Featherstone explained the widespread up-take of the vocabulary of "lifestyle" as being predicated on the marketer's mantra that rules no longer exist; there are only choices. Moreover, choices made by consuming individuals were what determined their individuality, their self-presentation, and ultimately their social identity. As such, this narrative of choice implied a move away from or beyond classed identities to a post-class social field in which status, affiliation, and ambition arose from and were shaped by the individual practices of the consuming self and sustained by a meritocratic model of social progress (Giddens 1991; Beck 1992; Lash and Urry 1994; Pakulski and Waters 1996). For example, advertising invites subjects to buy items because "it's all about you" or to "create your own legend." From this perspective, as Mark Tomlinson (1998: 2–3) explains, the social field as a complex and uneven formation becomes "flattened" out; the dominant vision is of a level arena in which all individuals can choose to consume and perform in ways which allow them to disaggregate from classed formations and other collectives. Or, put differently, social mobility and social success become predicated on individual decisions and are marked by the accoutrements of the consuming self. Karen Sternheimer, whose work addresses the pursuit of the American dream through media celebrity success, says we increasingly learn to "see ourselves as consumers first, workers second" (2011: 14).

Arguably at the intersection of all of these practices and social changes is an essentially gendered economy, one which has been significantly revised to take into account the changes cited above. So, for example, historically an enduring ideological characterization of men was as economic producers, industry workers, and income providers. Women were consumers, service workers, carers, and homemakers (see Savage 2000: 137). Connected to this was the inference that while men remade the world (and perhaps themselves) through work and public action, women essentially remade themselves and their far smaller and more socially restricted world of home, leisure, and family. This characterization was always dubious and open to contestation; it was also a social mapping that not only identified men and women as occupying different social, public, and private realms but also maintained that these roles were natural, proper, and socially desirable. At any rate, in the late twentieth to early twenty-first century the conventional divisions between "feminine" and "masculine" occupations, duties, and preoccupations are being eroded or redrawn in Western economies and the markers of gender identity are being renegotiated together with those of social class (see Attwood 2005). So, for instance, in consumerist terms, the cosmetics, fashion, and lifestyle industries target both women and men consumers, and men have colonized television lifestyle and makeover shows as experts and advisors. So, too, women are seen expressing ambitions to be successful in public arenas; many appear to thrive in the new post-industrial world of flexible work and consumer-based leisure. However, Angela McRobbie has astutely argued in her critique of the popular and political field of postfeminism and its compromised meshing with a neoliberal economic agenda that new forms of gender power have emerged "that seek to manage the requirements of the new global economy and the availability of a feminised workforce through producing and seeing changes for women" (2009: 7). She suggests that the instrumental subject positions available to young women in particular "as part of a process of substitution and displacement" merely *appear* to "offer possibilities for freedom and change in their social position and status" (2009: 7). These "freedoms" weave through neoliberal capitalist-fueled fantasies of a world in which all individuals can carve out upwardly mobile, securely employed lives enjoying political and social equality (see also Berlant 2011; Negra 2009).

As McRobbie's (2009: 128–34) discussion of the TV makeover shows of the early 2000s has shown, popular factual television has promoted and reinforced the allegedly liberated post-class, postfeminist experience, not only in images of the consuming embodied self, but also through representations of certain types of post-industrial work and meritocratic success. Images of women as entrepreneurs, innovators, and business leaders were also coming to the fore. As the reality TV arena became increasingly crowded and competitive it also mirrored these new models of competitive work and leisure. For example, reality participants often declare: "I'm not here to make friends, I'm here to win." This declaration is heard so routinely that YouTube users regularly upload annual "supercut" montages featuring pushy participants defiantly declaring their intention to succeed at any cost. These ongoing reconfigurations of gendered and classed identity in relation to work and leisure also play out in exaggerated form in constructed reality docusoaps. As such they can inspire both fascination and unease. Character, ambition, and consumerist self-production arguably mask felt inequities of gender or class via the pursuit of social success and status.

## *The Only Way Is Essex*: Essex Girl and Essex Man

Long before the advent of *TOWIE*, Essex was presented in journalism and television as a place in which certain formations of social class and gender were writ large. From the mid- to late 1980s onwards, as neoliberalism increasingly took hold of the political imaginary, Essex citizens were often rhetorically linked to new right conservative political values, to pushy social aspirations and flashy consumption. This landscape was populated in media mythology by the figures of so-called Essex Man and Essex Girl. Rather akin to the Italian American Guido characters who feature in *Jersey Shore*, Essex people became the focus of sharp-tongued disparagement of the kind usually reserved for those who dare to rise above their social class. They attracted critical reactions which, we have argued, revealed a distinct nervousness about the "don't care" aggressive entrepreneurialism with which they were associated, and the ways in which this was linked to shifts in class belonging and normative gender roles (Biressi and Nunn 2013).

In comic and political sketches Essex Man was most often associated with entrepreneurial money-making and boom economics. He was presented as someone who valued branded clothes and expensive cars, and showed little respect for his elders and betters. Far less associated with the world of work, Essex Girl was repeatedly presented as a figure of gross hyper-consumption and sexual exhibitionism. The usually misogynistic jokes frequently made about Essex Girls from the 1990s onwards relied on the audience's assumed commonly shared assumptions about class, consumerism, and (bad) taste. As research on class and gender (e.g. Skeggs 1997, 2004) has already highlighted, working-class women have always had to negotiate historically embedded and tricky notions of respectability and proper conduct. Essex Girls appeared to disrupt these conventions altogether by adopting a polished exterior and by generating economic and social worth through an overt and unembarrassed investment in their dress and personal appearance (see Skeggs 2005). As such, more recently, the Essex Girl has also been disparaged as a female "chav:" an insult similar to the US insult "white trash," used to yoke white working-class femininity to broader social anxieties about unconfined sexuality, misdirected consumption, and social nonconformity.

So when *TOWIE* arrived in 2010 British audiences already understood the significance of its Essex setting and the promise of a show offering a platform for Essex characters to play out their love lives, their leisure, and their ambitions in hyperbolic fashion. The show's introduction anticipates the excessive glamour referenced throughout, with a voiceover declaring: "This program contains flash cars, big watches and extreme posing." This is followed by a Bond movie pastiche featuring a glittering parade of silhouetted sharp-suited young men and sexy women, rounded off by the appearance of the *TOWIE* ensemble cast accessorized with jewels and Chihuahuas (one of the many references to Hollywood celebrity lifestyles). All of this is set to the 1988 pop song hit "The Only Way Is Up." Other series trailers and lead-ins feature country houses, golfing clubs, and nightclubs, and carry a wealth of signifiers of explicit and unembarrassed financial success, such as personalized car number plates, champagne, and Jacuzzis. The show features a regular cast in their twenties and early thirties; a supporting cast includes a few older relatives and extended friendship groups. Their "real-life" jobs are mostly situated in the leisure and entertainment industries, reportedly including employment as a nightclub promoter, models, a beautician, hair salon and fashion shop owners, a financial manager, and a property developer.

It is entertainment television and especially reality formats such as lifestyle makeover and talent competition shows such as *Pop Idol* and structured docusoaps such as *TOWIE* that reveal the shifting terrain of gender and class sketched out above. Self-presentation, self-branding, and self-promotion are fundamental to the success of participants, who function both as so-called ordinary people and as performers whose own future social advancement might depend upon their marketable appeal as celebrity subjects (Hearn 2008). Consequently *TOWIE* emphasizes style and appearance. As youth-focused television (in which very few older characters feature in any depth) both men and women seem to embrace wholeheartedly the importance of looking good and/or of undergoing makeovers to improve their appeal, whether they intend to run a successful nightclub or become a celebrity superstar. Diane Negra argues that this drive to look good for the purposes of social success is "one of the most distinctive features of the post-feminist era" (2009: 119). Negra suggests that an overwhelming social imperative to sustain an elaborate personal grooming regime runs alongside a "growing frankness" about sexuality. This frankness is most apparent in what Ariel Levy (2005) has referred to as "raunch culture," in which consumerism and media culture together insist that women should embrace, and are even empowered by, sexual exhibitionism. This wider cultural and indeed economic transformation is evidenced in what Negra (2009: 119) has called the "new treatment industries"—nail bars, day spas, bronzing parlors, and so forth. Such places have become a ubiquitous feature of pedestrian areas and shopping malls and feature heavily in shows such as *TOWIE*.

## Loveable, outrageous, loud, ambitious

The majority of *TOWIE* time is devoted to repetitious scenarios of pleasure, personal indulgence, and opportunities to party, naturally providing platforms for this kind of exhibitionism and self-management (see Woods 2012). The distinctive features of the postfeminist era as outlined by Negra, McRobbie, and others are vigorously celebrated and the new treatment industries in their minor (e.g. salons) and major (e.g. plastic surgery) forms feature prominently. For example, in Series 4 Lauren P. and her friend Chloe visit the "Make Yourself Amazing" cosmetic surgery center, where their initially serious and intimate conversation soon turns into humorous banter. Lauren consults with a plastic surgeon following a public health scare concerning PIP breast implants and learns that she will need a scan and possibly further surgery. Again, while she seems initially fearful, the scene soon shifts register when the women start joking around with specimen implants while being observed, with some bemusement, by the male middle-class professional surgeon. Scenes such as this, which counterpoint *TOWIE* characters with responsible outsiders (a common trope of the series), signal the absurdity of the characters' taste and lifestyle choices by implying a shallow understanding of the consequences of their actions. Nonetheless, the constant repetition of such scenes (for both men and women) may also normalize the wider field of beauty treatment and surgery as both necessary and trivial everyday practices. As Chloe makes clear when she confides in Lauren P. about the traumas of childbirth, whatever the situation, a woman should look her best and wear full make-up.

The ethos here is also of luxury life-styling as a reasonable expectation for young people and of "luxury commodities and experiences as transformative, renewing, and life-affirming" (Negra 2009: 125). The vitality and regenerative qualities of extravagance are most strikingly portrayed via the constant partying which forms the major set-pieces in *TOWIE*. No opportunity is overlooked to create spaces for play, including Halloween, Christmas, venue launches, vacations, and even a séance. For example, an episode in Series 2 follows Amy's 16-year-old gay cousin Harry as he plans—from inception to the big day—his spectacular fancy dress birthday party. Harry, who is too young to consume alcohol legally, nonetheless plans a huge affair with a bar, music, decorations, and high-end glamour. In *TOWIE* the party requires a celebrity-style reveal in which a cohort of semi-nude male models carry in Harry, dressed as performer Lady Gaga. The party then becomes the arena in which friendships are tested and love-matches formed.

While most *TOWIE* storylines follow group and pair friendships and romantic entanglements, a significant, albeit far smaller, number chart the pursuit of potentially lucrative successful employment, especially in the spheres of media and celebrity culture. The labor of *TOWIE* in terms of the work of the performers is amplified through the narrative pursuit of enduring public visibility outside and beyond the lifecycle of the series. For instance, the 2011 series sporadically followed the formation by four cast members of the all-girl pop group *Lola* (an acronym for loveable, outrageous, loud, ambitious), Lauren's placement at an agency as a recruiter of male models, and Amy's attempt to become a fashion model and Katie Price-style celebrity in her own right. These storylines emphasize preparation to secure these plum roles rather than the work involved in the careers themselves; preparation includes extensive salon treatments and endless playful speculation about future stardom.

Short scenes also highlight the negotiations involved as each individual tries to establish the right connections to succeed in the "real" world, rather than what we might think of as the "fake" world of *TOWIE*. So viewers witness Amy's disappointment when informed by a modeling agency that she is only suitable for men's "glamour" modeling (downmarket topless modeling associated with the tabloid press and therefore not her ideal choice) because her breast implants would not meet the requirements of its more upmarket advertising clients. She soon concedes that glamour work is her only option after the photographer persuades her that this is the route to fame. More serious hurdles in the workplace are also dealt with in cursory fashion. Viewers only briefly see, for instance, the devastation caused to Lauren G.'s salon after it is vandalized by a local citizen (Series 4), before the show moves on to its usual upbeat subject matter of relationships and parties. More positively, perhaps, viewers watch *Lola* being offered a chance to record a track and assemble a marketing portfolio by Universal Studios. Cast members are also intermittently filmed running small business enterprises such as a beauty salon (rather comically situated in the front room of a suburban house), a bijoux fashion boutique, and a nightclub. These environments usually offer amusing peeks into the leisure industries and provide even more opportunities for the deployment of the sexual double entendres which are a constant feature of the show. Shops such as the provisionally entitled "Lauren's LA Blow Bar" opened by Lauren G. in the 2012 series tend to serve more as intimate venues for the exchange of gossip (mostly but not always between women) rather than workplaces.

If *TOWIE* masks or denies the real labor of income generation and paid work, so, too, the felt reality of social class is highlighted only to be diminished and its implications dismissed. The show exhibits a knowing playfulness about social class and the changing contours of what were formerly working-class ways of life (or at least as these have been mythologized). Thus, the older generation, mainly grandparents, are established both as a link with the past and as an endearing but amusing connection to the present. Grandmothers Nanny Pat and Nanny Brighton usually make appearances to establish a dramatic contrast between a traditional British (working-class) past and the modern, glamorous seemingly classless or post-class Americanized present. This is most evident when Nanny Brighton arrives at Harry's fancy dress party perfectly attired as Queen Elizabeth (accompanied by the anthem "Rule Britannia") while the younger people wear extremely scanty contemporary costumes. Scenes such as the unannounced appearance of Nanny Pat at grandson Mark's glossy modern apartment, in which she arrives with her homemade bread pudding and a sympathetic ear, likewise signal the continuity of family affection and family values while providing evidence of dramatic social change. The striking incongruity of the two characters eating traditional thrifty comfort food in an affluent setting concludes with Mark, Nanny, and Jess (a member of *Lola*) drinking champagne to toast Jess' future success. Similarly, Nanny Brighton supposedly turns up unannounced to keep an eye on her grandson after his four-year relationship with his girlfriend breaks down. Having found him and the lads horsing about in their pajamas in the middle of the day, she declares: "Oh James, what are you doing? Mummy said, would I have a look in on you ... to make sure you are behaving yourself."

Playful class reflection also takes place in a scene in which Lydia announces to her mother Debbie (Series 4) that she intends to take elocution lessons. Lydia declares: "I've decided I no longer want to speak like an Essex girl." While social class and social expectations become the focus of their discussion, these are closely oriented around love relationships and family and the securing of a better class of life partner. Lydia explains, "I just really want my next man to be, like ... instead of being, like, 'Oh come on, love, I'll take you down Sugar Hut for a pint ... [adopts posh accent] oh Lydia let's go to the museum or go and see the opera.'" The discussion disintegrates into parody and laughter as they speculate about what would happen when Lydia's upper-class suitor was taken to meet the family. "Then what?" asks Debbie. "It will be like meeting the Fockers," referencing the successful culture-clash Hollywood film.

Radically differing social expectations regularly cause more serious disputes between Kirk, whose gender roles values are presented as being fairly conservative, and his ambitious girlfriend Amy (Series 2, 2011). In one scene Kirk remonstrates strongly with Amy for wanting to pursue glamour modeling: "It's a good thing, it's a good career, but do you want people just to have your pictures because you've got your bangers [breasts] out?" Amy makes clear that, regardless, she will do as she likes. Kirk also consults his mother Julie about Amy's preference for affluent settings and expensive nights out: "She likes all the nice restaurants and stuff but that ain't me. … She ain't up for, you know, cinema, cheap restaurants and stuff like that." Julie reassures him that he has to be himself in his relationships until she learns that he intends to take Amy to the zoo. "Take her up the drink [wine bar]," Julie advises. Despite this advice and Amy's lack of enthusiasm ("I think you should be taking me out for a nice dinner"), he persists, with disastrous consequences. Their zoo date only serves to highlight their contrasting values more starkly: she arrives in glamorous celebrity style, while he, according to Amy, dresses like a zoo-keeper.

## Conclusion

We have only briefly indicated here how structured reality shows such as *TOWIE* represent a distinct departure from the original docusoap format and how this impacts on the ways in which audiences and critics understand the roles and functions of its characters as classed and gendered figures. Su Holmes (2010: 251) recently noted the growing perception that the "ordinary" people who were once lionized as the ideal participants of these genres are now giving way to those who can offer a "'semi-professional' type of performance." If this is so, then the integrity of the performers is liable to be read quite differently now, compared to casts of the docusoaps of earlier decades. In the earlier docusoaps characters were judged on the basis of their authenticity and "realness" as (classed) individuals who were often working in unglamorous low-reward jobs in unremarkable settings. As already noted, the shows themselves were usually accepted as legitimate documentary, even though they relaxed the rules once governing the form. In the new structured reality shows, performers must engage with what might be called a post-reality TV calibration of the emotional, personal, and especially presentational skills required to be a popular character in the present moment. In other words, they no longer need to be genuine. Instead they must be entertaining.

More specifically, *TOWIE* is a social world placing a premium on hyper-groomed appearance. Elaborate and costly grooming is figured as a necessary everyday practice. As McRobbie (2009: 7, 124–5) has noted, young women have become "more autonomously feminized (and glamorized) in their class identity." They are encouraged to participate in consumer culture and makeover practices as the passport to individual recognition and social success. For young men, too, the *TOWIE* message is that the manufacture of the successful self demands paying attention to their self-presentation to a degree once only stereotypically associated with pampered femininity and with those for whom leisure was their main pastime. As noted above, for critics of the show, this overt and shameless attention to the self and to the exhibition of the self inspires an unease related to both class and gender. Performers are criticized for being classless (rather than post-class), unrespectable, and for refusing to conform to common standards of masculine and feminine behavior. But the skills and practices undertaken by *TOWIE* stars can also be read as necessary post-class competencies that enable them to be not only real Essex girls and guys but also to become successful actor-celebrities. Here performers work to create their own social advancement through their own self-fashioning and through their effective operation in the media, consumer, and service industries rather than in the more traditional arenas of meritocratic social advancement. We might say, then, that the characters in *TOWIE* (together with their obsessions, lifestyles, and conduct) are both ordinary and extraordinary. As such they inhabit, albeit in hyperbolic cartoon fashion, a post-class, postfeminist social, economic, and cultural field and one in which the pressures to perform will feel familiar to many.

# References

Allen, K. and H. Mendick (2012) "Keeping It Real? Social Class, Young People and Authenticity in Reality TV," *Sociology* 46(5): 1–17.

Attwood, F. (2005) "Inside Out: Men on the Home Front," *Journal of Consumer Culture* 5(1) (March): 87–107.

Beck, U. (1992) *The Risk Society*, London: Sage.

Berlant, L. (2011) *Cruel Optimism*, Durham, NC: Duke University Press.

Bignell, J. and J. Orlebar (2005) *The Television Handbook*, 3rd edition, London: Routledge.

Biressi, A. and H. Nunn (2005) *Reality TV: Realism and Revelation*, London: Wallflower.

——(2013) *Class and Contemporary British Culture*, London: Palgrave Macmillan.

Boorstin, D. (1992 [1962]) *The Image: A Guide to Pseudo-Events in America*, New York: Vintage.

Bruzzi, S. (2000) *New Documentary: A Critical Introduction*, London: Routledge.

Featherstone, M. (1987) "Lifestyle and Consumer Culture," *Theory, Culture & Society* 4: 55–70.

Giddens, A. (1991) *Modernity and Self-Identity*, Cambridge: Polity.

Grindstaff, L. (2011) "From *Jerry Springer* to *Jersey Shore*: The Cultural Politics of Class in/on US Reality Programming," in Beverly Skeggs and Helen Wood (eds.) *Real Class: Ordinary People and Reality Television across National Spaces*, London: British Film Institute, pp. 197–209.

Hearn, A. (2008) "Variations on the Branded Self: Theme, Invention, Improvisation and Inventory," in D. Hesmondhalgh and J. Toynbee (eds.) *The Media and Social Theory*, London: Routledge, pp. 194–210.

Holmes, S. (2010) "Reality TV and 'Ordinary People': Revisiting Celebrity, Performance, and Authenticity," in N. Carpentier and S. van Bauwel (eds.) *Trans-Reality TV: The Transgression of Reality, Genre, Politics and Audience*, Plymouth: Lexington Books, pp. 251–74.

Joyce, P. (ed.) (1995) *Class*, Oxford: Oxford University Press.

Kilborn, R. (2003) *Staging the Real: Factual TV Programming in the Age of Big Brother*, Manchester: Manchester University Press.

Klein, A. (2011) "The Hills, Jersey Shore and the Aesthetics of Class," in *Flow TV*. http://flowtv.org/2011/04/the-hills-jersey-shore-and-the-aesthetics-of-class/.

Lash, S. and J. Urry (1994) *Economies of Signs and Space*, London: Sage.

Leppert, A. and J. Wilson (2008) "Living the Hills Life: Lauren Conrad as Reality Star, Soap Opera Heroine and Brand," *Genders* 48. http://www.genders.org/g48/g48_leppertwilson.html.

Levy, A. (2005) *Female Chauvinist Pigs: Women and the Rise of Raunch Culture*, New York: Free Press.

McRobbie, A. (2009) *The Aftermath of Feminism: Gender, Culture and Social Change*, London: Sage.

Negra, D. (2009) *What a Girl Wants? Fantasizing the Reclamation of Self in Postfeminism*, London: Routledge.

Pakulski, J. and M. Waters (1996) *The Death of Class*, London: Sage.

Raeside, J. (2011) "A Different Kind of Reality TV." http://www.guardian.co.uk/tv-and-radio/2011/jun/01/reality-tv-only-way-essex.

Savage, M. (2000) *Class Analysis and Social Transformation*, Buckingham: Open University Press.

Skeggs, B. (1997) *Formations of Class and Gender: Becoming Respectable*, London: Sage.

——(2004) "The Re-branding of Class: Propertising Culture," in F. Devine, M. Savage, J. Scott, and R. Crompton (eds.) (2005) *Rethinking Class: Cultures, Identities and Lifestyles*, Basingstoke: Palgrave Macmillan, pp. 46–68.

——(2005) "The Making of Class and Gender through Visualizing Moral Subject Formation," *Sociology* 39(5): 965–82.

Sternheimer, K. (2011) *Celebrity Culture and the American Dream*, London: Routledge.

Tomlinson, M. (1998) "Lifestyle and Social Classes," CRIC Discussion Paper no. 9, Manchester: Centre for Research on Innovation and Competition/University of Manchester.

Tyler, I. (2007) "From 'The Me Decade' to 'The Me Millennium': The Cultural History of Narcissism," *International Journal of Cultural Studies* 10(3): 343–63.

Woods, F. (2012) "Classed Femininity, Performativity and British Structured Reality Programming," *Television and New Media* 13(6): 1–18.

# 25

# Society's emerging femininities

## Neoliberal, postfeminist, and hybrid identities on television in South Africa

## Shelley-Jean Bradfield

In the final episode of the miniseries[1] of *Society* (2007), which aired on one of South African Broadcasting Corporation's (SABC) two public service channels, Inno, a young, thin, and beautiful black woman who supplements her limited salary as a "television weather girl" with gifts from wealthy suitors, is pictured in her messy apartment surrounded by 67 pairs of designer shoes. Inno tries to take comfort from her possessions even as she eludes her landlord, unable to pay her rent. With its emphasis on the lives and interests of upper-middle-class women who live out the success of the African dream, *Society* has been compared to the HBO drama *Sex and the City* (1998–2004), with its portrayal of conspicuous consumption and highly sexualized representations (Brown 2009). Yet, as a show populated almost solely by black women, and incorporating the particularities of the South African context beyond its glamorous setting in Johannesburg, *Society* offers a unique perspective on the feminine possibilities available to women in post-apartheid South Africa.

The drama's national distinctiveness is further established in series two (2009–10) when Inno spends the night with her extended family in a working-class township. Afraid to stay alone after being held at gunpoint, Inno is forced to confront her economic inadequacies. Not only can she not come up with her rent or taxi fare, Inno cannot meet her family's demands to help purchase their electricity or groceries. Desperate, Inno sells exclusive rights to a tabloid to feature her celebrity. The contrast between Inno's elite status as a member of the professional and middle class in South Africa and her and her family's inability to make ends meet highlights the complexity of living in the current moment in South Africa. In 2009, alongside a rising middle class, more than 31 percent of South Africa's citizens lived in poverty (World Bank Development Research Group 2012). These scenes emphasize the country's post-apartheid neoliberal orientation, and the preference for individual solutions to social problems, evident through Inno's decision to sell her story, even though social and economic inequality is a systemic issue. Finally, although Inno's vignette suggests the show's postfeminist sensibility by constructing her as an active subject, plot developments reveal the fragility of her sexual power. Jealously confronting her at gunpoint about her promiscuity, one of Inno's suitors contains her subjectivity by treating her as a sexual possession. Thus she is positioned as a victim of patriarchal regulation and violence.

Building on the few television shows that have centered women's experiences in post-apartheid South Africa,[2] such as *Home Affairs* (2005–9) on SABC1 and *Madam & Eve* (2000–5) on e.tv, *Society* explores the relationships between four young, black professional women, brought together by the suicide of a high-school friend. Akua, a stockbroker, is defined by her high-power career, convertible sports car, and beautiful home. Despite her accomplishments Akua wants more from life; she volunteers at a local orphanage, hoping, with or without a husband, to adopt a baby. Lois, a doctor, is married to her high-school sweetheart, yet resents the pregnancy that delays their emigration to the US. Lois turns to alcohol given the stress of her estrangement from her "colored" (mixed race) family at her marriage to a black man. Her alcohol intake increases with news of an unplanned pregnancy and her increasing alienation from her husband after he learns of her high-school abortion. Beth, a private-school teacher, plays the role of the token black employee in an otherwise all-white school. She lives with her photographer partner, Thuli, who issues Beth an ultimatum to "come out" to their friends and her colleagues or put the long-term relationship of the two women at risk.

Drawing on multiple associations, the show's title refers to burial "societies" established by black communities during apartheid. Prevented from participating in formal banking and investment institutions, black people often organized burial societies comprised of friends, family, or community to amass funding for funerals and care for members who had lost family (Calvin and Coetzee 2009). The show's four women initially form a burial society to help fund the funeral of Dineo, who commits suicide in the first episode. After the funeral, Akua encourages her three friends to remain connected by converting the burial society into a *stokvel*, an informal savings group used to distribute total earnings to a different member at each successive period (Calvin and Coetzee 2009). *Society*'s title also alludes to the aspirations of the new black middle class—the society to which all four female protagonists belong, or desire to belong. This reference evokes national tensions between nation-building objectives intended to unite South Africans based on individual rights (established through the transition to independence) and subsequent neoliberal policies that favor elite interests, maintaining the status quo of a large underclass without rights or access to middle-class privileges.

Examining the text of *Society* for its racial, gender, and class concerns, I take up Simone de Beauvoir (1953) and Judith Lorber's (2004) position that the meanings of identity markers are socially constructed, contingent on their historical and geographical contexts, and continually adapting to new forces and circumstances. Because they are processual rather than biological, identities defined by performance communicate social hierarchies, limit performance possibilities, and respond to the circumstances in which they are generated. Rosalind Gill and Christina Scharff speak of plural "femininities" to question how performances of gender are "lived, experienced and represented" (Gill and Scharff 2011: 2). This chapter follows suit by examining how femininities in post-apartheid South Africa are mediated in shows such as *Society*. Which feminine practices are incorporated into the show? What new performances of femininities are constructed in response to changing political and economic circumstances? How do class expectations and racial categories influence the range of feminine identities represented? I argue that television images of black, middle-class women negotiate the contradictions of a transitional society by constructing individual choice and responsibility as the underlying assumption of citizenship, adopting a postfeminist sensibility of sexual choice and empowerment, and establishing a preference for the traditional values of community and family as desirable racial and ethnic practices in post-apartheid South Africa. I focus specifically on the universal thematics of individual choice, hard work as the guarantee of success, *de facto* expectations of individual material gain and consumption, the seeming absence of patriarchy where women have equal access to economic and political power, women's willingness to sexualize and exploit their bodies in the service of their careers or material gain, and women's susceptibility to surveillance and self-reinvention.

## Neoliberalism and the "new" middle class

As the most pervasive form of governance on the contemporary global stage, David Harvey defines neoliberalism as "a theory of political economic practices that proposes that human well-being can best be advanced by liberating individual entrepreneurial freedoms and skills within an institutional framework characterized by strong private property rights, free markets and free trade" (Harvey 2005: 2). As such, neoliberals advocate individual freedom through a roll back of state regulation and social welfare; an emphasis on profitability through privatization; and recognition and education of individuals as self-autonomous, rational subjects responsible for their own destinies rather than as members of a collective (see Gill and Scharff 2011).

Conceiving of consumers as active entrepreneurs with the right to consume, neoliberal policies define consumption as a productive practice of a successful economy and selfhood (Friedman 1957). Although formalized neoliberalism is relatively recent to South Africa, Deborah Posel (2010) sketches out the state's long history of distinguishing between racial groups through their capacity or freedom to consume. During apartheid, racial definitions functioned to regulate the right to consume by severely curtailing black people's access to consumer artifacts and credit, while expanding white capacity for conspicuous consumption and consumer credit. In the post-apartheid era, conspicuous consumption by black people readily acquires the status of symbolic liberation. Thus, although consumption has always been racialized in South Africa, consumption by the emerging black middle class is the moral imperative of patriotic citizenship in the new nation. The emergence of this class implies the success of neoliberal policies (Ives 2007).

The post-apartheid adoption of neoliberal practices occurred almost immediately after independence when Nelson Mandela's Reconstruction and Development Program (RDP) came under critical scrutiny. This policy had assigned responsibility to the state for social development and incorporating previously marginalized people groups into the formal economy. But threats to the economy and accusations of mismanagement pushed the state to embrace a more conservative economic strategy (Visser 2004). The government reduced state expenditure on social services, limited state intervention in the economy, fostered privatization, and addressed redistribution through a trickledown effect of privatized market growth (Visser 2004). Subsequently, Thabo Mbeki's government instituted a broad policy deracializing business owner-ship and management, regulating employment in favor of previously marginalized groups, and providing easier access to credit for black people, among other strategies to integrate black people into the mainstream economy (Iheduru 2004; Odhiambo 2008). By combining the competing objectives of profitability (neoliberalism) with economic deracialization (social equality), the state hoped to fulfill its election com-mitment to redistribute wealth without alienating white elites, and gain entry to the global marketplace, attracting international investment and encouraging job creation. While analysts disagree on the success of these antagonistic objectives (see Turok 2000), some scholars argue that the incremental growth since the 1990s in the number of black professionals, black executives, and black-controlled printing and publishing groups, as well as the value of stock market transactions by black investors, testifies to the "highly visible, increasingly vocal, and powerful group of black capitalists" (Iheduru 2004: 15).

## Postfeminism and its femininities

Arguing that Anglo-American media promulgate a postfeminist sensibility, Rosalind Gill traces the current moment's fascination with "femininity as a bodily property; the shift from objectification to subjectification; an emphasis upon self-surveillance, monitoring and self-discipline; a focus on individualism, choice and empowerment; the dominance of a makeover paradigm; and a resurgence of ideas about natural sexual difference" (Gill 2007: 147). Gill sees Western media's postfeminist sensibility as a response to feminism, with the postfeminist "entanglement of feminist and anti-feminist discourses" and notions of "autonomy, choice and self-improvement [that] sit side-by-side with surveillance, discipline and the vilification of those who make the 'wrong' 'choices'" and neoliberalism's ideal subject (Gill 2007: 163). Gill explains that the postfeminist and the neoliberal subject are both defined as autonomous rather than situated within constraining systems or institutional limits. The "auton-omous, calculating, self-regulating subject of neoliberalism bears a strong resem-blance to the active, freely choosing, self-reinventing subject of postfeminism" (Gill 2007: 163). Finally, both orientations construct women as their ideal subjects, subjects who require transformation and self-discipline, yet who are presented as choosing to regulate or transform themselves without coercion.

Of course, the histories of South African feminisms do not map directly onto those of the US or the UK, which Gill describes. South African media nevertheless appear to demonstrate a similar postfeminist sensibility towards female characters and women. Tom Odhiambo (2008) shows how two popular South African magazines, Drum and True Love, embody femininity as a property of the body, and the sub-jectification of women, demonstrated by beauty queens who experience instant fame in exchange for their willingness to sell consumable products, including their bodies. Moreover, television schedules exhibit a postfeminist sensibility by showcasing women in need of transformations through makeover shows such as Skin Deep and

*America's Next Top Model*; by trading on the increasing desirability of surveillance, particularly of women, in reality programming, evident in *Blame It On Fame* and *Cheaters*; by programming glamorous soap operas that promote conspicuous consumption and advance the aspirational trajectory of characters motivated by free choice, apparent in *The Bold and the Beautiful*, *Generations*, and *Isidingo*; and by integrating advertising practices to promote products and lifestyles between programming segments and embedded within shows, that flaunt femininity as a property of the body, emphasize the need to discipline the female body, and, above all, appeal to consumer choice as empowering for women.

## Society's emerging femininities

*Society*'s diverse protagonists suggest the potential of the show to expand the kinds of femininities mediated by television. Analyzing the ways in which the show takes up the ideology of neoliberalism in late capitalism, and exhibits a postfeminist sensibility through character story arcs, this chapter highlights the forms of femininity that emerge under these conditions. Neoliberalism's notion of subjectivity, defined through freedom of choice and individual autonomy, signals an ideological burden on individuals to determine their own destiny, and, importantly, to actively assume responsibility for failure, irrespective of larger systems and institutions that structure and limit their destinies. Akua's decision to marry Robert Woods, a 70-year-old, wealthy white divorcé, because he makes her happy, suggests the apparent freedom of South Africans to marry whomever they choose, unrestricted by apartheid miscegenation laws. Akua's resolve to exercise freedom of choice is further established through her willingness to marry Woods even though her friends, family, and soon-to-be stepchildren disapprove. Celebrating Akua's independence and decisiveness, if not approving of her choice, Efi, Akua's mother, congratulates her daughter on the wedding announcement: "You always know exactly what's right for you—*no matter what anybody says*. You are a beautiful, strong-willed woman and I love you, my baby!" (Series 2, Episode 26, my emphasis). Despite social disapproval, Efi affirms Akua's neoliberal femininity by celebrating her freedom to do as she pleases, and crediting her for her own success based on her decisions and practices.

In addition to bearing responsibility for their own successes and failures, the women on *Society* are expected to accept neoliberalism's account of the cause–effect relationship between hard work and success. When Akua is named junior partner of an investment company, the other partners support her appointment because, as one says: "Akua, don't worry, you so deserved it!" Another senior partner even more explicitly assures Akua that her promotion did not result from Black Economic Empowerment (BEE) policies, emphasizing, "You were made a partner of this firm because of your merit and your dedication to the company" (Series 1, Episode 4). Accentuating Akua's entrepreneurial subjectivity, rather than her black and female identities, the partner dismisses the state's attempt to redress apartheid's legacy of inequality through policies that benefit businesses that hire and promote employees from previously marginalized groups. As such, the show draws attention to the neoliberal ideal of meritocracy that rewards hard work with promotions and raises.

In contrast with Akua's financial and professional success coming on the heels of her hard work, Inno bears the brunt economically and socially of *not* choosing the endorsed route to success. Instead of locating supplemental employment opportunities to support her expensive tastes, Inno exploits her sexual desirability and relies on male lovers to pay for her extravagances. Even Inno's mother, a mean-spirited alcoholic, suspects that Inno needs something when she chooses to visit. When Inno illicitly withdraws R20,000 from the society's bank account, Inno's three friends turn their backs on her, holding her responsible for her own failures, including her notoriety as a "has been" among television casting agents. Corresponding with neo-liberal ideologies that hold individuals responsible for their own destinies, Inno is vilified by her friends and community.

*Society* largely depicts characters who achieve or aspire to upper-middle-class affluence or society. Although Inno struggles to pay her rent, she prizes wealthy lovers and expensive clothes, and accepts stolen credit cards from a loan shark with no regard to how she will repay the loans. Although the combination of Inno's expensive habits and her limited income finally disrupt the equilibrium of the society, the other three women exhibit similar expectations of unlimited consumption. Akua purchases a sports car just because she can afford one; Lois's husband presents her with a new van before their baby is born; and Beth casually supports her partner's expenses while she establishes her photography career. By showcasing the economic prosperity of middle-class black women in South Africa, *Society* promotes the neoliberal ideal of the achievability of the African dream, even when these aspirations require dramatic transformations for success.

Akin to the way that neoliberalism conceals racial, economic, and gender inequalities by playing up the economic prosperity of black women, postfeminist media images presume the triumph of feminist objectives and ignore ongoing discrimination against women in late capitalist South Africa. The conversation between a managing partner and Akua after she is named partner draws attention to the ideal of a meritocracy in which women are rewarded for their hard work. Remarking that promotions for women are still atypical, Akua's response underscores the need for continued feminist activism: "Why would I have a problem with [benefiting from Black Economic Empowerment policies]? BEE is there to make sure change takes place otherwise I doubt that someone like me will ever have a chance ... in this world. So go ahead, add four points to your score card, I have no problem being a BEE appointment."

A postfeminist sensibility also masks contemporary discrimination against non-normative sexualities by incorporating images of homosexuality while limiting such images to heterosexual couplings (see Battles and Hilton-Morrow 2002). Beth and her lesbian partner expand the range of femininities that are enacted, yet Beth's ongoing prejudices towards lesbians, and her unwillingness to reveal her sexuality to her friends and colleagues, reduces the threat of these images. Attending her first lesbian party after separating from Thuli, Beth confesses to Akua: "I'm not even sure I'm a lesbian without [Thuli]. ... I have such issues with lesbians ... there are things they do that still freak me out" (Series 2, Episode 11). When Akua concedes that she enjoyed the party, Beth proposes that she should have left Akua at the lesbian party, but first "dipped you in chocolate and thrown you to the lesbians!" Comparing lesbians to animals with voracious sexual appetites, Beth introduces contradictory impulses toward lesbianism in the show: proffering the potential of lesbian femininities but reducing these performances to traditional femininity rather than "butch" or transgendered presentations.

Inno and Akua present their bodies as highly stylized canvases, in line with a postfeminist ideology that asserts sexy bodies as "women's key (if not sole) source of identity" (Gill 2007: 149). The lithe, tall Inno is obsessed with designer clothes and skimpy shorts that reveal her heterosexual availability. As the only female investment broker in the firm, Akua also makes a fashion statement with her high-end feminine suits and expensive jewelry. Lois and Beth pay much less attention to their appearance, although Lois has had her curly hair relaxed and Beth wears a weave; both women dress professionally for their jobs. Significantly, all four women undergo a radical transformation over the course of the second series. Gill argues that a postfeminist sensibility targets women, who are led to believe that they need reinvention because "their life is lacking or flawed in some way" (2007: 156). After Thuli is beaten by two homophobic men, and Beth is robbed at a traffic light, Beth becomes frightened by her vulnerability. She enrolls in a self-defense course, shaves off her long hair weave, dresses more androgynously (ironically, wearing the khaki pants uniform of "butch" lesbians that she has criticized), and coaches a lesbian soccer team as part of her therapy. This process is typical of the makeover genre, in which subjects are required to admit their inadequacies (Beth's lesbianism) and undergo painful transformations (changing her body presentation and claiming her lesbian sexuality publicly) before being readmitted into middle-class society, evident through her father's reconciliatory acceptance of her sexuality (Tincknell 2011).

Motivated by her sense of isolation from friends and family, the workaholic Akua reads a self-help book and transforms herself into a party animal, seeking any opportunity to make friends and find a husband. Lois's reinvention is hinted at in the final episode when she checks herself into an addiction treatment facility, intending to confess her addictive personality, begin the painful process of sobriety, and regain the trust of her family and friends, ultimately re-entering her daughter's life. After several men threaten to violently exploit her willingness to sexualize her body for material gain, and she is abandoned by friends disgusted by her dishonesty, Inno admits that she needs to change her destiny. Reinventing herself through regular church attendance, a non-glamorous job at a call center, and living within her means, Inno aspires to fix her flaws so she will be reaccepted by her friends and society.

## Glocalization of desire

The globalizing forces of neoliberalism and postfeminism predict a global orientation toward the homogenized objectives of the autonomous individual, consumer sovereignty, and the pursuit of corporate profitability by any means. But local interests and interactions with global demands transform content and speak to traditions particular to regions and ethnicities. Such is the case in South Africa, where television is mandated to address the diversity and concerns of the country, and where the industry benefits from national cultural protectionist policies designed to enable the creation of locally produced cultural artifacts.

As a valued tool in the project of uniting a disparate nation, South African television (public service channels, private free-to-air, and private pay-TV channels) must meet content and linguistic requirements spelled out in the constitution and prescribed by the Independent Communications Authority of South Africa (ICASA). Obligated to represent the country's racial, ethnic, and linguistic diversity, and broadcast in all 11 official languages, television channels are required to air locally produced programming according to predetermined ICASA quotas (ICASA 2006). Despite the emphasis on local content, television channels continue to import programming. Purchasing content is much cheaper than producing it locally and the relatively small production industry cannot produce enough programming to supply the existing channels. As a consequence, television programming presents what Marwan Kraidy describes as "entangled articulations of global and local discourses," an amalgamation of local and global interests (1999: 471).

The concepts of glocalization and hybrid identities are particularly useful in considering the critical engagement of the global with the local and the mixed identities that are constructed along the interstices of the local and the global. Richard Giulianotti and Roland Robertson characterize glocalization as "the agency of quotidian social actors in critically engaging with and transforming global cultural phenomena in accordance with perceived local cultural needs as well as values and beliefs" (2006: 173). Their definition draws attention to the structural limits of the process of globalization and the agentive interactions between global cultural producers and artifacts, and local industries and audiences. In addition, Victor Roudometof explains that the concept of glocalization proposes the "possibility that individuals might not be consistent in their advocacy of [cosmopolitan and local] ideals, but that they might be displaying different degrees of such attitudes" (2005: 123). Communities and individuals select from a continuum of attitudes that are historically and geographically contingent rather than predetermined by global producers or products.

I use Roudometof's observation about the mixing of global and local interests to argue that the text prefers local or traditional values and beliefs (such as the nuclear family and community), although *Society* characters exhibit orientations informed by both global and local contexts and interests; the women display hybrid identities by adopting global attitudes of individual autonomy and conspicuous consumption to different degrees. Studying the development of Maronite identities in Lebanon, Kraidy explains how his participants fashioned their identities between the competing worldviews of tradition and modernity, and "adopted and rejected elements from both Arab and Western programs, underscoring symbolic leakage between the two worldviews" (2005: 467). The *Society* women likewise negotiate between the contending visions of global values and traditional practices.

Exhibiting a preference for traditional practices, *Society* establishes the centrality of family to the happiness and success of women's lives. Absorbed by her career and addiction, Lois neglects her marriage and motherhood. When Mandla threatens to leave her and take their daughter with him, Lois calls on her extended family to bring healing and reconciliation. Arranging a traditional "indaba," Lois invites her mother-in-law and two brothers, and her own mother to eat with her and Mandla and witness her confession, inviting them to offer advice and mediate between the spouses. Although Mandla does not cooperate, and eventually divorces Lois, her extended family offers crucial support for her rehabilitation.

Estranged from her parents and siblings because of her "choice" to live as a lesbian, Beth chooses to hide her sexual orientation from her friends and colleagues, hoping to avoid more rejections. When Beth eventually comes out at a Pride parade, she is disciplined for disregarding heterosexual norms and loses her teaching position and her long-term partner. Although she attempts to find healing by becoming a fighting machine, Beth recovers from her post-traumatic stress disorder through community support and volunteering opportunities at an NGO for lesbians. Also experiencing healing through group membership, Inno joins a Christian church and accepts responsibility for her precarious financial addictions as a means to turn her life around. Finding salvation through traditional avenues, Inno repairs her relationships and lands a job hosting on television, coming full circle.

Emphasizing the communal over the individual, the traditional over the modern, yet incorporating protagonists who define themselves through individualism and incorporate neoliberal and postfeminist ideals into their lives, *Society* offers a complicated view of femininity in the new South Africa. Through its story arcs the show proposes which performances of femininity are valued and which are disciplined. By providing representations of modern, individualistic characters, women are offered carte blanche to construct their own versions of femininity, focusing on their needs as women, and pursuing their dreams of equality. However, the neoliberal focus on the individual without corresponding attention to systemic constraints suggests that women are responsible for their own failures and not supported through equity policies. In addition, while the incorporation of multiple sexualities suggests greater acceptance of diverse femininities, the show's reinscription of heteronormativity demonstrates the limits of femininity. The postfeminist emphasis on the sexualized individual enables women to deploy their sexuality yet warns women, through Inno's story, that South Africa continues to be dangerous, as women remain objects of sexual violence. Finally, although *Society* presents women who embrace modern practices and desire access to a world of consumption and privilege, traditional beliefs and practices are also celebrated and permit women to perform a broader range of femininities. Constructing femininities that are particular to the South African context, *Society* negotiates global and local demands, generating hybrid identities that maneuver through the contending practices of tradition and modernity.

## Notes

1 *Society* first aired as a miniseries but was subsequently expanded into a series based on its popularity. In South Africa consecutive seasons of television shows are referred to as series.
2 The relative scarcity of female-centered programming can be explained partly by the country's emphasis on nation-building and uniting previously segregated groups, the relative infancy of the television industry, and the limited number of television outlets that rely on mass audiences rather than niche interests to attract viewers.

# References

Battles, K. and W. Hilton-Morrow (2002) "Gay Characters in Conventional Spaces: *Will and Grace* and the Situation Comedy Genre," *Critical Studies in Media Communication* 19(1): 87–105.

Beauvoir, S. de (1953) *The Second Sex*, translated from French by H. M. Parshley, New York: Knopf.

Brown, S. (2009) "Society returning to our screens?," TVSA. http://www.tvsa.co.za/shugasblogiwood/article11232.asp.

Calvin, B. and G. Coetzee (eds.) (2009) *A Review of the South African Microfinance Sector*. http://web.up.ac.za/sitefiles/file/1/3841/Volume%20II%20Section%20IV%20Special%20Products.pdf.

Friedman, M. (1957) *A Theory of the Consumption Function*, Princeton, NJ: Princeton University Press.

Gill, R. (2007) "Postfeminist Media Culture: Elements of a Sensibility," *European Journal of Cultural Studies* 10(2): 147–66.

Gill, R. and C. Scharff (2011) "Introduction," in R. Gill and C. Scharff (eds.) *New Femininities: Postfeminism, Neoliberalism and Subjectivity*, New York: Palgrave Macmillan, pp. 1–17.

Giulianotti, R. and R. Robertson (2006) "Glocalization, Globalization and Migration: The Case of Scottish Football Supporters in North America," *International Sociology* 21(2): 171–96.

Harvey, D. (2005) *A Brief History of Neoliberalism*, Oxford: Oxford University Press.

ICASA (2006) "South African Television Content Regulations, Notice 154 of 2006," in *Government Gazette* No. 28454, January 31, Cape Town: Government Gazette.

Iheduru, O. C. (2004) "Black Economic Power and Nation-Building in Post-Apartheid South Africa," *Journal of Modern African Studies* 42(1): 1–30.

Ives, S. (2007) "Mediating the Neoliberal Nation: Television in Post-Apartheid South Africa," *ACME* 6(1): 153–73.

Kraidy, M. M. (1999) "The Global, the Local, and the Hybrid: A Native Ethnography of Glocalization," *Critical Studies in Mass Communication* 16(4): 456–76.

——(2005) *Hybridity or the Cultural Logic of Globalization*, Philadelphia: Temple University Press.

Lorber, J. (2004) "Night to His Day: The Social Construction of Gender," in P. S. Rothenberg (ed.) *Race, Class and Gender in the United States*, New York: Worth Publishers, pp. 54–64.

Odhiambo, T. (2008) "The Black Female Body as a 'Consumer and a Consumable' in Current *Drum* and *True Love* Magazines in South Africa," *African Studies* 67(1): 71–80.

Posel, D. (2010) "Races to Consume: Revisiting South Africa's History of Race, Consumption and the Struggle for Freedom," *Ethnic and Racial Studies* 33(2): 157–75.

Roudometof, V. (2005) "Transnationalism, Cosmopolitanism and Glocalization," *Current Sociology* 53(1): 113–35.

Tincknell, E. (2011) "Scourging the Abject Body: *Ten Years Younger* and Fragmented Femininity under Neoliberalism," in R. Gill and C. Scharff (eds.) *New Femininities: Postfeminism, Neoliberalism and Subjectivity*, Basingstoke: Palgrave Macmillan, pp. 83–95.

Turok, B. (2000) "Black Economic Empowerment—Serving Elite or Mass Interests?," *New Agenda* [Cape Town] (Winter): 4–7.

Visser, W. (2004) "'Shifting RDP into Gear': The ANC Government's Dilemma in Providing an Equitable System of Social Security for the 'New' South Africa," in ITH Linzer Konferenz. Austria, September 17. Austria: International Conference of Labor and Social History, pp. 1–18.

World Bank Development Research Group (2012) *Poverty Headcount Ratio at $2 a Day (PPP) (% of Population)*. http://data.worldbank.org/indicator/SI.POV.2DAY.

# 26
# A nice bit of skirt and the talking head
## Sex, politics, and news

## *Karen Ross*

### Angela Merkel: Barbie doll or Iron Lady?

Merkel grimly submitted to an executive fashion makeover after the media sneered at her frumpy look; now she clearly relishes shining out in jewel-toned jackets from a forest of dark suits at G20 meetings. And, just once, she stunned the nation by wearing a deep blue evening dress with a fjord-like cleavage and pearls to an opera in Oslo. Quite possibly that was when a lot of Germans first woke up to the fact that their head of government was female. But, ordinarily, Merkel still wears less make-up and hairspray on the job than Silvio Berlusconi on vacation.

(Constanze Stelzenmüller, *Observer*, August 23, 2009: 33)

In the early 1990s, I stood as the Labour candidate in my local ward elections. I was rather amazed and not a little disconcerted with the news coverage I received, where the focus was on my haircut (short), my choice of footgear (Doc Martens), and my age (mid-thirties), but definitely *not* on my politics. In the years since, we have seen increasing numbers of women contest and then win top political jobs around the globe. They are often the first woman to ever hold that office in their country, and often in the vanguard of political and social innovation.

This chapter considers the immensely tricky relationship between gender, politics, and journalism, focusing primarily on the ways in which political women (and men) are represented in and by news media. I argue that, notwithstanding the more general slide toward infotainment, easy-chew news, and the priapic imperative, politics is still regarded as a job for the boys, literally. This is despite the growing success of women's global campaigns to become president or prime minister. Thus, women continue to be seen at best as a novelty, at worst an aberration in media discourse. In several elections where women were competing for the highest political office, their personal lives came under intense scrutiny, every detail examined for signs of deviancy or scandal, especially if they were unmarried or childfree (McGregor 1996; Comrie 2006; van Zoonen 2006; Trimble and Treiberg 2010). While the media's tabloid turn means that *all* politicians are more vulnerable to the salacious interests of journalists (see also Juntunen and Väliverronen 2010), women's more limited media coverage results in an overdetermined focus on the personal over political issues.

Determining why gender-differentiated coverage of politicians is such a global phenomenon and why journalists seem so out of step with voters—whose decision-making suggests a more sophisticated appreciation of women's political potential than that held by many journalists—is not straightforward. A variety of factors are in play including the circulation and routinization of gender-based stereotypes, the male-ordered nature of many newsroom environments, and the reliance on the "usual suspects" as sources and subjects for news discourse. This is not everywhere the case and some women politicians receive gender-neutral coverage and even "positive" coverage. With other coverage, women's political authority is not overtly undermined but they are cast as superwoman. While this is not necessarily demeaning, it nonetheless positions women by their sex rather than their political competencies. But mostly, news coverage of women is gendered. Given most women's lower status within political hierarchies compared to their male colleagues, for women to achieve the oxygen of media publicity is already more difficult. In some contexts, their novelty value works in their favor to boost media interest but, as we shall see, this is often a rather double-edged sword.

## Skirting *herstory*

While some significant work was undertaken on women and news in the 1970s and 1980s (see, e.g., Tuchman *et al.* 1978), much of that work focused on the representation of women as news objects. It discussed either how women typically appeared in news discourse (as victims, wives, and eye candy) or, more importantly, their *absence* from news. The 1990s saw the development of more nuanced analyses of news coverage of women politicians. In the vanguard of such scholarship was Kim Fridkin Khan whose studies of news coverage of US political candidates (Kahn 1991, 1992, 1994a, 1994b; Kahn and Goldenberg 1991; Kahn and Kenney 1997) constitutes an important milestone. Throughout the 1990s, other studies looked at news coverage of women politicians as election candidates but also their inclusion in news discourse outside the intense period of election coverage. The vast majority of these studies demonstrated the same two propensities: first, coverage of women was more likely to focus on personal attributes, including style, than their political positions; and, second, echoing Tuchman *et al.*'s iconic assertion of women's "symbolic annihilation," political women were largely absent from the news agenda (Braden 1996; Norris 1997b).

Moving into the 2000s, researchers continued to find the same kind of gender-based news coverage despite the strides which women politicians were making in the real world. These trends were witnessed across the West (Bystrom *et al.* 2001; Gallagher 2001; Banwart *et al.* 2003; Gidengil and Everitt 2005; Heldman *et al.* 2005). Not only were women politicians framed very differently in terms of the kinds of story topics in which they featured, not only was the focus more on the personal than the political, but the tone and orientation of news discourse were also different, often negative (Adcock 2010). Looking at the German Bundestag and Angela Merkel's candidacy, Semetko and Boomgaarden (2007) found that although she had more or less the same level of exposure as her male opponent, gender was still used as a device for framing stories. Some work, including my own, focused not just on the ways in which women (and men) politicians were represented in the media but also on how politicians themselves perceived both the media's coverage of themselves and their political colleagues, and how they cultivated their own media relationships (Strömbäck and Nord 2006; Cohen et al. 2008; Ross 2009). I found that politicians from the UK, Northern Ireland, New Zealand, Australia, and South Africa were unanimous in their condemnation of most journalistic practice on the grounds that they believed it damages both the image of politics and, more importantly, democracy itself (Ross 2002). Sex-based stereotypes used both to trivialize and objectify women politicians can affect women's decision to stand for elected office. Lovenduski and Norris (1996) argue that these can also inform voters' perceptions of candidates.

Work on women and news more generally demonstrates that women as objects and subjects of news occupy three primary positions, as eye candy, as victims, and as mothers (WACC 2010; Ross and Carter 2011). Rather worryingly, women politicians are similarly straitjacketed by news discourse framing them as bodies to be discussed, whose domestic arrangements are apparently more interesting than their policy statements, and whose coiffures are more newsworthy than their credentials. While journalists counter criticism by suggesting they are giving the public what they/we want, are we really so interested in politicians' stylists, their shoes, and their sartorial choices? A focus on these fripperies serves to trivialize women and undermine their potency as political actors, both actual and in waiting (Sreberny-Mohammadi and Ross 1996; Ward 2000; Sones et al. 2005; Stevens 2007). But it's not always a bad news story. A few researchers argue that women's distinctiveness as candidates actually plays out in their favor: their novelty value attracts more media attention (Banwart et al. 2003). But, as many women politicians told me (Ross 2002), they could easily grab a headline by wearing red stilettos, saying something vulgar, or behaving "like a man" and thus subverting the so-called norms of feminine behavior. If women can also be fitted into the "first of ... " category, especially at very senior levels, they will also be more newsworthy—but not always in a good or positive way.

## It's not *just* words

While women politicians are often trivialized by news discourse that disavows political presentation in favor of sartorial style, the use of specific naming strategies also works to undermine women's credibility. This was perfectly captured by the soubriquet of "Blair's Babes" given to the 101 Labour women who were elected as MPs in the 1997 British general election. The *Mirror* newspaper is credited with having originally coined the phrase in relation to several women celebrities who were planning to vote Labour in the 1997 election (Sones et al. 2005). The label was subsequently used to caption the photo of a victorious Tony Blair surrounded by "his" women. Some women did not, apparently, object to the label while others felt it undermined the historic significance of their success (Sones *et al.* 2005). Childs (2008) suggests that subsequent representations of women politicians were often inflected with references to those "babes," and journalists regularly used both the photo and the label to characterize those Labour women as "robotic" and syco-phantic (Cowley and Childs 2003). This notion of a male leader's harem has been mimicked by similar labels, including Cameron's cuties, Gordon's gals, and Nick's nymphets, a strategy which continues to trivialize women politicians and reduces them to a mere chorus line of simpering support (see also Mavin *et al.* 2010).

As well as the use of undermining language and a preoccupation with sartorial style, the media also like to discuss women and men politicians in relation to the traits which they are alleged to possess which suit them more or less to political office; here gender (in)appropriateness again comes into play. Among the first scholars to consider such second-level agenda-setting dimensions were McCombs *et al.* (1997), who argued that attributes regarded by journalists as salient then become salient on the public agenda. Traits associated with personality, morality, honesty, and intellectual prowess, as well as the more obvious ones such as leadership ability and political experience, all appear to be in the mix when voters consider potential candidates (McCombs and Estrada 1997; Kiousis 2005; Hayes 2011). Focusing on elections in the late 1990s, Devitt (2002) and Heldman *et al.* (2005) argue that women's person-ality traits are more scrutinized than male candidates. Major and Coleman's (2008) study of coverage of the Louisiana Governorship race in 2003, however, showed a reduction in gender (and race) stereotyped coverage, although it was still much in evidence. Studying mixed-sex congressional races from the 2008 cycle, Banwart (2010) shows that traditional trait stereotypes continue to be present in relation to voters' valuation of women candidates, although voters' beliefs about gender-specific policy areas were more complicated. As "masculine traits" are seen as more desirable in political leaders, this can lead to the overexposure of male candidates and the stereotyping of women in the opposite direction (Lawrence and Rose 2010).

## Jobs for the girls?

The period since 2000 has seen an unprecedented number of women contesting top jobs with mixed success and in 2012, a woman was the head of government in 20 countries (Inter-Parliamentary Union 2012). How, then, can we account for the news media's continuing stereotyping and marginalization of women political candidates? Again, some studies suggest that voters appear to prefer that presidential or prime ministerial candidates exhibit overtly "masculine" traits and behaviors (Huddy and Terkildsen 1993). Yet even that is not the whole story, since senior political women have often been criticized for being *too* macho. Treading the line between "gender-appropriate" behavior and demonstrating leadership qualities is a good trick to pull off (Jamieson 1995; Bligh *et al.* 2011; Ross and Comrie 2012). But sometimes circumstances are such that women do get it right, they do get the vote, and they do achieve senior political office. In the case of the news coverage of Michele Bachelet's (ultimately suc-cessful) attempt to become Chile's first woman president, while the coverage she received was quite different to that of her two main male rivals and was gender specific, it was not negative (Valenzuela and Correa 2009). This could have helped her win—i.e. if the public associated her with positive traits such as care and compassion, although she was also framed as less competent than her main rivals. However, on balance, her charisma and honesty apparently outweighed her lack of leadership experience. In addition, she started the election campaign as the frontrunner, which some commentators have argued is a considerable advantage (see Trimble 2007; Ibroscheva and Stover 2011), as is a pre-existing reputation as a strong leader (Horn Sheeler 2010).

## When sex and journalism collide

Several researchers argue that content is related to who produces it: we get what we get on the page or the website or the 6 O'Clock News because of who writes and edits the copy and files the story (Norris 1997a; de Bruin and Ross 2004; Lovenduski 2005; North 2009; Ayers and Lawson 2011; Chambers et al. 2004; Cochrane 2011; Rehkopf and Reinstadler 2011). If most of those people are men, then we get the news refracted through a male lens. This is not to say that we would get a remarkably different news agenda if more women worked as political journalists. It is to suggest, however, that many women have a different style and sensibility, have different experiences of the world, and bring differently inflected perspectives to their journalism (Steiner 1998; de Bruin 2000; de Bruin and Ross 2004; Rodgers and Thorson 2003; Melin-Higgins 2004; North 2009). Large newsrooms with a predominance of men staffers are said to produce a style of journalism which coheres around a male-ordered norm masquerading as "good" journalism (see also van Zoonen 1998; Robinson 2005). Others suggest that women journalists are more likely to use women sources and thus produce a differently nuanced journalism which includes more diverse viewpoints (Zoch and VanSlyke Turk 1998; Armstrong 2004). Given that many studies of news sources over the past 25 years suggest that men outnumber women in a ratio of 3:1 in terms not just of political voices but of all voices (see, e.g., Delano Brown et al. 1987; Shoemaker and Reese 1996; Liebler and Smith 1997; Ross 2007; WACC 2010), strategies encouraging a range of viewpoints which are both diverse and more reflective of "real" society are to be welcomed. A study of media coverage of the Chile presidential elections in 2005/6, which was won by Michele Bachelet, suggests that women reporters were more aware of Bachelet's "first woman" breakthrough than their male colleagues, explicitly mentioning her sex more often than male journalists (Valenzuela and Correa 2009). However, other work, including my own, suggests that the sex of journalists makes little difference to whether more women are used as sources, although women journalists appear to be more likely to write stories featuring women exclusively than men (Ross et al. 2013).

## Conclusion

Some scholars find evidence of some improvement in the media's coverage of women politicians over the past few decades. Nevertheless, as their candidacy becomes less of a novelty, such "improvements" come with some caveats. Whilst the *volume* of coverage may be improving in some situations, if the tone and content are still largely negative and stereotypical, then the truism that all publicity is good publicity must be turned on its head: bad publicity *is* bad for politicians and, as such, no publicity might be preferable. Women politicians remain obstinately "othered" by media discourse. They still require the prefix "woman" to mark them out as different to the traditional (male) politician, a strategy which even I feel compelled to use. Women are still undermined by journalists' continuing fascination with their coiffure, couture, and conjugal relations, and still ignored for their policy position.

Despite the highly gendered, unhelpful, and stereotypical ways in which news media continue to frame women politicians and candidates, the public continue to vote with their feet and elect women both to the ordinary rank and file of the Parliamentary benches but also to the top job, *pace* Dilma Rousseff (Brazil), Atifete Jahjaga (Kosovo), Helle Thorning-Schmidt (Denmark), Portia Simpson Miller (Jamaica), all of whom have been (newly) elected since January 2011. But the crucial issue here is that women often achieve their political ambitions *despite* news media, not *because* of them. Moreover, they are doing so because there is an increasing dissonance between the news media's agenda and our own, public one. This is absolutely not to argue that the media are irrelevant since this is palpably not true and the level of congruity between the media and the public's agenda remains strong. But it *is* to suggest that as citizens of the twenty-first century, we use an array of news sources and are less dependent on traditional media to frame the world for us than was the case for previous generations. So, does it really matter that news media represent women and men politicians and candidates differently? To some extent, the public's access to and use of personal and party political blogs, alternative news outlets, and various social media serve to mitigate the worst excesses of mainstream journalism by offering a variety of different perspectives. But mainstream news remains an important source of information for large parts of the population. The findings from 30-plus years of agenda-setting research provide compelling evidence that the media *can* set the agenda for what policy issues the public think are important and, more crucially, decide whose voices are important to hear. Gender does still matter. It matters not least because how politicians are perceived by the public has an impact on their political fate and one of the primary ways in which "the public" come to "know" politicians is through news media. Although the increasing number of women achieving the top political job gives the lie to the media's totalizing power to determine political fortunes, journalists are certainly not without influence and what they say and how they say it still have considerable importance in the lives of politicians and publics alike.

## References

Adcock, C. (2010) "The Politician, the Wife, the Citizen and Her Newspaper: Rethinking Women, Democracy and Media(ted) Representation," *Feminist Media Studies* 10(2): 135–60.

Armstrong, C. L. (2004) "The Influence of Reporter Gender on Source Selection in Newspaper Stories," *Journalism and Mass Communication Quarterly* 81(1): 139–54.

Ayers, E. and M. Lawson (2011) *A-Gendered Press*, London: ECHO.

Banwart, M. (2010) "Gender and Candidate Communication: Effects of Stereotypes in the 2008 Election," *American Behavioral Scientist* 54(3): 265–83.

Banwart, M. C., D. G. Bystrom, and T. Robertson (2003) "From the Primary to the General Election: A Comparative Analysis of Candidate Media Coverage in Mixed-gender 2000 Races for Governor and US Senate," *American Behavioral Scientist* 46(5): 658–76.

Bligh, M., M. Schlehofer, B. Casad, and A. Gaffney (2011) "Competent Enough, But Would You *Vote* for Her? Gender Stereotypes and Media Influences on Perceptions of Women Politicians," *Journal of Applied Social Psychology* 42(3): 560–97.

Braden, M. (1996) *Women, Politicians and the Media*, Lexington: University of Kentucky Press.

Bystrom, D. G., T. A. Robertson, and M. C. Banwart (2001) "Framing the Fight: An Analysis of Media Coverage of Female and Male Candidates in Primary Races for Governor and U.S. Senate in 2000," *American Behavioral Scientist* 44: 658–76.

Chambers, D., L. Steiner, and C. Fleming (2004) *Women and Journalism*, London: Routledge.

Childs, S. (2008) *Women and British Party Politics*, Oxford: Routledge.

Cochrane, K. (2011) "Women's Representation in Media: Who's Running the Show?," *Guardian*, December 6. http://www.guardian.co.uk/news/datablog/2011/dec/06/women-repre-sentation-media.

Cohen, J., Y. Tsfati, and T. Sheafer (2008) "The Influence of Presumed Media Influence in Politics: Do Politicians' Perceptions of Media Power Matter?," *Public Opinion Quarterly* 72 (2): 331–44.

Comrie, M. (2006) "The Media and Leadership," in R. Miller and M. Mintrom (eds.) *Political Leadership in New Zealand*, Auckland: Auckland University Press, pp. 175–95.

Cowley, P. and S. Childs (2003) "Too Spineless to Rebel? New Labour's Women MPs," *British Journal of Political Science* 33(3): 345–65.

de Bruin, M. (2000) "Gender, Organizational and Professional Identities in Journalism," *Journalism* 1(2): 239–60.

de Bruin, M. and K. Ross (eds.) (2004) *Gender and Newsroom Cultures: Identities at Work*, Cresskill, NJ: Hampton Press.

Delano Brown, J., C. R. Bybee, S. T. Wearden, and D. M. Straughan (1987) "Invisible Power: Newspaper News: Sources and the Limits of Diversity," *Journalism Quarterly* 64 (Spring): 50.

Devitt, J. (2002) "Framing Gender on the Campaign Trail: Female Gubernatorial Candidates and the Press," *Journalism and Mass Communication Quarterly* 79: 445–63.

Gallagher, M. (2001) *Gender Setting: New Agendas for Media Monitoring and Advocacy*, New York: Palgrave.

Gidengil, E. and J. Everitt (2005) "Conventional Coverage/Unconventional Politicians: Gender and Media Coverage of Canadian Leaders' Debates 1993, 1997, 2000," *Canadian Journal of Political Science* 36(3): 559–77.

Hayes, D. (2011) "When Gender and Party Collide: Stereotyping in Candidate Trait Attribution," *Politics & Gender* 7: 133–65.

Heldman, C., S. J. Carroll, and S. Olson (2005) "'She Brought Only a Skirt': Print Media Coverage of Elizabeth Dole's Bid for the Republican Presidential Nomination," *Political Communication* 22(2): 315–35.

Horn Sheeler, K. (2010) "Beauty Queens and Unruly Women in the Year of the Woman Governor: Jennifer Granholm and the Visibility of Leadership," *Women Studies in Communication* 33(1): 34–53.

Huddy, L. and N. Terkildsen (1993) "The Consequences of Gender Stereotypes for Women Candidates at Different Levels and Types of Office," *Political Research Quarterly* 46(3): 503–25.

Ibroscheva, E. and M. Stover (2011) "The Girls of Parliament: A Historical Analysis of the Press Coverage of Female Politicians in Bulgaria," in K. Ross (ed.) *The Handbook of Gender, Sex, and Media*, Chichester: John Wiley.

Inter-Parliamentary Union (2012) "Women in National Parliaments." http://www.ipu.org/wmn-e/world.htm.

Jamieson, K. H. (1995) *Beyond the Double Bind: Women and Leadership*, New York: Oxford University Press.

Juntunen, L. and E. Väliverronen (2010) "Politics of Sexting: Re-negotiating the Boundaries of Private and Public in Political Journalism," *Journalism Studies* 11(6): 817–31.

Kahn, K. F. (1991) "Senate Elections in the News: Examining Campaign Coverage," *Legislative Studies Quarterly* 16(3): 349–74.

——(1992) "Does Being Male Help? An Investigation of the Effects of Candidate Gender and Campaign Coverage on Evaluations of US Senate Candidate," *Journal of Politics* 54(2): 497–517.

——(1994a) "The Distorted Mirror: Press Coverage of Women Candidates for Statewide Office," *Journal of Politics* 56(1): 154–73.

——(1994b) "Does Gender Make a Difference? An Experimental Examination of Sex Stereotypes and Press Patterns in Statewide Campaigns," *American Journal of Political Science* 38(1): 162–95.

Kahn, K. F. and E. N. Goldenberg (1991) "Women Candidates in the News: An Examination of Gender Differences in US Senate Campaign Coverage," *Public Opinion Quarterly* 55: 180–99.

Kahn, K. F. and P. J. Kenney (1997) "A Model of Candidate Evaluations in Senate Elections: The Impact of Campaign Intensity," *Journal of Politics* 59(4): 1173–206.

Kiousis, S. (2005) "Compelling Arguments and Attitude Strength: Exploring the Impact of Second-level Agenda Setting on Public Opinion of Presidential Candidate Images," *Harvard International Journal of Press/Politics* 10(2): 3–27.

Lawrence, R. G. and M. Rose (2010). *Hillary Clinton's Race for the White House: Gender Politics and the Media on the Campaign Trail*, Boulder, CO: Lynne Rienner.

Liebler, C. M. and S. J. Smith (1997) "Tracking Gender Differences: A Comparative Analysis of Network Correspondents and Their Sources," *Journal of Broadcasting and Electronic Media* 41(1): 58–68.

Lovenduski, J. (2005) *Feminizing Politics*, Cambridge: Polity.

Lovenduski, J. and P. Norris (eds.) (1996) *Women in Politics*, Oxford: Oxford University Press.

McCombs, M. E. and G. Estrada (1997) "The News Media and the Pictures in Our Heads," in S. Iyengar and R. Reeves (eds.) *Do the Media Govern?*, London: Sage, pp. 237–47.

McCombs, M., J. P. Llamas, E. Lopez-Escobar, and F. Rey (1997) "Candidate Images in Spanish Elections: Second-level Agenda-setting Effects," *Journalism & Mass Communication Quarterly* 74: 703–16.

McGregor J. (1996) "Gender Politics and the News: The Search for a Beehive Bimbo-Boadicea," in J. McGregor (ed.) *Dangerous Democracy? News Media Politics in New Zealand*, Palmerston North: Dunmore, pp. 181–96.

Major, L. and R. Coleman (2008) "The Intersection of Race and Gender in Election Coverage: What Happens When the Candidates Don't Fit the Stereotypes?," *Howard Journal of Communications* 19(4): 315–33.

Mavin, S., P. Bryans, and R. Cunningham (2010) "Fed-up with Blair's Babes, Gordon's Gals, Cameron's Cuties, Nick's Nymphets: Challenging Gendered Media Representations of Women Political Leaders," *Gender in Management, An International Journal* 25(7): 550–69.

Melin-Higgins, M. (2004) "Coping with Journalism: Gendered Newsroom Culture," in Marjan de Bruin and Karen Ross (eds.) *Gender and Newsroom Cultures: Identities at Work*, Cresskill, NJ: Hampton Press, pp. 197–222.

Norris, P. (ed.) (1997a) *Women, Media and Politics*, Oxford: Oxford University Press.

——(1997b) "Women Leaders Worldwide: A Splash of Color in the Photo Op," in P. Norris (ed.) *Women, Media and Politics*, Oxford: Oxford University Press, pp. 149–65.

North, L. (2009) *The Gendered Newsroom: How Journalists Experience the Changing World of Media*, Cresskill, NJ: Hampton Press.

Rehkopf, F. and M. Reinstadler (2011) "All Equal in UK Newspaper Journalism?," *Cision (blog)*, March 8. FMalik1922http://blog.uk.cision.com/2011/03/women%E2%80%99s-day-2011-all-equal-in-uk-newspaper journalism/.

Robinson, G. (2004) "Gender in the Newsroom: Canadian Experiences," in M. de Bruin and K. Ross (eds.) *Gender and Newsroom Cultures: Identities at Work*, Cresskill, NJ: Hampton Press, pp. 181–96.

——(2005) *Gender, Journalism and Equity: Canadian, U.S. and European Perspectives*, Cresskill, NJ: Hampton Press.

Rodgers, S. and E. Thorson (2003) "A Socialization Perspective on Male and Female Reporting," *Journal of Communication* 53(4): 658–75.

Ross, K. (2002) *Women, Politics, Media: Uneasy Relations in Comparative Perspective*, Cresskill, NJ: Hampton Press.

——(2007) "The Journalist, the Housewife, the Citizen and the Press: Women and Men as Sources in Local News Narratives," *Journalism* 8(4): 449–73.

——(2009) *Gendered Media: Women, Men and Identity Politics*, Lanham, MD: Rowman & Littlefield.

Ross, K. and C. Carter (2011) "Women and News: A Long and Winding Road," *Media, Culture & Society* 33(8): 1148–65.

Ross, K. and M. Comrie (2012) "The Rules of the (Leadership) Game: Gender, Politics and News," *Journalism Studies* 13(8): 967–82.

Ross, K., E. Evans, L. Harrison, M. Shears, and K. Wadia (2013) "The Gender of News and News of Gender: Sex, Politics and Press Coverage of the 2010 British General Election," *International Journal of Press/Politics* 18(1): 3–20.

Semetko, H. A. and H. G. Boomgaarden (2007) "Reporting Germany's 2005 Bundestag Election Campaign: Was Gender an Issue?," *Press/Politics* 12(4): 154–71.

Shoemaker, P. J. and S. D. Reese (1996) *Mediating the Message: Theories of Influence on Mass Media Content*, 2nd edition, White Plains, NY: Longman.

Sones, B., M. Moran, and J. Lovenduski (2005) *Women in Parliament, The New Suffragettes*, London: Politicos.

Sreberny-Mohammadi, A. and K. Ross (1996) "Women MPs and the Media: Representing the Body Politic," in J. Lovenduski and P. Norris (eds.) *Women in Politics*, Oxford: Oxford University Press, pp. 105–17.

Steiner, L. (1998) "Newsroom Accounts of Power at Work," in C. Carter, G. Branston, and S. Allan (eds.) *News, Gender and Power*, London: Routledge, pp. 145–59.

Stevens, A. (2007) *Women, Power and Politics*, Basingstoke: Palgrave Macmillan.

Strömbäck, J. and L. W. Nord (2006) "Do Politicians Lead the Tango: A Study of the Relationship between Swedish Journalists and their Political Sources in the Context of Election Campaigns," *European Journal of Communication* 21(2): 147–64.

Trimble, L. (2007) "Gender, Political Leadership and Media Visibility: Globe and Mail Coverage of Conservative Party of Canada Leadership Contests," *Canadian Journal of Political Science* 40(4): 969–93.

Trimble, L. and N. Treiberg (2010) "'Either Way, There's Going to Be a Man in Charge': Media Representations of New Zealand Prime Minister Helen Clark," in R. Murray (ed.)

*Cracking the Highest Glass Ceiling: A Global Comparison of Women's Campaigns for Executive Office*, Santa Barbara, CA: Praeger.

Tuchman, G., Arlene Kaplan Daniels, and James Benét (1978) *Hearth and Home: Images of Women in the Mass Media*, New York: Oxford University Press.

Valenzuela, S. and T. Correa (2009) "Press Coverage and Public Opinion on Women Candidates: The Case of Chile's Michelle Bachelet," *International Communication Gazette* 71(3): 203–23.

van Zoonen, L. (1998) "One of the Girls? The Changing Gender of Journalism," in C. Carter, G. Branston, and S. Allan (eds.) *News, Gender and Power*, London: Routledge, pp. 33–46.

——(2006) "The Personal, the Political and the Popular: A Woman's Guide to Celebrity Politics," *European Journal of Cultural Studies* 9(3): 287–301.

WACC (2010) *Who Makes the News?*, London: World Association for Christian Communication.

Ward, L. (2000) "Learning from the 'Babe' Experience: How the Finest Hour Became a Fiasco," in A. Coote (ed.) *New Gender Agenda*, London: IPPR.

Zoch, L. M. and J. VanSlyke Turk (1998) "Women Making News: Gender as a Variable in Source Selection and Use," *Journalism and Mass Communication Quarterly* 75(4): 762–75.

# 27

# Transgender, transmedia, transnationality

## Chaz Bono in documentary and *Dancing with the Stars*

## Katherine Sender

Discussing the travelogue as an exemplary genre of transgender autobiography, Jay Prosser (1999) addresses what initially appear to be the genre's contradictory impulses: movement and specificity. Resisting polarized debates in transgender theory and politics between reactionary essentialism and progressive fluidity, Prosser does not counter movement with stasis, nor specificity with generality. He resists the temptation to see movement and specificity as oppositional, instead seeing "affiliation and specification as interconstitutive of each other and of transgender studies" (Prosser 1999: 87). Movement and specificity are particularly apt in considering the televised representations of Chaz Bono that appeared on US television and elsewhere in 2011. Bono's transgender narrative exemplifies movement, mobility, and travel and also reaffirms specificity, identification, and the importance of context. These dynamics not only describe the various iterations of Bono's transgender narrative but also reflect larger debates within communication and media studies about flows of content across platforms and regions. Movement, specificity, and their interconnections frame Bono's transition to and repositioning as a man, the various ways this trajectory was represented in different media forms, the circulation of his narrative across media platforms, and the transnational distribution of his story. Prosser's call to attend to both movement and specificity in transgender narratives intensifies the political significance of media scholars' discussions of transplatform and transnational media.

The range and rapidity of the circulation of Chaz Bono's transgender narrative can be understood in part from his lifetime in the media spotlight. Born as a girl in 1969 to Sonny Bono and Cher, Chastity appeared regularly on their comedy and music show *The Sonny & Cher Show*. Her mother's increasing fame as a pop icon and her father's move from music to politics as a Republican congressman (until his death in 1998) marked Chastity as an ongoing subject of tabloid gossip. Outed as a lesbian in 1995, she went on to work with various gay rights organizations. In 2009 Chaz made public his gender transition on *Entertainment Tonight* and on other media outlets.

Predicting the ongoing media interest in his transition, Bono decided to shape his own narrative in two documentaries, first *Becoming Chaz* and then *Being Chaz*. He approached World of Wonder, which had experience in gay, lesbian, bisexual, and transgender (GLBT) media production, including *TransGeneration*, *Ru Paul's Drag Race*, and *Ru Paul's Drag U*. Bono was a producer for the two documentaries that focus on his transition and appearance on *Dancing with the Stars* in the context of his home life with his fiancée, Jenny Elia. Oprah Winfrey's struggling cable channel, OWN, distributed both documentaries; and the publication of Bono's memoir, *Transition* (2011), coincided with the broadcast of the first documentary in May 2011.

In September 2011 ABC announced that Bono would compete on the thirteenth season of the extremely popular US reality television show *Dancing with the Stars* (*DWTS*). In addition to an openly gay host, Bruno Tonioli, this season also featured Carson Kressley of *Queer Eye* fame as a competitor, making this a very queer season. Predictably, right-wing groups charged that *DWTS* violated their expectations for "family television" (Cohen 2011). The popularity of the franchise around the world and Bono's fame as Cher's child made his story an international phenomenon. Although Bono was voted off after six episodes, both Bono and *Becoming Chaz* were celebrated with awards from the Gay and Lesbian Alliance Against Defamation.

Media coverage of Bono's transition can be contextualized within three frames: representations of transgender people in mainstream and marginal media, movements of transgender narratives across platforms, and transnational circuits of transgender media distribution and reception. I have argued that we can understand GLBT media representations according to their proximity to the media center—characterized by high financial investment, professionalism, institutionalization, and audience figures (Sender 2012). Texts produced at the media center are likely to be most normative: gender conforming, family oriented, non-sexual, and apolitical. At the margins of this center, the domain of reality television and small cable channels, we find more adventurous GLBT representations: lower budgets, flexible labor, and niche audiences both allow and demand riskier and more diverse images. Finally, at the periphery of these margins are self-funded media, such as web series, that are produced for microniche audiences, are not beholden to advertisers, and can circulate a wide range of GLBT images. This argument was mostly focused on making sense of gay and lesbian images; I investigate here whether it is similarly useful to understand the differences in Bono's transgender narrative between the media center (*DWTS*) and its margins (the documentaries).

This concentric model of media representation is predicated upon a highly diverse, mobile, multimodal system of media production and distribution, described by Henry Jenkins as "convergence culture" (Jenkins 2006). Whereas Jenkins's example was *The Matrix*, Bono's narrative also exemplifies transmedia storytelling, a story that "unfolds across multiple media platforms, with each new text making a distinctive and valuable contribution to the whole" (2006: 97–8). Each contribution to the larger story must be comprehensible as an individual iteration. Each must capitalize on the specificities of its medium: "A good transmedia franchise works to attract multiple constituencies by pitching the content somewhat differently in the different media" (2006: 98). Transmedia storytelling exemplifies the logic of intensively horizontally integrated media industries, where one megacorporation owns many different media production companies (film, television, video games, comics, and so on). The story of Bono's transition was not simultaneously engineered by one overarching media company, but Bono had a significant role in engineering his own "brand" across the media landscape, producing transmedia storytelling in traditional and online media. This research considers how Bono skillfully exploited transmedia to circulate his transgender narrative.

Bono also illustrates the transnational circulation of transgender celebrity. Reality television has proven especially mobile across media markets: It is cheap to produce and often very popular, its formats are designed to be readily adaptable across distinct locales, and its circuits of distribution are well established (see, for example, Kraidy and Sender 2011). Despite the increasing international distribution of media, and the burgeoning scholarship that accompanies this, relatively little has been written about the global circulation of gay and lesbian, let alone transgender, representations. Even Christopher Pullen's recent anthology (Pullen 2012), a welcome contribution, scarcely considers transgender media. Scholarly work on transgender media typically focuses on the representation of transgender people outside the West (see, for example, Bluck 2012); the dangers of imposing Western frames and terminologies on gender-variant people in non-Western countries (for example Halberstam 2012); or the potentials of online message boards for the constitution of a transnational transgender identity (Heinz 2012). Very little work addresses how transgender media narratives travel globally. This chapter, lastly, considers how official and unofficial global flows of media representations facilitate the international circulation of Bono's story of transition and transgender personhood.

This study investigates the production and circulation of representations of Bono in the two documentaries *Becoming Chaz* and *Being Chaz*; the six episodes of *DWTS* in which he was a contestant; his memoir, *Transition: The Story of How I Became a Man* (2011); televised media (US news programs, talk shows); print media (US and international newspapers and magazines); and online media. I do not offer a comprehensive account of all Bono's media appearances. Rather, I suggest the range in both platform and location of his transgender narrative from three linked perspectives: the scope of his transgender representation in the documentaries (marginal media) compared with *DWTS* (media center); transmedia proliferation; and the transnational circulation of his narrative.

## Transgender representation at the media margins and center

A concentric model of minority media representations would predict that transgender images at the center (*DWTS*) would be more conservative than those appearing on the margins of this center (*Becoming Chaz* and *Being Chaz*). What, however, would a conservative or progressive view of a transgender person look like? Scholarly consideration of transgender representation remains scarce; attention to female-to-male transgender representations is scarcer still, with the important exception of studies of Kimberly Pierce's film *Boys Don't Cry* (Halberstam 2001; Henderson 2001; Cooper 2002). Halberstam describes the debates about the ontology and politics of gender variance as a struggle between "a transsexuality that emerges from the mismatch of sex and gender," on one hand, and "a transgenderism that announces itself as an infinite array of gendered bodies," on the other (2012: 337). Halberstam's model for progressive transgender politics could be adopted for representations too: "at their best, transgender politics are part of a larger form of queer critique that destabilizes the foundations of heteronormativity and questions the relays of stability between gender, family and nation" (2012: 337). We could look at Bono's narrative to address the extent to which he is represented as embodying a "mismatch of sex and gender," typically addressed as being "trapped in the wrong body." At the same time, can he also occupy a mobile position in an "infinite array of gendered bodies"? If so, how does this mobility present itself? Do these images unsettle taken-for-granted roles of normative genders within the family? Is there more scope for a progressive destabilization of gender, family, and national norms in the more marginal media, the documentaries aired on OWN, than in *DWTS*, which is located at the epicenter of mainstream media production?

Both the documentaries and the reality show *DWTS* capitalize on the values fundamental to their genres: ordinariness, authenticity, and realism. This has particular value for gay and transgender representations (Pullen 2007): This is not an *image* of a trans person (usually played by a gender-normative actor) but testimony to the fact of transgender. The genres have important distinctions, however, and the success of both texts can be accounted for by their fidelity to the demands of their form. *DWTS* is highly entertaining, immediate, and routinized, on one hand, and *Becoming Chaz* and *Being Chaz* are intimate, confessional, and educational, on the other. These characteristics combine with the texts' proximity to the media center to shape their representation of Bono as a transgender man.

In the documentaries, reality show, memoir, and news media Bono represents himself as having been born into the wrong body. He describes himself as "a man trapped inside a female shell" (*Becoming Chaz*). Later, he introduces himself on the first episode of *DWTS*: "I'm Chaz Bono. I'm the first transgender star on *Dancing with the Stars*, which means that I was born with a female body, but I have transitioned and I am now a male." The point here is not to ascribe Bono to a position on some spectrum of gender essentialism. As Prosser asserts, the sense of being trapped in the wrong body is fundamentally felt by many gender-variant people: "My contention is that transsexuals continue to deploy the image of wrong embodiment [after it's medically strategic] because being trapped in the wrong body is simply what transsexuality feels like" (Prosser 1998: 69). Instead I am concerned with how this experience of being born in the wrong body is represented in the different texts, at the margins and center of media production.

*Becoming Chaz* echoes Prosser's study of the transgender travelogue: Bono is on a journey as he physically changes through hormone therapy, travels from Los Angeles to San Francisco to have surgery, and narratively constructs himself as a body-in-transition. He uses the documentary, and his body as evidence within it, to educate viewers about the physical aspects of female-to-male transition. We see him injecting testosterone, and teaching Elia how to do it; watch him prepare for and recover from surgery to have his breasts removed and his chest reconstructed. *Being Chaz* represents a different kind of journey: Bono's body is stabilizing in his male form and becomes a political tool for transgender visibility, not least as he documents his experience on *DWTS*. In both, the documentaries assert that the body is the cause of gender: we hear about the emotional and relational effects of taking testosterone, as both Bono and Elia adapt to his increased assertiveness and "male energy." Bono does not present his body in order to pass as biologically male; his is a visible transgender body. Bono apparently willingly assents to the demand by normatively gendered people that trans people must trade their body privacy for understanding, and is subjected to all sorts of prurient interest in order to account for his gender trajectory. In two of the televised interviews he and Elia are quizzed about how their sex life has changed since Bono's transition (*Nightline*, November 18, 2009; *Oprah*, May 9, 2011).

On *DWTS* Bono presents himself as having already transitioned, as "now male." Unlike the documentaries, in which he had more control over his image, *DWTS* suggests a struggle between him and the production apparatus about the status of his transgender body. Bono is consistently shown as inadequately masculine (Mocarski et al. 2012). Judge Tonioli patronizes Bono throughout the series, calling him a "penguin," an "Ewok," and a "teddy bear." Whereas the other men on the show—male celebrities and professional dancers—frequently appear in tight clothes or states of undress, Bono's body is covered by layers of clothing. Further, Bono struggles with physical injuries throughout the season, and is often shown icing an ankle or knee in preparation to dance. However, there is a tension between the live moments of the show and the prerecorded segments, where Bono has more control over his self-representation. In the episode that focuses on contestants' most memorable year, Bono chooses the song "Laugh at Me" written by his father, Sonny, saying, "If you have a problem with me, that's your problem, not mine. ... It's about being a different kind of man." In those parts of the show that Bono can shape, his self-presentation as a transitioned male is confident, however much some feedback on his live performance undermines this.

Different texts also treat Bono's position within family very differently. Bono's famous family underpins his narrative in each: in one news interview he talks about how he would have transitioned earlier but he was concerned about what effects the publicity would have on his family. Indeed, in her interview for *Becoming Chaz*, and thus somewhat early in his transition, Cher confesses that she wished Bono had transitioned "quietly." Bono's family is represented very differently in the documentaries and *DWTS*. *Becoming Chaz* and *Being Chaz* show Bono within a rich network of biological and chosen family. He lives with his fiancée and their cats and dogs; his aunts, grandmother, and soon-to-be-in-laws visit; he has a supportive stepmother and half-siblings; he is embedded in a 12-step network; his sponsor loaned him the money for his top surgery. In turn, he volunteers with Transforming Family, a local group that supports families with transgender children.

In contrast, the first documentary represents his relationship with Cher as significantly challenged by his transition. One intertitle in *Becoming Chaz* explains that Bono hasn't seen his mother since his top surgery. Cher struggles with pronouns and describes listening to Chaz's "old voice" on his answering machine and wanting to save it because she'd "never hear that voice again." By the time Bono performs on *DWTS* Cher has come around and is supportive of his transition and performance. In response to the hostile reception by the show's conservative viewers, Cher goes on the offensive on her Twitter feed, calling critics "stupid bigots." Although both the documentaries and *DWTS* emphasize Bono's family of origin, his extended familial network is entirely eclipsed in the mainstream show. The familiar shots of contestants' family and friends after each dance offer only the briefest glimpse of Elia; in one episode the camera lingers on a man I believe is Bono's publicist, leaving his fiancée out of the frame. In contrast, extended shots show the other contestants' partners, and when Cher attends the show the producers make a big deal of her response to Bono's performance. In *DWTS*, then, the traces of Cher's ambivalence are erased, as is the continuity of Elia's support; the biological family is reaffirmed.

Transgender offspring present a family crisis of a different order from that posed by gay and lesbian children. In the case of gay and lesbian children, the crisis is patrilineage: how to imagine future generations when biological reproduction cannot be taken for granted. With transgender children, however, the crisis is not for future generations but in this one: the pre-transition child is the dead child, the child the parent must let go of. In *Transition* Bono describes Cher's devastation at hearing that his voice had dropped as a result of testosterone treatments and her decision not to see him for a while. He writes, "I couldn't help but feel a little abandoned, especially after we had become so close again. I decided to take this request as a need to grieve the loss of her daughter" (Bono 2011: 209). Whereas *Becoming Chaz* engages with both Cher's and Bono's pain about the rupture in their relationship, and *Being Chaz* shows the gradual rebuilding of it, *DWTS* presents a seamless image of mother-bear solidarity—Cher defending her cub against the "haters." This is done at the expense of Bono's extensive and loving support network, not least Elia, whose status as Bono's partner is the subject of confusion. On *The Late Show with David Letterman* Cher says Bono had been a lesbian but is now a man. Letterman offers that Bono is "a *male* lesbian." Cher responds, "A male lesbian—no no! That doesn't work!" In contrast to the uncertainty of Elia's role, Cher's status as Bono's biologically tied, fiercely supportive mother is reaffirmed in these mainstream representations.

Needham (2009) is troubled by the reinstatement on television of normativity in gay as well as heterosexual families. He argues that the temporal rhythms of the medium—flow and scheduling, for example—affirm heteronormative domestic and familial representations and contexts of reception. Those representations of Bono appearing at the media center affirm Needham's analysis: shoring up the biological family represented by his relationship with his mother, Cher, and consistently invoking his close relationship with his father. Elia is marginalized both visually (*DWTS*'s inattention to her among the crowd) and narratively (Cher and Letterman can't imagine the status of Bono and Elia's relationship). The rhythm of a highly popular, rigorously formatted dance competion has space for neither biological family rupture nor queer affiliation. In the documentaries, however, Bono is suspended in an extended family connected by genes, law, love, friendship, and politics. His engagement with Elia might suggest an assumption of homonormative monogamous resolution, but this relationship is tense throughout. The documentaries do not evade the challenges posed to their commitment by Bono's transition, Jenny's drinking, and the stress involved in completing her Masters degree. The second documentary's closing scene shows Bono saying they are in "a very hard place." In the documentaries, distributed from the margins of the media center, non-normative family formations are privileged, their tensions and irresolutions affirmed.

Comparing the different presentations of Bono's body and family in the documentaries and *DWTS* enables a consideration of the possibilities for movement and specificity at the margins and center of media production. The conventions of both genres affirm his authenticity. His self-presentation as a high-profile transgender man offers uprecedented visibility in national and international media. A number of factors central to the production of each show, however, shape how his presentation ultimately appeared. Bono's central role in initiating and producing the documentaries, their generic conventions as "confessional" documentary (Pullen 2007: 11), their distribution on a new network shaped by Winfrey's brand of mediated intimacy combined to produce a text remarkable for its openness. I don't only mean in the sense of its frankness, but semiotically too: The emphasis here is on movement, irresolution, and ambivalence. In contrast, *DWTS* can be seen as a relatively closed text. The insistent rhythms of the show—episodic within the season, segmented within the episode, patterned in the to and fro of dance and audience response—leave little room for indeterminacy. Here Bono's gender status is achieved, his relationship with his mother affirmed. He trades control over his self-representation for the publicity that his appearance will bring. Rewatching *DWTS* alongside *Being Chaz*, which documents the process of being on the show, reveals that Bono had few illusions about the risks he was taking by participating in the competition, including those to his personal safety. The rigors of the program's structure, its position as one of the most popular shows on air, and much of the audience's likely unfamiliarity with transgender people mean that Bono has to present a body resolved, a narrative completed. This may be strategic essentialism: a political strategy that puts to one side a commitment to fluidity and irresolution that poststructuralism demands in favor of a unified identity necessary to make strong political claims. Whereas the documentaries can hold movement and specificity in tension, *DWTS* pictures specificity as the reaffirmation of gender and family stability.

## Transmedia, transnationality

Simply comparing Bono's self-presentations in the documentaries and *DWTS* does not account for the circulation of his transgender story across a wide range of media and national contexts. I am adapting Jenkins's productive phrase "transmedia storytelling" beyond his original sense, in which media companies control and disseminate the brand. I argue that Bono has controlled and proliferated his transgender storytelling—his brand—across multiple media platforms. His transmedia trajectory can be segmented into three relatively discrete periods. The first occurred with his initial coming out as transgender on the television show *Entertainment Tonight* in October 2009, when his first documentary was already underway. This precipitated a flurry of news media appearances, including on *Good Morning America* and *Nightline* soon thereafter. The second transmedia phase surrounded the premiere of *Becoming Chaz* and the simultaneous publication of his memoir in May 2011. In a skilled piece of cross-promotion, Oprah Winfrey leveraged her huge audience for the last season of her syndicated show *Oprah* (May 9, 2011) to market Bono's first documentary on her OWN channel the following day. Bono appeared in other mainstream television shows, including David Letterman's *Late Show* on May 11, 2011. Each interviewer respectfully probes Bono on the basics of transgender psychology and physiology; he patiently and articulately distinguishes gender identity from sexual identification, top surgery from mastectomy, and so on. Recalling his appearance on *Letterman*, Bono writes, "I was able to give David Letterman a transgender 101 lecture with millions of Americans watching" (2011: 242). Bono's story appeared in major print outlets, including a lengthy article in the *New York Times* describing Bono as a "reluctant transgender role model" (Wilson 2011), and a predictably family-oriented approach from Canada's *McLean's* magazine ("How Cher's Daughter Became Her Son," Johnson 2011). News of Bono's transition also circulated widely on the internet, with well-established GLBT media websites such as AfterEllen.com and AfterElton. com covering the story, as well as bloggers, vloggers, and Twitter feeds. Significant as this transmedia coverage was, while this news story originated in the domain of a marginal cable channel and memoir, Bono's story may have been a passing moment.

The attention garnered by Bono's documentaries and book was dwarfed by the news that he would be a contestant on *DWTS* in early September 2011. The *DWTS* casting choice precipitated predictable backlash in the blogosphere that inevitably fed back into a news media industry hungry for conflict (Reuters 2011). Conservative bloggers were outraged that this "family" show would cast both Bono and Kressley. *ABC News* gave Bono's story a lengthy treatment (September 2, 2011) leveraging the news to promote their own channel's *DWTS*: Bono and his dance partner discussed competing on the show and the accompanying vicious transphobia. Producers inevitably aired the views of right-wing critics, including a spokeswoman from an online pressure group, OneMillionMoms. This group boycotted the show, she said, because Bono's presence "will be very confusing for children and he should not be included in the cast." Bono utilized this media moment to emphasize the importance of his appearance on such a mainstream show: "This for me shows why it is so important for me to be on the show, because so little is known about transgender, there are so many completely inaccurate stereotypes and thoughts that people have." His publicist continues: Watching *DWTS* "is not going to make your kid transgender, but what it could do is save your kid's life because young transgender kids, kids with gender identity issues, have a huge suicide rate, and if they see one positive influence, one positive role model, this could save lives and that's why Chaz is here" (*ABC News* 2011). In addition to coverage in other major television shows, print media, and online sites, Twitter was also a major site of contestation. Cher used her extensive network of Twitter followers to call opponents of Bono's *DWTS* appearance "stupid bigots," a use of social media that made its way back into traditional news media (Cohen 2011).

These three phases of Bono's transmedia narrative suggest differences in the mobility of transgender biography according to proximity to the media center. Representations produced at the margins of the media center (the documentaries) had some potential to traverse both to the center and to the periphery. *DWTS*, however, located at the very center of media production, had more purchase across a wide range of platforms, not least because of the right-wing backlash against the show. However frustrating were the limits imposed on Bono's nuanced presentation of his transition in *DWTS*, this media opportunity gave Bono unprecedented publicity for transgender visibility.

The specificity of Bono's transmedia narrative across platforms is also reflected in the transnational trajectory of the various texts. *Becoming Chaz* premiered at the Sundance Film Festival in the US in 2011, and was then aired on OWN in the US and Canada, as was *Being Chaz* later in 2011. For reason of form and distribution circuits, these documentaries had relatively limited global mobility. In contrast, *DWTS* has become one of the most popular global brands, with local productions in more than 35 countries. The US season featuring Bono aired on the most highly rated Canadian channel, CTV (2011), as well as on Sky satellite in the UK (2012) and New Zealand's most popular channel, TV One (2011). Its distribution to New Zealand demonstrates the national specificity of transnational media trajectories, in both production and reception. New Zealand was one of the few places in which the Bono season of *DWTS* was aired: Because of the success of the show's local adaptations around the world, the US version had *less* international play than some other reality shows that are simply sold in their US version to other countries. New Zealand had produced a highly popular local version of the show from 2005 to 2009. It proved too expensive for such a small television market, however, and was canceled and replaced by the cheaper, already produced US version. Although the season was shown in few markets outside the US, news outlets in many other countries covered the story because of Cher's fame and *DWTS*'s popularity.

There was little public conservative backlash in New Zealand to Bono or *DWTS*. The national newspaper the *New Zealand Herald* ran a few short articles about Bono's appearance on *DWTS*, starting with a typically tabloid-style headline "Chaz Bono Wants a Penis" (*New Zealand Herald* 2011a). The paper kept the story alive over the coming weeks by covering Cher's appearance on the show, mentioning other contestants' responses, and making *DWTS* their TV "Pick of the Week" (*New Zealand Herald* 2011b, 2011c, 2011d). Despite the prurience of the *Herald*'s attention to Bono's body, other articles offer examples of solidarity: Cher's for her son, and fellow-contestant David Arquette's because of his relationship with his transgender sister, Alexis (who had her own moment of visibility on another reality show, *The Surreal Life*). The lack of reactionary opposition in New Zealand to Bono's appearance on *DWTS* may be explained by New Zealanders' familiarity with transgender images: Georgina Beyer was the world's first openly transgender politician elected to a national assembly (2005–7). New Zealand television has featured a long-running sketch comedy series by two openly lesbian cross-dressing sisters, the Topp Twins. Pearson argues that a tradition of Pasifika non-normative gender performance in New Zealand had a role in public acceptance of the Topp Twins, even in conservative regions of the country: "[R]eading transgender in New Zealand might owe a partial debt to Pacific conceptions of identity" (Pearson forthcoming: 19). The nonchalant reception in New Zealand of Bono on *DWTS* may have reflected a national familiarity with various iterations of gender variance in both political and popular fields. The international market for reality television facilitated a limited distribution of Bono's transgender narrative, the reception of which is particular to the countries in which this is circulated.

Prosser argues that the act of writing transgender travel memoirs is important in at least three ways: Transgender authors need to represent their transition; they demonstrate a commitment to movement—physical, geographical, and narrative—in their representation; and they emphasize representation itself as a journey. The story of Bono's transition across a wide variety of media platforms and some national contexts exemplifies the intersectionality of this approach. Transgender texts situated at different proximities to the media center are more or less free to work with the tensions between movement and specificity, with those at the media center narrowing towards stasis. The precise trajectories of transgender images across media platforms illustrate that transmedia flows are not equally accessible. The contested status of transgender narratives demands that we consider not only how texts circulate between the center and peripheries, but the specificities of their production at each location. Although contemporary global circuits facilitate unprecedented international distribution, the media economies and cultures of their reception are specific. Considering Bono's mediated self-presentation according to gender transition, shifting family configurations, migration across platform, and global flows demands commitment to movement, specificity, and their intersections. Transgender media cannot simply be celebrated for their inventive proliferation; the containment of those stories in their particular iterations, platforms, and locations must be considered.

## References

ABC News (2011) "Chaz Bono Under Fire for 'Dancing With the Stars' Season 13 Selection," September 2. http://www.youtube.com/watch?v=VS8EtnJRrq4.

Bluck, S. (2012) "Transsexual in Iran: A fatwa for freedom?," in C. Pullen (ed.) LGBT Transnational Identity and the Media, New York: Palgrave Macmillan.

Bono, C. (2011) Transition: The Story of How I Became a Man, New York: Dutton.

Cohen, A. (2011) "Transgender Celeb Gets Bad Raps from Dancing Critics," The Advertiser, September 3.

Cooper, B. (2002) "Boys Don't Cry and Female Masculinity: Reclaiming a Life and Dismantling the Politics of Normative Heterosexuality," Critical Studies in Media Communication 19: 44–63.

Halberstam, J. (2001) "The Transgender Gaze in Boys Don't Cry," Screen 42: 294–8.

——(2012) "Global Female Masculinities," Sexualities 15: 336–54.

Heinz, M. (2012) "Inscribing Transmale Discourses Online," International Communication Association Annual Conference, Phoenix, US.

Henderson, L. (2001) "The Class Character of Boys Don't Cry," Screen 42: 299–303.

Jenkins, H. (2006) Convergence Culture: Where Old and New Media Collide, New York: New York University Press.

Johnson, B. D. (2011) "How Cher's Daughter Became Her Son," Maclean's, Canada, April 26. http://www2.macleans.ca/2011/04/26/how-cher%E2%80%99s-daughter-became-her-son/.

Kraidy, M. and K. Sender (eds.) (2011) The Politics of Reality TV: Global Perspectives, New York: Routledge.

Mocarski, R., B. Emmons, R. Smallwood, and S. Butler (2012) "'A Different Kind of Man': Mediated Transgendered Subjectivity, Chaz Bono on Dancing with the Stars," International Communication Association Annual Conference, Phoenix, US.

Needham, G. (2009) "Scheduling Normativity: Television, the Family, and Queer Temporality," in G. Davis and G. Needham (eds.) Queer TV: Theories, Histories, Politics, London: Routledge.

New Zealand Herald (2011a) "Chaz Bono Wants a Penis," New Zealand Herald, September 1.

——(2011b) "Cher to Attend 'Dancing with the Stars' for Son Chaz," New Zealand Herald, September 8.

——(2011c) "David Arquette Can Relate to Chaz Bono," *New Zealand Herald*, September 20.

——(2011d) "TV Pick of the Week: Dancing with the Stars," *New Zealand Herald*, November 3.

Pearson, S. (forthcoming) "Televisual Transgender: Hybridizing the Mainstream in Pasifika New Zealand," in N. Besnier and K. Alexeyeff (eds.) *Gender on the Edge: Transgender, Gay, and Other Pacific Islanders*, Honolulu: University of Hawai'i Press.

Prosser, J. (1998) *Second Skins: The Body Narratives of Transsexuality*, New York: Columbia University Press.

——(1999) "Exceptional Locations: Transsexual Travelogues," in K. More and S. Whittle (eds.) *Reclaiming Genders: Transsexual Grammars at the Fin de Siecle*, London: Cassell.

Pullen, C. (2007) *Documenting Gay Men: Identity and Performance in Reality Television and Documentary Film*, London, McFarland & Company.

——(ed.) (2012) *LGBT Transnational Identity and the Media*, New York: Palgrave Macmillan.

Reuters (2011) "'Chaz Is Being Viciously Attacked': Cher," *National Post*, September 2.

Sender, K. (2012) "No Hard Feelings: Reflexivity and Queer Affect in the New Media Landscape," in K. Ross (ed.) *The Handbook of Gender, Sex, and Media*, Malden, MA: Blackwell.

Wilson, C. (2011) "The Reluctant Transgender Role Model," *New York Times*, May 8.

# 28

# Celebrity, gossip, privacy, and scandal

## *Milly Williamson*

Among the central debates regarding celebrity culture is whether modern fame has opened up the public sphere to people outside traditional hierarchies, and, if so, whether this opening is symptomatic of cultural decline. To some people, the burgeoning of celebrity marks a serious cultural demise (Boorstin 1961); an unprecedented deterioration in press standards and in its civic role (Franklin 1997; Langer 1998); or a symptom of a transition to a more ephemeral and "liquid" epoch (Bauman 2005). Celebrity culture, from this perspective, represents a trivialization of news content (Gitlin 1997) and demonstrates the troubling link between the news media and global entertainment industries. Others regard celebrity culture as part of an opening up of the public sphere, a democratic expansion of the categories of people who can take to the public stage (Ponce de Leon 2002; Connell 1992). Here journalism manifests concerns about social difference that are recognizable to audiences, rather than "remote and abstract" (Connell 1992: 82).

Gender is central to this debate. Given women's traditional or historical relegation to the private sphere, celebrity culture arguably provides women with increasing opportunity to take to the public stage in much greater numbers (Lumby 1997). Some also suggest that both reality TV and the turn to celebrity gossip in the news media are less a question of declining standards and more an example of the way that news media must now address a wider audience than the traditional (male) elite. The language of gossip that surrounds celebrity culture is considered to speak in the idiom of ordinary people and in particular to address the competences of women, previously excluded from the public realm (Hermes 1995; Shattuc 1997; van Zoonen 2006). A new public sphere, or counter public sphere, equated with these processes is regarded as more inclusive and participatory; it is arguably less elitist, less male dominated.

The appeal of this second argument is very strong, not least because some of those who bemoan the perceived decline of cultural standards do so on markedly elitist grounds. Indeed, prominent feminists have criticized Jürgen Habermas's (1991; originally published in German in 1962) conception of the public sphere, because it ignores the absence of women (and of the working class) from traditional public culture (Fraser 1990). Daniel Boorstin's work represents one of the earliest endorsements of the idea that celebrity culture represents cultural decline: He points to a mythical past where "heroes" attained fame through noble deeds. These figures, he argues, have been replaced with inauthentic, fabricated celebrities who are "well-known for their well-knowness" (Boorstin 1961: 58). The shift from public culture's celebration of the "idols of production" to the "idols of consumption" (Lowenthal 1961) is seen to mark a transition from a public emphasis on the world of work and industry (and higher values) to the world of leisure and consumption (and the celebration of notoriety and scandal) and a consequent decline in public culture. For Zygmunt Bauman (2005), today's celebrity (here today, gone tomorrow) is symptomatic of a shift from a solid modern era, which celebrated heroes who defended the nation, to a liquid modernity, which is inherently ephemeral and episodic. Unlike previous fame, which celebrated achievement, the current emphasis on celebrity scandal, "the cavalcade of celebrities, each one leaping out of nowhere only to sink shortly into oblivion, is eminently suited to marking the succession of episodes into which lifetimes are sliced" (Bauman 2005: 50). For Bauman, the shift from a culture of production to one of consumption, as represented by celebrity, may superficially seem to bring greater freedom, but actually makes our uncertainties and dissatisfactions more difficult to pin down. He argues that the episodic quality of liquid life actually makes more diffuse our desire for emancipation.

In contrast, some scholars celebrate the shattering of greatness and the demise of aura that is seen to reside in celebrity culture. For Ponce de Leon, the processes leading to current celebrity culture—such as the spread of democracy, the values of individualism, and the rise of a consumer market economy—"have steadily eroded all sources of authority, including the aura that formerly surrounded the 'great'" (Ponce de Leon 2002: 4).

One must not simply dismiss concerns about the increasing commodification of the news media or its corporate links to the global entertainment industry. Graeme Turner points to the "commercial alignment" between the news media, magazine industry, and the "promotional needs of the major entertainment organisations" (2004: 73). Furthermore, the view that entertainment has simply democratized public culture ignores the "massive concentration of symbolic power in media institutions," which in turn impacts on audiences' engagement with the media, itself an "uneven symbolic landscape" (Couldry 2003: 82). In light of a government inquiry into the phone hacking scandal at the tabloid *News of the World*, no one can ignore the corrupting influence on journalistic practices resulting from corporate news media's increasing emphasis on news of private scandal (involving both celebrities and ordinary people).

However, many of the claims about current celebrity culture—from either perspective outlined above—should be understood in the context of a much longer set of historical processes. Fame in any epoch is shaped by the social, economic, and historical moment; fame indicates the balance of social forces at any given time. It therefore can express the values supporting social power and is also sensitive to shifts in and challenges to power in any period. An historical examination of female celebrity reveals the deeply contradictory character of modern fame that persists. Fame has been permanently transformed by the transition to modern bourgeois society and the contradictions contained therein. It is rooted in values of social mobility, but shaped by the limits to actual social mobility, linked increasingly over two centuries to the economic imperatives of a market- and commodity-driven media, and yet appearing to express something beyond the economic, about identity, the self, individuality, and one's place in the world. This chapter offers an alternative critique of celebrity culture. By grounding this historically, it examines longstanding contradictions in fame that throw open to question the views either that today's celebrity culture is more focused on the private than in the past, or that a concentration on the personality is new (in the press or otherwise). Nor is it the case, I argue, that late twentieth- and early twenty-first-century celebrity culture is unique in admitting new classes of people into its ranks and thereby democratizing the public realm. Each of these processes has been in motion for over two centuries. Each expresses the transition to modernity, and the economic needs of commercial entertainment and media. Each is fettered therefore by the contradictions in the social transformations that gave birth to it, including, significantly, the changing sexual landscape and women's social position.

## The fame of women in the theater and the private/public paradox

The relationship between celebrity and public culture must be understood historically, including its contradictions. By the end of the eighteenth century, the cultural politics of fame and public prominence had altered drastically. This had begun to be attached to the modern values of fame now associated with contemporary celebrity: a celebration of individualism, an emphasis on personality, a keen interest in the private lives of public figures, and a focus on scandal. The definition of fame was changing because of the enormous political, economic, and social transformations of that period of history, a turbulent and contradictory time that was shaking the old order to its foundations. It was marked by widespread dissent across Europe. In 1789 the French National Assembly declared the abolition of feudalism and decreed the Declaration of the Rights of Man and the Citizen. This swept aside the power of the feudal monarchy and the clergy in France and replaced it with a system that was reaching (however faltering) for democracy, equality, and freedom. The reverberations of this revolutionary upheaval spread across Europe. A new social mobility gave rise to new ideologies of the self—crucially, the ideologies of individualism and of the common man (Rojek 2001). These new ways of understanding the self began shaping new modes of public prominence that broke with the aristocratic ideologies of the old order; but they also began to put into place new ideologies of belonging based on the increasing political power of the bourgeoisie. Nonetheless, European society saw the rise to fame and renown of people from many new walks of life, including, significantly, those associated with the incipient mass entertainment industries (commercial theater, amusement parks, and publishing). The possibility of fame for people from new social classes and the ideology of meritocracy emerge in this moment—not in the twentieth century. However, as the precursor to contemporary celebrity, these possibilities are severely limited by the commercial imperatives of the early media and also because normative values about different social roles for men and women became entrenched as the social and political power of the bourgeoisie solidified. Fame for women in the theater was won at a cost. Actresses' financial independence depended upon acquiescence to public insinuations about their sexuality. Meanwhile the press mercilessly targeted prominent women where accusations of sexual wrongdoing had been voiced.

The tumultuous final two decades of the eighteenth century coincided with a dramatic expansion of the reading public and saw the increase of printed material, the growth of the press, and new genres of publications such as magazines and pamphlets. There were increased means for disseminating information and the development of a national and even international public culture, although mass media in today's sense did not exist. The print culture of this time was multifaceted; it included radical and commercial presses, serious news, scandal, and even "penny dreadful" horror pamphlets. The commercial part of this print culture was from the outset obsessed with famous and notorious individuals; some say it was the age of the personality as much as it was the age of reason (Luckhurst and Moody 2005). Indeed, prominent individuals were known to pay for "puffs," columns in the commercial press that literally puffed up their reputation. Just as popular was the printing of scandal, the attempted destruction of reputations. And women were a favorite target, particularly when crime and sexuality could be linked. Two crime stories particularly caught the imagination of the British commercial press and its readers in the late eighteenth century: the stories of Caroline Rudd, on trial for forgery, and the Duchess of Kingston, on trial for bigamy (Moody 2007). Both were accused of adultery and of using sexuality to manipulate the opposite sex. Both trials produced a frenzy of interest, for each seemed to undermine the institution of marriage, to challenge society's basic assumptions about femininity, and to give expression to concerns about changing roles of women. These early cases also highlight the symbiotic relationship between the scandal mongering of the press and the activities in other spheres of culture. For instance, Samuel Foote (2010, 2011), a theater manager operating on the edge of legality himself (he built a reputation on the theater of mimicry and of sexual scandal mongering), drew on these two stories in his plays *The Cozeners* (1774) and *A Trip to Calais* (1775). Foote capitalized on the notoriety of these two women; the performance of his plays fueled the uproar, and contributed to the trial of the Duchess in 1776 becoming a huge society event, with tickets being sold for the then enormous sum of 20 guineas.

In this same period, the British theater, with a much longer commercial history than other European theaters, saw the establishment of a star system. Prominent actors from London's legitimate theater toured the provinces, where their appearances were used for marketing purposes. Many of these early theatrical stars were women, who, like other groups in society, found greater freedom as a result of the social upheavals of this period and the breaking up of traditional social roles. However, gender here provides one of the most salient examples of the contradictions of modern fame. The changing sexual landscape meant that for the first time women beyond the realms of the aristocracy were thrust into the public eye. But even so, the public definition of femininity was confined to the private realm. Despite the greater freedom they experienced, actresses were defined by their sexuality; insinuations of sexual scandal were the norm. Just as the commercial press exposed the private lives of notorious women, it also sexually satirized actresses at a time of growth in the theater.

The treatment of actresses by journalists and satirists echoes the preoccupations of the time, and indicates both the greater freedoms for women and the limits to that freedom. Again, celebrity culture is often lauded as an expression of growing democracy because new categories of people can take the public stage. This is partly true: Even in the late eighteenth century, before the emergence of celebrity circulated by mass media, the fame of actresses was part of a process of growing cultural democracy. But this is only one side of the coin: with fame came the notoriety that accompanied social uncertainty. That notoriety was located in ideas that upheld the subjugated position of women.

Furthermore, those critics who contrast the "serious" public culture of the past with contemporary scandal mongering frivolity, ignore the treatment meted out to many of the new entrants into the public arena—particularly women. Scandal and prurience are part of the cultural shift of bourgeois society, rather than a belated addendum. Also, rather than actresses entering the public domain *per se*, there was a blurring of the public and private realms in the lives of actresses, indeed the first blurring of the public/private boundary. In England, until 1660, women were banned from acting in the legitimate theater. However, by the mid- to late eighteenth century, women became indispensable to the commercial theater as actresses, writers, and theatrical managers (Nussbaum 2005: 149). Indeed, actresses were earning a living wage; many were the heads of households, which certainly upended accepted gender roles. However, this was accompanied by the widespread view that the theater had a corrupting influence and that women were both responsible for the corrupting influence of the theater and more susceptible to it. Actresses were considered to be immodest. Society assumed that "the woman who displayed herself on the public stage was probably a whore" (Nussbaum 2005: 152).

The "illusion of intimacy" (Schickel 2000), which is a central concern of film scholars' understanding of twentieth-century stardom, has its earliest expression in the late eighteenth-century theater and speaks of actresses' growing economic independence and, paradoxically, their simultaneous sexualization (Wanko 2003). Actresses' private lives were from the outset fodder for gossip in a way that the lives of male actors typically were not. Theater managers understood that blurring the line between public image and intimate knowledge could heighten an actress's marketability. Audiences encouraged actresses to reveal their intimate selves; male spectators often paid a fee to visit them backstage in the hope of gaining sexual favors. It made sense for actresses to participate in this "illusion of public intimacy:" in order to increase their fame and popularity, they deliberately tried to merge their theatrical persona with their private selves. They delivered prologues and epilogues whose secrets might entice audiences. Biographical materials about actresses also encouraged an illusion of public intimacy; memoirs published by actresses (almost always written by men) also blurred public image and private selves. Memoirs often "closely linked women with their stage characters, publicized personal scandals, intensified quarrels between players, and thus stimulated the patronage of the commercial theater" (Nussbaum 2005: 151). When Peg Woffington debuted as Macheath's moll in Gay's *Beggar's Opera*, her memoirist claimed that she "appeared to be the very Character she personated" (although at the time of the performance she was 12 years old) (Woffington 1760: 12). Restoration theater established a new kind of intimacy with famous performers that was predominantly centered on female sexuality. It also established illusions of public intimacy that began with insinuations of prostitution. So while expanded social roles for women allowed for greater freedom and public prominence, these were heavily constrained within discourses of sexuality. The paradoxes framing early actresses' fame are part of the shape of the whole of theatrical culture and portend key issues in mass mediated celebrity culture to come. This paradox is with us today, despite advances for women.

Throughout the nineteenth century, the role of the theatrical star became increasingly important. After 1843, when patent protection for legitimate theaters ended, respectable theater grew. So did the power of the theatrical star, who was often both actor and theatrical manager, including female actor managers. With their growing importance, women actor managers attempted to control their own public images and present a respectable self. The famous contralto Lucia Elizabeth Vestry managed the Olympic Theatre, where she successfully produced operatic burlesques in the 1830s; the Covent Garden; and, finally, with her husband Charles James Mathews, the Lyceum Theatre (1847–55). Madame Vestry was, however, the undisputed manager and Charles her able assistant.

Sarah Bernhardt, perhaps the most famous actress of the nineteenth century and the first established theatrical actress to "star" in film, managed the Théâtres de la Renaissance (1893–9). Bernhardt's career is a salient example of the nineteenth-century actress's oscillation between sexual scandal and respectability, which becomes a central theme in twentieth-century female fame. Her early career is marked by scandalous rumors of her sexual appetite and indiscretions. She had an affair with a Belgian nobleman; her only son was born out of wedlock. She was later rumored to have had a passionate affair with the French Impressionist painter Louise Abbéma, who is reputed to have dedicated one of her paintings to Bernhardt, on the anniversary of their romance. Later, while married to actor Aristedes Damala, a morphine addict, Bernhardt was rumored to have had an affair with the future King Edward VII. Although Bernhardt maintained a flamboyant lifestyle, however, she worked hard to move on from her courtesan past and to establish and manage a reputation as a serious, respectable actress. By the late 1870s, although the hint of scandal never entirely disappeared, her reputation was secure. Like other actor managers, she toured extensively and became an enormous success across the world, including in the US. By the beginning of the twentieth century, with an international reputation as the Divine Sarah, she took roles in early French films, such as *La Tosca* (1908). In her second (1912) film, she played Queen Elizabeth.

## Female celebrity and the cinema

In 1914 Adolph Zukor enjoyed huge success with Mary Pickford in *Tess of the Storm*. Promoting Pickford (and other players) as stars became central to his distribution strategy. By 1916 Zukor had the first vertically integrated film corporation, having gained control of Paramount Pictures and substantial holdings in first-run film exhibition theaters. He used stars like Pickford to create demand for his product. Mary Pickford's career reveals the ever-moving fortunes of female fame and its social import, with her rise to prominence in an industry that was quickly becoming a mature oligopoly. Pickford understood that she was one of Paramount's key assets and a valuable commodity for the promotion of film. Exhibitors were more interested in Pickford than Paramount. Accordingly, Pickford renegotiated her contract salary from $20,000 per year to $1,000 per week and half of all film distribution profits. Thus, the battles between studios and stars for control over profits and star image—so significant in the history of Hollywood—begin here with "Little Mary." Because the star product became such a central plank in the film industry's business strategy, studios put enormous effort into controlling those images, and, as in the case of theatrical actresses of the previous century, attempted to merge on-screen persona with off-screen personality. As with the theatrical stars of the previous century, considerable effort was taken to merge Pickford's screen persona and her off-screen personality. However, in contrast to the sexual scandal that surrounded female theatrical stars, film stars such as Pickford projected a wholesome girl-next-door image. Richard de Cordova argues that the regulation of the knowledge about film stars in the early twentieth century was an important part of the development of the star system and contributed enormously to the augmentation of the power of the cinema industry. He highlights an attempt to build an image of the cinema as a morally healthy institution, essentially a backlash against the theater and its private scandals (de Cordova 1990). This was the context for the production and management of Pickford's image. Her off-screen persona was that of a spunky, honest girl who was kind to everyone, but could stand up for herself. This image directly fed into her screen roles: She usually played a poor girl on the verge of blossoming womanhood. Even when her screen character fed the fantasy of social mobility and married into wealth, she was depicted as staying true to her roots.

The public image of "Little Mary" contrasts with her industry reputation, where she was renowned for her business acumen and her deep understanding of the film industry. She produced many highly successful films and was one of the founders of the United Artists, established to circumvent the distribution powers of the vertically integrated studios. Although her public image was constrained by the normative gender discourses embedded in American culture, Pickford had considerable prestige and industry power. Pickford herself built her unified on-screen/off-screen persona. In 1917, at the age of 24, Pickford produced *Poor Little Rich Girl*, in which she also starred. Later that same year, she produced and starred as a child character in *Rebecca of Sunnybrook* and *The Little Princess*. Important to Pickford's image of wholesome femininity was its anchoring in idealized American-ness and whiteness (Redmond 2007). Notably, star images in the early twentieth century were built on discourses of wholesome, white, middle America at a time when high levels of immigration to US cities (13.5 million by 1910) were being met by a campaign of Americanization; the idea of the "melting pot" masked a process of assimilation. Educational films such as *The Making of an American Citizen* (1912) and *The Making of America* (1920) were part of a broad attempt at building a homogeneous American culture, based on values represented in the film industry (and other media, such as the press and radio) by star images. When Pickford married Douglas Fairbanks, the very image of American masculinity—handsome, athletic, and funny—they became America's most celebrated couple, emblematic of an idealized American identity.

The career of the female star speaks volumes about the contradictions between the growing power of the commercial entertainment industries and the possibility for expanded participation in the surrounding mediated public sphere. Women celebrities found public prominence, and a few held powerful positions; but the nature of that public participation was circumscribed by, and subordinated to, the business needs of media industries growing in power and influence throughout the twentieth century. In each period, the female star was defined (and, as we have seen, those definitions alter in different historical moments) by the dominant ideas about femininity and gender roles, and, moreover, reinforced ideological constructions of gender.

## Female celebrity today

The media focus on celebrity has unquestionably expanded throughout the twentieth and twenty-first centuries, as new technology, commercially driven deregulation, and media mergers have produced a combined pressure to fill media content from a predictable source. Pseudo-events (Boorstin 1961) generated by the promotional strategies of celebrity culture and celebrity gossip provide just such content. How have female celebrities faired in this new environment? The picture is more complex than ever for a variety of media- and non-media-related reasons. The women's movement of the latter half of the twentieth century forced onto the social, political, and media agendas questions of female equality in law and representation. The range of roles for women in film and television dramatically expanded (see Tasker 1998). Feminist commentators have analyzed the extent to which the star/celebrity can control her own image (Epstein 2007; Kramer 2004; Feasy 2004; Williams 2007). Today the debate about the agency of female celebrities rests on the question of feminist representation, that is, the extent to which a female star's image supports or challenges normative gender expectations. This is a welcome outcome of the feminist movement of the 1970s, which put questions of gender inequality on the cultural and media map. However, scandal and sexuality continue to be central components in the public examination of female celebrity. Female sexuality continues to be a central component in discussions of the female stars and celebrities.

A new kind of celebrity has emerged from the expansion of reality television and the growth of the internet. The rise of the ordinary celebrity or self-made internet celebrity is sometimes seen as showing the ability of new technology to open up the public sphere to new groups of people. But is the mere fact that ordinary people are visible in celebrity culture a cause for celebrating the growing democracy of our culture, or is the content of that visibility an important question? Graeme Turner coined the term "the demotic turn" in order to question the claims about democratization that accompanied the increased media presence of ordinary people (Turner 2004, 2010). Certainly, the participation of non-dominant social groups in new media is a complex issue, involving uneven levels of participation and self-representation. But the media treatment of the "ordinary" celebrities on reality TV and the internet is revealing about contemporary balance of forces. Tabloid media treat most female "ordinary" celebrities with contempt and derision. For example, the mercifully now defunct *News of the World* filled abundant columns with scorn for "ordinary" celebrities. On February 24, 2008 the online edition ran a piece on the top ten Celebrity Chavs. "Chav" is a British term of abuse to describe working-class identity as lacking in taste, culture, or dignity. This all-female list was topped by Kerry Katona, the first UK female winner of *I'm a Celebrity Get Me Out Of Here*. At the time of her 2004 win Katona was heralded as an example of social mobility—an unpretentious working-class girl made good. Four years later the *News of the World* ridiculed her as "Chav No. 1." Number two on the list was Britney Spears, described as "trailer trash." Number five on the list was glamour model Jordan (Katie Price), whose "huge fake boobs" make her a "real contender for the chav crown." In a period of massive disparities between rich and poor, a decrease in social mobility, and the rise of anti-welfare, neoliberal politics, the derision heaped on largely female ordinary celebrities is not a boisterous shattering of the aura of fame. Instead it marks a return to open disdain for the working class in public culture, using tabloid-esque misogyny to make it "fun" and acceptable.

The history of female celebrity exemplifies the paradox of modern fame: It is both an expression of growing freedom and democracy and an example of the limits to both. Sexualized scandal is not new in the public sphere. Instead it is part of public culture that emerges with bourgeois society. Indeed, it expresses the contradictions at its heart—the persistent subjugation of women (among others) coinciding with an ideology of freedom and equality. The values attached to female celebrity are always shaped by the commercial needs of the businesses in which they are located and are tied to broader, socially circulating gender norms (and sometimes shifts in those norms). The meanings and social functions of celebrity are part of the historical process; and the continuities in the values attached to female fame are also set alongside their meanings in specific historical moments. However, we should not assume that the growth of celebrity and of the media enhances democratic public participation. What the treatment of ordinary female celebrities in today's media makes visible is the continuation of a social hierarchy based on class, race, and gender.

## References

Bauman, Z. (2005) *Liquid Life*, Cambridge: Polity.

Bloom, H. (ed.) (1998) *John Gay's The Beggar's Opera*, New York: Chelsea House.

Boorstin, D. J. (1961) *The Image: A Guide to Pseudo-Events in America*, New York: Altheneum.

Connell, I. (1992) "Personalities in the Popular Media," in P. Dahlgren and C. Sparks (eds.) *Journalism and Popular Culture*, London: Sage, pp. 64–85.

Couldry, N. (2003) *Media Rituals: A Critical Approach*, London and New York: Routledge.

de Cordova, R. (1990) *Picture Personalities: The Emergence of the Star System in America*, Urbana and Chicago: University of Illinois Press.

Epstein, R. (2007) "Sharon Stone in a Gap Turtle Neck," in S. Redmond and S. Holmes (eds.) *Stardom and Celebrity: A Reader*, London: Sage, pp. 206–18.

Feasy, R. (2004) "Stardom and Sharon Stone: Power as Masquerade," *Quarterly Review of Film and Video* 21(3): 199–207.

Foote, S. (2010) *The Cozeners: A Comedy in Three Acts*, London: The British Library; originally published by Mr. Colman, 1774.

——(2011) *A Trip To Calais: A Comedy in Three Acts*, London: British Library; originally published by Mr. Colman, 1775.

Franklin, B. (1997) *Newzak and the News Media*, London: Edward Arnold.

Fraser, N. (1990) "Rethinking the Public Sphere: A Contribution to the Critique of Actual Existing Democracy," *Social Text* 25/26: 56–80.

Gitlin, T. (1997) "The Anti-Political Populism of Cultural Studies," in M. Ferguson and P. Golding (eds.) *Cultural Studies in Question*, London: Sage, pp. 25–38.

Habermas, J. (1991) *The Structural Transformation of the Public Sphere: An Inquiry into a Category of Bourgeois Society*, translated by Thomas Burger with the assistance of Frederick Lawrence, Cambridge, MA: MIT Press.

Hermes, J. (1995) *Reading Women's Magazines: An Analysis of Everyday Media Use*, Cambridge: Polity.

Kramer, P. (2004) "The Fall and Rise of Sandra Bullock: Notes on Starmaking and Female Stardom in Contemporary Hollywood," in A. Willis (ed.) *Hollywood Film Stars and Beyond*, Manchester: Manchester University Press, pp. 89–112.

Langer, J. (1998) *Tabloid Television: Popular Journalism and the 'Other' News*, London: Routledge.

Lowenthal, L. (1961) *Literature, Popular Culture, and Society*, Englewood Cliffs, NJ: Prentice-Hall.

Luckhurst, M. and J. Moody (eds.) (2005) *Theatre and Celebrity in Britain, 1660–2000*, Basingstoke: Palgrave Macmillan.

Lumby, C. (1997) *Bad Girls: Media, Sex and Feminism in the 90s*, St. Leonards, NSW: Allen and Unwin.

Moody, J. (2007) *Illegitimate Theatre in London, 1770–1840*, Cambridge: Cambridge University Press.

Nussbaum, F. (2005) "Actresses and the Economics of Celebrity 1700–1800," in M. Luckhurst and J. Moody (eds.) (2005) *Theatre and Celebrity in Britain, 1660–2000*, Basingstoke: Palgrave Macmillan, pp. 149–68.

Ponce de Leon, C. L. (2002) *Self Exposure: Human Interest Journalism and the Emergence of Celebrity in America, 1890–1940*, Urbana and Chicago: University of Illinois Press.

Redmond, S. (2007) "The Whiteness of Stars: Looking at Kate Winslet's Unruly White Body," in S. Redmond and S. Holmes (eds.) *Stardom and Celebrity: A Reader*, London: Sage, pp. 263–74.

Rojek, C. (2001) *Celebrity*, London: Reaktion.

Schickel, R. (2000) *Intimate Strangers: The Culture of Celebrity*, Chicago: Ivan R. Dee.

Shattuc, J. M. (1997) *The Talking Cure: TV Talk Shows and Women*, New York and London: Routledge.

Tasker, Y. (1998) *Working Girls: Gender and Sexuality in Popular Cinema*, London: Routledge.

Turner, G. (2004) *Understanding Celebrity*, London: Sage.

——(2010) *Ordinary People and the Media: The Demotic Turn*, London: Sage.

Van Zoonen, L. (2006) "The Personal, the Political and the Popular: A Woman's Guide to Celebrity Politics," *European Journal of Cultural Studies* 9(3): 287–301.

Wanko, C. (2003) *Roles of Authority: Thespian Biography and Celebrity in Eighteenth-Century Britain*, Lubbock: Texas Tech University Press.

Williams, R. (2007) "From *Beyond Control* to in Control: Investigating Drew Barrymore's Feminist Agency/Authorship," in S. Redmond and S. Holmes (eds.) *Stardom and Celebrity: A Reader*, London: Sage, pp. 111–26.

Woffington, M. (1760) *Memoirs of the Celebrated Mrs. Woffington*, London: Lowe.

# 29

# "Shameless mums" and universal pedophiles

## Sexualization and commodification of children

## Sara Bragg

### The "sexualization of childhood" as global cause and participatory sport

In recent years, the "sexualization of childhood," and to some extent its "commercialization," has moved into the center of public policy and debate internationally. Raised as a concern at high-profile and official levels, the issue has brought together government departments, academic researchers, voluntary sector and pressure groups, teachers, children's authors, media commentators, media institutions, and more. In Britain, for example, the New Labour government of 1997–2010 commissioned a series of reports concerning children's online safety (Byron 2008), the commercialization of childhood (Buckingham 2009), and the sexualization of young people (Papadopoulos 2010). The Scottish parliament funded research into "sexualized" consumer goods available to children, such as Playboy merchandise (Buckingham et al. 2010). The UK Coalition government that came to power in 2010 commissioned a further review of the sexualization and commercialization of childhood (Bailey 2011). The American Psychological Association's (2007) review of the psychological literature on sexualization has been widely cited, as has a controversial Australian report (discussed further on pp. 324 and 326–7) entitled *Corporate Paedophilia* (Rush and La Nauze 2006). The latter apparently sparked an inquiry and reports by the Australian Senate (2008) and the Commissioner for Children and Young People in Western Australia (CCYPWA 2012). Duits and van Zoonen (2011) describe a 2008 proposal by the Dutch government for a policy against the sexualization of girls and young women. In France, Chantal Jouanno, a Senator and a former Minister for Sports, published a parliamentary report, *Against Hyper-sexualization: A New Fight for Equality*, in 2012. The same year a Polish politician, Joanna Skrzydlewska, presented the European parliament with 21 recommendations addressing the sexualization of girls. Sexualization and commercialization, often in relation to globalization processes, have been the focus of protests in countries beyond the Global North, including South Africa and India; in the state of Kerala, for example, Hindu fundamentalists have opposed celebrations of St. Valentine's day (Lukose 2009).

Despite controversies over the covert (but pervasive) influence of right-wing Christian evangelism, "sexualization" is generally presented as an issue for parents that is also "pro-women," sometimes even explicitly feminist. Yet, it is increasingly couched in the language of scientific "truths," particularly psychology, rather than feminism (Duits and van Zoonen 2011). Moreover, it "is big business," as Claire Charles remarks (2012: 317), discussing how Australian popular feminist commentators (such as Melinda Tankard Reist, Maggie Hamilton, and Dannielle Miller) have become mini-industries in their own right, selling books, courses, workshops, posters, and apps, and making frequent media appearances. Their American counterparts include Meenakshi Gigi Durham, Sharon Lamb and Lyn Brown, Diane Levin, and Jean Kilbourne, and in the UK Sue Palmer, Natasha Walters, Ed Mayo, and Agnes Nairn. Voluntary sector organizations, both secular and religious based, have taken action on sexualization, marketing to children, and commercial pressures on families. In 2010 the UK-based parenting website mumsnet launched a high-profile campaign aimed at retailers, "Let Girls Be Girls," endorsed by politicians of left and right.

Media institutions have themselves taken up the issue, as when a UK tabloid newspaper ran a short but successful crusade against a so-called "paedo bikini" in April 2010, or a UK television channel launched a campaign called "Stop Pimping Our Kids." More commonly, however, the media are identified as a key source and cause of the problem. Recent campaigns call for placing a ban, label, or "health warning" on airbrushed images; other campaigns oppose media "objectification" of women and propose "real role models."

One might also describe the debate about the sexualization of childhood as something of an international participatory sport, one well suited to the new media age. Anyone can take a stance, express views or mobilize campaigns via the internet. The issue is a standby for magazine and newspaper websites with space to fill. These sites regularly run opinion pieces, polls, and stories about allegedly "sexualizing" consumer items ("paedo bikinis," padded bras, or heels for eight-year-olds) or practices (the "shameless mum" whose daughter gets a fake tan, pole dances, has a makeover, and so on). Online forums provide a space for comments that reliably garner many responses. More often than not, these debates take the form of a "blame game," with blame apportioned between exploitative corporate behemoths and reckless consumers (in Britain often described as "chavvy," a pejorative slang word for white working class). One illustrative example: in June 2011, some 589 people responded to a "non-scientific" *Sydney Morning Herald* poll asking, "Who or what is to blame for the 'commercialization and sexualization' of childhood?" Twenty percent accused marketers and advertisers; 5 percent the media; 8 percent modern-day parenting; but 67 percent identified "all of the above." These debates, as I have argued elsewhere, should not be dismissed merely as "moral panics," but understood as part of the terrain on which shifts in notions of public and private, citizenship and ethical responsibilities, are negotiated (Bragg and Buckingham 2012).

The "sexualization of childhood" has achieved its public visibility and prominence despite, and no doubt in part because of, a lack of consensus about what the phrase means. Those taking a stance against "the sexualization of childhood" may be referring to quite different things, ranging from the provision of sexuality education, child trafficking or sexual abuse, teenage sexual activity, the inadequacy of internet regulation, the gender-stereotyped and/or age-(in)appropriate design and marketing of goods and services for children, the representation of women in advertising, and much else besides. Ignoring these divergences allows the public debate to proceed as if there is consensus that that sexualization exists, is negative, is the fault of some-body or something, and that children should be shielded from it. Nonetheless, a body of academic literature is cautioning against the "moral" register in which the debate is conducted; it highlights the analytical inadequacies of terms such as "sexualization" or "pornification," and challenges the evidence for its alleged harms or that children/childhoods are being "sexualized." The following sections discuss this work selectively, focusing on questions of media and gender.

## "Decline" and "fall" in narratives of childhood sexualization

The argument that contemporary culture is becoming increasingly "sexual" and/or "sexualized" is often bound up with a narrative of social decline and even nostalgia for a "golden age" located in an unspecified but always-already vanished past when things were not this way (Taylor 2010). Criticism of commercialization likewise constructs consumerism as a relatively recent alien invader of a previously sheltered world of childhood. These claims do not withstand historical scrutiny, however. Recent research argues cogently that consumer culture has not distorted childhood, but, rather, has constituted it and shaped how we come to understand and "know" it. For instance, Cross (2004) explores how the idea of childhood innocence has been used to promote and expand consumption. Cook (2003, 2004) shows that the US child market developed from the 1920s onwards by taking children seriously as "social actors;" in constructing them in increasingly age- and gender-differentiated ways, it offered influential resources through which both children and adults came to think about child identities and relations with others:

> Not wholly responsible for children's changing status, markets and the market culture of childhood nevertheless have been necessary to its realization. One cannot readily imagine moving from the "seen and not heard" Anglo childhood of the Victorian Era to the boisterous, in-your-face global childhood of electronic media society without a children's consumer culture to provide context and trajectory.
>
> (Cook 2003: 161)

Likewise, the commodification of children for adults' erotic contemplation is centuries old (Kincaid 1992; Higonnet 1998). While the *public visibility* of the issue and how it is defined may have changed, "sexualized" representations of children cannot be seen only as a consequence of contemporary consumerism (Buckingham 2009: 114). Egan and Hawkes (2008, 2010) highlight the class, race, and gender dimensions of earlier "sexual purity" campaigns to protect children's "innocence;" drawing on Foucault, they analyze the (sexual) regulation and surveillance of the child as one means through which emerging modern nation-states from the eighteenth century attempted to optimize the capacities of populations. Nonetheless, most academic commentators agree that recent decades have seen a "mainstreaming of sex" (Attwood 2009), involving the blurring of boundaries between the pornographic and the mainstream; new forms of sexual encounter (phone/cybersex); and a growth in commercial sex services and new spaces for sexual entertainment (e.g. escort agencies, lap dancing clubs and sex tours, internet sites). Even so, the meaning and precise interpretation of this "mainstreaming" are contested: Attwood's thoughtful overviews (2006, 2010) consider some nuanced analyses foregrounding the "democratization of desire" or processes of informalization and egalitarianism, exemplified by greater tolerance of sexual diversity, new forms of expertise and arenas for debating sex, the potential for even "objectifying" media forms and practices to embody transgressive female sexualities. Yet such alternative accounts receive scant attention in the public debate.

If "commercialization" implies a prior, non-commercial childhood, what "sexualization" implies about childhood sexuality is more ambiguous. The term is often preceded by the word "premature" and descriptions of children as either "innocent" or "growing up too fast." A standard definition of sexualization is "the imposition of adult sexuality on to children and young people before they are capable of dealing with it, mentally, emotionally or physically" (see, e.g., Papadopoulos 2010: 6). Childhood is here viewed through a normative "developmental" lens: children must pass through a number of stages that are paradoxically not only natural, but at the same time vulnerable to being disrupted. Adulthood is the end point of this process, secured by the presence of both sexuality and the "capability" of "dealing" with it.

Feminists have long since exposed the tyranny of childhood "innocence," a concept that slips between description and prescription (Kitzinger 1988). What Faulkner terms our cultural "innocence fetish" separates childhood and sexuality to the extent that any child who expresses or experiences sexuality is considered "fallen"—outside the domain of childhood and even denied the protection that their status as child is meant to bring (Jackson 1982; Egan and Hawkes 2010; Faulkner 2011).

Anti-sexualization campaigners do not necessarily endorse such a view of children. Rush and La Nauze, for example, acknowledge children's "slowly developing" sexuality (2006: 1). Nonetheless, as Simpson (2011) remarks, their account, like others, is permeated with value-laden distinctions between unhealthy, premature, or otherwise problematic forms of sexuality, and "healthy," timely, "appropriate" ones. Notions of "readiness," or of a misalignment between physical, mental, and emotional development, justifies adult protectionism. It also effectively prohibits children and young people from participating in the public debate about the issue: They can only echo pre-existing adult perspectives, because to disagree with them is simply evidence that they do not understand what is involved. "[W]hile children themselves *may believe* that they can understand and contextualise, say, a Playboy logo on a pencil case ... such encounters may be having a profound impact on attitudes and behaviour at an *unconscious* level" (Papadopoulos 2010: 29, my emphasis).

While the public debate refers to the "sexualization of childhood," in practice, as many commentators have observed, it focuses on girls. Girls are viewed as more "at risk" from sexualization processes than are boys, and affected in different ways, in part because of problematic assumptions about audiences' relationship to media representations, as discussed on p. 326. Such protectionism is only partial, however.

Egan and Hawkes (2008) compile the punitive labels used for girls who are considered "sexualized," including "skank," "prostitot," "kinderwhore," "sex bait," "sexually precocious," or "slutty," as well as dressing "like a stripper" or wearing "hooker chic," "skank chic," "dumpster chic," or "trailer park fashion." Similar class- and gender-based hostility is directed towards the parents (nearly always mothers), who are held to promote sexualization or commodification through their irresponsible consumption (Bragg and Buckingham 2012; Bragg 2012).

## Media texts and interpretations within the sexualization debate

Although accounts of sexualization differ, most scholars present it as a process that occurs because of, first, the nature of the symbols, objects, and representations (the culture) that surround children and, second, children's relationship with that culture. One target for concern is how new, less regulated, technologies enable children to access "adult" material not intended for them (ranging from music videos to pornography). While such anxieties recur with each successive new technology, critics also assert that the contemporary cultural landscape presents distinctive challenges. These include trends in marketing to children that emphasize gender (perhaps) to a greater extent than before, while they also de-differentiate in terms of age. Thus, clothes are often produced across a broader and lower age range (e.g. 7–15 years); styles and products targeted at adults are duplicated for children; girls' magazines, even for pre-teenagers, increasingly resemble women's magazines in style and content, with their emphases on celebrities, beauty, and fashion. In addition, some products previously more closely associated with adult markets and sexuality have migrated, sometimes actively repackaged as children's goods (as in trends for children's make-up sets) or just adopted by young consumers (such as Playboy merchandise). Vocabularies too have shifted. Words like "sexy" become more common or innuendo is used in selling goods, such as a temporary hair color called "One Night Stand" (see Buckingham et al. 2010).

Activists as well as academics identify various "negative" outcomes of this "sexualized culture," primarily for individuals. These include children (girls) *becoming* sexual, that is, developing a premature or inappropriate interest in sex or in "deviant" sexualities; seeing sexuality as a route to success; engaging in unsafe and other risky sexual practices or in "ladette" behavior; becoming obsessed with appearance, with cosmetic surgery, and/or with celebrity culture; suffering from "low self-esteem," poor body image, eating disorders and other addictions, or from impaired academic performance. "Sexualization" is also presented as an explanation for child sexual abuse, although not always with the blatant callousness of Palmer, who remarks, "When children dressed like dockside tarts throng the streets, it's hardly surprising that pedophilia thrives" (2007: 275). One can clearly identify here a victim-blaming discourse that feminists have long challenged in relation to rape.

One can also question the validity of the empirical evidence basis for other claims. Psychological research generalizes from studies with adults to children, often treats extreme cases as routine, and draws conclusions on the basis of some highly problematic experiments. In their vigorous debunking of this evidence, Egan and

Hawkes refer to an experiment in which girls were asked to sit math tests wearing bikinis (2008: 296; see also Buckingham 2009, 2011; Buckingham *et al.* 2010; Duits and van Zoonen 2011; Duschinsky 2010; Gill 2009; Lerum and Dworkin 2009; Lumby and Albury 2010; Rysst 2010; Smith and Attwood 2011; Vares *et al.* 2011).

However, since research cannot conclusively prove a "no harm" position, the idea of adopting a "precautionary principle" against sexualized goods and media has gained ground; for instance, Bailey (2011) espouses this position. We need instead to challenge the sexualization thesis by interrogating its assumptions and how it functions as an interpretive practice. How does it encourage us to understand culture and society, and the relationships between culture and identity or subjectivity?

Consider the quotations below:

> The world is *saturated* by more images today than at any other time in our modern history. Behind each of these images lies *a message* about expectations, values and ideals. Women are revered—and rewarded—for their physical attributes and both girls and boys are under pressure to emulate polarised gender stereotypes from a younger and younger age. ... [T]hese developments are having a profound impact, particularly on girls and young women. ...
>
> [I]t is important to look at the social scripts children are being influenced by and what makes children *susceptible* to them. ... *The predominant message for boys is to be sexually dominant and to *objectify* the female body. ... Sexualised ideals of young, thin, beauty ... [and] "airbrushing" photographs ... can lead people to *believe in a reality that does not exist*.
>
> (Papadopoulos 2010: 5, 7–8, my emphasis)

> A girl apparently aged *about ten* wears *a chain pulled like a choker* around her neck, with the ends dangling *where her cleavage would be if she were older*. Her *hot pink* tank top and black trousers hang slightly loosely from *her child's frame*. ... An *outsized* ring on one of her fingers *dominates* one hand. ... She adopts the *female full frontal pose* which is familiar to us from images of adult women models.
>
> (Rush and La Nauze 2006: vii, my emphasis)

Like Papadopoulos, anti-sexualization scholars and campaigners frequently describe what they perceive as the message(s) and values of contemporary media. In so doing, they imply that meaning is immanent—something already "in" the text—and simultaneously assert their authority to define what that meaning is. Media texts are seen as overwhelmingly powerful ("saturating" the consciousness of "susceptible" child audiences in particular); they function primarily to provide information about how the world is, therefore it is vital that they do not "distort" it, but are "accurate" and "realistic." Fantasy modalities, or failures to depict characters as fully rounded individuals, are morally reprehensible ("objectifying"). Culture here is akin to a virus, able to invade a susceptible host body (a child) on contact and produce disease (unwanted identities and subjectivities).

The second extract is a reading of an advertisement aimed at sustaining the authors' argument that it constitutes "corporate pedophilia." As Simpson (2011) remarks, images and objects need to be read as sexual to become sexualized. And language does more than describe or capture a pre-existing "reality"; it functions performatively to interpret and define it. Here, the vocabulary used is itself "sexual" in order to emphasize the sexual meanings identified in it. Relatedly, Duschinsky (2012) observes the inconsistency with which images of women are described as "hypersexualized," but equivalent images of men merely "hypermasculinized" and reinforcing the gender-specific effects ascribed to girls vs. boys.

Meaning relies on context. Thus any argument about the significance of media representations and consumer goods is simultaneously an argument about the genres and the cultural fields that should guide our interpretation. For Rush and La Nauze, the frame of reference is images of adult women with which we are already "familiar." In response, Lumby and Albury (2010) survey contemporary Australian girls' popular culture and representational traditions, from media to family photography. Set in this broader context, they argue, the kinds of poses and clothing condemned by Rush and La Nauze are in fact commonplace; this alters the "cultural messages" they can be said to carry:

> To assume that [children in images] are offering themselves up for an adult sexual gaze, or that their pose or clothing suggests that they understand and have internalised this gaze, is a claim for which we have been able to find no evidence. Child sexual abusers may, of course, read sexual invitations into images of children. They may read sexual invitations into the wearing of school uniforms or Speedo swimsuits, for that matter. We would argue, however, that the gaze of the pedophile is not the gaze reasonable adults bring to images of children.
>
> (Lumby and Albury 2010: 145)

Lumby and Albury's argument is compelling; it makes visible an issue that is left unspoken and under-analyzed in accounts of sexualization, which habitually assume that children's media should be read in relation to the conventions of adult media, including soft porn. Interestingly, a similar move is also made time and again in the kinds of online discussion forums mentioned above. Discussing the "paedo bikini" and its padded top, for example, many contributors recontextualized the issue by reinterpreting the product ("more like a thick lining"). They pointed out that similar ("trivial fashion") items were available everywhere, questioned the motivations behind targeting a downmarket chain store, and defended its consumers. One comment— "I go there 'cause am skint"—highlighted the socioeconomic positioning of the shop (see http://www.thesun.co.uk/sol/homepage/news/2931327/Primarks-padded-bikini-tops-for-kids-condemned.html?allComments=true). Deciding to whom one should listen in such cases may be a matter of class politics as much as aesthetic or moral judgment.

However, I am less convinced of the utility of Lumby and Albury's notion of a "reasonable adult" gaze, except as a convenient legal fiction, because it potentially shuts down the interesting questions that the issue of context opens up. In my view, their readings of images are more sophisticated and justifiable than those of the report's authors. Nonetheless, if those images cannot be said to be "sexual" in any simple way, by the same token nor can they be categorically "non-sexual." Foreclosing either possibility underplays the intense uncertainty and ambivalence surrounding images of children and questions of the adult gaze. The more we insist on the innocence of the asexual child, the more sexualized we as spectators become. Describing images of children as pornographic or sexual, and interpreting them "through the eyes of a pedophile," positions us as the potential pedophilic viewers we claim to abhor (Faulkner 2011; Lebeau 2008). Lebeau argues that representations of the child have been haunted since the inception of cinema itself, by the questions: "Is it sexual? Is it innocent?" (2008: 97). Modern audiences are likely to be unsettled by—for instance—the comedy turns of child star Shirley Temple as prostitute or exotic dancer, seen mimicking Mae West's drawl and swagger. It is difficult, Lebeau comments, not to wonder what the adult audience wants from this child; the question rebounds on us as the spectators of the image, as indeed it also should when it comes to the "sexualization and commercialization of childhood."

## Unsettling certainties, or why being or becoming "critical" is not the answer

The public debate about "sexualization" is problematic on many fronts. The multiplicity of concerns, fears, and interest groups proliferating around the issue has tended to obscure some unedifying politics, whether these be the fundamentalist agendas of the religious right, or the class antagonism and misogyny directed at those who consume the products or texts it stigmatizes (Duschinsky 2010). Here I have emphasized in particular the shortcomings of its interpretations of contemporary media and consumer culture, which tend to be simplistic, over-generalized, and undifferentiated: wherever it looks, it finds only the same old story—that "sex sells," for example. It is often unreflexive about the values and assumptions underlying these accounts, and authoritarian in privileging them over any others. Its arrogance extends to its often patronizing depictions of children as inherently more vulnerable to media and commercial influence than adults, notions that make it far too easy for children's own views to be ignored.

In response, I have brought a postmodern sensibility that insists on the indeterminacy and context-dependence of meaning. Politics and pedagogy around issues such as sexualization, I would argue, badly need these perspectives. It is common to hear campaigners call for programs of media or consumer literacy to enable children to become more "critical," even to "inoculate" them against undue influence. Those who dispute the sexualization thesis often make the point that children are not passive, but agentic and critical meaning makers of the culture around them.

Neither position is entirely helpful, however. The media do not cause our social ills in the direct way often assumed, so literacy will not ameliorate them. Nor will being critical "cure" children of their passionate attachments to disapproved cultural texts. Nor should it, because surely we seek to understand what we know and love (see Bragg 2001). At the same time, while acknowledging young people's prior competence is vital, it doesn't—yet—tell us how we might draw on it, and what else young people might want or need to learn. For, as Gill reminds us, citing Modleski, we are all victims of ideology at some level (2007: 73), which is only to say that we exist within culture, with culture understood as what is constituted within the practices of everyday life, rather than a contact disease carried by texts. The only way to be immune from cultural influence (and even then not always) is not to be interested in it, not to care, know, or understand anything about it. But then, of course, one has no authority either, which is perhaps why young people find it so easy to tune out adult laments. Why should they listen to anyone who can't tell Beyoncé from Rihanna, grunge from goth, Top Shop from New Look?

We do not therefore have to become experts in every aspect of youth culture, however. We need to conceptualize media and consumer culture as providing *resources*, not as sources of domination; to stop insisting that whatever we are already "familiar" with provides the only possible context for interpretation; and to become interested in what other people have to tell us. Asking others about the frames of reference through which they place and make sense of particular images or products will help us understand their existing skills, knowledge, and competence in negotiating cultural environments, and explain divergences of interpretation. Nonetheless, it doesn't foreclose dialogue about whether other frames (those adults supply) might also be applicable or insightful. As Simpson (2011) also suggests, acknowledging ambiguity—that meaning is indeterminate, that interpretation is an inevitably open-ended process—may allow us to tolerate the anxiety of thinking about childhood sexuality in terms of both agency and abuse, without one excluding the other. In turn, this avoids a consequence of the sexualization debate that we should be far more distraught about: that it risks denying children and young people any role as guide to or co-creator of the culture around us all.

# References

American Psychological Association (2007) *Report of the APA Task Force on the Sexualization of Girls*, Washington, DC: American Psychological Association. www.apa.org/pi/wpo/sexualization.htm.

Attwood, F. (2006) "Sexed up: Theorizing the Sexualization of Culture," *Sexualities* 9: 77–94.

——(ed.) (2009) *Mainstreaming Sex: The Sexualization of Western Culture*, London: I. B. Tauris.

——(2010) "Sexualization, Sex and Manners," *Sexualities* 13(6): 742–5.

Australian Senate (2008) *Sexualization of Children in the Contemporary Media*, Parliament of Australia. http://www.aph.gov.au_senate_committee_eca_ctte_sexualization_of_children.report_ c01.pdf.

Bailey, R. (2011) *Letting Children be Children: Report of an Independent Review of the Commercialisation and Sexualisation of Childhood*, London: Department for Education.

Bragg, S. (2001) "Perverse and Improper Pedagogies: The Case of Freddy's Fingers and Russell's Head," *The Velvet Light Trap* 48 (University of Texas Press): 68–80.

——(2012) "What I Heard about Sexualisation: Or, Conversations with My Inner Barbie," *Gender and Education* 24(3): 311–16.

Bragg, S. and D. Buckingham (2012) "Global Concerns, Local Negotiations and Moral Selves: Contemporary Parenting and the 'Sexualisation of Childhood' Debate," *Feminist Media Studies* (August 29). http://www.tandfonline.com/doi/abs/10.1080/14680777.2012.700523#. UgzEUNLqmSo.

Buckingham, D. (2009) *The Impact of the Commercial World on Children's Wellbeing: Report of an Independent Assessment*, London: DCSF/DCMS.

——(2011) *The Material Child: Growing up in Consumer Culture*, Cambridge and Malden, MA: Polity.

Buckingham, D., S. Bragg, R. Russell, and R. Willett (2010) *Sexualised Goods Aimed at Children: A Report to the Scottish Parliament Equal Opportunities Committee*, Glasgow: Scottish Parliament.

Byron, T. (2008) *The Byron Review: Safer Children in a Digital World*, London: DCSF.

Charles, C. E. (2012) "New Girl Heroes: The Rise of Popular Feminist Commentators in an Era of Sexualisation," *Gender and Education* 24(3): 317–23.

Commissioner for Children and Young People Western Australia (CCYPWA) (2012) *Sexualisation of Children*, Issues Paper 9, Commissioner for Children and Young People, Western Australia. http://www.ccyp.wa.gov.au/files/IssuesPapers/Issues%20Paper%20-%20Sexualisation%20of%20Children.pdf.

Cook, D. T. (2003) "Spatial Biographies of Children's Consumption: Market Places and Spaces of Childhood in the 1930s and Beyond," *Journal of Consumer Culture* 3: 147–69.

——(2004) *The Commodification of Childhood: The Children's Clothing Industry and the Rise of the Child Consumer*, Durham, NC: Duke University Press.

Cross, G. (2004) *The Cute and the Cool: Wondrous Innocence and Modern American Children's Culture*, New York: Oxford University Press

Duits, L. and L. van Zoonen (2011) "Coming to Terms with Sexualization," *European Journal of Cultural Studies* 14(5): 491–506.

Duschinsky, R. (2010) "Feminism, Sexualisation and Social Status," *Media International Australia* 135: 94–105.

——(2012) "The Gender of Sexualisation," paper presented at *Pornified?* Conference, December 1–2, Institute of Education, London.

Egan, R. and G. Hawkes (2008) "Endangered Girls and Incendiary Objects: Unpacking the Discourse on Sexualization," *Sexuality & Culture* 12(4): 291–311.

——(2010) *Theorizing the Sexual Child in Modernity*, Basingstoke: Palgrave Macmillan.

Faulkner, J. (2011) *The Importance of Being Innocent: Why We Worry about Children*, Cambridge: Cambridge University Press.

Gill, R. (2007) "Critical Respect: The Difficulties and Dilemmas of Agency and 'Choice' for Feminism: A Reply to Duits and van Zoonen," *European Journal of Women's Studies* 14(1): 69–80.

——(2009) "Beyond the 'Sexualization of Culture' Thesis," *Sexualities* 12(2): 137–60.

Higonnet, A. (1998) *Pictures of Innocence: The History and Crisis of Ideal Childhood*, London: Thames and Hudson.

Jackson, S. (1982) *Childhood and Sexuality*, Oxford: Blackwell.

Jouanno, C. (2012) *Contre l'Hypersexualisation, un nouveau combat pour l'égalité: Rapport parlementaire*, Ministère des Solidarités et de la Cohésion sociale.

Kincaid, J. R. (1992) *Child-loving: The Erotic Child and Victorian Culture*, New York and London: Routledge.

Kitzinger, J. (1988) "Defending Innocence: Ideologies of Childhood," *Feminist Review* 28: 77–87.

Lebeau, V. (2008) *Childhood and Cinema*, London: Reaktion Books.

Lerum, K. and S. L. Dworkin (2009) "'Bad Girls Rule': An Interdisciplinary Feminist Commentary on the Report of the APA Task Force on the Sexualization of Girls," *Journal of Sex Research* 46(4): 250–63.

Lukose, R. A. (2009) *Liberalization's Children: Gender, Youth, and Consumer Citizenship in Globalizing India*, Durham, NC and London: Duke University Press

Lumby, C. and K. Albury (2010) "Too Much? Too Young? The Sexualisation of Children Debate in Australia," *Media International Australia* 135: 141–52.

Palmer, S. (2007) *Toxic Childhood: How the Modern World Is Damaging Our Children and What We Can Do about It*, 2nd edition, London: Orion.

Papadopoulos, L. (2010) *Sexualisation of Young People Review*, London: DfEE.

Rush, E. and A. La Nauze (2006) *Corporate Paedophilia: Sexualisation of Children in Australia, Working paper no. 90*, Canberra: ACT: Australia Institute.

Rysst, M. (2010) "Girls, Bodies and Romance in the Light of a Presumed Sexualization of Childhood," *Girlhood Studies* 3(2): 69–88.

Simpson, B. (2011) "Sexualizing the Child: The Strange Case of Bill Henson, His 'Absolutely Revolting' Images and the Law of Childhood Innocence," *Sexualities* 14(3): 290–311.

Smith, C. and F. Attwood (2011) "Lamenting Sexualization: Research, Rhetoric and the Story of Young People's 'Sexualization' in the UK Home Office Review," *Sex Education* 11(3): 327–37.

Taylor, A. (2010) "Troubling Childhood Innocence: Reframing the Debate over the Media Sexualisation of Children," *Australasian Journal of Early Childhood* 35(1): 48–57.

Vares, T., S. Jackson, and R. Gill (2011) "Preteen Girls Read 'Tween' Popular Culture: Diversity, Complexity and Contradiction," *International Journal of Media and Cultural Politics* 7(2): 139–54.

# 30

# Glances, dances, romances

## An overview of gendered sexual narratives in teen drama series

## *Susan Berridge*

Issues of sexuality are central to the teen drama series genre. Programs focus on teenage characters as they mature; sexual development is key in marking this transition from childhood to adulthood. From lingering glances signaling attraction between characters, to first dates and kisses shortly afterwards, and then to the formation of monogamous, sexual relationships, the serial structure of these programs parallels the normative developmental narrative of sexuality. At the same time, the liminal teenage period is portrayed as particularly vulnerable; both male and female teenage characters' fallibility and vulnerability, including their vulnerability to sexual pressure, manipulation, and abuse, is a recurring and prominent theme of the genre. This chapter explores how this vulnerability is gendered and sexualized in significant ways.

Despite the centrality of issues of sexuality to the genre, little academic work has been done in this area. This omission is surprising given the pervasive anxiety that surrounds the sexualization of teenagers—particularly young girls—in contemporary popular culture more broadly. Instead, feminist and teen television scholarship has tended to focus quite narrowly on whether individual teenage characters (particularly heterosexual females) constitute appropriate role models for young viewers, categorizing images accordingly as either positive or negative (Pender 2002). This anxiety is often justified by an underlying assumption that these viewers are more susceptible to televisual imagery than adults and thus need guidance on how and what to watch (see Vint 2002). Yet, as Sarah Projansky observes, in relation to filmic depictions of teenage female sexuality, discussions of sexual violence are notably absent in pedagogical debates about the potential of teen texts to educate young viewers about appropriate (read progressive/feminist) models of sexuality (Projansky 2011: 101).

Trying to measure whether individual representations are positive is inherently problematic. First, this approach displays a patronizing and overly simplistic notion of viewer identification, assuming a direct cause-and-effect relationship between what viewers watch and how they subsequently behave. Challenging this view, audience studies reveal that, far from watching passively, teenagers engage actively with texts that are aimed at them (see, e.g., Brooker 2001). Second, this approach divorces individual representations from their context, leading to incomplete analyses. For example, the ambiguities inherent in long-running series become obscured, as do questions of genre. The rigidity of this approach is particularly ill suited to a genre in which the fallibility of teenage characters is a prominent theme. Most importantly, the relentless focus of much feminist teen television criticism on heroines in isolation means that this work cannot say anything broader about men, masculinity, and gender relations, thereby risking losing the political relevance of feminism (Boyle 2005).

Rather than replicating this positive/negative approach and measuring individual sexual representations against an elusive ideal, then, this chapter will consider the *kinds* of stories about teenage sexuality offered (or not) in teen drama series. It examines constructions of both female and male sexuality across the genre. To do so, I employ a structural methodology, mapping dominant generic sexual narratives across a number of US teen drama series. In the broader research (see Berridge 2010), I examine 11 US teen series from 1990 to 2008. The analysis drawn on here refers to *Beverly Hills 90210* (Fox, 1990–2000), *My So-Called Life* (ABC, 1994–5), *Buffy the Vampire Slayer* (The WB/UPN, 1997–2003), *Dawson's Creek* (The WB/CW, 1998–2003), *Freaks and Geeks* (NBC, 1999–2000), *Smallville* (The WB/CW, 2001–11), *The O.C.* (Fox, 2003–7), *One Tree Hill* (The WB/CW, 2003–12), *Veronica Mars* (UPN/The CW, 2004–7), *Friday Night Lights* (NBC, 2006–11), and *Gossip Girl* (The CW, 2007– continuing). This chapter also includes analysis of more contemporary teen series, including *Awkward.* (MTV, 2011– continuing), and *90210* (The CW, 2008– continuing), an updated version of the original *Beverly Hills*.

The patterns uncovered by a structural approach provide the starting point for a deeper analysis of the relationship between depictions of teenage gender and sexuality, as well as a discussion of the implications of these constructions of gendered sexuality on storylines explicitly involving sexual violence. Perhaps not surprisingly in a genre that emphasizes youthful vulnerability, sexual violence storylines are common (see Berridge 2010). Feminist activist Catherine MacKinnon (1996 [1983]) helpfully foregrounds the connections between dominant constructions of gender, sexuality, and power and male sexual violence against women. For MacKinnon, the social construction of heterosexuality, which institutionalizes male sexual dominance and female sexual submission, is the linchpin of gender inequality (1996: 185). I first identify the genre's dominant sexual norms, before considering the relationship between constructions of gendered sexuality and narratives of sexual violence.

## Boys will be boys, so lock up your daughters

Michelle Byers's (2007 [1998]) insightful analysis of constructions of gendered sexuality in *My So-Called Life* provides a useful precedent for mapping patterns across the televised depictions of sexuality. Adopting a structural approach, Byers argues that for each character central to the series, sexuality is rooted in a gender-appropriate stereotype (2007: 22). According to Byers, the three central female teens assume roles of "innocence" (referring to the protagonist, Angela (Claire Danes), who remains a virgin throughout the series), "promiscuity," and "conformity." The three core male teens occupy the roles of "traditional masculinity," "deviance," and "immaturity."

Byers argues that while these sexual roles are constricting for both male and female characters, the male teenagers have some potential for mobility. As she notes, in these constructions "the binary positioning of feminine and masculine sexualities is one wherein the feminine is ever the less powerful, the less sexual, the less free to choose, the one with the most to lose" (2007: 22). Male sexuality is portrayed as active, complex, and fluid in the series, while "girls can only choose between saying yes and no, knowing that to say no in this text is to forgo agency and to say yes almost always leads to loss" (2007: 22).

Notably, *My So-Called Life* is, in many ways, an exceptional case. Because the series was canceled after just one season, the teenagers' sexual identities are arguably more fixed than in longer-running series. In the program, Angela never loses her virginity and, thus, remains perpetually "innocent." In other teen drama series, characters can transcend the sexual roles initially written for them. However, what is striking from taking a structural approach to teenage sexuality across a number of teen series is that the *range* of roles available to characters remains largely the same as those identified by Byers. The starting point for most female teens is the "innocent." They then move on to the "conformist" by entering heterosexual monogamous relationships, as did, for example, Haley (Bethany Joy Lenz) in *One Tree Hill*. Alternatively, female teens may move from the "promiscuous" role to the "conformist" (see Serena [Blake Lively] in *Gossip Girl* or Jen [Michelle Williams] in *Dawson's Creek*). Less commonly, female characters move from the "conformist" to "promiscuity," but this trajectory is not portrayed in the programs as desirable. For example, in season three of *The O.C.*, central female teen Marissa (Mischa Barton) enters a casual sexual relationship with Volchok (Cam Gigandet), a peripheral male teen, who from the outset is coded as a "bad boy." Notably, Marissa begins dating him while dealing with the aftermath of her friend's death. At this point, she is drinking heavily and skipping school. Thus, their relationship is portrayed as part of a long chain of self-destructive behavior, culminating in Marissa's death when Volchok runs her car off the road in a jealous rage.

The dominance of gendered constructions of sexuality is reflected by narratives surrounding male and female characters losing their virginity. If they have not already lost their virginity before the series begins, male teens tend to do so early on in the first season. These loss-of-virginity narratives are typically episodic. As such, the lead up to or aftermath of this sexual encounter gets very little emphasis. Nothing suggests that males need to be emotionally "ready" to have sex. Instead, they are portrayed as ever-willing, regardless of who their sexual partner is, replicating the dominant stereotype that male sexuality is natural and uncontrollable, requiring no thought or emotion. Moreover, central male teens often verbally pressure their girlfriends into having sex. This is illustrated by an episode of *My So-Called Life* in which Angela's boyfriend, Jordan (Jared Leto), tries to push her into having sex. Significantly, his behavior is not framed as sexual violence by the program or diegetically by Angela. The episode focuses almost exclusively on whether Angela feels ready to have sex. In turn, Jordan is marginalized within the narrative and, thus, not held accountable for his pushiness. Instead, his behavior is framed as an expression of normative heterosexual relations, resonating with MacKinnon's argument that hegemonic constructions of heterosexuality underpin gender inequality (1996: 185).

This notion of teenage male sexuality as natural is reinforced by the permissive attitude of parents towards their sons having sex. This relaxed stance is illustrated in an episode from *The O.C.* (Episode 119, "The Heartbreak"), in which male teen Seth (Adam Brody) and his father Sandy (Peter Gallagher) discuss the aftermath of Seth losing his virginity and, specifically, Seth's concerns about his performance:

SANDY: Just because you're ready to go, it doesn't mean she is.
SETH: I'm always ready to go.
SANDY: [proudly] Well, you're my son. We Cohens are very sexual beings.
SETH: Oh my god.
SANDY: Virile! Get used to it.
SETH: [mutters] This is disgusting. Foreplay, huh?
SANDY: I'm telling you. The appetizer is as good as the main course.

Notably, this conversation is framed as a comedic moment in the series. Sandy is portrayed as unconcerned and proud of his son, implying that, for men, losing their virginity is a natural rite of passage.

Significantly here, both Sandy and Seth emphasize the *practical* aspects of sexual performance. In contrast, female teenagers frequently emphasize more emotional aspects of sex, such as concerns about being psychologically ready to lose their virginity or their fear of seeming sexually immature to their male partner. Great emphasis is placed on the importance of being "ready" for sex, choosing the right partner (someone who will respect them), and having sex for the right reasons. If these conditions are not met, it is suggested, sex will be psychologically damaging and certainly not pleasurable, reinforcing Byers's argument about the "innocence" of female teenage characters and indicating that their sexual vulnerability is a central generic theme. Even when all these conditions are met, female characters often face negative consequences for engaging in sexual activity, as I shall go on to discuss.

Season one of *Beverly Hills*, which aired from 1990 to 1991 (and is widely considered to be one of the earliest examples of a teen drama series), offers a particularly useful example of the differential narrative treatment of female and male teens losing their virginity through the experiences of twin protagonists Brandon (Jason Priestley) and Brenda (Shannon Doherty). Brandon's loss-of-virginity narrative is relegated to just one episode at the start of the season. Reinforcing the notion of male sexuality as a natural rite of passage, he loses his virginity in his bedroom to a non-recurring character while his parents are in the house. Although his mother is immediately heard to express some concern, she makes no attempt to stop him. Notably, her fears center on the implications for the girl rather than her own son. In contrast, Brenda's sexuality is much more heavily policed by her parents. When she does finally lose her virginity, after several episodes' worth of soul-searching and lengthy conversations with her girlfriends, she does so in the context of a long-term monogamous relationship in the more neutral space of a hotel room and without her parents' knowledge. The different spaces in which the twins lose their virginity suggests that different rules apply to male and female teenagers' sexual development.

Despite meeting all the "appropriate" conditions for losing her virginity—waiting until she is ready and choosing a partner who cares for her—Brenda, unlike her brother, still faces negative consequences. Darren Star, the creator of *Beverly Hills*, told an interviewer that this gendered bias was largely due to the network pressure he experienced after presenting Brenda's loss of virginity in a positive light (Itzkoff 2008). He explains, "The affiliates were scandalized—not because they had sex, but because Brenda was happy about it, and it didn't have any dire consequences" (Itzkoff 2008). As a result, Star was strongly advised to write an episode addressing these ramifications. Indicating the narrative weight placed on female teens losing their virginity, Brenda faces a pregnancy scare in the season one finale; in season two, the couple breaks up.

It would be wrong to assume that these storylines are always in the interest of educating teenage viewers about the perils of sex; they could equally serve to enhance dramatic tension. Indeed, these narratives often coincide with season finales, thereby creating climatic cliffhangers. Notably, however, pregnancy is framed as an exclusively *female* problem. In *Beverly Hills*, the pregnancy is framed very much as a story to do with Brenda rather than her boyfriend. It replicates the traditional notion that sex is a woman's responsibility and perpetuates the stereotype of male sexuality as something that men cannot control. While this example aired over two decades ago, these gendered sexual myths still prevail, as illustrated by a pregnancy storyline in the updated *90210*, which aired in 2009. In this narrative, ex-drug addict Adrianna (Jessica Lowndes) discovers she is pregnant while taking an HIV test. Significantly, due to her promiscuous past, she is not immediately certain who the father is. Two episodes thus focus solely on her reaction. Even when she does figure out the paternity, the male teenager in question is peripheral and unsupportive and, as such, the pregnancy is framed as solely her issue. Again, this resonates with Byers's argument that female teenagers face much more negative repercussions from engaging in sexual activity than do males.

The gendered differences surrounding the representation of teenage sexuality extend to other sexual narratives, including one-night stands and infidelity. When a central female character engages in a one-night stand, it rarely has much to do with active desire. Rather, these encounters occur because she is drunk, unhappy, lonely, or tricked into thinking the sex could lead to something more. The emotional aftermath of the experience commonly extends beyond the episode in which the sex takes place. In season two of *Dawson's Creek*, for example, a one-night stand between Jen and a male classmate occurs when Jen is in a particularly vulnerable state. In previous episodes, her grandfather has died and she has become increasingly isolated from her friends. Although Jen appears sexually in control leading up to the encounter, the following morning her regret is signaled through lingering facial close-ups after her classmate rejects her. While the negative aftermaths of these sexual narratives could be partially attributed to the moralizing aims of many teen drama series, it is significant that male teenagers typically have much more positive experiences. Reflecting the greater degree of sexual freedom afforded to males by patriarchal society, one-night stands involving central male characters are not much of a story. They largely take place because of male sexual desire, which is presented as uncontrollable and in need of release. This gendered inequality between representations of casual sex, which is embedded in the narrative organization, indicates a reluctance to depict active female sexuality as morally good and potentially pleasurable.

Narratives about sexual infidelity overlap considerably with those about one-night stands. Males face less negative consequences when they cheat on a partner and tend to be forgiven more quickly. For example, in *My So-Called Life*, Jordan cheats on Angela with her best friend and is forgiven relatively quickly. The assumption apparently is that "male heterosexuality, even irresponsible male heterosexuality, is perfectly acceptable at any age" (Byers 2007: 23–4). By contrast, females who cheat face much more serious repercussions, as indicated by the title of a *Friday Night Lights* episode, "It's Different for Girls," dealing with infidelity. Lyla (Minka Kelly), the girl who has cheated on her boyfriend, is ostracized by her female peers and faces extensive verbal bullying. In contrast, the boy she has cheated with (her boyfriend's best friend) remains relatively unscathed. Regardless of who is in a relationship and who has actually cheated, it is overwhelmingly the girl who is blamed, again reflecting the greater sexual freedom afforded to males in patriarchal society. These infidelity narratives suggest that females are more accountable for their sexual urges than males and, thus, should exercise more control.

The common narrative trope of female sexual activity followed by despair and regret persists across the genre, regardless of the era in which programs are broadcast. What has changed, however, is the way in which female teenage sexual empowerment is portrayed, indicating an engagement in contemporary series with postfeminist discourses. Highly sexually active teen girls have existed since the early days of the genre, but the way in which these females construct their sexuality has shifted. As Rosalind Gill argues, postfeminist culture invites girls as well as older women "to become a particular kind of self, and endowed with agency on condition that it is used to construct oneself as a subject closely resembling the heterosexual male fantasy that is found in pornography" (Gill 2007: 158). Early seasons of *One Tree Hill*, which aired from 2003 onwards, neatly illustrate this trend through the sexual experiences of Brooke (Sophia Bush) and Rachel (Danneel Harris). Brooke offers her naked body to a potential love interest in the backseat of his car, while Rachel submits provocative photos of herself in her underwear to a lads' magazine. Both teens are depicted in the series' early seasons as confident and assertive. Thus, their sexual objectification is portrayed as an active choice—*their* choice—rather than something done to them by men (Gill 2007). Here, the postfeminist notion of "individual choice" legitimates sexual objectification as a mode of female sexual empowerment (Pitcher 2006).

While I am not suggesting that teen series are reflective of reality, the genre's sexual representations intersect with broader discourses of teenage sexual culture, particularly in relation to female sexual agency. For example, Ariel Levy (2006) and Deborah Tolman (2005), both of whom interviewed teenage girls about their sexual identities, detected an absence of desire, agency, and pleasure in the way these girls discussed their sexual experiences. This pattern is reflected in the pilot of recent teen series *Awkward.*, in which protagonist Jenna (Ashley Rickards) loses her virginity to her long-term crush, Matty (Beau Mirchoff). Notably, Jenna's desire for Matty is clear, conveyed through her voiceover, lingering gaze, and awkwardness around him. Thus, when they have sex for the first time at summer camp, it is clearly consensual. And yet, significantly, there is no sexual pleasure on Jenna's part. Instead, the experience is portrayed as physically painful, illustrated by close-ups of Jenna's tearful facial expression. The sex results immediately in loss when Jenna realizes that Matty plans to ignore her publicly and that their encounter will not lead to the romantic relationship she dreamed of. Within the show's diegesis, then, sex, even if consensual, is not portrayed as a desirable option for teenage girls, reflecting Byers's argument about *My So-Called Life*: Saying yes to sex almost always results in loss for teenage girls (2007: 22).

Thus, although female teenagers in teen drama series are portrayed as increasingly sexually confident, their sexual agency almost always results in despair. Gill argues that to be critical of the postfeminist shift towards female sexual "empowerment" is "to point to the dangers of such representations of women in a culture in which sexual violence is endemic" (2007: 159). In *Awkward.*, Jenna's loss of virginity is consensual and certainly not framed as abusive. Nonetheless, traditional models of gendered sexuality, characterized by male sexual dominance and female sexual submission, contribute to and replicate uneven power relations between Jenna and Matty, leaving Jenna, in her own words, "rubbed raw and reeling."

Teen drama series construct the distinctions between male and female teenage sexuality as natural gender differences. Male sexuality is presented as natural, unstoppable, and something the male teen in question cannot control, thus removing all sense of culpability for his actions. In contrast, female sexuality is commonly portrayed as devoid of desire even when under the girl's control. This notion that females are more responsible for their sexual actions than males—and less entitled to sexual pleasure—has significant implications for sexual violence storylines across the genre, as I shall now discuss.

In teen series, sexual violence is framed overwhelmingly as a young woman's personal problem, rather than something that is done to her by men (Berridge 2011). These personal experiences are removed from the broader gendered social structures that enable and permit male sexual violence against women. Indeed, sexual violence is rarely dealt with as a form of gendered abuse in the programs and is instead used to highlight other issues, most commonly the vulnerability of female youth. In several storylines the sexual violence occurs in adult settings at night after the female teenager attempts to act and/or dress older than her age. For example, in the pilot of *My So-Called Life*, Rayanne (A. J. Langer) is sexually assaulted after she and Angela lie to Angela's parents, sneak out to an over-21s nightclub and drink alcohol in the car park. A similar pattern occurs in a 2003 *One Tree Hill* episode in which a central female high-school student is almost raped at a college party. While some storylines feature the negative consequences for male teenagers who try to act older than they are, these consequences are not sexually threatening. For example, the male protagonist of an equivalent storyline in season two of *Dawson's Creek* who ruins his sixteenth birthday by going to a club and getting drunk suffers no sexually threatening ramifications.

In the lead-up to the sexual attack, the narrative relentlessly and solely focuses on these female victims, emphasizing what they were wearing, drinking, and doing at the time of the assault. This narrative scrutiny of the female victim is notable when compared to the treatment of victims of other kinds of physical (non-sexual) violence across the genre. For example, when teenage characters are physically abused by their parent or guardian, the narrative does not dwell on their actions prior to the abuse. This reinforces the notion that females are more responsible for sexual activities than males. Indeed, male perpetrators are rarely held accountable for their actions. As peripheral characters, they typically disappear shortly after committing the abuse. Instead, these narratives often end with the female victim learning a lesson, thus placing the onus for change firmly on her rather than on the male perpetrator. Illustrating this, a season two episode of *Beverly Hills* featuring an attempted rape ends with the victim dressing less provocatively. Ultimately, then, sexual violence in these storylines acts as a didactic warning to (female) viewers about the perils of attempting to act or dress older than their age, rather than a warning about the potential dangers of normative constructions of gendered sexuality that promote male sexual dominance and female sexual submission.

Across the genre, connections are rarely made between hegemonic constructions of gendered sexuality and sexual violence. Perpetrators are marked as distinct from "normal" males in the series, suggesting that sexual violence is the domain of individual bad men and an isolated problem of an otherwise fully functioning patriarchy. Further restoring ideals of gendered sexuality, in these programs sexual violence often operates as a catalyst for heterosexual romantic relationships by creating a space for the display of ideal masculinity. An attempted rape narrative from season one of *Friday Night Lights* provides a useful example of how central male teens enact ideal masculinity by defending and protecting female victims. In this storyline, sexual violence operates to advance a romantic relationship between the victim, Tyra (Adrianne Palicki), and her male friend, Landry (Jesse Plemons). Following the attack, Tyra is cast as needing male protection. Landry provides this by soothing and physically protecting her when she is attacked again by the man who tried to rape her. Although Landry accidentally kills the perpetrator in the process, his use of violence here is legitimated as heroic by the series. In this way, the narrative restores rather than problematizes ideals of masculinity, thereby operating to reinforce the patriarchal status quo. Hegemonic ideals of gendered sexuality are further restored by the budding romance between Tyra and Landry, thus allowing the program to largely ignore wider questions about the relationship between gender, sexuality, and power.

## Conclusion

My central aim here has been to complicate the recurring critical feminist focus, which tends to categorize individual sexual representations in teen dramas as positive or negative. Instead, I consider the *kinds* of stories told (or not) about teenage sexuality in these programs, paying close attention to the intersection of gender with these narratives and exploring the implications of the genre's constructions of gendered sexuality on sexual violence narratives. My intention has been to provide a broad overview of gendered sexual narratives. While I acknowledge that specific plots in these series challenge these dominant norms, my aim has been to identify recurring patterns rather than individual contradictions. It may seem antithetical that this chapter, which stems in part from a frustration with the way in which teenage viewers are often assumed by feminist and television scholarship to be passive dupes, adopts a structural approach. Structuralism treats texts as if their meanings are given and fixed and only need to be uncovered. It restricts itself to textual analysis in order to determine these meanings and has been widely criticized by poststructuralists for overemphasizing the authority of the text over the agency of viewers. I certainly do not want to deny the possibility of resistant or oppositional readings to such sexual narratives. With their ensemble casts and interweaving storylines, teen drama series privilege multiple points of identification, and the small body of audience studies on teenagers and television reveals that these viewers make meaning and take pleasure from these programs in complex ways.

However, the patterns uncovered through a structural approach to generic sexual narratives point to the presence of *preferred* readings (Hall 1999 [1973]). Overall, the same kinds of stories about teenage sexuality recur again and again: storylines that are heavily gendered, perpetuating the dominant myth of male sexuality as natural and unstoppable, while reinforcing the idea that females are more responsible than males for their sexual actions. Television does not present an unmediated "window on the world," but rather, as Robert C. Allen explains, "it constructs representations of the world based on complex sets of conventions—conventions whose operations are largely hidden by their transparency" (1992: 7). By denaturalizing these repetitive narratives, which are so familiar they often go unnoticed, and by exposing the recurring gendered patterns in the genre's dominant sexual narratives, I hope I have rendered these storylines strange and raised questions about why these enduring structures prevail.

# References

Allen, R. C. (1992) *Channels of Discourse, Reassembled: Television and Contemporary Criticism*, 2nd edition, London: Routledge.

Berridge, S. (2010) "Serialised Sexual Violence in Teen Television Drama Series," unpublished Ph.D. thesis, University of Glasgow.

——(2011) "Personal Problems and Women's Issues: Episodic Sexual Violence Narratives in US Teen Drama Series," *Feminist Media Studies* 11(4): 467–81.

Boyle, K. (2005) "Feminism Without Men: Feminist Media Studies in a Post-Feminist Age," in J. Curran and M. Gurevitch (eds.) *Mass Media and Society*, 4th edition, London: Hodder Arnold, pp. 29–43.

Brooker, W. (2001) "Living on Dawson's Creek: Teen Viewers, Cultural Convergence, and the Television Overflow," *International Journal of Cultural Studies* 4(4): 456–72.

Byers, M. (2007 [1998]) "Gender/Sexuality/Desire: Subversion of Difference and Construction of Loss in Adolescent Drama of My *So-Called Life*," in D. Lavery and M. Byers (eds.) *Dear Angela: Remembering* My So-Called Life, Lanham, MD: Rowman & Littlefield, pp. 13–34.

Gill, R. (2007) "Postfeminist Media Culture: Elements of a Sensibility," *European Journal of Cultural Studies* 10(2): 147–66.

Hall, S. (1999 [1973]) "Encoding and Decoding in Television Discourse," in S. During (ed.) *The Cultural Studies Reader*, London: Routledge, pp. 507–17.

Itzkoff, D. (2008) "When Teenage Angst Had Its Own Zip Code," *New York Times*, August 29. http://www.nytimes.com/2008/08/31/arts/television/31itzk.html.

Levy, A. (2006) *Female Chauvinist Pigs: Women and the Rise of Raunch Culture*, New York and London: Free Press.

MacKinnon, C. (1996 [1983]) "Feminism, Marxism, Method and the State," in S. Jackson and S. Scott (eds.) *Feminism and Sexuality: A Reader*, Edinburgh: Edinburgh University Press.

Pender, P. (2002) "'I'm Buffy and You're … History': The Postmodern Politics of *Buffy*," in R. Wilcox and D. Lavery (eds.) *Fighting the Forces: What's at Stake in* Buffy the Vampire Slayer, London: Rowman & Littlefield, pp. 35–44.

Pitcher, K. (2006) "The Staging of Agency in *Girls Gone Wild*," *Critical Studies in Media Communication* 23(3): 200–18.

Projansky, S. (2011) "Girls' Sexualities in *The Sisterhood of the Travelling Pants* Universe: Feminist Challenges and Missed Opportunities," in H. Radner and R. Stringer (eds.) *Feminism at the Movies: Understanding Gender in Contemporary Popular Cinema*, London: Routledge,

Tolman, D. (2005) *Dilemmas of Desire: Teenage Girls Talk about Sexuality*, Cambridge, MA: Harvard University Press.

Vint, S. (2002) "'Killing Us Softly?' A Feminist Search for the 'Real' Buffy," *Slayage: The Online Journal of Buffy Studies*, April 5. www.slayage.tv.

# 31

# Smoothing the wrinkles

## Hollywood, "successful aging," and the new visibility of older female stars

## *Josephine Dolan*

For decades, feminist scholarship has consistently critiqued the patriarchal underpinnings of Hollywood's relationship with women, in terms of both its industrial practices and its representational systems. During its pioneering era, Hollywood was dominated by women who occupied every aspect of the filmmaking process, both off and on screen; but the consolidation of the studio system in the 1920s and 1930s served to reduce the scope of opportunities for women working in off-screen roles. Off screen, a pattern of gendered employment was effectively established, one that continues to confine women to so-called "feminine" crafts such as scriptwriting and costume. Celebrated exceptions like Ida Lupino, Dorothy Arzner, Nora Ephron, Nancy Meyers, and Kathryn Bigelow have found various ways to succeed as producers and directors in Hollywood's continuing male-dominated culture. More typically, as recently as 2011, "women comprised only 18% of directors, executive producers, cinematographers and editors working on the top 250 domestic grossing films" (Lauzen 2012: 1).

At the same time, on-screen representations came to be increasingly predicated on a gendered star system that privileges hetero-masculine desires, and are dominated by historically specific discourses of idealized and fetishized feminine beauty that, in turn, severely limit the number and types of roles available to women. As far back as 1973 Molly Haskell observed that the elision of beauty and youth that underpins Hollywood casting impacted upon the professional longevity of female stars, who, at the first visible signs of aging, were deemed "too old or over-ripe for a part," except as a marginalized mother or older sister. Meanwhile, the careers of their similarly aged male counterparts were, and continue to be, shored up by heteronormative romantic couplings with much younger female stars, both on and off screen (Haskell 1973: 14). Even more problematically, Hollywood's ostensible reflections on its own gendered and agist practices—represented in films such as *Sunset Boulevard* (Billy Wilder, 1950) and *Whatever Happened to Baby Jane?* (Robert Aldrich, 1962)—do little more than establish older female stars as abject objects of a pathological gaze (Dolan 2013).

This formulation of the pathological gaze derives from Foucault, whose *The Birth of the Clinic* (1973 [1963]) suggests that the doctor/patient encounter is structured by clinicians who seek the signs of disease and abnormality on a patient's body through prior knowledge of normal, healthy bodies. It is in knowing the signs of the healthy body that the clinician recognizes the symptoms of the abnormal, and can thus diagnose ill health. The clinical gaze is therefore split between knowledge of the normal and that of the pathological. The exercise of power by the clinician suggested here is exacerbated by the medical profession's authority to constitute the terms of the normal that are brought to bear in the scrutiny of the patient's body. Extrapolating from this, films such as *Sunset Boulevard* and *Whatever Happened to Baby Jane?* can be recognized as mobilizing a similar split gaze. This is a gaze that pathologizes the body of the older female star through its knowledge of a youthful norm that enables the signs of aging to be recognizable and readable; and these signs are constituted as symptoms of abnormality. Clearly, in its rendering of specific older female star bodies as pathological, this split gaze also constitutes an ideological tautology that serves to legitimate the generalized cinematic invisibility of older female stars.

Notably, other national film industries, such as that of the UK, have adopted Hollywood's narrative conventions in order to compete in the global film market. The reach of Hollywood's pathologizing, agist, and gendered representational system extends far beyond films made in Los Angeles, making "Hollywood" a globalized paradigm. Consequently, the pattern of refusing to cast older female stars in significant roles, or casting them as marginal characters or as abject pathological figures, has become a globalized cinematic practice. And, as Simone de Beauvoir (1972), Germaine Greer (1992), and Kathleen Woodward (1999) have variously suggested, the cinematic invisibility of older, post-menopausal women is symptomatic of a broader, highly pervasive, and endemic cultural marginality.

It is against this century-long backdrop of cinematic marginalization that a recent proliferation of acclaimed performances by older female stars can be recognized and registered as significant. Since circa 2000, nominations for best actress at the Academy Awards, Hollywood's annual celebration of its own highest achievements, suggest that a female star's fiftieth birthday no longer signals retirement. When Meryl Streep won the best actress accolade in 2011 for *The Iron Lady* (Phyllida Lloyd) it followed earlier nominations in 1999, 2002, 2006, 2008, and 2009 for *Music of the Heart* (Wes Craven), *Adaptation* (Spike Jonze), *The Devil Wears Prada* (David Frankel), *Doubt* (John Patrick Shanley), and *Julie and Julia* (Nora Ephron). Similarly, Helen Mirren's 2006 best actress award for her performance in *The Queen* (Stephen Frears) came to be bracketed by 2001 and 2004 nominations for *Gosford Park* (Robert Altman) and *The Last Station* (Michael Hoffman). Other older female stars who have been nominated for "best actress" are Judi Dench in 2001, 2005, and 2007 for *Iris* (Richard Eyre), *Mrs. Henderson Presents* (Stephen Frears), and *Notes on a Scandal* (Richard Eyre); Ellen Burstyn in 2000 for *Requiem for a Dream* (Darren Aronofsky); Diane Keaton in 2003 for *Something's Gotta Give* (Nancy Meyers); Annette Bening in 2005 and 2010 for *Being Julia* (István Szabó), and *The Kids Are All Right* (Lisa Cholodenko); Julie Christie in 2007 for *Away from Her* (Sarah Polley); and Glenn Close in 2011 for *Albert Nobbs* (Rodrigo Garcia). This new and celebrated visibility of older female stars can be, and should be, seen as an important breakthrough indicating that adjustments are taking place within Hollywood patriarchy and that the signs of age inscribed on the bodies of older female stars are no longer equated with a normalized invisibility and its associated pathologized visibility.

However, a closer study of older female stardom suggests that celebrations of this new visibility need to be carefully qualified. Theorists of stardom (see, e.g., Dyer 1979, 1987; Gledhill 1991) have long suggested that stars cannot be reduced to marketing and promotional strategies; or to the economic success of their films; or to the popularity of a given actress/actor; or indeed to the quality of their performances. Rather, as Richard Dyer suggests, stars need to be understood as "always extensive, multimedia, intertextual," and as complex and polysemic signifying systems that are fully implicated in the circulation and reproduction of dominant discourses and ideologies (1987: 3). Crucially, stars function as "embodiments of the social categories in which people are placed and through which they make sense of their lives, and indeed through which we make our lives—categories of class, gender, ethnicity, religion, sexual orientation and so on" (Dyer 1987: 18). In other words, stars make discursively produced identities seem as if they are biological, and hence essential, properties of the body.

It thus comes as no surprise that older female stars are typically positioned to embody idealized aging femininity within Hollywood's heteronormative sexual paradigm, though this is rarely articulated as active sexuality. Mostly, older female stars are cast in roles where their sexuality is repressed in some way. This occurs through religious convention in *Doubt*, illness in *The Last Station* and *Iris*, age-related lack of opportunity in *Mrs. Henderson Presents*, and the gender and sexual confusions of transvestism in *Albert Nobbs*. *Notes on a Scandal* is unusual in its depiction of lesbian desire, but this is effectively pathologized through its story of predatory sexual harassment. *Something's Gotta Give* is one of the few films suggesting positive and active female sexuality, although, as Sally Chivers (2011: 129–34) observes, the female protagonist, Erica (Diane Keaton), functions largely to secure aging masculinity within age-appropriate coupledom and to prop up Jack Nicholson's embodiment of aging virility. Clearly, then, apart from opportunities offered to older female stars, little has changed since Haskell first staged her trenchant critique of Hollywood's masculinist representational system.

Such masculinist reiterations are not the only problem due to the striking absence from this new visibility of aging stars like Angela Bassett and Whoopi Goldberg, whose youthful successes have already thrown into relief the acute marginalization of non-white actresses in the Hollywood paradigm (see, e.g., Tasker 1998). Whilst Bassett has been sidelined into less prestigious television roles, Goldberg is literally rendered invisible through recent performances in which she is heard rather than seen—as a documentary film narrator; or the voice of Stretch, an animated character in *Toy Story 3* (Lee Unkrich, 2010). Such exclusionary practices are highly problematic; not only because they marginalize non-white older stars, but because they also reproduce the ubiquitous and pernicious white, racial privilege that is normalized and rendered ideologically hegemonic through the embodiments of Hollywood's star system (Dyer 1997). If older female stars can be recognized as embodiments of a problematic and discursively produced, white, racial identity, what of old age itself? What does the new visibility of older female stars suggest about contemporary discourses of old age and what particular inscriptions of old age are embodied by older female stars? Moreover, does the new visibility of older female stars suggest that Hollywood has relinquished its pathologizing gaze?

## Embodiment and "successful aging"

More than 20 years ago, cultural gerontologists were identifying an emergent, regulatory discourse of "successful aging" (Rowe and Kahn 1997), subsequently summarized as being "the avoidance of disease or disease susceptibility, a high cognitive capacity, and active engagement with life" (Byrnes and Dillaway 2004: 67). This model of "successful aging" is now established as the commonsense alternative to, and remedy for, those accounts of burdensome and vulnerable old age that underpin gloomy predictions of the economic and emotional costs to the state, to communities, and to families of an aging population. Because of their capacity to naturalize discourse and ideology, stars offer an especially efficient mechanism through which to secure "successful aging" as hegemonic. Through both the characters they play and their continuing presence in the media circuits of contemporary culture, older stars function to make "successful aging" seem like "common sense."

Indeed, stars can be seen to play a part in the negotiation of "successful aging" itself. When the configuration first emerged it was associated with the promise of a leisured, golden retirement funded by a combination of state and private pensions. However, because of the global recession of 2008, the dream of leisured retirement has been deferred for the duration. Across the West, in the context of nationally variable retirement ages, the raising of official retirement ages has effectively extended working life for both men and women. One result has been the transformation of "successful aging" from being a discourse of leisured retirement to being a regulatory regime of the body "fit for work." With their continuing careers, all older stars can be seen to embody the deferment of retirement, while powerfully signifying the "fit for work" body. For female stars, however, the alignment between this version of "successful aging" and their old age bodies is not as straightforward as for their male counterparts. Older male stars have always been represented as employed, active, engaged, and hetero-virile and therefore readily available to embody the emergent discourses of "successful aging" and, hence, deferred retirement. But, in order for female stars to perform this function, they first must be removed from their persistent position of invisibility, or pathologized visibility, and be made available for visible celebration instead. In this context, then, the high profile of older female stars at the Academy Awards represents a crucial stage in achieving their alignment with, and embodiment of, formulations of "successful aging." However, because of women's complex engagement with paid work under patriarchy, and prevailing assumptions that women do not *really* retire because of continuing domestic responsibilities, there is less urgency that discourses of deferred retirement are ideologically secured through their inscription on the bodies of older female stars. My intention here is not to suggest that the work performed by older female stars does not lock into injunctions for working women to defer retirement from paid work. Rather, my aim is to register how the embodiment of successful aging is deflected through gender difference and the constitution of aging femininity.

The constitution of a feminized "successful aging" is most apparent when it becomes little more than an extension into old age of what Naomi Wolf (1990) terms "The Beauty Myth"; that is, a set of normalized and regulatory discourses of ideal feminine beauty implicitly privileging the appearance of youth over that of old age. This extension can be recognized in many highly publicized red carpet appearances by older female stars such as Cher, Susan Sarandon, Goldie Hawn, and Faye Dunaway, as much as the panoply of Oscar nominees listed above. Similarly, the old age extension of "The Beauty Myth" is reiterated in well-paid endorsements for L'Oreal cosmetics by Jane Fonda and Andie MacDowell, who repeatedly assure us that "We're worth it." Meanwhile, Nicole Kidman's curiously unfurrowed, immobile brow suggest that it is never too soon to smooth the wrinkles. Such stars foreground the prevalence of cosmetic interventions such as Botox and facelifts that effectively "youthify" the appearance of the female star's aging body, thus enabling them to embody a particularly feminine version of "successful aging."

However, the wrinkle-free face that signifies feminine "successful aging" is not solely dependent on cosmetics and surgical procedures. Vivian Sobchak notes an equal dependence on post-production techniques such as airbrushing and computer graphic transformations, what she terms the "second operation of plastic surgery" (1999: 206). The artifice of these transformations has led to consumer protests and legal action on both sides of the Atlantic. In 2012, the UK's Advertising Standards Authority ruled that the L'Oreal campaign faced up by Rachel Weisz was exaggerated and misleading and banned it, although the watchdog agency rejected complaints about a separate L'Oreal commercial for a moisturizer featuring a photograph of actress Jane Fonda (Reuters 2012). It also banned some Photoshopped cosmetics ads featuring Julia Roberts and Christy Turlington. After the National Advertising Division (NAD) of the Council of Better Business Bureaus ruled that a CoverGirl mascara ad was misleading, Procter & Gamble shut down the advertising. The NAD, which can issue rulings but cannot itself enforce them, said it was following the lead of its sister body in the UK.

The suspicion of the photographic image's unreliability makes "live" appearances by older female stars on chat shows and at red carpet events all the more powerful since it ostensibly bypasses the opportunity for "second operation of plastic surgery" and allows for the "successfully" aged body to be effectively displayed. Such "live" appearances also illuminate how the effort of smoothing the wrinkles is not confined to stars' faces. It also extends to bodies that are seemingly unmarked by pregnancy or overindulgence; characterized by slender legs, pert breasts, and buttocks; and displayed through revealing and figure-hugging dresses. While live appearances provide rich sites for exhibiting this feminine version of "successful aging," they pale in comparison when compared to the power of paparazzi images. Famously, in 2008, just months after receiving an Oscar for her performance in the title role of *The Queen*, a globally circulated paparazzi shot of a bikini-clad Helen Mirren established hers as the idealized benchmark of the older women's body, the embodiment of "senior sexiness" (see, e.g., *Mail Online* 2008). The power of such photographs resides in the absence of specific investments in preserving Mirren's image. In the paparazzi paradigm just as valuable is a shot breaking the "magic spell" of "cosmeceutical enhancement" (Sobchak 1999: 202) by revealing any signs of letting go (flab, body hair, stretch marks), the signs of maintenance (leaving the gym, leaving the beauty parlour, leaving the clinic), or signs of surgery (attempts to conceal scars, before and after images). Therefore, Mirren is completely distanced from those pre- or post-production enhancements of star imagery that underpin official promotion; the bikini image testifies to a "natural" achievement of "successful aging." Once discourse is rendered "natural" in this way, its ideological function is effaced and it readily enters into "common sense."

Crucially, while the discourses surrounding the Mirren bikini shot naturalize the "successfully aged" female body, there is no pretense that it should be effortless. The *Daily Mail* points out, "this was no retouched studio shot, with the only work to transform her toned body having been carried out during gruelling hours in the gym" (*Mail Online* 2008). Similarly, in 2011 during an interview on NBC's *Today* show, Jane Fonda forged a link between effort and "successful aging" when she rationalized her own election of plastic surgery despite having foresworn such procedures when she signed as the "aging face" of L'Oreal cosmetics five years earlier. In that "regretful" interview she said:

> It's important to exercise when you're younger. But it's like the number one ingredient for successful aging. … It's less about trying to look a certain way as being able to get up and down out of a chair, carry your grandkids, look over your shoulder when backing down a driveway. Staying independent as you can.
>
> (Fonda 2011)

Given that Fonda had just updated her trademark fitness videos it is tempting to accuse her of dissembling, of disavowing her own economic, emotional, and psychological investments in "successful aging." But this overlooks the interpellatory power of discourse by conflating the person Jane Fonda, who no doubt suffers all manner of anxieties about her aging body, with the star image Jane Fonda, whose signifying system both exploits and is exploited by ideologies of feminine beauty at their intersection with formations of "successful aging."

## "Successful aging" disrupted

All this echoes Sadie Wearing's (2007) formulation of "new aging," which is characterized by the increased visibility of the older female body and a concomitant desire to disavow the negative connotations of aging *per se*, while also avoiding the equally negative connotations of an overly youthful appearance epitomized by the damning phrase "mutton dressed as lamb." According to Wearing, recent representations of the aging female body attempt to "have it both ways" insofar as they "offer the fantasy of therapeutic rejuvenation while remaining firmly entrenched in a coercive and moralizing policing of aesthetic and gender norms" that "set the standards of both chronological decorum and time defiance regulating" (Wearing 2007: 304–5). Anxieties about "chronological decorum" are evident in the numerous "best and worst gown" web pages from both fans and "official" sources such as online newspapers that are annually published in the wake of each year's Academy Award ceremonies. For instance, adjudications of a failure to comply with time defiance regulation are implicit in Liz Jones's (2012) remarks that Meryl Streep's dress had "too much fabric" and highly explicit when Sun and Goto (2012) judge the dress to be "dated."

But where the adjudications of "chronological decorum" are brought to bear on Streep for the concealment of her flesh, Madonna is judged for the excessive exposure of hers, as typified by a gossip site's poll "Is it time for the material girl to wear more material?" (*Celebuzz* 2012). As Diane Railton and Paul Watson (2012) observe, the global circulation of similar discourses constitutes a radical shift from Madonna's image as the "material girl" of the 1980s, when her film- and music-derived popularity was at its peak, to her current incarnation as an aging pop diva. Always controversial because of her performance of pornographic gestures and use of fetishistic costume in the representational spaces of her music videos and films, she nonetheless mesmerized with her ability to switch between distinct sexed and gendered identities through her proud display of a well-toned body. This served to highlight gender performativity by unsettling naturalized assumptions that muscularity is a biological property of the male body. However, since reaching her fifties, Madonna has been increasingly vilified for exposing her flesh, a "tawdry embarrassment" (Fryer 2012).

Notably, the discourses surrounding Madonna's exposed flesh sharply contrast with those about Helen Mirren. The latter's "enviable curves and flat stomach" (*Mail Online* 2008) are heralded as an exemplary example of "senior sexiness"; Madonna is scorned because of her sinewy arms; gnarled, bony knees and "wrinkled and vein-ravaged hands that reveal she is battling to defy the signs of aging" (*Mail Online* 2007). Unlike Mirren, Madonna's skin is represented as bearing the signs of aging—it sags, it wrinkles, it is visibly veined. Therefore, Madonna's transgression of "chronological decorum" apparently is not produced by exposing flesh *per se*. Rather, the terms of transgression are defined through the *type* of flesh on show, and, by extension, by the signs of aging made visible. In short, Madonna displays the wrong kind of flesh to be allowed the burden of exposure. She apparently embodies an incipient old age that cannot be contained, controlled, managed, or concealed by the efforts of exercise or diet or cosmetics.

Two points must be made here. First, the contempt for Madonna's flesh reveals how little has really changed since the production of *Sunset Boulevard* and *Whatever Happened to Baby Jane?* The body of the aging female star can still be rendered the object of a pathologizing gaze if it fails the injunctions of "chronological decorum." This recognition usefully exposes the extent to which the new visibility of the older female star is contingent on conformity to "successful aging" agendas and contingent on the extent to which the star can embody and thus naturalize its ideologies. Second, the deployment of a pathological gaze onto the body of Madonna illuminates some of the cultural anxieties—both public and personal—that attend the feared collapse of "successful aging." Such anxieties can be recognized in the fantasy film *Stardust* (Matthew Vaughn, 2007), where Michelle Pfeiffer plays an ancient witch, Lamia, whose youthful appearance is shown to rely on endless replenishment by energy stolen from earthbound and embodied celestial stars. (The slippage between film and celestial stars is highly telling.) Notably, as Lamia's energy drains, her youthful beauty literally unravels and peels away, exposing the abject crone beneath. In this especially invidious representation of aging femininity, Pfeiffer, like Madonna, can be seen as embodying both the growing hegemony of cosmeceutical enhancement and the surrounding cultural anxieties about its vulnerability. Crucially, both Madonna and Pfeiffer disturbingly foreground anxieties about the provisionality of "successful aging," its propensity to rupture, to break down, to revert to an underlying and inevitable "*un*successful aging" that portends the final stages of life. Here flesh is not pathologized simply because it bears the signs of aging, but because those signs of aging are a potent reminder of our universal mortality.

In other instances the body of the older female star is inscribed with the cultural anxieties associated with other pathologized signs of aging such as mental decline. In 2007, somewhat disingenuously given that she was only 40, Nicole Kidman became the female face of Nintendo's Brain Training campaign. She announced, "I've quickly found that training my brain is a great way to keep my mind feeling young" (*Videogamer* 2007). As with the wrinkle-free brow, Kidman suggests that it is never too soon to forestall the ostensible decline into old age. This positions "keeping the mind young" as pivotal in achieving "successful aging." It is the counterpoint to its opposite, the failing, old age mind associated with conditions such as Alzheimer's and dementia—defined by that loss of cognitive capacity that precludes the active engagement with life crucial to "successful aging."

In recent years, representations of cognitive loss as both feared and fearful have been central to several highly acclaimed performances by older female stars: Judi Dench for *Iris*, Julie Christie for *Away from Her*, and Meryl Streep for *The Iron Lady*. In their treatment of older women as disturbed and disturbing, as objects of a pathologizing gaze, these films bear striking resemblances to representations of abject femininity in *Sunset Boulevard* and *Whatever Happened to Baby Jane?* However, where those earlier films very much reflected Hollywood's own neglect of its aging female stars, these more recent films take their bearings from current cultural anxieties about the vulnerable old age that lies beyond "successful aging." Sally Chivers (2011: 75) suggests that these anxieties are managed through a heightening and reconfiguring of Hollywood's heteronormative imperative through the intimacies and commitments of a loving care that supplants sexuality as the glue of coupledom. In some ways, this renders these films postfeminist in that they represent masculinity through terms akin to that of the caring "new man," while their chronological contemporaneity with second-wave feminism "proves" that feminist protest was never necessary in the first place. Equally, the films' reconfiguration of the emotional dynamics of heteronormative caring powerfully locates the care of vulnerable elderly people as a private, domestic concern in ways that ideologically efface state- and community-derived collective economic and emotional responsibilities.

Notably, this ideological work is produced through the on-screen abjection and pathologization of older female stars. However, this rarely bleeds into the female star's off-screen image because surrounding discourses emphasize performance and acting ability. As exemplified by Mirren, Christie, and Streep this typically culminates in highly publicized Academy Award nominations and associated red carpet appearances where their newly restored glamour forges a clear separation between abject character and celebrated star; in this way the character, and not the star, bears the burden of the pathological gaze. In other words, these stars are not positioned as the embodiment of cognitive loss, and, by extension, their ability to embody "successful aging" is not disrupted. This undoubtedly serves the interests of Hollywood, but it also suggests that "successful aging" has a privileged and protected status in the embodied ideologies of old age.

As this essay highlights, the new visibility of older female Hollywood stars is fully embedded in the production, reproduction, and embodiment of a complex nexus of feminized discourses of "successful aging" that incorporates and naturalizes ideologies of deferred retirement, cosmeceutical enhancement, and chronological decorum into longstanding formations of normative whiteness. Weaving through this are those pathologized ruptures to "successful aging" occasioned by signifiers of mortality inscribed on the flesh of older female stars and/or reproduced in their performances of abject, cognitive failure and which point to the broader cultural anxieties that attend Western demographics of aging. While the dynamic of this nexus serves to protect older female stars from alignment with pathologized abjection, it does so in ways that effectively privilege the terms of "successful aging." Effectively, the new visibility of older female stars is thus rendered conditional on conformity to "The Beauty Myth's" extension into old age and the effacement of potential ruptures to the ideological hegemony of "successful aging."

# References

Beauvoir, S. de (1972) *Old Age*, London: Andre Deutsch.

Byrnes, M. and H. Dillaway (2004) "Who Is 'Successful' at Aging? A Critique of the Literature and a Call for More Inclusive Perspectives," American Sociological Association meetings, San Francisco, CA, August 14.

*Celebuzz* (2012) "Age Appropriate? 53 Year Old Madonna Bears Bum at Music Festival." http://www.celebuzz.com/2012-03-26/age-appropriate-53-year-old-madonna-bares-bum-at-miami-music-festival-photos/.

Chivers, S. (2011) *The Silvering Screen: Old Age and Disability in Cinema*, Toronto, Buffalo and London: University of Toronto Press.

Dolan, J. (2013) "Firm and Hard: Stardom, Gender and the Troubling Embodiment of 'Successful Aging',￼" in J. I. Prieto-Arranz, P. Bastida-Rodríguez, C. Calafat-Ripoll, M. Fernández-Morales, and C. Suárez-Gómez (eds.) *De-Centring Cultural Studies: Past, Present and Future of Popular Culture*, Newcastle: Cambridge Scholars Press, pp. 217–46.

Dyer, R. (1979) *Stars*, London: British Film Institute.

——(1987) *Heavenly Bodies: Film Stars and Society*, London: Routledge.

——(1997) *White: Essays on Race and Culture*, London and New York: Routledge.

Fonda, J. (2011) *Today Interview*. http://today.msnbc.msn.com/id/45556326/ns/today-today_health/t/jane-fonda-why-i-chose-plastic-surgery/.

Foucault, M. (1973 [1963]) *The Birth of the Clinic: An Archaeology of Medical Perception*, London: Tavistock Publications.

Fryer, J. (2012) "Sorry Madge You're Now Just a Tawdry Embarrassment: She's a Fan. But after Sitting through the 53-year-old's Lewd, Expletive-ridden New Show, Jane Fryer Is Not Happy," *Mail Online*. http://www.dailymail.co.uk/news/article-2175666/Madonna-Hyde-Park-review-Sorry-Madge-youre-just-tawdry-embarrassment.html#ixzz22Bs6f36e.

Gledhill, C. (ed.) (1991) *Stardom: Industry of Desire*, London and New York: Routledge.

Greer, G. (1992) *The Change: Women, Ageing and the Menopause*, New York: Alfred A. Knopf.

Haskell, M. (1973) *From Reverence to Rape: The Treatment of Women in the Movies*, Chicago: University of Chicago Press.

Jones, L. (2012) "Oscars Fashion Review," *Mail Online*. http://www.dailymail.co.uk/femail/article-2107439/Oscars-fashion-review-2012-The-best-worst-red-carpet-dresses.html.

Lauzen, M. M. (2012) "The Celluloid Ceiling: Behind-the-scenes Employment of Women on the Top 250 Films." http://womenintvfilm.sdsu.edu/files/2011_Celluloid_Ceiling_Exec_Summ.pdf.

*Mail Online* (2007) "She's So Vein: The Very Veiny Hand of Madonna." http://www.daily-mail.co.uk/tvshowbiz/article-462819/Shes-vein-veiny-hand-Madonna.html.

——(2008) "Helen Mirren the Bikini Queen Reigns Supreme at 63." http://www.dailymail.co.uk/tvshowbiz/article-1035510/Helen-Mirren-bikini-queen-reigns-supreme-63.html.

Railton, D. and P. Watson (2012) "'She's So Vein': Madonna and the Drag of Aging," in J. Dolan and E. Tincknell (eds.) *Aging Feminities: Troubling Representations*, London: Cambridge Scholars Publishing, pp. 195–206.

Reuters (2012) "UK Bans 'Misleading' Rachel Weisz L'Oreal Advert." http://www.reuters.com/article/2012/02/01/us-rachelweisz-loreal-idUSTRE8100ZD20120201.

Rowe, J. W. and R. L. Kahn (1997) "Successful Aging," *The Gerontologist* 37: 433–41.

Sobchak, V. (1999) "Scary Women: Cinema, Surgery and Special Effects," in K. Woodward (ed.) *Figuring Age: Women, Bodies, Generations*, Bloomington and Indianapolis: Indiana University Press, pp. 200–11.

Sun, F. and Y. Goto (2012) *Time Entertainment On-line*. http://entertainment.time.com/2012/02/26/oscars-2012-the-best-and-worst-dressed/#meryl-streep-2.

Tasker, Y. (1998) *Working Girls: Gender, Sexuality and Popular Cinema*, London and New York: Routledge.

*Videogamer* (2007) "Nicole Kidman the New Face of Brain Training." http://www.videogamer.com/ds/more_brain_training/news/nicole_kidman_the_new_face_of_brain_training.html.

Wearing, S. (2007) "'Subjects of Rejuvenation': Aging in Postfeminist Culture," in Y. Tasker and D. Negra (eds.) *Interrogating Postfeminism: Gender and the Politics of Popular Culture*, Durham, NC and London: Duke University Press, pp. 277–310.

Wolf, N. (1990) *The Beauty Myth*, London: Vintage.

Woodward, K. (ed.) (1999) *Figuring Age: Women, Bodies, Generations*, Bloomington and Indianapolis: Indiana University Press.

# 32

# Perfect bodies, imperfect messages

## Media coverage of cosmetic surgery and ideal beauty

### *J. Robyn Goodman*

"It [the perfect body] is everywhere. I get *Cosmo*, *Vogue*, and all the girls are beautiful. And it's the same thing when I go home. Everyone in Miami is gorgeous. Living in Miami is like living in the magazine. All the girls are parading around with perfect bodies, and you don't ever get a break," said Brianna, a 21-year-old American student who was undergoing breast augmentation surgery. "I think [cosmetic surgery] makes you feel better about yourself, and I've seen that in a lot of girls. And I think it's [breast augmentation] a lot safer process now because they use saline, so in case it does pop, it's just salt water. It's not going to really kill you or anything. I'm going to be in pain, but what's a week compared to my whole life being happy."

Brianna's story is not uncommon. Over the past 20 years, the number of cosmetic surgeries[1] to fix perceived imperfections has grown drastically around the world. It has increased as much as 880 percent in some countries (e.g. www.surgery.org; www.factsanddetails.com/china). In 2010 alone, 18.5 million cosmetic procedures were carried out worldwide, with the US, Brazil, China, India, and Japan ranking in the top five (www.iasps.org). After controlling for population size, South Korea ranked number one, followed by Greece, Italy, Brazil, and Colombia (*Economist* 2012). In 2010, more than six million people had the five most common surgical procedures—liposuction, breast augmentation, blepharoplasty (removing excess skin from the eyelids), rhinoplasty, and abdominoplasty; and 7.3 million people had the five most common minimally invasive procedures—Botox, hyaluronic acid injections (e.g. Juvederm), fat injections, laser hair removal, and Intense Pulsed Light (IPL) laser treatment of the skin (www.isaps.org). However, countries vary in their preferences. For example, Brazilians are seven times more likely than other nationalities to have buttock procedures, whereas Greek men are ten times more likely to have penis enlargement (*Economist* 2012).

Approximately 90 percent of the procedures in Brazil, the United States, and China are done on women like Brianna (www.plasticsurgery.org; www.factsanddetails.com/china). In Canada and the US, adults aged 35 to 50 had the greatest number of procedures (Polonijo and Carpiano 2008; www.surgery.org). In contrast, most users in China are in their twenties; 62 percent of Koreans aged 25 to 29 have had cosmetic surgery (www.factsanddetails.com/china; Pais 2007). Desire for cosmetic surgery is likewise growing. Dove's 2004 global beauty survey found 25 percent of women would consider cosmetic surgery; 40 percent would contemplate it if safety were guaranteed and costs were lower (Ectoff *et al.* 2004). In Brazil, the US, and South Korea, as many as 65–80 percent of the population desire some form of cosmetic surgery (Pais 2007; de Andrade 2010; www.surgery.org).

This worldwide growth in and desire for cosmetic surgery flourish despite safety concerns and risks. For example, the death rate for abdominoplasty patients is 1 in 600; 1 of every 347 liposuction procedures produces major complications such as long-term swelling and unplanned hospitalization (Yoho *et al.* 2005). Between 15 and 20 percent of breast augmentation surgeries result in excessive hardness and noticeable distortion in the breast (Wolf 1991; www.fda.gov/cdrh/breastimplants/birisk.html). Even minimally invasive procedures have issues. In 30–40 percent of laser skin resurfacing patients, the treated skin is visibly darker than the surrounding skin (Tanzi and Alster 2008).

Researchers have outlined several reasons for the continuing growth, despite these risks and complications. An oversupply of plastic surgeons and growth in clinics specializing in cosmetic surgery in some countries have led surgeons to recruit consumers and offer procedures at low cost (Latteier 1998; Sullivan 2001; Swami *et al.* 2011). Patient-related factors include stronger approval of and desire for cosmetic surgery; an aging population wanting to maintain a youthful appearance; as well as low self-image, body dissatisfaction, mental health issues, vanity, and familial pressures (e.g. Latteier 1998; Ricciardelli and White 2011). Finally, media and society have helped establish a youthful, wrinkle-free, toned, lean body based on white European standards as the ideal for men and women (Hanabusa 2008; Adams 2009). Indeed, in many countries the body has become a status symbol, touted as the route to career, personal, social, and romantic success (Swami *et al.* 2011; Ricciardelli and White 2011).

This chapter emphasizes the media's role as an information source for and influence on cosmetic surgery and ideal beauty, since sociocultural pressures seem to be a major factor in cosmetic surgery's growth, with media serving as the strongest disseminator of these pressures (Latteier 1998). One study of breast augmentation patients found the top influences were magazines, television, and the internet (Walden *et al.* 2010). Interviews with cosmetic surgery patients further reveal media pressure. Brianna told me:

> We talk about whoever's on the cover of *Cosmopolitan*, *Vogue* or *Bazaar*. They are the ideal. They are super thin, have abs, big boobs. And I think it [the media ideal] causes people to criticize themselves more because they don't fit that [ideal].

## Media as information source

In the US, 83 percent of breast augmentation patients sought information in women's magazine articles, 71 percent on television, 50 percent in newspaper or news magazine articles, and 38 percent in magazine ads (Didie and Sarwer 2003). Showing how these ratios can vary by country, women in India primarily used television (61 percent), movies (12 percent), and newspapers/books (11 percent) (Patil *et al.* 2011). The internet is, not surprisingly, becoming the major information source. Approximately two-thirds of US and UK cosmetic surgery patients got the majority of their information from the internet; patients were 40 times more likely to start their information search on Google or a surgeon's website than with a physician (Nassab *et al.* 2010; Walden *et al.* 2010).

Print media coverage of cosmetic surgery largely focuses on types of procedures, who is having it and why, and the procedure's benefits (e.g. Adams 2009; Polonijo and Carpiano 2008). The content is overwhelmingly positive, suggesting surgery can improve mental and physical health. One-third of 171 US breast implant articles over the past 35 years named mental and physical benefits, while only eight emphasized risks, 35 percent mention no risks, and 28 percent characterized serious complication as uncommon (Sullivan 2001). Almost half the articles in Canadian women's magazines depicted cosmetic surgery as improving emotional health; 76 percent described negative emotional health before surgery; 71 percent described positive emotional health afterwards (Polonijo and Carpiano 2008).

Not surprisingly, then, Western print media often de-emphasize risks by underreporting them, as well as downplaying pain and discomfort, although they frequently mention negative effects such as pain and swelling (Adams 2009; Brooks 2004; Polonijo and Carpiano 2008). In Italy and Canada risks were discussed in newspapers and magazines less than 20 percent of the time, although the articles emphasized patients know about risks (Mondini *et al.* 1996; Polonijo and Carpiano 2008).

Magazines typically present cosmetic surgery in only a few ways, most often by portraying cosmetic surgery as a scientific wonder. Updates on trends and new technology present procedures in magical terms (Brooks 2004). Other themes include aging (aging is unnatural or a problem to be fixed), malleability (bodies are endlessly moldable, with each body part presented as diseased or flawed but easily correctable), and medicalization of the body (to make the body "normal," although the body part in question is already "normal" by medical standards) (Woodstock, 2001; Polonijo and Carpiano 2008).

First-person and especially celebrity accounts also have emerged as prominent in magazines. In the US, first-person accounts emphasize individuals' motivations for having surgery, praise patients' courage and candor, and present patients as empowered and rational (Sullivan 2001; Woodstock 2001; Brooks 2004). Canadian first-person accounts tend to profile two women—one with positive and one with negative emotional health prior to surgery but both experiencing positive outcomes after the surgery, including increased self-esteem, greater happiness, and a greater ability to attract a romantic partner (Polonijo and Carpiano 2008). Of course, celebrities may discuss positive and negative views on cosmetic surgery (Reid and Malone 2008; Rountree and Davis 2011). Korean celebrities, however, are apparently offered free surgery in exchange for promoting it (Davies and Han 2011).

Print articles have largely focused on Caucasian women under 40 years old (Polonijo and Carpiano 2008). When women of color are discussed, articles tended to normalize racial ambiguity by highlighting popular procedures to change racial characteristics, such as Asians' creaseless eyelids and Africans' wider noses. They further normalize the European beauty standard by presenting racial ambiguity as assimilation rather than erasure of racial identification (Adams 2009). Western media discuss women's cosmetic surgery in terms of vanity or improving mental or physical health, while stories about men give their rational justifications for their decisions (Adams 2009). UK television programs from the 1990s presented men as feeling shameful and hesitant; unlike breast augmentation for women, pectoral implants and penile augmentation were presented as frivolous and nonsensical (Davis 2002).

Reality television shows cosmetic surgery as a quick, easy, painless way to change the body so the authentic inner self matches the inauthentic outer self (Heyes 2007). Most follow a similar format. First are personalized stories describing contestants (almost exclusively women) as feeling tortured or disabled by their appearance, thereby causing the audience to sympathize and identify with contestants (Heyes 2007; Pitts-Taylor 2007). Few spend more than ten minutes of an hour-long show showing the surgical and healing processes. At the end, participants get new hairdos, make-up, and clothes so they can reveal their new self to the squeals of friends and family (George 2004). Thus, the on-screen transformation is framed as a Cinderella-like fairy tale in which unhappy individuals are magically transformed to live happily ever after (Heyes 2007; Pitts-Taylor 2007). However, plastic surgeons fear that these reality shows trivialize cosmetic surgery by emphasizing personal stories (American Society for Aesthetic Plastic Surgery 2003; George 2004). They make surgery and healing look easy, and present multiple surgeries as the norm and uncomplicated. Both are mis-leading and create unrealistic expectations (George 2004). What was once seen as a procedure for the rich, famous, or vain is now seen as attainable and palatable for the masses (George 2004).

According to Hanabusa (2008), Japanese Manga programs depict cosmetic surgery in ways similar to US reality television. Only female characters had cosmetic sur-gery, and in two of the three Manga programs, the women had surgery for career advancement and were rewarded with romance, much like reality television. The third Manga, however, questioned Japanese beauty norms. It starred an unattractive woman whose unique appearance inspired others to surgically alter their looks, making what was previously unattractive the new beauty ideal. More typically these media homogenize and normalize images of a standard ideal beauty and depict achievement of the ideal as the only route to success and happiness.

In the US from 1985 to 2004, cosmetic surgery ads focused on liposuction (54 percent), breast augmentation (39 percent), and facelifts (39 percent), although ads for Botox and laser resurfacing increased by 30 percent in that period (Hennink-Kaminski et al. 2010). Korean ads, however, largely focused on eliminating double chins and wrinkles (Davies and Han 2011). Despite focusing on different procedures, both countries' ads focused on fat removal (liposuction and double chins) and regaining youthful skin (facelift, eye/forehead wrinkles). Furthermore, because ads rarely mention risks, complications, recovery time, physician background, or costs, they lack important health information (Sullivan 2001; Hennink-Kaminski et al. 2010). For example, US studies have found that 80 percent of ads name a specific physician, but fewer than half mention board certification (Hennink-Kaminski et al. 2010). Few mention whether the surgical facility is accredited or warn that physician credentials and experience are important to ensure safe, satisfactory outcomes (Sullivan 2001).

Instead of health information, most ads focused on selling ideal beauty through sales appeals, visuals, and headlines. Hennink-Kaminski, Reid, and King (2010) found at least half the ads used a physical appearance appeal, encouraging outward transformation for the sake of beauty. One-third used an assurance appeal to encourage trust in the procedure and doctor, while 22 percent simply stated basic information such as office hours and procedures provided. Although sexual appeals (i.e. sex-related benefits) were used in only 20 percent of ads, sexual appeals have more than doubled since 1996 (Hennink-Kaminski et al. 2010). Of the ads with sexual appeals, 53 percent said surgery would increase one's self-esteem, 34 percent claimed increased sexual attractiveness, and 11 percent claimed increased sexual activity (Hennink-Kaminski and Reichert 2011).

Web studies are becoming particularly important given that two-thirds of US and UK cosmetic surgery patients got the majority of their information from the web (Nassab et al. 2010; Walden et al. 2010). In Korea, surgery is prolifically promoted, through more than 6,000 online communities, 47,000 blogs, and 3,000 social media pages (Davies and Han 2011). All the US websites used before-and-after photos and two-thirds used video; in contrast, 46 percent of UK sites used before-and-after photos and 26 percent used video (Nassab et al. 2011). However, in both countries, studies show complications were reported between 10 percent and 40 percent of the time, and less than 5 percent of sites discussed post-surgical care (Nassab et al. 2010; Nassab et al. 2011). Thus, the sites, particularly in the US, emphasized what cosmetic surgery could achieve more than pertinent procedure and risk information.

Luo (2012) studied 50 Chinese cosmetic surgery hospitals' websites, finding many photographs of happy, young, carefree female patients with the hospital's physicians, which she said downplayed the procedure's pain while emphasizing its ease. Furthermore, all the female "patients'" pictures depicted ideal beauty. The beauty ideal borrowed the Western ideal of large, rounded breasts, although China historically has regarded female breasts as functional, and the Western double eyelid fold, albeit with slight rather than deepset folds. Simultaneously, it constructed "Oriental beauty" by venerating classical Asian features—delicate, heart-shaped face and small chin (Luo 2012).

## Media exposure and influence

Research finding that people regard the media as an information source for cosmetic surgery and that news coverage emphasizes ideal beauty achievement, ease of procedures, and social, physical, and mental benefits rather than procedure and risk information does not itself provide evidence that the media affected the increase in cosmetic surgery. For this effect to happen, many have theorized individuals need to be exposed to numerous cosmetic surgery messages and internalize the ideal body first before an effect can occur. Thus, this section will address media exposure and internalization first and then direct media effects.

The number of cosmetic surgery ads, magazine and newspaper articles, and television shows featuring cosmetic surgery has significantly increased over time. This increase in media brings a high degree of exposure. According to one study of American college students, 52 percent read cosmetic surgery articles at least sometimes, and 71 percent saw cosmetic surgery-related TV programs at least sometimes (Delinsky 2005). In particular, exposure to cosmetic surgery messages predicts internalization of these messages for South Koreans (Park and Cho 2011). Other studies connect greater internalization of the media's appearance ideal to acceptance of and interest in cosmetic surgery, at least for Americans and Brazilians (Markey and Markey 2009; Swami et al. 2011). For instance, Henderson-King and Brooks (2009) found the more American women internalized the ideal body, the more likely it was that they considered cosmetic surgery and accepted cosmetic surgery as a way to increase body satisfaction and self-esteem, as well as achieve social and career success. Similarly, internalizing media messages was moderately associated with Korean students' attitudes toward cosmetic surgery (Swami et al. 2012). Thus, individuals are indeed internalizing media messages about ideal appearance and cosmetic surgery, and this internalization is usually associated with consideration and acceptance of cosmetic surgery.

Media influence is possible, given research indicating that women's exposure to cosmetic surgery ads, perceived media pressure to have cosmetic surgery, and higher media usage were all related to greater approval and likelihood of having cosmetic surgery (Delinsky 2005; Sarwer et al. 2005; Markey and Markey 2009, 2010; Swami 2009), Although patterns in media usage are approximately the same for women who have and have not had cosmetic surgery, the odds of having cosmetic surgery increased 18 percent with greater media usage (Eriksen and Goering 2011). Furthermore, women who watched cosmetic surgery reality television shows were more likely to desire cosmetic surgery, had more positive attitudes toward it, and perceived greater pressure to have it (Nabi 2009; Sperry et al. 2009). Women who made comparisons between themselves and the show's participants were more likely to have higher body dissatisfaction, greater body consciousness, and more likely to have invasive and minimally invasive procedures (Nabi 2009). In terms of health information, viewers felt significantly more knowledgeable about the procedures, risks, benefits, alternatives, and recovery time.

The aforementioned studies show only an association between media consumption and cosmetic surgery. However, several studies offer evidence that media exposure predicts endorsement and consideration of cosmetic surgery (Swami 2009). Women who frequently saw ideal beauty on television wanted larger breasts if they perceived themselves as small busted, or smaller breasts if they saw themselves as exceptionally large busted; moreover, media exposure predicted endorsement of breast augmentation (or reduction) surgery (Harrison 2003). More magazine and television use by middle-aged women was related to more positive attitudes toward cosmetic surgery, greater likelihood of having cosmetic surgery, and greater social motivation for having cosmetic surgery (Slevec and Tiggemann 2010). Whereas magazines had an indirect influence, greater television viewing directly influenced higher body dissatisfaction, greater appearance investment, and greater aging anxiety, which then influenced cosmetic surgery attitudes, likelihood, and motivation. Viewing cosmetic surgery reality television, other reality television shows, and entertainment news has been said to explain positive attitudes toward and a desire to undergo cosmetic surgery (Sperry *et al.* 2009; Markey and Markey 2010).

Delinsky (2005) found no differences among Caucasian, Asian, and black women's likelihood of having cosmetic surgery or in their media exposure to cosmetic surgery information, but black women were much less likely to approve of cosmetic surgery than Asian and Caucasian women. Greater cosmetic surgery media exposure also predicted greater approval and likelihood of having cosmetic surgery for all groups (Crockett *et al.* 2007). Men and women who watched and had positive views of cosmetic surgery reality television, moreover, were more likely to undergo both invasive and minimally invasive procedures (Nabi 2009; Markey and Markey 2010). Park and Cho (2011) found media exposure and interpersonal experiences with cosmetic surgery were the strongest predictors of future intention among young South Korean men and women.

## Conclusion

This chapter sought to understand media's role as an information source for and influence on cosmetic surgery and ideal beauty in light of the global growth in cosmetic surgery, despite noted safety issues. Although research indicates both an associational and a causal link between media exposure and attitudes toward and likelihood of undergoing cosmetic surgery, many still debate how much influence the media actually have, given that only a small percentage of people exposed to the media have actually undergone cosmetic surgery. At the very least, however, the evidence clearly shows three things. First, the media contribute to the normalization of cosmetic surgery through their increased coverage and the manner in which they discuss it. Most media emphasize "everybody" is having surgery these days, as well as how easily, painlessly, and magically we can be transformed into the ideal (Sullivan 2001). And even Brianna espouses this normalization when she says, "it's everywhere" and "more common now than in the 80s and 90s."

Second, the media disseminate an unattainable beauty ideal for women: a thin body, full breasts, big eyes, small nose, full lips, flawless skin, and high cheekbones (Cunningham *et al.* 1995; Sullivan 2001). All these attributes are hallmarks of youth, and all but thinness are considered global beauty ideals (Cunningham *et al.* 1995). With few inherently possessing all these traits but the established beauty ideal being presented as the route to economic, emotional, romantic, and social success, women feel compelled to undergo cosmetic procedures. Because many studies show this ideal is largely based on Caucasian appearance, racial and ethnic differences such as Africans' wider noses and Asians' single eyelids become symbols of difference that must be erased or, at the very least, "softened." Thus, the danger of disseminating a global beauty ideal based on a single race is its suggestion of racial/beauty superiority.

Third, the media's failure to adequately discuss risks and complications, coupled with their overemphasis on social and mental benefits, is particularly problematic given patients often use media as the only or the major source of cosmetic surgery information (e.g. Walden *et al.* 2010). Consequently, people are more likely to see cosmetic surgery as riskless or dismiss any risks they hear about. For example,

Brianna said that breast augmentation was safer because saline implants are "just salt water" and aren't "going to really kill you" if they pop. She further dismisses the risks when she calls complications "freak accidents" despite the fact that one of her friends had breast implant folding. Moreover, she knows breast cancer, which runs in her family, is harder to detect with implants, but she assures me placing the implant under the muscle makes detection a non-issue. This placement *may* improve the mammogram's image. But not all physicians agree on whether placement influences mammograms, and mammograms are still clearer without implants (Adamo 2012).

Furthermore, the media's overemphasis on benefits and dismissal of risks is misleading. For example, women with breast implants have a three times higher suicide rate than those without; 80 percent of cosmetic surgery patients suffer post-traumatic stress (Allen 2003; Naish 2011). Many patients also suffer depression, anxiety, and disappointment with their new look because they believed surgery would "solve dissatisfactions with their lives," which the media reaffirm (Naish 2011, para. 32). The media's current cosmetic surgery coverage, with its emphasis on entertainment and increasing sales rather than information on risks and complications, thus does the public a disservice. Because the media normalize cosmetic surgery, disseminate a specific (Caucasian) beauty ideal, and present youthful beauty as the way to get a better job, attract a romantic partner, and attain happiness, cosmetic surgery ultimately becomes an investment or even a necessity rather than a personal choice for those who want to improve their life and social status. This renders cosmetic surgery another form of social oppression, not a source of personal empowerment. Although cosmetic surgeons need to do a better job of psychological screening before surgery, the media—as a major information source—have a responsibility to fully present and equally emphasize both the benefits and the risks of cosmetic surgery.

## Note

1 Cosmetic surgery, the focus of this chapter, is defined as elective surgery to enhance one's beauty. Its purpose is purely aesthetic. Cosmetic surgery, which includes both surgical and minimally invasive procedures, differs from reconstructive surgery, done for medical or health reasons or to reconstruct body parts that have been disfigured in accidents.

## References

Adamo, C. G. (2012) "Mammograms & Breast Implants," March 7. http://www.implantinfo. com/breast_augmentation/Mammograms-Breast-Implants-364.aspx.

Adams, J. (2009) "Bodies of Change: A Comparative Analysis of Media Representations of Body Modification," *Sociological Perspectives* 52(1): 103–29.

Allen, C. (2003) "Plastic Surgery and Suicide," *Psychology Today*, October 1. http://www. psychologytoday.com/articles/200310/plastic-surgery-and-suicide.

American Society for Aesthetic Plastic Surgery (2003) "Plastic Surgery and 'Reality' TV: Real Life or Extreme Entertainment?," press release. http://www.surgery.org/media/news-releases/ plastic-surgery-and-reality-tv-real-life-or-extreme-entertainment.

Brooks, A. (2004) "Under the Knife and Proud of It: An Analysis of the Normalization of Cosmetic Surgery," *Critical Sociology* 30(2): 207–39.

Crockett, R. J., T. Pruzinsky, and J. A. Persing (2007) "The Influence of Plastic Surgery 'Reality TV' on Cosmetic Surgery Patient Expectations and Decision Making," *Plastic and Reconstructive Surgery* 120: 316–24.

Cunningham, M. R., A. R. Roberts, A. P. Barbee, P. B. Druen, and C. Wu (1995) "Their Ideas of Beauty Are, on the Whole, the Same as Ours: Consistency and Variability in the Cross-Cultural Perception of Female Physical Attractiveness," *Journal of Personality and Social Psychology* 68(2): 261–79.

Davies, G. and G. Han (2011) "Korean Cosmetic Surgery and Digital Publicity: Beauty by Korean Design," *Media International Australia* 141: 146–56.

Davis, K. (2002) "A Dubious Equality: Men, Women and Cosmetic Surgery," *Body & Society* 8(1): 49–65.

de Andrade, D. D. (2010) "On Norms and Bodies: Findings from Field Research on Cosmetic Surgery in Rio de Janeiro, Brazil," *Reproductive Health Matters* 18(35): 74–83.

Delinsky, S. S. (2005) "Cosmetic Surgery: A Common and Accepted Form of Self-Improvement?," *Journal of Applied Social Psychology* 35: 2012–28.

Didie, E. R. and D. B. Sarwer (2003) "Factors that Influence the Decision to Undergo Cosmetic Breast Augmentation," *Journal of Women's Health* 12(3): 241–53.

*Economist* (2012) "A Cut Above: Who Has the Most Plastic Surgery,"April 23.http://www.economist.com/blogs/graphicdetail/2012/04/daily-chart-13.

Ectoff, N., S. Orbach, J. Scott, and H. D'Agostino (2004) "The Real Truth about Beauty: A Global Report." http://www.scribd.com/doc/16653666/1/%E2%80%9CTHE-REAL-TRUTH-ABOUT-BEAUTY-A-GLOBAL-REPORT%E2%80%9D.

Eriksen, S. and S. Goering (2011) "A Test of the Agency Hypothesis in Women's Cosmetic Surgery Usage," *Sex Roles* 64: 888–901.

George, L. (2004) "TV Makes Cosmetic Surgery Seem Easy," April 26. http://www.thecanadianencyclopedia.com/PrinterFriendly.cfm?Params=M1ARTM0012598.

Hanabusa, M. (2008) "Reading Dual Meanings of Power on Young Women's Bodies: The Representation of Cosmetic Surgery in Japanese Manga," *International Research in Children's Literature* 1(1): 82–98.

Harrison, K. (2003) "Television Viewers' Ideal Body Proportions: The Case of the Curvaceously Thin Woman," *Sex Roles* 48: 255–64.

Henderson-King, D. and K. D. Brooks (2009) "Materialism, Sociocultural Appearance Messages, and Paternal Attitudes Predict College Women's Attitudes about Cosmetic Surgery," *Psychology of Women Quarterly* 33: 133–42.

Hennink-Kaminski, H. and T. Reichert (2011) "Using Sexual Appeals in Advertising to Sell Cosmetic Surgery: A Content Analysis from 1986 to 2007," *Sexuality & Culture* 15(1): 41–55.

Hennink-Kaminski, H., L. Reid, and K. King (2010) "The Content of Cosmetic Surgery Advertisements Placed in Large City Magazines, 1985–2004," *Journal of Current Issues and Research in Advertising* 32(2): 41–57.

Heyes, C. J. (2007) "Cosmetic Surgery and the Televisual Makeover," *Feminist Media Studies* 7(1): 17–32.

Latteier, C. (1998) *Breasts: The Women's Perspective on an American Obsession*, Binghampton, NY: Haworth Press.

Luo, W. (2012) "Selling Cosmetic Surgery and Beauty Ideals: The Female Body in the Web Sites of Chinese Hospitals," *Women's Studies in Communication* 35: 68–95.

Markey, C. N. and P. M. Markey (2009) "Sociocultural Correlates of Young Women's Desire to Obtain Cosmetic Surgery," *Sex Roles* 61: 158–66.

——(2010) "A Correlational and Experimental Examination of Reality Television Viewing and Interest in Cosmetic Surgery," *Body Image* 7(2): 165–71.

Mondini, S., A. Favaro, and P. Santonastaso (1996) "Eating Disorders and the Ideal of Feminine Beauty in Italian Newspapers and Magazines," *Eating Disorder Review* 4(2): 112–20.

Nabi, R. L. (2009) "Cosmetic Surgery Makeover Programs and Intentions to Undergo Cosmetic Enhancement: A Consideration of Three Models of Media Effects," *Human Communication Research* 35: 1–27.

Naish, J. (2011) "When Looks Can Kill," *Daily Mail*, January 25. http://www.dailymail.co.uk/femail/article-1349913/How-plastic-surgery-lead-self-loathing-disappointment-suicide.html?printingPage=true.

Nassab, R., H. Navsaria, S. Myers, and J. Frame (2011) "Online Marketing Strategies of Plastic Surgeons and Clinics: A Comparative Study of the United Kingdom and the United States," *Aesthetic Surgery Journal* 31(5): 566–71.

Nassab, R., N. Hamnett, K. Nelson, K. Simranjit, B. Greensill, S. Dhital, and A. Juma (2010) "Cosmetic Tourism: Public Opinion and Analysis of Information and Content Available on the Internet," *Aesthetic Surgery Journal* 30(3): 465–9.

Pais, J. (2007) "Half of Korean Women Have Undergone Plastic Surgery," February 22. http://twitchfilm.com/news/2007/02/half-of-korean-women-have-undergone-plastic-surgery.php.

Park, J. S. and C. Cho (2011) "Factors Explaining College Students' Intention to Receive Cosmetic Surgery in the Future: A Structural Equation Modeling Approach," *Journal of Medical Marketing* 11: 127–43.

Patil, S. B., S. M. Kale, N. Khare, S. Jaiswal, and S. Ingole (2011) "Aesthetic Surgery: Expanding Horizons: Concepts, Desires, and Fears of Rural Women in Central India," *Aesthetic Plastic Surgery* 35: 717–23.

Pitts-Taylor, V. (2007) *Surgery Junkies: Wellness and Pathology in Cosmetic Culture*, New Brunswick, NJ: Rutgers University Press.

Polonijo, A. N. and R. M. Carpiano (2008) "Representations of Cosmetic Surgery and Emotional Health in Women's Magazines in Canada," *Women's Health Issues* 18: 463–70.

Reid, A. J. and P. S. C. Malone (2008) "Plastic Surgery in the Press," *Journal of Plastic, Reconstructive & Aesthetic Surgery* 61: 866–9.

Ricciardelli, R. and P. White (2011) "Modifying the Body: Canadian Men's Perspectives on Appearance and Cosmetic Surgery," *The Qualitative Report* 16(4): 949–70.

Rountree, M. M., and L. Davis (2011) "A Dimensional Qualitative Research Approach to Understanding Medically Unnecessary Aesthetic Surgery," *Psychology & Marketing* 28(10): 1027–43.

Sarwer, D. B., T. F. Cash, L. Magee, E. F. Williams, J. K. Thompson, M. Roehrig, S. Tantleff-Dunn, A. K. Agliata, D. E. Wilfley, A. D. Amidon, D. A. Anderson, and M. Romanofski (2005) "College Students and Cosmetic Surgery: An Investigation of Experiences, Attitudes, and Body Image," *Plastic and Reconstructive Surgery* 115(3): 931–8.

Slevec, J. and M. Tiggemann (2010) "Attitudes toward Cosmetic Surgery in Middle-Aged Women: Body Image, Aging Anxiety, and the Media," *Psychology of Women Quarterly* 34: 65–74.

Sperry, S., J. K. Thompson, D. B. Sarwer, and T. F. Cash (2009) "Cosmetic Reality TV Viewership: Relations with Cosmetic Surgery Attitudes, Body Image, and Disordered Eating," *Annals of Plastic Surgery* 62(1): 7–12.

Sullivan, D. (2001) *Cosmetic Surgery: The Cutting Edge of Commercial Medicine in America*, New Brunswick, NJ: Rutgers University Press.

Swami, V. (2009) "Body Appreciation, Media Influence, and Weight Status Predict Consideration of Cosmetic Surgery among Female Undergraduates," *Body Image* 6(4): 315–17.

Swami, V., A. N. N. B. Campana, L. Ferreira, S. Barrett, A. S. Harris, and M. C. G. C. F. Tavares (2011) "The Acceptance of Cosmetic Surgery Scale: Initial Examination of Its Factor Structure and Correlates among Brazilian Adults," *Body Image* 8: 179–85.

Swami, V., C. Hwang, and J. Jung (2012) "Correlates of Acceptance of Cosmetic Surgery Scale among South Korean University Students," *Aesthetic Surgery Journal* 32(2): 220–9.

Tanzi, E. L. and T. S. Alster (2008) "Skin Resurfacing: Ablative Lasers, Chemical Peels, and Dermabrasion," in L. Goldsmith, S. Katz, B. Gilchrest, A. Paller, D. Leffell, and K. Wolff (eds.) *Fitzpatrick's Dermatology in General Medicine*, 7th edition., vol. 2, New York: McGraw-Hill Medical, pp. 2364–71.

Walden, J. L., G. Panagopoulous, and S. W. Shrader (2010) "Contemporary Decision Making and Perception in Patients Undergoing Cosmetic Breast Augmentation," *Aesthetic Surgery Journal* 30(3): 395–403.

Wolf, N. (1991) *The Beauty Myth: How Images of Beauty Are Used Against Women*, New York: William Morrow and Company.

Woodstock, L. (2001) "Skin Deep, Soul Deep: Mass Mediating Cosmetic Surgery in Popular Magazines, 1968–98," *The Communication Review* 4: 421–42.

Yoho, R. A., J. J. Romaine, and D. O'Neil (2005). "Review of the Liposuction, Abdominoplasty, and Face-lift Mortality and Morbidity Risk Literature," *Dermatological Surgery* 31: 733–43.

# 33

# Globalization, beauty regimes, and mediascapes in the New India

## Radhika Parameswaran

When black actor and comedian Chris Rock's young daughter asks, "Daddy, how come I don't have good hair," this celebrity parent undertakes a personal journey of enlightenment, as chronicled in the documentary film *Good Hair* (2009), to find answers. *Good Hair* tracks Rock's quest to untangle the social, economic, and historical strands of power and profit that convert hair from seemingly lifeless fiber into a pulsating and polymorphous signifier of beauty norms. Guiding viewers through a hectic itinerary, Rock visits beauty salons and barbershops, the spectacular Bronner Bros. International Hair Show in Atlanta, and, finally, the Venkateshwara Temple in Tirupathi, India. Here South Indian women sacrifice their hair, thereby supplying most of the prized raw material for the global hair extension industry. During his sojourn in India, the actor-comedian and concerned father advises a puzzled young Indian woman with long, thick black hair, tamed into a ponytail, to "run the other way" if she spots any black women in the vicinity. Rock's enactment of cruel comedy in this cross-cultural exchange portrays black women as simultaneously abject *and* predatory consumers of innocent Indian women's "good hair." The hidden raced, classed, and gendered flows of desire, dominance, commodities, and currency that fuel globalization—the economic processes that produce deeply interconnected modes of life in the industrialized world—also rise to the surface in this scene where the comedian's joke fails to register with a potential female "supplier" of good hair in India.

Taking the same journey as Rock, although in a constructive manner that refuses to reduce black women to objects of pity or ridicule, Esther Berry's academic analysis of globalization and the hairy politics of beauty probes the "global exchange of human hair, a business implicated in structuring First and Third World femininities, consumer and producer relations between the West and the rest, as hair is culled and then spun into a 'repulsive gift'—hair extensions—bestowed upon the scalps of a First World clientele" (2008: 64). Virgin Indian hair (unexposed to harsh chemicals) undergoes fumigation (ventilation and cleaning), de-pigmentation (stripping of black color), and finally re-pigmentation (dyeing in different colors) at the hands of the multinational company Great Lengths, headquartered in Rome, Italy. It thus changes into a "zombie commodity," a living-dead bodily organ that is understood to possess "a life force that is critical to maintaining or revitalizing Western femininity" (Berry 2008: 75). Berry's dissection of the global traffic in human hair as "a business in body parts" reveals the ugly underbelly of beauty: the exploitation of Third World women's bodies and labor for the benefit of First World women.

In the end, both Rock's film and Berry's deconstructive critique of Indian women's marginal positions in the global hair industry's supply chain offer important and timely, but nevertheless partial, glimpses into the ways in which commoditized beauty culture has traveled to the "New India," with "New" signaling India's trans-formation from a marginal Third World nation into an "emerging market" and a rising global power. For instance, viewers of Rock's *Good Hair* or Western readers of Berry's essay may not consider the possibility that wealthy and upper-class *Indian* women, including Bollywood celebrities, who are part of the privileged transnational elite, are likely to be consumers (even if they are not in the majority) of the very same hair extensions that endow First World women with beauty. Divine Diva India, an exclusive retailer of hair products in New Delhi, Bangalore, Mumbai, and Chennai, promises visitors to its website (http://www.divadivinehair.co.in/) that "any hair extension and wig product that is available in the international market is now available in India through Diva Divine; and in the remote chance that we do not have it, we will get it for you within 10–14 days." In the age of globalization and its uneven economic cleavages, there are First Worlds in almost every Third World nation, and vice versa. Global business and capitalist discourses of the last two decades have positioned India, the world's largest democracy, as a key player—along with Brazil, Russia, and China—in the global geopolitical arena. As such, India offers a cheap, educated, and skilled labor force for global manufacturing and service sectors, at the same time it dangles the promise of a vast differentiated consumer marketplace for an array of imported products, including high-end hair extensions, which return to India as "international goods" after raw Indian hair is processed and finished in Italy. India's entry into the economic and cultural circuits of globalization can be traced to the late 1980s, when Prime Minister Rajiv Gandhi first unveiled his vision for an economic revitalization process centered on the relaxation of import regulations—an incentive for multinationals to sell commodities and services catering to the middle classes (Parameswaran 2004). The Old India—with its Gandhian hangover of viewing conspicuous consumption as sinful, a socialist public ethos of poverty reduction, and a largely non-aligned (suspicious of the West) foreign policy—has gradually given way to the New India—with its embrace of affluent Western lifestyles *and* beauty products, a more capitalist and consumerist climate favoring the middle classes, and a pro-Western foreign policy outlook.

Taking into consideration India's metamorphosis into a lucrative site for global consumption and production, this chapter sketches a bird's-eye view of con-temporary beauty regimes in New India's burgeoning material and media economies. How has Western beauty culture—its commodities, media regimes, aesthetics, and cultural practices—migrated to the New India? Does the globalization of beauty cul-ture in a postcolonial nation mean homogenization and the erasure of national and local formations and identities? Are Indian consumers passive dupes of the global beauty industry's discourses and practices of cultural imperialism? This case study of India illustrates the complex and contradictory ways in which beauty culture gets caught up in the forces of economic globalization, cultural imperialism, nationalism, glocalization, and the agency of ordinary consumers and citizens.

## Globalization and beauty's political economy: parlors, products, pageants, and pictures

I am visiting my brother and his family in July 2010 in Hyderabad, my hometown. I left behind this sleepy and modest city in South India in 1990, when I left to study in America. Twenty years later, I am astonished to witness the dramatic changes in Hyderabad, which has become a busy hub for multinational business outsourcing. As I walk with my almost 18-year-old niece through her residential neighborhood, I notice signs for scores of beauty parlors posted in front of middle- and upper-middle-class homes. When I was growing up in Hyderabad in the 1980s, the city had only a few beauty parlors (run chiefly by Chinese immigrants), located primarily in the commercial district areas, and these exclusive parlors were patronized largely by wealthy and upper-class Indian women. The beauty parlor signs scattered around me in this neighborhood, two decades later, announced the arrival of two larger phenomena in globalizing India. On the consumption end, they indexed the aggressive seepage of beauty culture, its downward percolation through the intricate economic and cultural layers of India's socioeconomic structure. On the production end, they referenced the rise of middle-class Indian women's entrepreneurship in the beauty sector. Balancing their duties as mothers and wives in a patriarchal culture with their desire to bolster household incomes *and* gain a measure of economic independence, busy women owners and managers were operating these modest beauty enterprises out of their domestic spaces. My niece disdained these homegrown parlors as "ghatiya" (shoddy/shabby) establishments with untrained staff and "third-rate Indian products." Desiring guaranteed "sophisticated hair" for her birthday party, my niece instead led me to her preferred and more expensive temple of beauty, Vogue Salon, where young, well-dressed (read Western attire) English-speaking professionals offered their customers *imported* products from Europe and America. From the mid-1990s onwards, a spate of beauty merchandise from Western multinationals, including Revlon (USA), Maybelline (USA), L'Oreal (France), Reckitt Benckiser (UK), and Oriflame (Sweden), has flooded high-end salons (like Vogue), air-conditioned shopping centers, and middle- and upper-class homes in India, even as the multinational invasion also has spawned a spectrum of low-end imitators in the domestic beauty industry, an affordable product range typically found in modest neighborhood parlors and in public housing units, urban slums, and rural hamlets (Parameswaran 2001).

My niece's visit to this upscale parlor in Hyderabad also signaled the generational transformation in educated Indian women's guilt-free desire to participate in global consumer modernity. My mother (and my niece's grandmother) was an educated woman who worked outside the home as a teacher, but as a member of the post-colonial Gandhian urban middle class, she and her peers had frowned upon beauty parlors and their services as frivolous and narcissistic symbols of a decadent Western lifestyle. I fell somewhere in between. My refusal to trim my eyebrows aligned me with my mother and Old India, but then my shiny painted toenails, which my niece admired, earned me restricted membership in the upwardly mobile, post-Gandhian New India. These tidal changes in the generational currents of beauty culture, ranging from trimmed eyebrows and painted toenails to cosmetic surgery and fitness regimens, have left their impressions across India, as the news magazine *India Today* testifies: "Over 20 percent of the client turnover in cosmetics surgery and beauty clinics is the age group between 12 and 16 years" (Bhupta and Pai 2007). Documenting the growing trend of middle- and upper-class urban Indian children joining gyms, visiting beauty salons, and procuring the services of cosmetic surgeons, this magazine notes that the romp and play of some children's birthday parties have turned into adult-style beauty sessions with manicures, pedicures, tattoos, and hair-cuts: "Even birthday parties are no longer about streamers and frills. They are being celebrated in swish salons and spas across urban India. Manvi Singhee celebrated her sixth birthday in style at A Cut Above Children, an exclusive salon attached to the Savera Hotel in Chennai. With her girlfriends, Manvi had a beauty salon party where salon staff and therapists pampered their senses." Columnist Anjali Chhabria (2007) and author and journalist Anita Anand (2002) write that the guilt-free endor-sement of beauty culture has also encouraged a shift in middle-class girls' career aspirations, with many more young Indian women today expressing an interest in glamorous modeling and entertainment careers rather than the more service-oriented "nation-building professions" of Old India—engineering, medicine, or teaching.

As my niece and I walk towards the Vogue Salon located on the busy main highway, we run into a young woman carrying a small suitcase decorated with colorful newspaper images of local beauty queens. My niece introduces me to her acquain-tance with a quick explanation: "Shanti delivers beauty treatments." Shanti, a migrant factory worker from a nearby village, works part time as an itinerant beau-tician, visiting busy middle-class professional women in their homes on weekends and in the evenings. She proudly opens up her suitcase to show me a professional certificate and the tools of her trade. The growing demand for beauty services among the middle and upper classes—from adults to teenagers and children—has led to new forms of vocational education (beauty schools) and employment for the urban poor and for rural migrant women seeking a better life in Indian cities. Even large prison complexes in India have begun offering beauty training and rehabilitation classes for their female inmates with the intention of helping them secure employ-ment in beauty parlors and salons or as self-employed beauticians after their release (Parameswaran 2004). For poor young women like Shanti, whose mother worked as a maid in the village, getting trained and employed in the beauty trade represents a step up on the ladder of success.

Inside the plush Vogue Salon in Hyderabad, while beauticians work their magic to promote my niece's already "good hair" to "best hair" status, I leaf through dozens of women's magazines that stitch together a global "mediascape," a concept that Appadurai defines as "image-centered, narrative-based accounts of strips of reality," a fluid and shifting terrain of distant worlds and scripted fantasies that invite global audiences' imaginative inhabitation and stimulate "desire for acquisition and movement" (1996: 35–6). Mirroring the exponential growth in international beauty and fashion magazines in China since that neighboring country implemented open-door economic policies (Feng and Frith 2008), *Elle*, *Vogue*, *Cosmopolitan*, *Marie Claire*, and *Harper's Bazaar* have also arrived in the New India, expanding the palette of feminine subject positions available for young middle-class women whose mothers, as young women, had access to a much more limited menu of domestic magazine titles, namely, *Femina*, *Women's Era*, and *Savvy*. Unlike the Chinese versions of international magazines that are printed in Mandarin, the Indian versions are produced in English, a lasting and permanent legacy of India's historical status as a British colony. Beauty and fashion products, experts' advice columns, and beautiful (slim, young, and light-skinned) foreign and Indian supermodels and celebrities populate the glossy advertising and editorial pages of these magazines that cater to India's English-speaking middle classes, a consumer demographic that policymakers, marketers, and popular culture have promoted as the aspirational reference group for the rest of the nation. The internal logic of these magazines' intertextual representations, which feed upon and extend other global and local mediated worlds, leads readers sequentially towards a particular "ideoscape," an interlinked regime of femininity that sutures the "beautiful body" to ideologies and master-narratives of prosperity, power, and success (Appadurai 1996: 36).

Responding to competition from foreign magazines, the leading domestic magazine, *Femina*, has reinvented itself as the principal beltway for producing global beauty queens, whose smiling faces frequently adorn this magazine's covers and scores of advertisements, commercials, and billboards for beauty products. *Femina* magazine's staff manages the annual Miss India contest—a live spectacle touring major Indian cities—whose three finalists are automatically selected as India's representatives in the Miss World, Miss Universe, and Miss Asia-Pacific pageants. For example, since she won the Miss World contest in 1994, Aishwarya Rai has achieved unprecedented fame in the global mediascape as an international model, a Bollywood icon with hundreds of dedicated fan websites, and an occasional crossover actress in Hollywood. Her career certifies the beauty pageant's magnetic capacity to attract new and more expansive forms of stardom for its participants. The centrifugal force of these metropolitan national and global pageants, which are sponsored by a host of lifestyle and beauty merchants, radiates outward, with corporations harnessing local versions of beauty contests in small towns and villages as grassroots marketing and branding tools that can coach potential (still uninitiated) Indian consumers to assimilate the symbolic and material signposts that represent upward mobility (Parameswaran 2001). Local newspapers and general-interest magazines in New India's booming vernacular-language print media industry report on these contests, publishing visual collages of beauty queens in their crowns and sashes as they accept gift packages of cosmetics and personal care products from corporate representatives. Extending the shelf life of such images, women readers like Shanti, the young beautician, cut out and paste these photographs onto their "beauty suitcases."

My niece steps out of the inner bowels of Vogue Salon, her wavy extension-free hair cut in layers and straightened to simulate a Jennifer Aniston look. As she gently shakes her head from side to side she asks, "So, what do you think?" Her posed performance replayed for me the staple "before-and-after" moment, the much anticipated climactic achievement of beauty, that saturates makeover reality shows. Waving the cover of *Femina* magazine to show her the latest Miss India, I say, "Are you ready to compete for Miss World?" Wearing a playful, yet slightly anxious expression, she responds, "Nice hair, but not tall enough, a little too chubby, and I definitely need to be two shades lighter." We had just passed, at a bus stop outside the salon, a billboard for *Fair & Lovely* skin-lightening cream, a product category that accounts for about 40 percent of the Indian cosmetics market (Parameswaran and Cardoza 2009).

## "Firangi" (foreign) artifacts, "desi" (Indian) adaptations

The semiotic webs of beauty's commodity culture in post-liberalization India, the material lattice within which ordinary acts of everyday life—a short walk with my niece to a beauty salon—are suspended, point to a new wave of firangi (foreign) imperialism, a largely American conquest (with economic/capitalist, not territorial domination) of a South Asian nation that another Western power, the British, had already once conquered and ruled (with economic *and* formal territorial control). A perfunctory historical glance at these webs might suggest that my niece's Revlon and Clinique cosmetics in the New India are now getting stacked on top of her great grandmother's favorite Vinolia and Pears soaps, which reigned as coveted objects of luxury in colonial India. Yet, this simple and seemingly banal observation points to a blind spot in de-territorialized, grand theories of cultural imperialism, which some-times fail to account for the historically anchored ways in which globalization unfolds in different parts of the world. For example, the younger generation of *English-speaking* Indian citizens, beneficiaries of global outsourcing, who work at call centers and have a disposable income to purchase lifestyle commodities and ser-vices—cosmetics, fitness club memberships, branded clothing, glossy magazines, and beauty salon visits—are embedded in an emergent class formation whose linguistic skills and cultural competencies can be traced to India's nineteenth-century British colonial period (Parameswaran 2008).

The intersection of colonial history with contemporary globalization is one example of a South Asian particularity that helps us avoid the pitfalls of pursuing a singular "master theory" of globalization to explain or unravel the baffling and knotty empirical complexities of beauty culture in the New India. On the surface, the deluge of material artifacts of Western beauty, from billboards and pageants to cosmetics counters in supermarkets, presents evidence of American-style corporate beauty's standardizing force, its financial power to fabricate a homogeneous template for "global beauty" that erases national/local differences. There is no denying the potential for a fresh wave of Euro-American imperialism in India to the extent that one has to acknowledge the sheer presence and the grander scale and intensified circulation of foreign beauty commodities and the Westernized aesthetics and practices of beauty they may engineer. From the vantage point of such scholars as Schiller (2001) and Harindranath (2002), who have questioned easy dismissals of cultural imperialism, the material and cultural zones of beauty culture in contemporary India do exhibit layers of Western domination. The uneven contours of such layers are emerging out of colonial India's fault lines of gender, class, caste, and region. But, various agents and institutions with different investments are also harnessing beauty events/rituals and products to resuscitate and reinvent nationalism at a time when the Indian nation state has aggressively promoted "New India" as a desirable transnational signifier of "nationalist belonging" for the Diaspora and domestic citizens alike. In short, as Grewal (2005) has argued, the constructs of "nation" and national affiliation remain even more relevant today as political mobilizing tools and as affective resources for the articulation of consumer and citizen identities in the midst of globalization's aggressive excursions to Asia.

Commercial media and business and state elites celebrate victorious global Indian beauty queens as symbols of national pride (Parameswaran 2001), and these successful beauty queens stake out their claims to membership in a patriotic middle-class meritocracy that earns positive visibility for India on the global stage (Parameswaran 2004). Reinforcing nationalist sentiments, women's magazines' essentialist narratives praise Indian women's ethnic beauty—their full lips and big eyes—as superior to Western beauty (Reddy 2006) and domestic beauty companies' advertisements mine "ancient" Indian heritage and mythologies to affirm the authenticity of their products (Reddy 2006; Parameswaran and Cardoza 2009). For example, when multinational companies' skin-lightening products threatened the domination of local brands, domestic companies began to pursue ethnic marketing strategies with quasi-religious nationalist imagery to convince Indian women consumers that their "natural" indigenous products were more suited for Indian skin than the chemical artifice of Western cosmetic science. An advertisement for Hindustan Lever's Ayurvedic Fair & Lovely cream bears the headline "Discover the 5000 year old Ayurvedic secret to Fairness" and displays a sumptuous culinary smorgasbord of colorful herbs and spices arranged against a pure white background to evoke the symbolic flavors of pure, raw, and uncorrupted national culture. The very same Ayurvedic science, following in the wake of Yoga's overseas travels, shuttles westward as a form of "East to West counter-flow" (rather than the expected "imperialist West to East flow") under the more trendy corporate disguise of "Aveda," an American-based beauty company whose spiritual philosophy and products, according to its official website, are based in India's "ancient holistic system of healing that strives to create balance in body, mind and spirit." Matching the Western multinational Aveda's global aspirations, if not its revenues, Hindustan Lever, the ambitious Indian subsidiary of Unilever headquartered in Mumbai, exports its cosmetics to more than 38 countries in Asia and Africa, thus making visible another kind of regional counter-flow among non-Western nations.

Furthermore, echoing a larger trend of "glocalization" in imported media formats (from MTV programs to quiz shows like *Who Wants to Be a Millionaire?*), Western cosmetics companies and beauty magazines have had to "Indianize" their products to connect with consumers in the subcontinent. Indian models and Bollywood celebrities grace the covers of standardized international magazines and their advertising images. Indian staff and local columnists and experts, not media professionals located in the West, generate international magazines' localized editorial content on beauty. Translating white femininity for the hybrid visual vernacular of urban beauty culture in India, advertising agencies display white models in Indian clothes and jewelry in order to signify "India's economic self-confidence" and this postcolonial nation's equal cultural exchange with the West (Lakshmi 2008). Additionally, Eastern European models in India—whose faces "stare out from billboards, from the facades of glitzy glass-fronted malls, and from fashion magazines"—earn far less than local Indian celebrity spokespersons featured in advertising, namely, cricket and Bollywood superstars and Indian supermodels (Lakshmi 2008). Aishwarya Rai, a slim, light-skinned global Indian celebrity and not a white supermodel, was chosen as the alluring public face (2004–5) of L'Oreal's White Perfect cream in India. Straddling different worlds, Rai, who was anointed the "Most beautiful woman in the world" on the Oprah Show and on CBS's 60 Minutes in 2005, trades on her ambiguous racial coding *and* her flexible currency—approximating Western standards of beauty, epitomizing sartorial ideals of Indian beauty in Bollywood films, exemplifying the dutiful Indian daughter and wife in India and in the West, and embodying the patriotic-cosmopolitan global Indian citizen—to script a successful Indian version of transnational modernity that serves up different blends of the global and the local to suit the palates of different audiences (Osuri 2008; Parameswaran 2011). Similarly, it would be shortsighted to assume that widespread media images of light-skinned Indian supermodels and Bollywood celebrities, who approximate white standards of beauty, offer incontrovertible evidence of white supremacy and cultural imperialism in India (Parameswaran and Cardoza 2009). These "glocalized" images of feminine beauty instead amalgamate the glamorous allure of the foreign or "Western firangi" with the authentic and wholesome stamps of the national and the regional, or "desi."

The relevance of nation and national identity and these manifestations of "glocalization" do not negate or neutralize the theory of cultural imperialism and its specter of Western domination, but they do direct us towards the ongoing, located negotiations of beauty culture that are taking place on the ground in India and elsewhere among the creative forces of capitalism (transnational and domestic), nationalism, and local conceptions of feminine beauty. Teasing out the tethered geographical imaginations of India and the West that structure beauty's commodified terrain, Vanita Reddy (2006) astutely notes that the global-national beautiful Indian woman signifies a paradoxical site of cultural contestation at a time of rapid transition. This ambient, hybrid figure alternately affirms and disavows both Old India and the West as stable geographies to celebrate the ascendance of a cosmopolitan New India. Articulations of difference and heterogeneity jostle with sameness and homogeneity in the semiotic space of beauty's public culture in the New India. Defying the explanatory power of singular theories of globalization, these significations of beauty demand close and careful scrutiny of the global and the national in public discourses and images.

## Beauty, hybridity, and "real" women's agency in the New India

What do we make of L'Oreal's True Match Foundation Crème when a young South Indian woman, decked out in her traditional clothing and jewelry, applies it to her face to enhance her "Indian femininity"? I have the pleasure of witnessing my young niece's artistic performance in Hyderabad in 2010, the day after her visit to Vogue Salon, where poster after poster displays global Indian women dressed in professional

Western clothing. Contrary to the salon's promotion of a Westernized mediascape, my niece, dressed in an ornate silk gagra-choli (North Indian traditional clothing modified to reflect a trendy Bollywood style) sings traditional North Indian Hindustani music for family and friends gathered to celebrate her eighteenth birthday. The guests' plates are filled with idilis and chutney, iconic South Indian foods; and they drink Coca-Cola out of traditional steel-made glasses. These real-world iterations of hybridity, defined as cultural mixing and mingling in everyday life situations where eclectic cultural objects and practices converge in unexpected ways (Pieterse 2009), illuminate the modest (but important) agency of ordinary subjects, their ability to critically interpret beauty norms or appropriate beauty commodities in ways that resist, reinforce, or push against the hegemonic boundaries of social structures. Joining scores of other educated middle-class Indian women, women in my family consume an East–West style of ethnic fashion popularized by select beautiful-intellectual female celebrities (Nandita Das, Konkana Sen Sharma, and Barkha Dutt) and by the Indian clothing company Fabindia. We pair Fabindia's colorful blouses (kurtis) and scarves with Western-style pants or jeans to signify our modern "hybrid" identities. Voicing our consumer agency within constrained capitalist spaces, we amalgamate the need to be practical and mobile at work with the desire to possess and display a bicultural, not assimilated, form of cosmopolitan-authentic beauty.

What light does research on globalization and beauty shed on women's expressions of agency in the New India? For example, returning to the beginning of this chapter, we might ask a different set of questions about the Indian women who donate their hair at a Hindu temple. Do they expect to be admired for their courage in baring their "ugly" baldness in a culture that fetishizes long black hair as a marker of beauty? Do they feel victimized because corporations sell their "good hair" to affluent women without their consent or do they pity these women for their inadequacies? Exposing the deep cracks in ethnographic work on beauty in Asia and Africa, we have very little knowledge of Indian audiences' complicated responses to beauty's mediascapes. But, the scant existing work on women's voices and experiences disturbs the longstanding ethnocentric idea that non-Western women have no recourse to subjectivity outside of the positions of "passive dupe" or "hapless victim of patriarchy, global/local capitalism, and state power." The poor women childcare workers I interviewed in Delhi in 2009 were skeptical of one fantasy mediascape— television commercials—in the New India that links the use of skin-lightening creams with the instant rewards of marriage and permanent happiness (Parameswaran 2011). At the same time, they also disclosed that they did purchase these products, but combined them with more reliable home beauty remedies passed on by their mothers and grandmothers. Beauty contestants in the Miss India pageant endure a stringent training program geared to please a patriarchal/capitalist male gaze. Nevertheless, in a culture that offers few women choices for upward mobility, they also capitalize on the pageant's lessons and networking opportunities in entertainment and fashion industries to "advance their self-worth and class status" (Dewey 2008: 9). One group of college-educated women in Kolkata "aspire to look good" when they say they desire the thin female bodies that dominate domestic (Bollywood) and imported mediascapes. But, negotiating competing cultural ideals of femininity, they also reject the skinny, ultra-thin female archetype and express "ambivalence" about dieting *only* to achieve a normative appearance (Talukdar 2012: 110). Structures of power do not evaporate in these empirical accounts of beauty regimes, but they do acknowledge that the unruliness of everyday life cannot *always* be governed by *all* structures and by academic critiques *all* the time. While none of this research directly addresses Indian women whose invisible labor—their bodily production and donation of hair—sustains the global hair extension industry, it could lead us to speculate that these women's responses and experiences will most likely complicate any reductive and homogenizing predictions of singular theories of cultural imperialism, nationalism, feminism, or postcolonialism.

In conclusion, the meanings of beauty regimes and their mediascapes in globalization's New India ferment and come into being, not in isolation, but only through contexts that serve as catalysts to breed "beauty culture." The semiotics of beauty regimes cannot be shipped and sold in hermetically sealed jars. Beauty's varied global and local avatars—and their attendant texts, objects, narratives, and practices—in an altering India bear the imprints of history and emerge only in dialogue with the social and economic formations that surround them.

## Acknowledgments

The author thanks Carol Polsgrove for her insightful comments and editorial suggestions.

## References

Anand, A. (2002) *The Beauty Game*, Panchasheel Park, New Delhi: Penguin Books.

Appadurai, A. (1996) *Modernity at Large: Cultural Dimensions of Globalization*, Minneapolis: University of Minnesota Press.

Berry, E. (2008) "The Zombie Commodity: Hair and the Politics of Its Globalization," *Postcolonial Studies* 11(1): 63–84.

Bhupta, M. and A. Pai (2007) "No Kidding: A Makeover Trends in Teenagers in India," *India Today*, June 25. http://indiatoday.intoday.in/story/alarming-make-over-trends-and-custom-in-adolescents-in-india/1/155686.html.

Chhabria, A. (2007) "No Bar on Beauty: Adolescents: In a World of Romanticism," *India Today*, June 25. http://indiatoday.intoday.in/story/dr-anjali-chhabria-on-adolescents-glamour-and-fashion-magnetism/1/155689.html.

Dewey, S. (2008) *Making Miss India Miss World*, Syracuse, NY: Syracuse University Press.

Feng, Y. and K. Frith (2008) "The Growth of International Women's Magazines in China and the Role of Transnational Advertising," *Journal of Magazine and New Media Research* 10(1): 1–14.

Grewal, I. (2005) *Transnational America: Feminisms, Diasporas, Neo-liberalisms*, Durham, NC: Duke University Press.

Harindranath, R. (2002) "Reviving Cultural Imperialism: International Audiences, Global Capitalism, and the Transnational Elite," in S. Kumar and L. Parks (eds.) *Planet TV: A Global Television Reader*, New York: New York University Press.

Lakshmi, R. (2008) "In India's Huge Marketplace, Advertisers Find Fair Skin Sells," *Washington Post*, January 27. http://www.washingtonpost.com/wp-dyn/content/article/2008.

Osuri, G. (2008) "Ash-coloured Whiteness: The Transfiguration of Aishwarya Rai," *South Asian Popular Culture* 6(2): 109–23.

Parameswaran, R. (2001) "Global Media Events in India: Contests over Beauty, Gender, and Nation," *Journalism & Communication Monographs* 3(2): 53–105.

——(2004) "Global Queens, National Celebrities: Tales of Feminine Triumph in Post-liberalization India," *Critical Studies in Media Communication* 21(4): 346–70.

——(2008) "The Missing Sides of Globalization: Communication, Culture, and Postcolonial Critique," *Communication, Culture, and Critique* 1(8): 116–25.

——(2011) "E-raceing Color: Gender and Transnational Visual Economies of Beauty," in R. Hegde (ed.) *Circuits of Visibility: Gender and Transnational Media Cultures*, New York: New York University Press.

Parameswaran, R. and K. Cardoza (2009) "Melanin on the Margins: Advertising and the Cultural Politics of Fair/Light/White Beauty in India," *Journalism & Communication Monographs* 11(3): 213–74.

Pieterse, J. N. (2009) *Globalization and Culture: Global Melange*, Lanham, MD: Rowman & Littlefield.

Reddy, V. (2006) "The Nationalization of the Global Indian Woman: Geographies of Beauty in Femina," *South Asian Popular Culture* 4(1): 61–85.

Schiller, H. (2001) "Not Yet the Post-imperialist Era," in M. G. Durham and D. Kellner (eds.) *Media and Cultural Studies: Key Words*, Malden, MA: Blackwell.

Talukdar, J. (2012) "Thin but Not Skinny: Women Negotiating the Never-Too-Thin Body Ideal in Urban India," *Women's Studies International Forum* 35: 109–18.

# 34

# Narrative pleasure in *Homeland*

## The competing femininities of "rogue agents" and "terror wives"

## *Gargi Bhattacharyya*

### Securitization and everyday structures of feeling

Since the 2011 US assassination of Osama Bin Laden, the register in the rhetoric surrounding the war on terror has changed. The death of Bin Laden was presented—for the purposes of US electioneering—as a just conclusion to the nebulous war ignited by 9/11. However, despite this apparent endpoint, this phase of global conflict has led to an open use of many types of unpalatable practice (of illegal warfare, of extra-judicial process, of violence and repression) as allegedly necessary evils for the maintenance of state security (Meeropol 2005). Here I explore the way this shift in what is deemed acceptable and defensible in the conduct of "war," and the accompanying adaptation in understandings of what constitutes "war" (Bhatt 2012), is supported and complemented by popular media representations, including those referencing versions of feminism.

In writing before about the open secret of violence in the war on terror (Bhattacharyya 2008, 2009), I suggested that such an open secret constitutes a particular structure of feeling and governance that places audiences in the position of complicit witness. The war on terror has shifted popular narratives around torture, abuse, and the killing of civilians so that we are constantly reminded that these are supposedly necessary evils (see Dershowitz 2002). Such a project requires repeated reiteration of the logic of tolerating illegality in the pursuit of (our) safety.

Below I contrast the narrative workings of the first series of the immensely popular and influential television program *Homeland* with the representation of women associated with UK terrorist suspects. I argue that, in the name of the security state, we are witnessing a replaying of older mythologies of good and bad girls, and of domesticated and disorderly femininity, to recuperate some aspects of popular feminism for the purposes of securitization.

### The role of "feminism," the role of media

Feminism has been misused in pursuit of the war on terror (Puar 2007; Bhattacharyya 2008). My earlier project identified how a version of feminist rhetoric both was used to justify military intervention and came to inform the construction of the enemy and the practices of dehumanization defended as necessary evils in the battle against terror. Despite the changing formulation of the global war against terrorism, aspects of that misuse of feminism continue in the popular representation of security threats, including for the purposes of entertainment.

Some narrative constructions can mobilize a kind of feminist consciousness on the part of the viewer—with such a consciousness becoming central to the narrative pleasures of the text—and through this pursuit of narrative pleasure engage viewers in the logic of security. By the logic of security and securitization, I mean the framework of reasoning that subsumes most or all other governmental goals to that of consolidating safety in the most aggressive of manners, including the unlawful, and the accompanying process that reframes most or all other state activity in terms of its ability to contribute to this goal (see Fekete 2004). Such logics require a significant reworking of the relationship between citizen and state—and the repetition of particular structures of narrative could be seen as one aspect of this reworking of popular consciousness to create differently compliant citizens.

## Visual and other pleasures in the service of the security state

In revisiting some aspects of her groundbreaking essay "Visual Pleasure and Narrative Cinema," Laura Mulvey (2010) outlines the ambiguity that characterizes the central female figures in the work of Alfred Hitchcock. She admits that over the years she has come to the view that Hitchcock is not a misogynist (Mulvey 1975). Instead, she suggests:

> He uses cinema to reflect on, even analyse the way certain alluring fascinating female iconographies encapsulated particularly by the blonde ... have a particular symbiosis with the male protagonist's sexual anxieties as well as their desires.
>
> (Mulvey 2010)

Mulvey's earlier work sought to disrupt the pleasures of scopophilia and the illusion of narrative control, "to make way for a total negation of the ease and plenitude of the narrative fiction film" (1975: 7). Her more recent account offers a revision. Mulvey acknowledges that women on film may represent the beautiful objects of the male gaze, but simultaneously may suggest other meanings altogether, including acting as protagonists in narrative structures that unsettle patriarchal and other powers.

In 1975, Mulvey was clear that narrative agency is a central aspect of (male) spectators' power and pleasure:

> As the spectator identifies with the main male protagonist, he projects his look on to that of his like, his screen surrogate, so that the power of the male protagonist as he controls events coincides with the active power of the erotic look, both giving a satisfying sense of omnipotence.
>
> (Mulvey 1975: 11)

However, in her 2010 rereading, Mulvey argues that the explicit staging of feminine artifice brings another point of identification and potential disruption to the screen. Mulvey goes on to identify what she describes as the "two main attributes to the Hitchcock blonde"—a combination of artifice and fragility. This, Mulvey suggests, gives a constant sense of "an exterior, a masquerade." We, the audience, take pleasure in the visual representation of this femininity of high artifice, but we are simultaneously ambivalent towards "the domination of the male protagonist and of society more generally." Mulvey's account of the manner in which audiences can at once take pleasure in formulaic representations of femininity and yet be critical of the social construction of such gender norms suggests that audiences become engaged with the central female figure, despite her staged artifice, fragility, and, perhaps, unreliability. The "Hitchcock blonde" is a far from straightforward movie heroine—and yet audience pleasures may arise from ambivalence towards her.

I argue that these viewing practices—well established in audiences familiar with US and UK mass cinema and television—have trained media audiences to recognize and accommodate particular incarnations of feminine fragility and masquerade and to absorb such characteristics into a larger pleasure in the critique of improper domination. This schooling in how to read the ambivalence of feminine display under patriarchy enables audiences to identify with the ambivalence of feminine display in the service of the security state. In the process, displays of improper femininity can become an element of the authentication of the narrative voice seeking to uncover terrorist conspiracies—because we know from other genres that the apparently unreliable woman may be the only one able to piece together the workings of dangerous powers.

## Misunderstood hysterics in the service of the CIA

Analyzing the 1887 painting by Andre Brouillet of the famous physician Charcot presenting the renowned "hysteric," Blanche, Sander Gilman argues that Blanche models her performance of hysteria on the representation of the hysteric created by the physician and artist: she performs a textbook display of hysteria in a room decorated with instructive images of textbook displays of hysteria (Gilman 1993: 346). Gilman describes these teaching charts that cover the walls of wards and treatment rooms: "It is part of the world of the patient, a means through which to learn how to structure one's hysteria so as to make one an exemplary patient" (1993: 349). Embedded in Gilman's analysis is the understanding both that hysteria is a highly cultured and normative performance and that such performances can bring social recognition and reward, of a sort. The hysteric achieves a form of status and value, in part through participating in the process of being cured.

The society that creates the hysteric—and, importantly, the damaging conditions that cause hysteria—also rewards the proper performance of hysteria. Embodying the distressing fault lines of society can be a valued role, but, we learn from Gilman's account of Blanche, the display must be textbook perfect. The central character, rogue CIA agent Carrie, in *Homeland* is presented as just such a tolerated hysteric. Her erratic behavior and mental health condition are accommodated (to an extent) because her hysterical insights are recuperated into the service of the (security) state.

Yet when this same display pushes her to pursue meanings that cannot be spoken openly—because her analysis of a particular threat also uncovers the complicity of the US Vice-President and head of the CIA in illegal drone strikes against children—she is relegated to the space of the outcast hysteric.

The final scene of the first series of *Homeland* focuses on Carrie's contorted face as she submits to the electroshock therapy that she has decided is necessary if she is to manage her bipolar disorder. The image of the restrained woman receiving electro-convulsive shock therapy (ECT) is unsettlingly familiar, bringing together both our uncomfortably heightened knowledge of torture by electric shock and a mining of the well-established popular distaste towards such invasive treatments of mental health disorders (for a history of ECT, see Shorter and Healy 2007).

Earlier accounts revealed the racialized narratives that accompanied these stories of women and madness, so that hysteria could be regarded as not only an eruption of disorderly femininity but also an outcome of racial degeneracy, an eruption of contaminated blood—the physical assault of shock therapy made more legitimate by the suggestion that these subjects were in danger of becoming less than human (Gilman 2008). However, in the example of *Homeland* the focus is on femininity—and the discomfort for the audience of seeing such a dehumanizing submission chosen as a route for the unruly but insightful central character to become accepted as a reasonable human once more.

## Reclaiming hysteria for a securitized age

Feminist media studies has established, among other things, a sophisticated apparatus through which to analyze representations of women as symptom. Carrie echoes some well-established traits of the hysteric on film. She is presented as the physical unease of attempting to achieve security. We understand that it is the burden of feeling responsible for the nation's security that has broken her psyche in some way. Something that happened in Iraq haunts her subsequent choices. Yet we also learn that Carrie's bipolar disorder predates Iraq, runs in her family, and can be managed by medication if she chooses to take it. In fact, this unreason has its roots within the safe domesticity of the white family and nation, far away from the dangerous streets of Iraq.

Whereas a plethora of readings of the female hysteric have suggested that a symptomatic analysis of such displays can uncover the convoluted conspiracies of patriarchy (Bernheimer and Kahane 1990), Carrie's manic insight serves to reveal that the paranoid defenses of the security state are justified. Here validating the hysteric blurs into accepting the varied abuses of the security state and reframing our understanding of the world through the eyes of the over-zealous CIA agent. This is Carrie's own defense of her behavior and of her inability to view the world except through the lens of agent. All those around her, and the audience, suspect that her approach is wrong. She receives repeated warnings at work—to maintain proper boundaries, to follow procedure, to stay within the law—and she displays some behavior that seems designed to prove what an improper woman she is, not only single and childless, but dirty (she "washes" her armpits with a babywipe before attending a big event in Episode 1). She is also sexually manipulative, terrorizes children, and cannot consider the implications of her actions for the safety of her colleagues or herself.

Yet the overall lesson is that, however unlikeable, such behavior is necessary to maintain our collective safety. The unruly hysteric is an unexpected complement to the securitized state. The message from both is that dangerous enemies threaten us in our homes. If we wish to be defended against such threats, we must accept these various ugly behaviors carried out in our name.

Such a narrative continues one theme of the war on terror, that femininity and feminism—both female bodies and a discourse of women's rights—can become central elements of the project of securitization. What appears to be a development is the use of familiar tropes of women's unreason to serve as an alternative justification of irrational actions by the state. The femininity that serves the security state here is the unruly femininity of the hysteric. The too orderly femininity of the Muslim woman, or of the revert, or of the white woman who marries a revert are all marked as dangers.[1] In a worldview that considers Muslims excessively domestic and familial, old-fashioned bad girls become the embodiment of a kind of heroic patriotism.

## Narrative pleasures and ambivalence about domination

Carrie embodies key aspects of a pleasurably displaced experience of narrative. She takes up the central space of screen and story, she is the one piecing together an understanding of events, and therefore she is the guide to the developing plot for the audience. She is complicated and broken and seemingly unlovable, and so both the most human reference point for the audience and a complicated point of identification. The manner in which the audience is encouraged to maintain an emotional and moral ambivalence towards the character of Carrie shows how the logic of the security state is propagated as the only available mode of being in our time. By this, I do not mean that there is no other way to think, but that the ideological push towards securitization operates through this inhabiting of ambivalence and discomfort.

The denouement of series one brings together a number of elements of misbehavior by Carrie—the manic assembly of the timeline that identifies the gap in their suspect's activities, the dangerous insight that interrogation works by finding what it is that makes the subject of interrogation human, the tiny linking clue that could only be learned by hearing the semi-conscious sleep-talk of a suspect. It is hard to avoid the suggestion that all misconduct is justified if the case is solved, if the threat is disarmed. This, in fact, is close to how Carrie herself justifies unorthodox behavior. Without the theft and nocturnal ordering of stolen classified documents, there would be no revelatory insight into the pattern of Abu Nazir's activity. Without the seduction of the returning prisoner, the unguarded cry in the night of the lost child's name would never be heard. Without the interrogator's mind-set, a mind-set that seeks to exploit the weak points of the subject of interrogation, the significance of this hidden attachment to a dead child could not be understood. Each element of Carrie's misbehavior or dishonesty comes to be justified by the revelations of the plot. Yet she remains a markedly dangerous character, unable to make herself comprehensible to the custodians of reason in her working life.

## White widows and the refusal of narrative and other pleasures

Another incarnation of the white woman touched by terrorism is played out in one of the back stories of *Homeland*. The rich girl with the Arab boyfriend is a barely sketched character. In series one, what we "know" of her emerges only in Saul's interrogation by suggestion—in which he tells a story about privilege, containment, escape, and friendship in order to come the denouement that he too "fell in love with a brown girl." What we learn is why white girls might be considered a weak link in the national defense.

In 2012, seven years after the London bombings on public transport that killed 52 people, sections of the British press sought to reopen debates about allegiance, identity, and the source of terrorist threat through a series of pieces focusing on the wives of those suspected of the bombings. Such discussion served as a popular reference point to a larger and ongoing debate about the alleged "failure" of multiculturalism (see Mitchell 2004; Vertovec 2010). More interesting, for my purposes, is the reappearance of the white wife as a figure in the drama of terrorist threat. After the 7/7 bombings, debate centered on the question of how apparently normal and (most importantly) *integrated* young men could do such a thing to other Britons. The figure of the white woman touched by terrorism was quite marginal in the outcry and speculation that followed 7/7. However, in 2012, at around the time that *Homeland* was being screened in Britain, a story about the mysterious white wife of a bomber appeared in the press. Samantha Lewthwaite represented a number of favored reference points—daughter of a military family, badly affected by the break-up of her parents' marriage, becomes a Muslim at 15, allegedly after learning about Islam in religious studies lessons at school, marries fellow revert Jermaine Lindsay after they meet in an Islamic chatroom. Although she had described the London bombings as "abhorrent," in 2012 Lewthwaite's name became linked to investigations into planned bomb attacks in Kenya. While previously she may have represented familiar tropes, slightly updated to fit the preoccupations of our time—respectable woman who has fallen from grace, troubled outcome of a broken home, vulnerable victim of institutionalized multiculturalism, unsuspecting innocent groomed in an internet chatroom, transgressor of racial, and now also religious, boundaries—her new media incarnation seems to arise specifically from our time.

In a piece entitled "The Search for the White Widow," the *Telegraph* outlines the new lines of speculation swirling around a woman who may or may not be Samantha Lewthwaite, while admitting "a vacuum of verifiable fact" surrounding the various accusations repeated in the article. Central among these was the rumor that Lewthwaite is an Al-Qaeda financer, using her education and status as a white woman to carry out plots undetected. The *Telegraph* reporter acknowledges that Lewthwaite has become the object of the fantasies of various players:

> In fact, none of that is fact. Instead, it is part of the myth of Samantha Lewthwaite that seems to have taken hold, benefiting propagandists on both sides of East Africa's growing rift between security and terror.
>
> (Pflanz 2012)

She has been accused variously of being al-Qaeda's chief financier in the region, funding the recruitment and smuggling of Muslim youth to terror training camps in Somalia, and coaching her own all-women jihadist squad there. She has been linked with senior al-Qaeda commanders' alleged plots to attack Eton College and the Dorchester and Ritz hotels in London.

(Pflanz 2012)

Whoever the white widow is, she is imagined to derive her influence as a result of the trappings of a kind of female empowerment. Whiteness gives her status and mobility. She has money and can pay in cash, including her rent. She has had access to higher education—and this contributes to the rumors. She is mobile and can associate with a wide range of people, including a variety of men. In fact, none of the British press seemed able to confirm that the woman under discussion was, in fact, Samantha Lewthwaite. The uncertainty surrounding the identity of the white widow is a central component of her mythology.

Echoing earlier examples of racist agitation, the racially privileged woman is a site of considerable racist fantasy and anxiety. She embodies the permeable boundary of nation—because it is unruly and semi-civilized women who threaten to transgress the strictures against interracial contact, because they don't understand, because they are ruled by their bodies, because they are not themselves representative of the privileged group, because the second-class citizenship of women creates an opening for association and alliance with all sorts of lesser others. Women are attracted to exotic but lesser beings because they are soft-headed, lascivious, and dangerously open to identifying with the less-than-human.

In this instance, the contaminated/fallen white woman is somehow conspicuous yet invisible and made oddly glamorous, as if embracing Islam is a route to a version of jet-set celebrity lifestyle. Perhaps this recuperation into a kind of consumer feminism—an independent lady who pays her own way—is preferable to the apparently greater scandal that middle-class white girls might give up their previous lives to become hair-covering Muslim wives.

## The agent who knew too much

In the context of globalized English-speaking reception, the character of Carrie can be seen to continue longstanding tropes in the representation of white femininity. Close-ups of her face, framed significantly by a headscarf, anxiously looking upwards as she retreats from a threat that we cannot see, form one of the recurring images of the opening credits. Although Carrie is presented in a far more naturalistic and occasionally grotesque manner within the narrative episodes, this framing image echoes others from the history of cinema: The distressed face of the beautiful woman indicates the horror out of shot that remains beyond representation (for the significance of the close-up, see Doane 2003).

This trope remains central to the series—the troubled and misunderstood woman who finds herself trapped in a horror that is invisible to others. From *Rebecca* to Hitchcock to *I Know What You Did Last Summer*, global audiences are familiar with this well-worn cinematic construction of (largely) white femininity (Modleski 1988). For Carrie, the monster that only she can see is the incursion of international terrorism into the formerly safe space of the Western nation—and in common with other stories about apparently unstable heroines, the narrative tension arises from the audience's uncertainty about the reliability of this paranoid view. Yet, the denouement of series one consists, in part, of the realization that Carrie's reading of the world is true. Below I consider the implications of vindicating the hysterical voice for the purposes of security.

## Stories teach us how to understand and feel?

I have been interested in the role of popular narrative in the creation of everyday securitization. Although here I considered narratives from popular media, my long-standing interest is the narrative logics of security states and how we, as everyday citizens, come to insert ourselves into these narratives. There is an interplay between the stories of state practices and the stories of popular media, particularly in the construction of our shared investment in supporting security practices, including those that may appear unpalatable to our sense of our allegedly liberal democratic values. Popular narratives, whether presented as fictional entertainments or factual accounts of our world, offer a range of triggers to audiences. We might learn that this or that representation tells us what a terrorist looks like, or a patriot, or a victim, or an innocent bystander. Within this pantheon of characters, of course, there are intersections with other conventions of representation relating to other powerful constructions such as gender, nation, race, and class (see Poynting *et al.* 2004).

In earlier times, we learned to identify how gender dissonance or class resistance could be coded as threats to the nation, including national security. In our time, new mythologies emerge so that the femininity that protects and perpetuates the nation might entail serial monogamy, prioritizing paid employment as a central component of identity, and engaging in consumer practices deemed necessary to a market-friendly liberal feminism (see McRobbie 2008), or patriots may be those who prioritize the defense of the nation above pursuing class-based interests through industrial action (in 2012, members of the Public and Commercial Services Union, including staff from the UK Border Agency, pursuing industrial action in the run-up to the London Olympics were portrayed as unpatriotic and/or treacherous). These choices in relation to representing the characters of our imagined national and international drama remain important and continue to shape popular imagination even in these hyper-mediatized times.

However, the construction of narrative in popular media plays a particular and central role in positioning the audience as consenting to the logic and practices of the security state. This is not so simple a process as earlier depictions of propaganda where stories and pictures were designed to tell us what to think in the representational equivalent of a very loud voice or to construct clear character types to elicit sympathy or disgust as required, although plenty of these practices continue. The issue is the role of popular narrative in inculcating consent among audiences, not through an explicit set of choices but through the processes of narrative identification and understanding. Sometimes, as in the television series *Homeland*, following the plot demands that the viewer come to understand the constraints and imperatives motivating the agent of the security state—when each instance of bad behavior then comes to yield the information that pieces together the next important plot point, the overall implication of following the story is that all such behavior is justified. More than this, the ability to follow such narratives can rely on the audience learning to inhabit the logic of securitization. This is a way of learning about the world of terrorist threat by learning to see through the eyes of the rogue agent, the hysteric in service to the security state. In part through reference to familiar film conventions, an initially skeptical audience comes to recognize over the course of the film that the apparently unstable heroine is, in fact, the only one able to comprehend what is happening around her. In an age of securitization, this narrative structure can be redeployed to mobilize the audience's identification with the central character seeking to battle threats from terrorists that no one else can see. If the identification is grudging and the character unappealing, so much the better, because that is an important part of the lesson for the general public. You may not like these people, but you must appreciate the sense of what they are doing.

The white widows remind us that the weaknesses of femininity—including the liberated femininity that has benefited from the cultural trappings of liberal democracy—can lead to a dangerous and contaminating association with the monstrous. Carrie, on the other hand, demonstrates the ability of the security state to accommodate the insights of some feminisms. Carrie can remain an exemplar of unruly femininity—no phallic woman here—yet her feminine disorder serves to confirm the logic of the security state. As we learn, slowly and sometimes painfully, to hear the messages of the hysteric voice and to allow this uncomfortable performativity into our conception of what and who can be human, we also learn to see the enemies in our midst and the need to violate norms of decency in the pursuit of safety. The final scene in series one of Carrie's electric-shock grimace jolts the viewer into the realization that without her all knowledge of the plot disappears, invisible forever to those too steeped in the orthodoxies of accepted reason. When we long for her to be saved and vindicated, we are longing for the security state and, despite ourselves, all the horror that it entails.

## Note

1 Since, according to Islam, children are born with an innate sense of God, some people born in other religious traditions see their conversion to Islam as a "return." For this reason, many Muslims prefer to say that they have "reverted," rather than converted.

## References

Bernheimer, C. and C. Kahane (1990) *In Dora's Case: Freud, Hysteria, Feminism*, New York: Columbia University Press.
Bhatt, C. (2012) "Human Rights and the Transformations of War," *Sociology* 46(5): 813–28.

Bhattacharyya, G. (2008) *Dangerous Brown Men: Exploiting Sex, Violence and Feminism in the War on Terror*, London: Zed Books.

——(2009) "Spectatorship and the War on Terror: Creating Consensus through Global Audiences," Special Issue of *Globalizations*, "Globalization, Ethics and the War on Terror" 6(1) (March).

Dershowitz, A. (2002) *Why Terrorism Works: Understanding the Threat, Responding to the Challenge*, New Haven, CT: Yale University Press.

Doane, M. A. (2003) "The Close-Up: Scale and Detail in the Cinema," *Differences: A Journal of Feminist Cultural Studies* 14(3) (Fall): 89–111.

Fekete, L. (2004) "Anti-Muslim Racism and the European Security State," *Race and Class* 46(1): 3–29.

Gilman, S. (1993) "The Image of the Hysteric," in L. G. Sander, H. King, R. Porter, G. S. Rousseau, and E. Showalter (eds.) *Hysteria Beyond Freud*, Berkeley: University of California Press.

——(2008) "Electrotherapy and Mental Illness: Then and Now," *History of Psychiatry* 19(3): 339–57.

McRobbie, A. (2008) *The Aftermath of Feminism: Gender, Culture and Social Change*, London: Sage.

Meeropol, R. (2005) *America's Disappeared: Secret Imprisonment Detainees and the "War on Terror"*, New York: Seven Stories Press.

Mitchell, K. (2004) "Geographies of Identity: Multiculturalism Unplugged," *Progress in Human Geography* 28(5): 641–51.

Modleski, T. (1988) *The Women Who Knew Too Much: Hitchcock and Feminist Theory*, New York: Methuen.

Mulvey, L. (1975) "Visual Pleasure and Narrative Cinema," *Screen* 16(3) (Autumn): 6–18.

——(2010) "The Hitchcock Blonde." http://www.bfi.org.uk/live/video/310.

Nelson, J. S. (2003) "Four Forms of Terrorism: Horror, Dystopia, Thriller and Noir," *Poroi* 2 (1) (August).

Pflanz, M. (2012) "The Hunt for the White Widow," *Telegraph*, July 15. http://www.telegraph.co.uk/news/worldnews/africaandindianocean/somalia/9402087/The-hunt-for-the-white-widow.html.

Poynting, S., G. Noble, P. Tabar, and J. Collins (2004) *Bin Laden in the Suburbs: Criminalising the Arab Other*, Sydney: Institute of Criminology.

Puar, J. (2007) *Terrorist Assemblages: Homonationalism in Queer Times*, Durham, NC: Duke University Press.

Shorter, E. and D. Healy (2007) *Shock Therapy: A History of Electroconvulsive Treatment in Mental Illness*, Toronto: Toronto University Press.

Vertovec, S. (2010) "Towards Post-Multiculturalism? Changing Communities, Conditions and Contexts of Diversity," *International Social Science Journal* 61(199) (March): 83–95.

# 35

# Above the fold and beyond the veil

## Islamophobia in Western media

## *Nahed Eltantawy*

A quick Google image search for "Muslim women" brings up a sea of black—pictures of bodies covered in the traditional black abaya worn by many Muslim women, eyes peering out from black veils, and women dressed in black, holding machine guns. This sea of blackness has become the Western media's dominant portrayal of Muslim women. These images and the negative connotations in accompanying texts feed into mounting Islamophobia of the veil.[1]

The origins of the term Islamophobia are disputed (Allen 2005). Islamophobia as a term goes back to the nineteenth and early twentieth centuries, when it was used to describe European attitudes toward Islam and Muslims (Bravo López 2011). In the early 1990s, in describing the sociopolitical problems of Muslims in Britain, Tariq Modood defined Islamophobia as "a cultural sickness" (1992: 69). The 1997 Runnymede Trust Report on British Muslims was among the first to provide a detailed definition of Islamophobia:

> [Islamophobia] is recognizably similar to "xenophobia" and "europhobia," and is a useful shorthand way of referring to dread or hatred of Islam and, therefore, to fear or dislike of all or most Muslims. Such dread and dislike have existed in western countries and cultures for several centuries. In the last twenty years, however, the dislike has become more explicit, more extreme, and more dangerous. It is an ingredient of all sections of our media, and is prevalent in all sections of our society.
>
> (Runnymede Trust Commission on British Muslims
> and Islamophobia 1997: 1)

By extension, Islamophobia of the veil can be defined as "dread and dislike" combined with mystification of Muslim women's traditional hair covering worldwide.[2] Yet, similar to Islamophobia, this anxiety (and mystification) of the veil burgeoned over the years and intensified following 9/11. Many Western feminists and media pundits now view the veil as the ultimate sign of Muslim women's oppression. Westerners regard the veil as mysterious, secretive, and even dangerous and radical (Hoodfar 2003; El-Guindi 2005; Merali 2006). Western fears about the veil can be traced back to the European colonial era of the nineteenth and early twentieth centuries (Said 1979; Hoodfar 1993).

As Bullock explains, "For the western media, hijab, by and large, stands for oppression and as shorthand for all the horrors of Islam ... terrorism, violence, barbarity, and backwardness" (2000: 42). This chapter will show that negative portrayals of the veil continue in articles, opinion columns, and political cartoons in newspapers published across the US, Europe, Australia, and Canada.

## History of the veil

Although largely associated with Islam, the veil predates the Islamic era (Graham-Brown 1988; Ahmed 1993; El Guindi 1999; Hoodfar 2003; Macdonald 2006). Women donned veils in pre-Islamic Arabia, Greece, Assyria, the Balkans, and Byzantium. Veils were also worn in certain Jewish and Christian communities (Macdonald 2006: 8). The veil exists in many variations and continues to change in accordance with fashions throughout the years, although Western literature often presents veiling "as a uniform and static practice going back over 1,000 years" (Hoodfar 2003: 11).

In some countries, such as Iran, all women are required to cover their hair and body by wearing a long gown called the chador. In Saudi Arabia, the government requires all Saudi women to cover their face with a niqab and to wear a black robe-like gown over their clothes, known as the abaya. The majority of Muslim women who adopt hair or full-face veils, however, do so by choice. In countries like Egypt, Morocco, Syria, Lebanon, and Turkey, hijab varies and is not necessarily adopted by all Muslim women. The Muslim Brotherhood Party estimates that more than 70 percent of Egyptian women wear at least a headscarf (Sayare 2012).

Muslims who adopt head coverings do so for various reasons. Some women wear it to identify with Islam and be closer to God, while others adorn it as a form of beauty (Wikan 1982; Chatty 1997). Still other women don the hijab to bring attention to sexist messages about women's bodies and pressures to be thin (Ahmed 2011). Leila Ahmed (2011) found some women wear the hijab as confirmation of their pride in being Muslims, while others wear it because it is religiously required. Ahmed (2011) argues that, while veiling can be viewed as oppressive, for many Muslim women it is a way to show pride in their Muslim identity and to openly reject negative stereotypes. Some women wear it to hide their identity (Fernea 1965), while others adopt it to make a political statement. Historically, veiling was popular in political movements, as in the case of Egyptian women in the 1970s (El Guindi 2005). Similar pro-hijab movements were witnessed in the West, as a reaction to 9/11 Islamophobia. "Faced with a growing American public acceptance of the diatribe against Islam and Muslims, some young American-born Muslim women appear to have appropriated a century-old view of the hijab as a symbol of solidarity and resistance to efforts to eradicate the religion of Islam" (Haddad 2007: 254).

Contemporary veiling usually consists of a loose-fitting outfit (a dress or a blouse with a skirt or pants) along with a headscarf that can vary in its colors and wrapping style (El Guindi 2005). Yet the imaginary veil that most Westerners think of is an awkward, all-encompassing black cloak that hides the body and the face and is designed to hinder women's mobility (Dickey 1994). That a Google images search of "veils and Muslim women" brings up a sea of blackness therefore comes as no surprise.

Such depictions of veiling in the West are emphatically contested as problematic by many Muslim feminists (Ahmed 1993; El Guindi 2005; Merali 2006), who assert that, contrary to Western claims that the hijab is oppressive, Islam and the veil empower and liberate Muslim women. For example, Merali (2006: 174, 176) argues: "We come to attention because of our (perceived) negativity and become the subjects of discussion only when our mistreatment brings us to the notice of critical circles. ... The veil, burqa, chador, and headscarf are blurred into one symbolic entity; all Muslim women—their motivations, their beliefs and their aspirations—are generalized, despised, or simply denied legitimacy." After giving additional history and context about the veil and other coverings for Muslim women, this chapter will highlight some prominent, albeit unfortunate, examples of problematic news coverage of Muslim women, with special attention to editorial cartoons.

## The West and the veil

Western fascination with the Muslim "Other" is not new. Edward Said (1979) argued that a long tradition of false and romanticized images of Asia and the Middle East in Western culture served to justify Europe and America's colonial and imperial ambitions. He said a society builds up its identity more efficiently by imagining an Other. The binary opposition of "Orientalism" helped the West to define itself as culturally and intellectually superior, while the East, or the Orient, was imagined and reflected as culturally static and inferior.

Historically, Orientalism has represented Muslim women either as exotic and mysterious or as oppressed and backward. Colonial writings construct the Oriental woman as sensual and living in harems, the section of the house reserved for women of a Muslim household (Kabbani 1986). Additionally, colonial texts frequently represented Muslim women as sexually available, especially in the harem setting (Alloula 1986).

Such colonial depictions of Muslim women in the harem often included sexual fantasies of the Oriental *femme fatale*. Myra Macdonald (2006) finds such images in nineteenth-century paintings of Delacroix and Ingres, and the striptease "dance of the seven veils" in theatrical and cinematic performances; these continue in contemporary advertising and film. These sexualized images of the colonial era largely contributed to contemporary Islamophobia of the veil. "Even although the enticement of the shimmering diaphanous veil of screen representations may seem at the opposite end of any spectrum from the total obscurity of the burqa, the harem of the Western imaginary has left a legacy of mystique and sexual anticipation that still contributes to the veil's fascination" (Macdonald 2006: 11).

Extending this argument, Graham-Brown (2003) asserts that colonial texts, photographs, and paintings portrayed Orientalized women as possessions or playthings of men. The women were portrayed as passive and still; barred within the walls of the harem, awaiting the man who is the sole reason for their existence. Paradoxically, foreign men were not allowed into the harem, so such harem scenes were composed in a studio or were figments of an artist's imagination. Oddly, what Western colonizers viewed as oppressive, secluded, and erotic was perceived by Muslim women of the harem as educational, prestigious, and a source of pride (Afshar 2000; Mernissi 2003).

Today, images of the hijab, veil, chador, or burqa worn by Muslim women are not uncommon in news coverage across Europe, Australia, Canada, and the United States. In the years following 9/11, these images intensified. Pictures of burqa-clad Afghan women were quite common during and after the US war on Afghanistan. Having studied images of Afghan women on the *Time* news magazine website, Cloud (2004) concedes that Afghan women were mistreated under the Taliban, but asserts that these *Time* images do more than represent reality. Comparing these images to nineteenth-century British colonial discourses, she says Americans use these images to force their paternal gaze on others and, thus, define the Afghan woman "as the object of U.S. cultural hegemony" (Cloud 2004: 293). The specific sequence of the photos on the Time.com website suggests that until the US intervened to save them "Afghan women wandered in chaos or lived, invisible and indistinct, at the mercy and discretion of irrational autocratic men" (Cloud 2004: 294). Analysis of Associated Press photographs of Afghan women during and after the Taliban era likewise undermines US claims that the war on Afghanistan helped liberate Afghan women from their burqas, since the majority of photographs in the new post-Taliban era showed women still wearing burqas, suggesting a more complex version of Afghan women's liberation (Fahmy 2004).

## Contemporary depictions of the veil

In the decade since 9/11, Islamophobia remains widespread. Western media biases continue to fuel Islamophobia in general and of the veil specifically. At the least, these negative depictions confirm deep-rooted stereotypes and fail to provide accurate realities about followers of Islam. I argue that media misrepresentation can contribute to growing abhorrence and denunciation of Islam and Muslims. For example, Fox News is home to a number of right-wing shows that regularly confirm inaccurate Muslim stereotypes (Lean 2012). According to a 2011 Brookings Institution poll, 63 percent of Republicans and 66 percent of Tea Party affiliates agree with the position affirmed by Fox News that Islam contradicts US values, and nearly half of the Republicans who watch Fox News believe that Muslim Americans are trying to force Islamic Shari'a law as the "law of the land" (Jones *et al.* 2011; Lean 2012). A 2010 poll found that almost half of the US population holds "unfavorable" views of Islam, although more than half say they lack a basic understanding of Islam (*Washington Post*/ABC 2010: 2). A 2011 report suggests that European attitudes toward Islam are no different, since, with the exception of Portugal, "Europe is largely united in its rejection of Muslims" (Zick *et al.* 2011: 2).

These findings about Islamophobic media help foretell similarly problematic coverage of Muslim women. Western newspaper stories and editorial cartoons pay little attention to Muslim women who are not veiled, taking the veil to symbolize Islam. "The veil then, and not a woman, symbolizes Islam and its implied oppressiveness" (Gottschalk and Greenberg 2008: 54). Martin-Munoz describes the reductionist image of Muslim women prevalent in Western media: "The predominant image is of a passive, exotic, and veiled victim-woman who reacts to events instead of actively participating in them. She is an impersonal object of communal stereotypes that sustain cultural prejudices" (2010: para. 2).

Analysis of contemporary Western media depictions of Muslim women reveals that the media most commonly portray the Muslim woman as an enigma, an oppressed weakling; a faceless clone, or a Western Muslimah. Such consistent themes feed into Islamophobia of the veil.

## Enigma

Cartoons and news coverage highlighting the "enigma" theme revisit the long tradition of false and romanticized images of the Orient as described by Said (1979). The enigmatic Muslim woman is the Other who cannot speak and needs to be represented; she is exotic, mysterious, hidden, invisible, even inhuman, or traditional, oppressed, uneducated, backward, and inferior to men (Kabbani 1986; Mohanty et al. 1991; Lacsamana 1999). When reporters cannot see the person beneath the veil, especially when they are unable or unwilling to interview women, they are likely to stereotype. Political cartoonists usually use the niqab to minimize women's presence, voice, and agency: "This resonates with the idea that niqabi women are already oppressed, so why depict them with an agency that they do not have?" (Cervantes 2012: para. 4).

One article in The Australian suggested that some Muslim women "look like black ghosts in the niqab" (Dent 2003: 16). New York Times columnist Maureen Dowd described Saudi Arabian women as "faceless" and "ghostly" (2002: 11). The black abayas worn by some women have been termed by the Australian Advertiser as "shapeless robes" and by the Cleveland Plain Dealer as the "black baglike garment" (Harris 2001: 2; Marchetti 2003: J11). The San Francisco Chronicle said: "Sometimes you can see their faces. Sometimes just their eyes. Sometimes you see nothing at all of the humans beneath the black shrouds" (Ryan 2004: B1). Muslim women are also described in Scotland on Sunday as "peering dark-eyed from inside their burkhas" (Deerin 2004: 16). The Guardian's Polly Toynbee (2006) concludes that "the veil turns women into things," while a columnist for The Age, a daily broadsheet published in Melbourne, Australia (Haussegger 2010) asks, "What God demands men roam free while women wear a sackcloth that restricts their movement and dehumanizes them?" (para. 11).

Cartoonist Peter de Wit's (2008) "Burka Babes" series was born out of his famous comic strip "Sigmund," published in the Dutch daily de Volkskrant. One cartoon shows a group of Westerners close to the Statue of Liberty. Yet, instead of taking pictures of the monument, they take pictures with a burqa-clad woman (de Wit 2008: 18). Ironically, a description of the "Burka Babes" on de Wit's official website claims that the Dutch cartoonist "cleverly developed their personalities, turning them into real Burka Babes with surprisingly upbeat views on religion, men, and life in general." Yet, many of de Wit's cartoons depict these women as oppressed and shapeless, and not so upbeat. For example, one burqa-clad woman, when asked if she is looking forward to spring, responds: "Not sure, I'll have to ask my husband" (de Wit 2008: 13). In another, a "burka babe" is offended when a Muslim bearded man calls out to her, "Hi there, gorgeous"; however, when a second man utters, "Hi there, sexless object," she responds, "That's more like it" (de Wit 2008: 12).

### Oppressed weakling

Western reportage frequently depicts Muslim women as oppressed and in need of rescuing, preferably by a Westerner. As Abu-Lughod explains, "[O]ne of the most dangerous functions of these [Western] images of Middle Eastern or Muslim women is to enable many of us to imagine that these women need rescuing by us or by our governments" (2006: 6, para. 2). So, the veil is portrayed as oppressive, and women wearing it are depicted as weak, fragile, or oppressed by men and religion. Dario Castillejos's (2009) cartoon, for example, shows a woman whose black burqa is torn; a rope dangling out implies this is a way out of her burqa prison.[3] At other times, reporters or cartoonists blame Muslim men for such oppression. Jason Love's (2007) cartoon, for example, shows a Muslim husband telling a tourist: "I haven't named her yet," referring to his black-clad wife as if she's a pet.[4]

*New York Times* columnists have referred to Muslim women as "swaddled breeders under house arrest" (Dowd 2001: 13) and "treated like doormats" (Kristoff 2002: 31). Perhaps one of the harshest depictions of Muslim women as oppressed weaklings is a *Toronto Star* article titled "Lifting the Veil on Women's Enslavement." Michele Landsberg (2002) recalls how in Paris she saw an Arab man strolling in the "shimmering heat" in casual clothes and trailed by several children and two women in "stifling" black chadors. Landsberg declared: "Those dead, shuttered, hollow-eyed faces were the ugliest image of enslavement I have ever seen. ... To see women in a state of such abject abasement, paraded through the sophisticated City of Light, was literally sickening" (2002: A02). Not once in her article did Landsberg quote any Muslim women, veiled or non-veiled, to confirm whether they shared her views.

Indeed, Western reporters rarely quote veiled Muslim women. In 2005, Gallup pollsters interviewed more than 8,000 urban and rural Muslim women from eight predominantly Muslim countries (Mogahed 2006), and few women on their own mentioned gender inequality as a major problem. Even in Turkey and Lebanon, the most secularized of the eight countries, only 9–11 percent of those polled mentioned gender inequality among their top five concerns. Asked what they resented most about their own societies, most women mentioned a lack of unity among Muslim nations, violent extremism, and political and economic corruption. Asked what they resent most about Western societies, the majority mentioned pornography, promiscuity, and public indecency, which they see in Hollywood movies exported to the Muslim world. "So while the veil is often perceived by many in the West as a symbol of women's inferior cultural status in the Muslim world, in Muslim societies, the perceived lack of modesty portrayed in Western media is thought to signal women's degraded cultural status" (Mogahed 2006: 2).

## Faceless clone

As faceless clones, Muslim women are stripped of their individual identity. They are viewed as one large monolithic group sharing an identical outward appearance and presumed to share identical qualities and personalities. For example, a *Boston Globe* reporter interviewed three Iraqi sisters living in Dearborn, Michigan, about the Iraqi elections. Implying some surprise that the women had diverse opinions, the reporter said that although the three sisters wore nearly identical black abayas and headscarves, each had her own opinion on Iraq's future, with emphasis on equal rights for women (Ghannam 2003: A3).

This notion of Islam as monolithic emerged in a de Wit (2008) "Burka Babes" cartoon showing two women dressed identically in black abaya and burqa. One of them, standing in front of a broken mirror, tells the other, on the mirror's opposite side, "Thanks, my new mirror is being delivered tomorrow" (de Wit 2008: 52).

## Western Muslimah[5]

Not all news coverage of Muslim women is negative and Islamophobic, and presumably most journalists are not intentionally trying to create or confirm stereotypes. In their search for the truth, journalists often help correct stereotypes. This was especially true right after 9/11, when then President George W. Bush urged Americans not to take out their anger on Muslim Americans. Journalists embraced Bush's words. The subsequent coverage helped inform and educate people about Muslim practices and showed that Muslim Americans are hardworking, taxpaying neighbors and co-workers. Nevertheless, this type of coverage carries its own biases, including hailing Western Muslim women's liberal thinking and modern appearance, as if these women offer a more likeable version of Islam than their Muslim counterparts in the non-Western world. Descriptions like "Maverick Muslim Women Rip Veil off Religion's Traditional Gender Values" (Curiel 2005: F1) imply that the women mentioned in the article want to rip the figurative veils off their religious beliefs, like ripping off this much-contested literal veil. Depictions of this Western Muslimah are also evident in *The Australian*, which said: "Instead of donning black scarves and shapeless dresses to get closer to God, new hijab girls are customizing their Western wardrobes to match their newly acquired scarves and religiosity" (Dent 2003: 16). In the *Financial Times* Geraldine Brooks hailed young Muslim women from the US and Canada who are helping create an "American-style Islam" (2004: 26). Brooks applauded this "new Islam" as free of "the customs that are often the worst of the anti-women practices associated with the faith, such as female genital mutilation, face veiling and denial of the right to a life outside the home ... " (2004: 26). Other evidence of this preferred Western Muslimah include the New York *Daily News*'s congratulatory descriptions of non-veiled liberal Muslims living in the West. One was "a petite stylish woman with bright, black eyes"; another is dressed simply in jeans and black sweater, "her large brown eyes never break[ing] their gaze" (Lite 2005: 50).[6] Very few articles described other Muslim women in such detail, whether they wear the hijab or not. Such coverage is problematic in that it clearly favors the style of Muslim women who are modern, liberal, and live in the West; the message here is that these modern, Western-looking women are unlike the traditional backward, burqa-clad Other, to whom audiences can hardly relate.

## Conclusions

Western cartoons, news coverage, and columns continue to frequently represent Muslim women in one-dimensional terms. Western media often identify Muslim women by their veil and their oppression by Muslim men and religion. This reductionist view is "underpinned by an unconscious adherence to liberalism and modernization theory, compounded by an ignorance of any actual details about Muslim women's lives" (Bullock 2002: xv). Abu-Lughod argues that these images are bad for Muslim women in Western countries "because of the deadening effect they have on our capacity to appreciate the complexity and diversity of Muslim women's lives—as human beings" (2006: para. 2).

Muslim women are frustrated by being reduced to pieces of black cloth, viewed as women with headscarves "in need of salvation" (Navarro 2010: 112). After all, sexism and patriarchy exist in most societies at varying levels. Muslim women resent being caricatured and being represented by reporters who know little about Islam. Additionally, Muslim women in the West sometimes fear negative reactions because of their veils. Some American Muslim women abandoned the headscarf after 9/11, sometimes because they were concerned with reactions from work colleagues, strangers, and even other Muslims (Khalid 2011). A 2008 report validates these fears by describing Islamophobic crimes in Canada, France, the US, Sweden, Austria, and the United Kingdom (Human Rights First 2008).

Such one-dimensional and stereotyped depictions of the veil are also problematic because of the absence of Muslim women's voices. This skewed coverage should be corrected. After all, Muslim women are not going anywhere. The world's Muslim population is forecast to increase by 35 percent (at about twice the rate of non-Muslim populations) over the next 20 years, rising to 2.2 billion by 2030 (Grim and Karim 2011: 13). Hence, news that covers Muslim women as diverse human beings and that allows actual Muslim women to confirm or refute reporters' claims is necessary.

## Notes

1 The word veil refers to various forms of head and face coverings adopted by Muslim women. It can refer to a woman's headscarf, also known as *hijab* or *chador*. It can also refer to a full-face veil, known as *niqab* or *burqa*. In this chapter, the word veil refers to the full-face cover.

2 No statistics are available on the total number of Muslim women worldwide who wear a headscarf or full-face veil, although there are statistics on veiling in various Western countries. The French Interior Ministry estimates the number of full-face-veiled Muslim women close to 1,900 out of a total of four to six million French Muslims (Samuel 2011). Only a few hundred out of Belgium's 630,000 Muslims wear a burqa (Cendrowicz 2010). About 43 percent of the one million Muslim women in the US wear a headscarf (Pew Research Center 2007).

3 This burqa prison cartoon was published in a Mexican newspaper in 2009 and on cartoonmovement.com, a political cartoon syndication website created by a Dutch cartoonist (personal correspondence with Castillejos, December 17, 2012).
4 Love (personal correspondence, December 19, 2012) says the cartoon was also published in "hundreds of papers, magazines, websites, etc." The cartoon was accessed via cartoonstock.com.
5 *Muslimah* is the Arabic word for Muslim woman.
6 They have been dubbed "radical feminists" for their strong criticism of Islam (Al-Sini 2011).

# References

Abu-Lughod, L. (2006) "The Muslim Woman: The Power of Images and the Danger of Pity," *Eurozine*, September 1. http://www.eurozine.com/articles/2006-09-01-abulughod-en.html.
Afshar, H. (2000) "Age, Gender and Slavery in and out of the Persian Harem: A Different Story," *Ethnic & Racial Studies* 23(5): 905–16.
Ahmed, L. (1993) *Women and Gender in Islam: Historical Roots of a Modern Debate*, New Haven, CT: Yale University Press.
——(2011) "Feminism, Colonialism and Islamophobia: Treacherous Sympathy with Muslim Women," *Qantara.de*, August 18. http://en.qantara.de/Treacherous-Sympathy-with-Muslim-Women/16963c77/index.html.
Allen, C. (2005) *Islamophobia: Contested Concept in the Public Space*, Ph.D. dissertation, Department of Theology, University of Birmingham, Birmingham.
Alloula, M. (1986) *The Colonial Harem (Theory and History of Literature)*, vol. 21, Minneapolis: University of Minnesota Press.
Al-Sini, D. (2011) "The Trouble with Irshad Manji," *Riding the Tiger*, July 14. http://www.ridingthetiger.org/2011/07/14/trouble-with-irshad-manji.
Bravo López, F. (2011) "Towards a Definition of Islamophobia: Approximations of the Early Twentieth Century," *Ethnic and Racial Studies* 34: 556–73.
Brooks, G. (2004) "Double Jeopardy Muslim Women Can't Win: Flogged for Removing the Veil in Islamic Countries, Denied an Education for Keeping It on in Parts Yet They Are Emerging as Islam's Most Passionate Polemicists in the West," *Financial Times*, July 10: 26.
Bullock, K. (2000) "Challenging Media Representations of the Veil: Contemporary Muslim Women's Re-veiling Movement," *American Journal of Islamic Social Sciences* 17(3): 22–53.
——(2002) *Rethinking Muslim Women and the Veil: Challenging Historical and Modern Stereotypes*, Herndon, VA: International Institute of Islamic Thought.
Castillejos, D. (2009) "Escaping the Burqa," Cartoon, *Cartoon Movement*. http://www.cartoonmovement.com/cartoon/349.
Cendrowicz, L. (2010). "Belgium Moves Closer to Europe's First Burqa Ban," *Time*, April 3. http://www.time.com/time/world/article/0,8599,1977350,00.html.
Cervantes, E. A. (2012) "Women in Political Cartoons: How Are Muslim Women Doing in Political Cartoons?," *Muslimah Media Watch*, December 5. http://www.patheos.com/blogs/mmw/2012/01/how-are-muslim-women-doing-in-political-cartoons/.
Chatty, D. (1997) "The Burqa Face Cover: An Aspect of Dress in Southeastern Arabia," in N. Lindisfarne-Tapper and B. Ingham (eds.) *Languages of Dress in the Middle East*, Richmond: Curzon.
Cloud, D. L. (2004) "'To Veil the Threat of Terror': Afghan Women and the 'Clash of Civilizations' in the Imagery of the U.S. War on Terrorism," *Quarterly Journal of Speech* 90(3): 285–306.
Curiel, J. (2005) "Maverick Muslim Women Rip Veil off Religion's Traditional Gender Values," *San Francisco Chronicle*, August 28: F1.

de Wit, P. (2008) *Burka Babes*, Amsterdam: Uitgeverij De Harmonie.

——(n.d.) *Sigmund* official website. http://www.sigmund.nl/?p=burkababes_eng.

Deerin, C. (2004) "When Fear Hits Home," *Scotland on Sunday*, March 21: 16.

Dent, J. (2003) "Hail the New Veil," *The Australian*, December 12: 16.

Dickey, M. (1994) "Images of Muslim Women in Occidental Consciousness: Reality vs. Fiction," Honors thesis, Department of Sociology and Anthropology, Concordia University.

Dowd, M. (2001) "Liberties; Cleopatra and Osama," *New York Times*, November 18: 13.

——(2002) "Driving While Female," *New York Times*, November 17: 11.

El Guindi, F. (1999) *Veil: Modesty, Privacy and Resistance*, Oxford and New York: Berg.

——(2005) "Gendered Resistance, Feminist Veiling, Islamic Feminism," *Ahfad Journal* 22(1): 53–78.

Fahmy, S. (2004) "Picturing Afghan Women: A Content Analysis of AP Wire Photographs during the Taliban Regime and after the Fall of the Taliban Regime," *Gazette: The International Journal for Communication Studies* 66(2): 91–112.

Fernea, E. W. (1965) *Guests of the Sheik: An Ethnography of an Iraqi Village*, New York: Anchor.

Ghannam, J. (2003) "All Eyes on the Homeland in Detroit's Iraqi Community: Hope and Anxiety as Exiles Imagine Post-Hussein Era," *Boston Globe*, April 28: A3.

Gottschalk, P. and G. Greenberg (2008) *Islamophobia: Making Muslims the Enemy*, Lanham, MD: Rowman & Littlefield.

Graham-Brown, S. (1988) *Images of Women: The Portrayal of Women in Photography of the Middle East, 1860–1950*, New York: Columbia University Press.

——(2003) "The Seen, the Unseen, and the Imagined: Private and Public Lives," in R. Lewis and S. Mills (eds.) *Feminist Postcolonial Theory: A Reader*, New York: Routledge, pp. 502–19.

Grim, B. J. and M. S. Karim (2011) "The Future of the Global Muslim Population: Projections for 2010–30," *Pew Research Center Forum on Religion & Public Life*. http://www.pewforum.org/uploadedFiles/Topics/Religious_Affiliation/Muslim/FutureGlobalMuslimPopulation-WebPDF-Feb10.pdf.

Haddad, Y. Y. (2007) "The Post-9/11 *Hijab* as Icon," *Sociology of Religion* 68(3): 253–367.

Harris, S. (2001) "Muslim Mission Just a Walkover," *The Advertiser*, October 5: 2.

Haussegger, V. (2010) "The Burqa is a War on Women," *Age*, May 21. http://www.virginia haussegger.com.au/column_details.php?id=184.

Hoodfar, H. (1993) "The Veil in Their Minds and on Our Heads: The Persistence of Colonial Images of Muslim Women," *RFR/DRF* 22: 5–18.

——(2003) "More than Clothing: Veiling as an Adaptive Strategy," in S. S. Alvi, H. Hoodfar, and S. McDonough (eds.) *The Muslim Veil in North America*, Ontario: Women's Press, pp. 3–40.

Human Rights First (2008) "Violence against Muslims: 2008 Hate Crime Survey." http://www.oic-oci.org/uploads/File/humanrightsfirst-fd-080924-muslims-web.pdf.

Jones, R. P., D. Cox, W. A. Galston, and E. J. Dionne, Jr. (2011) "What It Means to be American: Attitudes in an Increasingly Diverse America Ten Years after 9/11," *Governance Studies at Brookings*. http://www.brookings.edu/~/media/research/files/reports/2011/9/06%20american%20attitudes/0906_american_attitudes.pdf.

Kabbani, R. (1986) *Europe's Myths of the Orient*, Bloomington: Indiana University Press.

Khalid, A. (2011) "Lifting the Veil: Muslim Women Explain Their Choice," *NPR*, April 21. http://www.npr.org/2011/04/21/135523680/lifting-the-veil-muslim-women-explain-their-choice.

Kristoff, N. (2002) "Iraq's Little Secret," *New York Times*, October 1: 31A.

Lacsamana, A. E. (1999) "Colonizing the South: Postmodernism, Desire, and Agency," *Socialist Review* 27: 95–106.

Landsberg, M. (2002) "Lifting the Veil on Women's Enslavement," *Toronto Star*, October 6: A02.

Lean, N. (2012) *The Islamophobia Industry: How the Right Manufactures Fear of Muslims*, New York: Pluto Press.

Lite, J. (2005) "Loosening Their Religion: Sick of Silence, Muslim Women Are Shaking up the Boy's Club," *Daily News*, March 3: 50.

Love, J. (2007) "Cartoon," *Ventura County Star*. http://www.cartoonstock.com/directory/r/religious_symbols_gifts.asp.

Macdonald, M. (2006) "Muslim Women and the Veil," *Feminist Media Studies* 6(1): 7–23.

Marchetti, D. (2003) "A Scary Story of Militants," *Plain Dealer*, June 8: J11.

Martin-Munoz, G. (2010) "The Arab World's Silent Feminist Revolution," *Project Syndicate*, December 9. http://www.project-syndicate.org/commentary/the-arab-world-s-silent-feminist-revolution.

Merali, A. (2006) "'Mad Woman in the Burqa': Muslim Women as Exemplar Feminists," *Hecate* 32(1): 173–98.

Mernissi, F. (2003) "The Meaning of Spatial Boundaries," in Reina Lewis and Sara Mills (eds.) *Feminist Postcolonial Theory*, New York: Routledge, pp. 489–501.

Modood, T. (1992) *Not Easy Being British*, Stoke on Trent: Runnymede Trust & Trentham Books.

Mogahed, D. (2006) "Perspectives of Women in the Muslim World," *The Gallup Center for Muslim Studies*. http://www.gallup.com/press/109699/perspectives-women-muslim-world.aspx.

Mohanty, C. T., A. Russo, and L. Torres (1991) *Third World Women and the Politics of Feminism*, Bloomington: Indiana University Press.

Navarro, L. (2010) "Islamophobia and Sexism: Muslim Women in the Western Mass Media," *Human Architecture: Journal of the Sociology of Self Knowledge* 8(2): 95–114.

Pew Research Center (2007) "Muslim Americans: Middle Class and Mostly Mainstream." http://pewresearch.org/files/old-assets/pdf/muslim-americans.pdf.

Runnymede Trust Commission on British Muslims and Islamophobia (1997) "Islamophobia: A Challenge for All of Us." http://www.runnymedetrust.org/publications/17/32.html.

Ryan, J. (2004) "The Error of Too Much Tolerance," *San Francisco Chronicle*, August 26: B1.

Said, E. (1979) *Orientalism*, New York: Vintage.

Samuel, H. (2011) "Burqa Ban: French Women Fined for Wearing Full-face Veil," *Telegraph*, September 22. http://www.telegraph.co.uk/news/worldnews/europe/france/8781241/Burka-ban-French-women-fined-for-wearing-full-face-veil.html.

Sayare, S. (2012) "Egypt Abuzz as Newsreader on State TV Wears Hijab," *New York Times*, September 2. http://www.nytimes.com/2012/09/03/world/middleeast/egypt-abuzz-as-woman-in-hijab-reads-news-on-state-tv.html?_r=0.

Toynbee, P. (2006 "Only a Fully Secular State Can Protect Women's Rights," *Guardian*, October 17. http://www.guardian.co.uk/commentisfree/2006/oct/17/comment.politics3.

*Washington Post*/ABC (2010) "Cordoba House Controversy Could Cause Political Risks," Poll on the Views of Islam. http://a.abcnews.go.com/images/US/ht_cordoba_house_100908.pdf.

Wikan, U. (1982) *Behind the Veil in Arabia*, Baltimore, MD: Johns Hopkins University Press.

Zick, A., B. Küpper, and A. Hövermann (2011) "Intolerance, Prejudice and Discrimination: A European Report," a study for the Friedrich Ebert Foundation. http://www.fes-gegen-rechtsextremismus.de/pdf_11/FES-Study-Intolerance-main-findings.pdf.

# 36

# Sport, media, and the gender-based insult

## David Rowe

### Sport, masculinization, and feminization

Since the institutional establishment of sport as a regulated, professionalized form of physical activity in the nineteenth century, sport has been a major focus of sex/ gender division and hierarchy. For example, in few other pursuits is highly invasive sex testing conducted in very public circumstances, as occurred recently in the case of the South African runner Caster Semenya (Cooky *et al.* 2012). Sex-based classification is integral to many, if not most, forms of sport, which in turn is the foundation of constructions of gender that, in the main, privilege dominant forms of masculinity over those of femininity (see Scraton and Flintoff 2002). This is not to argue that sport is entirely a male preserve. Many women are skilled participants and enthusiastic spectators. But sport's historical legacy as a sociocultural domain where men place themselves at the center and marginalize women remains resilient in its constructions of celebrated, exclusivist masculinity that both overtly and covertly tends to position femininity as subordinate, peripheral, sexualized, and even contemptible (McKay *et al.* 2000).

Sport remains a male-dominated institution—institutionally, economically, ideologically, and culturally—despite policies dedicated to eradicating sexual and gender inequality. Abundant empirical evidence attests to this inequality, ranging from the ownership and control of sports clubs and associations and the distribution of material rewards in sport, to the differential quantity and quality of media coverage of sportsmen and women (Hartmann and Pfister 2003; Bruce *et al.* 2010). The specific focus here, however, is the gender order inscribed within the language of professional male team contact sport in some instances that have garnered massive media attention. The media are especially important given their role in helping to reveal and circulate how gender power is exercised in male sport's everyday routines. Occasionally, especially during "live" sports contests watched by large and even global audiences, and in subsequent disciplinary and legal proceedings, broadcast footage and commentary across a range of media play key roles in indicating who said what to whom, and in shaping meaning and significance for wider gender relations.

Public evidence is increasing that the gender-based insult is routinely practiced even within those male team sports that are subjected to intense media and public scrutiny, and whose associations are officially mandated to eradicate prejudice and discrimination, and to foster respect among players, officials, and fans (such as the "Respect" and other social responsibility initiatives of Union des Associations Européennes de Football [UEFA], the governing body of European association football).

However, what is perhaps more shocking about the common resort to gender insult as a weapon is that it generally *fails* to shock or to incur widespread condemnation. In stark contrast to the consensually condemned racial insult, the comparative normalization of the sex/gender-based insult is often thrown into sharp relief during media sport scandals arising from confrontations in male team sports, where masculinist insults (based on the assumed innate superiority of aggressive maleness) are revealed as routine constituents of inter-player discourse. This observation by no means implies any diminution of the gravity of the offense of racialized denigration in sport, nor does it try to set up forms of denigration in competition with each other. Indeed, as will be argued on pp. 398–400, "race-" and gender-based insults are not infrequently combined in the exercise of a more comprehensive vilification of sporting opponents, and of those with whom they are materially and symbolically associated (see also Rowe 2010a). Nor do I suggest that sportswomen do not also sometimes insult each other (such as by using the common misogynistic term "slut" or through expressions of "violent femininity"—Gill 2007). The foci of this chapter, however, are the gendered power relationships within and surrounding sport that clearly persist beyond "plain sight" despite professed dedication to the eradication of gender inequality in sport, and in which the media are key players. Here the gender-based insult in sport is analyzed as a form of "power play" exercised through everyday, naturalized masculinization and feminization. It comes to light often only incidentally in pursuit of another kind of offense reported in the news and sports media.

## WAGS, scandals, and other media creations

The media, including the specialist sport and entertainment rounds and "beats" of journalism, are constantly involved in the "patrolling" of masculinity and femininity. For example, the focus on the so-called WAGS (wives and girlfriends) of elite sportsmen (as fictionalized in the now-discontinued British television drama *Footballers' Wives*) can be read as a tracing of the contemporary contours of male and female conjugal roles and, to some degree, as a re-instantiation of a more gendered traditional nuclear family division of labor, albeit one with a distinctively twenty-first-century celebrity consumption orientation. Here the media's concern is often with the "distraction" of elite sportsmen by women and its potentially debilitating impact on men's sports performance. Indeed, the classic patriarchal notion, which received "scientific" credibility in the nineteenth century, that sex with women (it does not contemplate male homosexuality) "drains" men of their athletic vitality continues to be reproduced (Rowe 2010b). Even where the WAG has her own high-profile career, as in the case of Victoria Beckham, wife of the world's most famous association footballer, David Beckham, the arrangement is usually set up as one of competition rather than complementarity or independence.

The tabloid news media, in particular, such as the now-closed British "scandal sheet" the *News of the World*, are deeply implicated in the exposure of cases of infidelity involving prominent sportsmen. Here the use of paparazzi photographers, private investigators, paid "confessions" by female participants, and unsavory or illegal practices, such as "blagging" (paying for confidential private information) and phone hacking, generate media scandals. The resultant prevailing images of promiscuous sportsmen and rapacious women combine prurience and moral condemnation. The most infamous of such male celebrity sport infidelity scandals is that of golfer Tiger Woods, whose scripted televised public apology was the BBC's lead story of the day (February 19, 2010), but there are many others, including basketball's Kobe Bryant and footballers Ryan Giggs and John Terry. Indeed, such scandals may now be said to constitute a media genre in their own right, at the heart of which is a concern with sexual conduct and gendered behavior.

Although these stories have political dimensions (including the politics of image management of heterosexual celebrity families, sexual desire, and gendered norms), they are principally concerned with salacious revelations within the private sphere. Of greater sociopolitical import, perhaps, is the gender-based sport insult that takes place and is partially captured in that manifestation of the mediated public sphere that is live, televised sport.

## Manifestations of masculinist insult discourse in sport

Masculinist insult discourse is mobilized in two common ways in sport. The first is to feminize the opponents by comparing them either to women, especially younger ones ("playing like a girl"), or, at one remove, to homosexual men (through insulting epithets such as "faggot"). The latter practice, alongside homophobia among some sports fans and administrators, and the reluctance of sponsors and advertisers to contract with gay and lesbian athletes, helps explain why sports professionals rarely "come out" (Anderson 2005). This phenomenon can be broadly understood as the exercise of an aggressive hegemonic masculinity (Connell 1987) that posits itself as inherently superior to femininity and to "feminized" forms of masculinity.

The insult involves likening male opponents to women (thereby signifying their athletic inferiority), or casting aspersions, usually of a sexual nature, on significant women in their lives, especially wives, girlfriends, mothers, and sisters (thereby signifying their social inferiority). News media have provided evidence of this practice in forensic detail through transcripts of captured or alleged conversations, but, at least in some of the most highly publicized cases, largely as a byproduct of another transgression. As noted above, in the current era the charge of racism in sport has been taken particularly seriously, it has been in pursuit of racial vilification that gender-based insults have been recorded. Indeed, race and gender may be entwined in significant ways.

One of the most conspicuous examples of this connection concerns the expulsion of the French captain Zinedine Zidane from the field of play for violent conduct during the 2006 FIFA World Cup Final in Germany. The image of Zidane headbutting Italian opponent Marco Materazzi in the chest was prominent across the world's media, alongside detailed speculation of the cause of this act; some newspapers even employed multilingual lip readers. The most dramatic explanation was that Zidane, a self-described "non-practicing Muslim" of Algerian descent, reacted violently when Materazzi called him the "son of a terrorist whore." This alleged insult, combining racial, religious, and sexual offense, was widely condemned in newspapers such as the UK's *Sun*, *Daily Star*, and *Daily Mail*, and, if proven, could be regarded as a case of sexual racism, which I define as combined, mutually reinforcing sexual and racial prejudice that, for example, links sexual promiscuity with "racial" genetic inheritance (Rowe 2010a). However, Materazzi subsequently successfully sued these newspapers for libel after this accusation was deemed unproven by the Disciplinary Committee of FIFA, the world governing body of association football. His only admission was that he had insulted Zidane's sister, although Zidane continued to insist that his mother was also subjected to "very hard words." A BBC interviewer began by saying to Zidane that "everyone" wants to know exactly what Materazzi said:

ZINEDINE ZIDANE:   They were very serious things, very personal things.

INTERVIEWER:   About your mother and your sister?

ZINEDINE ZIDANE:   Yes. They were very hard words. You hear them once and you try to move away. But then you hear them twice, and then a third time. … I am a man and some words are harder to hear than actions. I would rather have taken a blow to the face than hear that.

(BBC 2006: n.p.)

What was actually said in this exchange will never be known comprehensively, but the case suggests what appears to be the common use of gender-based insults in elite male sport.

Association football is by no means the only sport in which this phenomenon is apparent. For example, in early 2008 during a cricket Test match in Sydney, Indian cricketer Harbhajan Singh allegedly called Andrew Symonds, a UK-born Australian cricketer of African Caribbean and white parentage, a "monkey." This confrontation garnered enormous media coverage in India, Australia, and in other cricket-playing countries. It provoked similar attempts at multilingual lip reading to determine what was said: one suggestion was that Singh had actually called Symonds a "teri maki" (a term corresponding to "motherfucker" in Hindi), which had been misheard as "monkey" (Rowe 2011). Here, as with the Zidane–Materazzi case, the defense was that the alleged racial insult was "only" gender based; an offense which, if proven, would have incurred no comparable or, indeed, *any* likely sanction. Because of its standing as the "global game" and claim to be in the forefront of anti-discrimination and prejudice in sport (FIFA 2012), though, conflicts over accusations of vilification in football receive particular media prominence.

A striking example of the phenomenon of alleged racial, and uncontested gender, insults concerns the dispute arising from an on-field confrontation in 2011 between two English Premier League footballers—Liverpool's Luis Suarez and Manchester United's Patrice Evra—after which the latter alleged that he had been racially abused by the former. The following excerpt from the Independent Regulation Commission's disciplinary inquiry into the matter provides the flavor of their exchange:

> 178. Mr Evra stated that the goalmouth incident started when he addressed Mr Suarez, beginning with the phrase "Concha de tu hermana." According to the experts, the literal translation is "your sister's cunt" and it can be taken as a general swear word expressing anger, although the word "concha" is not as taboo as the English word "cunt." It is thus equivalent to "fucking hell" or "fuck me." If directed at someone in particular, it can also be understood as "[you] son of a bitch."
>
> 179. Assuming Mr Suarez responded with "Porque tu eres negro" [author comment: translated into English either as "because you are black" or, as Evra first interpreted it, "because you are a nigger"], this would be interpreted in Uruguay and other regions of Latin America as racially offensive. When the noun is used in the way described by Mr Evra, it is not a friendly form of address, but is used in an insulting way: it is given as the rationale for an act of physical aggression (the foul), as if the person deserved such an attack since they are black.
>
> (Independent Regulatory Commission of the
> Football Association 2011: 47)

In shifting between sexually oriented provocations concerning a male player's female family member and retaliatory racist and other forms of abuse, such documented on-field encounters reveal an underlying form of aggressive, ruthless sporting masculinity that is "writ large" when receiving intensive media coverage. While media commentators often express disapproval, both in reporting official disciplinary proceedings and in published opinion, both sports organizations and journalists tend to downplay the implicit process of masculinization and feminization that occurs through the apparently routine practice of gender-based insult between competitors. For example, in its summary and justification of the suspension of Suarez, the Commission noted:

> 441. The use by a footballer of insulting words, which include reference to another player's colour, is wholly unacceptable. It is wrong in principle. It is also wrong because footballers, such as Mr Suarez, are looked up to and admired by a great many football fans, especially young fans. If professional footballers use racially insulting language on a football pitch, this is likely to have a corrosive effect on young football fans, some of whom are the professional footballers of the future. It also has a potentially damaging effect on the wider football community and society generally.
>
> (Independent Regulatory Commission of the
> Football Association 2011: 109)

While insulting behavior by footballers is deplored, it is only "racially insulting language on a football pitch" that is detailed. Its "corrosive" and "damaging" effects are seemingly limited to the domain of "color," thereby leaving aside questions of gender. The "young football fans" who may become professional footballers are implicitly male, and the potential impact of gender-based abuse on both male *and* female fans/players is not articulated. FIFA's mission statement (2012) states: "We believe it is FIFA's responsibility to foster unity within the football world and to use football to promote solidarity, regardless of gender, ethnic background, faith or culture." Apparently, however, neither FIFA nor its affiliates like UEFA or the FA have much will to engage with gender at the level of everyday abuse among male football players. Notably, few journalists have sought to counteract this situation. British newspapers such as the *Daily Mail* (Lawton 2011) and *Daily Telegraph* (Winter 2011) barely noticed the offensive gendered dimension of their confrontation. As with the Zidane affair, the scandal focused on racism, with sexism treated as a second-order matter. The "race" and gender orders are made clear here, as well as the subordination of the latter to the former in terms of discursive prominence. Just as Materazzi's first-ascribed comments about Zidane's mother were generally focused on the epithet "terrorist" rather than "whore," and the accusation that Singh had called Symonds a "monkey" mitigated by the claim that he might in fact have said "motherfucker" in Hindi, there was apparently little concern about Evra's misogynistic reference to Suarez's sister, or of Materazzi to Zidane's. This muted response to insults such as "son of a bitch" and "motherfucker" used in an all-male sport environment, treating them as banal or in some way inevitable, illustrates the dominance of a certain mode of masculinity in the field of sport that suggests a degree of complicity among the ranks of another male-dominated occupation—sports journalism (Rowe 2007).

In another racial dispute in football, but one that entered a legal rather than a disciplinary process, the English Premier League club Chelsea's captain John Terry was accused of vilifying Queens Park Rangers player Anton Ferdinand by using "threatening, abusive or insulting words or behaviour or disorderly behaviour" likely to cause "harassment, alarm or distress" due to it being "racially aggravated." Once again, the accusation was that one player had combined racism and sexism in a single epithet—"fucking black cunt"—in insulting the other. During *Regina v. John Terry*, at the end of which the Senior District Judge of Westminster Magistrates' Court found the case against Terry unproven (following which the FA charged him in July 2012 with using insulting abusive words and/or behaviors, again highlighting the alleged racial dimension, that led to a fine and a four-match ban), the language used by the antagonists attracted considerable attention. Some newspapers and all broadcast media did not "spell out" the most offensive words used, apart from the one that incurred the allegation in the first instance—"black"; others, such as the *Guardian*, provided an unexpurgated account of what was said. With regard to the positioning of masculinity and femininity in the practice of professional male contact sport, the evidence was illuminating. As collated and laid out in many news stories, such as the one below (although with unusual candor), what might in other domains be regarded as conduct extraordinarily detrimental to respectful relationships between men and women was described as "mandatory":

> The truth is it is not particularly revelatory or shocking that footballers use the kind of language and sexual insults that filled courtroom number one.

Yet hearing the various exchanges dissected in these surroundings brought home just how trashy and puerile it all was. The one thing Terry and Ferdinand agreed upon was that being called "a cunt" was almost mandatory in football. Penny's [the Prosecutor] conclusion was that if referees applied the rule that abusive language merited a red card the average game would last "no longer than 10 minutes."

As well as the "shagging Bridge's missus' stuff" [a reference to a highly pub-licized alleged affair between Terry and a team-mate's partner], Terry said he had regularly heard his mother, Sue, being called a "slag." One of the QPR players had shouted something about her during a post-match coming together between the rival players in the tunnel. But Terry said he had heard this kind of abuse from 40,000 people sometimes. "My mum dated a guy from Liverpool for a while," he said. "The Liverpool fans made up a song that my mum 'loves Scouse cock.'" The average football match was depicted as a hateful place, where the crowds look for weakness and then attack with a zombie mentality.

(Taylor 2012)

This routinization of abuse is distinctly gendered. The indecencies used by players and fans alike construct a gender order in which women, both in the abstract and in roles as significant others, are systematically alienated from sport through the literally offensive use of language as a strategic weapon. The practice of abusive swearing was described as so common as to have become unremarkable for players themselves. Thus, "Mr Ferdinand told the court: 'It's handbags, innit—it's what happens on the pitch,' and said he shook hands with Mr Terry" (BBC 2012). The invocation of women through the "handbag" synecdoche (the object standing for the category "woman") provides another instance of unconscious, reflexive hierarchical gender sorting in sport. Thus, the idea that this everyday object associated with women is ineffectual in physical combat once again symbolically consigns them to the margins of sport, conceived as a domain of potent male warriors and impotent female combatants. This "automatically" produced gender hierarchy seemingly only becomes notable when provocative attacks on mothers, wives, girlfriends, and sisters are revealed in the context of complaints about racial and other forms of vilification. As one sports journalist reported about the Terry–Ferdinand case:

With courtroom deadpan delivery and forensic word-by-word deconstruction, the lingua franca of the pitch lost its pejorative power to shock, displaying instead a terrifying paucity of vocabulary possessed by our multimillionaire sports stars.

"You're an ugly cunt … (pause) … is that one of them [an on-pitch insult]?" inquired Penny of Terry, with unfortunate timing. "Common or garden swearwords, cunt, prick, fuck? That's normal, isn't it?"

Yes, replied Terry. Add in "fat", "ugly", and gestures that indicate bad breath, before the aforementioned C-word. "Cunt is fine," Ferdinand said in his evidence, but not if you added the word black, which took it to a whole new level.

(Conn 2012)

The aforementioned space between what is "fine" and what is at a "whole new level" of offense is to some extent marked also by the comments of two sports journalists, both of whom are from well-regarded broadsheet newspapers, and who found the exchanges between the players "trashy and puerile," with a "paucity of vocabulary," rather than symptomatic of a much more damaging phenomenon—deeply ingrained sexism.

This brief survey of the Terry–Ferdinand and similar cases shows that journalists rarely challenged the normalization of gender-based abuse in sport (in this case football). Indeed, the most telling critique (from a feminist academic) of the language of male sport was found in the letters page of the same newspaper (the *Guardian*) that included the two quotations immediately above, rather than the news or sports sections:

> What strikes me is the indifference with which the usage of the slang term for the female genitals goes without question in society at large. ... While acknowledging that some (not I) might argue there is a hierarchy of "isms," I find it hard to accept that using such derogatory terminology goes unquestioned. The racism is subject to a courtroom challenge, the sexism does not merit a mention.
>
> (Briggs 2012)

The key point here is that, while the news media do routinely decry the linguistic impoverishment and crudity of the gender-based insult in male-dominated sport, they rarely represent it as anything other than a rather unsavory but highly predictable product of a masculinist, competitive sport environment. What they signally fail to do is advance a deeper condemnation that would prompt a more telling analysis of sport's gender order—why is femininity invoked in the context of insulting provocations? And why is there so little concern with the alienation and marginalization of women through the common, if not routine, use of such language among sport and media organizations alike?

## Conclusion: gender and the "lost" media scandal

These conspicuous instances, which have been widely publicized, demonstrate the largely unconscious and unexamined reproduction of sport's historical domination by men. They arguably expose one notable way in which sport is implicated in the construction of asymmetries of masculine and feminine power through their naturalization in mediated popular culture. I selected these examples of gender-based insult in sport that attracted a great deal of media coverage and public attention for two principal reasons—they involved male sporting celebrities and allegations of racism on the field of play. At the time of the alleged offenses, millions of people around the world were watching events transpire in real time or on delay via a range of media devices—mainly television, but also on computer, tablet, and mobile telephone screens. In this sense, despite numerous witnesses, the "truth" of what occurred could not be easily discerned, and could only be teased out laboriously through claim and counterclaim.

These were, therefore, media scandals (Lull and Hinerman 1997) that compromised sport's moral and ethical order. Audiovisual material, media news, commentary and analysis (including the aforementioned multi- and monolingual lip reading), and disciplinary and court transcripts, provided a wealth of detail concerning how professional sportsmen lauded for their athletic prowess conduct themselves in language in practice. In all these cases, the focus of the scandal was racism, an ideology of domination that, like sexism, is also foundational within sport (Carrington 2010). As has already been stated, my emphasis on gender here is by no means an attempt to underplay the seriousness of racism, but is intended to reveal the ways in which one malign expression of power can come to overshadow another. It is clear that sports authorities take racism more seriously than sexism, particularly when one player directly abuses another in racial terms. Sexist abuse is generally at one remove—insulting the female associates of an opponent, or his relationships with them. It could be objected that the words used are simple "equal opportunity" indecencies—for example, evocations of male genitalia, such as "fucking knobhead" and "prick" (the "common or garden swearwords" described in court during the Terry case), were also used. Also, it might be said that women do not need condescending "protection" from "colorful," sexually graphic language; women often use it themselves—including against each other.

However, close attention to what was said—and *how* it was said in the cases described above—exposes the ways in which systematic denigration of women was regarded as normal. Thus, the homosocial environment of male contact sport can be described—at least in some instances and in some sporting contexts—as a site where women can be vilified *in their absence*. Gaye Tuchman's (1978) renowned refinement and application of the concept of "symbolic annihilation" to gender is pertinent here. Yet, crucially, this is an annihilation of a distinctive kind—one in which women are brought into the male sporting arena in language, only to be expelled from it via the association of femininity with degradation. In this respect, men perpetuate their domination of the institution of sport (as administrators and as athletes in most team and many individual sports), and another male-dominated institution, the media (especially the sports media), does little to intervene in this ideological process.

Finally, then, the responsibility of the media is brought into focus. Journalists and other commentators in these cases have consistently focused on the principal, more "spectacular" narrative—concerning racial abuse—but have failed to grasp the seriousness of the "secondary" one—the gender-based insult. The use of such language is treated as deplorable but orthodox and almost banal. As Taylor (2012) noted above, "The truth is it is not particularly revelatory or shocking that footballers use the kind of language and sexual insults that filled courtroom number one." Yet it could be argued that the routine nature of such discourse requires not just resigned disapproval by news media, but a vigorous questioning and challenge. Without such a response by (mostly male) sports journalists, including in the "quality" newspapers, and by journalists on the wider news rounds, criticisms of complacency, dereliction of duty, "herd following," and even complicity gain considerable weight. Such terms are no doubt offensive to journalists. But their reluctance to take offense on behalf of others (especially but not exclusively women) and to challenge the "business as normal" of sporting institutions (principally run by men) has helped install the gender-based insult and its implicit alienation of women as *de rigueur* among some of the most popular and prestigious male contact sports.

# References

Anderson, E. (2005) *In the Game: Gay Athletes and the Cult of Masculinity*, Albany: State University of New York Press.

BBC (BBC Online) (2006) "Zidane Explains," July 12. http://news.bbc.co.uk/sport2/hi/football/world_cup_2006/teams/france/5174758.stm.

——(2012) "John Terry and Anton Ferdinand: Disputed Remarks," July 10. http://www.bbc.co.uk/news/uk-england-18771554.

Briggs, J. (2012) "Letters: Football, Sexism and Homophobia," *Guardian*, July 12. http://www.guardian.co.uk/football/2012/jul/12/football-sexism-homphobia.

Bruce, T., J. Hovden, and P. Markula (eds.) (2010) *Sportswomen at the Olympics: A Global Content Analysis of Newspaper Coverage*, Rotterdam: Sense.

Carrington, B. (2010) *Race, Sport and Politics: The Sporting Black Diaspora*, London: Sage.

Conn, D. (2012) "John Terry Acquitted of Racism but Football Guilty of Too Much Abuse," *Guardian*, July 13. http://www.guardian.co.uk/football/2012/jul/13/john-terry-acquitted-racism?intcmp=239.

Connell, R. W. (1987) *Gender and Power*, Sydney: Allen and Unwin.

Cooky, C., R. Dycus, and S. L. Dworkin (2012) "'What Makes a Woman a Woman?' Versus 'Our First Lady of Sport': A Comparative Analysis of the United States and the South African Media Coverage of Caster Semenya," *Journal of Sport and Social Issues*, doi:10.1177/0193723512447940.

FIFA (2012) *Mission and Statutes*. http://www.fifa.com/aboutfifa/organisation/mission.html.

Gill, F. (2007) "'Violent' Femininity: Women Rugby Players and Gender Negotiation," *Women's Studies International Forum* 30(5): 416–26.

Hartmann, I. and G. Pfister (eds.) (2003) *Sport and Women: Social Issues in International Perspective*, London and New York: Routledge.

Independent Regulatory Commission of the Football Association (2011) *The Football Association and Luis Suarez: Reasons of the Regulatory Commission*. http://www.thefa.com/TheFA/Disciplinary/NewsAndFeatures/2011/~/media/Files/PDF/TheFA/Disciplinary/Written%20reasons/FA%20v%20Suarez%20Written%20Reasons%20of%20Regulatory%20Commission.ashx.

Lawton, M. (2011) "Guilty! Suarez Hit with EIGHT-match Ban and Huge Fine after Liverpool Star Racially Abused Evra," *Mail Online*, December 21. http://www.dailymail.co.uk/sport/football/article-2076452/Luis-Suarez-given-match-ban-race-row.html#ixzz22MBhQF00.

Lull, J. and S. Hinerman (eds.) (1997) *Media Scandals: Morality and Desire in the Popular Culture Marketplace*, Cambridge: Polity.

McKay, J., M. Messner, and D. Sabo (eds.) (2000) *Masculinities, Gender Relations, and Sport*, Thousand Oaks, CA: Sage.

Rowe, D. (2007) "Sports Journalism: Still the 'Toy Department' of the News Media?," *Journalism: Theory, Practice & Criticism* 8(4): 385–405.

——(2010a) "Stages of the Global: Media, Sport, Racialization and the Last Temptation of Zinedine Zidane," *International Review for the Sociology of Sport* 45(3): 355–71.

——(2010b) "Attention La Femme! Intimate Relationships and Male Sports Performance," in L. K. Fuller (ed.) *Sexual Sports Rhetoric: Global and Universal Contexts*, New York: Peter Lang, pp. 69–81.

——(2011) "The Televised Sport 'Monkey' Trial: 'Race' and the Politics of Postcolonial Cricket," *Sport in Society* 14(6): 786–98.

Scraton, S. and A. Flintoff (eds.) (2002) *Gender and Sport: A Reader*, London and New York: Routledge.

Taylor, D. (2012) "John Terry Is Cleared, but Football's Reputation Takes a Battering," *Guardian*, July 12. http://www.guardian.co.uk/football/2012/jul/13/john-terry-cleared-football-reputation?intcmp=239.

Tuchman, G. (1978) "Introduction: The Symbolic Annihilation of Women by the Mass Media," in G. Tuchman, A. K. Daniels, and J. Benét (eds.) *Hearth and Home: Images of Women in the Mass Media*, New York: Oxford University Press, pp. 3–38.

Winter, H. (2011) "The Issue Is Not Why Luis Suarez Said It, But Why Didn't He Know It Would Cause a Storm," *Telegraph*, December 20. http://www.telegraph.co.uk/sport/football/teams/manchester-united/8969367/The-issue-is-not-why-Luis-Suarez-said-it-but-why-didnt-he-know-it-would-cause-a-storm.html.

# Part IV

# MEDIA AUDIENCES, USERS, AND PROSUMERS

# 37

# Subjects of capacity?

## Reality TV and young women

## Laurie Ouellette

In 2009, the US MTV cable network launched the reality series *16 and Pregnant* as a "public education partnership" with the National Campaign to Prevent Teen and Unplanned Pregnancy, a Washington, DC-based nonprofit organization. The spinoff, *Teen Mom*, was launched later the same year with a similar mission of deterring early childbearing. Combining the conventions of observational documentary and teen soap opera, and adding confessionals and graphics to the mix, both productions generated high ratings (and enormous profits), even as they were also framed by public service announcements, therapeutic after-shows, study guides, and interactive websites emphasizing their purpose as "teachable moments" and "cautionary tales." As multiple seasons and sequels with new casts appeared, the "real-life" experiences of pregnant teenagers and young mothers became a staple theme of MTV programming, providing the raw material to encourage responsible sexual practices and life planning.

This chapter critically analyzes the partnership to educate the MTV audience as a means to reduce the rate of teenage pregnancy in the United States. My aim is not to dismiss the progressive possibilities of the initiative, but rather to situate it within institutional efforts to shape, reform, and "govern" television audiences and to unpack the political rationalities, gender dynamics, and contradictions involved in this mission. By treating teenage pregnancy as a problem to be solved by teaching young female television viewers to conduct themselves as "subjects of capacity" (McRobbie 2007), MTV and its partners downplay broader societal factors such as access to reproductive healthcare and conservative assaults on legal abortion and school-based sex education programs. However well intended, enlisting reality television as a tool of family planning also further intensifies the self-regulation of femininity in postfeminist neoliberal societies (McRobbie 2007, 2008). The campaign to discourage women from bearing children until they are self-sufficient and "responsible" goes hand in hand with the downsizing of federal welfare programs intended to assist low-income women and children in the United States since the 1990s and conveys the message that policies created to protect the rights of pregnant teenagers to public education and social services are no longer needed. MTV and its nonprofit partners define the appropriate choices and life trajectories for *all* women in middle-class terms that value delayed parenthood (Solinger 2000 [1992], 2001), and put the onus for achieving this version of female success on individuals conceived as the managers of their own fates and fortunes (Rose 1996) regardless of class, race, and ethnic differences. In this way, *16 and Pregnant* and *Teen Mom* discourage collective action of any kind, including feminist organizing for social change.

To understand the power dynamics of reality programs like *16 and Pregnant* and *Teen Mom*, a brief discussion of television audiences and the shifting concept of public service will be helpful. Toward that end, the following section situates MTV's partnership with the National Campaign to Prevent Teen and Unplanned Pregnancy within a broader history of efforts to guide, shape, and govern audiences, from the classic age of public service broadcasting to the fusion of commercial logic and citizenship training. I show how US reality television in particular has been stitched into dispersed campaigns to "empower" self-sufficient and responsible citizens, setting the stage for more analysis of "teachable moments" aimed specifically at young women and girls.

## Governing the audience

While *16 and Pregnant* and *Teen Mom* are conceived and packaged as commercial entertainment, MTV and its partners also accentuate the problem-solving nature of the series, going so far as to claim that reality television can be a highly effective form of birth control when it allows viewers to "see up close" and to "practically feel how difficult the whole process is" (Bates 2010). At a time when federal and state welfare programs intended to assist low-income people have been slashed and funding for contraception and abortion is under fire in the US due to conservative pressures, the notion that reality television can reduce pregnancy rates rests on having "teens demonstrate to their peers how hard it is to become responsible for a baby before you're really responsible for yourself." Cameras "follow the young mothers-to-be as they make tough decisions about their lives, like dropping out of high school, either because it's too exhausting or to escape being gossiped about." The viewer goes right into the delivery room, where plenty of "whimpers, gasps and grunts" convey the message that labor is painful. In the end, "pregnancy is the easy part—it's the parenthood that's really, really difficult," explains the National Campaign to Prevent Teen and Unplanned Pregnancy (Bates 2010). This point is further emphasized by "take away" messages in which the female characters speak directly to the audience and by televised therapy sessions with the cast aired after the episodes.

By showing the emotional, financial, and physical difficulties of early childbearing, *16 and Pregnant* and *Teen Mom* are apparently assumed to enable viewers (especially young women) to reflect on the costs, risks, and challenges of getting pregnant and plan their sexual behavior and life trajectories accordingly. To facilitate this, MTV also directs viewers to discussion templates, supplementary information, self-reflection exercises, quizzes, educational games (such as My Paper Boyfriend), and other digital resources provided by the National Campaign to Prevent Teen and Unplanned Pregnancy. Importantly, this pedagogical mode of address coexists within a dominant array of MTV programming (including other reality programs such as *Jersey Shore* and *The Real World*) in which scantily clad young women and men hang around in hot tubs and on the beach, party and "hook up" on a casual basis, usually with little reflection on birth control, let alone life plans. Women bear the burden of these mixed messages: While they are granted increased freedom to engage in sexual activity outside of marriage, they are also conceived as the primary subjects of corrective initiatives (such as *16 and Pregnant* and *Teen Mom*) that hold them responsible for their fertility (McRobbie 2007) and the long-term consequences of their sexual behaviors and choices (Ouellette forthcoming). Before examining this burden in more detail, considering how institutional constructions of the audience set the stage for particular power dynamics and contradictions is important.

In *Desperately Seeking the Audience* (1991), Ien Ang reminds us that the "audience" is an institutional construct—an abstraction used by television for its own purposes (see also Hartley 1992). This happens differently in commercial and public service broadcasting. Advertising-supported channels (such as MTV) have historically conceived their audience as a market to be "captured," whereas public broadcasters (such as the BBC in the United Kingdom or PBS in the United States) have conceived their audience as a public that must be "reformed, educated and informed" (Ang 1991: 28–9). The commercial model approaches programming as a means to attract the eyeballs of consumers; the public service model approaches programming as a "cultural technology" for achieving particular social and educational objectives, often related to liberal democratic ideals, such as creating an educated, cultured, and informed citizenry. Although classic public service aims are different from the imperative to "win" an audience for advertisers and shareholders, they are not necessarily less controlling. As Ang contends, there's a fine line between enlightenment and social management when television's purpose is to reform the public so that it can "better perform its democratic rights and duties" (1991: 28–9; see also Ouellette 2002).

MTV's partnership with the National Campaign to Prevent Teen and Unplanned Pregnancy combines elements of commercial and public service broadcasting. The commercial cable network conceives of the audience for all its programming, including *16 and Pregnant* and *Teen Mom*, as a market to be captured. At the same time, it works with the nonprofit agency to shape, guide, and improve a subset of the public—in this case, girls and young women. As the role of the state in the care and training of citizens has decreased under neoliberalism, corporations are expected to take up these roles. What Andrew Barry calls "ethical capitalism" (2004) has come to bear on the market-driven US television industry, as a range of networks and cable channels take up "do good" agendas that often correlate with the political rationales of privatization, the outsourcing of state powers and responsibilities, and personal responsibilization (Ouellette 2012). While broadcast and cable networks in the US are no longer required to provide formal public service programming as a result of deregulatory policies, many have nonetheless embraced low-cost educational and problem-solving objectives that can be woven into high-rated reality entertainment. This helps differentiate and brand channels as ethical and socially responsible in a cluttered media environment, at a time when problems ranging from breast cancer to environmental destruction are being taken up as high-profile causes by market-driven corporations. Often, the US television industry relies on private and public non-profit agencies to legitimate and manage its cause-oriented and educational agendas, a task that often includes disseminating supplementary resources online. Working hand in hand with the nonprofit sector, US television has in this sense become stitched into a neoliberal model of governing that sees the market as the best space for managing problems, and values commercially oriented public–private partnerships over direct state involvement in the social—including tax-funded public broadcasting.

Enlisting reality entertainment as a venue for problem solving and the production of citizens who can thrive under neoliberal conditions requires some unpacking in that reality television is often considered the antithesis of public service television. For instance, John Corner sees the surge of "factual entertainment" as a consequence of the demise of the public service tradition worldwide (2002; see also Born 2006). By fusing the conventions of soap opera, sitcoms, and other entertainment genres with news and documentary, reality entertainment downplays and "diverts" audiences from earlier civic objectives (such as citizenship formation), Corner contends. This may be true, but there's more to the story. If we are moving toward a "post-documentary" television culture, global trends of deregulation, public sector downsizing, and privatization have encouraged the development of other cultural technologies that can guide and shape citizens in new ways. In the United States, partnerships between commercial media industries, public agencies, and nonprofit organizations advancing objectives ranging from healthy eating to employment to recycling have proliferated. Within this context, many of the civic "functions" ascribed to the public service tradition have been radically reinterpreted and integrated into reality entertainment formats; 16 and Pregnant and Teen Mom exemplify these developments.

In Better Living through Reality TV: Television and Post-Welfare Citizenship (2008), James Hay and I argue that commercial reality entertainment plays a central role in circulating instructions, resources, techniques, and scripts for "good citizenship" in a free-market society such as the United States, where federal welfare policies since the 1990s have sought to reduce public assistance to the needy and personal responsibility for one's own welfare is legislated as a civic requirement. Many reality programs address their audience as consumers of voyeurism, affect, and spectacle, and, at the same time, as subjects who must be educated and reformed to meet the changing demands of neoliberal citizenship. This dual address is not surprising, given that reality television took cultural form amidst the neoliberal policies and reforms of the 1990s and beyond, including welfare reform, the outsourcing of state services, and rising expectations of personal responsibility. I suggest that the application of documentary techniques to the performance and evaluation of daily life makes reality television entertainment useful to strategies of "governing at a distance" that de-emphasize state responsibility and require us all to avoid dependency on government and manage our own health, prosperity, and well-being. In neoliberal societies such as the US, where the expectation is that corporations, nonprofits, and individuals can manage sociality more effectively and efficiently than the public sector, reality television's human subjects provide the basis of lessons on citizenship that reinforce these reforms.

The National Campaign to Prevent Teen and Unplanned Pregnancy legitimates the pedagogical value of 16 and Pregnant and Teen Mom, and attempts to influence and maximize the "effects" of the programs by linking viewers to a suggested interpretive framework and calls to action. Study guides and resources circulated through the National Campaign's websites and teen-oriented blogs downplay the commercial packaging of the programs and the pleasures they may offer viewers. These materials encourage viewers to evaluate the "real-life" conduct and relationships depicted on screen, weigh the costs of pregnancy for the characters and society, and reflect on their own behavior and life plans. These materials engage with audiences as a means of producing good citizen subjects who do not depend on society or undermine their potential by having children at a young age. While viewers are also directed to websites that do provide more practical information about birth control, the National Campaign's mission is not focused on facilitating access (the organization does not distribute or fund contraception). The main purpose of the study materials is to observe and evaluate others as a form of self-regulation. The following excerpt from a 16 and Pregnant study guide illustrates how a new configuration of public service hinges on the translation of specific objectives into the ethics and choices of individuals:

> Being a teen parent makes it a lot harder to reach your educational and financial goals. Is Gary ready to be the sole provider for his family? Will Amber be able to graduate from high school or go to college? More than half of teen moms never graduate from college and fewer than 2% finish college by age 30. How would it be different if they had waited a few more years before starting a family? Have you ever thought about how getting pregnant and having a baby might affect your future plans?
> (National Campaign to Prevent Teen and Unplanned Pregnancy n.d.a)

The implied "you" in this passage is female. On 16 and Pregnant and Teen Mom, and in the materials distributed online, boyfriends are shown to be immature, uncommitted, and unprepared to take responsibility for children (Gary in this episode is "addicted" to video games). The teenage mother is assumed to bear the final responsibility (and personal sacrifices) of childbearing. This gendering of responsibility—along with class and racial inequalities disavowed by the emphasis on individual choice and behavior—will be explored shortly. I first note the important similarities between US reality productions such as these and a more established attempt to educate television (and radio) audiences as a means to regulate the female body: the entertainment-education tradition.

## Mobilizing the audience

Entertainment-education refers to efforts by nonprofit agencies, researchers, and governments to use popular-culture techniques to disseminate information and guidance (often involving reproduction and health) to audiences in the developing world. This tradition is different from public broadcasting, which claims to provide educational and cultural resources for participation in democracy—a broad mission that has historically involved providing socially legitimated "sober" alternatives to mass amusements (Corner 2002). The behavioral objectives of entertainment-education are more specific and are often related to health, sanitation, family planning, and population control. Mass cultural forms are deployed as the "bait" for integrated educational messages in an attempt to bring about measurable attitudinal and behavioral changes in specifically targeted audiences. Organizations such as Population Communications International have long deployed radio and television soap opera to promote aims such as sexual responsibility and the use of birth control as a component of global public health campaigns (Greene and Breshears 2010). Similar to the MTV programs discussed here, proponents of entertainment-education embrace cultural conventions associated with a feminized mass audience: melodramatic narratives, strong emotional identifications, "realistic characters and plot lines that incorporate local beliefs and concerns" as instrumental to the conveyance of "facts" and the promotion of healthy behavior (2010: 189). In this respect, the "governance of women's reproductive and sexual health" hinges on the ability of "biopolitical media industries to transform women into media audiences" (2010: 187). Only as audiences for genres such as soap opera are women thought to be "knowable" and "targetable" as subjects of reform. In the entertainment-education tradition, mass cultural techniques are believed to be especially useful and necessary instruments for influencing uneducated female populations, and this assumption underscores the National Campaign to Prevent Teen and Unplanned Pregnancy's endorsement of and collaboration with 16 and Pregnant and Teen Mom as well.

Unlike the entertainment-education tradition, MTV's partnership with the National Campaign to Prevent Teen and Unplanned Pregnancy hinges on the possibilities of media interactivity. They do not assume the audience will necessarily absorb the desired message of the programs; supplemental online resources are also provided to encourage pedagogical and self-reflexive viewing practices. 16 and Pregnant and Teen Mom viewers are prompted to become "active" subjects who track down more information, visit websites, discuss the programs with their parents and/ or adults such as educators, and engage in self-shaping strategies. Media convergence enables an intensified relay between television audiences and citizen subjects who are called upon to "empower" themselves using the interactive resources available to them. This activity takes place within the framework of the MTV brand. In this sense nonprofit partners such as the National Campaign and TV viewers are also enlisted to help brand MTV as a socially conscious and responsible media corporation in the absence of formal public service mandates.

The growth of social marketing is also relevant here. Like entertainment-education, social marketing campaigns attempt to reform subjects in specific and measurable behaviorist ways, such as getting them to quit smoking (Balnaves and O'Regan 2002). Usually organized as collaborations between the commercial sector and nonprofit agencies, social marketing campaigns identify "audiences" in the hopes of intervening in their attitudes and behavior (2002: 19). Applying the techniques of advertising and promotion to the conduct of audiences, these campaigns are technologies of "subjectification": "targeted populations, who are simultaneously audiences, can be expected, if the campaign is successful, to diffuse, multiply and facilitate the take up of the behavioral norms and values being promoted" (2002: 19). Social marketing is assumed to be particularly effective in contexts where objectives are transparent, and audiences are invited to become "co-creators" of governmental objectives. In the US, social marketing has been integrated into reality entertainment promoting weight loss, recycling, delayed parenting, and other social objectives through the convergence of programming and interactive technologies, as with 16 and Pregnant and *Teen Mom*. What vary are the objectives, the targeted audiences/subjects, the agencies involved, and the political rationalities upon which the campaigns rest. I now turn to the specificity of these issues.

## The new sexual contract

On many MTV reality programs (including *The Real World* and *Jersey Shore*), young women are encouraged to flaunt their bodies and engage in (often casual) sexual activity while the cameras roll. This represents a partial shift away from standard mechanisms of female objectification and the "double standard." Women on these shows are not shamed for being sexually active. In some cases they outperform and "overpower" men in their sexual desires and prowess. Whether this constitutes a gain for women or merely a marketing ploy is not the subject of this chapter. My point is that profound anxieties about and attempts to qualify and "correct" these messages have coalesced around young women. If the women of reality television appear to enjoy a new sense of sexual pleasure and independence, initiatives like *16 and Pregnant* and *Teen Mom* suggest that such "freedom" hinges on young women's capacities to manage their sexual reproduction and life trajectories. Together, these strands of reality entertainment enforce what Angela McRobbie (2007) has termed the "new social contract."

McRobbie (2007) observes that having a "well-planned life" has become a requirement of femininity in neoliberal Western democracies. If some women have made gains in consumer visibility, access to work and education, and sexual independence, these hinge on a "normative" expectation of gainful employment as well as control over one's fertility. This new sexual contract is underscored by a "posting" logic in which social movements (feminism, civil rights) are assumed to have done their jobs, and all women are assumed capable of achieving gender-blind notions of "independence and self-reliance." The paradox is that doing so involves endless "self-monitoring," and in times of stress "therapy, counseling or guidance," for now more than ever young women are "intensively managed subjects of post-feminist, gender-aware biopolitical practices of new governmentality," says McRobbie. Within this context, the concept of "planned parenthood" become an imperative to "avoid early maternity" in order to become gainfully employed and economically self-sufficient and help "solve the welfare crisis" by avoiding state dependency (2007: 701). MTV's partnership with the National Campaign to Prevent Teen and Unwanted Pregnancy both exemplifies and contributes to these trends.

The Clinton administration created the National Campaign to Prevent Teen and Unplanned Pregnancy in 1996 as a component of welfare reform legislation (no public funding was involved). The 1996 Personal Responsibility Act formally ended welfare as an "entitlement" in the name of empowering citizens to help themselves, and teenage pregnancy was posited as a national epidemic closely linked to welfare dependency. A central component of the legislation involved helping "young people make responsible choices and delay parenting until they are financially and emotionally ready," in the words of then president Bill Clinton. This objective was joined by the mandate for everyone—whether male, female, young, old, white, black—to take responsibility for their own fates and fortunes. The pregnant teenager was characterized as someone who had failed to plan her life properly (including preparation for lifelong employment) but could no longer depend on the state for assistance.

Distancing itself from struggles over healthcare, control over one's body, access to abortion, funding for contraception, and other issues emphasized by feminists and organizations such as Planned Parenthood, the National Campaign to Prevent Teen and Unplanned Pregnancy embarked on a mission of curbing teenage pregnancy in the service of "reducing out of wedlock births, improving family well being, reducing tax payers burdens, reducing the need for abortion, reducing family turmoil and relationship conflict and helping women and men better plan their futures" (National Campaign to Prevent Teen and Unplanned Pregnancy n.d.b). By discussing teenage activity and endorsing birth control, the organization provided an alternative to conservative "abstinence until marriage" sex education policies that took hold in the United States in the 1980s. But it downplayed structural issues (including struggles over school policies) and perpetuated the neoliberal shift away from collective rights and a public safety net to rising expectations of personal responsibility and self-regulation.

The campaign's mission also exemplifies the shift away from the moral condemnation of premarital sexual activity (especially for girls and women) to a focus on personal development and citizenship training. Building on Nikolas Rose's (1996) suggestion that traditional codes of morality are declining, giving way to a rising emphasis on "ethics or work on the self," Sara Bragg recognizes the potentialities of an approach that invites young people to engage with themselves and take responsibility for their actions. However, she also cautions that the new "ethical" orientation of sex education, operating as it does within a neoliberal context, may not serve girls well (2006: 548–9). In the wake of diminished social programs and public support systems, approaches to sex education that regulate the interiority of young women, "inviting the display of the self and experiences, can easily become part of the same technology through which self-regulating and responsible individuals are created rather than a critique of such practices" (2006: 549). The "at risk" girl shadows the "can do" (educated, sexually empowered, confident) girl and she is "more harshly stigmatized and judged for her failure in getting pregnant given the opportunities allegedly available to young women now," Bragg points out (2006: 548). If young women do not pursue adoption, they are further subjected to judgments. As Ricki Solinger points out, an economic grid determines who is considered "fit" to be a mother: only those women who can afford to support a child and pay for middle-class "advantages" are thought to be appropriate consumers of "motherhood status" (2000: 239).

While the female subjects of 16 and Pregnant and Teen Mom frequently confess their failure to use birth control to parents and friends (one suspects these explanations are prompted by MTV), no moral shame for premarital sexual activity is bestowed upon them. Illustrating Bragg's point, the MTV productions define the "problem" of teen pregnancy as a matter of life planning. This approach is even more evident in the public service announcements, therapy check-ups, study guides, and online resources surrounding the shows. MTV does link the programs to National Campaign to Prevent Teen and Unplanned Pregnancy websites (including it'syoursexlife.org) that provide information for avoiding pregnancy and STD testing, and it has done this more as the seasons have progressed. But this is linked to the more fundamental objectives of instilling better choice-making and personal responsibility. Significantly, the choices made available to young women as subjects of lessons in capable life planning do not include abortion. Only one "very special" episode of *16 and Pregnant* has dealt with abortion, and the study materials downplay this option. No attention is paid to the availability (or not) of high-school programs, healthcare services, and public resources for teenage mothers. Adoption, on the other hand, is strongly advocated across the programs as the sufficient and rewarding future.

Racial and class inequalities are constructed as personal failures. On *16 and Pregnant* and *Teen Mom*, racial inequalities are presumed nonexistent and stereotypes of the black welfare mother are avoided. Socioeconomic hierarchies are similarly disavowed. The shows' regular inclusion of white middle-class girls suggests that anyone can get pregnant, but the difference between the viewer (the subject of capacity) and teenage mothers who fail to manage their situations evokes the binary construction of "can do" and "at risk" girls. Troubled female characters who drop out of high school, get into fights, and battle depression, alcoholism, smoking, run-ins with the police, and clashes with child welfare agencies tend to come from lower-income families. These characters represent the margins of the new governmentality discussed by McRobbie (2007). Conversely, the pregnant subjects who do graduate high school, attend college, and are recognized as good mothers tend to have educated parents who help out, family houses, cars, and other advantages. While class is an implied source of generational pathology, the capacity to overcome the obstacle of early parenting is presented as the result of individual behavior and choice. As subjects of capacity, young women are held solely accountable for their successes as well as their failures.

## Conclusion

Despite their potentially helpful progressive dimensions, campaigns to enlist reality entertainment as a solution to the problem of teenage pregnancy come at a high cost. MTV's partnership with the National Campaign to Prevent Teen and Unplanned Pregnancy de-emphasizes structural reforms (such as maintaining federal funding for Planned Parenthood, a national organization committed to providing affordable healthcare and abortion services) and places the onus to avoid pregnancy and delay parenting on individuals. The concept of "planned parenthood" (McRobbie 2007) has indeed become an imperative that is closely bound to postfeminist contradictions and middle-class norms about delayed parenting, as well as assumptions about personal responsibility in the age of shrinking social programs for pregnant teenagers and low-income families. MTV's ability to simultaneously make visible and profit from human subjects living out the realities of neoliberal capitalism brand it as committed to socially conscious goals, representing the changing face of public service television in the United States. *16 and Pregnant* and *Teen Mom* claim to empower female television viewers to become "subjects of capacity" by avoiding the mistakes of others and making the right choices about reproduction. However, these programs and the partners who support them discourage these same viewers from forming alliances with others in the ongoing struggle to secure access to legal abortion, affordable healthcare, and progressive sex education in the United States.

# References

Ang, I. (1991) *Desperately Seeking the Audience*, New York: Routledge.

Balnaves, M. and T. O'Regan (2002) "Governing Audiences," in M. Balnaves, T. O'Regan, and J. Sternberg (eds.) *Mobilising the Audience*, St. Lucia, Queensland: University of Queensland Press, pp. 10–28.

Barry, A. (2004) "Ethical Capitalism," in W. Larner and W. Walters (eds.) *Global Governmentality*, London: Sage, pp. 195–211.

Bates, K. (2010) "MTV's *Teen Mom* Makes for Teaching Moments," National Public Radio, August 10. http://www.wbur.org/npr/128626258/mtvs-teen-mom-makes-for-teaching-moments.

Born, G. (2006) "Digitalising Democracy," in J. Lloyd and J. Seaton (eds.) *What Can Be Done? Making the Media and Politics Better*, Oxford: Blackwell, pp. 102–23.

Bragg, S. (2006) "Young Women, the Media and Sex Education," *Feminist Media Studies* 6(4): 546–51.

Corner, J. (2002) "Performing the Real: Documentary Diversions," *Television New Media* 3(3): 255–69.

Greene, R. W. and D. Breshears (2010) "Biopolitical Media: Population, Communications International, and the Governing of Reproductive Health," in L. Reed and P. Saukko (eds.) *Governing the Female Body: Gender, Health, and Networks of Power*, Buffalo, NY: State University of New York Press, pp. 186–205.

Hartley, J. (1992) *Tele-ology: Studies in Television*, New York: Routledge.

McRobbie, A. (2007) "Top Girls: Young Women and the Post-Feminist Sexual Contract," *Cultural Studies* 21(4–5): 718–37.

——(2008) *The Aftermath of Feminism: Gender, Culture and Social Change*, London: Sage.

National Campaign to Prevent Teen and Unplanned Pregnancy (n.d.a) *16 and Pregnant: Season 1 Discussion Guides*. http://www.thenationalcampaign.org/resources/pdf/16-and-preg-discussion-guide.pdf.

——(n.d.b) "Responsible Behavior, Responsible Policies." http://www.thenationalcampaign.org/about-us/default.aspx.

Ouellette, L. (2002) *Viewers Like You? How Public TV Failed the People*, New York: Columbia University Press.

——(2012) "Citizen Brand: ABC and the Do Good Turn in U.S. Television," in R. Mukherjee and S. Banet-Weiser (eds.) *Commodity Activism: Cultural Resistance in Neoliberal Times*, New York: New York University Press, pp. 57–75.

——(forthcoming) "It's Not TV, It's Birth Control: Reality Television and the 'Problem' of Teenage Pregnancy," in B. Weber (ed.) *Reality Gendervision*, Durham, NC: Duke University Press.

Ouellette, L. and J. Hay (2008) *Better Living through Reality TV: Television and Post-Welfare Citizenship*, Malden, MA: Blackwell.

Rose, N. (1996) "Governing 'Advanced' Liberal Democracies," in A. Barry, T. Osbourne, and N. Rose (eds.) *Foucault and Political Reason: Liberalism, Neo-Liberalism and Rationalities of Government*, Chicago, University of Chicago Press, pp. 37–64.

Solinger, R. (2000 [1992]) *Wake up Little Susie: Single Pregnancy and Race before Roe v. Wade*, New York: Routledge.

——(2001) *Beggars and Choosers: How the Politics of Choice Shapes Adoption, Abortion, and Welfare in the United States*, New York: Hill and Wang.

# 38

# Telenovelas, gender, and genre

## *Esther Hamburger*

Brazilian telenovelas are prime-time soaps broadcast Monday through Saturday on commercial television. Unlike daytime soap operas, telenovelas have clear narrative beginnings and endings, with each story typically lasting from six to eight months. Although the recent popularization of DVDs, cable television, and the internet has diversified television, telenovelas remain the most popular and profitable national television genre. From 1976 onward, Brazilian television companies have exported telenovelas; the genre has become one of the most successful in the world. Although in Brazil male and female audiences watch telenovelas, the genre remains defined in gendered terms as feminine by producers, market researchers, and audiences. While their narratives contribute to shifting notions around gender roles, issues such as abortion remain taboo.

The different meanings telenovelas mobilize have through time prompted scholars around the world and across a range of academic disciplines to research the genre. They are of academic interest for their unique capacity to incorporate elements of popular culture—such as *literatura de cordel*, literally "string literature"—into an industrial product (Rowe and Schelling 1991). The potential political influence of telenovelas on audiences has been a recurrent topic of academic discussion (Mattelart and Mattelart 1990; Skidmore 1993; Vink 1988). Synergy between telenovelas, shifting gender relations and consumerism have also been described (Almeida 2003, 2012; Hamburger 1999, 2005).

Cinema is intrinsically related to the development of modern life (Charney and Schwartz 1995). Miriam Hansen (1999) coined the term *vernacular modernism* to refer to the mass appeal of Hollywood cinema, with its connection to consumerism, the production of taste and fashion, and the emergence of a gendered public sphere. In so doing Hansen has connected industrialized modernism to avant-garde modernist forms. In countries like Brazil, telenovelas can be understood in relation to Hansen's idea of vernacular modernism; these narratives are related to consumerism, to didactic display of technologies, and new means of transportation and communication. They are also in synergy with shifting notions of gender relations. With few exceptions the genre has reproduced race discrimination by favoring white casts (Araújo 2000).

This chapter discusses how telenovelas tend to blur gender and genre boundaries. They represent a typically feminine popular culture form which has dominated televisual prime time around the world, with storylines that often mobilize the nation.

In so doing, besides mobilizing national and transnational media fluxes, they provide suggestive material to question the binaries of feminine and masculine, melodrama and newscast, private and public, mass culture and modernism (Huyssen 1986). This chapter surveys the workings of telenovelas in an attempt to map this virtual space with its forms of gendered public life. I first discuss the history of television and the telenovela in Brazil and then look at the practices involved in their production, such as the proto interactive feedback process and audience control practices. Next, I look at the expansion of the feminine in telenovelas over time to raise questions about previous research on the genre and to suggest future research on the transnational dimensions of telenovela production and reception.

## Background history of television and telenovelas in Brazil

### Networks

On September 18, 1950, radio and newspaper tycoon Assis Chateaubriand launched television in Brazil. He named the country's first network Tupi after his radio network (Tupi being the main native population in Brazil). Although Tupi remained the dominant network through the 1950s and 1960s, other commercial stations appeared, including TV Rio, Bandeirantes, Record, and Excelsior. Even though the number of broadcasters increased rapidly, the number of households equipped with television sets did not initially follow at the same speed. For 20 years, television remained a restricted medium (Hamburger 1998).

Only after 1964, when a military coup imposed an authoritarian, nationalist government that lasted until 1985, did television consolidate into an industry (Ortiz 1987). The military considered television useful in supporting its doctrines of "national integration" and "national security." The government helped to foster and consolidate the medium, providing the microwave infrastructure for national broadcasting (1969), introducing PAL-M, a national color system (1973), and satellite communication. During the 1970s and 1980s, television reached large portions of the country, and the number of households with television began to significantly increase (Hamburger 1998).

The government also favored and helped to fund the "development" of a consumer market. Television advertisements helped to sell a wide range of consumer goods, contributing to the "modernization" of Brazil. In parallel to what was happening in theater, cinema, and music, the government controlled television content through rigid censorship. In the capital, Brasilia, a team of censors were responsible for approving television scripts before they were produced. Telenovela writers such as Gilberto Braga reported frequently traveling to Brasília to negotiate cuts in his scripts (Almeida and Araújo 1995).

In 1965, Roberto Marinho, owner of a Rio de Janeiro radio and newspaper group, inaugurated Globo Network. Globo extended Excelsior's first efforts in formalizing and professionalizing contracts and relations between television stations, their employees, advertising agents, research institutes, and government. In the 1970s, Globo became the most watched and the most profitable television network, a position it retains today. Globo established a fixed program grid that interspersed telenovelas with the news. In 1969, for the first time Brazilians in different regions of the country, and across class, age, and gender, shared the experience of receiving the same news and telenovelas. At that time illiteracy was still high, and radio was mainly local.

In 1980 Tupi went bankrupt. In 1981, the military granted the vacant frequency to Sílvio Santos, who founded SBT (Brazilian Television System). SBT broadcasts imported Latin American titles, including *Maria del Barrio* (1995–6). In 1983, Manchete Network began broadcasting on the frequency once occupied by Excelsior. In the early 1990s, Manchete briefly represented a threat to Globo's hegemony with a series of telenovelas. However, in 1999 it also went bankrupted and ceased broadcasting. In the early 2000s, Record Network, run by the fundamentalist Universal Church, was ranked as the second most popular national network due to, among other things, its production of telenovelas.

### Telenovelas

The first Brazilian telenovela was *Sua Vida me Pertence* (1951), aired twice a week on Tupi Network. In 1963, Excelsior Network introduced the Monday through Saturday prime-time telenovela slot. The format was immediately adopted by rival networks and marked the ascension of the transnational genre. Scripts written in one country would be rewritten and remade according to the number of installments and specific censorship and cultural policies in others. The first daily telenovela, *2–5499 Ocupado* (1963), was adapted in Brazil from an Argentine telenovela.

In 1964, TV TUPI and TV Rio aired *O Direito de Nascer*, adapted from a Cuban original script that had already been produced on both radio and television elsewhere. A transnational circuit of scripts was still in place when Globo hired Cuban exile Gloria Magadan to head the first Dramaturgy Department inside a network. Magadan insisted on writing and directing stories that were set in faraway places and times. In 1969, Globo fired Magadan, replacing her with Daniel Filho. Under his direction, Globo started to produce prime-time daily contemporary series that touched on current issues: The Brazilian telenovela sought "realism" as opposed to the "melodrama" made in other Latin American countries (Ortiz *et al.* 1988). In 1968, the Tupi Network aired *Beto Roquefeller*, an original Brazilian story that experimented with contemporary times, informal dialogue, and well-known places in São Paulo. *Beto Roquefeller* eschewed the heavy dramatic tone of its Latino relatives, inspiring the growth of "realist" Brazilian programs.

By the 1970s, telenovelas found international recognition (Marques de Melo 1991). Their increasingly global export suggested the possibility of diversification of transnational flows of information and culture (Varis 1988). At first, Brazil exported telenovelas to Portugal, then to several other capitalist countries in Latin America and eventually to socialist ones such as Cuba, China, and the Soviet Union. European and North American countries also imported the popular product. In the same decade, qualitative and quantitative audience research became central to the development of the television industry. Over the years, research has tended to be undertaken with affluent, metropolitan female viewers, who are considered to be important consumers. As such, quantitative ratings and audience opinion centrally shape the production of telenovelas, which privileges the program tastes of middle-class female urban viewers (Almeida 2003; Hamburger 1999, 2005; Hamburger and Almeida 2003, forthcoming).

## Researching the telenovela

Examination of the field of research on the telenovela demonstrates a wide interest in its ideological meanings. Early Brazilian studies tended to argue that the genre constructs politically conservative messages for its audiences, which serve to alienate them from society and reinforce patriarchal authority. Studies undertaken by foreign scholars have often stressed the critical and anti-hegemonic potential of the genre for audiences. These very different and perhaps irreconcilable findings may be the result of examining the genre in different political, economic, and cultural contexts, but may also reveal inadequacies in the research questions being posed (Hamburger 2002).

Although the narrow focus of studies undertaken to date tends to limit the understanding of telenovelas, it is nevertheless useful in that it provides an historical record of the genre where the lack of television archives substantially limits the scope of research. The absence of archives is also responsible for the main weakness of the existing studies; most focus on contemporary telenovelas at the time of broadcast and thus tend to produce limited understanding of the genre. Nonetheless, a growing plurality of research approaches now includes diachronic studies; the analysis of transnational flows of telenovelas; examination of the institutional structures of Brazilian television stations that produce telenovelas; ideological analysis of program content; and research on reception contexts, with some taking into account the relation between the telenovela text and its consumption.

Research has also investigated connections between the telenovela and the growth of related industries such as phonography, which disseminated soundtracks. Another link has been with the literary industry, which began to publish booklets adapted from scripts and/or books that have inspired plots (Ortiz 1987). Diachronic or historical quantitative and qualitative studies have sought to describe some of the longstanding conventions of the Brazilian genre. For instance, researchers have documented efforts to oppose, from within the industry, what they pejoratively classified as "Mexican melodrama" (Ortiz *et al.* 1988). In search of "realism," Brazilian writers have created national alternatives to replace what they considered to be vulgar, imported dramatic formulae; the national version of the genre would introduce references to ongoing "modernizing" processes, enlarging the scope of melodramatic conventions.

Michèle Mattelart and Armand Mattelart (1990) regard telenovelas in a largely positive light. The Brazilian case suggested possible ways of preserving national cultures and identities within the context of commercial television. Mattelart and Mattelart view Brazilian telenovela authors as "organic intellectuals" in the Gramscian sense: artists who could contribute to the creation of a "public-people" in a libertarian milieu. Dominique Wolton (1996) devotes a chapter to Brazilian telenovelas in his book about generalist television. Latin American scholars such as Colombian Jesús Martin-Barbero (Martin-Barbero and Munoz 1992; Martin-Barbero and Rey 2000) and Mexican Néstor García Canclini (1995) have validated the study of telenovelas and other cultural "hybrid" manifestations as important Latin American texts. But the gender dimensions of the genre remain marginal in scholarly discussions.

## Telenovelas and the feminine

Early studies took for granted the association between telenovelas and women viewers. During the 1970s and 1980s, Maria Rita Kehl (1979, 1986), Ondina Fachel Leal and R. Oliven (1988), Rosane Manhães Prado (1987), Sonia Novinsky Miceli (1974), and Jane Sarques (1986) variously combined research on female reception, analysis of government documents, and visual conventions. In general, these authors denounced the conservatism of the genre that invariably reinforced, in their view, subordinate and largely passive feminine roles. For example, research concludes that the kiss exhausts the erotic dimension of the relationships between the characters in the telenovela, featuring a limited iconography of love. Studies with female audiences verify their compliance with the imaginary transmitted by the telenovela, standardizing the domestic universe in a conventional bourgeois model: abundant, clean, and affluent households where women are responsible for domestic chores and the education of the children, while men work to bring money home. Analysis of narratives supports this point. For example in *Os Gigantes* (1979–80), the central character is an independent woman, a professional journalist working as an international correspondent in Italy who does not intend to start a family but instead to devote herself to her profession. Low ratings justified corporate pressure that was then put on scriptwriter Lauro César Muniz, who resigned after a controversial episode of the telenovela. Subjugated by her mother, the central female character returns to her home country to assist her dying brother, and to marry and generate an heir to the family fortune. Faced with this pressure, and becoming mentally unstable, the protagonist crashes in the plane she is flying. Her inclination toward personal freedom is embodied in her ability to pilot—an activity usually associated with men. The tragic end would have reinforced the non-legitimacy of her desire (Sarques 1986).

Two other early audience studies point to diverse possible readings of telenovela plots, revealing differences of interpretation by class and across large and smaller urban centers. Leal (1988) compared the reception of *Sol de Verão* (1982) among female domestic employers and employees, residents of wealthy and poor neighborhoods in Porto Alegre. She suggests that the domestic employer identifies with the protagonist who longs for freedom and breaks off her marriage with a husband who materially has supported her but has not satisfied her emotionally or sexually. However, the domestic employees did not identify with the decision of the middle-class woman character who left her marriage in order to pursue what their employers saw as more liberated relationships. This example shows how a telenovela might work as a shared repertoire through which different groups dispute their different understandings about ongoing and controversial processes of social change. Prado (1987) observes that women television viewers from the small town Cunha understand certain female characters in the telenovela *Roque Santeiro* (1985) as "independent"; they associated these characters with the freedom they longed for but which was available only to women in big cities, not to them.

Historical distance reveals how the realm of what is allowed and expected of women in Brazil in everyday life and in telenovelas has broadened to include the right to individual pleasure and to work, while, conversely, the complexity of male characters appears to be decreasing. Although early female protagonists ended up defeated, and over time telenovela narratives seem to have problematized the relationship with masculine authority. And, in the wider culture, the relaxation of television censorship has led to more liberal representations of the body and sensuality.

Examples of telenovelas dealing with the body as a base for identity—including sexual—transformation abound. Telenovelas also debate shifts in family structure and gender relations. Faria (1989) notes important connections between social transformation and the telenovela during the second half of the twentieth century. For example, childbirth rates have sharply decreased, despite the absence of a national family programming policy. Additionally, the entry of women into paid labor has been significant and rapid. Levels of urbanization also notably increased, linked to higher levels of migration, especially from the northeastern states of Brazil to slums in the outskirts of the metropolitan areas in the southeast of the country. At the same time, family structure models vary more widely due to the fragmentation of the nuclear family, an increase in the number of households led by women, and more recently growth in the number of people living alone (Berquó 1998; Faria and Potter 2002; McAnany 1992).

Telenovelas are organized around a theme of romantic relationships, which are seen to be increasingly fragile in the twenty-first century (Costa 2000). If we go back to the beginning of the 1970s, in telenovelas like *Irmãos Coragem* (1970) or *Selva de Pedra* (1972), the main characters were men torn between the love of two women who represented "traditional" or "modern" models of the Brazilian female ideal. At that time, sex before marriage always resulted in pregnancy and nuptials. In 1975, Sonia Braga exposes quite a lot of skin as *Gabriela*, the title character of a novel and of the telenovela. The camera follows from below the movement of the character who, having scaled a tall roof, crawls, her legs open, to retrieve a child's kite. It is a sensual pose admired by other characters who place themselves so as to enjoy the view—a privilege that viewers share thanks to the convenient positioning of the camera. In 1979, in the series *Malu Mulher*, a vertically stretched arm directs the viewer's gaze towards the movement of a feminine hand, tense and shut, which then opens to indicate orgasm. In this one scene, *Malu Mulher* moves the audience into the realm of bedroom intimacy to legitimize and praise female sexuality. Throughout the 1980s, the display of female and male bodies became more liberal. Nowadays scenes in bed are common in telenovelas. In 1983, *Guerra dos Sexos* used comedy to dramatize gender tensions involved in daily disputes between men and women. In 1988, *Vale Tudo* portrayed a villain businesswoman who was involved with a younger gigolo, and who became the most popular character in the story. In 1990, the telenovela *Barriga de Aluguel* problematized artificial insemination and the potential personal consequences of scientific interference in reproduction. The story portrayed the drama of a couple who hired a woman to receive artificial insemination of a lab-produced egg from their sperm and ovule. The biological father became involved with the surrogate and she became attached to the fetus. The question was:

Who should be considered as the actual mother of this artificially inseminated being, the woman who conceived or the woman in whose body it became a baby?

From the 1980s and into the 1990s, the balance between female and male characters shifted. Female characters became increasingly complex, while male characters became more two dimensional. Expressing his frustration, Brazilian actor Edson Cellulari observed that male roles were becoming secondary to those for women. Men's main role had turned into that of *beija-flor*, or "flower kisser" in a literal translation of the Portuguese word for hummingbird.

In 1990, Rede Manchete challenged the hegemony of Globo, investing in the production of telenovelas that questioned Globo's "modernizing" rhetoric. *Pantanal*, filmed in "the heart of Brazil," with long takes of landscapes crossed by transparent waters filled with naked women, presented an alternative to the "Brazil of the future" represented in Globo's telenovelas. *Pantanal*'s male protagonist has four sons. The success of the telenovela anticipated current ecological discourse by exalting an exotic west Brazilian landscape, instead of the usual eastern urban landscapes where modern, liberated consumerism was shown as a norm (Machado and Becker 2008; Hamburger 2005). Significantly, the move away from urban consumerism coincides with cultural aspiration for more stable families. The representation of weddings, which had been long abandoned by telenovelas, began to reappear to confirm the narrative desirability of happy endings. In 1996, Manchete produced *Xica da Silva*, a historical sensual telenovela set during colonial times of slavery. The recent broadcast of *Xica da Silva* in North America has brought to scholarly attention Brazilian telenovelas' sensual appeal (Benavides 2008).

In 2006, Record Network began to produce telenovelas which presented another version of the Brazilian contemporary urban daily life, one which included persistent social inequality and violence. *Vidas Opostas* (2006) brought the *favela* scene, drugs, and violence from contemporary cinema to television. Globo Network immediately replied with *Duas Caras* (2007), a story set in a studio *favela*, in a less violent and more optimistic setting. Recently, high audience ratings for Globo's *Avenida Brasil* (2012) suggest that despite the overall fall in television ratings telenovelas can still draw in large audiences and galvanize the country. With humor, this telenovela represents unusual family models now found in contemporary Brazil. For example, a contemporary telenovela family may be constituted by one man and three women, or two men and one pregnant woman.

## Future gender and telenovela research

Despite the current decrease in television audience ratings as one of the consequences of the diversification of the audiovisual domain, the telenovela remains a popular cultural form in Brazil. Recent studies challenge the view of telenovelas either as imposing retrogressive content on audiences or as a form largely resisted by viewers. Attention needs to turn to an examination of the ways in which the genre expresses ongoing social tensions in Brazilian society and how audiences make sense of the genre. Although telenovelas have become less popular with viewers, they retain their position as an important television genre, and a central site through which networks compete with one another for audiences.

Unlike classic Hollywood stories, telenovela narratives cannot be represented in linear progression performed by goal-oriented characters. The protagonist position, for example, often changes during the course of a story. A television genre commonly viewed as feminine became prime-time television and a legitimate arena to problematize issues of national imagination in romantic terms. Female characters have come to the forefront and female protagonists are often more complex and active characters than their male counterparts. Conversely, male domains seem to have become more narrow as male protagonists are often reduced to representations of sensual bodies. In the final part of this chapter, I formulate questions for further comparative transnational research on telenovelas, gender, and genre.

## Questions for future research on telenovelas, gender, and genre

The telenovela both captures and expresses new economic, social, and cultural fashions, the emergence of new electronic products, modes of communication and transport. As a privileged, national, electronic "window to the world," telenovelas often engage with controversial subjects, such as female orgasm, the social legitimacy of separation and divorce, gay marriage, and racial prejudice. At the same time, they are often centrally linked with the consumerism of their feminized audience members, linking stories to certain consumer goods, from fashions, to electronic gadgets, banks, and cars.

It is possible to follow a line of progressive liberalization in telenovelas around issues such as the fragmentation of the family, representations of sexuality, and expansion of the scope of life chances for women. However, greater opportunities for women in the workplace have not necessarily meant a redistribution of personal responsibilities between men and women in society; in general, women have kept their domestic obligations whilst also assuming responsibilities in their jobs.

Mapping different cases around the world might allow further thinking on the relationship between television series, governments, and gender relations. Moreover, the contrast between the visibility of certain issues and the invisibility of others— such as race, in the Brazilian case—might suggest different contours of virtual spaces around the world. Is the connection between television and liberalization present in other nations as well? Egypt seems to suggest a rather different relationship between "modernizing" television soaps, military government, and viewers. Here the military favored "modern" secular tales, which Muslim viewers resisted (Abu-Lughod 2005).

In Brazil, the telenovela's daily installments are broadcast while future "chapters" are being written, produced, and edited. This simultaneous production–broadcast–viewing feedback process favors television's incorporation of the ongoing debates, as well as the representation of the latest fashions, banks, cars, phones, airplane trips, computers, domestic appliances, and so on. Not all viewers have had equal opportunity to share feedback on storylines with telenovela producers. Until 1997, because of their assumed lack of consumer power, audience research has excluded viewers whom researchers classified as being at the bottom of the social scale ("class E") and viewers who did not live in one of the nine main metropolitan regions. Focus groups have been conducted only among upper-middle-class women in the two main cities. As such, audience research has tended to help consolidate the notion that the universe of television viewers was smaller, more affluent, and more feminine than it actually was. Gaps between the universe of imagined viewers and actual viewers provide striking insights about the ways in which Western *pluralist* theories and practices about desirable relations between media and society have been appropriated in an unequal, undemocratic situation (Hall 1982). It is possible to speculate that in Brazil this gap between the imagined and actual universe of viewers has favored the audience in the sense that it justified productions targeted at viewers who were imagined as more educated. Is this gap present in other nations and cultures too? What might be the theoretical and material consequences of these gaps for audiences and programming?

As "women's series" that are not confined to "women's television programming schedules," telenovelas dominate prime-time television in Brazil. In other countries, they are sometimes aired in timeslots that are regarded as "feminine," such as mornings or afternoons. In Portugal, Brazil, and in many other Latin American countries, telenovelas unexpectedly provide privileged, prime-time evening spaces for targeted advertising where they sell specific products and in the process facilitate a transition to "modern" forms of family structure and gender relations. They sell consumerism as a part of modern forms of life. Mapping broadcasters and timeslots in countries around the world could help researchers to better understand the different meanings these texts have in varying cultures and historical periods.

From different perspectives, reception studies have demonstrated that viewers' understanding of telenovelas does not necessarily coincide with the interpretations of critics. Telenovela reception studies confirm this, and now commonly explore the interplay of text, production, and viewing. Viewers appear to largely understand the genre as offering legitimate portrayals of a country and its people which nevertheless rarely correspond with their own experiences; instead, the representations of Brazilian life found in telenovelas are seen to relate to what some viewers regard as life in affluent parts of the country. Audiences appear to associate these narratives with a universe in which they would like to be included. Broadcast for free on national airwaves, the message seems to be: come to the center and take part in this inexorable move to "modern" times. Multiple identifications with stories, plots, and characters as well as criticisms of these aspects are possible. Thanks to a range of possible readings, telenovelas may provide a shared national repertoire through which many debates and anxieties are processed. Does this "femininization" of national virtual spaces occur elsewhere? How does it alter the politics and aesthetics of gender and genre?

# References

Abu-Lughod, L. (2005) *Dramas of Nationhood: The Politics of Television in Egypt*, Chicago and London: University of Chicago Press.

Almeida, C. J. M. and M. E. de Araújo (eds.) (1995) *A Televisão Brasileira Ao Vivo. Depoimentos De André Mendes De Almeida; Arthur Fontes; Cláudio Torres; Euclydes Marinho; Fatima*

Ali; Fernando Barbosa Lima; Gilberto Braga; Leonor Brasseres; Luiz Fernando Carvalho; Lucia Leme; Luiz Gleiser; Guel Arraes; Maria Teresa Souza Monteiro; Olga Curado; Otávio Florisbal; Patricio Mello; Paulo José; Ruberto Appel; Roberto Irineu Marinho; Roberto Muylaert; Sylvio Luiz, Rio de Janeiro: Imago.

Almeida, H. B. (2003) *Muitas Mais Cousas: Telenovela, Consumo e Gênero*, doctoral thesis, São Paulo: Anpocs/Edusc.

——(2012) "Trocando Em Miu?Dos—Ge?Nero e Sexualidade Na Tv a Partir De Malu Mulher," *Revista Brasileira de Ciências Sociais* 27(79): 125–37.

Araújo, J. Z. (2000) *A Negação Do Brasil: O Negro Na Telenovel a Brasileira*, São Paulo: Editora Senac.

Barros, L. C. M. de and L. Goldenstein (1996) "O Novo Capitalismo Brasileiro," *Gazeta Mercantil*, August 12.

Benavides, O. H. (2008) *Drugs, Thugs and Divas*, Austin: University of Texas Press.

Berquó, E. (1998) "Arranjos Familiares No Brasil: Uma Visão Demográfica," in Lilia Schwarcz (ed.) *História Da Vida Privada N. Iv*, São Paulo: Cia. das Letras, pp. 411–38.

Bourdon, J. (1994) "Alone in the Desert of 50 Million Viewers: Audience Ratings in French Television," *Media, Culture and Society* 16: 375–94.

Canclini, N. G. (1995) *Consumidores e Cidadãos: Conflitos Multiculturais Da Globalização*, Rio de Janeiro: UFRJ.

Charney, L. and V. R. Schwartz (1995) *Cinema and the Invention of Modern Life*. Berkely and Los Angeles, CA: University of California Press.

——(2010) *O Cinema E a Invenção Da Vida Moderna*, São Paulo: Cosac & Naify.

Costa, C. (2000) *Eu Compro Essa Mulher*, Rio de Janeiro: Jorge Zahar.

Eco, U. (1970) *Apocalípticos e Integrados*, São Paulo: Perspectiva.

Faria, V. (1989) "Políticas de governo e regulação da fecundidade: consequências não antecipadas e efeitos perversos," *Ciências Sociais Hoje*, São Paulo: Vértice, pp. 62–103.

Faria, V. E. and J. E. Potter (2002) "Televisão, Telenovelas e Queda De Fecundidade No Nordeste," *Novos Estudos Cebrap* 62 (March): 21–39.

Hall, S. (1982) "The Redescovery of Ideology," in M. Gurevitch, T. Bennet, and J. Woollacott (eds.) *Culture, Society and the Media*, New York: Methuen, pp. 56–90.

Hamburger, E. (1998) "Diluindo Fronteiras: As Novelas No Cotidiano," in Lilia Schwarcz (ed.) *História Da Vida Privada*, vol. 4, São Paulo: Cia das Letras, pp. 439–87.

——(1999) "Politics and Intimacy in Brazilian Telenovelas," unpublished Ph.D. dissertation, University of Chicago.

——(2002) "Indústria Cultural Brasileira Vista Daqui e De Fora," in S. Miceli (ed.) *O Que Ler Na Ciência Social Brasileira*, São Paulo and Brasília: ANPOCS/Editora Sumaré/Capes, pp. 53–84.

——(2005) *O Brasil Antenado, a Sociedade Da Novela*, Rio de Janeiro: Jorge Zahar Editor.

Hamburger, E. and H. B. de Almeida (2003) "Sociologia, Pesquisa De Mercado e Sexualidade Na Mídia: Audiências e Imagens," in S. Carrara, M. F. Gregori, and A. Piscitelli (eds.) *Sexualidade e Saberes*, São Paulo: UNICAMP, Campinas.

——(forthcoming) "Imagining TV Audiences in Brazil," in J. Bourdon and C. Méadel (eds.) *Measuring Television Audiences Globally: Deconstructing the Ratings Machine*, Basingstoke: Palgrave Macmillan.

Hansen, M. (1999) "The Mass Production of the Senses: Classical Cinema as Vernacular Modernism," *Modernism/Modernity* 6(2): 59–77.

Huyssen, A. (1986) *After the Great Divide: Modernism, Mass Culture, Post-Modernism*, Bloomington: Indiana University Press.

Kehl, M. R. (1979) "Novelas, Novelinhas e Novelões: Mil e Uma Noites para as Multidões," in E. Carvalho, M. R. Kehl, and S. Naves-Ribeiro (eds.) *Anos 70: Televisão*, Rio de Janeiro: Editora Europa.

——(1986) "Eu Vi Um Brasil Na Tv," in M. R. Kehl, A. H. da Costa, and I. F. Simões (eds.) *Um País No Ar: História Da Tv Brasileira Em Três Canais*, São Paulo: Brasiliense/FUNARTE.

Leal, O. F. and R. Oliven (1988) "Class Interpretations of a Soap Opera Narrative: The Case of the Brazilian Novela 'Summer Sun'," *Theory, Culture and Society* 5: 81–99.

McAnany, E. (1992) "The Telenovela and Social Change: A Brazilian Communication/Demography Challenge," in *Conference on the Telenovela and Social Change in Brazil*, University of Texas at Austin/Population Research Center.

Machado, A. and B. Becker (2008) *Pantanal, a Reinvenção Da Telenovela*, São Paulo: Educ.

Marques de Melo, J. (1991) *The Presence of the Brazilian Telenovelas in the International Market: Case Study of Globo Network*, São Paulo: Universidade de São Paulo.

Martin-Barbero, J. and S. Munoz (1992) *Television y Melodrama: Generos y Lecturas De La Telenovela en Colombia*, Bogota: Tercer Mundo Editores.

Martin-Barbero, J. and G. Rey (2000) *Os Exercícios Do Ver. São Paulo*, São Paulo: SENAC.

Mattelart, M. and A. Mattelart (1990) *The Carnival of Images: Brazilian Television Fiction*, translated from the French by David Buxton, New York: Bergin & Garvey.

Miceli, S. N. (1974) "A Imitação Da Vida," University of São Paulo.

Ortiz, R. (1987) *A Moderna Tradição Brasileira*, São Paulo: Brasiliense.

Ortiz, R., S. Borelli, and J. Ramos (1988) *Telenovela: História e Producão*, São Paulo: Brasiliense.

Prado, R. M. (1987) "Mulher De Novela e Mulher De Verdade—Estudo Sobre Cidade Pequena, Mulher e Telenovela," Master of Science dissertation, Museu Nacional/Universidade Federal do Rio de Janeiro.

Rowe, W. and V. Schelling (1991) *Memory and Modernity: Popular Culture in Latin America*, London: Verso.

Sarques, J. J. (1986) *A Ideologia Sexual Dos Gigantes*, Goiania: Editora da Universidade Federal de Goiás.

Skidmore, T. (ed.) (1993) *Television, Politics, and the Transition to Democracy in Latin America*, Washington, DC: Woodrow Wilson International Center for Scholars.

Varis, T. (1988) "Trends in International Television Flow," in C. Schneider and B. Wallis (eds.) *Global Television*, New York: Wedge Press, pp. 95–107.

Vink, N. (1988) *The Telenovela and Emancipation: A Study on Television and Social Change in Brazil*, Amsterdam: Royal Tropical Institute.

Wolton, D. (1996) *Elogio Do Grande Público*, São Paulo: Ática.

# 39

# Gendering and selling the female news audience in a digital age

## *Dustin Harp*

In those parts of the world with a free press—that is, free from government control—the news industry business model necessitates earning money to survive. Understanding this, we've grown accustomed to advertisements alongside news even though many of us realize certain conflicts between press freedom and the potential power advertisers have in subtly (and sometimes overtly) shaping news content. For example, a local newspaper might not run a negative exposé on a local business that buys weekly full-page advertisements. Less often discussed and understood is how historically and currently the placement of advertising and its relationship to news content and production reinforce patriarchal and stereotypical notions of gender, and position women (more so than men) as consumers to be sold to advertisers. Advertising has long driven journalistic choices in the packaging of news. In the United States newspaper publishers started in the 1890s segregating content related to women by creating special pages (Jordan 1938; Kitch 2002; Marzolf 1977). Women's pages were introduced in order to package and sell women readers as a group of consumers to advertisers. This practice of promoting news content to a gendered audience is not solely a US phenomenon, as evidenced by the number of women's sections in newspapers around the globe.

This chapter illuminates the history of the news industry's relationship to women readers before examining how the digital environment of news and information may or may not be changing this relationship. In examining the practice of packaging and presenting journalistic content for women within the context of digital media, the chapter asks, is women's content marginalized in the digital news and information era? And if so, what does this marginalization mean and why should we care?

## History and context

Historically, men throughout the world have had more access than women to education and, in turn, news and information. As such, men have been the keepers of the public sphere—as politicians, businessmen, and journalists. Traditional daily newspaper reporters have generally written stories with male readers in mind (Chambers *et al.* 2004; Isanovic 2006; Molotch 1978; Tuchman *et al.* 1978). In the United States, this changed in the 1890s when newspaper publisher Joseph Pulitzer began including pages in his newspapers specifically targeting a female audience (Harp 2007; Marzolf 1977). These women's pages, however, were created with a more troubling intent than simply informing women about the world around them. They were institutionalized into the newspaper in order to sell women consumers to advertisers. The timing of this development in the United States coincided with greater access to education for women, industrialization, and urbanization. Along with the growth of cities came department stores whose executives wanted to advertise to women, who had become the primary shoppers and spenders in households. Pulitzer hired female reporters and writers to create pages of content aimed specifically at women (Marzolf 1977). The content of women's pages dealt primarily with family and household—the domestic or feminine sphere. Consequently, while the rest of the newspaper, traditionally meant for men, treated readers as citizens, the women's pages constructed women as consumers (Harp 2007).

Women's pages remained a part of US newspapers for decades to come. While they were often thought to be silly and superficial, they also included serious stories. Recipes, advice columns, weddings, and high society news could be found on these pages, but they also raised serious issues, including birth control, child and spousal abuse, and divorce laws (Castleberry 1989; Marzolf 1977). Such broad topics illustrate one key problem with gender-partitioned pages: What exactly is women's news? Most typically industry insiders have defined it in terms of *women's issues*, meaning those issues of interest to women (Harp 2007). Not only is this a terribly narrowing and stereotypical means for understanding women's news, its vagueness offers little guidance to journalists and editors of these sections. Others in the industry have said women's news is an approach and style to reporting and writing: a human interest form of journalism (Harp 2007).

These vague definitions highlight another major problem with attempting to categorize news content for women. Essentially all things related to women have ended up in these sections, triggering the complaint that women's pages were a dumping ground or "ghetto" for stories that could very easily be considered news elsewhere in the paper (Goodman 1993; Lont 1995; Van Gelder 1974). For example, a book written by a woman might be reviewed for a women's section instead of the newspaper's regular book review section (Harp 2007). For those who wonder why anyone would have a problem with this placement, consider that fewer readers (particularly men) would see the book review. Consequently, fewer people become aware of and read the book; ultimately the book sales, popularity, and status of the author are lower than these might otherwise be.

Further, critics—including journalists and readers, feminists and non-feminists—have argued that if one section of a newspaper is designated for women, by default the other sections—international and local news, business and sports—are men's sections. This labeling of news proves problematic because it reinforces the notion that issues in the public sphere are men's issues. In setting up a separate section for women, the newspaper industry supported the public/masculine versus private/feminine notion, putting women in *their* place—in the home, caring, cooking, and cleaning for their family (unpaid labor) rather than in the workforce and political realm, where power and money can be attained. Moreover, these sections also undermined the careers of women journalists. Rather than being hired to edit and write for general news pages where pay, recognition, and readership were higher, women journalists were consigned to the "career ghetto" of the women's pages.

Arguments against such news content packaging—from readers, journalists, and media critics—are not unique to the US (Gakahu and Mukhongo 2007; Harp 2007) and have prompted many publishers and editors to rid their newspapers of these women's sections, or at least rename them (Guenin 1975; Marzolf 1977; Merritt and Gross 1978; Miller 1976). In the United States, a significant shift occurred when in 1969 the *Washington Post* and in 1970 the *Los Angeles Times* led a movement to discard women's pages in favor of what are now known as "lifestyle" pages (Mills 1988; Yang 1996). Not coincidentally, this change occurred during the height of the second-wave feminist movement, when feminists were calling for equality in and integration into all aspects of society (Harp 2007). With the transformation to lifestyle sections, editors were responding to such critiques by integrating "women's content" into all areas of the newspaper. However, evidence suggests that with these newly named sections (often regarded as nothing more than a name change) very little altered in terms of content by and for women throughout the news pages of US newspapers. Women ended up with less control over content as editors began hiring men to oversee lifestyle sections. Stories related to women actually declined: rather than being integrated into all areas of the newspaper, such content simply disappeared (Guenin 1975; Merritt and Gross 1978; Miller 1976).

Despite critiques of women's sections, not everyone welcomed their elimination. Many women, including feminists, argued they were necessary because they offered a place in the news where women had control of the content and gave voice to women's issues (Lueck and Chang 2002). In any case, the disappointment did not last long, as steadily declining female readerships led many in the news industry to reintroduce women's pages in the 1990s. Industry insiders argued and focus groups illustrated that the drop in readership occurred because women did not see themselves in the newspaper. As was the case when newspapers introduced women's pages in the first place, the readership decline was a concern not because of the industry's commitment to keeping women informed, but instead because of the need to secure a stable group of consumers to sell to advertisers (Harp 2007).

Today, news pages specifically targeting women are widely available around the world. Concurrently, feminists continue to debate the merits and drawbacks of gender-segregated news content (Gakahu and Mukhongo 2007; Lueck and Chang 2002). Despite arguments against them, such pages often prove popular with women readers. This is likely because issues of interest and stories about women are lacking in other sections of the news (Carter *et al.* 1998; Chambers *et al.* 2004; Isanovic 2006). Lack of content for women is partly a result, some maintain, of a male-dominated profession (Ross and Carter 2011). As of 2011 only about 37 percent of newspaper reporters, copy and layout editors, photographers, and supervisors in US newsrooms were women (Pugh Yi and Dearfield 2012), while in other countries around the world the percentage is much lower. The 2010 Global Media Monitoring Project found after monitoring 1,281 media outlets (television, newspapers, and radio stations) in 108 countries that women reported only 37 percent of the stories (WACC 2010). Further, females made up only 24 percent of news subjects or sources. No wonder the topic of marginalizing women's content and readers remains relevant.

## A market- and technology-driven system

News and information systems have changed significantly since women's sections were first introduced in the United States. While globally newspapers remain a central source of news for many, people are increasingly turning to online news using their mobile phones (Miller *et al.* 2012; Social Networking Popular Across Globe 2012). A digital divide—based on poverty, education, language, and computer literacy—exists and separates online news users from those who do not access the internet. In 2011, the percentage of the Indian population using the internet was only 10.2 percent, across Africa 13.5 percent, while in North America the number reached 78.6 percent (Internet World Stats 2011). The global divide also has been shaped along gender lines—women's lower access to the internet than men's is significant because "gender roles and relationships affect women's education, mobility, time, skills and resources" (UNESCO 2002: 11). Despite this digital divide, online news is becoming a primary source of information, particularly as technologies and access become less expensive. By the end of 2010 in the United States, "the Internet surpassed print newspapers as a source of national and international news" (Olmstead *et al.* 2012). While these numbers leave out a large portion of the world population, online news is likely to be a primary source of information for many people in the decades to come and is replacing much print news consumption.

In this new online environment much has changed. The old system of editors and reporters sending the news they choose (the gatekeeper model) to a waiting audience is dissolving. Now, instead, news consumers can be producers; everyday citizens with internet access and savvy can produce news content. This has led to a greater diversity of voices offering news and information, and the ability of consumers to choose their news—information that is important, relevant, or interesting to them. The multitude of information now available to online users can be both awe inspiring and overwhelming. Recognizable and reputable online news sources with a commitment to journalistic standards maintain an important space in this digital environment. Within this new media environment, and understanding the historical context of how the news industry has and continues to treat women as marginalized citizens (and primary consumers), are these online editors segregating content for women readers? And, if so, what consequences might that have in digital environments for readers following mainstream news?

Within the framework of democratic theory, newspapers have traditionally served as an instrument for an informed citizenry. This notion of newspapers' role in democracy formed the foundation for previous arguments against the gendered segregation of content. Newspapers should not label news about family, food, furnishings, and fashion as "women's content" and business and politics as men's. Newspapers should signify that the public and private spheres of our lives are important to both men and women. Online environments are nevertheless replete with niche marketed websites and gender-segregated content. The way people consume information has radically changed as audiences search and select news from sources throughout the web. Such changes call for a re-examination of how news is segregated online and a revisiting of previous arguments about gendered designations for content.

Content specifically targeting women (and just about any other demographic one can think of) abounds on the internet. The subject matter spans the serious to the silly, and the ideological to the superficial, often in the form of blogs. Many blogs target women through content deemed to be of interest to them—similar topics to those found in women's magazines and women's pages of newspapers. Particularly popular, and illustrating just how much of a niche market the internet has become, are "mommy blogs"—authored by mothers who blog in many forms and styles about their lives in the context of raising children. Traditional print magazines have also moved online. New citizen voices are mixing with traditional journalistic ones on the internet. With so much niche marketing, would it be bad for news and information sites to also structure content in this manner? Do those old arguments still hold weight?

## News and women online

The online news and information media landscape is quite varied and incredibly vast. My overview of online news as it relates to gendered content offers a broad rather than comprehensive impression of this environment in different parts of the world while attempting to detail some of the most read news websites.

The Chinese Xinhua News Agency website (xinhuanet.com) has no section specifically titled for women but, like so many newspapers in print and online throughout the world, it has a section titled "Fashion," with subsections including Beauty, Fitness, and Mothering. The news site of the *People's Daily* (people.com.cn), the official newspaper of the Chinese government, also includes a section titled "Fashion," whose audience is signified through its URL: lady.people.com.cn. Feng Huang Wang (ifeng.com), a news site based on Phoenix Television, a Hong Kong-based television broadcaster, has a Fashion section with a tagline reading "Chinese elite women preferred fashion portal." Three of the leading internet portals in China, including Xin Lang Wang (Sina.com) (one of the more popular sites where people get their news in China), So Hu (Sohu.com), and Netease/Wang Yi (163.com), each have sections specifically titled for women. Xin Lang Wang's section is "Female" and includes content on beauty, clothing, fashion, fitness, love and relationships, gossip, shopping, weddings, plastic surgery, and astrology. The other two portals, both with the section names "Women," have similar content.

According to Alexa.com, a web information company, the top news websites in Spanish and Portuguese are Brazil's UOL (www.uol.com.br), Brazil's Globo group (www.globo.com), all country-specific versions of the Terra portal (e.g. Brazil: terra. com.br; Chile: www.terra.cl; Spain: www.terra.es), Spain's *El País* newspaper (elpaís. com), and Mexico's *El Universal* newspaper (www.eluniversal.com.mx). Most of these are sites linked to a media group (e.g. the portal UOL in Brazil, the US's *New York Times* or Britain's the *Guardian*). Like the main news websites in China, most of these sites do not have a section explicitly named for women, most notably Brazil's

Globo group (as well as its main newspaper, *O Globo*, www.oglobo.globo.com). That said, all of the sites have a life/style section with content on topics typically seen as women's issues: beauty, family and parenting, relationships, fashion, health and diets, and cooking.

When women's sections did exist on Latin American websites, not surprisingly, "woman" or "women" (or some variation of it, such as "women's corner" or "between women") was a common name. In some cases, these sections explicitly linked women to lifestyle matters (e.g. Chile's emol.com has a "Trends & Women" section). The content most often found in these sections was traditionally feminine and similar to that in other parts of the world. At the same time, serious issues were addressed in these sections, such as domestic violence. Brazil's UOL had a subsection on weddings and Argentina's Clarin.com had one on work (including the work/family divide)—again, typical content for these women's sections.

The daily *Folha de São Paulo* (http://www.folha.uol.com.br/) is Brazil's newspaper of record. On its online homepage, the sections are clear—politics, world, economy, citizenship, sports, culture, F5 (entertainment news), technology, science, health, blogs, columns, and so on. The blog area lists 41 sections. They range from politics, street art, "the homosexual universe," to a kind of agony aunt giving advice on personal problems.

The daily *Público* (http://www.publico.pt/) is Portugal's newspaper of record, with typical news and section divides. The section "life&style" diversifies into seven additional areas, including beauty, family, and relationships. Not unusually, each section is primarily aimed at a female audience, illustrating how the change in name from the "woman's section" to "style" has not necessarily brought a conceptual change in the audience or in content.

Among US news websites with the highest traffic are the *Huffington Post*, the *New York Times*, the *Washington Post*, *Fox News*, and *CNN*, according to Alexa.com. The *Huffington Post* also publishes editions in Canada, the UK, France, Spain, Germany, Australia, and a growing list of other countries. The US version (launched in June 2011) includes segregated content for women, found under the "Voices" section, although it is also suggested for those searching under the "Style" tab. "Voices" includes other content areas with similar identity headings, including black, Latino, and gay voices. These are all, like women, marginalized groups in the United States—all maintain the position of "other" in relation to the normalized white heterosexual male.

In her blog, Margaret Wheeler Johnson, Women's Editor for the *Huffington Post*, described the vision for the "Voices" section a year after it launched. Admitting that there are good reasons against a women's section, but without addressing any of those critiques, she asks if this content determination creates a separate but equal space. She concludes: "We have a women's section because we really like identifying as female. Because we like its particular concerns" (Johnson 2012). Content in the women's section of the *Huffington Post* varies widely; it is organized under several subheadings, including Healthy Living, Weddings, Divorce, Style, Post 50, and Parents. An informal analysis over several days indicates that the content on these pages fits into a traditional understanding of lifestyle content, with few stories that would warrant space in hard news pages. As such, important stories do not appear on the homepage, but are instead designated women's news and *dumped* in that section. Interestingly, women's pages for the UK version tend to tackle more serious issues and less fashion and food.

The *New York Times* website runs an occasional series titled "Female Factor" containing stories supplied by the *International Herald Tribune* and dealing with women's issues across the globe. While the moniker is present on these stories, they are not found in a particular section, although they are often located in the "world" or "U.S." section. The *New York Times* online, like the *Washington Post* and most of the other highly read news sites in the United States, has a style section that targets women through fashion, home design, and food. The tone, images, and sources make clear that women are often the primary targets of the content. Most recently, in 2012, "She the People," a blog for women writing about politics and culture, launched on the *Washington Post*'s website.

## Revisiting the women's page in the online world

With the segregation of women's content moving online, current discussions echo those from the 1960s, when critics argued for the need to rid newspapers of the "women's pages" and place stories about women throughout the newspaper. One commentary that received quite a bit of attention (including being reposted on popular websites like Talking Points Memo and MsMagazine.com) was written in June 2010 by Ruth Rosen, a former columnist for the *Los Angeles Times* and *San Francisco Chronicle*. Rosen noted: "The good news is that [these sections] are no longer about society, cooking and fashion. Most are tough, smart, incisive, analytic and focus on events, trends or stories that the mainstream online news still ignores. The bad news is that they are not on the 'front page' where men might learn about women's lives" (Rosen 2010).

Today, some of the most highly read news and information sites on the web have separate sections for women. Rosen points to three highly read websites in the United States—Salon.com, with a section titled "Broadsheet," Slate.com, with "Double X," and PoliticsDaily.com's "Woman Up"—along with "50/50" found on the British online magazine website OpenDemocracy. Rosen often saw high-quality and important stories in these women's sections. Her main concern is that readers (both men and women) often cannot find important stories about women because they are buried within the layers of websites and not front and center with other important news. The possible consequences of marginalizing stories about "women's issues" are significant. "My concern is that gender equality will only emerge when men are educated about women's lives and when women stop being quarantined as 'the other'" (Rosen 2010).

Women's section editors and feminist critics have noted that women writers of gender-segregated online sections are often resigned to write for them (Harp 2007; Rosen 2010). Many appear to be happy to "have an oasis in which to offer a feminist perspective on the world events, where they don't have to fight editors who still view women as 'the other,' and where they can expose, debate, and re-think how we would re-organize the world 'if women really mattered'" (Rosen 2010). What these women are describing is a counter or alternative public sphere, a space where marginalized voices can freely discuss important issues outside of the masculine public sphere, where they have less power (Fraser 1990).

In January 2011, the topic of gender-segregated news became a popular (and contentious) topic when Salon.com ceased publishing "Broadsheet." The editor wrote, "No feature in Salon's history kicked up the amount of righteous dust and ad hominem rage as Broadsheet, which debuted in 2005. ... We're immensely proud of the role it's played raising intensely important questions about women's issues in politics, pop culture and way beyond" (Lauerman 2011). Readers responded to the news with lively debate. Many acknowledged the bind of these sections—both marginalizing women while providing a space and voice. Some readers expressed their sadness and anger in seeing Broadsheet go. Others cheered its demise. One reader summed up the contradiction inherent in these special sections: "It's hard to know what side to be on regarding Broadsheet" (Lauerman 2011).

In January 2012, Poynter.com (a journalism industry website) published an article titled "Should News Sites Have Separate (but Equal?) Spheres for Women's Content?" (Tenore 2012). The launching of The Washington Post's "She the People" blog spurred the piece by Mallary Jean Tenore, who asked Melinda Henneberger, editor of the new blog, about the criticism. Henneberger explained, "If being in a ghetto means I have the incredible privilege of bringing a bunch of incredibly talented women to one of the world's best newspapers to write about everything for an audience that includes everyone, then call it that if you want to, but never have I felt less cramped" (quoted in Tenore 2012).

## Conclusion

Very little has changed in the current digital news environment from previous generations in terms of arguments for and against separating "women's content" from the rest of the news. "Women's content" remains marginalized. What is discouraging and perhaps surprising is how long the issue has been relevant but unresolved. The push to integrate such content into all areas of news has failed. It is discouraging and shocking that women around the world still have so little voice in their news media, as journalists, sources, and as audiences.

What started, at least in the United States, as a drive to attract women readers to sell to advertisers, has become a standard means for attracting women readers to newspapers in a narrow and marginalized way. Stereotypical notions of "women's news" have been constructed and content segregated from the rest of the news for the sake of advertising revenue. Yet the role of advertising in all of this is more complicated in a digital age. People no longer decide where advertisements belong in a particular publication but rather various demographic and psychographic data signal a computer program to choose advertising based on a best guess of what might interest that particular reader. Advertising, then, is not (and never really has been) a valid explanation for packaging news this way. What remains consistent is that news organizations want to attract women readers so they can sell them to advertisers. Worldwide statistics—remember that women are 24 percent of news subjects and sources (WACC 2010)—deliver the discouraging news that women are not integrated into mainstream news content. In many cases publishers, editors, and reporters continue to employ a strategy developed more than a century ago as a means for providing women with content and advertisers with women consumers.

Arguments against packaging particular content for women, which have existed for decades and hold true in a digital age, are not a judgment of the content itself but of how society defines appropriate gender roles. To package content on a general news site for a particular and always marginalized group (women, blacks, Latinos, or gays) reinforces stereotypes, discrimination, and power structures. While women have online stand-alone women's news magazines—many with a progressive, feminist, and activist stance—too often in the online mainstream news and information environment special sections segregate them from the rest of the news. Success in the mainstream digital news environment would be women's news that is integrated, not segregated—a solution proposed decades ago for the print news world. Along with integration, success would be about powerful and challenging stories about women's status and equality in the world to regularly be front-page news. Reinforcing differences, divisions, and marginalization based on gender only further reinforces inequalities between men and women.

## Acknowledgments

Special thanks to Ingrid Bachmann, Lei Guo, and Tania Rosas-Moreno for their assistance in examining non-English news websites.

## References

Carter, C., G. Branston, and S. Allan (1998) *News, Gender and Power*, London: Routledge.

Castleberry, V. (1989) "Women in Journalism (Interview)," Washington Press Club Foundation, session 2. http://npc.press.org.

Chambers, D., L. Steiner, and C. Fleming (2004) *Women in Journalism*, New York: Routledge.

Fraser, N. (1990) "Rethinking the Public Sphere: A Contribution to the Critique of Actually Existing Democracy," *Social Text* 25/26: 56–80.

Gakahu, N. W. and L. L. Mukhongo (2007) "'Women's Pages' in Kenya's Newspapers: Implications for the Country's Development," *Gender & Development* 15(3): 425–34.

Goodman, E. (1993) "Symposium—Is the Media a Woman's Place," *Media Studies Journal: The Media and Women without Apology* 7(1–2): 49–67.

Guenin, Z. B. (1975) "Women's Pages in American Newspapers: Missing Out on Contemporary Content," *Journalism Quarterly* 52(1): 66–75.

Harp, D. (2007) *Desperately Seeking Women Readers: U.S. Newspapers and the Construction of a Female Readership*, New York: Lexington Books.

Internet World Stats (2011) http://www.internetworldstats.com/stats.htm.

Isanovic, A. (2006) "Media Discourse as a Male Domain: Gender Representation in the Daily Newspapers of Bosnia and Herzegovina, Croatia and Serbia," in N. Moranjak-Bamburać, T. Jusić, and A. Isanović (eds.) *Stereotyping Representation of Women in Print Media in South East Europe*, Sarajevo: Mediacentar.

Johnson, M. W. (2012) "Huffington Post Women: Why We Need a Women's Page." http://www.huffingtonpost.com/margaret-wheeler-johnson/huffington-post-women-why-womens-page_b_1593167.html.

Jordan, E. (1938) *Three Rousing Cheers*, New York: Appleton-Century.

Kitch, C. (2002) "Women in Journalism," in W. David Sloan and Lisa Mullikin Parcell (eds.) *American Journalism: History, Principles, Practices*, Jefferson, NC: McFarland.

Lauerman, K. (2011) "New Year's Changes at Salon Online." http://www.salon.com/2011/01/07/seitz_and_tcf/.

Lont, C. (1995) *Women and Media: Content/Careers/Criticism*, Belmont, CA: Wadsworth.

Lueck, T. and H. Chang (2002) "Tribune's 'WomaNews' Gives Voice to Women's Issues," *Newspaper Research Journal* 23(1): 59–72.

Marzolf, M. (1977) *Up from the Footnote: A History of Women Journalists*, New York: Hasting House.

Merritt, S. and H. Gross (1978) "Women's Page/Lifestyle Editors: Does Sex Make a Difference?," *Journalism Quarterly* 55(3): 508–14.

Miller, C., L. Rainie, K. Purcell, A. Mitchell, and T. Rosenstiel (2012) "How People Get Local News and Information in Different Communities," Pew Research Center's Pew internet. http://www.pewinternet.org/Reports/2012/Communities-and-Local-News.aspx.

Miller, S. (1976) "Changes in Women's/Lifestyle Sections," *Journalism Quarterly* 53: 641–7.

Mills, K. (1988) *A Place in the News: From the Women's Pages to the Front Pages*, New York: Dodd, Mead.

Molotch, H. L. (1978) "The News of Women and the Work of Men," in G. Tuchman, A. K. Daniels, and J. Bennett (eds.) *Hearth and Home: Images of Women in Mass Media*, New York: Oxford University Press.

Olmstead, K., J. Sasseen, A. Mitchell, and T. Rosenstiel (2012) "Digital: News Gains Audience but Loses Ground in Chase for Revenue," *The State of the News Media 2012*, The Pew Research Center's Project for Excellence in Journalism. http://stateofthemedia.org/2012/digital-news-gains-audience-but-loses-more-ground-in-chase-for-revenue/.

Pugh Yi, R. H. and C. T. Dearfield (2012) "The Status of Women in the U.S. Media," Women's Media Center website. http://wmc.3cdn.net/a6b2dc282c824e903a_arm6b0hk8.pdf.

Rosen, R. (2010) "Gender Apartheid Online," *Berkeley Daily Planet*, June 22. http://www.berkeleydailyplanet.com/issue/2010-06-22/article/35649?headline=Gender-Apartheid-Online-By-Ruth-Rosen.

Ross, K. and C. Carter (2011) "Women and News: A Long and Winding Road," *Media, Culture & Society* 33(8): 1148–65.

Social Networking Popular Across Globe (2012) Pew Research Center Global Attitudes Project. http://www.pewglobal.org/files/2012/12/Pew-Global-Attitudes-Project-Technology-Report-FINAL-December-12-2012.pdf.

Tenore, M. J. (2012) "Should News Sites Have Separate (but Equal?) Spheres for Women's Content?," Poynter, January 18, 2012. http://www.poynter.org/latest-news/top-stories/159647/live-chat-today-should-news-sites-have-separate-but-equal-spheres-for-womens-content/.

Tuchman, G., A. K. Daniels, and J. Bennett (eds.) (1978) *Hearth and Home: Images of Women in Mass Media*, New York: Oxford University Press.

UNESCO (2002) "Participation and Access of Women to the Media, and the Impact of Media on and Its Use as an Instrument for the Advancement and Power of Women." http://www.un.org/womenwatch/daw/egm/media2002/index.html.

Van Gelder, L. (1974) "Women's Pages: You Can't Make News out of a Silk Purse," *Ms.* (November): 112–26.

World Association for Christian Communication (WACC) (2010) "Who Makes the News?," Global Media Monitoring Project. http://www.whomakesthenews.org.

Yang, M. (1996) "Women's Pages or People's Pages: The Production of News for Women in the Washington Post in the 1950s," *Journalism & Mass Communication Quarterly* 73(2): 364–78.

# 40

# Looking beyond representation

## Situating the significance of gender portrayal within game play

## Christine Daviault and Gareth Schott

Over the last two decades, gender in gaming has been examined extensively, leading to a number of key observations. Scholars from a wide variety of fields of inquiry have noted a persistent lack of female characters in games and the sexist and unrealistic manner in which they are portrayed when they do appear in game-texts (e.g. Beasley and Stanley 2002; Dietz 1998; Dill *et al.* 2005; Downs and Smith 2010; Haninger and Thompson 2004; Ivory 2006; Provenzo 1991). These conclusions may explain why the number of female video game players has stagnated for years between 30 and 40 percent of total players in many countries, including the United States (ESA 2010).

The emergence and development of games studies as a dedicated field of research has led to a call to move beyond what Forsey calls "visualism"—the "disciplinary proclivity to elevate vision as the 'noblest sense'" (2010: 572)—as the focal point for exposing the mechanics by which older media texts operate. Game studies scholars were quick to warn against the assumption that games "present only one type of experience and foster one type of engagement" (Newman 2002: 1), such as proclamations as to what constitutes "girl-friendly" game design (Graner Ray 2004). A number of scholars have thus shifted their focus to *locate* and engage directly with women who *do* play in order to unearth the ways in which they negotiate game play in a gender-coded environment (Bryce and Rutter 2002; Daviault 2010; Royse *et al.* 2007; Schott and Horrell 2000; Taylor 2006). Typically, researchers have found that women consume games in a multiplicity of ways and their preferences are "highly contextual and therefore dependent on social, cultural, and other quotidian factors" (Jenson and de Castell 2010: 56).

Interestingly, despite this perceived gender imbalance, "most of the critical attention directed at questions of gaming and gender has focused on girls and women" (Carr 2006: 162). In comparison, very little attention has been paid to the importance of the representational qualities of game characters and their impact on male players (Kirkland 2009). In fact, many of the early research approaches have reflected a tendency and desire to glean a *universality* with regard to female preferences (Jenson and de Castell 2008). Any design features that appeared to either deter or appeal to female game players were regressed to produce a profile of the female gamer as distinct from male gamers. Looking at the last three decades of research on gender and gaming, Jenson and de Castell (2010) concluded that the methodological approaches used to conduct studies in this area have left few opportunities to challenge or reinterpret data that situate women as different in gaming culture.

In this chapter, we propose to look beyond representation and reassess the significance of gender portrayal as part of the wider experience of game play. After all, avatars are barely visible in games configured from the first-person perspective since the player embodies the character, thus only usually sees his or her hands in game play. Even in games that employ the third-person perspective, it can be argued that gender does not have as much of an impact on players as early research seemed to indicate. For example, with reference to one of the earliest and highest-profile female characters, Lara Croft of the *Tomb Raider* game franchise (Core Designs 1996–2013), Aarseth has stated that: "The dimensions of Lara Croft's body ... are irrelevant to me as a player because a different-looking body would not make me play differently. ... When I play, I don't even see her body, but see through it and past it" (2004: 46). This viewpoint echoes comments made by Vangie "Aurora" Beal (Clan PMS member and creator of gamegirlz.com), who said:

> When I play I don't really think in terms of man/woman, but when I go out and play with the ladies in my clan, I find it is a more "womanly" experience, but it is the social aspect that brings those feelings, not *the game* or the *game play* itself.
> (Schott and Thomas 2008: 41, my emphasis)

As Frasca has recognized, the "potential [of games] is not narrative, but simulation: the ability to represent dynamic systems" (2001: n.p.)—a quality that was employed by Carr's study of female players, which highlighted the need to understand the "relationships between taste, content, context and competence, in order to explore the multiple factors that feed into users' choices and contribute to the formation of gaming preferences" (2005: 466). We argue that the "experience" of play does not necessarily permit the player to engage in extensive interpretive work more commonly associated with other media and elevated in textual analysis. Indeed, the character of Lara Croft may have prompted a variety of readings (Jansz and Martis 2007; Kennedy 2002; Schleiner 2001), but textual analyses typically failed to locate the character within the context of player exploration, negotiation, and activation of the interactive matrices of a game-text, that also contains "semantic, narrative, figurative and strategic resources" (Ferri 2007: 3). Games are dynamic entities that remain "in potentia" until actualized by the player (Klastrup 2003). In doing so, they involve the player in recursive actions (Lauteren 2002) to produce polysemic performances and readings (Consalvo 2003). In other words, each play session is different and characters may be received very differently depending on the player and other factors. Dovey and Kennedy have also argued that in assessing a game "we cannot have recourse solely to its textual characteristics; we have to pay particular attention to the *moment* of its enactment as it is played" (2006: 4). A strong argument thus emerges, too, for reassessing the significance of representation in light of the configurative demands of game experience.

## Invasion of the private sphere and increased scrutiny

While digital games can be traced as far back as the 1950s, they did not really become a part of mainstream entertainment until the 1970s and 1980s with the proliferation of video arcades and the launch of the first domestic game consoles (Magnavox Odyssey in 1972; Atari 2600 in 1977; Nintendo Entertainment System in 1983; SEGA Master system in 1985; and Genesis in 1989). Early console versions of arcade games, such as *Pong* (Atari 1975) and *Space Invaders* (Atari 1980), aroused little criticism or concern due to their primitive game play and lack of characters. Even *Pac Man* (Namco 1980; ported by Atari 1982)—among the highest-grossing arcade games of all time (Kent 2001) and one of the first games to use characters—avoided criticism for its violence or sexism (although the later addition of Ms Pac Man gave us a Pac replete with a hair bow). Spatially and territorially, until game consoles became a common feature of home entertainment and personal computers achieved processing powers that were advanced enough to incorporate game play, gaming was still predominantly a public act to be found in the world of arcades, and by definition the realm of male teenagers and adults.

This started changing in the 1990s when video games began to attract attention for their more realistic violent and sexist content. This shift came as a result of a number of changes in the industry. First of all, the video game industry was fast becoming one of the most important leisure activities in the home (in the US, industry sales reached $5.1 billion in 1997) with a rise in purchases of home consoles and personal computers and a decline in the popularity of arcades. Advances in technology, including 3D graphics, multimedia, online gaming, and multiplayer capabilities allowed for the creation of more complex story arcs and environments as well as more human/ humanoid characters. These factors transformed what was once primarily in the public domain into an activity that was suddenly perceived as affecting much younger children in the home, leading to a significant shift in public perception.

In the US, parents, educators, and government officials became increasingly concerned with the impact of video games, arguing that they may be sending the wrong messages. The public outcry surrounding the computer game *Doom* (id Software 1993) is one of the most notorious examples of the time, with critics going as far as calling it a "mass murder simulator" (Irvine and Kincaid 1999) and blaming it for the Columbine High School massacre in 1999. Another infamous computer and console game released in 1996, *Duke Nukem 3D* (3D Realms), was blamed for promoting pornography, prostitution, and violence. What had been seen as a pastime firmly situated in the public sphere suddenly became a mainstream leisure activity accessible to children in the home and, as such, was viewed as a source of potential harm.

## Gender and video games

Over the next two decades, several scholars responded to these concerns and conducted comprehensive studies looking at the proportion, type, gender, and race of video game characters and evaluating their role and representation in games. Dietz, for example, examined the portrayal of women and the use of violent themes in

33 popular Nintendo and Sega Genesis games. She found that 41 percent of the games with characters did not have any female ones and "women [were] portrayed as sex objects" in 28 percent of these games. Almost half the games included violence directed at others, with 21 percent directed at women (Dietz 1998: 425). In 2003, Downs and Smith (2010: 727–28) examined a number of variables depicting overt sexuality (e.g. sexually revealing clothing, nudity, breast and waist size and unrealistic body proportion) in 60 console video games. They found a significantly higher proportion of male (86 percent) versus female (41 percent) characters, with more female characters shown in sexually revealing clothing (86 percent) compared to their male counterparts (11 percent) and a greater likeliness to display a small waist (40 percent vs. 1 percent).

No matter what variables they choose to focus on, all the studies examining character representation in video games reach similar conclusions, highlighting both a lack of female characters in video games and their sexualized portrayal when they are present (perceived as negatively affecting girls and women), as well as a preponderance of violent themes (perceived as adversely affecting boys and men). While the quantitative data collected by such studies offers an interesting snapshot of gender and video game characters, they tend to focus solely on female characters and issues of representation. In doing so, they forgo developing an understanding of games as a *process* (Kontour 2009). Kontour argues that games cannot be examined solely on the basis of representation, or essential characteristics involved in game play will be overlooked, such as the fact that games are not simply watched, they are played. This means "the action in a game unfolds largely according to user input rather than a fully predetermined set of static, recurring elements as one would expect to see in cinema or television"; moreover, games are played in a variety of contexts involving "various types of psycho-social interactions" (Kontour 2009: 12). Bryce and Rutter (2002) also warn against the temptation to extrapolate conclusions from discrete samples that fail to take into account how gender constructions presented in video games are dynamically consumed by players and can lead to a multiplicity of readings of femininity and masculinity. Thus, a contextualization of the significance of gender portrayal as part of the wider experience of game play is needed to place it at the moment of actualization. In other words, uncovering "the relationship between the structure of a game and the way people engage with that system" is necessary (Waern 2012: 1).

## Broadening the scope of game analysis

In response to the limitations of representational analyses, scholars have attempted to examine women's engagement with characters. Rather than focusing on what turns women away from gaming, such as sexist representation, many have instead chosen to analyze how women negotiate their participation in gaming culture. Schott and Horrell (2000) interviewed women gamers and observed their game play. They found that the participants had crafted playing styles and motivations of their own; their access to gaming and progression in the games they played were heavily negotiated within the male-coded environment of video games. Royse *et al.* (2007) also examined how women consume games and experience gaming through interviews and focus groups. They established that "power gamers, those playing from three to more than 10 hours weekly, were comfortable with technology and the integration of video games into their lives" (2007: 563) and while they "admit to the hypersexualization of some female images in games and the sexism of some male players, they have defined games successfully for themselves as being about pleasure, mastery and control" (2007: 564). Taylor (2003) agrees and argues that an important motivator for women gamers playing violent first-person shooting (FPS) games is that they give them the opportunity to challenge traditional gender expectations and explore aggressive behavior in a safe environment.

There is an obvious dichotomy between what is perceived in textual analyses of video game content as a deterrent to the inclusion of more girls and women in gaming culture—sexism, hypersexualized female characters, violence—and what actual female gamers experience. Daviault (2010) compared the approaches of two significant groups in gaming culture in the 1990s: "girls' games" companies launched by women to design games for girls and the "Quake girls," made up of female gamer clans playing the violent FPS game *Quake* (id Software 1996) online. She found that while both groups had similar goals of encouraging more girls and women to play video games, their approaches could not have been more different. The game developers aimed to create games for girls according to their perceived preferences, while the "Quake girls" rejected "traditional feminine values in order to enjoy playing the violent and highly competitive game *Quake* in an environment that was not only male dominated but hostile to the incursion of women" (2010: 67).

These various examinations of female gamer preferences clearly illustrate the need to place the experience of gaming within a broader context of player exploration, negotiation, and activation of the interactive matrix of the game-text (Ferri 2007: 3). In the early days of game studies as a field of research, ludologists (e.g. Aarseth, Eskelinen, Frasca) argued for the need to consider the input of the player on the game and to look at games as systems.

## Games as systems

While representational analyses have failed to encompass the greater experience of play, the ludology approach (study of games as rules) neglected to consider gender at all. Indeed, the theoretical and conceptual understanding of games as systems was initially achieved by consigning the player's role to little more than the predisposed need to act on games in order for a game to function as intended—in other words, to "exercise its effect" (Aarseth 1997: 127). While this approach had the benefit of accounting for the presence of the player—something that was missing in representational analyses—it reduced the player to an "unfree subject" (Gadamer 1960). The role of the player in game studies was thus initially suppressed due to the emphasis placed on how games are "facilitators that structure player behaviour" (Aarseth 2007: 130). The players, both "half-real" in the way they interact with real rules *while* imagining a fictional world (Juul 2005) and half-themselves "games rule us" (Aarseth 2007: 133), often appear absolved and subsumed by the game.

At the other extreme, Heide Smith (2006) describes how game research overstated what he has categorized as the "active player." Not determined by the "preferred reading" of the author/designer, instead it is the unrepresentative but "unexpected, aberrant, oppositional or directly subversive" (2006: 30–1) moments of play that are found interesting and then reported in research. Somewhere between these two poles remains a need for accounts of play that elucidate the *moments* in which ergodicity of the text—that is, a disposition or readiness to act—is translated into player action, informed by inimitable factors that bring experience, schemas, and command to the processes of interpretation and configuration.

## Moving beyond the representative

More recent research (van Vught *et al.* 2012) has begun to uncover a preference on the part of players to interpret the game and game environment from a configurative perspective. In other words, the way that the player can act on an interactive environment *through* a character is beginning to emerge as more significant than any representational qualities possessed by the character. This is quite different from the way that we assess non-interactive media. Indeed, the establishment of game studies was based on a premise that game play is a different kind of mediated activity, compared to other forms of media reception, in a desire to avoid the assimilation of games as an object of study into media and film studies as "experiential equivalents." This kind of media blindness (Hausken 2004) to the unique properties and demands of games is evident in regulation of game content (via classification) in which age-restriction is largely determined by the image on screen as the assumed principal communicative form that the player interprets (not configures). The rating process thus characterizes the audiovisual representation of content, leaving the role of interactivity and the way that content is encountered and processed by players severely underarticulated.

Multi-modality theory is a branch of social semiotics (Hodge and Kress 1988) that has fruitfully been applied to textual analysis of games precisely because it acknowledges how the communicative strata of games extend beyond representation (Schott and Burn 2007). What is watchable as screen output in games forms part of the orientational function of the text that will often point to a game's imperative mood: the need to act. Eskelinen (2001) has therefore stated that the most important relationship we have with a game is in the configurative act of playing. This leads us to argue in favor of examining what Lindley and Sennersten call the "competitive, rule constrained form of a game" (2006: 6), or Ermi and Mäyrä refer to as "challenge-based immersion" concerned with the balance of challenges and abilities (2005: n.p.).

On the other hand, Gee (2003) represents a high-profile game researcher arguing in favor of a process of identity construction in which a character's identity in a game becomes the identity that the player wants his character to have. Gee argues that players project their own values onto a character in a process called "projective identity." This comprises the fusion of a "virtual identity" (the identity of a virtual character in a virtual world) and a "real world identity" (the player's own identity). Although this proposal is somewhat appealing, controlling how a character performs does not necessarily mean that players also project their way of thinking, feeling, and knowing (i.e. their consciousness) onto a character. Acting for your character does not inevitably mean thinking for your character. Bruner (1986) helps to reinforce the notion of play as a configurative practice when he argues that a story is considered to be a combination of a "landscape of action" and a "landscape of consciousness." He states:

> Stories must construct two landscapes simultaneously. One is the landscape of action, where the constituents are the arguments of action: agent, intention or goal, situation, instrument, something corresponding to a "story grammar." The other landscape is the landscape of consciousness: what those involved in the action know, think, or feel, or do not know, think, or feel.
>
> (Bruner 1986: 14)

Although these two "landscapes" are essential to a story, some stories may focus more on the representation of action, whereas other stories focus more on the representation of consciousness. Now, it is safe to say video games focus primarily on the landscape of action. When we look at the textual clues we generate on the screen, they show only action, and consciousness seems to play no part whatsoever. As Juul argues, the interactive structure of games makes it "hard to create a game about emotions (or thoughts) because emotions are hard to implement in rules" (2005: 20). It is because we can act that the game focuses on allowing us to perform interesting actions that generally involve moving and manipulating objects. As Ryan has argued, it is simply more enjoyable to play the role of the dragon-slaying hero of Russian fairy tales than it is to play the role of Anna Karenina or Emma Bovary, because "involvement in the plot is not emotional, but rather a matter of exploring a world, solving problems, performing actions ... and above all dealing with interesting objects in a concrete environment" (2001: n.p.).

This is supported by Kirkland, who says the bodies we manipulate in video games "are not characters in a narrative; they are avatars in a game whose visual details soon become unimportant as players engage in the more pragmatic abstract processes of spatial navigation, weapons triangulation, and puzzle solution that the games demand" (2009: 168).

## Looking beyond representation

Video games have been examined as stories with characters and much has been written about the failings of these characters to offer a multiplicity of representations. They have also been studied visually in a similar manner to other forms of visual media, which failed to account for the interactive nature of games. In reaction to these traditional approaches, games have also been dissected as systems with rules that frame the experience of game play. While representational analyses reduced games mainly to their visual components, ludological analyses almost reduced players to automatons following the rules set by designers. As we have seen, both approaches failed to account for the more holistic and configurative way players actually experience the multiple facets of a game.

While gender is an important aspect of games representationally, it cannot be fully understood outside of the experience of game play. This dichotomy is illustrated by studies (e.g. Royse *et al.* 2007) showing that non-players are a lot more bothered by sexist gender portrayals than actual players, who, while they acknowledge the existence of sexism in gaming culture, focus a lot more on the experience of play and the manipulation of characters and the environment to compete and achieve goals.

Much has been written in the last two decades (see Jenson and de Castell 2010 for a summary) about the need to increase the proportion of women in technology-related fields. Video games have been presented as one option that might help girls familiarize themselves with technology. However, focusing solely on the sexist representation of women in games, seen as a barrier to the increased participation of women in gaming culture, may have been detrimental, as we have demonstrated in this chapter, to both a broader and more nuanced view of gender in games. While highlighting the failings of gender portrayal in video games is important, it is not sufficient in itself to draw conclusions as to what impact it might have on actual players. We need to go beyond representation; to push forward in re-evaluating the significance of gender portrayals in games in favor of a broader understanding of how players derive enjoyment and configure the gaming environment to their own ends.

# References

3D Realms (1996) *Duke Nukem 3D*, GT Interactive.

Aarseth, E. (1997) *Cybertext. Perspectives on Ergodic Literature*, London: Johns Hopkins University Press.

——(2004) "Genre Trouble: Narrativism and the Art of Simulation," in N. Wardrip-Fruin and P. Harrigan (eds.) *First Person: New Media as Story, Performance, and Game*, Cambridge, MA: MIT Press, pp. 45–55.

——(2007) "I Fought the Law: Transgressive Play and the Implied Player," *Proceedings of the Digital Game Research Association Conference: Situated Play*, Tokyo, Japan. www.digra.org/dl/db/07313.03489.pdf.

Atari (1975) *Pong*, Atari Inc.

——(1980) *Space Invaders*, Taito Corporation.

——(1982) *Pac Man*, Namco.

Beasley, B. and T. C. Stanley (2002) "Shirts vs. Skins: Clothing as an Indicator of Gender Role Stereotyping in Video Games," *Mass Communication & Society* 5(3): 279–93.

Bruner, J. (1986) *Actual Minds, Possible Worlds*, Cambridge, MA: Harvard University Press.

Bryce, J. and J. Rutter (2002) "Killing Like a Girl: Gendered Gaming and Girl Gamers' Visibility," in F. Mäyrä (ed.) *Computer Games and Digital Cultures Conference Proceedings*, Tampere, Finland: Tampere University Press, pp. 243–55.

Carr, D. (2005) "Context, Gaming Pleasures and Gendered Preferences," *Simulation and Gaming* 36(4): 464–82.

——(2006) "Games and Gender," in D. Carr, D. Buckingham, A. Burn, and G. Schott (eds.) *Computer Games: Text, Narrative, and Play*, Cambridge: Polity, pp. 162–78.

Consalvo, M. (2003) "Hot Dates and Fairy-Tale Romances: Studying Sexuality in Videogames," in J. P. Wolf and B. Perron (eds.) *The Video Game Theory Reader*, New York: Routledge.

Core Design (1996) *Tomb Raider*, Eidos.

Daviault, C. (2010) *Look Who's Pulling the Trigger Now: A Study of Girls'/Women's Relationship with Video Games*, Saarbrüken, Germany: LAP LAMBERT Academic Publishing.

Dietz, T. L. (1998) "An Examination of Violence and Gender Role Portrayals in Video Games: Implications for Gender Socialization and Aggressive Behavior," *Sex Roles* 38(5–6): 425–42.

Dill, K. E., D. A. Gentile, W. A., Richter, and J. C. Dill (2005) "Violence, Sex, Race and Age in Popular Video Games: A Content Analysis," in E. Cole and J. H. Daniel (eds.) *Featuring Females: Feminist Analyses of the Media*, Washington, DC: American Psychological Association, pp. 115–30.

Dovey, J. and H. Kennedy (2006) *Game Cultures: Computer Games as New Media*, Maidenhead: Open University Press.

Downs, E. and S. Smith (2010) "Keeping Abreast of Hypersexuality: A Video Game Character Content Analysis," *Sex Roles* 62(11): 721–33.

Ermi, L. and F. Mäyrä (2005) "Fundamental Components of the Gameplay Experience: Analysing Immersion," *Proceedings of the Digital Game Research Association Conference: Changing Views—Worlds in Play*, Vancouver, Canada. http://www.digra.org/dl/db/06276.41516.pdf.

ESA (2010) "2010 Sales, Demographic and Usage Data: Essential Facts about the Computer and Video Game Industry," *Entertainment Software Association*. http://www.theesa.com/facts/pdfs/ESA_Essential_Facts_2010.pdf.

Eskelinen, M. (2001) "The Gaming Situation," *Game Studies* 1(1). http://www.gamestudies.org/0101/eskelinen/.

Ferri, G. (2007) "Narrating Machines and Interactive Matrices: A Semiotic Common Ground for Game Studies," *Proceedings of the Digital Game Research Association Conference: Situated Play*, Tokyo, Japan. http://www.digra.org/dl/db/07311.02554.pdf.

Forsey, M. G. (2010) "Ethnography as Participant Listening," *Ethnography* 11(4): 558–72.

Frasca, G. (2001) "What Is Ludology? A Provisory Definition." http://www.ludology.org/2001/07/what-is-ludolog.html.

Gadamer, H.-G. (1960) *Truth and Method*, London: Sheed & Ward.

Gee, J. P. (2003) *What Video Games Have to Teach Us about Learning and Literacy*, New York: Palgrave Macmillan.

Graner Ray, S. G. (2004) *Gender Inclusive Game Design: Expanding the Market*, Hingham, MA: Charles River Media, Inc.

Haninger, K. and K. M. Thompson (2004) "Content and Ratings of Teen-rated Video Games," *Journal of the American Medical Association* 291(7): 856–65.

Hausken, L. (2004) "Textual Theory and Blind Spots in Media Studies," in M.-L. Ryan (ed.) *Narrative Across Media: The Language of Storytelling*, Lincoln: University of Nebraska Press, pp. 391–404.

Heide Smith, J. (2006) "Plans and Purposes: How Videogame Goals Shape Player Behaviour," unpublished doctoral dissertation, IT University of Copenhagen, Copenhagen.

Hodge, R. and G. Kress (1988) *Social Semiotics*, Cambridge: Polity.

id Software (1993) *Doom*, id Software.

——(1996) *Quake*, GT Interactive.

Irvine, R. and C. Kincaid (1999) "Video Games Can Kill," *Accuracy in Media*. http://www.aim.org/media-monitor/video-games-can-kill/.

Ivory, J. D. (2006) "Still a Man's Game: Gender Representation in Online Reviews of Video Games," *Mass Communication and Society* 9(1): 103–14.

Jansz, J. and R. G. Martis (2007) "The Lara Phenomenon: Powerful Female Characters in Video Games," *Sex Roles* 56(3–4): 141–8.

Jenson, J. and S. de Castell (2008) "Theorizing Gender and Digital Gameplay: Oversights, Accidents and Surprises," *Eludamos. Journal for Computer Game Culture* 2(1): 15–25.

——(2010) "Gender, Simulation, and Gaming: Research Review and Redirections," *Simulation Gaming* 41(1): 51–71.

Juul, J. (2005) *Half Real: Video Games between Real Rules and Fictional Worlds*, Cambridge, MA: MIT Press.

Kennedy, H. W. (2002) "Lara Croft: Feminist Icon or Cyberbimbo?," *Game Studies: The International Journal of Computer Game Research* 2(2). http://www.gamestudies.org/0202/kennedy/.

Kent, S. L. (2001) *The Ultimate History of Video Games: From Pong to Pokémon and Beyond ... The Story behind the Craze That Touched Our Lives and Changed the World*, New York: Three Rivers Press.

Kirkland, E. (2009) "Masculinity in Video Games: The Gendered Gameplay of Silent Hill," *Camera Obscura* 24(2): 161–83.

Klastrup, L. (2003) "Towards a Poetics of Virtual Worlds—Multi-user Textuality and the Emergence of Story," unpublished doctoral dissertation, IT University of Copenhagen, Copenhagen.

Kontour, K. (2009) "Revisiting Violent Videogame Research: Game Studies Perspectives on Aggression, Violence, Immersion, Interaction, and Textual Analysis," *Digital Culture & Education* 1(1): 6–30.

Lauteren, G. (2002) "The Pleasure of the Playable Text: Towards an Aesthetic Theory of Computer Games," in F. Mäyrä (ed.) *Computer Games and Digital Cultures Conference Proceedings*, Tampere, Finland: Tampere University Press, pp. 217–25.

Lindley, C. A. and C. C. Sennersten (2006) "A Cognitive Framework for the Analysis of Game Play: Tasks, Schemas and Attention Theory," *Proceedings of the Cognitive Science Society Conference: Workshop on the Cognitive Science of Games and Game Play*, Vancouver, Canada. https://picard.hgo.se/~game/images/d/da/CognitiveFrameworkGamePlayAnal.pdf.

Newman, J. (2002) "The Myth of the Ergodic Videogame," *Game Studies* 2(1). www.gamestudies.org/0102/newman/.

Provenzo, E. (1991) *Video Kids: Making Sense of Nintendo*, Cambridge, MA: Harvard University Press.

Royse, P., J. Lee, B. Undrahbuyan, M. Hopson, and M. Consalvo (2007) "Women and Games: Technologies of the Gendered Self," *New Media Society* 9(4): 555–76.

Ryan, M. L. (2001) "Beyond Myth and Methaphor—The Case of Narrative in Digital Media," *Game Studies* 1(1). http://www.gamestudies.org/0101/ryan/.

Schleiner, A.-M. (2001) "Does Lara Croft Wear Fake Polygons? Gender and Gender-Role Subversion in Computer Adventure Games," *Leonardo* 34(3): 221–6.

Schott, G. and A. Burn (2007) "Fan Art as a Function of Agency in Oddworld Fan-Culture," in A. Clarke and G. Mitchell (eds.) *Videogames and Art*, London: Intellect, pp. 238–54.

Schott, G. and K. Horrell (2000) "Girl Gamers and Their Relationship with the Gaming Culture," *Convergence* 6(4): 36–53.

Schott, G. and S. Thomas (2008) "The Impact of Nintendo's 'For Men' Advertising Campaign on a Potential Female Market," *Eludamos. Journal for Computer Game Culture* 2(1): 41–52.

Taylor, T. L. (2003) "Multiple Pleasures: Women and Online Gaming," *Convergence* 9(1): 21–46.

——(2006) *Play between Worlds: Exploring Online Game Culture*, Cambridge, MA: MIT Press.

van Vught, J., G. Schott, and R. Marczak (2012) "Understanding Player Experience: Finding a Useable Model for Game Classification," *Proceedings of the 8th Australasian Conference on Interactive Entertainment: Playing the System*, ACM Digital Library.

Waern, A. (2012) "Framing Games," *Proceedings of the Digital Game Research Association Nordic Conference: Experiencing Games: Games, Play and Players*, Tampere, Finland. www.digra.org/dl/db/12168.20295.pdf.

# 41

# Textual orientation
## Queer female fandom online

## *Julie Levin Russo*

At the end of 2011, an editorial column on the pop culture blog AfterEllen.com posed the question: "Does lesbian subtext still matter?" (Hogan 2012). AfterEllen—named in tribute to the 1997 milestone when both US comedian Ellen DeGeneres and her eponymous television sitcom character came out (*Ellen*, ABC 1994–8)—is a website that covers lesbian and bisexual women and characters in TV, film, entertainment, and independent media. This article exemplifies new questions facing LGBTQ audiences in the era of gay representation on mainstream television. In her book *All the Rage*, Susanna Danuta Walters chronicles the contradictions of what a 1995 *Entertainment Weekly* cover story famously called the "gay 90s," writing that while "visibility has indeed opened up public awareness and an appreciation of gay and lesbian rights, it has also circumscribed those rights into categories that may themselves become new kinds of 'closets'" (2003: 18). In the ensuing decade, the number and range of LGBTQ characters and figures in the mass media in the US has continued to grow, and so has the debate about the politics of representation.

In the aforementioned blog post, this debate is framed in terms of an opposition between "subtext"—homoerotic elements of characterization, narrative, *mise-en scène*, and their surrounding discourses—and "maintext"—explicit portrayals of LGBT individuals. In the several pages of reader comments on the AfterEllen post, some people insist on the social value of positive images. User WaxLionMonkeyBookends, for example, argues that "AfterEllen has a responsibility to passionately put itself behind projects that promote progressive visibility ... to openly encourage (or at least comment on) shows that DO portray gay women as maintext." Other commenters agree with the piece's author that "subtext matters because it creates a virtual playground for lesbian fans to interact with each other ... because lesbians can use that subtext, that chemistry between two female characters, to create their own versions of the story." Are we really, as WaxLionMonkeyBookends and others argue, on a path of historical evolution, wherein lesbians become ever more visible? Or do same-sex romances and same-sex subtext—relationships that are only implied or perceived to be more than platonic—serve different but simultaneously vital roles within our culture? Or might we wonder, rather, if the dichotomy this discussion posits between "subtext" and "maintext" is as transparent and unambiguous as it appears to be?

Growing gay visibility in the media is due not just to social change but also to industrial and technological change. The US broadcast model of network television has been under pressure for decades from innovations like cable (increasing the number of channels and competition between them) and the VCR (the first of many devices offering audiences more choice and control in scheduling TV viewing). The internet and digital video have only intensified these trends. In the context of pro-liferating channels and multiple streams of distribution (Lotz 2007), the industry has responded at the level of marketing and content by shifting toward "narrowcasting" (targeting ever more specific niche demographics) and distinction (promoting its legitimacy and status by dealing with controversial topics like sexuality) (Levine 2007). DeGeneres's sitcom was groundbreaking because it bucked a general trajectory whereby US TV's tentative ventures onto the delicate terrain of LGBT lead char-acters have migrated from premium channels (*Queer as Folk*, Showtime, 2000–5; *Six Feet Under*, HBO, 2001–5) to cable networks (*Queer Eye*, Bravo, 2003–7; *South of Nowhere*, The N, 2005–8) to prime time (*Glee*, Fox, 2009–; *Modern Family*, ABC, 2009–), while supplemented by new formations of fan networks and independent media online (Beirne 2007).

This chapter focuses on queer female fandom from its pre-digital roots to its pre-sent-day internet bounty, emphasizing issues surrounding its internal diversity and external dynamics. The term "queer" is complex and contradictory, straddling the continuum from identity politics—the idea that queer people should band together on the basis of common interests to advocate for recognition and rights—to radical refusal of this notion of a stable identity and other normative categories. The phe-nomenon of fandom asks us to consider the value of subtext, pausing at this moment of techno-cultural transformation to consider what we have to gain and to lose. In mainstream media, boosting the visibility of marginalized groups goes hand in hand with boosting their commercial profile. Through a survey of the history of fan communities, how they have been framed in terms of gender and sexuality, and their current exploits and conflicts, I will point to some of the vitality and multiplicity of queer female fandom that we should be wary of exchanging for business as usual.

## Female fandom

Debates about homoerotic subtext like the one at AfterEllen are attuned to a broader tradition of queer readings of mass culture. Film scholars have analyzed the veiled language of homosexual desire in classical Hollywood films, for example, reclaiming them as part of the history of LGBT media producers and audiences (Doty 2000). During the decades of the Motion Picture Production Code, a system of voluntary censorship governing lewd or immoral images in US cinema (primarily enforced 1934–64), explicit depictions of homosexuality were banned. According to Lynne Joyrich, this meant that alternative sexualities were "connotatively played" with the inadvertent effect that "homosexuality became impossible either to confirm or to disprove" (2001: 442). Although not all queer viewers consciously mobilize this legacy, we could say that lesbian fans of television programs like *Xena: Warrior Princess* (syndicated, 1995–2001) drew on this interpretive heritage to recognize their favorite show as a queer romance between lead characters Xena (Lucy Lawless) and Gabrielle (Renee O'Connor).

In counterpoint to the significance of popular media within LGBT communities, groups of predominantly heterosexual women are central to the history of media fandom. Since at least the 1970s, when the practice coalesced around *Star Trek* (NBC, 1966–9) and several other cult programs, enthusiasts have produced amateur fiction, art, and videos by borrowing from mass culture source texts. Before the popularization of the internet, these creative works ("fanworks") were primarily recorded in handmade magazines ("fanzines") and other analog formats and distributed at fan conventions or through the mail. Portrayals of a romantic and/or sexual relationship between two male characters quickly became a substantial genre; this tradition is known as "slash," since couples like the paradigmatic Kirk and Spock of *Star Trek* were abbreviated as "K/S." While fan fiction stories pairing two female characters and followings for female pairings have existed throughout this period, *Xena* was the first television program to spawn a large fandom with a lesbian relationship as its principal focus in the 1990s, after the advent of the web (Jones 2000). The rise of female slash—termed femslash, femmeslash, or girlslash, but also called subtext fic, altfic (from "alternative"), or saffic in its relatively autonomous communities—is thus intertwined with transitions in both "old" and "new" media.

One explanation for the late arrival of this formation is that few earlier television programs included two or more strong and complex central female characters. The internet's role in expanding the accessibility and diversity of fan fiction no doubt also contributed to femslash's critical mass. Fan subcultures have evolved along with the emergence of Usenet newsgroups, email lists, homemade sites, threaded forums, blogging services, and social networks (Coppa 2006). The web changed the tenor of fandom, increasing the magnitude and diversity of fan production and its visibility within mainstream culture, generating new interdependencies and tensions between fans and the entertainment industry.

An early example of how online communication extends popular debates about the politics of representation is *Xena* fandom. In 1997, a member of the newsgroup alt.tv.xena compiled answers to Frequently Asked Questions (FAQs) about "subtext" on the series, defining this term as "a subtle, underlying theme … [of] romantic innuendo between Xena and Gabrielle" (ATX 1998). In response to frequent harassment by homophobic skeptics (e.g. "All this subtext crap is pure bull. Xena's no lesbian"), fans of the couple offered "proof" in the form of "interviews with the cast and crew" of the program wherein they "flatly stated … that they put subtextual scenes and dialogue in the shows intentionally." This exchange around *Xena* in the late 1990s was a harbinger of the increasingly visible and direct contact between media consumers and professional producers that is one corollary of fandom's transition to the internet.

These histories of queer viewing and fan creativity provide the context for the debate at AfterEllen. But on what side of the line drawn there between lesbian representation and coy underground appeal would *Xena: Warrior Princess* fall? Defining when subtext crosses over into maintext has never been simple. And, in an era of complex interchanges across rapidly changing digital platforms, media aesthetics, labor systems, and individual and collective viewing practices, saying definitively how and where positive LGBT images appear is more difficult than ever. The same could be said for queer female fan communities, which are becoming interwoven with the increasingly diffuse proliferation of online fan activities. Today, popular femslash followings of couples on programs like *Grey's Anatomy* (ABC, 2005–), *Pretty Little Liars* (ABC Family, 2010–), *True Blood* (HBO, 2008–), and *Game of Thrones* (HBO, 2011–) have significant intersections with groups favoring male slash, "het" (heterosexual) fan fiction, or other fan works based on those shows. They occupy many of the same online platforms (including LiveJournal, Twitter, Tumblr, and Facebook). In some instances, an explicit lesbian couple coexists with subtextual favorites (on *Glee*, for example, Santana and Brittany are officially together but slashing Rachel and Quinn is equally common), just as onscreen heterosexual couples have always jockeyed for attention with fans' queer pairings. Thus, even delineating queer female fandom as an object of study—whether a particular mode of visibility or a particular online community—is increasingly complicated.

Little scholarship is yet available on femslash fandom (as distinct from lesbian representation), and with today's digital abundance, even generating reliable demographics of this population is difficult. But it is safe to say that it is still a small minority of overall fan participation. Nor is it easy to verify the degree to which established claims about slash and related fan practices apply to femslash configurations and the degree to which the latter are historically, subculturally, and erotically distinct. Although the presence of some straight men and straight women in femslash fandom is often discussed, the assumption among fans and critics is that queer women are its primary demographic.

This presumed correspondence between the sexualities portrayed in fan fiction and artwork and the sexualities of its readers and writers is a marked departure from the fascination with straight women writing gay male porn that characterizes much of the research on slash. Moreover, male slash implies a particular mode of reading that interfaces with the mass media's codes for representing masculinity: because affectionate gestures between men are taboo, onscreen instances of intimate male–male relationships appear charged with romance and eroticism. In the rarer cases where two female characters have a close relationship, their attachment may be expressed more freely but thus read less clearly as homoerotic. These factors—the particular inflection of women's engagement with televised women, the underrepresentation of female characters in the mass media, and the unique interpretive strategies involved in investing in femslash pairings—point to specificities of queer female fandom that warrant sustained analysis within the field of fan studies, to which I now turn.

## Fan studies

The history of divisions within fan communities that strongly align (ideologically and often demographically) with femininity vs. masculinity has been a pivotal topic of inquiry in media and cultural studies. This intensity speaks to the ways that the field of fan studies has been a key site for negotiating and extending questions about media audiences, gender, and sexuality. Before it reached the critical mass to constitute a distinct discipline in the 2000s, most research on media fandom was conducted under the umbrella of audience studies. Its typically qualitative, ethnographic method initially grew out of ideas developed within cultural studies, intersecting with reader response theory from literature, theories of spectatorship from film studies, and other novel approaches to analyzing popular culture (Busse and Gray 2011). A formative intervention in this period was the concept of the "active audience": Viewers and consumers, particularly those from marginalized groups, engage in a dynamic process of reception and interpretation that challenges the mass media's control over dominant messages and mythologies. Scholars were invested in resisting academia's hierarchies, which privileged high art while dismissing low culture, particularly since the suspect category of the popular is habitually feminized. In keeping with this agenda, they emphasized the possibilities for individual and collective resistance inherent in entertainment favored by women, ethnic minorities, the working class, youth, and so on.

Creative media fans—an especially passionate, articulate, and reflective subset of audiences, who literalize the activeness of reception by actually producing texts—were an attractive object for such research, and these predominantly female (not to mention white and middle-class) communities are often credited with a feminist critique of mass culture. The most cited works from this first phase of fan studies showcase its already interdisciplinary scope: science fiction author and critic Joanna Russ's 1985 essay "Pornography by Women, for Women, with Love"; Camille Bacon-Smith's 1991 ethnography on *Star Trek* fans, *Enterprising Women*; film theorist Constance Penley's 1991 analysis of slash in "Brownian Motion: Women, Tactics, and Technology"; literary scholar Janice Radway's influential 1987 study of female consumers of pulp novels, *Reading the Romance*; and the 1992 landmark cultural studies anthology *The Adoring Audience*. All of these works mobilize a feminist framework to foreground the complexities of heterosexual women's relationships to popular culture.

Henry Jenkins's book *Textual Poachers* most famously synthesized these perspectives and methodologies, presenting research on media fandom's communities and creative activities. Countering sexist and elitist "stereotypes of fans as cultural dupes, social misfits, and mindless consumers," Jenkins argues that they "become active participants in the construction and circulation of textual meanings" (1992: 23–4). But he concedes that "fans operate from a position of cultural marginality and social weakness ... lack direct access to the means of commercial cultural production and have only the most limited resources with which to influence the entertainment industry's decisions" (1992: 26). This relatively bounded and static economy of cultural, textual, and technological relationships between fan and corporate production was already obsolescing. An unanticipated weakness of Jenkins's project was its appearance just before the emergence of the worldwide web. Many of the observations and arguments of this early work would immediately need to be reassessed when growing access to online communication rapidly changed fandom's practices, demographics, and position in the larger cultural economy.

In an overview of "Fan Studies 101," Karen Hellekson observes that fan "[s]cholarship was slow to follow along as fans took to the Internet" (2009: 6). When published work did begin to catch up to the explosion of online fandom, its development was not organized or cohesive. Adding to this haphazard quality is the fact that "fan studies is a truly interdisciplinary field" incorporating approaches from "English and communication ... ethnography ... media, film, and television studies ... psychology ... law" (2009: 5). Hellekson worries that this dispersion may lead to intellectual amnesia, wherein "women-dominated, old-style active fans and their contributions are now in the process of being erased by studies of (male) online fandom, although recuperative work is underway" (2009: 5). Despite this trend, the late 1990s and early 2000s were a dynamic period in the evolution of both media fandom and its academic study. The expanding purview of the field responds to expanding participation in interactive fan behaviors among media consumers, rendering fan studies increasingly important to audience studies as a whole. And alongside this traditional emphasis on reception has been a move to analyze fanworks as aesthetic objects in their own right, while scholars in the area of industry studies also consider professional, legal, and technological developments in commercial media production as it evolves to incorporate fan positions and activities in more structured ways.

In their introduction to *Fandom: Identities and Communities in a Mediated World*, editors Jonathan Gray, Cornel Sandvoss, and C. Lee Harrington suggest that we have reached a "third wave" of fan studies, which takes into account the "empirical" end of fandoms as "subcultures" due to the "changing communication technologies and media texts [that] contribute to and reflect the increasing entrenchment of fan consumption in the structure of our everyday life" (2007: 8). In the more explicitly feminist anthology *Fan Fiction and Fan Communities in the Age of the Internet*, Karen Hellekson and Kristina Busse offer a less authoritative account of the field, emphasizing the multiplicity and fluidity of fan studies and its objects and underscoring "the dense intertextuality found in the creation of fan works of art and in fan academic discourse" (2006: 5–6). However we frame the ongoing project of fan studies, the discipline is clearly becoming more cohesive and legitimate with the rapid expansion of fan engagement, and as the entertainment industry increasingly absorbs fandom's characteristic patterns of interactivity as a dominant structuring principle. With its roots in communities of women and their production of explicit same-sex romances, gender and sexuality have been pivotal to the questions asked by fan studies and to its contributions to media audience research. Thinking about our present-day mediascape as and through fandom may be one route to understanding how it intersects axes of gender and sexuality.

## Gendering media convergence

Digital media and the internet have profoundly impacted the technological, industrial, and cultural organization of entertainment production and consumption. "Convergence" is a buzzword for these sweeping changes, and, in an academic context, it describes less the merging of distinct media than their proliferation and entanglement. Our understanding of this term in media studies is anchored by another influential book by Jenkins—*Convergence Culture* (2006). For Jenkins, convergence is not embodied in a unified technology or business but instead represents a paradigm shift—a move from medium-specific content toward content that flows across multiple media channels, toward the increased interdependence of communications systems, toward multiple ways of accessing media content, and toward ever more complex relations between top-down corporate media and bottom-up participatory culture.

(Jenkins 2006: 243)

Fandom remains at the heart of Jenkins's concerns. As such, he explicates convergence largely in terms of fan practices, cementing the centrality of fan production to broader discourses about media in transition. In contrast to the rather romantic tone of *Textual Poachers*, which framed fandom as a subculture resistant to the homogeneous and normative messages emanating from mainstream media, much current research is occupied with the corporate dimensions of this transformation. Jenkins sees no contradiction between "tactical collaboration" (2006: 250) with the media industry and his "critical utopian" (2006: 247) idea that "the emergence of new media technologies supports a democratic urge to allow more people to create and circulate media" (2006: 258). This collision of new market imperatives and participatory potentials is the site of mounting tensions and synergies between fans and commercial entertainment today.

Fans are not subversive by definition, but nor are the interests of fans and corporations necessarily commensurate. Conditions of increasing commodification and control raise the stakes of their negotiations, stressing traditional hierarchies of gender and sexuality, revealing new tensions around race, class, and nation. Despite the heterogeneity of the various patterns that constitute fandom, queer fan activities like slash have remained a key dimension of both media transformations and continuing academic research. Likewise, gender continues to be a central reference for popular, industrial, and scholarly conceptions of today's fans. Building on a long history of stereotyping mass culture as "feminine," media fans have been denigrated as overemotional and uncritical consumers. To recuperate its most avid audiences, the entertainment industry has chiefly promoted and pandered to a more "masculine" fan, one who is pictured as having discerning tastes, technological savvy, original contributions, and disposable income. I'd like to explore how corporate efforts to mobilize and monetize fan labor as a commercial force within convergence may affect queer female fan communities.

Jenkins readily admits that gender, sexuality, and other inequalities impact the shifting power relations of convergence. Of particular concern is the risk that the "mainstreaming of fandom" may privilege the activities and modalities that young, straight, white, affluent males are assumed to enjoy. One example from *Convergence Culture* is Lucasfilm's sponsored website for *Star Wars* fan films, Atomfilms.com. Jenkins points out that the rules for acceptable submissions "are anything but gender neutral"—legal stipulations banning "'fan fiction'—which attempts to expand on the *Star Wars* universe ... [and] copyrighted *Star Wars* music or video" effectively "create a two-tier system" resulting in the "invisibility of these mostly female-produced works" (2006: 154–6). Studying the rise of the masculinized fan as a protagonist for convergence as a cultural, industrial, and technological process, Suzanne Scott proposes that similar hierarchies may operate broadly, as "the fanboy's visibility is, in many cases, a byproduct of his complicity with industrially valued (that is to say, marketable or co-optable) modes of fannish participation" (2011: 12). If the "fanboy" is taking on the guise of social exemplar, coveted viewer, and model citizen of online "participatory culture," where does that leave "fangirl" production, pleasures, and communities?

## Queer, queerer, queerest

Femslash fans occupy a particularly delicate corner of this nexus of issues because of their partial but simultaneous overlap with traditions from creative fandom, LGBTQ fandom, gay civil rights, and independent media. Alongside debates about the role of gender in fan communities and the degree to which "fangirl" and "fanboy" stereotypes reflect demographic realities, academics and fans have considered whether slash is a "queer" phenomenon. Because fan fiction featuring male–male couples is predominantly produced by straight women, its authors and characters may have only minimal contact with LGBTQ identities and concerns as they play out in everyday life. In addition to the identitarian question of whether it's fair to call this phenomenon a queer community, the term queer invokes a political stance that resists normative models of sexuality and behavior. Is it reasonable to consider slash queer in this sense, or does this rehash outmoded celebrations of fandom as subversive?

Busse argues that of all the reasons slash has been called subversive (including its queering of mass cultural texts, openness about women's sexual agency and fantasies, and anti-capitalist "gift economy"), the most compelling are the interactions between its female readers and writers. Slashers' constant communication about and intertextual co-creation of erotic desires sustains a "homosocial environment ... [and] homoerotically charged relations" between women, "transcending the wide variety of the slashers' sexual identities" (2005: 105). Busse finds the term "queer" useful because it goes beyond "straight/gay dichotomies" and "moves from sexual identity based on object choice to practices including fantasy ... [and] allows for the various ways subjects identify within fantasy space" (2005: 121–2). On the other hand, fans are sensitive to a "discrepancy between performances of online queerness and lived queer experience" (Lothian et al. 2007: 107), with one participant ultimately describing slash fandom not as a "queer female space" per se but as "a space that invites queer potential" (2007: 109). The intersections of sexuality and textuality— the capacity to both eroticize the content and transform the structure of mass media—are crucial to the power and possibility of slash fanworks and communities.

Certainly some lesbian and bisexual-identifying women participate in the fluid configurations of male slash and in other iterations of fan production. In the case of femslash, however, women who are queer IRL ("in real life") are assumed to be in the majority. While slashers may at times cross over to appreciate media portrayals of gay male couples, femslash fandom has a stronger overlap with a personal and political desire for lesbian representation. Femslashers follow onscreen lesbian couples alongside their subtextual favorites and have often clamored for one of the latter characters to "come out" on television. In this sense, lesbian fans may contravene some of the gendered expectations of fangirl vs. fanboy tropes, which have been associated with a dichotomy between "transformational" vs. "affirmational" engagement as media viewers. Coined by a fan, these terms describe a pronounced opposition between creative media fans (the predominantly female authors of fan fiction), who are "all about laying hands upon the source and twisting it to [their] own purposes," and the "sanctioned fans," who "reaffirm the source material, attempt to divine authorial intent, or debate elements of the text while staying firmly within the established 'rules' of the fictional universe" (Scott 2011: 31–2). These poles have been tied to feminine and masculine modes of participation, respectively, with male-coded affirmational fans typically gaining more recognition and legitimacy from the media industry because they acknowledge the professionals' authority and play by the "rules." Lesbian fans who demand endorsements from actors and writers and onscreen storylines that reflect their desires are also behaving affirmationally. If the figure of the straight white male fan occupies a position of privilege, we can understand why fans who identify as queer women aspire to a similar position of positive visibility in mass culture.

The double bind fans face is that, within the corporate schemas of entertainment, mainstream visibility equates with profitability. The most vocal consumers of lesbian media, whether subtext or maintext, are constituted by the industry as part of the emerging "gay market" for advertising and products (Sender 2005). In the context of *Xena* fandom, Jeanne Hamming observes that "the internet ... has brought fan fiction to the immediate attention of television producers who have responded by incorporating fan material into production" (2001: §7). While many scholars have considered this a positive development in the direction of a more "democratic" participatory culture, Hamming cautions that "the circuit created between *Xena: Warrior Princess* and *Xena* slash fiction, between the production of the series (as commodity) and the production of slash confession (also as commodity), is, in short, a capitalist relation" (2001: §18). If the convergence of television and the internet has offered marginalized groups new opportunities to speak and intervene on the terrain of mass media, it's important to remember that bargains are being struck between established and emerging sites of cultural power. The development of LGBT audiences as a market niche with dedicated networks, programming, advertising, and online sensations parallels and intensifies the pattern established with African Americans, among others, in the post-broadcast era (Torres 2010). As long as we live in a capitalist society, this type of commodification will be a key dynamic by which marginalized groups gain mainstream visibility and acceptance. Even allowing for the importance of positive representation, we need to bear in mind the stakes and conditions of framing visibility in the corporate media's terms.

Similar questions to these animate the debate about subtext at AfterEllen with which I opened this chapter. Some commentators argue that an increasingly deliberate deployment of same-sex subtext is merely the industry's calculated attempt to capture slash fans and queer audiences without offering up explicit portrayals of gay characters. But femslashers assert that fans' creative communities hold value and pleasure outside the mainstream media's limited repertoire. The existence of such a lively comment thread speaks to the scope of texts, interpretations, and relationships that the web can support. Any doubters that femslash has become a significant force in fandom may have been impressed by the unexpected win of *Glee* characters Rachel

Berry and Quinn Fabray—who are not in one of the show's several overt gay relationships—in an E!Online poll to elect "TV's Top Couple" (Dos Santos 2012). They
were able to beat popular male slash couple Dean and Castiel from *Supernatural* as
well as *Glee* girlfriends Santana and Brittany. But amidst the excitement, let's
remember that an internet poll isn't democracy—and ultimately what distinguishes
slash within digital culture from the top-down economy of television is that you
don't have to choose between couples, sexualities, or stories in the first place.

# References

ATX, E. (1998) "The Subtext FAQ for alt.tv.xena," *Xenite.org*. http://web.archive.org/web/
20051031202026/http://www.xenite.org/faqs/subtext.html.

Bacon-Smith, C. (1991) *Enterprising Women: Television Fandom and the Creation of Popular Myth*,
Philadelphia: University of Pennsylvania Press.

Beirne, R. (2007) "Introduction," in *Televising Queer Women*, New York: Palgrave Macmillan,
pp. 1–16.

Busse, K. (2005) "'Digital Get Down': Postmodern Boy Band Slash and the Queer Female
Space," in C. Malcolm and J. Nyman (eds.) *Eros.Usa: Essays on the Culture and Literature of
Desire*, Gdansk: Gdansk University Press, pp. 103–25.

Busse, K. and J. Gray (2011) "Fan Cultures and Fan Communities," in V. Nightingale (ed.) *The
Handbook of Media Audiences*, New York: Blackwell, pp. 425–43.

Coppa, F. (2006) "A Brief History of Media Fandom," in K. Hellekson and K. Busse (eds.) *Fan
Fiction and Fan Communities in the Age of the Internet*, Jefferson, NC: McFarland, pp. 41–59.

Dos Santos, K. (2012) "TV's Top Couple Tournament: And the Winner Is ... ," *E!Online*.
http://www.eonline.com/news/294212/tv-s-top-couple-tournament-and-the-winner-is.

Doty, A. (2000) *Flaming Classics: Queering the Film Canon*, New York: Routledge.

Gray, J. A., C. L. Harrington, and C. Sandvoss (2007) "Introduction: Why Study Fans?," in
*Fandom: Identities and Communities in a Mediated World*, New York: New York University
Press, pp. 1–16.

Hamming, J. E. (2001) "Whatever Turns You On: Becoming-Lesbian and the Production of
Desire in the Xenaverse," *Genders* 34. http://www.genders.org/g34/g34_hamming.html.

Hellekson, K. (2009) "Fan Studies 101," *SFRA Review* 287: 5–7. http://khellekson.wordpress.
com/2009/03/29/fan-studies-101/.

Hellekson, K. and K. Busse (2006) "Introduction: Work in Progress," in *Fan Fiction and Fan
Communities in the Age of the Internet*, Jefferson, NC: McFarland, pp. 5–32.

Hogan, H. (2012) "Does Lesbian Subtext Still Matter?," *AfterEllen.com*. http://www.afterellen.
com/tv/does-lesbian-subtext-still-matter.

Jenkins, H. (1992) *Textual Poachers: Television Fans and Participatory Culture*, New York: Routledge.

——(2006) *Convergence Culture: Where Old and New Media Collide*, New York: New York
University Press.

Jones, S. G. (2000) "Histories, Fictions, and Xena: Warrior Princess," *Television and
New Media* 1: 403–18.

Joyrich, L. (2001) "Epistemology of the Console," *Critical Inquiry* 27(3): 439–67.

Levine, E. (2007) *Wallowing in Sex: The New Sexual Culture of 1970s American Television*,
Durham, NC: Duke University Press.

Lewis, L. A. (ed.) (1992) *The Adoring Audience: Fan Culture and Popular Media*, New York: Routledge.

Lothian, A., K. Busse, and R. A. Reid (2007) "'Yearning Void and Infinite Potential': Online
Slash Fandom as Queer Female Space," *English Language Notes* 42(5): 103–11.

Lotz, A. D. (2007) *The Television Will Be Revolutionized*, New York: New York University Press.

Penley, C. (1991) "Brownian Motion: Women, Tactics, and Technology," in C. Penley and A. Ross (eds.) *Technoculture*, Minneapolis: University of Minnesota Press, pp. 135–61.

Radway, J. (1987) *Reading the Romance: Women, Patriarchy, and Popular Literature*, New York: Verso.

Russ, J. (1985) "Pornography by Women, for Women, with Love," in *Magic Mommas, Trembling Sisters, Puritans & Perverts: Feminist Essays*, New York: Crossing Press, pp. 79–99.

Scott, S. (2011) "Revenge of the Fanboy: Convergence Culture and the Politics of Incorporation," unpublished dissertation, USC.

Sender, K. (2005) *Business, Not Politics: The Making of the Gay Market*, New York: Columbia University Press.

Torres, S. (2010) "Television and Race," in J. Wasco (ed.) *A Companion to Television*, New York: Blackwell, pp. 395–40.

Walters, S. D. (2003) *All the Rage: The Story of Gay Visibility in America*, Chicago: University of Chicago Press.

# 42

# Delivering the male—and more

## Fandom and media sport

## *Toby Miller*

Sport and the media have long exercised anxious minds keen to control unruly populations. A millennium ago, John of Salisbury warned that juggling, mime, and acting had negative impacts on "unoccupied minds ... pampered by the solace of some pleasure ... to their greater harm" (quoted in Zyvatkauskas 2007: 18). A few centuries later, Edward Said was equally concerned by such temptations:

> Consciousness of sports, with its scores and history and technique and all the rest of it, is at the level of sophistication that is almost terrifying ... investment is being made in those things that distract you from realities that are too complicated.
>
> (Said 1993: 23)

Umberto Eco explained this through the concept of sport cubed: The meaning of a sports event is multiplied, first by media coverage of it *per se*, then by coverage *of* that coverage. The effect is to distract audiences from social issues because they dwell on sporting gossip (Eco 1987: 162–4).

These venerable critiques are scientized when the psy-function (psychoanalysis, psychiatry, psychology, and psycho-pharmacology) joins the party, for example querying the impact of television coverage on viewers lest it affect the alleged capacity of sport to release individual tension and facilitate social cohesion, or diminish the quality of semen in young men due to the amount of time they lie around watching sport rather than playing it (Bernhardt *et al.* 1998; Gaskins *et al.* 2013).

Gender is profoundly implicated in these assumptions. For instance, when Janet Jackson's breast was momentarily exposed during the 2004 US National Football League (NFL) Super Bowl broadcast, it stimulated bizarre, even hysterical, media, public, and regulatory responses (Wenner 2004). The satirical paper *The Onion* cleverly mocked these anxious accounts of effects on audiences via a *faux* study of US youth: "No one who lived through that day is likely to forget the horror, said noted child therapist Dr. Eli Wasserbaum" ("U.S. Children Still Traumatized ... " 2005). Six years later, international football (soccer) stars Didier Drogba and Cristiano Ronaldo were featured on a *Vanity Fair* cover, attired only in underpants. Their appearance did not engage such moral panics, marking a trend that forms the backdrop to this chapter ("Don't Call It Soccer! … " 2010).

Who is the implied spectator to the bourgeois media's coverage of sport, given that newsrooms are largely male run, and coverage of sport focuses predominantly on men, but women viewers, readers, and listeners are active, numerous—and have been so from the first? After examining this contradictory story, I hone in on the rise, fall, and televisualization of football hooligans and wrestling fans. Their stories represent breach moments, occasions when cultures recalibrate because of changes to the economy of gender.

## The backdrop

The vast majority of scholarship on this topic is beholden to the psy-function, whose authors identify and measure activities inside people's heads in order to explain gender, spectatorship, and sport. They are particularly fascinated with relaxation, relief, arousal, aggression, entertainment, and identification—aged Aristotelian categories about drama that are newly invigorated with the marvel of modern, scientific labeling. A personal favorite is the "Sport Fan Motivation Scale." Such research typically finds that men watch more media sport than women, are more animated by it, and likelier to define themselves through it (Sloan 1989; Tang and Cooper 2012; Trail and James 2001; Wann 1995). This is deemed to occur because media sport offers shared experiences without profound intimacy (Arehart-Treichel 2012). Such *nostra* generally extrapolate from English-speaking studies undertaken in the Global North to essentialize spectatorship via an account of male sports fans as immature or at least biologically driven, their conduct determined by testosterone levels that shift with team success and failure on TV (Bernhardt *et al.* 1998).

Historical sociologist Norbert Elias borrows these psy-*données*, investigating changes in time and space that occurred when imperialist adventurers began the globalization of sport (Elias 1978; Elias and Dunning 1986). Elias's idea of a civilizing impulse deriving from that history is problematic, but his work has nevertheless stimulated some interesting microsociology. His followers have shown that the contemporary sporting body sends gendered messages via the media about discipline, mirroring, dominance, and communication (Maguire 1993). The disciplined sports body is remodeled through diet and training. The mirroring body functions as a machine of desire, encouraging mimetic conduct via the purchase of commodities. The dominant body exercises power through physical force. The communicative body is an expressive totality, balletic and beautiful, wracked and wrecked.

Investments in such bodies by the media help explain, and in turn are illuminated by, breach moments when sporting fantasies go wrong. Consider the fury unleashed on an Australian Olympic rower who engaged in a form of anti-nationalistic refusal by ceasing to perform towards the end of an event. The media accused her of being "un-Australian." Another example is the public grief and anger that erupt when the seemingly pure, meritocratic sporting body is shown to depend on illicit chemical and medical regimes. In each case, sporting journalism reacts with incredulity rather than penitence at its complicity with reactionary nationalism or industrialized competitiveness (Australian Crime Commission 2013; Lowden 2013; McKay and Roderick 2010).

## Alternative forms of thought

I depart from these orthodoxies, by focusing on political economy rather than psychological interiority. In place of a preoccupation with consciousness, I concentrate on the overt, public, and contested construction and conduct of spectatorship by corporations, governments, and supporters. The governing assumption is that there is no "real" response to be found among audiences, only incarnations of such responses by interested parties, be they academia, capital, the state, or fandom (Miller 2009).

For marketers in the Global North, young, affluent men are the most desirable media spectators. By contrast with other segments of the population, they watch little television, have protean preferences for brands, and earn sizeable incomes. They often love TV sport, which makes their interest in it disproportionately influential on programming (Commission on the Future of Women's Sport 2010: 7). For example, the US cable and satellite network Fox Soccer targets men aged 18–34 with annual household incomes of US$75,000 and above ("Fox Soccer ... " 2008).[1] The station boasts that three-quarters of its audience are male and half own their own homes.[2] Commercials provide textual hints about the network's plan for matching viewers to advertisers: its advertisements concentrate remorselessly on regaining and sustaining hair growth and erections, losing and hiding pimples and pounds, and becoming and adoring soldiers and sailors.

For an even more chauvinistic instance, we might consider coverage of the US Armed Forces Bowl, a college American football event sponsored by a helicopter manufacturer. The Bowl is designed to create goodwill towards corporate welfare through broad-brush suburbanite homologies constructed between sport, nation, and *matériel* (bombs, guns, and military transport). The contest is televised—and owned—by ESPN, Disney's sports channel, a network available in 194 countries and 15 languages. It features military recruiters preying on young spectators and showcases the "Great American Patriot Award" (Butterworth and Moskal 2009; Miller 2010).[3] Such events manufacture ideological links between nationalism and state violence, interpellating male audiences as sacrificial sons of glory. Unsurprisingly, studies of US TV sports fans indicate high levels of support for imperialist warmongering among white men (Stempel 2006).

Sometimes athletes' social and private lives become as important as their professional qualities, providing audiences with stereotypes of success, power, and beauty: "una imagen; pero no una imagen natural" (an image; but an unnatural one) that has been transmogrified "del icono ideográfico en icono normativo" (from an ideographic icon into a normative one) (Bueno 2002: 2). Sponsors pay sizeable sums to associate their products with such celebrities. By 2005, these endorsements were estimated at over $1 billion in the USA, based on a wager about fan interest in athletes' lifestyles that contractually favors reliability and decency but finds those qualities hard to separate from surprise headlines and excess. Such investment assumes that audiences seek to replicate stars' fetishized qualities by purchasing commodities associated with them. Marketing mavens call this "associative learning" (Thrall *et al.* 2008; Till *et al.* 2008). The tabloid media subsidize such transmogrifications because they are equally interested in celebrating and condemning stars, as official photo shoots of big heterosexual weddings are gradually displaced on magazine covers by unauthorized paparazzi shots of big masculine waistlines.

Clearly, the gendering of media audiences has to do with business strategies. These are subject to change as corporations target different demographic groups at different times, and the genre is becoming more inclusive in certain ways by contrast with its hyper-masculinist past. In Canada in the early 1990s, the beer company that owned the Sports Network (TSN) adopted "We deliver the male" as its cable TV motto. As late as 1998, an advertisement for ESPN promised "More tackles, less tutus" (TSN quoted in Sparks 1992: 330, 334; "There's Life Outside Sports ... " 1998). Women spectators felt excluded from TV's "discourse of [Australian] football" because their pleasurable voyeurism was not of interest to broadcasters (Poynton and Hartley 1990: 144). But commercial and cultural changes have exerted tremendous pressure on the gender normativity of sport, weakening the seemingly rock-solid maleness at its core, thanks to the weight of numbers.

Female US spectators have long tuned into the Olympics in large numbers. For example, the 1992 Winter Games drew 57 percent of its TV audience from women. Women's figure skating out-rated that year's men's baseball World Series and National Collegiate Athletic Association basketball championship game. The women's technical skating program at the 1994 Winter Games drew the fourth-highest ratings of any program in US history, while the 1998 National Basketball Association play-offs attracted more women to Game Seven of the Bulls–Pacers series than *Veronica's Closet* or *ER*. Every major professional men's league in the USA has a women's media marketing plan, and male spectatorship of TV sport in the USA is in decline, as more and more viewers turn to the History and Discovery channels. The perennial savior of network sportscasters, the NFL, saw 1998–9 and 1999–2000 ratings for *Monday Night Football* at record lows—and one-third of its audience was female. In 1999, more men aged 18–34 watched professional women's softball on ESPN2 than Arena football, the National Hockey League, or Major League Soccer. The NFL suffered a 13 percent decrease in TV ratings in the five seasons from 1997 and Disney exiled *Monday Night Football* from its broadcast network ABC to ESPN in 2006. The code increasingly relied on female viewers. By 2012, they made up 40 percent of its audience (Miller 2001, 2010; Oates 2012; Wenner and Gantz 1998).

NBC initiated "a female-inclusive sports subgenre" at the 1992 Summer Games, offering "private-life" histories of selected contestants, which may have had an effect on female audience numbers. In 1996, 50 percent of the US Olympic audience was adult women and 35 percent men, with women's gymnastics one of the most popular events and male boxing and wrestling edged out of prime time (though there remained a disproportionate address of men's sport). The network reported an increase of 26 percent in the number of women viewers aged 25–54 by comparison with the 1992 Games (Miller 2001). Nevertheless, female athletes continue to be depicted in US media coverage in passive roles by contrast with men (Buysse and Wolter 2013).

Something new is happening, as evidenced in the photograph of Drogba and Ronaldo's underwear. A further clue comes from ABC's coverage of Super Bowl 2000, which featured Giants cornerback Jason Seahorn in uniform pants during a pre-game show and reporter Meredith Vieira remarking that the sport is "all about the butt." This is not to say that the objectification of the male body is universally welcome or relevant, but it certainly compromises the hitherto powerful assumption of male spectatorship to sport (Nelson 2002; Weissman 2010).

Women currently comprise half of ESPN's US viewers (McBride 2011) and TSN, which undertook to "deliver the male" 20 years ago, now promises that "Sponsorship programs on TSN.ca can be tailored to your target audience."[4] The failure of *Sports Illustrated for Women*, published from 2000 to 2002, was attributed to the first George W. Bush recession, which affected advertising budgets. In 2010, ESPN launched espnW, a website targeting female fans that followed on a thrice-yearly magazine for women (Hueter 2010).[5] *The Onion* grotesquely but tellingly satirized stereotypical reactions to this development by suggesting the site would concentrate on

> Highlights that feature an explanation of the rules, what's happening, and who everyone is ... Team-by-team sensitivity ratings ... Message boards where a bunch of chicks can dyke it out like crazy ... Community feature where site users can discuss goings-on, share stories, and then secretly trash on each other in private chats ... [and] Somewhat less male-on-male eroticism.
> ("Features of the New espnW.com" 2010)

Television and web coverage of the 2012 Olympics attracted 80 percent of the US population, without significant social divisions, other than those following online, which was largely the province of the young (one billion worldwide). Already, well over half the US population connected with broadband uses it to follow sport. But a comparatively high proportion of women prefer sport on TV. Male fans appear to favor cell phones and tablets to laptops or desktops (Burst Media 2012; Pew Research Center for the People and the Press 2012).

In 1995, more women than men in the UK watched Wimbledon tennis on television, and the numbers were nearly equal for boxing. By 2009, the million people viewing England's Football Association Women's Cup Final out-rated numerous men's cricket, rugby, and football fixtures and the British Women's Open Golf drew larger audiences than the men's Ryder Cup contest between the US and Europe. Meanwhile, the vast majority of people watching women's sport on UK TV were men (Commission on the Future of Women's Sport 2010: 6–8; Miller 2001).

Gender distinctions and inequalities remain at play. The hyper-masculinity characteristic of newsrooms and the biases of sporting departments remain divisive issues in the gendered world of sports. In the USA, there are 48 male sportscasters for every female and 94 percent of sports editors are men, as are 90 percent of their assistants. The corollaries of journalistic inattention to female fans are clear (Adams and Tuggle 2004; Schreiber 2012). Their Australian media counterparts also continue to discriminate: in 2008–9, 9 percent of non-news TV was dedicated to women's sport. The figure was 86 percent for men's sports (Australian Sports Commission 2009: v).

TOBY MILLER

## Case studies

The psy-function and sociological accounts mentioned earlier have encountered some problems since the 1970s with their assumptions about sport as a means of safely expressing social tensions, thereby minimizing political conflict. Over the last 40 years, live football, for example, has frequently been a crucible of nationalistic, racist, misogynistic, and hyper-masculinist conduct by fans, in part responding to spiraling unemployment, a compromised welfare state, and emergent immigration and inter-ethnic issues that became tinderboxes with the arrival of people from former colonies (in small numbers) to deindustrializing European metropoles and the movement to cities of the poorest segments of Latin American society. In the UK, some football grounds became places to enact these tensions through white male heterosexual violence. Counter-measures have included all-seat stadia, individual profiling, life bans, Interpol information exchange, high ticket prices, checks on alcohol, separation of rival fans, ground security, fining or banning clubs for poor crowd control, and scheduling matches between local teams at lunch time to reduce drunkenness beforehand. The media were dual sites for playing out and resolving this gendered audience problem. Initially they provided sites for pundits and politicians to deride football fans as male monsters. Then, as new media technologies, most importantly satellite, came into play, proprietors corralled male audiences who had been priced out of buying tickets to games by purchasing the rights to show football on TV. More and more matches became available to watch, but in pubs and homes rather than in person (Pope 2011).

Liz Moor (2007) claims these developments should not be regarded as simply excluding people on a class basis through commodification. They have also stimulated new forms of gendered spectatorship, as pubs and sports bars have become crucial sites for collective, deterritorialized viewing (Eastman and Land 1997; Wenner 1998; for an historical view, see McCarthy 1995). A visit to a Dominican-targeted bar in Washington Heights during summer may see immigrant men viewing baseball games involving their countrymen on various televisions, while a Santa Monica British-style pub may offer football and rugby union on different walls at the same time, and a Clerkenwell gastro pub may provide one television set dedicated to La Liga and another to the Barclays Premier League (Cooper 1999).

Such viewing practices can be understood as intercultural. Néstor García Canclini (2004) demonstrates that mobile texts must be understood through three lenses: globalization also deglobalizes, in that it is not only about mobility and exchange, but also disconnectedness and exclusion; minorities frequently emerge transnationally, due to migration by people who continue to communicate, work, and consume through their languages of origin; but demographic minorities within sovereign states may not form permanent cultural minorities on their adopted terrain. Mobile subject positions of this kind are ambivalently received by the psy-function. On the one hand, public viewing is welcomed because it may diminish domestic struggles over economic and social deprivation. Conversely, it might reduce industrial productivity (Gantz 2012). The discourse is remorselessly tied to a conservative ethos of community, which signifies obedience and productivity.

Hooligans and dawdlers are not the only sports spectators who provoke mistrust. In the USA, the capitalist crisis that crystallized in the late 1970s found expression in

466

the controlled chaos of televised wrestling, which occupies a liminal status between sport and scripted entertainment. It is an exemplary site for the evaluation of male bodies reshaped by training, medication, and display—and for the derision of fans by the psy-function. Wrestling has long had a special place in the gendering of audiences in a way that seems to compromise its status as a sport, even though it handily indexes social change. Consider the now rather antique stories below. They come from the archive of Mass Observation, a strange blend of British Surrealism and questionnaire empiricism that gathered a vast array of data about ordinary life during the late 1930s and early 1940s. They illustrate that the sexualized gaze was alive in the earliest moments of media wrestling:

> No other sport has such fine husky specimens of manhood as wrestling. I find it such a change to see real he men after the spineless and insipid men one meets ordinarily—"A woman," 1938
>
> I love it because it brings back to me, I am 67 years of age, my young days when men were men and not the namby pamby, simpering, artificial, hair curling variety—"A man," 1938
>
> (quoted in Mass-Observation 1939: 133)

After great success with women viewers of 1940s and 1950s French and US television, wrestling lost its place on commercial networks, a victim of their decision to privilege male spectators' greater disposable incomes. The USA reintroduced the sport on cable in the 1980s, when deregulation enabled genre-based channels and encouraged lawless forms of representation; sport morphed into fiction (Geurens 1989; Sammond 2005). Wrestling's return involved a new address to women and revised rules. Quick falls, tightly circumscribed moves, and rigorous refereeing were forsaken. In their stead came a circus-like activity, dominated by absurd persons in silly costumes adopting exotic personae and acrobatic displays (Mazer 1998). Utopic cultural critics celebrated this as carnivalesque play with a gendered hierarchy that engaged mock hysteria among fans (Fiske 1987; Sammond 2005; Schimmel et al. 2007). But the psy-function worried that the genre's lawlessness had a deleterious effect on young audiences, encouraging wanton disobedience (Waxmonsky and Beresin 2001).

Both these cases urge us towards political-economic rather than conventional engagements with the idea of media audiences. Each case study illustrates the imperative to comprehend institutional aspects of manufacturing audiences in place of psy-function orthodoxy.

## Conclusion

In 1869, the Cincinnati Red Stockings baseball team song addressed the female gaze:

> The ladies want to know
> Who are those gallant men in
> Stockings red.
>
> (quoted in Schreier 1989: 104)

The Reds were on the money. Whether the sporting body is exposed in its bloodied, bowed, and beaten form or its triumphant, tall, and talented one, anxieties and hopes about audiences are never far away.

A century and a half on from Cincinnati gallantry, the internet has seen an efflorescence of women's sporting sites that both express female desire as per early baseball spectators and provide alternative perspectives. Sites run by and for women fans are impressive in their blend of organic interest and professional whimsy. *HerGameLife*, for instance, has over 200 female bloggers (Maria 2012).[6]

Of course, the internet is no more a utopia than its elderly and middle-aged media equivalents: for instance, in December 2012, Google offered 409,000 hits for "Soccer is gay," an anti-queer US cliché about anything that escapes popular ken.[7] Many such sites attack the sexuality of football's players and followers (Mercado 2008), although they also include *The Onion*'s parody of soccer coming out that mocks such attitudes, playing with gender.[8]

The above facts have resulted neither in gender equality in media coverage of sport nor in the valuation of men and women as subjects and objects of the gaze. Despite many women's fascination for sport, and repeated evidence that women's sport appeals to viewers across social categories, the resources dedicated by the international bourgeois media to such tastes remain largely structured in patriarchal dominance, privileging men as performers, commentators, sponsors, and spectators (Commission on the Future of Women's Sport 2010; Bruce 2013; López Díaz with Gallo Suárez 2011; Talleu 2011).

Sport and gender jumble together in a complex and protean weave of contradictory commodification. They cannot be kept apart and lead unstable lives: cheek by capital: torso by Totti, boot by Beckham. The paradox of sport, its simultaneously transcendent and imprisoning quality and profound capacity to allegorize, is most obvious, dangerous, and transformative regarding gender. With the advent of consumer capitalism and postmodern culture, the body has become an increasingly visible locus of desire. It's not just women who are objects of this gaze and suffer physical harm due to social expectations, and not just men who inspect the bodies of others for foibles, follicles, and fun.

These shifts are intimately connected to the fact that across the past three decades sport has become an international capitalist project. New pressures accompany the spoils. As part of the desire to address media spectators and capture their attention for advertisers, the body has become an object of lyrical rhapsody and gendered money. It is up for grabs as a sexual icon. Sculpted features, chiseled waistlines, well-appointed curves, dreamy eyes, administered hair, and an air of casual threat are the currency of the day. Like beauty and fitness of all kinds, stars will fade and the media will identify new names, new bodies, new Eros, new Euros. Drogba and Ronaldo in underwear will be shunted into the shadows, but someone will take up what they leave behind.

## Notes

1 Fox also undertakes surveillance of viewers on the web: http://surveys.researchresults.com/mrIWeb/mrIWeb.dll.
2 See http://www.cvadsales.com/network_fox_soccer.html.

3 See http://www.armedforcesbowl.com/military/great-american-patriot-award/.
4 See http://www.tsn.ca/contact/#advertsing_contact.
5 See http://espn.go.com/espnw/.
6 See http://www.hergamelife.com/about-her-game-life/.
7 See http://www.google.com.mx/search?q=%22soccer+is+gay%22&oq=%22soccer+is+gay%22&sugexp=chrome,mod=3&sourceid=chrome&ie=UTF-8.
8 See http://www.theonion.com/video/soccer-officially-announces-it-is-gay,17603/.

# References

Adams, T. and C. A. Tuggle (2004) "ESPN's SportsCenter and Coverage of Women's Athletics: 'It's a Boys' Club'," *Mass Communication & Society* 7(2): 237–48.

Arehart-Treichel, J. (2012) "Why Sports Evoke Passion, for Better or Worse," *Psychiatric News* 47(9): 13.

Australian Crime Commission (2013) *Organised Crime and Drugs in Sport*, Canberra: Australian Crime Commission.

Australian Sports Commission (2009) *Towards a Level Playing Field: Sport and Gender in Australian Media January 2008–July 2009*, Canberra: Australian Sports Commission.

Benkwitz, A. and G. Molnar (2012) "Interpreting and Exploring Football Fan Rivalries: An Overview," *Soccer & Society* 13(4): 479–94.

Bernhardt, P. C., J. M. Dabbs, Jr., and J. A. Fielden (1998) "Testosterone Changes during Vicarious Experiences of Winning and Losing among Fans at Sporting Events," *Physiology & Behavior* 65(1): 59–62.

Bruce, T. (2013) "Reflections on Communications and Sport: On Women and Femininities," *Communication and Sport*, DOI: 10.1177/2167479512472883.

Bueno, G. (2002) "La canonización de Marilyn Monroe," *El Catoblepas* 9: 2.

Burst M. (2012) *Sports Fans and Digital Media: A Scorecard on Preferences and Behaviors*, Boston: Burst Media.

Butterworth, M. L. and S. D. Moskal (2009) "American Football, Flags, and 'Fun': The Bell Helicopter Armed Forces Bowl and the Rhetorical Production of Militarism," *Communication, Culture & Critique* 2(4): 411–33.

Buysse, J. A. and S. Wolter (2013) "Gender Representation in 2010 NCAA Division I Media Guides: The Battle for Equity Was Only Temporarily Won," *Journal of Issues in Intercollegiate Athletics* 6: 1–21.

Commission on the Future of Women's Sport (2010) *Prime Time: The Case for Commercial Investment in Women's Sport*, London: Women's Sport and Fitness Foundation.

Cooper, M. (1999) "2-TV Beisbol: Ramirez and Sosa," *New York Times*, September 18: B1, B6.

"Don't Call It Soccer! How to Look Like a Football Phenomenon" (2010) *Vanity Fair*, May 24. http://www.vanityfair.com/online/beauty/2010/05/dont-call-it-soccer-how-to-look-like-a-football-phenomenon.

Earnheardt, A. C., P. M. Haridakis, and B. S. Hugenberg (eds.) (2012) *Sports Fans, Identity, and Socialization: Exploring the Fandemonium*, Lanham, MD: Lexington Books.

Eastman, S. T. and A. M. Land (1997) "The Best of Both Worlds: Sports Fans Find Good Seats at the Bar," *Journal of Sport & Social Issues* 21(2): 156–78.

Eco, U. (1987) *Travels in Hyperreality*, trans. William Weaver, London: Picador.

Elias, N. (1978) "On Transformations of Aggressiveness," *Theory and Society* 5(2): 229–42.

Elias, N. and E. Dunning (1986) *Quest for Excitement: Sport and Leisure in the Civilizing Process*, Oxford: Basil Blackwell.

"Features of the New espnW.com" (2010) *The Onion*, December 10. http://www.theonion. com/articles/features-of-the-new-espnwcom,18642/.

Fiske, John (1987) *Television Culture*, London: Routledge.

"Fox Soccer Channel Becomes an Official Nielsen[-]Rated Network Starting October 1" (2008) *Foxsports.com*, September 15. http://www.pr-inside.com/fox-soccer-channel-becomes-an-official-r807097.htm.

Gantz, W. (2012) "Reflections on Communication and Sport: On Fanship and Social Relationships," *Communication and Sport*, doi: 10.1177/2167479512467446.

García Canclini, N. (2004) *Diferentes, desiguales y desconectados: Mapas de la interculturalidad*, Barcelona: Editorial Gedisa.

Gaskins, A. J., J. Mendiola, Myriam Afeiche, Niels Jörgensen, Shanna H. Swan, and Jorge E. (2013) "Physical Activity and Television Watching in Relation to Semen Quality in Young Men," *British Medical Journal* (February), doi: 10.1136/bjsports-2012-091644.

Geurens, J.-P. (1989) "The Brainbusters: The Upside Down World of Television Wrestling," *Spectator* 9(2): 56–67.

Haspel, P.(2009) "Baltimore Colts and Diner Guys: Pro Sports Fandom and Social Identity in Barry Levinson's *Diner*," *Aethlon* 26(2): 59–73.

Hueter, M. (2010) "espnW: A Brand for Female Athletes," *Blogs with Balls*, October 4. http:// blogswithballs.com/2010/10/espnw-a-brand-for-female-athletes/.

López Díaz, P. with C. Gallo Suárez (2011) *Deporte y mujeres en los medios de comunicación: Sugerencias y recomendaciones*, Madrid: Consejo Superior de Deportes.

Lowden, D. (2013) "Don't Blame Sports Journalists for Missing Corruption Scandal," *The Conversation*, February 11. https://theconversation.edu.au/dont-blame-sports-journalists-for-missing-corruption-scandal-12115.

McBride, Kelly (2011) "Can a Sports Network Known for Its Male Brand Serve the Female Fan?," *Poynter.org*, December 26. http://www.poynter.org/latest-news/top-stories/157096/can-a-sports-network-known-for-its-male-brand-serve-the-female-fan/.

McCarthy, A. (1995) "'The Front Row Is Reserved for Scotch Drinkers': Early Television's Tavern Audiences," *Cinema Journal* 34(4): 31–49.

McCutcheon, L. E., R. Lange, and James Houran (2002) "Conceptualization and Measurement of Celebrity Worship," *British Journal of Psychology* 93(1): 67–87.

McKay, J. and M. Roderick (2010) "'Lay Down Sally': Media Narratives of Failure in Australian Sport," *Journal of Australian Studies* 34(3): 295–315.

Maguire, J. (1993) "Bodies, Sportscultures and Societies: A Critical Review of Some Theories in the Sociology of the Body," *International Review for the Sociology of Sport* 28(1): 33–52.

Maria (2012) "A Conversation with Men: Can You Relate?," *HerGameLife*, November 25. http://www.hergamelife.com/2012/11/a-conversation-with-men-can-you-relate/.

Markovits, A. S. and E. Albertson (2012) *Sportista: Female Fandom in the United States*, Philadelphia: Temple University Press.

Mass-Observation (1939) *Britain*, Harmondsworth: Penguin.

Mazer, S. (1998) *Professional Wrestling: Sport and Spectacle*, Jackson: University Press of Mississippi.

Mercado, M. (2008) "Why America Hates Soccer," *Football.co.uk*, March 25. http://www. football.co.uk/football_features/story_306.shtml.

Miller, T. (2001) *SportSex*, Philadelphia: Temple University Press.

——(2009) "Media Effects and Cultural Studies: A Contentious Relationship," in Robin L. Nabi and Mary Beth Oliver (eds.) *The Sage Handbook of Media Processes and Effects*, Thousand Oaks, CA: Sage Publications, pp. 131–43.

——(2010) *Television Studies: The Basics*, London: Routledge.

Moor, L. (2007) "Sport and Commodification: A Reflection on Key Concepts," *Journal of Sport & Social Issues* 31(2): 128–42.

Nelson, K. (2002) "The Erotic Gaze and Sports: An Ethnographic Consideration," *Journal of Sport History* 29(3): 407–12.

Oates, T. P. (2012) "Representing the Audience: The Gendered Politics of Sport Media," *Feminist Media Studies* 12(4): 603–7.

Pew Research Center for the People and the Press (2012) *High Marks for NBC's Coverage: Eight-in-Ten Following Olympics on TV or Digitally*, August 6. http://www.people-press.org/2012/08/06/eight-in-ten-following-olympics-on-tv-or-digitally/.

Pope, S. (2011) "'Like Pulling Down Durham Cathedral and Building a Brothel': Women as 'New Consumer' Fans?," *International Review for the Sociology of Sport* 46(4): 471–87.

Poynton, B. and J. Hartley (1990) "Male-Gazing: Australian Rules Football, Gender and Television," in Mary Ellen Brown (eds.) *Television and Women's Culture: The Politics of the Popular*, Sydney: Currency Press, pp. 144–57.

Said, E. (1993) "An Interview with Edward Said," *boundary 2* 20(1): 1–25.

Sammond, N. (ed.) (2005) *Steel Chair to the Heap: The Pleasure and Pain of Professional Wrestling*, Durham, NC: Duke University Press.

Schimmel, K. S., C. L. Harrington, and D. D. Bielby (2007) "Keep Your Fans to Yourself: The Disjuncture between Sport Studies' and Pop Culture Studies' Perspectives on Fandom," *Sport in Society* 10(4): 580–600.

Schreiber, K. (2012) "Why Don't We Watch More Women's Sports?" *Greatist*, August 2. http://greatist.com/fitness/women-sports-viewership-080212/.

Schreier, B. A. (1989) "Sporting Wear," in Claudia Brush Kidwell and Valerie Steele (eds.) *Men and Women: Dressing the Part*, Washington, DC: Smithsonian Institution Press, pp. 92–123.

Sloan, L. R. (1989) "The Motives of Sports Fans," in J. H. Goldstein (ed.) *Sports, Games, and Play: Social and Psychological Motivations*, 2nd edition, Hillsdale, NJ: Lawrence Erlbaum, pp. 175–240.

Sparks, R. (1992) "'Delivering the Male': Sports, Canadian Television, and the Making of TSN," *Canadian Journal of Communication* 17(1): 319–42.

Stempel, C. (2006) "Televised Sports, Masculinist Moral Capital, and Support for the U.S. Invasion of Iraq," *Journal of Sport & Social Issues* 30(1): 79–106.

Talleu, C. (2011) *Egalité homme-femme dans le sport: L'Accès des filles et des femmes aux pratiques sportives: Manuel de bonnes pratiques 2*, Strasburg: Conseil de l'Europe.

Tang, T. and R. Cooper (2012) "Gender, Sports, and New Media: Predictors of Viewing during the 2008 Beijing Olympics," *Journal of Broadcasting & Electronic Media* 56(1): 75–91.

"There's Life Outside Sports. There's Also Ballet" (1998) *Broadcasting and Cable*, May 11: 24–5.

Thrall, A. T., J. Lollio-Fahkreddine, Jon B., L. D., W. Herrin, Z. Paquette, R. Wenglinski, and A. Wyatt (2008) "Star Power: Celebrity Advocacy and the Evolution of the Public Sphere," *International Journal of Press/Politics* 13(4): 362–85.

Till, B. D., S. M. Stanley, and R. Priluck (2008) "Classical Conditioning and Celebrity Endorsers: An Examination of Belongingness and Resistance to Extinction," *Psychology & Marketing* 25(2): 179–96.

Trail, G. T. and J. D. James (2001) "The Motivation Scale for Sport Consumption: Assessment of the Scale's Psychometric Properties," *Journal of Sport Behavior* 24(1): 108–27.

"U.S. Children Still Traumatized One Year after Seeing Partially Exposed Breast on TV" (2005) *The Onion*, January 26. http://www.theonion.com/articles/us-children-still-traumatized-one-year-after-seein,1285/.

Wann, D. L. (1995) "Preliminary Validation of the Sport Fan Motivation Scale," *Journal of Sport & Social Issues* 19(4): 377–96.

Waxmonsky, J. and E. V. Beresin (2001) "Taking Professional Wrestling to the Mat: A Look at the Appeal and Potential Effects of Professional Wrestling on Children," *Academic Psychiatry* 25(2): 125–31.

Weed, M. (2008) "Exploring the Sport Spectator Experience: Virtual Football Spectatorship in the Pub," *Soccer & Society* 9(2): 189–97.

Weissman, N. (2010) "A Timely Message about Female Sports Fans," *Washington Post*, September 16. http://voices.washingtonpost.com/box-seats/2010/09/a_timely_message_about_ female.html.

Wenner, L. (1998) "In Search of the Sports Bar: Masculinity, Alcohol, Sports, and the Mediation of Public Space," in Geneviève Rail (ed.) *Sport and Postmodern Times*, Albany: State University of New York Press, pp. 302–32.

——(2004) "Recovering (from) Janet Jackson's Breast: Ethics and the Nexus of Media, Sports, and Management," *Journal of Sport Management* 18(4): 315–34.

Wenner, L. A. and W. Gantz (1998) "Watching Sports on Television: Audience Experience, Gender, Fanship, and Marriage," in Lawrence A. Wenner (ed.) *MediaSport*, London: Routledge, pp. 233–51.

Zyvatkauskas, C. (2007) "Theatre Critic," *Economist*, February 3: 18.

# 43
# Men's use of pornography
## *Matthew B. Ezzell*

Pornography is sometimes dismissed, celebrated, or problematized as fantasy (see, e.g., Kipnis 1996; Lehman 2006; Williams 2004). It has been argued that pornography reflects, shapes, and conditions the sexual imaginations and fantasies of consumers and, more broadly, those growing up within a social world in which pornography is neither fringe nor secret, but part and parcel of the mainstream culture (Dines 2010; Levy 2005; Paul 2005). And, yet, in important respects, pornography is not fantasy. The billions of dollars traded in national and international markets are real.[1] The women and men used in its production are real. What is done to those people is real. And the consumers who purchase or otherwise access pornographic material are real (Boyle 2000; Dworkin 1995; Jensen 2007). The majority of these consumers are heterosexual men.[2] While these men, the everyday consumers of pornography, have been the focus of much research, here I highlight the ways that men's choices to consume pornography function as an expression of patriarchal masculinity that reinforces sex inequality. I will outline the male pornography consumer and the material consumed, analyze men's choices in the context of patriarchy and global corporate capitalism, review existing research on the impact of men's consumption patterns, and discuss the promise of men's choices to resist. Who is the male pornography consumer, and what impact do his choices have on the world he inhabits?

## Everyman

In most Westernized countries, exposure to and consumption of pornographic material is now a nearly ubiquitous experience for young people, particularly for boys and young men. Males are more likely than females to consume pornography, to do so more frequently, and to view consumption in more favorable terms (Flood 2010; Johansson and Hammarén 2007; Sabina *et al.* 2008). Large numbers of children experience unwanted exposure to pornography online (Flood 2007, 2009; Wolak *et al.* 2006), but even more actively seek it out. For example, 90 percent of Canadian boys aged 13 and 14 reported accessing sexually explicit materials in 2006 (*ScienceDaily* 2007: see also Check 1995). Similarly high rates are found across the globe. Over 90 percent of boys surveyed in Baltic and Nordic countries reported being consumers of pornography (Mossige *et al.* 2007; see also Häggström-Nordin *et al.* 2006), in addition to 88 percent of Italian boys and young men (Romito and Beltramini 2011) and 87 percent of college-aged males in the US (Carroll *et al.* 2008). Studies in Australia (Flood 2007), Cambodia (Fordham 2006), and Taiwan (Lin and Lin 1996; Lo and Wei 2005) produced similar results. In this context, particularly in the absence of comprehensive sex and sexuality education in the school or the home (Sutton *et al.* 2002), pornography in many countries functions as a core component of many boys' and young men's gender and sexual socialization (Brown *et al.* 2006; Flood 2007, 2009, 2010; Peter and Valkenburg 2007). The consumer of pornography, it appears, is everyman.

## Men's choices: agents and dupes, consumers and consumed

The modern male pornography consumer is "both abuser and abused, consumer and consumed" (Whisnant 2010: 115). As he exercises agency through the active choice to consume commercial pornography, he simultaneously enacts patriarchal dominance through a compensatory manhood act (Schrock and Schwalbe 2009) and is targeted as a consumer under conditions of global corporate capitalism (Johnson 2010). Indeed, the ubiquitous and mainstreamed aspects of pornography exist alongside the fact that the most popular pornographic material is increasingly degrading (centered on the physical/emotional abuse and/or demoralization of an inferior other) and openly misogynist (see Jensen 2007). Content analysis of top-selling videos found over 88 percent of scenes involved acts of physical aggression—overwhelmingly against women—while over 48 percent involved verbal aggression (Bridges *et al.* 2010). Although boys and young men may not purposefully seek out violent or aggressive material when they first become consumers, interview data and content analysis of online forums suggest that exposure to "harsher" content is difficult to avoid (Flood 2007; Johnson 2010; Whisnant 2010). Moreover, many men's consumption follows a pattern of desensitization and escalation such that over time they actively look for more extreme material (Jensen 2007; Maltz and Maltz 2008; Paul 2005).

Given the explicitly degrading content of much mainstream pornography, consumers may have to face questions about their identities when they seek it out. Jensen frames the question as follows: "Why is this sexually pleasurable to you, and what kind of person does that make you?" (2002b: para. 21). Whisnant (2010) elucidates several identity-work strategies male consumers employ in online discussion forums in order to manage their sense of themselves as good people in the face of the pornography they consume. These include moral ambivalence (amoral critiques); palliative comparison ("I'm not *that* bad"); line-drawing ("I won't consume *that* pornography"); diminished responsibility (diffusing or displacing responsibility for the consequences of one's actions); blaming the victim ("she seems into it"); gender work (pornography makes you a "real man," but not a monster); and self-fragmentation (splitting the "porn self" from the "ethical self"). As she argues, the male consumer is "pregroomed" to accept overt misogyny through socialization into a mainstream culture in which men's violence against women is normalized across a variety of contexts (2010: 114; see also Dines 2010; Jensen 2002a, 2007). But he is explicitly groomed to make use of these types of identity-work strategies through participation in online forums in which consumers construct collective narratives around their porn use; the text and promotional materials that accompany pornographic products; and DVD commentary that "interprets the images" (Whisnant 2010: 123), explicitly coding acts as consensual and enjoyable for the women involved, even if they appear to be in pain. Speaking to this point, Bridges *et al.* (2010) found that 95 percent of those aggressed against in top-selling pornography videos responded with pleasure or neutrality. They argue that this "consensual depiction of aggression" risks "rendering true aggression against women invisible" (2010: 1080), while it simultaneously offers male consumers a resource in their identity-work ("blaming the victim").

As Johnson (2010) points out, men's choices to consume pornography do not occur in a vacuum. Instead, they take place within the context of patriarchy and capitalism. These systems "conspire to define the male consumer as a site of exploitation for the commercial pornography industry" (2010: 147). Under patriarchy, men across structural locations experience solidarity through shared control over women as a class. Up to and following the Industrial Revolution, capitalism served patriarchy by promoting women's economic and social dependence on men through low wages, essentially "buying off" economically exploited men by providing them control over women's domestic labor. In this way, women were doubly exploited— once through exploited labor in sex-segregated occupations and twice through unpaid labor in the home—as a way of promoting male dominance generally and male solidarity across the economic spectrum (Johnson 2010; see also Hartmann 1979).

Under global corporate capitalism, women have been drawn into the workforce as laborers and consumers, upsetting the previous symbiotic relationship that existed between patriarchy and industrial capitalism. This has threatened institutional male dominance by challenging economically exploited men's power over women interpersonally. In this context, not all men have equal access to the "patriarchal dividend," the advantages typically conferred on men as a group for enacting hegemonic masculinity (Connell 1987; Connell and Messerschmidt 2005). This creates the "male paradox of power" (Johnson 2010: 151): many men personally *feel* powerless at the same time that men are privileged as a class.

To deal with this paradox, many men look for ways to enact hegemonic masculinity through compensatory manhood acts—acts which signify "a capacity to exert control over one's self, the environment, and others" (Schrock and Schwalbe 2009: 286). The consumption of commercial pornography functions as a compensatory manhood act because it allows men across the economic spectrum micro-access to the performance of hegemonic masculinity, at the same time that it exploits them as consumers. For example, as Kimmel (2008) points out, the sexual mandate of hegemonic masculinity is unattainable, yet many young men feel entitled to sex and frustrated by women's perceived control of access to it. For young men in this context, consuming explicitly degrading and misogynistic commercial pornography "is a way to level the playing field just a little bit" (2008: 183). Pornography, then, functions in the way domestic power over women did under industrial capitalism.

The male consumer of pornography is caught up in a social and economic equation that provides a collective gain for men as a class but exacts an individual cost. This is not to equate the exploitation of women and men under the intersection of patriarchy and capitalism. As Johnson notes: "Women are harmed through men's choices even if those choices are bounded by systems of power that also diminish and harm men" (2010: 162). It is to point out, though, that under patriarchy and capitalism male consumers are both winners and losers.

## The impact of men's consumption of pornography

The bulk of social science research on pornography has focused on its effects, notably on consumers' attitudes and behaviors. Yet debates are ongoing regarding the effects of research and its usefulness (Boyle 2000; Jensen 2004; Thornburgh and Lin 2002). Experimental research, for example, can give us hints about the ways consumers interact with media, but it has limitations. Answers to questions about attitudes toward women, for example, do not necessarily speak to the enactment of any particular behaviors. Experiments also do not replicate the conditions of consuming pornography as part of a daily or weekly practice over the course of years. Further, experimental studies do not replicate the ways that boys and men use pornographic material to facilitate masturbation (Jensen 2007).

Effects research, thus, should be approached with caution; but even so, a review of existing studies can point us toward greater understanding. The effects of media consumption can be moderated by many factors: age, gender, sexual experiences, responses to/engagement with the material, specific content, and the context of exposure/consumption (Malamuth et al. 2012; Malamuth and Huppin 2005). Some researchers have found positive (Kimmel 1990; McKee 2007) or neutral (Garos et al. 2004; Luder et al. 2011) effects. For example, pornography can function as a form of sex education for young people, providing information about the human body and sexual practices, thus increasing a sense of sexual competence and liberalization and decreasing sexual shame (Brown et al. 2006; Huston et al. 1998; Johansson and Hammarén 2007; MacDonald 1990; McKee et al. 2008).

Other researchers, however, have questioned the lessons learned from this education, highlighting negative effects for at least some populations of consumers. In a thorough review of existing literature, Flood notes that pornography consumption can shift boys' and men's sexual practices and expectations, harm female partners' sense of intimacy, encourage sexualized and sexually objectifying understandings of girls and women, and intensify boys' and young men's acceptance of and participation in sexual violence (2010: 166–76). As an example, Malamuth, Addison, and Koss (2000) found that men who are predisposed to violence (i.e. men who are impulsive, hostile to women, and promiscuous) may seek out violent pornography, which, in turn, may increase their likelihood of engaging in sexually aggressive and controlling behavior. Indeed, interviews with convicted sex offenders suggest that adolescent exposure to pornography is a significant predictor of the elevation of violence in the perpetrators' attacks (Mancini et al. 2012). Other studies have found that boys and men who habitually consume pornography are more likely to describe women in sexual terms; to view women in stereotypical ways; to hold attitudes supportive of violence against women; and/or to engage in acts of violence against women (APA 2007; Bonino et al. 2006; Burns 2001; Check 1995; Frable et al. 1997; Hald et al. 2010). Pornography consumption is associated with having multiple sexual partners; paying for sex (Wright and Randall 2012); and lower levels of commitment in romantic relationships and higher likelihoods of infidelity (Lambert *et al.* 2012). Consumers of paraphilic pornography (BDSM, fetishism, bestiality, and/or violent/coercive pornography) are more likely to experience diminished overall sexual satisfaction due to suppressed empathy for their sexual partners (Štulhofer *et al.* 2010).

Interviews with consumers speak in concert with the empirical studies mentioned above. Based on a nationally representative poll and in-depth interviews with over 100 people in the US, Paul (2005) documents a range of self-identified personal effects of pornography consumption. Although some respondents highlighted positive effects, many men spoke to negative effects as well, including: objectifying women in and outside of pornography; habituation and desensitization; pushing sexual partners to try positions/practices seen in pornography; experiencing sex with partners as boring; dependence on pornography to facilitate masturbation; dependence on mental images of pornography to maintain erections during sex with a partner; pressuring women to have sex; and feelings of depression/lack of control. Echoing Paul's work, Maltz and Maltz (2008) highlight the ways that pornography consumption can negatively shape some users' sexual desires and practices, deaden libido and ability to perform sexually, and compromise users' ability to connect emotionally and sexually to partners (see also Dines 2010; Häggström-Nordin *et al.* 2006; Jensen 2007; Kimmel 2008: 185–9).

The impact of growing up in a sexualized culture on girls and women is well documented. A review of existing literature found ample evidence of negative effects related to cognitive functioning, physical and mental health, sexuality, and attitudes and beliefs (APA 2007; see also Dines 2010; Levin and Kilbourne 2008; Paul 2005). But research on women as the partners of male pornography consumers is also revealing. Both Maltz and Maltz (2008) and Paul (2005) highlight the sense of betrayal, inadequacy, rejection, lack of trust, and, if in the context of a relationship with children, fear for children that many female partners of male pornography consumers experience. Bergner and Bridges found a woman's discovery of a male partner's extensive pornography use was typically "traumatic" (2002: 195), altering her worldview in relation to (1) her relationship with her partner, (2) her view of her own worth/desirability, and (3) her view of the character of her partner. And in interviews with Canadian women, Shaw (2010) found that women clearly disliked their male partners' pornography use, but were often reluctant to speak out for fear of being seen as a "prude," old-fashioned, or anti-sex. The women stressed that this was not a matter of personal taste; it was rooted in their perceptions that the material "impacted negatively on their lives and on the lives of other women" (2010: 209).

Looking at the experiences of survivors of men's violence against women is also illuminating. Russell (1988) found that 32 percent of respondents from a random sample of women in the San Francisco area who reported experiences of wife rape had been asked to pose for pornography. Similarly, over 8 percent of the Canadian college women in DeKeseredy and Schwartz's (1998) study reported being forced to enact scenes from pornography. And in their survey of 100 survivors seeking services from rape crisis centers, Bergen and Bogle (2000) found that 40 percent of the women who knew their abuser consumed pornography said that the pornography was part of the abuse, with 12 percent of the total sample indicating that pornography was imitated during the abuse (see also Dines 2010: 95–8). This research does not speak to issues of causality, but it does "provide more evidence about how pornography plays a role in the sexual violence experienced by some women" (Bergen and Bogle 2000: 232). Put simply, media, as a reflection and shaper of social reality, matter.

## Men who refuse/resist

In closing, as Boyle argues, with pornography consumption among men at close to 90 percent in a range of countries, and with pornography more mainstreamed and normalized than ever, "it is the porn *refuser*, and not the consumer, who is truly marginalized" (2010: 144). This is the case in mainstream media coverage of pornography and its consumers, and it is the case in social science research. But importantly, men are organizing, from feminist perspectives and as allies to women, against the commercial pornography industry (Cochrane 2010; see also, www.stoppornculture. org, and www.antipornmen.org). More research on these men is needed. Their path (s) to "refusal," their experiences relating to others as friends, allies, and sexual partners, and their experiences constructing and enacting a sexuality against the commercial online pornography industry could suggest avenues for the construction of a different, arguably more humane, social world. Who is the male pornography refuser, and what impact do his choices have on the world he inhabits?

## Acknowledgments

The author would like to thank Bob Jensen and Beth Eck for thoughtful feedback on a draft of this chapter, in addition to Christine Ciccosanti for assistance in pulling together materials. He would also like to thank the editors of this collection for their insight and commitment to critical engagement on issues that matter.

## Notes

1 Accurate figures on the size and scope of the pornography industry are hard to nail down. The global industry has been estimated to be worth as much as $97 billion (Ropelato n.d.), with a US market worth $10 billion (Leung 2007). Others have criticized these figures as baseless, arguing that the global industry is too hard to adequately track and that the US market more accurately brings in $2–4 billion annually (Ackman 2001; Futrelle 2012). Regardless, the pornography industry is driven by a profit motive and has close ties to mainstream corporations and industries (Dines 2010: 47–58).

2 Gay, bisexual, trans, and pansexual men consume pornography; but, as consumers, these populations have been generally under-researched. One Norwegian study (Træen et al. 2006) found that gay/bisexual men reported higher consumption rates than heterosexual men. Sherman (1995) argues that gay male pornography (GMP) serves an important social function by providing a marginalized sexual population resources to lead self-affirming sexual lives (see, also, Hillier et al. 2001); yet, Crawford (1996) counters that Sherman is overly selective in his review and neglects a thorough analysis of power and coercion in GMP. On that point, Kendall (2004a, 2004b, 2004c) argues that GMP mimics hegemonic masculinity and reproduces sex inequality. Others argue that GMP racializes sex inequality

by disproportionately feminizing Asian men and hypersexualizing the black male body (see Dines 2006; Fung 1991; Hoang 2004). Still others (Duggan and McCreary 2004) say consumption of GMP by gay men was positively correlated with social physique anxiety.

# References

Ackman, D. (2001) "How Big Is Porn?," *Forbes.com*, May 25. http://www.forbes.com/2001/05/25/0524porn.html/.

American Psychological Association (APA) (2007) *Report of the APA Task Force on the Sexualization of Girls*, Washington, DC: APA.

Bergen, R. K. and K. A. Bogle (2000) "Exploring the Connection Between Pornography and Sexual Violence," *Violence and Victims* 15(3): 227–34.

Bergner, R. M. and A. J. Bridges (2002) "The Significance of Heavy Pornography Involvement for Romantic Partners: Research and Clinical Implications," *Journal of Sex and Marital Therapy* 28(5): 193–206.

Bonino, S., S. Ciairano, E. Rabaglietti, and E. Cattelino (2006) "Use of Pornography and Self-Reported Engagement in Sexual Violence among Adolescents," *European Journal of Developmental Psychology* 3(3): 265–88.

Boyle, K. (ed.) (2000) "The Pornography Debates: Beyond Cause and Effect," *Women's Studies International Forum* 23(2): 187–95.

——(2010) *Everyday Pornography*, New York: Routledge.

Bridges, A., R. Wosnitzer, E. Scharrer, C. Sun, and R. Liberman (2010) "Aggression and Sexual Behavior in Bestselling Pornography Videos: A Content Analysis Update," *Violence Against Women* 16(10): 1065–85.

Brown, J. D., K. L. L'Engle, C. J. Pardun, G. Guo, K. Kenneavy, and C. Jackson (2006) "Sexy Media Matter: Exposure to Sexual Content in Music, Movies, Television, and Magazines Predicts Black and White Adolescents' Sexual Behavior," *Pediatrics* 117(4): 1018–27.

Burns, R. J. (2001) "Male Internet Pornography Consumers and the Attitudes Toward Men and Women," unpublished Ph.D. thesis, University of Oklahoma.

Carroll, J. S., L. M. Padilla-Walker, L. J. Nelson, C. D. Olson, C. M. Barry, and S. D. Madsen (2008) "Generation XXX: Pornography Acceptance and Use among Emerging Adults," *Journal of Adolescent Research* 23(1): 6–30.

Check, J. (1995) "Teenage Training: The Effects of Pornography on Adolescent Males," in L. R. Lederer and R. Delgado (eds.) *The Price We Pay: The Case against Racist Speech, Hate Propaganda, and Pornography*, New York: Hill and Wang, pp. 89–91.

Cochrane, K. (2010) "The Men Who Believe Porn Is Wrong," *Guardian*, October 25. http://www.guardian.co.uk/culture/2010/oct/25/men-believe-porn-is-wrong.

Connell, R. W. (1987) *Gender and Power*, Palo Alto, CA: Stanford University Press.

Connell, R. W. and J. W. Messerschmidt (2005) "Hegemonic Masculinity: Rethinking the Concept," *Gender & Society* 19: 829–59.

Crawford, B. J. (1996) "Gay Does Not Necessarily Mean Good: A Critique of Jeffrey Sherman's 'Love Speech: The Social Utility of Pornography'," *American University Journal of Gender, Social Policy and the Law* 5(1): 9–20.

DeKeseredy, W. and M. Schwartz (1998) "Male Peer Support and Woman Abuse in Postsecondary School Courtship," in R. K. Bergen (ed.) *Issues in Intimate Violence*, Thousand Oaks, CA: Sage, pp. 83–96.

Dines, G. (2006) "The White Man's Burden: Gonzo Pornography and the Construction of Black Masculinity," *Yale Journal of Law and Feminism* 18(1): 283–97.

——(2010) *Pornland: How Porn Has Hijacked Our Sexuality*, Boston, MA: Beacon Press.

Duggan, S. J. and D. R. McCreary (2004) "Body Image, Eating Disorders, and the Drive for Muscularity in Gay and Heterosexual Men: The Influence of Media Images," in T. G. Morrison (ed.) *Eclectic Views on Gay Male Pornography: Pornucopia*, Binghampton, NY: Harrington Park Press, pp. 45–58.

Dworkin, A. (1995) "Pornography Happens to Women," in L. Lederer and R. Delgado (eds.) *The Price We Pay: The Case against Racist Speech, Hate Propaganda, and Pornography*, New York: Hill and Wang, pp. 181–93.

Flood, M. (2007) "Exposure to Pornography among Youth in Australia," *Journal of Sociology* 43(1): 45–60.

——(2009) "The Harms of Pornography Exposure among Children and Young People," *Child Abuse Review* 18(6): 384–400.

——(2010) "Young Men Using Pornography," in K. Boyle (ed.) *Everyday Pornography*, New York: Routledge, pp. 164–78.

Fordham, G. (2006) "'As If They Were Watching My Body': A Study of Pornography and the Development of Attitudes Towards Sex and Sexual Behaviour among Cambodian Youth," Cambodia: World Vision Cambodia. http://www.worldvision.org.kh/pdf/Pornography_Research_Report2006.pdf.

Frable, D., A. Johnson, and H. Kellman (1997) "Seeing Masculine Men, Sexy Women, and Gender Differences," *Journal of Personality* 65(2): 311–55.

Fung, R. (1991) "Looking for My Penis: The Eroticized Asian in Gay Video Porn," in Bad Object-Choices (ed.) *How Do I Look? Queer Film and Video*, Seattle, WA: Bay Press, pp. 145–68.

Futrelle, D. (2012) "Sex on the Internet: Sizing Up the Online Smut Economy," *Time Business: News and Views on the Economy, Markets, and Business*, April 4. http://business.time.com/2012/04/04/sex-on-the-internet-sizing-up-the-online-smut-economy/.

Garos, S., J. K. Bettan, A. Kluck, and A. Easton (2004) "Sexism and Pornography Use," *Journal of Psychology and Human Sexuality* 16(1): 69–96.

Häggström-Nordin, E., J. Sandberg, U. Hanson, and T. Tydén (2006) "'It's Everywhere': Young Swedish People's Thoughts and Reflections about Pornography," *Scandinavian Journal of Caring Sciences* 20(4): 386–93.

Hald, G. M., N. M. Malamuth, and C. Yuen (2010) "Pornography and Attitudes Supporting Violence against Women: Revisiting the Relationship in Nonexperimental Studies," *Aggressive Behavior* 36(1): 14–20.

Hartmann, H. I. (1979) "The Unhappy Marriage of Marxism and Feminism: Towards a More Progressive Union," *Capital & Class* 3(2): 1–33.

Hillier, L., C. Kurdas, and P. Horsley (2001) *"It's Just Easier": The Internet as a Safety-Net for Same Sex Attracted Young People*, Melbourne: Australian Research Centre in Sex, Health and Society, Latrobe University. http://www.latrobe.edu.au/ssay/assets/downloads/internetreport[1].pdf.

Hoang, N. T. (2004) "The Resurrection of Brandon Lee: The Making of a Gay Asian American Porn Star," in L. Williams (ed.) *Porn Studies*, Durham, NC: Duke University Press, pp. 223–70.

Huston, A., E. Wartella, and E. Donnerstein (1998) *Measuring the Effects of Sexual Content in the Media*, Menlo Park, CA: Henry J. Kaiser Family Foundation.

Jensen, R. (2002a) "Men's Pleasure, Women's Pain: A Dangerous Sexual Ethic Woven into the Cultural Fabric," *Fredricksburg Free Lance-Star*, September 1: D-1,3. http://uts.cc.utexas.edu/~rjensen/freelance/rapeisnormal.htm.

——(2002b) "You Are What You Eat: The Pervasive Porn Industry and What It Says about You and Your Desires," *Clamor* Magazine, pp. 54–9. http://uts.cc.utexas.edu/~rjensen/freelance/pornographyandmasculinity.htm.

——(2004) "Pornography and Sexual Violence," *VAWNet Applied Research Forum, National Online Resource Center on Violence Against Women*, July. http://new.vawnet.org/Assoc_Files_VAWnet/AR_PornAndSV.pdf.

——(2007) *Getting Off: Pornography and the End of Masculinity*, Cambridge, MA: South End Press.

Johansson, T. and N. Hammarén (2007) "Hegemonic Masculinity and Pornography: Young People's Attitudes Toward and Relations to Pornography," *Journal of Men's Studies* 15(1): 57–70.

Johnson, J. A. (2010) "To Catch a Curious Clicker: A Social Network Analysis of the Online Pornography Industry," in K. Boyle (ed.) *Everyday Pornography*, New York: Routledge, pp. 147–63.

Kendall, C. N. (2004a) "Educating Gay Male Youth: Since When Is Pornography a Path Towards Self-Respect?," in T. G. Morrison (ed.) *Eclectic Views on Gay Male Pornography: Pornucopia*, Binghampton, NY: Harrington Park Press, pp. 83–128.

——(2004b) *Gay Male Pornography: An Issue of Sex Discrimination*, Vancouver: UBC Press.

——(2004c) "Gay Male Pornography and Sexual Violence: A Sex Equity Perspective on Gay Male Rape and Partner Abuse," *McGill Law Journal* 49(4): 877–923.

Kimmel, M. (1990) "Introduction: Guilty Pleasures—Pornography in Men's Lives," in M. Kimmel (ed.) *Men Confront Pornography*, New York: Crown, pp. 1–22.

——(2008) *Guyland: The Perilous World Where Boys Become Men*, New York: HarperCollins.

Kipnis, L. (1996) *Bound and Gagged: Pornography and the Politics of Fantasy in America*, Durham, NC: Duke University Press.

Lambert, N. M., S. Negash, T. F. Stillman, S. B. Olmstead, and F. D. Fincham (2012) "A Love That Doesn't Last: Pornography Consumption and Weakened Commitment to One's Romantic Partner," *Journal of Social and Clinical Psychology* 31(4): 410–38.

Lehman, P. (ed.) (2006) *Pornography: Film and Culture*, New Brunswick, NJ: Rutgers University Press.

Leung, R. (2007) "Porn in the U.S.A.," *CBS News, 60 Minutes*, December 5. http://www.cbsnews.com/2100-18560_162-585049.html.

Levin, D. E. and J. Kilbourne (2008) *So Sexy, So Soon: The New Sexualized Childhood and What Parents Can Do to Protect Their Kids*, New York: Ballantine Books.

Levy, A. (2005) *Female Chauvinist Pigs: Women and the Rise of Raunch Culture*, New York: Free Press.

Lin, H. S. and S. H. Lin (1996) "Sexual Knowledge, Attitudes and Behavior of Taiwan High School and Junior College Students," paper presented at the Asian Sex Symposium, Taipei, Taiwan, July.

Lo, V. and R. Wei (2005) "Exposure to Internet Pornography and Taiwanese Adolescents' Sexual Attitudes and Behavior," *Journal of Broadcasting and Electronic Media* 49(2): 221–37.

Luder, M. T., I. Pittet, A. Berchtold, C. Akré, P. A. Michaud, and J. C. Suris (2011) "Associations between Online Pornography and Sexual Behavior among Adolescents: Myth or Reality?," *Archives of Sexual Behavior* 40(5): 1027–35.

MacDonald, S. (1990) "Confessions of a Feminist Porn Watcher," in M. Kimmel (ed.) *Men Confront Pornography*, New York: Crown, pp. 34–42.

McKee, A. (2007) "'Saying You've Been at Dad's Porn Book Is Part of Growing up': Youth, Pornography, and Education," *Metro Magazine* 155: 118–22.

McKee, A., K. Albury, and C. Lumby (2008) *The Porn Report*, Melbourne: Melbourne University Press.

Malamuth, N. and M. Huppin (2005) "Pornography and Teenagers: The Importance of Individual Differences," *Adolescent Medicine* 16(2): 315–26.

Malamuth, N. M., A. Addison, and M. Koss (2000) "Pornography and Sexual Aggression: Are There Reliable Effects and Can We Understand Them?," *Annual Review of Sex Research* 11(2): 26–91.

Malamuth, N. M., G. M. Hald, and M. Koss (2012) "Pornography, Individual Differences in Risk and Men's Acceptance of Violence against Women in a Representative Sample," *Sex Roles* 66(7–8): 427–39.

Maltz, L. and W. Maltz (2008) *The Porn Trap: The Essential Guide to Overcoming Problems Caused by Pornography*, New York: HarperCollins.

Mancini, C., A. Reckdenwald, and E. Beauregard (2012) "Pornographic Exposure Over the Lifecourse and the Severity of Sexual Offenses: Imitation and Cathartic Effects," *Journal of Criminal Justice* 40(1): 21–30.

Morrison, T. G. (ed.) (2004) *Eclectic Views on Gay Male Pornography: Pornucopia*, Binghampton, NY: Harrington Park Press.

Mossige, S., M. Ainsaar, and C. Svedin (eds.) (2007) *The Baltic Sea Regional Study on Adolescent Sexuality* (NOVA Rapport 18/2007), Oslo, Norway: Norwegian Social Research. http://www.nova.no/asset/2812/1/2812_1.pdf.

Paul, P. (2005) *Pornified: How Pornography Is Transforming Our Lives, Our Relationships, and Our Families*, New York: Macmillan.

Peter, J. and P. M. Valkenburg (2007) "Adolescents' Exposure to a Sexualized Media Environment and Their Notions of Women as Sex Objects," *Sex Roles* 56(5–6): 381–95.

Romito, P. and L. Beltramini (2011) "Watching Pornography: Gender Differences, Violence and Victimization. An Exploratory Study in Italy," *Violence Against Women* 17(10): 1313–26.

Ropelato, J. (n.d.). "Internet Pornography Statistics," *TopTenReviews*. http://internet-filter-review.toptenreviews.com/internet-pornography-statistics.html.

Russell, D. E. H. (1988) "Pornography and Rape: A Causal Model," *Political Psychology* 9: 41–73.

Sabina, C., J. Wolak, and D. Finkelhor (2008) "The Nature and Dynamics of Internet Pornography Exposure for Youth," *CyberPsychology and Behavior* 11(6): 691–3.

Schrock, D. and M. Schwalbe (2009) "Men, Masculinity, and Manhood Acts," *Annual Review of Sociology* 35: 277–95.

*ScienceDaily* (2007) "One in Three Boys Heavy Porn Users, Study Shows,", February 23. http://www.sciencedaily.com/releases/2007/02/070223142813.htm.

Shaw, S. M. (2010) "Men's Leisure and Women's Lives: The Impact of Pornography on Women," *Leisure Studies* 18(3): 197–212.

Sherman, J. G. (1995) "Love Speech: The Social Utility of Pornography," *Stanford Law Review* 47(4): 661–705.

Štulhofer, A., V. Buško, and I. Landripet (2010) "Pornography, Sexual Socialization, and Satisfaction among Young Men," *Archives of Sexual Behavior* 39(1): 168–78.

Sutton, M. J., J. D. Brown, K. M. Wilson, and J. D. Klein (2002), "Shaking the Tree of Knowledge for Forbidden Fruit: Where Adolescents Learn about Sexuality and Contraception," in J. D. Beown, J. R. Steele, and K. Walsh-Childers (eds.) *Sexual Teens, Sexual Media: Investigating Media's Influence on Adolescent Sexuality*, Mahwah, NJ: Lawrence Erlbaum Associates, pp. 25–55.

Thornburgh, D. and H. Lin (eds.) (2002) *Youth, Pornography, and the Internet*, Washington, DC: National Academy Press.

Træen, B., T. S. Nilsen, and H. Stigum (2006) "Use of Pornography in Traditional Media and on the Internet in Norway," *Journal of Sex Research* 43(3): 245–54.

Whisnant, R. (2010) "From Jekyll to Hyde: The Grooming of Male Pornography Consumers," in K. Boyle (ed.) *Everyday Pornography*, New York: Routledge, pp. 114–33.

Williams, L. (2004) *Porn Studies*, Durham, NC: Duke University Press.

Willis, P. (1977) *Learning to Labor: How Working Class Kids Get Working Class Jobs*, New York: Columbia University Press.

Wolak, J., K. Mitchell, and D. Finkelhor (2006) "Online Victimization of Youth: Five Years Later," National Center for Missing and Exploited Children. http://www.missingkids.com/en_US/publications/NC167.pdf.

Wright, P. J. and A. K. Randall (2012) "Internet Pornography Exposure and Risky Sexual Behavior among Adult Males in the United States," *Computers and Human Behavior* 28(4): 1410–16.

# 44

# Gender and social media

## Sexism, empowerment, or the irrelevance of gender?

## *Tanja Carstensen*

In the field of science and technology studies (STS), the idea that technologies—including media—are the results of negotiation processes and power struggles is not controversial. At the same time, it is no longer disputed that technological development does not follow its own logic, but rather is the outcome and materialization of social power relations (Bijker *et al.* 1987; MacKenzie and Wajcman 1985). Feminist technology researcher Judy Wajcman (2004) states that technologies are also related to the constitution of gender relations and gender-relevant developments. With the arrival of every new technology, social power relations and thus gender relations are renegotiated. Technology and media are not exclusive determinants of social changes, but they are not merely passive things either:

> Technology must be understood as part of the social fabric that holds society together ... , technological change is a contingent and heterogeneous process in which technology and society are mutually constituted.
>
> (Wajcman 2004: 106)

The relation of the internet and gender was also constituted mutually. During the early days of the internet in the 1990s, diverse and contrary expectations shaped perceptions about the internet and gender relations. Three very different prognoses were advanced that are still relevant (Carstensen 2008, 2009; see also van Zoonen 2002):

- One part of the discussion called attention to the internet as a male domain (Dorer 1997; Spender 1996). This view of the internet was influenced by the interpretation of the internet as "technical." The central reasons cited had to do with the close link between technology and masculinity; the delayed access of many women to the internet; androcentric content; and male-dominated discussions in forums and chatrooms (Herring 1996). The internet was considered to be riddled with the same inequalities and power relations as the "real world."

- Another view held that the internet was also linked to hopes and expectations of creating solidarity and closer connections among women. Plant (1997) retold the story of technology and gender, interpreting the net as feminine because it refers to female-connoted activities such as spinning, weaving, networking, and communication. Feminists discussed the possibilities of new public spaces and anticipated changes through the removal of the boundaries between the public and private spheres as well as between home and work, e.g. by telework (Consalvo and Paasonen 2002; Wajcman *et al.* 2010). In addition, global access to information and easier communication were recognized as having the potential to strengthen feminist politics (Harcourt 1999; Floyd *et al.* 2002).
- Additionally, some feminists, inspired by poststructuralist theories, developed utopian projects for a world beyond binary gender relations. Cyberfeminists hoped that the boundaries between technology and humans, as well as between men and women, would be broken down on the internet. Visions like Donna Haraway's "cyborg" (1991) encouraged people to imagine a world without gender. The possibility of anonymous communication via the internet and "gender swapping" in chatrooms and forums, where the "real" body is not present and identities could be invented anew, connected the internet with the hope for postmodern and deconstructive future designs in which gender relations would be in flux (Bruckman 1993; Turkle 1995).

Certainly it is no coincidence that these three hopes and fears reflect three of the most important paradigms of feminist theory: deficit, difference, and deconstruction. New media and technologies, in particular, have always been canvasses for current arguments and struggles (Carstensen 2008; van Zoonen 2002).

Pursuing the questions of whether the internet has reinforced gender inequality or whether it has strengthened feminist politics or even offered new spaces for identity experiments beyond stereotypical gender constructions, here I begin by reviewing gender relations during the "first" web. I then explore research that examines how gender relations may have changed with the emergence of social media. I will take into account issues of (un)equal access and use; the gendered interfaces and identities in social networks; the role of gender-sensitive users as prosumers; feminist campaigns; as well as antifeminist provocations in social media.

## A short overview of gender relations during the "first" web

During the early spread of the internet in the 1990s, a number of feminist researchers argued that the internet was a male domain. Access was shaped by substantial gender inequalities (Dorer 1997). Among the German-speaking areas of the web, women comprised only 6 percent of users in 1995 (Fittkau and Maaß Consulting 1995). The main users of the web were highly educated, young, white, and male.

Concerning patterns of usage, early studies identified a range of "typical male" and "typical female" uses. They showed, for example, that women used the internet in a more directed manner and less playfully. On mailing lists and in newsgroups, women read for more time than they spent writing their own contributions (Dorer 1997: 22). Herring (1996) identified different styles of online communication: a male adversarial

style in which the poster distanced himself from other participants, who were criticized, often while promoting his own importance; and a female style that displayed
features of deference, hedging, apology, asking questions rather than making assertions, and which also had a personal orientation that emphasized support of others.
Later results were less gender stereotypical, but still stated quantitative differences in
the duration and frequency of internet use. These differences can be best explained
not by "female usage patterns" but by socioeconomic factors such as income and
resources, available free time, as well as by a gender-segregated labor market that
offers women different possibilities to use the internet in professional contexts than
men (Bimber 2000; Winker 2005).

Gender and technology studies have emphasized the notion that gender relations have
an impact on the way technology and media are constructed and designed. Designers
(unconsciously) inscribe different views of female and male users and uses into technology, and by this they reproduce their ideas of gender relations. For instance,
gender difference is constructed through gender-specific design, through the way the
technology is put on the market, or through associations with gendered rooms and
spaces (e.g. kitchen, garage). A range of studies have shown how gender stereotypes
materialize in technology (for example the shaver; Berg and Lie 1993; Oudshoorn et al.
2002). Such "gender scripts" could also be found on the early web. The first studies
noted the male-influenced development context (military, science, hacker spaces) and
showed that the content was aimed at male interests (automobiles, computers, sports,
and pornography; see Dorer 1997). Other studies referred to the gender-stereotyped
design of digital cities (Rommes et al. 1999) or of representations in avatars (Bath
2003). At the same time, a great many spaces and communities for women and girls
arose in different countries (Schachtner and Winker 2005; Tillmann 2008).

The hopes of deconstructivist feminists that the internet might enable the
exploration of queer gender identities beyond the usual gender binary of masculine
and feminine were soon disappointed. Early studies showed that gender played a
significant role in virtual online communication. Instead of experimenting with
gender roles, a reliance on sexual difference seemed to be an important means of
orientation in anonymous communications. Many conversations began with the
question "a/s/l?" (age/sex/location) (Döring 2008: 127).

The hope that the internet would strengthen feminist politics also was not really
fulfilled in its nascent years. Although feminist projects used the internet for self-
presentation and information, the interactive opportunities that the web offered for opinion formation, mobilization, political action, and the development of critical counter-
publics remained negligible. Only some of the feminist websites offered a list of
more or less sorted hyperlinks on other feminist sites. Feminist information remained
widespread and unconnected on the web (Carstensen and Winker 2005). Thus, in the
early days of the internet, especially the positive expectations were disappointed.

## The "new" internet: social media and Web 2.0

Since the beginning of the widespread adoption of the internet in the 1990s, the
situation has changed a great deal—in terms of both gender relations and the web.

With the development of social networking sites such as Facebook and MySpace, weblogs, wikis, and video and music platforms, ideas of user participation, information exchange and sharing, democratization of knowledge, the removal of the sender/ recipient structure, community building, and new forms of cooperation and collaboration without hierarchies (O'Reilly 2005) have become reanimated. Many have predicted that this development will substantially increase the agency of users. As bloggers, wiki participants, and members of social networking sites, users generate content and applications and therein contribute to the construction and production of Web 2.0 media as active "prosumers," consumers who are increasingly involved in professional production processes (Bruns 2008; Toffler 1970). Alongside these hopes, there are also pessimistic estimations about the impact of social and mobile media on our lives. Turkle states a range of paradoxical developments: for example that people engaged in online communication have a continual connection but rarely have each other's full attention. She criticizes multi-tasking, constant and ubiquitous accessibility, and the decreasing quality of communication and social relations: "We go online because we are busy but end up spending more time with technology and less with each other" (Turkle 2011: 281).

Below, I investigate the gendered impacts of social media in light of issues such as access and use, the interfaces and identities in social networks, the role of prosumers, campaigns, and provocations in social media.

## Gendered access to and use of social media

In contrast to early statistics, the percentage of internet users in general, as well as female internet users more specifically, has increased enormously in recent years. A gender gap still exists but has decreased. In the USA, 80 percent of men and 76 percent of women were online in 2011 (PEW Internet & American Life Project 2012a); 81.5 percent of men and 70.5 percent of women were online in Germany in 2012. In terms of usage patterns, only a few differences appear; most of the internet services (social networks, email, etc.) are used equally. Exceptions are the use of chatrooms or listening to internet radio, areas in which men dominate. In Germany, the duration of daily internet use is also still different: men are online for 147 minutes and women for 118 minutes each day (Busemann and Gscheidle 2012). Regarding social media, 4 percent of German users use Twitter (men and women are equally represented) (Busemann and Gscheidle 2012; van Eimeren and Frees 2012). In the USA the percentage of Twitter users is higher but also nearly equal: 14 percent of male internet users and 15 percent of female. Use of Twitter via mobile phones is balanced at 9 percent of both genders in the USA (PEW Internet & American Life Project 2012b).

Gender relations among social networks also are nearly balanced: in Germany, for example, 42 percent of female internet users and 43 percent of male internet users have a profile in a private community. Professional networks are used by 9 percent of male internet users and 7 percent of female internet users (Busemann and Gscheidle 2012: 381). Twenty percent of German women and 27 percent of German men have mobile access to the internet (van Eimeren and Frees 2012: 368). With

24 percent of men owning a smartphone, their numbers are slightly higher than the 20 percent of women who own one (van Eimeren and Frees 2012: 367).

Wikipedia is used in a predominantly passive manner, but widely. In Germany, 75 percent of male internet users and 70 percent of female internet users consult it. But a large gender gap appears in terms of the contribution of women among the active authors. Only 6 percent of contributors were women (Merz and Döring 2010); according to Wikimedia, 10–15 percent are female (Herbold 2011) in Germany as well as in the USA (Cohen 2011). The reasons for this are as yet unclear. Some suppose the high barriers, restrictive rules, and the crude communication style in the community to be the causes.

Another key issue in internet use is the reorganization of time and space, which has a gender dimension, as it complicates the idea of a strict division between work and family. Negative impacts are perceived to result from extending working time into time normally reserved for family, for hopes of better work–life balance. Wajcman et al.'s (2010) study supports a positive view on this issue. Based on a representative survey of Australian employees recently undertaken, many of them appear to be using the internet for personal purposes during work time to a greater extent than the opposite. The authors conclude from this that new media are actually being used by many to improve their work–life balance.

## Social networks: gendered interfaces and identities

On social networking sites, users present themselves through a profile, which typically contains information about gender, date of birth, location, education and business data, interests and activities, as well as political, religious, and sexual attitudes. Social networks provide diverse functionalities to enable networking and communication with other members, to establish groups, and to have discussions.

Gender plays a significant role among the fields in the forms. Most of the networks force users to position themselves definitively by questioning gender explicitly. They constrain gender to a binary category and often define gender as a mandatory field. Analyses of the interfaces of social networking sites show that there are only a few networks that offer such possibilities as "unknown" or "other" to indicate gender, for example Last.fm or Flickr. On studiVZ, a student network in Germany, if users refuse to choose one of the two gender alternatives the following statement appears: "Only female or male entities can register with us!" (Wötzel-Herber 2008: 38). In the current version of Facebook, users are asked through a dropdown menu to "Select sex: Male/Female" and are requested to "Please select either Male or Female" if they refuse. Even if it is less surprising that social networks are interested in this information for targeted advertising, it is remarkable that gender is a mandatory field while other fields in the registration form do not necessarily have to be filled out. As in other studies of feminist technology and media research, the results show that binary gendered structures and norms of "typical" usage patterns and "normal" identities are inscribed into the interfaces of social networking sites.

The desire for clear gender identities also seems to be considerable on the part of many social media users. In contrast to earlier hopes and findings in internet research which viewed it as an assortment of "identity workshops," authenticity has now become the decisive norm—that is, presenting one's "real" identity and being encouraged to disclose as much information as possible about oneself. Gender appears to have become an especially important category in one's self-presentation (Manago *et al.* 2008; Wötzel-Herber 2008). However, other studies paint a more ambivalent picture. Van Doorn, van Zoonen, and Wyatt have investigated Dutch and Flemish blogs and state that one can observe different versions of femininity that have been used to create a heterogeneous interpretation of female gender identity. In blogs, multiple and diffuse performances of femininity are presented although they refer to real-life and everyday experiences. Users are constantly performing their gender in different ways as they post new entries (van Doorn *et al.* 2007).

Furthermore, we can also find subversive, ironic, and resistant usage patterns of social networking sites: for example, the practice of changing the gender indicator at every login. Others use queer images such as pictures of women with beards and therefore irritate common viewing patterns of gender stereotypes (Richard *et al.* 2010: 210–49).

## Gender-sensitive prosumers: struggles over design and content

Science and technology studies approaches emphasize that the design of technologies or media scripts is not closed; it remains flexible and cannot determine users' practices and identities completely. This also opens room for manoeuver with regard to gender:

> Users define whether things are useful, or maybe fun, what things are good for and for whom, whether they experience them as gendered and whether they find them useful to articulate and perform their (gender) identities. By interpreting and using technologies, users are active participants in shaping the gendering of artifacts.
>
> (Oudshoorn *et al.* 2002: 481)

In contrast to the early times of the internet, it is remarkable that binary, discriminatory, and stereotyped design has become an issue of negotiations among users (Carstensen 2012). On Facebook, Wikipedia, and MySpace feminist claims toward design and content have become a starting point for struggles. The technological opportunities to establish groups and to discuss and disseminate information are used to criticize gender-stereotyped design. For example, in 2007 the Facebook group "For a queer-positive Facebook … " was founded to lobby the site operators to add new features to the user profiles that would allow a more inclusive representation of a wide range of personal self-identities. For example, the dropdown menu for "sex" should be changed to "gender" and switched to a fill-in-the-blank format. Further, the group asks that people who select "in a relationship" should have the option of including multiple partners. However, attempts to change the registration forms failed. Although the group had more than 16,000 members in 2009 who supported this concern and contributed to a heated discussion, Facebook did not react.

Another case was the struggle on Facebook to fight for the right to publish breastfeeding photos. Referring to the terms of use that prohibit the publishing of naked breasts, Facebook began to delete a range of photos that featured breastfeeding mothers. In reaction, the group "Hey Facebook, breastfeeding is not obscene!" was founded. Soon it attracted more than 260,000 members and published more than 7,000 pictures of breastfeeding and resisted Facebook's demands. Feminist users carry out visible struggles, raise their voices in opposition to existing design, create trouble, and develop ideas for alternative design. Feminist agency to change forms in social network sites is limited, but at least this technology offers a great deal of space and agency in terms of discourse, protest, requests, and petitions (Carstensen 2012).

## Feminist campaigns and antifeminist provocations in social media

From its beginning, gender researchers have also investigated the question of whether or not the internet could strengthen worldwide solidarity among women, create critical counter-publics, improve participation, and increase the opportunities for feminist politics (Consalvo and Paasonen 2002). As mentioned above, early studies came to the conclusion that the nascent internet was reduced to its possibilities for information (Carstensen and Winker 2005). While only a few girls' and women's networks used the early internet for debating, with the emergence of social media the exchange of ideas and meanings became much easier. In blogs as well as on Twitter, Facebook, and other social networks, an active, intensively discursive, self-organized queer-feminist net culture arose. Social networking sites facilitate exchanges of information, discussions, and comments. They provide spaces for users to empower each other, to establish events and protests and mobilize for political action. The design of social media enables a dense interdependence of feminist discussions.

The issues discussed are broad and controversial. Feminists comment on and criticize current political issues that relate to gender, family, or equality politics; they publish thoughts about their lives as queers; as parents; mobilize for "slutwalks" challenging sexual objectifications and restrictions; demonstrate against the criminal convictions of the Russian feminist punk band Pussy Riot; and uncover situations of common-place sexism and male privilege. A number of feminist discussions in social media also deal with users' own privileges as white, educated, and non-disabled women; and they tackle questions of inclusion, exclusion, self-understanding, positioning, and so on.

For feminist campaigns, Twitter plays a particularly important role. For example, the #MooreandMe Twitter campaign illustrated just how successful feminist protest in Web 2.0 can be. Feminists started the #MooreandMe campaign in response to moviemaker Michael Moore and TV moderator Keith Olbermann's mischaracteriza-tions and outright dismissals of the rape allegations against Julian Assange. It employed the hashtag (a means of highlighting a topical issue or theme on Twitter) #MooreandMe and used the opportunity to address both men directly via Twitter. Both apologized one week later. Another example is the German speaking campaign #aufschrei ("outcry"), through which women collect and publish experiences of sexism and which have provoked expansive public and political debates far beyond Twitter.

At the same time, it should be noted that feminist net culture is as heterogeneous as other feminist cultures and initiatives. There are frequent attempts to create a common platform that will subsume all feminist activities on the web, but they always fail on account of lingering questions of how to define feminism, who may call themselves feminist, and what feminist aims should be.

The visibility of feminism on the web has increased in proportion to the recent successes of feminist campaigns. As a direct or indirect consequence, feminists have sometimes been confronted with aggressive and provocative attacks. For example, in August 2007, the existing entries on "Ladyfest" and "riot grrrl" on the German version of Wikipedia were suggested for deletion. The deletion of these entries was justified by one user due to them apparently lacking in relevance, quality, and significance. Subsequent responses argued for the relevance and quality of the entries. In the end, an administrator decided to keep them. However, in the English version of Wikipedia the attempt to implement a category for female superheroes failed. An internal vote defined the category as "unnecessary."

On blogs and Twitter in particular, so-called masculists often comment on feminist entries in sexist, racist, homophobic, and antifeminist ways. Feminists are confronted with attempts to eliminate feminist statements from the public eye by defamation or threats of violence or even death, as well as with "trolls," that is, people who post intentionally provocative messages in order to hurt or "flame" (i.e. verbally abuse) others. Feminists frequently discuss how to handle such comments. The main issue is whether it is more useful to delete them from their own blogs and ignore them or if it is a better strategy to collect and publish them in order to make the aggression and threats visible and public. Meanwhile, preliminary approaches are emerging to handle the problem in creative and empowering ways. For example, the American site Monetizing the Hate and the German site hatr.org collect such comments.

## Conclusions

Social media have become male domains in which gender stereotypes and inequalities are reinforced, but also have provided opportunities for the articulation of feminist politics, as well as providing new spaces beyond stereotypical gender constructions. Particularly regarding access and usage of social media, gender no longer seems to play a significant role. Research appears to find only a few gender differences in patterns of daily usage. At the same time, analyses of the design of the social networks show fixed gender scripts that reinforce the binary gender system. Although active users struggle against these scripts and resistant users experiment with ways to subvert them, the possibilities to intervene in the design of social media are restricted, contrary to the hopes of increased user agency. Furthermore, the volume and frequency of gender debates in social media have increased. The web now offers a greater range of forums where different people can meet and connect. Feminists who use social media become more visible, which may help to mobilize a broader audience for their aims. At the same time, however, feminist views are often met with greater rejection and aggression. In addition to such centralized domains as Facebook and Wikipedia, the rise of Twitter and blogs brought with them immense potential for decentralized networking and discussion, which supports the needs of feminist political activism.

Therefore, on the one hand, social media offer various technological opportunities and, on the other hand, users employ social media in different ways. Both shape the access, use, design, identities, and politics of the web. In this mutual process of constituting, users act across sexism, stereotypes, negotiations, gender irrelevance, and empowerment.

# References

Bath, C. (2003) "Einschreibungen von Geschlecht: Lassen sich Informationstechnologien feministisch gestalten?," in J. Weber and C. Bath (eds.) *Turbulente Körper, soziale Maschinen. Feministische Studien zur Technowissenschaftskultur*, Opladen: Leske & Budrich, pp. 75–95.

Berg, A. J. and M. Lie (1993) "Feminism and Constructivism: Do Artifacts Have Gender?," *Science, Technology and Human Values* 20(3): 332–51.

Bijker, W. E., T. P. Hughes, and T. J. Pinch (eds.) (1987) *The Social Construction of Technological Systems: New Directions in the Sociology and History of Technology*, Cambridge, MA: MIT Press.

Bimber, B. (2000) "Measuring the Gender Gap on the Internet," *Social Science Quarterly* 81(3): 868–76.

Bruckman, A. (1993) "Gender Swapping on the Internet," *Proc.INET'93*: EFC1–5.

Bruns, A. (2008) *Blogs, Wikipedia, Second Life, and Beyond: From Production to Produsage*, New York: Peter Lang.

Busemann, K. and C. Gscheidle (2012) "Web 2.0: Habitualisierung der Social Communities," *Media Perspektiven* 41(7–8): 380–90.

Carstensen, T. (2008) "Zur Ko-Konstruktion von Technik und Geschlecht in Diskursen über das Internet," in Alumni-Verein Hamburger Soziologinnen und Soziologen e.V. (ed.) *Lebendige Soziologie. Jahrbuch 2006/2007*, Hamburg, pp. 24–41.

——(2009) "Gender Trouble in Web 2.0: Gender Relations in Social Network Sites, Wikis and Weblogs," *International Journal of Gender, Science and Technology* 1(1). http://genderandset. open.ac.uk/index.php/genderandset/article/view/18.

——(2012) "Struggling for Feminist Design: The Role of Users in Producing and Constructing Web 2.0 Media," in E. Zobl and R. Drüeke (eds.) *Feminist Media: Participatory Spaces, Networks and Cultural Citizenship*, Bielefeld: Transcript, pp. 170–82.

Carstensen, T. and G. Winker (2005) "A Tool but not a Medium—Practical Use of the Internet in the Women's Movement," in J. Archibald, J. Emms, F. Grundy, J. Payne, and E. Turner (eds.) *The Gender Politics of ICT*, London: Middlesex University Press, pp. 149–62.

Cohen, N. (2011) "Define Gender Gap? Look Up Wikipedia's Contributor List," *New York Times*, January 30. www.nytimes.com/2011/01/31/business/media/31link.html.

Consalvo, M. and S. Paasonen (eds.) (2002) *Women and Everyday Uses of the Internet: Agency and Identity*, New York: Peter Lang.

Dorer, J. (1997) "Gendered Net: Ein Forschungsüberblick über den geschlechtsspezifischen Umgang mit neuen Kommunikationstechnologien," *Rundfunk und Fernsehen* 45(1): 19–29.

Döring, N. (2008) "Männlichkeit und Weiblichkeit im Netz: Dimensionen des Cyber-Gendering," in F. von Gross, W. Marotzki, and U. Sander (eds.) *Internet—Bildung—Gemeinschaft*, Wiesbaden: Verlag für Sozialwissenschaften, pp. 119–41.

Fittkau and Maaß Consulting (eds.) (1995) *1. WWW-Benutzer-Analyse W3B*. www.w3b.org/ ergebnisse/w3b1/.

Floyd, C., G. Kelkar, S. Klein-Franke, C. Kramarae, and C. Limpangog (eds.) (2002) *Feminist Challenges in the Information Age: Information as a Social Resource*, Opladen: Leske & Budrich.

Haraway, D. (1991) *Simians, Cyborgs, and Women: The Reinvention of Nature*, New York: Routledge.

Harcourt, W. (1999) Women@internet: Creating New Cultures in Cyberspace, New York: Zed Books.

Herbold, A. (2011) "Frauen im Netz: Sag doch auch mal was," Zeit online. February 7. www.zeit.de/digital/internet/2011-02/internet-frauen-maenner.

Herring, S. C. (1996) "Bringing Familiar Baggage to the New Frontier: Gender Differences in Computer-Mediated Communication," in V. J. Vitanza (ed.) CyberReader, Boston: Allyn & Bacon, pp. 144-54.

MacKenzie, D. and J. Wajcman (eds.) (1985) The Social Shaping of Technology: How the Refrigerator Got Its Hum, Milton Keynes and Philadelphia: Open University Press.

Manago, A. M., M. B. Graham, P. M. Greenfield, and G. Salimkhan (2008) "Self-presentation and Gender on MySpace," Journal of Applied Developmental Psychology 29(6): 446-58.

Merz, M. and N. Döring (2010) "Aktive Beteiligung an Wikipedia aus sozial-kognitiver Perspektive." www.purl.org/merz/20100926.

O'Reilly, T. (2005) "What Is Web 2.0. Design Patterns and Business Models for the Next Generation." www.oreilly.de/artikel/web20.html.

Oudshoorn, N., A. R. Saetnan, and M. Lie (2002) "On Gender and Things: Reflexions on an Exhibition on Gendered Artefacts," Women's Studies International Forum 25(4): 471-83.

Pew Internet & American Life Project (2012a) Digital Differences. http://pewinternet.org/~/media//Files/Reports/2012/PIP_Digital_differences_041312.pdf.

——(2012b) Twitter Use 2012. http://pewinternet.org/~/media//Files/Reports/2012/PIP_Twitter_Use_2012.pdf.

Plant, S. (1997) Zeroes and Ones: Digital Women and the New Technoculture, New York: Doubleday.

Richard, B., J. Grünwald, M. Recht, and N. Metz (2010) Flickernde Jugend—rauschende Bilder, Frankfurt and New York: Campus.

Rommes, E., E. van Oost, and N. Oudshoorn (1999) "Gender and the Design of a Digital City," Information Technology, Communication and Society 4(2): 476-95.

Schachtner, C. and G. Winker (eds.) (2005) Virtuelle Räume—neue Öffentlichkeiten, Frankfurt and New York: Campus.

Shade, L. R. (2002) Gender & Community in the Social Construction of the Internet, New York: Peter Lang.

Spender, D. (1996) Nattering on the Net, Toronto: Garamond Press.

Tillmann, A. (2008) Identitätsspielraum Internet, Weinheim and Munich: Juventa.

Toffler, A. (1970) Future Shock, London: Bodley Head.

Turkle, S. (1995) Life on the Screen: Identity in the Age of the Internet, New York: Simon & Schuster.

——(2011) Alone Together: Why We Expect More from Technology and Less from Each Other, New York: Basic Books.

van Doorn, N., L. van Zoonen, and S. Wyatt (2007) "Writing from Experience: Presentations of Gender Identity on Weblogs," European Journal of Women's Studies 14(2): 143-59.

van Eimeren, B. and B. Frees (2012) "76 Prozent der Deutschen online—neue Nutzungssituation durch mobile Endgeräte," Media Perspektiven 7-8: 362-79.

van Zoonen, L. (2002) "Gendering the Internet: Claims, Controversies and Cultures," European Journal of Communication 17(1): 5-23.

Wajcman, J. (2004) TechnoFeminism, Cambridge: Polity.

Wajcman, J., E. Rose, J. E. Brown, and M. Bittman (2010) "Enacting Virtual Connections between Work and Home," Journal of Sociology 46(3): 257-75.

Winker, G. (2005) "Internet Research from a Gender Perspective: Searching for Differentiated Use Patterns," in J. Archibald, J. Emms, F. Grundy, J. Payne, and E. Turner (eds.) The Gender Politics of ICT, London: Middlesex University Press, pp. 191-204.

Wötzel-Herber, H. (2008) Doing Me and the Others: Identitätskonstruktionen in Online-Communities. http://woetzel-herber.de/2009/02/22/doing-meand-the-others-identitatskonstruktionen-in-online-communities/.

# 45

# Slippery subjects

## Gender, meaning, and the Bollywood audience

## *Shakuntala Banaji*

### Debating gender and film spectatorship

Critical studies of gender representation in Hindi, most notably "Bollywood" films, are not uncommon, quite often focusing on male viewers of the genre. Such viewers are thought to identify predominantly with a limited number of sexist and heterosexist discursive positions, mapped out for them by the films. These discursive positions, defined here not simply as units of communication but also as structures of feeling and thinking expressed through visual and other language, which order experience and inflect behavior, are assumed to be fairly homogeneous across individual films and even across entire genres. In order to understand how and why this movement between assumptions about textual meaning-producing strategies and audience meaning-making takes place in relation to Hindi films, it is important to understand the history and background of studies of cinematic gender representation. Foremost, a concern about the direct effects of media on behavior has motivated a good many of the theorists writing in this area. Empirical studies of gender representation imply strongly that media images serve as "models" for readers and viewers; for instance, Kaul argues that

> The popularity of films, newspapers and television in India prompts speculation on the social consequences of such media portrayal: it is potentially very damaging. Not only is a patriarchal world order reinforced in the press, on the screen and in television serials, but the existing dichotomy of sex roles is perpetuated ... The relentlessly negative representation of women in India's media has had the effect of validating women's inferiority as real and natural. The end result can only be a progressive debilitation of women's self-image.
>
> (Kaul 1996: 261–2)

The triangular move from potentially "damaging" images of women in the media to the reinforcing of social discrimination and then on to a negative transformation of women's "self-image" takes place rather seamlessly. It appears not only logical but simply common sense. The facts of existence for a majority of India's women, mostly rural and poor or urban and poor, as well as the evidence garnered via research into media representation and used in Kaul's paper, make such a linkage seem all the more justified. Other researchers doing textual analysis of Hindi films (Chatterji 1998; Kazmi 1998; Mathur 2002; Nair 2002; Vishwanath 2002) have argued that the films support unjust, patriarchal regimes. These studies also imply that audiences, only rarely approached in person and that too in the most superficial ways (Derné 2000), participate in these social imaginaries. For instance, expressing the frustration of many feminists with the representation of women in commercial Indian films, Maithili Rao's essay "To Be a Woman" (1995) appears to speak both about films and for female spectators. In her words, "women's response to popular cinema is a ceaseless love–hate thraldom because the film image ostensibly celebrates her eroticism while reducing her to a passive sex-object" (1995: 241).

In this context, increased sexual "permissiveness" on the screen is seen as simply one more complicating factor in the chain of iconography which binds and degrades women. In this view, recent films fuse the traditional Hindi film dichotomies of "vamp/prostitute/dancing girl" and "chaste wife" within individual heroines and make the idea of "woman" merely more appealing to certain men. Meanwhile, heroines become less psychologically coherent. Male viewers would, apparently, previously have had to cheer for dancing girls and then to fall silent in respect for the loyal piety of the heroine. Now, according to Rao, these men are given license to imagine, beneath the demure sari, the sexual delights which the heroine displayed and *promised* when, as an unmarried youngster, she cavorted in "itsy bitsy fluff" or "disported in diaphanous saris under waterfalls" (1995: 243). It is thus the way in which Hindi commercial cinema appears to reinforce certain oppressive patterns of thought and self-image for women that comes across in Rao's essay as most deeply disturbing. She writes of the film *Aaina* (*Mirror*, Deepak Sareen, 1993) that "the condoning of psychic violence done to women [goes] largely unnoticed. Meekness and patience are rewarded whereas the ambitious woman's attempt to exploit her sexuality for personal fame [is] condemned as morally reprehensible" (1995: 253–4). In a similar vein, feminist film theorist Shoma A. Chatterji argues that, contrary to performing an "idealising" function, "myth" in Indian popular culture perpetuates images of women which are "beautiful" but in which their "inner strength"—if they have any—"mainly derives from a man, dead or alive—father, brother, husband or son" (1998: 49).

Most of these textual analyses endorse two theoretical premises of major relevance to our discussion in this chapter. The first premise, following Laura Mulvey's seminal essay on narrative cinema, suggests that all textual pleasure is predicated on the passive display of female bodies, fetishism, voyeurism, and the successful subordination of the female to the male gaze. The second insists that gender identities are formed and maintained within a simple binary of masculine and feminine sex roles. Problematically, however, all these studies fail to analyze, in more than vague and generalized terms, the mechanisms whereby such supposedly psychologically constitutive activity takes place. There is also an implicit acceptance that gender identities are more significant than other aspects of identity in the interpretation and enjoyment of media texts. Crudely put, when you watch and understand a Hindi film or other media text, you respond to it and interpret it first as a man or woman. Other aspects of your identity are thus either subsidiary or irrelevant to how you interpret films. However, put so bluntly, this seems a highly suspect and somewhat limiting conclusion. So, where else can we look for a framework which might shed light on the connections between Hindi film viewing, meaning, and gender identity?

Feminist social psychologist Lynne Segal takes issue with what she deems to be theoretical weaknesses in social psychological sex-role constructions of gender identity such as the ones we have just looked at. She suggests that there is no necessary "rational" movement from disenchantment with or even anger against the "oppressive" or obsolete structures of "patriarchal" life to social change and alteration of the gender order (Segal 1999). In effect, when we know something is bad for us, this does not always spur us to reject it immediately; nor, just because we do reject something and stop doing it, does this mean we are not aware that it might have negative consequences for us or for the world. Perhaps, then, what is required from a theory of gender that hopes to explain men's and women's relationship to media representation is a conception of subjectivity which does not assume a *consistent relationship* between action and emotion or between aspects of an individual's psychic identity. Some strands of poststructuralist feminism appear to present just such an account. The research presented in the following sections draws on such arguments for its conceptual framework in answering the seemingly straightforward questions: How do viewers of Hindi films interpret and respond to representations of masculinity and femininity in the movies they watch, and in what ways do their gender identities seem to be inflected by these interpretations?

## Audiences and meanings

While a range of audience studies of films has been carried out in the past decade (Austin 2002; Barker and Brooks 1998; Cherry 2002), those that deal significantly or exclusively with themes of masculinity, femininity, and gender are not so numerous. In line with the more dialectical view of gender identity and representation arrived at in the previous section, Kimberley Chabot Davis discusses how her audience ethnographies are informed by "anti-essentialist theories of subjectivity" and explains that she investigates "how multiple axes of identity can complicate a viewer or reader's positioning" (2003: 5). Chabot Davis finds from her audience study of responses to *Kiss of the Spider Woman* (the novel, film, and musical versions), the story of two men who meet in prison, that only half of the gay men interviewed identified with the effeminate gay character Molina; "many in fact identified with Valentin, the macho political prisoner who could be read as either straight or bisexual" (2003: 5). This finding complicates immediately the notion that audiences or individual spectators watch film sequences and unreflexively begin to copy particular gender roles. People do not automatically identify with characters who share their maleness or femaleness. Gender is conceptualized here as a series of discourses— structures of feeling and thinking about the self and the world which are expressed either verbally or visually—and material practices encompassing behaviors and actions towards fellow humans as well as the making of visual and verbal representations.

From her interview-based study of audience responses to the film *The Piano*, Chabot Davis concludes that "identification is an ideological process, rather than one that simply devolves from the female body or psyche." Indeed, "[f]eminist viewers of *The Piano* recognized that their identification and/or disidentification with the protagonist Ada was influenced by their own adherence to particular feminist ideologies" (Chabot Davis 2003: 6). The fact that these women self-identify as feminists might tempt researchers in a quantitative tradition to dismiss their discussions of viewing and identification as so far from the "norm" as to be meaningless in providing an explanatory framework for how spectatorship and identity are connected. I suggest, however, that their explicit acknowledgment of ideological worldviews simply makes it easier to understand their interpretation of films than it would be in the case of viewers who do not have the vocabulary to describe the ideological stances they hold and the discourses in which they nonetheless participate.

Iglesias-Prieto (2004) examines the Mexican film *Danzon* and the relationship of diverse groups of viewers to its depictions of class, gender, and sexuality. Her focus group discussions with young heterosexual men, gay men, lesbians, and heterosexual women from different class backgrounds reveal several common "reading patterns." These center on aspects of identity that are not simply to do with gender, although they do intersect with gender at various points. For instance: "the group composed of younger gay men spoke of the story of *Danzon* in a manner similar to that registered in women's groups. ... The possibility of change in a female character composes a subversive element that upsets the distribution of power in gender relations. For this group, Julia becomes a model in that she is congruent with what the younger gay men seem to admire" (2004: 183–4). Thus, both Chabot Davis's and Iglesias-Prieto's studies suggest that, in contrast to the emphasis on embedded or inherent meaning which comes from textual analysis, the same moments in a film, watched by different audience cohorts, can hold divergent meanings and symbolic references. They also suggest that identification is a conscious ideological choice for some viewers. So, how do these findings play out in the very different context of Hindi popular film viewing?

## Gender, sexuality, and Hindi film audiences

Over more than a decade now, I have conducted extended in-depth interviews with more than 100 young people and two dozen older adults in India and the UK about their media use and Hindi film viewing, particularly in relation to gender, sexuality, religion, and class. Interviews, which generally lasted between one and four hours and were conducted one on one or in pairs, have been analyzed thematically in the light of forms of discourse analysis stemming from social psychology (Henriques *et al.* 1984; Potter and Wetherell 1987). Thus, although aspects of viewer identity such as class, gender, and religion are seen as significant in inflecting experiences of life and film, interviewees' accounts of Hindi film viewing and use are presented here as part of a moment in cultural time and space that has absorbed and thus reflects key meanings, values, and discourses from its surrounding sites of culture. This chapter draws particularly on a small number of the extensive responses to questions about representation, gender, pleasure, and morality in a series of films in the late 1990s and through the 2000s. Following Miller and Glassner (1997: 101), the language of interviewing is not seen here as a straightforward reflection of an unproblematic reality experienced by the interviewees. Instead, interviews are seen as providing accounts of media experience, which are also constructions of self that can and do change at different points in time or in different viewing contexts.

Turning to the question of how discourses and representation of gender in Hindi films are actually interpreted and received, a series of clear themes and patterns emerges from my data. In line with the theoretical framework outlined, and going further than other work in this tradition, the opinions, beliefs, and actions of view- ers, as described by them during interviews, seemed frequently *at odds* with their purported judgments about courtship, sex, and marriage or masculinity, femininity, and sexuality in Hindi films. For instance, several unmarried female viewers, in both Asian and Western cities, who expressed deep enjoyment of film narratives about the importance of chastity and the sacrifice of daughters' personal desires in the face of parental authority or out of love/respect for fathers, were themselves engaged in clandestine sexual relationships and desirous of acceptance of these relationships by their parents (Banaji 2012 [2006]). While some of these interviewees even used the interview situations as therapeutic moments to analyze the differences between their avowed beliefs and pleasures in film narrative and their actual beliefs and actions, others remained unreflexive throughout. For instance, several young male viewers who claimed heterosexuality, having championed the rights of film heroines and real- life women to self-determination, described complacently how they acquiesced in the subordination of their own girlfriends'/wives' autonomy to their wishes or their families' supposed "traditions" and values. Thus, regardless of viewers' gender, age, religion, or location, they deployed *available discourses* for talking about gender, both on and off screen. While some of these were stereotypical (assuming the fixed and essential nature of gender identity) and some were quite clearly counter-stereotypical (assuming that men and women can become and be different from how they behave or appear at particular times), they frequently coexisted in accounts of viewing.

When I asked interviewees to discuss films about religion, politics, and romance, religion and nationalism intersected with gender and sexuality in their interpretations in interesting ways. Several male viewers who described themselves as gay were emphatic in insisting that, given the lack of plausible and coherent gay male characters, they identified comfortably with the experiences and choices of heroines on screen. One of these viewers maintained that he could not accept his own sexual attraction to men as "a permanent thing" and claimed he watched Hindi films in the hope that he would discover the way to be "a proper man, a proper Indian husband." At a later point in the interview, however, he criticized the overwhelming heteronormativity of Hindi films. Following a discussion of young people sacrificing their romantic love to make their families happy in the film *Hum Aapke Hain Koun*, he stated:

MANISH: ... I don't think they should do that. It's all about the strength of your love, I think. If you give up then you'll be upset later that you never tried. Like with my ex. It really upset me when that ended. If you sacrifice then you never know how much that person means to you until they've gone. ... the minute we met, we knew we were meant to be together. His feelings complemented mine. But now he's under pressure to get married. I mean, I think Hindi films put a kind of pressure, maybe like on the older generation, reminding them that they have to get their children married. ... Like it tells them they *have to* have a daughter-in-law. I think it does have an effect.

Another feature of talk about masculinity and sexuality was the tendency for some viewers to suggest that religious, national, or class groups to which they did not belong were the perpetrators of sexual violence and regressive practice. So, "only Pakistanis" or "only Westerners" or "only Muslims" or only "lower-class men" molest women or can be homosexual, while "only white girls" and "only Hindu girls" would wear short skirts or act in pornographic movies. During interviews, several of these viewers became aware of and then embarrassed by their own normative claims. Others recounted how these were beliefs that they or their families had held previously but that they themselves no longer held having experienced "real life." When asked how they could take pleasure in such prejudiced depictions and discourses on the Hindi film screen, they suggested that textual pleasures and ideological beliefs off screen are not coterminous. The complexities of these thoughts *are* seen in the following discussion with a 21-year-old British-Nepali Hindu, Padma, about a sequence in the film *Dilwale Dulhaniya Le Jayenge* when the hero first encounters the heroine on an intercontinental train:

PADMA:  When they first meet each other on the train, it's so cute [pause, laughing]. It's only because he's Shah Rukh Khan that I say that. He probably *is* harassing her, like it's too much when he puts his head in her lap! Any other Indian guy and I'd be going "*Excuse me!* What're you doing? That's harassment here!" Call the guard, get him kicked off the train! He is harassing her and you only accept it because it is a Hindi film. You know, "Oh it's a film!" I mean if that happened in real life, you'd be like, "Oh my God, No!" But that's the thing, isn't it, it takes you away from real life. [pause]

INTERVIEWER:  Does it?

PADMA:  I reckon that in some places that could encourage guys to try it on, you know what I'm saying, some countries [smiling] … I reckon that in places like Nepal, India, people go and see that in the cinema and they go "Hey, I'd like to be a bit of a hero."

This excerpt highlights a tendency amongst film audiences to position their own responses to film themes and representations in relation to existing discourses on gender, class, or sexuality which are prevalent in their family or national and community media environment. It is therefore interesting to get a sense of *who* viewers are while elaborating their interpretations. Smriti (14) and Champa (15) are best friends. Smriti is lower middle class, Champa middle middle class. The girls met at school. Several conversations with parents and children reveal that Smriti's mother thinks Champa's family is "snobbish" and "a bad influence"; Champa's mother casts Smriti's mother as "narrow-minded" and "old-fashioned":

SMRITI:  [I like Hindi films because] they show love affairs, teenage problems and foreign locations. I am interested in that and I'm not ashamed. Who else will tell us about that? I want to travel and get away from my life here. But my mamma says I have to study, study, study. What for? To end up in just such a place with some useless guy whom I hate and who tells me what to do?

INTERVIEWER:  That sounds sad. So you watch films to see how you can change what you think your future holds? [Silence.] Have you seen anything that you were excited by recently?

CHAMPA AND SMRITI:  All *Twilight* series! [they both groan]

SMRITI:  *Love Aaj Kal, Saathiyan, Three Idiots, Fire.*

INTERVIEWER:  You watched *Fire*?

CHAMPA:  My mom lets us watch her DVDs. It's a good film. Some people say it's not showing Indian values, because the two women, you know ... But I think it's *very* Indian. More than most of the Hindi movies set in big houses in Sydney and New York and London.

SMRITI:  And it was funny how the film showed the two-faced [hypocritical] men in the family. The servant. On one side they expect you to behave in such a way, modest, good daughter-in-law. On the other side they are wanting to have sex or watch pornos [both girls laughing loudly].

CHAMPA:  I don't like the films set in the villages. They are so slow and there is nothing to see.

INTERVIEWER:  Do you mean visually they don't please you?

CHAMPA:  No. I really feel uncomfortable. A girl like me would not fit in there.

SMRITI:  I love those films. She doesn't like the villages, but I do. I go every vacation to my native place.

This excerpt from the beginning of our interview shows both girls positioning themselves in relation to their parents' worldviews and those supposedly conveyed in films. They pick out themes of travel, place and modernity, sexuality and hypocrisy, class, and gender for comment. Participating in a world opened up to them partly by Champa's mother and her cosmopolitan attitude to adolescence, both girls can comment on sexuality, pornography, and other aspects of media culture. Smriti, while yearning for a lifting of the cultural constraints placed on her by her family's class, by their gender values and their communal identity, claims she is still able to enjoy fiction films set in villages. Champa and Smriti's discussion tightens the complicated knots between sexuality, gender, communal identity, and class that have emerged in previous studies (Banaji 2008; Rao 2007). This suggests both the insistent intersectionality of film viewers' identity and the problematic nature of a research question which try to detach one set of social discourses in films entirely from all others.

Other salient themes about identification and meaning making emerge from actual interviews with audience members. Of these, a significant one relates to the way in which the same sequence watched by different people or with different companions can provoke divergent emotions and interpretations from viewers of the same gender. For example, Kaveri (11) and Nimmi (12) are cousins. Kaveri's parents work as shop assistants; Nimmi's parents belong to the aspiring middle classes.

INTERVIEWER:  You were telling me about that film *Fashion* [dir. Madhur Bhandarkar]. I'm surprised you were allowed to watch that.

NIMMI:  I like to see films because then I know all the latest designs. I ask my mamma to get them for me; she does. I think it's nice to look good. And models [in English] look good.

KAVERI:  [smiling] I think my mamma took us to that picture because she wanted us to think about how you can spoil your life running after material things, running after more. But [shyly] Nimmi was very excited to see all the costumes.

NIMMI [Confident]: Why was everything so beautiful and shown again and again by the camera if we weren't supposed to like it? It was like an advert. [Pause] I would have a balance in my life, not like those models who take cigarettes all the time and drink Pepsi for breakfast. But I want to look good [whispers], sexy. Some costumes are so beautiful—girls should be able to choose how they dress.

KAVERI: Yes, I agree with her that on one side the films make bad and dirty things very beautiful to watch and then on the other side we are told don't do this, this is not good. So it is hard to know which one to believe. But that is why we have to follow our own upbringing. I know what is right, what is wrong. Designer clothes and high grades in class and lots of money do not make someone a good human being ...

Interconnected discourses drawn from strands of humanist, feminist, and post-feminist thought surface during this exchange. Although both girls are under 13 and from the same extended family, their thinking is very distinct: Kaveri accepts her parents' divergent worldview and sees it as a moral imperative to be her own person, to reject global youth culture as well as Hindi film representations of perfection or social success. Nimmi, whose parents would be disturbed at the notion of her wanting to appear "sexy" and yet who gratify her every request when it comes to clothing and make-up, finds the visual pleasures of looking at clothing and girls on screen too strong for any moral subtexts of condemnation to taint her enjoyment. Further, she uses Hindi films' displays of fashion consumption as a way of inspiring new outfits and styles for herself. Her cousin points out that brands are inscribed with problematic versions of femininity. This is something Nimmi is aware of but chooses to reinterpret as supporting her choice to clothe herself fashionably ("girls should be able to choose how they dress"). Both girls put a premium on imagination and freedom, but read Hindi film depictions of femininity, class, and fashion from apparently opposing consumerist and civic viewpoints. This leads one of them to express her freedom as freedom of choice as a young female citizen-consumer, and the other to see freedom as divergent thinking, leading to critique of a society dominated by capitalist representations of success. Neither of the girls commented on the various incidents of sexual manipulation, violence, and female self-harm in the film, which could arguably be seen as the film's most consistent representation of working life for female models. Let us set these young women's readings of the film *Fashion* beside Linda Williams's argument that in narrative cinema "[t]he woman's gaze is punished ... by narrative processes that transform curiosity and desire into masochistic fantasy" (2002: 61). This juxtaposition allows us to see that theorizations of ideological discourses and subtexts in films may well be useful tools for understanding power relations within the texts but are less stable and useful when it comes to understanding audience meaning making and subsequent behavior.

## Destigmatizing the audience

A significant strand of broadly feminist writing is theoretically wedded to the belief that the media purvey stereotypical sex roles which implicitly become part of viewers' own gender identities. In such accounts, the *effects* of media stereotypes on human identity are often immediate, monolithic, and almost unbounded. To a large extent, this chapter has rejected the premises of fixed, rational, and essential identities in favor of more nuanced explications of gender identity and media. While mindful of the importance of fantasy and the unconscious in shaping human identity, I move away from the notion of "roles" and the "unconscious" adoption of them. We thus reach a notion of subjectivity that allows greater agency (however problematic) and flexibility (albeit limited by specific experiences and material contexts) in viewers' interactions with the media. In tandem, I argue that the pleasures of Hindi film viewing are not convincingly linked by audience research to theorizations which suggest an unconscious absorption of retrograde messages. Indeed, detailed work with film audiences has shown that films are far more than the sites of cultural struggle, although they are always also implicated in social tensions and conflicts.

However much textual elaborations of gender representation might push us to this conclusion, film viewing is not an activity that occurs in a vacuum or an ideologically homogeneous goldfish bowl. This is not to say that media producers do not follow culturally limited parameters of predominant notions of gender difference; nor is it to suggest that there is a precise and scientific process whereby one can chart and describe events which occur when representations of gender in texts and readers meet. What studies of spectatorship should take on board, I suggest, is the more or less limited range of interpretive choices available to most viewers and the ways in which these choices may be constrained by structural and psychic intersections of class, ethnicity, and gender or other aspects of human identity. Although often equally worrying or retrograde, contextual and sociocultural identities and experiences *in addition to gender*—from race and ethnicity through geography to sexuality and class—play a crucial role in complicating and inflecting audiences' responses to, pleasures in, and uses of gender representation in Bollywood Hindi films.

# References

Austin, T. (2002) *Hollywood, Hype and Audiences: Selling and Watching Popular Films in the 1990s*, Manchester: Manchester University Press.

Banaji, S. (2012 [2006]) *Reading Bollywood: The Young Audience and Hindi Films*, Basingstoke: Palgrave Macmillan.

——(2008) "Fascist Imaginaries and Clandestine Critiques: Young Hindi Film Viewers Respond to Love, Violence and Xenophobia in Cross-Border Romances," in M. Bharat and N. Kumar (eds) *War, Enemy and Hindi Films: Filming the Line of Control*, New Delhi: Routledge, pp. 157–58.

Barker, M. and K. Brooks (1998) *Knowing Audiences: Judge Dredd, Its Friends, Fans and Foes*, Luton: University of Luton Press.

Buckingham, D. (ed.) (1993) *Reading Audiences: Young People and the Media*, Manchester and London: Manchester University Press.

Chabot Davis, K. (2003) "An Ethnography of Political Identification: The Birmingham School Meets Psychoanalytic Theory," *Journal for the Psychoanalysis of Culture and Society* 8(1): 3–11.

Chatterji, S. A. (1998) *Cinema Object: Woman: A Study of the Portrayal of Women in Indian Cinema*, Calcutta: Parumita Publications.

Cherry, B. (2002) "Refusing to Refuse the Look: Female Viewers of the Horror Film," in M. Jankovich (ed.) *Horror: The Film Reader*, London: Routledge, pp. 169–77.

Derné, S. (2000) *Movies, Masculinity and Modernity: An Ethnography of Men's Film-going in India*, Westport, CT and London: Greenwood Press.

Henriques, J., W. Hollway, C. Urwin, C. Venn, and V. Walkerdine (1984) *Changing the Subject: Psychology, Social Regulation and Subjectivity*, London: Methuen.

Iglesias-Prieto, N. (2004) "Gazes and Cinematic Readings of Gender: Danzon and Its Relationship to Its Audience," *Discourse* 23(1/2): 173–93.

Kaul, C. (1996) "Some Perspectives on Issues of Gender and the Indian Media," in N. Daković, D. Derman, and K. Ross (eds.) *Gender and Media*, Ankara: Med-Campus Project #A126 Publications.

Kazmi, N. (1998) *The Dream Merchants of Bollywood*, New Delhi: UBSPD.

Mathur, V. (2002) "Women in Indian Cinema: Fictional Constructs," in J. Jain and S. Rai (eds.) *Films and Feminism: Essays in Indian Cinema*, Jaipur and New Delhi: Rawat Publications, pp. 65–71.

Miller, J. and B. Glassner (1997) "The 'Inside' and the 'Outside': Finding Realities in Interviews," in D. Silverman (ed.) *Qualitative Research*, New York, London and New Delhi: Sage, pp. 125–39.

Mulvey, L. (1975) "Visual Pleasure and Narrative Cinema," *Screen* 16(3): 16–18.

Nair, B. (2002) "Female Bodies and the Male Gaze: Laura Mulvey and Hindi Cinema," in J. Jain and S. Rai (eds.) *Films and Feminism: Essays in Indian Cinema*, Jaipur and New Delhi: Rawat Publications, pp. 52–55.

Potter, J. and M. Wetherell (1987) *Discourse and Social Psychology: Beyond Attitudes and Behaviour*, London: Sage.

Rao, M. (1995) "To Be a Woman," in A. Vasudev (ed.) *Frames of Mind: Reflections on Indian Cinema*, New Delhi: UBSPD, pp. 37–40.

Rao, S. (2007) "The Globalization of Bollywood: An Ethnography of Non-Elite Audiences in India," *The Communication Review* 10(1): 57–76.

Segal, L. (1999) *Why Feminism?*, Cambridge: Polity.

Vishwanath, G. (2002) "Saffronizing the Silver Screen: The Right-Winged Nineties Film," in J. Jain and S. Rai (eds.) *Films and Feminism: Essays in Indian Cinema*, Jaipur and New Delhi: Rawat Publications, pp. 39–51.

Williams, L. (2002) "When the Woman Looks," in M. Jankovich (ed.) *Horror: The Film Reader*, London and New York: Routledge, pp. 61–6.

# 46

# Asian women audiences, Asian popular culture, and media globalization

## *Youna Kim*

What grasp do we have of the relationship between consumption of media and the shaping of individual lives and identities? What do we know about the experiences of women in Asia? This chapter explores women's everyday experiences of media in Asian countries in relation to contemporary contexts of wide-ranging social change and transition. The media involve the complex processes of social change and transition—from the conduct of everyday life, to the reflexive understanding of a global world, to the construction of new identities and a constant tension in its expression within the everyday. Based on my ongoing ethnographic media studies in global sites (Kim 2005, 2008, 2011, 2012), this chapter provides a critical analysis of the emerging consequences of media consumption in women's everyday lives at a time when the political, economic, and technological contexts in which the media operate are becoming increasingly global. I argue that media globalization in Asia needs to be recognized as a proliferating, indispensable, yet highly complex and contradictory resource for the construction of identity within everyday lived experience.

## Everyday reflexivity

The notion of reflexivity has been a crucial issue for social researchers in Western academic debates since the mid-1980s—notably in critical ethnography (Clifford and Marcus 1986) and feminist epistemology (Skeggs 1995)—emphasizing the necessity of reflecting on the research conditions (e.g. power relations) under which knowledge is produced. But what about the reflexivity of ordinary people? What about women in a culture where gender repression is supposedly pervasive? What is it about the globally connected media world that provides openings for ordinary women to make sense of their lives in critical ways? I consider reflexivity as the major mechanism of grasping a relationship between globalization, as a mediated cultural force, and experience, since reflexivity is precisely what is at work in the everyday experience of global media culture.

The media are central to everyday reflexivity—the capacity to monitor action and its contexts to keep in touch with the grounds of everyday life, self-confront uncertainties, and understand the relationships between cause and effect, yet never quite control the complex dynamics of everyday life. Reflexivity is an everyday practice. It is intrinsic to human activity since human beings routinely keep in touch with the grounds of what they do, what they think, and what they feel as a circular feedback mechanism. But a different and significant process in contemporary everyday life has changed the very nature of reflexivity by providing conditions for increased capacities for reflexivity "in the light of new information or knowledge" (Giddens 1991: 20). This involves the routine incorporation of new information or knowledge into environments of action that are thereby reconstituted or reorganized. Ordinary people have the ability to reflect on the social conditions of their existence and to change them accordingly, going beyond traditional markers and the givens of social order (Beck et al. 1994).

The question, however, is, to what extent and in what ways? Whose reflexivity? This reflexivity is experienced differently by different social subjects in different social locations, defining those societies as distinctive. Reflexivity needs not to be understood as a universal capacity of subjects or a "generalized experience that cuts across social divides," but to be understood in specific life world contexts where reflexivity arises unevenly and often ambiguously with competing reflexivities. We need to recognize situated reflexivity, specifying the different experiences of reflexivity situated within different social spaces. The degrees of reflexivity and its particular character and content may differ, since it is mediated by a remarkably high level of education in Confucian societies like Korea (Kim 2005); it operates at a more collective, rather than individual, level than in the West. It may also be influenced by the lack of the reflexive forms of media representation in a relatively rigid society such as China (Kim 2008).

Often, when local media productions in Asia largely fail to respond to the changing socioeconomic status and desire of people—youth and women in particular—it is transnational media culture that is instead appropriated for making contact with the diverse formations of culture and for making sense of what it means to be a modern self (Kim 2007, 2008). The media are not the only contributor to the process of reflexivity, but the degree of the media's contribution depends on what other sources of reflexivity might or might not be available and who can access and utilize them as meaningful resources. Notaby, unlike Euro-American societies, where people might draw on expert psychological knowledge in their understanding of the self, such models and sources may not be widely accessible and used among people in Asia. When other sources such as psychotherapy and self-help expertise are not readily available in the local circumstances of day-to-day life, transnational media programming can be appropriated for an implicit therapeutic function and self-analysis to deal with the cultures of everyday life. It is not just the media's ubiquity in everyday life, but also their unique and plausibly powerful capacity to affect the meaning making of everyday life experience, to trigger a heightened reflexive awareness of the world, which is arguably a key cultural dynamic and challenge. Although media consumption may not lead to dramatic social change in the short run, and although the importance of the transformations generated by the media in the long run are problematically obscured by the attention to short-run immediate effects (Martin-Barbero 2003), people's mundane changes, imagination, and critical reflection triggered by the media and expressed in the practices of everyday life can be the basis of social constitution (Kim 2008).

## Case study of Korean women

My ethnographic findings in Korea (Kim 2005, 2006) demonstrate that reflexivity is an integral process of media talk. Korean women's reflections of themselves and their worlds are major elements of the experiences of the media in daily life. I conducted fieldwork to include a varied sample of women in their twenties, thirties, and fifties from both working-class and middle-class backgrounds: six different socioeconomic categories, with seven women in each category. This case study draws on the accounts of the middle-class women in their twenties, because this younger age group demonstrated an active use of global television. Television programs stand as the dominant representations of global culture—including Hollywood movies, travel shows, dramas, and CNN:

> English is a must for employment (in Korea). I withdrew from the university for one year and went to Australia for an English course. To brush up English now, I keep the TV on and listen to CNN, drama, movies. Who would find CNN interesting? But it's good for a listening practice. I don't find American drama interesting, but it's best for learning spoken English.
> (ES, Korean woman, 22, university student in Korea)

> The completion of an English course abroad is a boost on the employment resume. So many students travel to America, Canada, Europe. In this globalizing society it may sound strange if you haven't been abroad. You have to travel abroad to join the conversation.
> (YK, Korean woman, 22, university student in Korea)

Transnational culture today tends to be tied to the job market. English, as a language of global modernity and a means of making a living, has become a crucial precondition for the women's attainment of well-paid work and economic independence. As a consequence, these young women learn English, whether they like it or not. English has emerged as a new form of cultural capital in globalizing modern Korea. Learning English and involving themselves with wider Western culture through travel and global television are distinctive characteristics of the lives of young middle-class women in Korea. Their openness towards new cultural experiences is increasingly self-reflexive, characterized by a search for "differences" rather than universalities. What is common to this experience is a "learning of the self" that is reflexively interpreted and understood by a contrast between imagined (Western) freedom and practical (Korean) restrictions. The following extract illustrates what some young Korean women mean by Western free lifestyles, and its details reveal some of the constraints on being free in Korean society:

In *Friends* [an American comedy drama], they often get together in the coffee shop and chat sitting comfortably on the sofa. None of them seem to worry about life or work. Everyday life is just ha-ha-ho-ho happy and simple. They don't seem to have a nice job, yet life is jolly. The long blond works in the coffee shop as a waitress. The tall stupid woman sings stupid songs. Did they go to university? Probably they did, they don't look smart though. In Korean society, if we are a university graduate and work in a coffee shop, people will think of us as a total loser. Not to mention parents' fury, "Have I sent you to university to see you work in a coffee shop?" None of their parents seem to compel, "Quit fooling around, get married and settle down!" In their culture it seems OK to fool around and enjoy a life. Because nobody interferes in their life. I like such free social atmosphere.

(JH, Korean woman, 22, university student in Korea)

This remark illuminates the media's great capacity for evoking reflexivity in an endless chain of referentiality, intersected with the microcosms of everyday life. In the context of new cultural experiences, Korean ways of life and traditional norms are interrogated and criticized. Young middle-class women commonly criticize, on the one hand, Korean gender models and appropriate forms of behavior predicated on rigidly defined matrimonial roles, family expectations, and direct parental control. On the other hand, they derive new interpretations of life through Western images of free lifestyles. Significantly, their yearning for Western freedom crystallizes around the meaning of "individualization," which is fundamentally incompatible with traditional family values:

I like Western people's free individualistic life. They are making their own life, while we are making life for others.

(ES, Korean woman, 22, university student in Korea)

I hate the [Korean] car commercial. It's so stupid—"My husband wanted to remodel the kitchen for me, but I wanted to get him a new car instead. For my husband's confidence." Then, the husband drives a car and the wife happily leans on his shoulder. I hate that commercial. I would earn money on my own, change the kitchen on my own, and drive my own car!

(BR, Korean woman, 21, university student in Korea)

By imagining different ways of living and being through experiences of the media, these young women struggle to invent a more self-responsible, self-determined, "emancipatory life politics" (Giddens 1991: 214), a politics of self-actualization, which is no longer obligatory and embedded in traditional gendered roles. It is a struggle to break free from the fixities of social rules, norms, and expectations to discover a new self, asking, "How should I live?" "What do I want in life?" This search for a new identity is played out in the midst of transcultural experience, in heightened awareness of thoughts and feelings. The intensified self-reflexivity signals a deliberately hopeful movement, a transformative quest for individualization.

## Female individualization

To what extent do women have control over their lives? The troubling signs of female individualization as they intersect with media culture have become a new arena of anxiety for women in contemporary Asia, including Korea, Japan, China, Taiwan, Singapore, and Indonesia (Kim 2012). Signs of female individualization have been proliferating as a defining feature of contemporary modes of gender identity, albeit untenable and ambivalent, within the discursive regime of self—embodied in regulatory practices in society, where individualism is not placed at the heart of its culture. Arguably, the media are central to the signs of emergent cultures of female individualization producing the alternative social, cultural, and symbolic relations women wish to live within and defining the kind of self they wish to become. Individualization is encountered and mediated through popular media imaginaries that are present and often intentionally used as resources for reflexivity and self-imagining. This also provides a condition for an increased awareness of cultural differences and of women's own positions in relation to global Others, new symbolic objects of identification and contestation.

In Asia from the 1980s onward, women have gained higher levels of education and the commensurate expectations have become a driving motor in the women's aspirations for work, economic power, independence, freedom, and self-fulfillment (Kim 2012). However, women often experience gendered labor market inequity, setting limits on patterns of participation, women's socioeconomic position on the margins of work systems, and thus the illusion of the language of choice that the new capacities of education appear to promise. The enlargement of choice can be particularly illusory for women in contemporary Asia, where often rigid gendered socioeconomic and cultural conditions persist and continue to structure labor market outcomes and lifestyles.

For example, in contemporary Korea 95.3 percent of women go to high school and 63 percent of the women go on to higher education. High-school education in Japan has also reached equal levels for men (96.0 percent) and women (96.7 percent), and 45.3 percent of the women advance to higher education. Young women in urban China, who were born in the era of the single-child policy, with the emphasis on individual success, become the focus of parental expectations and the products of a fiercely competitive education system, in which gender difference is not recognized. There is greater gender equality in education and the expansion of educational opportunities for urban middle-class women; therefore, gender inequality is often thought to be diminished or nonexistent at the educational level of the urban middle class.

Despite impressive levels of higher education in Korea, only 46.7 percent of female university graduates are employed, mostly in traditional female career tracks, non-managerial and secretarial positions in small firms. Korean women still earn only 76 percent of what men make, giving Korean women little economic security. Japanese women in full-time employment earn only 65 percent of male wages, which is far from economically rewarding or emotionally fulfilling. Japan's male-dominated labor system divides recruits into "career track positions" and "general clerical work," with 80 percent of women being hired in the second category (Kim 2012: 5). The perception of education has become "consumption," a thing to be consumed by Japanese women without any expectation as to the consequences. Middle-class women in urban China must compete for jobs in a post-socialist context, in which gender difference, officially denied in their school years, seems "suddenly very pronounced" (Kim 20012: 5).

Increasingly, educated women are choosing to invest their resources in their career, rather than in marriage and family. The average age of marriage for Japanese women increased from 24.5 in 1975 to 28.5 in 2008, making Japan one of the latest-marrying populations in the world (Kim 2012). Non-marriage for women has become common in many urban areas of East Asia (Jones 2005). The total fertility rate for Asia as a whole dropped from approximately 6 children per woman in the period 1950–5 to approximately 2.7 children per woman by 1995–2000 (Chan and Yeoh 2002). Low-fertility countries such as Japan and Korea are characterized by low gender equity, a robust marriage institution, and strong familism (Suzuki 2008). Korea, a typical case, shows one of the world's lowest birth rates, 1.15 (KWDI 2009), as a growing number of women delay marriage/family life in pursuit of employment and self-actualization. Amid these transformations, divorce rates have increased, although in some countries more radically and more quickly than in others. The Korean divorce rate has rapidly increased, from 5.8 percent in 1980 to 11.1 percent in 1990, 16.8 percent in 1995, 33 percent in 2000, and almost 50 percent today (KWDI 2009). Since the 1990s, the divorce rate in China has increased quickly in urban cities, with Beijing at 39 percent and Shanghai at 38 percent today (Sina 2010).

These indicators of the family at risk represent visible and provisional, if not permanent, cases of individualization. The social transformations in many parts of contemporary urban Asia appear to engender similar, but not the same, trends and consequences of individualization, which is notably linked to contemporary Western/European social theory in the processes of modernity. Individualization is characterized by a growing emphasis on individual autonomy and independence from traditions and social institutions. Women are now released from traditional gender roles, and find themselves forced to build up a "life of their own" by way of the labor market, training, and mobility (Beck and Beck-Gernsheim 2002). Confronted with a plurality of choices, individuals' life politics is organized around an increasingly reflexive and calculable mode of thinking to colonize the future with some degree of success (Giddens 1991). Family members form an elective relationship or a permanent do-it-yourself project, shifting from traditional expectations of "being there for others" to contemporary notions of "living one's own life" as a free and independent individual (Beck and Beck-Gernsheim 2002).

However, what it means to be a free and independent individual in Asian societies today is much more complex and paradoxical. The current growth in the number of single people and delayed marriage in pursuit of higher education and work can be seen as an indicator of precarious individualization, which may challenge the stability of family but not necessarily hold a privileging logic of self-invention and freedom. What does individualization mean in the context of the family? Traditional external constraints on marriage and family, the heteronormative expectation of marriage by 30 in East Asia, or much earlier in South Asia, have not progressively disappeared. The family, not the individual, is still the basic unit of social reproduction in Asia. Individualization, or family-oriented individualization, encompasses a much more complex and delicate, culture-bound balance between individual and family, whose values and practices differ significantly from the individualizing trends of the West. Oftentimes in Asia, an imagined future of individualization is simultaneously organized around the modalities of marriage and family. This is evident in the varying degrees to which transnational Asian women remain both autonomous from and dependent upon concrete familial relations in their diasporic existence and do not necessarily desire individual autonomy or freedom from the notions of marriage and family, even while continually transgressing national borders and producing new narratives of individual freedom (Kim 2011).

This unresolved identity of individualization serves as an important context within which the role of the media can be understood in its intersection with Asian transformations. Transnational flows of the media have emerged in globalizing Asia with a seeming emphasis on individualization and new heterogeneous choices within a neoliberal capitalist culture of freedom. Amidst the proliferation of the media, the seeming pluralization of choices in life and the deepening of the self, ongoing identity work is struggled over by women, who create the expressive possibilities for identity transformation but may also face considerable difficulties, may still not know which way they are going, or may potentially suffer from unintended consequences.

## Transnational mobility

The limitations and contradictions of female individualization in Asia, as discussed above, are continually salient yet unresolved, giving rise to transnational mobility as a temporary resolution and a form of departure from a socially expected, normative biography (see Kim 2010, 2011). Women are traveling out of Korea, Japan, and China for very different reasons than those that sent them into Diaspora only 20 years ago. From the mid-1980s onward, more and more women are leaving their country to experience life overseas either as tourists or as students, eventually surpassing the number of men engaging in foreign travel. These new generations of women, who depart from the usual marriage track, are markers of contemporary transnational mobility, constituting a new kind of Diaspora, a "knowledge Diaspora." Why do women move? How do the media play a role in this migration process?

The disjuncture between higher educational attainment and labor market inequity prevents the chances of individualization, yet simultaneously generates the individualized, choice-based narratives women tend to construct in talking about an imagined future of individualization. Despite the paradoxical outcomes and anxieties of where women actually stand regarding a move towards individualization, multiple ways of imagining such a possibility are widely available in mediated cultural domains, with proliferating resources for the mobilization of self. The media, mostly taken for granted, go along with diasporic subjects today. These new kinds of transnational networks, connections, and various capacities of mobility are now changing not only the scale and patterns of migration but also the nature of migrant experience and thinking. Importantly, a provisional nomadic sensibility ("willing to go anywhere for a while") has been facilitated by the mediation of rapidly evolving media technologies. Women's desire to move is constituted by the contradictory socioeconomic relations, as well as by the cultural-symbolic forms by which everyday life is lived out, rethought, and rearticulated in its intersection with the emergence of precarious individualized identities.

## Case study of Korean, Japanese, and Chinese women

This phenomenon above is frequently figured in Asian women's imagination of the West through the everyday media, as demonstrated in the following data from my ethnographic research (e.g. Korean, Japanese, and Chinese women in their twenties and early thirties) (see Kim 2010, 2011). The following case study offers insights into the implications of women's migration, with data drawn from personal in-depth interviews and diaries. I conducted interviews with 60 Asian women (20 Koreans, 20 Japanese, and 20 Chinese) who had been living and studying in the UK/London for three to seven years. The women were between 26 and 33 years: single women of middle-class and upper-class positions. Also, a panel of 30 diarists (10 Koreans, 10 Japanese, and 10 Chinese) was recruited and asked to write/email diaries about their experiences and to express in detail key issues raised from the interviews. This method was designed to generate biographical accounts from the women and incorporate a reflexive biographical analysis:

> My job might be OK, my life might be OK compared to my mother's [in Korea]. But I didn't feel happy, couldn't be satisfied with just that! I have bigger desires ... The more I got to know bigger things through the media, the more I thought about them.
> (CR, Korean woman, 31, moved from Korea to the UK for study)

> This [Korean drama] showed beautiful scenery of Cambridge and London where they met while studying. It's a typical romance, an illusion made by TV. But I wanted to believe that could happen. Life would feel different there ... I imagined myself and anticipated to go.
> (EJ, Korean woman, 29, moved from Korea to the UK for study)

Young Korean women appear to have more choices and capacities in life, higher education, and better material provisions compared to past generations, yet this does not necessarily translate into greater happiness. Expectations of satisfaction have risen, affected by what other people have or an insatiable endless desire to have, which occurs by the intrusion of cultural "Others" through the media and has the consequence of causing both rising expectations and rising frustrations. The construction of an autonomous illusion ("I wanted to believe that could happen"), the ability to create an illusion which is known to be false but felt to be true, suggests that the knowing individual creates the existence for herself in her imagination, as both actor and audience in her own drama. Considerable meaning is gained, not merely from the illusion, but from "imagining that illusion as actuality," mobilizing the self towards a hoped-for-future:

> Japanese women's magazines showed photo essays about experiences of travelling and living abroad, which inspired me a lot. ... A 30-year-old TV

announcer quit her job because old women are not considered suitable for that job in Japan. Her job was replaced by a younger woman. So she moved to Paris to study. ... Her photo essay shows, Paris is beautiful! The beautiful illusion arouses such a good feeling that you want to be there.

(YK, Japanese woman, 28, moved from Japan to the UK for study)

So sick and tired of office work [in Japan], one day I decided to do nothing and watched this film *Notting Hill*. Romance, freedom, laughter, London parks are so green! I felt, go there! It makes you feel something good can happen there ... You know that is an illusion but you want to believe that illusion and go.

(SW, Japanese woman, 30, moved from Japan to the UK for study)

The aestheticization and romanticization of Western cities is known to be false but felt to be true or suggestive of a possibility that "something good can happen there." A general awareness of the link between media consumption and physical displacement exists in the Japanese women's emotional investment in the media at a level of utopian sensibility. It is intertwined with good feelings the media embody and evoke. The media certainly construct an illusion or an image of something better that women's day-to-day lives do not provide. But it is the intelligently detectable illusion that is put to work by the knowing individuals with intentionality of knowledge: "You know that is an illusion but you want to believe that illusion and go."

Life in China is so competitive, crowded and stressful. People work so hard, try to survive and win in competitive society ... Bus is so crowded that you have to squeeze in. There is no space for yourself. I started the everyday with this crowded bus ... A bus ride in the West seemed fun, pleasant [on TV], people easily got on and got off. Wouldn't it be nice to live in that environment? I saw this empty bus on TV a long time ago but still remember ... Here, London bus is not crowded, most of time I can sit down and think. There is a space for thinking about myself.

(BB, Chinese woman, 27, moved from China to the UK for study)

This mediated experience can powerfully create and allow a space for the self to emerge in the fluidities of transnational imagination, while engaging with a newly found curiosity and a search for a new self that can be played out and actualized. Different ways to conceive the self are emerging in more individualist terms marked by an outward-looking reflexivity. Contemporary Chinese female identities are being shaped by cultural consumption within mediated transnational networks. Chinese women have been subject to different imaginary social spaces which enable them to reflect upon their lived experiences within the multiple and competing regimes of identification, expanding potentialities for self-invention that the divergent cultural experiences give rise to and mobilize.

## Conclusion

Increased reflexivity in everyday life is not only the outcome of education, but also significantly the consequence of the proliferation of sites of mediated experience offering wider contexts of knowledge and images concerning different discourses outside local networks of experience. The media have not just become sites where such reflexivity takes place, but actually provide the specific terms and forms of everyday talk and practice in the light of non-local knowledge. It is via the increased exposure to global "Others" and reflexive capacities that ordinary women make sense of life conditions which differ from their own and come to critically question the taken-for-grantedness of their own social order. Significantly, what is emerging here can be the problematization of society itself, the increasing awareness of its structural rigidity and discontents as well as the interrogatory attitude towards the surrounding world. Engagement with the transnational media constitutes a heightened awareness vis-à-vis gender, sexuality, class, social mobility, individualization, and so on.

The mediated experience can have the effect of transforming women's sense of self, of the world beyond and their imagined place in it, while mobilizing the sedimented always-already orientation towards displacement. Media culture is clearly one of the new, mundane, and prime sites in which self-reflexivity is operating continuously, and some knowing self-monitoring subjects are more likely than others to be reflexive about gender relations, inequalities, and oppression within the larger context of the mediated world. The often intended consequences of everyday media consumption on the part of women—not only deriving pleasure and gratification but also gaining routine access to alternative forms of knowledge—contribute to an increasing likelihood of a habitual reflexivity in a routine life, and, moreover, a transnational reflexivity, through which the self can be regularly examined, rethought and redefined, even if not always discursively accomplished. Such changes in awareness, knowledge, and the questioning attitude towards the world may not always lead to social transformation in the short run; but new possibilities may arise from this heightened capacity for critical reflection and questioning. This evolving reflexive project is not just a direct cause and effect in the speed of social and cultural change but an increasingly insistent and intense process of mediation.

# References

Beck, U. and E. Beck-Gernsheim (2002) *Individualization*, London: Sage.

Beck, U., A. Giddens, and S. Lash (1994) *Reflexive Modernization: Politics, Tradition and Aesthetics in the Modern Social Order*, Cambridge: Polity.

Chan, A. and B. Yeoh (2002) "Gender, Family and Fertility in Asia," *Asia-Pacific Population Journal* 17(2): 5–10.

Clifford, J. and G. Marcus (1986) *Writing Culture: The Poetics and Politics of Ethnography*, Berkeley: University of California Press.

Giddens, A. (1991) *Modernity and Self-identity: Self and Society in the Late Modern Age*, Cambridge: Polity.

Jones, G. (2005) "The Flight from Marriage in South-East and East Asia," *Journal of Comparative Family Studies* 36(1): 93–119.

Kim, Y. (2005) *Women, Television and Everyday Life in Korea: Journeys of Hope*, London and New York: Routledge.

——(2006) "How TV Mediates the Husband–Wife Relationship: A Korean Generation/Class/Emotion Analysis," *Feminist Media Studies* 6(2): 126–43.

——(2007) "The Rising East Asian Wave: Korean Media Go Global," in Daya Thussu (ed.) *Media on the Move: Global Flow and Contra Flow*, London and New York: Routledge, pp. 135–52.

——(2008) *Media Consumption and Everyday Life in Asia*, London and New York: Routledge.

——(2010) "Female Individualization?: Transnational Mobility and Media Consumption of Asian Women," *Media, Culture & Society* 32(1): 25–43.

——(2011) *Transnational Migration, Media and Identity of Asian Women: Diasporic Daughters*, London and New York: Routledge.

——(2012) *Women and the Media in Asia: The Precarious Self*, London and New York: Palgrave Macmillan.

KWDI (Korean Women's Development Institute) (2009) "Documents and Databases." http://www2.kwdi.re.kr.

Martin-Barbero, J. (2003) "Cultural Change: The Perception of the Media and the Mediation of Its Images," *Television & New Media* 4(1): 85–106.

Sina (2010) "Beijing Divorce Rate Skyrockets," Sina.com, February 8.

Skeggs, B. (1995) *Feminist Cultural Theory: Process and Production*, Manchester: Manchester University Press.

Suzuki, T. (2008) "Korea's Strong Familism and Lowest-Low Fertility," *International Journal of Japanese Sociology* 17(1): 30–41.

# 47

# Women as radio audiences in Africa

## Tanja Bosch

Radio is still the most widespread, accessible, and popular form of communication in many countries in Africa. The costs of radio content production are comparatively inexpensive, and access to radio receivers is higher and the cost much lower than for other devices, including television sets. Despite the increasing prevalence of new media, and in particular mobile phones, radio has retained its position as an important space for the production and dispersion of national political and cultural discourses. The growth of the talk radio format (e.g. in South Africa and Kenya) has resulted in the use of the medium for the development of a range of public spheres (based on gender, ethnicity, sexuality, social background, region, and so on). In Africa, this format has allowed diverse and sometimes geographically disparate audiences to engage in debate and deliberation, often resulting in the formation of public opinion on controversial matters of social and political importance. The primary stimulus in the growth of the talk radio format has been the changed political situation in these countries, more specifically a move to democratically elected systems of government. The growing international trend (particularly in the United States) of politically oriented talk radio in the late 1990s has also had a strong influence on development of the genre in different African countries.

Similarly, community radio stations in some parts of the continent have created spaces for the circulation of counter-discourses and discussions by subaltern publics. As a cheap and accessible medium, radio in Africa has thus demonstrated its utility for the production of democratic public spheres in a Habermasian sense, as well as the formation of public sphericules, as Todd Gitlin (1998) has argued. Jürgen Habermas's (1989) notion of the public sphere was a concept used to describe a space where citizens exchange ideas and discuss issues, engaging in deliberative debate in order to reach collective opinion on matters of public interest. While the original conceptualization of the term referred to dialogue in coffee houses and salons primarily in seventeenth-century Great Britain, where people (largely white, propertied men) congregated physically, the term "public sphere" has since been adapted to refer to virtual media spaces where audiences "congregrate" even though they might be geographically separated and distant. Gitlin (1998) argued against this notion of a single public sphere, instead putting forward the notion of public sphericules, comprising segments of the public sphere. In Gitlin's view, each constitutes its own deliberative assembly. Instead of one unified public sphere, the notion of public sphericules thus implies that several parallel public spheres may be constituted around various groups with particular interests.

Critics of the traditional theoretical notions of the public sphere, usually based on Habermas's conceptualizations and use of the concept, have pointed out its exclusion of minorities, including women. Nancy Fraser (1990), for example, put forward the notion of subaltern counter-publics, groups formed by marginalized communities excluded from the mainstream public sphere. In particular, women and members of low socioeconomic groups were excluded from the bourgeois public sphere, and formed their own public spheres, which Fraser (1990) referred to as counter-publics. Following up on this point, my chapter explores the gendered nature of these mediated public spheres in relation to African radio practices.

Using Sartre's (1991) concept of serial collectivity or seriality, I also consider women audiences as a collective, with a particular focus on how radio programming and listening reflect the diverse range of gender discourses in African cultural contexts. Sartre (1991) first developed the notion of seriality in his *Critique of Dialectical Reason*. Feminist scholar Iris Marion Young (1994) draws upon Sartre's idea in order to argue that women are not an innate group with actively shared goals, but rather a "series" of individuals, unified passively by existing circumstances, material conditions, or routine practices and habits, which might include radio listening.

I first provide a brief summary of the intersections between gender and theoretical understandings of the public sphere, including the notion of a feminist public sphere. I then move on to consider women and their engagement in (or absence from) the public sphere, with specific reference to radio. Here I explore instances of women coming together as a group to produce radio, reflecting on previous research exploring gender as a factor in the radio listening experience; as well as a brief summary of feminist research on radio. I then reflect on women's participation in the public spheres created by radio stations in Africa, to provide a conceptual foundation to the discussion. The chapter concludes with a brief discussion of women radio audiences and new media, exploring how the growth of mobile phones has changed women's private listening practices and created possibilities for new forms of mobility. An example of this is that the mobile phone has allowed travel outside the home, while allowing for the maintenance of contact with home via the phone. Besides spatial mobility, access to a mobile phone is often associated with greater levels of freedom and independence, leading to more contextual mobility.

## The gendered public sphere

If we consider radio as one platform that may be used to facilitate deliberative discussion and debate in the public sphere, conceived as a space for the communicative generation of public opinion, then on-air discussion exists to "discredit views that cannot withstand critical scrutiny and to assume the legitimacy of those that do ... Thus it matters who participates and on what terms" (Fraser 2007: 7). The Habermasian public sphere is a space, conceptually separate from the state, in which political participation is enacted through rational, deliberative talk, as citizens discuss and debate matters of common interest. Habermas described it as "a sphere which mediates between society and state, in which the public organizes itself as the bearer of public opinion" (1989: 136).

Critics of Habermas's concept have pointed to the flawed premise that everyone could participate freely; the discursive modes of the bourgeois public sphere informally excluded racial minorities, women, and the poor. Fraser (1990, 2007) proposed the concept of counter-publics to refer to the tendency for these minorities to form parallel discursive arenas where they invented and circulated counter-discourses. Similarly, Gitlin (1998) proposed the idea of public sphericules, segmented spheres of assimilation with their own dynamics and forms of constitution. Instead of one unified public sphere, there are instead a number of smaller, self-contained public sphericules, which are mini-public spheres existing side by side. While the concept of the public sphere did not originally refer to media, in modern society electronic and broadcast media have increasingly been seen to fulfill this role. Radio certainly, with its capacity for on-air national dialogue and the ability to engage listeners who can call in to participate in live discussions, may be regarded as one such vehicle for public sphere debate.

Historically speaking, the exclusion of women from the public sphere in Africa and elsewhere in the world increases the relevance in our consideration of women radio listeners in Africa. Various forms of radio broadcasts, from state-owned or public broadcasters to commercial stations and local community radio stations, can be seen to fulfill the vision and aspiration to build a truly democratic public sphere. Given the varying objectives of these stations, it is not possible to argue that each reflects a normative version of the Habermasian public sphere; instead local radio stations in rural villages, for example, might fulfill the requirements for Gitlin's public sphericules or Fraser's subaltern counter-publics. The latter bears some resemblance to what Rita Felski (1989) has referred to as the feminist counter-public sphere, running beside the mainstream public sphere, and which in this instance might refer to women's or feminist radio collectives, or radio programs deliberately labeled as "women's shows" which offer women-centered programming and public participation.

## Women, public sphere, radio

Regardless of the specific nature of the public spheres facilitated by various types of radio, in Africa women are largely conspicuous by their absence. In general, women's voices are largely missing from mainstream political discussion, with daytime programming on talk stations stereotypically targeting women in their coverage of "soft," "feminine" issues of the personal private sphere such as relationships, domestic chores (e.g. cooking), or childrearing. While over the years there may have been an increasing number of hosts on talk radio stations, generally anecdotal listening experiences seem to indicate that the role of women on music radio is limited to newscasters, weather announcers, or, more commonly, the secondary host to the primary DJ, who is usually male. Moreover, the increase in women presenters arose from stations' realization that it was commercially viable to target a female commodity audience.

While talking about women as radio audiences, it is important to keep in mind that women do not make up a homogeneous group. Recall that Young (1994) drew on Sartre's *Critique of Dialectical Reason* to reconceptualize women as a series rather than a group, which recognizes a level of social existence that is constrained and directed by existing material conditions. Women listeners are thus passively brought together by a radio station, unified by the routine practice of listening to the radio; and the term "women" is used in this essay without necessarily essentializing women as a group. "The collective of radio listeners is constituted by their individual orientation toward objects, in this case radios and their material possibilities of sound transmission. As listeners they are isolated, but nevertheless they are aware of being part of a series of radio listeners, of others listening simultaneously linked to them indirectly through broadcasting" (Young 1994: 725).

In some instances, women have come together as a group to produce radio, for example the Feminist Radio Collective in Peru (Ariola 1992), Feminist International Radio Endeavour (FIRE), an international grassroots women's community radio network (see Gatua *et al.* 2010), the Women's International Newsgathering Service (Wings), or a host of other examples, primarily located in the United States. Of course, a formal grouping of women does not imply a feminist agenda, as Young points out: "feminism is a particularly reflexive impulse of women grouping, women grouping as women in order to change or eliminate the structures that serialize them as women" (1994: 736). Similarly, programming targeted at women or dealing with issues traditionally perceived as primarily relevant to women (family, home, relationships, and fashion) is also not necessarily feminist in nature. In general, radio broadcasters tend to adopt a liberal-inclusionary feminism, which assumes that on-air references to women or what might be perceived as women's issues, frequently referred to as "gender issues," in some way address issues of rights. At the same time, though, as Barber points out, "performances do not just play to ready-made congregations of spectators which are out there awaiting address; they convene those congregations and by their mode of address assign them a certain position from which they receive the address. Thus performances, in the act of addressing audiences, constitute those audiences as a particular form of collectivity" (1997: 354).

## Feminist radio research

Early research into women and radio, primarily undertaken in the USA and in the UK, often focused on the lack of women employees in the industry, the positioning of women as passive and undemanding listeners, the limiting domestic and sexual boundaries set by the media, and the overwhelming culture of male producers and female consumers (Mitchell 2000). In general, women have been underrepresented in the media, in terms of both coverage and participation, particularly at high levels of management. Turning to research undertaken in Africa, an East Africa study showed that in 1994 fewer than 20 percent of journalists were women (Adagala 1994). A more recent global study across 60 countries, including several African nations, reveals that women only hold 27 percent of media management jobs (Byerly 2011). During the early days of radio women tended to occupy "behind the scenes" jobs but rarely hosting; and when they were on air it was to host female-oriented programming (Maki 2008).

Dorothy Hobson's (1980) ethnographic work explored the role of radio in the everyday lives of British housewives, arguing that radio helped structure and punctuate the working day, DJ chat provided listeners with company, and that listening to the radio helped them negotiate tensions caused by their isolated lives (cited in O'Sullivan and Lewis 2006). The music radio industry relies on the established notion of the stereotypical female listener who invites the male presenter into her home as "romantic visitors descending on a bored housewife" (Baehr and Ryan 1984, cited in Tacchi 1998). More recently, Tacchi (2000) found that gender was a central variable in radio listening experiences, with respondents presenting their listening in ways that were congruent with their understandings of masculinity and femininity. Here we see how existing gender discourses can be reinforced and transmitted via the media.

## African feminist radio research

Women are generally absent from the public spheres created by African radio stations, in their participation both as hosts and as callers. Here it seems as though even though radio is often consumed in the home, seen as the private space of women, the public airwaves remain a largely heterosexual male domain. Of course, only a small percentage of the total audience usually calls in to a radio station to participate in on-air discussions, but, even so, the percentage of women callers is generally much smaller in relation to male callers. When women do participate, they are usually economically (and therefore culturally) privileged—they participate predominantly in English and on English-medium radio stations.

To draw on the field of cultural geography, one might argue that the space of radio is experienced very differently by poor, working-class women, who might be said to occupy a space of "dis-belonging" on the radio. This is not unique to radio. McFadden has argued that the African press in general is exclusionary of the "expression, the experience and the opinion of women," demonizing those women who do not fit the conservative images of women perpetuated by those who control the media (1998: 655). The media, radio included, are thus overwhelmingly gendered spaces in which discourses of power operate to create acceptable, normative images of women, and to privilege some bodies over others. The performativity of gendered norms over the airwaves thus results in a latent surveillance and a propensity toward exclusion for women listeners. When listeners call in to offer political commentary, for example, women's voices are very rarely heard. Women infrequently speak out critically (or in any way for that matter) on political issues, and on-air political deliberation and debates are dominated by men. This lack of women's voices on air is usually as a result of the way in which programmers have imagined their audiences (Maki 2008).

Radio adds a dimension of sociability to the lives of individual listeners in their homes, experienced by them as part of the material culture of the home and contributing to the creation of the domestic environment (Tacchi 1998). But at the same time, we begin to see how gender relations and identities are constructed via the largely hegemonic space of the radio airwaves. Drawing on Maki's study of Canadian radio stations, one might similarly argue that in an African context it is through this "inclusion" of women that stations are able to maintain the boundaries of femininity and masculinity, and "through fun and flirty speech, imply that feminism has succeeded and is no longer useful" (2008: 7). This is a common phenomenon on stations, where gender banter reinforces the "differences" between the male and female hosts, with the female hosts both embodying femininity while also expected to prove themselves in a masculine role. As Maki demonstrates, this results in "fun and playful gender-based comedy, without seeming out of touch or offensive to their audiences" (2008: 7).

Even in the segmentation of programming, with issues related to relationships primarily targeting women listeners, this type of programming reflects an overwhelmingly normative version of sexuality, which is always heterosexual. In the Pink, a gay and lesbian radio program on a community radio station in South Africa, was one example of the potential for radio to subvert this norm. Unfortunately, the show only ran for a few years before it was discontinued (Bosch 2007). There have been no other documented instances of the use of radio in Africa to promote discussions about gay and lesbian identities. Everyday on-air discussions, particularly those that traditionally target women during daytime slots, rest on the unspoken assumption of heteronormativity.

## Conclusion

Women radio audiences in Africa may not be homogeneous given the diversity of the continent—research in Southern Africa raises issues related to the gendered state, colonial labor policies, violence, popular protest, and resistance; while scholarship in Central and East Africa has produced work on domesticity, marital and sexual relationships, livelihood options, and nationalist struggles; and scholarship from West Africa focuses on instances of resistance and grassroots activism, showing images of women's power and autonomy (Cornwall 2005). These disparate research foci reveal the diversity of gendered experiences around the continent.

However, despite this diversity, we might be able to argue for the emergence of a "serial collectivity" in how radio programming and listening perpetuate existing gender discourses, regardless of geographic context. Women are not necessarily constituted as a group—they do not listen to the radio for gender-specific programming or because of their sex or gender; but through societal discourses, transmitted via the radio airwaves, they come into formation as a series or a social collective, as radio discourse defines the acceptable limits of their roles and participation in society.

Historically women audiences primarily have been considered in one-dimensional ways, largely as consumers of daytime radio programming on matters pertaining to the private sphere. In the main, they have been conspicuous in their absence from deliberative dialogue and political discussion on radio talk shows; and, moreover, these shows often tend to perpetuate a hegemonic discourse of heteronormativity. However, the rise of mobile telephony has begun to open up the ways in which women engage and interact with radio stations via their mobile phones;

perhaps paving the way for new forms of mobility and interactivity in relation to social space.

There has been an explosion of cell phone use and penetration in Africa, with mobile phones in developing countries generally providing an alternative solution to the challenge of providing universal access to landline telephone services given the slow diffusion of fixed telecommunications networks (Moyo 2009). The African cell phone "explosion" began in South Africa in 1993 when the government granted national cell phone licenses to MTN South Africa Ltd and Vodacom Group (Pty) Ltd, which quickly built large customer bases by offering prepaid cell phone cards (Mbarika 2007). Today there are ten times as many mobile phones as landlines in sub-Saharan Africa, though it has some of the lowest levels of infrastructure investment in the world; 60 percent of the population have mobile phone coverage (Aker and Mbiti 2010). This growth of cell phones and the concomitant rise of the mobile internet have implications for radio consumption, particularly given the already dif-ferentially gendered ways in which men and women use technology. Across the continent, women widely consume radio, with many choosing to listen to community radio stations, though data are sparse concerning gendered access to or ownership of mobile phones (Fortune et al. 2011).

One study in the United States shows that the number of women listening to radio via media other than traditional radio sets, in particular using computers or mobile phones, has grown rapidly (Schmitt 2012). While there is little documented evidence that this is the case in Africa, the growth of mobile telephony might mean that women are increasingly using their mobile phones to engage in private listening practices, listening to preloaded music files or to radio stations of their choice—these may be FM stations, though increasingly internet radio is also a popular choice. Listening practices are developing away from the tradition of public participation via the radio set at the center of the village. In its place, particularly in more urbanized contexts, women are increasingly making personal and private choices with regard to their listening habits. Instead of participating in call-in radio shows by phoning in to the station, in future women will be widely using the SMS option, which allows their anonymity, to a degree. The growing use of online social media sites such as Facebook and Twitter by radio stations is also a factor in this convergence of new technologies and radio listening practices. While issues of the digital divide and differential access remain, these sites can be fairly easily accessed using mobile phones. The digital divide refers to uneven access to computers and the internet, and Africa still lags behind other regions in terms of access, with only 15.6 percent internet penetration and 7 percent of the world's internet users.[1] Within the continent there is also variable access to computers and the internet, with some countries more resourced than others, and access between rural and urban centers varying widely within these countries.

With the use of social networking sites, which often rely heavily on pictures/graphics and text (in the case of Facebook at least), radio is no longer a one-dimensional, "blind" medium. The potential for stations is to grow audiences and to strengthen the relationship with the audience but also to increase the involvement of minorities who have not participated in traditional ways. Traditional participation often involves a cost—posting a letter or making a telephone call; whereas the costs of engaging online are hidden. Moreover, the internet has created a new space for social communication, and people often communicate more freely in online spaces.

These issues raise several opportunities for future African feminist radio audience research, including trends in relation to women's use of traditional and mobile technology use. Uses and gratifications or similar approaches could be used to explore audiences' specific motivations for radio listening, with particular reference to existing programming options and delivery platforms. Ethnographic feminist techniques would reveal gender-specific radio listening practices.

## Note

1 http://www.internetworldstats.com/stats1.htm.

## References

Adagala, E. (1994) *Women's Access to Decision Making in and through the Media with Particular Reference to the East African Situation*, Nairobi: Women in Communication Trust.

Aker, J. and I. Mbiti (2010) "Mobile Phones and Economic Development in Africa," *Journal of Economic Perspectives* 24(3): 207–32.

Ambler, C. (2002) "Mass Media and Leisure in Africa," *International Journal of African Historical Studies* 35(1): 119–36.

Ariola, T. (1992) "The Feminist Radio Collective of Peru: Women ... on the Air," in B. Girard (ed.) *A Passion for Radio: Radio Waves and the Community*, Montreal and New York: Black Rose, pp. 114–20. http://comunica.org/passion/pdf/chapter11.pdf.

Barber, K. (1997) "Preliminary Notes on Audiences in Africa," *Africa: Journal of the International African Institute* 67(3): 347–62.

Bennett, J. and V. Reddy (2009) "Researching the Pedagogies in South African Higher Education," *International Journal of Sexual Health* 21(4): 239–52.

Bentley, K. (2004) "Women's Human Rights and the Feminisation of Poverty in South Africa," *Review of African Political Economy* 31(100): 247–61

Bosch, T. (2007) "In the Pink: Gay Radio in South Africa," *Feminist Media Studies* 7(3) (September): 225–38.

——(2011) "Young Women and 'Technologies of the Self': Social Networking and Sexualities," *Agenda* 25(4): 75–86.

——(2012) "Talk Radio and the Public Sphere," in Liz Gunner, Dumisani Moyo, and Dina Ligaga (eds.) *Radio in Africa: Cultures, Publics, Communities*, Johannesburg: Wits University Press.

Bosch, T. and S. Holland-Muter (2012) "Women Crossing the Line: Exploring the Politics of Gender and Sexuality on a University Campus," *Feminist Africa* 17: 82–90. http://agi.ac.za/sites/agi.ac.za/files/6_profile_women_crossing_the_line.pdf

Byerly, C. (2011) *Global Report on the Status of Women in the News Media*, Washington, DC: International Women's Media Foundation. iwmf.org/pdfs/IWMF-Global-Report-Summary.pdf.

Cornwall, A. (2005) "Introduction: Perspectives on Gender in Africa," in Andrea Cornwall (ed.) *Readings in Gender in Africa*, London: SOAS, pp. 1–17.

Felski, R. (1989) *Beyond Feminist Aesthetics: Feminist Literature and Social Change*, Cambridge, MA: Harvard University Press.

Fortune, F., C. Chungong, and A. Kessinger (2011) "Community Radio, Gender & ICTs in West Africa: How Women Are Engaging with Community Radio through Mobile Phone

Technologies," July. http://www.globalyouthdesk.org/index.php?option=com_k2&view=item&id=206&Itemid=63.

Fraser, N. (1990) "Rethinking the Public Sphere: A Contribution to the Critique of Actually Existing Democracy," *Social Text* 25/26: 56–80.

——(2007) "Special Section: Transnational Public Sphere: Transnationalising the Public Sphere: On the Legitimacy and Efficacy of Public Opinion in a Post-Westphalian World," *Theory Culture & Society* 24(4): 7–30.

Gatua, M. W., T. O. Patton, and Michael R. Brown (2010) "Giving Voice to Invisible Women: 'FIRE' as Model of a Successful Women's Community Radio in Africa," *Howard Journal of Communications* 21(2): 164–81.

Gitlin, T. (1998) "Public Sphere or Public Sphericules?," in T. Liebes and J. Curran (eds.) *Media, Ritual, Identity*, London: Routledge, pp. 168–75.

Habermas, J. (1989) *The Structural Transformation of the Public Sphere*, Cambridge, MA: MIT Press.

McFadden, P. (1998) "Examining Myths of a Democratic Media," *Review of African Political Economy* 25(78): 653–57.

Maki, C. (2008) "The Conservation of a Gender Fantasy: Women and Top 40 Radio in Montreal," unpublished MA thesis, McGill University. http://digitool.library.mcgill.ca/webclient/StreamGate?folder_id=0& dvs = 1377009935427~397.

Mbarika, V. (2007) "Africa Calling," *IEEE Spectrum*. http://www.spectrum.ieee.org/print/3426.

Mitchell, C. (2000) *Women and Radio: Airing Differences*, London: Routledge.

Moyo, L. (2009) "Digital Democracy: Enhancing the Public Sphere," in G. Creeber and R. Martin (eds.) *Digital Culture: Understanding New Media*, London: Open University, pp. 139–56.

Nelson, L. and J. Seager (2005) "Introduction," in L. Nelson and J. Seager (eds.) *A Companion to Feminist Geography*, Malden, MA: Blackwell, pp. 1–12.

O'Sullivan, S. and P. Lewis (2006) "Future Directions for Research on Radio Audiences." sites-test.uclouvain.be/rec/index.php/rec/article/view/5721/5441.

Posel, D. (2011) "'Getting the Nation Talking about Sex': Reflections on the Politics of Sexuality and Nation-building in Post-apartheid South Africa," in S. Tamale (ed.) *African Sexualities: A Reader*, Cape Town: Pambazuka Press, pp. 130–44.

Sartre, J. (1991) *Critique of Dialectical Reason, vol. 1: Theory of Practical Ensembles*, London: Verso.

Schmitt, M. (2012) "Mobile and Web Radio Listening Growing Strongly among Women, Alan Burns & Associates Study Finds." http://kurthanson.com/news/mobile-and-web-radio-listening-growing-strongly-among-women-alan-burns-associates-study-finds.

Spitulnik, D. (2002) "Mobile Machines and Fluid Audiences: Rethinking Reception through Zambian Radio Culture," in Faye Ginsburg, Lila Abu-Lughod, and Brian Larkin (eds.) *Media Worlds*, Berkeley and Los Angeles: University of California Press, pp. 337–54.

Tacchi, J. (1998) "Radio Texture: Between Self and Others," in Daniel Miller (ed.) *Material Cultures: Why Some Things Matter*, London: UCL Press, pp. 25–45.

——(2000) "Gender, Fantasy and Radio Consumption: An Ethnographic Case Study," in Caroline Mitchell (ed.) *Women and Radio: Airing Differences*, London: Routledge, pp. 152–66.

West, H. and J. Fair (1993) "Development Communication and Popular Resistance in Africa: An Examination of the Struggle over Tradition and Modernity through Media," *African Studies Review* 36(1): 91–114.

Young, I. M. (1994) "Gender as Seriality: Thinking about Women as a Social Collective," *Signs* 19(3): 713–38.

# 48

# Reading girlhood

## Opportunities for social literacy

## *Dawn H. Currie*

It has been more than 60 years since the French existentialist and feminist Simone de Beauvoir famously pronounced "One is not born, but rather becomes, woman" (2010 [1949]: 293). Following her lead, second-wave feminists asked: How does one born female become a "woman"? Establishing and distinguishing itself as a field of inquiry during the 1980s, over the decades feminist cultural studies has taken up this question. In North America, the UK, and elsewhere, researchers looked for—and found—scripts for womanhood in commercial media. Magazines produced for girls and women, in particular, have been fruitful sites for research on "femininity" as a sign through which idealized womanhood is normalized.

The findings of this extensive research on these media tend to be repetitive: as a distinct genre, "women's magazines" offer readers a narrow range of acceptable ways to "be a woman." There was widespread confirmation during the 1970s and 1980s that these magazines authorize a femininity based on white, heterosexual, middle-class ideals. The ideal woman continues to be represented as white, attractive to men, and preoccupied with romantic interests (see Barthel 1988; Ferguson 1983; Tuchman 1979; Winship 1987). Likewise, articles and advertisements in girls' magazines mutually reinforce the message that happiness is found in male approval, secured through a regimen of beautification (Currie 1999; Evans *et al.* 1991; Peirce 1990). Based on these findings, magazines for girls and women have been dismissed as "ideological": commentators claim that these media limit young readers' thinking about their life options.

Reflecting the popularity of sex-role theory that supported the establishment of girls' studies as a distinct field of inquiry during the mid-1990s, girl advocates characterized commercial media as damaging for readers, linking them to low levels of self-esteem, body dissatisfaction, and eating disorders as endemic among adolescent females, especially those from white, professional households (see AAUW 1991). Psychologists argued that girls were internalizing media messages that being nice, having the right look, and recognizing subtle social cues are vital to acceptance by others (Duke and Kreshel 1998: 50). Critics have documented the overtly sexual themes in commercial media for girls (APA 2007; Jackson 2005; Jackson and Westrupp 2010), fueling public concern over the "Lolita Effect": "a restrictive, hidebound, market-driven" set of behaviors that encourages girls to flaunt their sexuality in order to become the subject of the male gaze (Durham 2008: 39).

For the large part, research that fosters these kinds of claims about media effects has been based on documentation of the *content* of media produced for girls, in particular fashion and beauty magazines. Reflecting the emergence of audience studies, during the 1990s researchers began to ask how girls, as the intended readers of adolescent magazines, make sense of such texts. The context for this shift included recognition that readers may not take up media messages as intended because reading entails the active negotiation of meaning. Within this context, audience research moves away from documenting the content of media to the process of *reading*.

Exploring *how* girls read fashion and beauty magazines is far more challenging than documenting what they read. Despite the fact that Jackson and Westrupp describe the 1990s as "a pinnacle of research on girls' magazines" (2010: 359), scholarship on girls' reading of these magazines is surprisingly limited. Most studies employ small samples of white middle-class readers (for exceptions, see Duke 2000; Durham 1999). While the fieldwork for my study is now over a decade old (Currie 1999), in this chapter I revisit some of the data in order to explore how an understanding of girls' reading can contribute to growing interest in media literacy for girls. Although it is widely acknowledged that commercial media often engage youth to a far greater extent than mandated classroom curricula, exactly how to take advantage of these media remains understudied. My ongoing work with Deirdre Kelly explores how public school teachers might employ commercial media targeting youth in their classrooms to promote critical media literacy.

Teachers we studied claimed that among the challenges they face is the pleasure youth experience from the texts that they often want to use to demonstrate, for example, the racist and sexist nature of media produced for youth consumption. This pleasure can stifle discussion rather than engage learners in critical analysis. Our current research asks how pleasure works through texts such as commercial entertainment. As part of that study, here I explore how ideology operates in ways that naturalize not only representations of the social world, but also the pleasure that readers can take from participating in that naturalization. Based on my research on girls' reading of adolescent magazines, I consider how we might harness reading pleasure to promote the empowerment of girl readers. By "empowerment," I refer to an understanding of media production in ways that engage girls in the production of their own, alternative representations.

## The "girl talk" study

Research for my book *Girl Talk: Adolescent Magazines and Their Readers* explores how a diverse group of 91 girls between the ages of 13 and 17 read *Seventeen, YM, Teen,* and *Sassy* (Currie 1999).[1] I chose fashion and beauty magazines because they promote what feminist sociologist Dorothy Smith (1990) calls a textually mediated discourse of (white hetero) femininity. Such a discourse encourages girls to orient their behavior in ways that please boys, especially in terms of self-presentation.[2] By promising readers the accomplishment of a femininity that will secure them social approval, it can gain girls' complicity in practices of gendered subordination.

Analysis of magazine reading thus enabled me to study these texts as a venue for the operation of power.

This framing reflects my Marxist or materialist feminism as an approach that historicizes the production of social hierarchies such as gender in order to investigate their relationship to totalities such as capitalism, patriarchy, and globalization. Historically, such a commitment has given analytical primacy to "the social" rather than cultural dimensions of everyday life through the study of institutions (like family and school), institutionalized roles, and the way these institutions and roles operate to reconstitute the social world according to specific social interests. Beginning in the 1980s, materialist feminists began to question how the symbolic order does not (simply) reflect these totalities in ways that conventional "economic base/ideological superstructure" thinking implies but rather works to re/constitute these totalities. The power that interests me is that exercised not only as the mass production of ideological texts, but also by readers through their engagement with these texts. How do adolescent girls, rather than adult feminist commentators, engage with fashion and beauty magazines targeting them as readers?

At the time I was conducting fieldwork for *Girl Talk*, recognition of the polysemic (multiple possible meanings) nature of texts and emphasis on reader agency encouraged feminists to see "more than one story" about magazine reading. The new story concerned the pleasure (adult) women can take from texts that celebrate traditional womanhood without necessarily accepting the tenets of patriarchal culture. For example, while agreeing that commercial texts can be "bad" for women, Winship described the pleasure that she gained personally from reading women's magazines, arguing that "we frequently luxuriate in the advertising. ... we become involved in the fictions they create, but we know full well those commodities will not elicit the promised fictions" (1987: 55–6).[3] Such a claim implicitly locates pleasure outside history, politics, and the economy—processes central to Marxist feminist analyses. Perhaps ironically, feminism itself was seen as enabling this disconnect. Although new magazines continued to tie femininity to domesticity during the final decades of the twentieth century, the popularization of feminism was claimed to enable readers to recognize the hidden agenda of patriarchal culture and, as a result, to critically reflect on texts in a way not possible for a previous generation of women.

What interested me was that girls in my study, unlike these adult commentators, sought out magazines because they were deemed to refer to "real" people and "real" situations that teenagers face. Regardless of which title girls favored, it was described as "more realistic" than its rivals:

> *Teen* ... It's just more to my liking. It just seems more *realistic*. I think it deals more with the problems that people *actually* have.
>
> (Crystal, 17)

> And in *Seventeen*, the articles are better than YM. ... The ones in *Seventeen* are about like real life, or sometimes they're stories that people have wrote. And I like reading that. ... Things like this [showing interviewer]—they have happened to my friends or something.
>
> (Christina, 15)

*Sassy* is a little better than YM. I mean it's in the same category but it's a little better because they put real people on the cover and real people inside the magazine. ... *Sassy* seems to pride itself on being more realistic than the other magazines.

(Stephanie, 13)

While glossy fashion layouts might draw girls' attention near graduation, participants preferred to read advice columns about relationships, beauty, and health; quizzes; reader-authored columns such as "Say Anything" or "It Happened to Me!"; stuff about guys or about romance; and real-life stories or tragedies. This finding led me to ask what gives these particular texts reader appeal.

Noticeably, girls expressed satisfaction when they could recognize themselves or their friends in the text. Advice columns in particular were seen to offer this possibility: "[I read advice columns] when they might apply to you, or you think this is so similar to your friends ... Because if it is *happening* to you, you just want to know what you could do" (Nicole, 15). And: "I guess it's kind of corny but sometimes I'll read a letter and like, I thought it was a good idea—you know, what they wrote. ... Usually whoever is answering the letter, says what *I* kind of tend to think at the same time, so that's kind of nice" (Kelsey, 16).

In the case of 16-year-old Jasmine:

I like reading those question and answer things. Where people send in their problems and then this person answers them ... I like reading the questions better than the answers though. The questions, I find them interesting, but the answers, I don't even care to hear. I just like to hear what people are sending in.

(Jasmine, 16; also see Kehily 1999: 72)

These readings show how magazine texts help construct the bounds of "normal" adolescence. This construction is perhaps more transparent in quizzes, which mirror advice columns: "Want him to notice you?" "No Guy? Find out why," and "Are you in love?" Unlike advice columns, however, answers are (seemingly) open to negotiation. Posed as self-discovery, quizzes allow the reader to directly insert herself into the world constructed by the text—"Are you an emotional mess?" "Could you be a star?" "Are you a great date?" and so on. The self-assessment offered by these texts appealed to many girls: "I always take the quizzes ... Like 'Are you too sensitive?'—they have 10 questions and then your results under 'a,' 'b' and 'c'—I think those are neat!" (Amber, 15). And: "Like I don't think if I wrote one, like actually wrote out one of the quizzes my personality would change, but I would think inside of me how different I was and stuff. I think it just helps [readers] think better about themselves sometimes" (Alyssa, 16).

The format as much as the content of quizzes accounts for their popularity (Currie 2001: 274–6; also see Ostermann and Keller-Cohen 1998). For most quizzes scores are rated and evaluated according to where they fall on a range of desirable outcomes. For example, in the quiz "Are you a great date?" scores classify the reader according to whether she is a "date disaster," a "first-rate date," or a "first-date failure." The disaster date is chastised by the editor:

> Do you have to give your date such a hard time? Being overly demanding of the guy you're with can be a way of hiding your own insecurity. (You'll point out his flaws before he notices yours!) This is not healthy, says Kate M. Wachs, Ph.D., a psychologist.
>
> (YM, June/July 1993)

In contrast, the first-rate date is praised:

> You're warm, friendly and positive, three important qualities for a good date, according to Dr. Wachs. And you don't analyze every move your date makes. Plus, you're into meeting a lot of guys, so when Mr. Right comes along, you'll know enough about guys to recognize him.
>
> (YM, June/July 1993)

The first-date failure is given instructions to improve her date-ability, by "being herself":

> Guys will ask you once, but then they usually lose interest. Maybe that's because when you go on a date, you get nervous. Relax, and remember that dating is supposed to be fun. Open up and let him know what you'd like to do.
>
> (YM, June/July 1993)

When considering content, this quiz echoes advice elsewhere in YM. The ability to please boys as a desirable quality depends on not criticizing their behavior or analyzing their "every move." Readers are informed that girls with successful dates have "important qualities"; those who fail to be asked out for subsequent dates probably have "psychological problems," as testified by expert Dr. Kate M. Wachs. While prescribing qualities that will make the reader pleasing to boys is thus embedded in the text, the format of the text implies that the reader's ability to be dateable is a result of being well adjusted, because a "normal" girl will secure dates with boys. What is omitted from this text but was reported by girls in this study is the fact that some boys (often "popular" ones) date only girls who engage in sex.

My study of magazine advice columns locates the pleasure of reading these texts in their ability to construct a "knowing" reader; because advice is given in the form of self-help, the reader is invited to experience herself as an autonomous, self-determining subject (2001: 276–7; also see Jackson and Westrupp 2010). Such a subject fits into adolescent culture through competence in the everyday practices of "being a girl." Given what is at stake—belonging to the world of "normal" adolescence—it should not be surprising that participants claimed to read magazines because they are useful (also see Duke 2000; Durham 1999). As expressed by 15-year-old Nicole: "They [magazines] teach you a lot of things, like what you should do, what you should think. Sometimes they're really helpful." As Jamie (17 years old) explained: "I mean, a magazine is fine to look through, but you really don't want to pay for something that you're not going to sit down and actually use ... I want to have something that's going to *do* something [laughs] for me." This view of magazines as a source of useful knowledge was reinforced by the social nature of magazine reading. As in the case of Holm (1997), magazine reading could promote group solidarity:

> If we're reading the magazine we'll talk about stuff in it. Like quizzes. If there is a question-and-answer like "Dear Jill" and "Dear Jack"—which is the younger people's questions—we kind of read them and discuss them. Like if your boyfriend didn't talk to you or something and you don't know what to do and they [reader] asked what to do, then we'd start a conversation like "What would *you* do?"
>
> (Chelsea, 15)

Durham found that peer pressure to conform to group discussions could mute alternative or resistant readings (1999: 210).

In short, magazine reading engaged young readers in the construction of the world of "normal" adolescent femininity (also see Finders 1996; Jackson and Westrupp 2010). But this process was not seamless—participants were not passive consumers of texts. While seeking knowledge, girls approached the text as knowledgeable readers. Implicit in the interview excerpts above, girls brought lived experience to their reading. The result is more apparent when participants discussed glossy representations of (purportedly) everyday teenage life. During focus groups, girls were given an ad for a make-up kit being used at an all-girls pajama party: "Oh this is neat! Like being with friends and having fun. A typical 'girls' night.' This is a good one because all girls have been there" (Heather, 15). And: "This appeals to me because I can relate to this. Like I can relate to sitting around with your friends and everything. It looks like sort of an average—just getting ready to go out ... I can relate to the picture" (Kristen, 15). Similarly, 13-year-old Amanda stated: "It kind of shows people doing real things. I would do that." At the same time, by drawing on lived experience Jamie dismissed the same ad: "These are commercials we laugh at!" So did 15-year-old Faye: "It seems a bit fake to me! ... talking on the phone, curlers in your hair, like doing your make-up and laughing in your pajamas. Like it's so like TV—that's what they do on TV." Likewise, 17-year-old Margie reasoned:

> From a teenage point of view, from *my* teenage point of view, from where *I* am—this kind if thing doesn't happen, in this kind of sense. We will do this, teenage girls will do this, but we don't all look like this ... we wouldn't be this clean-cut, and looking this pretty—we'd be like no make-up, lying on the bed discussing things that we'd never discuss anywhere else.
>
> (Margie, 17)

In *Girl Talk* (1999) I refer to these negotiations as "comparison reading": girls often compared magazine texts to their everyday life. As seen above, the resulting comparison could lead readers to challenge the text. Given this role of lived experience in their critical assessments of ads, their responses to ads employing traditional icons of adult femininity—a diamond engagement ring, a bride, and a woman holding a newborn—are interesting: these representations took reading beyond participants' lived experiences. Despite the fact that girls in my study came from diverse backgrounds, virtually all participants read these images uncritically, employing stereotypical understandings of adult femininity. For the diamond ring: "I like this one ... he's really in love with her and it kind of shows" (Roshni, 17). An advertisement for Beautiful Perfume represented a woman in a white wedding gown: "I like that—it says what it means. They're advertising for Beautiful and she's in a wedding dress and you always think about a bride as beautiful" (Lindsey, 16). For Eternity Perfume, depicting a woman holding an infant: "Yeah. Like this is one of my favourite ones. ... I just think it's kind of cute and I think it really looks like a mom and daughter. ... It's kind of a loving picture" (Rachel, 14). While lived experience gave readers a resource that enabled them to challenge representations of their everyday life, for these ads readers drew upon ideologies of romantic love and motherhood to arrive at unambiguous meaning. It is significant that the picture of a woman holding an infant was not interpreted as a "mother and *child*," but as a "mother and *daughter*." In some cases, participants stated that there was no need to discuss these ads because they "said what they mean." In other words, heterosexual romance and motherhood were a "natural" reading; these readings "felt" right (Currie 1999: 128–39). They were an obvious source of pleasure that worked to suppress critical interrogation of the text. What might these readings tell us about media literacy for young female readers of commercial media?

## Toward a social literacy for girls

Given the content of commercial magazines for adolescent girls, often they have been dismissed by parents, teachers, and (mainstream) researchers alike as "fluff." One result is that reading them tends to take place outside the classroom, as "extra-curricular" learning beyond adult surveillance (see Kaplan and Cole 2003). Considering their pervasive social presence, educators are beginning to ask what is gained—and lost—by ignoring venues of such social significance among youth. There is growing interest in using popular culture as a vehicle for teaching media literacy (see Alvermann *et al.* 1999; Buckingham 2003; Kellner and Share 2005; Share 2009).[4] After all, the use of popular media would enable teachers to promote literacy from where youth "are at." Despite this interest, however, we know little about how to use popular culture in the classroom. Our current ongoing research is an attempt to help fill this gap. We can learn about media literacy for girls from the research described in this chapter.

Taken at face value, it is perhaps easy to agree with critics that adolescent fashion and beauty magazines have little redeeming value. One result is the tendency to adopt a "protectionist" stance towards girls' extracurricular reading. By protectionist, I refer to the move to censor girls' reading of popular culture or, at best, "inoculate" girls from its harmful effects through media literacy based on "ideology critique" (see Wasko 2008). Such a critique teaches girls about misrepresentation of their interests. Stereotyping might be used as a tool to point out how the femininity represented in advertising, for example, emphasizes how girls and women should look without paying attention to "what's beautiful on the inside." While one might not personally disagree with this criticism, a limitation of this approach is that it teaches girls to classify media on the basis of "bad" versus "good" representations. It fails to encourage girls to question the processes through which these representations come to dominate our thinking or the political context in which they are consumed. At the same time, this approach assumes that young people are passive consumers of texts. It thus tends to discount the pleasure that many girls experience when reading what adults deem to be "bad" texts. Media critique can then be experienced as criticism of "personal taste," diminishing the relevance of pedagogical efforts.

Interestingly, debates about girls' reading somewhat parallel the experiences of adult women readers during the 1980s. Although intended as constructive critique of commercial culture, much of the sex-role research spearheaded by feminist scholars worked to reaffirm everyday notions about the cultural and literary inferiority of "women's media"—fashion and beauty magazines, romance novels, and soap operas. Feminist cultural critics began to redeem women-centered texts as a valid source of women's entertainment, based on the argument that feminist critique of these media enables women to take pleasure without ascribing truth-value to their messages. As noted above, some of these critics came out of the closet as avid readers of the very venues that their scholarship derided. While validating women's reading pleasure, this pleasure was relegated to the realm of fantasy.

As evident in audience research, young readers do not always make the kinds of distinctions between fantasy and "reality" made by these feminist critics. There is ample evidence that girls find their magazines useful because they are seen to address real-life situations and real-life dilemmas. For these readers, magazines are a source of information about the social world and their place in it. Teaching about these media thus requires an approach that connects commercial media to girls' everyday lives. Rather than emphasizing the "unreal" status of magazine representations, media literacy needs to address the context of their production and consumption, encouraging young readers to question their own interaction with commercial texts (see Buckingham 2003). We refer to such an approach as promoting *social* literacy. Unlike *media* literacy, inquiry begins from the text but does not remain there. It encourages girls to raise the kind of questions we ourselves use as media researchers: Who does this text *think* you are? Who does this text *want* you to be? Why? Based on your experience of being a teenage girl, how might you rewrite the text? And so on. Such a line of inquiry parallels the kind of questioning that implicitly informed girls' reading in my research. Respecting young readers as knowledgeable can enhance the pleasure of reading that comes through "naming" experience. It also suggests that rather than the glossy photos that feminist teachers might like to subject to critique—those of brides and loving mothers—using representations typical of teenage life might be more fruitful.

By harnessing media literacy to girls' everyday knowledge, readings by engaged pupils will be far more diverse and complex than interpretations imposed by adult viewers seeking to "protect" them from harmful media effects. While it will likely generate the kinds of disagreements among girls that I report above from focus group discussions, disagreement itself is a pedagogical resource (see Gainer 2010; Rhymes 2011); debate over how to read images draws attention to the situated nature of meaning making and to the difference that difference (such as racialization, class, and family heritage) makes in the reception as well as production of texts—a lesson that could inform girls' own textual representations produced on social media sites (such as Facebook, for example). In this way, *social* literacy supports the empowerment of girls.

## Notes

1 I purposefully recruited girls from mixed ethnic and class backgrounds. Because I do not discuss the relevance of ethnicity or class in this chapter, I include only age in my descriptors. Each participant chose her pseudonym.
2 In this chapter "discourse" does not refer to merely text or speech, but also sets of rules and procedures that produce certain ways of thinking and acting. Discourses are socially embedded in our everyday practice and cannot be understood as simply, or purely, a "cultural" phenomenon (Gee 2005).
3 Feminist scholars are now much more aware that the "we" of much early feminist writing stands in for "white, educated" women.
4 Most literature uses the term "popular culture" to refer to commercial culture. Following Fiske (1989) I reserve the term "popular culture" for culture that is made "from below" by people for its use value rather than exchange value (as in the case of commercial culture).

## References

Alvermann, D. E., J. S. Moon, and M. C. Hagood (1999) "Approaches to Teaching Using Popular Culture and the Politics of Pleasure," *Popular Culture in the Classroom: Teaching and Researching Critical Media Literacy*, Newark, DE: International Reading Association, pp. 22–40.

American Association of University Women (AAUW) (1991) *Shortchanging Girls, Shortchanging America*, Washington, DC: American Association of University Women.

American Psychological Association (APA) (2007) *Report of the APA Task Force on the Sexualization of Girls*, Washington, DC: APA.

Barthel, D. (1988) *Putting on Appearances: Gender and Advertising*, Philadelphia: Temple University Press.

Beauvoir, S. de (2010 [1949]) *The Second Sex*, trans. Constance Borde and Sheila Malovany-Chevallier, London: Vintage.

Buckingham, D. (2003) *Media Education: Literacy, Learning and Contemporary Culture*, Cambridge: Polity.

Currie, D. H. (1999) *Girl Talk*, Toronto: University of Toronto Press.

——(2001) "Dear Abby: Advice Pages as a Site for the Operation of Power," *Feminist Theory* 2 (3): 259–81.

Duke, L. L. (2000) "Black in a Blond World: Race and Girls' Interpretations of the Feminine Ideal in Teen Magazines," *Journalism and Mass Communication Quarterly* 77(2): 367–92.

Duke, L. L. and P. J. Kreshel (1998) "Negotiating Femininity: Girls in Early Adolescence Read Teen Magazines," *Journal of Communication Inquiry* 22(1): 48–71.

Durham, G. M. (1999) "Girls, Media, and the Negotiation of Sexuality: A Study of Race, Class and Gender in Adolescent Peer Groups," *Journalism and Mass Communication Quarterly* 76(2): 193–216.

——(2008) *The Lolita Effect: The Media Sexualization of Young Girls and What We Can Do about It*, Woodstock, NY: The Overlook Press.

Evans, E. D., J. Rutberg, C. Sather, and C. Turner (1991) "Content Analysis of Contemporary Teen Magazines for Adolescent Females," *Youth & Society* 23(1): 99–120.

Ferguson, M. (1983) *Forever Feminine: Women's Magazines and the Cult of Femininity*, London: Heinemann.

Finders, M. J. (1996) "Queens and Teen Zines: Early Adolescent Females Reading Their Way Toward Adulthood," *Anthropology and Education Quarterly* 27(1): 71–89.

Fiske, J. (1989) *Understanding Popular Culture*, Boston: Unwin Hyman.

Gainer, J. S. (2010) "Critical Media Literacy in Middle School: Exploring the Politics of Representation," *Journal of Adolescent & Adult Literacy* 53(5): 364–73.

Gee, J. P. (2005) *Introduction to Discourse Analysis*, New York: Routledge.

Holm, G. (1997) "Public Texts/Private Conversations: Readings of a Teen Magazine from the Girls' Point of View," *Young* 5(3): 20–9.

Jackson, S. (2005) "I'm 15 and Desperate for Sex: 'Doing' and 'Undoing' Desire in Letters to a Teenage Magazine," *Feminism & Psychology* 15(3): 295–313.

Jackson, S. and E. Westrupp (2010) "Sex, Postfeminist Popular Culture and the Pre-teen Girl," *Sexualities* 13(3): 357–76.

Kaplan, E. B. and L. Cole (2003) "'I Want to Read Stuff on Boys:' White, Latina, and Black Girls Reading *Seventeen* Magazine and Encountering Adolescence," *Adolescence* 38(14): 141–59.

Kehily, M. J. (1999) "More Sugar?: Teenage Magazines, Gender Displays and Sexual Learning," *European Journal of Cultural Studies* 2(1): 65–88.

Kellner, D. and J. Share (2005) "Toward Critical Media Literacy: Core Concepts, Debates, Organizations and Policy," *Discourse: Studies in the Cultural Politics of Education* 26(3): 369–86.

Ostermann, A. C. and D. Keller-Cohen (1998) "'Good Girls Go to Heaven; Bad Girls ... ' Learn to be Good: Quizzes in American and Brazilian Teenage Girls' Magazines," *Discourse & Society* 9(4): 531–58.

Peirce, K. (1990) "A Feminist Theoretical Perspective on the Socialization of Teenage Girls through *Seventeen* Magazine," *Sex Roles* 23(9/10): 491–501.

Rhymes, B. (2011) "Deference, Denial, and Beyond: A Repertoire Approach to Mass Media and Schooling," *Review of Research in Education* 35(1): 208–38.

Share, J. (2009) "Young Children and Critical Media Literacy," in R. Hammer and D. Kellner (eds.) *Media/Cultural Studies: Critical Approaches*, New York: Peter Lang, pp. 126–51.

Smith, D. (1990) *Texts, Facts, and Femininity*, London: Routledge

Tuchman, G. (1979) "Women's Depiction by the Mass Media," *Signs: Journal of Women in Culture and Society* 4(3): 528–37.

Wasko, J. (2008) "The Commodification of Youth Culture," in K. Drotner and S. Livingstone (eds.) *The International Handbook of Children, Media, and Culture*, Thousand Oaks: Sage, pp. 461–75.

Winship, J. (1987) *Inside Women's Magazines*, London: Pandora.

——(1991) "The Impossibility of *Best*: Enterprise Meets Domesticity in the Practical Women's Magazines of the 1980s," *Cultural Studies* 5(2): 131–56.

# 49

# Investigating users' responses to Dove's "real beauty" strategy
## Feminism, freedom, and Facebook[1]

## *Dara Persis Murray*

This chapter considers the meanings of "real beauty" that are produced by a corporation (Dove) and negotiated by its targeted female demographic. First, I provide a feminist media studies analysis of the Dove Campaign for Real Beauty (CFRB), arguing that this branding strategy communicates problematic messages of beauty and feminism to audiences. Next, I consider the ways in which CFRB utilizes social media to engage users with its "real beauty" messaging, paying attention to their interpretations of "real beauty." Do audiences view it as a liberating beauty philosophy that resists the dominant ideology of beauty, or do they see it as an oppressive media strategy? In considering the production and consumption of "real beauty," I address their alliance with "a postfeminist sensibility" (Gill 2007), illuminating the positioning of "real beauty" at the nexus of contemporary meanings of beauty and feminist politics.

Along these lines, I argue that by viewing women's conflict with the dominant ideology of beauty as a market to exploit for capitalist aims, CFRB is a cause branding strategy. It merges messages of corporate "concern and commitment for a cause" (Cone 2000) with the participation of women, girls, feminists, and female advocacy organizations who have the same social goals, concealing its economic aims by blending corporate (Dove) and individual (female audiences') identities through interactions about the brand. This affords Dove the opportunity to attract and retain customers (especially those who self-identify as a "real beauty") and to seed its identity among them by drawing on their emotions, actions, and identities.

### CFRB as strategy

A decade ago, the Unilever Corporation reassessed its marketing strategy for Dove, Unilever's brand of personal care products. In so doing, it advanced a branding strategy to create a global image and heighten customer loyalty to the Dove brand around the world; while there were minor differences in the texts' language and images to account for cultural sensibilities, their meanings remained consistent. CFRB's US messaging and audience responses to it are examined here, as America was a CFRB launch site and is a major consumer market.

Appealing to women on national and local levels through mass media texts and grassroots efforts, respectively, Dove implemented CFRB to engage audiences with the brand in their daily lives, making it a "social, economic and existential reality" (Arvidsson 2006: 14). Through a variety of techniques, audiences were enlisted to bond ideologically and materially with Dove by associating and investing its brand name and identity with the corporation's value of "real beauty." Although CFRB addressed a societal issue (the problematics surrounding the dominant ideology of female beauty), the ways in which the strategy was advanced and managed by Unilever/Dove to produce its desired outcome (brand attachment) raise questions about individuals' agency in relation to corporate power (Arvidsson 2006). Among the issues are whether or how audiences experience individual power through their engagement with CFRB's messages.

CFRB was based on Dove's 2003 report, "The Real Truth about Beauty." The study involved the participation of 3,200 women, ages 18 through 64, in ten countries, in a 20–25-minute telephone interview. The researchers found that fewer than 2 percent of women felt beautiful; 75 percent wanted representations of women to reflect diversity through age, shape, and size; and 76 percent wanted the media to portray beauty as more than physical (Etcoff *et al.* 2004).

The research subjects' responses spoke to the knotty dynamics between the messages produced by the beauty industry (defined here as comprised of the fashion, cosmetics, and diet industries) and their consumption by female audiences in the twentieth and twenty-first centuries. Through their media representations, the beauty industry communicates a cultural norm for female beauty (the dominant ideology of beauty), which is characterized by ultra-thin, tall, youthful, and sexual bodies. The images and language that comprise such representations connect non-conformity—not looking like and/or not agreeing with the dominant ideology of beauty—with a woman's inability to fulfill her gender role or experience happiness (Bartky 1990). Women's and girls' pursuit of this norm has led to another cultural norm of disciplining the body through diet and exercise regimes; oftentimes, this self-monitoring leads to eating disorders, low self-esteem, and body image issues (Bordo 2003).

The research subjects' responses suggested an untapped market for Dove: women who desired a new philosophy of beauty. In line with their findings, Dove announced its challenge to the dominant ideology: its media texts (print and television advertisements, viral videos, online presence, billboards) would feature *real women* (Dove's terminology) whose appearance in shape, age, color, and size contrasts with that of typical professional models. According to Alessandro Manfredi, Dove's Global Brand Director, the research offered Dove "a great opportunity to differentiate the brand from every [other] beauty brand" (Fielding *et al.* 2008). This strategy afforded Dove the ability to brand its corporate identity as a problem solver, rather than a perpetuator, of the troubling messages of beauty identified by its research subjects.

## Producing CFRB: a feminist (approved) strategy?

The participation of women and girls in the production of CFRB may read as "feminist" among audiences as it demonstrates a coming together of women from various walks of life to subvert the dominant ideology of beauty. The nature of this advocacy suggests credibility for the "real beauty" philosophy and for CFRB's stated aim of realizing positive social change for individuals negotiating beauty messaging and for the beauty industry itself. Ostensibly, then, the feminist values of improving the lives of women and effecting change in oppressive patriarchal structures (Dworkin 1974) appear to underscore CFRB.

CFRB was shaped by the advertising agency Ogilvy & Mather. The team that constructed its texts included women in important positions: the agency's Chair and Chief Executive Officer, Shelly Lazarus (a graduate of Smith College, which lists numerous feminist icons among its alumni; she sat on Smith's Board of Trustees), two creative directors, an art director, a writer, and producer. Ogilvy reached out to Susie Orbach, author of *Fat Is a Feminist Issue*, who, along with three other women, directed CFRB's foundational report and much of its subsequent research.

In the US, CFRB also advanced its message via nonprofit girls' and women's organizations. Called "self-esteem" partners, the Girl Scouts, Girls Inc., and the Boys and Girls Clubs of America operated as spaces for public involvement in the Dove Self-Esteem Fund, a CFRB brand extension financed predominantly by Unilever and supplemented by individual and corporate donations. The Fund promotes CFRB's messages by facilitating a relationship between the corporation, girls, and their mothers/mentors in what appears to be a partnership for the common good: to change the societal perception of beauty and increase girls' self-esteem. The Fund was promoted through viral videos like "Evolution" and "True Colors" (for an analysis of these texts, see Murray 2013). Further, through the Fund's website and the partners' locations and events, girls and their mothers/mentors could participate in online and in-person workshops and access Dove-created "self-esteem toolkits" for girls and "parent kits" for mothers/mentors. The Woodhull Institute for Ethical Leadership, another CFRB partner, offered online programs to further women's professional and ethical development. Woodhull was co-founded by Naomi Wolf, author of *The Beauty Myth* (1991), a feminist critique of the beauty industry.

So, does all this endorsement from women who have broken the "glass ceiling" (by obtaining powerful industry positions) as well as nonprofit organizations that sponsor feminist and female advocacy mean that CFRB is a feminist-approved strategy? In turn, can CFRB be considered a "feminist" campaign? A response to these questions is complicated by the proposal that we live in a "postfeminist media culture" (Gill 2007: 249) wherein popular messages of feminism associate female empowerment with the marketplace, supporting corporate interests. Subsequently, the postfeminist position contends that gender equality has been achieved in the public sphere, a position that separates meanings of citizenship from civic engagement (McRobbie 2008: 533). In this light, Ogilvy CEO Lazarus has not publicly aligned herself with feminism but has been noted as having a "feminist love of economic empowerment" (Dyer 2004: 191). The participation of Woodhull/Wolf with CFRB corresponds with the "power feminist" position that Wolf advocated post-*The*

*Beauty Myth*, which has been characterized as contending that "capital [is] the primary means of solidarity among women" (Sorisio 1997: 139). In addition, CFRB's "self-esteem" partnerships, promoted in a manner suggestive of a feminist grassroots effort, may be a tactic to minimize the connection between Dove and Unilever's other brands, and perhaps even to distract attention away from Unilever's ownership structure. Suggesting fractured ideological credibility about the corporation's concern regarding the dominant ideology of beauty, Unilever also owns Slimfast (a diet plan), Fair & Lovely Fairness Cream (a skin lightening product), and Axe deodorant (whose texts objectify women).

Although CFRB may be viewed as an echo of feminist concerns by addressing the beauty industry's problematic representations of beauty, careful consideration is needed before identifying CFRB with a call to feminist arms. As the next section will reveal, CFRB's appropriation of feminist expressions and symbols afforded its producers the ability "to reincorporate the cultural power of feminism" (Goldman 1992: 130) and depoliticize the feminist message. Audiences may perceive themselves as rebels against the dominant ideology of beauty by agreeing with Dove's seemingly revolutionary endeavor, but their support instead highlights CFRB's well-executed co-option of feminism as a strategy to generate brand attachment.

## Revealing CFRB: freeing female audiences?

CFRB was carried out across numerous media texts (see Murray 2013), two of which are examined here: CFRB's manifesto (one of CFRB's introductory images) and an advertisement for Dove Firming Lotion (one of CFRB's product launches). The messages draw on key terms in feminist politics—liberation and oppression—to present "real beauty" as democratizing, thereby freeing women from the directives of the dominant ideology of female beauty. This examination, however, unearths messages of an unequal power relationship between female audiences and the brand, as well as meanings of "real" women which suggest that Dove is not the liberating agent it represents itself to be.

The use of feminist language and the representation of "real" women in the manifesto draw in audiences to identify with the text's messages. Arranged in a line, the "real" women exhibit physical attributes intended to signal a departure from the dominant ideology of beauty. They represent CFRB's target consumer who desires liberation and are also a source of identification for audiences, inviting them to be a "real beauty." Underneath their portraits is copy, stating:

> For too long, beauty has been defined by narrow, unattainable stereotypes. It's time to change all that. Because Dove believes real beauty comes in many shapes, sizes, colors and ages. It's why we started the campaign for real beauty. And why we hope you'll take part. Together, let's think, talk, debate and learn how to make beauty real again. Cast your vote at campaignforrealbeauty.com.
> (Dove Manifesto 2004)

While the "real" women accompany the copy, Dove's linguistic message indicates that it holds more importance, as it occupies more space than the women and concludes with a blue color whose length and vibrancy are more visually compelling than the women's portraits. Moreover, the copy emphasizes Dove as the organizer, catalyst, and vehicle for change in beauty messaging: "it's time to change all that … it's why we started the campaign for real beauty." The text thus positions Dove to usurp the power of women and the feminist movement in this mission of "real beauty." Importantly, the emphasis on interaction represented in the "Cast your vote" device suggests the feminist value of suffrage; however, CFRB is not an election. Casting one's vote indicates support for Dove's strategy.

Like the manifesto, CFRB's advertisement for its skin firming lotion depicts "real" women whose appearance contrasts with the dominant ideology of homogeneous female beauty. However, as my analysis reveals, the images and copy suggest that conformity is a feature of "real beauty," too. Visually, the women's positioning atop the copy takes a figurative stand against supermodel-style beauty. Supporting standard beauty messaging, though, the use of clothing (or, notably, the lack of it) on their bodies and their positioning suggest objectification of the women for the purpose of selling goods and the "real beauty" philosophy. They wear bras and underwear, undergarments signifying intimacy (perhaps of a sexual nature); this connotation is reinforced by the bodies' arrangement: the hip of one woman touches the abdomen near the genital area of the woman next to her, who leans to touch the woman behind her. The women thus present their bodies for the potential pleasure of audiences (for sexual and/or emotional enjoyment), much as professional models do.

Yet, the copy indicates that Dove liberates women by helping them to be "real," separating them from audiences who are oppressed by the dominant ideology. It reads:

> Let's face it, firming the thighs of a size 2 supermodel is no challenge. Real women have real curves. And according to women who tried new Dove Firming, it left their skin feeling firmer in just one week. What better way to celebrate the curves you were born with? New Dove Firming Lotion, Cream and Body Wash. For beautifully firm skin.
>
> (Dove Firming 2005)

Since "real" women have "beautifully firm skin," they are able to "celebrate" their "curves," as the product helps them to manage "the curves you [they] were born with." Thus, "real beauty" is attainable through the consumption of Dove products, reinforcing audiences' identity as a consumer. The "real" women support this interpretation by providing a product testimonial that intimates consumerism: "according to women who tried new Dove, it left their skin feeling firmer in just one week." Importantly, the "real" women, like the audience, need a product to change their "real" bodies, and their testimonials reflect the beginning of their journey to conformity—as "firm," "real" women. Their material consumption also highlights their ideological acceptance of Dove's inference that their bodies are flawed objects to be fixed by Dove, as well as their agreement with the "real beauty" doctrine that skin should be firm (a value echoing the dominant ideology of beauty). The "real" women, though, present empowered attitudes about showing their bodies, particularly regarding sexuality. Such attitudes can suggest their postfeminist subjectification by portraying sexual objectification as pleasurable. The intersection of being a "real beauty" and postfeminism is explored next.

## Consuming CFRB: fashioning postfeminists via Facebook

Examining how users understand Dove's brand messaging invites an analysis of their engagement in the practice of self-branding. Dove fuses users' consumption of and conversation about "real beauty" on Dove's Facebook channel, potentiating a shaping of each user's identity as a self-branded "real beauty" who underscores the internalization of and interaction with CFRB's meanings and representations. She also represents the highest degree of ideological and material attachment to the brand.

Dove has employed social media as part of CFRB since its 2004 launch, when audiences voted on the appearance of "real" women via interactive billboards. It increased its online presence in 2010 with the Dove Movement for Self-Esteem (a CFRB brand extension). Its Facebook channel promotes "real beauty" as the central value for socialization via postings on its wall, discussion boards, videos, photos, and so forth. Its "History by Year" section includes four significant company events, three of which are launches: the Dove Company (1957), CFRB (2004), and the Self-Esteem Fund (2006). The 2012 event celebrates Dove's social media milestone of five million members in its Facebook community, called "The Dove Real Women Community"; clicking on this milestone brings users to an announcement: that the Community is "committed to reaching 15 million girls by 2015" (Dove Facebook Channel 2012).

Examining how CFRB's social media tactics engage users on and around Facebook fleshes out a response to the question: Do users view "real beauty" as a liberating beauty philosophy that resists the dominant ideology of beauty, or do they see it as an oppressive media strategy? Linking this query to CFRB's postfeminist underpinnings, I consider whether users' self-branding as a "real beauty" suggests an alliance with many of the themes (noted in italics within the forthcoming discussion) that comprise "a postfeminist sensibility":

> The notion that femininity is a bodily property; the shift from objectification to subjectification; the emphasis upon self-surveillance, monitoring and discipline; a focus upon individualism, choice and empowerment; the dominance of a makeover paradigm; the articulation or entanglement of feminist and antifeminist ideas.
>
> (Gill 2007: 254)

Beyond its articles and coupons, Dove's channel encourages users to connect in substantive ways with the brand. Its descriptions of Dove products reinforce the dominant ideology, emphasizing that *femininity is a bodily property*. These assets include (but are not limited to) "beautiful skin" (soft, youthful, firm), "even skin tone," silky and "strong" hair, and hairless underarms and legs. Users often echo agreement with what this bodily notion of beauty means and view Dove as enabling them to achieve it, as in this comment: "stay[ing] so pretty n young love it every women should try it [Dove products]." Or, they may view Dove's communication as representing a norm for femininity that is desirable to their mate, for example: "fill [sic] soft That's what a man like for his women like to fill [sic] soft and silk."

In April 2012, CFRB launched "Show Us Your Skin," a US-based strategy that Dove calls its "largest campaign of real women" (PR Newswire 2012). Users upload a photo of themselves to Dove's company website or Facebook page to appear in an advertisement for Dove Body Washes and Beauty Bars. These advertisements include women's photos flashing on a Times Square billboard (with Dove emailing the women a screen shot of their image to share with others), the photos posted on Dove's company website, and their usage in Dove's digital texts. This tactic, supported by users' willing responses, elucidates *the shift from objectification to subjectification*, since "If you want to be a 'real' woman ... All you have to do is show off some skin" (Olson 2012). A review of Facebook comments suggests that women (18 years and older) relish the opportunity to reveal their bodies for Dove. Comments commonly reflect such sentiments as "Ok then my DOVE lol Yes, I'd love to model my skin for you." For Dove, the show of skin testifies to its product's benefits. Accordingly, women "are encouraged to wear a towel, tank top, pair of shorts, or a dress in their photo—anything that tastefully shows off their skin" (PR Newswire 2012). For women, even more telling than their agreement to model their skin in a way that suggests subjectification are their statements proclaiming their relationship with the brand. One wrote, "[I] love dove and being part of the Dove family! I'm in this ad." Another said, "This is such a WONDERFUL idea! Thank you for featuring me!!! = D." Involvement in these cases seems to be driven by an emotional connection to the brand as well as by the social acceptability that they may access through associating with it (for instance, achieving fame as a model, if ever so briefly).

CFRB's texts suggest that to have high self-esteem requires constant work by audiences. Along these lines, users place an *emphasis upon self-surveillance, monitoring, and discipline* related to emotional self-regulation. User comments suggest the same, stressing the importance of having inner beauty, at times privileging it over outer beauty. To wit: "Your dress size doesn't make you beautful [sic]. If you have a wonderful personality you are beautiful. It's not all about looks." The channel's "Dove Real Woman of the Month" reinforces this outlook. In response to the question about "when she feels most beautiful," one woman expressed, "When I'm being the best person I can be as a mother, as a sister, as a daughter, as a friend." Her statement, though, connects her identity to those outside of herself, subtly signaling their power to make assessments of her inner beauty that affirm or deny her own view of herself.

Dove's Facebook application "I'm Beautiful Because" indicates *a focus upon individualism, choice, and empowerment* through its request for users to reinforce the "real beauty" messaging as their empowered choice of a beauty philosophy. Completing a sentence that begins "I'm Beautiful Because," users acknowledge, for instance, "We are beautiful because we are original and can not be replaced" and "Beause [sic] u are unique." Importantly, by doing this, users confirm an ideological and material attachment to Dove that influences their self-perception due to the implicit acceptance that they are beautiful either because of Dove or because they use Dove. This may lead to a belief that materially supporting Dove is empowering: for example, one user pasted Dove's copy about the Fund ("Each time you buy Dove, you help us and our charitable partners provide inspiring self-esteem programming for girls") onto her Facebook post, with the consumer response of "Awesomeness! I'll keep purchasing! ;-)."

Dove's channel offers tips and tools for users to employ its products, oftentimes indicating a before/after change. It is the user's self-branding to be a "real" woman, however, that highlights the essence of *the dominance of a makeover paradigm*, as it requires the transformation of one's identity. This shift is part of being a "real beauty," as one user notes: "For the first time in a lifetime of hating myself ... I learned to love myself from the inside out, and I realized I no longer needed to define the size of my life by the size of my body ... or any other external value." Being a "real beauty" can be accomplished simply by a user linking her Facebook profile with Dove's channel to be part of "Dove Real Women: Our Community." In addition, many women call themselves a "Dove Girl"; this self-branding is passed down through families, as one user writes, "I AM ALSO A DOVE GIRL AS WELL AS MY 3 DAUGHTERS AGES 14,12&3."

In April 2012, Dove introduced a Facebook application in Australia that employs the concept of the makeover as well. "The Ad Makeover by Dove" invites users to replace problematic advertisements that target women's body insecurities with "positive" advertisements. Like the Dove manifesto, this strategy situates the corporation as the site for activism. The copy states:

> Give these ads a makeover: Ads like these prey on your insecurities and make you feel bad. Together we can do something about this. This application gives you the power to displace feel-bad ads with messages that help women feel beautiful instead. It works like this: You pick a message. You choose the target audience for your message. Then Dove starts outbidding the negative ads for ad space, letting women see your positive message instead.
>
> (Dove Facebook: The Ad Makeover 2012)

This Facebook application illustrates target advertising, a strategy for corporations to home in on their desired demographics. The women creating the user-generated advertisements can be viewed as CFRB content creators whose texts afford Dove a new way to reach its consumers. This opportunity for women to "make over" beauty industry advertisements thus amounts to corporate recruitment of their unpaid labor for its own benefit. And, since their advertisements are only available to users who activate the application, these women's voices will likely not be heard in the broader media culture. The copy about Dove's proactive position of "outbidding the negative ads for ad space" is also misleading, as Unilever purchases Facebook advertising space for the users' "positive" advertisements (which subsequently allots less space for "negative" advertisements), but the application does not actually replace existing problematic advertisements. This social media tactic thereby engages women to feel good about realizing social change through the corporation and reinforces their commitment to self-identify as a "real beauty." However, it leaves the messaging of the beauty industry intact and the women with an illusion of power.

The "Dove Real Woman Role Model" series underscores users' conflict with what may be popularly interpreted as feminist thought and practice. Dove's focus on role models is connected to women and girls becoming a "real beauty": namely, to "help girls develop a positive relationship with beauty, so beauty becomes a source of confidence, not anxiety." Dove highlights women whose "self-esteem stories" resonate with their messaging. To publicize them, Dove posts "tips" from the Role Model, such as: "There's no such thing as a 'boys' club. Girls can do anything boys can." Interestingly, however, these tips arouse controversy rather than solidarity. For instance, one user argued against what she interpreted as gender division, stating, "I believe men and women are equal but that doesn't mean they're the same. Nothing wrong with ... 'boys clubs' nothing wrong with girl's clubs either," while another said the tip was "feminist crap ... there's no need to put down boys/men just to empower girls/women." Despite their apparent rejection of the Role Model's views, users can nevertheless be a "real beauty," since they exhibit an *articulation or entanglement of feminist and antifeminist ideas*.

## Final thoughts

This chapter has considered Dove's messaging of "real beauty," arguing that it reframes—rather than challenges—the dominant ideology of beauty to heighten women's and girls' attachment to the Dove brand as a self-branded "real beauty." While users may consider CFRB a liberating beauty philosophy due to its stated resistance to the dominant ideology of beauty and its showcasing of "real" women with diverse sizes, colors, shapes, and ages, this "liberation" encourages women to enact "a postfeminist sensibility," underlining CFRB as an oppressive strategy. Moreover, "real beauty" as an individualized pursuit necessitates work on the self, a focus that detracts from the feminist argument for collective thinking and structural change. Due to CFRB's online popularity, however, it is important to ask whether being a "real beauty" may liberate users in other ways.

A potential outgrowth of user interaction with CFRB is the stimulation of critical thinking about how to effect social change for women and girls. As one user wrote: "Hey Dove! How about a campaign to teach young boys to value young girls/women no matter what they look like! I KNOW this would get to the HEART of the problem of low self-esteem in girls/women!" Yet, by inviting Dove to expand the scope of CFRB's messaging, the user promotes Dove as an authority on such topics (perhaps more so than herself), supporting the corporation to indoctrinate broader audiences.

Another possibility is that CFRB may prompt women to realize other social missions. One user devised an anti-bullying program, posting its description to see whether Dove would be interested in joining forces with her to "take a stand against bullying." Interestingly, some users utilize this space to voice their concerns about Dove's conflicting messages of social responsibility. One popular topic of contention is Dove's policy of animal testing, which poses conflict for users ("the only bad thing [about Dove] ... is that ITS [sic] TESTED ON ANIMALS!!!") or is a deal-breaker for their brand attachment ("I'm really depressed that yesterday I saw Dove on a list of companies that use animal testing ... I will have to switch").

In many ways, CFRB imparts conflicting messages of female empowerment that are attributable to its interlock with meanings of "postfeminist" liberation. Yet, CFRB as an oppressive branding and self-branding strategy is not interpreted as such by users. Women and girls willingly identify as a "real beauty," merging their "concern and commitment" with Dove's for a social cause as part of CFRB's cause branding strategy. In so doing, they align their values with acceptance of a corporate strategy that positions itself in the feminist role of advocate for social change, with Dove's representations of beauty (even its objectification of women) and Dove-approved behavior ("self-esteem"), and with the traditional female role of ideological and material consumer. Ultimately, CFRB reinforces women's and girls' relationship to consumer culture rather than facilitates the realization of self-empowerment or societal change.

## Note

1 Parts of this chapter have appeared as "Branding 'Real' Social Change in Dove's Campaign For Real Beauty," in *Feminist Media Studies* 13(1) (March 2013).

## References

Arvidsson, A. (2006) *Brands: Meaning and Value in Media Culture*, New York: Routledge.

Bartky, S. L. (1990) *Femininity and Domination: Studies in the Phenomenology of Oppression*, New York: Routledge.

Bordo, S. (2003) *Unbearable Weight: Feminism, Western Culture, and the Body*, Berkeley: University of California Press.

Cone, C. L. (2000) *Cause Branding in the 21st Century*. http://www.psaresearch.com/causebranding.html.

Dove Facebook Channel (2012) http://www.facebook.com/dove.

Dove Facebook: The Ad Makeover (2012) http://www.facebook.com/dove/app_268922816518670.

Dove Firming (2005) http://usatoday30.usatoday.com/money/advertising/2005-07-07-dove-usat_x.htm.

Dove Manifesto (2004) http://www.coloribus.com/adsarchive/prints/dove-skincare-products-dove-manifesto-6606505/.

Dworkin, A. (1974) *Woman Hating*, New York: E. P. Dutton.

Dyer, S. (2004) "Lifestyles of the Media Rich and Oligopolistic," in Peter Phillips (ed.) *Censored 2005: The Top 25 Censored Stories*, New York: Seven Stories Press, pp. 189–97.

Etcoff, N., S. Orbach, J. Scott, and H. D'Agostino (2004) "The Real Truth about Beauty: A Global Report." http://www.clubofamsterdam.com/contentarticles/52%20Beauty/dove_white_paper_final.pdf.

Fielding, D., D. Lewis, M. White, A. Manfredi, and L. Scott (2008) "Dove Campaign Roundtable," *Advertising & Society Review* 9(4). http://muse.jhu.edu/login?auth=0&type=summary&url=/journals/advertising_and_society_review/v009/9.4.fielding.html.

Gill, R. (2007) *Gender and the Media*, Cambridge: Polity.

Goldman, R. (1992) *Reading Ads Socially*, New York: Routledge.

Hearn, A. (2008) "'Meat, Mask, Burden': Probing the Contours of the Branded 'Self'," *Journal of Consumer Culture* 8(2): 197–217.

McRobbie, A. (2008) "Young Women and Consumer Culture: An Intervention," *Cultural Studies* 22(5): 531–50.

Murray, D. P. (2013) "Branding 'Real' Social Change in Dove's Campaign for Real Beauty," *Feminist Media Studies* 13(1): 83–101.

Olson, J. (2012) *Dove's "Real Woman" Campaign Opens to the Public*. http://kstp.com/article/stories/s2592520.shtml.

PR Newswire (2012) *Dove All Real Women to Appear in National Dove Ads*. http://www.multivu.com/mnr/55405-dove-show-us-your-skin-campaign-all-real-women.

Sorisio, C. (1997) "A Tale of Two Feminisms: Power and Victimization in Contemporary Feminist Debate," in L. Heywood and J. Drake (eds.) *Third Wave Agenda: Being Feminist, Doing Feminism*, Minneapolis: University of Minnesota Press, pp. 134–49.

Wolf, N. (1991) *The Beauty Myth*, New York: William Morrow & Company.

# 50

# Feminism in a postfeminist world

## Women discuss who's "hot"—and why we care—on the collegiate "Anonymous Confession Board"

*Andrea L. Press and Francesca Tripodi*

The recent media fascination with the best-selling trilogy *Fifty Shades of Grey*—what some have called "mommy porn"—illustrates that women's overt discussions of sexuality remain shocking in US culture. This is particularly true when those discussions transcend the bounds of "conventionality," however defined. In the case of *Fifty Shades of Grey*, it is the explicit sadomasochism of the sexual encounter which most notably shocks. Various feminist commentators in the blogosphere recoil at Ana's submissive role, concerned that the sadomasochistic sex scenes objectify women's bodies and encourage emotional and sexual dependence (DelVecchio 2012; Perez 2012). Others celebrate the negotiation of sexual fantasy between Christian and Ana, in which Ana can find pleasure in various forms of sexual experience (Debold 2012; Maya 2012; Roiphe 2012). These recent debates echo the feminist sex debates dating back to the Barnard Conference of 1980, during which anti-porn feminists clashed with "pro-sex" feminists.[1] The proliferation of sexually charged media, their mass consumption, and the increasingly participatory nature of new media forms, all of which characterize the contemporary media environment, usher in a new set of questions for feminist reception studies which are relevant to these longstanding concerns.

McRobbie (2008) argues that we have not updated the paradigms in feminist theory developed in the 1970s and 1980s to understand current "sex war" debates. The new media environment has changed the game. For one thing, the ubiquity of pornography in spaces frequented by children and women has complicated the issues for feminists. Noting not only the new media environment, but the targeting of women as the new consumers of pornography, and the increasing sexualization of girls and teens, McRobbie urges us to seriously reconsider the impact on women of a new and increasingly sexualized cultural environment, rather than falling back on what can seem with the advantage of hindsight an overly simplistic anti-censorship position adopted by feminists of an earlier era.

At issue in the "sex wars" was, and is, our attempt to keep women's welfare in view as we make arguments about many issues, including sex. McRobbie's frustration echoes Katha Pollitt, whose piece entitled "Women Who Love Republicans Who Hate Them" argues that women are the only group who "refuse to take collective insults seriously" (2012: 10) as she tries to explain why they garner such strong support from women given the strongly anti-woman Republican agenda on issues such as birth control, and abortion in the case of rape and incest.[2]

Both McRobbie's and Pollitt's comments highlight a general scholarly frustration within feminist media studies concerning the inability of feminist scholars to influence public debate. Much has been written about the "aftermath of feminism" in Western culture (Douglas 2010; McRobbie 2009; Tasker and Negra 2007). Studies show that, paradoxically, women identify with a series of feminist positions, though not with the label "feminist" (Houvouras and Carter 2008; Peltola et al. 2004; Scharff 2011). While women still care about concerns of gender equality raised by the second wave, they describe traditional feminism as constraining and no longer relevant (Houvouras and Carter 2008; McCabe 2005; Peltola et al. 2004; Stein 1997). Some young women appear to associate feminism with certain extreme second-wave positions (such as rejecting men, sex, and consumption, which constituted only a very small part of the movement). As a result, one trend is for women to identify with how they are *unlike* feminists of the past, rather than focusing on similarities (Baumgardner and Richards 2010), or on how to draw upon feminist theory and apply it to the contemporary period.

Nevertheless women often espouse viewpoints that many scholars and activists—if not the women themselves—would term "feminist." Our goal is to shed light on this actual operation of feminism in response to binary thinking that opposes "feminist" and "non-feminist" positions in a simplistic dichotomy. In a book project in progress, Press coins the term "feminism on the ground" to describe this simultaneous embrace and rejection of feminism.

## Feminism in the new media environment

New media offer a set of locales in which we can witness this intricate maneuvering between positions, sometimes in the public dialogic space afforded by blogs, social media, message boards, etc. Pioneering thinker boyd (2007) calls spaces such as Facebook or Myspace "mediated publics," which differ from unmediated spaces because they are persistent, replicable, searchable, and accessible by invisible audiences. These mediated public spaces offer opportunities for the expression of positions which characterize the current state of feminism.[3]

Mediated spaces have sometimes posed new threats to women and others, as well as opportunities for self-expression. This chapter explores discourses around sexuality, and women's sexual attractiveness, found in a heavily used online message board that draws the bulk of its audience from students at a state university; the same and similar boards are extremely popular at universities throughout the USA. On this campus, Collegiate ACB ("The Anonymous Confession Board for college students throughout the country to discuss anything") was widely read and very well known;

over half of respondents in our survey (more in our focus groups) had heard of the site, and of those who knew it 90 percent visited it at least occasionally. While use of the board was highest amongst first year students and members of fraternity and sorority organizations, in general at least casual use of the board is high across the student body. According to our research, the board is mostly used by the white and Asian students on campus, while often avoided by African American and Hispanic students. Most users appear to be heterosexual, although the gay male community has a limited but distinctive presence. We find that many, indeed most, of the posts on the board target and police the appearance and sexual behavior of straight white and Asian women.

While gay and straight men are discussed, the types of critiques leveled at women are rarely pointed in men's direction, establishing that the group "dominance" of straight white men continues, and, even more important, is still assumed, in some mediated public spaces. Alternately, this pattern might signify that the dominance of this group is so contested, that spaces such as these are part of the ongoing work needed to reproduce and re-establish this dominance. The posts by and about gay men are interesting. At times, they are criticized (like straight women) for not being thin ("I thought to be a [twink] you had to be skinny?" or "[FULL NAME] has the biggest gut I've ever seen."). Overall we don't think the parameters of "attractive-ness" are as narrow for gay men as for straight women, but certainly a degree of appearance policing was going on for gay men. Lesbians are invisible on the site, perhaps related to the belief of some users that women read the board, but post only to defend the reputations of their friends or themselves.

In any case, the message board illustrates the limits of "feminism on the ground." While women's bodies and sexual behavior are targeted for praise and critique over and over, few if any objections to these discourses are raised. In this chapter, we ask the following questions: How is it that feminist perspectives have been incorporated into the general public's beliefs about a series of issues, while support is given to the continued privilege of certain groups, in particular, as the board illustrates, straight white males? How do these contradictions inflect current discussions of sexuality which maintain a privileged male "politicking" of women?

The board we examine exists in some form on many campuses across the United States. Collegiate ACB has persisted since 2008 under a variety of names, including College ACB, Blipdar, and Juicy Campus. College (now called "Collegiate") ACB was launched in 2008 at Wesleyan University as a more anonymous alternative to Facebook—safer for posters, who are not subject to the dangers posed by the trace-ability of Facebook posts; but not for the subjects of posts, who often do not remain anonymous. While users can "report" information they find offensive, the process of getting offensive content removed—even content that contains specific names—can take days, and material is easily reposted. Content remains searchable for years, and has even followed the board through several sales and renaming of the website. It is privately controlled by owners seeking to turn a profit from the board and its activity, though when we spoke with the owner of one of the board's iterations ("Blipdar") he expressed doubts as to its profitability.

Thus, the site embodies boyd's (2007) tenets of mediated spaces: even when own-ership changes, the content persists, remains searchable (by title of post or content), can be "moved" to other mediated publics with a simple "cut and paste," and is read by hundreds of people who do not post content of their own. On these boards, current college students post about a variety of topics, including where to find good sandwiches; politics; and which fraternities or sororities to join. But even casual perusal of the boards reveals that the most popular threads posted concern the sexual attractiveness and behavior of students, particularly heterosexual white or Asian women, who are named, categorized, and discussed at a level of detail which is often very specific about their body parts, appearance, and sexual activity.

## Methods

We first analyzed several of the most popular threads on the board's different names (College ACB, Blipdar, and Collegiate ACB). We focused on issues concerning women that we found troubling and of interest from a feminist perspective, in particular sexual attractiveness conceptualized as "hotness," women's sexual prowess, and questionable female sexual behavior labeled as "sluttiness."[4] In conjunction with interpretive textual analysis of the posts in these subject areas, we conducted two preliminary focus groups of students on campus who were alternately familiar with, but sometimes unaware of, the sites.[5] Many indicated that if they did post to the site they would not tell anyone. Respondents were cognizant of the site's taboo nature. Those who reported not using it expressed surprise at the content—in particular the use of first and last names in explicitly sexual and/or defamatory comments and threads.

Our initial focus groups quickly made clear that students were reluctant in the presence of their peers to admit using the site. To combat this problem we designed an online, anonymous survey to examine how many people used the site on campus and to explore issues surrounding feminist response, or lack of it, to various posts on the board.[6] The survey was distributed in the first week of the 2011–12 academic year to large introductory-level courses and general student listservs. We received 379 out of 2,825 responses for an approximately 13.4 percent response rate, rather low but still sufficient for preliminary analysis.

We held one final focus group with members of a sorority familiar with the board to further examine trends in the quantitative data. We also visited a feminist theory class who commented on an earlier draft of this chapter, in class discussion and in class posts. In particular, we were interested in examining the emphasis on ratings of women that we noted on the site, and why the space was not a place for feminist expression to resist such posts. Throughout the research we communicated with several key student informants familiar with the site and its place on college campuses, and with the fraternity–sorority system.

## Discussion

We received a sometimes contradictory set of responses to our queries about how audiences read the sexualized comments made about women found on Collegiate ACB.

## Sexism

In a perhaps surprising use of a second-wave feminist term, many of our informants—particularly in our online survey—identify the particular way female sexuality is treated on Collegiate ACB overall as "sexist."[7] When pressed as to what they
mean, students respond in a number of ways. A typical reaction was that men and
women are treated unequally. Our survey showed that 92.2 percent of respondents,
both men and women, felt women were written about in a sexist or derogatory way;
only 61 percent felt that men were similarly written about—although perhaps that is
a surprisingly large egalitarian application of the "sexist" label to the treatment of
both genders.

Students overall talked explicitly about the systemic denigration of women, and
about the denigration of feminism, as another sexist aspect of the board, in addition
to the explicitly sexual comments about women. A typical post in this regard reads:
"Wanna hear a joke: Women's Rights." Also cited as sexist was specifically the
objectification of women: "People talk about [women's] breast size or how easy they
are to get into bed. There's probably less sexism toward men, but there are still
derogatory comments made."

## Hotness, fatness

Comments and jokes about women's bodies fuel and sustain Collegiate ACB.
Women's bodies are either praised or censured for alternately conforming or not to
the narrow, sexualized contours of acceptable appearance for women (and these
seem to be the thin, white, large-breasted parameters prized by mainstream media
culture). Which women are "hot" and which are "fat" or "not hot" ("has that girl
[gained] about 30 pounds since freshman year?" implies that she is "not hot")
become a constant source of commentary. The board often discusses sororities in
this fashion, including by ranking the "hottest girls" in specific sororities, and the
"hottest sororities" (those with the highest number of "hot" women); these are
continually listed, debated, and commented upon.

"Hotness" as a label came up often on the board and in our survey responses. But
when we tried to probe this issue in our focus groups, we got mixed responses. In
one group, women acknowledged the ubiquity of "hotness" rankings and discussions on the board, but did not object to them, even when we pressed the point. So
many posts engaged the "hotness" judgment that many women seemed inured to
being subjected to constant judgments about it, at least in our face-to-face conversations. Focus group participants made no specific objections to this type of "rating."
One woman in our sorority focus group, when pressed, said nothing was wrong with
this listing, because those listed were all women who in "fact" *were* hot. "Veracity"
made the list acceptable. *Why* would anyone object to a listing of girls who were
"hot" as long as the label truly applied to these women? Sorority women were in fact
happy to see that the board included a list of the "hot" women in their group, as the
presence of sexually attractive women—when known publicly—increased
group status, benefiting everybody. It was uniformly flattering, even if they themselves did not make the list. Yet their comments betray a sense of unease. For

example, we asked, "Do you object to this kind of ranking of girls? Does this make you angry?" One responded:

> Maybe it should but it doesn't, I guess because I don't know, it's almost like flattering. I'm like "yeah, that girl is really pretty and I like her too so yeah, if someone says your friend is pretty it's, it's because they're …

As the sorority group would gain status from being home to "hot" women, we wondered if it was perhaps simply the desire for status that determined their positive response to the "hotness" list, and discouraged feminist critique. This was a new sorority and probably in need of recognition and status. They couldn't afford to be critical of a system in which they were trying to excel.

### The judgment process: dual-edged

Yet, how women arrive on the "pretty" or "hot" list is opaque, and a part of the policing process. Our respondents explicitly mentioned that only the women who date a lot and "get noticed" tend to be on the "hottest" lists:

> SARAH:  They're the girls that guys notice. … They are pretty but they also go out a lot and I feel I like if you're not the person who goes out a lot even if you are pretty you're not going to be put on the most attractive girls list.
> JACKIE:  Because like you know if you go out a lot and you represent your sorority … if you make a name for yourself you're like that girl.

Women do not react to this with any sort of feminist anger, with the "Maybe it should but it doesn't …" position being a typical response, one indicating awareness that the system flouts feminist rules, but also distancing the speaker from feminist values. In general, people in our focus groups were not upset even when friends were ranked or judged by their physical appearance. Some seemed to define ranking as dangerous but only regarding unflattering posts or in response to debates about whether a particular woman was attractive or not:

> SARAH:  [I]t's just very unfortunate when people post on that group and someone will post right under it, No that person is not attractive.

These derogatory comments could easily lead into other kinds of criticisms, as in the case of women whose sexual behavior was described as "slutty," discussed on p. 549.

In this way, the women of our sorority focus group began to describe the slippery slope that was being constructed when women were ranked by their physical appearance. As the conversation above indicates, women who are listed as "hot" or "pretty" were labeled as such because they were the ones "who get noticed." When you're noticed, you can be easily criticized as well as praised, as Sarah notes in the comment above. This type of notoriety is what quickly takes women from "flattering" lists to those that respondents described as more harmful, that described them as sluts or, conversely, prudes.

For example, one woman mentioned that she had a friend who'd been the subject of some posts calling her a "fat slut." She found this post hurtful because, in her words, "*she's not fat*": clearly in the face of these insults she felt compelled to respond to the larger of the two; the "slut" aspect seemed to bother her less. But a "fat" girl can't be "hot" according to current gender standards, a negative status that might spill over to friends and sorority. The label of "fat" applied to a good friend, therefore, was damaging, and hence worth a defense. It crowded out the second derogatory term "slut," as we elaborate below. On a related point, when we asked women what types of posts they object to, positive and negative categories appeared to be confused. Notice of any sort is a dual-edged sword. People want to be noticed, but notice only comes in the context of judgments, whether positive or negative, about their bodies and sexual attractiveness. Despite themselves, women responded with trepidation towards negative judgments and relief—even joy—at the positive.

In sum, the unpopularity of feminism as an identity, coupled with young women's overall lack of familiarity with many second-wave feminist arguments, led to a kind of confusion about what a legitimate critique of the board's posts would look like. Women were happy when they or their friends received positive, though judgmental, attention. While they were dismayed by negative remarks, and sometimes fought back against them, they did not tend to object to the type of discourse that subjected women to continuing judgments and rankings. Even when the lack of similar rankings or ratings for men was pointed out, feminist-inspired objections were absent.

## Sluts

In addition to comments about women's bodies, women's sexual behavior was examined and criticized in many posts. Sexual experience and prowess are sometimes praised, sometimes denigrated. The "slut" label is almost as ubiquitous on the board as "hot," and was widely feared as an epithet. Often "slut" was linked to particular women's names and specific allegations around sexual activity. Entire threads documented who gave the "best blow jobs," who had the "kinkiest sex." In such posts positive or negative qualities sometimes could be ambiguous.

Being mentioned as a slut on ACB was not always taken as offensive. As one woman put it:

> I think that like if a girl was posted about on this site and it was about her blow job giving skills and they were positive comments, honestly I don't think she'd be upset. I'm so serious, vs., if she said that she was so bad in bed or whatever she'd be hurtin' more and want it off …

This echoes the above example in which women described a friend discussed on the site as a "fat slut." They were concerned about her being overweight, but not especially about the intimation she had been with "too many" men.

Praise for sexual prowess, however, follows a slippery slope descending into censure. Our focus group interviews showed that this kind of public labeling had concrete consequences in that women termed "hot" received, as many noted in our interviews, significantly more male attention *because* of these posts, which were widely read. Such women were sought out in public spaces—they had been labeled "hot." However, they also ran the risk of being labeled as "sluts" because of their excessive sexual activity, enabled in part—or at least suggested—by their public labeling. Both labels—"hot" and "slut"—therefore carried a potentially negative association.

## Culture police

We concluded that the site functioned overall to police female appearance and sexual behavior. The posts defined through a set of rules what should add up to "hot," while avoiding the negative label of "slut." Women should be thin and sexually attractive, but should not carry their sexual attractiveness, or sexy behavior, to extremes, lest they risk being labeled "slut." The distinctions between these categories requires constant vigilance if boundaries are to be maintained. This could account for women's seemingly obsessive attention to the board, as they seek reassurance that they and their friends are "getting right" a set of subtly shaded categories and boundaries which are difficult to separate in their judgments of their friends, enemies, rivals, and associates, and in their evaluation of themselves.

While men's sexual behavior is sometimes censured on Collegiate ACB as well, they do not come under the same type or degree of criticism leveled at women; certainly there is no comparable dissection of their bodies and "hot" appearance. Heterosexual white men seem, insofar as this can be determined from an anonymous message board, to be the policers; white and Asian women the policed. African American and Hispanic students apparently declined to participate on the board, largely due to concerns about lack of anonymity on campus given their smaller numbers. There are fewer predominantly African American and Hispanic fraternities than white ones, and minority students in our focus groups said they faced greater dangers than whites if their posts could be traced.

The legacy of feminism is in part a level of comfort with sexuality and perhaps, as McRobbie (2008) argues, an increased fluidity of the boundaries of heterosexuality. Yet, we witnessed precisely the opposite on Collegiate ACB and its predecessors, which seem to police these boundaries rather than to enable their fluidity. Douglas introduces the term "enlightened feminism" to describe an alternate perspective on young women's relationship to feminism. In her terms, feminism is assumed (Douglas 2010). Therefore, when sexist behavior—in our case, labeling and ranking women for their appearance and sexual activity, on a website that does not similarly label and rank men—occurs, it is accepted, with a "wink," because we can assume a certain level of feminism as its cultural context.

Yet we found less assumed feminism than simple incomprehension of feminism as a perspective, at least when applied to issues of ranking women's bodies and policing their sexual activity—issues that would rankle any second-waver. Our attempts to elicit a feminist critique of these issues, made in frustration, almost disbelief, fell largely on flat ears. While some survey respondents expressed a negative judgment of the sexism they witnessed on the board and labeled it as such, many did not. Our focus group interviews betrayed a notable lack of objection to these types of posts.

In a final attempt to provoke discussion of feminism in relation to these issues, we planted two posts we considered overtly "feminist" responses or critiques on two different threads on Collegiate ACB, one thread which referred to "hottest girls" and the other to "biggest boobs." Our post called the comments "sexist." What was interesting was the almost total lack of response to our criticism; we were ignored (no posts responded to us at all, and we received three "thumbs down" comments and no "thumbs up"). Rather than opening up a space for feminist critique and discussion, it was entirely silenced within the space and discourse of the board.

## Conclusion

Marwick and boyd (2011) ruminate on the potential imagined audience of different "tweeters" on the social media site Twitter. Perhaps Collegiate ACB is a site where those new to the college scene struggle over the collective "we" of students on a particular college campus. The "feminist" public sphere is particularly in search of a "we" in what is essentially a postfeminist—or at least, a post-second-wave feminist—age. The struggle over various versions of feminist identity—second wave, third wave, postfeminist, non-feminist—attests to the difficulty of forming a "we" posed by contested forms of feminist identity. For this reason, the treatment of feminist issues in the new mediated public spheres is made possible by ubiquitous social media and is crucially important for the terms of contemporary feminist debate. What we have found is that feminism is both denigrated and ever present; the "feminism on the ground" of the college students we interviewed was sometimes evident, yet more often hidden under a variety of perspectives that borrow from antifeminist, postfeminist, and "third-wave" feminist discourses.[8]

Our analysis raises several key issues which are difficult to parse given the current ambivalent and contradictory opinions concerning feminist issues espoused by our respondents. While it's tempting to invoke Pollitt's notion that "women are the only group" allowing, even at times supporting, collective insults, when responding to the absence of critical attitudes toward the rating of women it's too pat and simplistic a position to be explanatory. Most women think they know sexism when they see it. This is clear from our survey. From our focus groups we see that young women want to claim the freedom to be "hot," or to enjoy when friends and sorority sisters are so labeled, and to enjoy the status of associating with such women. Undeniable in the mass audience that the *Fifty Shades of Grey* trilogy enjoys is the presence of many women at least apparently enjoying sexual fantasies that feminists such as Catherine MacKinnon, Andrea Dworkin, and many others might find misogynistic.

But once again, as feminist media scholars, we are left yearning for media industries that highlight more and different choices for women. In a new media environment that supports *Feminista* and a plethora of other explicitly feminist blogs, why is Collegiate ACB the more used, more widely read forum on a wide variety of college campuses? Why were women in our focus groups literally scared to admit they read a feminist blog—one woman put it: "yes, I read blogs—NOT feminist blogs." The entrenched, enduring nature of sexism in our media culture is not natural—it is remarkable, and demands our continuing attention and analysis.[9]

## Notes

1 See Vance (1993) on the Barnard Conference, and McRobbie (2009) for commentary on these issues. See Dworkin and MacKinnon (1988) for their theory of pornography.
2 Denise Walsh points out (personal communication, October 2012) that self-hate is a long-standing issue for subordinated groups. Women are not the only group to vote against their own interests.
3 See websites such as Feminista, Thefbomb.org (younger feminist dialog), www.hercirclee-zine.com, www.themamafesto.com (feminist moms), www.blackademic.com.
4 In reproducing threads and postings from the boards, we disguise the actual names posted; at times we alter the words used so that the posts we quote cannot be traced. All focus group names are quoted pseudonymously.
5 Preliminary groups used volunteers from students in a class taught by Press. Remaining focus groups were comprised of students in a sorority who were familiar with the board.
6 The survey used Morgan's (1996) Feminism Scale—a sociopolitical tool to measure and assess gender role attitudes, goals of feminism, and feminist ideology.
7 The question asked in the online survey was: "Do you think women/men are written about in a sexist or derogatory way?" Students were asked to elaborate on the meaning of these terms. In the focus groups we tended to shy away from direct references to feminism or sexism to avoid biasing student responses. We did note, however, a tendency for students not to identify publicly with feminism; this might have influenced their responses in the more public focus group method, and might explain its occurrence more frequently online.
8 "Third-wave" feminism is sometimes seen as encouraging a new openness around issues of sexual appearance, activity, and expression (Baumgardner and Richards 2010; Hogeland 2001).
9 Ridgeway (2011) offers an interesting explanation for Pollitt, relevant to our analysis, of the specificity of gender domination. She links this to the relationship women have to men requiring constant association, and a constantly linked status.

## References

Baumgardner, J. and A. Richards (2010) *Manifesta [10th Anniversary Edition]: Young Women, Feminism, and the Future*, New York: Farrar, Straus & Giroux.

boyd, d. (2007) *Social Network Sites: Public, Private, or What?* http://apo.org.au/?q=node/4081.

Debold, E. (2012) "Too Many Shades of Grey," *Huffington Post*. http://www.huffingtonpost.com/elizabeth-debold/50-shades-of-grey_b_1459689.html.

DelVecchio, M. (2012) "Anti-Feminist Ideals in *Fifty Shades of Grey*," *Her Circle: A Magazine of Women's Creative Arts and Activism*. http://www.hercircleezine.com/2012/05/02/anti-feminist-ideals-in-fifty-shades-of-grey/.

Douglas, S. J. (2010) *Enlightened Sexism: The Seductive Message That Feminism's Work Is Done*, New York: Times Books.

Dworkin, A. (1981) *Pornography: Men Possessing Women*, New York: Perigee Books.

Dworkin, A. and C. A. MacKinnon (1988) *Pornography and Civil Rights: A New Day for Women's Equality*, Minneapolis: Organizing Against Pornography (734 E. Lake St., Minneapolis 55407).

Gill, R. (2007) "Postfeminist Media Culture: Elements of a Sensibility," *European Journal of Cultural Studies* 10(2): 147–66.

Gill, R. and C. Scharff (2011) *New Femininities: Postfeminism, Neoliberalism and Subjectivity*, London: Palgrave Macmillan.

Hogeland, L. M. (2001) "Against Generational Thinking, or, Some Things that 'Third-Wave' Feminism Isn't," *Women's Studies in Communication* 24(1): 107.

Houvouras, S. and J. C. Carter (2008) "The F Word: College Students' Definitions of a Feminist," *Sociological Forum* 23(2): 234–56.

Hudson, J. (2010) "Gay Teen Suicide Sparks Debate Over Cyber Bullying," *The Atlantic Wire*. http://www.theatlanticwire.com/national/2010/10/gay-teen-suicide-sparks-debate-over-cyber-bullying/22829/.

Kearney, M. C. (2006) *Girls Make Media*, London: Routledge.

McCabe, J. (2005) "What's in a Label? The Relationship between Feminist Self-Identification and 'Feminist' Attitudes among U.S. Women and Men," *Gender & Society* 19(4): 480–505.

McRobbie, A. (2008) "Pornographic Permutations," *Communication Review* 11(3): 225–36.

——(2009) *The Aftermath of Feminism: Gender, Culture and Social Change*, Los Angeles and London: Sage.

Marwick, A. and d. boyd (2011) "To See and Be Seen: Celebrity Practice on Twitter," *Convergence Convergence* 17(2): 139–58.

Maya (2012) "What Katie Roiphe Gets Wrong about 'Fifty Shades of Grey' and Fantasies of Sexual Submission." http://feministing.com/2012/04/16/what-katie-roiphe-gets-wrong-about-fifty-shades-of-grey-and-fantasies-of-sexual-submission/.

Morgan, B. L. (1996) "Putting the Feminism into Feminism Scales: Introduction of a Liberal Feminist Attitude and Ideology Scale (LFAIS)," *Sex Roles* 34(5–6): 359–90.

Peltola, P., M. A. Milkie, and S. Presser (2004) "The 'Feminist' Mystique: Feminist Identity in Three Generations of Women," *Gender & Society* 18(1): 122–44.

Perez, G. (2012) "Fifty Shades of Feminist Criticism," *Fifty Shades of Feminist Criticism*. http://fiftyshadesfeminist.wordpress.com/.

Pollitt, K. (2012) "Women Who Love Republicans Who Hate Them," *The Nation*, August 29. http://www.thenation.com/article/169630/women-who-love-republicans-who-hate-them#.

Ridgeway, C. L. (2011) *Framed by Gender: How Gender Inequality Persists in the Modern World*, New York: Oxford University Press.

Roiphe, K. (2012) "Spanking Goes Mainstream," *The Daily Beast*. http://www.thedailybeast.com/newsweek/2012/04/15/working-women-s-fantasies.html.

Scharff, C. (2011) *Repudiating Feminism: Young Women in a Neoliberal World*, Farnham and Burlington, VT: Ashgate.

Stein, A. (1997) *Sex and Sensibility: Stories of a Lesbian Generation*, Berkeley: University of California Press.

Tasker, Y. and D. Negra (eds.) (2007) *Interrogating Postfeminism: Gender and the Politics of Popular Culture*, Durham, NC: Duke University Press.

Vance, C. S. (ed.) (1993) *Pleasure and Danger: Exploring Female Sexuality*, London: Rivers Oram Press.

# 51

# Gendered networked visualities

## Locative camera phone cultures in Seoul, South Korea

## *Larissa Hjorth*

In a busy café in Seoul's trendy Gangnam area, a young woman drinks coffee. Far from bored or lonely, Soo touches her smartphone like an old friend. After "checking in" on Facebook to show others where she is, she begins to explore her various smartphone photo apps. Soo used to take self-portraits (*sel-ca*) and upload them to Korea's oldest social network site, Cyworld minihompy. However, with the rise of location-aware media like Facebook and Foursquare, she feels less compelled to share images of herself; instead she creates different images of her location. Sharing these ambient images among physically absent yet electronically co-present friends gives her comfort and joy. The sharing allows her to share moments—emotional gestures in a particular time and space—with friends in other co-present spaces. So, while Soo is in a café she also inhabits online spaces whereby physically absent friends are "absent presences" (Gergen 2002).

Soo and her friends take and share up to ten images a day. This is not unusual in Seoul's vibrant mediascape. They view it as a way to be creative and playful with friends when seeing them physically is impossible. The images create a way to both share and memorialize places and experiences. This sharing of ambient gestures via geo-tagged camera phone images also enables friends to catch up serendipitously. Today, Soo liked the shadow cast by the café's flowerpot. She moved through various photo apps until deciding on Instagram. She loved the way she could render the banal image of a flowerpot into something dreamy, whimsical, and of another era. The analogue aesthetics of the app reminded her of a Polaroid. She then uploaded the evocative image onto various social and locative media—Cyworld minihompy, Foursquare and Facebook. On Foursquare she noticed that one of her good friends, Mi-Hyun, had just checked into a café next door. She sent a message with her flowerpot image saying, "Is your view as good as this?" Reading the message almost instantaneously, Mi-Hyun laughed and moved next door to have coffee with Soo.

This vignette depicts a typical scenario in which locative-based services (LBS), referring to services that use Global Positioning Systems (GPS) to locate the user geographically and temporally, are reshaping camera phone practices. In this transformation, they are also reshaping users' experience with place as an overlay of different forms of information. With the added layer of LBS, information about the camera phone images—where and when they were taken—becomes automatic by default. On the one hand, this overlaying of the geographic with the social highlights that place has always mattered to mobile media (Ito 2003 [2002]; Hjorth 2005). Far from eroding place, mobile media amplify the complexities of place as something lived and imagined, geographic and yet psychological. LBS enable mobile media users to create and convey more complex details about a locality. On the other hand, LBS create new motivations for narrating a sense of place and the role of amateur and vernacular photography.

Shifts in contemporary amateur photography highlight the changes in how co-absent co-presence is navigated, performed, and represented. Last century it was the Kodak camera that epitomized amateur photography and played an important role in normalizing notions of the family as well as ritualizing events such as holidays; personal photography as central to the process of identity formation and memor-ialization (Gye 2007: 279). The shift towards camera phones not only changes how we capture, store, and disseminate images but also has "important repercussions for how we understand who we are and how we remember the past" (Gye 2007: 279).

For Daniel Palmer, smartphone photography is distinctive in various ways, with one key feature being the relationship between touch and the image in what he calls an "embodied visual intimacy" (2012: 88). While "touch has long been an important, but neglected, dimension in the history of photography ... the iPhone, held in the palm of the hand, reintroduces a visual intimacy to screen culture that is missing from the larger monitor screen" (2012: 88). The iPhone camera represents a new "universe of reference" whereby smartphones like the iPhone—with their attendant software applications like Instagram, Google Goggles, and Hipstamatic—have cre-ated new ways of thinking about camera phone practices as lying between image and information (Chesher 2012). As Chris Chesher notes, the iPhone "universe of refer-ence" disrupts the genealogy of mass amateur photography.

High-quality camera phones, along with the growth in distribution services via social and locative media, have given rise to new forms of visuality (Pink and Hjorth 2012). While first-generation photo sites like Flickr (Burgess 2007; Mørk Petersen 2009) played a key role in amateur and vernacular photography, the convergence of locative, social and mobile media is producing new types of visuality. These new types of co-present visuality overlay and interweave online and offline cartographies in different ways—maps that require us to consider locality in terms of co-presence rather than co-location (Beaulieu 2010). With the added dimensions of movement and touch becoming important features of camera phones the emphasis on net-worked is shifting to "emplaced" visuality. Images are emplaced in relation to what human geographer Tim Ingold (2008) has called a "meshwork" and entanglement of lines. Images themselves are part of such lines as they are inextricable from the camera and person who took them. In this sense camera phone images are not simply about what they represent (although they are also about that) but are additionally about what is behind, above, below, and to either side.

In the rise of camera phones, women have dominated. In the early uptake around the turn of the century, it was young women in Japan, South Korea, and China who symbolized these new visualities (Hjorth 2007, 2009; Lee 2005, 2009). As Dong-Hoo Lee (2005) notes, South Korean women were quick to embrace camera phone practices with such passion that some even decided to become professional photographers. Behind the stereotypes about camera phone users being narcissistic, these new visualities demonstrate women's changing roles in South Korea society and thus are a site for empowerment.

Although camera phone genres like self-portraiture have blossomed globally, especially with young women users (Hjorth 2007; Lee 2005), vernacular visualities are flourishing in ways that reflect a localized notion of place, social, and identity-making practices. Mobile media such as camera phones play a key role in constructing twenty-first-century user created content (UCC). In particular, mobile media practices have highlighted how relationships between gender, labor, and technology are paradoxically being reinforced (Fortunati 2009; Wajcman et al. 2009) and also potentially subverted (Hjorth 2009). On the one hand, we see more possibility for media empowerment, creativity, and sociality. On the other hand is the potential for more exploitation due the "wireless leash" capacity of mobile media to further blur public and private, online and offline, work and home spaces. Specifically, in the Asia-Pacific region—which has been home to much global production and consumption of mobile media—changing gendered labor practices are reflected in gendered UCC patterns (Hjorth 2009). In locations such as Seoul, the rise of camera phone practices has been synonymous with debates around young women's empowerment (Hjorth 2007; Lee 2005) and emergent forms of intimate politics and publics (Hjorth and Arnold 2013).

This chapter explores the changing role of camera phone practices as they become overlaid with LBS. This second generation of camera phone practices—epitomized by smartphone apps where LBS such as geotagging is often by default—sees new forms of visuality that, in turn, reflect changing representations of women. For the first generation of camera phone studies (Ito and Okabe 2003, 2005, 2006), networked sites like Flickr and YouTube were key to defining aesthetics such as "common banalities" (Mørk Petersen 2009) and "vernacular creativity" (Burgess 2007). However, with the growth in LBS like Foursquare that allows users to "check in" and upload pictures, the relationship between networked visuality and emplaced visuality gets complicated, especially for women. Whereas the first generation of camera phone practices noted gendered differences (Hjorth 2007; Lee 2005), through LBS these gendered visualities take on new dimensions—particularly in terms of their potential "stalker" elements (Gazzard 2011). While notions of privacy differ subject to sociocultural context, women are often victims of LBS's potential for stalking (Cincotta and Ashford 2011).

I explore some of the ambivalences around these emergent visualities and their relationship to gendered modes of performativity. Here, I am repurposing Judith Butler's (1991) notion of performativity in which gender is viewed not as natural or biological but socioculturally constructed through a series of expressions that are regulated. Against homogenized notions of women as a category, Butler argued for culturally and socially nuanced understandings. Feminist Italian scholar Leopoldina Fortunati (2009) argues that we must also account for age and class variations in gendered mobile media practice.

Known for its gendered mobile media innovation in both production and consumption (Hjorth 2007, 2009; Lee 2005), Seoul, South Korea provides a compelling case study for some of the pleasures and problems associated with the rise of location-aware media. Seoul also provides important examples of mobile media as democracy (Kim 2003) and, more recently, a growing ambivalence in light of governmental and corporate surveillance—highlighted by the arrest of bloggers for anti-government sentiment (such as the blogger Minerva) and the scandal over the illegal tracking of Samsung workers (Hjorth 2011a; Lee 2011; Wallace 2012).

This chapter draws on fieldwork done in 2009–12 as part of an Australian Research Council Discovery grant (*Online@AsiaPacific*) with Michael Arnold; we conducted ethnographies in Manila, Melbourne, Seoul, Singapore, Tokyo, and Shanghai. Respondents were recruited through universities, with ages ranging from 18 to 64 years old. The fieldwork consisted of focus groups, surveys, and in-depth interviews. Each year in each location we spoke to 60 respondents. Here I consider ways women use gamified LBS and camera phone images. I reflect upon the relationship between these new playful visualities and generational notions of privacy. I argue that LBS camera phone practices are taking on new gendered visual cartographies that both rehearse and revise traditional Korean notions of place (*bang*) and intimacy (*ilchon*).

## The case study of emplaced visuality: the place of LBS and gender in Korea

Korea offers many traditional and contemporary versions of the *bang* (space/room): *jimjilbang* (public bathhouse), *PC bang*, *DVD bang*, and *noraebang* (music room). Florence Chee (2005), in her ethnography on *PC bang* and the politics of online multiplayer games, argues that these are social spaces operating as "third spaces" between home and work. Hee-jeong Choi describes the *bang* as an independent space for the sharing of ideas that is "static in form, yet flexible in functionality" (2009: 93). In other words, the *bang* has no predetermined purpose; instead the occupants sharing the space actively determine the use.

The *ilchon* (intimacy) has similarly been repurposed by new media. In Korea's once dominant social network site Cyworld minihompy, friends are called *ilchon*, a Korean kinship concept traditionally used to denote one degree of distance from family members (i.e. one's mother is one chon) (Hjorth 2011a; Hjorth and Kim 2005). Popular with one-third of the population for over a decade, Cyworld had been recently overtaken by Facebook in Korea. From avatar customization to camera phone photo taking and sharing, young women's media practices dominated (Hjorth 2007; Lee 2005). However, uses of various types of representation, such as the adoption of *kawaii* culture (i.e. Japanese for cute), differ depending on the individual. Some women use the *kawaii* expression as an ironic gesture, others as code between friends (Hjorth 2009).

For some women respondents, creating and sharing visual cultures through LBS is about a type of girl culture. This girl culture included the use of cute *kawaii* culture (Hjorth 2009) to toy with gender stereotypes as well as evoke emotional responses. *Kawaii* gestures included cute cartoon characters as well as cute *sel-ca* expressions (whereby users hold the camera above their head and look up into the lens. This creates an image of big eyes and relatively small faces). Women respondents were more active not only in the amount of camera phone pictures they took but also in how many they uploaded to sites and also in their commenting on friends' images.

For the women interviewed, part of being a good friend was to respond to a friend's images, from "That looks lovely" to "Wish I were there!" Given the importance of commenting on friends' uploading of images, images rarely lack sociality. Sometimes this tacit etiquette around proving your friendship via image commentary meant that some respondents felt compelled to respond even when they had little to say. But through the act of commenting on images, respondents felt that they linked a co-present sense of place (*bang*) with intimacy (*ilchon*). By commenting on the images, the geotagged visual narratives were linked into a more complex notion of place as not merely geographic and temporal but also emotional and social.

For 30-year-old Kahyun, LBS are "girls' games" in which the in-built game play—i.e. in Foursquare users check in to receive badges—is added onto via unofficial game play. For Kahyun and her friends, playing Foursquare was less about the official game of winning badges and more about playing with camera phone images, commenting and socializing in playful ways. As Kahyun noted, "the games are an excuse in which we can catch up online. ... They create different dimensions to the offline space and provide more chances to socialize." For Kahyun, using LBS games is very much part of her generation's media usage. Her parents only used LBS like Google Maps; since they didn't take camera phone pictures, according to Kahyun, they didn't understand much of the references and contexts. LBS games provided Kahyun and her friends different ways to play with friends in other places. She viewed LBS as "games for girls" because they fostered camera phone sharing by overlaying sociality with place in innovative ways. As Kahyun notes,

> I use Daum Map, Four season, and ittime. I'm using it [LBS] like I would play a game. I let people check where I am or get points. Also I can see where I have visited and how many times I've been there. But my main interest is in socializing with friends in new and creative ways. And the potential to catch up offline by chance.
>
> (Kahyun, 30)

Women respondents spoke of taking and sharing camera phone pictures as engaging the geographic with the social—that is, creating a geosocial co-present experience. One 30-year-old woman, Soo-hyun, described using LBS as a way of narrating of place—by overlaying images and comments onto a place—as highly gendered:

> Usually, women users view it [LBS] as a game to be played and added onto. For example, they record comments or put photos of the places where they've been before. Or they use it [LBS] so that they can get points and coupons to use ... But, male users use it [LBS] to leave their footprints so they can find out how they moved in certain situations. Or check out women. I think they don't have big interests about getting coupons or recording histories through posting photos or comments.
>
> (Soo-hyun, 30)

For Soo, LBS like Facebook Places allow her to be co-present with friends elsewhere. She likes to leave comments when friends visit and take pictures of places. It is also a great way to "bump" into friends in her physical proximity. Soo states:

> My friends and I lead such hectic lives it can sometimes be impossible to catch up. But sometimes I see that a friend is nearby via Facebook Places and so we can share a quick coffee [face-to-face]. Commenting on people's photos is a great way to stay in perpetual contact. Sometimes I know that a friend has taken a picture just for me because of the content and message. Sharing pictures can make me feel closer with friends even when I can't see them [physically].
>
> (Soo-hyun, 30)

However, not all LBS games positively reflect Korean contemporary life. For some respondents LBS games reflected the increasing pressure for the young to be part of *Chalnajok* (Cho 2009). While "*Chal-na*" means "instant," "*jok*" refers to a tribe (Lee 2009). Users attributed their interest in taking and sharing pictures to the pressure to be part of the *Chalnajok*, in which mobile media play a key role. One woman, Nara Ara, aged 27 noted:

> Sometimes I don't want to take endless pictures and share them. I may be feeling sad or be having a bad hair day. But then when I get pictures from my friends this makes me want to return the feelings.
>
> (Nara Ara, 27)

Nara Ara's comments illustrate the compulsion for LBS camera phone sharing as part of gift-giving (Mauss 1954). Some of the earlier mobile media studies highlighted how practices such as SMS (short messaging service) reinforce sociocultural notions of power and repository by reflecting gift-giving rituals (Taylor and Harper 2003). These rituals around often-tacit etiquette regarding mobile media become even more complex when social and locative media are added to the mix. Many of the expectations were linked to women's age—younger respondents felt more compelled to comment on every image their friends posted, whereas older respondents were more likely to just comment on a few but in more detail. Sometimes they would use the excuse of commenting on a picture to let their friends know that they were thinking of them, or to reflect upon previous shared experiences. Nara Ara feels compelled to share because her friends share. This feeling of obligation plays an important role in the frequency of maintaining mobile media contact. Etiquette implies an expectation that mobile media users are "always on" and thus always responsive.

While LBS games provide more opportunity to catch up they also provide strangers with more information about users and their activities. This has led to website activists such as "Please Rob Me" which seek to alert people to the costs associated with location-awareness (www.pleaserobme.com). Kahyun did note that location-based games have the potential for surveillance, especially from strangers. She and her female friends were very careful about their privacy settings. This encouraged them to take less *sel-ca* and more abstract or ambient images of inanimate objects.

Claiming privacy issues, Kahyun said that she didn't share *sel-ca* via LBS contexts. When she was younger she loved taking *sel-ca* with friends and sharing via minihompy, but now she felt LBS was not a good context for it:

> As a woman I am conscious that leaving information about where I go isn't always a good thing. My friends and I now tend to share pictures of abstract and familiar objects rather than sel-ca. Uploading images of yourself in places is boring for friends and also gives strangers too much information.
>
> (Kahyun, 30)

Kahyun said such worries about stalking seemed to be less of an issue for the male players she knew. But this difference around privacy was not just between women and men users, but also generational. Typifying cultural, gender, and generational differences, Kahyun contrasted her parents' trust of the online, evident in their open use of social media, to her own generation, which often tried to create boundaries between different audiences (i.e. work/private, family/friends). For Kahyun, the role of social and mobile media in "collapsing contexts" (boyd 2010)—that is, the bleeding between different social groups (family, friends, and work colleagues), platforms, and media—meant that she and her friends often tried to distinguish the types of material they share with different audiences. She noted:

> My parents are very open in their use of Cyworld minihompy. But for me and my friends there are some things we share that we don't want everyone seeing, especially parents and grandparents. As they don't take many photos they don't understand the context and the references. So I prefer to edit my settings so that they can't see many of my photos, it's easier that way.
>
> (Kahyun, 30)

Not all surveillance is ominous. In fact, the rise of LBS has allowed parents to keep a "friendly eye" on children at a distance. This is a global phenomenon—current estimates are that over 80 million parents track their children via locative media (Sengupta 2012; Schofield Clark 2012; Schofield Clark and Sywyj 2012). For a 40-year-old father and mother, social and locative media helped keep an eye on their teenage daughter and her friends. Just like Japanese mothers, for whom the mobile phone functioned as a "mum in the pocket" (Matsuda 2009), the parents said they could be a "friendly, caring eye" in monitoring their daughter via minihompy and flags. This parental überveillance became important when one of their daughter's friends demonstrated suicidal tendencies: The parents intervened and created a parental network to help youth with emotional health issues. So, despite the dark side of surveillance as demonstrated in Korean corporate and government examples like the pseudonymous netizen Minerva (a blogger jailed for "predicting" President Lee's financial issues) and the Samsung SDI mobile tracking scandal (in which Samsung illegally tracked workers trying to organize a union meeting), locative media can enable familial benevolence.

As discussed by the women interviewed, camera phone images within LBS were intentionally meant to be ambient and creative. Many of these women had noted a sharp distinction in the types of images they took and shared: less *sel-ca* images and more poetic gestures—many tried to think creatively about how they represented the place. They wanted more than just a postcard image; instead they wanted to convey an emotion to other co-present friends about their experience. This motivation was clearly about revising Korean notions of place (*bang*) with intimates (*ilchon*). By using different smartphone photo apps, respondents tried to inscribe a sense of place with emotion. This practice is what anthropologist Sarah Pink identifies as the "multisensorality of images." That is, they are located in "the production and consumption of images as happening in movement, and consider them as components of configurations of place" (Pink 2011: 4). Drawing on Tim Ingold's (2008) conceptualization of place as "entanglement," Pink notes, "Thus, the 'event' where photographs are produced and consumed becomes not a meeting point in a network of connections but an intensity of entangled lines in movement ... a meshwork of moving things" (2011: 8). In this meshwork of moving things, LBS camera phone images help reinforce traditional notions of place, just as they help transform the relationship between experiencing and recording a place. A 28-year-old woman told us:

> Here [LBS games] place is clearly a shared experience, reflecting the Korean bang. I use it [LBS games] to share my feeling or beautiful photos with others whenever I visit new places. These pictures are about a feeling, a smell, a touch. Or sometimes I use it [LBS games] when I'm curious who is in the same place with me. ... I think using it [LBS] changes the way I record a place rather than the way I experience a place. Getting points or stickers makes me to think about the places more meaningfully.

What is especially pertinent in these comments is the fact that she said LBS "changes the way I *record* a place rather than the way I *experience* a place." This is a curious differentiation. Does not the recording of the place affect the way it is relived and re-experienced as part of mnemonic narrations? In this way, recording brings together the *social* and *spatial*, or, in the case of Korea, the *bang* and the *ilchon*. Here we see Ingrid Richardson and Rowan Wilken's (2012) post-phenomenological argument for understanding place as a series of "placings" overlaid with entangled forms of co-presence and moving information. Camera phone practices contribute to a changing relationship between performativity, memory, and place. Rather than operating to memorialize place, camera phone practices, especially through LBS networks, are creating playful performances around the movement of co-presence, place, and placing that are gendered. And these gendered playful visualities vis-à-vis gamified LBS require us to reflect upon the changing nature of location and information.

## Conclusion: locating the gender

While LBS have attracted much analysis recently, gender has been relatively overlooked—despite the fact that gender informs the nature of mobile media and gaming cultures. As a new form of UCC, LBS camera phone practices are demonstrating emerging forms of visual and geospatial cultures that are informed by localized gendered contexts. Although second-generation gamified LBS like Foursquare are in their infancy, this is an area of growing diversity and complexity within mobile media and communication. In particular, LBS are changing how we visualize intimate cartographies though shifting camera phone practices. These gendered images' visualities take on new dimensions—particularly in terms of the potential for stalking (Gazzard 2011). While Korean notions of privacy differ dramatically from the Anglophone context (Lee 2011), women are often the victims of stalking that LBS enable (Cincotta and Ashford 2011).

The increased proliferation of camera phone images encouraged by the way in which LBS link place and intimacy gives way to two directions. On the one hand, surveyed respondents often did not take pictures of themselves, mindful of how these geospatial visualities could be taken out of context by strangers. Constructing boundaries around different audiences played a key role in LBS camera phone practices as a relatively generational phenomenon. Just as camera phone genres like *sel-ca* are generational, so too are LBS camera phoneurs. On the other hand, through the deployment of photo apps, LBS camera phones evoke a "multisensorial" dimension of place to co-present intimates. This Korean context, then, suggests the need for sociocultural feminist readings of LBS and camera phone practices as these move into new cartographies of place-making overlaid with playful socialities.

## Acknowledgments

I would like to thank Jungyoun Moon.

## References

Beaulieu, A. (2010) "From Co-location to Co-presence: Shifts in the Use of Ethnography for the Study of Knowledge," *Social Studies of Science* 40(3): 453–70.

boyd, d. (2010) "Social Network Sites as Networked Publics: Affordances, Dynamics, and Implications," in Z. Papachararissi (ed.) *A Networked Self*, London: Routledge, pp. 39–58.

Burgess, J. E. (2007) "Vernacular Creativity and New Media," doctoral dissertation. http://eprints.qut.edu.au/16378/.

Butler, J. (1991) *Gender Trouble*, London: Routledge.

Chee, F. (2005) "Understanding Korean Experiences of Online Game Hype, Identity, and the Menace of the 'Wang-tta'," presented at DIGRA 2005 Conference: Changing Views: Worlds in Play, Canada.

Chesher, C. (2012) "Between Image and Information: The iPhone Camera in the History of Photography," in Larissa Hjorth, Jean Burgess, and Ingrid Richardson (eds.), *Studying Mobile Media: Cultural Technologies, Mobile Communication, and the iPhone*, New York: Routledge, pp. 98–117.

Cho, H.-J. (2009) "Youth and Technology in Seoul," presented at the *Inter-Asia Culture Typhoon Conference*, June, Tokyo.

Choi, H.-J. (2009) "The City, Self, and Connections: Transyouth and Urban Social Networking in Seoul," in S. Hemelryk Donald, T. Anderson, and D. Spry (eds.) *Youth, Society and Mobile Media in Asia*, London and New York: Routledge, pp. 88–107.

Cincotta, K. and K. Ashford (2011) "The New Privacy Predators," *Women's Health* (November). http://www.purehacking.com/sites/default/files/uploads/2011_11_00_Australian_Womens_Health_November.pdf.

de Souza e Silva, A. and J. Frith (2012) *Mobile Interfaces in Public Spaces: Locational Privacy, Control and Urban Sociability*, New York: Routledge.

de Souza e Silva, A. and L. Hjorth (2009) "Playful Urban Spaces: A Historical Approach to Mobile Games," *Simulation and Gaming* 40(5): 602–25.

Farman, J. (2011) *Mobile Interface Theory*, London: Routledge.

Fortunati, L. (2009) "Gender and the Mobile Phone," in G. Goggin and L. Hjorth (eds.) *Mobile Technologies: From Telecommunications to Media*, London: Routledge, pp. 23–34.

Gazzard, A. (2011) "Location, Location, Location: Collecting Space and Place in Mobile Media," *Convergence: The International Journal of Research into New Media Technologies* 17(4): 405–17.

Gergen, K. J. (2002) "The Challenge of Absent Presence," in J. E. Katz and M. Aakhus (eds.) *Perpetual Contact: Mobile Communication, Private Talk, Public Performance*, Cambridge: Cambridge University Press, pp. 227–41.

Gordon, E. and A. de Souza e Silva (2011) *Net Locality*, Chichester: John Wiley.

Gye, L. (2007) "Picture This," *Continuum: Journal of Media & Cultural Studies* 21(2): 279–88.

Hjorth, L. (2005) "Postal Presence: The Persistence of the Post Metaphor in Current SMS/MMS Practices," in *Fibreculture Journal* 6: Mobilities, New Social Intensities and the Coordinates of Digital Networks. http://journal.fibreculture.org/issue6/.

——(2007) "Snapshots of Almost Contact," *Continuum* 21(2): 227–38.

——(2009) *Mobile Media in the Asia-Pacific: Gender and the Art of Being Mobile*, London and New York: Routledge.

——(2011a) "Locating the Online: Creativity and User-created Content in Seoul," *Media International Australia* 141: 118–27.

——(2011b) "Mobile Spectres of Intimacy: The Gendered Role of Mobile Technologies in Love—Past, Present and Future," in R. Ling and S. Campbell (eds.) *The Mobile Communication Research Series*, vol. II: *Mobile Communication: Bringing Us Together or Tearing Us Apart?*, Edison, NJ: Transaction Books, pp. 37–60.

Hjorth, L. and M. Arnold (2013) *Online@AsiaPacific*, New York: Routledge.

Hjorth, L. and H. Kim (2005) "Being There and Being Here: Gendered Customising of Mobile 3G Practices through a Case Study in Seoul," *Convergence* 11(2): 49–55.

Hjorth, L., B. Na, and J.-S. Huhh (2009) "Games of Gender: A Case Study on Women Who Play Games in Seoul, South Korea," in L. Hjorth and D. Chan (eds.) *Gaming Cultures and Place in the Asia-Pacific Region*, London: Routledge, pp. 273–88.

Ingold, T. (2008) "Bindings against Boundaries: Entanglements of Life in an Open World," *Environment and Planning A* 40(8): 1796–810.

Ito, M. (2003 [2002]) "Mobiles and the Appropriation of Place," *Receiver* 8. http://academic.evergreen.edu/curricular/evs/readings/itoShort.pdf.

Ito, M. and D. Okabe (2003) "Camera Phones Changing the Definition of Picture-Worthy," *Japan Media Review*. www.ojr.org/japan/wireless/1062208524.php.

——(2005) "Intimate Visual Co-Presence," paper presented at Ubicomp, Takanawa Prince Hotel, Tokyo, Japan, September 11–14. www.itfisher.com/mito.

——(2006) "Everyday Contexts of Camera Phone Use: Steps Towards Technosocial Ethnographic Frameworks," in J. Höflich and M. Hartmann (eds.) *Mobile Communication in Everyday Life: An Ethnographic View*, Berlin: Frank and Timme, pp. 79–102.

Kim, S. D. (2003) "The Shaping of New Politics in the Era of Mobile and Cyber Communication," in K. Nyiri (ed.) *Mobile Democracy*, Vienna: Passagen Verlag, pp. 317–26.

Lee, D.-H. (2005) "Women's Creation of Camera Phone Culture," *Fibreculture Journal* 6. http://www.fibreculture.org/journal/issue6/issue6_donghoo_print.html.

——(2009) "Re-imaging Urban Space: Mobility, Connectivity, and a Sense of Place," in G. Goggin and L. Hjorth (eds.) *Mobile Technologies*, London and New York: Routledge, pp. 235–51.

Lee, K. S. (2011) "Interrogating 'Digital Korea': Mobile Phone Tracking and the Spatial Expansion of Labour Control," *Media International Australia* 141: 107–17.

Matsuda, M. (2009) "Mobile Media and the Transformation of the Family," in G. Goggin and L. Hjorth (eds.) *Mobile Technologies*, London and New York: Routledge, pp. 62–72.

Mauss, M. (1954) *The Gift*, London: Kegan Paul.

Mørk Petersen, S. (2009) "Common Banality: The Affective Character of Photo Sharing, Everyday Life and Produsage Cultures," unpublished Ph.D. thesis, ITU Copenhagen.

Palmer, D. S. V. (2012) "iPhone Photography: Mediating Visions of Social Space," in Larissa Hjorth, Jean Burgess, and Ingrid Richardson (eds.) *Studying Mobile Media: Cultural Technologies, Mobile Communication, and the iPhone*, New York: Routledge, pp. 85–97.

Pink, S. (2009) *Doing Sensory Ethnography*, London: Sage Publications.

——(2011) "Sensory Digital Photography: Re-thinking 'Moving' and the Image," *Visual Studies* 26(1): 4–13.

Pink, S. and L. Hjorth (2012) "Emplaced Cartographies: Reconceptualising Camera Phone Practices in an Age of Locative Media," *Media International Australia* 145: 145–55.

Richardson, I. and R. Wilken (2012) "Parerga of the Third Screen: Mobile Media, Place, and Presence," in R. Wilken and G. Goggin (eds.) *Mobile Technology and Place*, New York: Routledge, pp. 198–212.

Schofield Clark, L. (2012) *The Parent App: Understanding Families in the Digital Age*, New York: Oxford University Press.

Schofield Clark, L. and L. Sywyj (2012) "Mobile Intimacies among Refugee Teens and Their Parents," *Feminist Media Studies* 12(4): 485–95.

Sengupta, S. (2012) "'Big Brother'? No, It's Parents," *New York Times*, June 25. http://tinyurl.com/aysm5ud.

Taylor, A. and R. Harper (2003) "The Gift Of Gab? A Design Oriented Sociology of Young People's Use of Mobiles," *Journal of Computer Supported Cooperative Work* 12(3): 267–96.

Villi, M. (2010) "Visual Mobile Communication: Camera Phone Photo Messages as Ritual Communication and Mediated Presence," Academic dissertation, Aalto University School of Art and Design, Helsinki.

Wajcman, J., M. Bittman, and J. Brown (2009) "Intimate Connections: The Impact of the Mobile Phone on Work Life Boundaries," in G. Goggin and L. Hjorth (eds.) *Mobile Technologies*, London and New York: Routledge, pp. 9–22.

Wallace, R. (2012) "Free Speech Fight over Arrest of Seoul Satirist," *Weekend Australian*, April 7–8: 9.

# 52

# Gendering the Arab Spring

## Arab women journalists/activists, "cyberfeminism," and the sociopolitical revolution

## Sahar Khamis

Any observer of the so-called Arab Spring, the massive wave of political revolt that has been sweeping the Arab region since 2011, could not help but notice the visible role that women have been playing in it. Hundreds of thousands of Arab women throughout the region, including in some of the most traditional, conservative countries, like Yemen and Bahrain, took to the streets, alongside men, calling for an end to dictatorship and repression and demanding dignity and freedom (Khamis 2011; Radsch 2011, 2012). In doing so, they were not confining themselves to stereotypical gender roles, such as nurturing or supporting men in their struggle for freedom. Rather, they were often in the front lines of resistance, risking their lives, exposed to the dangers of arrest or assault. The Arab Spring unveiled "numerous examples of courageous Arab women heroes risking not only their reputation but also their physical safety for the sake of reform" (Al-Malki *et al.* 2012: 81).

However, beside this political struggle that has been, and still is, taking place in many parts of the Arab world an equally pressing *gender-specific* struggle is ongoing, namely: women's struggle to secure political and social gains despite many challenges, such as reactionary social forces, the rise of political Islam, the imposition of a top-down *cosmetic feminism*, which only serves those in power, and an *unsafe public space*, which poses the risk of rape, humiliation, and harassment. Although Arab women fought alongside men to overcome dictatorship and autocracy, "unlike men, women face two battles: the first for political change and the second to obtain a real change of their societal status to become fully equal to their male counterparts" (Alamm 2012: 14).

Here I explore, through in-depth personal interviews, how a group of young Arab women journalists/activists from Egypt, Syria, Libya, Yemen, and Bahrain are redefining activism, empowerment, and resistance, and their perceptions of the most important opportunities, threats, and uncertainties for women in their countries. Most importantly, I analyze their reliance on "cyberfeminism" (Daniels 2009; Fernandez *et al.* 2003; Gajjala 2003) to launch a parallel sociopolitical revolution, through mobilization, documentation, and education, to combat discrimination, harassment, and all forms of abuse.

## Redefining activism, empowerment, and resistance

I am an active journalist, not just a political activist … my first responsibility is deconstructing the passive citizen, through encouraging people to demand their political and social rights. As a woman activist, however, I have another responsibility, which is raising awareness about women's issues and helping them to fight for their rights. Both of these struggles, in my opinion, are ongoing and interrelated. You can't separate one from the other.
(Nada Al Wadi, personal interview, November 2, 2012, Washington, DC)

This was the answer that Bahraini journalist/activist Nada Al Wadi, who was forced to flee after being detained and threatened by Bahraini authorities due to her offline and online political activism, gave in response to the question: "How do you define activism?"Answering the same question, other journalists/activists endorsed a new form of grassroots activism that comes from women themselves; it is *bottom up*, rather than top down; *horizontal*, rather than vertical; and gives women a chance to make their voices heard. As Al Wadi puts it: "I don't want to speak for women, I want women to speak for themselves. That's the whole point!" Likewise, Honey Al Sayed, a Syrian journalist and former host of a popular radio show for seven years, who is currently based in the US after fleeing violence-torn Syria, describes her show's main mission as "giving women a platform to express their needs, fears, and demands, not telling them what to think, say, or do" (Honey Al Sayed, personal interview, October 10, 2012, Washington, DC).

It is for these reasons that these journalists/activists collectively denounced *state-manufactured activism* that is vertically imposed on women through structured political parties and organizations, or even co-opted nongovernmental organizations (NGOs), which operate under the governments' umbrella and are sponsored and supported by them. "These are all fake types of activism that do not truly represent the average Arab woman's goals, needs, or agenda. Women are becoming more aware and more skeptical of such efforts," explains Rihab Elhaj, a US-based Libyan activist and co-founder of the "New Libya Foundation," who worked earlier as a producer with *El Hurra* satellite television channel (Rihab Elhaj, personal interview, October 13, 2012, Washington, DC).

Answering the parallel question "Do you consider yourself to be an activist?" they all agreed that they are engaged in various forms of activism(s), both online and offline, and described themselves as: *ambassadors* of the truth, *agents* of positive change, and *prophets* of goodwill and kind deeds. As Elhaj puts it: "As a journalist with a good cause, my job is to engage in a new form of *jihad*, which doesn't take place in the battlefield, but rather in the social field, and doesn't rely on weapons, but rather on words."

With this understanding of activism comes a parallel definition of empowerment as women's ability to help themselves; rely on their own resources; and advocate for their own causes. In other words, they perceived empowerment as an indigenous and autonomous phenomenon which must be framed, operationalized, and carried out by women. As Yamine Hani, an Egyptian journalist/activist who works on the foreign desk at *Al Akhbar* national daily newspaper explains:

> Empowerment can only be self-defined and enacted by women themselves for themselves. It implies that women should not wait for others to do things for them. There is no such thing in history as someone granting you your rights on a silver plate. You have to earn them yourself. This is exactly what Arab women should do.
>
> (Yasmine Hani, personal interview, November 1, 2012, Washington, DC)

Hani adds:

> At the heart of this empowerment lies a sincere desire to get rid of the deeply entrenched culture of passivity, submission, and obedience, which has been passed on from one generation to the next, and which negatively impacted Arab women and hampered their progress for a long time, and to replace it with a new culture of free thinking and acting.

One point that all the interviewees agreed on was that "Arab women could be their own worst enemies," if they internalize their subordination; accept isolating and marginalizing themselves; decline to go out and fight for their rights; and fail to organize through effective grassroots movements and organizations. All the interviewees, however, denounced the uncritical borrowing of Western notions of feminism and empowerment (Khamis 2010), which ignore the specifics of Arab women's sociopolitical, cultural, and religious contexts. As Fahmia Al Fotih, a Yemeni journalist/activist who is an analyst with the UN Population Fund, puts it: "How can you simply import Western notions of feminism and empowerment which are born in the US or Europe and apply them blindly to a country which faces many serious political, social, economic, and infrastructural challenges like Yemen? How can this work?" (personal interview, Fahmia Al Fotih, October 2, 2012, Washington, DC). Similarly, all the other interviewees saw a need to contextualize Western notions of feminism and empowerment within the unique frameworks of their own societies, which impose different sets of constraints, challenges, and limitations on women. These include infrastructural and economic challenges, staggeringly high illiteracy rates among Arab women, the poor quality of education, reactionary social forces, patriarchy, and misogyny, which are more pressing in tribal, conservative societies, like Libya and Yemen, but are still existent in other countries, such as Egypt and Syria, which have a longer history of women's participation in political and social spheres.

As for their understanding of resistance, they saw it as a multi-folded process encompassing both political and social dimensions that are closely interlinked and interrelated (Khamis 2010). As Al Sayed explains:

> Our job as women activists and journalists *is politicizing the social and socializing the political by drawing attention to women's* specific needs, demands, and causes and making sure they are taken seriously and incorporated in laws and

legislations. For political reform to happen, social reform is also needed. They are parts of one interconnected, vicious circle.

Similarly, Hani remarks:

> Our battle is not just fought in Tahrir Square alongside men to oust a corrupt dictator and reform the political system, although we contributed significantly to this struggle. Our battle is also fought in everyday life, through our newspaper articles, media shows, online social media forums, and social circles, to demand our rights as women.

This multifaceted sociopolitical struggle asserts these women's position as members of a "subaltern counterpublic" (Fraser 1992) who are forming resistance communities in political and social domains, both online and offline. By doing so, they are establishing the missing link between private spheres, which have been traditionally (mis)perceived as the feminine domain, and public spheres, (mis)perceived as the masculine domain, through increasing the visibility of women's issues and cultivating support for them in the reordering of their transitioning societies.

## Three functions for "cyberfeminism": mobilization, documentation, and education

The remarkable role in the Arab Spring of "cyberactivism," defined as "the act of using the Internet to advance a political cause that is difficult to advance offline" (Howard 2011: 145), led these journalists/activists to draw upon "cyberfeminism," defined as "the innovative ways women are using digital technologies to re-engineer their lives" (Daniels 2009: 103), to raise awareness about women's issues and overcome the challenges confronting them.

We should avoid the (mis)perception that gender is a "unified category and, by implication, that digital technologies mean the same thing to all women across differences of race, class, sexuality" (Daniels 2009: 103). Nonetheless, "for many women, including themselves in these new technologies means including themselves in internetworked global feminism" (2009: 106). Furthermore, reliance on new technologies enables "the very people who are excluded from mainstream society ... to include themselves in these new technologies on their own terms" (2009: 106). The outcome of such an inclusion, as Gajjala puts it, is that "they can see themselves as protagonists of the revolution" (2003: 49). This best describes Arab women activists, both literally and metaphorically.

Taking into account these women's adoption of a grassroots, bottom-up, horizontal view of activism, it is only natural that they found new media, especially social media, to be the most effective and relevant tools to use, due to their immediacy, interactivity, accessibility, affordability, and wide reception by a diverse audience, both nationally and internationally (Bennett 2008; Coleman 2005). Therefore, they are not relying on an "'old' cyberfeminism, characterized by a utopian vision of a postcorporeal woman corrupting patriarchy" (Daniels 2009: 102), but instead a "new" cyberfeminism, which is more about "confronting the top-down from the bottom-up" (Fernandez *et al.* 2003: 22–3).

As Al Sayed remarks:

> These new media are the *people's media*, rather than the *government's media*, they put people in charge, allow their voices to be heard, and enable them to connect and spread their messages. This makes them especially suitable for supporting the causes of marginalized groups, such as women, minorities, and political dissidents.

Moreover, these new media were found to be especially helpful for women who live in socially segregated, traditional societies, such as Yemen, where women are largely excluded from the public sphere.

> Being online means giving women a *window* through which they can see, and be seen by, the rest of the world. This helps them overcome their social isolation, at least in the virtual world, through communicating with both men and women, a privilege they cannot enjoy in everyday life in Yemeni society.
>
> (Al Fotih)

A major challenge perceived by all the interviewees was the unsafe public space during and after the Arab Spring. This ranged from sexual harassment to physical violence and virginity testing in Egypt, detention and persecution in Bahrain, and rape on a massive scale in Syria and Libya. The purpose of such practices is intimidating women and discouraging their political participation. The women activists deployed three principal strategies, namely: mobilization, documentation, and education to overcome this challenge.

The mobilization strategy was evident in the efforts of Rihab Elhaj, who, with the help of other Libyan women activists, founded an online group named RAIL or "Rape and Abuse in Libya." The main purpose of this group, as Elhaj explains, is raising awareness about the magnitude of this serious problem; estimating the number of women who suffered from rape or abuse, which is not an easy task due to the social stigmatization that results in many of these cases going unreported; and securing help and support for these women, many of whom fled to refugee camps in neighboring Tunisia. "This online group helps us to coordinate our efforts, spread the word about this problem, connect with these women, and secure the needed help and support for them, whether in the form of medical services, psychological counseling, or financial assistance," Elhaj elucidates. Moreover, Elhaj, with the help of two other Libyan women activists, founded the "Libya Outreach" group online in February 2011, shortly after the eruption of the revolution, in an effort to inform the world about what was going on, in general, and what was happening to women, in particular, to boost international awareness about the many challenges confronting Libyan women, their deteriorating situation, and the possible ways through which they could be helped and supported. Likewise, Honey Al Sayed indicated that she is using her new program, which is broadcast online via Skype, through the new internet-based channel named "Syria-Li" (translated as "Syria is mine"), to rally international support for Syrian women who are rape victims and/or refugees, many of whom fled to neighboring Turkey, through increasing the visibility of these disadvantaged groups, both nationally and internationally, and disclosing their sufferings and hardships, in the hope of securing the needed medical, economic, and social support for them.

Both Elhaj and Al Sayed described their main job as being about securing maximum support for rape and abuse victims and/or refugees, who are by far the most vulnerable groups of women. They both acknowledged the difficulty of finding out the exact numbers of women who fall under these categories, reaching out to them, and providing them with the needed assistance. "It is for these reasons that social media play a crucial role in tackling these issues, due to their anonymity, accessibility, interactivity, and broad international reach," Al Sayed indicates.

The documentation strategy was clearly evident in the "eyewitness" accounts which some of these journalists/activists were able to obtain and upload online. For example, Yasmine Hani joined many protests that took place in Cairo, both during and after the revolution, and was able to capture powerful images of her fellow women protestors being beaten, harassed, or arrested and to upload them online via her Facebook page, in addition to tweeting about them. "I was lucky enough to be only tear gassed during these protests, but I used my cell phone and digital camera to document the brutality and abuse that some of my best women friends suffered from during street demonstrations and clashes in Cairo," Hani remarks. "The power of these new social media tools lies in their proliferating and snowballing effect. If I tag 40 people with these photos on Facebook, they will, in turn, tag another 40 or 50 people and so on, resulting in an expanding circle of receivers," she adds.

Hani also hails the immediacy of these social media tools, which ensures that important events will get instant coverage and attention at home and abroad:

> When the Egyptian activist Esraa Abdel Fattah was arrested in 2008, very few people knew about it at that time, as it was not tweeted or posted on Facebook. Therefore, it did not really attract enough attention or trigger strong reaction. However, when the Egyptian activist Asmaa' Mahfouz was arrested and subjected to a military trial after the revolution, everybody knew about it immediately, thanks to Twitter, and an international campaign was launched calling for her release. Eventually, she was "released with a hashtag," as some Western media outlets commented on the incident.

Likewise, the Bahraini journalist Nada Al Wadi was detained and questioned by the authorities, before fleeing the country, because she dared to use her cell phone and digital camera to document what was happening to her fellow citizens, and specifically Bahraini women activists, at the hands of security forces:

> I told the police officers who detained me and interrogated me that I was just doing my job as a journalist by recording these images, but they were not happy about it, of course. I wanted the whole world to see the bravery and courage of women, in a tiny, conservative, Gulf country, who flooded

the streets to protest and call for their basic human rights, and the violence, brutality, and arrest they were subjected to. I felt that documenting these incidents, through uploading them on Facebook, writing about them on my blog, and tweeting on them, so that the whole world will instantly see them, was at the heart of my responsibility, as a good citizen and a good journalist.

Finally, all the interviewees agreed that new social media could play an important educational role in combating this unsafe public space in two different ways, namely: educating women about their rights as citizens and empowering them with the tools and resources to fight for them, as well as educating society about the dangers of these negative practices against women and why they should be stopped.

The first type of education was best exemplified in the online-based "Hana Naas Center" (named after a Libyan woman activist who fought for women's rights). As one of its founders, Rihab Elhaj, explains, this aims to provide Libyan women with educational and employment opportunities, through scholarships, jobs, and funds for small projects. As Elhaj contends:

> As long as women are ignorant and economically dependent on men, they can never be empowered, and the cycle of humiliation and harassment is likely to go on. Educating women and helping them to be economically sufficient is the best way to empower them and, therefore, enable them to break this evil, vicious cycle.

As for educating society against these dangerous practices, Honey Al Sayed hailed the power of "positive media" used to tackle the most pressing challenges and problems facing society. As she stated:

> I always try through my programs, whether the one that I hosted on radio for seven years before or the new one that is broadcasted online via Skype, to spread a positive message by educating people about the dangers of malpractices against women, such as violence, harassment, and rape. I always host religious, legal, and medical experts to talk about these social ills and the best ways to fight them.

Likewise, interviewees mentioned that they use their journalistic skills, whether through mainstream media venues or via online-based citizen journalism, to speak against these negatives practices, raise awareness about them on a local, regional, and international scale, educate society about their hazardous ramifications, and empower women to stand up for themselves by reporting these incidents and seeking the needed help.

The above examples clearly reveal that "opportunities to apply considerable ... pressure for reforms are now available through digital media networks ... The next social movement may well launch demonstrations from desktops and cellular phones. It may write its own news and gain large audiences for it" (Bennett 2008: 20). They are also indicative of the existence of a high level of genuine, autonomous e-citizenship among these young Arab women activists, who were able to put forward their own agendas and make their voices heard. To do so, they were able to take advantage of the internet, which "appeals to autonomous e-citizens, who see it as a relatively free space in which untrammeled creativity and acephalous networks can flourish" (Coleman 2008: 192).

## Looking ahead: opportunities and threats

This chapter explored the multiple roles played by young Arab women journalists/ activists who used "cyberfeminism" to launch a parallel sociopolitical revolution, not only resisting dictatorship, autocracy, and corruption on the political level, but also fighting repression, violence, and harassment against women on the social level. Their activisms linked political and social domains, private and public spheres, local and global audiences, online and offline activities, as well as mainstream and citizen journalism. They worked to combat the unsafe public space that threatens Arab women, through the three strategies of mobilization, documentation, and education, using new social media tools.

Looking ahead, each of the interviewees saw clear opportunities for the advancement of women in their respective countries. However, they agreed that much more needs to be done to keep the heat on the governments in post-revolutionary countries and to positively shape the agendas of governments in favor of women's issues in the countries which are still struggling for freedom. One of the best opportunities they all saw was the overlap between the future of women's activism and youth activism. As Hani suggested:

> After the Arab Spring, youth and women could be said to be two sides of the same coin when it comes to activism. Youth constitute almost 70 percent of Arab societies. They are the critical mass, which is proactive, dynamic, and technologically savvy. They are creating closely intertwined circles of trust, both online and offline, that trickle down to wider segments of the public and are, therefore, capable of breaking the spiral of silence that once characterized Arab societies. Therefore, they are truly capable of shaping the future of their countries. Today, women are riding the same wagon with youth and heading in the right direction of reforming their societies. Young women are the gateway for change in Arab societies.

In this context, Hani hails the rise of young Arab women public opinion leaders, whose activism and leadership were enabled through combining online and offline efforts, such as Egyptian activists Nawara Negm, Esraa Abdel Fattah, and Asmaa' Mahfouz (Radsch 2012). According to Hani, the rise of these new public opinion leaders brought about new salience and support for women's issues. For example, Nawara Negm bravely discussed the issue of women's mass harassment on the streets of Cairo before the eruption of the Egyptian revolution, and the sensitive issue of subjecting female protesters to virginity testing after the revolution, which forced mainstream media to cover both issues (Al-Malki et al. 2012). This spillover in tackling women's issues from the realm of citizen journalism to the realm of mainstream journalism was perceived by all the interviewees as serving women's interests by drawing attention to their sufferings and challenges.

However, all the interviewees agreed that despite the significant role that women played in the Arab Spring, and the positive attention they received due to their prominent and heroic roles in it, real challenges confront Arab women and threaten their gains. One of these challenges was the shift from solidarity to fragmentation whereby the great historic moment of unity, which rallied all people together behind the one cause of ousting dictators and fighting for freedom, was replaced by a much more fragmented and divided political and social scene afterwards. According to Elhaj, "This poses the threat of marginalizing, or even stigmatizing, women activists, some of whom were labeled as too liberal or secular and, therefore, were excluded from playing significant political or social roles, especially in countries where Islamists gained power."

The rise of political Islam in transitioning countries, namely, Egypt, Tunisia, and Libya, was seen by all interviewees as a potential threat to women, albeit to varying degrees. Opinions ranged from a belief that a moderate form of Islam could be reconciled with the advancement of women's rights, since it is always up to women themselves to stand up for their causes and demand their rights, to doubt that such a reconciliation is possible, because they simply believed that Islam and feminism *cannot coexist.*

Representing the first position, Fahmia Al Fotih recalls how thousands of Yemeni women flooded the streets of San'aa and other cities in Yemen in clear defiance of the President's statement that it was un-Islamic for women to join public protests, alongside men. "Some of these women even raised banners stating that it was un-Islamic for the President to deprive people of their basic human rights, including the right to express themselves and to enjoy freedom." This demonstrates that "Arab leaders learned the hard way they risked the wrath of women if they played the religious card to block women's rights" (Al-Malki *et al.* 2012: 81). However, all the interviewees were of the view that the rise of political Islam poses the risk of a new form of top-down, cosmetic feminism, which neither represents Arab women nor reflects their agendas. This process of "tokenism" took different forms before and after the Arab Spring (Al-Malki *et al.* 2012). Before the Arab Spring, it was exhibited through what could be described as the *first lady syndrome*, which imposed an elitist, top-down feminism that didn't successfully trickle down to all women. Many of these first ladies "championed women's rights more for the international headlines than for meaningful structural change at home" (Al-Malki *et al.* 2012: 84). After the Arab Spring, it was manifested through turning women from active participants to *silent witnesses*, through appointing passive and unqualified women in newly formed councils and organizations to meet a certain quota and appease women's movements. As Al Wadi remarks, "There is no value in appointing women to decision-making positions, if they are not truly capable of taking decisions and acting as decision-makers."

There is also the parallel fear of women's issues drowning in the tide of post-revolutionary challenges in transitioning countries, like Egypt, Tunisia, and Libya, and the violent clashes and fierce struggles in countries which are still fighting for freedom, like Syria, and, to a lesser degree, Bahrain. The ultimate result could be reproducing the same old political and social structures, where women's "political talents have been systematically overlooked and … political participation has been systematically excluded" (Al-Malki *et al.* 2012: 101). This indicates a greater problem, the desire to divorce women's issues from the overall struggle for change and reform in these countries. As Al Sayed indicates, "Women's issues cannot be isolated from the wider political, economic, and social contexts, since they are part and parcel of the process of change and reform in transitioning countries."

In projecting the future role of new media in promoting women's rights, they were all confident about the continuing and expanding role of activist "cyberfeminism" as an effective tool in the struggle for women's rights. As Al Fotih puts it, "Just like there is no turning back on the political struggle to secure freedom, democracy, and justice in the Arab world, there is also no turning back on the use of online activism. It simply proved to be very successful and effective in bringing about change." However, there were also some fears associated with overreliance on new media, ranging from "online fatigue," as Elhaj puts it, due to information overload, to the fear of "substituting clicking for doing, which could give people a false sense of gratification," as Al Sayed remarks. This poses the potential risk of re-exploiting new media as safety valves, rather than using them as effective mobilization tools, as was the case before the eruption of the Arab Spring (Seib 2007).

Adopting a realistic approach is wise when contemplating the future of Arab women and their struggle for their rights after the Arab Spring. We should acknowledge the gains and opportunities, as well as the threats and challenges ahead. In predicting the role of cyberactivism, and especially "cyberfeminism," it would be equally wise to adopt an approach of "cyberrealism," which acknowledges that "the new capacities created by the Internet represent a potential that can be tapped under the right circumstance and that do empower more peripheral groups" (Muhlberger 2004: 226).

Adopting this approach necessitates acknowledging the relevance and importance of new media in aiding the process of sociopolitical change, while equally acknowledging some of the limitations of these new media in bringing about change, since they are potential catalysts for change, not magical tools. People create change, not technologies. This was clearly evident in the Arab Spring, with millions of citizens risking their lives in struggles for freedom and dignity. Likewise, only Arab women can bring about change, through bearing the burden and facing real risks in their struggle for their rights.

# References

Alamm, W. (2012) "Reflections on Women in the Arab Spring: Women's Voices from Around the World," March 5, Middle East Program: Woodrow Wilson International Center for Scholars. http://www.wilsoncenter.org/sites/default/files/International%20Women%27s%20Day%202012_4.pdf.

Al-Malki, A., D. Kaufer, S. Ishizaki, and K. Dreher (2012) *Arab Women in Arab News: Old Stereotypes and New Media*, Doha: Bloomsbury Qatar Foundation Publishing.

Bennett, W. L. (2008) "Changing Citizenship in the Digital Age," in W. L. Bennett (ed.) *Civic Life Online: Learning How Digital Media Can Engage Youth*, Cambridge, MA: MIT Press, pp. 1–24.

Coleman, S. (2005) "Blogs and the New Politics of Listening," *Political Quarterly* 76(2): 272–80.

——(2008) "Doing it for Themselves: Management versus Autonomy in Youth E-citizenship," in W. L. Bennett (ed.) *Civic Life Online: Learning How Digital Media Can Engage Youth*, Cambridge, MA: MIT Press, pp. 189–206.

Daniels, J. (2009) "Rethinking Cyberfeminism(s): Race, Gender and Embodiment," *Women's Studies Quarterly* 37(1&2): 101–24.

Fernandez, M., F. Wilding, and M. Wright (2003) (eds.) *Domain Errors! Cyberfeminist Practices*, Brooklyn, NY: Autonomedia.

Fraser, N. (1992) "Rethinking the Public Sphere," in C. Calhoun (ed.) *Habermas and the Public Sphere*, Cambridge, MA: MIT Press, pp. 109–42.

Gajjala, R. (2003) "South Asian Digital Diasporas and Cyberfeminist Webs: Negotiating Globalization, Nation, Gender, and Information Technology Design," *Contemporary South Asia* 12(1): 41–56.

Howard, P. N. (2011) *The Digital Origins of Dictatorship and Democracy: Information Technology and Political Islam*, Oxford: Oxford University Press.

Khamis, S. (2010) "Islamic Feminism in New Arab Media: Platforms for Self-Expression and Sites for Multiple Resistances," *Journal of Arab and Muslim Media Research* 3(3): 237–55.

——(2011) "The Arab 'Feminist' Spring?," *Feminist Studies* 37(3): 692–5.

Muhlberger, P. (2004) "Access, Skill, and Motivation in Online Political Discussion: Testing Cyberrealism," in P. Shane (ed.) *Democracy Online: The Prospects for Political Renewal through the Internet*, New York: Routledge, pp. 225–37.

Radsch, C. (2011) "Bahrain's Young Women Keep the Revolution Aloud." http://womensenews. org/story/leadership/110727/bahrains-young-women-keep-the-revolution-aloud.

——(2012) "Unveiling the Revolutionaries: Cyberactivism and the Role of Women in the Arab Uprisings," James A. Baker III Institute for Public Policy of Rice University. http:// bakerinstitute.org/publications/ITP-pub-CyberactivismAndWomen-051712.pdf.

Seib, P. (2007) "New Media and Prospects for Democratization," in P. Seib (ed.) *New Media and the New Middle East*, New York: Palgrave Macmillan, pp. 1–18.

# Part V

# GENDERED MEDIA FUTURES AND THE FUTURE OF GENDER

# 53

# Latinas on television and film

## Exploring the limits and possibilities of inclusion

### Angharad N. Valdivia

*Sleep Dealer*, the 2008 futurist film co-written and directed by Alex Rivera, focuses on a Mexican young man who sells his labor across the border and forges a trans-national Latino alliance with his metaphorical counterpart, a US Latino soldier. Both men operate in a cyborgian hybrid of technology and the body (Haraway 1991) in which their labor is virtually transported across borders to accomplish geopolitical and economic goals. Crucial to the plot, although nearly erased from this narrative, is Dolores Cruz, the woman who brings the young men together through treachery and love, a classic situation in which the Latina character serves the internally contradictory role of translator and traitor. In this sense, she is like Malinche, an iconic figure in Mexican and Chicano history—a woman who acted as translator/interpreter between the Spanish *conquistadores* and the Aztecs, but also betrayed the Aztecs (see Alarcón 1989). The sci-fi film plays widely in the film festival circuit, and it deserves wide circulation for the novel and trenchant manner in which it treats its themes: exploitation of the Global South for both its labor and its natural resources; border crossing; incorporation of technology into work and into the human body; and the quotidian militarization of space. Departing from narratives such as *Spanglish* (2004) that depict feminized border crossers as safe, consumable, and docile (Molina-Guzmán 2010), Rivera provides a traditional portrait of domestic, troubled, and submissive women in general and the Malinche/Dolores character in particular; the latter contributes to the story as the connecting thread, bringing the men together through seduction, betrayal, and, eventually, romantic love.

Similarly, another very popular ABC network prime-time show, *Modern Family*, foregrounds Gloria (Sofia Vergara), one of today's best-known US Latinas. Listed on the IMDb.com character list as second only to Ed O'Neill,[1] the patriarch and Gloria's husband in the show, Sofia plays the traditional trophy wife with a new millennium twist, a Latina who often acknowledges her relational ethnic placement vis-à-vis the rest of the mostly white cast. Gloria reiterates many of the stereotypical elements of Latina representation in the US: She is loud and often hysterical; she speaks English with a very thick accent; she is hypersexualized and curvaceous;[2] she has the long brown hair[3] and light brown skin of the idealized Latina body; and she not only has a child from a previous relationship, but also gives birth in the 2012 season, thus illustrating Latina fertility. A gay white homonormative couple, who adopt an Asian child, and a white postfeminist nuclear family round out this show's new versions of old narratives.

Rounding out the contemporary location of Latinidad—the process of being, becoming, and/or performing a Latina/o subjectivity—in film and television are Jennifer Lopez and Selena Gomez. Lopez re-energized her career with a two-year stint as a judge in the show *American Idol* and as co-hostess (with ex-husband Marc Anthony) of the dance contest show *¡Q'Viva! The Chosen*, in Spanish on Univision and in English on Fox network. Gomez, a teen sensation on Disney Channel and beyond, was named after the Tejana (Texan) star Selena. Gomez has branched out from her debut in the Disney Channel show *The Wizards of Waverly Place*. Gomez has become a recording star with her famous ex-boyfriend, Justin Bieber, and her best friend Demi Lovato, yet another Disney star; and a range of products market her brand to tween and teen audiences.

These examples illustrate the ruptures and continuities that turn up in exploring the limits and possibilities of inclusion of Latinas in television and film. These women stand in for the imagined nation. They track the interstices and struggles of the contemporary identity crisis that faces the United States, which formerly thought of itself as homogeneous or binary in composition (i.e. black and white). These themes cut across popular culture, whether in a Latina/o produced film about Latina/o issues, in a prime-time television show with a primarily Caucasian cast, or through the careers of two spectacular Latinas, that is, Latinas who are foregrounded in celebrity culture as singularly sexy and representing the excess of their embodied ethnicity (Molina-Guzmán 2010).[4] Latina representations circulate and reiterate traditional narratives about gender, race, sexuality, and nation that in turn trigger a range of recognizable audience responses and community reactions. Drawing on a history of representations and discourses of Latinidad primarily but not exclusively in the US, this chapter examines the different stages of representation of Latinas, the competing discourses that abounded at the end of the last century, and the rise in hybrid and ambiguous representations now appearing in the mainstream media.

In particular, I explore the implicit utopia that guides much of the research and activism about issues of production, discourse and representation, and audience and interpretation in ethnic studies in general and Latina/o studies in particular. The tension between a stereotype or easily recognizable discourse and an effacement or subtle presence places media producers in a difficult position. Which option within this difficult and untenable binary should they generate given that audiences' responses, recognitions, and potential reactions work within a discourse of implicit utopias that wants both the obvious and the subtle? Many mainstream producers, who undeniably function within an industry that foregrounds the profit motive, nonetheless sometimes attempt to create representations that extend, extenuate, or rupture previous tendencies. Latina/o audiences expect linear progress to address historical issues of exclusion and stereotyping as well as contemporary gains and to acknowledge their majority/minority status, especially since 2000, when the US Census declared Hispanics to be the most numerous minority group. Expectations apply to mainstream presence, such as Sofia Vergara in *Modern Family* and Selena Gomez, as well as in widely circulated Latina/o entertainment media, as evidenced in

*Sleep Dealer* and Jennifer Lopez on *¡Q'Viva!* Those involved in the production of media content must contend with audiences' implicit demands for the presence of identifiable people who go beyond stereotypes. At the center of it all are the representations (depoliticized, consumable bodies) that unite the producers with the audience and force questions such as: What will make them/us happy? When and under what circumstances will they/we feel that Latinas on television and film are included in a satisfactory manner, in a satisfying way? What will resolve the gender and racial discomfort of the mainstream (Molina-Guzmán 2010) *and* the expectations of the Latina/o audience? Where is that fine line between offensive and/or demeaning stereotype and the whitening of culture and/or flattening of difference?

Given these questions, a focus on mainstream representations makes sense for several reasons. The struggle over signification through the figure of woman as nation occurs in the mainstream culture because Latina/os, and other minoritized groups, seek a rightful place as core members of the culture—that is, included in and contributing to its core values and narratives. Latina feminist media studies scholars have convincingly argued that the struggle over the nation is significantly carried out through and over women's bodies in popular culture as well as other texts, such as laws and freeway signs (Shohat and Stam 1995; Ruiz 2002; Mendible 2007; Paredez 2009; Cepeda 2010; Molina-Guzmán 2010; Valdivia 2010). As Molina-Guzmán asserts: "Movies are informative of ideologically dominant and conflicted constructions Latina femininity, domesticity, and citizenship" (2010: 153). Similar analysis applies to television. Most importantly, in terms of the implicit utopia, being present at the center—that is, the mainstream—makes the figure of woman through television and film a central component of narratives about the nation in an ethnographic fashion (López 1991; Shohat and Stam 1995).

Analysis of Latinas and issues of Latinidad in mainstream popular culture helps us chart a path of inclusion and representation with seven stages: exclusion; minimal inclusion/symbolic annihilation; binary black/secondary and white/primary; single ethnicity or combined minoritized ethnicities in television shows and movies; multicultural palette; Latina protagonist through sexualization, hyperembodiment, or ambiguity and hybridity; and utopia. This chapter defines and clarifies these stages in their order of emergence. Nonetheless, they continue to coexist. Some of them have become less prominent with time, but their rise and wane chart the inevitable political winds that influence representation far more than any given population's proportion in and contribution to the nation.

## History

The first stage, exclusion, is more of an ideal extreme than a documented reality. Historically the "other" has been always present, if only by implication: White subjectivity only has meaning in relation to a "colored" other (Shohat and Stam 1995). Thus, even early US representations in film and later in television either implicitly or explicitly referenced Native Americans, African Americans, and/or some form of global other. These were usually in a sexualized and feminized form when desired, or masculine and violent when feared. Both forms represented threats to the national body politic. Understanding Latina/os in Hollywood film more specifically has been significantly advanced by the extensive research by Charles Ramirez Berg, Rosa Linda Fregoso, Carlos E. Cortés, and Mary Beltrán. Beltrán (2009) traced Latinas in film back to the silent era; she notes that the transition to sound opened up the sensory ability to assign an accent to Latinas, sometimes despite their ability to speak perfect English. The dark lady and spitfire, two of the most enduring Latina stereotypes, can be seen in this transition era in Hollywood film. Both types represent a form of symbolic annihilation (Tuchman *et al.* 1978) and thus point to the prevalence of that second stage, in which women, especially minority women, are represented in less than their proportion in the general population, and when represented they are marginalized, trivialized, or sensationalized, especially, in the Latina case, through hypersexuality. Symbolic annihilation, I should underscore, is a step up from absence: Symbolic presence is necessary before you can be further annihilated. Symbolic annihilation has been documented much more often in regard to African Americans than to Latina/os, though in hindsight some of the African Americans were Afrolatina/os. On television and film Latina/os continue to be underrepresented and trivialized in too many movies and shows to count. For instance, the character of Maria (Ana de la Reguera) in *Cowboys and Aliens* (2011) pretty much illustrates the marginal and nearly nameless part (everyone is called Maria) for a Latina in contemporary Hollywood film.

Particular recurring roles for Latina characters, such as the maid, illustrate the symbolic annihilation of the Latina, in this case as a domestic servant, often nameless, always working class, and many times with a thick accent. Variations of this role range from the more than 100 times that Lupe Ontiveros played a maid, to the role of Flor (played by the Spanish actress Paz Vega) in *Spanglish* (2004), as well as Marisa Ventura (Jennifer Lopez) in *Maid in Manhattan* (2002). Rosario (Shelley Morrison), in the long-running and much awarded[5] *Will & Grace*, represents a highly ironic and in-your-face rendition of the Latina maid. While not always a secondary character, as in *Maid in Manhattan*, the Latina domestic symbolically reduces Latinas to a marginal job. As Molina-Guzmán (2010) asserts, this symbolically colonizes the Latina.

The latest Latin boom, the one of the 1990s, is marked—again not metaphorically but literally—over Selena's dead body. Paredez's book *Selenidad* (2009) riffs on Gloria Anzaldúa's work by titling one section of a chapter "This Bridge Called My Corpse." Selena was killed in 1996 and the movie *Selena* came out in 1997—thus accomplishing simultaneously the near-canonization of Selena in the Latina/o imaginary and, through Selena's dead body, the crossover of Jennifer Lopez, who remains today Hollywood's reigning Latina. To be sure *Selena* ushered in a period beyond absence and somewhere between symbolic annihilation and something else. *Selena* represents a sanitized version of the late Tejana's life yet manages to foreground Jennifer Lopez's butt and begin the process of sexualization that continues to characterize that star's trajectory and much of Latina representation today. Simultaneously, however, *Selena* also represents a nearly postfeminist characterization of a Latina seeking to assert agency and control in the public limelight through performance and stylization of her body. Furthermore, the individualist remaking of the self also positions this representation of Selena in the neoliberal realm, as nearly all agency and remaking are transferred from a governmental or social sphere to that of the risk-taking individual.

Following that latest Latin boom, we begin to see an expansion of the black and white binary into inclusion of Latinas in three types of movies and shows: those centering on a single ethnicity; dyads; and within a multicultural palette that often includes Latina/os as well as Asian Americans. For the first option, we see a range of family-oriented television shows with a wide range of Latina/o characters; this is evidenced by *George Lopez* (2002–7). For the second option of dyads, the tendency until recently had been black/secondary and white/primary, such as in the now iconic television show *I Spy* (1965–8) in which Bill Cosby played sidekick to Robert Culp. Sidekicks were often male; only recently, in the wake of the second stage of the women's movement, were they female. As expected, until recently, with many shows featuring a female protagonist and her sidekick, both were white; *Cagney and Lacey* (1981–8) exemplifies this trend. But *Chelsea Lately* claims to be the first late night show to have a Latino sidekick in Chuy Brown. Accordingly, major Hollywood films are also including a brawny Latina sidekick alongside the brainy protagonist. For instance, Milla Jovovich (Alice) and Michelle Rodriguez (Rain Ocampo) form a duo in *Resident Evil* (2002), which sits in that recent genre of movies based on a digital game. Often, the sidekick appears in the form of an ambiguous character, someone who can be interpreted as white or as a range of ethnicities from white to light black, depending on the viewer's decision. Thus, in this second subcategory are characters such as Miranda Sanchez (Lalaine), who was Lizzie McGuire's faithful sidekick in that popular television show on the Disney channel (2001–4), and the two sidekicks to the white protagonist Anne Marie (Kate Bosworth) in *Blue Crush* (2002), all three ambiguous ethnics. We can infer Latinidad into the characters of Miranda and Eden (Michelle Rodriguez), although they can also be interpreted as white. In the case of the ambiguous ethnic Lena (Sanoe Lake), we can infer some type of ethnicity—or none at all if we are so inclined.

For the third option of multicultural palette, following the Latin boom of the 1990s, Latinas begin to appear among secondary characters. In various iterations of the children's television show *Barney* (1992–2009), a cast of roughly ten children—including Selena Gomez and Demi Lovato in Seasons 7 and 8—provided a multicultural palette of secondary characters, in addition to main characters Barney the purple dinosaur and his dinosaur friends. Another Disney franchise, *The Cheetah Girls* (2003, 2006, and 2008), included a multicultural palette girl group with a Latina character, Chanel (Adrienne Bailon). Chanel is definitely Latina, as marked by her occasional dialogue in Spanish; furthermore, in developing the character, discussion explicitly mentions her Latina mother and her personal Latinidad. On the other hand, she refuses to reveal her specificity within Latinidad—in a way similar to *Dora the Explorer*, whose specific provenance is likewise never mentioned in the long-running television show. Other prime-time US television shows such as *Ugly Betty* (2006–10) and *Desperate Housewives* (2004–12) feature Latina protagonists within a cast that foregrounds whites and includes other ethnicities. Identifiable Latinas, with Latina histories and ethnic issues, are now a part of some large casts much more so than in the previous wave of television hits such as *Friends* (1994–2004), a show widely criticized for its unswerving whiteness.

Another version of Latina inclusion, in large or small casts, is more subtle in its representation of Latinidad. For instance, the hugely successful *High School Musical*

(HSM, 2006, 2007, and 2008) brought back the musical as a popular genre combined with a multicultural palette. Moreover HSM highlights the new form of the ambiguous Latina. Gabriella Montez (Vanessa Hudgens), the female part of the main romantic couple in HSM, is so subtly Latina that only after six years did some of my girls studies colleagues notice her ethnicity. Similarly to Eden in Blue Crush, audiences can infer her ethnicity from her tough girl approach (Beltrán 2004) and accent, as well as in relation to the normative whiteness of the Anne Marie character and the ambiguous Asian Islander ethnicity of Lena, the third part of the girl group. Likewise, in the Wizards of Waverly Place (2007–12) Selena Gomez plays the part of Alex, short for Alexandra, with María Canals Barrera playing the role of her mother, Theresa. While very few episodes contain elements of Latinidad, such as a quinceañera party, both of their names are Anglicized—Alexandra instead of Alejandra and Theresa instead of Teresa, which serves to sustain the ambiguity of their ethnicity. We find ambiguous ethnics, including Cloe, the subtle Latina, in the mediated doll line[6] Bratz and its television shows and the Hollywood feature-length film Bratz: The Movie (2007) (Valdivia 2011b). There is little Latinidad and ethnicity to Cloe other than a lively Latin soundtrack playing in her kitchen to alert those looking for it that we are in a Latina/o household and, therefore, that Cloe is Latina. The fact is that the ambiguity of these Latinas is accomplished through very subtle signifiers. The pattern emerging here is that these Latinas are represented so subtly in the multicultural cast as to be ambiguously Latinas, or ambiguously ethnic for that matter. Inescapably, the representation of Latinas in the mainstream slips into the arena of the ambiguous. In turn, this often dips into the hybrid, which is also an area of indefinite and unidentifiable ethnic mixture. As I have argued elsewhere (Valdivia 2009, 2011a, 2011b), hybridity speaks to the widespread population and cultural[7] mixtures that go against the narratives of authenticity so dear and politically central to ethnic rights movements yet so untenable according to biological data. The tension between a strategic essentialism necessary for mobilization and group cohesion versus scientifically and culturally demonstrable porosity seeps into the internally contradictory representations and audience reactions to these representations. Moreover, ambiguity is a highly economical way to address audiences, as it seeks to interpellate a range of ethnicities and nationalities without antagonizing those who still hold on to notions of white centrality. Finally, ambiguity once more returns our race and ethnic spectrum to lightness, thereby once again pushing blackness to the margins.

## What do we want?

The abbreviated history of the many overlapping stages of Latina representation on film and television illustrates the fact that Latinas appear in popular culture in a heterogeneity of possibilities. The question remains, what do we want from Latina/os on the screen? Do we regard any of these options as optimal? Or are we—Latina/os and others who are interested in those social justice issues turning on production, representation, and interpretation of media and cinema—striving for a null hypothesis? I do not mean to excuse major Hollywood film and television studios that are often part of global conglomerates, but would anything they produce contemporarily or might produce in the near future satisfy activists and community groups and individuals? What is our implicit utopia?

We do not want stereotypes, which, whether positive or negative, are usually simplistic and undesirable. The old stereotypes of the dark lady and spitfire are still morphing, now having become gang members and hypersexual spectacular bodies; but these reproduce a perspective of Latinas as aberrant, abnormal, and undesirable members of the body politic. We prefer complex characters that suggest the diversity and heterogeneity of characters within Latinidad. Yet, although we disdain stereotypes, we want some form of recognizable Latina presence. Moreover, if that presence is too subtle we complain that she has been whitened, assimilated, and flattened. So we argue for authenticity—a concept that is used to police the borders around ethnic identity but a concept that is unsustainable by the documented hybridity of populations and cultures. This takes us to a position in which we acknowledge that hybridity is not only omnipresent, but so prevalent that it describes us all. Meanwhile, we want to be able to figure out who is what. Viewers of *Dora the Explorer* debate the protagonist's exact Latina roots endlessly on blogs (Harewood and Valdivia 2005). Despite our own inability, as members of the audience in our everyday lived experience, to determine people's cultural, ethnic, and national roots, we demand this of mainstream media. Furthermore, we argue for upward mobility (Dávila 2008) even as we continue to code working-class representations as more authentic.

This multiple ambivalence, I suggest, harks back to our inescapably hybrid history, subjectivity, and culture. What is Latina/o is both specific and general; it contains "pure" elements and blends in with other nations and cultures. Do we keep arguing for inclusion at the center? After all, given our presence and contributions, we deserve to be and in some ways are at the center. And do we keep arguing for difference, some sort of identifiable and discernible difference that speaks to presence without total dilution? Our representational politics (which of course takes up issues of production and interpretation) implies separatism, something we also stand against, since it means a perpetual marginalization.

Presence is a goal accomplished: Sofia Vergara, Jennifer Lopez, Selena Gomez, and the ubiquitous Latina domestic speak to that. What *specific* type of presence we want is what we have not clearly articulated in a positive sense—meaning as something more than what we do not like. The trivialization and marginalization of symbolic annihilation, while it was an early way station, is not utopia. Thus, the Latina domestic is not our goal, even if it acknowledges our presence and contribution to the labor pool. *Maid in Manhattan* promotes the maid protagonist to managerial status; yet, it does so through the body, and booty, of Jennifer Lopez, a spectacular and sexualized Latina. According to Beltrán, the new Latina action hero, roles that both Lopez and Michelle Rodriguez have taken on, enacts "*spectacular heterosexuality*" (2004: 198, emphasis in original), thus making "the transgression of aggression more palatable" (2004: 198). The famous embodied and sexualized Latinas, when coded as such, perform much more aggressive roles than their white counterparts.

Once we move to the terrain of the ambiguous and the hybrid, the tension between presence, belonging, and identifiability becomes more pronounced. Are the Alex and Gabriella characters in *Wizards* and *HSM*, respectively, the goal toward

ANGHARAD N. VALDIVIA

which the Latina/o population has been aiming? Does this subtle representation mean that Latinas are part of the national imaginary? Or does the need for "Latina-dar," drawing on the concept of Gaydar—the need for insider knowledge about gay culture to be able to identify a narrative or representation as invoking gay cultural forms—mean that all traces of Latinidad are so subsumed as to make these images yet another instance of the whitewashing of cultural diversity?

## Conclusion

While proportional representation has yet to be achieved in regards to Latinas in film and television, the history of representation includes many stages, all of which still coexist and overlap. The continuation of these stages, including ones with inter-ethnic casts and protagonists, demonstrates that television and film have not remained uninfluenced by demographic shifts. Programmers have had to acknowledge greater population diversity in an effort to appeal to shifting audiences. As well, the production of Latina/o themed movies and television shows suggests a growing base of Latina/o producers with the resources and ethnic pride to make contributions to mainstream popular culture. As Latina/o audiences we want authenticity and recognition outside of stereotypes and with acknowledgment of belonging. We want themes that focus on the Latina/o experience linked to and included with general themes about US culture and society.

On another level of internal contradiction, Báez (2008) and others have documented the Latina audiences' desire for both the beauty of the Latina and wholesome non-sexualized images. Yet, a third level of tension pits the celebration of the varieties of music and food within Latinidad, as heterogeneous as these are, against the desire for a terrain of signification that aspires to intellectual and artistic "belonging." Pride in working-class status also rubs against the upwardly mobile segment of the Latina/o population striving for inclusion in the mainstream, of media and education, politics and society at large. We have reached a point where we might want to take some time and effort to explicitly articulate our utopia lest we keep spinning our wheels criticizing the wide range of representations currently circulating in film and television. The figure of woman as signifier of the nation applies to and through ethnicity. The demographic trends within the US generate a dynamic wherein symbolic, and therefore material, contestation will be worked through the bodies of spectacular and everyday Latinas. How the inclusion is accomplished and measured from within and without Latinidad will be a measure of the ability of the US to acknowledge its diverse population and culture.

## Notes

1 O'Neill is probably most famous for his role as the father in the long-running sitcom *Married with Children*.
2 In terms of Latina representation she has the classic Coca-Cola bottle (Báez 2008) or guitar shape (Beltrán 2009).

586

3 Actually Sofia Vergara has light brown, nearly blonde hair but producers encouraged her to dye it dark brown so as not to confuse the mainstream audience's expectation that all Latinas have brown hair.
4 I am greatly influenced by the work of Molina-Guzmán (2010) about the relation between the few spectacular Latinas and everyday bodies and experiences of the majority of working-class Latinas.
5 This show earned many GLADD (Gay and Lesbian Alliance Against Defamation) awards for its representation of gay people.
6 A mediated doll line includes dolls as part of a synergized brand system that includes media elements such as television shows, movies, online presence, popular music discs and downloads, digital games, etc., in addition to other products ranging from food to clothing and furniture.
7 Population mixture refers to DNA and cultural mixture to the culture produced by those mixed DNA people.

# References

Alarcón, N. (1989) "Traddutora, Traditora: A Paradigmatic Figure of Chicana Feminism," *Cultural Critique* 13: 57–87.

Báez, J. (2008) "Mexican American Women Talk Back: Audience Responses to Representations of Latinidad in US Advertising," in A. N. Valdivia (ed.) *Latina/o Communication Studies Today*, New York: Peter Lang, pp. 257–82.

Beltrán, M. (2004) "Más Macha: The New Latina Action Hero," in Yvonne Tasker (ed.) *Action and Adventure Cinema*, London: Routledge, pp. 186–200.

——(2009) *Latina/o Stars in U.S. Eyes: The Making and Meanings of Film and TV Stardom*, Urbana: University of Illinois Press.

Cepeda, M. E. (2010) *Musical ImagiNation: U.S.–Colombian Identity and the Latin Music Boom*, New York: New York University Press.

Dávila, A. M. (2008) *Latino Spin: Public Image and the Whitewashing of Race*, New York: New York University Press.

Goldberg, D. T. (2009) *The Threat of Race: Reflections on Racial Neoliberalism*, Malden, MA: Wiley-Blackwell.

Haraway, D. J. (1991) *Simians, Cyborgs, and Women: The Reinvention of Nature*, New York: Routledge.

Harewood, S. J. and A. N. Valdivia (2005) "Exploring Dora: Re-embodied Latinidad on the Web," in S. R. Mazzarella (ed.) *Girl Wide Web: Girls, the Internet, and the Negotiation of Identity*, New York: Peter Lang.

López, A. M. (1991) "Are All Latins from Manhattan? Hollywood, Ethnography, and Cultural Colonialism," in L. D. Friedman (ed.) *Unspeakable Images: Ethnicity and the American Cinema*, Urbana: University of Illinois, pp. 404–24.

Mendible, M. (ed.) (2007) *From Bananas to Buttocks: The Latina Body in Popular Film and Culture*, Austin: University of Texas Press.

Molina-Guzmán, I. (2010) *Dangerous Curves: Latina Bodies in the Media*, New York: New York University Press.

Paredez, D. (2009) *Selenidad: Selena, Latinos, and the Performance of Memory*, Durham, NC: Duke University Press.

Ruiz, M. V. (2002) "Border Narratives, HIV/AIDS, and Latina/o Health in the United States: A Cultural Analysis," *Feminist Media Studies* 2(1): 81–96.

Shohat, E. and R. Stam (1995) *Unthinking Eurocentrism: Multiculturalism and the Media*, London and New York: Routledge.

Tuchman, G., A. K. Daniels, and J. Benet (eds.) (1978) *Hearth and Home: Images of Women in the Mass Media*, New York: Oxford University Press.

Valdivia, A. N. (2009) "Living in a Hybrid Material World: Girls, Ethnicity and Doll Products," *Girlhood Studies: An Interdisciplinary Journal* 1(3): 173–93.

——(2010) *Latina/os and the Media*, Cambridge: Polity.

——(2011a) "Transnationalism, Hybridity, and Latinidad: Gendered Discourses of Ethnicity," in R. Hegde (ed.) *Circuits of Visibility: Gender and Transnational Media Cultures*, New York: New York University Press.

——(2011b) "This Tween Bridge over my Latina Girl Back: US Mainstream Negotiates Ethnicity," in M. C. Kearney (ed.) *Mediated Girlhoods*, New York: Peter Lang, pp. 93–109.

# 54

# Postfeminist sexual culture

## Rosalind Gill

Over the last decade, "porno chic," the "pornification" of society, and the "sexualization of culture" have become major topics of concern in news media, in policy arenas, and in academic study. The notions of "pornification" and "sexualization" capture the growing sense of Western societies as saturated by sexual representations and discourses, and in which pornography has become increasingly influential, permeating mainstream media and contemporary culture. Porn stars have emerged as best-selling authors and celebrities; a "porno chic" aesthetic can be seen in fashion, music videos, and advertising; and practices once associated with the sex industry—for example lap dancing and pole dancing—have become newly respectable, promoted as a regular feature of corporate entertainment or recreational activity. This shift speaks to something more than the idea that "sex has become the big story" (Plummer 1995: 4). As Feona Attwood has noted, it denotes a range of things:

> a contemporary preoccupation with sexual values, practices and identities; the public shift to more permissive sexual attitudes; the proliferation of sexual texts; the emergence of new forms of sexual experience; the apparent breakdown of rules, categories and regulations designed to keep the obscene at bay; [and the] fondness for the scandals, controversies and panics around sex.
>
> (Attwood 2006: 77)

This chapter gives an overview of some of the key feminist perspectives on sexualization, to highlight areas of debate and indicate directions for future research. It is worth noting that debates about the sexualization of culture constitute a complicated and contested terrain, one suffused with strong feelings, and frequently polarized. Too often the field seems distorted by the long shadows of earlier debates. Regarding the "sex wars" or "porn wars" of the early 1980s, Drucilla Cornell (2000) has argued that every feminist was made to take a position or was forcibly allocated one. Unlike academic domains that do not attract such passion, academic writing about sexualization is characterized by heightened emotion and a distinctively "performative" quality in which scholars rhetorically conjure "harm," claim authority, express "concern," present themselves in a favorable light, defend against particular readings of their argument, etc. My own—no less rhetorical but perennially uncomfortable—position here, as someone who is neither anti-sex nor anti-porn, is not sanguine or celebratory about the modes of sexism (and racism, classism, and heteronormativity) at work in contemporary "sexualized" culture. Sex positive but anti-sexism, I remain suspicious about the rhetorical/performative work—and the epistemic violence—done by such labels; I have consistently advocated complicating polarized positions in the emerging "sexualization wars."

## The sexualization of culture?

Anxieties and concerns about sexualization have come to the fore in recent years across several spheres. They can be seen in influential reports from think tanks (e.g. Rush and La Nauze 2006; APA 2007; Fawcett Society 2009), government reports (e.g. Byron 2008; Buckingham *et al.* 2010; Papadopoulos 2010; Bailey 2011); activist campaigns (for example to change the licensing laws for lap dancing clubs), as well as a variety of well-publicized popular books (e.g. Levy 2005; Durham 2009; Levin and Kilbourne 2009). The titles of reports, books, and feature articles signal some of the contours of the anxieties—particularly those concerning children—e.g. "so sexy, so soon" or "too much, too young." Concerns have centered on the direct sexualization of children in, for example, the resurgence of the child beauty pageant, as well as on the persistent interpellation of children in sexual terms, often evidenced by the marketing to younger and younger girls of "sexualized" clothing, such as padded bras and G-string knickers. More broadly, anxieties are expressed about the increasing volume and intensity of "sexualized" material in the media, which leads, it is argued, to a raft of harms for girls and women, including poor attainment at school, depression, low self-esteem, and eating disorders (APA 2007).

Media coverage of these discussions of "sexualization" has been extensive, but the media occupy a contradictory position. They are best thought of in multiple terms as a key site of sexualization, of concerns about sexualization, and, furthermore, of *concerns about concerns* about sexualization. At least in the UK, newspapers are replete with "sexualized" representations (pictures of semi-naked women, "sexy" stories, adverts for telephone sex lines, etc.); they have also been a central location for critical discussions of "sexualization"—with certain newspapers taking the role of "moral guardians," with repeated articles about the dangers of sexualized culture. These are frequently accompanied by multiple pictures of the offending content—as seen in the *Daily Mail*'s outraged coverage of the TV talent show *The X Factor*: the newspaper reproduced several stills from the program's allegedly shocking and inappropriate dance routines—including some which had apparently not even been aired. Newspapers also produce a different kind of article, which I call the "sexualization fatigue think piece." Here journalists adopt a superior, world-weary tone of boredom about the banality of the sexualization debates, and/or worry about the harm of moral panics; they suggest that the elevated public concern about sexualization either distracts from more important issues (e.g. poverty) or lends legitimacy to increased surveillance of the individual or regulation of the media. We should be wary, then, of examining the media only as a site of sexualization—and be aware of its complicated, multiple positionings.

## Feminist perspectives on "sexualization"

Different and diverse feminist positions engage with the sexualization of culture. Some contemporary radical feminist arguments are reminiscent of the second-wave anti-pornography perspectives of Andrea Dworkin (1981) and Catherine MacKinnon (e.g. Dworkin and MacKinnon 1988). Sheila Jeffreys's (2009) *The Industrial Vagina* is an impassioned polemic against the "global sex trade" that connects the mainstreaming of pornography to military prostitution, sex tourism, and the trafficking of women and children. Gail Dines (2010) connects the "gonzo" porn that dominates the internet to the wider hypersexualized culture (see also Tankard Reist 2009).

Other—contrasting—third-wave positions build from the sex-positive feminism of the same period (Califia 1994; Juffer 1998; Johnson 2002; Jenkins and Church Gibson 2003) to offer more optimistic views of sexualization grounded in understandings of women not as victims but instead as producers and consumers of "sexual" material—in ways that break significantly with constructions of women as passive and asexual (Lumby 1997; Smith 2007; Attwood 2009). "A whole series of signifiers are linked to promote a new, liberated, contemporary sexuality for women; sex is stylish, a source of physical pleasure, a means of creating identity, a form of body work, self-expression, a quest for individual fulfilment" (Attwood 2006: 86).

A further distinctive feminist perspective explores contemporary sexualization as a postfeminist and neoliberal phenomenon linked to consumerism and discourses of celebrity, choice, and empowerment (Coleman 2008; Gill 2008; Munford 2009; Whitehead and Kurz 2009; Ringrose and Eriksson Barajas 2011). Some see in contemporary sexualized culture not a more feminist sexual future but a turning backwards (Whelehan 2000), a "retro sexism" (Williamson 2003) in which objectifying representations of women are wrapped up in a feisty discourse of fake empowerment (Levy 2005).

None of this latter work sits comfortably in the old "anti-porn" versus "sex positive" binary. Much of it is explicitly pro-sex, but its target of critique is the way in which sexualization, power, and commerce intersect—often at the expense of the possibilities of exploring, experimenting, and celebrating diverse sexualities.

Looking at media portrayals of women, my own work (Gill 2008, 2009a; Harvey and Gill 2011a, 2011b) has charted a shift from "objectification" to "sexual subjectification." Women are no longer depicted as passive sex objects, but hailed as confident, freely choosing, seemingly empowered sexual subjects. I examine the exclusions of this change—only some women (young, slim, attractive) are accorded sexual subjecthood—and the shift in subjectivity it invites/requires. Developing the Foucaultian notion of "technologies of selfhood," I see contemporary sexualized, consumerist, and neoliberal societies as calling forth a new postfeminist feminine subject who is incited to be compulsorily sexy and always "up for it." Given a corresponding shift in the sexual representation of men's bodies in the media, I have also examined how young men respond to the increasingly idealized and eroticized representation of the male body (Gill *et al.* 2000; Gill 2011; see also Evans *et al.* 2010).

These divergent feminist approaches have generated a wide range of debates and points of contestation. Three important areas of tension relate to media influence and audience agency, power and difference, and what can be "done" about sexualization, with media literacy offered as a kind of panacea.

## Media influence: beyond victims and agents

Many of the debates about sexualization hinge, in different ways, on an understanding of the effects of a putatively "sexualized" culture, and individuals' capacities to resist, refuse, or resignify its meanings—notions often treated in shorthand as instances of "agency" or "empowerment." Underlying these debates are profoundly different understandings of the media and its influence. On one side is the dominant, US tradition, with its roots in psychology, which sees (sexualized) media as negatively affecting individuals' attitudes, beliefs, and behaviors. Media emerge here as homogeneous, monolithic, and all powerful: *The Media*, rather than a diversity of different media, platforms, genres, and productions, with—presumably—different kinds of representations of girls and young women, and, moreover, in which girls are increasingly involved as active producers, not merely consumers. Such a view can be seen in the APA's Task Force on the Sexualization of Girls (APA 2007); its report on time spent "with the media" made no distinctions between different kinds of media and how they are used, e.g. watching a documentary versus reading a magazine versus playing an online game versus updating a Facebook profile.

At its heart is the notion of media audiences as passive dupes who unquestioningly and uncritically absorb media messages "hypodermically" injected into them. Influence is characterized almost exclusively in terms of "mimicry" and "imitation." For example, Sharon Lamb and Zoë Peterson (2012) ask, "Why do girls imitate sexualized media and how conscious is this imitation?" They speculate on the meanings and pleasures of imitation but do not question the idea that this *is* the fundamental psychological process at issue in girls' engagement with the media. Moreover, when discussed in relation to the media, young women emerge as isolated, atomized, passive individuals, rather than engaged social actors embedded in family, friendship, school, and many other networks. Individuals often are treated as tabulae rasae (who, without the media, presumably would freely go on to develop a "healthy" sexuality). A particularly problematic idea of childhood innocence is frequently mobilized in debates about children and sexualization (e.g. Buckingham 2000; Egan and Hawkes 2008)

A contrasting tradition of research is found in some audience media and cultural studies scholarship (e.g. Radway 1984; Ang 1985; Hermes 1995; Gauntlett and Hill 1999). This research often starts agnostic about the putative intensification of sexualization; it sees the media more positively as offering "tools to think with" (Bragg and Buckingham 2009) rather than as agents of harm. Framed partly as a response to the psychological tradition, this work critiques media effects and presents audiences as active, knowledgeable, sophisticated, and critical users or consumers of media (Buckingham and Bragg 2004; Smith 2007; Jackson and Vares 2011).

David Buckingham and Sara Bragg champion the view that children are not naïve or incompetent consumers but use a range of critical skills and perspectives when interpreting sexual content. Moreover, children's responses to sexual imagery display "a well-developed understanding of how such images are constructed and manipulated," and children and young people are "literate" and "highly critical" consumers (Buckingham and Bragg 2004: 238). This sees children as actively deciding how far to engage with sexualized culture.

Such research is important in exploring the diverse meanings people give to engagements with media and in according proper respect to audiences, particularly children and young people. At times, however, this research can offer overly optimistic readings—seeing autonomy and choice and resistance everywhere. Bragg and Buckingham present young people as "autonomous, calculating and self-regulating entities in control of their own quest for knowledge in relation to sex and sexual material" (2009: 136) and able to make their own decisions, judgments, and choices. These apparently extend even to the "choice" of whether to be a child: "the media are creating new ways of being a child—not corrupting but confronting young people with choices about whether to remain a child or whether and when to enter the 'adult' world of sexual media" (2009: 136). Here, then, "child" becomes simply another discursive identity category, which subjects can choose or choose not to inhabit—as if that choice were fully within their control.

Perhaps reacting against the negative focus on "harms," this research emphasizes both the "pleasures" of sexualized culture and how problematic meanings may be resisted. For example, Holland and Attwood argue that women participating in pole dancing classes "resisted" the idea of objectification and "reworked" traditional indicators of femininity "into experiences of sexual agency and power" (2009: 177).

The difference between this and more "critical" readings may come down to an attitude or affective disposition, a tendency to read optimistically or pessimistically. But it also raises theoretical and methodological concerns, notably the tendency to take at face value interviewees' statements rather than seeing them as themselves performative. Moreover, with important exceptions (e.g. Ang 1985; Walkerdine 1997a, 1997b), the tradition relies on the assumption that respondents are "transparent to themselves"— i.e. able to excavate and lay bare their feelings and influences, as if they were entirely rational unitary subjects. Such a perspective is no more able than is the "effects" tradition to understand the complicated terrain of desire, intimacy, and sexuality. We need new psychosocial perspectives that move beyond the idea of both dupes/victims and autonomous agents, and we need more sophisticated formulations of the complex relationship between media and individuals, between culture and subjectivity.

### Power and difference: thinking intersectionally about sexualization

Although notions of agency and empowerment animate debates about "sexualization," the literature rarely considers power. Curiously, empowerment is treated as an individualized phenomenon which, although clearly connected to gender and age, is not related analytically to issues of power, inequality, or oppression. Why is sexualization so infrequently connected to sexism or to racism, to class inequality or homophobia? These questions relate to my concerns about the utility of the notion of "sexualization." While they appear to speak to something apparently new and real, the notions of "sexualization" or "pornification" or "raunch" (McNair 2002; Levy 2005) are rife with problems. The terms are too general. They are difficult to operationalize and therefore to use analytically. They tend to homogenize, ignoring differences and obscuring the fact that different people are "sexualized" in different ways and with different meanings. Sexualization does not operate outside of processes of gendering, racialization, and classing, and works within a visual economy that remains profoundly ageist, (dis)ablist, and heteronormative (Gill 2009b). Furthermore, the terms seem to pull us back into a moral domain, rather than one of politics or ethics—they pull towards judgments about "explicitness" and "exposure" rather than questions about equality or justice. Might it not be more productive to talk about sexism rather than sexualization? For all their force in animating and inspiring a new generation of feminists (Banyard 2010), I worry too that these terms reinstate the terms of the "sex wars" of the 1980s, with their familiar polarizations and discomfiting alliances between pro-censorship feminists and right-wing religious organizations (Cornell 2000).

This is worsened by the profoundly classed, racialized, and heteronormative framing of the debates themselves, whose privileged object of anxiety and "concern" has been the white, Western, middle-class, girl-child, sometimes figured as a "typical 13-year-old girl"—able-bodied, Anglo-American, presumed heterosexual (APA 2007; Lamb and Peterson 2012). This figure is repeatedly mobilized in academic, policy, and media reports and comes to constitute or define who is "at risk" (Harris 2004: 13). She becomes discursively overdetermined to such an extent that her specificity is rendered invisible: She is always already (pre)figured, she shapes what becomes thinkable about "sexualization." What if we changed her gender or ethnicity, or thought of her as a lesbian or as living with a disability? This would open new ways of thinking—sexual experiences might not be framed so strongly in terms of risk and danger.

More broadly, we urgently need an intersectional approach to the complex nexus of sex, media, and power. Avtar Brah and Ann Phoenix explain that intersectionality signifies:

> The complex, irreducible, varied and variable effects which ensue when multiple axes of differentiation—economic, political, cultural, psychic, subjective and experiential—intersect in historically specific contexts. The concept emphasizes that different dimensions of social life cannot be separated out into discrete and pure strands.
>
> (Brah and Phoenix 2004: 76)

This, then, is a call to think about "sexualization" and sexual empowerment *with* sexism, racism, ageism, classism, homophobia, (dis)ablism, and also to think transnationally (Imre *et al.* 2009). Besides *integrating* sexism with other axes of power and difference, it is also a matter of facing up to the complex dynamics and complicities in play in the current moment—precisely those complicities that repeatedly locate white, middle-class, heterosexual North American girls as the privileged subjects of the debate.

### Responding to "sexualization": beyond "media literacy"

How should we respond to "sexualization"? What should we say about the growing status of "media literacy" as an apparent panacea? The notion of media literacy as a Good Thing is fast taking on the status of common sense. There is a European Charter for media literacy. UNESCO pledges that "empowerment of young people through information and media literacy is an important prerequisite for fostering equitable access to information and knowledge, and building inclusive knowledge societies" (UNESCO 2006, quoted in Lunt and Livingstone 2012). Who could object to young people (indeed all people) getting the tools to deconstruct and critique media messages so they have a healthy skepticism? What's not to like?

One problem with media literacy is the implicit understanding of subjectivity on which it rests. The project of critique, dissection, comparison, and deconstruction relies on a model of the subject as unified and rational; it operates largely as a cognitive process. The idea seems to be that if someone is media literate—if they can discourse critically on an image's or text's aims and techniques—they will somehow be inoculated or protected against its otherwise harmful effects. It relies upon the idea of subjectivity as coherent, rather than split or contradictory, with the assumption that affect follows knowledge in rather a neat and obedient manner. I question this contention.

My research with Sue Jackson and Tiina Vares (e.g. Jackson *et al.* 2013; Vares *et al.* 2011) challenges the easy celebration of media literacy. The "tween" girls we studied show varying degrees of media literacy, with some of them extremely critical consumers of media, even from the age of ten. They are familiar with the language of critique and take pleasure in "unpacking" media images to reveal their artifice. In particular the girls enjoyed displaying their awareness that media images are constructed, with many exchanges about techniques such as airbrushing, the use of Photoshop, or the difference between magazines' "before and after" shots, in which "*everything* had changed," not just the area of the body that "should" have done.

Some girls discussed their anger about "anorexic models," girls in magazines with "perfect skin," and, more broadly, the gap between media images of girls and young women and those in the real world. They were contemptuous of the idea that celebrity endorsements would persuade them to buy any particular product. Indeed, in many senses the girls seemed archetypal media literate subjects—knowing, critical appraisers of adverts, magazines, and a whole variety of other genres. Yet despite this—despite an extraordinarily sophisticated vocabulary of critique—they said media representations still got to them, still had an ability to hurt them, still—as they repeatedly told us—made them "feel bad" or "feel sad" and/or made them long to look a particular way or to own a particular product. In other words, the girls' ability to produce subtle and sometimes angry decodings of media content did not seem to displace alternative, powerful responses to what they saw, read, and heard. The girls did not seem to feel "better" or more "empowered" by dint of their knowledge of media practices. They might enjoy showing off this knowledge but it did not negate or change other, often painful, feelings. In some cases, having the knowledge made them feel even more trapped—by the sense that they understood how it all worked: They saw through the "fake-ness" (as they put it), yet still felt they had to live up to the particular images of beauty they were fed.

Another objection is found in a critique of the way that media literacy forces the work of deconstructing media back on to individuals. This is part of a wider shift in power and governance towards greater self-governmentality, in which individuals are constituted as self-governing subjects. In relation to media regulation it can be seen at a policy level (at least in the UK): with a move away from state regulation and an increasing focus on media literate individuals self-regulating in relation to media content (Arthurs 2004). Media literacy thus becomes an *individual obligation*; we are made responsible for our own engagements with media—both what we use and how we engage. To champion media literacy, then, is to endorse this shift in power, and to make individuals responsible for the work of thinking critically and deconstructing media content. But it also, surely, espouses a kind of defeatism, for it suggests that media cannot be changed. All that can be changed is how we engage with them. Thus young people are asked to come equipped with tools to deconstruct sexism; young women are exhorted to become better at dissecting media's "sexualized" images and critiquing harmful images.

Why have we (feminists) become so quietist? When did engaging with sexist media seem to call out for an ever more sophisticated and literate media user, rather than a campaign to stamp out sexism? Have we given up on changing the world, to focus only on tweaking our critical orientations to it? As well as being part of a wider shift in the operation of power, I take this issue to be deeply gendered, part of the "postfeminist problem" in which gender inequality is no longer taken very seriously in Northern/Western developed societies, is not felt to be a "real" problem or form of oppression (see Gill 2007). Quite rightly, we do not respond to racism in the media with calls to educate young black people to better deconstruct racist images. On the contrary, we work to eradicate racism; we speak of its institutional nature, as a structural feature endemic to many organizations, including media (Downing and Husband 2005; Rattansi 2007). Yet issues pertaining to gender, sexuality, and sexualization show little evidence of such a robust response. Instead, calls for media literacy education imply that an informed populace of "critical" young women is the best that can be hoped for. Perhaps ironically, this focus can itself seem sexist, not only because it treats gender oppression as trivial, but also because it emphasizes the requirement for girls and young women to work on the self, to perfect the ways they engage with media, to become ever more responsible neoliberal subjects. Might it not be time to get angry again, to try to change the world? Media literacy as a kind of catch-all solution to "sexualization" needs to be interrogated.

## Conclusion

The term "sexualization" speaks to a variety of phenomena, perceived changes in culture, and significant shifts in representational practices over the last two decades, e.g. the increased visibility of eroticized depictions of the male body in public space and the "postfeminist" return to displaying a sexualized female body in the media. However, as an analytical category it has limited usefulness. It polarizes debate and accentuates division. It pushes moralistic rather than political responses to representational culture. It flattens and homogenizes significant differences in the way bodies are figured and materialized in the media. I am repeatedly struck by the "lifted out" quality of debates about sexualization—removed from the messy, complicated, power-suffused sites of everyday life (e.g. schools) and anchored only in a number of endlessly recirculated hyperreal (in Baudrillard's terms) examples, such as child beauty pageants or the sale of items of "inappropriate" clothing. The tools and vocabularies supplied by "sexualization" do not now offer us leverage to think, act, and intervene. We must go beyond both the "effects" and the "critical readers" paradigms, to develop more nuanced, psychosocial engagements that push past the familiar figures of the cultural dope or the autonomous, freely choosing agent. We need to think further about power and difference. And in moving from scholarship to activism or policy response, we need to question whether "media literacy" is the best way to respond to a media and a wider culture that remain characterized by stark inequality and injustice.

# References

American Psychological Association (APA) (2007) *Report of the APA Task Force on the Sexualization of Girls*, Washington, DC: APA.

Ang, I. (1985) *Watching Dallas: Soap Opera and the Melodramatic Imagination*, London: Methuen.

Arthurs, J. (2004) *Television and Sexuality: Regulation and the Politics of Taste*, Maidenhead: Open University Press.

Attwood, F. (2006) "Sexed Up: Theorizing the Sexualization of Culture," *Sexualities* 9(1): 77–94.

——(2009) *Mainstreaming Sex: The Sexualization of Western Culture*, London and New York: I. B. Tauris.

Bailey, R. (2011) *Letting Children Be Children: The Report of an Independent Review of the Commercialisation and Sexualisation of Children*, London: Department of Education

Banyard, K. (2010) *The Equality Illusion: The Truth about Women and Men Today*, London: Faber & Faber.

Bragg, S. and D. Buckingham (2002) *Young People and Sexual Content on Television*, London: Broadcasting Standards Commission.

——(2009) "Too Much Too Young? Young People, Sexual Media and Learning," in F. Attwood (ed.) *Mainstreaming Sex: The Sexualization of Western Culture*, London: I. B. Tauris.

Brah, Avtar and Ann Phoenix (2004) "Ain't I a Woman? Revisiting Intersectionality," *Journal of International Women's Studies* 5(3) (May): 75–86.

Buckingham, D. (2000) *After the Death of Childhood: Growing up in the Age of Electronic Media*, Cambridge: Polity.

Buckingham, D. and S. Bragg (2004) *Young People, Sex and the Media*, Basingstoke: Palgrave Macmillan.

Buckingham, David, Rebekah Willett, Sara Bragg, and Rachel Russell (2010) *Sexualised Goods Aimed at Children: A Report to the Scottish Parliament Equal Opportunities Committee*, Edinburgh: Scottish Parliament Equal Opportunities Committee.

Byron, T. (2008) *Safer Children in a Digital World: The Report of the Byron Review*, London: Department for Children, Schools and Families, and the Department for Culture, Media and Sport.

Califia, P. (1994) *Public Sex*, Pittsburgh: Cleiss Press.

Church Gibson, P. (ed.) (1993) *More Dirty Looks: Gender, and Power*, London: BFI.

Coleman, R. (2008) "The Becoming of Bodies: Girls, Media Effects and Body Image," *Feminist Media Studies* 8(2): 163–80.

Cornell, D. (2000) *Feminism and Pornography*, Oxford: Oxford University Press.

Dines, G. (2010) *Pornland: How Porn Has Hijacked Our Sexuality*, Boston: Beacon Press

Downing, J. and C. Husband (2005) *Representing Race: Racisms, Ethnicity and the Media*, London: Sage.

Durham, M. G. (2009) *The Lolita Effect: The Media Sexualization of Young Girls and What We Can Do about It*, London and New York: Duckworth Overlook.

Dworkin, A. (1981) *Pornography: Men Possessing Women*, New York: Plume/Penguin Publishing.

Dworkin, A. and C. MacKinnon (1988) *Pornography and Civil Rights: A New Day for Women's Equality*, Minneapolis: Organizing Against Pornography.

Egan, D. and G. Hawkes (2008) "Girls, Sexuality and the Strange Carnalities of Advertisements," *Australian Feminist Studies* 23: 307–22.

Evans, A., S. Riley, and A. Shankar (2010) "Technologies of Sexiness: Theorizing Women's Engagement in the Sexualization of Culture," *Feminism & Psychology* 20: 1–18. doi: 10.1177/0959353509351854.

Fawcett Society (2009) *Corporate Sexism: The Sex Industry's Infiltration of the Modern Workplace*, London: Fawcett.

Gauntlett, D. and A. Hill (1999) *TV Living: Television, Culture and Everyday Life*, London: Routledge.

Gill, R. (2007) *Gender and the Media*, Cambridge: Polity.

——(2008) "Empowerment/Sexism: Figuring Female Sexual Agency in Contemporary Advertising," *Feminism & Psychology* 18(1): 35–60.

——(2009a) "Supersexualize Me! Advertising, (Post)feminism and 'the Midriffs'," in F. B. Attwood (ed.) *Mainstreaming Sex: The Sexualization of Culture*, London and New York: I. B. Tauris.

——(2009b) "Beyond the 'Sexualization of Culture' Thesis: An Intersectional Analysis of 'Sixpacks', 'Midriffs' and 'Hot Lesbians' in Advertising," *Sexualities* 12: 137–60.

——(2011) "Bend It Like Beckham? The Challenges of Reading Gender in Visual Culture," in P. Reavey (ed.) *Visual Psychologies*, London and New York: Routledge.

——(2012) "Media, Empowerment and the 'Sexualization of Culture' Debates," *Sex Roles* 66: 736–45.

Gill, R., K. Henwood, and C. Maclean (2000) "The Tyranny of the 'Sixpack?': Understanding Men's Responses to Representations of the Male Body in Popular Culture," in C. Squire (ed.) *Culture in Psychology*, London: Routledge.

Harris, Anita (2004) *Future Girl: Young Women in the 21st Century*, London and New York: Routledge.

Harvey, L. and R. Gill (2011a) "Spicing It Up: Sexual Entrepreneurs and *The Sex Inspectors*," in R. Gill and C. Scharff (eds.) *New Femininities: Postfeminism, Neoliberalism and Subjectivity*, Basingstoke: Palgrave Macmillan.

——(2011b) "*The Sex Inspectors*: Self-help, Makeover and Mediated Sex," in K. Ross (ed.) *Handbook on Gender, Sexualities and Media*, Oxford: Blackwell.

Hermes, J. (1995) *Reading Women's Magazines: An Analysis of Everyday Media Use*, Cambridge: Polity.

Holland, S. and F. Attwood (2009) "Keeping Fit in 6 Inch Heels: The Mainstreaming of Pole Dancing," in F. Attwood (ed.) *Mainstreaming Sex: The Sexualization of Western Culture*, London: I. B. Tauris.

Imre, A., K. Mariniak, and A. O'Healy (2009) "Transcultural Mediations and Transnational Politics of Difference," *Feminist Media Studies* 9: 385–90. Doi: 10.1080/14680770903232961.

Jackson, S. and T. Vares (2011) "Media 'Sluts': 'Tween' Girls' Negotiations of Postfeminist Sexual Subjectivities in Popular Culture," in R. Gill and C. Scharff (eds.) *New Femininities: Postfeminism, Neoliberalism and Subjectivity*, Basingstoke: Palgrave Macmillan.

Jackson, S., T. Vares, and R. Gill (2013) "'The Whole Playboy Mansion Image': Girls Fashioning and Fashioned Selves within a Postfeminist Culture," *Feminism & Psychology* 23: 143–62.

Jeffreys, S. (2009) *The Industrial Vagina: The Political Economy of the Global Sex Trade*, London: Routledge.

Jenkins, H. and P. C. Gibson (2003) *More Dirty Looks: Gender, Pornography & Power*, London: BFI.

Johnson, M. L. (2002) *Jane Sexes It Up: True Confessions of Feminist Desire*, New York: Four Walls Eight Windows.

Juffer, J. (1998) *At Home with Pornography*, New York: New York University Press.

Lamb, S. and Z. Peterson (2012) "Adolescent Girls' Sexual Empowerment: Two Feminists Explore the Concept," *Sex Roles* 66 (11/12): 703–12.

Levin, D. E. and J. Kilbourne (2009) *So Sexy So Soon: The New Sexualized Childhood and What Parents Can Do to Protect Their Kids*, New York: Ballantine Books.

Levy, A. (2005) *Female Chauvinist Pigs: Women and the Rise of Raunch Culture*, New York: Free Press.

Lumby, C. (1997) *Bad Girls: Media, Sex and Feminism in the 90s*, London: Allen & Unwin.

Lunt, P. and S. Livingstone (2012) *Media Regulation*. London: Sage.

McNair, B. (2002) *Striptease Culture: Sex, Media and the Democratization of Desire*, London: Routledge.

Munford, R. (2009) "BUST-ing the Third Wave: Barbies, Blow Jobs and Girlie Feminism," in F. Attwood (ed.) *Mainstreaming Sex: The Sexualization of Western Culture*, London: I. B. Tauris.

Papadopoulos, L. (2010) *Sexualization of Young People Review*, London: UK Home Office. http://www.homeoffice.gov.uk/documents/Sexualization-young-people.

Plummer, K. (1995) *Telling Sexual Stories: Power, Change and Social Worlds*, London: Routledge.

Radway, Janice (1984) *Reading the Romance*, Chapel Hill, NC: The University of North Carolina Press.

Rattansi, A. (2007) *Racism: A Very Short Introduction*, Oxford: Oxford University Press.

Ringrose, J. and K. Eriksson Barajas (2011) "Gendered Risks and Opportunities? Exploring Teen Girls' Digitised Sexual Identity in Postfeminist Media Contexts," *International Journal of Media and Cultural Politics* 7(2): 121–38.

Rush, E. and A. La Nauze (2006) *Corporate Paedophilia: Sexualization of Children in Australia*, Canberra: The Australia Institute.

Smith, C. (2007) *One for the Girls: The Pleasures and Practices of Reading Women's Porn*, Bristol: Intellect Books.

Tankard Reist, M. (ed.) (2009) *Getting Real: Challenging the Sexualization of Girls*, Melbourne: Spinifex.

Vares, T., S. Jackson, and R. Gill (2011) "Preteen Girls Read 'Tween' Popular Culture: Diversity, Complexity and Contradiction," *International Journal of Media & Cultural Politics* 7: 139–54. Doi: 10.1386/macp.7.2.139_1.

Walkerdine, V. (1997a) *Daddy's Girl: Young Girls and Popular Culture*, Basingstoke: Macmillan.

——(1997b) "Video Replay: Families, Films and Fantasy," in V. Burgin, J. Donald, and C. Kaplan (eds.) *Formations of Fantasy*, London: Methuen.

Whelehan, I. (2000) *Overloaded Popular Culture and the Future of Feminism*, London: Women's Press.

Whitehead, K. and T. Kurz (2009) "Empowerment and the Pole," *Feminism & Psychology* 19(2): 224–44.

Williamson, J. (2003) "Sexism with an Alibi," *Guardian*, May 31.

# 55

# Post-postfeminism

## Catharine Lumby

In her definitive essay "Postfeminism," Sarah Gamble notes that the term "post-feminism" originated in the early 1980s in the news and other popular media. She says media commentators typically used the term to indicate "joyous liberation from the ideological shackles of a hopelessly outdated feminist movement" (Gamble 2006: 36). A clear, if highly unsympathetic, example of this understanding of the term can be found in Susan Faludi's best-selling book, *Backlash: The Undeclared War Against Women* (1991), in which she names postfeminism as covertly hostile to the broader aims of the women's movement. As Gamble explains:

> For Faludi, postfeminism *is* the backlash, and its triumph lies in its ability to define itself as an ironic, pseudo-intellectual critique on the feminist move-ment, rather than an overtly hostile response to it. In a society which largely defines itself through media-inspired images, women are easily persuaded that feminism is unfashionable, passé, and therefore not worthy of serious consideration. "We're all 'post-feminist' now, they assert, meaning not that women have arrived at equal justice and moved beyond it, but simply that they themselves are beyond even pretending to care."
>
> (Gamble 2006: 38)

While this accurately describes the way the term was first used in popular parlance, it does not, as Gamble herself goes on to argue, begin to account for the multidimensional meanings later attributed to the term. Indeed, like the term "postmodernism," the term "postfeminism" quickly came to operate less as a descriptor in both popular and academic contexts than as a lightning rod for debates about the purpose, politics, and relevance of feminism. As feminist media studies scholar L. S. Kim (2001) notes, there are three main points of reference for understanding the term. First, it refers to a simple generational division between second wavers and younger feminists, who do not feel the same need that older generations did to sign onto feminism in the first place. Second, it can refer to a backlash against feminism based on the idea that feminist goals have already been achieved and so are no longer relevant to young women. Third, it refers to a far more nuanced and theoretical framework for thinking with and through feminist ideas; this is allied to a philosophical shift in the contemporary humanities in the turn to poststructuralism, a diverse theoretical frame-work drawing on continental philosophers such as Michel Foucault and Jacques Derrida (Kim 2001: 321). To understand the heat these debates generated and the investments that protagonists and antagonists brought to them, and before exploring these debates in detail, framing them in historical terms is important.

Feminism has always been a site of intense rifts, of debates over the movement's relationship to sexuality, class, race, and colonialism, as well as to theory and appropriate forms of activism. In the most general terms, second-wave feminism, spawned in the late 1960s, had split by the early 1970s. Pronounced divides emerged between liberal feminists (who believed that equality with men and freedom from discrimination and violence could be achieved within liberal democracy), socialist feminists (who aligned the oppression of women with the social injustices of capitalism), and radical feminists (who saw patriarchy as the primary form of oppression and often promoted separatism). As the feminist movement began to make inroads in public law and policy, a division also began to emerge between "grassroots" feminist activists and feminists who were regarded as removed from everyday struggles because of their privileged status in the corporate, government, or university sectors (Morris 1988). This is not to say that these rifts are necessarily always problematic or to suggest that feminism should be driven by consensus. As I have argued elsewhere, rifts can be productive as long as all parties engaged manage their differences with a respectful ethics of engagement—by respect for difference and a willingness to learn from the perspectives and experiences of others (Lumby 1997).

Complicating an already heterogeneous picture of feminism was the emergence in the early 1990s of a group of feminist authors who either espoused or were labeled as proponents of "third-wave feminism." In some cases, the term was used merely in a generational sense. US author Naomi Wolf's best-selling book *The Beauty Myth* (1991) was in no sense a departure from critiques routinely mounted by second-wave feminists of the way women were valued by their appearance and sexual desirability to men. However, the author herself, who became an international celebrity on its publication, was hailed as a harbinger of the bold new generation. The early 1990s also saw the publication of a host of influential books written by women who identified themselves as feminists but who had major quarrels with some of the legacies of second-wave feminism. Katie Roiphe (1993) attacked what she sees as the "zoo-keeper school" of feminism, which, according to her, regarded men as animals and women as perpetual victims. Rene Denfeld argued in *The New Victorians* that contemporary feminism was dominated by a puritanical ethos: "Today's feminists have created an overarching theory that blames male sexuality for the world's woes" (1995: 11). These books became associated with an alleged generational split between original second-wave feminists and the generation that followed in their footsteps. In some exchanges, "third-wave" feminists were pitted against their generational forebears as either agents provocateurs or ungrateful daughters.

Updating her classic study of women, *Damned Whores and God's Police*, Australian feminist Anne Summers included a new chapter titled "Letter to the Next Generation" (1994). This expresses concern for young women who during the 1980s regarded older feminists as utterly remote from them and their lives:

> We were, after all, a mere generation apart. ... So why did they look at us through such unsympathetic eyes? Was it us, or was it them? Was this just a generation gap—or something more profound?
>
> (Summers 1994: 505)

Her chapter drew strong responses from younger feminists who argued that many women in the next generation were committed to the feminist cause and said Summers had misinterpreted their desire to debate feminist ideals. In a collection titled *Talking Up: Young Women's Take on Feminism*, editors Rosamund Else-Mitchell and Naomi Flutter write:

> Anne Summers dared young women to talk back. As one of the gatekeepers of public debate, she tossed us the key and beckoned. However, we did not wish to "seize control" nor "tweak noses", nor declare our feminisms newer, better or more relevant than those of older women.
>
> (Else-Mitchell and Flutter 1998: xi)

Postfeminism is a set of discourses that move back and forth between the popular and the scholarly. Its significance can only be understood by looking at its use and contestation in both arenas.

### Postfeminism and poststructuralism

In an iconic essay published in 2004, leading feminist media studies scholar Angela McRobbie explored the implications of a world in which,

> If we turn attention to some of the participatory dynamics in leisure and everyday life which see young women endorse (or else refuse to condemn) the ironic normalisation of pornography, where they indicate their approval of and desire to be pin up girls for the centrefolds of the soft porn "lad mags," where it is not at all unusual to pass young women in the street wearing T-shirts bearing phrases such as "Porn Queen" or "Pay To Touch" across the breasts, and where in the UK at least young women quite happily attend lap dancing clubs (perhaps as a test of their sophistication and "cool"), we are witness to a hyper-culture of commercial sexuality, one aspect of which is the repudiation of a feminism invoked only to be summarily dismissed.
>
> (McRobbie 2004: 259)

McRobbie's argument is far more nuanced than the standard claims that young women have repudiated feminism because they have been simple-mindedly misled and corrupted by popular culture. She nonetheless concludes that postfeminism is a term which "positively draws on and invokes feminism as that which can be taken into account" and suggests "that equality is achieved" (McRobbie 2004: 255). McRobbie's framing of postfeminism echoes that of feminist media studies scholar Tania Modleski. In *Feminism without Women*, Modleski argues that media texts associated with postfeminism, ranging from popular books on feminism to news articles, "in proclaiming and assuming the advent of postfeminism, are actually engaged in negating the critiques and undermining the goals of feminism—in effect, delivering us back into a pre-feminist world" (1991: 3). Of course, McRobbie's position on young women's ability to negotiate popular culture with agency may well have shifted in response to what she perceives as a qualitative change in the sexualized representation of women—that contemporary popular culture is increasingly sexualized in ways that have seen a return to crude sexist stereotyping cloaked in irony.

Other scholars, however, say the term postfeminism implies a more complex relationship to second-wave feminism than these critiques contend. In *Postfeminisms*, Ann Brooks argues that feminism is:

> a useful conceptual frame of reference encompassing the intersection of feminism with a number of other anti-foundationalist movements including postmodernism, post-structuralism and post-colonialism. Post-feminism represents, as Yeatman (1994: 49) claims, feminisms "coming of age," its maturity into a confident body of theory and politics, representing pluralism and difference and reflecting on its position in relation to other philosophical and political movements similarly demanding change.
>
> (Brooks 1997: 1)

At the heart of Brooks's thesis is the notion that postfeminism announces a conceptual shift in feminist thinking away from an emphasis on equality, and towards a recognition of the importance of difference. In academic debates, according to Brooks, postfeminism denotes not a depoliticization of feminist theory or activity but rather an enrichment of feminist theory which has resulted from contact with the conceptual work underpinning other contemporary movements for broader social change.

Brooks traces what she sees as a paradigm shift in the focus of much feminist scholarly thinking to the influence, on one hand, of an engagement with key poststructuralist thinkers and, on the other, to challenges to feminism presented by women of color. Both forms of engagement, she argues, led to a questioning of the use of essentialist or universal frameworks in feminist thinking. She cites bell hooks, who asserted: "Race and class identity create differences in quality of life, social status and lifestyle that take precedence over the common experience women share—differences that are rarely transcended" (hooks 1984: 4).

Poststructuralist theory, which has also influenced postcolonial theory and postmodernist theories, describes a complex set of conceptual challenges to the way liberal humanists conceive of power, identity, and the self. Key thinkers include French philosophers Michel Foucault, Gilles Deleuze, and Jacques Derrida. Foundational poststructuralist feminist thinkers include Luce Irigaray, Hélène Cixous, Julia Kristeva, Judith Butler, Gayatri Chakravorty Spivak, and Meaghan Morris. The array of thinkers and concepts central to the poststructuralist turn in feminist thinking is far too broad to analyze in detail here. If one thing links them, however, it is a concern to move away from universalizing and homogenizing accounts of how power, sex, and gender operate. This is not to say that all feminist thinkers who have been influenced by poststructuralist thought agree that they are postfeminist or that they see the term as useful for feminist thought and activism. Indeed, the poststructuralist turn in feminist theory arguably opened up as many questions as it answered. As Anna Yeatman notes following the turn to poststructuralism: "feminism lies on the cusp of a paradigm revolution and the features of the alternative emergent paradigm are not yet clear" (1990: 284). What some of those features of that emergent paradigm might be is a subject I'll return to when we explore the question of whether we have moved beyond the putative feminist/postfeminist divide into a new "post-postfeminist" phase.

## Media studies and postfeminism

Entering the twenty-first century, feminist theory and practice was marked, as Amanda Lotz argues, by "confusion and contradiction." She wrote:

> Surveying the terrain of both feminist theory and popular discussion of feminism, we seem to have entered an alternate language universe where words can simultaneously connote a meaning and its opposite, where labels are more significant than the theory behind the labels. This is the contemporary theoretical context in which scholars deliberate feminism, anti-feminism, postfeminism, third-wave feminism, women-of-color feminism, and power feminism, to name but a few.
>
> (Lotz 2001: 105)

Lotz's critical point is that lack of shared understanding of postfeminism raises particular concern because "media criticism provides some of the most expansive theoretical explorations of postfeminism" (2001: 106). Her point is that, in scholarly terms, postfeminism has little precision but is often used as a broad descriptor which assumes a consensus about its meaning that doesn't exist. At the very least, scholars must unpack their understanding of the term and explain how they differ from other scholars in their understanding of the term's meaning and usefulness.

Reference points for both popular and scholarly commentators in these debates throughout the past two decades have been television and filmic texts which have increasingly depicted female characters as assertive, career focused, sexually active, and, in some cases, the physical equals of male protagonists. Analyzing some of the iconic television programs that were tagged with the "postfeminist" label, such as *Sex and the City*, *Ally McBeal*, and *Xena: Warrior Princess*, Kim (2001) explores the nuances of the relationship between a genuine backlash against feminism and an emergent postfeminism that might frame a different account of female sexuality and power following the (always partial) successes of second-wave feminism in the developed world. She says postfeminist television criticism needs to offer an account of both race and class, and thereby move beyond a "white and upper middle class" framework for picturing women and their struggles with life, identity, and power. She writes:

> Television criticism has consistently accounted for and analyzed female characters and female viewers and the choices that they have. Emerging from the (second-wave) feminist movement, television criticism shares the goals of deconstructing systems of power and systems of representation. Now that we are, apparently, in a postfeminist era, I think a kind of postfeminist television criticism must also emerge.
>
> (Kim 2001: 331)

Like a range of other scholars who have studied the new wave of allegedly "post-feminist" characters depicted in programs such as *Ally McBeal* and *Sex in the City*, Kim criticizes what she broadly sees as the superficiality of accounts suggesting that these shows depict powerful women who control their own destiny.

Over the past two decades, many feminist media studies scholars have been profoundly influenced not only by poststructuralist analyses but also by cultural studies theories that emerged out of work done in the 1960s and 1970s at the Centre for Contemporary Cultural Studies at the University of Birmingham. The Centre drove a shift away from both a liberal humanist dismissal of popular culture as unworthy of serious study and earlier Marxist analyses which, at their most simplistic, framed popular culture as a kind of mass sedative distracting the working classes with narratives designed to mask their oppression. The focus of cultural studies shifted away from studies of what popular culture, including popular media, was doing *to* people to a focus on what people were doing *with* it.

In feminist cultural studies terms, this focus on quotidian pleasures led to renewed appreciation of genres that were once derided as either trashy or antifeminist, including romance novels and women's magazines (Modleski 1984; Radway 1984; McRobbie 1991). Analyzing *Cleo*, a still published Australian magazine set up in 1972 to compete with *Cosmo*, and that at the time featured a nude male centerfold, Megan Le Masurier argues that the magazine translated "feminism into a language 'ordinary' women could relate to—the language of popular feminism" (2010: 216). *Cleo* included much of the same material as *Cosmopolitan* magazine. Yet it also ran long features on issues important to the Women's Liberation agenda (Le Masurier 2007). Le Masurier takes the term "popular feminism" from Joanne Hollows and Rachel Moseley, who have argued that "it was through popular culture that most women came to an awareness and understanding of feminism" (Le Masurier 2010: 217).

Many feminist and/or postfeminist scholars have explored media representations of women in order to discern how they match up to feminist ideals of a given era. Le Masurier takes a more nuanced approach to the way representations flow between readers or viewers and the text:

> Popular feminism can describe more than just the representations (or misrepresentations) of an "authentic" feminism *in* popular media. It can be understood as a cultural space, a flow of communication, where producers, readers, feminist issues/sensibilities and text can interact. ... My reading of *Cleo* as a magazine of popular feminism goes against the grain of the received wisdom that women's magazines in this period were full of "deep conservatism" when it came to feminism (McRobbie 1999: 46). And it goes against the grain of histories of the second wave that position the women's movement as solely existing outside and in opposition to popular media.
>
> (Le Masurier 2010: 218)

By analyzing readers' letters to *Cleo* published over 13 years, Le Masurier makes a critical intervention in much of the media studies debates over whether popular television shows, movies, or magazines constitute sufficiently feminist texts and/or whether they can be recuperated by reference to postfeminism. The past two decades, for example, have spawned considerable debate about television shows such as *Buffy the Vampire Slayer*, *Sex and the City*, *Ally McBeal*, and *LA Law* (Lotz 2001; Arthurs 2003; Gerhard 2005). Much of this work has focused on the narratives and characters depicted in these shows rather than on studying the diverse modes of their reception. Le Masurier (2010) shifts our gaze from texts to readers and the complexities of their relationships with the magazine. While acknowledging the limitations of using readers' letters as an empirical base—given that editors may well have selected letters that reflected their own views—Le Masurier advocates that scholars find ways to account for the voices of ordinary women and their responses to the emerging second-wave movement of the time. *Cleo* is currently less focused on explicitly feminist issues. Notably, she does not, however, suggest that we adopt a purely "celebratory" approach to popular culture and its consumption. Rather, she suggests, the interactions between readers, viewers, and texts are more complex than this. The pleasures available to women, even to feminists, in popular culture are necessarily complicated by their own circumstances and the opportunities for socioeconomic and personal agency that they may or may not have experienced in their own lives.

## Beyond the feminist and postfeminist binary

In her book *Yes Means Yes*, Kath Albury explores the diversity of sexual practices and personal values that describe heterosexuality. An Australian scholar who focuses on sexuality, she does not shy away from the subject of sexual violence and assault; however, she also focuses on "the kinds of sex that heterosexual women say 'yes' to" (Albury 2002: viii). Albury's account of the diversity of heterosexual practices and pleasures is a critique of heteronormative discourses merely taking for granted that sex is something heterosexual men "do" to women and that the repertoire of heterosexual practices is straightforward and "normal." Her book can be neatly characterized neither as "feminist" in the second-wave sense nor as "postfeminist." Albury engages with and critiques a broad array of feminist theories and activist positions in relation to their framing of heterosexuality while firmly positioning herself within a feminist politics.

Albury advocates moving away from simple binaries that position issues and politics in terms of an either/or. She says "being sex-positive requires acceptance of shaky ground, ambivalence and the constant renegotiation of sexual identities" (Albury 2002: 39). She shows, however, that attention to ambivalence and ongoing renegotiation of identity does not equate to a rejection of a fundamental concern with ethics or a denial that women's capacity to negotiate is constrained by economic, social, and political circumstances. Popular culture, like everyday life, is often a site of ambivalent pleasure for women, heterosexual or not.

Like Le Masurier, Albury focuses on an issue that has historically divided feminists and certainly defined putative feminist/postfeminist debate in media studies: the opposition between woman as sexual object and as sexual subject. Postfeminism has often been criticized as making false claims about female autonomy. As Rosalind Gill wrote, "the figure of the autonomous, active, desiring subject" that we find in many contemporary popular representations of women in advertising, television, film and magazines is really "objectification in new and more pernicious guise" (2003: 105).

Feona Attwood explores this very question in detail in an analysis of billboards that have attracted enormous public controversy in the UK. Among these was an advertisement for *Opium* perfume featuring Sophie Dahl lying naked on her back, and a Wonderbra campaign. The tagline read "Hello boys." Attwood draws out the multiple accounts of these ads, from traditional feminist concerns about the objectification of the female body for the benefit of the male gaze, to accounts of these ads as playing to younger women more than men with their tongue-in-cheek hedonism. Attwood is less interested in whose response to the ads is "right" or whose is "wrong" than in the way these ads act as "a locus for discussion about sexuality and its representation" (2007: 16). Attempts to engage with debates about women's sexual subjectivity and their sexual objectification in the contemporary era, she suggests, must always acknowledge that, at least in the Western world, feminism is not standing on the outside of "postfeminism" looking in. Feminist perspectives are now fundamental to every public dialogue about gender, representation, and sexuality, as illustrated by examinations of public debates across the world about advertisements featuring women (Lumby 1997).

Popular media representations of women, then, and the pleasures women may or may not take in them cannot be neatly boxed as either authentically "feminist" or flippantly "postfeminist." In the Western world, at least, second-wave feminism has made fundamental inroads in law, public policy, and education. Feminism is a force to be reckoned with. It is reflected in popular media—even as it is contested. This is not to imply that feminists of any persuasion should ever take for granted the legal and social reforms fought for by second-wave feminists in fields as diverse as abortion law, discrimination in education and employment, and domestic violence and sexual assault. It does, however, require an acknowledgment that feminist perspectives are now fundamentally part of any debate about women's representation or rights, at least in the Western world.

## Less lip, more listening

So what would feminist media studies look like if we could move beyond the feminist/postfeminist divide that continues to stalk so much scholarship in the field? At the risk of asking a question that may seem utopian or even simplistic: Could feminist media studies scholars of all theoretical persuasions and political identities agree to disagree and spend more time learning from each other's differences?

One might start by identifying the issues that blister the skin of feminist debate and periodically erupt into unproductively heated, divisive, and often very public debates. Here I mean the panels and media articles that trade in battle metaphors to suggest feminists are engaged in "generational feuds" or are locked in "wars" over pornography, raunch culture, or scholarly theory. Inevitably, such alleged combat over the meaning and purpose of feminism provides journalists the opportunity to run yet another cover story asking "Is Feminism Dead?"

Beginning a conversation about the sticking points in feminist media studies, I suggest, requires careful attention to the speaking positions all of us adopt, whether they are based on generational experience, class, race, sexuality, or any other determinant of identity. In particular, it means being aware of the forms of power available to us (as well as being aware of how, why, and when others are disempowered). In terms feminists have borrowed from Foucault, this means recognizing that power and knowledge are never separable and that there is no way of "speaking the truth" as an outsider to power. In simple terms, this suggests that all speaking positions—dominant, submissive, victimized, or ostentatiously reasonable—are always laced with their own claims to authority.

Meaghan Morris (1988), a feminist cultural and media studies scholar, has been writing insightfully about this question of speaking position for more than three decades, asking what's at stake in defining feminist politics in relation to an assumed "we" or against an assumed "other." She says feminist media and cultural studies scholars need to pay careful attention both to speaking position and to where and how their work rubs up against its objects of study. Morris offers feminist media studies scholars a double challenge:

> On one hand, she asks us to critically and rigorously interrogate the terms in which we frame the work of feminism and our claims to "represent" that project. On the other, she warns against descending into the kind of theoretical navel-gazing that amounts to polishing beautiful theories and leaving them to shine on a shelf.

(Lumby 2011: 96)

Morris consistently demonstrates that we should always be suspicious of universalizing claims to "know" when it comes to politics, theory, or our objects of study.

Perhaps another way to understand this challenge is to see that it's not just a matter of *speaking* positions—it's a matter of *listening* positions. Feminist media studies, at its best, requires us to pay close attention to the cultural, spatial, and temporal location of the texts and audiences we study. It is not a matter of bringing a given set of feminist concerns or theoretical constructs to an object of study. It is about being open to having those concerns or constructs *changed* by what we encounter. When we listen actively to what others are saying, we may learn to hear more clearly how we sound when we speak to them.

# References

Albury, K. (2002) *Yes Means Yes: Getting Explicit about Heterosex*, Sydney: Allen and Unwin.
Arthurs, J. (2003) "Sex and the City and Consumer Culture: Remediating Postfeminist Drama," *Feminist Media Studies* 3(1): 83–98.
Attwood, F. (2007) "Pornography and Objectification," *Feminist Media Studies* 4(1): 7–19.
Brooks, A. (1997) *Postfeminisms: Feminism, Cultural Theory and Cultural Forms*, London and New York: Routledge.
Denfeld, R. (1995) *The New Victorians: A Young Woman's Challenge to the Old Feminist Order*, New York: Warner Books.
Else-Mitchell, R. and N. Flutter (1998) "Introduction," in R. Else-Mitchell and N. Flutter (eds.) *Talking Up: Young Women's Take on Feminism*, North Melbourne: Spinifex Press, pp. xi–xxiii.

Faludi, S. (1991) *Backlash: The Undeclared War Against Women*, New York: Crown.

Gamble, S. (2006) "Postfeminism," in S. Gamble (ed.) *The Routledge Companion to Feminism and Postfeminism*, London and New York: Routledge, pp. 36–45.

Gerhard, J. (2005) "Sex and the City," *Feminist Media Studies* 5(1): 37–49.

Gill, R. (2003) "From Sexual Objectification to Sexual Subjectification: The Resexualisation of Women's Bodies in the Media," *Feminist Media Studies* 3(1): 100–5.

hooks, b. (1984) *Feminist Theory: From Margin to Centre*, Boston: South End Press.

Kim, L. S. (2001) "'Sex and the Single Girl' in Postfeminism: The F Word on Television," *Television New Media* 2: 319–34.

Le Masurier, M. (2007) "My Other, My Self: Cleo Magazine and Feminism in 1970s Australia," *Australian Feminist Studies* 22(53): 191–211.

——(2010) "Reading the Flesh," *Feminist Media Studies* 11(2): 215–29.

Lotz, A. (2001) "Postfeminist Television Criticism: Rehabilitating Critical Terms and Identifying Postfeminist Attributes," *Feminist Media Studies* 1(1): 105–21.

Lumby, C. (1997) *Bad Girls: The Media, Sex and Feminism in the 90s*, Sydney: Allen and Unwin.

——(2011) "Past the Post in Feminist Media Studies," *Feminist Media Studies* 11(1): 95–100.

McRobbie, A. (1991) *Feminism and Youth Culture: From "Jackie" to "Just Seventeen,"* London: Macmillan.

——(2004) "Post-feminism and Popular Culture," *Feminist Media Studies* 4(3): 255–64.

Modleski, T. (1984) *Loving with a Vengeance: Mass-Produced Fantasies for Women*, London and New York: Methuen.

——(1991) *Feminism without Women: Culture and Criticism in a "Postfeminist" Age*, New York: Routledge.

Morris, M. (1988) "Politics Now (Anxieties of a Petty-Bourgeois Intellectual)," in M. Morris, *The Pirate's Fiancée: Feminism, Reading, Postmodernism*, London and New York: Verso, pp. 173–86.

Radway, J. (1984) *Reading the Romance: Women, Patriarchy and Popular Literature*, London: University of North Carolina Press.

Roiphe, K. (1993) *The Morning After: Sex, Fear and Feminism*, Boston, New York, Toronto and London: Little, Brown and Company.

Summers, A. (1994) *Damned Whores and God's Police*, Melbourne: Penguin Books.

Wolf, N. (1991) *The Beauty Myth*, Toronto: Vintage Books.

Yeatman, A. (1990) "A Feminist Theory of Social Differentiation," in L. Nicholson (ed.) *Feminism/Postmodernism*, New York and London: Routledge.

# 56

# Policing the crisis of masculinity

## Media and masculinity at the dawn of the new century

## Brenton J. Malin

In the 1990s, popular and academic sources began to notice an apparent change in Western ideals of masculinity. In the US, diverse voices expressed dissatisfaction with the so-called traditional manhood that had characterized the 1980s, seeing its emphasis on hyper-masculine toughness and emotional control as dangerous to both individual men and the wider culture. Reminiscent of the "consciousness-raising sessions" that had been popular with women in the 1970s, Robert Bly's (1990) book *Iron John* encouraged the formation of groups that brought men together to share their feelings about manhood. That same year, the right-wing religious group the Promise Keepers first met, filling a football stadium with men prepared to discuss how hyper-masculinity encroached on their spiritual and family lives. Noting similar reactions elsewhere in the US and throughout Europe, starting in the mid-1990s, journalists commented that an apparent "crisis of masculinity" had taken root not only in the US, but also in England, Australia, and Scotland (Lewis 1995; Raven 1998; Greig 2004). By 2003, one could write, as did one British journalist, "we all know that there's a crisis of masculinity throughout the Western world" (Sawyer 2003: 6).

This popular sense of masculine crisis connected to several decades of academic and political work in identity politics, in which scholars and activists sought to challenge some of the oppressive power of traditional, white, heterosexual masculinity. Although the rhetoric of masculine crisis has a much longer history—its US roots dating back to the founding of the country (Rotundo 1993; Bederman 1995; Kimmel 1996)—the critiques provided by second-wave feminists created an especially self-conscious conversation about the troubles of traditional manhood (Malin 2005; Ehrenreich 1983). Traditional masculinity, like its convergent identities of whiteness, heterosexuality, and middle-classness, operates under a cloak of invisibility that provides a variety of privileges. Those who fall outside of these dominant categories are "marked" such that they can speak only as their particular identity and can thus always be dismissed for holding a "minority opinion." In contrast, those occupying the category of traditional masculinity—at least to the extent that they can—are "unmarked"; they speak from a universal position of general citizen (Butler 1990, 1993; Warner 1994). Recognizing how identity politics began to challenge this unmarked status, Lauren Berlant wrote: "Today many formerly iconic citizens who used to feel undefensive and unfettered feel truly exposed and vulnerable. ... They sense that they now have *identities*, when it used to be just other people who had them" (1997: 2). In calling attention to dominant masculinity as an identity, the identity politics of the late twentieth century challenged its privileged invisibility.

This chapter traces responses to this rhetoric of masculine crisis from the 1990s into the early twenty-first century. As the idea of masculine crisis entered the popular consciousness, media producers and journalists responded in a range of often conflicted ways. In the US media, for example, a version of presumably sensitive, new age masculinity emerged. This "new man" offered an alternative to traditional representations of masculinity, albeit without straying too far from dominant conceptions of manhood. This had parallels in the British "metrosexual," most famously exemplified by football player David Beckham. Such images used the vulnerability that Berlant identified as a particular kind of marketing tool, crafting a presumably less traditional version of maleness that was still highly marketable. If these 1990s images embraced a presumed masculine sensitivity, however, a range of early twenty-first-century representations frame masculine vulnerability as a kind of reverse discrimination, using the rhetoric of masculine crisis even more aggressively to reclaim traditional notions of masculinity. Exploring this developing history helps to demonstrate the elasticity of the rhetoric of masculine crisis, of mediated representations of manhood, and of dominant conceptions of Western masculinity itself.

## Sheep in wolves' clothing

In the US, the presumably sensitive masculinity of the 1990s stood out for its stark contrast to the hyper-masculine images of the 1980s. As Susan Jeffords (1994) has illustrated, the Reagan era saw the predominance of a hard-bodied hero whose hyper-masculine toughness was its central feature. Hollywood figures such as Arnold Schwarzenegger exemplified this particular version of traditional masculinity. Their violent, muscled bodies and their denial of emotion—with the exception of anger, which they expressed freely—reflected many tenets of masculinity that later critics would react against.

In step with the gender critiques of the 1990s, Schwarzenegger's image began to change. In the 1990 film *Kindergarten Cop* Schwarzenegger plays a hard-boiled undercover cop who is "softened" by his interaction with a classroom full of cute kindergartners. In the 1994 film *Junior*, he even gives birth. According to a news article from 1998, the popularity of Leonardo DiCaprio, the "baby-faced, androgynous 23 year old in *Titanic*," and of fellow Hollywood figures such as Matt Damon, Keanu Reeves, and Johnny Depp demonstrated a new generation's "rebellion against troglodyte macho archetypes" (Holden 1998: 2A, 20). The character Ross, played by David Schwimmer, in the 1990s American television situation comedy *Friends* won similar praise for his sensitivity. A *Newsweek* article calling him an "unlikely hunk" refers to him as "the melancholy X-er, Hamlet-like in his agonizing over whether it's manly for a guy to use fabric softener" (Marin 1995: 68).

The new man found popularity elsewhere as well. A 1990 news article in Australia imagined the positive changes that would result from the new man's sensitivity. "Out will go the overworked true-blue Aussie and other nationalistic themes. ... In comes romance and the caring, sharing, nurturing, yet masculine man (for New Man is definitely not a wimp)" (Anderson 1990: 6). Although the new man became a topic of discussion in England in the 1980s (Gill 2003), as with much of the West, this figure also held an important place in the 1990s. The television talk show *Men Talk*, broadcast on Channel 4 beginning in 1992, was created by Eleanor Stephens, who had served as an editor for the feminist magazine *Spare Rib* and had been part of the collective that published *Our Bodies Ourselves* (Robinson 2005). On this program, which Stephens conceived as an attempt to get men "to take responsibility for their sexual and emotional behavior" (Robinson 2005: 36), a group of men sat around discussing their feelings and relationships in ways reminiscent of a 1970s consciousness-raising session. A 1998 story in the UK's *Daily Mail* identified what its author called the Woman-Man, who "phones, just for a chat. He cries, openly, during romantic movies. He intuitively knows when something is upsetting his wife, instead of shouting 'You're mad' and dashing off to the golf club." Famous Women-Men mentioned in the article include Tony Blair, David Beckham, Hugh Grant, and English singer-songwriter Robbie Williams (Taylor and Persaud 1998: 28–9). Such discussions prompted British writer A. A. Gill to assert that the modern British man "must be girlie, caring and emoting, or you are a football hooligan, paparazzo, paedophile or rapist" ("Women: Talking Dirty" 1998: 4).

For all of the talk of his sensitivity and "newness," the 1990s new man reinforced a number of traditional masculine ideals. For example, the new man represented in much mainstream media was decidedly—and sometimes extremely—heterosexual. For all of his supposed unlikely hunkiness, Ross's *Friends* storylines were inevitably about his relationships with women, especially his pursuit of and then on-again off-again relationship with fellow main character Rachel, played by Jennifer Aniston. DiCaprio's character Jack in *Titanic* was not so androgynous that the film couldn't be driven by his romantic relationship with Rose (Kate Winslet). Similarly, *Men Talk* inevitably focused on men's relationships with women; the show's host, Richard Jobson, asked such questions as "Do men really like women?" "Can we please them?" "And is it really worth the effort?" (Berkmann 1992: 36). Finally, the new man discussed and represented in these popular sources was inevitably white—reproducing another characteristic of traditional masculinity (Gill 2003; Malin 2005).

Indeed, with the exception of his alleged emotional expressiveness, the new man reiterated most of the dominant categories of traditional, hegemonic masculinity. He was white, heterosexual, and, at minimum, middle class—or at least enjoying middle-class cultural capital, as is the case with DiCaprio's Jack in *Titanic*. Despite his supposed lower-class status, Jack is extremely knowledgeable about both classic and contemporary art (Malin 2005). The supposed vulnerability of the new man allowed him a kind of pass regarding the larger ideologies of masculinity in which he took part. Richard Jobson summed this up in an interview about *Men Talk* in which he expressed his loathing for a range of typically masculine qualities. Highlighting what he saw as the dilemma of the vulnerable new masculinity, Jobson explained: "The things I hate about being a guy also give me pleasure. ... I enjoy looking at women as objects of desire but I also see it as a loathsome quality. I hate it, but then again, I kinda enjoy it. Then I hate myself for enjoying it. It's a terrible conflict." Suggesting that it was his "desire to change" that redeemed him, in part, from this conflict (Cohen 1992: 20), Jobson captured the general character that made the new man seem to many popular commentators to be a way through the 1990s crisis of masculinity. The struggles of the new man were represented within a frame of vulnerability and emotional sincerity that was itself counter to traditional notions of masculine stoicism. In adopting a kind of self-loathing awkwardness, the new man needed to change very little about his traditional masculinity.

## Parody, irony, and rehabilitation

The political flexibility of the 1990s new man—which allowed for the simultaneous rejection and rejuvenation of a range of traditionally masculine traits—is perhaps most clearly represented by the fact that this new masculinity could serve the aims of both a supposedly neo-feminist television program (Stephens's Men Talk) and the right-wing Christian men's group the Promise Keepers. In his book Real Men Worship, Promise Keeper LaMar Boschman (1996) argued that men's "cultural conditioning" had created problems for their religious and personal lives. Of course, the culturally constructed nature of masculinity and gender more generally was and is an important concept within progressive critiques of identity. Recognizing the constructed nature of masculinity—which long relied upon an assumed naturalness—can highlight the vulnerability of masculinity, suggesting that men, too, suffer as a result of patriarchy. Since the 1960s, this argument had served opposing men's movements and conceptions of masculine crisis, one self-consciously pro-feminist and one advocating an antifeminist men's rights position that claimed that men were taken advantage of in divorce proceedings and elsewhere (Malin 2005). In stressing masculine sensitivity and emotional expression—alongside various rehabilitations of traditional maleness—the mainstream new men of the 1990s had folded these men's movements together. Both DiCaprio and the Promise Keepers could be emotional and hyper-masculine—in all of its traditional features—allowing their emotionality to occlude these more oppressive characteristics.

Moving into the later 1990s and early twenty-first century, the new man would give way to other, though no less conflicted, representations of masculinity. In England, for instance, popular and scholarly sources noted the arrival of "the new lad," who, in contrast to the earlier new man, explicitly embraced political incorrectness, flaunting traditional male characteristics, especially in regards to sexualizing women (Gill 2003). If the new man had taken issue with the objectification of women—even while maintaining his utter heterosexuality—the new lad dropped any pretense of this less objectifying gaze. Maxim magazine, founded in England in 1995 and the US in 1998, featured page after page of scantily clad women in highly sexualized poses. Apparently pushing back against the sensitivity of the new man, this neo-traditional manhood explicitly celebrated much that the new man supposedly loathed.

Just as the new man was not the simple rejection of traditional masculinity it appeared to be, the less politically correct manhood of the late 1990s and early twenty-first century did not simply champion traditional masculinity without question. The often extreme versions of masculinity depicted in this later period maintained a measure of irony as well. The US television program *The Man Show*, for instance, which ran from 1999 to 2004 on the cable television network Comedy Central, featured non-hard-bodied comedians Adam Corolla and Jimmy Kimmel. Both men offered over-the-top images of scantily clad women in their "Juggy dance squad" and constantly joked about their own male inadequacies. Given the absurdity of the show's sketches, which included a mock advertisement for curare-tipped blow darts intended to incapacitate one's wife in order to avoid doing household chores, it was difficult not to see the program as a kind of parody of traditional manhood. Still, as the "Juggies" danced across the stage to the cheers of the male studio audience, *The Man Show* hyperbolically celebrated the stereotypically masculine gaze and the power imbalances that accompany its objectification.

The British television program *The Office* (2001–3), produced by Ricky Gervais, offered a more challenging representation of masculinity. As Tara Brabazon has argued, "*The Office* men are desperate, clingy, aggressive, demanding, and demeaning" (2005: 15). Gervais's character, David Brent, the regional manager of the paper company in which the mock-reality program takes place, offers a representation of masculinity uncomfortably aware of the identity politics of the previous decade. Despite David's professed sensitivity to a variety of minority groups, his various attempts at political correctness inevitably end up insulting the groups he claims to value. For example, after a photograph of David's head on a pornographic image of a woman circulates around the office, he tries with limited success to express his disdain of the objectification of the picture:

> Well. I'm angry. And not because I'm in it, but because it degrades women, which I hate. And the culprit, whoever he is, is in this room. Or she, it could be a woman. Women are as filthy as men. Not naming any names—I don't know any—but women are dirty.

In another scene, in trying to defend the lack of ethnic minorities in the office, David explains: "I haven't got a sign on the door that says white people only, you know. I don't care if you're black, brown, yellow. Orientals make very good workers, for example."

David's accidental incorrectness is matched only by his failure at many aspects of traditional manhood. As if having a pornographic picture of yourself passed around by the workers who report to you is not bad enough, David's employees are otherwise insubordinate and mocking. His boss questions both his leadership ability and his manhood. When David fails to downsize his office as directed, she tells him, "If you're not man enough to do your own job, I will do it for you." David's character offers a hyper-real parody of masculinity of the post-industrial age, in which men have to prove themselves in an almost exclusively white-collar environment. This shift away from manual labor had been seen as detrimental to traditional manhood at least since 1950s era discussions of the "man in the gray flannel suit" (Ehrenreich

1983; Kimmel 1996; Malin 2005). In hyperbolizing the awkward fit between hyper-masculinity and the twenty-first-century office, David's character and *The Office* more broadly pointed to the fragile vulnerabilities that underwrote this vision of manhood.

Other versions of this ironic masculinity took less explicitly comedic forms. Mafia boss Tony Soprano, of the HBO series *The Sopranos*, offered his own extremes of hyper-masculine toughness punctuated by moments of relative vulnerability. Moving from beating up his enemies in one scene to unloading his feelings on the couch of his therapist, Dr. Melfi, in another, Soprano was, in his own words, "the sad clown: laughing on the outside, crying on the inside." Indeed, one of Soprano's observations from the pilot episode of the program captured the conflicted emotional turmoil that centered his character's representation:

> Nowadays, everybody's gotta go to shrinks, and counselors, and go on *Sally Jessy Raphael* and talk about their problems. What happened to Gary Cooper? The strong, silent type. That was an American. He wasn't in touch with his feelings. He just did what he had to do. See, what they didn't know was once they got Gary Cooper in touch with his feelings that they wouldn't be able to shut him up!

In another scene set in an old church, Soprano tells his daughter: "Stone and marble workers that came over here from Italy built this place." Pointing to the same kind of post-industrial climate that centers *The Office*, he continues, "Go out now and find two guys who can put decent grout around the bathtub." Here and elsewhere, Soprano is presented as in tension with the versions of masculinity that gained so much attention in the early 1990s.

Unlike David Brent, Soprano, with the exception of his visits to Dr. Melfi, is a paragon of traditional masculinity. He owns a strip club (the Bada Bing), smokes cigars, sleeps with a variety of women, and lashes out in all of the violent ways one would expect from a mob boss. Far from making Soprano an object of ridicule, however, mainstream critics read this hyper-masculinity as a sign of the show's realism and depth. Noting the increased violence in Season 3 of *The Sopranos*, *New York Times* critic James Caryn wrote that "making the brutality more explicit was the only way to remain true to the complex reality of Tony's life, and it was worth doing" (2001: E1). *Washington Post* critic Tom Shales likewise argued that the realism of the program made it an "elegant, dark drama about a suburban mobster" (2001: C1). The US cable program *The Shield*, shown on the FX network from 2002 to 2008, offered a similarly hyper-masculine anti-hero in its main character, corrupt police officer Vic Mackey, and won similar critical praise for its presumed realism (Malin 2010). Don Draper's hypersexual character on the American program *Mad Men* would receive enormous critical acclaim as well (Tyree 2010; Carew 2011; Falkof 2012). The hyper-masculinity criticized at the beginning of the 1990s had come to be celebrated for its presumed emotional realism and depth, with Mackey and Draper, like Soprano, offering a version of tough, aggressive manhood punctuated by brief moments of emotionality.

That hyper-masculine figures Soprano, Mackey, and Draper could garner such acclaim testifies to the conflicted status of millennial masculinity (David Brent's non-politically correct gaffes were acclaimed for their realism as well). Soprano presented a powerful image of traditional masculinity with just enough self-reflexivity to make it seem not only acceptable, but deeply intelligent. As with the new man of the 1990s, in Soprano an image of vulnerability—in Soprano's case, amounting to sharing his feelings with Dr. Melfi or spending time with his family—played alongside one of heterosexuality, whiteness, and aggression. Of course, Soprano typically seemed much more aggressive than he did vulnerable. On *Friends* there was little fear that Ross would put someone in the hospital; less still the graveyard.

Mark Crispin Miller's (1988) thoughts on irony in television are helpful in thinking about how these shows use self-reflexivity to redeem certain features of traditional masculinity. Miller argued that American television was dominated by a kind of *prophylactic irony* (1988: 15) in which viewers and the larger culture adopted a guise of knowing distance. This preventive or protective action allowed a variety of ideologies to go unchallenged. This kind of irony was demonstrated when America's Fox television network produced *The Simpsons*, a television program that made fun of television and the Fox network itself. Positioned as ironic viewers, audiences for *The Simpsons* could watch the program with a level of disdain for its parent network, all the while helping both program and network succeed.

*The Sopranos*, *The Shield*, *Mad Men*, *The Man Show*, and, to a lesser extent, *The Office* placed viewers in an ironic relationship to traditional male values, encouraging them to think about the problems and vulnerabilities of these values at the same time as they were celebrated. If Miller's prophylactic irony suggests a kind of protection of established values, these programs engaged in a more antagonistic form of *anaphylactic irony*. *Phylaxis* comes from the Greek word for watching or guarding. *Anaphylactic*, then, refers to an exaggerated reaction or hypersensitivity to a foreign substance. The neo-traditional masculine programs of the early twenty-first century did not simply stand guard. These programs struck out aggressively—often, but not always, in humorous ways—at a variety of forces against which men were presumed to struggle. If new men such as Ross embraced their presumed vulnerability, assuming a sensitivity that allowed them to carry on a range of traditional values, for Soprano vulnerability became both evidence of the struggles of masculinity and the very thing to be struggled against. As millennial men lashed out against women, minorities, and the broader effeminizing effects of the larger culture, they accused them of making men vulnerable in the first place. In the process, they celebrated a vision of masculinity no less traditional than the hard body of the Reagan era. Millennial manhood offered a new version of traditional masculinity made strong precisely through its conflicted masculine vulnerabilities.

The rehabilitative power of anaphylactic irony becomes still clearer when viewed in its logical extremes. For instance, the terrorist attacks of September 11 created a range of discussions of masculine vulnerability, sensitivity, and aggression. Writing for *Slate*, William Saletan (2001) offered a highly gendered analogy in order to suggest why Americans should not attempt to understand or make sense of the attackers' motives, comparing the US to a "battered wife" and the terrorists to her battering husband: "What are you doing that causes him to react this way? You hope that by identifying and avoiding the offending behavior, you can regain domestic peace and a sense of control. You're deluding yourself. As long as your husband decides which of your acts will earn you a beating, he's the master, and you're the slave." This sense of profound vulnerability—which ignored the larger power differentials between the terrorists and the US—would be matched only by a highly masculine call for aggression. Condemning what he ridiculed as an overly sensitive response to the attacks, *Time* contributor Lance Morrow (2001) wrote: "For once let's not have grief counselors standing by with banal consolations. ... A day cannot live in infamy without rage. Let's have rage." Profoundly vulnerable *and* full of rage, the post-September 11 American image shared much with the conflicted men of the early twenty-first century.

Without the sense of parody that accompanied these masculine representations, however, these September 11 voices offered a kind of post-ironic masculinity—as conflicted in its imagery as it was convinced of its utter sincerity. The same sort of aggressive, if unreflective, ironic masculinity would dominate the media programs of Rush Limbaugh and Glenn Beck, whose rancor against "Feminazis" looked much like the extreme satire of *The Man Show*. Addressing Sandra Fluke, a Georgetown University law student involved in a campaign to require the university's health plan to provide birth control, Limbaugh called her a "slut" and a "prostitute" who was arguing that "she must be paid to have sex" (*The Rush Limbaugh Show*, February 29, 2011). Although Limbaugh eventually "apologized" after a number of his advertisers withdrew, his show continued much of this same rhetoric, building on a formula he had followed throughout the history of the program. Glenn Beck offered similar views regarding women, although his were frequently interlaced with tearful expressions of supposed concern for the values of his country. Limbaugh and Beck were their own representations of the sad clown, offering up a kind of failed, fallen masculinity, struggling to make its way in the new millennium. Like Tony Soprano, they used this presumed vulnerability to justify a variety of hyper-masculine attacks.

## Between men and media representations

A caller to Limbaugh's radio program shortly after his comments about Sandra Fluke expressed gratitude for Limbaugh's perspective on women. "Dan" explained that when he was in high school in the mid-1990s, he "was a very confused and unhappy young man because they tried to teach us that men and women were identical, and liberal and feminist social engineering, you know, they had me very confused. They taught me that the way I was raised to be a gentleman and open a door for a woman was demeaning to a woman. That being a man and asking a woman out was domineering and aggressive" (*The Rush Limbaugh Show*, March 5, 2011). Limbaugh's attacks on Fluke resonated with Dan's feelings of frustration. Dan had presumably been raised as a new man and now wanted to lash out—with Limbaugh—via the anaphylactic masculinity of the new millennium.

Dan's experiences notwithstanding, actual men need not identify with these masculine representations for them to have an impact or importance. The so-called "crisis of masculinity" has very little basis in reality if we think of it in terms of economic and political power, as Western men continue to hold such power in abundance. Still, the rhetoric of masculine crisis can strongly influence what kinds of stories get told, how we represent important events (such as September 11), and who is treated as having legitimate authority to speak (presumably the real sufferers, such as Limbaugh, rather than someone like Sandra Fluke). Via this rhetoric, masculinity tends to become a flattened image of aggression and vulnerability in which men can only be aggressive, vulnerable, or some awkward combination of the two.

Tracing Western mediated masculinity from the 1990s to the early twenty-first century suggests how the mainstream media have negotiated the sense of masculine vulnerability that took center stage at the dawn of the millennium. While shining a light on this vulnerability can have and has had the effect of highlighting the fragile nature of masculinity as a concept, it has also been used to buttress traditional notions of masculinity, often in extremely aggressive forms. The media's inability to think beyond these fairly narrow stereotypes of aggression and vulnerability highlights mainstream Western culture's utter lack of creativity in thinking about and representing masculinity. This is tied to the economic and political safety of traditional images themselves, which in maintaining the status quo do not risk upsetting the advertisers, investors, and others with a stake in the brand identities and profitability of the mainstream media.

# References

Anderson, K. (1990) "Is It the Age of the New Man?," *Sunday Mail* (Brisbane), April 15: 6.

Bederman, G. (1995) *Manliness and Civilization: A Cultural History of Gender and Race in the United States, 1880–1917*, Chicago: University of Chicago Press.

Berkmann, M. (1992) "New Men on an Ego Trip," *Daily Mail*, August 21: 36.

Berlant, L. G. (1997) *The Queen of America Goes to Washington City: Essays on Sex and Citizenship*, Durham, NC: Duke University Press.

Bly, R. (1990) *Iron John: A Book about Men*, Reading, MA: Addison-Wesley.

Boschman, L. (1996) *Real Men Worship*, Ann Arbor, MI: Vine Books.

Brabazon, T. (2005) "'What Have You Ever Done on the Telly?' The Office, (Post) Reality Television and (Post) Work," *International Journal of Cultural Studies* 8: 101–17.

Butler, J. (1990) *Gender Trouble: Feminism and the Subversion of Identity*, New York: Routledge.

——(1993) *Bodies That Matter: On the Discursive Limits of "Sex,"* New York: Routledge.

Carew, A. (2011) "*Mad Men* Plus Ça Change," *Metro* 169: 126–9.

Caryn, J. (2001) "'The Sopranos': Brutally Honest," *New York Times*, May 22: E1.

Cohen, D. (1992) "On the Torture of Being a Man," *Independent*, September 16: 20.

Ehrenreich, B. (1983) *The Hearts of Men: American Dreams and the Flight from Commitment*, Garden City, NY: Anchor Press.

Falkof, N. (2012) "The Father, the Failure and the Self-Made Man: Masculinity in *Mad Men*," *Critical Quarterly* 54: 31–45.

Gill, R. (2003) "Power and the Production of Subjects: A Genealogy of the New Man and the New Lad," in B. Benwell (ed.) *Masculinity and Men's Lifestyle Magazines*, Oxford: Blackwell/ Sociological Review.

Greig, B. (2004) "Here Is the Real Masculinity Crisis," *The Age*, April 2: 15.

Holden, S. (1998) "Hollywood, Sex, and Sad Estrangement," *New York Times*, May 3: 2A, 20.

Jeffords, S. (1994) *Hard Bodies: Hollywood Masculinity in the Reagan Era*, New Brunswick, NJ: Rutgers University Press.

Kimmel, M. S. (1996) *Manhood in America: A Cultural History*, New York: Free Press.

Lewis, P. (1995) "Men Behaving Badly as Macho Bastions Crumble," *Scotland on Sunday*, August 20: 14.

Malin, B. J. (2005) *American Masculinity under Clinton: Popular Media and the Nineties "Crisis of Masculinity,"* New York: Peter Lang.

——(2010) "Viral Manhood: Niche Marketing, Hardboiled Detectives, and the Economics of Masculinity," *Media Culture & Society* 32: 373–89.

Marin, R. (1995) "Triumph of a Coffee Bar Hamlet," *Newsweek*, April 24: 68.

Miller, M. C. (1988) *Boxed In: The Culture of TV*, Evanston, IL: Northwestern University Press.

Morrow, L. (2001) "The Case for Rage and Retribution," *Time*, September 14: 48.

Raven, C. (1998) "Women: Belt up Boys," *Guardian*, August 24: 6.

Robinson, T. (2005) "Obituary: Eleanor Stephens: Feminist TV Journalist Who Brought a Fresh Eye to Sex and Food," *Guardian*, December 9: 36.

Rotundo, E. A. (1993) *American Manhood: Transformations in Masculinity from the Revolution to the Modern Era*, New York: Basic Books.

Saletan, W. (2001) "Truth or Consequences," *Slate.com* [Online], September 20.

Sawyer, M. (2003) "We All Know That There's a Crisis of Masculinity throughout the Western World," *The Mirror*, June 14: 6.

Shales, T. (2001) "Criminal Elegant: 'The Sopranos' Heightens Reality," *Washington Post*, May 12: C1.

Taylor, S. and R. Persaud (1998) "Are You a Man-Woman? ( ... And Is Your Loved One Really a Woman-Man?)," *Daily Mail*, December 2: 28–9.

Tyree, J. M. (2010) "No Fun: Debunking the 1960s in Mad Men and A Serious Man," *Film Quarterly* 63: 33–9.

Warner, M. (1994) "The Mass Subject and the Mass Public," in D. J. Calhoun (ed.) *Habermas and the Public Sphere*, Cambridge, MA: MIT Press.

"Women: Talking Dirty" (1998) *Guardian*, July 2: 4.

# 57
# Glassy architectures in journalism

## Linda Steiner

Many theories have been proposed to explain why more women are not news media executives and why, as either journalists or leaders of news organizations, women have not had more impact on journalism. Using data about US news media, this chapter considers several concepts used to explain (none convincingly) why women and men should behave differently, but seemingly do not, when producing news content or running newsrooms. For several decades, when any single newsroom had only one or two women reporters, the leading theory was that when women are present only as tokens they cannot challenge prevailing practices, so cannot achieve significant organizational change. Meanwhile, the assumption was that media representations have major impact, that representations reflect their makers, and that when women could, they would want to produce different kinds of content. Now that women are at least one-third of newsroom staffs, the paucity of women at the upper echelons of media industry organizations is a popular explanation for newsrooms' resistance to new ways of doing journalism. It's more complicated, however.

### Gender in the newsroom: the statistics

A progressive nonprofit that works to make women visible and powerful in media, the Women's Media Center, amassed statistics from several sources with regard to roles of women in US media in 2012 (Klos 2013):

- Regarding major newspapers' coverage of the last US presidential election, men's front-page bylines outnumbered women's by nearly 3 to 1.
- At newspapers, women were 18 percent of publishers and held 34.2 percent of supervisory positions. Women held 37 percent of all job categories; women of color are 6 percent of newsroom staffs.
- Men were far more likely than women to be quoted (across news platforms), including with respect to abortion, birth control, and women's rights.
- At both legacy and online news sites, women are often relegated to "pink topics"—food, family, furniture, and fashion.

- On Sunday TV talk shows, women were 25–29 percent of roundtable guests.
- Seven of 100 honorees on the Daily Beast's Digital Power Index were women.
- Women were 30 percent of television news directors.
- Women directed 39 percent of documentaries shown at major festivals.
- Women were 20 percent of radio news directors. One woman—the conservative Laura Ingraham—was among the ten most important radio talk show hosts.

## The historic glass door

At least before the second-wave women's movement took hold, the widely perceived problem for women was that media organizations had a "glass door" (Hassink and Russo 2010): Women stood on the outside looking in, but could not get inside. If they were hired, to continue the architectural metaphors, they remained on a sticky floor; at best they climbed a frustrating pink ladder essentially leading them nowhere. The writer Nora Ephron (2010) described working, in 1962, at *Newsweek*: "If you were a college graduate (like me) who had worked on your college newspaper (like me) and you were a girl (like me), they hired you as a mail girl. If you were a boy (unlike me) with exactly the same qualifications, they hired you as a reporter and sent you to a bureau." Ephron moved from mail girl to clipper to fact-checker, without noticing *Newsweek*'s "brilliantly institutionalized" sexism, before getting a job at the *New York Post*.

Women rarely still celebrate the pink ladder. The Pink Ladders website collects stories about women ascending pink ladders while integrating personal and work life "into a fully blended experience" (http://pinkladders.com). More typically, even women who have found satisfaction in the media's pink ghetto, or climbed to the top of the women's pages, have resented the constraints. Some women have overtly resisted. In 1970, 46 *Newsweek* women filed the first class-action sex-discrimination lawsuit; their action against the magazine's "caste system" (Povich 2012: 3) came, ironically, the same day as *Newsweek*'s cover story on the feminist movement. Sex- and race-based discrimination suits soon followed elsewhere, first at Time Inc. magazines, and then at the *Washington Post*, *Newsday*, the *Detroit News*, and the *Baltimore Sun*. In 1977 *Reader's Digest* agreed to pay $1.5 million to 2,600 women employees. The *New York Times* promised $200,000 to 550 women and a new affirmative-action plan (and probably retains the best record of hiring women). Lynn Povich became *Newsweek*'s first woman senior editor in 1975. Yet, women still encounter significant sexism. As Povich says, cultural transformation is harder than legal reform.

## The notion of critical mass

Finding that isolation prohibited women from offering new visions or implementing new management methods, Rosabeth Moss Kanter (1977) proposed that once (but not before) women were about one-third of an organization women could form alliances, support one another, and affect group culture. This notion of critical mass, which nuclear physicists use to refer to the quantity needed to start a chain reaction, became hugely popular among feminists and underwrote their optimism. Once women reached "critical mass" in a work environment, activists thought, they would change their institutions. Media and journalism scholars likewise argued that women should be hired because, once hired in sufficient numbers (again, this was usually estimated to be around 30 percent), they would redefine news and reform news organizations. Once women reporters reached this irreversible turning point, they would produce, and women would get, more, and more accurate, news coverage. Meanwhile, lack of critical mass was often referenced to explain why women's work was not (yet) more different from men's. One woman columnist said: "You have to have 'the rule of three' functioning before there will consistently be impact. If there is just one woman in a story conference or editorial page meeting, you have to blend in. If there are two, you compete for attention. When there are three women, you reach a critical mass" (quoted in Mills 1997: 45).

Once women journalists approached or surpassed 30 percent of newsrooms, the search began in earnest for evidence of the difference they made. For example, data suggest (summarized in Steiner 2012) that women are more likely to use a greater diversity of sources, going beyond officials and political and social elites to cite non-elites and nongovernmental or unofficial figures, including women. The evidence is not overwhelming, however; large-scale surveys do not show significant gender differences, including in ethics (see, e.g., Weaver et al. 2007). Whether this is a matter of organization-specific factors, socialization of women into prevailing definitions of newsworthiness originated by men, or dictates from the top, women do not overturn newsroom conventions or volunteer a distinctly woman's perspective.[1]

The Global Media Monitoring Project (GMMP) continues to show not only slow progress around the world since 1995, but also a paucity of women's voices in news media content. Its 2010 report analyzed data from 1,281 newspapers, television, and radio stations in 108 countries. Women reported 37 percent of all stories; women did 52 percent of television stories, 36 percent of the online news stories, and 45 percent of radio stories (WACC 2010). Consistent with previous GMMP data, 28 percent of news subjects in stories reported by women were women, in contrast to 22 percent in stories reported by men. Up from 2005, 13 percent of all stories focused specifically on women; 6 percent highlighted issues of gender equality or inequality. Seven percent of stories reported by women challenged stereotypes, in contrast to 4 percent of stories by men; 35 percent of stories by women reporters reinforced stereotypes, compared to 42 percent of stories reported by men. With women reporting more than one-third of all stories, the data thus argue against critical mass. In any case, since most stories are both assigned and edited, differences in topics and approach perhaps say more about assignment and editorial processes than individual choice.

Ironically, achieving critical mass briefly provoked hysteria that journalism was becoming a pink ghetto (Beasley and Theus 1988). This claim that women's successful incursion into journalism inevitably would undermine journalism, including by lowering salaries and thereby pushing out men, borrowed from findings about other pink ghetto or pink collar jobs such as childcare, nursing, and secretarial work. Since jobs typically associated with women tend to be lower in status and pay than those of men, when a domain shifts from male to female dominated its pay and prestige fall in a vicious circle, thus facilitating the entry of more women. Notably, only slightly better are the velvet ghettos, that is, spheres employing mainly women, who in this case are high profile (implying affirmative action, diversity, and progressiveness), albeit essentially powerless. Indeed, in the mid-1980s public relations "slid" into a velvet ghetto, dominated by women, as men left for higher-status, higher-pay jobs. Meanwhile, having hired many women in their public relations divisions, corporations were less pressured to hire women in more influential jobs. For some years, two-thirds or more of PR practitioners in the US have been women (Toth *et al.* 1998). Other research similarly indicates that, generally, managers earn less when their subordinates, peers, or supervisors are largely women (and younger), at least once women hit a 50 percent threshold; women in women-dominated industries and workplaces also suffer pay inequities (Pollard 2006).

As it turns out, the decrease in journalism's pay and status should be connected to interrelated changes in technology, a general de-skilling of journalism, and the emergence of online and citizen projects, and a corresponding (if not resulting) decline in newspapers. Journalism has become neither a pink nor a velvet ghetto. In any case, theories regarding the pink ghetto and critical mass are conceptually and empirically weak. At best these endorse a kind of double bind for women, whatever the domain—politics, business, or journalism—requiring women to bring something distinctive to the table and to be an advocate for an agenda, but simultaneously to uphold journalism's professional ideology and value system. Women journalists appear to have opted for professionalism but they chafe at the expectations that they report differently than do men.

## The glass ceiling in leadership

In the 1980s, attention shifted to women's difficulties getting into high-level, high-status, and high-paying jobs. That is, the issue became the glass ceiling, an invisible barrier to promotion to leadership positions, such that, in the US, white and African American women can "see" elite positions but cannot attain them.[2] Among Fortune 500 companies, women constituted only 3.6 percent of the chief executive officers, 6 percent of the highest-paying positions, 16 percent of the corporate officers, and 16.6 percent of the board members (Catalyst 2012). More specifically, in 2012 the CEOs of the top 15 media corporations (a mix of print, online, television, and radio) were all men; only 17 percent of their board members were women. Global news media research found glass ceilings for women in 20 of 59 nations studied, with women holding 27 percent of the top management jobs (Byerly 2011).

The Federal Glass Ceiling Commission's (1995) report identified several barriers in businesses that could be relevant to news organizations, including recruiting practices that fail to seek out women and minorities, a prevailing white male culture, unfair performance and evaluation standards, sexist treatment, stereotyping and harassment by colleagues, lack of family-friendly policies, and lack of role models. Highlighting the problem for women of a long, slow track to promotion, the Commission also criticized "pipeline" barriers—lack of mentoring and of management training, clustering women in staff positions that don't lead to the top. While some say not enough women are in the pipeline, others contend that credentialed, trained women are being unjustly held back from advancement by unacknowledged "leaks" or "blockages" in the pipes. The Commission's report in 1995, when 97 percent of the senior managers of the largest 1,000 companies were white men, noted that under-lying all of these barriers may be the fear of many white men that they were losing control of their advancement opportunities.

Usually, the term "glass ceiling" is attributed to Gay Bryant, a magazine editor (*Family Circle* and *Working Woman*), who first used the term during a 1984 interview. Later Bryant expanded on the related problem of getting stuck in middle management, called a "sticky ladder":

> Women may already be in middle management, but the steps from there up to the senior hierarchy are likely to be slow and painstakingly small. Partly because corporations are structured as pyramids, with many middle managers trying to move up into the few available spots, and partly because of con-tinuing, though more subtle, discrimination, a lot of women are hitting a "glass ceiling" and finding they can rise no further.
>
> (Bryant 1985: 19)

The intersection of the glass ceiling with critical mass, then, suggests women are artificially and wrongly prevented from moving into decision-making positions where they would, and could, buck male norms. The "topping-out factor" suggests that what matters most is having women at the very top, with three remaining the magic number. One study of corporate boards found that "a critical mass of three or more women can cause a fundamental change in the boardroom and enhance corporate governance" (Kramer *et al.* 2006). The Thirty Percent Coalition, a US advocacy organization of business leaders and women's groups, insists that corporate boards with a "critical mass" of at least three women have richer discussions, better decision-making, more collaborative management, and stronger organization (http://www.30per-centcoalition.org/). The Supreme Court is similarly offered as a perfect example: One woman Justice is newsworthy as a "first"; two is better but still an exception; and once three women sit on the Court, they stop being unusual (White House Project 2009).

Applied to journalism leadership, the idea was that only when women attained high-level management and executive positions in critical mass could they undo the newsroom's macho culture and encourage news serving women. The paucity of women executives and editors and publishers would explain why women were not bringing about significant changes, despite their presence as reporters. This was consistent with David Manning White's (1950) study of a single wire editor whose personal and even idiosyncratic beliefs of newsworthiness shaped the news. The Glass Ceiling Commission said something similar in 1995: lack of ownership of media outlets by minorities and women negatively impacts news reporting; greater diversity at the top could reduce stereotyping.

The glass ceiling is not absolutely impenetrable.[3] But women attempting to breach the organizational and/or cultural barriers risk serious injury from the broken glass; women close to the glass ceiling experience the greatest pay gap. As it turns out, some research connects overall wage gaps not so much to the gender gap at top levels, but rather to a "glass escalator" that quickly and smoothly transports white men through the organizational ranks (Smith 2012). As a result, white men retain a wage, benefits, and promotion advantage at each level of authority, such that wage gaps are wider between white men and other groups even for employees who report to women and minorities. Other group differences are important, too. For example, women journalists, especially executives, are significantly less likely than men to live with a partner or have children, just as, among US executives, 90 percent of men but 65 percent of women have children; and women are twice as likely as men to delay having children (Pollard 2005; Robinson 2005).

Notably, as with the issue of women journalists, rhetoric about women's leadership has shifted from fairness and equality to women's superiority. A research institute says Fortune 500 companies with high percentages of women officers are generally more profitable because appointing women to the board signals that the company is already doing well; moreover, women bring new skills to the mix (Curtis 2012). Women leaders were rated by peers, bosses, and other associates as better overall leaders than their male counterparts, but scored especially higher than men on integrity and "nurturing" competencies such as building relationships (Zenger and Folkman 2012).

Such celebrations of women's profound impact as executives notwithstanding, newsroom gatekeeping did not change with "Ms. Gates," nor do women newsroom executives generally promote other women. One so-called Ms. Gates selected few stories dealing with women's issues or featuring women as the main subject or main source and she denied that gender regularly influenced her decision-making (Bleske 1991). Women and men editors and television news directors seem to make similar decisions (Burks and Stone 1993). Likewise finding no significant gender differences among managers regarding coverage of political figures' private lives, Splichal and Garrison (2000) concluded that managers are rewarded for conformity and adapting to newsroom culture. Somewhat later studies also found that editor gender made little difference to which topics were covered, although women-headed newspapers tended to focus on positive stories and to treat reporters with gender equity slightly more often than newspapers headed by men (Craft and Wanta 2004). At a March 27, 2013 panel on "Diversity in a Digital Age" held at the University of Maryland, Mary Bryne, managing editor for sports at USA Today, bragged that she had personally selected for publication the cheesecake photographs of a coach's wife. Photographs of the bikini-clad former model would bring "clicks" from the audience, Bryne said, "and I need clicks."

One explanation for this failure to find gender difference is simply that running a major news organization—and earning profits when profits are rare—requires the same logic of women and men. One might also argue that women and men who make it to the top have learned the same professional ideology and values. Alternatively, women leaders' difficulties in counteracting a male-dominated culture have been said to reflect lack of critical mass at the top. Yet, even when women held the top four leadership positions at the Sarasota (FL) Herald-Tribune—more than meeting the standard for critical mass—its news content did not differ much from newspapers led by men, although it placed a high value on teamwork, collaboration, and family–work balance (Everbach 2006). That said, Gallagher correctly ridicules fears that women are already invading and feminizing journalism's upper echelons:

> It is as if one woman at the top is as much as the system can absorb without being thrown into a paroxysm of professional anguish about the potential

effects on status, salaries, self-esteem of "feminization." ... The "one at a time" mentality vis-à-vis women in senior editorial management precludes the possibility of women building up the kind of power base necessary for real change either in terms of journalistic output or in the way the institutions of journalism are organized.

(Gallagher 2001)

## The glass cliff

Michelle Ryan and Alex Haslam (2007) analyze the "glass cliff." The glass ceiling's obverse, this predicts that leadership positions awarded to women carry greater risks of failure. Women do not always fail as executives, of course; but they seem more often to be asked to accept difficult jobs before getting enough information and tools, or where no one is likely to succeed. Moreover, when women fail, their poor performance is attributed to their sex/gender. Even when performing exactly the same leadership roles as men, women managers are often under greater scrutiny and criticism and tend to be evaluated less favorably. In contrast, men are more likely to advise men friends and colleagues to stay away from doomed projects. In part as a result, men are more likely to turn down overly risky jobs; they win safer and more secure jobs. When men fail in those top jobs, their masculinity is not treated as causal. Eagly and Karau (2002) speculate that the incongruity between two qualities—seeming womanly and managerial—causes less favorable evaluations of both women's leadership potential and women leaders' actual behaviors, putting women leaders in a lose–lose situation. If their behavior confirms stereotypes about women, they do not seem to be proper leaders; if their behavior is consistent with leadership stereotypes, they are not thought of as proper women.

According to Ryan and Haslam, women are overrepresented in precarious leadership positions not because of hostile sexism or a desire to see women fail, but because employers regard traditionally feminine traits such as sympathy, understanding, and intuition as particularly important for struggling companies. Sexists and non-sexists (and women and men) are equally likely to put women on glass cliffs. Perhaps it is a combination of benign sexism—the notion of doing women a favor, which also protects the power brokers from charges of overt discrimination—as well as the notions that women are more expendable (easier to get rid of) and have greater scapegoat potential (easier to blame for problems they may not have directly caused). This tendency to "think crisis—think female" would surely seem to apply to news organizations. Indeed, the recent appointment of Marissa Mayer as CEO of the troubled Yahoo may exemplify the glass cliff.[4]

## Conclusion: new spins on old debates

Public opinion data indicated that most—overall, 89 percent of those polled—US women and men express readiness to see women take the highest leadership positions across all ten sectors studied, from academia and business to media (White

House Project 2009).[5] Indeed, 96 percent were confident women could succeed as heads of film and television studios and as newspaper editors.

Ironically, this expressed comfort level was accompanied by the misperception that women are already widely enjoying leadership roles across major employment sectors, equally with men. But if the public opinion exaggerates the extent of women's leadership, women *are* working across media fields—just as women have entered other public spheres, including in elite positions in business, government, nonprofits, and politics. This is true even of the journalism beats once nearly monopolized by men, such as science, technology, economics, and even sports and war reporting. Arguably news content has changed over the last several decades. Perhaps this represents the cumulative effect of feminists pushing for changes, major economic, societal, and political transformations, including in gender relations, and in journalism itself. Van Zoonen (1998) properly emphasizes how news organizations "feminized" in order to attract new markets, such as working women. Whether this continues to change reporting—and whether the same gender differences will persist in the twenty-first century—is a different question.

Women do not enjoy statistical parity in terms of their journalistic employment across all genres, beats, and platforms. Among the many issues is the continuing marginalization of women's work (including the journalistic beats associated with women) as "soft" and unimportant. This circular and self-fulfilling problem, both real and perceptual, undermines what could otherwise be faster improvements in women journalists' pay, status, and leadership opportunities.

Moreover, women reporters also still confront significant sexism, including crude and repugnant sexist behavior, although they rarely complain of it. A very quickly growing Tumblr site (http://saidtoladyjournos.tumblr.com/) collects sexist, patronizing, and boorish remarks made to women journalists; these comments reveal how sources and colleagues treat women journalists as either brainless and dainty or, more often, sexual partners. Exposing most clearly the vulnerability of women journalists is the case of CBS correspondent Lara Logan, who had long been subjected to sexist commentary about her physical beauty. That was not the worst of it, of course: Logan was sexually assaulted by a mob in Cairo in February 2011. Learning of the attack, several women war reporters admitted that they never told anyone of being sexually assaulted, lest they be sent home.

Moreover, while women are now about 37 percent of all US journalists, they are half of the rookies, and less likely than men to be married and have children, suggesting that they leave in greater numbers—apparently when they are interested in having children (Robinson 2005). "This career is not conducive to having a family," one woman reporter said (Weaver et al. 2007: 122). US women who quit journalism blamed low salaries, the daily grind, lack of mentoring, and especially ability to spend time with their families (Everbach and Flournoy 2007). Indeed, compared to men, women journalists experience more stress—more exhaustion and work pressures interfering with personal lives—although lower levels of professional efficacy and burnout (Reinardy 2009).

Of course, the crucial challenge of juggling work and family is not specific to high-level journalism jobs or even to media jobs more generally. Recent years have seen yet another eruption of furious controversy and ferment over women and work. Explaining why she quit the State Department, Anne-Marie Slaughter (2012) asserted that women "still can't have it all." Slaughter vigorously refuted what she called the feminist mythology that women could juggle high-level work with family and parenting responsibilities if they were sufficiently committed, married the right person (she noted that an actively helpful, supportive mate is necessary but not sufficient), and correctly sequenced things. Meanwhile, criticizing those who would discourage women from trying to reach the top, Sheryl Sandberg (2013), Facebook's chief operating officer and its first woman board member, calls on women to "lean in" to their careers. At the other extreme, journalist Hannah Rosin (2012) argues that "traditionally" feminine attributes, like empathy, patience, and flexibility, make women perfect for the new global economy. According to her, that women around the world still don't get equal pay for equal work, much less achieve leadership positions, is merely the last artifact of a vanishing age. Finally, Warren Farrell (2005) says women choose to give up pay in exchange for overall greater happiness and personal growth, safety, flexibility, shorter hours, and proximity to home. These advantages lead to more competition for these jobs and thus lower pay. In contrast, he says, men's trade-offs include working more hours; taking more hazardous assignments; agreeing to move to undesirable locations; and training for more technical jobs and higher-pay jobs.

In my view, binary understandings of gender are problematic on several fronts. First, they ignore how sexism and discrimination can still prevent women from getting good jobs—ones that provide for a sense of satisfaction, with fair pay, and flexibility. Changing journalism's hard-driving, intense work culture could allow for more flexible hours, working from home, and a reevaluation of family responsibilities, which would benefit both women and men across the pay/status hierarchy. Replacing the recurrent and now banal mommy wars, which only prey upon middle class women's anxieties (Rivers 2007), with a few daddy wars could be helpful.

Static ideas of gender, even ones that ostensibly acknowledge the social constructedness of gender, not only presume but demand implausible distinctions between men and women, ignoring politics, sexuality, race, culture, and geography. Responding to complaints by *New York Times* staff about then-executive editor Jill Abramson (as uncaring, absent/disengaged, or impatient), her managing editor Dean Baquet defended Abramson by vigorously criticizing the "really easy caricature ... of the bitchy woman" versus the calmer guy (Byers 2013). This seems reasonable: The *Times*'s top person is neither saintly nor bitchy. In making the issue gender instead of equity, the dichotomy in topics does not serve women reporters, who are uncomfortably and even unfairly expected to cover (and to want to cover) women's interests, which are at best vaguely defined, and to do so in some distinctively but universalized womanly way. Meanwhile, to simultaneously uphold journalism principles and reform them. Journalists and news audiences—in their very real diversity—are better served when a rich variety of approaches are developed to give serious consideration to a range of topics, from human rights to consumer finance, from war to parenthood.

## Notes

1 Women working for pan-Arab news media intentionally repress their emotions and profess detachment, to reaffirm their professional commitment to objectivity, while men colleagues allow expressions of attachment and empathy (Mellor 2012).

2 African American men do not face that glass ceiling (Cotter *et al.* 2001).

3 The "glass ceiling" generated related concepts. Similar to the "sticky floor," "glass walls" are barriers blocking lateral movement from low-paying domains to ones with opportunity for advancement. The "concrete wall" and "concrete ceiling" represent the compounding barriers facing many minority women. The "glass closet" invokes the exclusion of gay men and lesbians, while "celluloid ceiling" denotes a paucity of women in creative positions in Hollywood. "Bamboo ceilings" block East Asian Americans, while "gray ceilings" denote the problem for Generation Xers unable to advance given the numbers of baby boomers ahead of them. No wonder a website for women executives is called "The Glass Hammer" (http://www.theglasshammer.com/).

4 If anyone doubted the company was troubled, it became explicit when Mayer, as one of her early decisions, ended telecommuting for employees, at least until the "crisis" passes.

5 The lowest ranking was in the military: 70 percent expressed comfort with women as generals.

# References

Beasley, M. and K. T. Theus (1988) *The New Majority: A Look at What the Preponderance of Women in Journalism Education Means to the Schools and to the Profession*, Lanham, MD: University Press of America.

Bleske, G. L. (1991) "Ms. Gates Takes Over: An Updated Version of a 1949 Case Study," *Newspaper Research Journal* 12: 88–97.

Bryant, G. (1985) *The Working Woman Report*, New York: Simon & Schuster.

Burks, K. K. and V. A. Stone (1993) "Career-related Characteristics of Male and Female News Directors," *Journalism Quarterly* 70: 542–9.

Byerly, C. (2011) "Global Report on Women in the News Media. International Women's Media Foundation." http://iwmf.org/pdfs/IWMF-Global-Report-Summary.pdf.

Byers, D. (2013) "Turbulence at *The Times*," *Politico*, April 23. http://www.politico.com/story/2013/04/new-york-times-turbulence-90544_Page2.html.

Catalyst (2012) "U.S. Women in Business: Pyramids." http://www.catalyst.org/publication/132/us-women-in-business.

Cotter, D. A., J. M. Hermsen, S. Ovadia, and R. Vanneman (2001) "The Glass Ceiling Effect," *Social Forces* 80(2): 655–81.

Craft, S. and W. Wanta (2004) "Women in the Newsroom: Influences of Female Editors and Reporters on the News Agenda," *Journalism & Mass Communication Quarterly* 81: 124–38.

Curtis, M. (2012) "Does Gender Diversity Improve Performance?," July 31. https://infocus.credit-suisse.com/app/article/index.cfm?fuseaction=OpenArticle&aoid=360157&lang=EN.

Eagly, A. H. and S. J. Karau (2002) "Role Congruity Theory of Prejudice toward Female Leaders," *Psychological Review* 109: 573–98.

Ephron, N. (2010) "The Graduate," *Elle*, November 10. http://www.elle.com/pop-culture/reviews/the-graduate-nora-ephron.

Everbach, T. (2006) "The Culture of a Women-Led Newspaper: An Ethnographic Study of the *Sarasota Herald-Tribune*," *Journalism & Mass Communication Quarterly* 83: 477–93.

Everbach, T. and C. Flournoy (2007) "For Better Pay, Work Conditions," *Newspaper Research Journal* 28(3): 52–63.

Farrell, W. (2005) *Why Men Earn More*, New York: American Management Association.

Federal Glass Ceiling Commission (1995) *Good for Business: Making Full Use of the Nation's Capital*, Washington, DC: Federal Glass Ceiling Commission.

Gallagher, M. (2001) "Reporting on Gender in Journalism: Why Do So Few Women Reach the Top?," *Nieman Reports*, Winter. http://www.nieman.harvard.edu/reportsitem.aspx?id=101542.

Hassink, W. H. J. and G. Russo (2010) "The Glass Door: The Gender Composition of Newly-Hired Workers across Hierarchical Job Levels," Tjalling C. Koopmans Research Institute #4858. http://forumonpublicpolicy.com/archive07/pollard.pdf.

Kanter, R. M. (1977) *Men and Women of the Corporation*, New York: Basic Books.

Klos, D. M. (2013) "The Status of Women in the U.S. Media 2013," The Women's Media Center. http://www.womensmediacenter.com/.

Kramer, V. W., A. M. Konrad, and S. Erkut (2006) "Critical Mass on Corporate Boards: Why Three or More Women Enhance Governance," WCW 11, Wellesley Centers for Women.

Mellor, N. (2012) "Hearts of Steel: Female Journalists Reflecting on Their Professional Ethics," *Feminist Media Studies* 12(2): 180–213.

Mills, K. (1997) "What Difference Do Women Journalists Make?," in P. Norris (ed.) *Women, Media, and Politics*, New York: Oxford University Press, pp. 41–55.

Pollard, P. L. (2005) "A Critical Analysis of the Glass Ceiling Phenomenon." http://wfnetwork.bc.edu/encyclopedia_template.php?id=871.

——(2006) "A Critical Analysis of Gender Based Workplace Challenges Facing Women: Gender and Compensation," *Forum on Public Policy*. http://forumonpublicpolicy.com/archive07/pollard.pdf.

Povich, L. (2012) *The Good Girls Revolt: How the Women of Newsweek Sued Their Bosses and Changed the Workplace*, New York: Public Affairs.

Reinardy, S. (2009) "Female Journalists More Likely to Leave Newspapers," *Newspaper Research Journal* 30(3): 42–57.

Rivers, C. (2007) *Selling Anxiety: How the News Media Scare Women*, Hanover, NH: University Press of New England.

Robinson, G. J. (2005) *Gender, Journalism and Equity: Canadian, US and European Experiences*, Cresskill, NJ: Hampton Press.

Rosin, H. (2012) *The End of Men and the Rise of Women*, New York: Riverhead Books.

Ryan, M. K. and S. A. Haslam (2007) "The Glass Cliff: Exploring the Dynamics Surrounding Women's Appointment to Precarious Leadership Positions," *Academy of Management Review* 32: 549–72.

Sandberg, S. (2013) *Lean In: Women, Work, and the Will to Lead*, New York: Knopf.

Slaughter, A.-M. (2012) "Why Women Still Can't Have It All," *The Atlantic*, July/August. http://www.theatlantic.com/magazine/archive/2012/07/why-women-still-cant-have-it-all/309020/.

Smith, R. A. (2012) "Money, Benefits, and Power: A Test of the Glass Ceiling and Glass Escalator Hypotheses," *Annals of the American Academy of Political and Social Science* 639: 149–72.

Splichal, S. and B. Garrison (2000) "Covering Public Officials: Gender and Privacy Issue Differences," *Journal of Mass Media Ethics* 15: 167–79.

Steiner, L. (2012) "Failed Theories: Explaining Gender Difference in Journalism," *Review of Communication* 12: 201–23.

Toth, E. L., S. A. Serini, D. K. Wright, and A. Emig (1998) "Trends in Public Relations Roles: 1990–95," *Public Relations Review* 24: 145–63.

van Zoonen, L. (1998) "One of the Girls?: The Changing Gender of Journalism," in C. Carter, G. Branston, and S. Allan (eds.) *News, Gender and Power*, New York: Routledge, pp. 33–46.

Weaver, D. H., R. A. Beam, B. J. Brownlee, P. S. Voakes, and G. C. Wilhoit (2007) *The American Journalist in the 21st Century: U.S. News People at the Dawn of a New Millennium*, Mahwah, NJ: Erlbaum.

White, D. M. (1950) "The 'Gate Keeper': A Case Study in the Selection of News," *Journalism Quarterly* 27: 383–91.

White House Project (2009) "Benchmarking Women's Leadership." http://www.in.gov/icw/files/benchmark_wom_leadership.pdf.

World Association for Christian Communication (WACC) (2010) *Who Makes the News?*, London: World Association for Christian Communication. www.whomakesthe news.org.

Zenger, J. and J. Folkman (2012) "Are Women Better Leaders than Men?," Harvard Business Review Blog, March 15. http://blogs.hbr.org/cs/2012/03/a_study_in_leadership_women_ do.html.

# 58

# Intersectionality, digital identities, and migrant youths

## Moroccan Dutch youths as digital space invaders

### Koen Leurs and Sandra Ponzanesi

*Kop of Munt* (in English, *Head or Tail*) is a nine-minute movie uploaded on You-Tube. The video is accompanied by a tagline explaining that *Head or Tail* offers a sketch of the day Moroccans left the Netherlands en masse. The video was made in October 2009 by MUNT, a collective of Moroccan Dutch young professionals. Its multiple uploads have attracted 450,000 online views so far, spurring a heated debate in mainstream Dutch news media. The video presents an exaggerated inventory of the consequences—at least according to prevailing stereotypes about Moroccans—of what the Netherlands would look like if people of Moroccan descent left the country: Newspaper delivery stagnates because white Dutch youths do not want to take up low-paid paperboy jobs; theater performances by Moroccan Dutch artists are canceled; barbershops close down; newspaper opinion sections are left empty because Islamization, the headscarf, and street crime cease to exist; taxis become scarce; social housing projects are abandoned; prisons are put up for sale because they are untenanted; satellite dishes—often mistakenly seen as emblematic symbols of segregation and the failure of integration—disappear from view; and requests for social services decline. The very exaggerations of the online video counter anti-immigration sentiments and Islamophobia by exposing the absurdities in the Dutch debate. *Kop of Munt* references *Die Stadt ohne Juden*, a 1924 film suggesting what would happen if Jews disappeared from Vienna, and *A Day Without a Mexican*, a 2004 film depicting what would happen if all Mexicans left California. The video teases out pre-set ideas about Moroccan Dutchness, offering a new take on the positive contribution of migration and fostering greater intercultural understanding. Islamophobia in the Netherlands targets the Moroccan Dutch community, especially after the 2004 political murder of controversial Dutch filmmaker Theo van Gogh by the Moroccan Dutch Mohammed Bouyeri.[1] That assassination was itself interpreted in the light of the September 11, 2001 Islamic fundamentalist attacks in New York. Spearheaded by former Dutch Member of Parliament Geert Wilders and his Freedom Party PVV and abetted by sensationalist commercial news media, both national policy and media discourse deny "Moroccan youth" (who are often born in the Netherlands) the Dutch national identity. They are dismissed as a danger, problem, financial burden, or nuisance. Moroccan Dutch boys are assumed to be "street terrorists" and/or Muslim fundamentalists; girls are constructed as either unemancipated or oppressed by Islam and in need of rescue.[2]

Discrimination is not fueled solely by unidirectional gendered, raced, or age-based exclusionary claims. Rather, singling out any one of these categories obscures others. Feminist theorizing about intersections allows us to move past additive conceptualizations of gender, race, age, class, sexuality, etc. to understand these not as singular or unitary attributes but instead always entangled. Building on an analogy between discrimination and traffic in an intersection, moving in all four directions, Kimberlé Crenshaw notes, "If an accident happens in an intersection, it can be caused by cars traveling from any number of directions and, sometimes, from all of them" (1989: 149). *Kop of Munt* illustrates how injuries to Moroccan Dutch people result from a complex configuration of gender, race, religious, age, and generation discrimination.

The concept of intersectionality problematizes identification as emerging from multiple axes of categorization that coexist and co-construct identity. This chapter charts the advantages of intersectional approaches by focusing on migrant youths' use of digital media for the articulation of their online identities. First, having surveyed the literature, we advocate moving both beyond isolationist approaches to the study of digital identities and beyond mainstream understandings of digital culture as either liberating (utopian perspectives) or disenfranchising (techno-deterministic approaches to digital media). Intersectional feminist studies of migration and technologies allow for exploring the more nuanced and fluid realm of online worlds without losing sight of how power relationships get reorganized and reformed online.

Analyzing the digital practices of Moroccan Dutch youths, we take uneven participation in digital spaces as an entry point. Online forums and hypertextual linkages on online social networking sites show how intersectionality works online. Because this theoretical paradigm does not fully account for the multiple axes of belonging, we propose an innovative way of thinking about intersecting digital spatial hierarchies and their subversion by bringing postcolonial theory to bear on the complex interface between online and offline worlds. Fieldwork was conducted as part of Wired Up, a collaborative, international research project aimed at understanding the multifarious implications of digital media use among migrant youths (www.uu.nl/wiredup). Besides participant observation across different platforms, we circulated questionnaires among 1,408 Dutch youths (including 344 Moroccan Dutch youths), and conducted in-depth interviews with 43 Moroccan Dutch youths 12 to 18 years old.

## Beyond the digital divide

Difference, inequality, and hierarchies in/of the internet have first and foremost been analyzed in terms of digital divides. Scholarship initially focused on the material divides in terms of ownership of hardware and internet access across geographic scales and across markers of difference: The rich, overdeveloped parts of the world are highly connected, while underdeveloped countries are disconnected. Ownership and access is spread across distinct axes of differentiation: men, youths, whites, and upper classes are better connected in comparison with women, elderly, non-whites, and working/lower classes. The term digital divide is ideologically loaded, particularly its proposal that once the gap is closed a "computer revolution" will take place, spreading democracy and promoting equality (Murelli and Okot-Uma 2002). The second wave of scholarship focused on skills and literacies needed to find information, again finding gaps between the "information haves" and the "information have-nots" operating at geographical and personal markers of difference (Selwyn 2004).

Social media applications promise users a presence online. Acknowledging unevenness in people's contribution to digital culture is urgent, because these so-called Web 2.0 platforms promise that users can control their own representations. The question, however, is whether everyone can equally participate and contribute. Main target audiences for major internet applications again are young, white, middle- and upper-class men, mostly located in the Western world (Donnelly 2011; Graham 2011; Nakamura and Chow-White 2012). Platform templates, drop-down menu options, and user majorities configure symbolic grammars of difference by virtue of the dominant user practices and norms that emerge within these digital spaces. These new, uncharted developments beg for analysis that considers interlocking and interrelating forms of oppression and agency.

## Intersectionality goes online: from isolationist to the intersectional study of digital identities

Few intersectional studies on digital embodiment, subjectivities, and identities are currently available. Singular axes of differentiation are typically studied in isolation. Techno-determinist new media theorists initially proclaimed the internet, as a parallel world of cyberspace, would be liberatory in its core, enabling users to establish progressive and civic communities (Barlow 1996; Rheingold 2002). Feminist technology scholars at first followed this positive stream of thought. For example, Sherry Turkle (1997) noted that users could "bend" their gender. Providing a way out of gender and technological determinism, Donna Haraway (1991 [1985]) developed the metaphor of the "cyborg" to tease out more inclusive woman–technology relations. Katherine Hayles's *My Mother Was a Computer* (2005) and Judy Wajcman's *Technofeminism* (2004) similarly read gender and technology as shaping one another.

Critical race scholars scrutinized how technologies shape ideas on race. Beth Kolko, Lisa Nakamura, and Gilbert Rodman (2000) and Lisa Nakamura and Peter A. Chow-White (2012) challenged race-blind understanding of digital cultures. Daniel Miller and Don Slater (2000) and Myria Georgiou (2006) account for the impact of digital technologies on the lives of migrants. Gary Bunt (2009) and Lorne L. Dawson and Douglas Cowan (2004) address how digital technologies shape religious practices and perceptions.

A focus on intersectional sociocultural configurations of subordination and agency urges scholars interested in internet practices to localize how various previously hidden categories—such as age, gender, sexuality, race, ethnicity, class, generation, and religion—may interrelate and impact differently. This makes visible how people are differentially positioned and differentially position themselves (Yuval-Davis 2006), and also reveals broader structural inequalities that travel from the offline to the online realm. Danger remains in using intersectionality as a "catch-all phrase." For example, some social scientists use intersectionality more as a "buzzword," by combining different singular categories, rather than accounting for the heterogeneity and hierarchies within and across categories (Davis 2008). Arguing that its potential paradoxically lies in its ambiguity, Kathy Davis cautions that "the world around us is always more complicated and contradictory than we ever could have anticipated." Intersectionality does not offer a "normative straitjacket" or fixed set of protocols for feminist inquiry; rather it stimulates innovative, explorative, and accountable feminist research practice (Davis 2008: 79).

Indeed, various postcolonial and feminist media and technology scholars have recognized the urgency of taking up an intersectional approach. Emphasizing that contemporary technologized bodies are "not simply *any* body," Pramod Nayar asserts: "Bodies are raced, gendered, and classed, and situated in particular social, economic, and cultural contexts" (2010: 66). Adrienne Shaw demonstrates how intersectional thinking fosters a situated understanding of the articulation of identity among video game players who are "not solely male, not heterosexual and not white/Anglo identified" (2012: 39). She shows how identifying as a gamer emerges alongside and in dialogue with the dominant young, heterosexual, white/Anglo, and male gamer market. Lynette Kvasny, Eileen Trauth, and Alison Morgan mobilize the perspective to surface internal differences among and within categories: "While women are typically treated as a homogenous group in gender and IT research, intersectionality presents the theoretical argument for examining within group variation with respect to how women are exposed to, experience and respond to the generalized, group-level exercise of power" (2009: 111). Studying computer adoption among working-class mothers from ethnic minority communities in the UK, Helen Kennedy highlights how her informants displayed "digital diversity" by identifying against imposed labels, technological expectations, and prioritized community notions (2005: 483). The value of intersectionality thus goes beyond the invocation of a list of axes. It situates everyday internet-based practices in local contexts as part of revealing and narrating micro-politics.

## Moroccan Dutch youths' differential identity performativity

Studies of acculturation show that the generation which has migrated is primarily oriented towards acquiring a solid social-economic position, while identity issues play a large role for their descendants (Berry *et al.* 2006). For example, Meenakshi Durham describes the complex journeys of second-generation young people: "the psychological transition of adolescence, already charged in terms of gender and sexuality, is then imbricated with the conundrums of the other transition—the diaspora identity that demands delicate negotiations of race/ethnicity, nation, class, language, culture and history" (2004: 141).

Feminist and migration scholars have found generational and gendered double standards: different expectations, roles and norms surround migrant boys and girls. Moroccan Dutch youths' gender and sexual identification can similarly be seen as an arena for power struggles. Moroccan Dutch boys are often permitted "a wider radius of action" outside the home, while "girls still face the most restrictions," as gatekeepers to maintaining the family honor; girls spend more leisure time indoors with female friends (Pels and de Haan 2003: 61). Parents may seek to protect their children from "'outside' spaces of socialization," such as Dutch regimes of upbringing (de Haan 2012: 333). Although the majority of Moroccan Dutch people present themselves as Muslim, the way religiosity is practiced differs from their parents. Islamic religious practice is becoming a more private individual experience among Moroccan Dutch youths (Phalet and Wal 2004: 39). Nonetheless, two broad and prejudiced discourses maintain influence over the lives of Moroccan Dutch Muslim women (Piela 2012: 2–3). In the (neo-)Orientalist discourse, Muslim women, especially those wearing the hijab, are represented as backward, irrational, silent, and sub-jugated by Muslim male oppressors (Said 1979; Afshar 2008). In the conservative patriarchal Islamist discourse, women are also essentialized, albeit differently. This discourse foregrounds Western women as sex objects, in contrast to Muslim women granted rights within their families by Islam (Piela 2012).

Issues of discrimination, Islamophobia, age, generation, diaspora, and religion and youth culture complicate their process of coming of age. As *Kop of Munt* illustrates, internet practices can reveal how various axes of difference are negotiated and subverted. For example, having found that "Moroccan-Dutch girls have to struggle against western stereotypes and against the restrictions they encounter within their families and communities," Lenie Brouwer (2006) argues that online girls can "demonstrate counterviews towards the dominant western image of Muslim women as well as to their own communities."

## Digital space invaders

In *Space Invaders: Race, Gender and Bodies Out of Place*, Nirmal Puwar explains that space is never neutral; every space has its own template. She examined institutionalized phy-sical spaces in Britain, such as Parliament, the civil service, and academia. Spaces are guided by their own norms, expectations, and protocols that are usually oriented towards "white male bodies." Spaces thus hold "privileged and reserved positions" for certain people, thus considering other bodies as "out of place." Puwar sees an "increased presence of women and racial minorities in public spaces" previously dominated by white men. But, she argues, they sometimes remain "space invaders" when confronted with the dominant norms (2004: 33). Extending the notion of invading to the digital space helps unearth the complex dynamics of how the body is reinscribed online. Following Puwar, we ask, what happens when Moroccan Dutch youths take up "privileged positions" not reserved for them across digital space?

Digital interface decisions and user majorities reserve certain dominant consumer, national, gender, ethnic, and racial positions. Consider, for example, the keywords that the Google Netherlands search engine associates with "Marokkanen" (the Dutch word for Moroccans). Upon typing a word in the search box, Google automatically provides ("auto-completes") search query suggestions. The auto-complete algorithm offers query suggestions in a drop-down list, predicting behavior based on previous queries of Google users, site traffic, page visits, and recently crawled websites. The search query suggestions are illustrative of some of the ways Moroccan Dutch youths are allocated particular stereotypical positions.[3]

The suggestions that appeared can be translated from Dutch as follows: "Moroccans must die," "Moroccans Veenendaal," and "Moroccans must exit the country." The first and third suggestions point the Google user towards right-wing neo-Nazi websites—mostly discussion forums—where extremists share disturbing views on migration, Islam, and the multicultural society. The auto-complete suggestion linking Moroccans to Veenendaal reinforces the emphasis on negative incidents (including robberies, violence, and disturbances) related to the Moroccan Dutch population in the majority Orthodox Christian town of Veenendaal. Simultaneously, Google Image Search results appear below the suggestions. The four images emphasize aggressive masculine street culture by depicting groups of Moroccan Dutch boys in the streets as dangerous loiterers. The inclusion of a policeman in one of the images accentuates Moroccan Dutch boys as troublemakers. The auto-complete and image search algorithms emphasize gendered, ethnic, religion-based exclusionary associations of Moroccan Dutch people.

Peer-produced norms also operate as exclusionary mechanisms. Oussema, a 15-year-old interviewee, recalled witnessing people keeping a firm grip on their purses when anxiously encountering him in the supermarket. Nor are these processes restricted to the offline world. Oussema says he often encounters racism and stigmatization while playing video games. The first-person shooter game Counter Strike lets players talk to each other through their microphones and headsets. Having introduced himself in the game by saying, "I am a Moroccan, I am a Muslim," Oussema painfully described being cursed by white Dutch opponents who called him a "terrorist." During an interview, Safae, 18, explained that a friend who covers her hair with a veil uploaded a picture on the Dutch social networking site Hyves; afterwards somebody sent her a message: "We live in 2010, a headscarf is out-dated, and it's something of the past." Targeting the headscarf as a hyper-visible marker of difference, white (secularized) Christian user-generated norms operate as digital "othering" mechanisms.

Thus, digital spaces are not merely mute or external backdrops of identity formation. Rather, they are distinct expressive cultures filled with intersectional ideologies, hierarchies, and politics. How do subjects on the wrong side of the templated and peer-produced digital divide invade prescriptive spaces transforming them from within and also creating alternative platforms for communication and belonging? By exploring two strategies—securing communicative spaces of their own and publishing hypertextual selves—we highlight how identity categories are not fixed straitjackets that can be imposed top down or simply subverted from below. An intersectional approach helps to unearth the interdependences between categories such as nationality, gender, race, ethnicity, class, religion, and age as normative impositions but also as fluid categories that can be constantly reconfigured and reinvented online through the appropriation of technological affordances.

## A corner of their own

Our survey findings indicate a distinct preference among ethnic minorities in the Netherlands for engaging with online message boards: Moroccan Dutch youths visit discussion boards more than white Dutch youths (Leurs 2012). Forums such as Marokko.nl are felt as safe spaces to connect with fellow Moroccan Dutch youths (Leurs *et al.* 2012). Naoul, a 16-year-old girl, says Marokko.nl "is your own circle, with all those Moroccan things"; she adds, "the people there are like you, that's nice." As a corner of their own, these sites create a space where an ethnic minority becomes the majority. Symbolic grammars of difference can be unpacked here among a receptive and even dedicated audience. Boundary markers include Moroccan images and symbols such as photos taken in Morocco, Arabic typing, as well as visual references to Islam like a minaret and the Quran, as well as photos of veiled women. Furthermore, in the discussions users can reframe dominant stereotypical racial and Islamophobic views circulating in news media. Sixteen-year-old Nevra finds that "different stories" are shared on internet forums, where "there is often negative talk about Moroccan youths, I find that youths there can say what they want, showing it is not all bad." Besides ethnic repositioning, notions of gender, religion, and sexuality are also negotiated. Bibi, 16, reports visiting Marokko.nl to discuss issues of sexuality in the context of marriage; she would rather turn to the online community to talk about the first night after marriage instead of bringing the topic up with her parents. She said, "With the Muslim faith when you have the first day you are not to oppose your husband and just do 'it.' And [about] these things I'm definitely not going to my parents, 'Mom, dad, listen, is that the case.'" Fifteen-year-old Meryam turns to Marokko.nl to read about personal stories that people have shared, including about Islam. She says that some Islamic rules and principles are not available in the Quran or other printed books, "but they might be available on the Internet." Participating in online forums, girls report a greater sense of freedom for discussing the sometimes stringent social-cultural codes of socialization of their parents, and wider Moroccan Dutch and/or Islamic community. The interviewees, however, not only connect with fellow members of the Moroccan Dutch community, but also forge connections with majority groups and interests.

## Hypertextual selves

Social networking sites (SNSs) like Facebook and the Dutch Hyves allow users to publish hyperlinks on their personal profile pages; they can list preferences, join groups, and express affiliations with interest-based communities. Donna Haraway recognized that hypertext emphasizes establishing connections; it neither foregrounds nor forecloses certain areas of the internet. Approaching profile pages from the perspective of hypertext enables "inquiry into which connections matter, why, and for whom" (Haraway 1997: 128–30). This way, hypertext can be grasped as a concept, empirical material, and a means of intervention, which we employ to innovatively map Moroccan Dutch traversals and connections across and between categories of difference.

Figure 58.1 shows the icons of the groups to which 13-year-old Midia hyperlinks on her Hyves profile page. She connects to a variety of groups ranging from feminist interests ("Women in Charge"), gender and ethnic solidarity ("Moroccan girls hyves"), Dutch nationalism ("I love Holland"), to food cultures relating to both

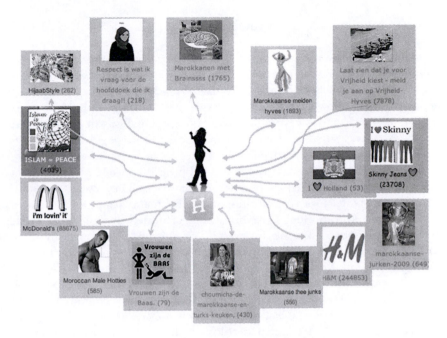

*Figure 58.1* Hyves groups that Midia links to on her Hyves profile page (April 15, 2009)

migration backgrounds ("Choumicha, the Moroccan and Turkish kitchen," "Moroccan tea junky") as well as global junk food ("McDonald's"). She expresses her religious attachments ("Hijaab Style," "Islam = Peace," "Respect is what I ask for the head-scarf that I'm wearing"), and publishes her preference for different clothing styles ranging from Moroccan dresses ("Moroccan dresses 2009") to global fashion trends ("Skinny Jeans love" and the brand "H&M"). Additionally she joined the groups "Moroccan Male Hotties" and "Show you choose for Freedom—sign up for the Freedom-Hyves." These groups vary in member-size, from 53 members of the group "I love Holland" to 244,853 members of "H&M."

The hyperlinked icons are published on Midia's profile and these different visual statements cover a wide spectrum of affiliations. Hypertext becomes a discursive space of encounter. The intersectional multiplicity of her personal gender, sexual, diaspora, religious, ethnic, and youth cultural trajectory becomes visible. Midia actively revalues her social and symbolic embeddings. She connects the categories of Islam and Dutch nationalism, which are dominantly framed as irreconcilable by Dutch right-wing politicians, while countering negative perceptions of Islam as a violent religion and also making a plea for greater tolerance of veiling practices among Muslim girls. Simultaneously she reframes the veil as a stylish fashion element. The representative profile page shows unexpected hypertextual coalitions of migrant youth as space invaders: they align with majority groups through affiliating with global youth food preferences, activism, and clothing styles. Rather than continuing migrant cultural legacies, migrant youth are actively transforming those in ways that resonate with the dominant local and global youth cultures in which they grow up.

## Conclusions

Digital identities emerge not as a set of unitary categories. Rather, when organized cartographically, they reveal entanglements with different axes of differentiation. Intersectional online micro-politics can be usefully mapped onto broader structural offline inequalities, allowing scholars to move past utopian online/offline binary thinking, as well as to move beyond additive conceptualizations of gender, ethnicity, age, class, sexuality, and so on, to understand these not as singular or unitary attributes but instead as always interdependent. However, to avoid re-essentializing categories of difference online, we recall Nirmal Puwar's concept of space invaders. Space invaders are considered as bodies out of place. They cross, trespass, and invade institutional settings typically populated by mainstream, white, male, elite bodies. Women and minorities have, however, permeated those through top-down governmental practices (like the integration of minorities through multicultural policies) and bottom-up approaches by creating countercultures and entering the no-go spaces through social climbing and education. Illustratively, the video *Kop of Munt* satirically proposes the erasure of all Moroccan Dutch bodies out of space in the Netherlands, which—instead of a positive reordering—causes emptiness, chaos, and unruliness, as migrants play crucial roles in Dutch society.

Our detecting of new tactics to decolonize digital spaces moves beyond the studies on digital divide which originally marked the exclusion of the have-nots, but thereby retained the inferiority of gendered, ethnic, and elderly bodies in online spaces. The example of Moroccan Dutch digital identifications here shows how bodies out of space offline enter the digital realm to renegotiate their place along (1) minoritarian lines on discussion boards and (2) majoritarian lines on social networking sites. Digital migrant youths' identities emerge online as multi-layered individual paths navigating through and across the affordances and restrictions of digital media spaces.

## Acknowledgments

The authors acknowledge input from Alison Harvey and Tamara Shepherd.

## Notes

1 Van Gogh, in collaboration with Ayaan Hirsi Ali, produced the film *Submission* (2004), which shows a woman wearing a see-through chador, her naked body painted with verses from the Quran.
2 Moroccan Dutch people make up some 2.1 percent of the total Dutch population of 16.6 million. After Turkish Dutch people they are the largest ethnic minority. Some 47 percent migrated to the Netherlands after the 1960s, when demand grew for guest workers in Northern Europe; the others were born in the Netherlands, after their parents had migrated (CBS 2011).
3 The search, on May 29, 2012, used Mozilla Firefox with "Private Browsing" enabled and without being logged in to a Google account and without having previously searched for the topic.

# References

Afshar, H. (2008) "Can I See Your Hair. Choice, Agency, and Attitudes," *Ethnic and Racial Studies* 31(2): 411–27.

Barlow, J. P. (1996) "A Declaration of the Independence of Cyberspace," *Electronic Frontier Foundation*. https://projects.eff.org/~barlow/Declaration-Final.html.

Berry, J. W., J. S. Phinney, D. L. Sam, and P. Vedder (2006) *Immigrant Youth in Cultural Transition*, Mahwah, NJ: Lawrence Erlbaum Associates.

Brouwer, L. (2006) "Giving Voice to Dutch Moroccan Girls on the Internet," *Global Media Journal* 5(9). http://lass.calumet.purdue.edu/cca/gmj/fa06/gmj_fa06_brouwer.htm.

Bunt, G. (2009) *iMuslims*, Chapel Hill: University of North Carolina Press.

CBS (2011) "CBS Statline," *Statistics Netherlands*. http://statline.cbs.nl/statweb/?LA=en.

Crenshaw, K. (1989) "Demarginalizing the Intersection of Race and Sex," *University of Chicago Legal Forum*: 139–67.

Davis, K. (2008) "Intersectionality as Buzzword," *Feminist Theory* 9(1): 67–85.

Dawson, L. L. and D. E. Cowan (eds.) (2004) *Online: Finding Faith on the Internet*, New York: Routledge.

de Haan, M. J. (2012) "Immigrant Learning," in K. S. Gallagher, R. Goodyear, D. Brewer, and R. Rueda (eds.) *Urban Education: A Model for Leadership and Policy*, New York: Routledge.

Donnelly, A. M. (2011) "Read My Profile," in M. Ames and S. Burcon (eds.) *Women and Language*, Jefferson, NC: McFarland.

Durham, M. G. (2004) "Constructing the 'New Ethnicities'," *Critical Studies in Media Communication* 21(2): 140–61.

Georgiou, M. (2006) *Diaspora, Identity and the Media*, Cresskill, NJ: Hampton Press.

Graham, M. (2011) "The Spatialities of the Digital Divide," *Progress in Development Studies* 11(3): 211–27.

Haraway, D. (1991 [1985]) "A Manifesto for Cyborgs," in D. Haraway, *Simians, Cyborgs and Women: The Reinvention of Nature*, New York: Routledge.

——(1997) *Modest Witness@Second Millenium*, New York: Routledge.

Hayles, K. (2005) *My Mother Was a Computer*, Chicago: University of Chicago Press.

Kennedy, H. (2005) "Subjective Intersections in the Face of the Machine," *European Journal of Women's Studies* 12(4): 471–87.

Kolko, B., L. Nakamura, and G. Rodman (eds.) (2000) *Race in Cyberspace*, New York: Routledge.

*Kop of Munt* (2009) [online video] Directed by MUNT, the Netherlands: Jiskfilm. http://www.youtube.com/watch?v=wNhiIe3g70s.

Kvasny, L., E. M. Trauth, and A. Morgan (2009) "Power Relations in IT Education and Work," *Journal of Information, Communication & Ethics in Society* 7(2/3): 96–118.

Leurs, K. (2012) *Digital Passages: Moroccan-Dutch Youths Performing Diaspora, Gender and Youth Cultural Identities across Digital Space*, Ph.D. dissertation, Utrecht University. http://igitur-archive.library.uu.nl/dissertations/2012-0614-200543/leurs.pdf.

Leurs, K., E. Midden, and S. Ponzanesi (2012) "Digital Multiculturalism in the Netherlands: Religious, Ethnic, and Gender Positioning by Moroccan-Dutch Youth," *Religion and Gender* 2(1): 150–75. http://www.religionandgender.org/index.php/rg/article/download/36/pdf_1.

Miller, D. and D. Slater (2000) *The Internet: An Ethnographic Approach*, Oxford: Berg.

Murelli, E. and R. W. O. Okot-Uma (2002) *Breaking the Digital Divide*, London: Commonwealth Secretariat.

Nakamura, L. and P. Chow-White (2012) "Introduction," in L. Nakamura and P. Chow-White (eds.) *Race after the Internet*, New York: Routledge.

Nayar, P. K. (2010) *Introduction to New Media and Cybercultures*, Oxford: Wiley-Blackwell.

Pels, T. and M. J. de Haan (2003) *Continuity and Change in Moroccan Socialization*, Utrecht: Verwey-Jonker Instituut/Utrecht University.

Phalet, K. and J. ter Wal (eds.) (2004) *Moslim in Nederland* [Muslim in the Netherlands], The Hague: SCP.

Piela, A. (2012) *Muslim Women Online*, London: Routledge.

Puwar, N. (2004) *Space Invaders: Race, Gender and Bodies Out of Place*, Oxford: Berg.

Rheingold, H. (2002) *Smart Mobs*, Cambridge: Perseus Books.

Said, E. (1979) *Orientalism*, New York: Vintage Books.

Selwyn, N. (2004) "Reconsidering Political and Popular Understandings of the Digital Divide," *New Media & Society* 6: 341–62.

Shaw, A. (2012) "Do You Identify as a Gamer?," *New Media & Society* 14(1): 28–44.

Turkle, S. (1997) *Life On the Screen*, New York: Touchstone.

Wajcman, J. (2004) *Technofeminism*, Cambridge: John Wiley and Sons.

Yuval-Davis, N. (2006) "Intersectionality and Feminist Politics," *European Journal of Women's Studies* 13(3): 193–209.

# 59

# Online popular anti-sexism political action in the UK and USA

## The importance of collaborative anger for social change

## Cynthia Carter

> Anger is a fuel. You need it to launch a rocket. But if all you have is fuel without any complex internal mechanism directing it, you don't have a rocket. You have a bomb.
> (Schwartz 2006)

Until very recently, many feminist media scholars were loath to use the term "sexist" to describe the treatment of women working in media industries, the representation of women (and men) across a range of media texts, or audiences' uncritical responses to that media content. The reasons for this were wholly understandable, given that the notion of sexism appeared to have been thoroughly robbed of its power of political critique in the latter years of second-wave feminism, used as it was too widely and generally. Some feminists felt uncomfortable using the word, as Rosalind Gill (2011: 61) suggests in recounting a 2005 story about a young woman who asked feminist media critic Judith Williamson what might be done to address the ongoing issue of sexism in advertising. Many feminists had, in Williamson's view, allowed others to co-opt and deride the notion of sexism, often turning it upside down in order to accuse feminists of being "uptight," "frigid," or "humourless" (Gill 2011: 61).

My sense is that by the late 1990s and through much of the last decade, few feminists thought that the term "sexist" had consequential analytical or political purchase. As Gill suggests, it seemed to belong to another era of feminism, one that tended to take the "softly softly" approach to encouraging the media to portray women more "positively," or, alternatively, representing a strongly radical position that pitted men against women in simplistic ways, which many feminists regarded as a vestige of the past (see also Dean 2010; Attenborough 2012). What I find particularly interesting is Williamson's conclusion that if we are going to tackle what appears to be increasing sexism in media, we should "simply start using the term again" (Gill 2011: 61). This would allow feminist media scholars and activists to put media sexism back on the scholarly and public agenda (see also Walter 2010). As Gill suggests by the title of her article "Sexism Reloaded, or, It's Time to Get Angry Again!," a cursory look at online political activism around gender issues clearly demonstrates that there is a great deal of anger over sexist stereotyping and gender pay gaps in media industries. Those who think equality has been won and that feminism is therefore unnecessary are angry about the resurgence of feminist criticism, while still others feel that men can't win even when they try to support feminism.

Despite the establishment of wide-ranging legal reforms in both the UK and US (as is also the case in most countries, to varying degrees, around the world) that were intended to bring women and men economic, social, political, and personal equality, now, in the second decade of the twenty-first century, we're still dealing with resistance to the inclusion of women in the public sphere on equal terms with men. Moreover, calls for men to become more responsible for care and domestic labor in the private sphere also continue to meet resistance. Of course, if the term "sexism" is to have any political purchase it needs some redefinition in order to repoliticize it for today's cultural, technological, and political realities. As Gill suggests:

> [I]f we think about sexism not as a single, unchanging "thing" (e.g., a set of relatively stable stereotypes), but instead reconceptualize it as an *agile, dynamic, changing and diverse set of malleable representations and practices of power*, how could it be anything less than *urgent* to have this term in our critical vocabulary? Surely part of the project of feminist media studies is—or should be—about understanding and illuminating the varied ways in which sexism (and its intersections with other axes of power) operates through the media.
>
> (Gill 2011: 62)

With these points in mind I would like to highlight some of the important and interesting ways in which the term "sexism" is being redefined and used in and through online popular anti-sexist political action. Such activities are contributing to rethinking media sexism along the lines Gill identifies. They include interrogation of the ways in which sexism is reproduced through cultural production; intervention in debates around the emergence of postfeminism; engagement with media sexualization; reclaiming the intellectual projects of ideology and discourse critique in order to address gender and power; acknowledgment of the absolute requirement for developing the notion of sexism through an intersectional critique where gender is linked to "race," sexuality, class, disability, generation, and so forth; and political in both its macro (polity) and micro (everyday life) forms. It is also vital to ensure that feminist theory and political activism never again become as decoupled as they were in the 1980s, a situation which led to debilitating fissures between academics and activists that had disastrous consequences for the women's movement.

One encouraging sign that this debilitating situation will not repeat itself is the recent rise of student activism on an ever-growing number of UK university campuses (and elsewhere in the world), with many citing the rise of "lad culture" as one of the main objects of their protests. As the *Guardian* newspaper journalist Emily Hilton (2013) notes, "women are fighting back—or at least that's what the recent surge in the number of student feminist societies suggests. Students at the Universities of Westminster, Durham, Liverpool, Gloucestershire, Central Lancashire and King's College London have each set up feminist societies in the last 12 months." It's not just women who are engaged in such political action. Men also want to challenge the view that feminism is no longer relevant and are actively refusing the sexism of "lad culture" even as many of their male peers appear to be embracing it (Hilton 2013). Some men realize that challenging restrictive forms of femininity and masculinity and supporting feminist aims, in the long run, is in men's interests, too. The path in this journey, however, is not smooth.

In what follows, I provide several case studies of current online popular anti-sexist activism in order to highlight how the notion of sexism is currently developing, as well as the extent to which it provides a focus for many political activities. Most are drawn from initiatives established in the UK and US. This in no way is to suggest that such online activism is only occurring in these places; nothing could be further from the truth. Increasingly, women and men are finding that social media, in particular, facilitate both online and offline feminist political engagement around the globe, as, for example, with the so-called "Arab Spring." The reasons for this are obvious: the internet can quickly facilitate connections between like-minded people and political activities and allow them to bypass traditional lines of communication (mainstream media) and political lobbying.

## Making a difference together

I am struck by how much online anti-sexist action is now taking place. Indeed, I had to make difficult decisions as to which initiatives to focus on in this chapter. I chose "Miss Representation," which combines a documentary with a media literacy curriculum for the purpose of raising awareness and promoting activism centered on the ways in which mainstream media representations of girls and women inhibit them from reaching their full potential in life. The Good Men Project is committed to exploring what it means to be a "good man" in the twenty-first century. Both of these projects were initiated by not-for-profit organizations originating from the US. I also will describe the Women's Room, an organization compiling a database of female experts across the widest range of professions, disciplines, topics, and issues; and the Everyday Sexism Project, a Twitter initiative asking women to tweet past and current experiences of sexism in their lives to highlight the range and extent of everyday sexism. Finally, I include two British petition-based political actions with similar aims: No More Page Three, and Turn Your Back on Page 3 (TYBOP3), both committed to ridding *The Sun* of its daily picture of a topless woman (although models can be as young as 16), which has been published in that tabloid newspaper since 1970.

Had I the space to address other types of gender activism, I would have included a fast-growing arena of intervention in discussions around sexism, namely feminist online zines such as *The F Word* and *Week Women*, both based in the UK, blogs like *Feminist Current* from Canada, feminist blogs in the UK such as *Feminista* and *Hollaback!*, or longstanding feminist online communities such as *Feminist.com*, established in the US but which now has a global reach. A broader discussion also would include magazines that have been campaigning for gender equality for decades, such as the American *Ms.* and *Off Our Backs*, as well as those that had ceased publication but are now returning, such as the UK's *Spare Rib* magazine, relaunched in 2013. The case studies focused on here are organized into three broad types: education; expert voices; and campaigning.

## Educational

Miss Representation and the Good Men Project are not-for-profit educational organizations based in the US. Both began with the aim of raising public awareness about gender issues. The former recently became more campaign oriented, while the latter has established itself primarily as an online campaigning magazine with a strong orientation toward reader discussion.

### *Miss Representation*

Miss Representation.org, founded in 2011 by US filmmaker and advocate Jennifer Siebel Newsom, is, in its website's words, a "social action campaign, and media organization established to shift people's consciousness, inspire individual and community action, and ultimately transform culture so everyone, regardless of gender, age or circumstance can fulfill their potential" (Miss Representation n.d.). The organization began life on the back of a 2011 film by the same name that was launched at the Sundance Film Festival and then shown on the Oprah Winfrey Network (OWN). The purpose of the film, as Newsom indicated in an interview with Marianne Schnall (2011) for Huff Post's "Women" section was to spark wide public discussion about women in American society. In Newsom's view, the feminine had become devalued in society and women's voices marginalized in the public sphere. She believed that her intervention through the film, which features the stories of teenage girls, interviews with politicians, journalists, entertainers, academics, and activists, as well as examples of sexism in the media and statistics about women's status in society, would expose the ongoing objectification of women. The film, insists Schnall, shows how mainstream media representations of girls and women results in

> valuing them only for their youth, beauty and sexuality [which] can lead to the suppression of women who are rendered voiceless, disempowered, dehumanized and objectified. This ultimately leads to preventing them from realizing their full potential to the detriment of themselves, our democracy, and society.
>
> (Schnall 2011)

In Newsom's view, the media are a "huge pedagogical force of communication" which establish cultural values and norms around gender, thus limiting girls' and women's potential. Challenging contemporary gender representation marks an important arena of political activism. The film does not simply provide a negative critique of the American media but instead offers "concrete solutions and hope, and ... there's a comprehensive action campaign as part of this" (Schnall 2011).

Miss Representation's website reflects both an educative and campaigning strategy for keeping the public conversation going about gender and representation. The website also offers information about where the film is currently being screened, and a gender-focused media literacy curriculum that can be purchased by schools and universities. A blog features stories about Miss Representation's social media campaigning and Take Action, which is the face of its campaigning efforts. These include #notbuyingit; a "Media We Like" feature, which encourages people to share examples of best media practices in gender representation on Pinterest; "Conversation Starters," online guides for young people and their families to download to start family discussions about gender issues; advice on how to make a YouTube clip; a "House Party Kit" to be used in a screening with family or friends; "Weekly Action Alerts," which are emails outlining one specific campaigning action; "Gender Equality Principles," designed to be used by companies to ensure gender equality in the workplace; general "Resources and Tools for Action" that can be employed to organize local campaigns; and links to Miss Representation's Twitter, Facebook, and Pinterest interfaces.

## The Good Men Project

The Good Men Foundation, initiated in 2009 by the successful entrepreneur Tom Matlock, is a nonprofit organization "dedicated to helping organizations that provide educational, social, financial and legal support to men and boys at risk" (Wikipedia n.d.). A central initiative of the Foundation is the Good Men Project (TGMP), which began with a documentary featuring men talking about "defining moments" in their lives, and an accompanying anthology on the same subject (Good Men Project n.d.). Having focused primarily on career and earning money to provide for his family, when his son was only six months old Matlack faced the breakdown of his marriage and eventual divorce. This was his own "defining moment," which provoked his recognition that his focus on career success had left no room in his life to be a good husband and father. Some years later, he realized that many other men were in a similar position and decided to make a documentary that would "spark a national conversation about what it means to be a good man in the 21st century" (The Editors 2013). In the four years since its launch it has become a "diverse, multi-faceted media company and media-based social platform" (Good Men Project n.d.).

TGMP sees itself as a community exploring the fast-changing role of men in contemporary American society (many contributors to the site also increasingly come from outside the US; see also Penny 2013 and Poole 2013 for a discussion of the "crisis in masculinity"). The community blogs and comments on a wide range of issues, including fatherhood, sex, parenting, work, politics, sport, pornography, war, ethics, and family. Often quite difficult subjects, including those that many still consider to be taboo, including homosexuality, emotions, health issues, feminism, challenging violence in sport, and racism, are addressed. As the TGMP site states:

> Our content reflects the multidimensionality of men—we are alternatively funny and serious, provocative and thoughtful, earnest and light-hearted. We search far and wide for new stories and new voices from the "front lines

of modern manhood." And we do it without moralizing and without caricaturizing our audience; we let guys be guys, but we do it while challenging confining cultural notions of what a "real man" must be.

(Good Men Project n.d.)

Matlack stepped down from his position on the TGMP in April 2013 (see The Editors 2013) just two days after posting the blog entry on the TGMP "What's a Guy to Do?" In the piece, Matlack criticized Catherine Rempell's *New York Times* article where she argued that, rather than expecting women to "lean in" so as to advance their careers, what is needed is more men who pull their weight at home. While admitting that men are still in positions of great power in the world, Matlack said that they are also struggling to understand the changing position of men in the twenty-first century. His frustration with those who would criticize men for wanting to break out of restrictive masculine roles and redefine what it means to be a man is evident. The breaking point, however, was criticism aimed at him after what he admits was a stupid mistake on his part—writing about women and make-up for the Room for Debate. This blog post sparked sharp rebukes from a number of feminist bloggers, including Amanda Marcotte on the *Slate* website, and Meghan Murphy, founder and editor of the blog *Feminist Current*. These two feminist writers expressed what is still a burning resentment and anger amongst some feminists with regard to male initiatives attempting to contribute to debates around gender. Murphy wrote a blistering reproach:

So here's the thing, Tom. Feminism doesn't want you. The last thing we need is some rich, white dude explaining to us how REAL liberation should happen. You've proven yourself over and over again to be a sexist douche who thinks feminists are bashing all men simply because they call YOU out on your bullshit. YOU are part of the problem.

(Murphy 2013)

Murphy's view has been challenged by others, such as the US feminist activist Lauren Rankin (2013), who argues that feminism needs men who can be allies, support feminists without sidelining them, and challenge the sexism of their male friends and colleagues. As Rankin concludes, men can be feminists because "feminism isn't a label, but an action. ... Men are not the target; patriarchy is."

## Expert voices

Research initiatives such as the Global Media Monitoring Project, which has surveyed the world's news media in five-year intervals since 1995, have consistently shown that men make up the majority of authoritative sources used by journalists around the world. The persistent view is that journalists, politicians, and others have few women upon whose expertise they can draw. Feminists argue that the dearth of authoritative women's voices in the news silences and disenfranchises them within democratic society. The UK's The Women's Room addresses this concern by establishing a database of women experts across a wide range of topics, issues, and professions.

## The Women's Room

In November 2012, British feminists Caroline Criado-Perez and Catherine Smith co-founded the website The Women's Room to challenge the view that insufficient expertise exists amongst women to be used to inform and enrich public debate. The month before Criado-Perez had noted that, for two days in a row, the influential daily news program the *Today* program on BBC Radio 4 invited all-male panels of experts to talk about breast cancer and teenage contraception. Despite strong criticisms from the public, producers claimed that they were unable to find female experts on these issues. Criado-Perez thought this was "the most ridiculous thing I've ever heard" (Driscoll 2013). The next step was to set up a Twitter account asking women to come forward to help establish a database of female experts, and within minutes, apparently, she was inundated with responses (Driscoll 2013).

The notion of expertise shaping the website is wide—with Criado-Perez and Smith keen to avoid simply reinventing "expertise," this time with white, middle-class women. Instead, the aim is to broadly define "expertise" so as to be more inclusive of the broadest possible range of voices. As Criado-Perez notes, "Experts are not just people with academic expertise or professional qualifications, everyone has had experiences and are able to add an interesting or worthwhile dimension to a subject" (Driscoll 2013). As of June 2013, over 2,500 women had registered as experts on the Women's Room website. On the homepage is a large button that journalists can click to "find an expert." The project also monitors the media through its feature "MediaWatch" for examples of both best and worst practices regarding the representation of women, as well as media stories about the project. "Forums" is a message board encouraging women to connect to discuss issues, and there are web links to other activist groups. Concludes Criado-Perez, "I hope that Media Watch will work as a carrot and a stick. We can celebrate programmes that are getting it right. But also equally to come down hard when they have an all-male panel to discuss something" (Driscoll 2013).

## Campaigning

Direct campaigning refers to specific initiatives that grow out of the desire to address media sexism, which activists target while encouraging others to contribute by sharing everyday experiences of sexism, online petitions, writing letters to politicians and news organizations, and so forth.

### The Everyday Sexism Project

UK-based activist Laura Bates set up the Everyday Sexism Project on Twitter and on the web without funding or publicity in April 2012 in order to document women's everyday experiences of sexism. At first, she thought that it might mainly attract friends and serve as a space for sharing such experiences. Eighteen months later, it had collected over 50,000 entries from 19 countries.

Very quickly, opportunities to write about the project arose through the UK online news sites for the *Guardian* and the *Independent* as well as newspapers and magazines around the world. Because funding for the fast-growing project was coming from Bates's personal income, she very quickly encountered difficulty in managing it, along with the growing number of requests for her to speak to various organizations. Although almost all of the feedback about the project was positive, she also received misogynistic responses. One was: "You experience sexism because women are inferior in every single way to men. The only reason you have been put on this planet is so we can fuck you." The message ended, "Please die" (Bates 2013). Many other hateful messages were sent, but Bates was surrounded by supportive women and men who helped her to persevere. As Bates (2013) notes, "Anyone who describes feminism as an in-fighting, back-biting movement has clearly never been as lucky as I was, at those lowest moments, to discover the strength and kindness, advice and support of so many other women and men." She is now helped by university lecturer Emer O'Toole and a team of eight volunteers who collate the 1,000 or so entries each week that are offered via Twitter and the website. The project's next aim is to secure funding in order to build its profile as an educational archive that can be searched by topic and location.

## No More Page Three

Writer and actor Lucy Anne Holmes started the No More Page Three campaign in the summer of 2012 to lobby *The Sun*'s editor, Dominic Mohan, to drop the image of a topless young woman on page 3 of the newspaper, a feature launched in the newspaper in 1970. It is unacceptable, in Holmes's view, that the most prominent image of a woman in the UK's largest circulation daily newspaper is that of a semi-nude woman. The continuing existence of Page 3, she asserts, disrespects the achievements of women. As Holmes contends:

> It's about what we should say to young women and girls—daughters, nieces, sisters, friends and work colleagues, about where to obtain their self-esteem. Page Three teaches them that a woman's worth is all about the way she looks and her sexual availability to men. We like to think that worth is about achievements, aspirations, values, and relationships. There's not much about that in the newspapers.
>
> (Holmes 2013)

A central feature of the campaign has been to ask Members of Parliament (MPs) to sign a letter to *The Sun*'s editor asking him to cease publishing Page 3. In 2012, a total of 113 MPs (43.2 percent of all female MPs and 17.4 percent of all MPs) supported this initiative. Additionally, Holmes's campaign, which now has around ten volunteers helping to run the website and social media platforms, has gained institutional support from the UK Girl Guides, UK Feminista, Women's Aid, Rape Crisis Centre Ireland, the Everyday Sexism Project, The Women's Room, Turn Your Back on Page 3, and many others.

### *Turn Your Back on Page 3*

Turn Your Back on Page 3 also advocates getting rid of *The Sun*'s "Page 3 Girl." In 2009, after reading former Labour MP Clare Short's book *Dear Clare ... This Is What Women Think about Page 3*, Francine Hoenderkamp decided to mount this campaign. While acknowledging that other feminist organizations, such as Object, were already challenging sexism in the media, in her view a specific drive was needed to pick up where Short left off two decades before when she attempted to pass a bill through Parliament to ban Page 3. Like Lucy Holmes of the *No More Page Three* campaign, Hoenderkamp's concern is that such imagery reinforces the notion that women are sexual objects. She says:

> So prevalent is the presentation of women as submissive "sex objects" in the British press and media, might society have been brainwashed into believing that girls and women exist purely for men's sexual gratification and titillation? If society does believe this, then that certainly could help explain these shockingly low rape-conviction rates.
>
> (Hoenderkamp 2009)

In 2011, Object and TYBOP3 collaborated to put together a submission to the Leveson Inquiry into the culture, practice, and ethics of the press. They produced evidence about the sexism rife in the British press and its potential harms to women and men. They concluded that the Inquiry offered the British public a "unique opportunity to ensure that the hyper-sexualisation and objectification of women in our tabloid press is placed firmly on the agenda as we work together for a print-based media which is socially responsible and which adheres to common principles of equality" (Object and Turn Your Back on Page 3 2011).

## Conclusion

Joan Smith (2013) argues that since the 2008 economic crisis in the UK women have been disproportionately affected. The 2010 General Election resulted in a Coalition government that has cut government welfare spending and public service employment (where high numbers of women work). The UK's Women's Resource Centre, which comprises 42 women's and human rights groups, recently published its report "Women's Equality in the UK—A Health Check," which concludes that if welfare spending and public service employment are cut further the suffering of all but the most wealthy women will intensify. The government is a signatory to the United Nations Convention on the Elimination of All Forms of Discrimination against Women (CEDAW). Government ministers maintain that the UK has in place robust equality laws to ensure social mobility and equal opportunities. However, Vivien Hayes, chief executive of the Women's Resource Centre, claims that such laws are not making a significant impact on improving women's lives:

> The reality for women living in the UK is that there is incomplete realisation of these rights and serious attitudinal and behavioural barriers to substantive equality for all women.
>
> (Vivien Hayes quoted in Bates 2013: 9)

Such changes are fueling considerable anger not only in the UK but also around the world. At the same time, resentment is growing over the ways in which feminist arguments around women's empowerment have been co-opted by Western capitalist societies in ways that are not welcomed by all—for example in a growing emphasis on women's sexuality in media culture and in the culture more widely.

In a 2012 TED.com discussion on the importance of anger (Palmer 2012), one particular contribution seems to illustrate my point about the potential usefulness of anger in rethinking and re-operationalizing the notion of sexism. "Barry" suggested:

> My anger usually erupts from two causes. When I get repeatedly frustrated, the inner anger builds until I shout at the world and, often, at myself. This is childish, but I have not been able to completely control it without causing side effects that are even more destructive, so I just let it out and apologize later.
>
> The second cause is a perceived injustice and not always against myself. I have learned to control this anger and use it to positive ends. This form of anger is very valuable. This form of anger can be used to back down a predator or start a revolution, or perhaps lead to election reform.
>
> ("Barry" quoted in Palmer 2012)

This chapter has examined a range of online anti-sexism political activism in order to demonstrate the ways in which such actions are drawing upon individual and collective anger to bring about greater gender justice. This review of only a handful of such activities makes clear that anger is largely being used for productive and positive ends. The future of media and gender activism depends upon continuing collaboration and support for such aims and challenging those instances where anger is used to divide, derail, and destroy the political solidarity needed for such ends.

# References

Attenborough, F. (2012) "Sexism Reloaded … or Sexism Re-presented? Irrelevant Precision and the British Press," *Feminist Media Studies*. DOI:10.1080/14680777.2012.700524. http://dx.doi.org/10.1080/14680777.2012.700524.

Bates, L. (2013) "The Everyday Sexism Project: A Year of Shouting Back." http://www.guardian.co.uk/lifeandstyle/the-womens-blog-with-jane-martinson/2013/apr/16/everyday-sexism-project-shouting-back.

Dean, J. (2010) "Feminism in the Papers: Contested Feminisms in the British Quality Press," *Feminist Media Studies* 10(4): 391–407.

Driscoll, B. (2013) "The Women's Room Co-Founder, Caroline Criado-Perez, On Female Experts," *Feminism and Media*, March 15. http://www.huffingtonpost.co.uk/2013/03/15/co-founder-of-the-womens-room-caroline-criado-perez_n_2882480.html.

Editors, The (2013) "On Tom Matlack and the Good Men Project," April 9. http://goodmenproject.com/press/on-tom-matlack-and-the-good-men-project/.

Gill, R. (2011) "Sexism Reloaded, or, It's Time to Get Angry Again!," *Feminist Media Studies* 11(1): 61–72.

Good Men Project (n.d.) "About." http://goodmenproject.com/about/.

Hilton, E. (2013) "Is 'Lad Culture' Causing a Surge in Student Feminist Societies?," *Guardian*, May 8. http://www.guardian.co.uk/education/2013/may/08/lad-culture-student-feminism.

Hoenderkamp, F. (2009) "Turn Your Back on Page 3," *The F Word*. http://www.thefword.org.uk/features/2009/08/dear_clare_i_ha.

Holmes, Lucy Anne (2013) "FAQs," No More Page 3. http://nomorepage3.org/faqs/.

Marcotte, A. (2013) "Also, My Wife's Morning Breath Smells Like Cinnamon Buns," *Slate*, January 2. http://www.slate.com/blogs/xx_factor/2013/01/02/natural_beauty_more_oppressive_than_makeup.html.

Miss Representation (n.d.) "About Us." http://www.missrepresentation.org/about-us/.

Murphy, M. (2013) "Tom Matlack: Victim of Feminism," *Feministcurrent*, April 7. http://feministcurrent.com/7476/tom-matlack-victim-of-feminism/.

Object and Turn Your Back on Page 3 (2011) "OBJECT and Turn Your Back on Page 3 Joint Submission to the Leveson Inquiry," December. http://www.object.org.uk/files/The%20Leveson%20Inquiry%20-%20OBJECT%20and%20Turn%20Your%20Back%20on%20Page%203%20Joint%20Submission%282%29.pdf.

Palmer, B. (2012) "The Importance of Anger: A Conversation on TED.com," June 27. http://www.ted.com/conversations/12258/the_importance_of_anger.html.

Penny, L. (2013) "We Need to Talk about Masculinity," *Guardian*, May 16. http://www.guardian.co.uk/commentisfree/2013/may/16/masculinity-crisis-men?INTCMP=SRCH.

Poole, G. (2013) "How Tackling the 'Crisis of Masculinity' Creates a Crisis for Feminism," Comment is Free, Guardian.co.uk.

Rankin, L. (2013) "Feminism Needs Men Too," *Policymic*. http://www.policymic.com/articles/41655/feminism-needs-men-too.

Schnall, M. (2011) "Miss Representation: An Interview with Writer & Director Jennifer Siebel Newsom," October 20. http://www.huffingtonpost.com/marianne-schnall/miss-representation-a-gro_b_1017303.html.

Schwartz, G. (2006) "Anger Management: Anger Doesn't Have to Be a Bad Thing. You Just Need to Know When It's Best to Use It," *Men's Health*, June 15. http://www.menshealth.com/best-life/show-anger-or-stay-calm.

Smith, J. (2013) *The Public Woman*, London: Westbourne Press.

Walter, N. (2010) *Living Dolls: The Return of Sexism*, London: Virago.

Wikipedia (n.d.) "Tom Matlack." http://en.wikipedia.org/wiki/Tom_Matlack.

# INDEX

*16 and Pregnant* 14, 409–17, 418
2 Live Crew 38
*50 Shades of Grey* 261, 543, 551
*A Single Man* 45, 47, 48

ABC 16, 301, 309, 333, 450, 451, 453, 464–65, 579; *ABC News* 307, 387
abjection 12, 37, 342–43, 348–50, 363, 389
abortion 281, 409, 410, 416–19, 544, 607, 620
Abramson, Jill 628
abuse: child 322, 325, 327, 329, 431; class 319; of power/corruption 249, 377; physical 374, racial 13, 399, 403; sexual 332, 338–39, 474, 477–78, 569–70; substance 215; women/gendered 3, 13, 16, 32, 38, 47, 236, 400–403, 431, 490, 566,
Academy Awards 48–49, 58, 343, 345, 348–49
activism: anti-capitalist 4, 9; corporate based 540; feminist 3, 15, 16, 28, 30, 109, 211, 245–56, 285, 490, 565–75, 601, 603, 643–53; gay 73, 88; global 222–23, 229–30, 233–44; grassroots 4, 17, 519; Latino/a 580, 597; state-manufactured 10, 245–56; youth 639
actresses 75, 316, 343–44, 346, 367, 582; *see also* film, stars; theater
adbusting 234
adolescence 499, 526, 635
Adult Film Association of America (AFAA) 215
advertising: behavioral 158–59; content 28, 157, 271, 369–70, 525, 586; executives 26, 53, 158, 430; industry/agency 27, 152, 161–62, 164–65, 535; revenue 9, 34, 124, 437; strategy 175 238, 284, 346, 414, 427, 465, 529, 540; *see also* merchandizing
aesthetics: ambivalent 85; choice 138, 237, 327, 545; DIY 234; porn 589; Westernized 364, 368, 511
Afghanistan 26, 96, 387

Africa 15, 79, 112, 355, 358, 369, 371, 398, 433, 514–22; Central Africa 514, 519; East Africa 379, 517, 519; North Africa 78, 82, 223; South Africa 11, 108, 112–13, 129, 280–89, 292, 321, 395, 514–22; West Africa 93, 227, 519
African American 120, 458, 545, 550, 581–82, 623, 629
AfterEllen.com 307, 450
agency: activist 234; audience 16, 64, 161–62, 340, 474, 501, 525, 591; children's 192, 194, 329, 337; consumer 365, 474, 534; feminist 238–40, 241, 242, 489, 606; intersectionality 74, 634; narrative 375; porn 76, 211, 215, 474; sexual 2, 262–63, 337–38, 457, 592–93, 603; social media 486, 489–90, 634; women's 28, 33, 55, 262, 318, 337, 370–72, 388, 457, 603, 606; women of color 78, 582
agenda setting 23, 291, 293–95, 318, 651; *see also* news
aggression 39, 44, 180, 194, 399, 462, 474–75, 490, 585, 616–18
aging: celebrities 342–51; process 12, 354, 357; women 342
Ai Xiaoming 252
Alexa.com 434–35
Algeria 398
All-China Women's Federation (ACWF) 246
*Ally McBeal* 604–6
Al-Qaeda 379–80; *see also* terrorism
alternative media: as strategy, 109; feminist/women's 111, 233–34, 241
*America's Next Top Model* 77, 284
American Civil Liberties Union (ACLU) 217
*American Psycho* 47–49
Americanization 117, 317
androgyny/androcentric 286, 611, 483, 612
Ang, Ien 61, 411

Ann Summers (retailer) 261–63
anorexia 192, 193, 595; *see also* body, dissatisfaction; body, image; eating disorders
anti-sexism 18, 590, 643–53; *see also* sexism
Anzaldúa, Gloria 85–86, 94, 582
APA Task Force on the Sexualization of Girls 592
apartheid 11, 280–82, 284
Arab Spring 223, 254, 565–75, 645
artist and repertoire (A&R) 7, 122, 128, 129, 130, 131, 134
Association for Progressive Communications (APC) 226, 229
athletes: gay/lesbian 397; male 13, 403, 463; female 3; *see also* individual names
attractive/attractiveness, sexual 16, 182, 201–2, 356, 523, 544–50, 591; unattractive 182, 194, 355
audience: activist 234; assumptions 34–35, 122, 169–71, 175, 463–64, 518–19; commodity/target 14, 109, 120–22, 141, 149, 157–65, 409, 414–15, 458, 464–67, 584, 634; definition 67, 123, 287, 374, 514–17, 592; effects 37, 328, 376, 381, 461; engagement 15, 270, 312, 315, 376, 413, 454; labor 159–61; specialized 11, 123, 301, 450, 580–86; *see also* audience ratings, audience studies; commodification; feminine/femininity, gendered, masculine/masculinity; news; prosumers
audience studies 11, 16, 25, 61–68, 106, 371, 494; feminist 63–68, 521, 608; reception 74–75, 85, 140, 425–27; examples 68, 76–77, 422–23, 495–501, 505–11
audience ratings: systems 159–61, 163–65; measurements 421, 423, 425, 464
Australia: gays/lesbians 86–88; government 321; masculinity 610; media 8, 104–5; 201, 387–88, 435, 540; porn 215–16
*Australian Advertiser* 388
Australian Sex Party (ASP) 216
Austria 239, 240, 243, 391
authenticity: 17, 67, 186, 204, 306; as criterion/value 11, 206–7, 303, 488, 584–86; emotional 140
avatar 8, 173, 176, 372, 441, 446, 485, 557
*Awkward.* 333, 337–38
Axciom 158, 163

Bachelet, Michele 293–94
Bacon-Smith, Camille 64, 454
Bagdikian, Ben 116, 120
Bahrain 16, 229, 565, 566, 569, 570, 573

Barbie doll 181, 290
BBC (British Broadcasting Corporation) 397, 398, 401, 411, 649
*Beauty Myth* 12, 346, 350, 535–36, 601; *see also* Wolf, Naomi
beauty: Chinese 434, contests 283, 366–67, 369, 371, 590, 596; ideal/ideology 2, 12, 15, 142, 182, 533, 535–38, 541, 627, 646; gay 84–85, 325–26, 342–51, 352–62; Indian 363–73; industry 365–66, 368, 534, 535, 540; Latina 586; magazines 15, 367, 369, 435, 524–26, 529–30; Muslim 385; normative 182, 355, 363–64, 370, 371, 534, 595; parlors/salons 12, 271, 275, 286, 347, 363–73; products 12, 367, 369, 371; "Real Beauty" 16, 27, 533–42; wrinkles 342–51, 353, 355; *see also* Dove
Beckham, David 46, 397, 468, 611, 612
*Becoming Chaz* 301–6, 308
behavior: aggressive 444, 616, class 270; consumer 158–59, 161–64, 203, 206, 636; effect of media 12, 14, 33–34, 413–14, 417, 444, 476, 493, 541; feminine 65, 109, 130–32, 135, 184, 278, 292, 325, 376–78, 382, 495, 500, 506, 523–24, 626; masculine 65, 131–32, 203, 206, 278, 293, 527, 612; online 8, 158, 165; racist 397, 399–400; sexist 627, 643–53; sexual 16, 214, 216, 265, 334, 397, 410–13, 417, 457, 545–48, 549–50, 592, 612
*Beijing Declaration and Platform for Action* 27, 29, 223–26, 230, 250
*Being Chaz* 301–6, 308
Bell Company/AT&T 55–56
Berlant, Lauren 272, 611
Bernhardt, Sarah 316
Bertelsmann Music Group 108, 111, 118
*Beverly Hills 90210* 333, 335–36, 339
Beyoncé 78, 329
Bigelow, Kathryn 42–43, 342
Laden, Osama bin 374
biopolitics 6, 82, 89
birth control 410–16, 431, 544, 617, 620, 649
bisexuality 3, 11, 81, 226, 301, 450, 457, 478, 495
Blair, Tony 292, 612
blogs/blogging: anti-feminist 490; in China 249; democratic/feminist potential 2, 9, 233–34, 239, 295, 486, 489–90, 551, 557, 645, 648; fan/user generated 148, 452, 486; girls/women 182, 222, 412, 434, 468, 488; impact on work 150–51; men's 647; microblogging 16, 251; news 307, 356, 435; *see also* mommy blogs
Bobo, Jacqueline 64, 74

body: Chicana/Latina 78, 579, 582, 585; covering/hiding 384–94; dissatisfaction 353, 357, 523; female/feminine 28, 51–52, 64, 96, 265, 28–4, 337, 344–49, 413, 424, 484, 495, 534, 540, 546, 607; gay/queer 85; gendered 94, 636–37; healthy 343, 345, 348, 353, 462, 540; image 325, 353, 534; 540, male/masculine 4, 15, 42–43, 48, 63, 84, 262, 348, 462, 465, 468, 479, 591, 596, 616, 636; perfect 352–62, 367, 443; racialized 71, 85, 95–96, 182, 479, 546, 635, 637; sexualized 95, 98, 181–82, 211, 214, 219, 260, 265–66, 283, 286, 326, 337, 424, 441, 443, 476, 479, 546, 591, 596; transgendered 300–310, *see also* eating disorders; anorexia; aging
Bollywood 15, 364, 367, 369–71, 493–501
Bono, Chaz (Chastity Bono) 11, 300–310
Bono, Sonny 300, 304
Botox 346, 352, 355; *see also* cosmetic surgery; plastic surgery
bourgeois society/public sphere 11, 14, 246, 312–13, 315, 319, 423, 462, 468, 515–16
boys: boy culture 184; toys 184–6; images 179–86; normative 214; risk to 2, 28–29, 190–98; sexualization of 2, 12
branding 157, 204, 274, 367, 533–42; *see also* Dove, Campaign for Real Beauty
Brazil 295; 352, 364, 419–29; cosmetic surgery 352–53, 357; news websites 434–35; television audiences 14, 419, 425–26; television companies 14, 419–29; *see also* telenovelas
breasts 208, 266, 277, 303, 346, 356–58, 443, 461, 489, 547, 602; and breast augmentation 12, 274–75, 352, 353–55, 357, 359; breast cancer 411, 649; breastfeeding 489; *see also* cosmetic surgery; plastic surgery
British: colonialism 367–68, 387; cultural studies 66, 74; magazines 201–10, 239, 436; Muslims 384; press 34, 314, 379–80, 397, 400, 651; television 11, 269–79, 396, 614
*Buffy the Vampire Slayer* 39, 182, 333, 606
bullying 8, 192–93, 337; anti-bullying 541; online bullying 192, 194–97
burqa 26, 386–89, 390–92; *see also* chador; headscarf; hijab; niqab; veil/veiling
Bush, George W. 390, 465
Butler, Judith 169, 556, 603, 610–11

*Cagney and Lacey* 583
call center work 59, 98, 153, 286, 368

*Call of Duty* 171
Cambodia 88, 474
camera phone 16, 554–64; and iPhone 555; smartphone 487, 554, 556, 561; *see also* phones, mobile; phones, cell; Locative-based services (LBS);
Campaign for Real Beauty *see* Dove
campaigns, feminist 18, 29, 35–36, 96, 113, 202, 207–8, 229, 230, 233, 243, 247, 250, 252–53, 484, 486, 489–90, 535; gay 6, 86, 88; grassroots 9, 222; marketing 8, 175–76, 346, 349; online safety 228; pressure group 322–24, 326, 328, 409–18; political 290, 294; *see also* National Campaign to Prevent Teen and Unplanned Pregnancy
Canada 106, 153, 183, 217, 307–8, 352, 354, 385, 387, 390n1, 435, 464, 505, 645
capitalism: colonial 94; commodity 97, 124; ethical 411; global 6, 25, 94, 248, 370–71, 473–74; system 110, 119, 208–9, 238, 241, 468, 475, 525, 601; *see also* neoliberalism
cartoons: children's 162, 184; political 13, 385–88, 391
caste 75, 368, 621
*Castleville* 8, 168, 169, 171, 174–76
CBS 216, 370, 627, 640
CEO (chief executive officer) 216, 535, 623, 626
chador 26, 385, 386, 387, 389, 391, 640; *see also* burqa; headscarf; hijab; niqab; veil/veiling
chav 273, 319, 322; *see also* white trash
Cher 300, 304–7, 346
chick lit 98, 185
Child Online Protection Act (COPA) 217, 219
child sexual abuse/ trafficking 322, 325
childhood: commercialization 12, 321–31; developmental models 324; gendered 184, 186, 190, 324; innocence/purity 323, 592; sexualization 12, 321–31
Children Prevention Pornography Act (CPPA) 217
Chile 111, 294, 434
China: beauty 356; as economy 97, 504; exoticized 83; global power 98, 153, 352–53, 364, 367, 401; internet/news 434; women 507–11, 555
choice: consumer 284, 451, 474, 500, 520, 538, 539; individual 5, 26, 27, 214, 229, 263, 271, 282–84, 337, 359, 385, 413, 417, 507, 509, 538–39, 622; sexual 11, 120, 211, 213, 216, 218, 263, 265, 282, 288, 337, 457, 474, 591, 593

Christie, Julie 343, 349
CIA (Central Intelligence Agency) 376–78
cinema *see* film; Mulvey, Laura
citizen 95, 276, 282, 295, 313, 317,
  365, 368–70, 375, 381, 411–15, 431,
  433–34, 514, 516, 566, 570–71, 574,
  610–11; citizenship 282, 322, 365,
  380, 410, 412, 416, 435, 535, 581;
  consumer citizen 94, 97, 500; e-citizen
  457, 571–72, 623, 643–53
citizen journalism 571–73
class/social class: in Africa 280–86, 518; in
  Brazil 422–23, 427; in China 248, 252; in
  India 364–71, 496–501; in Korea 505–10;
  and media use 556, 568, 635, 649; men 15,
  455; middle 18, 24–25, 44, 47, 54–56, 176,
  237, 594, 612; mobility 57; Netherlands
  633–34; status/difference 63, 68, 107,
  173–75, 203–4; 227, 269–78, 328, 381, 417,
  466, 593, 603–4; women 72, 475; working
  11, 119, 319, 322, 325, 585–87; *see also*
  intersectional identity;
*Cleo* 605–6
Clinton, Bill 415
Close, Glenn 43, 343
*CNN* 435, 505
Collegiate "Anonymous Confession Board"
  (ACB) 16, 543–53
Collins, Patricia Hill 73
Colombia 352
comics 153, 240, 302
commerce 16, 36, 118, 144, 162, 163, 212,
  259–68, 591
commercial sex (sex retailing) 259–68; *see
  also* commerce; prostitution
commercialization 12, 182, 190, 214, 223,
  259–68, 321–31
commodification: audience 7, 154, 158–65,
  458, 466–68; gendered 14, 35, 229, 238,
  266–67; of news 302; self 204; youth 75,
  321–25
communication, online 452, 454, 484–86,
Communications Decency Act (CDA) 217
community: global 96, 98; local media 61,
  234, 514, 517–20; online 453, 486–87, 538,
  647; polity/neighborhood 56, 148, 186,
  217–18, 237, 368, 580, 585; queer 121,
  457, 545; as value/sense 11, 54, 118, 123,
  204, 241, 282, 287–88, 466, 635
confession boards *see* Collegiate ABC
conformity/non-conformity 120, 273, 333,
  348, 350, 534, 537, 625
conglomerates/conglomeration: global
  108–9, 111–12, 116–17, 584; marketing
  117–20, 213; media 7, 16, 118–23; music

116; sexuality 16, 121–24; women's
  participation 105, 108
Congress (US) 112, 217, 222, 224, 293, 300
conservative values: of business 111; family/
  gender 68, 214, 259, 410, 416, 518;
  feminism 26–27; transgenders 302–4,
  307–8; *see also* neoliberalism
conservative politics: in nation states 236,
  273, 282, 565, 567, 570, 621, 636; *see also*
  Republican Party; Tea Party
consumer/consumption 7: and behavior
  158; citizen 94, 97–98, 369, 500; culture
  11–12, 25, 97, 121, 269, 277, 312, 323,
  327–29, 365, 468, 542; gendered 119, 202,
  380, 415; goods 321–22, 327, 426; ICTs
  149, industries/markets 63, 158, 163–64,
  214, 363–64, 420, 536–37; porn 212–13,
  263, 265, 267, 473–75, 478; tastes 138,
  218, 233, 284–86, 371, 426
convergence: culture 118, 301; media/
  technology 211, 223, 413, 455–56, 458,
  520, 555
*Cops* 34
cosmetic feminism 565, 573
cosmetic surgery 12, 274, 325, 352–62, 366;
  and facelift 346, 355; *see also* plastic
  surgery; breast augmentation
*Cosmo, Cosmopolitan* 352, 353, 367, 605
cosmopolitanism 10, 86, 97–98, 245, 287,
  370–71, 499
counter-public, feminist 10, 245–56, 489;
  subaltern 515, 516
creative class 152
Crenshaw, Kimberlé 38, 72, 73, 86–86, 94,
  633
cricket 370, 398, 465
crisis of masculinity 5, 9, 18, 49, 83, 203,
  610–19; *see also* masculine/masculinity
critical mass 452, 454, 572, 621–25
Croft, Lara 172, 441
Cuba 48, 421
cult of domesticity 54, 59
cultural imperialism 12, 108, 117, 365, 368,
  370, 372
cyberbullying 192, 195, 197
cyberfeminism 16, 565–76,
cyborg 484, 579, 634; *see also* Haraway,
  Donna
Cyworld 554, 557, 560

*Daily Mail* 347, 398, 400, 590, 612
*Daily Mirror* 292, 494
*Dancing With the Stars (DWTS)* 11, 300–310
*Danzon* 496
data-mining 8, 158, 161, 163–65

*Dawson's Creek* 333–34, 336, 338
de Beauvoir, Simone 64, 281, 343, 523
Degeneres, Ellen 450–51
democracy/democratization: in China 245,
   248; cosmopolitan 10, 245; deliberative
   514–16, 519; in India 364; in Korea 557;
   liberal 38, 601; online 239, 486;
   participatory 61, 413; role of media 433;
   women 11, 315, 346; *see also* public sphere
Dench, Judi 43, 343, 349
Deng Xiaoping 245, 248,
Deng Yujiao 250–51, 253
Derrida, Jacques 600, 603
desire: female 12, 119, 261, 337–38, 346,
   423, 440, 468, 500, 509, 586; male 36, 336,
   602, 613; politics of 97–98, 324; queer/
   sexuality 6, 89, 344, 451, 593; Western
   and Oriental 81–83, 286, 363
Desmond, Richard 216
*Desperate Housewives* 583
Diaspora 369, 509, 635–36, 639
DiCaprio, Leonardo 611, 613
*Die Stadt ohne Juden* 632
diets 348, 462, 534, 536
*(Different Worlds) Same Heartbeats* 235, 244
digital 3, 218–19, 233, 621, 625; and culture
   18, 218–19, 430–39, 440–49, 459, 583,
   633–34; divide 520, 633–34, 640; identities
   632–42; industries 110, 161; literacy/media
   8, 123, 214, 453, 455, 633; media studies
   118, 182; migrants 632–42, policy 9,
   211–32; revolution 120; space 636–37,
   638; technology 97–98, 190–200, 212,
   214, 451, 485, 568, 570–71, 634
Digital Millennium Copyright Act 117
Dines, Gail 37, 214, 473, 474, 477–79, 591
discourse: of aging 345, 347; of difference
   206; feminist/postfeminist 26–27;
   globalization 94–95, 223, 466; insults
   396–97, 403; liberalism/choice 120; media/
   news 11, 18, 28, 99, 229, 291–93, 295, 519,
   524, 580–81, 633; policy 224, 226–27;
   rights 88, 378, 636; sexuality 82, 84,
   261–65; working class 204
Disney/Walt Disney 108–9, 181, 580, 583
divorce 284, 426, 431, 435, 508, 613, 647
documentary 85, 252, 269–70, 277, 300–310,
   344, 363, 409, 412, 592, 645, 647
docusoap 11, 269–79
do-it-yourself (DIY) 10, 122, 234, 238–42
domestic violence 32–36, 250, 435, 607; *see
   also* sexual violence, violence against
   women
domesticity 53, 54, 59, 89, 377, 519,
   525, 581

dominance, male 333, 338–39, 400, 462, 468,
   474–75
*Dora the Explorer* 181–82, 583, 585
Dove, Campaign for Real Beauty (CFRB) 16,
   27, 533–42; *see also* beauty, ideal
Drogba, Didier 461, 465, 468
Dworkin, Andrea 326, 473, 535, 551–52, 591
Dyer, Richard 42, 344, 535

eating disorders 325, 523, 534, 590; *see also*
   anorexia; body, image
education 27; in Arab countries 372, 567; in
   Asia 96, 507–8, 510–11; as demographic
   variable 52, 56, 74, 152–53, 487; gender
   (ed) 18, 646; secondary 54–56, 112, 149,
   380, 423, 230–31, 607; vocational 366; *see
   also* media, education/literacy; sex
   education
Egypt 16, 229, 385, 426, 565, 567, 569, 573
*El País* (Spain) 434
*El Universal* (Mexico) 434
eLance 149, 153
elections 283, 290–99, 537, 620, 651–52
Electronic Privacy Information Center
   (EPIC) 217
*Ellen* 450; *see also* DeGeneres, Ellen
empowerment: Arab activist 16, 565–67;
   cosmopolitan 116; girls 14, 71, 337–38,
   524, 531; via ICTs 225, 227, 239, 241, 491,
   556; (post)feminist ideal 5, 11, 26–27, 209,
   214, 261–62, 282–85, 535, 538–42, 552,
   591–94
End User License Agreements 162
*Entertainment Tonight* 300, 306
entertainment: commercial/corporate 11, 17,
   58, 222, 274, 313, 318, 452, 454–56;
   entertainment-education 413–14; games/
   leisure 442; jobs 152, 366, 371; for Latinas
   580; with news 311–12, 337, 359, 396, 435;
   sex/sexuality 3, 324, 589; value/formats
   138, 269, 410–12, 467; women's 454,
   524, 530
Ephron, Nora 342–43, 621
Eros Association 215–16
ESPN 109, 463–65
*Esquire* 202
essentialism 85, 300, 303, 306, 584
ethics 85, 413, 416, 594, 601, 606, 622,
   647, 651
ethnicity: in Africa 514; in diasporas 615; *see
   also* intersectional identity; Latinas
ethnography 77; in Asia 75, 371, 503–5; fan
   170, 545–5, 557; Latinas 581; in media
   industry 7; as method 25, 66–67, 78, 140,
   545; reflexivity 503; women's 15, 518

EU Kids Online 8, 190–200
European Commission/European Union 1, 71, 110, 113, 198
Everyday Sexism Project 645, 649–50
Evra, Patrice 399
Excelsior 420, 421
executives: Black 283; gaming 176; media 57, 138–39, 141; music 118, 122–23, 127, 129, 131; news 18, 620, 624–26
exhibitionism, sexual 181, 273, 274
e-zines 9, 233, 234; see also zines

Facebook: affordances 8, 486–88, 544, 557, 570–71, 638, 647; corporate pages 16, 520, 538–40; Facebook Places 559; games and apps 168–72, 176, 554; lesbian fans 453, 488–89; philosophy 149, 157, 161–62, 489; privacy 228, 545; structures 163, 490
Faludi, Susan 203, 600
fame: celebrity culture 11, 311–13; desire for 270, 275, 283, 494; women 314–19
family: in Asia 250, 365, 371, 498–99, 506, 508–9, 557, 560; career/work 55, 133, 152, 423–24, 432, 487, 623, 625, 627–28; gender roles 65, 149, 194, 272, 304, 396, 431, 435, 647; in Germany 25; images 64, 424–25, 555, 616; patriarchal 39; same sex 88, 182; in South Africa 11, 276, 280–88; values 86 208, 216, 301, 303, 583; violence and relationships 34, 150, 175, 198, 270, 305–7, 416, 610, 636
Family Television 61–62, 65
fans 14, 140, 367, 450–60, 462, 463; fan studies 453–55; see also slash; sports, fan markets
fantasy 56, 82–83, 501, 530; and capitalist 272; games 171; Oriental 82–83, 386; racist 380; sexual/porn 266–67, 326, 337, 457, 473, 543, 551; sports 462; women's 457, 317, 347, 500
fanzines 64, 452
fashion: industry 48, 98, 143, 152, 213, 272, 589, 620; magazine/content 15, 325, 367, 370–71, 434–36, 500, 517, 524–25, 529–30; products 185; style 286, 419, 639
fat 27, 352, 355, 401, 535, 547, 549
Fattah, Esraa Abdel 229, 570, 572
Federal Communication Commission (FCC) 112, 117
Federal Glass Ceiling Commission 624
feminine/femininity: aging 344–45, 349; behaviors/characteristics 9, 28, 53, 55, 59, 65, 168–69, 182, 292, 382, 538, 626, 628; child/teen 85, 179, 528; and colonialism 83; desire 119, 334, 593; disorderly 13,
374, 376–78, 382; ethnic/racialized 75–77, 123, 317, 581; ideal/normative 2, 24, 380–82, 409, 415, 523, 529; in India 367, 369–71, 495–97, 500; genres 37, 66, 172, 208, 260, 314, 419–20, 423–24, 426–27, 431, 435, 444, 518, 524; ICTs 484–85; skills/job roles 58, 183, 342; subjectivity 444
Feminine Mystique 24
feminism/feminists: activists 2, 15, 92, 202, 207, 211, 217, 228, 410, 416, 533–36, 627, 643–45, 651–52; in China 10, 245–54; cyberfeminists 484, 634, 648; male 203, 478, 648; Muslim 386; philosophy 5, 214, 503, 535, 541, 544–46, 620–28; politics 484–85, 490, 496, 628; research/scholars/critics 3, 7, 17–18, 23–30, 32, 36, 61–68, 72–79, 85, 94, 105–7, 109, 113, 139–40, 150, 157, 169, 223–25, 261, 263, 318, 325, 332–33, 436, 454, 500, 525, 530, 533, 544, 635; types of 63, 183, 349, 432, 517, 523, 547, 591, 601, 610; see also postfeminism
feminine/masculine binary 2, 4, 14, 63, 68, 272, 278, 397, 402, 420, 478, 494, 533, 568; and ideals 346–47, 376; in sport 395–97, 400
feminist media: content 9–10, 233–43, 436, 438, 485, 488–90, 515–18, 612–13, 645, 650
feminization 83, 395–96, 399, 625–27; and of labor 5, 51–58
femme fatale 43, 386
Ferdinand, Anton 400–402
fiction: detective, 39; vs fact 269, 375, 467; fan 452–53; genre 85, 235; as mystique 24; romance/erotic 260; science fiction 43, 171, 454, 456–57; see also slash
Fight Club 47, 49
film: depictions 35–36, 76, 180, 343–44, 632, 646; exoticizing 82–83; fan-produced 455–56, gaze and reception 36–37, 64, 348–49, 375, 496; labor context 7, 12, 57–59, 85, 138–44, 151, 153, 215, 342, 627; Latina 17, 77, 579–86; masculinity 5, 42–49, 611–12; stars 315–18; see also aging; Bollywood; Disney; Hollywood
Flickr 148, 487, 555, 556
Fonda, Jane 346–47
football/soccer 204, 206, 396, 398–402, 461–66, 610–12
For Him Magazine/FHM 204–7
Fortune 500 623, 625
Foucault, Michel 82, 235, 323, 343, 591, 600, 603, 608
Foursquare 554, 556, 558, 561

*Fox News* 387, 435
Fox Soccer 463, 468
France 108, 313, 321, 365, 391, 435
Francis, Joe 216
Fraser, Nancy 27, 245–47, 311, 437, 515–16, 568
Free Speech Coalition (FSC) 215
*Friday Night Lights* 333, 337, 339
Friedan, Betty 23–24; *see also Feminine Mystique*
*Friends* 506, 583, 611–12, 616

*Game of Thrones* 453
games/gaming: children's 84, 191, 143; gendered 2, 168–76, 179, 440–47; gendered production of 8, 117, 142, 170, 447; location-based (LBS) 558–61; racism 637; spectatorship 466; studies 440, 444, 445; as third space 557; *see also* sports
gatekeeping, news 7, 625
gays and lesbians: audiences 46, 120–22, 458, 496–97, 545; black men 75, 85; GLBT 11, 301, 307; media/ownership 120–21, 301, 519; media images 11, 302–3, 450, 495; politics 88, 300; porn 6, 81, 84, 216–17, 453; post-gay idea 81–82, 88–89; sexuality 48, 87; *see also* lesbians; queer; same-sex marriage; slash
Gay and Lesbian Alliance Against Defamation 301, 587
gaze: adult 327–28; female 467–68, 500; male 36–37, 44, 49, 95, 140, 181–82, 371, 375, 468, 494, 524, 607, 613, 614; pathological 342–45, 348, 349–50; *see also* Mulvey, Laura
gender *see* intersectional identity
gender (in)equality 27, 29, 225, 333, 436, 544; and achievement of 67, 389, 535, 596, 647; in Asia 507; ICTs 7–8, 15, 484; media role 112–13, 622; sport 13, 395–96, 468; workplace 127, 130, 135, 137–43
Gender Media Action (GMA) 246, 248, 251–53
gender roles *see* feminine/femininity, masculine/masculinity
gendered violence *see* sexual violence
geopolitics 75, 95–96, 364, 579
Gerbner, George 23–24
Germany 25, 87, 108, 398, 435, 486–87, 489–90
Gill, Rosalind: on feminism/postfeminism 26, 28, 203, 282–83, 337–38, 535, 606, 643–44; masculinities 25; parenting 133; sexism/sexualization 17, 28, 194, 213, 261–62; workplace 135, 152
Girl Scouts/Girl Guides 535, 650

girls: as consumers 184–86; girl culture 119, 122, 557; games 2, 85; girlfriends 175–76, 264, 276–77, 366, 396–97, 401, 459, 497; girls/teen media 12, 14–16, risk 8–9, 190–98; representation 179–83; sexualization 2; *see also* boys/boyhood
Gitlin, Todd 311, 514, 515, 516
glass ceiling 1, 57, 535, 620–30; glass cliff 626; glass closet 629; glass door 621; glass escalator 624; glass hammer 629; glass wall 629
*Glee* 120, 451, 453, 458–59
global capitalism/economy 6, 93, 94, 98, 224, 248, 272, 628
Global Gender Gap Report 27
Global Information Infrastructure (GII) 222–32
Global Media Monitoring Project (GMMP) 5, 29, 432, 622, 648
globalization 82–84, 87, 89, 287, 525; and beauty 370–72; economic processes 363–64; ICTs 6–7, 247; media 15, 466, 503; sex issues 35, 321
Globo Network 420–21, 425, 434–35
glocalization 12, 286–88, 365, 369–70
Goldberg, Whoopi 344
Gomez, Selena 580, 583, 584, 585
*Good Morning America* 306
Google 222, 226, 354, 384, 386, 468, 555, 558, 636–37, 640
Gosling, Ryan 45–46
gossip 148; celebrity 300, 311–18, 348; gendered 59, 276, 300, 434; at work 53, 58
*Gossip Girl* 333–34
GQ 201, 203–4
Greece 352, 385
Greer, Germaine 343
grooming: personal 11, 49, 53, 202, 204, 274, 277; sexual 379; socialization 474
Grupo Televisa 108, 111
Guinea 93

Habermas, Jürgen 245–47, 516; *see also* Public sphere
harassment, sexual 16, 162, 194, 197, 229, 249, 344, 452, 498, 565, 566, 569, 571, 572, 623; *see also* sexual violence; violence against women
Haraway, Donna 579, 634, 638; *see also* cyberfeminism
*Harper's Bazaar* 367
Haskell, Molly 12, 342, 344
headscarf 78, 380, 385, 386, 391, 632, 637, 639; *see also* burqa; chador; hijab; niqab; veil/veiling

health: emotional/mental 215, 353, 354, 376–77, 412, 413, 477, 560; physical 27, 56, 112, 204, 343, 354, 355, 356, 357, 359, 435, 526, 647; public 215, 274, 322, 414; sexual 86, 215, 414, 617

hegemony 111, 118, 170, 349, 350, 387, 421, 425

*HerGameLife* 468

heteronormativity 8, 95, 606; in families/ relationships 305, 342, 397, 508; gender roles 163, 229, 240, 288, 594; media content 497, 519–20; v. queers 87–88, 303; sexuality 344, 349

heterosexual/heterosexuality 262, 333–34, 585, 597; and conflation 24, 73, 523; in content 83, 173–76; heterosexism 15, 121, 493; and homosexuality 88, 121; men's 206, 265, 337, 473, 550, 610–13, 616, 635; prejudices 83, 288; sexualization 10, 44, 386, 519, 606; women 260–63, 452–54, 529

hijab 26, 385–87, 390–91, 636; *see also* birqa; chador; headscarf; niqab; veil/veiling

hip hop 38, 78, 122

Hispanic 545, 550, 580; *see also* Latinidad

Hollywood 12, 32, 36, 37, 39, 43, 45, 117, 118, 139, 142, 153, 274, 276, 317, 342–51, 367, 389, 419, 426, 451, 505, 582, 583, 584, 611, 629

*Homeland* 13, 374–83

homonationalism 6, 81, 88–89

homophobia 7, 85, 87–88, 97, 116, 236, 397, 593, 594

homosociality 132, 261, 265, 403, 457

Hong Kong 251, 434

hooks, bell 75, 603

human rights 9, 27, 88, 223, 224, 229, 252, 391, 571, 573, 628, 651

*Hustler* 213, 216, 265–67

hybridity 11, 120, 269, 280–89, 369, 370–71, 423, 579–81, 584–85

hyperlocal media 120, 116

hypermasculinization 18, 327, 613, 615

hypersexualization 591; of black men 85; of girls 182, 229; of women 181, 214, 327, 444, 579, 582

hysteria, feminine 376, 377–82, 467, 579

identity: brand/corporate 533–34; class 271, 273, 277, 281, 319, 499, 603–4, 607; community/social 163, 228, 243, 312, 457, 499, 509, 539, 556; consumer 537–38, 540; familial/domestic 555; feminist 549, 551; gender 2–3, 8, 15, 23–24, 30, 66, 74–77, 94, 99, 140, 157, 179, 185, 224, 263, 272–73, 281, 307–8, 381, 484, 488, 494–97, 499, 501, 503, 506–7, 607, 613; identity politics 451, 610–11, 614; masculine 1, 49, 203, 205, 474–75, 610–13, 635; Muslim 385, 390; national 77–78, 580, 633; racial/ ethnic 6, 37, 77, 79, 81–91, 239, 240, 281, 317, 344, 370, 379–80, 386, 580, 585, 603, 635; real world 445, 488; sexual 6, 78, 120–21, 157, 213, 229, 286, 326, 424, 457, 499, 591, 606–7, 635; transgender 206, 302; virtual 445, 637; youth 593, 607, 635–36; *see also* intersectional identity; queer, identity

ideology 6, 26, 61, 95–96, 165, 319, 328, 524–25, 529, 595–96, 624; and beauty 12, 350, 529, 533–40; China 248–49; of choice 5, 96; gendered 54, 68, 137, 214, 272, 343–45, 349, 395, 403; media role 24, 77, 422, 498, 500, 523; postfeminist 17, 286, 600; professional 523, 625; racial 75; Western neoliberal 82, 88, 284, 313

immigration/immigrants 34, 36, 71, 73, 77–78, 93, 95, 317, 365, 466, 632

incest 34, 36, 236, 544

India 12–12, 71, 75, 97, 98, 106, 108, 153, 225, 321, 352, 354, 363–73, 398, 433, 493–502; *see also* New India

individualism: and choice 538–39; individualization 506–9; postfeminist 283; dividing women 27, 262; Western 245, 288, 312–13

Indonesia 507

Information and communications technologies (ICTs) 7, 110, 190, 224, 226, 227

information society 7, 147–56, 198, 223, 227

Instagram 8, 157, 554, 555

insult: class 273; gender-based 395–205; racial 396, 398; *see also* abuse, racial; abuse, women

integration, social 95, 211, 632, 640

International Women's Media Foundation 108

internet 3, 419; and audience/users 161; celebrity 318; children 2, 9, 190–200, 217, 322; in China 245–56, 434; cosmetic surgery 353–54; digital divide 433, 633; digital media studies 118; feminist 14, 236, 239, 483–92, 565–75, 643–53; governance/ policy 9, 222–32; identities 632–42; masculinity 47; pornography 37, 212–13, 216–17, 324, 591; queer 14, 307, 450–60; radio 28, 520–21; sexism 208, 543–53; sexual violence 34; women 2, 110, 379, 433–34, 468; work/labor 632–42

interns, media 59, 148
intersectional identity (class, ethnicity, gender, race, sexuality); 3, 5–8, 10, 13, 15, 34–35, 52, 59, 61–63, 66, 71–79, 82–88, 93–96, 116, 123, 147, 151, 154, 161, 164, 170, 190, 197, 247, 263–64, 344, 381, 410, 413, 456, 497, 501, 512, 514, 568, 580, 601, 607, 614, 628, 633, 637, 640, 644, 653–55, 657
intersectionality 239, 242, 594, 632–42, 644
intertextuality 344, 367, 457
intimacy 593; in Korea 16, 557–58; media/mediated 45, 54, 234, 306, 462, 555; men/women 36, 47, 476, 537; public 315–16
Iraq 26, 377, 390
Islam 26, 379–80, 382, 384–94, 565, 573, 636–39; and Islamization 632; Islamophobia 18, 78, 384–94, 632, 636, 638; women/girls 98, 633
Italy 219, 240, 352, 354, 364, 423, 615

Jameson, Jenna 38, 264
Japan 117, 153–54, 247, 260, 352, 355, 507–12, 555, 557, 560
Jenkins, Henry 67, 301, 306, 454–56, 591
Jersey Shore 14, 270–71, 273, 410, 415
journalism: institution of 124, 311, 620–27; music 128; political 11, 290–95; reportage 2, 273, 437; sports 396, 403, 462; women's 430–37; see also feminization
journalists: Arab women 16, 565–75; coverage of individuals 11, 43, 314–15; on feminism 253, 607, 610–11, 628; on Muslims 388–91; on sex 35, 76, 590; sports 11, 400–403; women 18, 37, 294, 430–37, 620–28; work 151

Kanter, Rosabeth Moss 514, 621
Kenya 379
Kimmel, Michael 203, 475, 476, 477, 610, 615
Kop of Munt (Head or Tail) 632, 633, 636, 640
Korea 16, 117, 352–58, 504–12, 554–64

L'Oreal cosmetics 346–47, 365, 370
labor market 51, 54–57, 59, 150, 153, 203, 485, 507–9
language: feminist 233, 236–37, 242, 536, 605; racist 82, 399–402; sexist 25, 293, 322, 327, 395, 403
lap dancing 17, 324, 589, 590, 602

Latin America 29, 77, 98, 110, 111–12, 399, 421
Latinidad 75, 77, 580, 581, 583–86; music 122–23; Latina/o Studies 17, 123, 580; women 181, 579–88
leadership 127, 245, 247–49, 293, 294, 572, 614, 623–28
Lebanon 287, 385, 389
legislation 28–29, 147, 222, 228, 250, 415
lesbians: activism 300; athletes 397; attitudes to 3, 87–88, 302; images 11, 285–88, 344, 545; LGBTQ 450–60; media 81, 100–101, 301, 450–53, 457–58, 519; nonwestern 98; romances 450; romance fiction 455
liberalism/liberalization 7, 223, 245, 249, 380–82; post-liberalism 368; West 390–91, 411, 424–26; see also neoliberalism
Libya 16, 565–67, 569, 573
Lievrouw, Leah 233–39, 243
lifestyle 270–72, 284, 380, 603; and choices 27, 162, 274–75, 368; lifestyle pages/magazines 84, 87, 432, 435; male 152; Western 12, 97–98, 364, 366, 505–6
Limbaugh, Rush 617–18
liposuction 12, 352–53, 355; see also cosmetic surgery; plastic surgery
literacy: digital 191, 225, 227, 433; privacy 229; social 530–31; subcultural/cultural 10, 241–42; see also media, literacy/education
Loaded 204–5, 208
location based services (LBS) 16, 554–64; see also gaming; surveillance
Lolita Effect 181, 523
London bombings (2005) 379
Lopez, Jennifer 78, 123, 580, 581–82, 585
Los Angeles Times 432, 436
luxury 98, 175, 259–60, 263, 275, 368

MacKinnon, Catherine 44, 333, 551, 591
Mad Men 48, 615, 616
Madonna 75, 96, 348–49,
magazines 3, 38, 51, 61, 107, 111, 138, 172, 207, 233, 283, 302, 307, 312, 314, 353, 354, 366, 387, 392, 436, 464, 621, 650; feminist 234, 240, 436, 612, 645–46; gaming 175; gay 87; girls'/teenage 15–16, 207, 325, 523–33, 592, 595; lads 9, 201, 203–7, 337; men's 9, 201–11, 613; new man 9, 202–5; queer 81, 84, 235; quizzes 410, 526, 528; women's 24, 34, 63–64, 203, 206–7, 325, 353–54, 357, 366–70, 434, 438, 465, 510–11, 523, 525, 530, 605–6, 624; see also e-zines; fanzines; zines
Maid in Manhattan 582, 585

makeover: advertising, 540; paradigm 11, 269, 277, 283, 290, 538, 540; shows 272–74, 283–84, 286, 368
male body; see body, male/masculine
male gaze; see gaze, male; Mulvey, Laura; scopophilia
manga 153–54, 355; *see also* Japan
marketing: careers 128; to children 322–25, 590; to gays 120, 123; of porn 212–14; sex-segregated 55, 98, 169–70, 175, 202–3, 206, 238, 260, 264–65, 464, 611; social 414; targeted 8, 158–59, 161, 164–65, 369, 434, 451
marriage 314; and anti-gay laws 73, ideals/ rights 174, 247, 371, 411, 424, 509, 638; interracial 73, 281; rates 508; *see also* same sex marriage
masculine/masculinity: black 74–75; crisis of 2, 5, 9, 47–49, 83, 610–14, 617, 647; culture 132, 265; dominant conceptions 2, 15, 17–18, 42–44, 66, 202–8, 317, 353, 359, 473, 475, 610–18; gay 84; new man 9, 202–5, 349, 611–14, 616–17; "old man" 9, 202; in music 122–23, 128; socialized in boys 8, 179, 183; violence 32, 36–39; *see also* body, male/masculine; boys; feminine/ masculine binary; hyper-masculinity; identity, masculine; power, male
masculinization 140, 228, 395–96, 399
*Maxim* 204, 207, 613
Mayer, Marissa 626, 629
McChesney, Robert 111, 116, 120, 157, 211
McQueen, Steve 45–47
McRobbie, Angela: on consumerism 381; on postfeminism 26–27, 214, 272, 274, 277, 409, 525; on sexual freedom 415, 417, 543–44, 550, 552, 602, 605; on workers 58, 152
media: children 2, 8–9, 12, 68, 109, 179–89, 190–200, 207–8, 217, 321–31, 442, 461, 473, 543, 560, 583, 590, 592–93; education/literacy 16, 17, 29, 68, 523–32, 591, 594–97, 645, 647; global 23, 92–101, 108, 116–17, 153, 214, 219, 367, 503; hyperlocal 116, 120; effects 118, 356, 524, 530, 592; institutions 3, 224, 312, 321–22; production 1, 13, 58–59, 67, 74, 118, 123, 233, 237, 239, 242–43, 301–32, 306–7, 455, 504, 524; *see also* specific media
mediascapes 363–73
mediation, parental 190–200
Meehan, Eileen 6, 109, 141, 160, 163–65, 224
melodrama 14, 65, 269, 414, 420–22
*Men Talk* 612–13

merchandizing 8, 98, 179–89, 321, 325, 365
meritocracy 271–72, 278, 284–85, 313, 369, 462
Merkel, Angela 290, 292
Mexico 108, 111, 153, 434
Middle East 82, 223, 229, 386, 389
*Migrazine* 239–40
military: Brazil 420–21; China 247; Egypt 426, 570; justification 96, 375; porn 217, 591; sports 463
Mirren, Helen 353, 346–49
misogyny: hip hop 38; porn 551; public/anti-feminist 319, 474–75, 650; and sex 328; sports 400, 466, 696; televised 39, 273
*Miss Representation* 645–47
mobile media 2–3, 223–24, 486, 555–57, 559–62; *see also* camera phones
mobile telephones 402; *see also* camera phones; cell phones
mobility: class 56–57, 585; globalized 6, 466, 509; in India 371; queer/transgender 81–82, 86–89, 300, 307–8; social 271, 313, 319; whiteness 380; women's 11, 53, 334, 386, 508, 515; *see also* travel
mobilization 6, 29, 223, 485, 509, 566, 568–71, 574, 584
modeling: glamour models 275, 277, 366–67, 369–70, 499–500, 537, 595; industry/ women's work 143, 274; male 275; Page 3 girls 645
models: business 157–58, 165, 185, 212, 430, 451; economic 27, 112, 411–12; role 623, 307, 322, 332, 506, 540–44
modernization/modernity 115; and consumption 25, 97, 365, 419; liquid 312–13; as unequal/gendered 84, 94; Western/globalized 6, 94, 98, 287–88, 370, 505, 508
Modleski, Tania 140, 171–72, 174, 328, 381, 602, 605
mommy blogs 222, 434; *see also* blogs/ blogging
moral panics 54, 186, 197, 219, 322, 462, 590
morality: in China 248–50; codes 416; moralizing 17, 198, 323, 336, 416, 451, 500, 596; of nation-state 35, 282; positions 26, 86, 184, 327, 474, 494; regulating teens'/women's 56, 336, 347, 590, 594
Morley, David 61, 63, 65–66
Moroccan-Dutch 18, 78, 385, 632–42
Morris, Meaghan 601, 603, 608
mothers 54–56, 535; and blaming/mocking 322, 325, 397, 401, 416; differences from fathers 195; as market 164; mommy wars 628; in news 292;

surveillance 560; teen 14, 18, 409; and work 25, 132–33, 297, 365; *see also* work–life balance
MTV 270, 333, 369, 409–18
multicultural/multiculturalism 84, 86, 581, 583–84, 637, 640
Mulvey, Laura 36, 42, 44, 375–76; *see also* gaze, male; scopophilia; spectator
Muslim: anti-modern trope 95–96, 378–80, 633–39; feminists and Islam 563–74; as market 98; Muslimah 388, 390, 392; prejudice 71, 78, 633; Western imagery 13, 26, 379–81, 384–91, 638; *see also* Islamophobia
*My So-Called Life* 333–34, 337–38
MySpace 486, 488, 544
mythology: cowboy 43, 45, 49; emerging/media 381, 454; heroic 312; sexuality 35, 181, 273, 336, 340; about women 379–80, 494, 628; working class 276; *see also* Beauty Myth

narrowcasting 161, 164–65, 451
National Campaign to Prevent Teen and Unplanned Pregnancy 409–18
National Football League (NFL) 461, 464
nationalism: African 519; Brazilian 420; Chinese 247; Dutch 638–39; heteronormativity 95; Indian 12, 365, 369–72, 497; masculinity and sexism 214, 612; nation-building 281, 288, 366; in sports 462–63, 466
Native Americans 182
NBC 333, 452, 464
neoliberalism 48, 411–12, 596; and capitalism/economy 88, 92–93, 97, 105, 110–12, 118–19, 223, 239, 242, 272, 280–86; choice/freedom 26–27, 62, 120, 284–88, 416–17, 509, 591; feminism 27, 415; queer 6, 61, 88–89; values 11, 14, 269, 319; *see also* capitalism; liberalism/liberalization
Netherlands 18, 78, 632–42
netizens 250, 254, 560
New India 12, 363–73; *see also* India
new media: characteristics 234–42; gender/family relations 484, 487, 543; labor conditions 7, 58–59, 133, 152, 433; laws/regulation 117; participatory/feminist potential 2, 13, 118, 234, 318, 322, 452, 456, 543, 551, 568, 574, 634; social/political 16; *see also* Facebook; internet; social media
new social movements (NSMs) 61, 233, 241, 243

*New York Times* 307, 388–89, 434–36, 615, 621, 628, 648
New Zealand 4, 292, 308
news 5–6, 11, 303–4, 306, 308, 311–12, 314, 412, 622, 632, 638; audience 430–39, 628; crime 36, 314; discourse/language 11, 402–3; editors 57, 620, 625; feminist 28, 253, 600; newsgroups 61, 452, 484; newsroom cultures 18, 620, 622–27; online 11, 162, 251, 253, 307, 571, 620; ownership 105–15, 121, 311–12, 650; publishers 14, 57, 620; representations 13, 18, 29, 64, 77, 106, 213, 290–99, 356, 384–94, 622, 625, 627, 648; sexual violence 32–41, 93; sources 620, 622, 648–49; sports 398, 400–403; women's content 14, 430–39, 620; *see also* journalists; newspapers
*News of the World* 312, 318–19, 397
newspapers: advice columns 367, 431, 526; beauty coverage 354, 367; conglomeration 111–12; Indian 493; online 433–34, 650; sexual content 34, 208; 590, 650; tabloid 203, 207; women's employment 620, 622–25; *see also* journalism; journalists; gays/lesbians; news; queer; sports
*Newsweek* 611, 621
*Nightline* 304, 306
Nintendo 171, 175, 442–43
niqab 385, 388, 391; *see also* burqa; chador; headscarf; hijab; veil/veiling
*No More Page Three* 645, 650
normalization 343–44, 487, 526–28; and ageism 344, 346; commercial sex 267; femininity 523; gender hierarchy 94, 183, 381, 403, 464; heterosexuality 305, 606; masculinity 194, 206–8, 435; porn 194, 213, 478; racism 344; violence 33, 37, 339, 474
*Nuts* 204–6

objectification 593; of men 465; through sex 37, 43–44, 202, 204, 214, 261, 267; v. subjection 214, 283, 337, 538–39, 591; of women 9, 32, 36, 38, 206, 211, 322, 415, 537, 547, 606–7, 613–14, 646, 651
Occupy Wall Street 223, 254
oDesk 149, 153
*One Tree Hill* 333–35, 337–38
online risk; *see* risk, online
*Oprah*/Oprah Winfrey Network (OWN) 76, 172, 301, 304, 306, 370, 646
Oriental sex 81–91
Orientalism 82–84, 95–96, 356, 386, 636

othering 65, 78, 83–84, 94, 98, 386; and colonialism 71; queer 78; by race/ethnicity 3, 17, 173, 388, 391, 585, 637
outsourcing 5, 153, 365, 368, 411–12

Pakistan 96, 498
paparazzi 346, 397, 464
parenthood 132–33, 135, 409–10, 415, 417, 628; *see also* mother/motherhood; father/fatherhood
Parliament (UK) 207, 636, 650–51
patriarchy 25, 345, 376–77; and capitalism 64, 109–10, 371, 473, 475–76, 525; feminist critique 235, 342, 535, 601, 645; hierarchy 39, 42, 365, 468, 536; invisibility 282; men in 15, 66, 336–39, 396, 473–75, 613; reinforced by media 5, 42, 86, 344, 422, 430, 493–95; sexualization/violence 35, 339, 391
pay gap 1, 110, 152, 624
PBS 120, 411
pedophiles 322, 327, 327–28, 612
*People* 38, 203
Peru 34, 111, 517
Pfeiffer, Michelle 348–49
phone hacking scandal (UK) 312, 397
phones: camera 16, 554–64; cell/mobile 172, 465, 520, 570; *see also* mobile media; photography
photography 163, 561; amateur 555; content 205, 326–27, 346, 356, 367, 397, 625; women's employment 139, 151, 285, 412
Pickford, Mary 316–17
pink tropes: aisles 195; ghetto 621–23; tourism 86
Pinterest 8, 157, 647
Planned Parenthood 416–17
plastic surgery 274, 346–47, 355, 434; *see also* cosmetic surgery
*Playboy* 38, 202, 213, 215, 321, 324–25,
pleasure: audience 184, 340, 413, 457–58, 496, 537, 501; female culture 59, 148, 154, 182, 212; gaming 444; individual 424; narrative 32, 36, 44, 140, 374–83, 497; popular culture 17, 75, 274, 605–7, 512; reading 16, 530; sexual 10, 12, 37, 213–14, 219, 260–64, 266–67, 337–38, 415, 475, 537, 543, 591–93, 613; textual 67, 494, 498, 524–25, 527, 529–30; visual 32, 36, 44, 140, 500
pluralism 427, 603
*Pocahontas* 181–82
pole dancing 10, 17, 260–62, 589, 593
policymaking 7, 28, 107–8, 113, 157, 225–27, 248–49, 251

politicians 215–16, 430, 466, 639, 646, 648–49; men 290–99; transgender 308; women 11, 290–99, 321–22
politics 246, 433, 435–36; and class 157, 203, 327; feminist 233–44, 250, 252, 484–85, 489–90, 525, 533, 536, 546, 600, 603, 606, 608; gender 302, 397, 427, 497, 506, 508; sexual 328, 556; symbolic politics 29; *see also* identity politics; representation
Pollitt, Katha 544, 551
pornography 267, 325; child 217; culture 10, 389, 442, 491, 543, 591, 602, 607; industry 9, 38, 76, 211–119, 263; men's consumption 15, 473–78; objectification 202; online 191–93, 197; porn chic 589; porn refuser 478; violence 5, 32, 37
pornification 213, 323, 589, 593
Portugal 387, 421, 427, 435
postcolonialism 18, 75, 81–84, 94, 239, 364–65, 369, 372, 603, 633, 635
postfeminism: analysis of gender 269, 271; v. feminism 16–17, 600–7; sensibility 4, 11, 97–98, 214, 254, 280–86, 349, 409, 417, 533, 537–38, 541, 551, 600–7; sexual culture 96, 337–38, 589–97; women's choices 272
post-gay 81, 82, 88–89
postmodernism 81, 83, 88, 233, 235, 328, 468, 484
poststructuralism 62–63, 306, 339, 484, 495, 600, 602–5
power feminism 182, 535, 604; *see also* Wolf, Naomi
power, male 36, 42; and female 43, 66
preferred reading 340, 445; *see also* readers
pregnancy 14, 281, 336, 346, 409–18, 424–25
prime-time (television) 32, 38, 57, 419, 421, 426–27, 579–80, 583
privacy: rights 9, 218, 223–24, 246–50; value 54, 212, 304, 559–60, 562; violations 4, 556–57
pro-sex feminism 543, 591
prostitution 35–36, 259, 263, 267, 316, 442, 591
prosumption/prosumers 4, 13, 67, 150, 409–19, 486–92
protectionism 16, 96, 286, 324, 529
public opinion 247, 249, 254, 514–16, 572, 626–27
public relations/PR 123, 205, 538–39, 623
public service broadcasting 410–11
public sphere 11, 164, 179, 184–85, 215, 245, 311, 318–19, 397, 430–31, 442, 514–15; alternative 436; counter 245, 311, 436;

feminist 246–48, 436, 515, 551; gendered 419–20, 515–16, 535, 569, 644, 646; online 249

public sphericules 514–16; *see also* Gitlin, Todd

psychology 185; and entertainment content 45; impact 109, 347, 363, 495, 527, 592; news emphasis 12, 359; psy-function 461–62, 466–67; therapy/research 66, 206, 321–22, 325, 327, 496, 504, 569, 635

queer: fandom 14, 450–59; identity 6, 81–86, 485, 488; labor 116; media 120–23, 235–36, 238–41; multiple oppressions 75, 78, 84; music/queercore 7, 122–23; net culture 489; sexuality 81; theory 72–73, 81–86, 94, 98, 118–20, 303; *see also* identities, queer; mobility, queer; othering
*Queer Eye for the Straight Guy* 301, 451

race: activism 239, 601; discrimination/ racism 72–74, 160, 181, 396–97, 419; essentialized 173, 358, 400, 603–4; hierarchy 11, 61, 319; in hiring 143; media images/reception 74–76, 227, 237, 426, 456, 501, 580; nationalism 95; race/ post-race theory 81–82, 85–89, 634; *see also* ethnicity; intersectional identity
radio: audiences 15, 78, 413–14, 486, 514–21; in Brazil 420–21; feminist/ women's 28, 234, 566, 571; ownership 109, 111–12, 122; talk format 15, 514, 516; women's employment 57, 128, 433, 621–23
Radway, Janice 61, 63, 65–66, 454, 592, 605
*Rambo* 42, 44
rape: culture 2, 477; images/coverage 33–34, 36–38, 98, 250, 265, 339; war crime 32, 36, 569–71; *see also* sexual violence; violence, against women
raunch culture 274, 607
readers 314, 596, 605–6; girls 16, 500, 543–50; feminist 234, 241; as market 14, 264, 430–31, 437; magazine 201–8, 367, 523; studies 61–66, 74; women's news 431–33, 436–37; types 65–66, 74, 121, 340, 441, 445, 453, 496; *see also* preferred reading
Reagan, Ronald 111, 611, 616
reality television: celebrity 301–8, 318; and domestic violence 34; makeover 355–57, 368; neoliberal agenda 409–17; police 32, 34–35; women 284, 311; *see also* docusoap

reception studies: and political economy 124, 309; examples 270, 301–5, 380, 420; theories 74–75, 95, 140, 423, 427, 454–55, 543, 606; *see also* audience
Record Network 421, 425
reflexivity 85, 414, 504–5, 616; everyday 503–8, 512; feminist 517; lack of 12, 328, 401, 495–97
Refn, Winding 45–46
reform: economic 111–12, 248, 412, 415, educational 409, 411–12, 414; legal/ regulatory 34, 88, 111–12, 621, 644; media 117, 121, 124, 622, 628; political 56, 223, 412, 417, 565, 568, 652; social 568, 571–72, 574, 607
refugees 6, 76, 87–88, 569–70
religion: Christianity 288, 322, 385, 613, 637; Hinduism, 15, 398, 493–501; as identity marker 52, 58, 362, 632, 638; Islam 26, 379–80, 382, 384–94, 565, 573, 632–33, 636–39; as issue 497
Republican Party 216, 300, 544; *see also* Tea Party
resistance: class 381; cultural 16, 24, 170, 454, 541, 593, 644; institutional 620–31; labor 59; political 94, 109, 238, 519, 565–75; religious 385; social 248, 644
respectability 17, 54, 59, 78, 213, 215,-16, 273, 278, 316, 379, 589
*Return to Ravenhearst* 171, 174
Revlon 365, 368
Riot grrrl 7, 122, 237–38, 490
risk: children 8–9, 190–200, 324–25, 329, 594; cosmetic or plastic surgery 12, 352–62; business/economic 7, 11, 105–15, 141, 144, 201–2, 301, 582, 618, 624, 626; health/ personal 215, 306, 410, 416–17, 475, 565, 574, 647; political 16, 333, 565–75
Ronaldo, Cristiano 461, 468
rugby 465–66
Russia 108, 240, 364
Rwanda 36

sadomasochism 37, 543; *see also 50 Shades of Grey*; pornography
Said, Edward 82, 385–86, 388, 461, 636; *see also* Orientalism; othering
Salon.com 436–37
same sex marriage 73, 81, 86, 88, 426
*San Francisco Chronicle* 388, 436
*Sassy* 524, 526
Saudi Arabia 385, 388
scandal: celebrity 6, 290–99, 312; corporate 557, 560; sexual 11, 82, 290–99, 589; sports 2–3, 396–403; women as 380

Schiller, Herbert 108, 116, 368
Schmitz, Ka 240–41
scopophilia 44, 375; *see also* audience; gaze, male; Mulvey, Laura; spectator
screenwriters 58, 140–41
*Secret Diary of a Call Girl* 263
secularization 96, 322, 389, 426, 573, 637
security: communication 9, 230; digital 224, 227–29; economic 507; employment 152; national/state 13, 374–83, 420, 570
self-help 286, 504, 527
semiotics 66, 306, 368, 370, 372, 445
Serbia 214
*Seventeen* 524–25
*Sex and the City* (SATC) 10, 43, 49, 259–61, 263, 267, 280, 604, 606,
sex doll 266
sex education 409–18, 476
sex industry 35, 211–21, 259–68, 589; *see also* commercial sex; prostitution
sex mainstreaming 2, 37–38, 211–21, 324, 473–74, 478, 547, 589
sex roles 5, 140, 495, 523, 530; *see also* gender roles; stereotypes
sex segregation 4, 58, 130, 137
sex toys 10, 259–69; dildo/vibrator 10, 259–62, 266–67
sex trafficking 32, 35, 229, 322, 591; *see also* prostitution; sex work
sex wars 524–4, 589, 594
sex work 10, 267, 32, 215, 263–64; strip clubs/strippers 325, 615; *see also* prostitution
sexism 28, 63; anti campaigns 18, 207, 643–52; critiques 16, 236, 139, 447, 489, 547, 550–51, 591; employment 50, 130, 214, 621, 626–28; institutionalized 160, 170; intersectional theorizing 24, 74, 85, 391, 400, 593–96; media/online 67, 198, 206; profit risk 7, 116–24; sports/games 402–3, 442; *see also* anti-sexism; heterosexism
sex-segregation 4, 57–58, 130, 137
sexting, sexual messaging 8–9, 192–95, 229, 265, 267
sexual assault 32–41, 93, 607; *see also* rape; sexual violence; violence against women
sexual entitlement 262, 265
sexual objectification; *see* objectification
sexual violence 12, 32–39; blaming victims 2, 474, 476, 498; porn industry/images 211, 215, 477–78; power 93, 250–51; representations 5, 71, 76, 93, 98, 191, 288, 333–34, 338, 358–59; teaching/activism 198, 226, 251, 332,

571, 606; *see also* domestic violence
sexuality 593, 596, 607; ambiguous 44, 46; children/teen 12, 181, 193–94, 324–25, 329, 332–40, 524, 592, 635, 638; exploitation of 119–24, 214, 259–60, 267, 443, 537, 602; gay/queer/radical 6, 48, 81–88, 240–41, 447; ideologies 35; men 194, 337, 340, 468, 598, 601; representations/topic 5, 7, 46, 116, 237, 273–74, 285–86, 351, 457, 543–50, 646; research 81, 454–55, 496–97, 501, 607; women 264, 288, 314–18, 344, 349, 424, 426, 494, 591, 604, 652; *see* children; female; gay; intersectional identity; lesbian; male; Oriental sex; queer; trans
sexualization 219; of women/people of color 76, 79, 81, 86, 95, 214, 581–82, 585–86; of culture 10, 17, 213, 260, 325–28, 589–96; desexualization 83; girls'/children's 12, 181, 321–29, 332, 543, 590–93; effects 2, 582; in games/toys/sports 46, 172, 182, 261, 395, 443–44; marketing uses 238, 262, 321; media 202–3, 213–14, 264–65, 280, 579, 613
Shakira 77, 123
*Shame* 45–46, 48
Sina.com 251, 253, 434, 508
Singapore 84, 507, 557
Singh, Harbhajan 398, 400
Skype 569, 571
slash fiction 452–54, 456–59; and femslash 452–53, 457–58; femmeslash 452; girlslash 452; male 453; *see also* fans/fandom; fiction
*Sleep Dealer* 579, 581
slut 2, 265, 325, 396; and Slut Walk 2, 489, 546, 548–50, 617
SMS 520, 559
soap opera 426; and feminine genre 66–67, 172, 414, 530; prime-time 65, 419; targeted consumption 162, 284; *see also* docusoap; telenovela
social media 2; children's use 191; corporate/gendered exploitation 8, 118, 149, 157–65, 533–41; feminist/activist uses 10, 15–16, 223, 229, 2253, 489–90, 551–52, 568–72, 647–50; informational 356; for play 16; politics/policy 224–25, 228, 634–35; social marketing 414; women's uses 222, 484–87, 520, 531, 544; *see also* Facebook, Twitter
social movements: Arab women's 566–68, 571, 577; grassroots 9, 118, 208, 233–34, 238, 249–51, 519, 536, 601; identity

politics 84; new social movement (NSM) theory 233–43

social networking (SNSs): activist 249, 251–53, 486, 489, 520; identity uses 18, 198, 487–88, 633, 637–40; problems 53, 84, 193–98, 229; sharing 559

*Society* 280–89

South Africa 11, 108, 129, 280–89, 292, 321, 395, 514–22

Soviet Union; *see* Russia

*Space Invaders* 442, 636

Spain 29, 240, 434–35

*Spanglish* 579, 582

*Spare Rib* 612, 646

spatiality 7, 18, 83, 148, 153, 442, 446, 515, 561–62, 608, 633

spectator 14–15, 44, 85, 315, 328, 375, 395, 454, 462–68, 493–502, 517; *see also* audience; gaze; male; Mulvey, Laura; scopophilia

Spivak, Gayatri Chakravorty 94, 603

sports: denigration of women 2–3, 13, 396–404, 625; fan market 164; gay 397; gender differentiation 184, 464–68; heroes 463–64; male dominated 395, 403, 495; Olympics 381, 462, 464–65; scandals 397, 402–3; *see also* journalists, sports; lesbian, athletes; *see also* by individual sports

stag parties 264–65

*Star Trek* 452, 454

stereotypes: class 164, 417; fans 454, 457; gamer 171; gender 9, 35, 63, 132, 135, 137, 141–43, 159, 163, 179, 182, 185, 197–98, 253, 291, 293, 295, 323, 326, 333, 430, 484–85, 488, 490–91, 497, 501, 557, 565; Islam 385, 387–88, 391, 638; men/masculinity 18, 65, 131, 179, 213, 334, 336, 614, 618; racial 17, 34, 76, 83–84, 164, 388, 581, 293, 417, 438, 579–82, 585–86, 632, 636–37; sex-roles 25, 140, 143, 292, 500; sexual 194, 292, 334, 336; transgender 307; women/femininity 8, 11, 17, 24, 32, 42–43, 65, 106, 110, 127, 168–69, 172, 174–76, 179, 183, 277, 295, 385, 387–88, 391, 431, 437–38, 456, 476, 516, 518, 529, 536, 556, 579–82, 585–86, 603, 622–24, 626, 644

Stewart, Martha 8, 168–69, 174–76

Stop Online Piracy Act (SOPA) 222–23, 230

Strauss-Kahn, Dominique 6, 93

subaltern counter-publics 10, 245–56, 489, 515–16; *see also* Fraser, Nancy

subcultures/subcultural 10, 61, 81, 121, 235–37, 242, 452–53, 455–56; *see also* fans

subjectification 286, 414, 537–39, 591; *see also* objectification

subjectivity 44, 174, 284, 326, 595; feminine 44, 66, 76, 281, 284, 371, 495, 580, 585, 591, 593; gender 78, 501, 580, 585; queer 87, 119; race 76, 284, 580–81, 585; sexual 607

subtext: film 500; homoerotic 14, 450–60; moral 500

suicide 47–48, 281, 307, 359

Summers, Anne 600–602

Sundance Film Festival 308, 646

*Sunset Boulevard* 342–43, 348–49

Super Bowl (NFL) 461, 465,

Supreme Court (US) 139, 217, 624

surveillance: corporate/government 59, 557; by friends/family 559–60; policy 9, 230; practices 158, 163, 228–29, 518; sexual 82, 214, 282–84, 518, 529, 538–39

Sweden 129, 185, 186, 229, 365, 391

symbolic: annihilation 23, 32, 119–20, 291, 403, 581–82, 585; colonization 77; grammars 634, 638; rupture 77; *see also* Tuchman, Gaye

Symonds, Andrew 398–400

Syria 16, 385, 565–67, 569–70, 573

tabloids 205; and campaigning 322; gossip 300; sexism/sexist 207, 318, 651; style 11, 203, 275, 290, 308, 319; *see* Page 3 girls; *News of the World*

Taiwan 474, 507,

Taliban 96, 387

taste: queer 123; popular/cultural 121, 138, 270, 295, 419, 530; typecasting 142, 441; working class 273, 319

Tea Party 387; *see also* Republican Party

technology 183, 416, 579; and communication/media 54–55, 63, 77–78, 94, 97, 99, 142, 147–56, 201, 212–15, 318, 354, 520–21, 556, 623, 627; cultural 14, 411; gaming 442, 444, 447; internet/online 190, 198, 201, 212–15, 217, 325, 354, 433–38, 455–56, 483–92, 634–35

*Teen* 524–25

teen drama 12, 332–41

*Teen Mom* 14, 409–18

telecommuting/teleworking 150, 484, 629

*Telegraph* 379, 400

telenovelas 14, 419–29

telephone; *see* camera phones; phones, mobile/cell
television: *see* names of specific programs; docusoaps; prime-time; reality television; teen drama; telenovelas
terrorism 13, 26, 95–96, 371–83; *see also* enemy; war
Terry, John 397, 400–403
Thatcher, Margaret 111
*The Color Purple* 64, 74
*The Australian* 388, 390
*The Good Men Project* 645–48
*The Guardian* 71, 400, 402, 434, 644, 650
*The L Word* 77, 81
*The Late Show with David Letterman* 305, 307
*The O.C.* 333, 335
*The Onion* 461, 465
*The Only Way Is Essex (TOWIE)* 11, 269–79
*The Piano* 495–96
*The Real World* 410, 415
*The Simpsons* 182, 616
*The Sopranos* 615–16
*The Sun* 398, 645
*The Women's Room* 645, 648–50
theater 58, 109, 148, 313–17, 420, 632
third wave 10, 182–83, 551, 591, 601, 604; *see also* feminism
Third World 111, 363–64
*Time/Time Warner* 108, 118, 387, 617, 621
*Times of India* 108
*Titanic* 611–12
torture 36, 374–83
trafficking; *see* sex trafficking
transgender 11, 81, 226, 300–310
transmedia 300–310
transnationalism 4, 6, 9, 10, 29, 116, 245–47, 364, 369–70, 579; and feminism 3, 6, 10, 92–101, 236, 242–43; media 116–17, 119–20, 122–23, 131, 243, 300–302, 308, 420–22, 426, 504–5, 509, 511–12; mobility 509–10; toy industry 185
transsexuality 87, 259, 264, 302–3
travel 81, 87, 300, 308, 498–99, 509, 515; *see also* mobility, globalized
TSN 464–65
Tuchman, Gaye 23, 139–40, 291, 431, 523, 582; *see also* symbolic, annihilation
Tumblr 148, 222, 453, 627,
Turkle, Sherrie 484, 486, 634
TV Rio 420–21
Twitter 8, 157, 164, 228, 486; activist/community 229, 453, 489–90, 570, 645, 647, 649; celebrity use 304, 307

UOL (Brazil) 434–35
urbanization 99, 424, 431
user-generated content 8, 118, 148, 192, 222; *see also* citizen journalism

van Zoonen, Liesbet 28, 63–66, 224, 290, 294, 311, 321–22, 326, 483–84, 488, 627
VCR 62, 451
veil/veiling 13, 26, 95–96, 384–94, 637–39; *see also* burqa; chador; headscarf; niqab
velvet ghetto 623
Viacom 108, 121
victim, victimization 5, 13, 32–41, 93, 96, 182, 198, 219, 263, 281, 291–92, 325, 338–39, 371, 379, 381, 388, 474–75, 556, 562, 570, 591–93, 601, 608; *see also* rape; sexual violence; veil/veiling
Vietnam 88, 153
violence: media 1, 5, 29, 45, 32–41, 71, 112, 332–41, 425, 442–44, 494, 500, 615; male 466, 473–82, 615, 647; online/social media 162, 230, 490; racial 76, 83; symbolic violence 29; against women 29, 32, 71, 112, 226, 229–30, 239, 333, 338, 474, 476–77; *see also* sexual violence; violence against women; violence, state
violence, state 71, 74, 374–83, 463, 519, 565–75
virgin/virginity 333–38, 569, 572
visuality 16, 555–57
Vivendi 108
*Vogue* 352–53, 367; Vogue Salon 365–67, 370

war 32, 34, 36, 95, 171, 233, 247, 387, 627–28, 647; *see also* Afghanistan; Iraq; war on terror
war on terror 13, 26, 95, 374–83
*Washington Post* 387, 432, 435–36, 615, 621
Web 2.0 485–86, 489, 634
weblogs 233, 239, 486; *see also* blogs/blogging
weddings 149, 173, 270, 284, 425, 431, 434–35, 464, 529
welfare, welfare state 228, 282, 319, 409, 410, 412, 415, 417, 466, 651
*Whatever Happened to Baby Jane?* 242–43, 348–49
white trash 273; *see also* chav
whiteness 78–79, 85, 98, 173–75, 239, 317, 350, 583–84, 610, 616
Wii 171, 175–76
Wikipedia 2, 148, 222, 487–88, 490, 647
Winfrey, Oprah; *see* Oprah/Oprah Winfrey Network (OWN)

Wired Up 633
*Wizards of Waverly Place* 580, 584
Wolf, Naomi 346, 353, 535
womanhood 8, 73, 169, 174–76, 317, 523, 525
women's eNews 28
women's/girls' media genres 61–70, 269–79,
  280–89, 300–310, 311–20, 332–41, 352–62,
  363–73, 409–18, 419–29, 503–13, 514–22,
  523–42; *see also* beauty, magazines;
  docusoap; lifestyle, lifestyle magazines/
  pages; magazines, girls'/teenage;
  magazines, women's; soap opera
women's issues; *see* news, women's content
women's movement; *see* feminism
Women's News Network 28
women's pages; *see* news, women's pages
women's rights 16, 223, 229–30, 246–47,
  250–51, 378, 547, 571, 573–74, 620
work–life balance 170, 487
World Conference on Women (UN)
  223, 248

World Summit on the Information Society
  (WSIS) 223, 225–27, 230
wrestling 462, 464, 467
Writers Guild of America 140–41

*Xena: Warrior Princess* 452, 458, 604
Xin Lang Wang (Sina.com) 251, 253,
  434
Xinhua News Agency 434

Yemen 16, 565, 567, 569, 573
YM 424–27
YouTube 8, 148, 157, 270–72,
  556, 647
Yusufzai, Malala 96

Zidane, Zinedine 398, 400
zines 234–39, 240–42, 645; *see also* e-zines
*Zoo* 205–6
Zynga 168–69, 175